Merriam-Webster's
Compact
Spanish-English
Dictionary

Merriam-Webster, Incorporated
Springfield, Massachusetts

A GENUINE MERRIAM-WEBSTER

The name *Webster* alone is no guarantee of excellence. It is used by a number of publishers and may serve mainly to mislead an unwary buyer.

Merriam-Webster™ is the name you should look for when you consider the purchase of dictionaries or other fine reference books. It carries the reputation of a company that has been publishing since 1831 and is your assurance of quality and authority.

Contents

Preface   4a

Conjugation of Spanish Verbs   6a

Irregular English Verbs   18a

Abbreviations in this Work   23a

Pronunciation Symbols   24a

Spanish-English Dictionary   **1**

English-Spanish Dictionary   **187**

Common Spanish Abbreviations   417

Spanish Numbers   422

English Numbers   424

Preface

This Spanish-English Dictionary is a concise reference to the core vocabulary of Spanish and English. Its 40,000 entries and over 50,000 translations provide up-to-date coverage of the basic vocabulary and idioms in both languages. In addition, the book includes many specifically Latin-American words and phrases.

IPA (International Phonetic Alphabet) pronunciations are given for all English words. Included as well are tables of irregular verbs in both languages and the most common Spanish and English abbreviations.

This book shares many details of presentation with larger Spanish-English Dictionaries, but for reasons of conciseness it also has a number of features uniquely its own. Users need to be familiar with the following major features of this dictionary.

Main entries follow one another in strict alphabetical order, without regard to intervening spaces or hyphens. The Spanish letter combinations *ch* and *ll* are alphabetized within the letters *C* and *L*; however, the Spanish letter *ñ* is alphabetized separately between *N* and *O*.

Homographs (words spelled the same but having different meanings or parts of speech) are run on at a single main entry if they are closely related. Run-on homograph entries are replaced in the text by a boldfaced swung dash (as **haber** . . . *v aux* . . . — ∼ *nm* . . .). Homographs of distinctly different origin (as **date**[1] and **date**[2]) are given separate entries.

Run-on entries for related words that are not homographs may also follow the main entry. Thus we have the main entry **calcular** *vt* followed by run-on entries for — **calculador, -dora** *adj* . . . — **calculadora** *nf* . . . and — **cálculo** *nm*. However, if a related word falls later in the alphabet than a following unrelated main entry, it will be entered at its own place; **ear** and its run-on — **eardrum** precede the main entry **earl** which is followed by the main entry **earlobe**.

Variant spellings appear at the main entry separated by *or* (as **judgment** *or* **judgement, paralyze** *or Brit* **paralyse,** and **cacahuate** *or* **cacahuete**).

Inflected forms of English verbs, adjectives, adverbs, and nouns are shown when they are irregular (as **wage . . . waged; waging; ride . . . rode; ridden; good . . . better; best;** and **fly . . .** *n, pl* **flies**) or when there might be doubt about their spelling (as **ego . . .** *n, pl* **egos**). Inflected forms of Spanish irregular verbs are shown in the section Conjugation of Spanish Verbs on page 6a; numerical references to this table are included at the main entry (as **poseer** {20} *vt*). Irregular plurals of Spanish nouns or adjectives are shown at the main entry (as **ladrón, -drona** *n, mpl* **-drones**).

Cross-references are provided to lead the user to the appropriate main entry (as **mice → mouse** and **sobrestimar → sobreestimar**).

Pronunciation information is either given explicitly or implied for all English words. Pronunciation of Spanish words is assumed to be regular and is generally omitted; it is included, however, for certain foreign borrowings (as **pizza** ['pitsa, 'pisa]). A full list of the pronunciation symbols used appears on page 24a.

The grammatical function of entry words is indicated by an italic **functional label** (as *vt, adj,* and *nm*). Italic **usage labels** may be added at the entry or sense as well (as **timbre** *nm* . . . **4** *Lat* : postage stamp, **center** *or Brit* **centre** . . . *n* . . ., or **garra** *nf* . . . **2** *fam* : hand, paw). These labels are also included in the translations (as **bag** *n* . . . **2** HANDBAG : bolso *m,* cartera *f Lat*).

Usage notes are occasionally placed before a translation to clarify meaning or use (as **que** *conj* . . . **2** (*in comparisons*) : than).

Synonyms may appear before the translation word(s) in order to provide context for the meaning of an entry word or sense (as **sitio** *nm* . . . **2** ESPACIO : room, space; or **meet** . . . *vt* . . . **2** SATISFY : satisfacer).

Bold notes are sometimes used before a translation to introduce a plural sense or a common phrase using the main entry word (as **mueble** *nm* . . . **2 ~s** *nmpl* : furniture, furnishings, or **call** . . . *vt* . . . **2 ~ off** : cancelar). Note that when an entry word is repeated in a bold note, it is replaced by a swung dash.

Conjugation of Spanish Verbs

Simple Tenses

Tense	Regular Verbs Ending in -AR hablar	
PRESENT INDICATIVE	hablo	hablamos
	hablas	habláis
	habla	hablan
PRESENT SUBJUNCTIVE	hable	hablemos
	hables	habléis
	hable	hablen
PRETERIT INDICATIVE	hablé	hablamos
	hablaste	hablasteis
	habló	hablaron
IMPERFECT INDICATIVE	hablaba	hablábamos
	hablabas	hablabais
	hablaba	hablaban
IMPERFECT SUBJUNCTIVE	hablara	habláramos
	hablaras	hablarais
	hablara	hablaran
	or	
	hablase	hablásemos
	hablases	hablaseis
	hablase	hablasen
FUTURE INDICATIVE	hablaré	hablaremos
	hablarás	hablaréis
	hablará	hablarán
FUTURE SUBJUNCTIVE	hablare	habláremos
	hablares	hablareis
	hablare	hablaren
CONDITIONAL	hablaría	hablaríamos
	hablarías	hablaríais
	hablaría	hablarían
IMPERATIVE		hablemos
	habla	hablad
	hable	hablen
PRESENT PARTICIPLE (GERUND)	hablando	
PAST PARTICIPLE	hablado	

Regular Verbs Ending in -ER		Regular Verbs Ending in -IR	
comer		vivir	
como	comemos	vivo	vivimos
comes	coméis	vives	vivís
come	comen	vive	viven
coma	comamos	viva	vivamos
comas	comáis	vivas	viváis
coma	coman	viva	vivan
comí	comimos	viví	vivimos
comiste	comisteis	viviste	vivisteis
comió	comieron	vivió	vivieron
comía	comíamos	vivía	vivíamos
comías	comíais	vivías	vivíais
comía	comían	vivía	vivían
comiera	comiéramos	viviera	viviéramos
comieras	comierais	vivieras	vivierais
comiera	comieran	viviera	vivieran
or		*or*	
comiese	comiésemos	viviese	viviésemos
comieses	comieseis	vivieses	vivieseis
comiese	comiesen	viviese	viviesen
comeré	comeremos	viviré	viviremos
comerás	comeréis	vivirás	viviréis
comerá	comerán	vivirá	vivirán
comiere	comiéremos	viviere	viviéremos
comieres	comiereis	vivieres	viviereis
comiere	comieren	viviere	vivieren
comería	comeríamos	viviría	viviríamos
comerías	comeríais	vivirías	viviríais
comería	comerían	viviría	vivirían
	comamos		vivamos
come	comed	vive	vivid
coma	coman	viva	vivan
comiendo		viviendo	
comido		vivido	

Compound Tenses

1. Perfect Tenses

The perfect tenses are formed with *haber* and the past participle:

PRESENT PERFECT

> he hablado, etc. (*indicative*);
> haya hablado, etc. (*subjunctive*)

PAST PERFECT

> había hablado, etc. (*indicative*);
> hubiera hablado, etc. (*subjunctive*)
> *or*
> hubiese hablado, etc. (*subjunctive*)

PRETERIT PERFECT

> hube hablado, etc. (*indicative*)

FUTURE PERFECT

> habré hablado, etc. (*indicative*)

CONDITIONAL PERFECT

> habría hablado, etc. (*indicative*)

2. Progressive Tenses

The progressive tenses are formed with *estar* and the present participle:

PRESENT PROGRESSIVE

> estoy llamando, etc. (*indicative*);
> esté llamando, etc. (*subjunctive*)

IMPERFECT PROGRESSIVE

> estaba llamando, etc. (*indicative*);
> estuviera llamando, etc. (*subjunctive*)
> *or*
> estuviese llamando, etc. (*subjunctive*)

PRETERIT PROGRESSIVE

> estuve llamando, etc. (*indicative*)

FUTURE PROGRESSIVE

> estaré llamando, etc. (*indicative*)

CONDITIONAL PROGRESSIVE
    estaría llamando, etc. (*indicative*)

PRESENT PERFECT PROGRESSIVE
    he estado llamando, etc. (*indicative*);
    haya estado llamando, etc. (*subjunctive*)

PAST PERFECT PROGRESSIVE
    había estado llamando, etc. (*indicative*);
    hubiera estado llamando, etc. (*subjunctive*)
    or
    hubiese estado llamando, etc. (*subjunctive*)

Irregular Verbs

    The *imperfect subjunctive*, the *future subjunctive*, the *conditional*, and most forms of the *imperative* are not included in the model conjugations, but can be derived as follows:

    The *imperfect subjunctive* and the *future subjunctive* are formed from the third person plural form of the preterit tense by removing the last syllable (*-ron*) and adding the appropriate suffix:

PRETERIT INDICATIVE, THIRD PERSON PLURAL (querer)	quisieron
IMPERFECT SUBJUNCTIVE (querer)	quisiera, quisieras, etc. *or* quisiese, quisieses, etc.
FUTURE SUBJUNCTIVE (querer)	quisiere, quisieres, etc.

The conditional uses the same stem as the future indicative:

FUTURE INDICATIVE (poner)	pondré, pondrás, etc.
CONDITIONAL (poner)	pondría, pondrías, etc.

    The third person singular, first person plural, and third person plural forms of the *imperative* are the same as the corresponding forms of the present subjunctive.

    The second person singular form of the *imperative* is generally the same as the third person singular of the present indicative. Exceptions are noted in the model conjugations list.

    The second person plural *(vosotros)* form of the *imperative* is formed by removing the final *-r* of the infinitive form and adding a *-d* (ex.: *oír* → *oíd*).

Model Conjugations of Irregular Verbs

The model conjugations below include the following simple tenses: the *present indicative* (*IND*), the *present subjunctive* (*SUBJ*), the *preterit indicative* (*PRET*), the *imperfect indicative* (*IMPF*), the *future indicative* (*FUT*), the second person singular form of the *imperative* (*IMPER*) when it differs from the third person singular of the present indicative, the *gerund* or *present participle* (*PRP*), and the *past participle* (*PP*). Each set of conjugations is preceded by the corresponding infinitive form of the verb, shown in bold type. Only tenses containing irregularities are listed, and the irregular verb forms within each tense are displayed in bold type.

Each irregular verb entry in the Spanish-English section of this dictionary is cross-referenced by number to one of the following model conjugations. These cross-reference numbers are shown in curly braces { } immediately following the entry's functional label.

1 **abolir** *(defective verb)* : *IND* abolimos, abolís *(other forms not used)*; *SUBJ (not used)*; *IMPER (only second person plural is used)*

2 **abrir** : *PP* abierto

3 **actuar** : *IND* **actúo, actúas, actúa**, actuamos, actuáis, **actúan**; *SUBJ* **actúe, actúes, actúe**, actuemos, actuéis, **actúen**; *IMPER* **actúa**

4 **adquirir** : *IND* **adquiero, adquieres, adquiere**, adquirimos, adquirís, **adquieren**; *SUBJ* **adquiera, adquieras, adquiera**, adquiramos, adquiráis, **adquieran**; *IMPER* **adquiere**

5 **airar** : *IND* **aíro, aíras, aíra**, airamos, airáis, **aíran**; *SUBJ* **aíre, aíres, aíre**, airemos, airéis, **aíren**; *IMPER* **aíra**

6 **andar** : *PRET* **anduve, anduviste, anduvo, anduvimos, anduvisteis, anduvieron**

7 **asir** : *IND* **asgo**, ases, ase, asimos, asís, asen; *SUBJ* **asga, asgas, asga, asgamos, asgáis, asgan**

8 **aunar** : *IND* **aúno, aúnas, aúna,** aunamos, aunáis, **aúnan;** *SUBJ* **aúne, aúnes, aúne,** aunemos, aunéis, **aúnen;** *IMPER* **aúna**

9 **avergonzar** : *IND* **avergüenzo, avergüenzas, avergüenza,** avergonzamos, avergonzáis, **avergüenzan;** *SUBJ* **avergüence, avergüences, avergüence, avergoncemos, avergoncéis, avergüencen;** *PRET* **avergoncé;** *IMPER* **avergüenza**

10 **averiguar** : *SUBJ* **averigüe, averigües, averigüe, averigüemos, averigüéis, averigüen;** *PRET* **averigüé,** averiguaste, averiguó, averiguamos, averiguasteis, averiguaron

11 **bendecir** : *IND* **bendigo, bendices, bendice,** bendecimos, bendecís, **bendicen;** *SUBJ* **bendiga, bendigas, bendiga, bendigamos, bendigáis, bendigan;** *PRET* **bendije, bendijiste, bendijo, bendijimos, bendijisteis, bendijeron;** *IMPER* **bendice**

12 **caber** : *IND* **quepo,** cabes, cabe, cabemos, cabéis, caben; *SUBJ* **quepa, quepas, quepa, quepamos, quepáis, quepan;** *PRET* **cupe, cupiste, cupo, cupimos, cupisteis, cupieron;** *FUT* **cabré, cabrás, cabrá, cabremos, cabréis, cabrán**

13 **caer** : *IND* **caigo,** caes, cae, caemos, caéis, caen; *SUBJ* **caiga, caigas, caiga, caigamos, caigáis, caigan;** *PRET* caí, **caíste,** cayó, caímos, caísteis, cayeron; *PRP* cayendo; *PP* caído

14 **cocer** : *IND* **cuezo, cueces, cuece,** cocemos, cocéis, **cuecen;** *SUBJ* **cueza, cuezas, cueza, cozamos, cozáis, cuezan;** *IMPER* **cuece**

15 **coger** : *IND* **cojo,** coges, coge, cogemos, cogéis, cogen; *SUBJ* **coja, cojas, coja, cojamos, cojáis, cojan**

16 **colgar** : *IND* **cuelgo, cuelgas, cuelga,** colgamos, colgáis, **cuelgan;** *SUBJ* **cuelgue, cuelgues, cuelgue, colguemos, colguéis, cuelguen;** *PRET* **colgué,** colgaste, colgó, colgamos, colgasteis, colgaron; *IMPER* **cuelga**

17 **concernir** *(defective verb; used only in the third person singular and plural of the present indicative, present subjunctive, and imperfect subjunctive)* see 25 **discernir**

18 **conocer** : *IND* **conozco,** conoces, conoce, conocemos, conocéis, conocen; *SUBJ* **conozca, conozcas, conozca, conozcamos, conozcáis, conozcan**

19 **contar** : *IND* **cuento, cuentas, cuenta,** contamos, contáis, **cuentan;** *SUBJ* **cuente, cuentes, cuente,** contemos, contéis, **cuenten;** *IMPER* **cuenta**

20 **creer** : *PRET* creí, **creíste, creyó, creímos, creísteis, creyeron;** *PRP* **creyendo;** *PP* **creído**

21 **cruzar** : *SUBJ* **cruce, cruces, cruce, crucemos, crucéis, crucen;** *PRET* **crucé,** cruzaste, cruzó, cruzamos, cruzasteis, cruzaron

22 **dar** : *IND* **doy,** das, da, damos, **dais,** dan; *SUBJ* **dé,** des, **dé,** demos, **deis,** den; *PRET* **di, diste, dio, dimos, disteis, dieron**

23 **decir** : *IND* **digo, dices, dice,** decimos, decís, **dicen;** *SUBJ* **diga, digas, diga, digamos, digáis, digan;** *PRET* **dije, dijiste, dijo, dijimos, dijisteis, dijeron;** *FUT* **diré, dirás, dirá, diremos, diréis, dirán;** *IMPER* **di;** *PRP* **diciendo;** *PP* **dicho**

24 **delinquir** : *IND* **delinco,** delinques, delinque, delinquimos, delinquís, delinquen; *SUBJ* **delinca, delincas, delinca, delincamos, delincáis, delincan**

25 **discernir** : *IND* **discierno, disciernes, discierne,** discernimos, discernís, **disciernen;** *SUBJ* **discierna, disciernas, discierna,** discernamos, discernáis, **disciernan;** *IMPER* **discierne**

26 **distinguir** : *IND* **distingo,** distingues, distingue, distinguimos, distinguís, distinguen; *SUBJ* **distinga, distingas, distinga, distingamos, distingáis, distingan**

27 **dormir** : *IND* **duermo, duermes, duerme,** dormimos, dormís, **duermen;** *SUBJ* **duerma, duermas, duerma, durmamos, durmáis, duerman;** *PRET* dormí, dormiste, **durmió,** dormimos, dormisteis, **durmieron;** *IMPER* **duerme;** *PRP* **durmiendo**

28 **elegir** : *IND* **elijo, eliges, elige,** elegimos, elegís, **eligen;** *SUBJ* **elija, elijas, elija, elijamos, elijáis, elijan;** *PRET* elegí, elegiste, **eligió,** elegimos, elegisteis, **eligieron;** *IMPER* **elige;** *PRP* **eligiendo**

29 **empezar** : *IND* **empiezo, empiezas, empieza,** empezamos, empezáis, **empiezan;** *SUBJ* **empiece, empieces, empiece, empecemos, empecéis, empiecen;** *PRET* **empecé,** empezaste, empezó, empezamos, empezasteis, empezaron; *IMPER* **empieza**

30 **enraizar** : *IND* **enraízo, enraízas, enraíza,** enraizamos, enraizáis, **enraízan;** *SUBJ* **enraíce, enraíces, enraíce, enraicemos, enraicéis, enraícen;** *PRET* **enraicé,** enraizaste, enraizó, enraizamos, enraizasteis, enraizaron; *IMPER* **enraíza**

31 **erguir** : *IND* **irgo** *or* **yergo, irgues** *or* **yergues, irgue** *or* **yergue,** erguimos, erguís, **irguen** *or* **yerguen;** *SUBJ* **irga** *or* **yerga, irgas** *or* **yergas, irga** *or* **yerga, irgamos, irgáis, irgan** *or* **yergan;** *PRET* erguí, erguiste, **irguió,** erguimos, erguisteis, **irguieron;** *IMPER* **irgue** *or* **yergue;** *PRP* **irguiendo**

32 **errar** : *IND* **yerro, yerras, yerra,** erramos, erráis, **yerran;** *SUBJ* **yerre, yerres, yerre,** erremos, erréis, **yerren;** *IMPER* **yerra**

33 **escribir** : *PP* **escrito**

34 **estar** : *IND* **estoy, estás, está,** estamos, estáis, **están;** *SUBJ* **esté, estés, esté,** estemos, estéis, **estén;** *PRET* **estuve, estuviste, estuvo, estuvimos, estuvisteis, estuvieron;** *IMPER* **está**

35 **exigir** : *IND* **exijo,** exiges, exige, exigimos, exigís, exigen; *SUBJ* **exija, exijas, exija, exijamos, exijáis, exijan**

36 **forzar** : *IND* **fuerzo, fuerzas, fuerza,** forzamos, forzáis, **fuerzan;** *SUBJ* **fuerce, fuerces, fuerce, forcemos, forcéis, fuercen;** *PRET* **forcé,** forzaste, forzó, forzamos, forzasteis, forzaron; *IMPER* **fuerza**

37 **freír** : *IND* **frío, fríes, fríe, freímos,** freís, **fríen;** *SUBJ* **fría, frías, fría, friamos, friáis, frían;** *PRET* freí, **freíste, frió, freímos, freísteis, frieron;** *IMPER* **fríe;** *PRP* **friendo;** *PP* **frito**

38 **gruñir** : *PRET* gruñí, gruñiste, **gruñó,** gruñimos, gruñisteis, **gruñeron;** *PRP* **gruñendo**

39 **haber** : *IND* **he, has, ha, hemos,** habéis, **han;** *SUBJ* **haya, hayas, haya, hayamos, hayáis, hayan;** *PRET* **hube, hubiste, hubo, hubimos, hubisteis, hubieron;** *FUT* **habré, habrás, habrá, habremos, habréis, habrán;** *IMPER* **he**

40 **hacer** : *IND* **hago,** haces, hace, hacemos, hacéis, hacen; *SUBJ* **haga, hagas, haga, hagamos, hagáis, hagan;** *PRET* **hice, hiciste, hizo, hicimos, hicisteis, hicieron;** *FUT* **haré, harás, hará, haremos, haréis, harán;** *IMPER* **haz;** *PP* **hecho**

41 **huir** : *IND* **huyo, huyes, huye,** huimos, huís, **huyen;** *SUBJ* **huya, huyas, huya, huyamos, huyáis, huyan;** *PRET* huí, huiste, **huyó,** huimos, huisteis, **huyeron;** *IMPER* **huye;** *PRP* **huyendo**

42 **imprimir** : *PP* **impreso**

43 **ir** : *IND* **voy, vas, va, vamos, vais, van;** *SUBJ* **vaya, vayas, vaya, vayamos, vayáis, vayan;** *PRET* **fui, fuiste, fue, fuimos, fuisteis, fueron;** *IMPF* **iba, ibas, iba, íbamos, ibais, iban;** *IMPER* **ve;** *PRP* **yendo;** *PP* **ido**

44 **jugar** : *IND* **juego, juegas, juega,** jugamos, jugáis, **juegan;** *SUBJ* **juegue, juegues, juegue, juguemos, juguéis, jueguen;** *PRET* **jugué,** jugaste, jugó, jugamos, jugasteis, jugaron; *IMPER* **juega**

45 **lucir** : *IND* **luzco,** luces, luce, lucimos, lucís, lucen; *SUBJ* **luzca, luzcas, luzca, luzcamos, luzcáis, luzcan**

46 **morir** : *IND* **muero, mueres, muere,** morimos, morís,

mueren; *SUBJ* **muera, mueras, muera,** muramos, muráis,
mueran; *PRET* morí, moriste, **murió,** morimos, moristeis,
murieron; *IMPER* **muere;** *PRP* **muriendo;** *PP* **muerto**

47 **mover :** *IND* **muevo, mueves, mueve,** movemos, movéis,
mueven; *SUBJ* **mueva, muevas, mueva,** movamos, mováis,
muevan; *IMPER* **mueve**

48 **nacer :** *IND* **nazco,** naces, nace, nacemos, nacéis, nacen; *SUBJ*
nazca, nazcas, nazca, nazcamos, nazcáis, nazcan

49 **negar :** *IND* **niego, niegas, niega,** negamos, negáis, **niegan;**
SUBJ **niegue, niegues, niegue, neguemos, neguéis, nieguen;**
PRET **negué,** negaste, negó, negamos, negasteis, negaron; *IMPER*
niega

50 **oír :** *IND* **oigo, oyes, oye, oímos,** oís, **oyen;** *SUBJ* **oiga, oigas,
oiga, oigamos, oigáis, oigan;** *PRET* oí, **oíste, oyó, oímos,
oísteis, oyeron;** *IMPER* **oye;** *PRP* **oyendo;** *PP* **oído**

51 **oler :** *IND* **huelo, hueles, huele,** olemos, oléis, **huelen;** *SUBJ*
huela, huelas, huela, olamos, oláis, **huelan;** *IMPER* **huele**

52 **pagar :** *SUBJ* **pague, pagues, pague, paguemos, paguéis,
paguen;** *PRET* **pagué,** pagaste, pagó, pagamos, pagasteis, pa-
garon

53 **parecer :** *IND* **parezco,** pareces, parece, parecemos, parecéis,
parecen; *SUBJ* **parezca, parezcas, parezca, parezcamos,
parezcáis, parezcan**

54 **pedir :** *IND* **pido, pides, pide,** pedimos, pedís, **piden;** *SUBJ*
pida, pidas, pida, pidamos, pidáis, pidan; *PRET* pedí, pediste,
pidió, pedimos, pedisteis, **pidieron;** *IMPER* **pide;** *PRP* **pidiendo**

55 **pensar :** *IND* **pienso, piensas, piensa,** pensamos, penséis,
piensan; *SUBJ* **piense, pienses, piense,** pensemos, penséis,
piensen; *IMPER* **piensa**

56 **perder :** *IND* **pierdo, pierdes, pierde,** perdemos, perdéis, **pier-
den;** *SUBJ* **pierda, pierdas, pierda,** perdamos, perdáis, **pier-
dan;** *IMPER* **pierde**

57 **placer :** *IND* **plazco,** places, place, placemos, placéis, placen;
SUBJ **plazca, plazcas, plazca, plazcamos, plazcáis, plazcan;**
PRET plací, placiste, plació *or* **plugo,** placimos, placisteis, pla-
cieron *or* **pluguieron**

58 **poder :** *IND* **puedo, puedes, puede,** podemos, podéis, **pueden;**
SUBJ **pueda, puedas, pueda,** podamos, podáis, **puedan;** *PRET*

pude, pudiste, pudo, pudimos, pudisteis, pudieron; *FUT* **podré, podrás, podrá, podremos, podréis, podrán;** *IMPER* **puede;** *PRP* **pudiendo**

59 **podrir** *or* **pudrir :** *PP* **podrido** (*all other forms based on* pu-drir)

60 **poner :** *IND* **pongo,** pones, pone, ponemos, ponéis, ponen; *SUBJ* **ponga, pongas, ponga, pongamos, pongáis, pongan;** *PRET* **puse, pusiste, puso, pusimos, pusisteis, pusieron;** *FUT* **pondré, pondrás, pondrá, pondremos, pondréis, pondrán;** *IMPER* **pon;** *PP* **puesto**

61 **producir :** *IND* **produzco,** produces, produce, producimos, producís, producen; *SUBJ* **produzca, produzcas, produzca, produzcamos, produzcáis, produzcan;** *PRET* **produje, produjiste, produjo, produjimos, produjisteis, produjeron**

62 **prohibir :** *IND* **prohíbo, prohíbes, prohíbe,** prohibimos, prohibís, **prohíben;** *SUBJ* **prohíba, prohíbas, prohíba,** prohibamos, prohibáis, **prohíban;** *IMPER* **prohíbe**

63 **proveer :** *PRET* **proveí, proveíste, proveyó, proveímos, proveísteis, proveyeron;** *PRP* **proveyendo;** *PP* **provisto**

64 **querer :** *IND* **quiero, quieres, quiere,** queremos, queréis, **quieren;** *SUBJ* **quiera, quieras, quiera,** queramos, queráis, **quieran;** *PRET* **quise, quisiste, quiso, quisimos, quisisteis, quisieron;** *FUT* **querré, querrás, querrá, querremos, querréis, querrán;** *IMPER* **quiere**

65 **raer :** *IND* **rao** *or* **raigo** *or* **rayo,** raes, rae, raemos, raéis, raen; *SUBJ* **raiga** *or* **raya, raigas** *or* **rayas, raiga** *or* **raya, raigamos** *or* **rayamos, raigáis** *or* **rayáis, raigan** *or* **rayan;** *PRET* **raí, raíste, rayó, raímos, raísteis, rayeron;** *PRP* **rayendo;** *PP* **raído**

66 **reír :** *IND* **río, ríes, ríe, reímos,** reís, **ríen;** *SUBJ* **ría, rías, ría, riamos, riáis, rían;** *PRET* **reí, reíste, rió, reímos, reísteis, rieron;** *IMPER* **ríe;** *PRP* **riendo;** *PP* **reído**

67 **reñir :** *IND* **riño, riñes, riñe,** reñimos, reñís, **riñen;** *SUBJ* **riña, riñas, riña, riñamos, riñáis, riñan;** *PRET* reñí, reñiste, **riñó,** reñimos, reñisteis, **riñeron;** *PRP* **riñendo**

68 **reunir :** *IND* **reúno, reúnes, reúne,** reunimos, reunís, **reúnen;** *SUBJ* **reúna, reúnas, reúna,** reunamos, reunáis, **reúnan;** *IMPER* **reúne**

69 **roer :** *IND* **roo** *or* **roigo** *or* **royo,** roes, roe, roemos, roéis, roen;

SUBJ roa *or* **roiga** *or* **roya,** roas *or* **roigas** *or* **royas,** roa *or* **roiga** *or* **roya,** roamos *or* **roigamos** *or* **royamos,** roáis *or* **roigáis** *or* **royáis,** roan *or* **roigan** *or* **royan;** *PRET* roí, **roíste, royó, roí-mos, roísteis, royeron;** *PRP* **royendo;** *PP* **roído**

70 **romper** : *PP* **roto**

71 **saber** : *IND* **sé,** sabes, sabe, sabemos, sabéis, saben; *SUBJ* **sepa, sepas, sepa, sepamos, sepáis, sepan;** *PRET* **supe, supiste, supo, supimos, supisteis, supieron;** *FUT* **sabré, sabrás, sabrá, sabremos, sabréis, sabrán**

72 **sacar** : *SUBJ* **saque, saques, saque, saquemos, saquéis, saquen;** *PRET* **saqué,** sacaste, sacó, sacamos, sacasteis, sacaron

73 **salir** : *IND* **salgo,** sales, sale, salimos, salís, salen; *SUBJ* **salga, salgas, salga, salgamos, salgáis, salgan;** *FUT* **saldré, saldrás, saldrá, saldremos, saldréis, saldrán;** *IMPER* **sal**

74 **satisfacer** : *IND* **satisfago,** satisfaces, satisface, satisfacemos, satisfacéis, satisfacen; *SUBJ* **satisfaga, satisfagas, satisfaga, satisfagamos, satisfagáis, satisfagan;** *PRET* **satisfice, satisfi-ciste, satisfizo, satisficimos, satificisteis, satisficieron;** *FUT* **satisfaré, satisfarás, satisfará, satisfaremos, satisfaréis, satisfarán;** *IMPER* **satisfaz** *or* **satisface;** *PP* **satisfecho**

75 **seguir** : *IND* **sigo, sigues, sigue,** seguimos, seguís, **siguen;** *SUBJ* **siga, sigas, siga, sigamos, sigáis, sigan;** *PRET* seguí, seguiste, **siguió,** seguimos, seguisteis, **siguieron;** *IMPER* **sigue;** *PRP* **si-guiendo**

76 **sentir** : *IND* **siento, sientes, siente,** sentimos, sentís, **sienten;** *SUBJ* **sienta, sientas, sienta, sintamos, sintáis, sientan;** *PRET* sentí, sentiste, **sintió,** sentimos, sentisteis, **sintieron;** *IMPER* **siente;** *PRP* **sintiendo**

77 **ser** : *IND* **soy, eres, es, somos, sois, son;** *SUBJ* **sea, seas, sea, seamos, seáis, sean;** *PRET* **fui, fuiste, fue, fuimos, fuisteis, fueron;** *IMPF* **era, eras, era, éramos, erais, eran;** *IMPER* **sé;** *PRP* **siendo;** *PP* **sido**

78 **soler** *(defective verb; used only in the present, preterit, and im-perfect indicative, and the present and imperfect subjunctive) see* 47 **mover**

79 **tañer** : *PRET* tañí, tañiste, **tañó,** tañimos, tañisteis, **tañeron;** *PRP* **tañendo**

80 **tener** : *IND* **tengo, tienes, tiene,** tenemos, tenéis, **tienen;** *SUBJ* **tenga, tengas, tenga, tengamos, tengáis, tengan;** *PRET* **tuve,**

tuviste, tuvo, tuvimos, tuvisteis, tuvieron; *FUT* tendré, tendrás, tendrá, tendremos, tendréis, tendrán; *IMPER* ten

81 **traer** : *IND* **traigo,** traes, trae, traemos, traéis, traen; *SUBJ* **traiga, traigas, traiga, traigamos, traigáis, traigan;** *PRET* **traje, trajiste, trajo, trajimos, trajisteis, trajeron;** *PRP* **trayendo;** *PP* **traído**

82 **trocar** : *IND* **trueco, truecas, trueca,** trocamos, trocáis, **truecan;** *SUBJ* **trueque, trueques, trueque, troquemos, troquéis, truequen;** *PRET* **troqué,** trocaste, trocó, trocamos, trocasteis, trocaron; *IMPER* **trueca**

83 **uncir** : *IND* **unzo,** unces, unce, uncimos, uncís, uncen; *SUBJ* **unza, unzas, unza, unzamos, unzáis, unzan**

84 **valer** : *IND* **valgo,** vales, vale, valemos, valéis, valen; *SUBJ* **valga, valgas, valga, valgamos, valgáis, valgan;** *FUT* **valdré, valdrás, valdrá, valdremos, valdréis, valdrán**

85 **variar** : *IND* **varío, varías, varía,** variamos, variáis, **varían;** *SUBJ* **varíe, varíes, varíe,** variemos, variéis, **varíen;** *IMPER* **varía**

86 **vencer** : *IND* **venzo,** vences, vence, vencemos, vencéis, vencen; *SUBJ* **venza, venzas, venza, venzamos, venzáis, venzan**

87 **venir** : *IND* **vengo, vienes, viene,** venimos, venís, **vienen;** *SUBJ* **venga, vengas, venga, vengamos, vengáis, vengan;** *PRET* **vine, viniste, vino, vinimos, vinisteis, vinieron;** *FUT* **vendré, vendrás, vendrá, vendremos, vendréis, vendrán;** *IMPER* **ven;** *PRP* **viniendo**

88 **ver** : *IND* **veo, ves, ve, vemos, veis, ven;** *PRET* **vi, viste, vio,** vimos, visteis, vieron; *IMPER* **ve;** *PRP* **viendo;** *PP* **visto**

89 **volver** : *IND* **vuelvo, vuelves, vuelve,** volvemos, volvéis, **vuelven;** *SUBJ* **vuelva, vuelvas, vuelva,** volvamos, volváis, **vuelvan;** *IMPER* **vuelve;** *PP* **vuelto**

90 **yacer** : *IND* **yazco** *or* **yazgo** *or* **yago,** yaces, yace, yacemos, yacéis, yacen; *SUBJ* **yazca** *or* **yazga** *or* **yaga, yazcas** *or* **yazgas** *or* **yagas, yazca** *or* **yazga** *or* **yaga, yazcamos** *or* **yazgamos** *or* **yagamos, yazcáis** *or* **yazgáis** *or* **yagáis, yazcan** *or* **yazgan** *or* **yagan;** *IMPER* **yace** *or* **yaz**

Irregular English Verbs

INFINITIVE	PAST	PAST PARTICIPLE
arise	arose	arisen
awake	awoke	awoken *or* awaked
be	was, were	been
bear	bore	borne
beat	beat	beaten *or* beat
become	became	become
befall	befell	befallen
begin	began	begun
behold	beheld	beheld
bend	bent	bent
beseech	beseeched *or* besought	beseeched *or* besought
beset	beset	beset
bet	bet	bet
bid	bade *or* bid	bidden *or* bid
bind	bound	bound
bite	bit	bitten
bleed	bled	bled
blow	blew	blown
break	broke	broken
breed	bred	bred
bring	brought	brought
build	built	built
burn	burned *or* burnt	burned *or* burnt
burst	burst	burst
buy	bought	bought
can	could	—
cast	cast	cast
catch	caught	caught
choose	chose	chosen
cling	clung	clung
come	came	come
cost	cost	cost
creep	crept	crept
cut	cut	cut
deal	dealt	dealt
dig	dug	dug
do	did	done
draw	drew	drawn

INFINITIVE	PAST	PAST PARTICIPLE
dream	dreamed *or* dreamt	dreamed *or* dreamt
drink	drank	drunk *or* drank
drive	drove	driven
dwell	dwelled *or* dwelt	dwelled *or* dwelt
eat	ate	eaten
fall	fell	fallen
feed	fed	fed
feel	felt	felt
fight	fought	fought
find	found	found
flee	fled	fled
fling	flung	flung
fly	flew	flown
forbid	forbade	forbidden
forecast	forecast	forecast
forego	forewent	foregone
foresee	foresaw	foreseen
foretell	foretold	foretold
forget	forgot	forgotten *or* forgot
forgive	forgave	forgiven
forsake	forsook	forsaken
freeze	froze	frozen
get	got	got *or* gotten
give	gave	given
go	went	gone
grind	ground	ground
grow	grew	grown
hang	hung	hung
have	had	had
hear	heard	heard
hide	hid	hidden *or* hid
hit	hit	hit
hold	held	held
hurt	hurt	hurt
keep	kept	kept
kneel	knelt *or* kneeled	knelt *or* kneeled
know	knew	known
lay	laid	laid
lead	led	led
lean	leaned	leaned
leap	leaped *or* leapt	leaped *or* leapt
learn	learned	learned

INFINITIVE	PAST	PAST PARTICIPLE
leave	left	left
lend	lent	lent
let	let	let
lie	lay	lain
light	lit *or* lighted	lit *or* lighted
lose	lost	lost
make	made	made
may	might	—
mean	meant	meant
meet	met	met
mow	mowed	mowed *or* mown
pay	paid	paid
put	put	put
quit	quit	quit
read	read	read
rend	rent	rent
rid	rid	rid
ride	rode	ridden
ring	rang	rung
rise	rose	risen
run	ran	run
saw	sawed	sawed *or* sawn
say	said	said
see	saw	seen
seek	sought	sought
sell	sold	sold
send	sent	sent
set	set	set
shake	shook	shaken
shall	should	—
shear	sheared	sheared *or* shorn
shed	shed	shed
shine	shone *or* shined	shone *or* shined
shoot	shot	shot
show	showed	shown *or* showed
shrink	shrank *or* shrunk	shrunk *or* shrunken
shut	shut	shut
sing	sang *or* sung	sung
sink	sank *or* sunk	sunk
sit	sat	sat
slay	slew	slain
sleep	slept	slept

INFINITIVE	PAST	PAST PARTICIPLE
slide	slid	slid
sling	slung	slung
smell	smelled *or* smelt	smelled *or* smelt
sow	sowed	sown *or* sowed
speak	spoke	spoken
speed	sped *or* speeded	sped *or* speeded
spell	spelled	spelled
spend	spent	spent
spill	spilled	spilled
spin	spun	spun
spit	spit *or* spat	spit *or* spat
split	split	split
spoil	spoiled	spoiled
spread	spread	spread
spring	sprang *or* sprung	sprung
stand	stood	stood
steal	stole	stolen
stick	stuck	stuck
sting	stung	stung
stink	stank *or* stunk	stunk
stride	strode	stridden
strike	struck	struck
swear	swore	sworn
sweep	swept	swept
swell	swelled	swelled *or* swollen
swim	swam	swum
swing	swung	swung
take	took	taken
teach	taught	taught
tear	tore	torn
tell	told	told
think	thought	thought
throw	threw	thrown
thrust	thrust	thrust
tread	trod	trodden *or* trod
wake	woke	woken *or* waked
waylay	waylaid	waylaid
wear	wore	worn
weave	wove *or* weaved	woven *or* weaved
wed	wedded	wedded
weep	wept	wept
will	would	—

INFINITIVE	PAST	PAST PARTICIPLE
win	won	won
wind	wound	wound
withdraw	withdrew	withdrawn
withhold	withheld	withheld
withstand	withstood	withstood
wring	wrung	wrung
write	wrote	written

Abbreviations in this Work

adj	adjective	*nmf*	masculine or feminine noun
adv	adverb		
adv	adverbial phrase	*nmfpl*	plural noun invariable for gender
algn	alguien (someone)		
art	article	*nmfs & pl*	noun invariable for both gender and number
Brit	Great Britain		
conj	conjunction	*nmpl*	masculine plural noun
conj phr	conjunctive phrase	*nms & pl*	invariable singular or plural masculine noun
esp	especially		
etc	et cetera	*npl*	plural noun
f	feminine	*ns & pl*	noun invariable for plural
fam	familiar or colloquial		
fpl	feminine plural	*pl*	plural
interj	interjection	*pp*	past participle
Lat	Latin America	*prep*	preposition
m	masculine	*prep phr*	prepositional phrase
mf	masculine or feminine	*pron*	pronoun
mpl	masculine plural	*s.o.*	someone
n	noun	*sth*	something
nf	feminine noun	*usu*	usually
nfpl	feminine plural noun	*v*	verb
nfs & pl	invariable singular or plural feminine noun	*v aux*	auxiliary verb
		vi	intransitive verb
nm	masculine noun	*v impers*	impersonal verb
		vr	reflexive verb
		vt	transitive verb

Pronunciation Symbols

VOWELS

æ	ask, bat, glad
ɑ	cot, bomb
a	*New England* aunt, *British* ask, glass, *Spanish* casa
ɛ	egg, bet, fed
ə	about, javelin, Alabama
ə	when italicized as in əl, əm, ən, indicates a syllabic pronunciation of the consonant as in bottle, prism, button
i	very, any, thirty, *Spanish* piña
i:	eat, bead, bee
ɪ	id, bid, pit
o	Ohio, yellower, potato, *Spanish* óvalo
o:	oats, own, zone, blow
ɔ	awl, maul, caught, paw
ʊ	sure, should, could
u:	boot, few, coo
ʌ	under, putt, bud
eɪ	eight, wade, bay
aɪ	ice, bite, tie
aʊ	out, gown, plow
ɔɪ	oyster, coil, boy
ː	indicates that the preceding vowel is long. Long vowels are almost always diphthongs in English, but not in Spanish.

CONSONANTS

b	baby, labor, cab
d	day, ready, kid
dʒ	just, badger, fudge
ð	then, either, bathe
f	foe, tough, buff
g	go, bigger, bag
h	hot, aha
j	yes, vineyard
k	cat, keep, lacquer, flock
l	law, hollow, boil
m	mat, hemp, hammer, rim
n	new, tent, tenor, run
ŋ	rung, hang, swinger
p	pay, lapse, top
r	rope, burn, tar
s	sad, mist, kiss
ʃ	shoe, mission, slush
t	toe, button, mat
t̬	indicates that some speakers of English pronounce this sound as a voiced alveolar flap [ɾ], as in later, catty, battle
tʃ	choose, batch
θ	thin, ether, bath
v	vat, never, cave
w	wet, software
z	zoo, easy, buzz
ʒ	azure, beige
h, k, *p, t*	when italicized indicate sounds which are present in the pronunciation of some speakers of English but absent in the pronunciation of others, so that *whence* ['hwɛns] can be pronounced as ['hwɛns], ['hwɛnts], ['wɛnts], or ['wɛns]

STRESS MARKS

'	high stress	**pen**manship
ˌ	low stress	penman**ship**

Spanish-English
Dictionary

A

a[1] *nf* : a, first letter of the Spanish alphabet

a[2] *prep* **1** : to **2** ~ **las dos** : at two o'clock **3 al día siguiente** : (on) the following day **4** ~ **pied** : on foot **5 de lunes** ~ **viernes** : from Monday until Friday **6 tres veces** ~ **la semana** : three times per week **7** ~ **la** : in the manner of, like

abadía *nf* : abbey

abajo *adv* **1** : down, below, downstairs **2** ~ **de** *Lat* : under, beneath **3 de** ~ : (at the) bottom **4 hacia** ~ : downwards

abalanzarse {21} *vr* : hurl oneself, rush

abandonar *vt* **1** : abandon, leave **2** RENUNCIAR A : give up — **abandonarse** *vr* **1** : neglect oneself **2** ~ **a** : give oneself over to — **abandonado, -da** *adj* **1** : abandoned, deserted **2** DESCUIDADO : neglected **3** DESALIÑADO : slovenly — **abandono** *nm* **1** : abandonment, neglect **2 por** ~ : by default

abanico *nm* : fan — **abanicar** {72} *vt* : fan

abaratar *vt* : lower the price of — **abaratarse** *vr* : become cheaper

abarcar {72} *vt* **1** : cover, embrace **2** *Lat* : monopolize

abarrotar *vt* : pack, cram — **abarrotes** *nmpl Lat* **1** : groceries **2 tienda de** ~ : grocery store

abastecer {53} *vt* : supply, stock — **abastecimiento** *nm* : supply, provisions — **abasto** *nm* **1** : supply **2 no dar** ~ **a** : be unable to cope with

abatir {72} *v* : knock down, shoot down **2** DEPRIMIR : depress — **abatirse** *vr* **1** : get depressed **2** ~ **sobre** : swoop down on — **abatido, -da** *adj* : dejected, depressed — **abatimiento** *nm* : depression, dejection

abdicar {72} *v* : abdicate — **abdicación** *nf, pl* **-ciones** : abdication

abdomen *nm, pl* **-dómenes** : abdomen — **abdominal** *adj* : abdominal

abecé *nm* : ABC — **abecedario** *nm* : alphabet

abedul *nm* : birch

abeja *nf* : bee — **abejorro** *nm* : bumblebee

aberración *nf, pl* **-ciones** : aberration

abertura *nf* : opening

abeto *nm* : fir (tree)

abierto, -ta *adj* : open

abigarrado, -da *adj* : multicolored

abismo *nm* : abyss, chasm — **abismal** *adj* : vast, enormous

abjurar *vi* ~ **de** : abjure

ablandar *vt* : soften (up) — **ablandarse** *vr* : soften

abnegarse {49} *vr* : deny oneself — **abnegado, -da** *adj* : self-sacrificing — **abnegación** *nf, pl* **-ciones** : self-denial

abochornar *vt* : embarrass — **abochornarse** *vr* : get embarrassed

abofetear *vt* : slap

abogado, -da *n* : lawyer — **abogacía** *nf* : legal profession — **abogar** {52} *vi* ~ **por** : plead for, defend

abolengo *nm* : lineage

abolir {1} *vt* : abolish — **abolición** *nf, pl* **-ciones** : abolition

abollar *vt* : dent — **abolladura** *nf* : dent

abominar *vt* : abominate — **abominable** *adj* : abominable — **abominación** *nf, pl* **-ciones** : abomination

abonar *vt* **1** : pay (a bill, etc.) **2** : fertilize (the soil) — **abonarse** *vr* : subscribe — **abonado, -da** *n* : subscriber — **abono** *nm* **1** : payment, installment **2** FERTILIZANTE : fertilizer **3** : season ticket (to the theater, etc.)

abordar *vt* **1** : tackle (a problem) **2** : accost, approach (a person) **3** *Lat* : board — **abordaje** *nm* : boarding

aborigen *nmf, pl* **-rígenes** : aborigine — ~ *adj* : aboriginal, native

aborrecer {53} *vt* : abhor, detest — **aborrecible** *adj* : hateful — **aborrecimiento** *nm* : loathing

abortar *vi* : have a miscarriage — *vt* : abort — **aborto** *nm* : abortion, miscarriage

abotonar *vt* : button — **abotonarse** *vr* : button up

abovedado, -da *adj* : vaulted

abrasar *vt* : burn, scorch — **abrasarse** *vr* : burn up — **abrasador, -dora** *adj* : burning

abrasivo, -va *adj* : abrasive — **abrasivo** *nm* : abrasive

abrazar {21} *vt* : hug, embrace — **abrazarse** *vr* : embrace — **abraza-**

dera *nf* : clamp — **abrazo** *nm* : hug, embrace

abrebotellas *nms & pl* : bottle opener — **abrelatas** *nms & pl* : can opener

abrevadero *nm* : watering trough

abreviar *vt* **1** : shorten, abridge **2** : abbreviate (a word) — **abreviación** *nf, pl* **-ciones** : shortening — **abreviatura** *nf* : abbreviation

abridor *nm* : bottle opener, can opener

abrigar {52} *vt* **1** : wrap up (in clothing) **2** ALBERGAR : cherish, harbor — **abrigarse** *vr* : dress warmly — **abrigado, -da** *adj* **1** : sheltered **2** : warm, wrapped up (of persons) — **abrigo** *nm* **1** : coat, overcoat **2** REFUGIO : shelter, refuge

abril *nm* : April

abrillantar *vt* : polish, shine

abrir {2} *vt* **1** : open **2** : unlock, undo — *vi* : open up — **abrirse** *vr* **1** : open up **2** : clear up (of weather)

abrochar *vt* : button, fasten — **abrocharse** *vr* : fasten, do up

abrogar {52} *vt* : annul, repeal

abrumar *vt* : overwhelm — **abrumador, -dora** *adj* : overwhelming, oppressive

abrupto, -ta *adj* **1** ESCARPADO : steep **2** ÁSPERO : rugged, harsh **3** REPENTINO : abrupt

absceso *nm* : abscess

absolución *nf, pl* **-ciones 1** : absolution **2** : acquittal (in law)

absoluto, -ta *adj* **1** : absolute, unconditional **2 en absoluto** : not at all — **absolutamente** *adv* : absolutely

absolver {89} *vt* **1** : absolve **2** : acquit (in law)

absorber *vt* **1** : absorb **2** : take up (time, energy, etc.) — **absorbente** *adj* **1** : absorbent **2** INTERESANTE : absorbing — **absorción** *nf, pl* **-ciones** : absorption — **absorto, -ta** *adj* : absorbed, engrossed

abstemio, -mia *adj* : abstemious — ~ *n* : teetotaler

abstenerse {80} *vr* : abstain, refrain — **abstención** *nf, pl* **-ciones** : abstention — **abstinencia** *nf* : abstinence

abstracción *nf, pl* **-ciones** : abstraction — **abstracto, -ta** *adj* : abstract — **abstraer** {81} *vt* : abstract — **abstraerse** *vr* : lose oneself in thought — **abstraído, -da** *adj* : preoccupied

absurdo, -da *adj* : absurd, ridiculous — **absurdo** *nm* : absurdity

abuchear *vt* : boo, jeer — **abucheo** *nm* : booing

abuelo, -la *n* **1** : grandfather, grand-

mother **2 abuelos** *nmpl* : grandparents

abulia *nf* : apathy, lethargy

abultar *vi* : bulge, be bulky — *vt* : enlarge, expand — **abultado, -da** *adj* : bulky

abundar *vi* : abound, be plentiful — **abundancia** *nf* : abundance — **abundante** *adj* : abundant

aburrir *vt* : bore — **aburrirse** *vr* : get bored — **aburrido, -da** *adj* **1** : bored **2** TEDIOSO : boring — **aburrimiento** *nm* : boredom

abusar *vi* **1** : go too far **2** ~ **de** : abuse — **abusivo, -va** *adj* : outrageous, excessive — **abuso** *nm* : abuse

abyecto, -ta *adj* : abject, wretched

acá *adv* : here, over here

acabar *vi* **1** : finish, end **2** ~ **de** : have just (done something) **3** ~ **con** : put an end to **4** ~ **por** : end up (doing sth) — *vt* : finish — **acabarse** *vr* : come to an end — **acabado, -da** *adj* **1** : finished, perfect **2** AGOTADO : old, worn-out — **acabado** *nm* : finish

academia *nf* : academy — **académico, -ca** *adj* : academic

acaecer {53} *vi* : happen, occur

acallar *vt* : quiet, silence

acalorar *vt* : stir up, excite — **acalorarse** *vr* : get worked up — **acalorado, -da** *adj* : emotional, heated

acampar *vi* : camp — **acampada** *nf* **ir de** ~ : go camping

acanalado, -da *adj* **1** : grooved **2** : corrugated (of iron, etc.)

acantilado *nm* : cliff

acaparar *vt* **1** : hoard **2** MONOPOLIZAR : monopolize

acápite *nm Lat* : paragraph

acariciar *vt* **1** : caress **2** : cherish (hopes, ideas, etc.)

ácaro *nm* : mite

acarrear *vt* **1** : haul, carry **2** OCASIONAR : give rise to — **acarreo** *nm* : transport

acaso *adv* **1** : perhaps, maybe **2 por si** ~ : just in case

acatar *vt* : comply with, respect — **acatamiento** *nm* : compliance, respect

acatarrarse *vr* : catch a cold

acaudalado, -da *adj* : wealthy, rich

acaudillar *vt* : lead

acceder *vi* **1** : agree **2** ~ **a** : gain access to, enter

acceso *nm* **1** : access **2** ENTRADA : entrance **3** : attack, bout (of an illness) — **accesible** *adj* : accessible

accesorio *nm* : accessory — **accesorio, -ria** *adj* : incidental

accidentado, -da *adj* **1** : eventful, turbulent **2** : rough, uneven (of land, etc.) **3** HERIDO : injured — **~** *n* : accident victim

accidental *adj* : accidental — **accidentarse** *vr* : have an accident — **accidente** *nm* **1** : accident **2** : unevenness (of land)

acción *nf, pl* **-ciones 1** : action **2** ACTO : act, deed **3** : share, stock (in finance) — **accionar** *vt* : activate — *vi* : gesticulate — **accionista** *nmf* : stockholder

acebo *nm* : holly

acechar *vt* : watch, stalk — **acecho** *nm* **estar al ~ por** : be on the lookout for

aceite *nm* : oil — **aceitar** *vt* : oil — **aceitera** *nf* **1** : oilcan **2** : cruet (in cookery) **3** *Lat* : oil refinery — **aceitoso, -sa** *adj* : oily

aceituna *nf* : olive

acelerar *v* : accelerate — **acelerarse** *vr* : hurry up — **aceleración** *nf, pl* **-ciones** : acceleration — **acelerador** *nm* : accelerator

acelga *nf* : (Swiss) chard

acentuar {3} *vt* **1** : accent **2** ENFATIZAR : emphasize, stress — **acentuarse** *vr* : stand out — **acento** *nm* **1** : accent **2** ÉNFASIS : stress, emphasis

acepción *nf, pl* **-ciones** : sense, meaning

aceptar *vt* : accept — **aceptable** *adj* : acceptable — **aceptación** *nf, pl* **-ciones 1** : acceptance **2** ÉXITO : success

acequia *nf* : irrigation ditch

acera *nf* : sidewalk

acerbo, -ba *adj* : harsh, caustic

acerca *prep* **~ de** : about, concerning

acercar {72} *vt* : bring near or closer — **acercarse** *vr* : approach, draw near

acero *nm* **1** : steel **2** **~ inoxidable** : stainless steel

acérrimo, -ma *adj* **1** : staunch, steadfast **2** : bitter (of an enemy)

acertar {55} *vt* : guess correctly — *vi* **1** ATINAR : be accurate **2** **~ a** : manage to — **acertado, -da** *adj* : correct, accurate

acertijo *nm* : riddle

acervo *nm* : heritage

acetona *nf* : acetone, nail-polish remover

achacar {72} *vt* : attribute, impute

achacoso, -sa *adj* : sickly

achaparrado, -da *adj* : squat, stocky

achaque *nm* : aches and pains

achatar *vt* : flatten

achicar {72} *vt* **1** : make smaller **2** ACOBARDAR : intimidate **3** : bail out

(water) — **achicarse** *vr* : become intimidated

achicharrar *vt* : scorch, burn to a crisp

achicoria *nf* : chicory

aciago, -ga *adj* : fateful, unlucky

acicalar *vt* : dress up, adorn — **acicalarse** *vr* : get dressed up

acicate *nm* **1** : spur **2** INCENTIVO : incentive

ácido, -da *adj* : acid, sour — **acidez** *nf, pl* **-deces** : acidity — **ácido** *nm* : acid

acierto *nm* **1** : correct answer **2** HABILIDAD : skill, sound judgment

aclamar *vt* : acclaim — **aclamación** *nf, pl* **-ciones** : acclaim, applause

aclarar *vt* **1** CLARIFICAR : clarify, explain **2** : rinse (clothing) **3** **~ la voz** : clear one's throat — *vi* : clear up — **aclararse** *vr* : become clear — **aclaración** *nf, pl* **-ciones** : explanation — **aclaratorio, -ria** *adj* : explanatory

aclimatar *vt* : acclimatize — **aclimatarse** *vr* **~ a** : get used to — **aclimatación** *nf, pl* **-ciones** : acclimatization

acné *nm* : acne

acobardar *vt* : intimidate — **acobardarse** *vr* : become frightened

acodarse *vr* **~ en** : lean (one's elbows) on

acoger {15} *vt* **1** REFUGIAR : shelter **2** RECIBIR : receive, welcome — **acogerse** *vr* **1** : take refuge **2** **~ a** : resort to — **acogedor, -dora** *adj* : cozy, welcoming — **acogida** *nf* **1** : welcome **2** REFUGIO : refuge

acolchar *vt* : pad

acólito *nm* MONAGUILLO : altar boy

acometer *vt* **1** : attack **2** EMPRENDER : undertake — *vi* **~ contra** : rush against — **acometida** *nf* : attack, assault

acomodar *vt* **1** ADAPTAR : adjust **2** COLOCAR : put, make a place for — **acomodarse** *vr* **1** : settle in **2** **~ a** : adapt to — **acomodado, -da** *adj* : well-to-do — **acomodaticio, -cia** *adj* : accommodating, obliging — **acomodo** *nm* : job, position

acompañar *vt* **1** : accompany **2** ADJUNTAR : enclose — **acompañamiento** *nm* : accompaniment — **acompañante** *nmf* **1** COMPAÑERO : companion **2** : accompanist (in music)

acompasado, -da *adj* : rhythmic, measured

acondicionar *vt* : fit out, equip — **acondicionado, -da** *adj* : equipped

acongojar *vt* : distress, upset — **acongojarse** *vr* : get upset

aconsejar *vt* : advise — **aconsejable** *adj* : advisable

acontecer {53} *vi* : occur, happen — **acontecimiento** *nm* : event

acopiar *vt* : gather, collect — **acopio** *nm* : collection, stock

acoplar *vt* : couple, connect — **acoplarse** *vr* : fit together — **acoplamiento** *nm* : connection, coupling

acorazado, -da *adj* : armored — **acorazado** *nm* : battleship

acordar {19} *vt* **1** : agree (on) **2** *Lat* : award — **acordarse** *vr* : remember

acorde *adj* **1** : in agreement **2** ~ **con** : in keeping with — ~ *nm* : chord (in music)

acordeón *nm, pl* **-deones** : accordion

acordonar *vt* **1** : cordon off **2** : lace up (shoes)

acorralar *vt* : corner, corral

acortar *vt* : shorten, cut short — **acortarse** *vr* : get shorter

acosar *vt* : hound, harass — **acoso** *nm* : harassment

acostar {19} *vt* : put to bed — **acostarse** *vr* **1** : go to bed **2** TUMBARSE : lie down

acostumbrar *vt* : accustom — *vi* ~ **a** : be in the habit of — **acostumbrarse** *vr* ~ **a** : get used to — **acostumbrado, -da** *adj* **1** HABITUADO : accustomed **2** HABITUAL : usual

acotar *vt* **1** ANOTAR : annotate **2** DELIMITAR : mark off (land) — **acotación** *nf, pl* **-ciones** : marginal note — **acotado, -da** *adj* : enclosed

acre *adj* **1** : pungent **2** MORDAZ : harsh, biting

acrecentar {55} *vt* : increase — **acrecentamiento** *nm* : growth, increase

acreditar *vt* **1** : accredit, authorize **2** PROBAR : prove — **acreditarse** *vr* : prove oneself — **acreditado, -da** *adj* **1** : reputable **2** : accredited (in politics, etc.)

acreedor, -dora *adj* : worthy — ~ *n* : creditor

acribillar *vt* **1** : riddle, pepper **2** ~ **a** : harass with

acrílico *nm* : acrylic

acrimonia *nf or* **acritud** *nf* **1** : pungency **2** RESENTIMIENTO : bitterness, acrimony

acrobacia *nf* : acrobatics — **acróbata** *nmf* : acrobat — **acrobático, -ca** *adj* : acrobatic

acta *nf* **1** : certificate **2** : minutes *pl* (of a meeting)

actitud *nf* **1** : attitude **2** POSTURA : posture, position

activar *vt* **1** : activate **2** ESTIMULAR : stimulate, speed up — **actividad** *nf* : activity — **activo, -va** *adj* : active — **activo** *nm* : assets *pl*

acto *nm* **1** ACCIÓN : act, deed **2** : act (in theater) **3** en el ~ : right away

actor *nm* : actor — **actriz** *nf, pl* **-trices** : actress

actual *adj* : present, current — **actualidad** *nf* **1** : present time **2** ~**es** *nfpl* : current affairs — **actualizar** {21} *vt* : modernize — **actualización** *nf, pl* **-ciones** : modernization — **actualmente** *adv* : at present, nowadays

actuar {3} *vi* **1** : act, perform **2** ~ **de** : act as

acuarela *nf* : watercolor

acuario *nm* : aquarium

acuartelar *vt* : quarter (troops)

acuático, -ca *adj* : aquatic, water

acuchillar *vt* : knife, stab

acudir *vi* **1** : go, come **2** ~ **a** : be present at, attend **3** ~ **a** : turn to

acueducto *nm* : aqueduct

acuerdo *nm* **1** : agreement **2** de ~ : OK, all right **3** de ~ con : in accordance with **4** estar de ~ : agree

acumular *vt* : accumulate — **acumularse** *vr* : pile up — **acumulación** *nf, pl* **-ciones** : accumulation — **acumulador** *nm* : storage battery — **acumulativo, -va** *adj* : cumulative

acunar *vt* : rock

acuñar *vt* **1** : mint (money) **2** : coin (a word)

acuoso, -sa *adj* : watery

acupuntura *nf* : acupuncture

acurrucarse {72} *vr* : curl up, nestle

acusar *vt* **1** : accuse **2** MOSTRAR : reveal, show — **acusación** *nf, pl* **-ciones** : accusation, charge — **acusado, -da** *adj* : prominent, marked — ~ *n* : defendant

acuse *nm* ~ **de recibo** : acknowledgment of receipt

acústica *nf* : acoustics — **acústico, -ca** *adj* : acoustic

adagio *nm* **1** REFRÁN : adage, proverb **2** : adagio (in music)

adaptar *vt* **1** : adapt **2** AJUSTAR : adjust, fit — **adaptarse** *vr* ~ **a** : adapt to — **adaptable** *adj* : adaptable — **adaptación** *nf, pl* **-ciones** : adaptation — **adaptador** *nm* : adapter (in electricity)

adecuar {8} *vt* : adapt, make suitable — **adecuarse** *vr* ~ **a** : be appropriate for — **adecuado, -da** *adj* : suitable, appropriate

adelantar *vt* **1** : advance, move forward **2** PASAR : overtake **3** : pay in advance — **adelantarse** *vr* **1** : move forward, get ahead **2** : be fast (of a clock) — **adelantado, -da** *adj* **1** : advanced, ahead **2** : fast (of a clock) **3 por ~** : in advance — **adelante** *adv* **1** : ahead, forward **2** ¡~! : come in! **3 más ~** : later on, further on — **adelanto** *nm* **1** : advance **2** *or* **~ de dinero** : advance payment

adelgazar {21} *vt* : make thin — *vi* : lose weight

ademán *nm, pl* **-manes 1** GESTO : gesture **2 ~es** *nmpl* : manners **3 en ~ de** : as if to

además *adv* **1** : besides, furthermore **2 ~ de** : in addition to, as well as

adentro *adv* **1** : inside, within — **adentrarse** *vr* **~ en** : go into, get inside of

adepto, -ta *n* : follower, supporter

aderezar {21} *vt* **1** : season, dress — **aderezo** *nm* : dressing, seasoning

adeudar *vt* **1** : debit **2** DEBER : owe — **adeudo** *nm* **1** DÉBITO : debit **2** *Lat* : debt

adherirse {76} *vr* : adhere, stick — **adherencia** *nf* : adherence — **adhesión** *nf, pl* **-siones 1** : adhesion **2** APOYO : support — **adhesivo, -va** *adj* : adhesive — **adhesivo** *nm* : adhesive

adición *nf, pl* **-ciones** : addition — **adicional** *adj* : additional

adicto, -ta *adj* : addicted — **~** *n* : addict

adiestrar *vt* : train

adinerado, -da *adj* : wealthy

adiós *nm, pl* **adioses 1** : farewell **2** ¡~! : good-bye!

aditamento *nm* : attachment, accessory

aditivo *nm* : additive

adivinar *vt* **1** : guess **2** PREDECIR : foretell — **adivinación** *nf, pl* **-ciones** : guessing, prediction — **adivinanza** *nf* : riddle — **adivino, -na** *n* : fortune-teller

adjetivo *nm* : adjective

adjudicar {72} *vt* : award — **adjudicarse** *vr* : appropriate — **adjudicación** *nf, pl* **-ciones** : awarding

adjuntar *vt* : enclose (with a letter, etc.) — **adjunto, -ta** *adj* : enclosed, attached — **~** *n* : assistant

administración *nf, pl* **-ciones 1** : administration **2** : administering (of a drug, etc.) **3** DIRECCIÓN : management — **administrador, -dora** *n* : administrator, manager — **administrar** *vt* **1** : manage, run **2** : administer (a drug, etc.) — **administrativo, -va** *adj* : administrative

admirar *vt* : admire — **admirarse** *vr* : be amazed — **admirable** *adj* : admirable — **admiración** *nf, pl* **-ciones 1** : admiration **2** ASOMBRO : amazement — **admirador, -dora** *n* : admirer

admitir *vt* **1** : admit **2** ACEPTAR : accept — **admisible** *adj* : admissible, acceptable — **admisión** *nf, pl* **-siones 1** : admission **2** ACEPTACIÓN : acceptance

ADN *nm* : DNA

adobe *nm* : adobe

adobo *nm* : marinade

adoctrinar *vt* : indoctrinate — **adoctrinamiento** *nm* : indoctrination

adolecer {53} *vi* **~ de** : suffer from

adolescente *adj & nmf* : adolescent — **adolescencia** *nf* : adolescence

adonde *conj* : where

adónde *adv* : where

adoptar *vt* : adopt (a child), take (a decision) — **adopción** *nf, pl* **-ciones** : adoption — **adoptivo, -va** *adj* : adopted, adoptive

adoquín *nm, pl* **-quines** : cobblestone

adorar *vt* : adore, worship — **adorable** *adj* : adorable — **adoración** *nf, pl* **-ciones** : adoration, worship

adormecer {53} *vt* **1** : make sleepy **2** ENTUMECER : numb — **adormecerse** *vr* : doze off — **adormecimiento** *nm* : drowsiness — **adormilarse** *vr* : doze

adornar *vt* : decorate, adorn — **adorno** *nm* : ornament, decoration

adquirir {4} *vt* **1** : acquire **2** COMPRAR : purchase — **adquisición** *nf, pl* **-ciones 1** : acquisition **2** COMPRA : purchase

adrede *adv* : intentionally, on purpose

adscribir {33} *vt* : assign, appoint

aduana *nf* : customs (office) — **aduanero, -ra** *adj* : customs — **~** *n* : customs officer

aducir {61} *vt* : cite, put forward

adueñarse *vr* **~ de** : take possession of

adular *vt* : flatter — **adulación** *nf, pl* **-ciones** : adulation, flattery — **adulador, -dora** *adj* : flattering — **~** *n* : flatterer

adulterar *vt* : adulterate

adulterio *nm* : adultery — **adúltero, -ra** *n* : adulterer

adulto, -ta *adj & n* : adult

adusto, -ta *adj* : stern, severe

advenedizo, -za *n* : upstart

advenimiento *nm* : advent, arrival

adverbio *nm* : adverb — **adverbial** *adj* : adverbial

adversario, -ria *n* : adversary, opponent — **adverso, -sa** *adj* : adverse — **adversidad** *nf* : adversity

advertir {76} *vt* **1** AVISAR : warn **2** NOTAR : notice — **advertencia** *nf* : warning

adviento *nm* : Advent

adyacente *adj* : adjacent

aéreo, -rea *adj* : aerial, air

aerobic *nm* : aerobics *pl*

aerodinámico, -ca *adj* : aerodynamic

aeródromo *nm* : airfield

aerolínea *nf* : airline

aeromozo, -za *n* : flight attendant, steward *m*, stewardess *f*

aeronave *nf* : aircraft

aeropuerto *nm* : airport

aerosol *nm* : aerosol, spray

afable *adj* : affable — **afabilidad** *nf* : affability

afán *nm, pl* **afanes 1** ANHELO : eagerness **2** EMPEÑO : effort, hard work — **afanarse** *vr* : toil — **afanosamente** *adv* : industriously, busily — **afanoso, -sa** *adj* **1** : eager **2** TRABAJOSO : arduous

afear *vt* : make ugly, disfigure

afección *nf, pl* **-ciones** : ailment, complaint

afectar *vt* : affect — **afectación** *nf, pl* **-ciones** : affectation — **afectado, -da** *adj* : affected

afectivo, -va *adj* : emotional

afecto *nm* : affection — **afecto, -ta** *adj* ~ **a** : fond of — **afectuoso, -sa** *adj* : affectionate, caring

afeitar *vt* : shave — **afeitarse** *vr* : shave — **afeitada** *nf* : shave

afeminado, -da *adj* : effeminate

aferrarse {55} *vr* : cling, hold on

afianzar {21} *vt* : secure, strengthen — **afianzarse** *vr* : become established

afiche *nm Lat* : poster

afición *nf, pl* **-ciones 1** : penchant, fondness **2** PASATIEMPO : hobby — **aficionado, -da** *n* **1** ENTUSIASTA : enthusiast, fan **2** AMATEUR : amateur — **aficionarse** *vr* ~ **a** : become interested in

afilar *vt* : sharpen — **afilado, -da** *adj* : sharp — **afilador** *nm* : sharpener

afiliarse *vr* ~ **a** : join, become a member of — **afiliación** *nf, pl* **-ciones** : affiliation — **afiliado, -da** *adj* : affiliated

afín *adj, pl* **afines** : related, similar — **afinidad** *nf* : affinity, similarity

afinar *vt* **1** : tune **2** PULIR : perfect, refine

afirmar *vt* **1** : state, affirm **2** REFORZAR : strengthen — **afirmación** *nf, pl* **-ciones** : statement, affirmation — **afirmativo, -va** *adj* : affirmative

afligir {35} *vt* **1** : afflict **2** APENAR : distress — **afligirse** *vr* : grieve — **aflicción** *nf, pl* **-ciones** : grief, sorrow — **afligido -da** *adj* : sorrowful, distressed

aflojar *vt* : loosen, slacken — *vi* : ease up — **aflojarse** *vr* : become loose, slacken

aflorar *vi* : come to the surface, emerge — **afloramiento** *nm* : outcrop

afluencia *nf* : influx — **afluente** *nm* : tributary

afortunado, -da *adj* : fortunate, lucky — **afortunadamente** *adv* : fortunately

afrentar *vt* : insult — **afrenta** *nf* : affront, insult

africano, -na *adj* : African

afrontar *vt* : confront, face

afuera *adv* **1** : out **2** : outside, outdoors — **afueras** *nfpl* : outskirts

agachar *vt* : lower — **agacharse** *vr* : crouch, stoop

agalla *nf* **1** BRANQUIA : gill **2 tener** ~**s** *fam* : have guts

agarrar *vt* **1** ASIR : grasp **2** *Lat* : catch — **agarrarse** *vr* : hold on, cling — **agarradera** *nf Lat* : handle — **agarrado, -da** *adj fam* : stingy — **agarre** *nm* : grip, grasp — **agarrón** *nm, pl* **-rones** : tug, pull

agasajar *vt* : fête, wine and dine — **agasajo** *nm* : lavish attention

agave *nm* : agave

agazaparse *vr* : crouch down

agencia *nf* : agency, office — **agente** *nmf* : agent, officer

agenda *nf* **1** : agenda **2** LIBRETA : notebook

ágil *adj* : agile — **agilidad** *nf* : agility

agitar *vt* **1** : agitate, shake **2** : wave, flap (wings, etc.) **3** PERTURBAR : stir up — **agitarse** *vr* **1** : toss about **2** INQUIETARSE : get upset — **agitación** *nf, pl* **-ciones** : agitation, shaking **3** INTRANQUILIDAD : restlessness — **agitado, -da** *adj* **1** : agitated, excited **2** : choppy, rough (of the sea)

aglomerar *vt* : amass — **aglomerarse** *vr* : crowd together

agnóstico, -ca *adj & n* : agnostic

agobiar *vt* **1** : oppress **2** ABRUMAR : overwhelm — **agobiado, -da** *adj* : weary, weighed down — **agobiante** *adj* : oppressing, oppressive

agonizar {21} *vi* : be dying — **agonía** *nf* **1** : death throes **2** PENA : agony — **agonizante** *adj* : dying

agorero, -ra *adj* : ominous

agostar *vt* : wither

agosto *nm* : August

agotar *vt* **1** : deplete, use up **2** CANSAR : exhaust, weary — **agotarse** *vr* **1**

: run out, give out **2** CANSARSE : get tired — **agotado, -da** *adj* **1** CANSADO : exhausted **2** : sold out — **agotador, -dora** *adj* : exhausting — **agotamiento** *nm* : exhaustion

agraciado, -da *adj* **1** : attractive **2** AFORTUNADO : fortunate

agradar *vi* : be pleasing — **agradable** *adj* : pleasant, agreeable — **agrado** *nm* **1** : taste, liking **2 con ~** : with pleasure

agradecer {53} *vt* : be grateful for, thank — **agradecido, -da** *adj* : grateful — **agradecimiento** *nm* : gratitude

agrandar *vt* : enlarge — **agrandarse** *vr* : grow larger

agrario, -ria *adj* : agrarian, agricultural

agravar *vt* **1** : make heavier **2** EMPEORAR : aggravate, worsen — **agravarse** *vr* : get worse

agraviar *vt* : insult — **agravio** *nm* : insult

agredir {1} *vt* : attack

agregar {52} *vt* : add, attach — **agregado, -da** *n* : attaché — **agregado** *nm* : aggregate

agresión *nf, pl* **-siones** : aggression, attack — **agresividad** *nf* : aggressiveness — **agresivo, -va** *adj* : aggressive — **agresor, -sora** *n* : aggressor, attacker

agreste *adj* : rugged, wild

agriar *vt* : sour — **agriarse** *vr* **1** : turn sour (of milk, etc.) **2** : become embittered

agrícola *adj* : agricultural — **agricultura** *nf* : agriculture, farming — **agricultor, -tora** *n* : farmer

agridulce *adj* **1** : bittersweet **2** : sweet-and-sour (in cooking)

agrietar *vt* : crack — **agrietarse** *vr* **1** : crack **2** : chap

agrimensor, -sora *n* : surveyor

agrio, agria *adj* : sour

agrupar *vt* : group together — **agruparse** *vr* : form a group — **agrupación** *nf, pl* **-ciones** : group, association — **agrupamiento** *nm* : grouping

agua *nf* **1** : water **2 ~ oxigenada** : hydrogen peroxide **3 ~s negras** *or* **~s residuales** : sewage

aguacate *nm* : avocado

aguacero *nm* : downpour

aguado, -da *adj* **1** : watery **2** *Lat fam* : soft, flabby — **aguar** {10} *vt* **1** : water down, dilute **2 ~ la fiesta** *fam* : spoil the party

aguafuerte *nm* : etching

aguanieve *nf* : sleet

aguantar *vt* **1** SOPORTAR : bear, with-

stand **2** SOSTENER : hold — *vi* : hold out, last — **aguantarse** *vr* **1** : resign oneself **2** CONTENERSE : restrain oneself — **aguante** *nm* **1** : patience **2** RESISTENCIA : endurance

aguardar *vt* : await

aguardiente *nm* : clear brandy

aguarrás *nm* : turpentine

agudo, -da *adj* **1** : acute, sharp **2** : shrill, high-pitched (in music) — **agudeza** *nf* **1** : sharpness **2** : witticism

agüero *nm* : augury, omen

aguijón *nm, pl* **-jones 1** : stinger (of an insect) **2** ESTÍMULO : goad, stimulus — **aguijonear** *vt* : goad

águila *nf* : eagle

aguja *nf* **1** : needle **2** : hand (of a clock) **3** : spire (of a church)

agujero *nm* : hole

agujeta *nf* **1** *Lat* : shoelace **2 ~s** *nfpl* : (muscular) stiffness

aguzar {21} *vt* **1** : sharpen **2 ~ el oído** : prick up one's ears

ahí *adv* **1** : there **2 por ~** : somewhere, thereabouts

ahijado, -da *n* : godchild, godson *m*, goddaughter *f*

ahínco *nm* : eagerness, zeal

ahogar {52} *vt* **1** : drown **2** ASFIXIAR : smother — **ahogarse** *vr* : drown — **ahogo** *nm* : breathlessness

ahondar *vt* : deepen — *vi* : elaborate, go into detail

ahora *adv* **1** : now **2 ~ mismo** : right now

ahorcar {72} *vt* : hang, kill by hanging — **ahorcarse** *vr* : hang oneself

ahorita *adv* *Lat fam* : right now

ahorrar *vt* : save, spare — *vi* : save up — **ahorrarse** *vr* : spare oneself — **ahorro** *nm* : saving

ahuecar {72} *vt* **1** : hollow out **2** : cup (one's hands)

ahumar {8} *vt* : smoke, cure — **ahumado, -da** *adj* : smoked

ahuyentar *vt* : scare away, chase away

airado, -da *adj* : irate, angry

aire *nm* **1** : air **2 ~ acondicionado** : air-conditioning **3 al ~ libre** : in the open air, outdoors — **airear** *vt* : air, air out

aislar {5} *vt* **1** : isolate **2** : insulate (in electricity) — **aislamiento** *nm* **1** : isolation **2** : (electrical) insulation

ajar *vt* **1** : crumple, wrinkle **2** ESTROPEAR : spoil

ajedrez *nm* : chess

ajeno, -na *adj* **1** : someone else's **2** EXTRAÑO : alien **3 ~ a** : foreign to

ajetreado, -da *adj* : hectic, busy —

ajetrearse *vr* : bustle about — **ajetreo** *nm* : hustle and bustle

ají *nm, pl* **ajíes** *Lat* : chili pepper

ajo *nm* : garlic

ajustar *vt* 1 : adjust, adapt 2 ACORDAR : agree on 3 SALDAR : settle — **ajustarse** *vr* : fit, conform — **ajustable** *adj* : adjustable — **ajustado, -da** *adj* 1 : close, tight 2 CEÑIDO : tight-fitting — **ajuste** *nm* : adjustment

ajusticiar *vt* : execute, put to death

al (*contraction of* **a** *and* **el**) → **a²**

ala *nf* 1 : wing 2 : brim (of a hat)

alabanza *nf* : praise — **alabar** *vt* : praise

alacena *nf* : cupboard, larder

alacrán *nm, pl* **-cranes** : scorpion

alado, -da *adj* : winged

alambre *nm* : wire

alameda *nf* 1 : poplar grove 2 : tree-lined avenue — **álamo** *nm* : poplar

alarde *nm* : show, display — **alardear** *vi* : boast

alargar {52} *vt* 1 : extend, lengthen 2 PROLONGAR : prolong — **alargarse** *vr* : become longer — **alargador** *nm* : extension cord

alarido *nm* : howl, shriek

alarmar *vt* : alarm — **alarma** *nf* : alarm — **alarmante** *adj* : alarming

alba *nf* : dawn

albahaca *nf* : basil

albañil *nm* : bricklayer, mason

albaricoque *nm* : apricot

albedrío *nm* **libre ~** : free will

alberca *nf* 1 : reservoir, tank 2 *Lat* : swimming pool

albergar {52} *vt* : house, lodge — **albergue** *nm* 1 : lodging 2 REFUGIO : shelter 3 **~ juvenil** : youth hostel

albóndiga *nf* : meatball

alborear *v impers* : dawn — **albor** *nm* : dawning — **alborada** *nf* : dawn

alborotar *vt* : excite, stir up — *vi* : make a racket — **alborotarse** *vr* : get excited — **alborotado, -da** *adj* : excited, agitated — **alborotador, -dora** *n* : agitator, rioter — **alboroto** *nm* : ruckus

alborozar {21} *vt* : gladden — **alborozo** *nm* : joy

álbum *nm* : album

alcachofa *nf* : artichoke

alcalde, -desa *n* : mayor

alcance *nm* 1 : reach 2 ÁMBITO : range, scope

alcancía *nf* : money box

alcantarilla *nf* : sewer, drain

alcanzar {21} *vt* 1 : reach 2 LLEGAR A : catch up with 3 LOGRAR : achieve, attain — *vi* 1 : suffice, be enough 2 **~ a** : manage to

alcaparra *nf* : caper

alcázar *nm* : fortress, castle

alce *nm* : moose, European elk

alcoba *nf* : bedroom

alcohol *nm* : alcohol — **alcohólico, -ca** *adj & n* : alcoholic — **alcoholismo** *nm* : alcoholism

aldaba *nf* : door knocker

aldea *nf* : village — **aldeano, -na** *n* : villager

aleación *nf, pl* **-ciones** : alloy

aleatorio, -ria *adj* : random

aleccionar *vt* : instruct, teach

aledaño, -ña *adj* : bordering — **aledaños** *nmpl* : outskirts

alegar {52} *vt* : assert, allege — *vi Lat* : argue — **alegato** *nm* 1 : allegation (in law) 2 *Lat* : argument

alegoría *nf* : allegory — **alegórico, -ca** *adj* : allegorical

alegrar *vt* : make happy, cheer up — **alegrarse** *vr* : be glad — **alegre** *adj* 1 CONTENTO : glad, happy 2 : colorful, bright — **alegremente** *adv* : happily — **alegría** *nf* : joy, cheer

alejar *vt* 1 : remove, move away 2 ENAJENAR : estrange — **alejarse** *vr* : move away, drift apart — **alejado, -da** *adj* : remote — **alejamiento** *nm* 1 : removal 2 : estrangement (of persons)

alemán, -mana *adj, mpl* **-manes** : German — **alemán** *nm* : German (language)

alentar {55} *vt* : encourage — **alentador, -dora** *adj* : encouraging

alergia *nf* : allergy — **alérgico, -ca** *adj* : allergic

alero *nm* : eaves *pl*

alertar *vt* : alert — **alerta** *adv* : on the alert — **alerta** *adj & nf* : alert

aleta *nf* 1 : fin, flipper 2 : small wing

alevosía *nf* : treachery — **alevoso, -sa** *adj* : treacherous

alfabeto *nm* : alphabet — **alfabético, -ca** *adj* : alphabetical — **alfabetismo** *nm* : literacy — **alfabetizar** {21} *vt* 1 : teach literacy 2 : alphabetize

alfalfa *nf* : alfalfa

alfarería *nf* : pottery

alféizar *nm* : sill, windowsill

alfil *nm* : bishop (in chess)

alfiler *nm* 1 : pin 2 BROCHE : brooch — **alfiletero** *nm* : pincushion

alfombra *nf* : carpet, rug — **alfombrilla** *nf* : small rug, mat

alga *nf* : seaweed

álgebra *nf* : algebra

algo *pron* **1** : something **2** ~ **de** : some, a little — ~ *adv* : somewhat, rather

algodón *nm, pl* **-dones** : cotton

alguacil *nm* : constable, bailiff

alguien *pron* : somebody, someone

alguno, -na *adj* (**algún** *before masculine singular nouns*) **1** : some, any **2** (*in negative constructions*) : not any, not at all **3 algunas veces** : sometimes — ~ *pron* **1** : one, someone, somebody **2 algunos, -nas** *pron pl* : some, a few

alhaja *nf* : jewel

alharaca *nf* : fuss

aliado, -da *n* : ally — ~ *adj* : allied — **alianza** *nf* : alliance — **aliarse** {85} *vr* : form an alliance

alias *adv & nm* : alias

alicaído, -da *adj* : depressed

alicates *nmpl* : pliers

aliciente *nm* **1** : incentive **2** : attraction (to a place)

alienar *vt* : alienate — **alienación** *nf, pl* **-ciones** : alienation

aliento *nm* **1** : breath **2** ÁNIMO : encouragement, strength

aligerar *vt* **1** : lighten **2** APRESURAR : hasten, quicken

alimaña *nf* : pest, vermin

alimentar *vt* : feed, nourish — **alimentarse** *vr* ~ **con** : live on — **alimentación** *nf, pl* **-ciones** **1** : feeding **2** NUTRICIÓN : nourishment — **alimenticio, -cia** *adj* : nourishing — **alimento** *nm* : food, nourishment

alinear *vt* : align, line up — **alinearse** *vr* ~ **con** : align oneself with — **alineación** *nf, pl* **-ciones** **1** : alignment **2** : lineup (in sports)

aliño *nm* : dressing, seasoning — **aliñar** *vt* : season, dress

alisar *vt* : smooth

alistarse *vr* : join up, enlist — **alistamiento** *nm* : enlistment

aliviar *vt* : relieve, soothe — **aliviarse** *vr* : recover, get better — **alivio** *nm* : relief

aljibe *nm* : cistern, tank

allá *adv* **1** : there, over there **2 más** ~ : farther away **3 más** ~ **de** : beyond

allanar *vt* **1** : smooth, level out **2** *Spain* : break into (a house) **3** *Lat* : raid — **allanamiento** *nm* **1** *Spain* : breaking and entering **2** *Lat* : raid

allegado, -da *n* : close friend, relation

allí *adv* : there, over there

alma *nf* : soul

almacén *nm, pl* **-cenes** **1** : warehouse **2** *Lat* : shop, store **3 grandes almacenes** : department store — **alma-**

cenamiento *or* **almacenaje** *nm* : storage — **almacenar** *vt* : store

almádena *nf* : sledgehammer

almanaque *nm* : almanac

almeja *nf* : clam

almendra *nf* **1** : almond **2** : kernel (of nuts, fruit, etc.)

almiar *nm* : haystack

almíbar *nm* : syrup

almidón *nm, pl* **-dones** : starch — **almidonar** *vt* : starch

almirante *nm* : admiral

almohada *nf* : pillow — **almohadilla** *nf* : small pillow, pad — **almohadón** *nm, pl* **-dones** : bolster, large cushion

almorranas *nfpl* : hemorrhoids, piles

almorzar {36} *vi* : have lunch — *vt* : have for lunch — **almuerzo** *nm* : lunch

alocado, -da *adj* : crazy, wild

áloe *or* **aloe** *nm* : aloe

alojar *vt* : house, lodge — **alojarse** *vr* : lodge, room — **alojamiento** *nm* : lodging, accommodations *pl*

alondra *nf* : lark

alpaca *nf* : alpaca

alpinismo *nm* : mountain climbing — **alpinista** *nmf* : mountain climber

alpiste *nm* : birdseed

alquilar *vt* : rent, lease — **alquilarse** *vr* : be for rent — **alquiler** *nm* : rent, rental

alquitrán *nm, pl* **-tranes** : tar

alrededor *adv* **1** : around, about **2** ~ **de** : approximately — **alrededor de** *prep phr* : around — **alrededores** *nmpl* : outskirts

alta *nf* : discharge (of a patient)

altanería *nf* : haughtiness — **altanero, -ra** *adj* : haughty

altar *nm* : altar

altavoz *nm, pl* **-voces** : loudspeaker

alterar *vt* **1** : alter, modify **2** PERTURBAR : disturb — **alterarse** *vr* : get upset — **alteración** *nf, pl* **-ciones** **1** : alteration **2** ALBOROTO : disturbance — **alterado, -da** *adj* : upset

altercado *nm* : altercation, argument

alternar *vi* **1** : alternate **2** ~ **con** : socialize with — *vt* : alternate — **alternarse** *vr* : take turns — **alternativa** *nf* : alternative — **alternativo, -va** *adj* : alternating, alternative — **alterno, -na** *adj* : alternate

Alteza *nf* : Highness

altiplano *nm* : high plateau

altitud *nf* : altitude

altivez *nf, pl* **-veces** : haughtiness — **altivo, -va** *adj* : haughty

alto, -ta *adj* **1** : tall, high **2** RUIDOSO

: loud — **alto** *adv* **1** ARRIBA : high **2**
: loud, loudly — ~ *nm* **1** ALTURA
: height, elevation **2** : stop, halt — ~
interj : halt!, stop! — **altoparlante** *nm*
Lat : loudspeaker
altruista *adj* : altruistic — **altruismo**
nm : altruism
altura *nf* **1** : height **2** ALTITUD : altitude
3 a la ~ de : near, up by
alubia *nf* : kidney bean
alucinar *vi* : hallucinate — **alucinación**
nf, pl **-ciones** : hallucination
alud *nm* : avalanche
aludir *vi* : allude, refer — **aludido, -da**
adj **darse por ~** : take it personally
alumbrar *vt* **1** : light, illuminate **2** PARIR
: give birth to — **alumbrado** *nm*
: (electric) lighting — **alumbramien-**
to *nm* : childbirth
aluminio *nm* : aluminum
alumno, -na *n* : pupil, student
alusión *nf, pl* **-siones** : allusion
aluvión *nm, pl* **-viones** : flood, barrage
alzar {21} *vt* : lift, raise — **alzarse** *vr*
: rise (up) — **alza** *nf* : rise — **alza-**
miento *nm* : uprising
ama → amo
amabilidad *nf* : kindness — **amable**
adj : kind, nice
amaestrar *vt* : train
amagar {52} *vt* **1** : show signs of **2**
AMENAZAR : threaten — *vi* : be imminent — **amago** *nm* **1** INDICIO : sign **2**
AMENAZA : threat
amainar *vi* : abate
amamantar *v* : breast-feed, nurse
amanecer {53} *v impers* : dawn — *vi*
: wake up — ~ *nm* : dawn, daybreak
amanerado *adj* : affected, mannered
amansar *vt* **1** : tame **2** APACIGUAR
: soothe — **amansarse** *vr* : calm down
amante *adj* ~ **de** : fond of — ~ *nmf*
: lover
amañar *vt* : rig, tamper with
amapola *nf* : poppy
amar *vt* : love
amargar {52} *vt* : make bitter — **amar-**
gado, -da *adj* : embittered — **amar-**
go, -ga *adj* : bitter — **amargo** *nm*
: bitterness — **amargura** *nf* : bitterness, grief
amarillo, -lla *adj* : yellow — **amarillo**
nm : yellow
amarrar *vt* **1** : moor **2** ATAR : tie up
amasar *vt* **1** : knead **2** : amass (a fortune, etc.)
amateur *adj & nmf* : amateur
amatista *nf* : amethyst
ambages *nmpl* **sin ~** : without hesitation, straight to the point

ámbar *nm* : amber
ambición *nf, pl* **-ciones** : ambition —
ambicionar *vt* : aspire to — **ambi-**
cioso, -sa *adj* : ambitious
ambiente *nm* **1** AIRE : atmosphere **2**
MEDIO : environment, surroundings *pl*
— **ambiental** *adj* : environmental
ambigüedad *nf* : ambiguity — **am-**
biguo, -gua *adj* : ambiguous
ámbito *nm* : domain, sphere
ambos, -bas *adj & pron* : both
ambulancia *nf* : ambulance
ambulante *adj* : traveling, itinerant
ameba *nf* : amoeba
amedrentar *vt* : intimidate
amén *nm* **1** : amen **2** ~ **de** : in addition
to
amenazar {21} *vt* : threaten — **ame-**
naza *nf* : threat, menace
amenizar {21} *vt* : make pleasant, enliven — **ameno, -na** *adj* : pleasant
americano, -na *adj* : American
ameritar *vt Lat* : deserve
ametralladora *nf* : machine gun
amianto *nm* : asbestos
amiba → ameba
amígdala *nf* : tonsil — **amigdalitis** *nf*
: tonsilitis
amigo, -ga *adj* : friendly, close — ~ *n*
: friend — **amigable** *adj* : friendly
amilanar *vt* : daunt — **amilanarse** *vr*
: lose heart
aminorar *vt* : diminish
amistad *nf* : friendship — **amistoso,**
-sa *adj* : friendly
amnesia *nf* : amnesia
amnistía *nf* : amnesty
amo, ama *n* **1** : master *m*, mistress *f* **2**
ama de casa : homemaker, house-
wife **3 ama de llaves** : housekeeper
amodorrado, -da *adj* : drowsy
amolar {19} *vt* **1** : grind, sharpen **2** MO-
LESTAR : annoy
amoldar *vt* : adapt, adjust —
amoldarse *vr* ~ **a** : adapt to
amonestar *vt* : admonish, warn —
amonestación *nf, pl* **-ciones** : admo-
nition, warning
amoníaco *or* **amoniaco** *nm* : ammonia
amontonar *vt* : pile up — **amon-**
tonarse *vr* : pile up (of things), form a
crowd (of persons)
amor *nm* : love
amordazar {21} *vt* : gag
amorío *nm* : love affair — **amoroso,**
-sa *adj* **1** : loving **2** *Lat* : sweet, lovable
amortado, -da *adj* : black-and-blue
amortiguar {10} *vt* : muffle, soften,
tone down — **amortiguador** *nm*
: shock absorber

amortizar {21} *vt* : pay off — **amortización** *nf* : repayment
amotinar *vt* : incite (to riot) — **amotinarse** *vr* : riot, rebel
amparar *vt* : shelter, protect — **ampararse** *vr* 1 ~ **de** : take shelter from 2 ~ **en** : have recourse to — **amparo** *nm* : refuge, protection
ampliar {85} *vt* 1 : expand 2 : enlarge (a photograph) — **ampliación** *nf, pl* **-ciones** 1 : expansion, enlargement 2 : extension (of a building)
amplificar {72} *vt* : amplify — **amplificador** *nm* : amplifier
amplio, -plia *adj* : broad, wide, ample — **amplitud** *nf* 1 : breadth, extent 2 ESPACIOSIDAD : spaciousness
ampolla *nf* 1 : blister 2 : vial, ampoule — **ampollarse** *vr* : blister
ampuloso, -sa *adj* : pompous
amputar *vt* : amputate — **amputación** *nf, pl* **-ciones** : amputation
amueblar *vt* : furnish (a house, etc.)
amurallar *vt* : wall in
anacardo *nm* : cashew nut
anaconda *nf* : anaconda
anacrónico, -ca *adj* : anachronistic — **anacronismo** *nm* : anachronism
ánade *nmf* : duck
anagrama *nm* : anagram
anales *nmpl* : annals
analfabeto, -ta *adj & n* : illiterate — **analfabetismo** *nm* : illiteracy
analgésico *nm* : painkiller, analgesic
analizar {21} *vt* : analyze — **análisis** *nm* : analysis — **analítico, -ca** *adj* : analytical, analytic
analogía *nf* : analogy — **análogo, -ga** *adj* : analogous
ananá *or* **ananás** *nm, pl* **-nás** : pineapple
anaquel *nm* : shelf
anaranjado, -da *adj* : orange-colored
anarquía *nf* : anarchy — **anarquista** *adj & nmf* : anarchist
anatomía *nf* : anatomy — **anatómico, -ca** *adj* : anatomic, anatomical
anca *nf* 1 : haunch 2 ~**s de rana** : frogs' legs
ancestral *adj* : ancestral
ancho, -cha *adj* : wide, broad, ample — **ancho** *nm* : width
anchoa *nf* : anchovy
anchura *nf* : width, breadth
anciano, -na *adj* : aged, elderly — ~ *n* : elderly person
ancla *nf* : anchor — **anclar** *v* : anchor
andadas *nfpl* 1 : tracks 2 **volver a las** ~ : go back to one's old ways
andadura *nf* : walking, journey

andaluz, -luza *adj & n, mpl* **-luces** : Andalusian
andamio *nm* : scaffold
andanada *nf* 1 : volley 2 **soltar una** ~ : reprimand
andanzas *nfpl* : adventures
andar {6} *vi* 1 CAMINAR : walk 2 IR : go, travel 3 FUNCIONAR : run, work 4 ~ **en** : rummage around in 5 ~ **por** : be approximately — *vt* : cover, travel — ~ *nm* : gait, walk
andén *nm, pl* **-denes** 1 : (train) platform 2 *Lat* : sidewalk
andino, -na *adj* : Andean
andorrano, -na *adj* : Andorran
andrajos *nmpl* : tatters — **andrajoso, -sa** *adj* : ragged
anécdota *nf* : anecdote
anegar {52} *vt* : flood — **anegarse** *vr* 1 : be flooded 2 AHOGARSE : drown
anemia *nf* : anemia — **anémico, -ca** *adj* : anemic
anestesia *nf* : anesthesia — **anestésico, -ca** *adj* : anesthetic — **anestésico** *nm* : anesthetic
anexar *vt* : annex, attach — **anexo, -xa** *adj* : attached — **anexo** *nm* : annex
anfibio, -bia *adj* : amphibious — **anfibio** *nm* : amphibian
anfiteatro *nm* : amphitheater
anfitrión, -triona *n, mpl* **-triones** : host, hostess *f*
ángel *nm* : angel — **angelical** *adj* : angelic, angelical
angloparlante *adj* : English-speaking
anglosajón, -jona *adj, mpl* **-jones** : Anglo-Saxon
angosto, -ta *adj* : narrow
anguila *nf* : eel
ángulo *nm* 1 : angle 2 ESQUINA : corner — **angular** *adj* : angular — **anguloso, -sa** *adj* : angular
angustiar *vt* 1 : anguish, distress 2 INQUIETAR : worry — **angustiarse** *vr* : get upset — **angustia** *nf* 1 : anguish 2 INQUIETUD : worry — **angustioso, -sa** *adj* 1 : anguished 2 INQUIETANTE : distressing
anhelar *vt* : yearn for, crave — **anhelante** *adj* : yearning, longing — **anhelo** *nm* : longing
anidar *vi* : nest
anillo *nm* : ring
ánima *n* : soul
animación *nf, pl* **-ciones** 1 VIVEZA : liveliness 2 BULLICIO : hustle and bustle — **animado, -da** *adj* : cheerful, animated — **animador, -dora** *n* 1 : (television) host 2 : cheerleader

animadversión *nf, pl* **-siones** : animosity

animal *nm* : animal — **~** *nmf* : brute, beast — **~** *adj* : brutish

animar *vt* **1** ALENTAR : encourage **2** ALEGAR : cheer up — **animarse** *vr* **1** : liven up **2 ~ a** : get up the nerve to

ánimo *nm* **1** : spirit, soul **2** HUMOR : mood, spirits *pl* **3** ALIENTO : encouragement

animosidad *nf* : animosity, ill will

animoso, -sa *adj* : spirited, brave

aniquilar *vt* : annihilate — **aniquilación** *n, pl* **-ciones** : annihilation

anís *nm* : anise

aniversario *nm* : anniversary

ano *nm* : anus

anoche *adv* : last night

anochecer {53} *vi* : get dark — **~** *nm* : dusk, nightfall

anodino, -na *adj* : insipid, dull

anomalía *nf* : anomaly

anonadado, -da *adj* : dumbfounded

anónimo, -ma *adj* : anonymous — **anonimato** *nm* : anonymity

anorexia *nf* : anorexia

anormal *adj* : abnormal — **anormalidad** *nf* : abnormality

anotar *vt* **1** : annotate **2** APUNTAR : jot down — **anotación** *nf, pl* **-ciones** : annotation, note

anquilosarse *vr* **1** : become paralyzed **2** ESTANCARSE : stagnate — **anquilosamiento** *nm* **1** : paralysis **2** ESTANCAMIENTO : stagnation

ansiar {85} *vt* : long for — **ansia** *nf* **1** INQUIETUD : uneasiness **2** ANGUSTIA : anguish **3** ANHELO : longing — **ansiedad** *nf* : anxiety — **ansioso, -sa** *adj* **1** : anxious **2** DESEOSO : eager

antagónico, -ca *adj* : antagonistic — **antagonismo** *nm* : antagonism — **antagonista** *nmf* : antagonist

antaño *adv* : yesteryear, long ago

antártico, -ca *adj* : antarctic

ante[1] *nm* **1** : elk, moose **2** GAMUZA : suede

ante[2] *prep* **1** : before, in front of **2** : in view of **3 ~ todo** : above all

anteanoche *adv* : the night before last

anteayer *adv* : the day before yesterday

antebrazo *nm* : forearm

anteceder *vt* : precede — **antecedente** *adj* : previous, prior — **~** *nm* : precedent — **antecesor, -sora** *n* **1** : ancestor **2** PREDECESOR : predecessor

antedicho, -cha *adj* : aforesaid

antelación *nf, pl* **-ciones 1** : advance notice **2 con ~** : in advance

antemano *adv* **de ~** : beforehand

antena *nf* : antenna

antenoche → anteanoche

anteojos *nmpl* **1** : glasses, eyeglasses **2 ~ bifocales** : bifocals

antepasado, -da *n* : ancestor

antepecho *nm* : ledge

antepenúltimo, -ma *adj* : third from last

anteponer {60} *vt* **1** : place before **2** PREFERIR : prefer

anterior *adj* **1** : previous, earlier **2** DELANTERO : front — **anterioridad** *nf* **con ~** : beforehand, in advance — **anteriormente** *adv* : previously

antes *adv* **1** : before, earlier **2** ANTERIORMENTE : previously **3** PRIMERO : first **4** MEJOR : rather **5 ~ de** : before, previous to **6 ~ que** : before

antesala *nf* : waiting room

antiaéreo, -rea *adj* : antiaircraft

antibiótico *nm* : antibiotic

anticipar *vt* **1** : move up (a date, etc.) **2** : pay in advance — **anticiparse** *vr* **1** : be early **2** ADELANTARSE : get ahead — **anticipación** *nf, pl* **-ciones 1** : anticipation **2 con ~** : in advance — **anticipado, -da** *adj* **1** : advance, early **2 por ~** : in advance — **anticipo** *nm* **1** : advance (payment) **2** : foretaste

anticoncepción *nf, pl* **-ciones** : contraception — **anticonceptivo, -va** *adj* : contraceptive — **anticonceptivo** *nm* : contraceptive

anticongelante *nm* : antifreeze

anticuado, -da *adj* : antiquated, outdated

anticuario, -ria *n* : antique dealer — **anticuario** *nm* : antique shop

anticuerpo *nm* : antibody

antídoto *nm* : antidote

antier → anteayer

antiestético, -ca *adj* : unsightly

antifaz *nm, pl* **-faces** : mask

antífona *nf* : anthem

antigualla *nf* : relic, old thing

antiguo, -gua *adj* **1** : ancient, old **2** ANTERIOR : former **3** ANTICUADO : old-fashioned **4 muebles antiguos** : antique furniture — **antiguamente** *adv* **1** : long ago **2** ANTES : formerly — **antigüedad** *nf* **1** : antiquity **2** : seniority (in the workplace) **3 ~es** *nfpl* : antiques

antihigiénico, -ca *adj* : unsanitary

antihistamínico *nm* : antihistamine

antiinflamatorio, -ria *adj* : anti-inflammatory

antílope *nm* : antelope

antinatural *adj* : unnatural

antipatía *nf* : aversion, dislike — **antipático, -ca** *adj* : unpleasant
antirreglamentario, -ria *adj* : unlawful
antirrobo, -ba *adj* : antitheft
antisemita *adj* : anti-Semitic — **antisemitismo** *nm* : anti-Semitism
antiséptico, -ca *adj* : antiseptic — **antiséptico** *nm* : antiseptic
antisocial *adj* : antisocial
antítesis *nf* : antithesis
antojarse *vr* 1 APETECER : crave 2 PARECER : seem, appear — **antojadizo, -za** *adj* : capricious — **antojo** *nm* : whim, craving
antología *nf* : anthology
antorcha *nf* : torch
antro *nm* : dive, den
antropófago, -ga *nmf* : cannibal
antropología *nf* : anthropology
anual *adj* : annual, yearly — **anualidad** *nf* : annuity — **anuario** *nm* : yearbook, annual
anudar *vt* : knot — **anudarse** *vr* : tie, knot
anular *vt* 1 : annul, cancel — **anulación** *nf, pl* **-ciones** : annulment, cancellation
anunciar *vt* 1 : announce 2 : advertise (products) — **anunciante** *nmf* : advertiser — **anuncio** *nm* 1 : announcement 2 *or* ~ **publicitario** : advertisement
anzuelo *nm* 1 : fishhook 2 **morder el** ~ : take the bait
añadir *vt* : add — **añadidura** *nf* 1 : additive, addition 2 **por** ~ : in addition, furthermore
añejo, -ja *adj* : aged, vintage
añicos *nmpl* **hacer(se)** ~ : smash to pieces
añil *adj & nm* : indigo (color)
año *nm* 1 : year 2 **Año Nuevo** : New Year
añorar *vt* : long for, miss — **añoranza** *nf* : nostalgia
añoso, -sa *adj* : aged, old
aorta *nf* : aorta
apabullar *vt* : overwhelm
apacentar {55} *vt* : pasture, graze
apachurrar *vt Lat* : crush
apacible *adj* : gentle, mild
apaciguar {10} *vt* : appease, pacify — **apaciguarse** *vr* : calm down
apadrinar *vt* 1 : be a godparent to 2 : sponsor (an artist, etc.)
apagar {52} *vt* 1 : turn or switch off 2 EXTINGUIR : extinguish, put out — **apagarse** *vr* 1 EXTINGUIRSE : go out 2 : die down — **apagado, -da** *adj* 1 : off, out 2 : dull, subdued (of colors, sounds, etc.) — **apagador** *nm Lat*

: (light) switch — **apagón** *nm, pl* **-gones** : blackout
apalancar {72} *vt* 1 LEVANTAR : jack up 2 ABRIR : pry open — **apalancamiento** *nm* : leverage
apalear *vt* : beat up, thrash
aparador *nm* 1 : sideboard 2 *Lat* : shop window
aparato *nm* 1 : machine, appliance, apparatus 2 : system (in anatomy) 3 OSTENTACIÓN : ostentation — **aparatoso, -sa** *adj* 1 : ostentatious 2 ESPECTACULAR : spectacular
aparcar {72} *v Spain* : park — **aparcamiento** *nm Spain* 1 : parking 2 : parking lot
aparcero, -ra *n* : sharecropper
aparear *vt* : mate, pair up — **aparearse** *vr* : mate
aparecer {53} *vi* 1 : appear 2 PRESENTARSE : show up — **aparecerse** *vr* : appear
aparejar *vt* 1 : rig (a ship) 2 : harness (an animal) — **aparejado, -da** *adj* **llevar** ~ : entail — **aparejo** *nm* 1 : equipment, gear 2 : harness (for an animal) 3 : rigging (for a ship)
aparentar *vt* 1 : seem 2 FINGIR : feign — **aparente** *adj* : apparent, seeming
aparición *nf, pl* **-ciones** 1 : appearance 2 FANTASMA : apparition — **apariencia** *nf* 1 : appearance, look 2 **en** ~ : apparently
apartado *nm* 1 : section, paragraph 2 ~ **postal** : post office box
apartamento *nm* : apartment
apartar *vt* 1 ALEJAR : move away 2 SEPARAR : set aside, separate — **apartarse** *vr* 1 : move away 2 DESVIARSE : stray — **aparte** *adv* 1 : apart, separately 2 ADEMÁS : besides
apasionar *vt* : excite, fascinate — **apasionarse** *vr* : get excited — **apasionado, -da** *adj* : passionate, excited — **apasionante** *adj* : exciting
apatía *nf* : apathy — **apático, -ca** *adj* : apathetic
apearse *vr* 1 : dismount 2 : get out of or off (a vehicle)
apedrear *vt* : stone
apegarse {52} *vr* ~ **a** : become attached to, grow fond of — **apegado, -da** *adj* : devoted — **apego** *nm* : fondness
apelar *vi* 1 : appeal 2 ~ **a** : resort to — **apelación** *nf, pl* **-ciones** : appeal
apellido *nm* : last name, surname — **apellidarse** *vr* : have for a last name
apenar *vt* : sadden — **apenarse** *vr* 1 : grieve 2 *Lat* : become embarrassed

apenas *adv* : hardly, scarcely — ~ *conj* : as soon as

apéndice *nm* : appendix — **apendicitis** *nf* : appendicitis

apercibir *vt* **1** : warn **2** *Lat* : notice — **apercibirse** *vr* ~ **de** : notice — **apercibimiento** *nm* : warning

aperitivo *nm* **1** : appetizer **2** : aperitif

apero *nm* : tool, implement

apertura *nf* : opening

apesadumbrar *vt* : sadden — **apesadumbrarse** *vr* : be weighed down

apestar *vi* : stink — **apestoso, -sa** *adj* : stinking, foul

apetecer {53} *vt* : crave, long for — **apetecible** *adj* : appealing

apetito *nm* : appetite — **apetitoso, -sa** *adj* : appetizing

ápice *nm* **1** : apex, summit **2** PIZCA : bit, smidgen

apilar *vt* : pile up — **apilarse** *vr* : pile up

apiñar *vt* : pack, cram — **apiñarse** *vr* : crowd together

apio *nm* : celery

apisonadora *nf* : steamroller

aplacar {72} *vt* : appease, placate — **aplacarse** *vr* : calm down

aplanar *vt* : flatten, level

aplastar *vt* : crush — **aplastante** *adj* : overwhelming

aplaudir *v* : applaud — **aplauso** *nm* **1** : applause **2** : acclaim

aplazar {21} *vt* : postpone, defer — **aplazamiento** *nm* : postponement

aplicar {72} *vt* : apply — **aplicarse** *vr* : apply oneself — **aplicable** *adj* : applicable — **aplicación** *nf, pl* **-ciones** : application — **aplicado, -da** *adj* : diligent

aplomo *nm* : aplomb

apocarse {72} *vr* : belittle oneself — **apocado, -da** *adj* : timid — **apocamiento** *nm* : timidity

apodar *vt* : nickname

apoderar *vt* : empower — **apoderarse** *vr* ~ **de** : seize — **apoderado, -da** *n* : agent, proxy

apodo *nm* : nickname

apogeo *nm* : peak, height

apología *nf* : defense, apology

apoplegía *nf* : stroke, apoplexy

aporrear *vt* : bang on, beat

aportar *vt* : contribute — **aportación** *nf, pl* **-ciones** : contribution

apostar[1] {19} *v* : bet, wager

apostar[2] *vt* : station, post

apostillar *vt* : annotate — **apostilla** *nf* : note

apóstol *nm* : apostle

apóstrofo *nm* : apostrophe

apostura *nf* : elegance, grace

apoyar *vt* **1** : support **2** INCLINAR : lean, rest — **apoyarse** *vr* ~ **en** : lean on, rest on — **apoyo** *nm* : support

apreciar *vt* ESTIMAR : appreciate **2** EVALUAR : appraise — **apreciable** *adj* : considerable — **apreciación** *nf, pl* **-ciones 1** : appreciation **2** VALORACIÓN : appraisal — **aprecio** *nm* **1** : appraisal **2** ESTIMA : esteem

aprehender *vt* : apprehend — **aprehensión** *nf, pl* **-siones** : apprehension, capture

apremiar *vt* : urge — *vi* : be urgent — **apremiante** *adj* : pressing, urgent — **apremio** *nm* : urgency

aprender *v* : learn — **aprenderse** *vr* : memorize

aprendiz, -diza *n, mpl* **-dices** : apprentice, trainee — **aprendizaje** *nm* : apprenticeship

aprensión *nf, pl* **-siones** : apprehension, dread — **aprensivo, -va** *adj* : apprehensive

apresar *vt* : capture, seize — **apresamiento** *nm* : seizure, capture

aprestar *vt* : make ready — **aprestarse** *vr* : get ready

apresurar *vt* : speed up — **apresurarse** *vr* : hurry — **apresuradamente** *adv* : hurriedly, hastily — **apresurado, -da** *adj* : in a rush

apretar {55} *vt* **1** : press, push (a button) **2** : tighten (a knot, etc.) **3** ESTRECHAR : squeeze — *vi* **1** : press (down) **2** : fit too tightly — **apretón** *nm, pl* **-tones 1** : squeeze **2** ~ **de manos** : handshake — **apretado, -da** *adj* **1** : tight **2** *fam* : tightfisted

aprieto *nm* : predicament, jam

aprisa *adv* : quickly

aprisionar *vt* : imprison

aprobar {19} *vt* **1** : approve of **2** : pass (an exam, etc.) — *vi* : pass — **aprobación** *nf, pl* **-ciones** : approval

apropiarse *vr* ~ **de** : take possession of, appropriate — **apropiación** *nf, pl* **-ciones** : appropriation — **apropiado, -da** *adj* : appropriate

aprovechar *vt* : take advantage of, make good use of — *vi* : be of use — **aprovecharse** *vr* ~ **de** : take advantage of — **aprovechado, -da** *adj* **1** : diligent **2** OPORTUNISTA : opportunistic

aproximar *vt* : bring closer — **aproximarse** *vr* : approach — **aproximación** *nf, pl* **-ciones** : approximation — **aproximadamente** *adv*

: approximately — **aproximado, -da** *adj* : approximate

apto, -ta *adj* 1 : suitable 2 CAPAZ : capable — **aptitud** *nf* : aptitude, capability

apuesta *nf* : bet, wager

apuesto, -ta *adj* : elegant, good-looking

apuntalar *vt* : prop up, shore up

apuntar *vt* 1 : aim, point 2 ANOTAR : jot down 3 SEÑALAR : point at 4 : prompt (in theater) — **apuntarse** *vr* 1 : sign up 2 : score, chalk up (a victory, etc.) — **apunte** *nm* : note

apuñalar *vt* : stab

apurar *vt* 1 : hurry, rush 2 AGOTAR : use up 3 PREOCUPAR : trouble — **apurarse** *vr* 1 : worry 2 *Lat* : hurry up — **apuradamente** *adv* : with difficulty — **apurado, -da** *adj* 1 : needy 2 DIFÍCIL : difficult 3 *Lat* : rushed — **apuro** *nm* 1 : predicament, jam 2 *Lat* : hurry

aquejar *vt* : afflict

aquel, aquella *adj, mpl* **aquellos** : that, those

aquél, aquélla *pron, mpl* **aquéllos** 1 : that (one), those (ones) 2 : the former

aquello *pron* : that, that matter

aquí *adv* 1 : here 2 AHORA : now 3 **por ~** : hereabouts

aquietar *vt* : calm — **aquietarse** *vr* : calm down

ara *nf* 1 : altar 2 **en ~s de** : for the sake of

árabe *adj* : Arab, Arabic — **~** *nm* : Arabic (language)

arado *nm* : plow

arancel *nm* : tariff

arándano *nm* : blueberry

araña *nf* 1 : spider 2 LÁMPARA : chandelier

arañar *v* : scratch, claw — **arañazo** *nm* : scratch

arar *v* : plow

arbitrar *v* 1 : arbitrate 2 : referee, umpire (in sports) — **arbitraje** *nm* : arbitration — **arbitrario, -ria** *adj* : arbitrary — **arbitrio** *nm* 1 : (free) will 2 JUICIO : judgment — **árbitro, -tra** *n* 1 : arbitrator 2 : referee, umpire (in sports)

árbol *nm* : tree — **arboleda** *nf* : grove

arbusto *nm* : shrub, bush

arca *nf* 1 : ark 2 COFRE : chest

arcada *nf* 1 : arcade 2 **~s** *nfpl* : retching

arcaico, -ca *adj* : archaic

arcano, -na *adj* : arcane, secret

arce *nm* : maple tree

archipiélago *nm* : archipelago

archivar *vt* : file — **archivador** *nm* : filing cabinet — **archivo** *nm* 1 : file 2 : archives *pl*

arcilla *nf* : clay

arco *nm* 1 : arch 2 : bow (in sports, music, etc.) 3 : arc (in geometry) 4 **~ iris** : rainbow

arder *vi* : burn

ardid *nm* : scheme, ruse

ardiente *adj* 1 : burning 2 FOGOSO : ardent

ardilla *nf* 1 : squirrel 2 **~ listada** : chipmunk

ardor *nm* 1 : burning 2 ENTUSIASMO : passion, ardor

arduo, -dua *adj* : arduous

área *nf* : area

arena *nf* 1 : sand 2 PALESTRA : arena — **arenoso, -sa** *adj* : sandy, gritty

arenque *nm* : herring

arete *nm* *Lat* : earring

argamasa *nf* : mortar

argentino, -na *adj* : Argentinian, Argentine

argolla *nf* : hoop, ring

argot *nm* : slang

argüir {41} *vt* 1 : argue 2 DEMOSTRAR : prove, show — *vi* : argue

argumentar *vt* : argue, contend — **argumentación** *nf, pl* **-ciones** : (line of) argument — **argumento** *nm* 1 : argument, reasoning 2 TRAMA : plot, story line

árido, -da *adj* : dry, arid — **aridez** *nf, pl* **-deces** : aridity

arisco, -ca *adj* : surly

aristocracia *nf* : aristocracy — **aristócrata** *nmf* : aristocrat — **aristocrático, -ca** *adj* : aristocratic

aritmética *nf* : arithmetic — **aritmético, -ca** *adj* : arithmetic, arithmetical

armar *vt* 1 : arm 2 MONTAR : assemble — **arma** *nf* 1 : arm, weapon 2 **~ de fuego** : firearm — **armada** *nf* : navy — **armado, -da** *adj* : armed — **armadura** *nf* 1 : armor 2 ARMAZÓN : framework — **armamento** *nm* : armament, arms *pl*

armario *nm* 1 : (clothes) closet 2 : cupboard, cabinet

armazón *nmf, pl* **-zones** : frame, framework

armisticio *nm* : armistice

armonizar {21} *vt* 1 : harmonize 2 : reconcile (differences, etc.) — *vi* : harmonize, go together — **armonía** *nf* : harmony — **armónica** *nf* : harmonica — **armónico, -ca** *adj* : harmonic — **armonioso, -sa** *adj* : harmonious

arnés *nm, pl* **-neses** : harness

aro *nm* 1 : hoop, ring 2 *Lat* : earring
aroma *nm* : aroma, scent — **aromático, -ca** *adj* : aromatic
arpa *nf* : harp
arpón *nm, pl* **-pones** : harpoon
arquear *vt* : arch, bend — **arquearse** *vr* : bend, bow
arqueología *nf* : archaeology — **arqueológico, -ca** *adj* : archaeological — **arqueólogo, -ga** *n* : archaeologist
arquero, -ra *n* 1 : archer 2 PORTERO : goalkeeper, goalie
arquetipo *nm* : archetype
arquitectura *nf* : architecture — **arquitecto, -ta** *n* : architect — **arquitectónico, -ca** *adj* : architectural
arrabal *nm* 1 : slum 2 **~es** *nmpl* : outskirts
arracimarse *vr* : cluster together
arraigar {52} *vi* : take root, become established — **arraigarse** *vr* : settle down — **arraigado, -da** *adj* : deeply rooted, well established — **arraigo** *nm* : roots *pl*
arrancar {72} *vt* 1 : pull out, tear off 2 : start (an engine), boot (a computer) — *vi* 1 : start an engine 2 : get going — **arranque** *nm* 1 : starter (of a car) 2 ARREBATO : outburst 3 **punto de ~** : starting point
arrasar *vt* 1 : destroy, devastate 2 LLENAR : fill to the brim
arrastrar *vt* 1 : drag 2 ATRAER : draw, attract — *vi* : hang down, trail — **arrastrarse** *vr* 1 : crawl, creep 2 HUMILLARSE : grovel — **arrastre** *nm* 1 : dragging 2 : trawling (for fish)
arrear *vt* : urge on
arrebatar *vt* 1 : snatch, seize 2 CAUTIVAR : captivate — **arrebatarse** *vr* : get carried away — **arrebatado, -da** *adj* : hotheaded, rash — **arrebato** *nm* : outburst
arreciar *vi* : intensify, worsen
arrecife *nm* : reef
arreglar *vt* 1 COMPONER : fix 2 ORDENAR : tidy up 3 SOLUCIONAR : solve, work out — **arreglarse** *vr* 1 : get dressed (up) 2 **arreglárselas** *fam* : get by, manage — **arreglado, -da** *adj* 1 : fixed, repaired 2 ORDENADO : tidy 3 SOLUCIONADO : settled, sorted out 4 ATAVIADO : smart, dressed-up — **arreglo** *nm* 1 : arrangement 2 REPARACIÓN : repair 3 ACUERDO : agreement
arremangarse {52} *vr* : roll up one's sleeves
arremeter *vi* : attack, charge — **arremetida** *nf* : attack, onslaught

arremolinarse *vr* 1 : crowd around, mill about 2 : swirl (about)
arrendar {55} *vt* : rent, lease — **arrendador, -dora** *n* : landlord, landlady *f* — **arrendamiento** *nm* : rent, rental — **arrendatario, -ria** *n* : tenant, renter
arrepentirse {76} *vr* 1 : regret, be sorry 2 : repent (for one's sins) — **arrepentido, -da** *adj* : repentant — **arrepentimiento** *nm* : regret, repentance
arrestar *vt* : arrest, detain — **arresto** *nm* : arrest
arriar *vt* : lower
arriba *adv* 1 (*indicating position*) : above, overhead 2 (*indicating direction*) : up, upwards 3 : upstairs (of a house) 4 **~ de** : more than 5 **de ~ abajo** : from top to bottom
arribar *vi* 1 : arrive 2 : dock, put into port — **arribista** *nmf* : parvenu, upstart — **arribo** *nm* : arrival
arriendo → **arrendimiento**
arriesgar {52} *vt* : risk, venture — **arriesgarse** *vr* : take a chance — **arriesgado, -da** *adj* : risky
arrimar *vt* : bring closer, draw near — **arrimarse** *vr* : approach
arrinconar *vt* 1 : corner, box in 2 ABANDONAR : push aside
arrobar *vt* : entrance — **arrobarse** *vr* : be enraptured — **arrobamiento** *nm* : rapture, ecstasy
arrodillarse *vr* : kneel (down)
arrogancia *nf* : arrogance — **arrogante** *adj* : arrogant
arrojar *vt* 1 : hurl, cast 2 EMITIR : give off, spew out 3 PRODUCIR : yield — **arrojarse** *vr* : throw oneself — **arrojado, -da** *adj* : daring — **arrojo** *nm* : boldness, courage
arrollar *vt* 1 : sweep away 2 DERROTAR : crush, overwhelm 3 : run over (with a vehicle) — **arrollador, -dora** *adj* : overwhelming
arropar *vt* : clothe, cover (up) — **arroparse** *vr* : wrap oneself up
arroyo *nm* 1 RIACHUELO : stream 2 : gutter (in a street)
arroz *nm, pl* **arroces** : rice
arrugar {52} *vt* : wrinkle, crease — **arrugarse** *vr* : get wrinkled — **arruga** *nf* : wrinkle, crease
arruinar *vt* : ruin, wreck — **arruinarse** *vr* 1 : be ruined 2 EMPOBRECERSE : go bankrupt
arrullar *vt* : lull to sleep — *vi* : coo — **arrullo** *nm* 1 : lullaby 2 : cooing (of doves)
arrumbar *vt* : lay aside
arsenal *nm* : arsenal

arsénico nm : arsenic
arte nmf (usually m in singular, f in plural) **1** : art **2** HABILIDAD : skill **3** ASTUCIA : cunning, cleverness **4** → **bello**
artefacto nm : artifact, device
arteria nf : artery
artesanía nm **1** : craftsmanship **2** : handicrafts pl — **artesanal** adj : handmade — **artesano, -na** n : artisan, craftsman
ártico, -ca adj : arctic
articular vt : articulate — **articulación** nf, pl **-ciones 1** : articulation, pronunciation **2** COYUNTURA : joint
artículo nm **1** : article **2** ∼s de **primera necesidad** : essentials **3** ∼s **de tocador** : toiletries
artífice nmf : artisan, craftsman
artificial adj : artificial
artificio nm **1** HABILIDAD : skill **2** APARATO : device **3** ARDID : artifice, ruse — **artificioso, -sa** adj : cunning, deceptive
artillería nf : artillery
artilugio nm : gadget
artimaña nf : ruse, trick
artista nmf **1** : artist **2** ACTOR : actor, actress f — **artístico, -ca** adj : artistic
artritis nms & pl : arthritis — **artrítico, -ca** adj : arthritic
arveja nf Lat : pea
arzobispo nm : archbishop
as nm : ace
asa nf : handle
asado, -da adj : roasted, grilled — **asado** nm : roast — **asador** nm : spit — **asaduras** nfpl : offal, entrails
asalariado, -da n : wage earner — ∼ adj : salaried
asaltar vt **1** : assault **2** ROBAR : mug, rob — **asaltante** nmf **1** : assailant **2** ATRACADOR : mugger, robber — **asalto** nm **1** : assault **2** ROBO : mugging, robbery
asamblea nf : assembly, meeting
asar vt : roast, grill — **asarse** vr fam : roast, feel the heat
asbesto nm : asbestos
ascender {56} vi **1** : ascend, rise up **2** : be promoted (in a job) **3** ∼ a : amount to — vt : promote — **ascendencia** nf : ancestry, descent — **ascendiente** nmf : ancestor — ∼ nm : influence — **ascensión** nf, pl **-siones** : ascent — **ascenso** nm **1** : ascent, rise **2** : promotion (in a job) — **ascensor** nm : elevator
asco nm **1** : disgust **2 hacer** ∼s **de** : turn up one's nose at **3 me da** ∼ : it makes me sick

ascua nf **1** : ember **2 estar en** ∼s fam : be on edge
asear vt : clean, tidy up — **asearse** vr : get cleaned up — **aseado, -da** adj : clean, tidy
asediar vt **1** : besiege **2** ACOSAR : harass — **asedio** nm **1** : siege **2** ACOSO : harassment
asegurar vt **1** : assure **2** FIJAR : secure **3** : insure (a car, house, etc.) — **asegurarse** vr : make sure
asemejarse vr **1** : be similar **2** ∼ a : look like, resemble
asentar {55} vt **1** : set down **2** INSTALAR : set up, establish **3** Lat : state — **asentarse** vr **1** : settle **2** ESTABLECERSE : settle down — **asentado, -da** adj : settled, established
asentir {76} vi : assent, agree — **asentimiento** nm : assent
aseo nm : cleanliness
asequible adj : accessible, attainable
aserrar {55} vt : saw — **aserradero** nm : sawmill — **aserrín** nm, pl **-rrines** : sawdust
asesinar vt **1** : murder **2** : assassinate — **asesinato** nm **1** : murder **2** : assassination — **asesino, -na** n **1** : murderer, killer **2** : assassin
asesorar vt : advise, counsel — **asesorarse** vr ∼ **de** : consult — **asesor, -sora** n : advisor, consultant — **asesoramiento** nm : advice, counsel
asestar {55} vt **1** : aim (a weapon) **2** : deal (a blow)
aseverar vt : assert — **aseveración** nf, pl **-ciones** : assertion
asfalto nm : asphalt
asfixiar vt : asphyxiate, suffocate — **asfixiarse** vr : suffocate — **asfixia** nf : asphyxiation, suffocation
así adv **1** : like this, like that, thus **2** ∼ **de** : so, that (much) **3** ∼ **que** : so, therefore **4** ∼ **que** : as soon as **5** ∼ **como** : as well as — ∼ adj : such, like that — ∼ conj AUNQUE : even though
asiático, -ca adj : Asian, Asiatic
asidero nm : handle
asiduo, -dua adj : frequent, regular
asiento nm : seat
asignar vt **1** : assign, allocate **2** DESTINAR : appoint — **asignación** nf, pl **-ciones 1** : assignment **2** SUELDO : salary, pay — **asignatura** nf : subject, course
asilo nm **1** : asylum, home **2** REFUGIO : refuge, shelter — **asilado, -da** n : inmate
asimilar vt : assimilate — **asimilarse** vr ∼ a : resemble

asimismo *adv* **1** : similarly, likewise **2** TAMBIÉN : as well, also

asir {7} *vt* : seize, grasp — **asirse** *vr* ~ **a** : cling to

asistir *vi* ~ **a** : attend, be present at — *vt* : assist — **asistencia** *nf* **1** : attendance **2** AYUDA : assistance — **asistente** *nmf* **1** : assistant **2** los ~**s** : those present

asma *nf* : asthma — **asmático, -ca** *adj* : asthmatic

asno *nm* : ass, donkey

asociar *vt* : associate — **asociarse** *vr* **1** : form a partnership **2** ~ **a** : join, become a member of — **asociación** *nf, pl* **-ciones** : association — **asociado, -da** *adj* : associate, associated — ~ *n* : associate, partner

asolar {19} *vt* : devastate

asomar *vt* : show, stick out — *vi* : appear, show — **asomarse** *vr* **1** : appear **2** : stick one's head out (of a window)

asombrar *vt* : amaze, astonish — **asombrarse** *vr* : be amazed — **asombro** *nm* : amazement, astonishment — **asombroso, -sa** *adj* : amazing, astonishing

asomo *nm* **1** : hint, trace **2** ni por ~ : by no means

aspaviento *nm* : exaggerated gestures, fuss

aspecto *nm* **1** : aspect **2** APARIENCIA : appearance, look

áspero, -ra *adj* : rough, harsh — **aspereza** *nf* : roughness, harshness

aspersión *nf, pl* **-siones** : sprinkling — **aspersor** *nm* : sprinkler

aspiración *nf, pl* **-ciones** **1** : breathing in **2** ANHELO : aspiration

aspiradora *nf* : vacuum cleaner

aspirar *vi* ~ **a** : aspire to — *vt* : inhale, breathe in — **aspirante** *nmf* : applicant, candidate

aspirina *nf* : aspirin

asquear *vt* : sicken, disgust

asquerosidad *nf* : filth, foulness — **asqueroso, -sa** *adj* : disgusting, sickening

asta *nf* **1** : flagpole **2** CUERNO : antler, horn **3** : shaft (of a spear) — **astado, -da** *adj* : horned

asterisco *nm* : asterisk

asteroide *nm* : asteroid

astigmatismo *nm* : astigmatism

astillar *vt* : splinter — **astilla** *nf* : splinter, chip

astillero *nm* : shipyard

astral *adj* : astral

astringente *adj & nm* : astringent

astro *nm* **1** : heavenly body **2** : star (of movies, etc.)

astrología *nf* : astrology

astronauta *nmf* : astronaut — **astronáutica** *nf* : astronautics

astronave *nf* : spaceship

astronomía *nf* : astronomy — **astronómico, -ca** *adj* : astronomical — **astrónomo, -ma** *n* : astronomer

astucia *nf* **1** : astuteness **2** ARDID : cunning, guile — **astuto, -ta** *adj* **1** : astute **2** TAIMADO : crafty

asueto *nm* : time off, break

asumir *vt* : assume — **asunción** *nf, pl* **-ciones** : assumption

asunto *nm* **1** : matter, affair **2** NEGOCIO : business

asustar *vt* : scare, frighten — **asustarse** *vr* ~ **de** : be frightened of — **asustadizo, -za** *adj* : jumpy, skittish — **asustado, -da** *adj* : frightened, afraid

atacar {72} *v* : attack — **atacante** *nmf* : attacker

atado *nm* : bundle

atadura *nf* : tie, bond

atajar *vt* : block, cut off — *vi* ~ **por** : take a shortcut through — **atajo** *nm* : shortcut

atañer {79} *vi* ~ **a** : concern, have to do with

ataque *nm* **1** : attack, assault **2** ACCESO : fit **3** ~ **de nervios** : nervous breakdown

atar *vt* : tie up, tie down — **atarse** *vr* : tie (up)

atardecer {53} *v impers* : get dark — ~ *nm* : late afternoon, dusk

atareado, -da *adj* : busy

atascar {72} *vt* **1** : block, clog **2** ESTORBAR : hinder — **atascarse** *vr* **1** OBSTRUIRSE : become obstructed **2** : get bogged down — **atasco** *nm* **1** : blockage **2** EMBOTELLAMIENTO : traffic jam

ataúd *nm* : coffin

ataviar {85} *vt* : dress (up) — **ataviarse** *vr* : dress up — **atavío** *nm* : attire

atemorizar {21} *vt* : frighten — **atemorizarse** *vr* : get scared

atención *nf, pl* **-ciones** **1** : attention **2** prestar ~ : pay attention **3** llamar la ~ : attract attention — ~ *interj* : attention!, watch out!

atender {56} *vt* **1** : attend to **2** CUIDAR : look after **3** : heed (advice, etc.) — *vi* : pay attention

atenerse {80} *vr* ~ **a** : abide by

atentamente *adv* **1** : attentively **2** le saluda ~ : sincerely yours

atentar {55} *vi* ~ **contra** : make an attempt on — **atentado** *nm* : attack

atento, -ta *adj* **1** : attentive, mindful **2** CORTÉS : courteous

atenuar {3} *vt* **1** : dim (lights), tone down (colors, etc.) **2** DISMINUIR : lessen — **atenuante** *nmf* : extenuating circumstances

ateo, atea *adj* : atheistic — ~ *n* : atheist

aterciopelado, -da *adj* : velvety, downy

aterido, -da *adj* : frozen stiff

aterrar {55} *vt* : terrify — **aterrador, -dora** *adj* : terrifying

aterrizar {21} *vi* : land — **aterrizaje** *nm* : landing

aterrorizar {21} *vt* : terrify

atesorar *vt* : hoard, amass

atestar {55} *vt* **1** : crowd, pack **2** : testify to (in law) — **atestado, -da** *adj* : stuffed, packed

atestiguar {10} *vt* : testify to

atiborrar *vt* : stuff, cram — **atiborrarse** *vr* : stuff oneself

ático *nm* **1** : penthouse **2** DESVÁN : attic

atildado, -da *adj* : smart, neat

atinar *vi* : be on target

atípico, -ca *adj* : atypical

atirantar *vt* : tighten

atisbar *vt* **1** : spy on **2** VISLUMBRAR : catch a glimpse of — **atisbo** *nm* : sign, hint

atizar {21} *vt* **1** : poke (a fire) **2** : rouse, stir up (passions, etc.) — **atizador** *nm* : poker

atlántico, -ca *adj* : Atlantic

atlas *nm* : atlas

atleta *nmf* : athlete — **atlético, -ca** *adj* : athletic — **atletismo** *nm* : athletics

atmósfera *nf* : atmosphere — **atmosférico, -ca** *adj* : atmospheric

atolondrado, -da *adj* **1** : scatterbrained **2** ATURDIDO : bewildered, dazed

átomo *nm* : atom — **atómico, -ca** *adj* : atomic — **atomizador** *nm* : atomizer

atónito, -ta *adj* : astonished, amazed

atontar *vt* : stun, daze

atorar *vt* : block — **atorarse** *vr* : get stuck

atormentar *vt* : torment, torture — **atormentarse** *vr* : torment oneself, agonize — **atormentador, -dora** *n* : tormenter

atornillar *vt* : screw

atorrante *nmf Lat* : bum, loafer

atosigar {52} *vt* : harass, annoy

atracar {72} *vi* : dock, land — *vt* : hold up, mug — **atracarse** *vr fam* ~ **de** : gorge oneself with — **atracadero** *nm* : dock, pier — **atracador, -dora** *n* : robber, mugger

atracción *nf, pl* **-ciones** : attraction

atraco *nm* : holdup, robbery

atractivo, -va *adj* : attractive — **atractivo** *nm* : attraction, appeal

atraer {81} *vt* : attract

atragantarse *vr* : choke

atrancar {72} *vt* : block, bar — **atrancarse** *vr* : get blocked, get stuck

atrapar *vt* : trap, capture

atrás *adv* **1** DETRÁS : back, behind **2** ANTES : before, earlier **3 para** ~ *or* **hacia** ~ : backwards

atrasar *vt* **1** : put back (a clock) **2** DEMORAR : delay — *vi* : lose time — **atrasarse** *vr* : fall behind — **atrasado, -da** *adj* **1** : late, overdue **2** : backward (of countries, etc.) **3** : slow (of a clock) — **atraso** *nm* **1** RETRASO : delay **2** : backwardness **3** ~**s** *nmpl* : arrears

atravesar {55} *vt* **1** CRUZAR : cross **2** TRASPASAR : pierce **3** : lay across (a road, etc.) **4** : go through (a situation) — **atravesarse** *vr* : be in the way

atrayente *adj* : attractive

atreverse *vr* : dare — **atrevido, -da** *adj* **1** : bold **2** INSOLENTE : insolent — **atrevimiento** *nm* **1** : boldness **2** DESCARO : insolence

atribuir {41} *vt* **1** : attribute **2** : confer (powers, etc.) — **atribuirse** *vr* : take credit for

atribular *vt* : afflict, trouble

atributo *nm* : attribute

atrincherar *vt* : entrench — **atrincherarse** *vr* : dig oneself in

atrocidad *nf* : atrocity

atronador, -dora *adj* : thunderous

atropellar *vt* **1** : run over **2** : violate, abuse (a person) — **atropellarse** *vr* : rush — **atropellado, -da** *adj* : hasty — **atropello** *nm* : abuse, outrage

atroz *adj, pl* **atroces** : atrocious

atuendo *nm* : attire

atufar *vt* : vex — **atufarse** *vr* : get angry

atún *nm, pl* **atunes** : tuna

aturdir *vt* **1** : stun, shock **2** CONFUNDIR : bewilder — **aturdido, -da** *adj* : dazed, bewildered

audaz *adj, pl* **-daces** : bold, daring — **audacia** *nf* : boldness, audacity

audible *adj* : audible

audición *nf, pl* **-ciones 1** : hearing **2** : audition (in theater, etc.)

audiencia *nf* : audience

audífono *nm* **1** : hearing aid **2** ~**s** *nmpl* *Lat* : headphones, earphones

audiovisual *adj* : audiovisual

auditar *vt* : audit — **auditor, -tora** *n* : auditor

auditorio *nm* **1** : auditorium **2** PÚBLICO : audience

auge *nm* **1** : peak **2** : (economic) boom

augurar *vt* : predict, foretell — **augurio** *nm* : omen

augusto, -ta *adj* : august

aula *nf* : classroom

aullar {8} *vi* : howl — **aullido** *nm* : howl

aumentar *vt* : increase, raise — *vi* : increase, grow — **aumento** *nm* : increase, rise

aun *adv* **1** : even **2** ~ **así** : even so

aún *adv* **1** : still, yet **2 más** ~ : furthermore

aunar {8} *vt* : join, combine — **aunarse** *vr* : unite

aunque *conj* **1** : though, although, even if **2** ~ **sea** : at least

aureola *nf* **1** : halo **2** FAMA : aura

auricular *nm* **1** : telephone receiver **2** ~**es** *nmpl* : headphones

aurora *nf* : dawn

ausentarse *vr* : leave, go away — **ausencia** *nf* : absence — **ausente** *adj* : absent — ~ *nmf* **1** : absentee **2** : missing person (in law)

auspicios *nmpl* : sponsorship, auspices

austero, -ra *adj* : austere — **austeridad** *nf* : austerity

austral *adj* : southern

australiano, -na *adj* : Australian

austriaco *or* **austríaco, -ca** *adj* : Austrian

auténtico, -ca *adj* : authentic, genuine — **autenticidad** *nf* : authenticity

auto *nm* : auto, car

autoayuda *nf* : self-help

autobiografía *nf* : autobiography — **autobiográfico, -ca** *adj* : autobiographical

autobús *nm, pl* **-buses** : bus

autocompasión *nf* : self-pity

autocontrol *nm* : self-control

autocracia *nf* : autocracy

autóctono, -na *adj* : indigenous, native

autodefensa *nf* : self-defense

autodidacta *adj* : self-taught

autodisciplina *nf* : self-discipline

autoestop → **autostop**

autografiar *vt* : autograph — **autógrafo** *nm* : autograph

autómata *nm* : automaton

automático, -ca *adj* : automatic — **automatización** *nf, pl* **-ciones** : automation — **automatizar** {21} *vt* : automate

automotor, -triz *adj, fpl* **-trices** : self-propelled

automóvil *nm* : automobile — **automovilista** *nmf* : motorist — **automovilístico, -ca** *adj* : automobile, car

autonomía *nf* : autonomy — **autónomo, -ma** *adj* : autonomous

autopista *nf* : expressway, highway

autopropulsado, -da *adj* : self-propelled

autopsia *nf* : autopsy

autor, -tora *n* **1** : author **2** : perpetrator (of a crime)

autoridad *nf* : authority — **autoritario, -ria** *adj* : authoritarian

autorizar {21} *vt* : authorize, approve — **autorización** *nf, pl* **-ciones** : authorization — **autorizado, -da** *adj* **1** PERMITIDO : authorized **2** : authoritative

autorretrato *nm* : self-portrait

autoservicio *nm* **1** : self-service restaurant **2** SUPERMERCADO : supermarket

autostop *nm* **1** : hitchhiking **2 hacer** ~ : hitchhike — **autostopista** *nmf* : hitchhiker

autosuficiente *adj* : self-sufficient

auxiliar *vt* : aid, assist — ~ *adj* : auxiliary — ~ *nmf* **1** : assistant, helper **2** ~ **de vuelo** : flight attendant — **auxilio** *nm* **1** : aid, assistance **2 primeros** ~**s** : first aid

avalancha *nf* : avalanche

avalar *vt* : guarantee, endorse — **aval** *nm* : guarantee, endorsement

avanzar {21} *v* : advance, move forward — **avance** *nm* : advance — **avanzado, -da** *adj* : advanced

avaricia *nf* : greed, avarice — **avaricioso, -sa** *adj* : avaricious, greedy — **avaro, -ra** *adj* : miserly — ~ *n* : miser

avasallar *vt* : overpower, subjugate — **avasallador, -dora** *adj* : overwhelming

ave *nf* : bird

avecinarse *vr* : approach

avecindarse *vr* : settle, take up residence

avellana *nf* : hazelnut

avena *nf* **1** : oats *pl* **2** *or* **harina de** ~ : oatmeal

avenida *nf* : avenue

avenir {87} *vt* : reconcile, harmonize — **avenirse** *vr* : agree, come to terms

aventajar *vt* : be ahead of, surpass

aventar {55} *vt* **1** : fan **2** : winnow (grain) **3** *Lat* : throw, toss

aventurar *vt* : venture, risk — **aventurarse** *vr* : take a risk — **aventura** *nf* **1** : adventure **2** RIESGO : risk **3** AMORÍO : love affair — **aventurado, -da** *adj*

: risky — **aventurero, -ra** *adj* : adventurous — ~ *n* : adventurer

avergonzar {9} *vt* : shame, embarrass — **avergonzarse** *vr* : be ashamed, be embarrassed

averiar {85} *vt* : damage — **averiarse** *vr* : break down — **avería** *nf* **1** : damage **2** : breakdown (of an automobile) — **averiado, -da** *adj* **1** : damaged, faulty **2** : broken down (of an automobile)

averiguar {10} *vt* **1** : find out **2** INVESTIGAR : investigate — **averiguación** *nf, pl* **-ciones** : investigation, inquiry

aversión *nf, pl* **-siones** : aversion, dislike

avestruz *nm, pl* **-truces** : ostrich

aviación *nf, pl* **-ciones** : aviation — **aviador, -dora** *n* : aviator

aviar {85} *vt* : prepare, make ready

ávido, -da *adj* : eager, avid — **avidez** *nf, pl* **-deces** : eagerness

avío *nm* **1** : preparation, provision **2** ~**s** *nmpl* : gear, equipment

avión *nm, pl* **aviones** : airplane — **avioneta** *nf* : light airplane

avisar *vt* **1** : notify **2** ADVERTIR : warn — **aviso** *nm* **1** : notice **2** ADVERTENCIA : warning **3** *Lat* : advertisement, ad **4** **estar sobre** ~ : be on the alert

avispa *nf* : wasp — **avispón** *nm, pl* **-pones** : hornet

avispado, -da *adj fam* : clever, sharp

avistar *vt* : catch sight of

avivar *vt* **1** : enliven, brighten **2** : arouse (desire, etc.) **3** : intensify (pain)

axila *nf* : underarm, armpit

axioma *nm* : axiom

ay *interj* **1** : oh! **2** : ouch!, ow!

ayer *adv* : yesterday — ~ *nm* : yesteryear, days gone by

ayote *nm Lat* : pumpkin

ayudar *vt* : help, assist — **ayudarse** *vr* ~ **de** : make use of — **ayuda** *nf* : help, assistance — **ayudante** *nmf* : helper, assistant

ayunar *vi* : fast — **ayunas** *nfpl* **en** ~ : fasting — **ayuno** *nm* : fast

ayuntamiento *nm* **1** : town hall, city hall (building) **2** : town or city council

azabache *nm* : jet

azada *nf* : hoe — **azadonar** *vt* : hoe

azafata *nf* : stewardess *f*

azafrán *nm, pl* **-franes** : saffron

azalea *nf* : azalea

azar *nm* **1** : chance **2 al** ~ : at random — **azaroso, -sa** *adj* : hazardous (of a journey, etc.), eventful (of a life)

azorar *vt* **1** : alarm **2** DESCONCERTAR : embarrass — **azorarse** *vr* : get embarrassed

azotar *vt* : beat, whip — **azote** *nm* **1** LÁTIGO : whip, lash **2** CALAMIDAD : scourge

azotea *nf* : flat or terraced roof

azteca *adj* : Aztec

azúcar *nmf* : sugar — **azucarado, -da** *adj* : sugary — **azucarera** *nf* : sugar bowl — **azucarero, -ra** *adj* : sugar

azufre *nm* : sulphur

azul *adj & nm* : blue — **azulado, -da** *adj* : bluish

azulejo *nm* **1** : ceramic tile **2** *Lat* : bluebird

azur *n* : azure, sky blue

azuzar {21} *vt* : incite, urge on

B

b *nf* : b, second letter of the Spanish alphabet

babear *vi* : drool, slobber — **baba** *nf* : saliva, drool

babel *nmf* : bedlam

babero *nm* : bib

babor *nm* : port (side)

babosa *nf* : slug — **baboso, -sa** *adj* **1** : slimy **2** *Lat fam* : silly

babucha *nf* : slipper

babuino *nm* : baboon

bacalao *nm* : cod

bache *nm* **1** : pothole, rut **2** DIFICULTADES : bad time

bachiller *nmf* : high school graduate — **bachillerato** *nm* : high school diploma

bacon *nm Spain* : bacon

bacteria *nf* : bacterium

bagaje *nm* : baggage, luggage

bagatela *nf* : trinket

bagre *nm* : catfish

bahía *nf* : bay

bailar *v* : dance — **bailarín, -rina** *n, mpl* **-rines** : dancer — **baile** *nm* **1** : dance **2** FIESTA : dance party, ball

bajar *vt* **1** : bring down, lower **2** DESCENDER : go down, come down — *vi* : descend, drop — **bajarse** *vr* ~ **de** : get out of, get off — **baja** *nf* **1** : fall, drop **2** CESE : dismissal **3** PERMISO : sick leave **4** : (military) casualty — **bajada** *nf* **1** : descent, drop **2** PENDIENTE : slope

bajeza *nf* : lowness, meanness

bajío *nm* : sandbank, shoal

bajo, -ja *adj* **1** : low, lower **2** : short (in stature) **3** : soft, faint (of sounds) **4** VIL : base, vile — **bajo** *adv* **1** : low **2** habla más ~ : speak more softly — ~ *nm* **1** : ground floor **2** DOBLADILLO : hem **3** : bass (in music) — ~ *prep* : under, below — **bajón** *nm, pl* **-jones** : sharp drop, slump

bala *nf* **1** : bullet **2** : bale (of cotton, etc.)

balada *nf* : ballad

balancear *vt* **1** : balance **2** : swing (one's arms, etc.), rock (a boat) — **balancearse** *vr* : swing, sway — **balance** *nm* **1** : balance **2** : balance sheet — **balanceo** *nm* : swaying, rocking

balancín *nm, pl* **-cines 1** : seesaw **2** MECEDORA : rocking chair

balanza *nf* : scales *pl*, balance

balar *vi* : bleat

balaustrada *nf* : balustrade, banister

balazo *nm* **1** DISPARO : shot **2** : bullet wound

balbucear *vi* **1** : stammer, stutter **2** : babble (of a baby) — **balbuceo** *nm* : stammering, muttering, babbling

balcón *nm, pl* **-cones** : balcony

balde *nm* **1** : bucket, pail **2 en** ~ : in vain

baldío, -día *adj* **1** : uncultivated **2** INÚTIL : useless — **baldío** *nm* : wasteland

baldosa *nf* : floor tile

balear *vt Lat* : shoot (at) — **baleo** *nm Lat* : shot, shooting

balido *nm* : bleat

balín *nm, pl* **-lines** : pellet

balística *nf* : ballistics — **balístico, -ca** *adj* : ballistic

baliza *nf* **1** : buoy **2** : beacon (for aircraft)

ballena *nf* : whale

ballesta *nf* **1** : crossbow **2** : spring (of an automobile)

ballet *nm* : ballet

balneario *nm* : spa

balompié *nm* : soccer

balón *nm, pl* **-lones** : ball — **baloncesto** *nm* : basketball — **balonvolea** *nm* : volleyball

balsa *nf* **1** : raft **2** ESTANQUE : pond, pool

bálsamo *nm* : balsam, balm — **balsámico, -ca** *adj* : soothing

baluarte *nm* : bulwark, bastion

bambolear *vi* : sway, swing — **bambolearse** *vr* : sway, rock

bambú *nm, pl* **-búes** *or* **-bús** : bamboo

banal *adj* : banal

banana *nf Lat* : banana — **banano** *nm Lat* : banana

banca *nf* **1** : banking **2** BANCO : bench — **bancario, -ria** *adj* : bank, banking

— **bancarrota** *nf* : bankruptcy —

banco *nm* **1** : bank **2** BANCA : stool, bench, pew **3** : school (of fish)

banda *nf* **1** : band, strip **2** : band (in music) **3** PANDILLA : gang **4** : flock (of birds) **5** ~ **sonora** : sound track — **bandada** *nf* : flock (of birds), school (of fish)

bandazo *nm* : lurch

bandeja *nf* : tray, platter

bandera *nf* : flag, banner

banderilla *nf* : banderilla

banderín *nm, pl* **-rines** : pennant, small flag

bandido, -da *n* : bandit

bando *nm* **1** : proclamation, edict **2** PARTIDO : faction, side

bandolero, -ra *n* : bandit

banjo *nm* : banjo

banquero, -ra *n* : banker

banqueta *nf* **1** : stool, footstool **2** *Lat* : sidewalk

banquete *nm* : banquet

bañar *vt* **1** : bathe, wash **2** SUMERGIR : immerse **3** CUBRIR : coat, cover — **bañarse** *vr* **1** : take a bath **2** : go swimming — **bañera** *nf* : bathtub — **bañista** *nmf* : bather — **baño** *nm* **1** : bath, swim **2** BAÑERA : bathtub **3** ¿donde está el ~? : where is the bathroom? **4** ~ **María** : double boiler

baqueta *nf* **1** : ramrod **2** ~**s** *nfpl* : drumsticks

bar *nm* : bar, tavern

barajar *vt* **1** : shuffle (cards) **2** CONSIDERAR : consider — **baraja** *nf* : deck of cards

baranda *nf* : rail, railing — **barandal** *nm* : handrail, banister

barato, -ta *adj* : cheap — **barato** *adv* : cheap, cheaply — **barata** *nf Lat* : sale, bargain — **baratija** *nf* : trinket — **baratillo** *nm* : secondhand store, flea market

barba *nf* **1** : beard, stubble **2** BARBILLA : chin

barbacoa *nf* : barbecue

barbaridad *nf* **1** : barbarity, cruelty **2** ¡qué ~! : that's outrageous! — **barbarie** *nf* : barbarism, savagery — **bárbaro, -ra** *adj* : barbaric

barbecho *nm* : fallow land

barbero, -ra *n* : barber — **barbería** *nf* : barbershop

barbilla *nf* : chin

barbudo, -da *adj* : bearded

barca *nf* **1** : boat **2** ~ **de pasaje** : ferryboat — **barcaza** *nf* : barge — **barco** *nm* : boat, ship

barítono *nm* : baritone

barman *nm* : bartender

barnizar {21} *vt* **1** : varnish **2** : glaze (ceramics) — **barniz** *nm, pl* **-nices 1** : varnish **2** : glaze (on ceramics)

barómetro *nm* : barometer

barón *nm, pl* **-rones** : baron — **baronesa** *nf* : baroness

barquero *nm* : boatman

barquillo *nm* : wafer, cone

barra *nf* **1** : bar, rod, stick **2** : counter (of a bar, etc.)

barraca *nf* **1** : hut, cabin **2** CASETA : booth, stall

barranco *nm or* **barranca** *nf* : ravine, gorge, gully

barredera *nf* : street-sweeping machine

barrenar *vt* : drill — **barrena** *nf* : drill, auger

barrer *v* : sweep

barrera *nf* : barrier

barreta *nf* : crowbar

barriada *nf* : district, quarter

barrica *nf* : cask, keg

barricada *nf* : barricade

barrido *nm* : sweep, sweeping

barriga *nf* : belly

barril *nm* **1** : barrel, keg **2 de ~** : draft

barrio *nm* **1** : neighborhood **2 ~ bajo** : slums *pl*

barro *nm* **1** : mud **2** ARCILLA : clay **3** GRANO : pimple, blackhead — **barroso, -sa** *adj* : muddy

barrote *nm* : bar (on a window)

barrunto *nm* **1** : suspicion **2** INDICIO : sign, indication

bártulos *nmpl* : things, belongings

barullo *nm* : racket, ruckus

basa *nf* : base, pedestal — **basar** *vt* : base — **basarse** *vr* **~ en** : be based on

báscula *nf* : scales *pl*

base *nf* **1** : base **2** FUNDAMENTO : basis, foundation **3 ~ de datos** : database — **básico, -ca** *adj* : basic

basquetbol *or* **básquetbol** *nm Lat* : basketball

bastar *vi* : be enough, suffice — **bastante** *adv* **1** : fairly, rather **2** SUFICIENTE : enough — *~ adj* : enough, sufficient — *~ pron* : enough

bastardo, -da *adj & n* : bastard

bastidor *nm* **1** : frame **2** : wing (in theater) **3 entre ~es** : behind the scenes, backstage

bastilla *nf* : hem

bastión *nf, pl* **-tiones** : bastion, stronghold

basto, -ta *adj* : coarse, rough

bastón *nm, pl* **-tones 1** : cane, walking stick **2** : baton (in parades)

basura *nf* : garbage, rubbish — **basurero, -ra** *n* : garbage collector

bata *nf* **1** : bathrobe, housecoat **2** : smock (of a doctor, laboratory worker, etc.)

batallar *vi* : battle, fight — **batalla** *nf* **1** : battle, fight, struggle **2 de ~** : ordinary, everyday — **batallón** *nm, pl* **-llones** : battalion

batata *nf* : yam, sweet potato

batear *v* : bat, hit — **bate** *nm* : baseball bat — **bateador, -dora** *n* : batter, hitter

batería *nf* **1** : battery **2** : drums *pl* **3 ~ de cocina** : kitchen utensils *pl*

batir *vt* **1** : beat, whip **2** DERRIBAR : knock down — **batirse** *vr* : fight — **batido** *nm* : milk shake — **batidor** *nm* : eggbeater, whisk — **batidora** *nf* : electric mixer

batuta *nf* : baton

baúl *nm* : trunk, chest

bautismo *nm* : baptism — **bautismal** *adj* : baptismal — **bautizar** {21} *vt* : baptize — **bautizo** *nm* : baptism, christening

baya *nf* : berry

bayeta *nf* : cleaning cloth

bayoneta *nf* : bayonet

bazar *nm* : bazaar

bazo *nm* : spleen

bazofia *nf fam* : rubbish, hogwash

beato, -ta *adj* : blessed

bebé *nm* : baby

beber *v* : drink — **bebedero** *nm* : watering trough — **bebedor, -dora** *n* : (heavy) drinker — **bebida** *nf* : drink, beverage — **bebido, -da** *adj* : drunk

beca *nf* : grant, scholarship

becerro, -rra *n* : calf

befa *nf* : jeer, taunt

beige *adj & nm* : beige

beisbol *or* **béisbol** *nm* : baseball — **beisbolista** *nmf* : baseball player

beldad *nf* : beauty

belén *nf, pl* **-lenes** : Nativity scene

belga *adj* : Belgian

beliceño, -ña *adj* : Belizean

bélico, -ca *adj* : military, war — **belicoso, -sa** *adj* : warlike

beligerancia *nf* : belligerence — **beligerante** *adj & nmf* : belligerent

belleza *nf* : beauty — **bello, -lla** *adj* **1** : beautiful **2 bellas artes** : fine arts

bellota *nf* : acorn

bemol *adj & nm* : flat (in music)

bendecir {11} *vt* **1** : bless **2 ~ la mesa** : say grace — **bendición** *nf, pl* **-ciones** : benediction, blessing — **bendito, -ta** *adj* **1** : blessed, holy **2** DI-

CHOSO : fortunate **3 ¡bendito sea Dios!** : thank goodness!
benefactor, -tora *n* : benefactor
beneficiar *vt* : benefit, assist — **beneficiarse** *vr* : benefit, profit — **beneficiario, -ria** *n* : beneficiary — **beneficio** *nm* **1** : gain, profit **2** BIEN : benefit — **beneficioso, -sa** *adj* : beneficial — **benéfico, -ca** *adj* : charitable
benemérito, -ta *adj* : worthy
beneplácito *nm* : approval, consent
benévolo, -la *adj* : benevolent, kind — **benevolencia** *nf* : benevolence, kindness
bengala *nf or* **luz de ~** : flare
benigno, -na *adj* **1** : mild **2** : benign (in medicine) — **benignidad** *nf* : mildness, kindness
benjamín, -mina *n, mpl* **-mines** : youngest child
beodo, -da *adj & n* : drunk
berenjena *nf* : eggplant
berrear *vi* **1** : bellow, low **2** : bawl, howl (of a person) — **berrido** *nm* **1** : bellowing **2** : howl, scream (of a person)
berro *nm* : watercress
berza *nf* : cabbage
besar *vt* : kiss — **besarse** *vr* : kiss (each other) — **beso** *nm* : kiss
bestia *nf* : beast, animal — **bestial** *adj* : bestial, brutal — **bestialidad** *nf* : brutality
betabel *nm Lat* : beet
betún *nm, pl* **-tunes** : shoe polish
bianual *adj* : biannual
biberón *nm, pl* **-rones** : baby's bottle
Biblia *nf* : Bible — **bíblico, -ca** *adj* : biblical
bibliografía *nf* : bibliography — **bibliográfico, -ca** *adj* : bibliographic, bibliographical
biblioteca *nf* : library — **bibliotecario, -ria** *n* : librarian
bicarbonato *nm* **~ de soda** : baking soda
bicentenario *nm* : bicentennial
bíceps *nms & pl* : biceps
bicho *nm* : small animal, bug
bicicleta *nf* : bicycle — **bici** *nf fam* : bike
bicolor *adj* : two-tone
bidón *nm, pl* **-dones** : large can, drum
bien *adv* **1** : well, good **2** CORRECTAMENTE : correctly, right **3** MUY : very, quite **4** DE BUENA GANA : willingly **5 ~ que** : although **6 más ~** : rather — **bien** *adj* **1** : all right, well **2** AGRADABLE : pleasant, nice **3** SATISFACTORIO : satisfactory **4** CORRECTO : correct, right — **bien** *nm* **1** : good **2 ~es** *nmpl* : property, goods

bienal *adj & nf* : biennial
bienaventurado, -da *adj* : blessed, fortunate
bienestar *nm* : welfare, well-being
bienhechor, -chora *n* : benefactor
bienintencionado, -da *adj* : well-meaning
bienvenido, -da *adj* : welcome — **bienvenida** *nf* **1** : welcome **2 dar la ~ a** : welcome (s.o.)
bife *nm Lat* : steak
bifocales *nmpl* : bifocals
bifurcarse {72} *vr* : fork — **bifurcación** *nf, pl* **-ciones** : fork, branch
bigamia *nf* : bigamy
bigote *nm* **1** : mustache **2 ~s** *nmpl* : whiskers (of an animal)
bikini *nm* : bikini
bilingüe *adj* : bilingual
bilis *nf* : bile
billar *nm* : pool, billiards
billete *nm* **1** : bill, banknote **2** BOLETO : ticket — **billetera** *nf* : billfold, wallet
billón *nm, pl* **-llones** : trillion
bimensual, -suale *adj* : twice a month — **bimestral** *adj* : bimonthly
binario, -ria *adj* : binary
bingo *nm* : bingo
binoculares *nmpl* : binoculars
biodegradable *adj* : biodegradable
biofísica *nf* : biophysics
biografía *nf* : biography — **biográfico, -ca** *adj* : biographical — **biógrafo, -fa** *n* : biographer
biología *nf* : biology — **biológico, -ca** *adj* : biological, biologic — **biólogo, -ga** *n* : biologist
biombo *nm* : folding screen
biomecánica *nf* : biomechanics
biopsia *nf* : biopsy
bioquímica *nf* : biochemistry — **bioquímico, -ca** *adj* : biochemical
biotecnología *nf* : biotechnology
bipartidista *adj* : bipartisan
bípedo *nm* : biped
biquini → bikini
birlar *vt fam* : swipe, pinch
bis *adv* **1** : twice (in music) **2** : A (in an address) — **~** *nm* : encore
bisabuelo, -la *n* : great-grandfather *m*, great-grandmother *f*
bisagra *nf* : hinge
bisecar {72} *vt* : bisect
biselar *vt* : bevel
bisexual *adj* : bisexual
bisiesto *adj* **año ~** : leap year
bisnieto, -ta *n* : great-grandson *m*, great-granddaughter *f*
bisonte *nm* : bison, buffalo
bisoño, -ña *n* : novice

bistec *nm* : steak
bisturí *nm* : scalpel
bisutería *nf* : costume jewelry
bit *nm* : bit (unit of information)
bizco, -ca *adj* : cross-eyed
bizcocho *nm* : sponge cake
bizquear *vi* : squint — **bizquera** *nf*
: squint
blanco, -ca *adj* : white — **blanco, -ca** *n*
: white person — **blanco** *nm* **1** : white
2 DIANA : target, bull's-eye **3** : blank
(space) — **blancura** *nf* : whiteness
blandir {1} *vt* : wave, brandish
blando, -da *adj* **1** : soft, tender **2** DÉBIL
: weak-willed **3** INDULGENTE : lenient
— **blandura** *nf* **1** : softness, tenderness **2** DEBILIDAD : weakness **3** INDUL-
GENCIA : leniency
blanquear *vt* **1** : whiten, bleach **2**
: launder (money) — *vi* : turn white —
blanqueador *nm Lat* : bleach
blasfemar *vi* : blaspheme — **blasfemia**
nf : blasphemy — **blasfemo, -ma** *adj*
: blasphemous
bledo *nm* **no me importa un ~** *fam* : I
couldn't care less
blindaje *nm* : armor, armor plating —
blindado, -da *adj* : armored
bloc *nm, pl* **blocs** *Lat* : (writing) pad
bloquear *vt* **1** OBSTRUIR : block, obstruct
2 : blockade — **bloque** *nm* **1** : block **2**
: bloc (in politics) — **bloqueo** *nm* **1**
OBSTRUCCIÓN : blockage **2** : blockade
blusa *nf* : blouse — **blusón** *nm, pl*
-sones : smock
boato *nm* : showiness
bobina *nf* : bobbin, reel
bobo, -ba *adj* : silly, stupid — *~ n*
: fool, simpleton
boca *nf* **1** : mouth **2** ENTRADA : entrance
3 ~ arriba : faceup **4 ~ abajo** : facedown, prone **5 ~ de riego** : hydrant
bocacalle *nf* : entrance (to a street)
bocado *nm* **1** : bite, mouthful **2** : bit (of
a bridle) — **bocadillo** *nm Spain*
: sandwich
bocajarro *nm* **a ~** : point-blank
bocallave *nf* : keyhole
bocanada *nf* **1** : swallow, swig **2** : puff,
gust (of smoke, wind, etc.)
boceto *nm* : sketch, outline
bochorno *nm* **1** VERGÜENZA : embarrassment **2** : muggy weather — **bochornoso, -sa** *adj* **1** VERGONZOSO
: embarrassing **2** : muggy, sultry
bocina *nf* **1** : horn **2** : mouthpiece (of a
telephone) — **bocinazo** *nm* : honk,
toot
boda *nf* : wedding
bodega *nf* **1** : wine cellar **2** : warehouse

3 : hold (of a ship or airplane) **4** *Lat*
: grocery store
bofetear *vt* : slap — **bofetada** *nf or*
bofetón *nm* : slap (in the face)
boga *nf* : fashion, vogue
bohemio, -mia *adj & n* : bohemian
boicotear *vt* : boycott — **boicot** *nm, pl*
-cots : boycott
boina *nf* : beret
bola *nf* **1** : ball **2** *fam* : fib
bolera *nf* : bowling alley
boleta *nf Lat* : ticket — **boletería** *nf Lat*
: ticket office
boletín *nm, pl* **-tines 1** : bulletin **2 ~**
de noticias : news release
boleto *nm* : ticket
boliche *nm* **1** : bowling **2** BOLERA
: bowling alley
bolígrafo *nm* : ballpoint pen
bolillo *nm* : bobbin
boliviano, -na *adj* : Bolivian
bollo *nm* : bun, sweet roll
bolo *nm* **1** : bowling pin **2 ~s** *nmpl*
: bowling
bolsa *nf* **1** : bag **2** *Lat* : pocketbook,
purse **3 la Bolsa** : the stock market —
bolsillo *nm* : pocket — **bolso** *nm*
Spain : pocketbook, handbag
bomba *nf* **1** : bomb **2 ~ de gasolina**
: gas pump
bombachos *nmpl* : baggy trousers
bombardear *vt* : bomb, bombard —
bombardeo *nm* : bombing, bombard-
ment — **bombardero** *nm* : bomber
(airplane)
bombear *vt* : pump — **bombero, -ra** *n*
: firefighter
bombilla *nf* : lightbulb — **bombillo** *nm*
Lat : lightbulb
bombo *nm* **1** : bass drum **2 a ~s y**
platillos : with a great fanfare
bombón *nm, pl* **-bones** : candy, chocolate
bonachón, -chona *adj, mpl* **-chones**
fam : good-natured
bonanza *nf* **1** : fair weather (at sea) **2**
PROSPERIDAD : prosperity
bondad *nf* : goodness, kindness —
bondadoso, -sa *adj* : kind, good
boniato *nm* : sweet potato
bonificación *nf, pl* **-ciones 1** : bonus,
extra **2** DESCUENTO : discount
bonito, -ta *adj* : pretty, lovely
bono *nm* **1** : bond **2** VALE : voucher
boquear *vi* : gasp — **boqueada** *nf*
: gasp
boquerón *nm, pl* **-rones** : anchovy
boquete *nm* : gap, opening
boquiabierto, -ta *adj* : open-mouthed,
speechless

boquilla *nf* : mouthpiece (of a musical instrument)

borbollar *vi* : bubble

borbotar *or* **borbotear** *vi* : boil, bubble, gurgle — **borbotón** *nm*, *pl* -**tones** 1 : spurt 2 **salir a borbotones** : gush out

bordar *v* : embroider — **bordado** *nm* : embroidery, needlework

borde *nm* 1 : border, edge 2 **al ~ de** : on the verge of — **bordear** *vt* : border — **bordillo** *nm* : curb

bordo *nm* **a ~** : aboard, on board

borla *nf* 1 : pom-pom, tassel 2 : powder puff

borracho, -cha *adj & n* : drunk — **borrachera** *nf* : drunkenness

borrar *vt* : erase, blot out — **borrador** *nm* 1 : rough draft 2 : eraser (for a blackboard)

borrascoso, -sa *adj* : stormy

borrego, -ga *n* : lamb, sheep — **borrego** *nm Lat* : false rumor, hoax

borrón *nm*, *pl* -**rrones** 1 : smudge, blot 2 **~ y cuenta nueva** : let's forget about it — **borroso, -sa** *adj* 1 : blurry, smudgy 2 INDISTINTO : vague, hazy

bosque *nm* : woods, forest — **boscoso, -sa** *adj* : wooded

bosquejar *vt* : sketch (out) — **bosquejo** *nm* : outline, sketch

bostezar {21} *vi* : yawn — **bostezo** *nm* : yawn

bota *nf* : boot

botánica *nf* : botany — **botánico, -ca** *adj* : botanical

botar *vt* 1 : throw, hurl 2 *Lat* : throw away 3 : launch (a ship) — *vi* : bounce

bote *nm* 1 : small boat 2 *Spain* : can 3 TARRO : jar 4 SALTO : bounce, jump

botella *nf* : bottle

botín *nm*, *pl* -**tines** 1 : ankle boot 2 DESPOJOS : booty, plunder

botiquín *nm*, *pl* -**quines** 1 : medicine cabinet 2 : first-aid kit

botón *nm*, *pl* -**tones** 1 : button 2 YEMA : bud — **botones** *nmfs & pl* : bellhop

botulismo *nm* : botulism

boutique *nf* : boutique

bóveda *nf* : vault

boxear *vi* : box — **boxeador, -dora** *n* : boxer — **boxeo** *nm* : boxing

boya *nf* : buoy — **boyante** *adj* 1 : buoyant 2 PRÓSPERO : prosperous, thriving

bozal *nm* 1 : muzzle 2 : halter (for a horse)

bracear *vi* 1 : wave one's arms 2 NADAR : swim, crawl

bracero, -ra *n* : day laborer

bragas *nf Spain* : panties

bragueta *nf* : fly, pants zipper

braille *adj & nm* : braille

bramante *nm* : twine, string

bramar *vi* 1 : bellow, roar 2 : howl (of the wind) — **bramido** *nm* : bellow, roar

brandy *nm* : brandy

branquia *nf* : gill

brasa *nf* : ember

brasier *nm Lat* : brassiere

brasileño, -ña *adj* : Brazilian

bravata *nf* 1 : boast, bravado 2 AMENAZO : threat

bravo, -va *adj* 1 : fierce, savage 2 : rough (of the sea) 3 *Lat* : angry — *interj* : bravo!, well done! — **bravura** *nf* 1 FEROCIDAD : fierceness 2 VALENTÍA : bravery

braza *nf* 1 : breaststroke 2 : fathom (measurement) — **brazada** *nf* : stroke (in swimming)

brazalete *nm* 1 : bracelet 2 : (cloth) armband

brazo *nm* 1 : arm 2 : branch (of a river, etc.) 3 **~ derecho** : right-hand man 4 **~s** *nmpl* : hands, laborers

brea *nf* : tar

brebaje *nm* : concoction

brecha *nf* : breach, gap

brécol *nm* : broccoli

bregar {52} *vi* 1 LUCHAR : struggle 2 TRABAJAR : work hard — **brega** *nf* **andar a la ~** : struggle

breña *nf or* **breñal** *nm* : scrubland, brush

breve *adj* 1 : brief, short 2 **en ~** : shortly, in short — **brevedad** *nf* : brevity, shortness — **brevemente** *adv* : briefly

brezal *nm* : moor, heath — **brezo** *nm* : heather

bricolaje *or* **bricolage** *nm* : do-it-yourself

brida *nf* : bridle

brigada *nf* 1 : brigade 2 EQUIPO : gang, team, squad

brillar *vi* : shine, sparkle — **brillante** *adj* : brilliant, shiny — **~** *nm* : diamond — **brillantez** *nf* : brilliance — **brillo** *nm* 1 : luster, shine 2 ESPLENDOR : splendor — **brilloso, -sa** *adj* : shiny

brincar {72} *vi* : jump about, frolic — **brinco** *nm* : jump, skip

brindar *vi* : drink a toast — *vt* : offer, provide — **brindarse** *vr* : offer one's assistance — **brindis** *nm* : drink, toast

brío *nm* 1 : force, determination 2 ÁNIMO : spirit, verve — **brioso, -sa** *adj* : spirited, lively

brisa *nf* : breeze

británico, -ca *adj* : British
brizna *nf* **1** : strand, thread **2** : blade (of grass)
brocado *nm* : brocade
brocha *nf* : paintbrush
broche *nm* **1** : fastener, clasp **2** ALFILER : brooch
brocheta *nf* : skewer
brócoli *nm* : broccoli
bromear *vi* : joke, fool around — **broma** *nf* : joke, prank — **bromista** *adj* : fun-loving, joking — ~ *nmf* : joker, prankster
bronca *nf fam* : fight, row
bronce *nm* : bronze — **bronceado, -da** *adj* : suntanned — **bronceado** *nm* : tan — **broncearse** *vr* : get a suntan
bronco, -ca *adj* **1** : harsh, rough **2** : untamed, wild (of a horse)
bronquitis *nf* : bronchitis
broqueta *nf* : skewer
brotar *vi* **1** : bud, sprout **2** : stream, gush (of a river, tears, etc.) **3** : arise (of feelings, etc.) **4** : break out (in medicine) — **brote** *nm* **1** : outbreak **2** : sprout, bud, shoot (of plants)
brujería *nf* : witchcraft — **bruja** *nf* **1** : witch **2** *fam* : old hag — **brujo** *nm* : warlock, sorcerer — **brujo, -ja** *adj* : bewitching
brújula *nf* : compass
bruma *nf* : haze, mist — **brumoso, -sa** *adj* : hazy, misty
bruñir {38} *vt* : burnish, polish
brusco, -ca *adj* **1** SÚBITO : sudden, abrupt **2** TOSCO : brusque, rough — **brusquedad** *nf* : abruptness, brusqueness
brutal *adj* : brutal — **brutalidad** *nf* : brutality
bruto, -ta *adj* **1** : brutish, stupid **2** : crude (of petroleum, etc.), uncut (of diamonds) **3 peso** ~ : gross weight — ~ *n* : brute
bucal *adj* : oral
bucear *vi* **1** : dive, swim underwater **2** ~ **en** : delve into — **buceo** *nm* : (underwater) diving
bucle *nm* : curl
budín *nm, pl* **-dines** : pudding
budismo *nm* : Buddhism — **budista** *adj & nmf* : Buddhist
buenamente *adv* **1** : easily **2** VOLUNTARIAMENTE : willingly
buenaventura *nf* **1** : good luck **2 decir la** ~ **a uno** : tell s.o.'s fortune
bueno, -na *adj* (**buen** *before masculine singular nouns*) **1** : good **2** AMABLE : kind **3** APROPIADO : appropriate **4** SALUDABLE : well, healthy **5** : nice, fine (of weather) **6 buenos días** : hello, good day **7 buenas noches** : good night **8 buenas tardes** : good afternoon, good evening — **bueno** *interj* : OK!, all right!
buey *nm* : ox, steer
búfalo *nm* : buffalo
bufanda *nf* : scarf
bufar *vi* : snort — **bufido** *nm* : snort
bufet *or* **bufé** *nm* : buffet-style meal
bufete *nm* **1** : law practice **2** MESA : writing desk
bufo, -fa *adj* : comic — **bufón, -fona** *n, mpl* **-fones** : buffoon, jester — **bufonada** *nf* : wisecrack
buhardilla *nf* : attic, garret
búho *nm* : owl
buitre *nm* : vulture
bujía *nf* : spark plug
bulbo *nm* : bulb (of a plant)
bulevar *nm* : boulevard
búlgaro, -ra *adj* : Bulgarian
bulla *nf* : uproar, racket
bulldozer *nm* : bulldozer
bullicio *nm* **1** : uproar **2** AJETREO : hustle and bustle — **bullicioso, -sa** *adj* : noisy, boisterous
bullir {38} *vi* **1** : boil **2** AJETREARSE : bustle, stir
bulto *nm* **1** : package, bundle **2** VOLUMEN : bulk, size **3** FORMA : form, shape **4** PROTUBERANCIA : lump, swelling
bumerán *nm, pl* **-ranes** : boomerang
buñuelo *nm* : fried pastry
buque *nm* : ship
burbujear *vi* : bubble — **burbuja** *nf* : bubble
burdel *nm* : brothel
burdo, -da *adj* : coarse, rough
burgués, -guesa *adj & n, mpl* **-gueses** : bourgeois — **burguesía** *nf* : bourgeoisie
burlar *vt* : trick, deceive — **burlarse** *vr* ~ **de** : make fun of — **burla** *nf* **1** MOFA : mockery, ridicule **2** BROMA : joke, trick
burlesco, -ca *adj* : comic, funny
burlón, -lona *adj, mpl* **-lones** : mocking
burocracia *nf* : bureaucracy — **burócrata** *nmf* : bureaucrat — **burocrático, -ca** *adj* : bureaucratic
burro, -rra *n* **1** : donkey **2** *fam* : dunce — ~ *adj* : stupid — **burro** *nm* **1** : sawhorse **2** *Lat* : stepladder
bus *nm* : bus
buscar {72} *vt* **1** : look for, seek **2 ir a** ~ **a uno** : fetch s.o. — *vi* : search — **busca** *nf* : search — **búsqueda** *nf* : search

busto *nm* : bust (in sculpture)
butaca *nf* 1 : armchair 2 : (theater) seat
butano *nm* : butane

buzo *nm* : diver
buzón *nm, pl* **-zones** : mailbox
byte ['bait] *nm* : byte

C

c *nf* : c, third letter of the Spanish alphabet
cabal *adj* 1 : exact 2 COMPLETO : complete — **cabales** *nmpl* **no estar en sus ~** : not be in one's right mind
cabalgar {52} *vi* : ride — **cabalgata** *nf* : cavalcade
caballa *nf* : mackerel
caballería *nf* 1 : cavalry 2 CABALLO : horse, mount — **caballeriza** *nf* : stable
caballero *nm* 1 : gentleman 2 : knight (rank) — **caballerosidad** *nf* : chivalry — **caballeroso, -sa** *adj* : chivalrous
caballete *nm* 1 : ridge (of a roof) 2 : easel (for a canvas) 3 : bridge (of the nose)
caballito *nm* 1 : rocking horse 2 **~s** *nmpl* : merry-go-round
caballo *nm* 1 : horse 2 : knight (in chess) 3 **~ de fuerza** : horsepower
cabaña *nf* : cabin, hut
cabaret *nm, pl* **-rets** : nightclub, cabaret
cabecear *vi* 1 : shake one's head, nod 2 : pitch, lurch (of a boat)
cabecera *nf* 1 : head (of a bed, etc.) 2 : heading (in a text) 3 **médico de ~** : family doctor
cabecilla *nmf* : ringleader
cabello *nm* : hair — **cabelludo, -da** *adj* : hairy
caber {12} *vi* 1 : fit, go (into) 2 **no cabe duda** : there's no doubt
cabestro *nm* : halter
cabeza *nf* 1 : head 2 **de ~** : head first — **cabezada** *nf* 1 : butt (of the head) 2 **dar ~s** : nod off
cabezal *nm* : bolster, headrest
cabida *nf* 1 : room, capacity 2 **dar ~ a** : accomodate, find room for
cabina *nf* 1 : booth 2 : cab (of a truck, etc.) 3 : cabin, cockpit (of an airplane)
cabizbajo, -ja *adj* : downcast
cable *nm* : cable
cabo *nm* 1 : end, stub 2 TROZO : bit 3 : corporal (in the military) 4 : cape (in geography) 5 **al fin y al ~** : after all 6 **llevar a ~** : carry out, do
cabra *nf* : goat

cabriola *nf* 1 : leap, skip 2 **hacer ~s** : prance around
cabrito *nm* : kid (goat)
cacahuate *or* **cacahuete** *nm* : peanut
cacao *nm* 1 : cacao (tree) 2 : cocoa (drink)
cacarear *vi* : crow, cackle — *vt fam* : boast about
cacería *nf* : hunt
cacerola *nf* : pan, saucepan
cacharro *nm* 1 *fam* : thing, piece of junk 2 *fam* : jalopy 3 **~s** *nmpl* : pots and pans
cachear *vt* : search, frisk
cachemir *nm or* **cachemira** *nf* : cashmere
cachete *nm Lat* : cheek — **cachetada** *nf Lat* : slap
cacho *nm* 1 *fam* : piece, bit 2 *Lat* : horn
cachorro, -rra *n* 1 : cub 2 PERRITO : puppy
cactus *or* **cacto** *nm* : cactus
cada *adj* : each, every
cadalso *nm* : scaffold
cadáver *nm* : corpse
cadena *nf* 1 : chain 2 : (television) channel 3 **~ de montaje** : assembly line
cadencia *nf* : cadence
cadera *nf* : hip
cadete *nmf* : cadet
caducar {72} *vi* : expire — **caducidad** *nf* : expiration
caer {13} *vi* 1 : fall, drop 2 **~ bien a uno** : be to one's liking 3 **dejar ~** : drop 4 **me cae bien** : I like her, I like him — **caerse** *vr* : drop, fall (down)
café *nm* 1 : coffee 2 : café — **~** *adj Lat* : brown — **cafetera** *nf* : coffeepot — **cafetería** *nf* : coffee shop, cafeteria — **cafeína** *nf* : caffeine
caída *nf* 1 : fall, drop 2 PENDIENTE : slope
caimán *nm, pl* **-manes** : alligator
caja *nf* 1 : box, case 2 : checkout counter, cashier's desk (in a store) 3 **~ fuerte** : safe 4 **~ registradora** : cash register — **cajero, -ra** *n* 1 : cashier 2 : (bank) teller — **cajetilla** *nf* : pack (of cigarettes) — **cajón** *nm, pl* **-jones** 1

: drawer (in furniture) **2** : large box, crate

cajuela *nf Lat* : trunk (of a car)

cal *nf* : lime

cala *nf* : cove

calabaza *nf* **1** : pumpkin, squash, gourd **2 dar ~s a** *fam* : give the brush-off to — **calabacín** *nm, pl* **-cines** *or* **calabacita** *nf Lat* : zucchini

calabozo *nm* **1** : prison **2** CELDA : cell

calamar *nm* : squid

calambre *nm* **1** ESPASMO : cramp **2** : (electric) shock

calamidad *nf* : calamity

calar *vt* **1** : soak (through) **2** PERFORAR : pierce — **calarse** *vr* : get drenched

calavera *nf* : skull

calcar {72} *vt* **1** : trace **2** IMITAR : copy, imitate

calcetín *nm, pl* **-tines** : sock

calcinar *vt* : char

calcio *nm* : calcium

calcomanía *nf* : decal

calcular *vt* : calculate, estimate — **calculador, -dora** *adj* : calculating — **calculadora** *nf* : calculator — **cálculo** *nm* **1** : calculation **2** : calculus (in mathematics and medicine) **3 ~ biliar** : gallstone

caldera *nf* **1** : cauldron **2** : boiler (for heating, etc.) — **caldo** *nm* : broth, stock

calefacción *nf, pl* **-ciones** : heating, heat

calendario *nm* : calendar

calentar {55} *vt* : heat (up), warm (up) — **calentarse** *vr* : get warm, heat up — **calentador** *nm* : heater — **calentura** *nf* : temperature, fever

calibre *nm* **1** : caliber **2** DIÁMETRO : bore, diameter — **calibrar** *vt* : calibrate

calidad *nf* **1** : quality **2 en ~ de** : as, in the capacity of

cálido, -da *adj* : hot, warm

calidoscopio *nm* : kaleidoscope

caliente *adj* **1** : hot **2** ACALORADO : heated, fiery

calificar {72} *vt* **1** : qualify **2** EVALUAR : rate **3** : grade (an exam, etc.) — **calificación** *nf, pl* **-ciones** **1** : qualification **2** EVALUACIÓN : rating **3** NOTA : grade — **calificativo, -va** *adj* : qualifying — **calificativo** *nm* : qualifier, epithet

caligrafía *nf* : penmanship

calistenia *nf* : calisthenics

cáliz *nm, pl* **-lices** : chalice

caliza *nf* : limestone

callar *vi* : keep quiet, be silent — *vt* **1** : silence, hush **2** OCULTAR : keep secret — **callarse** *vr* : remain silent — **callado, -da** *adj* : quiet, silent

calle *nf* : street, road — **callejear** *vi* : wander about the streets — **callejero, -ra** *adj* **1** : street **2 perro callejero** : stray dog — **callejón** *nm, pl* **-jones** **1** : alley **2 ~ sin salida** : dead-end street

callo *nm* : callus, corn

calma *nf* : calm, quiet — **calmante** *adj* : soothing — *~ nm* : tranquilizer — **calmar** *vt* : calm, soothe — **calmarse** *vr* : calm down — **calmo, -ma** *adj Lat* : calm — **calmoso, -sa** *adj* **1** : calm **2** LENTO : slow

calor *nm* **1** : heat, warmth **2 tener ~** : be hot — **caloría** *nf* : calorie

calumnia *nf* : slander, libel — **calumniar** *vt* : slander, libel

caluroso, -sa *adj* **1** : hot **2** : warm, enthusiastic (of applause, etc.)

calvo, -va *adj* : bald — **calvicie** *nf* : baldness

calza *nf* : wedge

calzada *nf* : roadway

calzado *nm* : footwear — **calzar** {21} *vt* **1** : wear (shoes) **2** : put shoes on (s.o.)

calzones *nmpl Lat* : panties — **calzoncillos** *nmpl* : underpants, briefs

cama *nf* : bed

camada *nf* : litter, brood

camafeo *nm* : cameo

cámara *nf* **1** : chamber **2** *or* **~ fotográfica** : camera **3** : house (in government)

camarada *nmf* : comrade — **camaradería** *nf* : camaraderie

camarero, -ra *n* **1** : waiter, waitress *f* **2** : steward *m*, stewardess *f* (on a ship, etc.) — **camarera** *nf* : chambermaid *f*

camarón *nm, pl* **-rones** : shrimp

camarote *nm* : cabin, stateroom

cambiar *vt* **1** : change **2** CANJEAR : exchange — *vi* **1** : change **2** : shift gears (of an automobile) — **cambiarse** *vr* **1** : change (clothing) **2** : move (to a new address) — **cambiable** *adj* : changeable — **cambio** *nm* **1** : change **2** CANJE : exchange **3 en ~** : on the other hand

camelio *nm* : camel

camilla *nf* : stretcher — **camillero** *nm* : orderly (in a hospital)

caminar *vi* : walk — *vt* : cover (a distance) — **caminata** *nf* : hike

camino *nm* **1** : road, path **2** RUTA : way **3 a medio ~** : halfway (there) **4 ponerse en ~** : set out

camión *nm, pl* **-miones** **1** : truck **2** *Lat*

: bus — **camionero, -ra** n 1 : truck driver 2 Lat : bus driver — **camioneta** nm : light truck, van
camisa nf 1 : shirt 2 ~ **de fuerza** : straitjacket — **camiseta** nf : T-shirt, undershirt — **camisón** nm, pl **-sones** : nightshirt, nightgown
camorra nf fam : fight, trouble
camote nm Lat : sweet potato
campamento nm : camp
campana nf : bell — **campanada** nf : stroke (of a bell), peal — **campanario** nm : bell tower — **campanilla** nf : (small) bell
campaña nf 1 : countryside 2 : (military or political) campaign
campeón, -peona n, mpl **-peones** : champion — **campeonato** nm : championship
campesino, -na n : peasant, farm laborer — **campestre** adj : rural, rustic
camping nm 1 : campsite 2 hacer ~ : go camping
campiña nf : countryside
campo nm 1 : field 2 CAMPIÑA : countryside, country 3 CAMPAMENTO : camp
camuflaje nm : camouflage — **camuflar** vt : camouflage
cana nf : gray hair
canadiense adj : Canadian
canal nm 1 : canal 2 MEDIO : channel 3 : (radio or television) channel — **canalizar** {21} vt : channel
canalete nm : paddle (of a canoe)
canalla nf : rabble — ~ nmf fam : swine, bastard
canapé nm 1 : canapé 2 SOFÁ : sofa, couch
canario nm : canary
canasta nf : basket — **canasto** nm : large basket
cancelar vt 1 : cancel 2 : pay off, settle (a debt) — **cancelación** nf, pl **-ciones** 1 : cancellation 2 : payment in full (of a debt)
cáncer nm : cancer — **canceroso, -sa** adj : cancerous
cancha nf : court, field (for sports)
canciller nm : chancellor
canción nf, pl **-ciones** 1 : song 2 ~ de cuna : lullaby — **cancionero** nm : songbook
candado nm : padlock
candela nf : candle — **candelabro** nm : candelabra — **candelero** nm 1 : candlestick 2 estar en el ~ : be in the limelight
candente adj : red-hot

candidato, -ta n : candidate — **candidatura** nf : candidacy
cándido, -da adj : naïve — **candidez** nf 1 : simplicity 2 INGENUIDAD : naïveté
candil nm : oil lamp — **candilejas** nfpl : footlights
candor nm : naïveté, innocence
canela nf : cinnamon
cangrejo nm : crab
canguro nm : kangaroo
caníbal nmf : cannibal — **canibalismo** nm : cannibalism
canicas nfpl : (game of) marbles
canino, -na adj : canine — **canino** nm : canine (tooth)
canjear vt : exchange — **canje** nm : exchange, trade
cano, -na adj : gray, gray-haired
canoa nf : canoe
canon nm, pl **cánones** : canon
canonizar {21} vt : canonize
canoso, -sa adj : gray, gray-haired
cansar vt : tire (out) — vi : be tiring — **cansarse** vr : get tired — **cansado, -da** adj 1 : tired 2 PESADO : tiresome — **cansancio** nm : fatigue, weariness
cantalupo nm : cantaloupe
cantar v : sing — ~ nm : song — **cantante** nmf : singer
cántaro nm 1 : pitcher, jug 2 llover a ~s fam : rain cats and dogs
cantera nf : quarry (excavation)
cantidad nf 1 : quantity, amount 2 una ~ de : lots of
cantimplora nf : canteen, water bottle
cantina nf 1 : canteen, cafeteria 2 Lat : tavern, bar
canto nm 1 : singing, song 2 BORDE, LADO : edge 3 de ~ : on end, sideways 4 ~ rodado : boulder — **cantor, -tora** adj 1 : singing 2 pájaro ~ : songbird — ~ n : singer
caña nf 1 : cane, reed 2 ~ de pescar : fishing pole
cáñamo nm : hemp
cañería nf : pipes, piping — **caño** nm 1 : pipe 2 : spout (of a fountain) — **cañón** nm, pl **-ñones** 1 : cannon 2 : barrel (of a gun) 3 : canyon (in geography)
caoba nf : mahogany
caos nm : chaos — **caótico, -ca** adj : chaotic
capa nf 1 : cape, cloak 2 : coat (of paint, etc.), coating (in cooking) 3 ESTRATO : layer, stratum 4 : (social) class
capacidad nf 1 : capacity 2 APTITUD : ability
capacitar vt : train, qualify — **capacitación** nf, pl **-ciones** : training

caparazón *nm, pl* **-zones** : shell
capataz *nmf, pl* **-taces** : foreman
capaz *adj, pl* **-paces 1** : capable, able **2**
ESPACIOSO : spacious
capellán *nm, pl* **-llanes** : chaplain
capilla *nf* : chapel
capital *adj* **1** : capital **2** PRINCIPAL
: chief, principal — ∼ *nm* : capital
(assets) — ∼ *nf* : capital (city) —
capitalismo *nm* : capitalism — **capitalista** *adj & nmf* : capitalist, capitalistic — **capitalizar** {21} *vt* : capitalize
capitán, -tana *n, mpl* **-tanes** : captain
capitolio *nm* : capitol
capitular *vi* : capitulate, surrender —
capitulación *nf, pl* **-ciones** : surrender
capítulo *nm* : chapter
capó *nm* : hood (of a car)
capote *nm* : cloak, cape
capricho *nm* : whim, caprice — **caprichoso, -sa** *adj* : whimsical, capricious
cápsula *nf* : capsule
captar *vt* **1** : grasp **2** ATRAER : gain, attract (interest, etc.) **3** : harness (waters)
capturar *vt* : capture, seize — **captura** *nf* : capture, seizure
capucha *nf* : hood (of clothing)
capullo *nm* **1** : cocoon **2** : (flower) bud
caqui *adj & nm* : khaki
cara *nf* **1** : face **2** ASPECTO : appearance
3 *fam* : nerve, gall **4** ∼ **a** *or* **de** ∼ **a**
: facing
carabina *nf* : carbine
caracol *nm* **1** : snail **2** *Lat* : conch **3**
RIZO : curl
carácter *nm, pl* **-racteres 1** : character
2 ÍNDOLE : nature — **característica** *nf*
: characteristic — **característico, -ca**
adj : characteristic — **caracterizar**
{21} *vt* : characterize
caramba *interj* : oh my!, good grief!
carámbano *nm* : icicle
caramelo *nm* **1** : caramel **2** DULCE
: candy
carátula *nf* **1** CARETA : mask **2** : jacket
(of a record, etc.) **3** *Lat* : face (of a
watch)
caravana *nf* **1** : caravan **2** REMOLQUE
: trailer
caray → **caramba**
carbohidrato *nm* : carbohydrate
carbón *nm, pl* **-bones 1** : coal **2** : charcoal (for drawing) — **carboncillo** *nm*
: charcoal — **carbonero, -ra** *adj* : coal
— **carbonizar** {21} *vt* : char — **carbono** *nm* : carbon — **carburador** *nm*
: carburetor — **carburante** *nm* : fuel
carcajada *nf* : loud laugh, guffaw

cárcel *nf* : jail, prison — **carcelero, -ra**
n : jailer
carcinógeno *nm* : carcinogen
carcomer *vt* : eat away at — **carcomido, -da** *adj* : worm-eaten
cardenal *nm* **1** : cardinal **2** CONTUSIÓN
: bruise
cardíaco *or* **cardiaco, -ca** *adj* : cardiac,
heart
cárdigan *nm, pl* **-gans** : cardigan
cardinal *adj* : cardinal
cardiólogo, -ga *n* : cardiologist
cardo *nm* : thistle
carear *vt* : bring face-to-face
carecer {53} *vi* ∼ **de** : lack — **carencia** *nf* : lack, want — **carente** *adj* ∼
de : lacking (in)
carestía *nf* **1** : high cost **2** ESCASEZ
: dearth, scarcity
careta *nf* : mask
cargar {52} *vt* **1** : load **2** : charge (a battery, a purchase, etc.) **3** LLEVAR : carry
4 ∼ **de** : burden with — *vi* **1** : load **2**
∼ **con** : pick up, carry away — **carga**
nf **1** : load **2** CARGAMENTO : freight,
cargo **3** RESPONSABILIDAD : burden **4**
: charge (in electricity, etc.) — **cargado, -da** *adj* **1** : loaded, burdened **2** PESADO : heavy, stuffy **3** : charged (of a
battery) **4** FUERTE : strong, concentrated — **cargamento** *nm* : cargo, load —
cargo *nm* **1** : charge **2** PUESTO : position, office
cariarse *vr* : decay (of teeth)
caribe *adj* : Caribbean
caricatura *nf* **1** : caricature **2** : (political) cartoon — **caricaturizar** *vt* : caricature
caricia *nf* : caress
caridad *nf* **1** : charity **2** LIMOSNA : alms
pl
caries *nfs & pl* : cavity (in a tooth)
cariño *nm* : affection, love — **cariñoso, -sa** *adj* : affectionate, loving
carisma *nf* : charisma — **carismático,
-ca** *adj* : charismatic
caritativo, -va *adj* : charitable
cariz *nm, pl* **-rices** : appearance, aspect
carmesí *adj & nm* : crimson
carmín *nm, pl* **-mines** *or* ∼ **de labios**
: lipstick
carnada *nf* : bait
carnal *adj* **1** : carnal **2** primo ∼ : first
cousin
carnaval *nm* : carnival
carne *nf* **1** : meat **2** : flesh (of persons or
fruits) **3** ∼ **de cerdo** : pork **4** ∼ **de
gallina** : goose bumps **5** ∼ **de ternera** : veal
carné *nm* → **carnet**

carnero *nm* **1** : ram, sheep **2** : mutton (in cooking)

carnet *nm* **1** ～ **de conducir** : driver's license **2** ～ **de identidad** : identification card, ID

carnicería *nf* **1** : butcher shop **2** MATANZA : slaughter — **carnicero, -ra** *n* : butcher

carnívoro, -ra *adj* : carnivorous — **carnívoro** *nm* : carnivore

carnoso, -sa *adj* : fleshy

caro, -ra *adj* **1** : expensive **2** QUERIDO : dear — **caro** *adv* : dearly

carpa *nf* **1** : carp **2** TIENDA : tent

carpeta *nf* : folder

carpintería *nf* : carpentry — **carpintero, -ra** *n* : carpenter

carraspear *vi* : clear one's throat — **carraspera** *nf* **1** : hoarseness **2 tener** ～ : have a frog in one's throat

carrera *nf* **1** : running, run **2** COMPETICIÓN : race **3** : course (of studies) **4** PROFESIÓN : career, profession

carreta *nf* : cart, wagon

carrete *nm* : reel, spool

carretera *nf* : highway, road

carretilla *nf* : wheelbarrow

carril *nm* **1** : lane (of a road) **2** : rail (for a railroad)

carrillo *nm* : cheek

carrito *nm* : cart, trolley

carrizo *nm* : reed

carro *nm* **1** : wagon, cart **2** *Lat* : automobile, car — **carrocería** *nf* : body (of an automobile)

carroña *nf* : carrion

carroza *nf* **1** : carriage **2** : float (in a parade)

carruaje *nm* : carriage

carrusel *nm* : merry-go-round, carousel

carta *nf* **1** : letter **2** NAIPE : playing card **3** : charter (of an organization, etc.) **4** MENÚ : menu **5** MAPA : map, chart

cartel *nm* : poster, bill — **cartelera** *nf* : billboard

cartera *nf* **1** : briefcase **2** BILLETERA : wallet **3** *Lat* : pocketbook, handbag — **carterista** *nmf* : pickpocket

cartero, -ra *nm* : mail carrier, mailman *m*

cartílago *nm* : cartilage

cartilla *nf* **1** : primer, reader **2** : booklet, record (of a savings account, etc.)

cartón *nm, pl* **-tones 1** : cardboard **2** : carton (of cigarettes, etc.)

cartucho *nm* : cartridge

casa *nf* **1** : house **2** HOGAR : home **3** EMPRESA : company, firm **4** ～ **flotante** : houseboat

casar *vt* : marry — *vi* : go together,

match up — **casarse** *vr* **1** : get married **2** ～ **con** : marry — **casado, -da** *adj* : married — **casamiento** *nm* **1** : marriage **2** BODA : wedding

cascabel *nm* : small bell

cascada *nf* : waterfall

cascanueces *nms & pl* : nutcracker

cascar {72} *vt* : crack (a shell, etc.) — **cascarse** *vr* : crack, chip — **cáscara** *nf* : skin, peel, shell — **cascarón** *nm, pl* **-rones** : eggshell

casco *nm* **1** : helmet **2** : hull (of a boat) **3** : hoof (of a horse) **4** : fragment (of ceramics, etc.) **5** : center (of a town) **6** ENVASE : empty bottle

caserío *nm* **1** *Spain* : country house **2** POBLADO : hamlet

casero, -ra *adj* **1** : homemade **2** DOMÉSTICO : domestic, household — ～ *n* : landlord, landlady *f*

caseta *nf* : booth, stall

casete → **cassette**

casi *adv* **1** : almost, nearly **2** (*in negative phrases*) : hardly

casilla *nf* **1** : compartment, pigeonhole **2** CASETA : booth **3** : box (on a form)

casino *nm* **1** : casino **2** : (social) club

caso *nm* **1** : case **2 en** ～ **de** : in the event of **3 hacer** ～ : pay attention **4 no venir al** ～ : be beside the point

caspa *nf* : dandruff

cassette *nmf* : cassette

casta *nf* **1** : lineage, descent **2** : breed (of animals) **3** : caste (in India)

castaña *nf* : chestnut

castañetear *vi* : chatter (of teeth)

castaño, -ña *adj* : chestnut (color)

castañuela *nf* : castanet

castellano *nm* : Spanish, Castilian (language)

castidad *nf* : chastity

castigar {52} *vt* **1** : punish **2** : penalize (in sports) — **castigo** *nm* **1** : punishment **2** : penalty (in sports)

castillo *nm* : castle

casto, -ta *adj* : chaste, pure — **castizo, -za** *adj* : pure, traditional (in style)

castor *nm* : beaver

castrar *vt* : castrate

castrense *adj* : military

casual *adj* : chance, accidental — **casualidad** *nf* **1** : coincidence **2 por** ～ *or* **de** ～ : by chance — **casualmente** *adv* : by chance

cataclismo *nm* : cataclysm

catalán, -lana *adj, mpl* **-lanes** : Catalan — **catalán** *nm* : Catalan (language)

catalizador *nm* : catalyst

catalogar {52} *vt* : catalog, classify — **catálogo** *nm* : catalog

catapulta nf : catapult

catar vt : taste, sample

catarata nf 1 : waterfall 2 : cataract (in medicine)

catarro nm RESFRIADO : cold

catástrofe nf : catastrophe, disaster — **catastrófico, -ca** adj : catastrophic, disastrous

catecismo nm : catechism

cátedra nf : chair (at a university)

catedral nf : cathedral

catedrático, -ca n : professor

categoría nf 1 : category 2 RANGO : rank 3 de ~ : first-rate — **categórico, -ca** adj : categorical

católico, -ca adj & n : Catholic — **catolicismo** nm : Catholicism

catorce adj & nm : fourteen — **catorceavo** nm : fourteenth

catre nm : cot

cauce nm 1 : riverbed 2 VÍA : channel, means pl

caucho nm : rubber

caución nf, pl **-ciones** : security, guarantee

caudal nm 1 : volume of water, flow 2 RIQUEZA : wealth

caudillo nm : leader, commander

causar vt : cause, provoke — **causa** nf 1 : cause 2 RAZÓN : reason 3 : case (in law) 4 a ~ de : because of

cáustico, -ca adj : caustic

cautela nf : caution — **cauteloso, -sa** adj : cautious — **cautelosamente** adv : cautiously, warily

cautivar vt 1 : capture 2 ENCANTAR : captivate — **cautiverio** nm : captivity — **cautivo, -va** adj & n : captive

cauto, -ta adj : cautious

cavar v : dig

caverna nf : cavern, cave

cavidad nf : cavity

cavilar vi : ponder

cayado nm : crook, staff

cazar {21} vt 1 : hunt 2 ATRAPAR : catch, bag — vi : go hunting — **caza** nf 1 : hunt, hunting 2 : game (animals) — **cazador, -dora** n : hunter

cazo nm 1 : saucepan 2 CUCHARÓN : ladle — **cazuela** nf : casserole

CD nm : CD, compact disc

cebada nf : barley

cebar vt 1 : bait 2 : feed, fatten (animals) 3 : prime (a firearm, etc.) — **cebo** nm 1 CARNADA : bait 2 : charge (of a firearm)

cebolla nf : onion — **cebolleta** nf : scallion, green onion — **cebollino** nm : chive

cebra nf : zebra

cecear vi : lisp — **ceceo** nm : lisp

cedazo nm : sieve

ceder vi 1 : yield, give way 2 DISMINUIR : diminish, abate — vt : cede, hand over

cedro nm : cedar

cédula nf : document, certificate

cegar {49} vt 1 : blind 2 TAPAR : block, stop up — vi : be blinded, go blind — **ceguera** nf : blindness

ceja nf : eyebrow

cejar vi : give in, back down

celada nf : trap, ambush

celador, -dora n : guard, warden

celda nf : cell (of a jail)

celebrar vt 1 : celebrate 2 : hold (a meeting), say (Mass) 3 ALEGRARSE DE : be happy about — **celebrarse** vr : take place — **celebración** nf, pl **-ciones** : celebration — **célebre** adj : famous, celebrated — **celebridad** nf : celebrity

celeridad nf : swiftness, speed

celeste adj 1 : celestial, heavenly 2 or azul ~ : sky blue — **celestial** adj : celestial, heavenly

celibato nm : celibacy — **célibe** adj : celibate

celo nm 1 : zeal 2 en ~ : in heat 3 ~s nmpl : jealousy 4 tener ~s : be jealous

celofán nm, pl **-fanes** : cellophane

celoso, -sa adj 1 : jealous 2 DILIGENTE : zealous

célula nf : cell — **celular** adj : cellular

celulosa nf : cellulose

cementerio nm : cemetery

cemento nm 1 : cement 2 ~ armado : reinforced concrete

cena nf : supper, dinner

cenagal nm : bog, quagmire — **cenagoso** adj : swampy

cenar vi : have dinner, have supper — vt : have for dinner or supper

cenicero nm : ashtray

cenit nm : zenith

ceniza nf : ash

censo nm : census

censurar vt 1 : censor 2 REPROBAR : censure, criticize — **censura** nf 1 : censorship 2 REPROBACIÓN : censure, criticism

centavo nm 1 : cent 2 : centavo (unit of currency)

centellear vi : sparkle, twinkle — **centella** nf 1 : flash 2 CHISPA : spark — **centelleo** nm : twinkling, sparkle

centenar nm : hundred — **centenario** nm : centennial

centeno nm : rye

centésimo, -ma adj : hundredth
centígrado adj : centigrade, Celsius
centigramo nm : centigram
centímetro nm : centimeter
centinela nmf : sentinel, sentry
central adj : central — ~ nf : main office, headquarters — **centralita** nf : switchboard — **centralizar** {21} vt : centralize
centrar vt : center — **centrarse** vr ~ **en** : focus on — **céntrico, -ca** adj : central — **centro** nm 1 : center 2 : downtown (of a city) 3 ~ **de mesa** : centerpiece
centroamericano, -na adj : Central American
ceñir {67} vt 1 : encircle 2 : fit (s.o.) tightly — **ceñirse** vr ~ **a** : limit oneself to — **ceñido, -da** adj : tight
ceño nm 1 : frown 2 **fruncir el** ~ : knit one's brow, frown
cepillo nm 1 : brush 2 : (carpenter's) plane 3 ~ **de dientes** : toothbrush — **cepillar** vt 1 : brush 2 : plane (wood)
cera nf 1 : wax, beeswax 2 : floor wax, furniture wax
cerámica nf 1 : ceramics pl 2 : (piece of) pottery
cerca[1] nf : fence — **cercado** nm : enclosure
cerca[2] adv 1 : close, near 2 ~ **de** : near, close to 3 ~ **de** : nearly, almost — **cercano, -na** adj : near, close — **cercanía** nf 1 : proximity 2 ~s nfpl : outskirts
cercar {72} vt 1 : fence in 2 RODEAR : surround
cerciorarse vr ~ **de** : make sure of
cerco nm 1 : circle, ring 2 ASEDIO : siege 3 Lat : fence
cerda nf : bristle
cerdo nm 1 : pig, hog 2 ~ **macho** : boar
cereal adj & nm : cereal
cerebro nm : brain — **cerebral** adj : cerebral
ceremonia nf : ceremony — **ceremonial** adj : ceremonial — **ceremonioso, -sa** adj : ceremonious
cereza nf : cherry
cerilla nf : match — **cerillo** nm Lat : match
cerner {56} or **cernir** vt : sift — **cernerse** vr 1 : hover 2 ~ **sobre** : loom over — **cernidor** nm : sieve
cero nm : zero
cerrar {55} vt 1 : close, shut 2 : turn off (a faucet, etc.) 3 : bring to an end — vi 1 : close up, lock up 2 : close down (a business, etc.) — **cerrarse** vr 1

: close, shut 2 TERMINAR : come to a close, end — **cerrado, -da** adj 1 : closed, shut, locked 2 : overcast (of weather) 3 : sharp (of a curve) 4 : thick, broad (of an accent) — **cerradura** nf : lock — **cerrajero, -ra** n : locksmith
cerro nm : hill
cerrojo nm : bolt, latch
certamen nm, pl **-támenes** : competition, contest
certero, -ra adj : accurate, precise
certeza nf : certainty — **certidumbre** nf : certainty
certificar {72} vt 1 : certify 2 : register (mail) — **certificado, -da** adj : certified, registered — **certificado** nm : certificate
cervato nm : fawn
cerveza nf 1 : beer 2 ~ **de barril** : draft beer — **cervecería** nf 1 : brewery 2 BAR : beer hall, bar
cesar vi : cease, stop — vt : dismiss, lay off — **cesación** nf, pl **-ciones** : cessation, suspension — **cesante** adj 1 : laid off 2 Lat : unemployed — **cesantía** nf Lat : unemployment
cesárea nf : cesarean (section)
cese nm 1 : cessation, stop 2 DESTITUCIÓN : dismissal
césped nm : lawn, grass
cesta nf : basket — **cesto** nm 1 : (large) basket 2 ~ **de basura** : wastebasket
cetro nm : scepter
chabacano nm Lat : apricot
chabola nf Spain : shack, shanty
chacal nm : jackal
cháchara nf fam : gabbing, chatter
chacra nf Lat : (small) farm
chafar vt fam : flatten, crush
chal nm : shawl
chaleco nm : vest
chalet nm Spain : house
chalupa nf 1 : small boat 2 Lat : small stuffed tortilla
chamarra nf : jacket
chamba nf Lat fam : job
champaña or **champán** nm : champagne
champiñón nm, pl **-ñones** : mushroom
champú nm, pl **-pús** or **-púes** : shampoo
chamuscar {72} vt : scorch
chance nm Lat : chance, opportunity
chancho nm Lat : pig
chanclos nmpl : galoshes
chantaje nm : blackmail — **chantajear** vt : blackmail
chanza nf : joke, jest
chapa nf 1 : sheet, plate 2 INSIGNIA : badge — **chapado, -da** adj 1 : plated

2 chapado a la antigua : old-fashioned
chaparrón *nm, pl* **-rrones** : downpour
chapotear *vi* : splash
chapucero, -ra *adj* : shoddy, sloppy — **chapuza** *nf* : botched job
chapuzón *nm, pl* **-zones** : dip, short swim
chaqueta *nf* : jacket
charca *nf* : pond — **charco** *nm* : puddle
charlar *vi* : chat — **charla** *nf* : chat, talk — **charlatán, -tana** *adj, mpl* **-tanes** : talkative — ~ *n* 1 : chatterbox 2 FARSANTE : charlatan
charol *nm* 1 : patent leather 2 BARNIZ : varnish
chasco *nm* 1 : trick, joke 2 DECEPCIÓN : disappointment
chasis *nms & pl* : chassis
chasquear *vt* 1 : click (the tongue), snap (one's fingers) 2 : crack (a whip) — **chasquido** *nm* 1 : click, snap 2 : crack (of a whip)
chatarra *nf* : scrap (metal)
chato, -ta *adj* 1 : pug-nosed 2 APLANADO : flat
chauvinismo *nm* : chauvinism — **chauvinista** *adj* : chauvinist, chauvinistic
chaval, -vala *n fam* : kid, boy *m*, girl *f*
checo, -ca *adj* : Czech — **checo** *nm* : Czech (language)
chef *nm* : chef
cheque *nm* : check — **chequera** *nf* : checkbook
chequear *vt Lat* 1 : check, inspect, verify 2 : check in (baggage) — **chequeo** *nm* 1 : (medical) checkup 2 *Lat* : check, inspection
chica → **chico**
chicano, -na *adj* : Chicano, Mexican-American
chícharo *nm Lat* : pea
chicharrón *nm, pl* **-rrones** : pork rind
chichón *nm, pl* **-chones** : bump
chicle *nm* : chewing gum
chico, -ca *adj* : little, small — ~ *n* : child, boy *m*, girl *f*
chiflar *vt* : whistle at, boo — *vi Lat* : whistle — **chiflado, -da** *adj fam* : crazy, nuts — **chiflido** *nm* : whistling
chile *nm* : chili pepper
chileno, -na *adj* : Chilean
chillar *vi* 1 : shriek, scream 2 CHIRRIAR : screech, squeal — **chillido** *nm* 1 : scream 2 CHIRRIDO : screech, squeal — **chillón, -llona** *adj, mpl* **-llones** : shrill, loud
chimenea *nf* 1 : chimney 2 HOGAR : fireplace

chimpancé *nm* : chimpanzee
chinche *nf* : bedbug
chino, -na *adj* : Chinese — **chino** *nm* : Chinese (language)
chiquillo, -lla *n* : kid, child
chiquito, -ta *adj* : tiny — ~ *n* : little child, tot
chiribita *nf* : spark
chiripa *nf* 1 : fluke 2 **de** ~ : by sheer luck
chirivia *nf* : parsnip
chirriar {85} *vi* 1 : squeak, creak 2 : screech (of brakes, etc.) — **chirrido** *nm* 1 : squeak, creak 2 : screech (of brakes)
chisme *nm* : (piece of) gossip — **chismear** *vi* : gossip — **chismoso, -sa** *adj* : gossipy — ~ *n* : gossip
chispear *vi* : spark — **chispa** *nf* : spark
chisporrotear *vi* : crackle, sizzle — **chisporroteo** *nm* : crackle
chiste *nm* : joke, funny story — **chistoso, -sa** *adj* : funny, witty
chivo, -va *n* : kid, young goat
chocar {72} *vi* 1 : crash, collide 2 ENFRENTARSE : clash — **chocante** *adj* 1 : striking, shocking 2 *Lat* : unpleasant, rude
choclo *nm Lat* : ear of corn, corncob
chocolate *nm* : chocolate
chofer *or* **chófer** *nm* 1 : chauffeur 2 CONDUCTOR : driver
choque *nm* 1 : shock 2 : crash, collision (of vehicles) 3 CONFLICTO : clash
chorizo *nm* : chorizo, sausage
chorrear *vi* 1 : drip 2 BROTAR : pour out, gush — **chorro** *nm* 1 : stream, jet 2 HILO : trickle
chovinismo → **chauvinismo**
choza *nf* : hut, shack
chubasco *nm* : downpour, squall
chuchería *nf* 1 : knickknack, trinket 2 DULCE : sweet
chueco, -ca *adj Lat* : crooked
chuleta *nf* : cutlet, chop
chulo, -la *adj fam* : cute, pretty
chupar *vt* 1 : suck 2 ABSORBER : absorb 3 *fam* : guzzle — *vi* : suckle — **chupada** *nf* : suck, sucking — **chupete** *nm* 1 : pacifier 2 *Lat* : lollipop
churro *nm* 1 : fried dough 2 *fam* : botch, mess
chusco, -ca *adj* : funny
chusma *nf* : riffraff, rabble
chutar *vi* : shoot (in soccer)
cianuro *nm* : cyanide
cicatriz *nf, pl* **-trices** : scar — **cicatrizar** {21} *vi* : form a scar, heal
cíclico, -ca *adj* : cyclical
ciclismo *nm* : cycling — **ciclista** *nmf* : cyclist

ciclo *nm* : cycle
ciclón *nm, pl* **-clones** : cyclone
ciego, -ga *adj* : blind — **ciegamente** *adv* : blindly
cielo *nm* **1** : sky **2** : heaven (in religion)
ciempiés *nms & pl* : centipede
cien *adj* : a hundred, hundred — ~ *nm* : one hundred
ciénaga *nf* : swamp, bog
ciencia *nf* **1** : science **2 a ~ cierta** : for a fact
cieno *nm* : mire, mud, silt
científico, -ca *adj* : scientific — ~ *n* : scientist
ciento *adj (used in compound numbers)* : one hundred — ~ *nm* **1** : hundred, group of a hundred **2 por ~** : percent
cierre *nm* **1** : closing, closure **2** BROCHE : fastener, clasp
cierto, -ta *adj* **1** : true **2** SEGURO : certain **3 por ~** : as a matter of fact
ciervo, -va *n* : deer, stag *m*, hind *f*
cifra *nf* **1** : number, figure **2** : sum (of money, etc.) **3** CLAVE : code, cipher — **cifrar** *vt* **1** : write in code **2 ~ la esperanza en** : pin all one's hopes on
cigarrillo *nm* : cigarette — **cigarro** *nm* **1** : cigarette **2** PURO : cigar
cigüeña *nf* : stork
cilantro *nm* : cilantro, coriander
cilindro *nm* : cylinder — **cilíndrico, -ca** *adj* : cylindrical
cima *nf* : peak, summit
címbalo *nm* : cymbal
cimbrar *or* **cimbrear** *vt* : shake, rock — **cimbrarse** *or* **cimbrearse** *vr* : sway
cimentar {55} *vt* **1** : lay the foundation of **2** : cement, strengthen (relations, etc.) — **cimientos** *nmpl* : base, foundation(s)
cinc *nm* : zinc
cincel *nm* : chisel — **cincelar** *vt* : chisel
cinco *adj & nm* : five
cincuenta *adj & nm* : fifty — **cincuentavo, -va** *adj* : fiftieth — **cincuentavo** *nm* : fiftieth
cine *nm* : cinema, movies *pl* — **cinematográfico, -ca** *adj* : movie, film
cínico, -ca *adj* : cynical — ~ *n* : cynic — **cinismo** *nm* : cynicism
cinta *nf* **1** : ribbon, band **2 ~ adhesiva** : adhesive tape **3 ~ métrica** : tape measure **4 ~ magnetofónica** : magnetic tape
cinto *nm* : belt, girdle — **cintura** *nf* : waist — **cinturón** *nm, pl* **-rones 1** : belt **2 ~ de seguridad** : seat belt
ciprés *nm, pl* **-preses** : cypress
circo *nm* : circus
circuito *nm* : circuit

circulación *nf, pl* **-ciones 1** : circulation **2** TRÁFICO : traffic — **circular** *vi* **1** : circulate **2** : drive (a vehicle) — ~ *adj* : circular
círculo *nm* : circle
circuncidar *vt* : circumcise — **circuncisión** *nf, pl* **-siones** : circumcision
circundar *vt* : surround
circunferencia *nf* : circumference
circunscribir {33} *vt* : confine, limit — **circunscribirse** *vr* ~ **a** : limit oneself to — **circunscripción** *nf, pl* **-ciones** : district, constituency
circunspecto, -ta *adj* : circumspect, cautious
circunstancia *nf* : circumstance — **circunstancial** *adj* : chance — **circunstante** *nmf* **1** : bystander **2 los ~s** : those present
circunvalación *nf, pl* **-ciones 1** : encircling **2 carretera de ~** : bypass
cirio *nm* : candle
ciruela *nf* **1** : plum **2 ~ pasa** : prune
cirugía *nf* : surgery — **cirujano, -na** *n* : surgeon
cisma *nf* : schism
cisne *nm* : swan
cisterna *nf* : cistern
cita *nf* **1** : appointment, date **2** REFERENCIA : quote, quotation — **citación** *nf, pl* **-ciones** : summons — **citar** *vt* **1** : quote, cite **2** CONVOCAR : make an appointment with **3** : summon (in law) — **citarse** *vr* ~ **con** : arrange to meet
cítrico *nm* : citrus (fruit)
ciudad *nf* : city, town — **ciudadano, -na** *n* **1** : citizen **2** HABITANTE : resident — **ciudadanía** *nf* : citizenship
cívico, -ca *adj* : civic
civil *adj* : civil — ~ *nmf* : civilian — **civilidad** *nf* : civility — **civilización** *nf, pl* **-ciones** : civilization — **civilizar** {21} *vt* : civilize
cizaña *nf* : discord, rift
clamar *vi* : clamor, cry out — **clamor** *nm* : clamor, outcry — **clamoroso, -sa** *adj* : clamorous, loud
clan *nm* : clan
clandestino, -na *adj* : clandestine, secret
clara *nf* : egg white
claraboya *nf* : skylight
claramente *adv* : clearly
clarear *v impers* **1** : dawn **2** ACLARAR : clear up — *vi* : be transparent
claridad *nf* **1** : clarity, clearness **2** LUZ : light
clarificar {72} *vt* : clarify — **clarificación** *nf, pl* **-ciones** : clarification
clarín *nm, pl* **-rines** : bugle

clarinete *nm* : clarinet
clarividente *adj* **1** : clairvoyant **2** PER-
SPICAZ : perspicacious — **clarividen-
cia** *nf* **1** : clairvoyance **2** PERSPICACIA
: farsightedness
claro *adv* **1** : clearly **2** POR SUPUESTO : of
course, surely — ∼ *nm* **1** : clearing,
glade **2** ∼ **de luna** : moonlight —
claro, -ra *adj* **1** : clear, bright **2** : light
(of colors) **3** EVIDENTE : clear, evident
clase *nf* **1** class **2** TIPO : sort, kind
clásico, -ca *adj* : classic, classical —
clásico *nm* : classic
clasificar {72} *vt* **1** : classify, sort out **2**
: rate, rank (a hotel, a team, etc.) —
clasificarse *vr* : qualify (in competi-
tions) — **clasificación** *nf, pl* **-ciones**
1 : classification **2** : league (in sports)
claudicar {72} *vi* : back down
claustro *nm* : cloister
claustrofobia *nf* : claustrophobia —
claustrofóbico, -ca *adj* : claustropho-
bic
cláusula *nf* : clause
clausurar *v* : close (down) — **clausu-
ra** *nf* : closure, closing
clavado *nm Lat* : dive
clavar *vt* **1** : nail, hammer **2** HINCAR
: drive in, plunge
clave *nf* **1** CIFRA : code **2** SOLUCIÓN : key
3 : clef (in music) — ∼ *adj* : key
clavel *nm* : carnation
clavicémbalo *nm* : harpsichord
clavícula *nf* : collarbone
clavija *nf* **1** : peg, pin **2** : (electric) plug
clavo *nm* **1** : nail **2** : clove (spice)
claxon *nm, pl* **cláxones** : horn (of an
automobile)
clemencia *nf* : clemency, mercy —
clemente *adj* : merciful
clerical *adj* : clerical — **clérigo, -ga**
n : clergyman, cleric — **clero** *nm*
: clergy
cliché *nm* **1** : cliché **2** : negative (of a
photograph)
cliente, -ta *n* : customer, client — **clientela** *nf* : clientele, customers *pl*
clima *nm* **1** : climate **2** AMBIENTE : atmosphere — **climático, -ca** *adj* : cli-
matic
climatizar {21} *vt* : air-condition —
climatizado, -da *adj* : air-conditioned
clímax *nm* : climax
clínica *nf* : clinic — **clínico, -ca** *adj*
: clinical
clip *nm, pl* **clips** : (paper) clip
cloaca *nf* : sewer
cloquear *vi* : cluck — **cloqueo** *nm*
: cluck, clucking
cloro *nm* : chlorine

clóset *nm Lat, pl* **clósets** : (built-in)
closet, cupboard
club *nm* : club
coacción *nf, pl* **-ciones** : coercion —
coaccionar *vt* : coerce
coagular *v* : clot, coagulate — **coagularse** *vr* : coagulate — **coágulo** *nm*
: clot
coalición *nf, pl* **-ciones** : coalition
coartada *nf* : alibi
coartar *vt* : restrict, limit
cobarde *nmf* : coward — ∼ *adj* : cowardly — **cobardía** *nf* : cowardice
cobaya *nf* : guinea pig
cobertizo *nm* : shelter, shed
cobertor *nm* : bedspread
cobertura *nf* **1** : cover **2** : coverage (of
news, etc.)
cobijar *vt* : shelter — **cobijarse** *vr*
: take shelter — **cobija** *nf Lat* : blanket
— **cobijo** *nm* : shelter
cobra *nf* : cobra
cobrar *vt* **1** : charge, collect **2** : earn (a
salary, etc.) **3** ADQUIRIR : acquire, gain
4 : cash (a check) — *vi* : be paid —
cobrador, -dora *n* **1** : collector **2**
: conductor (of a bus, etc.)
cobre *nm* : copper
cobro *nm* : collection (of money), cash-
ing (of a check)
cocaína *nf* : cocaine
cocción *nf, pl* **-ciones** : cooking
cocear *vi* : kick
cocer {14} *vt* **1** : cook **2** HERVIR : boil
coche *nm* **1** : car, automobile **2** : coach
(of a train) **3** *or* ∼ **de caballos** : carriage **4** ∼ **fúnebre** : hearse —
cochecito *nm* : baby carriage, stroller
— **cochera** *nf* : garage, carport
cochino, -na *n* **1** : pig, hog — ∼ *adj*
fam : dirty, filthy — **cochinada** *nf*
fam : dirty thing — **cochinillo** *nm*
: piglet
cocido, -da *adj* **1** : boiled, cooked **2**
bien ∼ : well-done — **cocido** *nm*
: stew
cociente *nm* : quotient
cocina *nf* **1** : kitchen **2** : (kitchen) stove
3 : (art of) cooking, cuisine — **cocinar** *v* : cook — **cocinero, -ra** *n* : cook,
chef
coco *nm* : coconut
cocodrilo *nm* : crocodile
coctel *or* **cóctel** *nm* **1** : cocktail **2** FIES-
TA : cocktail party
codazo *nm* **1** : nudge **2 dar un** ∼ **a**
: elbow, nudge
codicia *nf* : greed — **codiciar** *vt* : covet
— **codicioso, -sa** *adj* : covetous,
greedy

código *nm* **1** : code **2** ~ **postal** : zip code **3** ~ **morse** : Morse code

codo *nm* : elbow

codorniz *nf*, *pl* **-nices** : quail

coexistir *vi* : coexist

cofre *nm* : chest, coffer

coger {15} *vt* **1** : take (hold of) **2** ATRA-PAR : catch **3** : pick up (from the ground) **4** : pick (fruit, etc.) — **cogerse** *vr* : hold on

cohechar *vt* : bribe — **cohecho** *nm* : bribe, bribery

coherencia *nf* : coherence — **coherente** *adj* : coherent — **cohesión** *nf*, *pl* **-siones** : cohesion

cohete *nm* : rocket

cohibir {62} *vt* **1** : restrict **2** : inhibit (a person) — **cohibirse** *vr* : feel inhibited — **cohibido, -da** *adj* : inhibited, shy

coincidir *vi* **1** : coincide **2** ~ **con** : agree with — **coincidencia** *nf* : coincidence

cojear *vi* **1** : limp **2** : wobble (of furniture, etc.) — **cojera** *nf* : limp

cojín *nm*, *pl* **-jines** : cushion — **cojinete** *nm* **1** : pad, cushion **2** : bearing (of a machine)

cojo, -ja *adj* **1** : lame **2** : wobbly (of furniture) — ~ *n* : lame person

col *nf* **1** : cabbage **2** ~ **de Bruselas** : Brussels sprout

cola *nf* **1** : tail **2** FILA : line (of people) **3** : end (of a line) **4** PEGAMENTO : glue **5** ~ **de caballo** : ponytail

colaborar *vi* : collaborate — **colaboración** *nf*, *pl* **-ciones** : collaboration — **colaborador, -dora** *n* **1** : collaborator **2** : contributor (to a periodical)

colada *nf Spain* **1** : laundry **2 hacer la** ~ : do the washing

colador *nm* : colander, strainer

colapso *nm* : collapse

colar {19} *vt* : strain, filter — **colarse** *vr* : sneak in, gate-crash

colcha *nf* : bedspread, quilt — **colchón** *nm*, *pl* **-chones** : mattress — **colchoneta** *nf* : mat

colear *vi* : wag its tail

colección *nf*, *pl* **-ciones** : collection — **coleccionar** *vt* : collect — **coleccionista** *nmf* : collector — **colecta** *nf* : collection (of donations)

colectividad *nf* : community — **colectivo, -va** *adj* : collective — **colectivo** *nm* **1** : collective **2** *Lat* : city bus

colector *nm* : sewer

colega *nmf* : colleague

colegio *nm* **1** : school **2** : (professional) college — **colegial, -giala** *n* : schoolboy *m*, schoolgirl *f*

colegir {28} *vt* : gather

cólera *nm* **1** : cholera — ~ *nf* : anger, rage — **colérico, -ca** *adj* **1** : bad-tempered **2** FURIOSO : angry

colesterol *nm* : cholesterol

coleta *nf* : pigtail

colgar {16} *vt* **1** : hang **2** : hang up (a telephone) **3** : hang out (laundry) — *vi* : hang up — **colgante** *adj* : hanging — ~ *nm* : pendant

colibrí *nm* : hummingbird

cólico *nm* : colic

coliflor *nf* : cauliflower

colilla *nf* : (cigarette) butt

colina *nf* : hill

colindar *vi* ~ **con** : be adjacent to — **colindante** *adj* : adjacent

coliseo *nm* : coliseum

colisión *nf*, *pl* **-siones** : collision — **colisionar** *vi* ~ **contra** : collide with

collar *nm* **1** : necklace **2** : collar (for pets)

colmar *vt* **1** : fill to the brim **2** : fulfill (a wish, etc.) **3** ~ **de** : shower with — **colmado, -da** *adj* : heaping

colmena *nf* : beehive

colmillo *nm* **1** : canine (tooth) **2** : fang (of a dog, etc.), tusk (of an elephant)

colmo *nm* **1** : height, limit **2 ¡eso es el** ~ **!** : that's the last straw!

colocar {72} *vt* **1** PONER : place, put **2** : find a job for — **colocarse** *vr* **1** SITUARSE : position oneself **2** : get a job — **colocación** *nf*, *pl* **-ciones 1** : placement, placing **2** EMPLEO : position, job

colombiano, -na *adj* : Colombian

colon *nm* : (intestinal) colon

colonia *nf* **1** : colony **2** PERFUME : cologne **3** *Lat* : residential area — **colonial** *adj* : colonial — **colonizar** {21} *vt* : colonize — **colonización** *nf*, *pl* **-ciones** : colonization — **colono, -na** *n* : settler, colonist

coloquial *adj* : colloquial — **coloquio** *nm* **1** : talk, discussion **2** CONGRESO : conference

color *nm* : color — **colorado, -da** *adj* : red — **colorear** *vt* : color — **colorete** *nm* : rouge — **colorido** *nm* : colors *pl*, coloring

colosal *adj* : colossal

columna *nf* **1** : column **2** ~ **vertebral** : spine, backbone — **columnista** *nmf* : columnist

columpiar *vt* : push (on a swing) — **columpiarse** *vr* : swing — **columpio** *nm* : swing

coma¹ *nm* : coma

coma² *nf* : comma

comadre *nf* **1** : godmother of one's child, mother of one's godchild **2** *fam*

: (female) friend — **comadrear** *vi fam* : gossip

comadreja *nf* : weasel

comadrona *nf* : midwife

comandancia *nf* : command headquarters, command — **comandante** *nmf* 1 : commander 2 : major (in the military) — **comando** *nm* 1 : commando 2 *Lat* : command

comarca *nf* : region, area

combar *vt* : bend, curve

combatir *vt* : combat, fight against — *vi* : fight — **combate** *nm* 1 : combat 2 : fight (in boxing) — **combatiente** *nmf* : combatant, fighter

combinar *vt* 1 : combine 2 : put together, match (colors, etc.) — **combinarse** *vr* : get together — **combinación** *nf, pl* **-ciones** 1 : combination 2 : connection (in travel)

combustible *nm* : fuel — **~** *adj* : combustible — **combustión** *nf, pl* **-tiones** : combustion

comedia *nf* : comedy

comedido, -da *adj* : moderate

comedor *nm* : dining room

comensal *nmf* : diner, dinner guest

comentar *vt* 1 : comment on, discuss 2 MENCIONAR : mention — **comentario** *nm* 1 : comment, remark 2 ANÁLISIS : commentary — **comentarista** *nmf* : commentator

comenzar {29} *v* : begin, start

comer *vt* 1 : eat 2 *fam* : eat up, eat into — *vi* 1 : eat 2 CENAR : have a meal 3 **dar de ~** : feed — **comerse** *vr* : eat up

comercio *nm* 1 : commerce, trade 2 NEGOCIO : business — **comercial** *adj* : commercial — **comercializar** {21} *vt* : market — **comerciante** *nmf* : merchant, dealer — **comerciar** *vi* : do business, trade

comestible *adj* : edible — **comestibles** *nmpl* : groceries, food

cometa *nm* : comet — **~** *nf* : kite

cometer *vt* 1 : commit 2 **~ un error** : make a mistake — **cometido** *nm* : assignment, task

comezón *nf, pl* **-zones** : itchiness, itching

comicios *nmpl* : elections

cómico, -ca *adj* : comic, comical — **~** *n* : comic, comedian

comida *nf* 1 ALIMENTO : food 2 *Spain* : lunch 3 *Lat* : dinner 4 **tres ~s al día** : three meals a day

comienzo *nm* : beginning

comillas *nfpl* : quotation marks

comino *nm* : cumin

comisario, -ria *n* : commissioner — **comisaría** *nf* : police station

comisión *nf, pl* **-siones** 1 : commission 2 COMITÉ : committee

comité *nm* : committee

como *conj* 1 : as, since 2 **sí** : if — **~** *prep* 1 : like, as 2 **así ~** : as well as — **~** *adv* 1 : as 2 APROXIMADAMENTE : around, about

cómo *adv* 1 : how 2 **~ no** : by all means 3 **¿~ te llamas?** : what's your name?

cómoda *nf* : chest of drawers

comodidad *nf* : comfort, convenience

comodín *nm, pl* **-dines** : joker (in playing cards)

cómodo, -da *adj* 1 : comfortable 2 ÚTIL : handy, convenient

comoquiera *adv* 1 : in any way 2 **~ que** : however

compacto, -ta *adj* : compact

compadecer {53} *vt* : feel sorry for — **compadecerse** *vr* **~ de** : take pity on

compadre *nm* 1 : godfather of one's child, father of one's godchild 2 *fam* : buddy

compañero, -ra *n* : companion, partner — **compañerismo** *nm* : companionship

compañía *nf* : company

comparar *vt* : compare — **comparable** *adj* : comparable — **comparación** *nf, pl* **-ciones** : comparison — **comparativo, -va** *adj* : comparative

comparecer *vt* : appear (before a court, etc.)

compartimiento *or* **compartimento** *nm* : compartment

compartir *vt* : share

compás *nm, pl* **-pases** 1 : compass 2 : rhythm, time (in music)

compasión *nf, pl* **-siones** : compassion, pity — **compasivo, -va** *adj* : compassionate

compatible *adj* : compatible — **compatibilidad** *nf* : compatibility

compatriota *nmf* : compatriot, fellow countryman

compeler *vt* : compel

compendiar *vt* : summarize — **compendio** *nm* : summary

compensar *vt* : compensate for — **compensación** *nf, pl* **-ciones** : compensation

competir {54} *vi* : compete — **competencia** *nf* 1 : competition, rivalry 2 CAPACIDAD : competence — **competente** *adj* : competent — **competición** *nf, pl* **-ciones** : competition — **competidor, -dora** *n* : competitor

compilar *vt* : compile
compinche *nmf fam* : friend, chum
complacer {57} *vt* : please — **complacerse** *vr* ~ **en** : take pleasure in — **complaciente** *adj* : obliging, helpful
complejidad *nf* : complexity — **complejo, -ja** *adj* : complex — **complejo** *nm* : complex
complementar *vt* : complement — **complementario, -ria** *adj* : complementary — **complemento** *nm* 1 : complement 2 : object (in grammar)
completar *vt* : complete — **completo, -ta** *adj* 1 : complete 2 PERFECTO : perfect 3 LLENO : full — **completamente** *adv* : completely
complexión *nf, pl* **-xiones** : constitution, build
complicar {72} *vt* 1 : complicate 2 IMPLICAR : involve — **complicación** *nf, pl* **-ciones** : complication — **complicado, -da** *adj* : complicated, complex
cómplice *nmf* : accomplice — ~ *adj* : conspiratorial, knowing
complot *nm, pl* **-plots** : conspiracy, plot
componer {60} *vt* 1 : make up, compose 2 : compose, write (a song) 3 ARREGLAR : fix, repair — **componerse** *vr* ~ **de** : consist of — **componente** *adj & nm* : component, constituent
comportarse *vr* : behave — **comportamiento** *nm* : behavior
composición *nf, pl* **-ciones** : composition — **compositor, -tora** *n* : composer, songwriter
compostura *nf* 1 : composure 2 REPARACIÓN : repair
comprar *vt* : buy, purchase — **compra** *nf* 1 : purchase 2 **ir de** ~**s** : go shopping — **comprador, -dora** *n* : buyer, shopper
comprender *vt* 1 : comprehend, understand 2 ABARCAR : cover, include — **comprensible** *adj* : understandable — **comprensión** *nf, pl* **-siones** : understanding — **comprensivo, -va** *adj* : understanding
compresa *nf* 1 : compress 2 *or* ~ **higiénica** : sanitary napkin
compresión *nf, pl* **-siones** : compression — **comprimido** *nm* : pill, tablet — **comprimir** *vt* : compress
comprobar {19} *vt* 1 VERIFICAR : check 2 DEMOSTRAR : prove — **comprobación** *nf, pl* **-ciones** : verification, check — **comprobante** *nm* 1 : proof 2 RECIBO : receipt, voucher
comprometer *vt* 1 : compromise 2 ARRIESGAR : jeopardize 3 OBLIGAR : com-

mit, put under obligation — **comprometerse** *vr* 1 : commit oneself 2 ~ **con** : get engaged to — **comprometedor, -dora** *adj* : compromising — **comprometido, -da** *adj* 1 : compromising, awkward 2 : engaged (to be married) — **compromiso** *nm* 1 : obligation, commitment 2 : (marriage) engagement 3 ACUERDO : agreement 4 APURO : awkward situation
compuesto, -ta *adj* 1 : compound 2 ~ **de** : made up of, consisting of — **compuesto** *nm* : compound
compulsivo, -va *adj* : compelling, urgent
computar *vt* : compute, calculate — **computadora** *nf or* **computador** *nm* 1 : computer 2 ~ **portátil** : laptop computer — **cómputo** *nm* : calculation
comulgar {52} *vi* : receive Communion
común *adj, pl* **-munes** 1 : common 2 ~ **y corriente** : ordinary 3 **por lo** ~ : generally
comuna *nf* : commune — **comunal** *adj* : communal
comunicar {72} *vt* : communicate — **comunicarse** *vr* 1 : communicate 2 ~ **con** : get in touch with — **comunicación** *nf, pl* **-ciones** : communication — **comunicado** *nm* : communiqué — **comunicativo, -va** *adj* : communicative
comunidad *nf* : community
comunión *nf, pl* **-niones** : communion, Communion
comunismo *nm* : Communism — **comunista** *adj & nmf* : Communist
con *prep* 1 : with 2 A PESAR DE : in spite of 3 *(before an infinitive)* : by 4 ~ **(tal) que** : so long as
cóncavo, -va *adj* : concave
concebir {54} *v* : conceive — **concebible** *adj* : conceivable
conceder *vt* 1 : grant, bestow 2 ADMITIR : concede
concejal, -jala *n* : councilman, alderman
concentrar *vt* : concentrate — **concentrarse** *vr* : concentrate — **concentración** *nf, pl* **-ciones** : concentration
concepción *nf, pl* **-ciones** : conception — **concepto** *nm* 1 : concept 2 OPINIÓN : opinion
concernir {17} *vi* ~ **a** : concern — **concerniente** *adj* ~ **a** : concerning
concertar {55} *vt* 1 : arrange, coordinate 2 *(used before an infinitive)* : agree 3 : harmonize (in music) — *vi* : be in harmony

concesión *nf, pl* **-siones 1** : concession **2** : awarding (of prizes, etc.)

concha *nf* : shell

conciencia *nf* **1** : conscience **2** CONOCIMIENTO : consciousness, awareness — **concientizar** {21} *vt Lat* : make aware — **concientizarse** *vr Lat* ∼ **de** : realize

concienzudo, -da *adj* : conscientious

concierto *nm* **1** : concert **2** : concerto (musical composition)

conciliar *vt* : reconcile — **conciliación** *nf, pl* **-ciones** : reconciliation

concilio *nm* : council

conciso, -sa *adj* : concise

conciudadano, -na *n* : fellow citizen

concluir {41} *vt* : conclude — *vi* : come to an end — **conclusión** *nf, pl* **-siones** : conclusion — **concluyente** *adj* : conclusive

concordar {19} *vi* : agree — *vt* : reconcile — **concordancia** *nf* : agreement — **concordia** *nf* : harmony, concord

concretar *vt* : make concrete, specify — **concretarse** *vr* : become definite, take shape — **concreto, -ta** *adj* **1** : concrete **2** DETERMINADO : specific **3** **en** ∼ : specifically — **concreto** *nm Lat* : concrete

concurrir *vi* **1** : come together, meet **2** ∼ **a** : take part in — **concurrencia** *nf* : audience, turnout — **concurrido, -da** *adj* : busy, crowded

concursar *vi* : compete, participate — **concursante** *nmf* : competitor — **concurso** *nm* **1** : competition **2** CONCURRENCIA : gathering **3** AYUDA : help, cooperation

condado *nm* : county

conde, -desa *n* : count *m*, countess *f*

condenar *vt* **1** : condemn, damn **2** : sentence (a criminal) — **condena** *nf* **1** : condemnation **2** SENTENCIA : sentence — **condenación** *nf, pl* **-ciones** : condemnation, damnation

condensar *vt* : condense — **condensación** *nf, pl* **-ciones** : condensation

condesa *nf* → **conde**

condescender {56} *vi* **1** : acquiesce, agree **2** ∼ **a** : condescend to — **condescendiente** *adj* : condescending

condición *nf, pl* **-ciones 1** : condition, state **2** CALIDAD : capacity, position — **condicional** *adj* : conditional

condimento *nm* : condiment, seasoning

condolerse {47} *vr* : sympathize — **condolencia** *nf* : condolence

condominio *nm* **1** : joint ownership **2** *Lat* : condominium

condón *nm, pl* **-dones** : condom

conducir {61} *vt* **1** DIRIGIR : direct, lead **2** MANEJAR : drive — *vi* **1** : drive **2** ∼ **a** : lead to — **conducirse** *vr* : behave

conducta *nf* : behavior, conduct

conducto *nm* : conduit, duct

conductor, -tora *n* : driver

conectar *vt* **1** : connect **2** ENCHUFAR : plug in — *vi* : connect

conejo, -ja *n* : rabbit — **conejera** *nf* : (rabbit) hutch

conexión *nf, pl* **-xiones** : connection — **conexo, -xa** *adj* : connected

confabularse *vr* : conspire, plot

confeccionar *vt* : make (up), prepare — **confección** *nf, pl* **-ciones 1** : making, preparation **2** : tailoring, dressmaking

confederación *nf, pl* **-ciones** : confederation

conferencia *nf* **1** : lecture **2** REUNIÓN : conference

conferir {76} *vt* : confer, bestow

confesar {55} *v* : confess — **confesarse** *vr* : go to confession — **confesión** *nf, pl* **-siones 1** : confession **2** CREDO : religion, creed

confeti *nm* : confetti

confiar {85} *vi* : trust — *vt* : entrust — **confiable** *adj* : trustworthy, reliable — **confiado, -da** *adj* **1** : confident **2** CRÉDULO : trusting — **confianza** *nf* **1** : trust **2** : confidence (in oneself)

confidencia *nf* : confidence, secret — **confidencial** *adj* : confidential — **confidencialidad** *nf* : confidentiality — **confidente** *nmf* **1** : confidant, confidante *f* **2** : (police) informer

configuración *nf, pl* **-ciones** : configuration, shape

confín *nm, pl* **-fines** : boundary, limit — **confinar** *vt* **1** : confine **2** DESTERRAR : exile

confirmar *vt* : confirm — **confirmación** *nf, pl* **-ciones** : confirmation

confiscar {72} *vt* : confiscate

confitería *nm* : candy store

confitura *nf* : jam

conflagración *nf, pl* **-ciones 1** : war, conflict **2** INCENDIO : fire

conflicto *nm* : conflict

confluencia *nf* : junction, confluence

conformar *vt* : shape, make up — **conformarse** *vr* **1** RESIGNARSE : resign oneself **2** ∼ **con** : content oneself with — **conforme** *adj* **1** : content, satisfied **2** ∼ **a** : in accordance with — ∼ *conj* : as — **conformidad** *nf* **1** : agreement **2** RESIGNACIÓN : resignation

confortar *vt* : comfort — **confortable** *adj* : comfortable

confrontar *vt* **1** : confront **2** COMPARAR : compare — *vi* : border — **confrontarse** *vr* ～ **con** : face up to — **confrontación** *nf, pl* **-ciones** : confrontation

confundir *vt* : confuse, mix up — **confundirse** *vr* : make a mistake, be confused — **confusión** *nf, pl* **-siones** : confusion — **confuso, -sa** *adj* **1** : confused **2** INDISTINTO : hazy, indistinct — **congelar** *vt* : freeze — **congelarse** *vr* : freeze — **congelación** *nf, pl* **-ciones** : freezing — **congelado, -da** *adj* : frozen — **congelador** *nm* : freezer

congeniar *vi* : get along

congestión *nf, pl* **-tiones** : congestion — **congestionado, -da** *adj* : congested

congoja *nf* : anguish, grief

congraciarse *vr* : ingratiate oneself

congratular *vt* : congratulate

congregar {52} *vt* : bring together — **congregarse** *vr* : congregate — **congregación** *nf, pl* **-ciones** : congregation, gathering

congreso *nm* : congress — **congresista** *nmf* : member of congress

conjeturar *vt* : guess, conjecture — **conjetura** *nf* : guess, conjecture

conjugar {52} *vt* : conjugate — **conjugación** *nf, pl* **-ciones** : conjugation

conjunción *nf, pl* **-ciones** : conjunction

conjunto, -ta *adj* : joint — **conjunto** *nm* **1** : collection **2** : outfit (of clothing) **3** GRUPO : band **4 en** ～ : as a whole

conjurar *vt* : ward off — *vi* : conspire, plot

conllevar *vt* : entail

conmemorar *vt* : commemorate — **conmemoración** *nf, pl* **-ciones** : commemoration — **conmemorativo, -va** *adj* : commemorative

conmigo *pron* : with me

conminar *vt* : threaten

conmiseración *nf, pl* **-ciones** : pity, commiseration

conmocionar *vt* : shock — **conmoción** *nf, pl* **-ciones 1** : shock, upheaval **2** *or* ～ **cerebral** : concussion

conmover {47} *vt* **1** : move, touch **2** SACUDIR : shake (up) — **conmoverse** *vr* : be moved — **conmovedor, -dora** *adj* : moving, touching

conmutador *nm* **1** : (electric) switch **2** *Lat* : switchboard

cono *nm* : cone

conocer {18} *vt* **1** : know **2** : meet (a person), get to know (a city, etc.) **3** RECONOCER : recognize — **conocerse** *vr* **1** : meet, get to know each other **2** : know oneself — **conocedor, -dora** *adj & n* : expert — **conocido, -da** *adj* : well-known — ～ *n* : acquaintance — **conocimiento** *nm* **1** : knowledge **2** SENTIDO : consciousness

conque *conj* : so

conquistar *vt* : conquer — **conquista** *nf* : conquest — **conquistador, -dora** *adj* : conquering — **conquistador** *nm* : conqueror

consabido, -da *adj* **1** : well-known **2** HABITUAL : usual

consagrar *vt* **1** : consecrate **2** DEDICAR : devote — **consagración** *nf, pl* **-ciones** : consecration

consciencia *nf* → **conciencia** — **consciente** *adj* : conscious, aware

consecución *nf, pl* **-ciones** : attainment

consecuencia *nf* **1** : consequence **2 en** ～ : accordingly — **consecuente** *adj* : consistent

consecutivo, -va *adj* : consecutive

conseguir {75} *vt* **1** : get, obtain **2** ～ **hacer algo** : manage to do sth

consejo *nm* **1** : advice, counsel **2** : council (assembly) — **consejero, -ra** *n* : adviser, counselor

consenso *nm* : consensus

consentir {76} *vt* **1** : allow, permit **2** MIMAR : pamper, spoil — *vi* : consent — **consentimiento** *nm* : consent, permission

conserje *nmf* : caretaker, janitor

conservar *vt* **1** : preserve **2** GUARDAR : keep, conserve — **conservarse** *vr* : keep — **conserva** *nf* **1** : preserve(s) **2** ～**s** *nfpl* : canned goods — **conservación** *nf, pl* **-ciones** : conservation, preservation — **conservador, -dora** *adj & n* : conservative — **conservatorio** *nm* : conservatory

considerar *vt* **1** : consider **2** RESPETAR : respect — **considerable** *adj* : considerable — **consideración** *nf, pl* **-ciones 1** : consideration **2** RESPETO : respect — **considerado, -da** *adj* **1** : considerate **2** RESPETADO : respected

consigna *nf* **1** ESLOGAN : slogan **2** ORDEN : orders **3** : checkroom (for baggage)

consigo *pron* : with her, with him, with you, with oneself

consiguiente *adj* **1** : consequent **2 por** ～ : consequently

consistir *vi* ~ **en 1** : consist of **2** : lie in, consist in — **consistencia** *nf* : consistency — **consistente** *adj* **1** : firm, solid **2** ~ **en** : consisting of

consolar {19} *vt* : console, comfort — **consolarse** *vr* : console oneself — **consolación** *nf, pl* **-ciones** : consolation

consolidar *vt* : consolidate — **consolidación** *nf, pl* **-ciones** : consolidation

consomé *nm* : consommé

consonante *adj* : consonant, harmonious — ~ *nf* : consonant

consorcio *nm* : consortium

conspirar *vi* : conspire, plot — **conspiración** *nf, pl* **-ciones** : conspiracy — **conspirador, -dora** *n* : conspirator

constancia *nf* **1** : record, evidence **2** PERSEVERANCIA : perseverance — **constante** *adj* : constant — **constantemente** *adv* : constantly, continually

constar *vi* **1** : be evident, be clear **2** ~ **de** : consist of

constatar *vt* **1** : verify **2** AFIRMAR : state, affirm

constelación *nf, pl* **-ciones** : constellation

consternación *nf, pl* **-ciones** : consternation

constipado, -da *adj* **estar** ~ : have a cold — **constipado** *nm* : cold — **constiparse** *vr* : catch a cold

constituir {41} *vt* **1** FORMAR : constitute, form **2** FUNDAR : establish, set up — **constituirse** *vr* ~ **en** : set oneself up as — **constitución** *nf, pl* **-ciones** : constitution — **constitucional** *adj* : constitutional — **constitutivo, -va** *adj* : constituent — **constituyente** *adj* & *nm* : constituent

constreñir {67} *vt* **1** : force, compel **2** RESTRINGIR : restrict, limit

construir {41} *vt* : build, construct — **construcción** *nf, pl* **-ciones** : construction, building — **constructivo, -va** *adj* : constructive — **constructor, -tora** *n* : builder

consuelo *nm* : consolation, comfort

consuetudinario, -ria *adj* : customary

cónsul *nmf* : consul — **consulado** *nm* : consulate

consultar *vt* : consult — **consulta** *nf* : consultation — **consultor, -tora** *n* : consultant — **consultorio** *nm* : office (of a doctor or dentist)

consumar *vt* **1** : consummate, complete **2** : commit (a crime)

consumir *vt* : consume — **consumirse** *vr* : waste away — **consumición** *nf, pl* **-ciones 1** : consumption **2** : drink (in a restaurant) — **consumido, -da** *adj* : thin, emaciated — **consumidor, -dora** *n* : consumer — **consumo** *nm* : consumption

contabilidad *nf* **1** : accounting, bookkeeping **2** : accountancy (profession) — **contable** *nmf Spain* : accountant, bookkeeper

contactar *vi* ~ **con** : get in touch with, contact — **contacto** *nm* : contact

contado, -da *adj* : numbered, few — **contado** *nm* **al** ~ : (in) cash

contador, -dora *n Lat* : accountant — **contador** *nm* : meter

contagiar *vt* **1** : infect **2** : transmit (a disease) — **contagiarse** *vr* **1** : be contagious **2** : become infected (with a disease) — **contagio** *nm* : contagion, infection — **contagioso, -sa** *adj* : contagious, infectious

contaminar *vt* : contaminate, pollute — **contaminación** *nf, pl* **-ciones** : contamination, pollution

contar {19} *vt* **1** : count **2** NARRAR : tell — *vi* **1** : count **2** ~ **con** : rely on, count on

contemplar *vt* **1** MIRAR : look at, behold **2** CONSIDERAR : contemplate — **contemplación** *nf, pl* **-ciones** : contemplation

contemporáneo, -nea *adj* & *n* : contemporary

contender {56} *vi* : contend, compete — **contendiente** *nmf* : competitor

contener {80} *vt* **1** : contain **2** RESTRINGIR : restrain, hold back — **contenerse** *vr* : restrain oneself — **contenedor** *nm* : container — **contenido, -da** *adj* : restrained — **contenido** *nm* : contents *pl*

contentar *vt* : please, make happy — **contentarse** *vr* ~ **con** : be satisfied with — **contento, -ta** *adj* : glad, happy, contented

contestar *vt* : answer — *vi* : reply, answer back — **contestación** *nf, pl* **-ciones** : answer, reply

contexto *nm* : context

contienda *nf* **1** COMBATE : dispute, fight **2** COMPETICIÓN : contest

contigo *pron* : with you

contiguo, -gua *adj* : adjacent

continente *nm* : continent — **continental** *adj* : continental

contingencia *nf* : contingency — **contingente** *adj* & *nm* : contingent

continuar {3} *v* : continue — **continuación** *nf, pl* **-ciones 1** : continuation **2 a** ~ : next, then — **continuidad** *nf* : continuity — **continuo, -nua** *adj* **1**

: continuous, steady **2** FRECUENTE
: continual

contorno *nm* **1** : outline **2** ~**s** *nmpl*
: surrounding area

contorsión *nf, pl* -**siones** : contortion

contra *prep* **1** : against **2 en** ~ : against
— ~ *nm* **los pros y los** ~**s** : the pros
and cons

contraatacar {72} *v* : counterattack —
contraataque *nm* : counterattack

contrabajo *nm* : double bass

contrabalancear *vt* : counterbalance

contrabandista *nmf* : smuggler —
contrabando *nm* **1** : smuggling **2**
: contraband (goods)

contracción *nf, pl* -**ciones** : contraction

contrachapado *nm* : plywood

contradecir {11} *vt* : contradict —
contradicción *nf, pl* -**ciones** : contradiction — **contradictorio, -ria** *adj*
: contradictory

contraer {81} *vt* **1** : contract **2** ~ **matrimonio** : get married — **contraerse**
vr : contract, tighten up

contrafuerte *nm* : buttress

contragolpe *nm* : backlash

contralto *nmf* : contralto

contrapartida *nf* : compensation

contrapelo: a ~ *adv phr* : the wrong
way

contrapeso *nm* : counterbalance

contraponer {60} *vt* **1** : counter, oppose **2** COMPARAR : compare

contraproducente *adj* : counterproductive

contrariar {85} *vt* **1** : oppose **2** MO-
LESTAR : vex, annoy — **contrariedad**
nf **1** : obstacle **2** DISGUSTO : annoyance
— **contrario, -ria** *adj* **1** OPUESTO : opposite **2 al contrario** : on the contrary
3 ser ~ **a** : be opposed to

contrarrestar *vt* : counteract

contrasentido *nm* : contradiction (in
terms)

contraseña *nf* : password

contrastar *vt* **1** : check, verify **2** RESIS-
TIR : resist — *vi* : contrast — **contraste** *nm* : contrast

contratar *vt* **1** : contract for **2** : hire, engage (workers)

contratiempo *nm* **1** : mishap **2** DIFICUL-
TAD : setback

contrato *nm* : contract — **contratista**
nmf : contractor

contraventana *nf* : shutter

contribuir {41} *vi* **1** : contribute **2** : pay
taxes — **contribución** *nf, pl* -**ciones 1**
: contribution **2** IMPUESTO : tax — **contribuyente** *nmf* **1** : contributor **2** : taxpayer

contrincante *nmf* : opponent

contrito, -ta *adj* : contrite

controlar *vt* : control **2** COMPROBAR
: monitor, check — **control** *nm* **1**
: control **2** VERIFICACIÓN : inspection,
check — **controlador, -dora** *n* : con-
troller

controversia *nf* : controversy

contundente *adj* **1** : blunt **2** : forceful,
convincing (of arguments, etc.)

contusión *nf, pl* -**siones** : bruise

convalecencia *nf* : convalescence —
convaleciente *adj & nmf* : convalescent

convencer {86} *vt* : convince, persuade — **convencerse** *vr* : be convinced — **convencimiento** *nm* : conviction, belief

convención *nf, pl* -**ciones** : convention
— **convencional** *adj* : conventional

convenir {87} *vi* **1** : be suitable, be advisable **2** ~ **en** : agree on — **conveniencia** *nf* **1** : convenience **2** : suitability (of an action, etc.) — **conveniente**
adj **1** : convenient **2** ACONSEJABLE
: suitable, advisable **3** PROVECHOSO
: useful — **convenio** *nm* : agreement,
pact

convento *nm* : convent, monastery

converger {15} *or* **convergir** *vi* : converge

conversar *vi* : converse, talk — **conversación** *nf, pl* -**ciones** : conversation

conversión *nf, pl* -**siones** : conversion
— **converso, -sa** *n* : convert

convertir {76} *vt* : convert — **convertirse** *vr* ~ **en** : turn into — **convertible** *adj & nm* : convertible

convexo, -xa *adj* : convex

convicción *nf, pl* -**ciones** : conviction
— **convicto, -ta** *adj* : convicted

convidar *vt* : invite — **convidado, -da**
n : guest

convincente *adj* : convincing

convite *nm* **1** : invitation **2** : banquet

convivir *vi* : live together — **conviven-
cia** *nf* : coexistence, living together

convocar {72} *vt* : convoke, call together

convulsión *nf, pl* -**siones 1** : convulsion **2** TRASTORNO : upheaval — **convulsivo, -va** *adj* : convulsive

conyugal *adj* : conjugal — **cónyuge**
nmf : spouse, partner

coñac *nm* : cognac, brandy

cooperar *vi* : cooperate — **cooperación** *nf, pl* -**ciones** : cooperation
— **cooperativa** *nf* : cooperative, coop — **cooperativo, -va** *adj* : cooperative

coordenada *nf* : coordinate

coordinar *vt* : coordinate — **coordinación** *nf, pl* **-ciones** : coordination — **coordinador, -dora** *n* : coordinator

copa *nf* **1** : glass, goblet **2** : cup (in sports) **3 tomar una ~** : have a drink

copia *nf* : copy — **copiar** *vt* : copy

copioso, -sa *adj* : copious, abundant

copla *nf* **1** : (popular) song **2** ESTROFA : verse, stanza

copo *nm* **1** : flake **2** *or* **~ de nieve** : snowflake

coquetear *vi* : flirt — **coqueteo** *nm* : flirting, flirtation — **coqueto, -ta** *adj* : flirtatious — **~** *n* : flirt

coraje *nm* **1** : valor, courage **2** IRA : anger

coral[1] *nm* : coral

coral[2] *adj* : choral — **~** *nf* : choir, chorale

Corán *nm* **el ~** : the Koran

coraza *nf* **1** : armor plating **2** : shell

corazón *nm, pl* **-zones 1** : heart **2** : core (of fruit) **3 mi ~** : my darling — **corazonada** *nf* **1** : hunch **2** IMPULSO : impulse

corbata *nf* : tie, necktie

corchete *nm* **1** : hook and eye, clasp **2** : square bracket (punctuation mark)

corcho *nm* : cork

cordel *nm* : cord, string

cordero *nm* : lamb

cordial *adj* : cordial — **cordialidad** *nf* : cordiality

cordillera *nf* : mountain range

córdoba *nf* : córdoba (Nicaraguan unit of currency)

cordón *nm, pl* **-dones 1** : cord **2 ~ policial** : (police) cordon **3 cordones** *nmpl* : shoelaces

cordura *nf* : sanity

corear *vt* : chant

coreografía *nf* : choreography

cornamenta *nf* : antlers *pl*

corneta *nf* : bugle

coro *nm* **1** : chorus **2** : (church) choir

corona *nf* **1** : crown **2** : wreath, garland (of flowers) — **coronación** *nf, pl* **-ciones** : coronation — **coronar** *vt* : crown

coronel *nm* : colonel

coronilla *nf* **1** : crown (of the head) **2 estar hasta la ~** : be fed up

corporación *nf, pl* **-ciones** : corporation

corporal *adj* : corporal, bodily

corporativo, -va *adj* : corporate

corpulento, -ta *adj* : stout

corral *nm* **1** : farmyard **2** : pen, corral (for animals) **3** *or* **corralito** : playpen

correa *nf* **1** : strap, belt **2** : leash (for a dog, etc.)

corrección *nf, pl* **-ciones 1** : correction **2** : correctness, propriety (of manners) — **correccional** *nm* : reformatory — **correctivo, -va** *adj* : corrective — **correcto, -ta** *adj* **1** : correct, right **2** CORTÉS : polite

corredizo, -za *adj* : sliding

corredor, -dora *n* **1** : runner, racer **2** AGENTE : agent, broker — **corredor** *nm* : corridor, hallway

corregir {28} *vt* : correct — **corregirse** *vr* : mend one's ways

correlación *nf, pl* **-ciones** : correlation

correo *nm* **1** : mail **2 ~ aéreo** : airmail

correr *vi* **1** : run, race **2** : flow (of a river, etc.) **3** : pass (of time) — *vt* **1** : run **2** RECORRER : travel over, cover **3** : draw (curtains) — **correrse** *vr* **1** : move along **2** : run (of colors)

corresponder *vi* **1** : correspond **2** PERTENECER : belong **3** ENCAJAR : fit **4 ~ a** : reciprocate, repay — **corresponderse** *vr* : write to each other — **correspondencia** *nf* **1** : correspondence **2** : connection (of a train, etc.) — **correspondiente** *adj* : corresponding, respective — **corresponsal** *nmf* : correspondent

corretear *vi* : run about, scamper

corrida *nf* **1** : run **2** *or* **~ de toros** : bullfight — **corrido, -da** *adj* **1** : straight, continuous **2** *fam* : worldly

corriente *adj* **1** : current **2** NORMAL : common, ordinary **3** : running (of water, etc.) — **~** *nf* **1** : current (of water, electricity, etc.), draft (of air) **2** TENDENCIA : tendency, trend — **~** *nm* **al ~ 1** : up-to-date **2** ENTERADO : aware, informed

corrillo *nm* : clique, circle — **corro** *nm* : ring, circle (of people)

corroborar *vt* : corroborate

corroer {69} *vt* **1** : corrode (of metals) **2** : erode, wear away — **corroerse** *vr* : corrode

corromper *vt* **1** : corrupt **2** PUDRIR : rot — **corrompido, -da** *adj* : corrupt

corrosión *nf, pl* **-siones** : corrosion — **corrosivo, -va** *adj* : corrosive

corrupción *nf, pl* **-ciones 1** : corruption **2** DESCOMPOSICIÓN : decay, rot — **corrupto, -ta** *adj* : corrupt

corsé *nm* : corset

cortar *vt* **1** : cut **2** RECORTAR : cut out **3** QUITAR : cut off — *vi* : cut — **cortarse** *vr* **1** : cut oneself **2** : be cut off (on the telephone) **3** : curdle (of milk) **4 ~ el pelo** : have one's hair cut — **cortada**

nf Lat : cut — **cortante** *adj* : cutting, sharp

cortauñas *nms & pl* : nail clippers

corte[1] *nm* **1** : cutting **2** ESTILO : cut, style **3** ~ **de pelo** : haircut

corte[2] *nf* **1** : court **2 hacer la** ~ **a** : court, woo — **cortejar** *vt* : court, woo

cortejo *nm* **1** : entourage **2** NOVIAZGO : courtship **3** ~ **fúnebre** : funeral procession

cortés *adj* : courteous, polite — **cortesía** *nf* : courtesy, politeness

corteza *nf* **1** : bark **2** : crust (of bread) **3** : rind, peel (of fruit)

cortina *nm* : curtain

corto, -ta *adj* **1** : short **2** ESCASO : scarce **3** *fam* : timid, shy **4** ~ **de vista** : nearsighted — **cortocircuito** *nm* : short circuit

corvo, -va *adj* : curved, bent

cosa *nf* **1** : thing **2** ASUNTO : matter, affair **3** ~ **de** : about **4 poca** ~ : nothing much

cosechar *v* : harvest, reap — **cosecha** *nf* **1** : harvest, crop **2** : vintage (of wine)

coser *v* : sew

cosmético, -ca *adj* : cosmetic — **cosmético** *nm* : cosmetic

cósmico, -ca *adj* : cosmic

cosmopolita *adj* : cosmopolitan

cosmos *nms* : cosmos

cosquillas *nfpl* **1** : tickling **2 hacer** ~ : tickle — **cosquilleo** *nm* : tickling sensation, tingle

costa *nf* **1** : coast, shore **2 a toda** ~ : at any cost

costado *nm* **1** : side **2 al** ~ : alongside

costar {19} *v* : cost

costarricense *or* **costarriqueño, -ña** *adj* : Costa Rican

coste *nm* → **costo** — **costear** *vt* : pay for

costero, -ra *adj* : coastal

costilla *nf* **1** : rib **2** CHULETA : chop, cutlet

costo *nm* : cost, price — **costoso, -sa** *adj* : costly

costra *nf* : scab

costumbre *nf* **1** : custom, habit **2 de** ~ : usual

costura *nf* **1** : sewing, dressmaking **2** PUNTADAS : seam — **costurera** *nf* : dressmaker

cotejar *vt* : compare

cotidiano, -na *adj* : daily

cotizar {21} *vt* : quote, set a price on — **cotización** *nf, pl* **-ciones** : quotation, price — **cotizado, -da** *adj* : in demand

coto *nm* : enclosure, reserve

cotorra *nf* **1** : small parrot **2** *fam* : chatterbox — **cotorrear** *vi fam* : chatter, gab

coyote *nm* : coyote

coyuntura *nf* **1** : joint **2** SITUACIÓN : situation, moment

coz *nm, pl* **coces** : kick (of an animal)

cráneo *nf* : cranium, skull

cráter *nm* : crater

crear *vt* : create — **creación** *nf, pl* **-ciones** : creation — **creativo, -va** *adj* : creative — **creador, -dora** *n* : creator

crecer {53} *vi* **1** : grow **2** AUMENTAR : increase — **crecido, -da** *adj* **1** : fullgrown **2** : large (of numbers) — **creciente** *adj* **1** : growing, increasing **2** : crescent (of the moon) — **crecimiento** *nm* **1** : growth **2** AUMENTO : increase

credenciales *nfpl* : credentials

credibilidad *nf* : credibility

crédito *nm* : credit

credo *nm* : creed

crédulo, -la *adj* : credulous, gullible

creer {20} *v* **1** : believe **2** SUPONER : suppose, think — **creerse** *vr* : regard oneself as — **creencia** *nf* : belief — **creíble** *adj* : believable, credible — **creído, -da** *adj fam* : conceited

crema *nf* : cream

cremación *nf, pl* **-ciones** : cremation

cremallera *nf* : zipper

cremoso, -sa *adj* : creamy

crepe *nmf* : crepe, pancake

crepitar *vi* : crackle

crepúsculo *nm* : twilight, dusk

crespo, -pa *adj* : curly, frizzy

crespón *nm, pl* **-pones** : crepe (fabric)

cresta *nf* **1** : crest **2** : comb (of a rooster)

cretino, -na *n* : cretin

creyente *nmf* : believer

criar {85} *vt* **1** : nurse (a baby) **2** EDUCAR : bring up, rear **3** : raise, breed (animals) — **cría** *nf* **1** : breeding, rearing **2** : young animal — **criadero** *nm* : farm, hatchery — **criado, -da** *n* : servant, maid *f* — **criador, -dora** *n* : breeder — **crianza** *nf* : upbringing, rearing

criatura *nf* **1** : creature **2** NIÑO : baby, child

crimen *nm, pl* **crímenes** : crime — **criminal** *adj & nmf* : criminal

críquet *nm* : cricket (game)

crin *nf* : mane

criollo, -lla *adj & n* : Creole

cripta *nf* : crypt

crisantemo *nm* : chrysanthemum

crisis *nf* **1** : crisis **2** ~ **nerviosa** : nervous breakdown

crispar *vt* **1** : tense (muscles), clench (one's fist) **2** IRRITAR : irritate, set on edge — **crisparse** *vr* : tense up

cristal *nm* **1** : crystal **2** VIDRIO : glass, piece of glass — **cristalería** *nf* : glassware — **cristalino, -na** *adj* : crystalline — **cristalino** *nm* : lens (of the eye) — **cristalizar** {21} *vi* : crystallize

cristiano, -na *adj & n* : Christian — **cristianismo** *nm* : Christianity — **Cristo** *nm* : Christ

criterio *nm* **1** : criterion **2** JUICIO : judgment, opinion

criticar {72} *vt* : criticize — **crítica** *nf* **1** : criticism **2** RESEÑA : review, critique — **crítico, -ca** *adj* : critical — ~ *n* : critic, reviewer

croar *vi* : croak

cromo *nm* : chromium, chrome

cromosoma *nm* : chromosome

crónica *nf* **1** : chronicle **2** : (news) report

crónico, -ca *adj* : chronic

cronista *nmf* : reporter, newscaster

cronología *nf* : chronology — **cronológico, -ca** *adj* : chronological

cronometro *vt* : time, clock — **cronómetro** *nm* : chronometer, stopwatch

croqueta *nf* : croquette

croquis *nm & pl* : (rough) sketch

cruce *nm* **1** : crossing **2** : crossroads, intersection **3** ~ **peatonal** : crosswalk

crucero *nm* **1** : cruise **2** : cruiser (ship)

crucial *adj* : crucial

crucificar {72} *vt* : crucify — **crucifijo** *nm* : crucifix — **crucifixión** *nf, pl* **-fixiones** : crucifixion

crucigrama *nm* : crossword puzzle

crudo, -da *adj* **1** : harsh, crude **2** : raw (of food) — **crudo** *nm* : crude oil

cruel *adj* : cruel — **crueldad** *nf* : cruelty

crujir *vi* **1** : rustle, creak, crackle, crunch — **crujido** *nm* : rustle, creak, crackle, crunch — **crujiente** *adj* : crunchy, crisp

cruzar {21} *vt* **1** : cross **2** : exchange (words) — **cruzarse** *vr* **1** : intersect **2** : pass each other — **cruz** *nf, pl* **cruces** : cross — **cruzada** *nf* : crusade — **cruzado, -da** *adj* : crossed — **cruzado** *nm* : crusader

cuaderno *nm* : notebook

cuadra *nf* **1** : stable **2** *Lat* : (city) block

cuadrado, -da *adj* : square — **cuadrado** *nm* : square

cuadragésimo, -ma *adj* : fortieth, forty- — ~ *n* : fortieth, forty- (in a series)

cuadrar *vi* **1** : conform, agree **2** : add up, tally (numbers) — *vt* : square — **cuadrarse** *vr* : stand at attention

cuadrilátero *nm* **1** : quadrilateral **2** : ring (in sports)

cuadrilla *nf* : gang, group

cuadro *nm* **1** : square **2** PINTURA : painting **3** DESCRIPCIÓN : picture, description **4** : staff, management (of an organization) **5** CUADRADO : check, square **6** : (baseball) diamond

cuadrúpedo *nm* : quadruped

cuadruple *adj* : quadruple — **cuadruplicar** {72} *vt* : quadruple

cuajar *vi* **1** : curdle **2** COAGULAR : clot, coagulate **3** : set (of pudding, etc.) **4** AFIANZARSE : catch on — *vt* **1** : curdle **2** ~ **de** : fill with

cual *pron* **1 el** ~, **la** ~, **los** ~**es, las** ~**es** : who, whom, which **2 lo** ~ : which **3 cada** ~ : everyone, everybody — ~ *prep* : like, as

cuál *pron* : which (one), what (one) — ~ *adj* : which, what

cualidad *nf* : quality, trait

cualquiera (**cualquier** *before nouns*) *adj, pl* **cualesquiera** : any, whatever — ~ *pron, pl* **cualesquiera** : anyone, whatever

cuán *adv* : how

cuando *conj* **1** : when **2** SI : since, if **3** ~ **más** : at the most **4 de vez en** ~ : from time to time — ~ *prep* : during, at the time of

cuándo *adv* **1** : when **2 ¿desde** ~? : since when?

cuantía *nf* **1** : quantity, extent **2** IMPORTANCIA : importance — **cuantioso, -sa** *adj* : abundant, considerable

cuanto *adv* **1** : as much as **2** ~ **antes** : as soon as possible **3 en** ~ : as soon as **4 en** ~ **a** : as for, as regards — **cuanto, -ta** *adj* : as many, whatever — ~ *pron* **1** : as much as, all that, everything **2 unos cuantos, unas cuantas** : a few

cuánto *adv* : how much, how many — **cuánto, -ta** *adj* : how much, how many — ~ *pron* : how much, how many

cuarenta *adj & nm* : forty — **cuarentavo, -va** *adj* : fortieth — **cuarentavo** *nm* : fortieth

cuarentena *nf* : quarantine

Cuaresma *nf* : Lent

cuartear *vt* : quarter, divide up — **cuartearse** *vr* : crack, split

cuartel *nm* **1** : barracks *pl* **2** ~ **general** : headquarters **3 no dar** ~ : show no mercy

cuarteto *nm* : quartet
cuarto, -ta *adj* : fourth — ～ *n* : fourth (in a series) — **cuarto** *nm* 1 : quarter, fourth 2 HABITACIÓN : room
cuarzo *nm* : quartz
cuatro *adj & nm* : four — **cuatrocientos, -tas** *adj* : four hundred — **cuatrocientos** *nms & pl* : four hundred
cuba *nf* : cask, barrel
cubano, -na *adj* : Cuban
cubeta *nf* 1 : keg, cask 2 *Lat* : pail, bucket
cúbico, -ca *adj* : cubic, cubed — **cubículo** *nm* : cubicle
cubierta *nf* 1 : cover, covering 2 : (automobile) tire 3 : deck (of a ship) — **cubierto** *nm* 1 : cutlery, place setting 2 a ～ : under cover
cubo *nm* 1 : cube 2 *Spain* : pail, bucket 3 : hub (of a wheel)
cubrecama *nm* : bedspread
cubrir {2} *vt* : cover — **cubrirse** *vr* 1 : cover oneself 2 : cloud over
cucaracha *nf* : cockroach
cuchara *nf* : spoon — **cucharada** *nf* : spoonful — **cucharilla** *or* **cucharita** *nf* : teaspoon — **cucharón** *nm, pl* **-rones** : ladle
cuchichear *vi* : whisper — **cuchicheo** *nm* : whisper
cuchilla *nf* 1 : (kitchen) knife 2 ～ **de afeitar** : razor blade — **cuchillada** *nf* : stab, knife wound — **cuchillo** *nm* : knife
cuclillas *nfpl* **en** ～ : squatting, crouching
cuco *nm* : cuckoo — **cuco, -ca** *adj fam* : pretty, cute
cucurucho *nm* : ice-cream cone
cuello *nm* 1 : neck 2 : collar (of clothing)
cuenca *nf* 1 : river basin 2 : (eye) socket — **cuenco** *nm* : bowl CONCAVIDAD : hollow
cuenta *nf* 1 : calculation, count 2 : (bank) account 3 FACTURA : check, bill 4 : bead (for a necklace, etc.) 5 **darse** ～ : realize 6 **tener en** ～ : bear in mind
cuento *nm* 1 : story, tale 2 ～ **de hadas** : fairy tale
cuerda *nf* 1 : cord, rope, string 2 ～s **vocales** : vocal cords 3 **dar** ～ **a** : wind up
cuerdo, -da *adj* : sane, sensible
cuerno *nm* 1 : horn 2 : antlers *pl* (of a deer)
cuero *nm* 1 : leather, hide 2 ～ **cabelludo** : scalp
cuerpo *nm* 1 : body 2 : corps (in the military, etc.)

cuervo *nm* : crow
cuesta *nf* 1 : slope 2 a ～s : on one's back 3 ～ **abajo** : downhill 4 ～ **arriba** : uphill
cuestión *nf, pl* **-tiones** : matter, affair — **cuestionar** *vt* : question — **cuestionario** *nm* 1 : questionnaire 2 : quiz (in school)
cueva *nf* : cave
cuidar *vt* 1 : take care of, look after 2 : pay attention to (details, etc.) — *vi* 1 ～ **de** : look after 2 ～ **de que** : make sure that — **cuidarse** *vr* : take care of oneself — **cuidado** *nm* 1 : care 2 PREOCUPACIÓN : worry, concern 3 **tener** ～ : be careful 4 **¡cuidado!** : watch out!, careful! — **cuidadoso, -sa** *adj* : careful — **cuidadosamente** *adv* : carefully
culata *nf* : butt (of a gun) — **culatazo** *nf* : kick, recoil
culebra *nf* : snake
culinario, -ria *adj* : culinary
culminar *vi* : culminate — **culminación** *nf, pl* **-ciones** : culmination
culo *nm fam* : backside, bottom
culpa *nf* 1 : fault, blame 2 PECADO : sin 3 **echar la** ～ **a** : blame 4 **tener la** ～ : be at fault — **culpabilidad** *nf* : guilt — **culpable** *adj* : guilty — ～ *nmf* : culprit, guilty party — **culpar** *vt* : blame
cultivar *vt* : cultivate — **cultivo** *nm* 1 : farming, cultivation 2 ～s : crops
culto, -ta *adj* : cultured, educated — **culto** *nm* 1 : worship 2 : (religious) cult — **cultura** *nf* : culture — **cultural** *adj* : cultural
cumbre *nf* : summit, top
cumpleaños *nms & pl* : birthday
cumplido, -da *adj* 1 : complete, full 2 CORTÉS : courteous — **cumplido** *nm* : compliment, courtesy
cumplimentar *vt* 1 : congratulate 2 CUMPLIR : carry out — **cumplimiento** *nm* : carrying out, performance
cumplir *vt* 1 : accomplish, carry out 2 : keep (a promise), observe (a law, etc.) 3 : reach (a given age) — *vi* 1 : expire, fall due 2 ～ **con el deber** : do one's duty — **cumplirse** *vr* 1 : expire 2 REALIZARSE : come true
cúmulo *nm* 1 : heap, pile 2 : cumulus (cloud)
cuna *nf* 1 : cradle 2 ORIGEN : birthplace
cundir *vi* 1 PROPAGARSE : spread, propagate 2 : go a long way
cuneta *nf* : ditch (in a road), gutter (in a street)
cuña *nf* : wedge

cuñado, -da *n* : brother-in-law *m*, sister-in-law *f*

cuota *nf* **1** : fee, dues **2** CUPO : quota **3** *Lat* : installment, payment

cupo *nm* **1** : quota, share **2** *Lat* : capacity, room

cupón *nm*, *pl* **-pones** : coupon

cúpula *nf* : dome, cupola

cura *nf* : cure, treatment — ~ *nm* : priest — **curación** *nf*, *pl* **-ciones** : healing — **curar** *vt* **1** : cure **2** : dress (a wound) **3** CURTIR : tan (hides) — **curarse** *vr* : get well

curiosear *vi* **1** : snoop, pry **2** : browse (in a store) — *vt* : look over — **curiosidad** *nf* : curiosity — **curioso, -sa** *adj* **1** : curious, inquisitive **2** RARO : unusual, strange

currículum *nm*, *pl* **-lums** *or* **currículo** *nm* : résumé, curriculum vitae

cursar *vt* **1** : take (a course), study **2** ENVIAR : send, pass on

cursi *adj fam* : affected, pretentious

cursiva *nf* : italics *pl*

curso *nm* **1** : course **2** : (school) year **3** en ~ : under way **4** en ~ : current

curtir *vt* **1** : tan **2** : harden (skin, features, etc.) — **curtiduría** *nf* : tannery

curva *nf* **1** : curve, bend **2** ~ **de nivel** : contour — **curvo, -va** *adj* : curved, bent

cúspide *nf* : apex, peak

custodia *nf* : custody — **custodiar** *vt* : guard, look after — **custodio, -dia** *n* : guardian

cutáneo, -nea *adj* : skin

cutícula *nf* : cuticle

cutis *nms & pl* : skin, complexion

cuyo, -ya *adj* **1** : whose, of whom, of which **2 en cuyo caso** : in which case

D

d *nf* : d, fourth letter of the Spanish alphabet

dádiva *nf* : gift, handout — **dadivoso, -sa** *adj* : generous

dado, -da *adj* **1** : given **2 dado que** : provided that, since — **dados** *nmpl* : dice

daga *nf* : dagger

daltónico, -ca *adj* : color-blind

dama *nf* **1** : lady **2** ~s *nfpl* : checkers

damnificar {72} *vt* : damage, injure

danés, -nesa *adj* : Danish — **danés** *nm* : Danish (language)

danzar {21} *v* : dance — **danza** *nf* : dance, dancing

dañar *vt* : damage, harm — **dañarse** *vr* **1** : be damaged **2** : hurt oneself — **dañino, -na** *adj* : harmful — **daño** *nm* **1** : damage, harm **2** ~s **y perjuicios** : damages

dar {22} *vt* **1** : give **2** PRODUCIR : yield, produce **3** : strike (the hour) **4** MOSTRAR : show — *vi* **1** ~ **como** : consider, regard as **2** ~ **con** : run into, meet **3** ~ **contra** : knock against **4** ~ **para** : be enough for — **darse** *vr* **1** : happen **2** ~ **contra** : bump into **3** ~ **por** : consider oneself **4 dárselas de** : pose as

dardo *nm* : dart

dársena *nf* : dock

datar *vt* : date — *vi* ~ **de** : date from

dátil *nm* : date (fruit)

dato *nm* **1** : fact **2** ~s *nmpl* : data

de *prep* **1** : of **2** ~ **Managua** : from Managua **3** ~ **niño** : as a child **4** ~ **noche** : at night **5 las tres** ~ **la mañana** : three o'clock in the morning **6 más** ~ **10** : more than 10

deambular *vi* : wander about, stroll

debajo *adv* **1** : underneath **2** ~ **de** : under, underneath **3 por** ~ : below, beneath

debatir *vt* : debate — **debatirse** *vr* : struggle — **debate** *nm* : debate

deber *vt* : owe — *v aux* **1** : have to, should **2** (*expressing probability*) : must — **deberse** *vr* ~ **a** : be due to — ~ *nm* **1** : duty **2** ~**es** *nmpl* : homework — **debido, -da** *adj* ~ **a** : due to, owing to

débil *adj* : weak, feeble — **debilidad** *nf* : weakness — **debilitar** *vt* : weaken — **debilitarse** *vr* : get weak — **débilmente** *adv* : weakly, faintly

débito *nm* **1** : debit **2** DEUDA : debt

debutar *vi* : debut — **debut** *nm*, *pl* ~**s** : debut — **debutante** *nf* : debutante *f*

década *nf* : decade

decadencia *nf* : decadence — **decadente** *adj* : decadent

decaer {13} *vi* : decline, weaken

decano, -na *n* : dean

decapitar *vt* : behead

decena *nf* : ten, about ten

decencia *nf* : decency

decenio *nm* : decade

decente *adj* : decent

decepcionar vt : disappoint — **decepción** nf, pl **-ciones** : disappointment
decibelio or **decibel** nm : decibel
decidir vt : decide, determine — vi : decide — **decidirse** vr : make up one's mind — **decididamente** adv : definitely, decidedly — **decidido, -da** adj : determined, resolute
decimal adj : decimal
décimo, -ma adj & n : tenth
decimoctavo, -va adj : eighteenth — ~ n : eighteenth (in a series)
decimocuarto, -ta adj : fourteenth — ~ n : fourteenth (in a series)
decimonoveno, -na or **decimonono, -na** adj : nineteenth — ~ n : nineteenth (in a series)
decimoquinto, -ta adj : fifteenth — ~ n : fifteenth (in a series)
decimoséptimo, -ma adj : seventeenth — ~ n : seventeenth (in a series)
decimosexto, -ta adj : sixteenth — ~ n : sixteenth (in a series)
decimotercero, -ra adj : thirteenth — ~ n : thirteenth (in a series)
decir {23} vt 1 : say 2 CONTAR : tell 3 es ~ : that is to say 4 querer ~ : mean — **decirse** vr 1 : tell oneself 2 ¿cómo se dice...en español? : how do you say...in Spanish? — ~ nm : saying, expression
decisión nf, pl **-siones** : decision — **decisivo, -va** adj : decisive
declarar vt : declare — vi : testify — **declararse** vr 1 : declare oneself 2 : break out (of a fire, an epidemic, etc.) — **declaración** nf, pl **-ciones** : statement
declinar v : decline
declive nm 1 : decline 2 PENDIENTE : slope
decolorar vt : bleach — **decolorarse** vr : fade
decoración nf, pl **-ciones** : decoration — **decorado** nm : stage set — **decorar** vt : decorate — **decorativo, -va** adj : decorative
decoro nm : decency, decorum — **decoroso, -sa** adj : decent, proper
decrecer {53} vi : decrease
decrépito, -ta adj : decrepit
decretar vt : decree — **decreto** nm : decree
dedal nm : thimble
dedicar {72} vt : dedicate — **dedicarse** vr ~ a : devote oneself to — **dedicación** nf, pl **-ciones** : dedication — **dedicatoria** nf : dedication, inscription
dedo nm 1 : finger 2 ~ del pie : toe

deducir {61} vt 1 INFERIR : deduce 2 DESCONTAR : deduct — **deducción** nf, pl **-ciones** : deduction
defecar {72} vi : defecate
defecto nm : defect — **defectuoso, -sa** adj : defective, faulty
defender {56} vt : defend — **defenderse** vr : defend oneself — **defensa** nf : defense — **defensiva** nf : defensive — **defensivo, -va** adj : defensive — **defensor, -sora** n 1 : defender 2 or **abogado defensor** : defense counsel
deferencia nf : deference — **deferente** adj : deferential
deficiencia nf : deficiency — **deficiente** adj : deficient
déficit nm, pl **-cits** : deficit
definir vt : define — **definición** nf, pl **-ciones** : definition — **definitivo, -va** adj 1 : definitive 2 en definitiva : in short
deformar vt 1 : deform 2 : distort (the truth, etc.) — **deformación** nf, pl **-ciones** : distortion — **deforme** adj : deformed — **deformidad** nf : deformity
defraudar vt 1 : defraud 2 DECEPCIONAR : disappoint
degenerar vi : degenerate — **degenerado, -da** adj : degenerate
degradar vt 1 : degrade 2 : demote (in the military)
degustar vt : taste
dehesa nf : pasture
deidad nf : deity
dejar vt 1 : leave 2 ABANDONAR : abandon 3 PERMITIR : allow — vi ~ de : quit — **dejado, -da** adj : slovenly, careless
dejo nm 1 : aftertaste 2 : (regional) accent
delantal nm : apron
delante adv 1 : ahead 2 ~ de : in front of
delantera nf 1 : front 2 tomar la ~ : take the lead — **delantero, -ra** adj : front, forward — ~ n : forward (in sports)
delatar vt : denounce, inform against
delegar {52} vt : delegate — **delegación** nf, pl **-ciones** : delegation — **delegado, -da** n : delegate, representative
deleitar vt : delight, please — **deleite** nm : delight
deletrear vi : spell (out)
delfín nm, pl **-fines** : dolphin
delgado, -da adj : thin
deliberar vi : deliberate — **deliberación** nf, pl **-ciones** : deliberation

— **deliberado, -da** *adj* : deliberate, intentional

delicadeza *nf* 1 : delicacy, daintiness 2 SUAVIDAD : gentleness 3 TACTO : tact — **delicado, -da** *adj* 1 : delicate 2 SENSIBLE : sensible 3 DISCRETO : tactful

delicia *nf* : delight — **delicioso, -sa** *adj* 1 : delightful 2 RICO : delicious

delictivo, -va *adj* : criminal

delimitar *vt* : define, set the boundaries of

delincuencia *nf* : delinquency, crime — **delincuente** *adj & nmf* : delinquent, criminal — **delinquir** {24} *vi* : break the law

delirante *adj* : delirious — **delirar** *vi* 1 : be delirious 2 ~ **por** *fam* : rave about — **delirio** *nm* 1 : delirium 2 ~ **de grandeza** : delusions of grandeur

delito *nm* : crime

delta *nm* : delta

demacrado, -da *adj* : emaciated

demandar *vt* 1 : sue 2 PEDIR : demand 3 *Lat* : require — **demanda** *nf* 1 : lawsuit 2 PETICIÓN : request 3 **la oferta y la** ~ : supply and demand — **demandante** *nmf* : plaintiff

demás *adj* : rest of the, other — ~ *pron* 1 **lo (la, los, las)** ~ : the rest, others 2 **por** ~ : extremely 3 **por lo** ~ : otherwise 4 **y** ~ : and so on

demasiado *adv* 1 : too 2 : too much — ~ *adj* : too much, too many

demencia *nf* : madness — **demente** *adj* : insane, mad

democracia *nf* : democracy — **demócrata** *nmf* : democrat — **democrático, -ca** *adj* : democratic

demoler {47} *vt* : demolish — **demolición** *nf, pl* **-ciones** : demolition

demonio *nm* : devil, demon

demorar *v* : delay — **demorarse** *vr* : take a long time — **demora** *nf* : delay

demostrar {19} *vt* 1 : demonstrate 2 MOSTRAR : show — **demostración** *nf, pl* **-ciones** : demonstration

demudar *vt* : change, alter

denegar {49} *vt* : deny, refuse — **denegación** *nf, pl* **-ciones** : denial, refusal

denigrar *vt* 1 : denigrate 2 INJURIAR : insult

denominador *nm* : denominator

denotar *vt* : denote, show

densidad *nf* : density — **denso, -sa** *adj* : dense

dental *adj* : dental — **dentado, -da** *adj* : toothed, notched — **dentadura** *nf* ~ **postiza** : dentures *pl* — **dentífrico** *nm* : toothpaste — **dentista** *nmf* : dentist

dentro *adv* 1 : in, inside 2 ~ **de poco** : soon, shortly 3 **por** ~ : inside

denuedo *nm* : courage

denunciar *vt* 1 : denounce 2 : report (a crime) — **denuncia** *nf* 1 : accusation 2 : (police) report

departamento *nm* 1 : department 2 *Lat* : apartment

depender *vi* 1 : depend 2 ~ **de** : depend on — **dependencia** *nf* 1 : dependence, dependency 2 SUCURSAL : branch office — **dependiente** *adj* : dependent — **dependiente, -ta** *n* : clerk, salesperson

deplorar *vt* : deplore, regret

deponer {60} *vt* : remove from office, depose

deportar *vt* : deport — **deportación** *nf, pl* **-ciones** : deportation

deporte *nm* : sport, sports *pl* — **deportista** *nmf* : sportsman *m*, sportswoman *f* — **deportivo, -va** *adj* 1 : sporty 2 **artículos deportivos** : sporting goods

depositar *vt* 1 : put, place 2 : deposit (in a bank, etc.) — **depósito** *nm* 1 : deposit 2 ALMACÉN : warehouse

depravado, -da *adj* : depraved

depreciarse *vr* : depreciate — **depreciación** *nf* : depreciation

depredador *nm* : predator

deprimir *vt* : depress — **deprimirse** *vr* : get depressed — **depresión** *nf, pl* **-siones** : depression

derecha *nf* 1 : right side 2 : right wing (in politics) — **derechista** *adj* : rightwing — **derecho** *nm* 1 : right 2 LEY : law — ~ *adv* : straight — **derecho, -cha** *adj* 1 : right, right-hand 2 VERTICAL : upright 3 RECTO : straight

deriva *nf* 1 : drift 2 **a la** ~ : adrift — **derivación** *nf, pl* **-ciones** : derivation — **derivar** *vi* 1 : drift 2 ~ **de** : derive from

derramamiento *nm* ~ **de sangre** : bloodshed

derramar *vt* 1 : spill 2 : shed (tears, blood) — **derramarse** *vr* : overflow — **derrame** *nm* 1 : spilling 2 : discharge, hemorrhage

derrapar *vi* : skid — **derrape** *nm* : skid

derretir {54} *vt* : melt, thaw — **derretirse** *vr* 1 : melt, thaw 2 ~ **por** *fam* : be crazy about

derribar *vt* 1 : demolish 2 : bring down (a plane, a tree, etc.) 3 : overthrow (a government, etc.)

derrocar {72} *vt* : overthrow

derrochar *vt* : waste, squander — **der-**

rochador, -dora n : spendthrift — **derroche** nm : extravagance, waste
derrotar vt : defeat — **derrota** nf : defeat
derruir {41} vt : demolish, tear down
derrumbar vt : demolish, knock down — **derrumbarse** vr : collapse, break down — **derrumbamiento** nm : collapse — **derrumbe** nm : collapse
desabotonar vt : unbutton, undo
desabrido, -da adj : bland
desabrochar vt : unbutton, undo — **desabrocharse** vr : come undone
desacato nm 1 : disrespect 2 : contempt (of court) — **desacatar** vt : defy, disobey
desacertado, -da adj : mistaken, wrong — **desacertar** {55} vi : be mistaken — **desacierto** nm : mistake, error
desaconsejar vt : advise against — **desaconsejable** adj : inadvisable
desacreditar vt : discredit
desactivar vt : deactivate
desacuerdo nm : disagreement
desafiar {85} vt : defy, challenge — **desafiante** adj : defiant
desafilado, -da adj : blunt
desafinado, -da adj : out-of-tune, off-key
desafío nm : challenge, defiance
desafortunado, -da adj : unfortunate — **desafortunadamente** adv : unfortunately
desagradar vt : displease — **desagradable** adj : disagreeable, unpleasant
desagradecido, -da adj : ungrateful
desagrado nm 1 : displeasure 2 **con ~** : reluctantly
desagravio nm : amends, reparation
desagregarse {52} vr : disintegrate
desaguar {10} vi : drain, empty — **desagüe** nm 1 : drainage 2 : drain (of a sink, etc.)
desahogar {52} vt 1 : relieve 2 : give vent to (anger, etc.) — **desahogarse** vr : let off steam, unburden oneself — **desahogado, -da** adj 1 : roomy 2 ADINERADO : comfortable, well-off — **desahogo** nm 1 : relief 2 **con ~** : comfortably
desahuciar vt 1 : deprive of hope 2 DESALOJAR : evict — **desahucio** nm : eviction
desaire nm : snub, rebuff — **desairar** vt : snub, slight
desalentar {55} vt : discourage — **desaliento** nm : discouragement
desaliñado, -da adj : slovenly
desalmado, -da adj : heartless, cruel

desalojar vt 1 : evacuate 2 DESAHUCIAR : evict
desamparar vt : abandon — **desamparo** nm : abandonment, desertion
desamueblado, -da adj : unfurnished
desangrarse vr : lose blood, bleed to death
desanimar vt : discourage — **desanimarse** vr : get discouraged — **desanimado, -da** adj : downhearted, despondent — **desánimo** nm : discouragement
desanudar vt : untie
desaparecer {53} vi : disappear — **desaparecido, -da** n : missing person — **desaparición** nf, pl -**ciones** : disappearance
desapasionado, -da adj : dispassionate
desapego nm : indifference
desapercebido, -da adj : unnoticed
desaprobar {19} vt : disapprove of — **desaprobación** nf, pl -**ciones** : disapproval
desaprovechar vt : waste
desarmar vt 1 : disarm 2 DESMONTAR : dismantle, take apart — **desarme** nm : disarmament
desarraigar {52} vt : uproot, root out
desarreglar vt 1 : mess up 2 : disrupt (plans, etc.) — **desarreglado, -da** adj : disorganized — **desarreglo** nm : untidiness, disorder
desarrollar vt : develop — **desarrollarse** vr : take place — **desarrollo** nm : development
desarticular vt 1 : break up, dismantle 2 : dislocate (a bone)
desaseado, -da adj 1 : dirty 2 DESORDENADO : messy
desastre nm : disaster — **desastroso, -sa** adj : disastrous
desatar vt 1 : undo, untie 2 : unleash (passions) — **desatarse** vr 1 : come undone 2 DESENCADENARSE : break out, erupt
desatascar {72} vt : unclog
desatender {56} vt 1 : disregard 2 : neglect (an obligation, etc.) — **desatento, -ta** adj : inattentive
desatinado, -da adj : foolish, silly
desautorizado, -da adj : unauthorized
desavenencia nf : disagreement
desayunar vi : have breakfast — vt : have for breakfast — **desayuno** nm : breakfast
desbancar {72} vt : oust
desbarajuste nm : disorder, confusion
desbaratar vt : ruin, destroy — **desbaratarse** vr : fall apart

desbocarse {72} *vr* : run away, bolt
desbordar *vt* **1** : overflow **2** : exceed
(limits) — **desbordarse** *vr* : overflow
— **desbordamiento** *nm* : overflow
descabellado, -da *adj* : crazy
descafeinado, -da *adj* : decaffeinated
descalabrar *vt* : hit on the head —
descalabro *nm* : misfortune, setback
descalificar {72} *vt* : disqualify —
descalificación *nf, pl* **-ciones** : disqualification
descalzarse {21} *vr* : take off one's
shoes — **descalzo, -za** *adj* : barefoot
descaminar *vt* : mislead, lead astray
descansar *v* : rest — **descanso** *nm* **1**
: rest **2** : landing (of a staircase) **3** : intermission (in theater), halftime (in
sports)
descapotable *adj & nm* : convertible
descarado, -da *adj* : insolent, shameless
descargar {52} *vt* **1** : unload **2** : discharge (a firearm, etc.) — **descarga**
nf **1** : unloading **2** : discharge (of a
firearm, of electricity, etc.) — **descar-
go** *nm* **1** : unloading **2** : discharge (of
a duty, etc.) **3** : defense (in law)
descarnado, -da *adj* : scrawny, gaunt
descaro *nm* : insolence, nerve
descarrilar *vi* : derail — **descarrilarse**
vr : be derailed
descartar *vt* : reject — **descartarse** *vr*
: discard
descascarar *vt* : peel, shell, husk
descender {56} *vt* **1** : go down **2** BAJAR
: lower — *vi* **1** : descend **2** ~ **de** : be
descended from — **descendencia** *nf*
1 : descendants *pl* **2** LINAJE : lineage,
descent — **descendiente** *nmf* : descendant — **descenso** *nm* **1** : descent
2 : drop, fall (in level, in temperature,
etc.)
descifrar *vt* : decipher, decode
descolgar {16} *vt* **1** : take down **2**
: pick up, answer (the telephone)
descolorarse *vr* : fade — **descolorido,
-da** *adj* : faded, discolored
descomponer {60} *vt* : break down —
descomponerse *vr* **1** : rot, decompose **2** *Lat* : break down — **descompuesto, -ta** *adj Lat* : out of order
descomunal *adj* : enormous
desconcertar {55} *vt* : disconcert,
confuse — **desconcertante** *adj* : confusing — **desconcierto** *nm* : confusion, bewilderment
desconectar *vt* : disconnect
desconfiar {85} *vi* ~ **de** : distrust —
desconfiado, -da *adj* : distrustful —
desconfianza *nf* : distrust

descongelar *vt* **1** : thaw, defrost **2** : un-
freeze (assets)
descongestionante *nm* : decongestant
desconocer {18} *vt* : not know, fail to
recognize — **desconocido, -da** *adj*
: unknown — ~ *n* : stranger
desconsiderado, -da *adj* : inconsiderate
desconsolar *vt* : distress — **desconsolado, -da** *adj* : heartbroken — **de-
sconsuelo** *nm* : grief, sorrow
descontar {19} *vt* : discount
descontento, -ta *adj* : dissatisfied —
descontento *nm* : discontent
descontinuar *vt* : discontinue
descorazonado, -da *adj* : discouraged
descorrer *vt* : draw back
descortés *adj, pl* **-teses** : rude — **descortesía** *nf* : discourtesy, rudeness
descoyuntar *vt* : dislocate
descrédito *nm* : discredit
descremado, -da *adj* : nonfat, skim
describir {33} *vt* : describe — **descripción** *nf, pl* **-ciones** : description —
descriptivo, -va *adj* : descriptive
descubierto, -ta *adj* **1** : exposed, un-
covered **2 al descubierto** : in the
open — **descubierto** *nm* : deficit,
overdraft
descubrir {2} *vt* **1** : discover **2** REVE-
LAR : reveal — **descubrimiento** *nm*
: discovery
descuento *nm* : discount
descuidar *vt* : neglect — **descuidarse**
vr **1** : be careless **2** ABANDONARSE : let
oneself go — **descuidado, -da** *adj* **1**
: careless, sloppy **2** DESATENDIDO
: neglected — **descuido** *nm* : neglect,
carelessness
desde *prep* **1** : from (a place), since (a
time) **2** ~ **luego** : of course
desdén *nm* : scorn, disdain — **desdeñar** *vt* : scorn — **desdeñoso, -sa**
adj : disdainful
desdicha *nf* **1** : misery **2** DESGRACIA
: misfortune — **desdichado, -da** *adj*
: unfortunate, unhappy
desear *vt* : wish, want — **deseable** *adj*
: desirable
desecar *vt* : dry up
desechar *vt* **1** : throw away **2** RECHAZ-
AR : reject — **desechable** *adj* : disposable — **desechos** *nmpl* : rubbish
desembarazarse {21} *vr* ~ **de** : get
rid of
desembarcar {72} *vi* : disembark — *vt*
: unload — **desembarcadero** *nm*
: jetty, landing pier — **desembarco**
nm : landing
desembocar {72} *vi* ~ **en 1** : flow

into **2** : lead to (a result) — **desembo-cadura** nf **1** : mouth (of a river) **2** : opening, end (of a street)

desembolsar vt : pay out — **desembolso** nm : payment, outlay

desembragar vi : disengage the clutch

desempacar {72} v Lat : unpack

desempate nm : tiebreaker

desempeñar vt **1** : play (a role) **2** : redeem (from a pawnshop) — **desempeñarse** vr : get out of debt

desempleo nm : unemployment — **desempleado, -da** adj : unemployed

desempolvar vt : dust

desencadenar vt **1** : unchain **2** : trigger, unleash (protests, crises, etc.) — **desencadenarse** vr : break loose

desencajar vt **1** : dislocate **2** DESCONECTAR : disconnect

desencanto nm : disillusionment

desenchufar vt : disconnect, unplug

desenfadado, -da adj : carefree, confident — **desenfado** nm : confidence, ease

desenfrenado, -da adj : unrestrained — **desenfreno** nm : abandon, lack of restraint

desenganchar vt : unhook

desengañar vt : disillusion — **desengaño** nm : disappointment

desenlace nm : ending, outcome

desenmarañar vt : disentangle

desenmascarar vt : unmask

desenredar vt : untangle — **desenredarse** vr ~ **de** : extricate oneself from

desenrollar vt : unroll, unwind

desentenderse {56} vr ~ **de** : want nothing to do with

desenterrar {55} vt : dig up, disinter

desentonar vi **1** : be out of tune **2** : clash (of colors, etc.)

desenvoltura nf : confidence, ease

desenvolver {89} vt : unfold, unwrap — **desenvolverse** vr : unfold, develop

desenvuelto, -ta adj : confident, self-assured

deseo nm : desire — **deseoso, -sa** adj : eager, anxious

desequilibrar vt : throw off balance — **desequilibrado, -da** adj : unbalanced — **desequilibrio** nm : imbalance

desertar vt : desert — **deserción** nf, pl **-ciones** : desertion — **desertor, -tora** n : deserter

desesperar vt : exasperate — vi : despair — **desesperarse** vr : become exasperated — **desesperación** nf, pl **-ciones** : desperation, despair — **desesperado, -da** adj : desperate, hopeless

desestimar vt : reject

desfalcar {72} vt : embezzle — **desfalco** nm : embezzlement

desfallecer {53} vi **1** : weaken **2** DESMAYARSE : faint

desfavorable adj : unfavorable

desfigurar vt **1** : disfigure, mar **2** : distort (the truth)

desfiladero nm : mountain pass, gorge

desfilar vi : march, parade — **desfile** nm : parade, procession

desfogar {52} vt : vent — **desfogarse** vr : let off steam

desgajar vt : tear off, break apart — **desgajarse** vr : come off

desgana nf **1** : lack of appetite **2** : lack of enthusiasm, reluctance

desgarbado, -da adj : gawky, ungainly

desgarrar vt : tear, rip — **desgarrador, -dora** adj : heartbreaking — **desgarro** nm : tear

desgastar vt : wear away, wear down — **desgaste** nm : deterioration, wear and tear

desgracia nf **1** : misfortune **2** caer en ~ : fall into disgrace **3** por ~ : unfortunately — **desgraciadamente** adv : unfortunately — **desgraciado, -da** adj : unfortunate

deshabitado, -da adj : uninhabited

deshacer {40} vt **1** : undo **2** DESTRUIR : destroy, ruin **3** DISOLVER : dissolve **4** : break (an agreement), cancel (plans, etc.) — **deshacerse** vr **1** : come undone **2** ~ **de** : get rid of **3** ~ **en** : lavish, heap (praise, etc.) — **deshecho, -cha** adj **1** : undone **2** DESTROZADO : destroyed, ruined

desheredar vt : disinherit

deshidratar vt : dehydrate

deshielo nm : thaw

deshilachar vt : unravel — **deshilacharse** vr : fray

deshonesto, -ta adj : dishonest

deshonrar vt : dishonor, disgrace — **deshonra** nf : dishonor — **deshonroso, -sa** adj : dishonorable

deshuesar vt **1** : pit (a fruit) **2** : bone, debone (meat)

desidia nf **1** : indolence **2** DESASEO : sloppiness

desierto, -ta adj : deserted, uninhabited — **desierto** nm : desert

designar vt : designate — **designación** nf, pl **-ciones** : appointment (to an office, etc.)

designio nm : plan

desigual adj **1** : unequal **2** DISPAREJO

: uneven — **desigualdad** *nf* : inequality

desilusionar *vt* : disappoint, disillusion — **desilusión** *nf*, *pl* **-siones** : disappointment, disillusionment

desinfectar *vt* : disinfect — **desinfectante** *adj & nm* : disinfectant

desinflar *vt* : deflate — **desinflarse** *vr* : deflate, go flat

desinhibido, -da *adj* : uninhibited

desintegrar *vt* : disintegrate — **desintegrarse** *vr* : disintegrate — **desintegración** *nf*, *pl* **-ciones** : disintegration

desinteresado, -da *adj* : unselfish, generous — **desinterés** *nm* : unselfishness

desistir *vi* ~ **de** : give up

desleal *adj* : disloyal — **deslealtad** *nf* : disloyalty

desleír {66} *vt* : dilute, dissolve

desligar {52} *vt* **1** : untie **2** SEPARAR : separate — **desligarse** *vr* : extricate oneself

desliz *nm*, *pl* **-lices** : slip, mistake — **deslizar** {21} *vt* : slide, slip — **deslizarse** *vr* : slide, glide

deslucido, -da *adj* : dingy, tarnished

deslumbrar *vt* : dazzle — **deslumbrante** *adj* : dazzling, blinding

deslustrar *vt* : tarnish, dull

desmán *nm*, *pl* **-manes** : outrage, excess

desmandarse *vr* : get out of hand

desmantelar *vt* : dismantle

desmañado, -da *adj* : clumsy

desmayar *vi* : lose heart — **desmayarse** *vr* : faint — **desmayo** *nm* : faint

desmedido, -da *adj* : excessive

desmejorar *vt* : impair — *vi* : deteriorate

desmemoriado, -da *adj* : forgetful

desmentir {76} *vt* : deny — **desmentido** *nm* : denial

desmenuzar {21} *vt* **1** : crumble **2** EXAMINAR : scrutinize — **desmenuzarse** *vr* : crumble

desmerecer {53} *vt* : be unworthy of — *vi* : decline in value

desmesurado, -da *adj* : excessive

desmigajar *vi* : crumble

desmontar *vt* **1** : dismantle, take apart **2** ALLANAR : level — *vi* : dismount

desmoralizar {21} *vt* : demoralize

desmoronarse *vr* : crumble

desnivel *nm* : unevenness

desnudar *vt* : undress, strip — **desnudarse** *vr* : get undressed — **desnudez** *nf*, *pl* **-deces** : nudity, nakedness — **desnudo, -da** *adj* : nude, naked — **desnudo** *nm* : nude

desnutrición *nf*, *pl* **-ciones** : malnutrition

desobedecer {53} *v* : disobey — **desobediencia** *nf* : disobedience — **desobediente** *adj* : disobedient

desocupar *vt* : empty, vacate — **desocupado, -da** *adj* **1** : vacant **2** DESEMPLEADO : unemployed

desodorante *adj & nm* : deodorant

desolado, -da *adj* **1** : desolate **2** DESCONSOLADO : devastated, distressed — **desolación** *nf*, *pl* **-ciones** : desolation

desorden *nm*, *pl* **desórdenes** : disorder, mess — **desordenado, -da** *adj* : untidy — **desordenadamente** *adv* : in a disorderly way

desorganizar {21} *vt* : disorganize — **desorganización** *nf*, *pl* **-ciones** : disorganization

desorientar *vt* : disorient, confuse — **desorientarse** *vr* : lose one's way

desovar *vi* : spawn

despachar *vt* **1** : deal with (a task, etc.) **2** ENVIAR : dispatch, send **3** : wait on, serve (customers) — **despacho** *nm* **1** : dispatch, shipment **2** OFICINA : office

despacio *adv* : slowly

desparramar *vt* : spill, scatter, spread

despavorido, -da *adj* : terrified

despecho *nm* **1** : spite **2 a** ~ **de** : despite, in spite of

despectivo, -va *adj* **1** : pejorative **2** DESPRECIATIVO : contemptuous

despedazar {21} *vt* : tear apart

despedir {54} *vt* **1** : see off **2** DESTITUIR : dismiss, fire **3** DESPRENDER : emit — **despedirse** *vr* : say good-bye — **despedida** *nf* : farewell, good-bye

despegar {52} *vt* : detach, unstick — *vi* : take off — **despegado, -da** *adj* : cold, distant — **despegue** *nm* : take-off

despeinar *vt* : ruffle (hair) — **despeinado, -da** *adj* : disheveled, unkempt

despejar *vt* : clear, free — *vi* : clear up — **despejado, -da** *adj* **1** : clear, fair **2** LÚCIDO : clear-headed

despellejar *vt* : skin (an animal)

despensa *nf* : pantry, larder

despeñadero *nm* : precipice

desperdiciar *vt* : waste — **desperdicio** *nm* **1** : waste **2** ~**s** *nmpl* : scraps

desperfecto *nm* : flaw, defect

despertar {55} *vi* : awaken, wake up — *vt* : wake, rouse — **despertador** *nm* : alarm clock

despiadado, -da *adj* : pitiless, merciless

despido *nm* : dismissal, layoff
despierto, -ta *adj* : awake
despilfarrar *vt* : squander — **despilfarrador, -dora** *n* : spendthrift — **despilfarro** *nm* : extravagance, wastefulness
despistar *vt* : throw off the track, confuse — **despistarse** *vr* : lose one's way — **despistado, -da** *adj* **1** : absentminded **2** DESORIENTADO : confused — **despiste** *nm* **1** : absentmindedness **2** ERROR : mistake
desplazar {21} *vt* : displace — **desplazarse** *vr* : travel
desplegar {49} *vt* : unfold, spread out — **despliegue** *nm* : display
desplomarse *vr* : collapse
desplumar *vt* **1** : pluck **2** *fam* : fleece
despoblado, -da *adj* : uninhabited, deserted — **despoblado** *nm* : deserted area
despojar *vt* : strip, deprive — **despojos** *nmpl* **1** : plunder **2** RESTOS : remains, scraps
desportillar *vt* : chip — **desportillarse** *vr* : chip — **desportilladura** *nf* : chip, nick
despota *nmf* : despot
despotricar *vi* : rant (and rave)
despreciar *vt* : despise, scorn — **despreciable** *adj* **1** : despicable **2** **una cantidad** ~ : a negligible amount — **desprecio** *nm* : disdain, scorn
desprender *vt* **1** : detach, remove **2** EMITIR : give off — **desprenderse** *vr* **1** : come off **2** DEDUCIRSE : be inferred, follow — **desprendimiento** *nm* ~ **de tierras** : landslide
despreocupado, -da *adj* : carefree, unconcerned
desprestigiar *vt* : discredit — **desprestigiarse** *vr* : lose face
desprevenido, -da *adj* : unprepared
desproporcionado, -da : out of proportion
despropósito *nm* : (piece of) nonsense, absurdity
desprovisto, -ta *adj* ~ **de** : lacking in
después *adv* **1** : afterward **2** ENTONCES : then, next **3** ~ **de** : after **4 después (de) que** : after **5** ~ **de todo** : after all
despuntado, -da *adj* : blunt, dull
desquiciar *vt* : drive crazy
desquitarse *vr* **1** : retaliate **2** ~ **con** : take it out on, get back at — **desquite** *nm* : revenge
destacar {72} *vt* : emphasize — *vi* : stand out — **destacado, -da** *adj* : outstanding
destapar *vt* : open, uncover — **destapador** *nm* *Lat* : bottle opener

destartalado, -da *adj* : dilapidated
destellar *vi* : flash, sparkle — **destello** *nm* : sparkle, twinkle, flash
destemplado, -da *adj* **1** : out of tune **2** MAL : out of sorts **3** : unpleasant (of weather)
desteñir {67} *vt* : fade, bleach — *vi* : run, fade — **desteñirse** *vr* : fade
desterrar {55} *vt* : banish, exile — **desterrado, -da** *n* : exile
destetar *vt* : wean
destiempo *adv* **a** ~ : at the wrong time
destierro *nm* : exile
destilar *vt* : distill — **destilería** *nf* : distillery
destinar *vt* **1** : assign, allocate **2** NOMBRAR : appoint — **destinado, -da** *adj* : destined — **destinatario, -ria** *n* : addressee — **destino** *nm* **1** : destiny **2** RUMBO : destination
destituir {41} *vt* : dismiss — **destitución** *nf*, *pl* **-ciones** : dismissal
destornillar *vt* : unscrew — **destornillador** *nm* : screwdriver
destreza *nf* : skill, dexterity
destrozar {21} *vt* : destroy, wreck — **destrozos** *nmpl* : damage, destruction
destrucción *nf*, *pl* **-ciones** : destruction — **destructivo, -va** *adj* : destructive — **destruir** {41} *vt* : destroy
desunir *vt* : split, divide
desusado, -da *adj* **1** : obsolete **2** INSÓLITO : unusual — **desuso** *nm* **caer en** ~ : fall into disuse
desvaído, -da *adj* **1** : pale, washed-out **2** BORROSO : vague, blurred
desvalido, -da *adj* : destitute, needy
desvalijar *vt* : rob
desván *nm*, *pl* **-vanes** : attic
desvanecer {53} *vt* : make disappear — **desvanecerse** *vr* **1** : vanish **2** DESMAYARSE : faint
desvariar {85} *vi* : be delirious — **desvarío** *nm* : delirium
desvelar *vt* : keep awake — **desvelarse** *vr* : stay awake — **desvelo** *nm* **1** : sleeplessness **2** ~ **s** *nmpl* : efforts
desvencijado, -da *adj* : dilapidated, rickety
desventaja *nf* : disadvantage
desventura *nf* : misfortune
desvergonzado, -da *adj* : shameless — **desvergüenza** *nf* : shamelessness
desvestir {54} *vt* : undress — **desvestirse** *vr* : get undressed
desviación *nf*, *pl* **-ciones 1** : deviation **2** : detour (in a road) — **desviar** {85} *vt* : divert, deflect — **desviarse** *vr* **1** : branch off **2** APARTARSE : stray — **desvío** *nm* : diversion, detour

detallar *vt* : detail — **detallado, -da** *adj*
: detailed, thorough — **detalle** *nm* **1**
: detail **2 al ~** : retail — **detallista** *adj*
: retail — **~** *nmf* : retailer
detectar *vt* : detect — **detective** *nmf*
: detective
detener {80} *vt* **1** : arrest, detain **2**
PARAR : stop **3** RETRASAR : delay — **detenerse** *vr* **1** : stop **2** DEMORARSE
: linger — **detención** *nf, pl* **-ciones**
: arrest, detention
detergente *nm* : detergent
deteriorar *vt* : damage — **deteriorarse**
vr : wear out, deteriorate — **deteriorado, -da** *adj* : damaged, worn — **deterioro** *nm* : deterioration, damage
determinar *vt* **1** : determine **2** MOTIVAR
: bring about **3** DECIDIR : decide — **de-
terminarse** *vr* : decide — **determinación** *nf, pl* **-ciones 1** : determination **2 tomar una ~** : make a decision
— **determinado, -da** *adj* **1** : determined **2** ESPECÍFICO : specific
detestar *vt* : detest
detonar *vi* : explode, detonate — **detonación** *nf, pl* **-ciones** : detonation
detrás *adv* **1** : behind **2 ~ de** : in back
of **3 por ~** : from behind
detrimento *nm* **en ~ de** : to the detriment of
deuda *nf* : debt — **deudor, -dora** *n*
: debtor
devaluar {3} *vt* : devalue — **devalu-
arse** *vr* : depreciate
devastar — **devastate** — **devastador,
-dora** *adj* : devastating
devenir {87} *vi* **1** : come about **2 ~ en**
: become, turn into
devoción *nf, pl* **-ciones** : devotion
devolución *nf, pl* **-ciones** : return
devolver {89} *vt* **1** RESTITUIR : give
back **2** : refund, pay back — *vi* : vomit
— **devolverse** *vr Lat* : return, come
back
devorar *vt* : devour
devoto, -ta *adj* : devout — **~** *n* : devotee
día *nm* **1** : day **2** : daytime **3 al ~** : up-
to-date **4 en pleno ~** : in broad day-
light
diabetes *nf* : diabetes — **diabético, -ca**
adj & *n* : diabetic
diablo *nm* : devil — **diablillo** *nm* : imp,
rascal — **diablura** *nf* : prank — **diabólico, -ca** *adj* : diabolic, diabolical
diafragma *nm* : diaphragm
diagnosticar {72} *vt* : diagnose — **diagnóstico, -ca** *adj* : diagnostic — **diagnóstico** *nm* : diagnosis
diagonal *adj* & *nf* : diagonal

diagrama *nm* : diagram
dial *nm* : dial (of a radio, etc.)
dialecto *nm* : dialect
dialogar {52} *vi* : have a talk — **diálogo** *nm* : dialogue
diamante *nm* : diamond
diámetro *nm* : diameter
diana *nf* **1** : reveille **2** BLANCO : target,
bull's-eye
diario, -ria *adj* : daily — **diario** *nm* **1**
: diary **2** PERIÓDICO : newspaper —
diariamente *adv* : daily
diarrea *nf* : diarrhea
dibujar *vt* **1** : draw **2** DESCRIBIR : portray
— **dibujante** *nmf* : draftsman *m*,
draftswoman *f* — **dibujo** *nm* **1** : drawing **2 ~s animados** : (animated) car-
toons
diccionario *nm* : dictionary
dicha *nf* **1** ALEGRÍA : happiness **2**
SUERTE : good luck — **dicho** *nm* : saying, proverb — **dichoso, -sa** *adj* **1**
: happy **2** AFORTUNADO : lucky
diciembre *nm* : December
dictar *vt* **1** : dictate **2** : pronounce (a
sentence), deliver (a speech) — **dicta-
do** *nm* : dictation — **dictador, -dora** *n*
: dictator — **dictadura** *nf* : dictatorship
diecinueve *adj* & *nm* : nineteen —
diecinueveavo, -va *adj* : nineteenth
dieciocho *adj* & *nm* : eighteen —
dieciochoavo, -va *or* **dieciochavo,
-va** *adj* : eighteenth
dieciséis *adj* & *nm* : sixteen — **dieciseisavo, -va** *adj* : sixteenth
diecisiete *adj* & *nm* : seventeen —
diecisieteavo, -va *adj* : seventeenth
diente *nm* **1** : tooth **2** : prong, tine (of a
fork, etc.) **3 ~ de ajo** : clove of garlic
4 ~ de león : dandelion
diesel ['disel] *adj* & *nm* : diesel
diestra *nf* : right hand — **diestro, -tra**
adj **1** : right **2** HÁBIL : skillful
dieta *nf* : diet — **dietético, -ca** *adj* : di-
etetic, dietary
diez *adj* & *nm, pl* **dieces** : ten
difamar *vt* : slander, libel — **difamación** *nf, pl* **-ciones** : slander, libel
diferencia *nf* : difference — **diferenciar** *vt* : distinguish between — **difer-
enciarse** *vr* : differ — **diferente** *adj*
: different
diferir {76} *vt* : postpone — *vi* : differ
difícil *adj* : difficult — **dificultad** *nf*
: difficulty — **dificultar** *vt* : hinder,
obstruct
difteria *nf* : diphtheria
difundir *vt* **1** : spread (out) **2** : broadcast
(television, etc.)

difunto, -ta *adj & n* : deceased
difusión *nf, pl* **-siones** : spreading
digerir {76} *vt* : digest — **digerible** *adj* : digestible — **digestión** *nf, pl* **-tiones** : digestion — **digestivo, -va** *adj* : digestive
dígito *nm* : digit — **digital** *adj* : digital
dignarse *vr* ~ **á** : deign to
dignatario, -ria *n* : dignitary — **dignidad** *nf* : dignity — **digno, -na** *adj* : worthy
digresión *nf, pl* **-ciones** : digression
dilapidar *vt* : waste, squander
dilatar *vt* **1** : expand, dilate **2** PROLONGAR : prolong **3** POSPONER : postpone
dilema *nm* : dilemma
diligencia *nf* **1** : diligence **2** TRÁMITE : procedure, task — **diligente** *adj* : diligent
diluir {41} *vt* : dilute
diluvio *nm* **1** : flood **2** LLUVIA : downpour
dimensión *nf, pl* **-siones** : dimension
diminuto, -ta *adj* : minute, tiny
dimitir *vi* : resign — **dimisión** *nf, pl* **-siones** : resignation
dinámico, -ca *adj* : dynamic
dinamita *nf* : dynamite
dínamo *or* **dinamo** *nmf* : dynamo
dinastía *nf* : dynasty
dineral *nm* : large sum, fortune
dinero *nm* : money
dinosaurio *nm* : dinosaur
diócesis *nfs & pl* : diocese
dios, diosa *n* : god, goddess *f* — **Dios** *nm* : God
diploma *nm* : diploma — **diplomado, -da** *adj* : qualified, trained
diplomacia *nf* : diplomacy — **diplomático, -ca** *adj* : diplomatic — ~ *n* : diplomat
diputación *nf, pl* **-ciones** : delegation — **diputado, -da** *n* : delegate
dique *nm* : dike
dirección *nf, pl* **-ciones 1** : address **2** SENTIDO : direction **3** GESTIÓN : management **4** : steering (of an automobile) — **direccional** *nf Lat* : turn signal, blinker — **directa** *nf* : high gear — **directiva** *nf* : board of directors — **directivo, -va** *adj* : managerial — ~ *n* : manager, director — **directo, -ta** *adj* **1** : direct **2** DERECHO : straight — **director, -tora** *n* **1** : director, manager **2** : conductor (of an orchestra) — **directorio** *nm* : directory — **directriz** *nf, pl* **-trices** : guideline
dirigencia *nf* : leaders *pl*, leadership — **dirigente** *nmf* : director, leader
dirigible *nm* : dirigible, blimp

dirigir {35} *vt* **1** : direct, lead **2** : address (a letter, etc.) **3** ENCAMINAR : aim **4** : conduct (music) — **dirigirse** *vr* **1** ~ **a** : go towards **2** ~ **a algn** : speak to s.o., write to s.o.
discernir {25} *vt* : discern, distinguish — **discernimiento** *nm* : discernment
disciplinar *vt* : discipline — **disciplina** *nf* : discipline
discípulo, -la *n* : disciple, follower
disco *nm* **1** : disc, disk **2** : discus (in sports) **3** ~ **compacto** : compact disc
discordante *adj* : discordant — **discordia** *nf* : discord
discoteca *nf* : disco, discotheque
discreción *nf, pl* **-ciones** : discretion
discrepancia *nf* **1** : discrepancy **2** DESACUERDO : disagreement — **discrepar** *vi* : differ, disagree
discreto, -ta *adj* : discreet
discriminar *vt* **1** : discriminate against **2** DISTINGUIR : distinguish — **discriminación** *nf, pl* **-ciones** : discrimination
disculpar *vt* : excuse, pardon — **disculparse** *vr* : apologize — **disculpa** *nf* **1** : apology **2** EXCUSA : excuse
discurrir *vi* **1** : pass, go by **2** REFLEXIONAR : ponder, reflect
discurso *nm* : speech, discourse
discutir *vt* **1** : discuss **2** CUESTIONAR : dispute — *vi* : argue — **discusión** *nf, pl* **-siones 1** : discussion **2** DISPUTA : argument — **discutible** *adj* : debatable
disecar {72} *vt* : dissect — **disección** *nf, pl* **-ciones** : dissection
diseminar *vt* : disseminate, spread
disentería *nf* : dysentery
disentir {76} *vi* ~ **de** : disagree with — **disentimiento** *nm* : disagreement, dissent
diseñar *vt* : design — **diseñador, -dora** *n* : designer — **diseño** *nm* : design
disertación *nf, pl* **-ciones 1** : lecture **2** : (written) dissertation
disfrazar {21} *vt* : disguise — **disfrazarse** *vr* ~ **de** : disguise oneself as — **disfraz** *nm, pl* **-fraces 1** : disguise **2** : costume (for a party, etc.)
disfrutar *vt* : enjoy — *vi* : enjoy oneself
disgustar *vt* : upset, annoy — **disgustarse** *vr* **1** : get annoyed **2** ENEMISTARSE : fall out (with s.o.) — **disgusto** *nm* **1** : annoyance, displeasure **2** RIÑA : quarrel
disidente *adj & nmf* : dissident
disimular *vt* : conceal, hide — *vi* : pretend — **disimulo** *nm* : pretense
disipar *vt* **1** : dispel **2** DERROCHAR : squander

diskette [di'sket] *nm* : floppy disk, diskette

dislexia *nf* : dyslexia — **disléxico, -ca** *adj* : dyslexic

dislocar {72} *vt* : dislocate — **dislocarse** *vr* : become dislocated

disminuir {41} *vt* : reduce — *vi* : decrease, drop — **disminución** *nf, pl* **-ciones** : decrease

disociar *vt* : dissociate

disolver {89} *vt* : dissolve — **disolverse** *vr* : dissolve

disparar *vi* : shoot, fire — *vt* : shoot — **dispararse** *vr* : shoot up, skyrocket

disparatado, -da *adj* : absurd — **disparate** *nm* : nonsense, silly thing

disparejo, -ja *adj* : uneven — **disparidad** *nf* : difference, disparity

disparo *nm* : shot

dispensar *vt* 1 : dispense, distribute 2 DISCULPAR : excuse

dispersar *vt* : disperse, scatter — **dispersarse** *vr* : disperse — **dispersión** *nf, pl* **-siones** : scattering

disponer {60} *vt* 1 : arrange, lay out 2 ORDENAR : decide, stipulate — *vi* ~ **de** : have at one's disposal — **disponerse** *vr* ~ **a** : be ready to — **disponibilidad** *nf* : availability — **disponible** *adj* : available

disposición *nf, pl* **-ciones** 1 : arrangement 2 APTITUD : aptitude 3 : order, provision (in law) 4 **a** ~ **de** : at the disposal of

dispositivo *nm* : device, mechanism

dispuesto, -ta *adj* : prepared, ready

disputar *vi* 1 : argue 2 COMPETIR : compete — *vt* : dispute — **disputa** *nf* : dispute, argument

disquete → **diskette**

distanciar *vt* : space out — **distanciarse** *vr* : grow apart — **distancia** *nf* : distance — **distante** *adj* : distant

distinguir {26} *vt* : distinguish — **distinguirse** *vr* : distinguish oneself, stand out — **distinción** *nf, pl* **-ciones** : distinction — **distintivo, -va** *adj* : distinctive — **distinto, -ta** *adj* 1 : different 2 CLARO : distinct, clear

distorsión *nf, pl* **-siones** : distortion

distraer {81} *vt* 1 : distract 2 DIVERTIR : entertain — **distraerse** *vr* 1 : get distracted 2 ENTRETENERSE : amuse oneself — **distracción** *nf, pl* **-ciones** 1 : amusement 2 DESPISTE : absentmindedness — **distraído, -da** *adj* : distracted, absentminded

distribuir {41} *vt* : distribute — **distribución** *nf, pl* **-ciones** : distribution — **distribuidor, -dora** *n* : distributor

distrito *nm* : district

disturbio *nm* : disturbance

disuadir *vt* : dissuade, discourage — **disuasivo, -va** *adj* : deterrent

diurno, -na *adj* : day, daytime

divagar {52} *vi* : digress

diván *nm, pl* **-vanes** : divan, couch

divergir {35} *vi* 1 : diverge 2 ~ **en** : differ on

diversidad *nf* : diversity

diversificar {72} *vt* : diversify

diversión *nf, pl* **-siones** : fun, entertainment

diverso, -sa *adj* : diverse

divertir {76} *vt* : entertain — **divertirse** *vr* : enjoy oneself, have fun — **divertido, -da** *adj* : entertaining

dividendo *nm* : dividend

dividir *vt* 1 : divide 2 REPARTIR : distribute

divinidad *nf* : divinity — **divino, -na** *adj* : divine

divisa *nf* 1 : currency 2 EMBLEMA : emblem

divisar *vt* : discern, make out

división *nf, pl* **-siones** : division — **divisor** *nm* : denominator

divorciar *vt* : divorce — **divorciarse** *vr* : get a divorce — **divorciado, -da** *n* : divorcé *m*, divorcée *f* — **divorcio** *nm* : divorce

divulgar {52} *vt* 1 : divulge, reveal 2 PROPAGAR : spread, circulate

dizque *adv Lat* : supposedly, apparently

doblar *vt* 1 : double 2 PLEGAR : fold 3 : turn (a corner) 4 : dub (a film) — *vi* 1 : turn — **doblarse** *vr* 1 : double over 2 ~ **a** : give in to — **dobladillo** *nm* : hem — **doble** *adj & nm* : double — ~ *nmf* : stand-in, double — **doblemente** *adv* : doubly — **doblegar** {52} *vt* : force to yield — **doblegarse** *vr* : give in — **doblez** *nm, pl* **-bleces** : fold, crease

doce *adj & nm* : twelve — **doceavo, -va** *adj* : twelfth — **docena** *nf* : dozen

docente *adj* : teaching

dócil *adj* : docile

doctor, -tora *n* : doctor — **doctorado** *nm* : doctorate

doctrina *nf* : doctrine

documentar *vt* : document — **documentación** *nf, pl* **-ciones** : documentation — **documental** *adj & nm* : documentary — **documento** *nm* : document

dogma *nm* : dogma — **dogmático, -ca** *adj* : dogmatic

dólar *nm* : dollar

doler {47} *vi* **1** : hurt **2** me duelen los pies : my feet hurt — **dolerse** *vr* ~ de : complain about — **dolor** *nm* **1** : pain PENA : grief **3** ~ de cabeza : headache **4** ~ de estómago : stomachache — **dolorido, -da 1** : sore **2** AFLIGIDO : hurt — **doloroso, -sa** *adj* : painful

domar *vt* : tame, break in

domesticar {72} *vt* : domesticate, tame — **doméstico, -ca** *adj* : domestic

domicilio *nm* : home, residence

dominar *vt* **1** : dominate, control **2** : master (a subject, a language, etc.) — **dominarse** *vr* : control oneself — **dominación** *nf, pl* -**ciones** : domination — **dominante** *adj* : dominant

domingo *nm* : Sunday — **dominical** *adj periódico* ~ : Sunday newspaper

dominio *nm* **1** : authority **2** : mastery (of a subject) **3** TERRITORIO : domain

dominó *nm, pl* -**nós** : dominoes *pl* (game)

don[1] *nm* : courtesy title preceding a man's first name

don[2] *nm* **1** : gift **2** TALENTO : talent — **donación** *nf, pl* -**ciones** : donation — **donador, -dora** *n* : donor

donaire *nm* : grace, charm

donar *vt* : donate — **donante** *nmf* : donor — **donativo** *nm* : donation

donde *conj* : where — ~ *prep Lat* : over by

dónde *adv* **1** : where **2** ¿de ~ eres? : where are you from? **3** ¿por ~? : whereabouts?

dondequiera *adv* **1** : anywhere **2** ~ que : wherever, everywhere

doña *nf* : courtesy title preceding a woman's first name

doquier *adv por* ~ : everywhere

dorar *vt* **1** : gild **2** : brown (food) — **dorado, -da** *adj* : gold, golden

dormir {27} *vt* : put to sleep — *vi* : sleep — **dormirse** *vr* : fall asleep — **dormido, -da** *adj* **1** : asleep **2** ENTUMECIDO : numb — **dormilón, -lona** *n* : sleepyhead, late riser — **dormitar** *vi* : doze — **dormitorio** *nm* **1** : bedroom **2** : dormitory (in a college)

dorso *nm* : back

dos *adj & nm* : two — **doscientos, -tas** *adj* : two hundred — **doscientos** *nms & pl* : two hundred

dosel *nm* : canopy

dosis *nfs & pl* : dose, dosage

dotar *vt* **1** : provide, equip **2** ~ de

: endow with — **dotación** *nf, pl* -**ciones 1** : endowment, funding **2** PERSONAL : personnel — **dote** *nf* **1** : dowry **2** ~s *nfpl* : gift, talent

dragar {52} *vt* : dredge — **draga** *nf* : dredge

dragón *nm, pl* -**gones** : dragon

drama *nm* : drama — **dramático, -ca** *adj* : dramatic — **dramatizar** {21} *vt* : dramatize — **dramaturgo, -ga** *n* : dramatist, playwright

drástico, -ca *adj* : drastic

drenar *vt* : drain — **drenaje** *nm* : drainage

droga *nf* : drug — **drogadicto, -ta** *n* : drug addict — **drogar** {52} *vt* : drug — **drogarse** *vr* : take drugs — **droguería** *nf* : drugstore

dromedario *nm* : dromedary

dual *adj* : dual

ducha *nf* : shower — **ducharse** *vr* : take a shower

ducho, -cha *adj* : experienced, skilled

duda *nf* : doubt — **dudar** *vt* : doubt — *vi* ~ **en** : hesitate to — **dudoso, -sa** *adj* **1** : doubtful **2** SOSPECHOSO : questionable

duelo *nm* **1** : duel **2** LUTO : mourning

duende *nm* : elf, imp

dueño, -na *n* **1** : owner **2** : landlord, landlady *f*

dulce *adj* **1** : sweet **2** : fresh (of water) **3** SUAVE : mild, gentle — ~ *nm* : candy, sweet — **dulzura** *nf* : sweetness

duna *nf* : dune

dúo *nm* : duo, duet

duodécimo, -ma *adj* : twelfth — ~ *n* : twelfth (in a series)

dúplex *nms & pl* : duplex (apartment)

duplicar {72} *vt* **1** : double **2** : duplicate, copy (a document, etc.) — **duplicado, -da** *adj* : duplicate — **duplicado** *nm* : copy

duque *nm* : duke — **duquesa** *nf* : duchess

durabilidad *nf* : durability

duración *nf, pl* -**ciones** : duration, length

duradero, -ra *adj* : durable, lasting

durante *prep* **1** : during **2** ~ una hora : for an hour

durar *vi* : endure, last

durazno *nm Lat* : peach

duro *adv* : hard — **duro, -ra** *adj* **1** : hard **2** SEVERO : harsh — **dureza** *nf* **1** : hardness **2** SEVERIDAD : harshness

E

e[1] *nf* : e, fifth letter of the Spanish alphabet

e[2] *conj* (*used instead of* **y** *before words beginning with* **i** *or* **hi**) : and

ebanista *nmf* : cabinetmaker

ébano *nm* : ebony

ebrio, -bria *adj* : drunk

ebullición *nf, pl* **-ciones** : boiling

echar *vt* **1** : throw, cast **2** EXPULSAR : expel, dismiss **3** : give off, emit (smoke, sparks, etc.) **4** BROTAR : sprout **5** PONER : put (on) **6** ~ **a perder** : spoil, ruin **7** ~ **de menos** : miss — **echarse** *vr* **1** : throw oneself **2** ACOSTARSE : lie down **3** ~ **a** : start (to)

eclesiástico, -ca *adj* : ecclesiastic — ~ *nm* : clergyman

eclipse *nm* : eclipse — **eclipsar** *vi* : eclipse

eco *nm* : echo

ecología *nf* : ecology — **ecológico, -ca** *adj* : ecological — **ecologista** *nmf* : ecologist

economía *nf* **1** : economy **2** : economics (science) — **economico, -ca** *adj* **1** : economic, economical **2** BARATO : inexpensive — **economista** *nmf* : economist — **economizar** {21} *v* : save

ecosistema *nm* : ecosystem

ecuación *nf, pl* **-ciones** : equation

ecuador *nm* : equator

ecuánime *adj* **1** : even-tempered **2** : impartial (in law)

ecuatoriano, -na *adj* : Ecuadorian, Ecuadorean, Ecuadoran

ecuestre *adj* : equestrian

edad *nf* **1** : age **2 Edad Media** : Middle Ages *pl* **3 ¿qué** ~ **tienes?** : how old are you?

edición *nf, pl* **-ciones** **1** : publishing, publication **2** : edition (of a book, etc.)

edicto *nm* : edict

edificar {72} *vt* : build — **edificio** *nm* : building

editar *vt* **1** : publish **2** : edit (a film, a text, etc.) — **editor, -tora** *n* **1** : publisher **2** : editor — **editorial** *adj* : publishing — ~ *nm* : editorial — ~ *nf* : publishing house

edredón *nm, pl* **-dones** : (down) comforter, duvet

educar {72} *vt* **1** : educate **2** CRIAR : bring up, raise **3** : train (the body, the voice, etc.) — **educación** *nf, pl* **-ciones** **1** : education **2** MODALES : (good) manners *pl* — **educado, -da** *adj* : polite — **educador, -dora** *n* : educator — **educativo, -va** *adj* : educational

efectivo, -va *adj* **1** : effective **2** REAL : real — **efectivo** *nm* : cash — **efectivamente** *adv* **1** : really **2** POR SUPUESTO : yes, indeed — **efecto** *nm* **1** : effect **2 en** ~ : in fact **3** ~**s** *nmpl* : goods, property — **efectuar** {3} *vt* : bring about, carry out

efervescente *adj* : effervescent — **efervescencia** *nf* : effervescence

eficaz *adj, pl* **-caces** **1** : effective **2** EFICIENTE : efficient — **eficacia** *nf* **1** : effectiveness **2** EFICIENCIA : efficiency

eficiente *adj* : efficient — **eficiencia** *nf* : efficiency

efímero, -ra *adj* : ephemeral

efusivo, -va *adj* : effusive

egipcio, -cia *adj* : Egyptian

ego *nm* : ego — **egocéntrico, -ca** *adj* : egocentric — **egoísmo** *nm* : egoism — **egoísta** *adj* : egoistic — ~ *nmf* : egoist

egresar *vi* : graduate — **egresado, -da** *n* : graduate — **egreso** *nm* : graduation, commencement

eje *nm* **1** : axis **2** : axle (of a wheel, etc.)

ejecutar *vt* **1** : execute, put to death **2** REALIZAR : carry out — **ejecución** *nf, pl* **-ciones** : execution

ejecutivo, -va *adj & n* : executive

ejemplar *adj* : exemplary — ~ *nm* **1** : copy, issue **2** EJEMPLO : example — **ejemplificar** {72} *vt* : exemplify — **ejemplo** *nm* **1** : example **2 por** ~ : for example

ejercer {86} *vt* **1** : practice (a profession) **2** : exercise (a right, etc.) — *vi* ~ **de** : practice as, work as — **ejercicio** *nm* **1** : exercise **2** : practice (of a profession, etc.)

ejército *nm* : army

el, la *art, pl* **los, las** : the — **el** *pron* (*referring to masculine nouns*) **1** : the one **2** ~ **que** : he who, whoever, the one that

él *pron* : he, him

elaborar *vt* **1** : manufacture, produce **2** : draw up (a plan, etc.)

elástico, -ca *adj* : elastic — **elástico** *nm* : elastic — **elasticidad** *nf* : elasticity

elección *nf, pl* **-ciones 1** : election **2** SELECCIÓN : choice — **elector, -tora** *n* : voter — **electorado** *nm* : electorate — **electoral** *adj* : electoral

electricidad *nf* : electricity — **eléctrico, -ca** *adj* : electric, electrical — **electricista** *nmf* : electrician — **electrificar** {72} *vt* : electrify — **electrizar** {21} *vt* : electrify, thrill — **electrocutar** *vt* : electrocute

electrodo *nm* : electrode

electrodoméstico *nm* : electric appliance

electromagnético, -ca *adj* : electromagnetic

electrón *nm, pl* **-trones** : electron — **electrónico, -ca** *adj* : electronic — **electrónica** *nf* : electronics

elefante, -ta *n* : elephant

elegante *adj* : elegant — **elegancia** *nf* : elegance

elegía *nf* : elegy

elegir {28} *vt* **1** : elect **2** ESCOGER : choose, select — **elegible** *adj* : eligible

elemento *nm* : element — **elemental** *adj* **1** : elementary, basic **2** ESENCIAL : fundamental

elenco *nm* : cast (of actors)

elevar *vt* **1** : raise, lift **2** ASCENDER : elevate (in a hierarchy), promote — **elevarse** *vr* : rise — **elevación** *nf, pl* **-ciones** : elevation — **elevador** *nm* **1** : hoist **2** *Lat* : elevator

eliminar *vt* : eliminate — **eliminación** *nf, pl* **-ciones** : elimination

elipse *nf* : ellipse — **elíptico, -ca** *adj* : elliptical, elliptic

elite *or* **élite** *nf* : elite

elixir *or* **elíxir** *nm* : elixir

ella *pron* : she, her — **ello** *pron* : it — **ellos, ellas** *pron pl* **1** : they, them **2 de ellos, de ellas** : theirs

elocuente *adj* : eloquent — **elocuencia** *nf* : eloquence

elogiar *vt* : praise — **elogio** *nm* : praise

eludir *vt* : avoid, elude

emanar *vi* ~ **de** : emanate from

emancipar *vt* : emancipate — **emanciparse** *vr* : free oneself — **emancipación** *nf, pl* **-ciones** : emancipation

embadurnar *vt* : smear, daub

embajada *nf* : embassy — **embajador, -dora** *n* : ambassador

embalar *vt* : wrap up, pack — **embalaje** *nm* : packing

embaldosar *vt* : pave with tiles

embalsamar *vt* : embalm

embalse *nm* : dam, reservoir

embarazar {21} *vt* **1** : make pregnant **2** IMPEDIR : restrict, hamper — **embarazada** *adj* : pregnant — **embarazo** *nm* **1** : pregnancy **2** IMPEDIMENTO : hindrance, obstacle — **embarazoso, -sa** *adj* : embarrassing

embarcar {72} *vt* : load — **embarcarse** *vr* : embark, board — **embarcación** *nf, pl* **-ciones** : boat, craft — **embarcadero** *nm* : pier, jetty — **embarco** *nm* : embarkation

embargar {52} *vt* **1** : seize, impound **2** : overwhelm (with emotion, etc.) — **embargo** *nm* **1** : embargo **2** : seizure (in law) **3 sin** ~ : nevertheless

embarque *nm* : loading (of goods), boarding (of passengers)

embarrancar {72} *vi* : run aground

embarullarse *vr fam* : get mixed up

embaucar {72} *vt* : trick, swindle — **embaucador, -dora** *n* : swindler

embeber *vt* : absorb — *vi* : shrink — **embeberse** *vr* : become absorbed

embelesar *vt* : enchant, delight — **embelesado, -da** *adj* : spellbound

embellecer {53} *vt* : embellish, beautify

embestir {54} *vt* : attack, charge at — *vi* : charge, attack — **embestida** *nf* **1** : attack **2** : charge (of a bull)

emblema *nm* : emblem

embobar *vt* : amaze, fascinate

embocadura *nf* **1** : mouth (of a river, etc.) **2** : mouthpiece (of an instrument)

émbolo *nm* : piston

embolsarse *vr* : put in one's pocket

emborracharse *vr* : get drunk

emborronar *vt* **1** : smudge, blot **2** GARABATEAR : scribble

emboscar {72} *vt* : ambush — **emboscada** *nf* : ambush

embotar *vt* : dull, blunt

embotellar *vt* : bottle (up) — **embotellamiento** *nm* : traffic jam

embrague *nm* : clutch — **embragar** {52} *vi* : engage the clutch

embriagarse {52} *vr* : get drunk — **embriagado, -da** *adj* : intoxicated, drunk — **embriagador, -dora** *adj* : intoxicating — **embriaguez** *nf* : drunkenness

embrión *nm, pl* **-briones** : embryo

embrollo *nm* : tangle, confusion

embrujar *vt* : bewitch — **embrujo** *nm* : spell, curse

embrutecer *vt* : brutalize

embudo *nm* : funnel

embuste *nm* : lie — **embustero, -ra** *adj*
: lying — ~ *n* : liar, cheat
embutir *vt* : stuff — **embutido** *nm*
: sausage, cold meat
emergencia *nf* : emergency
emerger {15} *vi* : emerge, appear
emigrar *vi* **1** : emigrate **2** : migrate (of
animals) — **emigración** *nf, pl*
-ciones 1 : emigration **2** : migration
(of animals) — **emigrante** *adj & nmf*
: emigrant
eminente *adj* : eminent — **eminencia**
nf : eminence
emitir *vt* **1** : emit **2** EXPRESAR : express
(an opinion, etc.) **3** : broadcast (on
radio or television) **4** : issue (money,
stamps, etc.) — **emisión** *nf, pl* **-siones**
1 : emission **2** : broadcast (on radio or
television) **3** : issue (of money, etc.) —
emisora *nf* : radio station
emoción *nf, pl* **-ciones** : emotion —
emocional *adj* : emotional — **emocionante** *adj* **1** : moving, touching **2**
APASIONANTE : exciting, thrilling —
emocionar *vt* **1** : move, touch **2** APA-
SIONAR : excite, thrill — **emocionarse**
vr **1** : be moved **2** APASIONARSE : get
excited — **emotivo, -va** *adj* **1** : emotional **2** CONMOVEDOR : moving
empacar {72} *vt Lat* : pack
empachar *vt* : give indigestion to —
empacharse *vr* : get indigestion —
empacho *nm* : indigestion
empadronarse *vr* : register to vote
empalagoso, -sa *adj* : excessively
sweet, cloying
empalizada *nf* : palisade (fence)
empalmar *vt* : connect, link — *vi*
: meet, converge — **empalme** *nm* **1**
: connection, link **2** : junction (of a
railroad, etc.)
empanada *nf* : pie, turnover — **em-
panadilla** *nf* : meat or seafood pie
empanar *vt* : bread (in cooking)
empantanar *vt* : flood — **empanta-
narse** *vr* **1** : become flooded **2** : get
bogged down
empañar *vt* **1** : steam (up) **2** : tarnish
(one's reputation, etc.) — **empañarse**
vr : fog up
empapar *vt* : soak — **empaparse** *vr*
: get soaking wet
empapelar *vt* : wallpaper
empaquetar *vt* : pack, package
emparedado, -da *adj* : walled in, con-
fined — **emparedado** *nm* : sandwich
emparejar *vt* : match up, pair — **em-
parejarse** *vr* : pair off
emparentado, -da *adj* : related, kindred

empastar *vt* : fill (a tooth) — **empaste**
nm : filling
empatar *vi* : result in a draw, be tied —
empate *nm* : draw, tie
empedernido, -da *adj* : inveterate,
hardened
empedrar {55} *vt* : pave (with stones)
— **empedrado** *nm* : paving, pavement
empeine *nm* : instep
empeñar *vt* : pawn — **empeñarse** *vr* **1**
: insist, persist **2** ENDEUDARSE : go into
debt **3** ~ **en** : make an effort to —
empeñado, -da *adj* **1** : determined,
committed **2** ENDEUDADO : in debt —
empeño *nm* **1** : determination, effort
2 casa de ~**s** : pawnshop
empeorar *vi* : get worse — *vt* : make
worse
empequeñecer {53} *vt* : diminish,
make smaller
emperador *nm* : emperor — **emperatriz** *nf, pl* **-trices** : empress
empezar {29} *v* : start, begin
empinar *vt* : raise — **empinarse** *vr*
: stand on tiptoe — **empinado, -da** *adj*
: steep
empírico, -ca *adj* : empirical
emplasto *nm* : poultice
emplazar {21} *vt* **1** : summon, subpoena **2** SITUAR : place, locate — **em-
plazamiento** *nm* **1** : location, site **2**
CITACIÓN : summons, subpoena
emplear *vt* **1** : employ **2** USAR : use —
emplearse *vr* **1** : get a job **2** USARSE
: be used — **empleado, -da** *n* : employee — **empleador, -dora** *n* : employer — **empleo** *nm* **1** : occupation,
job **2** USO : use
empobrecer {53} *vt* : impoverish —
empobrecerse *vr* : become poor
empollar *vi* : brood (eggs) — *vt* : incubate
empolvarse *vr* : powder one's face
empotrar *vt* : fit, build into — **empotrado, -da** *adj* : built-in
emprender *vt* : undertake, begin —
emprendedor, -dora *adj* : enterprising
empresa *nf* **1** COMPAÑIA : company,
firm **2** TAREA : undertaking — **empre-
sarial** *adj* : business, managerial —
empresario, -ria *n* **1** : businessman *m*,
businesswoman *f* **2** : impresario (in
theater), promoter (in sports)
empujar *v* : push — **empuje** *nm* : impetus, drive — **empujón** *nm, pl* **-jones**
: push, shove
empuñar *vt* : grasp, take hold of
emular *vt* : emulate
en *prep* **1** : in **2** DENTRO DE : into, inside

(of) **3** SOBRE : on **4** ~ **avión** : by plane **5** ~ **casa** : at home

enajenar *vt* : alienate — **enajenación** *nf, pl* **-ciones** : alienation

enagua *nf* : slip, petticoat

enaltecer {53} *vt* : praise, extol

enamorar *vt* : win the love of — **enamorarse** *vr* : fall in love — **enamorado, -da** *adj* : in love — ~ *n* : lover, sweetheart

enano, -na *adj & n* : dwarf

enarbolar *vt* **1** : hoist, raise **2** : brandish (arms, etc.)

enardecer {53} *vt* : stir up, excite

encabezar {21} *vt* **1** : head, lead **2** : put a heading on (an article, a list, etc.) — **encabezamiento** *nm* **1** : heading **2** : headline (in a newspaper)

encabritarse *vr* : rear up

encadenar *vt* **1** : chain, tie (up) **2** ENLAZAR : connect, link

encajar *vt* : fit (together) — *vi* **1** : fit **2** CUADRAR : conform, tally — **encaje** *nm* : lace

encalar *vt* : whitewash

encallar *vi* : run aground

encaminar *vt* : direct, aim — **encaminarse** *vr* ~ **a** : head for — **encaminado, -da** *adj* ~ **a** : aimed at, designed to

encandilar *vt* : dazzle

encanecer {53} *vi* : turn gray

encantar *vt* : enchant, bewitch — *vi* **me encanta esta canción** : I love this song — **encantado, -da** *adj* **1** : delighted **2** HECHIZADO : bewitched — **encantador, -dora** *adj* : charming, delightful — **encantamiento** *nm* : enchantment, spell — **encanto** *nm* **1** : charm, fascination **2** HECHIZO : spell

encapotarse *vr* : cloud over — **encapotado, -da** *adj* : overcast

encapricharse *vr* ~ **con** : be infatuated with

encapuchado, -da *adj* : hooded

encaramar *vt* : lift up — **encaramarse** *vr* ~ **a** : climb up on

encarar *vt* : face, confront

encarcelar *vt* : imprison — **encarcelamiento** *nm* : imprisonment

encarecer {53} *vt* : increase, raise (price, value, etc.) — **encarecerse** *vr* : become more expensive

encargar {52} *vt* **1** : put in charge of **2** PEDIR : order — **encargarse** *vr* ~ **de** : take charge of — **encargado, -da** *adj* : in charge — ~ *n* : manager, person in charge — **encargo** *nm* **1** : errand **2** TAREA : assignment, task **3** PEDIDO : order

encariñarse *vr* ~ **con** : become fond of

encarnar *vt* : embody — **encarnación** *nf, pl* **-ciones** : embodiment — **encarnado, -da** *adj* **1** : incarnate **2** ROJO : red

encarnizarse {21} *vr* ~ **con** : attack viciously — **encarnizado, -da** *adj* : bitter, bloody

encarrilar *vt* : put on the right track

encasillar *vt* : pigeonhole

encauzar {21} *vt* : channel

encender {56} *vt* **1** : light, set fire to **2** PRENDER : switch on, start **3** AVIVAR : arouse (passions, etc.) — **encenderse** *vr* **1** : get excited **2** RUBORIZARSE : blush — **encendedor** *nm* : lighter — **encendido, -da** *adj* : lit, on — **encendido** *nm* : ignition (switch)

encerar *vt* : wax, polish — **encerado, -da** *adj* : waxed — **encerado** *nm* : blackboard

encerrar {55} *vt* **1** : lock up, shut away **2** CONTENER : contain

encestar *vi* : score (in basketball)

enchilada *nf* : enchilada

enchufar *vt* : plug in, connect — **enchufe** *nm* : plug, socket

encía *nf* : gum (tissue)

encíclica *nf* : encyclical

enciclopedia *nf* : encyclopedia — **enciclopédico, -ca** *adj* : encyclopedic

encierro *nm* **1** : confinement **2** : sit-in (at a university, etc.)

encima *adv* **1** : on top **2** ADEMÁS : as well, besides **3** ~ **de** : on, over, on top of **4** **por** ~ **de** : above, beyond

encinta *adj* : pregnant

enclenque *adj* : weak, sickly

encoger {15} *v* : shrink — **encogerse** *vr* **1** : shrink **2** : cower, cringe **3** ~ **de hombros** : shrug (one's shoulders) — **encogido, -da** *adj* **1** : shrunken **2** TÍMIDO : shy

encolar *vt* : glue, stick

encolerizar {21} *vt* : enrage, infuriate — **encolerizarse** *vr* : get angry

encomendar {55} *vt* : entrust

encomienda *nf* **1** : charge, mission **2** *Lat* : parcel

encono *nm* : rancor, animosity

encontrar {19} *vt* **1** : find **2** : meet, encounter (difficulties, etc.) — **encontrarse** *vr* **1** : meet **2** HALLARSE : find oneself, be — **encontrado, -da** *adj* : contrary, opposing

encorvar *vt* : bend, curve — **encorvarse** *vr* : bend over, stoop

encrespar *vt* **1** : curl **2** IRRITAR : irritate — **encresparse** *vr* **1** : curl one's hair

2 IRRITARSE : get annoyed **3** : become choppy (of the sea)
encrucijada *nf* : crossroads
encuadernar *vt* : bind (a book) — **encuadernación** *nf, pl* **-ciones** : bookbinding
encuadrar *vt* **1** : frame **2** ENCAJAR : fit **3** COMPRENDER : contain, include
encubrir {2} *vt* : conceal, cover (up) — **encubierto, -ta** *adj* : covert — **encubrimiento** *nm* : cover-up
encuentro *nm* : meeting, encounter
encuestar *vt* : poll, take a survey of — **encuesta** *nf* **1** : investigation, inquiry **2** SONDEO : survey — **encuestador, -dora** *n* : pollster
encumbrado, -da *adj* : eminent, distinguished
encurtir *vt* : pickle
endeble *adj* : weak, feeble — **endeblez** *nf* : weakness, frailty
endemoniado, -da *adj* : wicked
enderezar {21} *vt* **1** : straighten (out) **2** : put upright, stand on end
endeudarse *vr* : go into debt — **endeudado, -da** *adj* : indebted, in debt — **endeudamiento** *nm* : debt
endiablado, -da *adj* **1** : wicked, diabolical **2** : complicated, difficult
endibia *or* **endivia** *nf* : endive
endosar *vt* : endorse — **endoso** *nm* : endorsement
endulzar {21} *vt* **1** : sweeten **2** : soften, mellow (a tone, a response, etc.) — **endulzante** *nm* : sweetener
endurecer {53} *vt* : harden — **endurecerse** *vr* : become hardened
enema *nm* : enema
enemigo, -ga *adj* : hostile — ~ *n* : enemy — **enemistad** *nf* : enmity — **enemistar** *vt* : make enemies of — **enemistarse** *vr* ~ **con** : fall out with
energía *nf* : energy — **enérgico, -ca** *adj* : energetic, vigorous, forceful
enero *nm* : January
enervar *vt* **1** : enervate, weaken **2** *fam* : get on one's nerves
enésimo, -ma *adj* **por enésima vez** : for the umpteenth time
enfadar *vt* : annoy, make angry — **enfadarse** *vr* : get annoyed — **enfado** *nm* : anger, annoyance — **enfadoso, -sa** *adj* : annoying
enfatizar {21} *vt* : emphasize — **énfasis** *nms & pl* : emphasis — **enfático, -ca** *adj* : emphatic
enfermar *vt* : make sick — *vi* : get sick — **enfermedad** *nf* : sickness, disease — **enfermería** *nf* : infirmary — **enfermero, -ra** *n* : nurse — **enfermizo, -za**

adj : sickly — **enfermo, -ma** *adj* : sick — ~ *n* : sick person, patient
enflaquecer {53} *vi* : lose weight
enfocar {72} *vt* **1** : focus (on) **2** : consider (a problem, etc.) — **enfoque** *nm* : focus
enfrascarse {72} *vr* ~ **en** : immerse oneself in, get caught up in
enfrentar *vt* **1** : confront, face **2** : bring face to face — **enfrentarse** *vr* ~ **con** : confront, clash with — **enfrente** *adv* **1** : opposite **2** ~ **de** : in front of
enfriar {85} *vt* : chill, cool — **enfriarse** *vr* **1** : get cold **2** RESFRIARSE : catch a cold — **enfriamiento** *nm* **1** : cooling off **2** CATARRO : cold
enfurecer {53} *vt* : infuriate — **enfurecerse** *vr* : fly into a rage
enfurruñarse *vr fam* : sulk
engalanar *vt* : decorate — **engalanarse** *vr* : dress up
enganchar *vt* : hook, snag, catch — **engancharse** *vr* **1** : get caught **2** ALISTARSE : enlist
engañar *vt* **1** EMBAUCAR : trick, deceive **2** : cheat on, be unfaithful to — **engañarse** *vr* **1** : deceive oneself **2** EQUIVOCARSE : be mistaken — **engaño** *nm* : deception, deceit — **engañoso, -sa** *adj* : deceptive, deceitful
engatusar *vt* : coax, cajole
engendrar *vt* **1** : beget **2** : engender, give rise to (suspicions, etc.)
englobar *vt* : include, embrace
engomar *vt* : glue
engordar *vt* : fatten — *vi* : gain weight
engorroso, -sa *adj* : bothersome
engranar *v* : mesh, engage — **engranaje** *nm* : gears *pl*
engrandecer {53} *vt* **1** : enlarge **2** ENALTECER : exalt
engrapar *vt Lat* : staple — **engrapadora** *nf Lat* : stapler
engrasar *vt* : lubricate, grease — **engrase** *nm* : lubrication
engreído, -da *adj* : conceited
engrosar {19} *vt* : swell — *vi* : gain weight
engrudo *nm* : paste
engullir {38} *vt* : gulp down, gobble up
enhebrar *vt* : thread
enhorabuena *nf* : congratulations *pl*
enigma *nm* : enigma — **enigmático, -ca** *adj* : enigmatic
enjabonar *vt* : soap (up), lather
enjaezar {21} *vt* : harness
enjalbegar {52} *vt* : whitewash
enjambrar *vi* : swarm — **enjambre** *nm* : swarm
enjaular *vt* **1** : cage **2** *fam* : jail

enjuagar {52} *vt* : rinse — **enjuague** *nm* **1** : rinse **2** ∼ **bucal** : mouthwash

enjugar {52} *vt* **1** : wipe away (tears) **2** : wipe out (debt)

enjuiclar *vt* **1** : prosecute **2** JUZGAR : try

enjuto, -ta *adj* : gaunt, lean

enlace *nm* **1** : bond, link **2** : junction (of a highway, etc.)

enlatar *vt* : can

enlazar {21} *vt* : join, link — *vi* ∼ **con** : link up with

enlistarse *vr Lat* : enlist

enlodar *vt* : cover with mud

enloquecer {53} *vt* : drive crazy — **enloquecerse** *vr* : go crazy

enlosar *vt* : pave, tile

enlutarse *vr* : go into mourning

enmarañar *vt* **1** : tangle **2** COMPLICAR : complicate **3** CONFUNDIR : confuse — **enmarañarse** *vr* **1** : get tangled up **2** CONFUNDIRSE : become confused

enmarcar {72} *vt* : frame

enmascarar *vt* : mask

enmendar {55} *vt* **1** : amend **2** CORREGIR : emend, correct — **enmendarse** *vr* : mend one's ways — **enmienda** *nf* **1** : amendment **2** CORRECCIÓN : correction

enmohecerse {53} *vr* **1** : become moldy **2** OXIDARSE : rust

enmudecer {53} *vt* : silence — *vi* : fall silent

ennegrecer {53} *vt* : blacken

ennoblecer {53} *vt* : ennoble, dignify

enojar *vt* **1** : anger **2** MOLESTAR : annoy — **enojarse** *vr* ∼ **con** : get upset with — **enojo** *nm* **1** : anger **2** MOLESTIA : annoyance — **enojoso, -sa** *adj* : annoying

enorgullecer {53} *vt* : make proud — **enorgullecerse** *vr* ∼ **de** : pride oneself on

enorme *adj* : enormous — **enormemente** *adv* : enormously, extremely — **enormidad** *nf* : enormity

enraizar {30} *vi* : take root

enredadera *nf* : climbing plant, vine

enredar *vt* **1** : tangle up, entangle **2** CONFUNDIR : confuse **3** IMPLICAR : involve — **enredarse** *vr* **1** : become entangled **2** ∼ **en** : get mixed up in — **enredo** *nm* **1** : tangle **2** EMBROLLO : confusion, mess — **enredoso, -sa** *adj* : tangled up, complicated

enrejado *nm* **1** : railing **2** REJILLA : grating, grille **3** : trellis (for plants)

enrevesado, -da *adj* : complicated

enriquecer {53} *vt* : enrich — **enriquecerse** *vr* : get rich

enrojecer {53} *vt* : redden — **enrojecerse** *vr* : blush

enrolar *vt* : enlist — **enrolarse** *vr* ∼ **en** : enlist in

enrollar *vt* : roll up, coil

enroscar {72} *vt* **1** : roll up **2** ATORNILLAR : screw in

ensalada *nf* : salad

ensalzar {21} *vt* : praise

ensamblar *vt* : assemble, fit together

ensanchar *vt* **1** : widen **2** AMPLIAR : expand — **ensanche** *nm* **1** : widening **2** : (urban) expansion, development

ensangrentado, -da *adj* : bloody, bloodstained

ensañarse *vr* : act cruelly

ensartar *vt* : string, thread

ensayar *vi* : rehearse — *vt* : try out, test — **ensayo** *nm* **1** : essay **2** PRUEBA : trial, test **3** : rehearsal (in theater, etc.)

enseguida *adv* : right away, immediately

ensenada *nf* : inlet, cove

enseñar *vt* **1** : teach **2** MOSTRAR : show — **enseñanza** *nf* **1** EDUCACIÓN : education **2** INSTRUCCIÓN : teaching

enseres *nmpl* **1** : equipment **2** ∼ **domésticos** : household goods

ensillar *vt* : saddle (up)

ensimismarse *vr* : lose oneself in thought

ensombrecer {53} *vt* : cast a shadow over, darken

ensoñación *nf, pl* **-ciones** : fantasy, daydream

ensordecer {53} *vt* : deafen — *vi* : go deaf — **ensordecedor, -dora** *adj* : deafening

ensortijar *vt* : curl

ensuciar *vt* : soil — **ensuciarse** *vr* : get dirty

ensueño *nm* : daydream, fantasy

entablar *vt* : initiate, start

entallar *vt* : tailor, fit (clothing) — *vi* : fit

entarimado *nm* : floorboards, flooring

ente *nm* **1** : being **2** ORGANISMO : body, organization

entender {56} *vt* **1** : understand **2** OPINAR : think, believe — *vi* **1** : understand **2** ∼ **de** : know about, be good at — **entenderse** *vr* **1** : understand each other **2** LLEVARSE BIEN : get along well — ∼ *nm* **a mi** ∼ : in my opinion — **entendido, -da** *adj* **1** : understood **2 eso se da por** ∼ : that goes without saying **3 tener** ∼ : be under the impression — **entendimiento** *nm* **1** : understanding **2** INTELIGENCIA : intellect

enterar *vt* : inform — **enterarse** *vr* : find out, learn — **enterado, -da** *adj* : well-informed

entereza *nf* **1** HONRADEZ : integrity **2** FORTALEZA : fortitude **3** FIRMEZA : resolve

enternecer {53} *vt* : move, touch

entero, -ra *adj* **1** : whole **2** TOTAL : absolute, total **3** INTACTO : intact — **entero** *nm* : integer, whole number

enterrar {55} *vt* : bury

entibiar *vt* : cool (down) — **entibiarse** *vr* : become lukewarm

entidad *nf* **1** : entity **2** ORGANIZACIÓN : body, organization

entierro *nm* **1** : burial **2** : funeral (ceremony)

entomología *nf* : entomology — **entomólogo, -ga** *n* : entomologist

entonar *vt* : sing, intone — *vi* : be in tune

entonces *adv* **1** : then **2 desde ~** : since then

entornado, -da *adj* : half-closed, ajar

entorno *nm* : surroundings *pl*, environment

entorpecer {53} *vt* **1** : hinder, obstruct **2** : numb, dull (wits, reactions, etc.)

entrada *nf* **1** : entrance, entry **2** BILLETE : ticket **3** COMIENZO : beginning **4** : inning (in baseball) **5 ~s** *nfpl* : income **6 tener ~s** : have a receding hairline

entraña *nf* **1** : core, heart **2 ~s** *nfpl* VÍSCERAS : entrails, innards — **entrañable** *adj* : close, intimate — **entrañar** *vt* : involve

entrar *vi* **1** : enter **2** EMPEZAR : begin — *vt* : introduce, bring in

entre *prep* **1** : between **2** : among

entreabrir {2} *vt* : leave ajar — **entreabierto, -ta** *adj* : half-open, ajar

entreacto *nm* : intermission

entrecejo nm fruncir el ~ : knit one's brows, frown

entrecortado, -da *adj* : faltering (of the voice), labored (of breathing)

entrecruzar {21} *vi* : intertwine

entredicho *nm* : doubt, question

entregar {52} *vt* : deliver, hand over — **entregarse** *vr* : surrender — **entrega** *nf* **1** : delivery **2** DEDICACIÓN : dedication, devotion **3 ~ inicial** : down payment

entrelazar {21} *vt* : intertwine — **entrelazarse** *vr* : become intertwined

entremés *nm, pl* **-meses 1** : hors d'oeuvre **2** : short play (in theater)

entremeterse → entrometerse

entremezclar *vt* : mix (up)

entrenar *vt* : train, drill — **entrenarse** *vr* : train — **entrenador, -dora** *n* : trainer, coach — **entranamiento** *nm* : training

entrepierna *nf* : crotch

entresacar {72} *vt* : pick out, select

entresuelo *nm* : mezzanine

entretanto *adv* : meanwhile — **~** *nm* **en el ~** : in the meantime

entretener {80} *vt* **1** : entertain **2** DESPISTAR : distract **3** RETRASAR : delay, hold up — **entretenerse** *vr* **1** : amuse oneself **2** DEMORARSE : dawdle — **entretenido, -da** *adj* : entertaining — **entretenimiento** *nm* **1** : entertainment, amusement **2** PASATIEMPO : pastime

entrever {88} *vt* : catch a glimpse of, make out

entrevistar *vt* : interview — **entrevista** *nf* : interview — **entrevistador, -dora** *n* : interviewer

entristecer {53} *vt* : sadden

entrometerse *vr* : interfere — **entrometido, -da** *adj* : meddling, nosy — *n* : meddler

entroncar {72} *vi* : be related, be connected

entumecer {53} *vt* : make numb — **entumecerse** *vr* : go numb — **entumecido, -da** *adj* **1** : numb **2** : stiff (of muscles, etc.)

enturbiar *vt* : cloud — **enturbiarse** *vr* : become cloudy

entusiasmar *vt* : fill with enthusiasm — **entusiasmarse** *vr* : get excited — **entusiasmo** *nm* : enthusiasm — **entusiasta** *adj* : enthusiastic — **~** *nmf* : enthusiast

enumerar *vt* : enumerate, list — **enumeración** *nf, pl* **-ciones** : enumeration, count

enunciar *vt* : enunciate — **enunciación** *nf, pl* **-ciones** : enunciation

envalentonar *vt* : make bold, encourage — **envalentonarse** *vr* : be brave

envanecerse {53} *vr* : become vain

envasar *vt* **1** : package **2** : bottle, can — **envase** *nm* **1** : packaging **2** RECIPIENTE : container **3** : jar, bottle, can

envejecer {53} *v* : age — **envejecido, -da** *adj* : aged, old — **envejecimiento** *nm* : aging

envenenar *vt* : poison — **envenenamiento** *nm* : poisoning

envergadura *nf* **1** ALCANCE : scope **2** : span (of wings, etc.)

envés *nm, pl* **-veses** : reverse side

enviar {85} *vt* : send — **enviado, -da** *n* : envoy, correspondent

envidiar *vt* : envy — **envidia** *nf* : envy,

jealousy — **envidioso, -sa** *adj* : jealous, envious

envilecer {53} *vt* : degrade, debase — **envilecimiento** *nm* : degradation

envío *nm* **1** : sending, shipment **2** : remittance (of funds)

enviudar *vi* : be widowed

envolver {89} *vt* **1** : wrap **2** RODEAR : surround **3** IMPLICAR : involve — **envoltorio** *nm or* **envoltura** *nf* : wrapping, wrapper

enyesar *vt* **1** : plaster **2** ESCAYOLAR : put in a plaster cast

enzima *nf* : enzyme

épico, -ca *adj* : epic — **épica** *nf* : epic

epidemia *nf* : epidemic — **epidémico, -ca** *adj* : epidemic

epilepsia *nf* : epilepsy — **epiléptico, -ca** *adj & n* : epileptic

epílogo *nm* : epilogue

episodio *nm* : episode

epitafio *nm* : epitaph

epíteto *nm* : epithet

época *nf* **1** : epoch, period **2** ESTACIÓN : season

epopeya *nf* : epic poem

equidad *nf* : equity, justice

equilátero, -ra *adj* : equilateral

equilibrar *vt* : balance — **equilibrado, -da** *adj* : well-balanced — **equilibrio** *nm* **1** : balance, equilibrium **2** JUICIO : good sense

equinoccio *nm* : equinox

equipaje *nm* : baggage, luggage

equipar *vt* : equip

equiparar *vt* **1** IGUALAR : make equal **2** COMPARAR : compare — **equiparable** *adj* : comparable

equipo *nm* **1** : equipment **2** : team, crew (in sports, etc.)

equitación *nf, pl* **-ciones** : horseback riding

equitativo, -va *adj* : equitable, fair, just

equivaler {84} *vi* : be equivalent — **equivalencia** *nf* : equivalence — **equivalente** *adj & nm* : equivalent

equivocar {72} *vt* : mistake, confuse — **equivocarse** *vr* : make a mistake — **equivocación** *nf, pl* **-ciones** : error, mistake — **equivocado, -da** *adj* : mistaken, wrong

equívoco, -ca *adj* : ambiguous — **equívoco** *nm* : misunderstanding

era *nf* : era

erario *nm* : public treasury, funds *pl*

erección *nf, pl* **-ciones** : erection

erguir {31} *vt* : raise, lift — **erguirse** *vr* : rise (up) — **erguido, -da** *adj* : erect, upright

erigir {35} *vt* : build, erect — **erigirse** *vr* ~ **en** : set oneself up as

erizarse {21} *vr* : bristle, stand on end — **erizado, -da** *adj* : bristly

erizo *nm* **1** : hedgehog **2** ~ **de mar** : sea urchin

ermitaño, -ña *n* : hermit

erosionar *vt* : erode — **erosión** *nf, pl* **-siones** : erosion

erótico, -ca *adj* : erotic

erradicar {72} *vt* : eradicate

errar {32} *vt* : miss — *vi* **1** : be wrong, be mistaken **2** VAGAR : wander — **errado, -da** *adj Lat* : wrong, mistaken

errata *nf* : misprint

errático, -ca *adj* : erratic

error *nm* : error — **erróneo, -nea** *adj* : erroneous, mistaken

eructar *vi* : belch, burp — **eructo** *nm* : belch, burp

erudito, -ta *adj* : erudite, learned

erupción *nf, pl* **-ciones 1** : eruption **2** SARPULLIDO : rash

esa, ésa → **ese, ése**

esbelto, -ta *adj* : slender, slim

esbozar {21} *vt* : sketch, outline — **esbozo** *nm* : sketch, outline

escabechar *vt* : pickle — **escabeche** *nm* : brine (for pickling)

escabel *nm* : footstool

escabroso, -sa *adj* **1** : rugged, rough **2** ESPINOSO : thorny, difficult **3** ATREVIDO : shocking, risqué

escabullirse {38} *vr* : slip away, escape

escalar *vt* : climb, scale — *vi* : escalate — **escala** *nf* **1** : scale **2** ESCALERA : ladder **3** : stopover (of an airplane, etc.) — **escalada** *nf* : ascent, climb — **escalador, -dora** *n* ALPINISTA : mountain climber

escaldar *vt* : scald

escalera *nf* **1** : stairs *pl*, staircase **2** ESCALA : ladder **3** ~ **mecánica** : escalator

escalfar *vt* : poach

escalinata *nf* : flight of stairs

escalofrío *nm* : shiver, chill — **escalofriante** *adj* : chilling, horrifying

escalonar *vt* **1** : stagger, spread out **2** : terrace (land) — **escalón** *nm, pl* **-lones** : step, rung

escama *nf* **1** : scale (of fish or reptiles) **2** : flake (of skin) — **escamoso, -sa** *adj* : scaly

escamotear *vt* **1** : conceal **2** ~ **algo a algn** : rob s.o. of sth

escandalizar {21} *vt* : scandalize — **escandalizarse** *vr* : be shocked — **escándalo** *nm* **1** : scandal **2** ALBOROTO : scene, commotion — **escandaloso,**

-sa *adj* **1** : shocking, scandalous **2** RUI-
DOSO : noisy

escandinavo, -va *adj* : Scandinavian

escáner *nm* : scanner

escaño *nm* **1** : seat (in a legislative
body) **2** BANCO : bench

escapar *vi* : escape, run away — **escaparse** *vr* **1** : escape **2** : leak out (of
gas, water, etc.) — **escapada** *nf* : escape

escaparate *nm* : store window

escapatoria *nf* : loophole, way out

escape *nm* **1** : leak (of gas, water, etc.)
2 : exhaust (from a vehicle)

escarabajo *nm* : beetle

escarbar *vt* **1** : dig, scratch, poke **2** ~
en : pry into

escarcha *nf* : frost (on a surface)

escarlata *adj & nf* : scarlet — **escarlatina** *nf* : scarlet fever

escarmentar {55} *vi* : learn one's lesson — **escarmiento** *nm* : lesson, punishment

escarnecer {53} *vt* : ridicule, mock —
escarnio *nm* : ridicule, mockery

escarola *nf* : escarole, endive

escarpa *nf* : steep slope — **escarpado,
-da** *adj* : steep

escasear *vi* : be scarce — **escasez** *nf,
pl* **-seces** : shortage, scarcity — **escaso, -sa** *adj* **1** : scarce **2** ~ **de** : short of

escatimar *vt* : be sparing with, skimp
on

escayolar *vt* : put in a plaster cast —
escayola *nf* **1** : plaster (for casts) **2**
: plaster cast

escena *nf* **1** : scene **2** ESCENARIO : stage
— **escenario** *nm* **1** : setting, scene **2**
ESCENA : stage — **escénico, -ca** *adj*
: scenic

escepticismo *nm* : skepticism — **escéptico, -ca** *adj* : skeptical — ~ *n*
: skeptic

esclarecer {53} *vt* : shed light on, clarify

esclavo, -va *n* : slave — **esclavitud** *nf*
: slavery — **esclavizar** {21} *vt* : enslave

esclerosis *nf* ~ **múltiple** : multiple
sclerosis

esclusa *nf* : floodgate, lock (of a canal)

escoba *nf* : broom

escocer {14} *vi* : sting

escocés, -cesa *adj, mpl* **-ceses 1**
: Scottish, plaid — **escocés** *nm, pl* **-ceses** : Scotch (whiskey)

escoger {15} *vt* : choose — **escogido,
-da** *adj* : choice, select

escolar *adj* : school — ~ *nmf* : student, pupil

escolta *nmf* : escort — **escoltar** *vt* : escort, accompany

escombros *nmpl* : ruins, rubble

esconder *vt* : hide, conceal — **esconderse** *vr* : hide — **escondidas** *nfpl* **1**
Lat : hide-and-seek **2 a** ~ : secretly,
in secret — **escondite** *nm* **1** : hiding
place **2** : hide-and-seek (game) — **es-
condrijo** *nm* : hiding place

escopeta *nf* : shotgun

escoplo *nm* : chisel

escoria *nf* **1** : slag **2** : dregs *pl* (of society, etc.)

escorpión *nm, pl* **-piones** : scorpion

escote *nm* **1** : (low) neckline **2 pagar a
~** : go Dutch

escotilla *nf* : hatchway

escribir {33} *v* : write — **escribirse** *vr*
1 : write to one another, correspond **2**
: be spelled — **escribiente** *nmf* : clerk
— **escrito, -ta** *adj* : written — **escritos** *nmpl* : writings — **escritor,
-tora** *n* : writer — **escritorio** *nm*
: desk — **escritura** *nf* **1** : handwriting
2 : deed (in law)

escroto *nm* : scrotum

escrúpulo *nm* : scruple — **escrupuloso, -sa** *adj* : scrupulous

escrutar *vt* **1** : scrutinize **2** : count
(votes) — **escrutinio** *nm* **1** : scrutiny **2**
: count (of votes)

escuadra *nf* **1** : square (instrument) **2**
: fleet (of ships), squad (in the military) — **escuadrón** *nm, pl* **-drones**
: squadron

escuálido, -da *adj* **1** : skinny **2** SUCIO
: squalid

escuchar *vt* **1** : listen to **2** *Lat* : hear —
vi : listen

escudo *nm* **1** : shield **2** *or* ~ **de armas**
: coat of arms

escudriñar *vt* : scrutinize, examine

escuela *nf* : school

escueto, -ta *adj* : plain, simple

esculpir *v* : sculpt — **escultor, -tora** *n*
: sculptor — **escultura** *nf* : sculpture

escupir *v* : spit

escurrir *vt* **1** : drain **2** : wring out
(clothes) — *vi* **1** : drain **2** : drip-dry (of
clothes) — **escurrirse** *vr* **1** : drain **2**
fam : slip away — **escurridizo, -da**
adj : slippery, evasive — **escurridor**
nm **1** : dish drainer **2** COLADOR : colander

ese, esa *adj, mpl* **esos** : that, those

ése, ésa *pron, mpl* **ésos** : that one,
those ones *pl*

esencia *nf* : essence — **esencial** *adj*
: essential

esfera *nf* 1 : sphere 2 : dial (of a watch) — **esférico, -ca** *adj* : spherical

esfinge *nf* : sphinx

esforzar {36} *vt* : strain — **esforzarse** *vr* : make an effort — **esfuerzo** *nm* : effort

esfumarse *vr* : fade away, vanish

esgrimir *vt* 1 : brandish, wield 2 : make use of (an argument, etc.) — **esgrima** *nf* 1 : fencing 2 **hacer ~** : fence

esguince *nm* : sprain, strain

eslabonar *vt* : link, connect — **eslabón** *nm, pl* **-bones** : link

eslavo, -va *adj* : Slavic

eslogan *nm, pl* **-lóganes** : slogan

esmaltar *vt* : enamel — **esmalte** *nm* 1 : enamel 2 **~ de uñas** : nail polish

esmerado, -da *adj* : careful

esmeralda *nf* : emerald

esmerarse *vr* : take great care

esmeril *nm* : emery

esmoquin *nm, pl* **-móquines** : tuxedo

esnob *nmf, pl* **esnobs** : snob — **~** *adj* : snobbish

eso *pron* (*neuter*) 1 : that 2 **¡~ es!** : that's it!, that's right! 3 **en ~** : at that point, then

esófago *nm* : esophagus

esos, ésos → ese, ése

espabilarse *vr* 1 : wake up 2 **DARSE PRISA** : get moving — **espabilado, -da** *adj* 1 : awake 2 **LISTO** : bright, clever

espaciar *vt* : space out, spread out — **espacial** *adj* : space — **espacio** *nm* 1 : space 2 **~ exterior** : outer space — **espacioso, -sa** *adj* : spacious

espada *nf* 1 : sword 2 **~s** *nfpl* : spades (in playing cards)

espagueti *nm or* **espaguetis** *nmpl* : spaghetti

espalda *nf* 1 : back 2 **~ s** *nfpl* : shoulders, back

espantar *vt* : scare, frighten — **espantarse** *vr* : become frightened — **espantajo** *nm or* **espantapájaros** *nms & pl* : scarecrow — **espanto** *nm* : fright, fear — **espantoso, -sa** *adj* 1 : frightening, horrific 2 **TERRIBLE** : awful, terrible

español, -ñola *adj* : Spanish — **español** *nm* : Spanish (language)

esparadrapo *nm* : adhesive bandage

esparcir {83} *vt* : scatter, spread — **esparcirse** *vr* 1 : be scattered, spread out 2 **DIVERTIRSE** : enjoy oneself

espárrago *nm* : asparagus

espasmo *nm* : spasm — **espasmódico, -ca** *adj* : spasmodic

espátula *nf* : spatula

especia *nf* : spice

especial *adj & nm* : special — **especialidad** *nf* : specialty — **especialista** *nmf* : specialist — **especializarse** {21} *vr* **~ en** : specialize in — **especialmente** *adv* : especially

especie *nf* 1 : species 2 **CLASE** : type, kind

especificar {72} *vt* : specify — **especificación** *nf, pl* **-ciones** : specification — **específico, -ca** *adj* : specific

espécimen *nm, pl* **especímenes** : specimen

espectáculo *nm* 1 : show, performance 2 **VISIÓN** : spectacle, view — **espectacular** *adj* : spectacular — **espectador, -dora** *n* : spectator

espectro *nm* 1 : spectrum 2 **FANTASMA** : ghost

especulación *nf, pl* **-ciones** : speculation

espejo *nm* : mirror — **espejismo** *nm* 1 : mirage 2 **ILUSIÓN** : illusion

espeluznante *adj* : terrifying, hairraising

esperar *vt* 1 : wait for 2 **CONTAR CON** : expect 3 **~ que** : hope (that) — *vi* : wait — **espera** *nf* : wait — **esperanza** *nf* : hope, expectation — **esperanzado, -da** *adj* : hopeful — **esperanzar** {21} *vt* : give hope to

esperma *nmf* 1 : sperm 2 **~ de ballena** : blubber

esperpento *nm* : (grotesque) sight, fright

espesar *vt* : thicken — **espesarse** *vr* : thicken — **espeso, -sa** *adj* : thick, heavy — **espesor** *nm* : thickness, density — **espesura** *nf* 1 **ESPESOR** : thickness 2 : thicket

espetar *vt* : blurt (out)

espiar {85} *vt* : spy on — *vi* : spy — **espía** *nmf* : spy

espiga *nf* : ear (of wheat, etc.)

espina *nf* 1 : thorn 2 : (fish) bone 3 **~ dorsal** : spine, backbone

espinaca *nf* 1 : spinach (plant) 2 **~s** *nfpl* : spinach (food)

espinazo *nm* : spine, backbone

espinilla *nf* 1 : shin 2 **GRANO** : blackhead, pimple

espinoso, -sa *adj* 1 : prickly 2 : bony (of fish) 3 : difficult, thorny (of problems, etc.)

espionaje *nm* : espionage

espiral *adj & nf* : spiral

espirar *v* : breathe out, exhale

espíritu *nm* 1 : spirit 2 **Espíritu Santo** : Holy Spirit — **espiritual** *adj* : spiritual — **espiritualidad** *nf* : spirituality

espita *nf* : spigot, faucet

espléndido, -da *adj* 1 : splendid 2 **GE-**

NEROSO : lavish — **esplendor** *nm*
: splendor

espliego *nm* : lavender

espolear *vt* : spur on

espoleta *nf* : fuse

espolvorear *vt* : sprinkle, dust

esponja *nf* 1 : sponge 2 **tirar la ~**
: throw in the towel — **esponjoso,
-sa** *adj* : spongy

espontaneidad *nf* : spontaneity —
espontáneo, -nea *adj* : spontaneous

espora *nf* : spore

esporádico, -ca *adj* : sporadic

esposo, -sa *n* : spouse, wife *f*, husband
m — **esposar** *vt* : handcuff — **esposas** *nfpl* : handcuffs

esprintar *vi* : sprint (in sports) — **esprint** *nm* : sprint

espuela *nf* : spur

espumar *vt* : skim — **espuma** *nf* 1
: foam, froth 2 : (soap) lather 3 : head
(on beer) — **espumoso, -sa** *adj* 1
: foamy, frothy 2 : sparkling (of wine)

esqueleto *nm* : skeleton

esquema *nf* : outline, sketch

esquí *nm* 1 : ski 2 : skiing (sport) 3 **~
acuático** : waterskiing — **esquiador,
-dora** *n* : skier — **esquiar** {85} *vi* : ski

esquilar *vt* : shear

esquimal *adj* : Eskimo

esquina *nf* : corner

esquirol *nm* : strikebreaker, scab

esquivar *vt* 1 : evade, dodge (a blow) 2
EVITAR : avoid — **esquivo, -va** *adj*
: shy, elusive

esquizofrenia *nf* : schizophrenia — **esquizofrénico, -ca** *adj & n* : schizophrenic

esta, ésta → este¹, éste

estable *adj* : stable — **estabilidad** *nf*
: stability — **estabilizar** {21} *vt* : stabilize

establecer {53} *vt* : establish — **establecerse** *vr* : establish oneself, settle —
establecimiento *nm* : establishment

establo *nm* : stable

estaca *nf* : stake — **estacada** *nf* 1
: (picket) fence 2 **dejar en la ~**
: leave in a lurch

estación *nf, pl* **-ciones** 1 : season 2 **~
de servicio** : gas station — **estacionar** *v* : park — **estacionamiento**
nm : parking — **estacionario, -ria** *adj*
: stationary

estadía *nf Lat* : stay

estadio *nm* 1 : stadium 2 FASE : phase,
stage

estadista *nmf* : statesman

estadística *nf* : statistics — **estadístico, -ca** *adj* : statistical

estado *nm* 1 : state 2 **~ civil** : marital
status

estadounidense *adj & nmf* : American
(from the United States)

estafar *vt* : swindle, defraud — **estafa**
nf : swindle, fraud — **estafador,
-dora** *n* : cheat, swindler

estallar *vi* 1 : explode 2 : break out (of
war, an epidemic, etc.) 3 **~ en llamas** : burst into flames — **estallido**
nm 1 : explosion 2 : report (of a gun) 3
: outbreak (of war, etc.)

estampar *vt* : stamp, print — **estampa**
nf 1 : print, illustration 2 ASPECTO : appearance — **estampado, -da** *adj*
: printed

estampida *nf* : stampede

estampilla *nf* : stamp

estancarse {72} *vr* 1 : stagnate 2
: come to a halt — **estancado, -da** *adj*
: stagnant

estancia *nf* 1 : stay 2 HABITACIÓN
: (large) room 3 *Lat* : (cattle) ranch

estanco, -ca *adj* : watertight

estándar *adj & nm* : standard — **estandarizar** {21} *vt* : standardize

estandarte *nm* : standard, banner

estanque *nm* 1 : pool, pond 2 : reservoir (for irrigation)

estante *nm* : shelf — **estantería** *nf*
: shelves *pl*, bookcase

estaño *nm* : tin

estar {34} *v aux* : be — *vi* 1 : be 2 : be
at home 3 QUEDARSE : stay, remain
4 **¿cómo estás?** : how are you? 5 **~
a** : cost 6 **~ bien (mal)** : be well
(sick) 7 **~ para** : be in the mood for 8
~ por : be in favor of 9 **~ por** : be
about to — **estarse** *vr* : stay, remain

estarcir {83} *vt* : stencil

estárter *nm* : choke (of an automobile)

estatal *adj* : state, national

estático, -ca *adj* 1 : static 2 INMÓVIL
: unmoving, still — **estática** *nf* : static

estatua *nf* : statue

estatura *nf* : height

estatus *nm* : status, prestige

estatuto *nm* : statute — **estatutario,
-ria** *adj* : statutory

este¹, esta *adj, mpl* **estos** : this, these

este² *adj* : eastern, east — **este** *nm* 1
: east 2 : east wind 3 **el Este** : the Orient

éste, ésta *pron, mpl* **éstos** 1 : this one,
these ones *pl* 2 : the latter

estela *nf* 1 : wake (of a ship) 2 : trail (of
smoke, etc.)

estera *nf* : mat

estéreo *adj & nm* : stereo — **estereofónico, -ca** *adj* : stereophonic

estereotipo *nm* : stereotype
estéril *adj* **1** : sterile **2** : infertile — **esterilidad** *nf* **1** : sterility **2** : infertility — **esterilizar** {21} *vt* : sterilize
estética *nf* : aesthetics — **estético, -ca** *adj* : aesthetic
estiércol *nm* : dung, manure
estigma *nm* : stigma — **estigmatizar** {21} *vt* : stigmatize
estilarse {21} *vr* : be in fashion
estilo *nm* **1** : style **2** MANERA : fashion, manner — **estilista** *nmf* : stylist
estima *nf* : esteem, regard — **estimación** *nf*, *pl* **-ciones 1** : esteem **2** VALORACIÓN : estimate — **estimado, -da** *adj* **Estimado señor** : Dear Sir —
estimar *vt* **1** : esteem, respect **2** VALORAR : value, estimate **3** CONSIDERAR : consider
estimular *vt* **1** : stimulate **2** ALENTAR : encourage — **estimulante** *adj* : stimulating — **~** *nm* : stimulant — **estímulo** *nm* : stimulus
estío *nm* : summertime
estipular *vt* : stipulate
estirar *vt* : stretch (out), extend — **estirado, -da** *adj* **1** : stretched, extended **2** ALTANERO : stuck-up, haughty — **estiramiento** *nm* **~ facial** : face-lift — **estirón** *nm*, *pl* **-rones** : pull, tug
estirpe *nf* : lineage, stock
estival *adj* : summer
esto *pron* (*neuter*) **1** : this **2 en ~** : at this point **3 por ~** : for this reason
estofa *nf* **1** : class, quality **2 de baja ~** : low-class
estofar *vt* : stew — **estofado** *nm* : stew
estoicismo *nm* : stoicism — **estoico, -ca** *adj* : stoic, stoical — **~** *n* : stoic
estómago *nm* : stomach — **estomacal** *adj* : stomach
estorbar *vt* : obstruct — *vi* : get in the way — **estorbo** *nm* **1** : obstacle **2** MOLESTIA : nuisance
estornino *nm* : starling
estornudar *vi* : sneeze — **estornudo** *nm* : sneeze
estos, éstos → este, éste
estrabismo *nm* : squint
estrado *nm* : platform, stage
estrafalario, -ria *adj* : eccentric, bizarre
estragar {52} *vt* : devastate — **estragos** *nmpl* **1** : ravages **2 hacer ~ en** *or* **causar ~ entre** : wreak havoc with
estragón *nm* : tarragon
estrangular *vt* : strangle — **estrangulación** *nf* : strangulation
estratagema *nf* : stratagem
estrategia *nf* : strategy — **estratégico, -ca** *adj* : strategic

estrato *nm* : stratum
estratosfera *nf* : stratosphere
estrechar *vt* **1** : narrow **2** : strengthen (a bond) **3** ABRAZAR : embrace **4 ~ la mano a uno** : shake s.o.'s hand — **estrecharse** *vr* : narrow — **estrechez** *nf*, *pl* **-checes 1** : narrowness **2** **estrecheces** *nfpl* : financial problems — **estrecho, -cha** *adj* **1** : tight, narrow **2** ÍNTIMO : close — **estrecho** *nm* : strait
estrella *nf* **1** : star **2** DESTINO : destiny **3 ~ de mar** : starfish — **estrellado, -da** *adj* **1** : starry **2** : star-shaped
estrellar *v* : crash — **estrellarse** *vr* **~ contre** : smash into
estremecer {53} *vt* : cause to shudder — *vi* : tremble, shake — **estremecerse** *vr* : shudder, shiver (with emotion) — **estremecimiento** *nm* : shaking, shivering
estrenar *vt* **1** : use for the first time **2** : premiere, open (a film, etc.) — **estrenarse** *vr* : make one's debut — **estreno** *nm* : debut, premiere
estreñirse {67} *vr* : be constipated — **estreñimiento** *nm* : constipation
estrépito *nm* : clamor, din — **estrepitoso, -sa** *adj* : noisy, clamorous
estrés *nm*, *pl* **estreses** : stress — **estresante** *adj* : stressful — **estresar** *vt* : stress (out)
estría *nf* : groove
estribaciones *nfpl* : foothills
estribar *vi* **~ en** : stem from, lie in
estribillo *nm* : refrain, chorus
estribo *nm* **1** : stirrup **2** : running board (of a vehicle) **3** CONTRAFUERTE : buttress **4 perder los ~s** : lose one's temper
estribor *nm* : starboard
estricto, -ta *adj* : strict
estridente *adj* : strident, shrill
estrofa *nf* : stanza, verse
estropajo *nm* : scouring pad
estropear *vt* **1** : ruin, spoil **2** DAÑAR : damage — **estropearse** *vr* **1** : go bad **2** AVERIARSE : break down — **estropicio** *nm* : damage, havoc
estructura *nf* : structure — **estructural** *adj* : structural
estruendo *nm* : din, roar — **estruendoso, -sa** *adj* : thunderous
estrujar *vt* : squeeze
estuario *nm* : estuary
estuche *nm* : kit, case
estuco *nm* : stucco
estudiar *v* : study — **estudiante** *nmf* : student — **estudiantil** *adj* : student — **estudio** *nm* **1** : study **2** OFICINA

: studio, office **3 ~s** *nmpl* : studies, education — **estudioso, -sa** *adj* : studious

estufa *nf* : stove, heater

estupefaciente *adj & nm* : narcotic — **estupefacto, -ta** *adj* : astonished

estupendo, -da *adj* : stupendous, marvelous

estúpido, -da *adj* : stupid — **estupidez** *nf, pl* **-deces** : stupidity

estupor *nm* **1** : stupor **2** ASOMBRO : amazement

etapa *nf* : stage, phase

etcétera : et cetera, and so on

éter *nm* : ether

etéreo, -rea *adj* : ethereal

eterno, -na *adj* : eternal — **eternidad** *nf* : eternity — **eternizarse** {21} *vr* : take forever

ética *nf* : ethics — **ético, -ca** *adj* : ethical

etimología *nf* : etymology

etíope *adj* : Ethiopian

etiqueta *nf* **1** : tag, label **2** PROTOCOLO : etiquette **3 de ~** : formal, dressy — **etiquetar** *vt* : label

étnico, -ca *adj* : ethnic

eucalipto *nm* : eucalyptus

Eucaristía *nf* : Eucharist, communion

eufemismo *nm* : euphemism — **eufemístico, -ca** *adj* : euphemistic

euforia *nf* : euphoria — **eufórico, -ca** *adj* : euphoric

europeo, -pea *adj* : European

eutanasia *nf* : euthanasia

evacuar *vt* : evacuate, vacate — *vi* : have a bowel movement — **evacuación** *nf, pl* **-ciones** : evacuation

evadir *vt* : evade, avoid — **evadirse** *vr* : escape

evaluar {3} *vt* : evaluate — **evaluación** *nf, pl* **-ciones** : evaluation

evangelio *nm* : gospel — **evangélico, -ca** *adj* : evangelical — **evangelismo** *nm* : evangelism

evaporar *vt* : evaporate — **evaporarse** *vr* : evaporate, disappear — **evaporación** *nf, pl* **-ciones** : evaporation

evasión *nf, pl* **-siones 1** : evasion **2** FUGA : escape — **evasiva** *nf* : excuse, pretext — **evasivo, -va** *adj* : evasive

evento *nm* : event

eventual *adj* **1** : temporary **2** POSIBLE : possible — **eventualidad** *nf* : possibility, eventuality

evidencia *nf* **1** : evidence, proof **2 poner en ~** : demonstrate — **evidenciar** *vt* : demonstrate, show — **evidente** *adj* : evident — **evidentemente** *adj* : evidently, apparently

evitar *vt* **1** : avoid **2** IMPEDIR : prevent — **evitable** *adj* : avoidable

evocar {72} *vt* : evoke

evolución *nf, pl* **-ciones** : evolution — **evolucionar** *vi* : evolve

exacerbar *vt* **1** : exacerbate **2** IRRITAR : irritate

exacto, -ta *adj* : precise, exact — **exactamente** *adv* : exactly — **exactitud** *nf* : precision, accuracy

exagerar *v* : exaggerate — **exageración** *nf, pl* **-ciones** : exaggeration — **exagerado, -da** *adj* : exaggerated

exaltar *vt* **1** : exalt, extol **2** EXCITAR : excite, arouse — **exaltarse** *vr* : get worked-up — **exaltado, -da** *adj* : worked up, hotheaded

examen *nm, pl* **exámenes 1** : examination, test **2** ANÁLISIS : investigation — **examinar** *vt* **1** : examine **2** ESTUDIAR : study, inspect — **examinarse** *vr* : take an exam

exánime *adj* : lifeless

exasperar *vt* : exasperate, irritate — **exasperación** *nf, pl* **-ciones** : exasperation

excavar *v* : excavate — **excavación** *nf, pl* **-ciones** : excavation

exceder *vt* : exceed, surpass — **excederse** *vr* : go too far — **excedente** *adj & nm* : surplus, excess

excelente *adj* : excellent — **excelencia** *nf* **1** : excellence **2 Su Excelencia** : His/Her Excellency

excéntrico, -ca *adj & n* : eccentric — **excentricidad** *nf* : eccentricity

excepción *nf, pl* **-ciones** : exception — **excepcional** *adj* : exceptional

excepto *prep* : except (for) — **exceptuar** {3} *vt* : exclude, except

exceso *nm* **1** : excess **2 ~ de velocidad** : speeding — **excesivo, -va** *adj* : excessive

excitar *vt* : excite, arouse — **excitarse** *vr* : get excited — **excitable** *adj* : excitable — **excitación** *nf, pl* **-ciones** : excitement, agitation, arousal — **excitante** *adj* : exciting

exclamar *v* : exclaim — **exclamación** *nf, pl* **-ciones** : exclamation

excluir {41} *vt* : exclude — **exclusión** *nf, pl* **-siones** : exclusion — **exclusivo, -va** *adj* : exclusive

excomulgar {52} *vt* : excommunicate — **excomunión** *nf, pl* **-niones** : excommunication

excremento *nm* : excrement

exculpar *vt* : exonerate

excursión *nf, pl* **-siones** : excursion —

excursionista *nmf* **1** : tourist, sightseer **2** : hiker

excusar *vt* **1** : excuse **2** EXIMIR : exempt — **excusarse** *vr* : apologize — **excusa** *nf* **1** : excuse **2** DISCULPA : apology

exento, -ta *adj* : exempt

exequias *nfpl* : funeral rites

exhalar *vt* **1** : exhale **2** : give off (an odor, etc.)

exhaustivo, -va *adj* : exhaustive — **exhausto, -ta** *adj* : exhausted, worn-out

exhibir *vt* : exhibit, show — **exhibición** *nf, pl* **-ciones** : exhibition

exhortar *vt* : exhort, admonish

exigir {35} *vt* : demand, require — **exigencia** *nf* : demand, requirement — **exigente** *adj* : demanding

exiguo, -gua *adj* : meager

exiliar *vt* : exile — **exiliarse** *vr* : go into exile — **exiliado, -da** *adj* : exiled, in exile — **~** *n* : exile — **exilio** *nm* : exile

eximir *vt* : exempt

existir *vi* : exist — **existencia** *nf* **1** : existence **2 ~s** *nfpl* MERCANCÍA : goods, stock — **existente** *adj* : existing

éxito *nm* **1** : success, hit **2 tener ~** : be successful — **exitoso, -sa** *adj Lat* : successful

éxodo *nm* : exodus

exorbitante *adj* : exorbitant

exorcizar {21} *vt* : exorcize — **exorcismo** *nm* : exorcism

exótico, -ca *adj* : exotic

expandir *vt* : expand — **expandirse** *vr* : spread — **expansión** *nf, pl* **-siones** : expansion — **expansivo, -va** *adj* : expansive

expatriarse {85} *vr* **1** : emigrate **2** EXILIARSE : go into exile — **expatriado, -da** *adj & n* : expatriate

expectativa *nf* **1** : expectation, hope **2 ~s** *nfpl* : prospects

expedición *nf, pl* **-ciones** : expedition

expediente *nm* **1** : expedient **2** DOCUMENTOS : file, record **3** INVESTIGACIÓN : inquiry, proceedings

expedir {54} *vt* **1** : issue **2** ENVIAR : dispatch — **expedito, -ta** *adj* : free, clear

expeler *vt* : expel, eject

expendedor, -dora *n* : dealer, seller

expensas *nfpl* **1** : expenses **2 a ~ de** : at the expense of

experiencia *nf* : experience

experimentar *vi* : experiment — *vt* **1** : experiment with, test out **2** SENTIR : experience, feel — **experimentado, -da** *adj* : experienced — **experimental** *adj* : experimental — **experimento** *nm* : experiment

experto, -ta *adj & n* : expert

expiar {85} *vt* : atone for

expirar *vi* **1** : expire **2** MORIR : die

explayar *vt* : extend — **explayarse** *vr* **1** : spread out **2** HABLAR : speak at length

explicar {72} *vt* **1** : explain — **explicarse** *vr* : understand — **explicación** *nf, pl* **-ciones** : explanation — **explicativo, -va** *adj* : explanatory

explícito, -ta *adj* : explicit

explorar *vt* : explore — **exploración** *nf, pl* **-ciones** : exploration — **explorador, -dora** *n* : explorer, scout — **exploratorio, -ria** *adj* : exploratory

explosión *nf, pl* **-siones** **1** : explosion **2** : outburst (of anger, laughter, etc.) — **explosivo, -va** *adj* : explosive — **explosivo** *nm* : explosive

explotar *vt* **1** : exploit **2** : operate, run (a factory, etc.), work (a mine) — *vi* : explode — **explotación** *nf, pl* **-ciones** **1** : exploitation **2** : running (of a business), working (of a mine)

exponer {60} *vt* **1** : expose **2** : explain, set out (ideas, theories, etc.) **3** EXHIBIR : exhibit, display — *vi* : exhibit — **exponerse** *vr* **~ a** : expose oneself to

exportar *vt* : export — **exportaciones** *nfpl* : exports — **exportador, -dora** *n* : exporter

exposición *nf, pl* **-ciones** **1** : exposure **2** : exhibition (of objects, art, etc.) **3** : exposition, setting out (of ideas, etc.) — **expositor, -tora** *n* **1** : exhibitor **2** : exponent (of a theory, etc.)

exprés *nms & pl* **1** : express (train) **2 or café ~** : espresso

expresamente *adv* : expressly, on purpose

expresar *vt* : express — **expresarse** *vr* : express oneself — **expresión** *nf, pl* **-siones** : expression — **expresivo, -va** *adj* **1** : expressive **2** CARIÑOSO : affectionate

expreso, -sa *adj* : express — **expreso** *nm* : express train, express

exprimir *vt* **1** : squeeze **2** EXPLOTAR : exploit — **exprimidor** *nm* : squeezer, juicer

expuesto, -ta *adj* **1** : exposed **2** PELIGROSO : risky, dangerous

expulsar *vt* : expel, eject — **expulsión** *nf, pl* **-siones** : expulsion

exquisito, -ta *adj* **1** : exquisite **2** RICO : delicious — **exquisitez** *nf* **1** : exquisiteness **2** : delicacy, special dish

éxtasis *nms & pl* : ecstasy — **extático, -ta** *adj* : ecstatic

extender {56} *vt* **1** : spread out **2** : draw up (a document), write out (a check)

— **extenderse** *vr* **1** : extend, spread **2**
DURAR : last — **extendido, -da** *adj* **1**
: widespread **2** : outstretched (of arms,
wings, etc.)
extensamente *adv* : extensively
extensión *nf, pl* **-siones 1** : extension **2**
AMPLITUD : expanse **3** ALCANCE : range,
extent — **extenso, -sa** *adj* : extensive
extenuar {3} *vt* : exhaust, tire out
exterior *adj* **1** : exterior, external **2**
EXTRANJERO : foreign — ~ *nm* **1** : outside **2 en el** ~ : abroad — **exteri-
orizar** {21} *vt* : show, reveal — **exteriormente** *adv* : outwardly, externally
exterminar *vt* : exterminate — **exterminación** *nf, pl* **-ciones** : extermination
— **exterminio** *nm* : extermination
externo, -na *adj* : external
extinguir {26} *vt* **1** : extinguish (a fire)
2 : put an end to, wipe out — **extinguirse** *vr* **1** : go out (of fire, light, etc.)
2 : become extinct — **extinción** *nf, pl*
-ciones : extinction — **extinguidor**
nm Lat : fire extinguisher — **extinto,
-ta** *adj* : extinct — **extintor** *nm* : fire
extinguisher
extirpar *vt* : remove, eradicate
extorsión *nf, pl* **-siones 1** : extortion **2**
MOLESTIA : trouble
extra *adv* : extra — ~ *adj* **1** ADICIONAL
: additional **2** : top-quality — ~ *nmf*
: extra (in movies) — ~ *nm* : extra
(expense)
extraditar *vt* : extradite
extraer {81} *vt* : extract — **extracción**
nf, pl **-ciones** : extraction — **extracto**
nm **1** : extract **2** RESUMEN : abstract,
summary

extranjero, -ra *adj* : foreign — ~ *n*
: foreigner — **extranjero** *nm* : foreign
countries *pl*
extrañar *vt* : miss (someone) — **ex-
trañarse** *vr* : be surprised — **ex-
trañeza** *nf* : surprise — **extraño, -ña**
adj **1** : foreign **2** RARO : strange, odd
— ~ *n* : stranger
extraoficial *adj* : unofficial
extraordinario, -ria *adj* : extraordinary
extrasensorial *adj* : extrasensory
extraterrestre *adj & nmf* : extraterrestrial
extravagante *adj* : extravagant, outrageous — **extravagancia** *nf* : extravagance, outlandishness
extraviar {85} *vt* : lose, misplace — **extraviarse** *vr* : get lost — **extravío** *nm*
: loss
extremar *vt* : carry to extremes — **ex-
tremarse** *vr* : do one's utmost — **extremadamente** *adv* : extremely — **ex-
tremado, -da** *adj* : extreme —
extremidad *nf* **1** : tip, end **2** ~**es** *nfpl*
: extremities — **extremista** *adj & nmf*
: extremist — **extremo, -ma** *adj* **1**
: extreme **2 en caso** ~ : as a last resort — **extremo** *nm* **1** : end **2 en** ~
: in the extreme, extremely **3 en ulti-
mo** ~ : as a last resort
extrovertido -da *adj* : extroverted —
~ *n* : extrovert
exuberante *adj* : exuberant — **exuberancia** *nf* : exuberance
exudar *vt* : exude
eyacular *vi* : ejaculate — **eyaculación**
nf, pl **-ciones** : ejaculation

F

f *nf* : f, sixth letter of the Spanish alphabet
fabricar {72} *vt* **1** : manufacture **2** CON-
STRUIR : build, construct **3** INVENTAR
: fabricate — **fábrica** *nf* : factory —
fabricación *nf, pl* **-ciones** : manufacture — **fabricante** *nmf* : manufacturer
fábula *nf* **1** : fable **2** MENTIRA : story, lie
fabuloso, -sa *adj* : fabulous
facción *nf, pl* **-ciones 1** : faction **2**
~**es** *nfpl* RASGOS : features
faceta *nf* : facet
facha *nf* : appearance, look
fachada *nf* : façade
facial *adj* : facial
fácil *adj* **1** : easy **2** PROBABLE : likely —
fácilmente *adv* : easily, readily —

facilidad *nf* **1** : facility, ease **2** ~**es**
nfpl : facilities, services — **facilitar** *vt*
1 : facilitate **2** PROPORCIONAR : provide, supply
facsímil *or* **facsímile** *nm* **1** COPIA : facsimile, copy **2** : fax
factible *adj* : feasible
factor *nm* : factor
factoría *nf* : factory
factura *nf* **1** : bill, invoice **2** HECHURA
: making, manufacture — **facturar** *vt*
1 : bill for **2** : check in (baggage, etc.)
facultad *nf* **1** : faculty, ability **2** AUTORI-
DAD : authority **3** : school (of a university) — **facultativo, -va** *adj* : optional
faena *nf* **1** : task, job **2** ~**s domésticas**
: housework

fagot *nm* : bassoon

faisán *nm, pl* **-sanes** : pheasant

faja *nf* **1** : sash **2** : girdle, corset **3** : strip (of land)

fajo *nm* : bundle, sheaf

falda *nf* **1** : skirt **2** : side, slope (of a mountain)

falible *adj* : fallible

fálico, -ca *adj* : phallic

fallar *vi* : fail, go wrong — *vt* **1** : pronounce judgment on **2** ERRAR : miss — **falla** *nf* **1** : flaw, defect **2** : (geological) fault

fallecer {53} *vi* : pass away, die — **fallecimiento** *nm* : demise, death

fallido, -da *adj* : failed, unsuccessful

fallo *nm* **1** : error **2** SENTENCIA : sentence, verdict

falo *nm* : phallus, penis

falsear *vt* : falsify, distort — **falsedad** *nf* **1** : falseness **2** MENTIRA : falsehood, lie — **falsificación** *nf, pl* **-ciones** : forgery, fake — **falsificador, -dora** *n* : forger — **falsificar** {72} *vt* **1** : counterfeit, forge **2** ALTERAR : falsify — **falso, -sa** *adj* **1** : false, untrue **2** FALSIFICADO : counterfeit, forged

falta *nf* **1** CARENCIA : lack **2** DEFECTO : defect, fault, error **3** AUSENCIA : absence **4** : offense, misdemeanor (in law) **5** : foul (in sports) **6** hacer ~ : be lacking, be needed **7** sin ~ : without fail — **faltar** *vi* **1** : be lacking, be needed **2** : be missing **3** QUEDAR : remain, be left **4** ¡no faltaba más! : don't mention it! — **falto, -ta** *adj* ~ de : lacking (in)

fama *nf* **1** : fame **2** REPUTACIÓN : reputation

famélico, -ca *adj* : starving

familia *nf* : family — **familiar** *adj* **1** : familial, family **2** CONOCIDO : familiar **3** : informal (of language, etc.) — ~ *nmf* : relation, relative — **familiaridad** *nf* : familiarity — **familiarizarse** {21} *vr* ~ con : familiarize oneself with

famoso, -sa *adj* : famous

fanático, -ca *adj* : fanatic, fanatical — ~ *n* : fanatic — **fanatismo** *nm* : fanaticism

fanfarria *nf* : fanfare

fanfarrón, -rrona *adj, mpl* **-rrones** *fam* : boastful — ~ *n* *fam* : braggart — **fanfarronear** *vi* : boast, brag

fango *nm* : mud, mire — **fangoso, -sa** *adj* : muddy

fantasear *vi* : fantasize, daydream — **fantasía** *nf* **1** : fantasy **2** IMAGINACIÓN : imagination

fantasma *nm* : ghost, phantom — **fantasmal** *adj* : ghostly

fantástico, -ca *adj* : fantastic

fardo *nm* : bundle

farfullar *v* : jabber, gabble

farmacéutico, -ca *adj* : pharmaceutical — ~ *n* : pharmacist — **farmacia** *nf* : drugstore, pharmacy

faro *nm* **1** : lighthouse **2** : headlight (of an automobile) — **farol** *nm* **1** LINTERNA : lantern **2** FAROLA : streetlight — **farola** *nf* **1** : lamppost **2** FAROL : streetlight

farsa *nf* : farce — **farsante** *nmf* : charlatan, fraud

fascículo *nm* : installment, part (of a publication)

fascinar *vt* : fascinate — **fascinación** *nf, pl* **-ciones** : fascination — **fascinante** *adj* : fascinating

fascismo *nm* : fascism — **fascista** *adj & nmf* : fascist

fase *nf* : phase

fastidiar *vt* : annoy, bother — *vi* : be annoying or bothersome — **fastidio** *nm* : annoyance — **fastidioso, -sa** *adj* : annoying, bothersome

fatal *adj* **1** : fateful **2** MORTAL : fatal **3** *fam* : awful, terrible — **fatalidad** *nf* **1** : fate, destiny **2** DESGRACIA : misfortune

fatídico, -ca *adj* : fateful, momentous

fatiga *nf* : fatigue — **fatigado, -da** *adj* : weary, tired — **fatigar** {52} *vt* : tire — **fatigarse** *vr* : get tired — **fatigoso, -sa** *adj* : fatiguing, tiring

fatuo, -tua *adj* **1** : fatuous **2** PRESUMIDO : conceited

fauna *nf* : fauna

favor *nm* **1** : favor **2 a** ~ **de** : in favor of **3 por** ~ : please — **favorable** *adj* **1** : favorable **2 ser** ~ **a** : be in favor of — **favorecedor, -dora** *adj* : flattering — **favorecer** {53} *vt* **1** AYUDAR : favor **2** : look well on, suit — **favoritismo** *nm* : favoritism — **favorito, -ta** *adj & n* : favorite

fax *nm* : fax — **faxear** *vt* : fax

faz *nf, pl* **faces** : face, countenance

fe *nf* **1** : faith **2 dar** ~ **de** : bear witness to **3 de buena** ~ : in good faith

fealdad *nf* : ugliness

febrero *nm* : February

febril *adj* : feverish

fecha *nf* **1** : date **2** ~ **de caducidad** *or* ~ **de vencimiento** : expiration date **3** ~ **límite** : deadline — **fechar** *vt* : date, put a date on

fechoría *nf* : misdeed

fécula *nf* : starch (in food)

fecundar *vt* **1** : fertilize (an egg) **2** : make fertile — **fecundo, -da** *adj* : fertile

federación *nf, pl* **-ciones** : federation — **federal** *adj* : federal

felicidad *nf* 1 : happiness 2 ¡~**es!** : best wishes!, congratulations!, happy birthday! — **felicitación** *nf, pl* **-ciones** : congratulation — **felicitar** *vt* : congratulate — **felicitarse** *vr* ~ **de** : be glad about

feligrés, -gresa *n, mpl* **-greses** : parishioner

felino, -na *adj & n* : feline

feliz *adj, pl* **-lices** 1 : happy 2 AFORTUNADO : fortunate 3 **Feliz Navidad** : Merry Christmas

felpa *nf* 1 : plush 2 : terry cloth (for towels, etc.)

felpudo *nm* : doormat

femenino, -na *adj* 1 : feminine 2 : female (in biology) — **femenino** *nm* : feminine (in grammar) — **feminelidad** *nf* : femininity — **feminismo** *nm* : feminism — **feminista** *adj & nmf* : feminist

fenómeno *nm* : phenomenon — **fenomenal** *adj* 1 : phenomenal 2 *fam* : fantastic, terrific

feo, fea *adj* 1 : ugly 2 DESAGRADABLE : unpleasant, nasty

féretro *nm* : coffin

feria *nf* 1 : fair, market 2 FIESTA : festival, holiday 3 *Lat fam* : small change — **feriado, -da** *adj* **día feriado** : public holiday

fermentar *v* : ferment — **fermentación** *nf, pl* **-ciones** : fermentation — **fermento** *nm* : ferment

feroz *adj, pl* **-roces** : ferocious, fierce — **ferocidad** *nf* : ferocity, fierceness

férreo, -rrea *adj* 1 : iron 2 **vía férrea** : railroad track

ferretería *nf* : hardware store

ferrocarril *nm* : railroad, railway — **ferroviario, -ria** *adj* : rail, railroad

ferry *nm, pl* **ferrys** : ferry

fértil *adj* : fertile, fruitful — **fertilidad** *nf* : fertility — **fertilizante** *nm* : fertilizer — **fertilizar** *vt* : fertilize

fervor *nm* : fervor, zeal — **ferviente** *adj* : fervent

festejar *vt* 1 : celebrate 2 AGASAJAR : entertain, wine and dine — **festejo** *nm* : celebration, festivity

festín *nm, pl* **-tines** : banquet, feast

festival *nm* : festival — **festividad** *nf* : festivity — **festivo, -va** *adj* 1 : festive 2 **día festivo** : holiday

fetiche *nm* : fetish

fétido, -da *adj* : foul-smelling, fetid

feto *nm* : fetus — **fetal** *adj* : fetal

feudal *adj* : feudal

fiable *adj* : reliable — **fiabilidad** *nf* : reliability

fiado, -da *adj* : on credit — **fiador, -dora** *n* : bondsman, guarantor

fiambres *nfpl* : cold cuts

fianza *nf* 1 : bail, bond 2 **dar** ~ : pay a deposit

fiar {85} *vt* 1 : guarantee 2 : sell on credit — *vi* **ser de** ~ : be trustworthy — **fiarse** *vr* ~ **de** : place trust in

fiasco *nm* : fiasco

fibra *nf* 1 : fiber 2 ~ **de vidrio** : fiberglass

ficción *nf, pl* **-ciones** : fiction

ficha *nf* 1 : token 2 TARJETA : index card 3 : counter, chip (in games) — **fichar** *vt* : file, index — **fichero** *nm* 1 : card file 2 : filing cabinet

ficticio, -cia *adj* : fictitious

fidedigno, -na *adj* : reliable, trustworthy

fidelidad *nf* : fidelity, faithfulness

fideo *nm* : noodle

fiebre *nf* 1 : fever 2 ~ **del heno** : hay fever 3 ~ **palúdica** : malaria

fiel *adj* 1 : faithful, loyal 2 PRECISO : accurate, reliable — ~ *nm* 1 : pointer (of a scale) 2 **los** ~**es** : the faithful — **fielmente** *adv* : faithfully

fieltro *nm* : felt

fiero, -ra *adj* : fierce, ferocious — **fiera** *nf* : wild animal, beast

fierro *nm Lat* : iron (bar)

fiesta *nf* 1 : party 2 DIA FESTIVO : holiday, feast day

figura *nf* 1 : figure 2 FORMA : shape, form — **figurar** *vi* 1 : figure (in), be included (among) 2 DESTACAR : stand out — *vt* : represent — **figurarse** *vr* : imagine

fijar *vt* 1 : fasten, affix 2 CONCRETAR : set, fix — **fijarse** *vr* 1 : settle 2 ~ **en** : notice, pay attention to — **fijo, -ja** *adj* 1 : fixed, firm 2 PERMANENTE : permanent

fila *nf* 1 : line, file, row 2 **ponerse en** ~ : line up

filantropía *nf* : philanthropy — **filantrópico, -ca** *adj* : philanthropic — **filántropo, -pa** *n* : philanthropist

filatelia *nf* : philately, stamp collecting

filete *nm* : fillet

filial *adj* : filial — ~ *nf* : affiliate, subsidiary

filigrana *nf* 1 : filigree 2 : watermark (on paper)

filipino, -na *adj* : Filipino

filmar *vt* : film, shoot — **filme** *or* **film** *nm* : film, movie

filo *nm* 1 : edge 2 **dar** ~ **a** : sharpen

filón *nm, pl* **-lones** 1 : vein (of minerals) 2 *fam* : gold mine

filoso, -sa *adj Lat* : sharp

filosofía *nf* : philosophy — **filosófico, -ca** *adj* : philosophical — **filósofo, -fa** *n* : philosopher

filtrar *v* : filter — **filtrarse** *vr* : leak out, seep through — **filtro** *nm* : filter

fin *nm* 1 : end 2 OBJETIVO : purpose, aim 3 **en** ~ : well, in short 4 ~ **de semana** : weekend 5 **por** ~ : finally, at last

final *adj* : final — ~ *nm* : end, conclusion — ~ *nf* : final (in sports) — **finalidad** *nf* : purpose, aim — **finalista** *nmf* : finalist — **finalizar** {21} *v* : finish, end — **finalmente** *adv* : finally

financiar *vt* : finance, fund — **financiero, -ra** *adj* : financial — ~ *n* : financier — **finanzas** *nfpl* : finance

finca *nf* 1 : farm, ranch 2 *Lat* : country house

fingir {35} *v* : feign, pretend — **fingido, -da** *adj* : false, feigned

finito, -ta *adj* : finite

finlandés, -desa *adj* : Finnish

fino, -na *adj* 1 : fine 2 DELGADO : slender 3 REFINADO : refined 4 AGUDO : sharp, keen — **finura** *nf* 1 : fineness 2 REFINAMIENTO : refinement

firma *nf* 1 : signature 2 : (act of) signing 3 EMPRESA : firm, company

firmamento *nm* : firmament, sky

firmar *v* : sign

firme *adj* 1 : firm, resolute 2 ESTABLE : steady, stable — **firmeza** *nf* 1 : strength, resolve 2 ESTABILIDAD : firmness, stability

fiscal *adj* : fiscal — ~ *nmf* : district attorney — **fisco** *nm* : (national) treasury

fisgar {52} *vt* : pry into — *vi* : pry — **fisgón, -gona** *n, mpl* -**gones** : snoop, busybody

física *nf* : physics — **físico, -ca** *adj* : physical — ~ *n* : physicist — **físico** *nm* : physique

fisiología *nf* : physiology — **fisiológico, -ca** *adj* : physiological — **fisiólogo, -ga** *n* : physiologist

fisioterapia *nf* : physical therapy — **fisioterapeuta** *nmf* : physical therapist

fisonomía *nf* : features *pl*, appearance

fisura *nf* : fissure

fláccido, -da *or* **flácido, -da** *adj* : flaccid, flabby

flaco, -ca *adj* 1 : thin, skinny 2 DÉBIL : weak

flagrante *adj* : flagrant

flamante *adj* 1 : bright, brilliant 2 NUEVO : brand-new

flamenco, -ca *adj* 1 : flamenco (of music or dance) 2 : Flemish — **fla-**

menco *nm* 1 : flamingo 2 : flamenco (music or dance)

flaquear *vi* : weaken, flag — **flaqueza** *nf* 1 : thinness 2 DEBILIDAD : weakness

flash *nm* : flash

flatulencia *nf* : flatulence

flauta *nf* 1 : flute 2 ~ **dulce** : recorder — **flautín** *nm, pl* -**tines** : piccolo — **flautista** *nmf* : flutist

flecha *nf* : arrow

fleco *nm* 1 : fringe 2 *Lat* : bangs *pl*

flema *nf* : phlegm — **flemático, -ca** *adj* : phlegmatic

flequillo *nm* : bangs *pl*

fletar *vt* 1 : charter, rent 2 *Lat* : transport — **flete** *nm* 1 : charter 2 : shipping (charges) 3 *Lat* : transport, freight

flexible *adj* : flexible — **flexibilidad** *nf* : flexibility

flirtear *vi* : flirt

flojo, -ja *adj* 1 SUELTO : loose, slack 2 DÉBIL : weak 3 PEREZOSO : lazy — **flojera** *nf fam* : lethargy

flor *nf* : flower — **flora** *nf* : flora — **floral** *adj* : floral — **floreado, -da** *adj* : flowered — **florear** *vi Lat* : flower, bloom — **florecer** {53} *vi* 1 : bloom, blossom 2 PROSPERAR : flourish — **floreciente** *adj* : flourishing — **florero** *nm* : vase — **florido, -da** *adj* : flowery — **florista** *nmf* : florist — **floritura** *nf* : frill, flourish

flota *nf* : fleet

flotar *vi* : float — **flotador** *nm* 1 : float 2 : life preserver (for a swimmer) — **flotante** *adj* : floating, buoyant — **flote: a** ~ *adv phr* : afloat

flotilla *nf* : flotilla, fleet

fluctuar {3} *vi* : fluctuate — **fluctuación** *nf, pl* -**ciones** : fluctuation

fluir {41} *vi* : flow — **fluidez** *nf* 1 : fluidity 2 : fluency (of language, etc.) — **fluido, -da** *adj* 1 : fluid 2 : fluent (of language) — **fluido** *nm* : fluid — **flujo** *nm* : flow

fluorescente *adj* : fluorescent

fluoruro *nm* : fluoride

fluvial *adj* : river

fobia *nf* : phobia

foca *nf* : seal (animal)

foco *nm* 1 : focus 2 : spotlight, floodlight (in theater, etc.) 3 *Lat* : lightbulb

fofo, -fa *adj* : flabby

fogata *nf* : bonfire

fogón *nm, pl* -**gones** : burner

fogoso, -sa *adj* : ardent

folklore *nm* : folklore — **folklórico, -ca** *adj* : folk, traditional

follaje *nm* : foliage

folleto *nm* : pamphlet, leaflet

fomentar *vt* : promote, encourage — **fo-mento** *nm* : promotion, encourage-ment

fonda *nf* : boarding house

fondear *vt* : sound out, examine — *vi* : anchor

fondillos *nmpl* : seat (of pants, etc.)

fondo *nm* **1** : bottom **2** : rear, back, end **3** PROFUNDIDAD : depth **4** : background (of a painting, etc.) **5** *Lat* : slip, petti-coat **6** ~s *nmpl* : funds, resources **7 a** ~ : thoroughly, in depth **8 en el** ~ : deep down

fonético, -ca *adj* : phonetic — **fonética** *nf* : phonetics

fontanería *nf Spain* : plumbing — **fontanero, -ra** *n Spain* : plumber

footing ['fuˌtɪŋ] *nm* **1** : jogging **2 hacer** ~ : jog

forajido, -da *n* : bandit, outlaw

foráneo, -nea *adj* : foreign, strange

forastero, -ra *n* : stranger, outsider

forcejear *vi* : struggle — **forcejeo** *nm* : struggle

forense *adj* : forensic

forja *nf* : forge — **forjar** *vt* **1** : forge **2** CREAR, FORMAR : build up, create

forma *nf* **1** : form, shape **2** MANERA : manner, way **3 en** ~ : fit, healthy **4** ~s *nfpl* : appearances, conventions — **formación** *nf, pl* **-ciones 1** : for-mation **2** EDUCACIÓN : training

formal *adj* **1** : formal **2** SERIO : serious **FIABLE** : dependable, reliable — **for-malidad** *nf* **1** : formality **2** SERIEDAD : seriousness **3** FIABILIDAD : reliability

formar *vt* **1** : form, shape **2** CONSTITUIR : constitute **3** EDUCAR : train, educate — **formarse** *vr* **1** DESARROLLARSE : develop, take shape **2** EDUCARSE : be educated

formato *nm* : format

formidable *adj* **1** : tremendous **2** *fam* : fantastic, terrific

fórmula *nf* : formula

formular *vt* **1** : formulate, draw up **2** : make, lodge (a complaint, etc.)

formulario *nm* : form

fornido, -da *adj* : well-built, burly

foro *nm* : forum

forraje *nm* : forage, fodder — **forrajear** *vi* : forage

forrar *vt* **1** : line (a garment) **2** : cover (a book) — **forro** *nm* **1** : lining **2** CUBIER-TA : book cover

fortalecer {53} *vt* : strengthen — **for-taleza** *nf* **1** : fortress **2** FUERZA : strength **3** : (moral) fortitude

fortificar {72} *vt* : fortify — **fortifi-cación** *nf, pl* **-ciones** : fortification

fortuito, -ta *adj* : fortuitous, chance

fortuna *nf* **1** SUERTE : fortune, luck **2** RIQUEZA : wealth, fortune **3 por** ~ : fortunately

forzar {36} *vt* **1** : force **2** : strain (one's eyes) — **forzosamente** *adv* : neces-sarily — **forzoso, -sa** *adj* : necessary, inevitable

fosa *nf* **1** : pit, ditch **2** TUMBA : grave **3** ~s **nasales** : nostrils

fósforo *nm* **1** : phosphorus **2** CERILLA : match — **fosforescente** *adj* : phos-phorescent

fósil *nm* : fossil

foso *nm* **1** : ditch **2** : pit (of a theater) **3** : moat (of a castle)

foto *nf* : photo

fotocopia *nf* : photocopy — **fotocopi-adora** *nf* : photocopier — **fotocopiar** *vt* : photocopy

fotogénico, -ca *adj* : photogenic

fotografía *nf* **1** : photography **2** : photo-graph, picture — **fotografiar** {85} *vt* : photograph — **fotográfico, -ca** *adj* : photographic — **fotógrafo, -fa** *n* : photographer

fotosíntesis *nf* : photosynthesis

fracasar *vi* : fail — **fracaso** *nm* : failure

fracción *nf, pl* **-ciones 1** : fraction **2** : faction (in politics) — **frac-cionamiento** *nm Lat* : housing devel-opment

fractura *nf* : fracture — **fracturarse** *vr* : fracture, break (a bone)

fragancia *nf* : fragrance, scent — **fra-gante** *adj* : fragrant

fragata *nf* : frigate

frágil *adj* **1** : fragile **2** DÉBIL : frail, deli-cate — **fragilidad** *nf* **1** : fragility **2** DE-BILIDAD : frailty

fragmento *nm* : fragment

fragor *nm* : clamor, din

fragoso, -sa *adj* : rough, rugged

fragua *nf* : forge — **fraguar** {10} *vt* **1** : forge **2** IDEAR : concoct — *vi* : hard-en, solidify

fraile *nm* : friar, monk

frambuesa *nf* : raspberry

francés, -cesa *adj, mpl* **-ceses** : French — **francés** *nm* : French (language)

franco, -ca *adj* **1** : frank, candid **2** : free (in commerce) — **franco** *nm* : franc

francotirador, -dora *n* : sniper

franela *nf* : flannel

franja *nf* **1** : stripe, band **2** FLECO : fringe

franquear *vt* **1** : clear (a path, etc.) **2** : cross over (a doorstep, etc.) **3** : pay postage on (mail) — **franqueo** *nm* : postage

franqueza *nf* : frankness
frasco *nm* : small bottle, vial, flask
frase *nf* 1 : phrase 2 ORACIÓN : sentence
fraternal *adj* : brotherly, fraternal — **fraternidad** *nf* : brotherhood, fraternity — **fraternizar** {21} *vi* : fraternize — **fraterno, -na** *adj* : brotherly, fraternal
fraude *nm* : fraud — **fraudulento, -ta** *adj* : fraudulent
fray *nm* (*used in titles*) : brother, friar
frazada *nf Lat* : blanket
frecuencia *nf* 1 : frequency 2 con ~ : often, frequently — **frecuentar** *vt* : frequent, haunt — **frecuente** *adj* : frequent
fregadero *nm* : kitchen sink
fregar {49} *vt* 1 : scrub, wash 2 *Lat fam* : annoy — *vi Lat fam* : be a pest
freír {37} *vt* : fry
fregona *nf Spain* : mop
frenar *vt* 1 : brake 2 RESTRINGIR : curb, check
frenesí *nm* : frenzy — **frenético, -ca** *adj* : frantic, frenzied
freno *nm* 1 : brake 2 : bit (of a bridle) 3 CONTROL : check, restraint
frente *nm* 1 : front 2 : facade (of a building) 3 al ~ de : at the head of 4 ~ a : opposite 5 de ~ : (facing) forward 6 hacer ~ a : face up to, brave — ~ *nf* : forehead
fresa *nf* : strawberry
fresco, -ca *adj* 1 : fresh 2 FRÍO : cool 3 *fam* : insolent, nervy — **fresco** *nm* 1 : fresh air 2 FRESCURA : coolness 3 : fresco (art or painting) — **frescor** *nm* : coolness, cool air — **frescura** *nf* 1 : freshness 2 FRÍO : coolness 3 *fam* : nerve, insolence
fresno *nm* : ash (tree)
frialdad *nf* 1 : coldness 2 INDIFERENCIA : indifference
fricción *nf, pl* **-ciones** 1 : friction 2 MASAJE : rubbing, massage — **friccionar** *vt* : rub
frigidez *nf* : frigidity
frigorífico *nm Spain* : refrigerator
frijol *nm Lat* : bean
frío, fría *adj* 1 : cold 2 INDIFERENTE : cool, indifferent — **frío** *nm* 1 : cold 2 INDIFERENCIA : coldness, indifference 3 hacer ~ : be cold (outside) 4 tener ~ : be cold, feel cold
frito, -ta *adj* 1 : fried 2 *fam* : fed up
frívolo, -la *adj* : frivolous — **frivolidad** *nf* : frivolity
fronda *nf* 1 : frond 2 *or* ~s *nfpl* : foliage — **frondoso, -sa** *adj* : leafy
frontera *nf* : border, frontier — **fronterizo, -za** *adj* : border, on the border — **frontero, -ra** *adj* : facing, opposite
frotar *vt* : rub — **frotarse** *vr* ~ las manos : rub one's hands
fructífero, -ra *adj* : fruitful
frugal *adj* : frugal, thrifty — **frugalidad** *adj* : frugality
fruncir {83} *vt* 1 : gather (in pleats) 2 ~ el ceño : frown 3 ~ la boca : purse one's lips
frustrar *vt* : frustrate — **frustrarse** *vr* : fail — **frustración** *nf, pl* **-ciones** : frustration — **frustrado, -da** *adj* 1 : frustrated 2 FRACASADO : failed, unsuccessful — **frustrante** *adj* : frustrating
fruta *nf* : fruit — **frutilla** *nf Lat* : strawberry — **fruto** *nm* 1 : fruit 2 RESULTADO : result, consequence
fucsia *adj & nm* : fuchsia
fuego *nm* 1 : fire 2 : flame, burner (on a stove) 3 ~s artificiales *nmpl* : fireworks 4 ¿tienes fuego? : have you got a light?
fuelle *nm* : bellows
fuente *nf* 1 : fountain 2 MANANTIAL : spring 3 ORIGEN : source 4 PLATO : platter, serving dish
fuera *adv* 1 : outside, out 2 : abroad, away 3 ~ de : outside of, beyond 4 ~ de : aside from, in addition to
fuerte *adj* 1 : strong 2 : bright (of colors), loud (of sounds) 3 EXTREMO : intense 4 DURO : hard — ~ *adv* 1 : strongly, hard 2 : loudly 3 MUCHO : abundantly, a lot — ~ *nm* 1 : fort 2 ESPECIALIDAD : strong point
fuerza *nf* 1 : strength 2 VIOLENCIA : force 3 PODER : power, might 4 ~s armadas *nfpl* : armed forces 5 a ~ de : by dint of 6 a la ~ : necessarily
fuga *nf* 1 : flight, escape 2 : fugue (in music) 3 ESCAPE : leak — **fugarse** {52} *vr* : flee, run away — **fugaz** *adj, pl* **-gaces** : fleeting — **fugitivo, -va** *adj & n* : fugitive
fulano, -na *n* : so-and-so, what's-his-name, what's-her-name
fulgor *nm* : brilliance, splendor
fulminar *vt* 1 : strike with lightning 2 : strike down (with an illness, etc.) — **fulminante** *adj* : devastating
fumar *v* : smoke — **fumarse** *vr* 1 : smoke 2 *fam* : squander — **fumador, -dora** *n* : smoker
funámbulo, -la *n* : tightrope walker
función *nf, pl* **-ciones** 1 : function 2 TRABAJOS : duties *pl* 3 : performance, show (in theater) — **funcional** *adj* : functional — **funcionamiento** *nm* 1

: functioning **2 en ～** : in operation —
funcionar vi **1** : function, run, work
2 no funciona : out of order —
funcionario, -ria n : civil servant, official
funda nf **1** : cover, sheath **2** or **～ de almohada** : pillowcase
fundar vt **1** ESTABLECER : found, establish **2** BASAR : base — **fundarse** vr **～
en** : be based on — **fundación** nf, pl
-ciones : foundation — **fundador,
-dora** n : founder — **fundamental** adj
: fundamental, basic — **fundamentalmente** adv : basically — **fundamentar** vt **1** : lay the foundations for **2**
BASAR : base — **fundamento** nm **1**
: foundation **2 ～s** nmpl : fundamentals
fundir vt **1** : melt down, smelt **2** FUSIO-
NAR : fuse, merge — **fundirse** vr **1**
: blend, merge **2** DERRETIRSE : melt **3**
: burn out (of a lightbulb) — **fundi-
ción** nf, pl **-ciones 1** : smelting **2**
: foundry
fúnebre adj **1** : funeral **2** LÚGUBRE
: gloomy
funeral adj : funeral, funerary — **～** nm
1 : funeral **2 ～es** nmpl EXEQUIAS : fu-

neral (rites) — **funeraria** nf : funeral
home
funesto, ta adj : terrible, disastrous
fungir {35} vi Lat : act, function
furgón nm, pl **-gones 1** : van, truck **2**
: freight car (of a train) **3 ～ de cola**
: caboose — **furgoneta** nf : van
furia nf **1** CÓLERA : fury, rage **2** VIOLEN-
CIA : violence — **furibundo, -da** adj
: furious — **furioso, -sa** adj **1** : furious, irate **2** INTENSO : intense, violent
— **furor** nm : fury
furtivo, -va adj : furtive
furúnculo nm : boil
fuselaje nm : fuselage
fusible nm : fuse
fusil nm : rifle — **fusilar** vt : shoot (by
firing squad)
fusión nf, pl **-siones 1** : fusion **2** UNIÓN
: union, merger — **fusionar** vt **1** : fuse
2 UNIR : merge — **fusionarse** vr
: merge
futbol or **fútbol** nm **1** : soccer **2 ～
americano** : football — **futbolista**
nmf : soccer player, football player
fútil adj : trifling, trivial
futuro, -ra adj : future — **futuro** nm
: future

G

g nf : g, seventh letter of the Spanish alphabet
gabán nm, pl **-banes** : topcoat, overcoat
gabardina nf **1** : trench coat, raincoat **2**
: gabardine (fabric)
gabinete nm **1** : cabinet (in government) **2** : (professional) office
gacela nf : gazelle
gaceta nf : gazette
gachas nfpl : porridge
gacho, -cha adj : drooping
gaélico, -ca adj : Gaelic
gafas nfpl **1** : eyeglasses **2 ～ de sol**
: sunglasses
gaita nf : bagpipes pl
gajo nm : segment (of fruit)
gala nf **1** : gala **2 de ～** : formal **3 hacer
～ de** : display, show off **4 ～s** nfpl
: finery
galáctico, -ca adj : galactic
galán nm, pl **-lanes 1** : leading man (in
theater) **2** fam : boyfriend
galante adj : gallant — **galantear** vt
: court, woo — **galantería** nf **1** : gal-
lantry **2** CUMPLIDO : compliment
galápago nm : (aquatic) turtle

galardón nm, pl **-dones** : reward
galaxia nf : galaxy
galera nf : galley
galería nf **1** : corridor **2** : gallery, balcony (in a theater)
galés, -lesa adj, mpl **-leses** : Welsh
galgo nm : greyhound
galimatías nms & pl : gibberish
gallardía nf **1** : bravery **2** ELEGAN-
CIA : elegance — **gallardo, -da** adj **1**
: brave **2** APUESTO : elegant, good-
looking
gallego, -ga adj : Galician
galleta nf **1** : (sweet) cookie **2** : (salted)
cracker
gallina nf **1** : hen **2 ～ de Guinea**
: guinea fowl — **gallinero** nm : hen-
house, (chicken) coop — **gallo** nm
: rooster, cock
galón nm, pl **-lones 1** : gallon **2** : stripe
(military insignia)
galopar vi : gallop — **galope** nm : gallop
galvanizar {21} vt : galvanize
gama nf **1** : range, spectrum **2** : scale (in
music)
gamba nf : large shrimp, prawn

gamuza *nf* **1** : chamois (animal) **2** : chamois (leather), suede

gana *nf* **1** : desire, wish **2** APETITO : appetite **3 de buena ~** : willingly, heartily **4 de mala ~** : unwillingly **5 no me da la ~** : I don't feel like it **6 tener ~s de** : feel like, be in the mood for

ganado *nm* **1** : cattle *pl*, livestock **2 ~ ovino** : sheep *pl* **3 ~ porcino** : swine *pl* — **ganadería** *nf* **1** : cattle raising **2** GANADO : livestock

ganador, -dora *adj* : winning — **~** *n* : winner

ganancia *nf* : profit

ganar *vt* **1** : earn **2** : win (in games, etc.) **3** CONSEGUIR : gain **4** ADQUERIR : get, obtain **5 ~ a algn** : win over s.o., beat s.o. — *vi* : win — **ganarse** *vr* **1** : win, gain **2 ~ la vida** : make a living

gancho *nm* **1** : hook **2** HORQUILLA : hairpin **3** *Lat* : (clothes) hanger

gandul, -dula *adj & n fam* : good-for-nothing — **gandul** *nm Lat* : pigeon pea

ganga *nf* : bargain

gangrena *nf* : gangrene

gángster *nmf* : gangster

ganso, -sa *n* : goose, gander *m* — **gansada** *nf* : silly thing, nonsense

gañir {38} *vi* : yelp — **gañido** *nm* : yelp

garabatear *v* : scribble — **garabato** *nm* : scribble

garaje *nm* : garage

garantizar {21} *vt* : guarantee — **garante** *nmf* : guarantor — **garantía** *nf* **1** : guarantee, warranty **2** FIANZA : surety

garapiñar *vt* : candy (fruits, etc.)

garbanzo *nm* : chickpea, garbanzo

garbo *nm* : grace, elegance — **garboso, -sa** *adj* : graceful, elegant

gardenia *nf* : gardenia

garfio *nm* : hook, gaff

garganta *nf* **1** : throat **2** CUELLO : neck **3** DESFILADERO : ravine, gorge — **gargantilla** *nf* : necklace

gárgara *nf* **1** : gargling, gargle **2 hacer ~s** : gargle

gárgola *nf* : gargoyle

garita *nf* **1** : sentry box **2** CABAÑA : cabin, hut

garito *nm* : gambling den

garra *nf* **1** : claw, talon **2** *fam* : hand, paw

garrafa *nf* : decanter, carafe — **garrafón** *nm, pl* **-fones** : large decanter or bottle

garrapata *nf* : tick

garrocha *nf* **1** : lance, pike **2** *Lat* : pole (in sports)

garrote *nm* : club, cudgel

garúa *nf Lat* : drizzle

garza *nf* : heron

gas *nm* **1** : gas **2 ~ lacrimógeno** : tear gas

gasa *nf* : gauze

gaseosa *nf* : soda, soft drink

gasolina *nf* : gasoline, gas — **gasoil** *or* **gasóleo** *nm* : diesel fuel — **gasolinera** *nf* : gas station, service station

gastar *vt* **1** : spend **2** CONSUMIR : consume, use up **3** DESPERDICIAR : squander, waste — **gastarse** *vr* **1** : spend **2** DETERIORARSE : wear out — **gastado, -da** *adj* **1** : spent **2** : worn-out (of clothing, etc.) — **gastador, -dora** *n* : spendthrift — **gasto** *nm* **1** : expense, expenditure **2 ~s generales** : overhead

gástrico, -ca *adj* : gastric

gastronomía *nf* : gastronomy — **gastrónomo, -ma** *n* : gourmet

gatas: a ~ *adv phr* : on all fours

gatear *vi* : crawl, creep

gatillo *nm* : trigger — **gatillero** *nm Mex* : gunman

gato, -ta *n* : cat — **gatito, -ta** *n* : kitten — **gato** *nm* : jack (for an automobile)

gaucho *nm* : gaucho

gaveta *nf* : drawer

gavilla *nf* **1** : sheaf **2** PANDILLA : gang

gaviota *nf* : gull, seagull

gay ['ge, 'gai] *adj* : gay (homosexual)

gaza *nf* : loop

gazpacho *nm* : gazpacho

géiser *nm* : geyser

gelatina *nf* : gelatin

gema *nf* : gem

gemelo, -la *adj & n* : twin — **gemelo** *nm* **1** : cuff link **2 ~s** *nmpl* : binoculars

gemir {54} *vi* : moan, groan, whine — **gemido** *nm* : moan, groan, whine

gen *or* **gene** *nm* : gene

genealogía *nf* : genealogy — **genealógico, -ca** *adj* : genealogical

generación *nf, pl* **-ciones** : generation

generador *nm* : generator

general *adj* **1** : general **2 en ~** *or* **por lo ~** : in general, generally — **~** *nmf* : general — **generalidad** *nf* **1** : generalization **2** MAYORÍA : majority — **generalizar** {21} *vi* : generalize — *vt* : spread (out) — **generalizarse** *vr* : become widespread — **generalmente** *adv* : usually, generally

generar *vt* : generate

género *nm* **1** : kind, sort **2** : gender (in

grammar) **3 ~ humano** : human race
— **genérico, -ca** *adj* : generic
generoso, -sa *adj* **1** : generous, unselfish **2** : ample (in quantity) — **generosidad** *nf* : generosity
génesis *nfs & pl* : genesis
genética *nf* : genetics — **genético, -ca**
adj : genetic
genial *adj* **1** : brilliant **2** ESTUPENDO
: great, terrific
genio *nm* **1** : genius **2** CARÁCTER : temper, disposition **3** : genie (in mythology)
genital *adj* : genital — **genitales** *nmpl*
: genitals
genocidio *nm* : genocide
gente *nf* **1** : people **2** *fam* : relatives *pl*,
folks *pl* **3 ser buena ~** : be nice, be
kind
gentil *adj* **1** AMABLE : kind **2** : gentile
(in religion) — **gentileza** *nf* : kindness, courtesy
gentío *nm* : crowd, mob
gentuza *nf* : riffraff, rabble
genuflexión *nf, pl* -**xiones** : genuflec-
tion
genuino, -na *adj* : genuine
geografía *nf* : geography — **geográfi-
co, -ca** *adj* : geographic, geographical
geología *nf* : geology — **geológico,
-ca** *adj* : geologic, geological
geometría *nf* : geometry — **geométrico, -ca** *adj* : geometric, geometrical
geranio *nm* : geranium
gerencia *nf* : management — **gerente**
nmf : manager
geriatría *nf* : geriatrics — **geriátrico,
-ca** *adj* : geriatric
germen *nm, pl* **gérmenes** : germ
germinar *vi* : germinate, sprout
gestación *nf, pl* -**ciones** : gestation
gesticular *vi* : gesticulate, gesture —
gesticulación *nf, pl* -**ciones** : gestic-
ulation
gestión *nf, pl* -**tiones 1** : procedure, step
2 ADMINISTRACIÓN : management —
gestionar *vt* **1** : negotiate, work towards **2** ADMINISTRAR : manage, handle
gesto *nm* **1** : gesture **2** : (facial) expression **3** MUECA : grimace
gigante *adj & nm* : giant — **gigantesco, -ca** *adj* : gigantic
gimnasia *nf* : gymnastics — **gimnasio**
nm : gymnasium, gym — **gimnasta**
nmf : gymnast
gimotear *vi* : whine, whimper
ginebra *nf* : gin
ginecología *nf* : gynecology — **gine-
cólogo, -ga** *n* : gynecologist
gira *nf* : tour

girar *vi* : turn (around), revolve — *vt* **1**
: turn, twist, rotate **2** : draft (checks) **3**
: transfer (funds)
girasol *nm* : sunflower
giratorio, -ria *adj* : revolving
giro *nm* **1** : turn, rotation **2** LOCUCIÓN
: expression **3 ~ bancario** : bank
draft **4 ~ postal** : money order
giroscopio *nm* : gyroscope
gis *nm Lat* : chalk
gitano, -na *adj & n* : Gypsy
glaciar *nm* : glacier — **glacial** *adj* : glacial, icy
gladiador *nm* : gladiator
glándula *nf* : gland
glasear *vt* : glaze, ice (cake, etc.) —
glaseado *nm* : icing
glicerina *nf* : glycerin
globo *nm* **1** : globe **2** : balloon **3 ~ ocular** : eyeball — **global** *adj* **1** : global
2 TOTAL : total, overall
glóbulo *nm* : blood cell, corpuscle
gloria *nf* : glory
glorieta *nf* **1** : bower, arbor **2** *Spain* : rotary, traffic circle
glorificar {72} *vt* : glorify
glorioso, -sa *adj* : glorious
glosario *nm* : glossary
glosa *nf* : glucose
gnomo ['nomo] *nm* : gnome
gobernar {55} *v* **1** : govern, rule **2** DIRI-
GIR : direct, manage **3** : steer (a boat,
etc.) — **gobernación** *nf, pl* -**ciones**
: governing, government — **gobernador, -dora** *n* : governor — **gobernante** *adj* : ruling, governing — **~** *n*
: ruler, leader — **gobierno** *nm* : government
goce *nm* : enjoyment
gol *nm* : goal (in sports)
golf *nm* : golf — **golfista** *nmf* : golfer
golfo *nm* : gulf
golondrina *nf* **1** : swallow **2 ~ de mar**
: tern
golosina *nf* : sweet, candy — **goloso,
-sa** *adj* : fond of sweets
golpe *nm* **1** : blow **2** PUÑETAZO : punch
3 : knock (on a door, etc.) **4 de ~**
: suddenly **5 de un ~** : all at once **6
~ de estado** : coup d'etat — **gol-
pear** *vt* **1** : hit, punch **2** : slam, bang (a
door, etc.) — *vi* : knock (at a door)
goma *nf* **1** CAUCHO : rubber **2** PEGAMEN-
TO : glue **3** *or* **~ elástica** : rubber
band **4 ~ de mascar** : chewing gum
5 ~ de borrar : eraser
gong *nm* : gong

gordo, -da *adj* **1** : fat, plump **2** GRUESO
: thick **3** : fatty (of meat) **4** *fam* : big,
serious — **~** *n* : fat person — **gorda**
nf Lat : thick corn tortilla — **gordo** *nm*
1 GRASA : fat **2** : jackpot (in a lottery)
— **gordura** *nf* : fatness, flab
gorgotear *vi* : gurgle, bubble
gorila *nm* : gorilla
gorjear *vi* **1** : chirp, tweet **2** : gurgle (of
a baby) — **gorjeo** *nm* : chirping
gorra *nf* **1** : cap, bonnet **2** de **~** *fam*
: for free
gorrear *vt fam* : bum, scrounge
gorrión *nm*, *pl* **-rriones** : sparrow
gorro *nm* **1** : cap, bonnet **2** de **~** *fam*
: for free
gota *nf* **1** : drop **2** : gout (in medicine)
— **gotear** *vi* : drip, leak — **goteo** *nm*
: drip, dripping — **gotera** *nf* : leak
gótico, -ca *adj* : Gothic
gozar {21} *vi* **1** : enjoy oneself **2 ~** de
algo : enjoy sth
gozne *nm* : hinge
gozo *nm* **1** : joy **2** PLACER : enjoyment,
pleasure — **gozoso, -sa** *adj* : joyful,
glad
grabar *vt* **1** : engrave **2** : record, tape —
grabación *nf*, *pl* **-ciones** : recording
— **grabado** *nm* : engraving — **grabadora** *nf* : tape recorder
gracia *nf* **1** : grace **2** FAVOR : favor, kindness **3** HUMOR : humor, wit **4 ~s** *nfpl*
: thanks **5** ¡(muchas) **~s!** : thank you
(very much)! — **gracioso, -sa** *adj*
: funny, amusing
grada *nf* **1** : step, stair **2** : row (in a theater, etc.) **3 ~s** *nfpl* : bleachers,
grandstand — **gradación** *nf*, *pl*
-ciones : gradation, scale — **gradería**
nf : rows *pl*, stands *pl* — **grado** *nm* **1**
: degree **2** : grade (in school) **3** de
buen ~ : willingly
graduar {3} *vt* **1** : regulate, adjust **2**
MARCAR : calibrate **3** : confer a degree
on (in education) — **graduarse** *vr*
: graduate (from a school) — **grad-
uación** *nf*, *pl* **-ciones 1** : graduation **2**
: alcohol content, proof — **graduado,
-da** *n* : graduate — **gradual** *adj* : gradual — **gradualmente** *adv* : little by
little, gradually
gráfico, -ca *adj* : graphic — **gráfica** *nf*
: graph — **gráfico** *nm* **1** : graph **2**
: graphic (in computers)
gragea *nf* : pill, tablet
grajo *nm* : rook (bird)
gramática *nf* : grammar — **gramatical**
adj : grammatical
gramo *nm* : gram

gran → grande
grana *nf* : scarlet
granada *nf* **1** : pomegranate **2** : grenade
(in the military)
granate *nm* : garnet
grande *adj* (**gran** *before singular
nouns*) **1** : large, big **2** ALTO : tall **3**
: great (in quality, intensity, etc.) **4** *Lat*
: grown-up — **grandeza** *nf* **1** : greatness **2** NOBLEZA : nobility — **grandiosidad** *nf* : grandeur — **grandioso, -sa**
adj : grand, magnificent
granel: a **~** *adv phr* **1** : in bulk **2** : in
abundance
granero *nm* : barn, granary
granito *nm* : granite
granizar {21} *v impers* : hail — **grani-
zada** *nf* : hailstorm — **granizado** *nm*
: iced drink — **granizo** *nm* : hail
granja *nf* : farm — **granjero, -ra** *n*
: farmer
grano *nm* **1** : grain **2** SEMILLA : seed **3**
: (coffee) bean **4** BARRO : pimple
granuja *nmf* : rascal
grapa *nf* : staple — **grapadora** *nf* : stapler — **grapar** *vt* : staple
grasa *nf* **1** : grease **2** : fat (in cooking,
etc.) — **grasiento, -ta** *adj* : greasy, oily
— **graso, -sa** *adj* : fatty, greasy, oily —
grasoso, -sa *adj Lat* : greasy, oily
gratificar {72} *vt* **1** : give a tip or bonus
to **2** SATISFACER : gratify, satisfy —
gratificación *nf*, *pl* **-ciones 1** : bonus,
tip, reward **2** SATISFACCIÓN : gratifica-
tion
gratis *adv & adj* : free
gratitud *nf* : gratitude
grato, -ta *adj* : pleasant, agreeable
gratuito, -ta *adj* **1** : gratuitous, unwarranted **2** GRATIS : free
grava *nf* : gravel
gravar *vt* **1** : tax **2** CARGAR : burden —
gravamen *nm*, *pl* **-vámenes 1** : burden, obligation **2** IMPUESTO : tax
grave *adj* **1** : grave, serious **2** : deep,
low (of a voice, etc.) — **gravedad** *nf*
: gravity
gravilla *nf* : gravel
gravitar *vi* **1** : gravitate **2 ~ sobre**
: weigh on — **gravitación** *nf*, *pl*
-ciones : gravitation
gravoso, -sa *adj* : costly, burdensome
graznar *vi* : caw, quack, honk —
graznido *nm* : caw, quack, honk
gregario, -ria *adj* : gregarious
gremio *nm* : guild, (trade) union
greñas *nfpl* : shaggy hair, mop
griego, -ga *adj* : Greek — **griego** *nm*
: Greek (language)
grieta *nf* : crack, crevice

grifo *nm Spain* : faucet, tap

grillete *nm* : shackle

grillo *nm* **1** : cricket **2 ~s** *nmpl* : fetters, shackles

grima *nf* **dar ~** : annoy, irritate

gringo, -ga *adj & n Lat fam* : Yankee, gringo

gripe *nf or* **gripa** *nf Lat* : flu, influenza

gris *adj & nm* : gray

gritar *v* : shout, scream, cry — **grito** *nm* **1** : shout, scream, cry **2 dar ~s** : shout

grosella *nf* : currant

grosería *nf* **1** : vulgar remark **2** DESCORTESÍA : rudeness — **grosero, -ra** *adj* **1** : coarse, vulgar **2** DESCORTÉS : rude

grosor *nm* : thickness

grotesco, -ca *adj* : grotesque, hideous

grúa *nf* : crane, derrick

grueso, -sa *adj* **1** : thick **2** CORPULENTO : stout, heavy — **gruesa** *nf* : gross — **grueso** *nm* **1** GROSOR : thickness **2** : main body, mass **3 en ~** : wholesale

grulla *nf* : crane (bird)

grumo *nm* : lump, clot — **grumoso, -sa** *adj* : lumpy

gruñir {38} *vi* **1** : growl, grunt **2** *fam* : grumble — **gruñido** *nm* **1** : growl, grunt **2** *fam* : grumble — **gruñón, -ñona** *adj, mpl* **-ñones** *fam* : grumpy, grouchy — **~** *n fam* : grouch

grupa *nf* : rump, hindquarters *pl*

grupo *nm* : group

gruta *nf* : grotto

guacamayo *nm or* **guacamaya** *nf Lat* : macaw

guacamole *nm* : guacamole

guadaña *nf* : scythe

guagua *nf Lat* **1** : baby **2** AUTOBÚS : bus

guajalote, -ta *or* **guajolote, -ta** *n Lat* : turkey

guante *nm* : glove

guapo, -pa *adj* : handsome, good-looking

guaraní *nm* : Guarani (language of Paraguay)

guarda *nmf* **1** : keeper, custodian **2** GUARDIÁN : security guard — **guardabarros** *nms & pl* : fender — **guardabosque** *nmf* : forest ranger — **guardacostas** *nmfs & pl* : coast guard vessel — **guardaespaldas** *nmfs & pl* : bodyguard — **guardameta** *nmf* : goalkeeper — **guardapolvo** *nm* : overalls *pl* — **guardar** *vt* **1** : keep **2** PROTEGER : guard, protect **3** RESERVAR : save — **guardarse** *vr* **~ de 1** : refrain from **2** : guard against — **guardarropa** *nm* **1**

: cloakroom, checkroom **2** ARMARIO : wardrobe

guardería *nf* : nursery, day-care center

guardia *nf* **1** : guard, vigilence **2** TURNO : duty, watch — **~** *nmf* **1** : guard **2** *or* **~ municipal** : police officer — **guardián, -diana** *n, mpl* **-dianes 1** : guardian, keeper **2** GUARDA : security guard

guarecer {53} *vt* : shelter, protect — **guarecerse** *vr* : take shelter

guarida *nf* **1** : den, lair (of animals) **2** : hideout (of persons)

guarnecer {53} *vt* **1** : adorn, garnish **2** : garrison (an area) — **guarnición** *nf, pl* **-ciones 1** : garnish, trimming **2** : (military) garrison

guasa *nf fam* **1** : joke **2 de ~** : in jest — **guasón, -sona** *adj, mpl* **-sones** *fam* : joking, witty — **~** *n fam* : joker

guatemalteco, -ca *adj* : Guatemalan

guayaba *nf* : guava

gubernamental *or* **gubernativo, -va** *adj* : governmental

guepardo *nm* : cheetah

güero, -ra *adj Lat* : blond, fair

guerra *nf* **1** : war, warfare **2** LUCHA : conflict, struggle — **guerrear** *vi* : wage war — **guerrero, -ra** *adj* **1** : war, fighting **2** BELICOSO : warlike — **~** *n* : warrior — **guerrilla** *nf* : guerrilla warfare — **guerrillero, -ra** *adj & n* : guerrilla

gueto *nm* : ghetto

guiar {85} *vt* **1** : guide, lead **2** ACONSEJAR : advise — **guiarse** *vr* : be guided by, go by — **guía** *nf* **1** : guidebook **2** ORIENTACIÓN : guidance — **~** *nmf* : guide, leader

guijarro *nm* : pebble

guillotina *nf* : guillotine

guinda *nf* : morello (cherry)

guiñar *vi* : wink — **guiño** *nm* : wink

guión *nm, pl* **guiones 1** : script, screenplay **2** : hyphen, dash (in punctuation) — **guionista** *nmf* : scriptwriter, screenwriter

guirnalda *nf* : garland

guisa *nf* **1** : manner, fashion **2 a ~ de** : by way of **3 de tal ~** : in such a way

guisado *nm* : stew

guisante *nm* : pea

guisar *vt* : cook — **guiso** *nm* : stew, casserole

guitarra *nf* : guitar — **guitarrista** *nmf* : guitarist

gula *nf* : gluttony

gusano *nm* **1** : worm **2** : maggot (larva)

gustar *vt* **1** : taste **2** *Lat* : like — *vi* **1** : be pleasing **2 como guste** : as you like **3**

me gustan los dulces : I like sweets
— **gusto** *nm* **1** : taste **2** PLACER : pleasure, liking **3 a** ~ : comfortable, at ease **4 al** ~ : to taste **5 mucho** ~

: pleased to meet you — **gustoso, -sa** *adj* **1** : tasty **2** AGRADABLE : pleasant **3 hacer algo** ~ : do sth willingly
gutural *adj* : guttural

H

h *nf* : h, eighth letter of the Spanish alphabet
haba *nf* : broad bean
habanero, -ra *adj* : Havanan — **habano** *nm* : Havana cigar
haber {39} *v aux* **1** : have, has **2** ~ **de** : must — *v impers* **1 hay** : there is, there are **2 hay que** : it is necessary (to) **3 ¿qué hay?** *or* **¿qué hubo?** : how's it going? — ~ *nm* **1** : assets *pl* **2** : credit side (in accounting) **3** ~**es** *nmpl* : income, earnings
habichuela *nf* **1** : bean **2** ~ **verde** : string bean
hábil *adj* **1** : able, skillful **2** LISTO : clever **3 horas** ~**es** : business hours — **habilidad** *nf* : ability, skill
habilitar *vt* **1** : equip, furnish **2** AUTORIZAR : authorize
habitar *vt* : inhabit — *vi* : reside, dwell — **habitable** *adj* : habitable, inhabitable — **habitación** *nf, pl* **-ciones 1** : room, bedroom **2** MORADA : dwelling, abode **3** : habitat (in biology) — **habitante** *nmf* : inhabitant, resident — **hábitat** *nm* : habitat
hábito *nm* : habit — **habitual** *adj* : habitual, usual — **habituar** {3} *vt* : accustom, habituate — **habituarse** *vr* ~ **a** : get used to
hablar *vi* **1** : speak, talk **2** ~ **de** : mention, talk about **3** ~ **con** : talk to, speak with — *vt* **1** : speak (a language) **2** DISCUTIR : discuss — **hablarse** *vr* **1** : speak to each other **2 se habla inglés** : English spoken — **habla** *nf* **1** : speech **2** IDIOMA : language, dialect **3 de** ~ **inglesa** : English-speaking — **hablador, -dora** *adj* : talkative — ~ *n* : chatterbox — **habladuría** *nf* **1** : rumor **2** ~**s** *nfpl* : gossip — **hablante** *nmf* : speaker
hacedor, -dora *n* : creator, maker
hacendado, -da *n* : landowner, rancher
hacer {40} *vt* **1** : do, perform **2** CONSTRUIR, CREAR : make **3** OBLIGAR : force, oblige — *vi* : act — *v impers* **1** ~ **calor/viento** : be hot/be windy **2** ~ **falta** : be necessary **3 hace mucho tiempo** : a long time ago **4 no lo hace** : it doesn't matter — **hacerse** *vr* **1**

VOLVERSE : become **2** : pretend (to be) **3** ~ **a** : get used to **4 se hace tarde** : it's getting late
hacha *nf* **1** : hatchet, ax **2** ANTORCHA : torch
hachís *nm* : hashish
hacia *prep* **1** : toward, towards **2** CERCA DE : near, around, about **3** ~ **abajo** : downward **4** ~ **adelante** : forward
hacienda *nf* **1** : estate, ranch **2** BIENES : property **3** *Lat* : livestock **4 Hacienda** : department of revenue
hacinar *vt* : stack
hada *nf* : fairy
hado *nm* : fate
halagar {52} *vt* : flatter — **halagador, -dora** *adj* : flattering — **halago** *nm* : flattery — **halagüeño, -ña** *adj* **1** : flattering **2** PROMETEDOR : promising
halcón *nm, pl* **-cones** : hawk, falcon
halibut *nm, pl* **-buts** : halibut
hálito *nm* : breath
hallar *vt* **1** : find **2** DESCUBRIR : discover, find out — **hallarse** *vr* : be, find oneself — **hallazgo** *nm* : discovery, find
halo *nm* : halo
hamaca *nf* : hammock
hambre *nf* **1** : hunger **2** INANICIÓN : starvation, famine **3 tener** ~ : be hungry — **hambriento, -ta** *adj* : hungry, starving — **hambruna** *nf* : famine
hamburguesa *nf* : hamburger
hampa *nf* : underworld — **hampón, -pona** *n, mpl* **-pones** : criminal, thug
hámster *nm* : hamster
hándicap *nm* : handicap (in sports)
hangar *nm* : hangar
haragán, -gana *adj, mpl* **-ganes** : lazy, idle — ~ *n* : slacker, idler — **haraganear** : be lazy, loaf
harapiento, -ta *adj* : ragged, in rags — **harapos** *nmpl* : rags, tatters
harina *nf* : flour
hartar *vt* **1** : glut, satiate **2** FASTIDIAR : annoy — **hartarse** *vr* **1** : gorge oneself **2** CANSARSE : get fed up — **harto, -ta** *adj* **1** : full, satiated **2** CANSADO : tired, fed up — **harto** *adv* : extremely, very — **hartura** *nf* **1** : surfeit **2** ABUNDANCIA : abundance, plenty
hasta *prep* **1** : until, up until (in time) **2**

: as far as, up to (in space) **3** ¡∼
luego! : see you later! **4** ∼ **que** : until
— ∼ *adv* : even

hastiar {85} *vt* **1** : make weary, bore **2**
ASQUEAR : sicken — **hastiarse** *vr* ∼
de : get tired of — **hastío** *nm* **1** : weariness, tedium **2** REPUGNANCIA : disgust

hato *nm* **1** : flock, herd **2** : bundle (of
possessions)

haya *nf* : beech

haz *nm, pl* **haces 1** : bundle, sheaf **2**
: beam (of light)

hazaña *nf* : feat, exploit

hazmerreír *nm fam* : laughingstock

he {39} *v impers* ∼ **aquí** : here is, here
are, behold

hebilla *nf* : buckle

hebra *nf* : strand, thread

hebreo, -brea *adj* : Hebrew — **hebreo**
nm : Hebrew (language)

hecatombe *nm* : disaster

hechizo *nm* **1** : spell **2** ENCANTO : charm,
fascination — **hechicería** *nf* : sorcery,
witchcraft — **hechicero, -ra** *n* : sorcerer, sorceress *f* — **hechizar** {21} *vt* **1**
: bewitch **2** CAUTIVAR : charm

hecho, -cha *adj* **1** : made, done **2**
: ready-to-wear (of clothing) **3** ∼ **y**
derecho : full-fledged, mature —
hecho *nm* **1** : fact **2** SUCESO : event **3**
ACTO : act, deed **4 de** ∼ : in fact —
hechura *nf* **1** : making, creation **2**
FORMA : shape, form **3** : build (of the
body) **4** ARTESANÍA : workmanship

heder {56} *vi* : stink, reek — **hediondez** *nf, pl* **-deces** : stench — **hediondo, -da** *adj* : stinking — **hedor** *nm*
: stench

helar {55} *v* : freeze — **helarse** *vr*
: freeze up, freeze over — **helado, -da**
adj **1** : freezing cold **2** CONGELADO
: frozen — **helada** *nf* : frost —
heladería *nf* : ice-cream parlor —
helado *nm* : ice cream — **heladora** *nf*
: freezer

helecho *nm* : fern

hélice *nf* **1** : propeller **2** ESPIRAL : spiral,
helix

helicóptero *nm* : helicopter

helio *nm* : helium

hembra *nf* **1** : female **2** MUJER : woman

hemisferio *nm* : hemisphere

hemorragia *nf* **1** : hemorrhage **2** ∼
nasal : nosebleed

hemorroides *nfpl* : hemorrhoids, piles

henchir {54} *vt* : stuff, fill

hender {56} *vt* : cleave, split — **hendidura** *nf* : crevice, fissure

henequén *nm, pl* **-quenes** : sisal

heno *nm* : hay

hepatitis *nf* : hepatitis

heraldo *nm* : herald

herbolario, -ria *n* : herbalist

heredar *vt* : inherit — **heredad** *nm*
: rural property, estate — **heredero,
-ra** *n* : heir, heiress *f* — **hereditario,
-ria** *adj* : hereditary

hereje *nmf* : heretic — **herejía** *nf*
: heresy

herencia *nf* **1** : inheritance **2** : heredity
(in biology)

herir {76} *vt* **1** : injure, wound **2** : hurt
(feelings, pride, etc.) — **herida** *nf* : injury, wound — **herido, -da** *adj* **1** : injured, wounded **2** : hurt (of feelings,
pride, etc.) — ∼ *n* : injured person,
casualty

hermano, -na *n* : brother *m*, sister *f* —
hermanastro, -tra *n* : half brother *m*,
half sister *f* — **hermandad** *nf* : brotherhood

hermético, -ca *adj* : hermetic, watertight

hermoso, -sa *adj* : beautiful, lovely —
hermosura *nf* : beauty

hernia *nf* : hernia

héroe *nm* : hero — **heroico, -ca** *adj*
: heroic — **heroína** *nf* **1** : heroine **2**
: heroin (narcotic) — **heroísmo** *nm*
: heroism

herradura *nf* : horseshoe

herramienta *nf* : tool

herrero, -ra *n* : blacksmith

herrumbre *nf* : rust

hervir {76} *v* : boil — **hervidero** *nm* **1**
: mass, swarm **2** : hotbed (of intrigue,
etc.) — **hervidor** *nm* : kettle — **hervor**
nm **1** : boiling **2** ENTUSIASMO : fervor,
ardor

heterogéneo, -nea *adj* : heterogeneous

heterosexual *adj & nmf* : heterosexual

hexágono *nm* : hexagon — **hexagonal**
adj : hexagonal

hez *nf, pl* **heces** : dregs *pl*, scum

hiato *nm* : hiatus

hibernar *vi* : hibernate — **hibernación**
nf, pl **-ciones** : hibernation

híbrido, -da *adj* : hybrid — **híbrido** *nm*
: hybrid

hidalgo, -ga *n* : nobleman *m*, noblewoman *f*

hidratante *adj* : moisturizing

hidrato *nm* ∼ **de carbono** : carbohydrate

hidráulico, -ca *adj* : hydraulic

hidroavión *nm, pl* **-aviones** : seaplane

hidroeléctrico, -ca *adj* : hydroelectric

hidrofobia *nf* : rabies

hidrógeno *nm* : hydrogen

hidroplano *nm* : hydroplane

hiedra *nf* 1 : ivy 2 ∼ **venenosa** : poison ivy
hiel *nm* 1 : bile 2 AMARGURA : bitterness
hielo *nm* 1 : ice 2 FRIALDAD : coldness 3 **romper el** ∼ : break the ice
hiena *nf* : hyena
hierba *nf* 1 : herb 2 CÉSPED : grass 3 **mala** ∼ : weed — **hierbabuena** *nf* : mint
hierro *nm* 1 : iron 2 ∼ **fundido** : cast iron
hígado *nm* : liver
higiene *nf* : hygiene — **higiénico, -ca** *adj* : hygienic
higo *nm* : fig
hijo, -ja *n* 1 : son *m*, daughter *f* 2 **hijos** *nmpl* : children, offspring — **hijastro, -tra** *n* : stepson *m*, stepdaughter *f*
hilar *v* 1 : spin 2 ∼ **delgado** : split hairs — **hilado** *nm* : yarn, thread
hilaridad *nf* : hilarity
hilera *nf* : file, row
hilo *nm* 1 : thread 2 LINO : linen 3 ALAMBRE : wire 4 : trickle (of water, etc.) 5 ∼ **dental** : dental floss
hilvanar *vt* 1 : baste, tack 2 : put together (ideas, etc.)
himno *nm* 1 : hymn 2 ∼ **nacional** : national anthem
hincapié *nm* **hacer** ∼ **en** : emphasize, stress
hincar {72} *vt* : drive in, plunge — **hincarse** *vr* ∼ **de rodillas** : kneel (down)
hinchar *vt Spain* : inflate, blow up — **hincharse** *vr* 1 : swell (up) 2 *Spain fam* : stuff oneself — **hinchado, -da** *adj* 1 : swollen 2 POMPOSO : pompous — **hinchazón** *nf*, *pl* **-zones** : swelling
hindú *adj & nmf* : Hindu — **hinduismo** *nm* : Hinduism
hinojo *nm* : fennel
hiperactivo, -va *adj* : hyperactive
hipersensible *adj* : oversensitive
hipertensión *nf*, *pl* **-siones** : hypertension, high blood pressure
hípico, -ca *adj* : equestrian, horse
hipil → **huipil**
hipnosis *nfs & pl* : hypnosis — **hipnótico, -ca** *adj* : hypnotic — **hipnotismo** *nm* : hypnotism — **hipnotizador, -dora** *n* : hypnotist — **hipnotizar** {21} *vt* : hypnotize
hipo *nm* 1 : hiccup, hiccups *pl* 2 **tener** ∼ : have hiccups
hipocondríaco, -ca *adj* : hypochondriacal — ∼ *n* : hypochondriac
hipocresía *nf* : hypocrisy — **hipócrita** *adj* : hypocritical — ∼ *nmf* : hypocrite

hipodérmico, -ca *adj* : hypodermic
hipódromo *nm* : racetrack
hipopótamo *nm* : hippopotamus
hipoteca *nf* : mortgage — **hipotecar** {72} *vt* : mortgage
hipótesis *nfs & pl* : hypothesis — **hipotético, -ca** *adj* : hypothetical
hiriente *adj* : hurtful, offensive
hirsuto, -ta *adj* 1 : hairy 2 : bristly, wiry (of hair)
hirviente *adj* : boiling
hispano, -na *or* **hispánico, -ca** *adj & n* : Hispanic — **hispanoamericano, -na** *adj* : Latin-American — ∼ *n* : Latin American — **hispanohablante** *or* **hispanoparlante** *adj* : Spanish-speaking
histeria *nf* : hysteria — **histérico, -ca** *adj* : hysterical — **histerismo** *nm* : hysteria
historia *nf* 1 : history 2 CUENTO : story — **historiador, -dora** *n* : historian — **historial** *nm* : record, background — **histórico, -ca** *adj* 1 : historical 2 IMPORTANTE : historic, important — **historieta** *nf* : comic strip
hito *nm* : milestone, landmark
hocico *nm* : snout, muzzle
hockey ['hoke, -ki] *nm* : hockey
hogar *nm* 1 : home 2 CHIMENEA : hearth, fireplace — **hogareño, -ña** *adj* 1 : home-loving 2 DOMÉSTICO : home, domestic
hoguera *nf* : bonfire
hoja *nf* 1 : leaf 2 : sheet (of paper) 3 ∼ **de afeitar** : razor blade — **hojalata** *nf* : tinplate — **hojaldre** *nm* : puff pastry — **hojear** *vt* : leaf through — **hojuela** *nf Lat* : flake
hola *interj* : hello!, hi!
holandés, -desa *adj*, *mpl* **-deses** : Dutch
holgado, -da *adj* 1 : loose, baggy 2 : comfortable (of an economic situation, a victory, etc.) — **holgazán, -zana** *adj*, *mpl* **-zanes** : lazy — ∼ *n* : slacker, idler — **holgazanear** *vi* : laze about, loaf — **holgura** *nf* 1 : looseness 2 BIENESTAR : comfort, ease
hollín *nm*, *pl* **-llines** : soot
holocausto *nm* : holocaust
hombre *nm* 1 : man 2 **el** ∼ : mankind 3 ∼ **de estado** : statesman 4 ∼ **de negocios** : businessman
hombrera *nf* 1 : shoulder pad 2 : epaulet (of a uniform)
hombría *nf* : manliness
hombro *nm* : shoulder
hombruno, -na *adj* : mannish

homenaje *nm* **1** : homage **2 rendir ~ a** : pay tribute to
homeopatía *nf* : homeopathy
homicidio *nm* : homicide, murder — **homicida** *adj* : homicidal, murderous — **~** *nmf* : murderer
homogéneo, -nea *adj* : homogeneous
homólogo, -ga *adj* : equivalent — **~** *n* : counterpart
homosexual *adj & nmf* : homosexual — **homosexualidad** *nf* : homosexuality
hondo, -da *adj* : deep — **hondo** *adv* : deeply — **hondonada** *nf* : hollow — **hondura** *nf* : depth
hondureño, -ña *adj* : Honduran
honesto, -ta *adj* : decent, honorable — **honestidad** *nf* : honesty, integrity
hongo *nm* **1** : mushroom **2** : fungus (in botany and medicine)
honor *nm* : honor — **honorable** *adj* : honorable — **honorario, -ria** *adj* : honorary — **honorarios** *nmpl* : payment, fee — **honra** *nf* : honor — **honradez** *nf, pl* **-deces** : honesty, integrity — **honrado, -da** *adj* : honest, upright — **honrar** *vt* : honor — **honrarse** *vr* : be honored — **honroso, -sa** *adj* : honorable
hora *nf* **1** : hour **2** : (specific) time **3** CITA : appointment **4 a la última ~** : at the last minute **5 ~ punta** : rush hour **6 media ~** : half an hour **7 ¿qué ~ es?** : what time is it? **8 ~ de oficina** : office hours **9 ~s extraordinarias** : overtime
horario *nm* : schedule, timetable
horca *nf* **1** : gallows *pl* **2** : pitchfork (in agriculture)
horcajadas: a ~ *adv phr* : astride
horda *nf* : horde
horizonte *nm* : horizon — **horizontal** *adj* : horizontal
horma *nf* **1** : form, mold, last **2** : shoe tree
hormiga *nf* : ant
hormigón *nm, pl* **-gones** : concrete
hormigueo *nm* : tingling, pins and needles
hormiguero *nm* **1** : anthill **2** : swarm (of people)
hormona *nf* : hormone
horno *nm* **1** : oven (for cooking) **2** : small furnace, kiln — **hornada** *nf* : batch — **hornear** *vt* : bake — **hornillo** *nf* : portable stove
horóscopo *nm* : horoscope
horquilla *nf* **1** : hairpin, bobby pin **2** HORCA : pitchfork
horrendo, -da *adj* : horrendous, awful

— **horrible** *adj* : horrible — **horripilante** *adj* : horrifying — **horror** *nm* **1** : horror, dread **2** ATROCIDAD : atrocity — **horrorizar** {21} *vt* : horrify, terrify — **horrorizarse** *vr* : be horrified — **horroroso, -sa** *adj* : horrifying, dreadful
hortaliza *nf* : (garden) vegetable — **hortelano, -na** *n* : truck farmer — **horticultura** *nf* : horticulture
hosco, -ca *adj* : sullen, gloomy
hospedar *vt* : put up, lodge — **hospedarse** *vr* : stay, lodge — **hospedaje** *nm* : lodging
hospital *nm* : hospital — **hospitalario, -ria** *adj* : hospitable — **hospitalidad** *nf* : hospitality — **hospitalizar** {21} *vt* : hospitalize
hostería *nf* : small hotel, inn
hostia *nf* : host (in religion)
hostigar {52} *vt* **1** : whip **2** ACOSAR : harass, pester
hostil *adj* : hostile — **hostilidad** *nf* : hostility
hotel *nm* : hotel — **hotelero, -ra** *adj* : hotel — **~** *n* : hotel manager, hotelier
hoy *adv* **1** : today **2 de ~ en adelante** : from now on **3 ~ (en) día** : nowadays **4 ~ mismo** : this very day
hoyo *nm* : hole — **hoyuelo** *nm* : dimple
hoz *nf, pl* **hoces** : sickle
huarache *nm* : huarache (sandal)
hueco, -ca *adj* **1** : hollow, empty **2** ESPONJOSO : soft, spongy **3** RESONANTE : resonant — **hueco** *nm* **1** : hollow, cavity **2** : recess (in a wall, etc.) **3 ~ de escalera** : stairwell
huelga *nf* **1** : strike **2 declararse en ~** : go on strike — **huelguista** *nmf* : striker
huella *nf* **1** : footprint **2** VESTIGIO : track, mark **3 ~ digital** *or* **~ dactilar** : fingerprint
huérfano, -na *n* : orphan — **~** *adj* : orphaned
huerta *nf* : truck farm — **huerto** *nm* **1** : vegetable garden **2** : (fruit) orchard
hueso *nm* **1** : bone **2** : pit, stone (of a fruit)
huésped, -peda *n* : guest — **huésped** *nm* : host (organism)
huesudo, -da *adj* : bony
huevo *nm* **1** : egg **2 ~s estrellados** : fried eggs **3 ~s revueltos** : scrambled eggs — **hueva** *nf* : roe
huida *nf* : flight, escape — **huidizo, -za** *adj* **1** : shy **2** FUGAZ : fleeting
huipil *nm Lat* : traditional embroidered blouse or dress

huir {41} *vi* **1** : escape, flee **2** ~ **de** : shun, avoid

hule *nm* **1** : oilcloth **2** *Lat* : rubber

humano, -na *adj* **1** : human **2** COMPASIVO : humane — **humano** *nm* : human (being) — **humanidad** *nf* **1** : humanity, mankind **2** BENEVOLENCIA : humaneness **3** ~es *nfpl* : humanities — **humanismo** *nm* : humanism — **humanista** *nmf* : humanist — **humanitario, -ria** *adj* & *n* : humanitarian

humear *vi* : smoke, steam — **humareda** *nf* : cloud of smoke

humedad *nf* **1** : dampness **2** : humidity (in meteorology) — **humedecer** {53} *vt* : moisten, dampen — **humedecerse** *vr* : become moist — **húmedo, -da** *adj* **1** : moist, damp **2** : humid (in meteorology)

humildad *nf* : humility — **humilde** *adj* : humble — **humillación** *nf*, *pl* -ciones : humiliation — **humillante** *adj* : humiliating — **humillar** *vt* : humiliate — **humillarse** *vr* : humble oneself

humo *nm* **1** : smoke, steam, fumes **2** ~s *nmpl* : airs, conceit

humor *nm* **1** : mood, temper **2** GRACIA : humor **3 de buen** ~ : in a good mood — **humorismo** *nm* : humor, wit — **humorista** *nmf* : humorist, comedian — **humorístico, -ca** *adj* : humorous

hundir *vt* **1** : sink **2** : destroy, ruin (a building, plans, etc.) — **hundirse** *vr* **1** : sink **2** DERRUMBARSE : collapse — **hundido, -da** *adj* : sunken — **hundimiento** *nm* **1** : sinking **2** DERRUMBE : collapse

húngaro, -ra *adj* : Hungarian

huracán *nm*, *pl* -canes : hurricane

huraño, -ña *adj* : unsociable

hurgar {52} *vi* ~ **en** : rummage around in

hurón *nm*, *pl* -rones : ferret

hurra *interj* : hurrah!, hooray!

hurtadillas: a ~ *adv phr* : stealthily, on the sly

hurtar *vt* : steal — **hurto** *nm* **1** ROBO : theft **2** : stolen property

husmear *vt* : sniff out, pry into — *vi* : nose around

huy *interj* : ow!, ouch!

I

i *nf* : i, ninth letter of the Spanish alphabet

ibérico, -ca *adj* : Iberian — **ibero, -ra** *or* **íbero, -ra** *adj* : Iberian

iceberg *nm*, *pl* -bergs : iceberg

icono *nm* : icon

ictericia *nf* : jaundice

ida *nf* **1** : outward journey **2** ~ **y vuelta** : round-trip **3** ~s **y venidas** : comings and goings

idea *nf* **1** : idea **2** OPINIÓN : opinion

ideal *adj* & *nm* : ideal — **idealismo** *nm* : idealism — **idealista** *adj* : idealistic — ~ *nmf* : idealist — **idealizar** {21} *vt* : idealize

idear *vt* : devise, think up

ídem *nm* : the same, ditto

identidad *nf* : identity — **idéntico, -ca** *adj* : identical — **identificar** {72} *vt* : identify — **identificarse** *vr* **1** : identify oneself **2** ~ **con** : identify with — **identificación** *nf*, *pl* -ciones : identification

ideología *nf* : ideology — **ideológico, -ca** *adj* : ideological

idílico, -ca *adj* : idyllic

idioma *nm* : language — **idiomático, -ca** *adj* : idiomatic

idiosincrasia *nf* : idiosyncrasy — **idiosincrásico, -ca** *adj* : idiosyncratic

idiota *adj* : idiotic — ~ *nmf* : idiot — **idiotez** *nf* : idiocy

ídolo *nm* : idol — **idolatrar** *vt* : idolize — **idolatría** *nf* : idolatry

idóneo, -nea *adj* : suitable, fitting — **idoneidad** *nf* : fitness, suitability

iglesia *nf* : church

iglú *nm* : igloo

ignición *nf*, *pl* -ciones : ignition

ignífugo, -ga *adj* : fire-resistant, fireproof

ignorar *vt* **1** : ignore **2** DESCONOCER : be unaware of — **ignorancia** *nf* : ignorance — **ignorante** *adj* : ignorant — ~ *nmf* : ignorant person

igual *adv* **1** : in the same way **2 por** ~ : equally — ~ *adj* **1** : equal **2** IDÉNTICO : the same **3** LISO : smooth, even **4** SEMEJANTE : similar — ~ *nmf* : equal, peer — **igualar** *vt* **1** : make equal **2** : be equal to **3** NIVELAR : level (off) — **igualdad** *nf* **1** : equality **2** UNIFORMI-

DAD : uniformity — **igualmente** adv : likewise

iguana nf : iguana

ijada nf : flank

ilegal adj : illegal

ilegible adj : illegible

ilegítimo, -ma adj : illegitimate — **ile-gitimidad** nf : illegitimacy

ileso, -sa adj : unharmed

ilícito, -ta adj : illicit

ilimitado, -da adj : unlimited

ilógico, -ca adj : illogical

iluminar vt : illuminate — **iluminarse** vr : light up — **iluminación** nf, pl -ciones 1 : illumination 2 ALUMBRADO : lighting

ilusionar vt : excite — **ilusionarse** vr : get one's hopes up — **ilusión** nf, pl -siones 1 : illusion 2 ESPERANZA : hope — **ilusionado, -da** adj : excited

iluso -sa adj : naïve, gullible — ～ n : dreamer, visionary — **ilusorio, -ria** adj : illusory

ilustrar vt 1 : illustrate 2 ACLARAR : explain — **ilustración** nf, pl -ciones 1 : illustration 2 SABER : learning 3 **la Ilustración** : the Enlightenment — **ilustrado, -da** adj 1 : illustrated 2 ERUDITO : learned — **ilustrador, -dora** n : illustrator

ilustre adj : illustrious

imagen nf, pl **imágenes** : image, picture

imaginar vt : imagine — **imaginarse** vr : imagine — **imaginación** nf, pl -ciones : imagination — **imaginario, -ria** adj : imaginary — **imaginativo, -va** adj : imaginative

imán nm, pl **imanes** : magnet — **imantar** vt : magnetize

imbécil adj : stupid, idiotic — ～ nmf : idiot

imborrable adj : indelible

imbuir {41} vt ～ **de** : imbue with

imitar vt 1 COPIAR : imitate, copy 2 : impersonate — **imitación** nf, pl -ciones 1 COPIA : imitation, copy 2 : impersonation — **imitador, -dora** n : impersonator

impaciencia nf : impatience — **impacientar** vt : make impatient, exasperate —**impacientarse** vr : grow impatient — **impaciente** adj : impatient

impacto nm : impact

impar adj : odd — ～ nm : odd number

imparcial adj : impartial — **imparcialidad** nf : impartiality

impartir vt : impart, give

impasible adj : impassive

impasse nm : impasse

impávido, -da adj : fearless

impecable adj : impeccable, spotless

impedir {54} vt 1 : prevent 2 DIFICULTAR : impede, hinder — **impedido, -da** adj : disabled — **impedimento** nm : obstacle, impediment

impeler vt : drive, propel

impenetrable adj : impenetrable

impenitente adj : unrepentant

impensable adj : unthinkable — **impensado, -da** adj : unexpected

imperar vi 1 : reign, rule 2 PREDOMINAR : prevail — **imperante** adj : prevailing

imperativo, -va adj : imperative — **imperativo** nm : imperative

imperceptible adj : imperceptible

imperdible nm : safety pin

imperdonable adj : unforgivable

imperfección nf, pl -ciones : imperfection — **imperfecto, -ta** adj : imperfect — **imperfecto** nm : imperfect (tense)

imperial adj : imperial — **imperialismo** nm : imperialism — **imperialista** adj & nmf : imperialist

impericia nf : lack of skill

imperio nm 1 : empire 2 DOMINIO : rule — **imperioso, -sa** adj 1 : imperious 2 URGENTE : pressing, urgent

impermeable adj 1 : waterproof 2 ～ **a** : impervious to — ～ nm : raincoat

impersonal adj : impersonal

impertinente adj : impertinent — **impertinencia** nf : impertinence

ímpetu nm 1 : impetus 2 ENERGÍA : energy, vigor 3 VIOLENCIA : force — **impetuoso, -sa** adj : impetuous — **impetuosidad** nf : impetuosity

impío, -pía adj : impious, ungodly

implacable adj : implacable

implantar vt 1 : implant 2 ESTABLECER : establish, introduce

implemento nm Lat : implement, tool

implicar {72} vt 1 : involve, implicate 2 SIGNIFICAR : imply — **implicación** nf, pl -ciones : implication

implícito, -ta adj : implicit

implorar vt : implore

imponer {60} vt 1 : impose 2 : command (respect, etc.) — vi : be imposing — **imponerse** vr 1 : assert oneself, command respect 2 PREVALECER : prevail — **imponente** adj : imposing, impressive — **imponible** adj : taxable

impopular adj : unpopular — **impopularidad** nf : unpopularity

importación nf, pl -ciones 1 : importation 2 **importaciones** nfpl : imports — **importado, -da** adj : imported — **importador, -dora** adj : importing — ～ n : importer

importancia *nf* : importance — **importante** *adj* : important — **importar** *vi* 1 : matter, be important 2 **no me importa** : I don't care — *vt* 1 : import 2 ASCENDER A : amount to, cost

importe *nm* 1 : price 2 CANTIDAD : sum, amount

importunar *vt* : bother — **importuno, -na** *adj* 1 : inopportune 2 MOLESTO : bothersome

imposible *adj* : impossible — **imposibilidad** *nf* : impossibility

imposición *nf, pl* -**ciones** 1 : imposition 2 IMPUESTO : tax

impostor, -tora *n* : impostor

impotente *adj* : powerless, impotent — **impotencia** *nf* : impotence

impracticable *adj* 1 : impracticable 2 INTRANSITABLE : impassable

impreciso, -sa *adj* : vague, imprecise — **imprecisión** *nf, pl* -**siones** 1 : vagueness 2 ERROR : inaccuracy

impredecible *adj* : unpredictable

impregnar *vt* : impregnate

imprenta *nf* 1 : printing 2 : printing shop, press

imprescindible *adj* : essential, indispensable

impresión *nf, pl* -**siones** 1 : impression 2 IMPRENTA : printing — **impresionable** *adj* : impressionable — **impresionante** *adj* : impressive — **impresionar** *vt* 1 : impress 2 CONMOVER : affect, move — *vi* : make an impression — **impresionarse** *vr* 1 : be impressed 2 CONMOVERSE : be affected

impreso, -sa *adj* : printed — **impreso** *nm* 1 FORMULARIO : form 2 ~**s** *nmpl* : printed matter — **impresor, -sora** *n* : printer — **impresora** *nf* : (computer) printer

imprevisible *adj* : unforeseeable — **imprevisto, -ta** *adj* : unexpected, unforeseen

imprimir {42} *vt* 1 : print 2 DAR : impart, give

improbable *adj* : improbable — **improbabilidad** *nf* : improbability

improcedente *adj* : inappropriate

improductivo, -va *adj* : unproductive

improperio *nm* : insult

impropio, -pia *adj* 1 : inappropriate 2 INCORRECTO : incorrect

improvisar *v* : improvise — **improvisado, -da** *adj* : improvised, impromptu — **improvisación** *nf, pl* -**ciones** : improvisation — **improviso: de** ~ *adv phr* : suddenly

imprudente *adj* : imprudent, rash —

imprudencia *nf* : imprudence, carelessness

impúdico, -ca *adj* : shameless, indecent

impuesto *nm* 1 : tax 2 ~ **sobre la renta** : income tax

impugnar *vt* : challenge, contest

impulsar *vt* : propel, drive — **impulsividad** *nf* : impulsiveness — **impulsivo, -va** *adj* : impulsive — **impulso** *nm* 1 : drive, thrust 2 MOTIVACIÓN : impulse

impune *adj* : unpunished — **impunidad** *nf* : impunity

impuro, -ra *adj* : impure — **impureza** *nf* : impurity

imputar *vt* : impute, attribute

inacabable *adj* : interminable, endless

inaccesible *adj* : inaccessible

inaceptable *adj* : unacceptable

inactivo, -va *adj* : inactive — **inactividad** *nf* : inactivity

inadaptado, -da *adj* : maladjusted — ~ *n* : misfit

inadecuado, -da *adj* 1 : inadequate 2 INAPROPIADO : inappropriate

inadmisible *adj* : inadmissible

inadvertido, -da *adj* 1 : unnoticed 2 DISTRAÍDO : distracted — **inadvertencia** *nf* : oversight

inagotable *adj* : inexhaustible

inaguantable *adj* : unbearable

inalámbrico, -ca *adj* : wireless, cordless

inalcanzable *adj* : unreachable, unattainable

inalterable *adj* 1 : unchangeable 2 : impassive (of character) 3 : fast (of colors)

inanición *nf, pl* -**ciones** : starvation, famine

inanimado, -da *adj* : inanimate

inaplicable *adj* : inapplicable

inapreciable *adj* : imperceptible

inapropiado, -da *adj* : inappropriate

inarticulado, -da *adj* : inarticulate

inasequible *adj* : unattainable

inaudito, -ta *adj* : unheard-of, unprecedented

inaugurar *vt* : inaugurate — **inauguración** *nf, pl* -**ciones** : inauguration — **inaugural** *adj* : inaugural

inca *adj* : Inca, Incan

incalculable *adj* : incalculable

incandescencia *nf* : incandescence — **incandescente** *adj* : incandescent

incansable *adj* : tireless

incapacitar *vt* : incapacitate, disable — **incapacidad** *nf* : incapacity, inability — **incapaz** *adj, pl* -**paces** : incapable

incautar *vt* : confiscate, seize

incendiar *vt* : set fire to, burn (down) — **incendiarse** *vr* : catch fire — **incendiario, -ria** *adj* : incendiary — ~ *n* : arsonist — **incendio** *nm* 1 : fire 2 ~ **premeditado** : arson
incentivo *nm* : incentive
incertidumbre *nf* : uncertainty
incesante *adj* : incessant
incesto *nm* : incest — **incestuoso, -sa** *adj* : incestuous
incidencia *nf* 1 : impact 2 SUCESO : incident — **incidental** *adj* : incidental — **incidente** *nm* : incident
incidir *vi* ~ **en** 1 : fall into (a habit, mistake, etc.) 2 INFLUIR EN : affect, influence
incienso *nm* : incense
incierto, -ta *adj* : uncertain
incinerar *vt* 1 : incinerate 2 : cremate (a corpse) — **incineración** *nf*, *pl* **-ciones** 1 : incineration 2 : cremation (of a corpse) — **incinerador** *nm* : incinerator
incipiente *adj* : incipient
incisión *nf*, *pl* **-siones** : incision
incisivo, -va *adj* : incisive — **incisivo** *nm* : incisor
incitar *vt* : incite, rouse
incivilizado, -da *adj* : uncivilized
inclinar *vt* : tilt, lean — **inclinarse** *vr* 1 : lean (over) 2 ~ **a** : be inclined to — **inclinación** *nf*, *pl* **-ciones** 1 : inclination 2 LADEAR : incline, tilt
incluir {41} *vt* 1 : include 2 ADJUNTAR : enclose — **inclusión** *nf*, *pl* **-siones** : inclusion — **inclusive** *adv* : up to and including — **inclusivo, -va** *adj* : inclusive — **incluso** *adv* : even, in fact — **incluso, -sa** *adj* : enclosed
incógnito, -ta *adj* 1 : unknown 2 **de** ~ : incognito
incoherente *adj* : incoherent — **incoherencia** *nf* : incoherence
incoloro, -ra *adj* : colorless
incombustible *adj* : fireproof
incomible *adj* : inedible
incomodar *vt* 1 : inconvenience 2 ENFADAR : bother, annoy — **incomodarse** *vr* 1 : take the trouble 2 ENFADARSE : get annoyed — **incomodidad** *nf* : discomfort — **incómodo, -da** *adj* 1 : uncomfortable 2 INCONVENIENTE : inconvenient, awkward
incomparable *adj* : incomparable
incompatible *adj* : incompatible — **incompatibilidad** *nf* : incompatibility
incompetente *adj* : incompetent — **incompetencia** *nf* : incompetence
incompleto, -ta *adj* : incomplete

incomprendido, -da *adj* : misunderstood — **incomprensible** *adj* : incomprehensible — **incomprensión** *nf*, *pl* **-siones** : lack of understanding
incomunicado, -da *adj* 1 : isolated 2 : in solitary confinement
inconcebible *adj* : inconceivable
inconcluso, -sa *adj* : unfinished
incondicional *adj* : unconditional
inconformista *adj* & *nmf* : nonconformist
inconfundible *adj* : unmistakable
incongruente *adj* : incongruous
inconmensurable *adj* : vast, immeasurable
inconsciente *adj* 1 : unconscious, unaware 2 IRREFLEXIVO : reckless — ~ *nm* **el** ~ : the unconscious — **inconsciencia** *nf* 1 : unconsciousness 2 INSENSATEZ : thoughtlessness
inconsecuente *adj* : inconsistent — **inconsecuencia** *nf* : inconsistency
inconsiderado, -da *adj* : inconsiderate
inconsistente *adj* 1 : flimsy 2 : watery (of a sauce, etc.) 3 : inconsistent (of an argument) — **inconsistencia** *nf* : inconsistency
inconsolable *adj* : inconsolable
inconstante *adj* : changeable, unreliable — **inconstancia** *nf* : inconstancy
inconstitucional *adj* : unconstitutional
incontable *adj* : countless
incontenible *adj* : irrepressible
incontestable *adj* : indisputable
incontinente *adj* : incontinent — **incontinencia** *nf* : incontinence
inconveniente *adj* 1 : inconvenient 2 INAPROPIADO : inappropriate — ~ *nm* : obstacle, problem — **inconveniencia** *nf* 1 : inconvenience 2 : tactless remark
incorporar *vt* 1 AGREGAR : incorporate, add 2 : mix (in cooking) — **incorporarse** *vr* 1 : sit up 2 ~ **a** : join — **incorporación** *nf*, *pl* **-ciones** : incorporation
incorrecto, -ta *adj* 1 : incorrect 2 DESCORTÉS : impolite
incorregible *adj* : incorrigible
incrédulo, -la *adj* : incredulous — **incredulidad** *nf* : incredulity, disbelief
increíble *adj* : incredible, unbelievable
incrementar *vt* : increase — **incremento** *nm* : increase
incriminar *vt* 1 : incriminate 2 ACUSAR : accuse
incrustar *vt* : set, inlay — **incrustarse** *vr* : become embedded
incubar *vt* : incubate — **incubadora** *nf* : incubator

incuestionable *adj* : unquestionable
inculcar {72} *vt* : instill
inculpar *vt* : accuse, charge
inculto, -ta *adj* 1 : uneducated 2 : uncultivated (of land)
incumplimiento *nm* 1 : noncompliance 2 ~ **de contrato** : breach of contract
incurable *adj* : incurable
incurrir *vi* ~ **en** 1 : incur (expenses, etc.) 2 : fall into, commit (crimes)
incursión *nf, pl* **-siones** : raid
indagar {52} *vt* : investigate — **indagación** *nf, pl* **-ciones** : investigation
indebido, -da *adj* : undue
indecente *adj* : indecent, obscene — **indecencia** *nf* : indecency, obscenity
indecible *adj* : inexpressible
indecisión *nf, pl* **-siones** : indecision — **indeciso, -sa** *adj* 1 : undecided 2 IRRESOLUTO : indecisive
indefenso, -sa *adj* : defenseless, helpless
indefinido, -da *adj* : indefinite — **indefinidamente** *adv* : indefinitely
indeleble *adj* : indelible
indemnizar {21} *vt* : indemnify, compensate — **indemnización** *nf, pl* **-ciones** : compensation
independiente *adj* : independent — **independencia** *nf* : independence — **independizarse** {21} *vr* : become independent
indescifrable *adj* : indecipherable
indescriptible *adj* : indescribable
indeseable *adj* : undesirable
indestructible *adj* : indestructible
indeterminado, -da *adj* : indeterminate
indicar {72} *vt* 1 : indicate 2 MOSTRAR : show — **indicación** *nf, pl* **-ciones** 1 : sign, indication 2 **indicaciones** *nfpl* : directions — **indicador** *nm* 1 : sign, signal 2 : gauge, dial, meter — **indicativo, -va** *adj* : indicative — **indicativo** *nm* : indicative (mood)
índice *nm* 1 : indication 2 : index (of a book, etc.) 3 : index finger 4 ~ **de natalidad** : birth rate
indicio *nm* : indication, sign
indiferente *adj* 1 : indifferent 2 **me es** ~ : it doesn't matter to me — **indiferencia** *nf* : indifference
indígena *adj* : indigenous, native — ~ *nmf* : native
indigente *adj & nmf* : indigent — **indigencia** *nf* : poverty
indigestión *nf, pl* **-tiones** : indigestion — **indigesto, -ta** *adj* : indigestible
indignar *vt* : outrage, infuriate — **indignarse** *vr* : become indignant — **indignación** *nf, pl* **-ciones** : indignation

— **indignado, -da** *adj* : indignant — **indignidad** *nf* : indignity — **indigno, -na** *adj* : unworthy
indio, -dia *adj* 1 : American Indian 2 : Indian (from India)
indirecta *nf* 1 : hint 2 **lanzar una** ~ : drop a hint — **indirecto, -ta** *adj* : indirect
indisciplina *nf* : lack of discipline — **indisciplinado, -da** *adj* : undisciplined
indiscreto, -ta *adj* : indiscreet — **indiscreción** *nf, pl* **-ciones** 1 : indiscretion 2 : tactless remark
indiscriminado, -da *adj* : indiscriminate
indiscutible *adj* : indisputable
indispensable *adj* : indispensable
indisponer {60} *vt* 1 : upset, make ill 2 ENEMISTAR : set against, set at odds — **indisponerse** *vr* 1 : become ill 2 ~ **con** : fall out with — **indisposición** *nf, pl* **-ciones** : indisposition, illness — **indispuesto, -ta** *adj* : unwell, indisposed
indistinto, -ta *adj* : indistinct
individual *adj* : individual — **individualidad** *nf* : individuality — **individualizar** {21} *vt* : individualize — **individuo** *nm* : individual
indivisible *adj* : indivisible
índole *nf* 1 : nature, character 2 TIPO : type, kind
indolente *adj* : indolent, lazy — **indolencia** *nf* : indolence, laziness
indoloro, -ra *adj* : painless
indómito, -ta *adj* : indomitable
indonesio, -sia *adj* : Indonesian
inducir {61} *vt* 1 : induce 2 DEDUCIR : infer
indudable *adj* : beyond doubt — **indudablemente** *adv* : undoubtedly
indulgente *adj* : indulgent — **indulgencia** *nf* : indulgence
indultar *vt* : pardon, reprieve — **indulto** *nm* : pardon, reprieve
industria *nf* : industry — **industrial** *adj* : industrial — ~ *nmf* : industrialist, manufacturer — **industrialización** *nf, pl* **-ciones** : industrialization — **industrializar** {21} *vt* : industrialize — **industrioso, -sa** *adj* : industrious
inédito, -ta *adj* : unpublished
inefable *adj* : inexpressible
ineficaz *adj, pl* **-caces** 1 : ineffective 2 INEFICIENTE : inefficient
ineficiente *adj* : inefficient — **ineficiencia** *nf* : inefficiency
inelegible *adj* : ineligible

ineludible *adj* : unavoidable, inescapable

inepto, -ta *adj* : inept — **ineptitud** *nf* : ineptitude

inequívoco, -ca *adj* : unequivocal

inercia *nf* : inertia

inerme *adj* : unarmed, defenseless

inerte *adj* : inert

inesperado, -da *adj* : unexpected

inestable *adj* : unstable — **inestabilidad** *nf* : instability

inevitable *adj* : inevitable

inexacto, -ta *adj* **1** : inexact **2** INCORRECTO : incorrect, wrong

inexistente *adj* : nonexistent

inexorable *adj* : inexorable

inexperiencia *nf* : inexperience — **inexperto, -ta** *adj* : inexperienced, unskilled

inexplicable *adj* : inexplicable

infalible *adj* : infallible

infame *adj* **1** : infamous, vile **2** *fam* : horrible — **infamia** *nf* : infamy, disgrace

infancia *nf* : infancy — **infanta** *nf* : infanta, princess — **infante** *nm* **1** : infante, prince **2** : infantryman (in the military) — **infantería** *nf* : infantry — **infantil** *adj* **1** : child's, children's **2** INMADURO : childish

infarto *nm* : heart attack

infatigable *adj* : tireless

infectar *vt* : infect — **infectarse** *vr* : become infected — **infección** *nf, pl* **-ciones** : infection — **infeccioso, -sa** *adj* : infectious — **infecto, -ta** *adj* **1** : infected **2** : foul, sickening

infecundo, -da *adj* : infertile

infeliz *adj, pl* **-lices** : unhappy — **infelicidad** *nf* : unhappiness

inferior *adj & nmf* : inferior — **inferioridad** *nf* : inferiority

inferir {76} *vt* **1** DEDUCIR : infer **2** : cause (harm or injury)

infernal *adj* : infernal, hellish

infestar *vt* : infest

infiel *adj* : unfaithful — **infidelidad** *nf* : infidelity

infierno *nm* **1** : hell **2 el quinto ~** *fam* : the middle of nowhere

infiltrar *vt* : infiltrate — **infiltrarse** *vr* : infiltrate

infinidad *nf* **1** : infinity **2 una ~ de** : countless — **infinitivo** *nm* : infinitive — **infinito, -ta** *adj* : infinite — **infinito** *nm* : infinity

inflación *nf, pl* **-ciones** : inflation — **inflacionario, -ria** *or* **inflacionista** *adj* : inflationary

inflamar *vt* : inflame — **inflamable** *adj* : flammable, inflammable — **inflamación** *nf, pl* **-ciones** : inflammation — **inflamatorio, -ria** *adj* : inflammatory

inflar *vt* **1** : inflate **2** EXAGERAR : exaggerate — **inflarse** *vr* **~ de** : swell (up) with

inflexible *adj* : inflexible — **inflexión** *nf, pl* **-xiones** : inflection

infligir {35} *vt* : inflict

influencia *nf* : influence — **influenciar** → influir

influenza *nf* : influenza

influir {41} *vt* : influence — *vi* **~ en** *or* **~ sobre** : have an influence on — **infl**ujo** *nm* : influence — **influyente** *adj* : influential

información *nf, pl* **-ciones** **1** : information **2** NOTICIAS : news **3** : directory assistance (on the telephone)

informal *adj* **1** : informal **2** IRRESPONSABLE : unreliable

informar *v* **1** : inform — **informarse** *vr* : get information, find out — **informante** *nmf* : informant — **informática** *nf* : information technology — **informativo, -va** *adj* : informative — **informatizar** {21} *vt* : computerize

informe *adj* : shapeless — **~** *nm* **1** : report **2 ~s** *nmpl* : information, data **3 ~s** *nmpl* : references (for employment)

infortunado, -da *adj* : unfortunate — **infortunio** *nm* : misfortune

infracción *nf, pl* **-ciones** : violation, infraction

infraestructura *nf* : infrastructure

infrahumano, -na *adj* : subhuman

infranqueable *adj* **1** : impassable **2** INSUPERABLE : insurmountable

infrarrojo, -ja *adj* : infrared

infrecuente *adj* : infrequent

infringir {35} *vt* : infringe

infructuoso, -sa *adj* : fruitless

infundado, -da *adj* : unfounded, baseless

infundir *vt* : instill, infuse — **infusión** *nf, pl* **-siones** : infusion

ingeniar *vt* : invent, think up

ingeniería *nf* : engineering — **ingeniero, -ra** *n* : engineer

ingenio *nm* **1** : ingenuity **2** AGUDEZA : wit **3** MÁQUINA : device, apparatus **4 ~ azucarero** *Lat* : sugar refinery — **ingenioso, -sa** *adj* **1** : ingenious **2** AGUDO : clever, witty — **ingeniosamente** *adv* : cleverly

ingenuidad *nf* : naïveté, ingenuousness — **ingenuo, -nua** *adj* : naive

ingerir {76} *vt* : ingest, consume

ingle *nf* : groin

inglés, -glesa *adj, mpl* **-gleses** : English — **inglés** *nm* : English (language)

ingrato, -ta *adj* **1** : ungrateful **2 un trabajo ingrato** : a thankless task — **ingratitud** *nf* : ingratitude

ingrediente *nm* : ingredient

ingresar *vt* : deposit — *vi* ~ **en** : enter, be admitted into, join — **ingreso** *nm* **1** : entrance, entry **2** : admission (into a hospital, etc.) **3** ~**s** *nmpl* : income, earnings

inhábil *adj* **1** : unskillful, clumsy **2** ~ **para** : unsuited for — **inhabilidad** *nf* : unskillfulness

inhabitable *adj* : uninhabitable — **inhabitado, -da** *adj* : uninhabited

inhalar *vt* : inhale — **inhalación** *nf* : inhalation

inherente *adj* : inherent

inhibir *vt* : inhibit — **inhibición** *nf, pl* **-ciones** : inhibition

inhóspito, -ta *adj* : inhospitable

inhumano, -na *adj* : inhuman, inhumane — **inhumanidad** *nf* : inhumanity

iniciar *vt* : initiate, begin — **iniciación** *nf, pl* **-ciones** **1** : initiation **2** COMIENZO : beginning — **inicial** *adj & nf* : initial — **iniciativa** *nf* : initiative — **inicio** *nm* : start, beginning

inigualado, -da *adj* : unequaled

ininterrumpido, -da *adj* : uninterrupted

injerirse {76} *vr* : interfere — **injerencia** *nf* : interference

injertar *vt* : graft — **injerto** *nm* : graft

injuriar *vt* : insult — **injuria** *nf* : insult — **injurioso, -sa** *adj* : insulting, abusive

injusticia *nf* : injustice, unfairness — **injusto, -ta** *adj* : unfair, unjust

inmaculado, -da *adj* : immaculate

inmaduro, -ra *adj* **1** : immature **2** : unripe (of fruit) — **inmadurez** *nf* : immaturity

inmediaciones *nfpl* : surrounding area

inmediato, -ta *adj* **1** : immediate **2** CONTIGUO : adjoining **3 de** ~ : immediately, right away **4** ~ **a** : next to, close to — **inmediatamente** *adv* : immediately

inmejorable *adj* : excellent

inmenso, -sa *adj* : immense, vast — **inmensidad** *nf* : immensity

inmerecido, -da *adj* : undeserved

inmersión *nf, pl* **-siones** : immersion

inmigrar *vi* : immigrate — **inmigración** *nf, pl* **-ciones** : immigration — **inmigrante** *adj & nmf* : immigrant

inminente *adj* : imminent, impending — **inminencia** *nf* : imminence

inmiscuirse {41} *vr* : interfere

inmobiliario, -ria *adj* : real estate, property

inmodesto, -ta *adj* : immodest

inmoral *adj* : immoral — **inmoralidad** *nf* : immorality

inmortal *adj & nmf* : immortal — **inmortalidad** *nf* : immortality

inmóvil *adj* : motionless, still — **inmovilizar** {21} *vt* : immobilize

inmueble *nm* : building, property

inmundicia *nf* : filth, trash — **inmundo, -da** *adj* : dirty, filthy

inmunizar {21} *vt* : immunize — **inmune** *adj* : immune — **inmunidad** *nf* : immunity — **inmunización** *nf, pl* **-ciones** : immunization

inmutable *adj* : unchangeable

innato, -ta *adj* : innate

innecesario, -ria *adj* : unnecessary, needless

innegable *adj* : undeniable

innoble *adj* : ignoble

innovar *vt* : introduce — *vi* : innovate — **innovación** *nf, pl* **-ciones** : innovation — **innovador, -dora** *adj* : innovative — ~ *n* : innovator

innumerable *adj* : innumerable

inocencia *nf* : innocence — **inocente** *adj & nmf* : innocent — **inocentón, -tona** *adj, mpl* **-tones** : naive — ~ *n* : simpleton, dupe

inocular *vt* : inoculate — **inoculación** *nf, pl* **-ciones** : inoculation

inocuo, -cua *adj* : innocuous

inodoro, -ra *adj* : odorless — **inodoro** *nm* : toilet

inofensivo, -va *adj* : inoffensive, harmless

inolvidable *adj* : unforgettable

inoperable *adj* : inoperable

inoperante *adj* : ineffective

inopinado, -da *adj* : unexpected

inoportuno, -na *adj* : untimely, inopportune

inorgánico, -ca *adj* : inorganic

inoxidable *adj* **1** : rustproof **2 acero** ~ : stainless steel

inquebrantable *adj* : unwavering

inquietar *vt* : disturb, worry — **inquietarse** *vr* : worry — **inquietante** *adj* : disturbing, worrisome — **inquieto, -ta** *adj* : anxious, worried — **inquietud** *nf* : anxiety, worry

inquilino, -na *n* : tenant

inquirir {4} *vi* : make inquiries — *vt* : investigate

insaciable *adj* : insatiable

insalubre *adj* : unhealthy

insatisfecho, -cha *adj* 1 : unsatisfied 2 DESCONTENTO : dissatisfied

inscribir {33} *vt* 1 : enroll, register 2 GRABAR : inscribe, engrave — **inscribirse** *vr* : register — **inscripción** *nf, pl* **-ciones** 1 : inscription 2 REGISTRO : registration

insecto *nm* : insect — **insecticida** *nm* : insecticide

inseguro, -ra *adj* 1 : insecure 2 PELIGROSO : unsafe 3 DUDOSO : uncertain — **inseguridad** *nf* 1 : insecurity 2 PELIGRO : lack of safety 3 DUDA : uncertainty

inseminar *vt* : inseminate — **inseminación** *nf, pl* **-ciones** : insemination

insensato, -ta *adj* : senseless, foolish — **insensatez** *nf* : foolishness, thoughtlessness

insensible *adj* 1 : insensitive, unfeeling 2 : numb (in medicine) 3 IMPERCEPTIBLE : imperceptible — **insensibilidad** *nf* : insensitivity

inseparable *adj* : inseparable

insertar *vt* : insert

insidia *nf* : snare, trap — **insidioso, -sa** *adj* : insidious

insigne *adj* : noted, famous

insignia *nf* 1 : insignia, badge 2 BANDERA : flag

insignificante *adj* : insignificant, negligible

insincero, -ra *adj* : insincere

insinuar {3} *vt* : insinuate — **insinuarse** *vr* ~ **en** : worm one's way into — **insinuación** *nf, pl* **-ciones** : insinuation — **insinuante** *adj* : insinuating, suggestive

insípido, -da *adj* : insipid

insistir *v* : insist — **insistencia** *nf* : insistence — **insistente** *adj* : insistent

insociable *adj* : unsociable

insolación *nf, pl* **-ciones** : sunstroke

insolencia *nf* : insolence — **insolente** *adj* : insolent

insólito, -ta *adj* : rare, unusual

insoluble *adj* : insoluble

insolvencia *nf* : insolvency, bankruptcy — **insolvente** *adj* : insolvent, bankrupt

insomnio *nm* : insomnia — **insomne** *nmf* : insomniac

insondable *adj* : unfathomable

insonorizado, -da *adj* : soundproof

insoportable *adj* : unbearable

insospechado, -da *adj* : unexpected

insostenible *adj* : untenable

inspeccionar *vt* : inspect — **inspección** *nf, pl* **-ciones** : inspection — **inspector, -tora** *n* : inspector

inspirar *vt* : inspire — *vi* : inhale — **inspirarse** *vr* : be inspired — **inspiración** *nf, pl* **-ciones** 1 : inspiration 2 RESPIRACIÓN : inhalation — **inspirador, -dora** *adj* : inspirational

instalar *vt* : install — **instalarse** *vr* : settle — **instalación** *nf, pl* **-ciones** : installation

instancia *nf* 1 : request 2 **en última ~** : ultimately, as a last resort

instantáneo, -nea *adj* : instantaneous, instant — **instantánea** *nf* : snapshot — **instante** *nm* 1 : instant 2 **a cada ~** : frequently, all the time 3 **al ~** : immediately

instar *vt* : urge, press

instaurar *vt* : establish — **instauración** *nf, pl* **-ciones** : establishment

instigar {52} *vt* : incite, instigate — **instigador, -dora** *n* : instigator

instinto *nm* : instinct — **instintivo, -va** *adj* : instinctive

institución *nf, pl* **-ciones** : institution — **institucional** *adj* : institutional — **institucionalizar** {21} *vt* : institutionalize — **instituir** {41} *vt* : institute, establish — **instituto** *nm* : institute — **institutriz** *nf, pl* **-trices** : governess

instruir {41} *vt* : instruct — **instrucción** *nf, pl* **-ciones** 1 : instruction 2 **instrucciones** *nfpl* : instructions, directions — **instructivo, -va** *adj* : instructive — **instructor, -tora** *n* : instructor

instrumento *nm* : instrument — **instrumental** *adj* : instrumental

insubordinarse *vr* : rebel — **insubordinado, -da** *adj* : insubordinate — **insubordinación** *nf, pl* **-ciones** : insubordination

insuficiente *adj* : insufficient, inadequate — **insuficiencia** *nf* 1 : insufficiency, inadequacy 2 ~ **cardíaca** : heart failure

insufrible *adj* : insufferable

insular *adj* : insular, island

insulina *nf* : insulin

insulso, -sa *adj* 1 : insipid, bland 2 SOSO : dull

insultar *vt* : insult — **insultante** *adj* : insulting — **insulto** *nm* : insult

insuperable *adj* : insurmountable

insurgente *adj & nmf* : insurgent

insurrección *nf, pl* **-ciones** : insurrection, uprising

intachable *adj* : irreproachable

intacto, -ta *adj* : intact

intangible *adj* : intangible

integrar *vt* : integrate — **integrarse** *vr* : become integrated — **integración**

nf, pl **-ciones** : integration — **integral** *adj* **1** : integral **2** **pan ~** : whole grain bread — **íntegro, -gra** *adj* **1** : honest, upright **2** ENTERO : whole, complete — **integridad** *nf* **1** RECTITUD : integrity **2** TOTALIDAD : wholeness

intelecto *nm* : intellect — **intelectual** *adj & nmf* : intellectual

inteligencia *nf* : intelligence — **inteligente** *adj* : intelligent — **inteligible** *adj* : intelligible

intemperie *nf* **a la ~** : in the open air, outside

intempestivo, -va *adj* : untimely, inopportune

intención *nf, pl* **-ciones** : intention, intent — **intencionado, -da** *adj* **1** : intended **2** **bien ~** : well-meaning **3** **mal ~** : malicious — **intencional** *adj* : intentional

intensidad *nf* : intensity — **intensificar** {72} *vt* : intensify — **intensificarse** *vr* : intensify — **intensivo, -va** *adj* : intensive — **intenso, -sa** *adj* : intense

intentar *vt* : attempt, try — **intento** *nm* **1** : intention **2** TENTATIVA : attempt

interactuar {3} *vi* : interact — **interacción** *nf, pl* **-ciones** : interaction — **interactivo, -va** *adj* : interactive

intercalar *vt* : insert, intersperse

intercambio *nm* : exchange — **intercambiable** *adj* : interchangeable — **intercambiar** *vt* : exchange, trade

interceder *vi* : intercede

interceptar *vt* : intercept — **interceptión** *nf, pl* **-ciones** : interception

intercesión *nf, pl* **-siones** : intercession

interés *nm, pl* **-reses** : interest — **interesado, -da** *adj* **1** : interested **2** EGOÍSTA : selfish — **interesante** *adj* : interesting — **interesar** *vt* : interest — *vi* : be of interest — **interesarse** *vr* : take an interest

interfaz *nf, pl* **-faces** : interface

interferir {76} *vi* : interfere — *vt* : interfere with — **interferencia** *nf* : interference

interino, -na *adj* : temporary, interim — **interinamente** *adv* : inwardly

interior *adj* : interior, inner — **~** *nm* : interior, inside — **interiormente** *adv* : inwardly

interjección *nf, pl* **-ciones** : interjection

interlocutor, -tora *n* : speaker

intermediario, -ria *adj & n* : intermediary

intermedio, -dia *adj* : intermediate — **intermedio** *nm* : intermission

interminable *adj* : interminable, endless

intermisión *nf, pl* **-siones** : intermission, pause

intermitente *adj* : intermittent — **~** *nm* : blinker, turn signal

internacional *adj* : international

internar *vt* : commit, confine — **internarse** *vr* : penetrate — **internado** *nm* : boarding school — **interno, -na** *adj* : internal — **~** *n* **1** : boarder **2** : inmate (in a jail, etc.)

interponer {60} *vt* : interpose — **interponerse** *vr* : intervene

interpretar *vt* **1** : interpret **2** : play, perform (in theater, etc.) — **interpretación** *nf, pl* **-ciones** : interpretation — **intérprete** *nmf* **1** TRADUCTOR : interpreter **2** : performer (of music)

interrogar {52} *vt* : interrogate, question — **interrogación** *nf, pl* **-ciones** **1** : interrogation **2** **signo de ~** : question mark — **interrogativo, -va** *adj* : interrogative — **interrogatorio** *nm* : interrogation, questioning

interrumpir *v* : interrupt — **interrupción** *nf, pl* **-ciones** : interruption — **interruptor** *nm* : (electrical) switch

intersección *nf, pl* **-ciones** : intersection

intervalo *nm* : interval

intervenir {87} *vi* **1** : take part **2** MEDIAR : intervene — *vt* **1** : tap (a telephone) **2** INSPECCIONAR : audit **3** OPERAR : operate on — **intervención** *nf, pl* **-ciones** **1** : intervention **2** : audit (in business) **3** *or* **~ quirúrgica** : operation — **interventor, -tora** *n* : inspector, auditor

intestino *nm* : intestine — **intestinal** *adj* : intestinal

intimar *vi* **~ con** : become friendly with — **intimidad** *nf* **1** : private life **2** AMISTAD : intimacy

intimidar *vt* : intimidate

íntimo, -ma *adj* **1** : intimate, close **2** PRIVADO : private

intolerable *adj* : intolerable — **intolerancia** *nf* : intolerance — **intolerante** *adj* : intolerant

intoxicar {72} *vt* : poison — **intoxicación** *nf, pl* **-ciones** : poisoning

intranquilizar {21} *vt* : make uneasy — **intranquilizarse** *vr* : be anxious — **intranquilidad** *nf* : uneasiness, anxiety — **intranquilo, -la** *adj* : uneasy, worried

intransigente *adj* : unyielding, intransigent

intransitable *adj* : impassable

intransitivo, -va *adj* : intransitive
intrascendente *adj* : unimportant, insignificant
intravenoso, -sa *adj* : intravenous
intrépido, -da *adj* : intrepid, fearless
intrigar {52} *v* : intrigue — **intriga** *nf* : intrigue — **intrigante** *adj* : intriguing
intrincado, -da *adj* : intricate, involved
intrínseco, -ca *adj* : intrinsic — **intrínsecament** *adv* : intrinsically, inherently
introducción *nf, pl* **-ciones** : introduction — **introducir** {61} *vt* 1 : introduce 2 METER : insert — **introducirse** *vr ~* **en** : penetrate, get into — **introductorio, -ria** *adj* : introductory
intromisión *nf, pl* **-siones** : interference
introvertido, -da *adj* : introverted — *~ n* : introvert
intrusión *nf, pl* **-siones** : intrusion — **intruso, -sa** *adj* : intrusive — *~ n* : intruder
intuir {41} *vt* : sense — **intuición** *nf, pl* **-ciones** : intuition — **intuitivo, -va** *adj* : intuitive
inundar *vt* : flood — **inundarse** *vr ~* **de** : be inundated with — **inundación** *nf, pl* **-ciones** : flood
inusitado, -da *adj* : unusual, uncommon
inútil *adj* 1 : useless 2 INVÁLIDO : disabled — **inutilidad** *nf* : uselessness — **inutilizar** {21} *vt* 1 : make useless 2 INCAPACITAR : disable
invadir *vt* : invade
invalidez *nf, pl* **-deces** 1 : invalidity 2 : disability (in medicine) — **inválido, -da** *adj & n* : invalid
invalorable *adj Lat* : invaluable
invariable *adj* : invariable
invasión *nf, pl* **-siones** : invasion — **invasor, -sora** *adj* : invading — *~ n* : invader
invencible *adj* : invincible
inventar *vt* 1 : invent 2 : fabricate, make up (a word, an excuse, etc.) — **invención** *nf, pl* **-ciones** 1 : invention 2 MENTIRA : lie, fabrication
inventario *nm* : inventory
inventiva *nf* : inventiveness — **inventivo, -va** *adj* : inventive — **inventor, -tora** *n* : inventor
invernadero *nm* : greenhouse
invernal *adj* : winter
inverosímil *adj* : unlikely
inversión *nf, pl* **-siones** 1 : inversion, reversal 2 : investment (of money, time, etc.)

inverso, -sa *adj* 1 : inverse 2 CONTRARIO : opposite 3 **a la inversa** : the other way around, inversely
inversor, -sora *n* : investor
invertebrado, -da *adj* : invertebrate — **invertebrado** *nm* : invertebrate
invertir {76} *vt* 1 : invert, reverse 2 : invest (money, time, etc.) — *vi* : make an investment
investidura *nf* : investiture
investigar {52} *vt* 1 : investigate 2 ESTUDIAR : research — *vi ~* **sobre** : do research into — **investigación** *nf, pl* **-ciones** 1 : investigation 2 ESTUDIO : research — **investigador, -dora** *n* : investigator, researcher
investir {54} *vt* : invest
inveterado, -da *adj* : deep-seated, inveterate
invicto, -ta *adj* : undefeated
invierno *nm* : winter
invisible *adj* : invisible — **invisibilidad** *nf* : invisibility
invitar *vt* : invite — **invitación** *nf, pl* **-ciones** : invitation — **invitado, -da** *n* : guest
invocar {72} *vt* : invoke — **invocación** *nf, pl* **-ciones** : invocation
involuntario, -ria *adj* : involuntary
invulnerable *adj* : invulnerable
inyectar *vt* : inject — **inyección** *nf, pl* **-ciones** : injection, shot — **inyectado, -da** *adj* **ojos inyectados** : bloodshot eyes
ion *nm* : ion — **ionizar** {21} *vt* : ionize
Ir {43} *vi* 1 : go 2 FUNCIONAR : work, function 3 CONVENIR : suit 4 **¿cómo te va?** : how are you? 5 *~* **con prisa** : be in a hurry 6 *~* **por** : follow, go along 7 **vamos** : let's go — *v aux* 1 *~* **a** : be going to, be about to 2 *~* **caminando** : take a walk 3 **vamos a ver** : we shall see — **irse** *vr* : go away, be gone
ira *nf* : rage, anger — **iracundo, -da** *adj* : irate, angry
iraní *adj* : Iranian
iraquí *adj* : Iraqi
iris *nms & pl* 1 : iris (of the eye) 2 **arco** *~* : rainbow
irlandés, -desa *adj, mpl* **-deses** : Irish
ironía *nf* : irony — **irónico, -ca** *adj* : ironic, ironical
irracional *adj* : irrational
irradiar *vt* : radiate, irradiate
irrazonable *adj* : unreasonable
irreal *adj* : unreal
irreconciliable *adj* : irreconcilable
irreconocible *adj* : unrecognizable
irrecuperable *adj* : irretrievable

irreductible *adj* : unyielding
irreemplazable *adj* : irreplaceable
irreflexivo, -va *adj* : rash, unthinking
irrefutable *adj* : irrefutable
irregular *adj* : irregular — **irregularidad** *nf* : irregularity
irrelevante *adj* : irrelevant
irreparable *adj* : irreparable
irreprimible *adj* : irrepressible
irreprochable *adj* : irreproachable
irresistible *adj* : irresistible
irresoluto, -ta *adj* : indecisive, irresolute
irrespetuoso, -sa *adj* : disrespectful
irresponsable *adj* : irresponsible — **irresponsabilidad** *nf* : irresponsibility
irreverente *adj* : irreverent
irreversible *adj* : irreversible
irrevocable *adj* : irrevocable
irrigar {52} *vt* : irrigate — **irrigación** *nf, pl* **-ciones** : irrigation

irrisorio, -ria *adj* : laughable, ridiculous
irritar *vt* : irritate — **irritarse** *vr* : get annoyed — **irritable** *adj* : irritable — **irritación** *nf, pl* **-ciones** : irritation — **irritante** *adj* : irritating
irrompible *adj* : unbreakable
irrumpir *vi* ~ **en** : burst into
isla *nf* : island
islámico, -ca *adj* : Islamic, Muslim
islandés, -desa *adj, mpl* **-deses** : Icelandic
isleño, -ña *n* : islander
israelí *adj* : Israeli
istmo *nm* : isthmus
italiano, -na *adj* : Italian — **italiano** *nm* : Italian (language)
itinerario *nm* : itinerary
izar {21} *vt* : hoist, raise
izquierda *nf* : left — **izquierdista** *adj & nmf* : leftist — **izquierdo, -da** *adj* : left

J

J *nf* : j, tenth letter of the Spanish alphabet
jabalí *nm, pl* **-líes** : wild boar
jabalina *nf* : javelin
jabón *nm, pl* **-bones** : soap — **jabonar** *vt* : soap (up) — **jabonera** *nf* : soap dish — **jabonoso, -sa** *adj* : soapy
jaca *nf* : pony
jacinto *nm* : hyacinth
jactarse *vr* : boast, brag — **jactancia** *nf* : boastfulness, bragging — **jactancioso, -sa** *adj* : boastful
jadear *vi* : pant, gasp — **jadeante** *adj* : panting, breathless — **jadeo** *nm* : gasp, panting
jaez *nm, pl* **jaeces** 1 : harness 2 **jaeces** *nmpl* : trappings
jaguar *nm* : jaguar
jaiba *nf Lat* : crab
jalapeño *nm Lat* : jalapeño pepper
jalar *v Lat* : pull, tug
jalea *nf* : jelly
jaleo *nm fam* 1 : uproar, racket 2 **armar un** ~ : raise a ruckus
jalón *nm, pl* **-lones** *Lat* : pull, tug
jamaicano, -na *or* **jamaiquino, -na** *adj* : Jamaican
jamás *adv* 1 : never 2 **para siempre** ~ : for ever and ever
jamelgo *nm* : nag (horse)
jamón *nm, pl* **-mones** 1 : ham 2 ~ **serrano** : cured ham
Januká *nmf* : Hanukkah

japonés, -nesa *adj, mpl* **-neses** : Japanese — **japonés** *nm* : Japanese (language)
jaque *nm* 1 : check (in chess) 2 ~ **mate** : checkmate
jaqueca *nf* : headache, migraine
jarabe *nm* : syrup
jardín *nm, pl* **-dines** 1 : garden 2 ~ **infantil** *or* ~ **de niños** *Lat* : kindergarten — **jardinería** *nf* : gardening — **jardinero, -ra** *n* : gardener
jarra *nf* : pitcher, jug — **jarro** *nm* : pitcher — **jarrón** *nm, pl* **-rrones** : vase
jaula *nf* : cage
jauría *nf* : pack of hounds
jazmín *nm, pl* **-mines** : jasmine
jazz ['jas, 'dʒas] *nm* : jazz
jeans ['jins, 'dʒins] *nmpl* : jeans
jefe, -fa *n* 1 : chief, leader 2 PATRÓN : boss 3 ~ **de cocina** : chef — **jefatura** *nf* 1 : leadership 2 SEDE : headquarters
jengibre *nm* : ginger
jeque *nm* : sheikh, sheik
jerarquía *nf* 1 : hierarchy 2 RANGO : rank — **jerárquico, -ca** *adj* : hierarchical
jerez *nm, pl* **-reces** : sherry
jerga *nf* 1 : coarse cloth 2 ARGOT : jargon, slang
jerigonza *nf* 1 : jargon 2 GALIMATÍAS : gibberish

jeringa *or* **jeringuilla** *nf* : syringe — **jeringar** {52} *vt fam* : annoy, pester
jeroglífico *nm* : hieroglyphic
jersey *nm*, *pl* **-seys** : jersey
jesuita *adj* & *nm* : Jesuit
Jesús *nm* : Jesus
jilguero *nm* : goldfinch
jinete *nmf* : horseman, horsewoman *f*, rider
jirafa *nf* : giraffe
jirón *nm*, *pl* **-rones** : shred, tatter
jitomate *nm Lat* : tomato
jockey ['jɔki, 'dʒɔ-] *nmf*, *pl* **-keys** [-kis] : jockey
jocoso, -sa *adj* : humorous, jocular
jofaina *nf* : washbowl
jolgorio *nm* : merrymaking
jornada *nf* 1 : day's journey 2 : working day — **jornal** *nm* : day's pay — **jornalero, -ra** *n* : day laborer
joroba *nf* : hump — **jorobado, -da** *adj* : hunchbacked, humpbacked — **~** *n* : hunchback — **jorobar** *vt fam* : annoy
jota *nf* 1 : iota, jot 2 **no veo ni ~** : I can't see a thing
joven *adj*, *pl* **jóvenes** : young — **~** *nmf* : young man *m*, young woman *f*, youth
jovial *adj* : jovial, cheerful
joya *nf* : jewel — **joyería** *nf* : jewelry store — **joyero, -ra** *n* : jeweler — **joyero** *nm* : jewelry box
juanete *nm* : bunion
jubilación *nf*, *pl* **-ciones** : retirement — **jubilado, -da** *adj* : retired — **~** *nmf* : retiree — **jubilar** *vt* : retire, pension off — **jubilarse** *vr* : retire — **jubileo** *nm* : jubilee
júbilo *nm* : joy, jubilation — **jubiloso, -sa** *adj* : joyous, jubilant
judaísmo *nm* : Judaism
judía *nf* 1 : bean 2 *or* **~ verde** : green bean, string bean
judicial *adj* : judicial
judío, -día *adj* : Jewish — **~** *n* : Jew
judo ['juðo, 'dʒu-] *nm* : judo
juego *nm* 1 : game 2 : playing (of children, etc.) 3 *or* **~s de azar** : gambling 4 CONJUNTO : set 5 **estar en ~** : be at stake 6 **fuera de ~** : offside (in sports) 7 **hacer ~** : go together, match 8 **~ de manos** : conjuring trick 9 **poner en ~** : bring into play
juerga *nf fam* : spree, binge
jueves *nms* & *pl* : Thursday
juez *nmf*, *pl* **jueces** 1 : judge 2 ÁRBITRO : umpire, referee

jugar {44} *vi* 1 : play 2 : gamble (in a casino, etc.) 3 APOSTAR : bet 4 **~ (al) tenis** : play tennis — *vt* : play — **jugarse** *vr* : risk, gamble (away) — **jugada** *nf* 1 : play, move 2 TRETA : (dirty) trick — **jugador, -dora** *n* 1 : player 2 : gambler
juglar *nm* : minstrel
jugo *nm* 1 : juice 2 SUSTANCIA : substance, essence — **jugoso, -sa** *adj* 1 : juicy 2 SUSTANCIAL : substantial, important
juguete *nm* : toy — **juguetear** *vi* : play — **juguetería** *nf* : toy store — **juguetón, -tona** *adj*, *mpl* **-tones** : playful
juicio *nm* 1 : judgment 2 RAZÓN : reason, sense 3 **a mi ~** : in my opinion — **juicioso, -sa** *adj* : wise, sensible
julio *nm* : July
junco *nm* : reed, rush
jungla *nf* : jungle
junio *nm* : June
juntar *vt* 1 UNIR : join, unite 2 REUNIR : collect — **juntarse** *vr* 1 : join (together) 2 REUNIRSE : meet, get together — **junta** *nf* 1 : board, committee 2 REUNIÓN : meeting 3 : (political) junta 4 : joint, gasket — **junto, -ta** *adj* 1 : joined 2 PRÓXIMO : close, adjacent 3 (*used adverbially*) : together 4 **~ a** : next to 5 **~ con** : together with — **juntura** *nf* : joint
Júpiter *nm* : Jupiter
jurar *v* 1 : swear 2 **~ en falso** : commit perjury — **jurado** *nm* 1 : jury 2 : juror, member of a jury — **juramento** *nm* : oath
jurídico, -ca *adj* : legal
jurisdicción *nf*, *pl* **-ciones** : jurisdiction
jurisprudencia *nf* : jurisprudence
justamente *adv* 1 : fairly, justly 2 PRECISAMENTE : precisely, exactly
justicia *nf* : justice, fairness
justificar {72} *vt* 1 : justify 2 DISCULPAR : excuse, vindicate — **justificación** *nf*, *pl* **-ciones** : justification
justo, -ta *adj* 1 : just, fair 2 EXACTO : exact 3 APRETADO : tight — **justo** *adv* 1 : just, exactly 2 **~ a tiempo** : just in time
juvenil *adj* : youthful — **juventud** *nf* 1 : youth 2 JÓVENES : young people
juzgar {52} *vt* 1 : try (a case in court) 2 ESTIMAR : judge, consider 3 **a ~ por** : judging by — **juzgado** *nm* : court, tribunal

K

k *nf* : k, eleventh letter of the Spanish alphabet

kaki → **caqui**

karate *or* **kárate** *nm* : karate

kilo *nm* : kilo — **kilogramo** *nm* : kilogram

kilómetro *nm* : kilometer — **kilometraje** *nm* : distance in kilometers, mileage — **kilométrico, -ca** *adj fam* : endless

kilovatio *nm* : kilowatt

kiosco *nm* → **quiosco**

L

l *nf* : l, twelfth letter of the Spanish alphabet

la *pron* **1** : her, it **2** (*formal*) : you **3** ~ **que** : the one who — ~ *art* → **el**

laberinto *nm* : labyrinth, maze

labia *nf fam* : gift of gab

labio *nm* : lip

labor *nf* **1** : work, labor **2** TAREA : task **3** ~**es domésticas** : housework — **laborable** *adj* **día** ~ : business day — **laborar** *vi* : work — **laboratorio** *nm* : laboratory, lab — **laborioso, -sa** *adj* : laborious

labrar *vt* **1** : cultivate, till **2** : work (metals), carve (stone, wood) **3** CAUSAR : cause, bring about — **labrado, -da** *adj* **1** : cultivated, tilled **2** : carved, wrought — **labrador, -dora** *n* : farmer — **labranza** *nf* : farming

laca *nf* **1** : lacquer **2** : hair spray

lacayo *nm* : lackey

lacerar *vt* : lacerate

lacio, -cia *adj* **1** : limp **2** : straight (of hair)

lacónico, -ca *adj* : laconic

lacra *nf* : scar

lacrar *vt* : seal — **lacre** *nm* : sealing wax

lacrimógeno, -na *adj* **gas lacrimógeno** : tear gas — **lacrimoso, -sa** *adj* : tearful

lácteo, -tea *adj* **1** : dairy **2 Vía Láctea** : Milky Way

ladear *vt* : tilt — **ladearse** *vr* : lean

ladera *nf* : slope, hillside

ladino, -na *adj* : crafty

lado *nm* **1** : side **2 al** ~ : next door, nearby **3 al** ~ **de** : beside, next to **4 de** ~ : sideways **5 por otro** ~ : on the other hand **6 por todos** ~**s** : everywhere, all around

ladrar *vi* : bark — **ladrido** *nm* : bark

ladrillo *nm* : brick

ladrón, -drona *n, mpl* -**drones** : thief

lagarto *nm* : lizard — **lagartija** *nf* : (small) lizard

lago *nm* : lake

lágrima *nf* : tear

laguna *nf* **1** : lagoon **2** VACÍO : gap

laico, -ca *adj* : lay, secular — ~ *n* : layman *m*, layperson

lamentar *vt* **1** : regret, be sorry about **2 lo lamento** : I'm sorry — **lamentarse** *vr* : lament — **lamentable** *adj* **1** : deplorable **2** TRISTE : sad, pitiful — **lamento** *nm* : lament, moan

lamer *vt* **1** : lick **2** : lap (against) — **lamida** *nf* : lick

lámina *nf* **1** PLANCHA : sheet **2** DIBUJO : plate, illustration — **laminar** *vt* : laminate

lámpara *nf* : lamp

lampiño, -ña *adj* : beardless, hairless

lana *nf* **1** : wool **2 de** ~ : woolen

lance *nm* **1** : event, incident **2** : throw (of dice, etc.) **3** RIÑA : quarrel

lanceta *nf* : lancet

lancha *nf* **1** : boat, launch **2** ~ **motora** : motorboat

langosta *nf* **1** : lobster **2** : locust (insect) — **langostino** *nm* : prawn, crayfish

languidecer {53} *vi* : languish — **languidez** *nf, pl* -**deces** : languor — **lánguido, -da** *adj* : languid, listless

lanilla *nf* : nap (of fabric)

lanudo, -da *adj* : woolly

lanza *nf* : spear, lance

lanzar {21} *vt* **1** : throw **2** : shoot (a glance), give (a sigh, etc.) **3** : launch (a missile, a project) — **lanzarse** *vr* : throw oneself — **lanzamiento** *nm* : throwing, launching

lapicero *nm* : (mechanical) pencil

lápida *nf* : tombstone

lapidar vt : stone
lápiz nm, pl **-pices 1** : pencil **2 ~ de labios** : lipstick
lapso nm : lapse (of time) — **lapsus** nms & pl : lapse, slip (of the tongue)
largar {52} vt **1** AFLOJAR : loosen, slacken **2** fam : give — **largarse** vr fam : go away, beat it — **largo, -ga** adj **1** : long **2 a la larga** : in the long run **3 a lo largo** : lengthwise **4 a lo largo de** : along — **largo** nm : length — **largometraje** nm : feature film — **largueza** nf : generosity
laringe nf : larynx — **laringitis** nfs & pl : laryngitis
larva nf : larva
las → **el**
lascivo, -va adj : lascivious, lewd
láser nm : laser
lastimar vt : hurt — **lastimarse** vr : hurt oneself — **lástima** nf **1** : pity **2 dar ~** : be pitiful **3 me dan ~!** : I feel sorry for them **4 ¡qué ~!** : what a shame! — **lastimero, -ra** adj : pitiful, wretched — **lastimoso, -sa** adj : pitiful, terrible
lastre nm : ballast
lata nf **1** : tinplate **2** : (tin) can **3** fam : nuisance, bore **4 dar (la) lata a** fam : bother, annoy
latente adj : latent
lateral adj : side, lateral
latido nm **1** : beat, throb **2 ~ del corazón** : heartbeat
latifundio nm : large estate
látigo nm : whip — **latigazo** nm : lash
latín nm : Latin (language)
latino, -na adj **1** : Latin **2** : Latin-American — **~** n : Latin American — **latinoamericano, -na** adj : Latin-American — **~** n : Latin American
latir vi : beat, throb
latitud nf : latitude
latón nm, pl **-tones** : brass
latoso, -sa adj fam : annoying
laúd nm : lute
laudable adj : laudable
laureado, -da adj : prize-winning
laurel nm **1** : laurel **2** : bay leaf (in cooking)
lava nf : lava
lavar vt : wash — **lavarse** vr **1** : wash oneself **2 ~ las manos** : wash one's hands — **lavable** adj : washable — **lavabo** nm **1** : sink **2** RETRETE : lavatory, toilet — **lavadero** nm : laundry room — **lavado** nm : wash, washing — **lavadora** nf : washing machine — **lavamanos** nms & pl : washbowl — **lavandería** nf : laundry (service) — **lavaplatos** nms & pl **1** : dishwasher **2**

Lat : kitchen sink — **lavativa** nf : enema — **lavatorio** nm : lavatory, washroom — **lavavajillas** nms & pl : dishwasher
laxante adj & nm : laxative — **laxo, -xa** adj : loose
lazo nm **1** VÍNCULO : link, bond **2** LAZADA : bow **3** : lasso, lariat — **lazada** nf : bow, loop
le pron **1** : (to) her, (to) him, (to) it **2** (formal) : (to) you **3** (as direct object) : him, you
leal adj : loyal, faithful — **lealtad** nf : loyalty, allegiance
lebrel nm : hound
lección nf, pl **-ciones 1** : lesson **2** : lecture (in a classroom)
leche nf **1** : milk **2 ~ descremada** or **~ desnatada** : skim milk **3 ~ en polvo** : powdered milk — **lechera** nf : milk jug — **lechería** nf : dairy store — **lechero, -ra** adj : dairy — **~** n : milkman m, milk dealer
lecho nm : bed
lechón, -chona n, mpl **-chones** : suckling pig
lechoso, -sa adj : milky
lechuga nf : lettuce
lechuza nf : owl
lector, -tora n : reader — **lectura** nf **1** : reading **2** ESCRITOS : reading matter
leer {20} v : read
legación nf, pl **-ciones** : legation
legado nm **1** : legacy **2** ENVIADO : legate, emissary
legajo nm : dossier, file
legal adj : legal — **legalidad** nf : legality — **legalizar** {21} vt : legalize — **legalización** nf, pl **-ciones** : legalization
legar {52} vt : bequeath
legendario, -ria adj : legendary
legible adj : legible
legión nf, pl **-giones** : legion — **legionario, -ria** n : legionnaire
legislar vi : legislate — **legislación** nf, pl **-ciones** : legislation — **legislador, -dora** n : legislator — **legislatura** nf : legislature
legítimo, -ma adj **1** : legitimate **2** GENUINO : authentic — **legitimidad** nf : legitimacy
lego, -ga adj **1** : secular, lay **2** IGNORANTE : ignorant — **~** n : layman m, layperson
legua nf : league
legumbre nf : vegetable
leído, -da adj : well-read
lejano, -na adj : distant, far away — **lejanía** nf : distance
lejía nf : bleach

lejos *adv* 1 : far (away) 2 a lo ∼ : in the distance 3 de ∼ *or* desde ∼ : from afar 4 ∼ de : far from
lelo, -la *adj* : silly, stupid
lema *nm* : motto
lencería *nf* 1 : linen 2 : (women's) lingerie
lengua *nf* 1 : tongue 2 IDIOMA : language 3 morderse la ∼ : hold one's tongue
lenguado *nm* : sole, flounder
lenguaje *nm* : language
lengüeta *nf* 1 : tongue (of a shoe) 2 : reed (of a musical instrument)
lengüetada *nf* beber a ∼s : lap (up)
lente *nmf* 1 : lens 2 ∼s *nmpl* : eyeglasses 3 ∼s de contacto : contact lenses
lenteja *nf* : lentil — **lentejuela** *nf* : sequin
lento, -ta *adj* : slow — **lento** *adv* : slowly — **lentitud** *nf* : slowness
leña *nf* : firewood — **leñador, -dora** *n* : lumberjack, woodcutter — **leño** *nm* : log
león, -ona *n, mpl* **leones** : lion, lioness *f*
leopardo *nm* : leopard
leotardo *nm* : leotard, tights *pl*
lepra *nf* : leprosy — **leproso, -sa** *n* : leper
lerdo, -da *adj* 1 TORPE : clumsy 2 TONTO : slow-witted
les *pron* 1 : (to) them, (to) you 2 (*as direct object*) : them, you
lesbiano, -na *adj* : lesbian — **lesbiana** *nf* : lesbian — **lesbianismo** *nm* : lesbianism
lesión *nf, pl* -**siones** : lesion, wound — **lesionado, -da** *adj* : injured, wounded — **lesionar** *vt* 1 : injure, wound 2 DAÑAR : damage
letal *adj* : lethal
letanía *nf* : litany
letárgico, -ca *adj* : lethargic — **letargo** *nm* : lethargy
letra *nf* 1 : letter 2 ESCRITURA : handwriting 3 : lyrics *pl* (of a song) 4 ∼ de cambio : bill of exchange 5 ∼s *nfpl* : arts — **letrado, -da** *adj* : learned — **letrero** *nm* : sign, notice
letrina *nf* : latrine
leucemia *nf* : leukemia
levadizo, -za *adj* puente levadizo : drawbridge
levadura *nf* 1 : yeast 2 ∼ en polvo : baking powder
levantar *vt* 1 : lift, raise 2 RECOGER : pick up 3 CONSTRUIR : erect, put up 4 ENCENDER : rouse, stir up 5 ∼ la mesa *Lat* : clear the table — **levan-**

tarse *vr* 1 : rise, stand up 2 : get out of bed 3 SUBLEVARSE : rise up — **levantamiento** *nm* 1 : raising, lifting 2 SUBLEVACIÓN : uprising
levante *nm* 1 : east 2 : east wind
levar *vt* ∼ anclas : weigh anchor
leve *adj* 1 : light, slight 2 : minor, trivial (of wounds, sins, etc.) — **levedad** *nf* : lightness — **levemente** *adv* : lightly, slightly
léxico *nm* : vocabulary, lexicon
ley *nf* 1 : law 2 de (buena) ∼ : genuine, pure (of metals)
leyenda *nf* 1 : legend 2 : caption (of an illustration, etc.)
liar {85} *vt* 1 : bind, tie (up) 2 : roll (a cigarette) 3 CONFUNDIR : confuse, muddle — **liarse** *vr* : get mixed up
libanés, -nesa *adj, mpl* -**neses** : Lebanese
libelo *nm* 1 : libel 2 : petition (in court)
libélula *nf* : dragonfly
liberación *nf, pl* -**ciones** : liberation, deliverance
liberal *adj & nmf* : liberal — **liberalidad** *nf* : generosity, liberality
liberar *vt* : liberate, free — **libertad** *nf* 1 : freedom, liberty 2 ∼ bajo fianza : bail 3 ∼ condicional : parole 4 en ∼ : free — **libertar** *vt* : set free
libertinaje *nm* : licentiousness — **libertino, -na** *n* : libertine
libido *nf* : libido
libio, -bia *adj* : Libyan
libra *nf* 1 : pound 2 ∼ esterlina : pound sterling
librar *vt* 1 : free, save 2 : wage, fight (a battle) 3 : draw, issue (a check, etc.) — **librarse** *vr* ∼ de : free oneself from, get rid of
libre *adj* 1 : free 2 : unoccupied (of space), spare (of time) 3 al aire ∼ : in the open air 4 ∼ de impuestos : tax-free
librea *nf* : livery
libro *nm* 1 : book 2 ∼ de bolsillo : paperback — **librería** *nf* : bookstore — **librero, -ra** *n* : bookseller — **librero** *nm Lat* : bookcase — **libreta** *nf* : notebook
licencia *nf* 1 : license, permit 2 PERMISO : permission 3 : (military) leave — **licenciado, -da** *n* 1 : graduate 2 *Lat* : lawyer — **licenciar** *vt* : dismiss, discharge — **licenciarse** *vr* : graduate — **licenciatura** *nf* : degree
licencioso, -sa *adj* : licentious
liceo *nm* : high school
licitar *vt* : bid for

lícito, -ta *adj* **1** : lawful, legal **2** JUSTO : just, fair
licor *nm* **1** : liquor **2** : liqueur — **licor- era** *nf* : decanter
licuadora *nf* : blender — **licuado** *nm* : milk shake — **licuar** {3} *vt* : liquefy
lid *nf* **1** : fight **2 en buena ~** : fair and square
líder *adj* : leading — **~** *nmf* : leader — **liderato** *or* **liderazgo** *nm* : leadership
lidia *nf* : bullfight — **lidiar** *v* : fight
liebre *nf* : hare
lienzo *nm* **1** : cotton or linen cloth **2** : canvas (for a painting) **3** PARED : wall
liga *nf* **1** : league **2** *Lat* : rubber band **3** : garter (for stockings) — **ligadura** *nf* **1** ATADURA : tie, bond **2** : ligature (in medicine or music) — **ligamento** *nm* : ligament — **ligar** {52} *vt* : bind, tie (up)
ligero, -ra *adj* **1** : light, lightweight **2** LEVE : slight **3** ÁGIL : agile **4** FRÍVOLO : lighthearted, superficial — **ligera- mente** *adv* : lightly, slightly — **ligereza** *nf* **1** : lightness **2** : flippancy (of character), thoughtlessness (of actions) **3** AGILIDAD : agility
lija *nf* : sandpaper — **lijar** *vt* : sand
lila *nf* : lilac
lima *nf* **1** : file **2** : lime (fruit) **3 ~ para uñas** : nail file — **limar** *vt* : file
limbo *nm* : limbo
limitar *vt* : limit — *vi* **~ con** : border on — **limitación** *nf, pl* **-ciones** : limitation, limit — **límite** *nm* **1** : limit **2** CONFÍN : boundary, border **3 ~ de ve- locidad** : speed limit **4 ~ fecha** : deadline — **limítrofe** *adj* : bordering
limo *nm* : slime, mud
limón *nm, pl* **-mones 1** : lemon **2 ~ verde** *Lat* : lime — **limonada** *nf* : lemonade
limosna *nf* **1** : alms **2 pedir ~** : beg — **limosnero, -ra** *n* : beggar
limpiabotas *nmfs & pl* : bootblack
limpiaparabrisas *nms & pl* : wind- shield wiper
limpiar *vt* **1** : clean, wipe (away) **2 ~ en seco** : dry-clean — **limpieza** *nf* **1** : cleanliness **2** : (act of) cleaning — **limpio** *adv* : cleanly, fairly — **limpio, -pia** *adj* **1** : clean, neat **2** HONRADO : honest **3** NETO : net, clear
limusina *nf* : limousine
linaje *nm* : lineage, ancestry
linaza *nf* : linseed
lince *nm* : lynx
linchar *vt* : lynch
lindar *vi* **~ con** : border on — **lindante**

adj : bordering — **linde** *nmf or* **lin- dero** *nm* : boundary
lindo, -da *adj* **1** : pretty, lovely **2 de lo lindo** *fam* : a lot
línea *nf* **1** : line **2 ~ de conducta** : course of action **3 en ~** : on-line **4 guardar la ~** : watch one's figure — **lineal** *adj* : linear
lingote *nm* : ingot
lingüista *nmf* : linguist — **lingüística** *nf* : linguistics — **lingüístico, -ca** *adj* : linguistic
linimento *nm* : liniment
lino *nm* **1** : flax (plant) **2** : linen (fabric)
linóleo *nm* : linoleum
linterna *nf* **1** FAROL : lantern **2** : flash- light
lío *nm* **1** : bundle **2** *fam* : mess, trouble **3** *fam* : (love) affair
liofilizar {21} *vt* : freeze-dry
liquen *nm* : lichen
liquidar *vt* **1** : liquefy **2** : liquidate (mer- chandise, etc.) **3** : settle, pay off (a debt, etc.) — **liquidación** *nf, pl* **-ciones 1** : liquidation **2** REBAJA : clearance sale — **líquido, -da** *adj* **1** : liquid **2** NETO : net — **líquido** *nm* : liquid
lira *nf* : lyre
lírico, -ca *adj* : lyric, lyrical — **lírica** *nf* : lyric poetry
lirio *nm* : iris
lisiado, -da *adj* : disabled — **~** *n* : dis- abled person — **lisiar** *vt* : disable, cripple
liso, -sa *adj* **1** : smooth **2** PLANO : flat **3** SENCILLO : plain **4 pelo ~** : straight hair
lisonjear *vt* : flatter — **lisonja** *nf* : flat- tery
lista *nf* **1** : stripe **2** ENUMERACIÓN : list **3** : menu (in a restaurant) — **listado, -da** *adj* : striped
listo, -ta *adj* **1** : clever, smart **2** PREPARADO : ready
listón *nm, pl* **-tones 1** : ribbon **2** : strip (of wood)
lisura *nf* : smoothness
litera *nf* : bunk bed, berth
literal *adj* : literal
literatura *nf* : literature — **literario, -ria** *adj* : literary
litigar {52} *vi* : litigate — **litigio** *nm* **1** : litigation **2 en ~** : in dispute
litografía *nf* **1** : lithography **2** : litho- graph (picture)
litoral *adj* : coastal — **~** *nm* : shore, seaboard
litro *nm* : liter

liturgia *nf* : liturgy — **litúrgico, -ca** *adj* : liturgical

liviano, -na *adj* 1 LIGERO : light 2 INCONSTANTE : fickle

lívido, -da *adj* : livid

llaga *nf* : sore, wound

llama *nf* 1 : flame 2 : llama (animal)

llamar *vt* 1 : call 2 : call up (on the telephone) — *vi* 1 : phone, call 2 : knock, ring (at the door) — **llamarse** *vr* 1 : be called 2 ¿cómo te llamas? : what's your name? — **llamada** *nf* : call — **llamado, -da** *adj* : named, called — **llamamiento** *nm* : call, appeal

llamarada *nf* 1 : blaze 2 : flushing (of the face)

llamativo, -va *adj* : flashy, showy

llamear *vi* : flame, blaze

llano, -na *adj* 1 : flat 2 : straightforward (of a person, a message, etc.) 3 SENCILLO : plain, simple — **llano** *nm* : plain — **llaneza** *nf* : simplicity

llanta *nf* 1 : rim (of a wheel) 2 *Lat* : tire

llanto *nm* : crying, weeping

llanura *nf* : plain

llave *nf* 1 : key 2 *Lat* : faucet 3 INTERRUPTOR : switch 4 cerrar con ~ : lock 5 ~ inglesa : monkey wrench — **llavero** *nm* : key chain

llegar {52} *vi* 1 : arrive, come 2 ALCANZAR : reach 3 BASTAR : be enough 4 ~ a : manage to 5 ~ a ser : become — **llegada** *nf* : arrival

llenar *vt* : fill (up), fill in — **lleno, -na** *adj* 1 : full 2 de lleno : completely — **lleno** *nm* : full house

llevar *vt* 1 : take, carry 2 CONDUCIR : lead 3 : wear (clothing, etc.) 4 TENER : have 5 llevo una hora aquí : I've been here for an hour — **llevarse** *vr* 1 : take (away) 2 ~ bien : get along well — **llevadero, -ra** *adj* : bearable

llorar *vi* : cry, weep — **lloriquear** *vi* : whimper, whine — **lloro** *nm* : crying — **llorón, -rona** *n, mpl* -rones : crybaby, whiner — **lloroso, -sa** *adj* : tearful

llover {47} *v impers* : rain — **llovizna** *nf* : drizzle — **lloviznar** *v impers* : drizzle

lluvia *nf* : rain — **lluvioso, -sa** *adj* : rainy

lo *pron* 1 : him, it 2 (*formal, masculine*) : you 3 ~ que : what, that which — ~ *art* 1 : the 2 ~ mejor : the best (part) 3 sé ~ bueno que eres : I know how good you are

loa *nf* : praise — **loable** *adj* : praiseworthy — **loar** *vt* : praise

lobo, -ba *n* : wolf

lóbrego, -ga *adj* : gloomy

lóbulo *nm* : lobe

local *adj* : local — ~ *nm* : premises *pl* — **localidad** *nf* : town, locality — **localizar** {21} *vt* 1 : localize 2 ENCONTRAR : locate — **localizarse** *vr* : be located

loción *nf, pl* -**ciones** : lotion

loco, -ca *adj* 1 : crazy, insane 2 a lo loco : wildly, recklessly 3 volverse ~ : go mad — ~ *n* 1 : crazy person, lunatic 2 hacerse el loco : act the fool

locomoción *nf, pl* -**ciones** : locomotion — **locomotora** *nf* : engine, locomotive

locuaz *adj, pl* -**cuaces** : talkative, loquacious

locución *nf, pl* -**ciones** : expression, phrase

locura *nf* 1 : insanity, madness 2 INSENSATEZ : crazy act, folly

locutor, -tora *n* : announcer

locutorio *nm* : phone booth

lodo *nm* : mud — **lodazal** *nm* : quagmire

logaritmo *nm* : logarithm

lógica *nf* : logic — **lógico, -ca** *adj* : logical — **logística** *nf* : logistics *pl*

logotipo *nm* : logo

lograr *vt* 1 : achieve, attain 2 CONSEGUIR : get, obtain 3 ~ hacer : manage to do — **logro** *nm* : achievement, success

loma *nf* : hill, hillock

lombriz *nf, pl* -**brices** : worm

lomo *nm* 1 : back (of an animal) 2 : spine (of a book) 3 ~ de cerdo : pork loin

lona *nf* : canvas

loncha *nf* : slice (of bacon, etc.)

lonche *nm Lat* : lunch — **lonchería** *nf Lat* : luncheonette

longaniza *nf* : sausage

longevidad *nf* : longevity — **longevo, -va** *adj* : long-lived

longitud *nf* 1 : longitude 2 LARGO : length

lonja → **loncha**

loro *nm* : parrot

los, las *pron* 1 : them 2 : you 3 los que, las que : those who, the ones who — **los** *art* → **el**

losa *nf* 1 : flagstone 2 *or* ~ sepulcral : tombstone

lote *nm* 1 : batch, lot 2 *Lat* : plot of land

lotería *nf* : lottery

loto *nm* : lotus

loza *nf* : crockery, earthenware

lozano, -na *adj* 1 : healthy-looking, vigorous 2 : luxuriant (of plants) — **lozanía** *nf* 1 : (youthful) vigor 2 : luxuriance (of plants)

lubricar {72} *vt* : lubricate — **lubri-**

cante *adj* : lubricating — ~ *nm* : lubricant
lucero *nm* : bright star
luchar *vi* **1** : fight, struggle **2** : wrestle (in sports) — **lucha** *nf* **1** : struggle, fight **2** : wrestling (sport) — **luchador, -dora** *n* : fighter, wrestler
lucidez *nf, pl* **-deces** : lucidity — **lúcido, -da** *adj* : lucid
lucido, -da *adj* : magnificent, splendid
luciérnaga *nf* : firefly, glowworm
lucir {45} *vi* **1** : shine **2** *Lat* : appear, seem — *vt* **1** : wear, sport **2** OSTENTAR : show off — **lucirse** *vr* **1** : shine, excel **2** PRESUMIR : show off — **lucimiento** *nm* **1** : brilliance **2** ÉXITO : brilliant performance, success
lucrativo, -va *adj* : lucrative — **lucro** *nm* : profit
luego *adv* **1** : then **2** : later (on) **3 desde** ~ : of course **4 ¡hasta** ~**!** : see you later! **5** ~ **que** : as soon as — ~ *conj* : therefore
lugar *nm* **1** : place **2** ESPACIO : space, room **3 dar** ~ **a** : give rise to **4 en** ~ **de** : instead of **5 tener** ~ : take place

lugarteniente *nmf* : deputy
lúgubre *adj* : gloomy
lujo *nm* **1** : luxury **2 de** ~ : deluxe — **lujoso, -sa** *adj* : luxurious
lujuria *nf* : lust
lumbre *nf* **1** : fire **2 poner en la** ~ : put on the stove
luminoso, -sa *adj* : shining, luminous
luna *nf* **1** : moon **2** : (window) glass **3** ESPEJO : mirror **4** ~ **de miel** : honeymoon — **lunar** *adj* : lunar — ~ *nm* : mole, beauty spot
lunes *nms & pl* : Monday
lupa *nf* : magnifying glass
lúpulo *nm* : hops
lustrar *vt* : shine, polish — **lustre** *nm* **1** BRILLO : luster, shine **2** ESPLENDOR : glory — **lustroso, -sa** *adj* : lustrous, shiny
luto *nm* **1** : mourning **2 estar de** ~ : be in mourning
luxación *nf, pl* **-ciones** : dislocation
luz *nf, pl* **luces 1** : light **2** : lighting (in a room, etc.) **3** *fam* : electricity **4 a la** ~ **de** : in light of **5 dar a** ~ : give birth **6 sacar a la** ~ : bring to light

M

m *nf* : m, 13th letter of the Spanish alphabet
macabro, -bra *adj* : macabre
macarrón *nm, pl* **-rrones 1** : macaroon **2 macarrones** *nmpl* : macaroni
maceta *nf* : flowerpot
machacar {72} *vt* : crush, grind — *vi* ~ **sobre** : go on about — **machacón, -cona** *adj, mpl* **-cones** : tiresome, boring
machete *nm* : machete — **machetear** *vt* : hack with a machete
macho *adj* **1** : male **2** *fam* : macho — ~ *nm* **1** : male **2** *fam* : he-man — **machista** *nm* : male chauvinist
machucar {72} *vt* **1** : beat, crush **2** : bruise (fruit)
macizo, -za *adj* : solid — **macizo** *nm* ~ **de flores** : flower bed
mácula *nf* : stain
madeja *nf* : skein, hank
madera *nf* **1** : wood **2** : lumber (for construction) **3** ~ **dura** : hardwood — **madero** *nm* : piece of lumber, plank
madre *nf* **1** : mother **2** ~ **política** : mother-in-law — **madrastra** *nf* : stepmother
madreselva *nf* : honeysuckle

madriguera *nf* : burrow, den
madrileño, -ña *adj* : of or from Madrid
madrina *nf* **1** : godmother **2** : bridesmaid (at a wedding)
madrugada *nf* **1** : dawn, daybreak — **madrugador, -dora** *n* : early riser
madurar *v* **1** : mature **2** : ripen (of fruit) — **madurez** *nf, pl* **-reces 1** : maturity **2** : ripeness (of fruit) — **maduro, -ra** *adj* **1** : mature **2** : ripe (of fruit)
maestría *nf* : mastery, skill — **maestro, -tra** *adj* : masterly, skilled — ~ *n* **1** : teacher (in grammar school) **2** EXPERTO : expert, master
Mafia *nf* : Mafia
magia *nf* : magic — **mágico, -ca** *adj* : magic, magical
magisterio *nm* : teachers *pl*, teaching profession
magistrado, -da *n* : magistrate, judge
magistral *adj* **1** : masterful **2** : magisterial (of an attitude, etc.)
magnánimo, -ma *adj* : magnanimous — **magnanimidad** *nf* : magnanimity
magnate *nmf* : magnate, tycoon
magnesia *nf* : magnesia — **magnesio** *nm* : magnesium
magnético, -ca *adj* : magnetic — **mag-**

netismo *nm* : magnetism — **magneti-zar** {21} *vt* : magnetize
magnetófono *nm* : tape recorder
magnificencia *nf* : magnificence — **magnífico, -ca** *adj* : magnificent
magnitud *nf* : magnitude
magnolia *nf* : magnolia
mago, -ga *n* 1 : magician 2 **los Reyes Magos** : the Magi
magro, -gra *adj* 1 : lean 2 MEZQUINO : poor, meager
magullar *vt* : bruise — **magulladura** *nf* : bruise
mahometano, -na *adj* : Islamic, Muslim — **~** *n* : Muslim
maicena *nf* : cornstarch
maíz *nm* : corn
maja *nf* : pestle
majadero, -ra *adj* : foolish, silly — **~** *n* : fool
majar *vt* : crush
majestad *nf* 1 : majesty 2 **Su Majestad** : His/Her Majesty — **majestuoso, -sa** *adj* : majestic
majo, -ja *adj* 1 : nice 2 GUAPO : good-looking
mal *adv* 1 : badly, poorly 2 INCORRECTAMENTE : incorrectly 3 DIFÍCILMENTE : with difficulty, hardly 4 **de ~ en peor** : from bad to worse 5 **menos ~** : it's just as well — **~** *nm* 1 : evil 2 DAÑO : harm, damage 3 ENFERMEDAD : illness — **~** *adj* → **malo**
malabarismo *nm* : juggling — **malabarista** *nmf* : juggler
malacostumbrar *vt* : spoil, pamper — **malacostumbrado, -da** *adj* : spoiled
malaria *nf* : malaria
malasio, -sia *adj* : Malaysian
malaventura *nf* : misfortune — **malaventurado, -da** *adj* : unfortunate
malayo, -ya *adj* : Malay, Malayan
malcriado, -da *adj* : bad-mannered, spoiled
maldad *nf* 1 : evil 2 : evil deed
maldecir {11} *vt* : curse, damn — *vi* 1 : curse, swear 2 **~ de** : speak ill of — **maldición** *nf, pl* **-ciones** : curse — **maldito, -ta** *adj fam* : damned
maleable *adj* : malleable
maleante *nmf* : crook
malecón *nm, pl* **-cones** : jetty
maleducado, -da *adj* : rude
maleficio *nm* : curse — **maléfico, -ca** *adj* : evil, harmful
malentendido *nm* : misunderstanding
malestar *nm* 1 : discomfort 2 INQUIETUD : uneasiness
maleta *nf* 1 : suitcase 2 **hacer la ~** : pack one's bags — **maletero, -ra** *n*

: porter — **maletero** *nm* : trunk (of an automobile) — **maletín** *nm, pl* **-tines** 1 PORTAFOLIO : briefcase 2 : overnight bag
malévolo, -la *adj* : malevolent — **malevolencia** *nf* : malevolence
maleza *nf* 1 : underbrush 2 MALAS HIERBAS : weeds *pl*
malgastar *vt* : waste, squander
malhablado, -da *adj* : foul-mouthed
malhechor, -chora *n* : criminal, delinquent
malhumorado, -da *adj* : bad-tempered, cross
malicia *nf* : malice — **malicioso, -sa** *adj* : malicious
maligno, -na *adj* 1 : malignant 2 PERNICIOSO : harmful, evil
malla *nf* 1 : mesh 2 **~s** *nfpl* : tights
malo, -la *adj* (**mal** *before masculine singular nouns*) 1 : bad 2 : poor (in quality) 3 ENFERMO : unwell 4 **estar de malas** : be in a bad mood — **~** *n* : villain, bad guy (in movies, etc.)
malograr *vt* : waste — **malograrse** *vr* 1 FRACASAR : fail 2 : die young — **malogro** *nm* : failure
maloliente *adj* : smelly
malpensado, -da *adj* : malicious, nasty
malsano, -na *adj* : unhealthy
malsonante *adj* : rude
malta *nf* : malt
maltratar *vt* : mistreat
maltrecho, -cha *adj* : battered
malvado, -da *adj* : evil, wicked
malvavisco *nm* : marshmallow
malversar *vt* : embezzle — **malversación** *nf, pl* **-ciones** : embezzlement
mama *nf* : teat (of an animal), breast (of a woman)
mamá *nf fam* : mom, mama
mamar *vi* 1 : suckle 2 **dar de ~ a** : breast-feed — *vt* 1 : suckle, nurse 2 : learn from childhood, grow up with — **mamario, -ria** *adj* : mammary
mamarracho *nm fam* : mess, sight
mambo *nm* : mambo
mamífero, -ra *adj* : mammalian — **mamífero** *nm* : mammal
mamografía *nf* : mammogram
mampara *nf* : screen, room divider
mampostería *nf* : masonry
manada *nf* 1 : flock, herd, pack 2 **en ~** : in droves
manar *vi* 1 : flow 2 **~ en** : be rich in — **manantial** *nm* 1 : spring 2 ORIGEN : source
manchar *vt* 1 : stain, spot, mark 2 : tarnish (a reputation, etc.) — **mancharse** *vr* : get dirty — **mancha** *nf* : stain

mancillar *vt* : sully, stain

manco, -ca *adj* : one-armed, one-handed

mancomunar *vt* : combine, join — **mancomunarse** *vr* : unite — **mancomunidad** *nf* : union

mandar *vt* **1** : command, order **2** ENVIAR : send **3** *Lat* : hurl, throw — *vt* **1** : be in charge **2 ¿mande?** *Lat* : yes?, pardon? — **mandadero, -ra** *nm* : messenger — **mandado** *nm* : errand — **mandamiento** *nm* **1** : order, warrant **2** : commandment (in religion)

mandarina *nf* : mandarin orange, tangerine

mandato *nm* **1** : term of office **2** ORDEN : mandate — **mandatario, -ria** *n* **1** : leader (in politics) **2** : agent (in law)

mandíbula *nf* : jaw, jawbone

mandil *nm* : apron

mando *nm* **1** : command, leadership **2 al ~ de** : in charge of **3 ~ a distancia** : remote control

mandolina *nf* : mandolin

mandón, -dona *adj, mpl* **-dones** : bossy

manecilla *nf* : hand (of a clock), pointer

manejar *vt* **1** : handle, operate **2** : manage (a business, etc.) **3** : manipulate (a person) **4** *Lat* : drive (a car) — **manejarse** *vr* **1** : manage, get by **2** *Lat* : behave — **manejo** *nm* **1** : handling, use **2** : management (of a business, etc.)

manera *nf* **1** : way, manner **2 de ~ que** : so that **3 de ninguna ~** : by no means **4 de todas ~s** : anyway

manga *nf* **1** : sleeve **2** MANGUERA : hose

mango *nm* **1** : hilt, handle **2** : mango (fruit)

mangonear *vt fam* : boss around — *vi* **1** : be bossy **2** HOLGAZANEAR : loaf, fool around

manguera *nf* : hose

maní *nm, pl* **-níes** *Lat* : peanut

manía *nf* **1** : mania, obsession **2** MODA PASAJERA : craze, fad **3** ANTIPATÍA : dislike — **maníaco, -ca** *adj* : maniacal — **~** *n* : maniac

maniatar *vt* : tie the hands of

maniático, -ca *adj* : obsessive, fussy — **~** *n* : fussy person, fanatic

manicomio *nm* : insane asylum

manicura *nf* : manicure — **manicuro, -ra** *n* : manicurist

manido, -da *adj* : stale, hackneyed

manifestar {55} *vt* **1** : demonstrate, show **2** DECLARAR : express, declare — **manifestarse** *vr* **1** : become evident **2** : demonstrate (in politics) — **manifestación** *nf, pl* **-ciones 1** : manifestation, sign **2** : demonstration (in politics) — **manifestante** *nmf* : protester, demonstrator — **manifiesto, -ta** *adj* : manifest, evident — **manifiesto** *nm* : manifesto

manija *nf* : handle

manillar *nm* : handlebars *pl*

maniobra *nf* : maneuver — **maniobrar** *v* : maneuver

manipular *vt* **1** : manipulate **2** MANEJAR : handle — **manipulación** *nf, pl* **-ciones** : manipulation

maniquí *nmf, pl* **-quíes** : mannequin, model — **~** *nm* : mannequin, dummy

manirroto, -ta *adj* : extravagant — **~** *n* : spendthrift

manivela *nf* : crank

manjar *nm* : delicacy, special dish

mano *nf* **1** : hand **2** : coat (of paint, etc.) **3 a ~** *or* **a la ~** : at hand, nearby **4 dar la ~** : shake hands **5 de segunda ~** : secondhand **6 ~ de obra** : labor, manpower

manojo *nm* : bunch

manopla *nf* : mitten

manosear *vt* **1** : handle excessively **2** : fondle (a person)

manotazo *nm* : slap

mansalva: a ~ *adv phr* : at close range, without risk

mansarda *nf* : attic

mansedumbre *nf* **1** : gentleness **2** : tameness (of an animal)

mansión *nf, pl* **-siones** : mansion

manso, -sa *adj* **1** : gentle **2** : tame (of an animal)

manta *nf* **1** : blanket **2** *Lat* : poncho

manteca *nf* : lard, fat — **mantecoso, -sa** *adj* : greasy

mantel *nm* : tablecloth — **mantelería** *nf* : table linen

mantener {80} *vt* **1** : support **2** CONSERVAR : preserve **3** : keep up, maintain (relations, correspondence, etc.) **4** AFIRMAR : affirm — **mantenerse** *vr* **1** : support oneself **2 ~ firme** : hold one's ground — **mantenimiento** *nm* **1** : maintenance **2** SUSTENTO : sustenance

mantequilla *nf* : butter — **mantequera** *nf* : churn — **mantequería** *nf* : dairy

mantilla *nf* : mantilla

manto *nm* : cloak

mantón *nm, pl* **-tones** : shawl

manual *adj* : manual — **~** *nm* : manual, handbook

manubrio *nm* **1** : handle, crank **2** *Lat* : handlebars *pl*

manufactura *nf* **1** : manufacture **2** FÁBRICA : factory

manuscrito *nm* : manuscript — **manuscrito, -ta** *adj* : handwritten

manutención *nf, pl* **-ciones** : maintenance

manzana *nf* **1** : apple **2** : (city) block — **manzanar** *nm* : apple orchard — **manzano** *nm* : apple tree

maña *nf* **1** : skill **2** ASTUCIA : cunning, guile

mañana *adv* : tomorrow — ~ *nm* **el** ~ : the future — ~ *nf* : morning

mañoso, -sa *adj* **1** : skillful **2** *Lat* : finicky

mapa *nm* : map — **mapamundi** *nm* : map of the world

mapache *nm* : raccoon

maqueta *nf* : model, mock-up

maquillaje *nm* : makeup — **maquillarse** *vr* : put on makeup

máquina *nf* **1** : machine **2** LOCOMOTORA : locomotive **3 a toda** ~ : at full speed **4** ~ **de escribir** : typewriter — **maquinación** *nf, pl* **-ciones** : machination — **maquinal** *adj* : mechanical — **maquinaria** *nf* **1** : machinery **2** : mechanism, works *pl* (of a watch, etc.) — **maquinilla** *nf* : small machine — **maquinista** *nmf* **1** : machinist **2** : (railroad) engineer

mar *nmf* **1** : sea **2 alta** ~ : high seas *pl*

maraca *nf* : maraca

maraña *nf* **1** : thicket **2** ENREDO : tangle, mess

maratón *nm, pl* **-tones** : marathon

maravilla *nf* **1** : wonder, marvel **2** : marigold (flower) — **maravillar** *vt* : astonish — **maravillarse** *vr* : be amazed — **maravilloso, -sa** *adj* : marvelous

marca *nf* **1** : mark **2** : brand (on livestock) **3** *or* ~ **de fábrica** : trademark **4** : record (in sports) — **marcado, -da** *adj* : marked — **marcador** *nm* **1** : scoreboard **2** *Lat* : marker, felttipped pen

marcapasos *nms & pl* : pacemaker

marcar {72} *vt* **1** : mark **2** : brand (livestock) **3** INDICAR : indicate, show **4** : dial (a telephone, etc.) **5** : score (in sports) — *vi* **1** : score **2** : dial (on the telephone, etc.)

marchar *vi* **1** : go **2** CAMINAR : walk **3** FUNCIONAR : work, run — **marcharse** *vr* : leave, go — **marcha** *nf* **1** : march **2** PASO : pace, speed **3** : gear (of an automobile) **4 poner en** ~ : put in motion

marchitarse *vr* : wither, wilt — **marchito, -ta** *adj* : withered

marcial *adj* : martial, military

marco *nm* **1** : frame **2** : goalposts *pl* (in sports) **3** ENTORNO : setting, framework

marea *nf* : tide — **marear** *vt* **1** : make nauseous or dizzy **2** CONFUNDIR : confuse — **marearse** *vr* **1** : become nauseated or dizzy **2** CONFUNDIRSE : get confused — **mareado, -da** *adj* **1** : sick, nauseous **2** ATURDIDO : dazed, dizzy

maremoto *nm* : tidal wave

mareo *nm* **1** : nausea, seasickness **2** VÉRTIGO : dizziness

marfil *nm* : ivory

margarina *nf* : margarine

margarita *nf* : daisy

margen *nm, pl* **márgenes 1** : edge, border **2** : margin (of a page, etc.) — **marginado, -da** *adj* **1** : alienated **2 clases marginadas** : underclass — ~ *n* : outcast — **marginal** *adj* : marginal — **marginar** *vt* : ostracize, exclude

mariachi *nm* : mariachi musician or band

maridaje *nm* : marriage, union — **marido** *nm* : husband

marihuana *or* **mariguana** *or* **marijuana** *nf* : marijuana

marimba *nf* : marimba

marina *nf* **1** : coast **2** *or* ~ **de guerra** : navy, fleet

marinada *nf* : marinade — **marinar** *vt* : marinate

marinero, -ra *adj* **1** : sea, marine **2** : seaworthy (of a ship) — **marinero** *nm* : sailor — **marino, -na** *adj* : marine — **marino** *nm* : seaman, sailor

marioneta *nf* : puppet, marionette

mariposa *nf* **1** : butterfly **2** ~ **nocturna** : moth

mariquita *nf* : ladybug

marisco *nm* **1** : shellfish **2** ~**s** *nmpl* : seafood

marisma *nf* : salt marsh

marítimo, -ma *adj* : maritime, shipping

mármol *nm* : marble

marmota *nf* ~ **de América** : groundhog

marquesina *nf* : marquee, (glass) canopy

marrano, -na *n* **1** : pig, hog **2** *fam* : slob

marrar *vt* : miss (a target) — *vi* : fail

marrón *adj & nm, pl* **-rrones** : brown

marroquí *adj* : Moroccan

marsopa *nf* : porpoise

marsupial *nm* : marsupial

Marte *nm* : Mars

martes *nms & pl* : Tuesday

martillo *nm* **1** : hammer **2** ~ **neumáti-**

co : jackhammer — **martillar** or **martillear** v : hammer

mártir nmf : martyr — **martirio** nm : martyrdom — **martirizar** {21} vt 1 : martyr 2 ATORMENTAR : torment

marxismo nm : Marxism — **marxista** adj & nmf : Marxist

marzo nm : March

mas conj : but

más adv 1 : more 2 **el/la/lo ~** : (the) most 3 (in negative constructions) : (any) longer 4 **¡qué día ~ bonito!** : what a beautiful day! — **~** adj 1 : more 2 : most 3 **¿quién ~?** : who else? — **~** prep : plus — **~** pron 1 a **lo ~** : at most 2 **de ~** : extra, spare 3 **o ~ o menos** : more or less 4 **¿tienes ~?** : do you have more?

masa nf 1 : mass, volume 2 : dough (in cooking) 3 **~s** : people, masses

masacre nf : massacre

masaje nm : massage — **masajear** vt : massage

mascar {72} v : chew

máscara nf : mask — **mascarada** nf : masquerade — **mascarilla** nf : mask (in medecine, etc.)

mascota nf : mascot

masculino, -na adj 1 : masculine, male 2 VARONIL : manly 3 : masculine (in grammar) — **masculinidad** nf : masculinity

mascullar v : mumble

masilla nf : putty

masivo, -va adj : mass, large-scale

masón nm, pl **-sones** : Mason, Freemason — **masónico, -ca** adj : Masonic

masoquismo nm : masochism — **masoquista** adj : masochistic — **~** nmf : masochist

masticar {72} v : chew

mástil nm 1 : mast 2 ASTA : flagpole 3 : neck (of a stringed instrument)

mastín nm, pl **-tines** : mastiff

masturbarse vr : masturbate — **masturbación** nf, pl **-ciones** : masturbation

mata nf : bush, shrub

matadero nm : slaughterhouse

matador nf : matador, bullfighter

matamoscas nms & pl : flyswatter

matar vt 1 : kill 2 : slaughter (animals) — **matarse** vr 1 : be killed 2 SUICIDARSE : commit suicide — **matanza** nf : slaughter, killing

matasanos nms & pl fam : quack

matasellos nms & pl : postmark

mate adj : matte, dull — **~** nm 1 : maté 2 **jaque ~** : checkmate

matemáticas nfpl : mathematics — **matemático, -ca** adj : mathematical — **~** n : mathematician

materia nf 1 ASUNTO : matter 2 MATERIAL : material — **material** adj 1 : material 2 **daños ~es** : property damage — **~** nm 1 : material 2 EQUIPO : equipment, gear — **materialismo** nm : materialism — **materialista** adj : materialistic — **materializar** {21} vt : bring to fruition — **materializarse** vr : materialize — **materialmente** adv : absolutely

maternal adj : maternal — **maternidad** nf 1 : motherhood 2 : maternity hospital — **materno, -na** adj 1 : maternal 2 **lengua materna** : mother tongue

matinal adj : morning

matinée or **matiné** nf : matinee

matiz nm, pl **-tices** 1 : nuance 2 : hue, shade (of colors) — **matizar** {21} vt 1 : blend (colors) 2 : qualify (a statement, etc.) 3 **~ de** : tinge with

matón nm, pl **-tones** 1 : bully 2 CRIMINAL : gangster, hoodlum

matorral nm : thicket

matraca nf 1 : rattle, noisemaker 2 **dar la ~ a** : pester

matriarcado nm : matriarchy

matrícula nf 1 : list, roll, register 2 INSCRIPCIÓN : registration 3 : license plate (of an automobile) — **matricular** vt : register — **matricularse** vr : register, matriculate

matrimonio nm 1 : marriage 2 PAREJA : (married) couple — **matrimonial** adj : marital

matriz nf, pl **-trices** 1 : matrix 2 : uterus, womb (in anatomy)

matrona nf : matron

matutino, -na adj : morning

maullar {8} vi : meow — **maullido** nm : meow

maxilar nm : jaw, jawbone

máxima nf : maxim

máxime adv : especially

máximo, -ma adj : maximum, highest — **máximo** nm 1 : maximum 2 **al ~** : to the full

maya adj : Mayan

mayo nm : May

mayonesa nf : mayonnaise

mayor adj 1 (comparative of **grande**) : bigger, larger, greater, older 2 (superlative of **grande**) : biggest, largest, greatest, oldest 3 **al por ~** : wholesale 4 **~ de edad** : of (legal) age — **~** nmf 1 : major (in the military) 2 ADULTO : adult 3 **~es** nmfpl : grown-ups — **mayoral** nm : foreman

mayordomo *nm* : butler
mayoreo *nm Lat* : wholesale
mayoría *nf* : majority
mayorista *adj* : wholesale — ~ *nmf* : wholesaler
mayormente *adv* : primarily
mayúscula *nf* : capital letter — **mayúsculo, -la** *adj* **1** : capital, uppercase **2 un fallo mayúsculo** : a terrible mistake
maza *nf* : mace (weapon)
mazapán *nm, pl* -**panes** : marzipan
mazmorra *nf* : dungeon
mazo *nm* **1** : mallet **2** MAJA : pestle
mazorca *nf* ~ **de maíz** : corncob
me *pron* **1** (*direct object*) : me **2** (*indirect object*) : to me, for me, from me **3** (*reflexive*) : myself, to myself, for myself, from myself
mecánica *nf* : mechanics — **mecánico, -ca** *adj* : mechanical — ~ *n* : mechanic
mecanismo *nm* : mechanism — **mecanización** *nf, pl* -**ciones** : mechanization — **mecanizar** {21} *vt* : mechanize
mecanografiar {85} *vt* : type — **mecanografía** *nf* : typing — **mecanógrafo, -fa** *n* : typist
mecate *nm Lat* : rope
mecedora *nf* : rocking chair
mecenas *nmfs & pl* : patron, sponsor — **mecenazgo** *nm* : patronage, sponsorship
mecer {86} *vt* **1** : rock **2** : push (on a swing) — **mecerse** *vr* : rock, swing
mecha *nf* **1** : fuse (of a bomb, etc.) **2** : wick (of a candle)
mechero *nm* **1** : burner **2** *Spain* : cigarette lighter
mechón *nm, pl* -**chones** : lock (of hair)
medalla *nf* : medal — **medallón** *nm, pl* -**llones** **1** : medallion **2** : locket (jewelry)
media *nf* **1** : average **2** ~s *nfpl* : stockings **3 a** ~s : by halves, halfway
mediación *nf, pl* -**ciones** : mediation
mediado, -da *adj* **1** : half full, half empty, half over **2** : halfway through — **mediados** *nmpl* **a** ~ **de** : halfway through, in the middle of
mediador, -dora *n* : mediator
medialuna *nf* **1** : crescent **2** : croissant (pastry)
medianamente *adv* : fairly
medianero, -ra *adj* **pared medianera** : dividing wall
mediano, -na *adj* **1** : medium, average **2** MEDIOCRE : mediocre
medianoche *nf* : midnight
mediante *prep* : through, by means of

mediar *vi* **1** : be in the middle **2** INTERVENIR : mediate **3** ~ **entre** : be between
medicación *nf, pl* -**ciones** : medication — **medicamento** *nm* : medicine — **medicar** {72} *vt* : medicate — **medicarse** *vr* : take medicine — **medicina** *nf* : medicine — **medicinal** *adj* : medicinal
medición *nf, pl* -**ciones** : measurement
médico, -ca *adj* : medical — ~ *n* : doctor, physician
medida *nf* **1** : measurement, measure **2** MODERACIÓN : moderation **3** GRADO : extent, degree **4 tomar** ~s : take steps — **medidor** *nm Lat* : meter, gauge
medieval *adj* : medieval
medio, -dia *adj* **1** : half **2** MEDIANO : average **3 una media hora** : half an hour **4 la clase media** : the middle class — **medio** *adv* : half — ~ *nm* **1** : half **2** MANERA : means *pl*, way **3 en** ~ **de** : in the middle of **4** ~ **ambiente** : environment **5** ~s *nmpl* : means, resources
mediocre *adj* : mediocre, average — **mediocridad** *nf* : mediocrity
mediodía *nm* : noon, midday
medioevo *nm* : Middle Ages
medir {54} *vt* **1** : measure **2** CONSIDERAR : weigh, consider — **medirse** *vr* : be moderate
meditar *vi* : meditate, contemplate — *vt* **1** : think over, consider **2** PLANEAR : plan, work out — **meditación** *nf, pl* -**ciones** : meditation
mediterráneo, -nea *adj* : Mediterranean
medrar *vt* : flourish, thrive
medroso, -sa *adj* : fearful
médula *nf* **1** : marrow **2** ~ **espinal** : spinal cord
medusa *nf* : jellyfish
megabyte *nm* : megabyte
megáfono *nm* : megaphone
mejicano → **mexicano**
mejilla *nf* : cheek
mejillón *nm, pl* -**llones** : mussel
mejor *adv* **1** (*comparative*) : better **2** (*superlative*) : best **3 a lo** ~ : maybe, perhaps — ~ *adj* **1** (*comparative of* **bueno** *or* **bien**) : better **2** (*superlative of* **bueno** *or* **bien**) : best **3 lo** ~ : the best thing **4 tanto** ~ : so much the better — **mejora** *nf* : improvement
mejorana *nf* : marjoram
mejorar *vt* : improve — *vi* : improve, get better
mejunje *nm* : concoction, brew

melancolía *nf* : melancholy — **melancólico, -ca** *adj* : melancholic, melancholy

melaza *nf* : molasses

melena *nf* **1** : long hair **2** : mane (of a lion)

melindroso, -sa *adj* **1** : affected **2** *Lat* : finicky

mella *nf* : chip, nick — **mellado, -da** *adj* : chipped, jagged

mellizo, -za *adj & n* : twin

melocotón *nm, pl* **-tones** : peach

melodía *nf* : melody — **melódico, -ca** *adj* : melodic

melodrama *nm* : melodrama — **melodramático, -ca** *adj* : melodramatic

melón *nm, pl* **-lones** : melon

meloso, -sa *adj* **1** : sweet, honeyed **2** EMPALAGOSO : cloying

membrana *nf* : membrane

membrete *nm* : letterhead, heading

membrillo *nm* : quince

membrudo, -da *adj* : muscular, burly

memorable *adj* : memorable

memorándum *or* **memorando** *nm, pl* **-dums** *or* **-dos** **1** : memorandum **2** AGENDA : notebook

memoria *nf* **1** : memory **2** RECUERDO : remembrance **3** INFORME : report **4** **de ~** : by heart **5** **~s** *nfpl* : memoirs — **memorizar** {21} *vt* : memorize

mena *nf* : ore

menaje *nm* : household goods *pl*, furnishings *pl*

mencionar *vt* : mention, refer to — **mención** *nf, pl* **-ciones** : mention

mendaz *adj, pl* **-daces** : lying

mendigar {52} *vi* : beg — *vt* : beg for — **mendicidad** *nf* : begging — **mendigo, -ga** *n* : beggar

mendrugo *nm* : crust (of bread)

menear *vt* **1** : move, shake **2** : sway (one's hips) **3** : wag (a tail) — **menearse** *vr* **1** : sway, shake, move **2** *fam* : hurry up

menester *nm* **ser ~** : be necessary — **menestroso, -sa** *adj* : needy

menguar *vt* : diminish, lessen — *vi* **1** : decline, decrease **2** : wane (of the moon) — **mengua** *nf* : decrease, decline

menopausia *nf* : menopause

menor *adj* **1** (*comparative of* **pequeño**) : smaller, lesser, younger **2** (*superlative of* **pequeño**) : smallest, least, youngest **3** : minor (in music) **4 al por ~** : retail — *nmf* : minor, juvenile

menos *adv* **1** (*comparative*) : less **2** (*superlative*) : least **3 ~ de** : fewer than — **~** *adj* **1** (*comparative*) : less, fewer **2** (*superlative*) : least, fewest — **~** *prep* **1** : minus **2** EXCEPTO : except — **~** *pron* **1** : less, fewer **2 al ~** *or* **por lo ~** : at least **3 a ~ que** : unless —

menoscabar *vt* **1** : lessen **2** ESTROPEAR : harm, damage — **menospreciar** *vt* **1** DESPRECIAR : scorn **2** SUBESTIMAR : undervalue — **menosprecio** *nm* : contempt

mensaje *nm* : message — **mensajero, -ra** *n* : messenger

menso, -sa *adj* *Lat fam* : foolish, stupid

menstruar {3} *vi* : menstruate — **menstruación** *nf* : menstruation

mensual *adj* : monthly — **mensualidad** *nf* **1** : monthly payment **2** : monthly salary

mensurable *adj* : measurable

menta *nf* **1** : mint, peppermint **2 ~ verde** : spearmint

mental *adj* : mental — **mentalidad** *nf* : mentality

mentar {55} *vt* : mention, name

mente *nf* : mind

mentir {76} *vi* : lie — **mentira** *nf* : lie — **mentirilla** *nf* : fib — **mentiroso, -sa** *adj* : lying — **~** *n* : liar

mentís *nms & pl* : denial

mentol *nm* : menthol

mentón *nm, pl* **-tones** : chin

menú *nm, pl* **-nús** : menu

menudear *vi* : occur frequently — **menudeo** *nm* *Lat* : retail, retailing

menudillos *nmpl* : giblets

menudo, -da *adj* **1** : small, insignificant **2 a ~** : often

meñique *nm* *or* **dedo ~** : little finger, pinkie

meollo *nm* **1** : marrow **2** ESENCIA : essence, core

mercado *nm* **1** : market **2 ~ de valores** : stock market — **mercadería** *nf* : merchandise, goods *pl*

mercancía *nf* : merchandise, goods *pl* — **mercante** *nmf* : merchant, dealer — **mercantil** *adj* : commercial

mercenario, -ria *adj & n* : mercenary

mercería *nf* : notions store

mercurio *nm* : mercury

Mercurio *nm* : Mercury (planet)

merecer {53} *vt* : deserve — *vi* : be worthy — **merecedor, -dora** *adj* : deserving, worthy — **merecido** *nm* **recibir su ~** : get one's just deserts

merendar {55} *vi* : have an afternoon snack — *vt* : have as an afternoon snack — **merendero** *nm* **1** : snack bar **2** : picnic area

merengue *nm* **1** : meringue **2** : merengue (dance)

meridiano, -na *adj* **1** : midday **2** CLARO : crystal-clear — **meridiano** *nm* : meridian — **meridional** *adj* : southern

merienda *nf* : afternoon snack, tea

mérito *nm* : merit, worth — **meritorio, -ria** *adj* : deserving — ~ *n* : intern, trainee

mermar *vi* : decrease — *vt* : reduce, cut down — **merma** *nf* : decrease

mermelada *nf* : marmalade, jam

mero, -ra *adj* **1** : mere, simple **2** *Lat fam* (*used as an intensifier*) : very, real — **mero** *adv Lat fam* **1** : nearly, almost **2** **aquí** ~ : right here

merodear *vi* **1** : maraud **2** ~ **por** : prowl about (a place)

mes *nm* : month

mesa *nf* **1** : table **2** COMITÉ : committee, board

mesarse *vr* ~ **los cabellos** : tear one's hair

meseta *nf* : plateau

Mesías *nm* : Messiah

mesilla *nf* : small table

mesón *nm, pl* **-sones** : inn — **mesonero, -ra** *nm* : innkeeper

mestizo, -za *adj* **1** : of mixed ancestry **2** HÍBRIDO : hybrid — ~ *n* : person of mixed ancestry

mesura *nf* : moderation — **mesurado, -da** *adj* : moderate, restrained

meta *nf* : goal, objective

metabolismo *nm* : metabolism

metafísica *nf* : metaphysics — **metafísico, -ca** *adj* : metaphysical

metáfora *nf* : metaphor — **metafórico, -ca** *adj* : metaphoric, metaphorical

metal *nm* **1** : metal **2** : brass section (in an orchestra) — **metálico, -ca** *adj* : metallic, metal — **metalurgia** *nf* : metallurgy

metamorfosis *nfs & pl* : metamorphosis

metano *nm* : methane

metedura *nf* ~ **de pata** *fam* : blunder

meteoro *nm* : meteor — **meteórico, -ca** *adj* : meteoric — **meteorito** *nm* : meteorite — **meteorología** *nf* : meteorology — **meteorólogo, -ga** *adj* : meteorological, meteorologic — ~ *n* : meteorologist

meter *vt* **1** : put (in) **2** : place (in a job, etc.) **3** ENREDAR : involve **4** CAUSAR : make, cause **5** : spread (a rumor) **6** *Lat* : strike (a blow) — **meterse** *vr* **1** : get in, enter **2** ~ **en** : get involved in, meddle in **3** ~ **con** *fam* : pick a fight with

meticuloso, -sa *adj* : meticulous

método *nm* : method — **metódico, -ca**

adj : methodical — **metodología** *nf* : methodology

metomentodo *nmf fam* : busybody

metralla *nf* : shrapnel — **metralleta** *nf* : submachine gun

métrico, -ca *adj* : metric, metrical

metro *nm* **1** : meter **2** : subway (train)

metrópoli *nf or* **metrópolis** *nfs & pl* : metropolis — **metropolitano, -na** *adj* : metropolitan

mexicano, -na *adj* : Mexican — **mexicoamericano, -na** *adj* : Mexican-American

mezcla *nf* **1** : mixture **2** ARGAMASA : mortar — **mezclar** *vt* **1** : mix, blend **2** CONFUNDIR : mix up, muddle **3** INVOLUCRAR : involve — **mezclarse** *vr* **1** : get mixed up **2** : mingle (socially) — **mezcolanza** *nf* : mixture

mezclilla *nf Lat* : denim

mezquino, -na *adj* **1** : mean, petty **2** ESCASO : meager — **mezquindad** *nf* : meanness, stinginess

mezquita *nf* : mosque

mezquite *nm* : mesquite

mi *adj* : my

mí *pron* **1** : me **2** *or* ~ **mismo,** ~ **misma** : myself **3 a** ~ **no me importa** : it doesn't matter to me

miajas → **migajas**

miau *nm* : meow

mica *nf* : mica

mico *nm* : (long-tailed) monkey

microbio *nm* : microbe, germ — **microbiología** *nf* : microbiology

microbús *nm, pl* **-buses** : minibus

microcosmos *nms & pl* : microcosm

microfilm *nm, pl* **-films** : microfilm

micrófono *nm* : microphone

microondas *nms & pl* : microwave (oven)

microorganismo *nm* : microorganism

microscopio *nm* : microscope — **microscópico, -ca** *adj* : microscopic

miedo *nm* **1** : fear **2 dar** ~ : be frightening — **miedoso, -sa** *adj* : fearful

miel *nf* : honey

miembro *nm* **1** : member **2** EXTREMIDAD : limb, extremity

mientras *adv or* ~ **tanto** : meanwhile, in the meantime — ~ *conj* **1** : while, as **2** ~ **que** : while, whereas **3** ~ **viva** : as long as I live

miércoles *nms & pl* : Wednesday

mies *nf* : (ripe) corn, grain

miga *nf* : crumb — **migajas** *nfpl* **1** : breadcrumbs **2** SOBRAS : leftovers

migración *nf, pl* **-ciones** : migration

migraña *nf* : migraine

migrar *vi* : migrate

mijo *nm* : millet

mil *adj & nm* : thousand

milagro *nm* : miracle — **milagroso, -sa** *adj* : miraculous

milenio *nm* : millennium

milésimo, -ma *adj* : thousandth

milicia *nf* **1** : militia **2** : military (service)

miligramo *nm* : milligram

mililitro *nm* : milliliter

milímetro *nm* : millimeter

militante *adj & nmf* : militant

militar *adj* : military — **~** *nmf* : soldier — **militarizar** {21} *vt* : militarize

milla *nf* : mile

millar *nm* : thousand

millón *nm, pl* **-llones 1** : million **2 mil millones** : billion — **millonario, -ria** *n* : millionaire — **millonésimo, -ma** *adj* : millionth

mimar *vt* : pamper, spoil

mimbre *nm* : wicker

mímica *nf* **1** : mime, sign language **2** IMITACIÓN : mimicry

mimo *nm* : pampering — **~** *nmf* : mime

mina *nf* **1** : mine **2** : lead (for pencils) — **minar** *vt* **1** : mine **2** DEBILITAR : undermine

mineral *adj* : mineral — **~** *nm* **1** : mineral **2** : ore (of a metal)

minería *nf* : mining — **minero, -ra** *adj* : mining — **~** *n* : miner

miniatura *nf* : miniature

minifalda *nf* : miniskirt

minifundio *nm* : small farm

minimizar {21} *vt* : minimize

mínimo, -ma *adj* **1** : minimum **2** MINÚSCULO : minute **3 en lo más ~** : in the slightest — **mínimo** *nm* : minimum

minino, -na *n fam* : pussycat

ministerio *nm* : ministry — **ministro, -tra** *n* **1** : minister, secretary **2 primer ministro** : prime minister

minoría *nf* : minority

minorista *adj* : retail — **~** *nmf* : retailer

minoritario, -ria *adj* : minority

minucia *nf* : trifle, small detail — **minucioso, -sa** *adj* **1** : detailed **2** METICULOSO : thorough

minué *nm* : minuet

minúsculo, -la *adj* : minuscule, tiny

minusvalía *nf* : handicap, disability — **minusválido, -da** *adj* : disabled

minuta *nf* **1** : bill, fee **2** BORRADOR : rough draft

minuto *nm* : minute — **minutero** *nm* : minute hand

mío, mía *adj* **1** : mine **2 una amiga mía** : a friend of mine — **~** *pron* **el mío, la mía** : mine, my own

miope *adj* : nearsighted

mirar *vt* **1** : look at **2** OBSERVAR : watch **3** CONSIDERAR : consider — *vi* **1** : look **2 ~ a** : face, overlook **3 ~ por** : look after — **mirarse** *vr* **1** : look at oneself **2** : look at each other — **mira** *nf* **1** : sight (of a firearm or instrument) **2** INTENCIÓN : aim, objective — **mirada** *nf* : look — **mirado, -da** *adj* **1** : careful **2** CONSIDERADO : considerate **3 bien ~** : well thought of — **mirador** *nm* **1** BALCÓN : balcony **2** : lookout, vantage point — **miramiento** *nm* : consideration

mirlo *nm* : blackbird

misa *nf* : Mass

miscelánea *nf* : miscellany

miserable *adj* **1** : poor **2** LASTIMOSO : miserable, wretched — **miseria** *nf* **1** : poverty **2** DESGRACIA : misfortune, misery

misericordia *nf* : mercy — **misericordioso, -sa** *adj* : merciful

mísero, -ra *adj* : wretched, miserable

misil *nm* : missile

misión *nf, pl* **-siones** : mission — **misionero, -ra** *adj & n* : missionary

mismo *adv* (used for emphasis) : right, exactly — **mismo, -ma** *adj* **1** : same **2** (used for emphasis) : very **3** : -self **4 por lo ~** : for that reason

misoginia *nf* : misogyny — **misógino** *nm* : misogynist

misterio *nm* : mystery — **misterioso, -sa** *adj* : mysterious

mística *nf* : mysticism — **místico, -ca** *adj* : mystic, mystical — **~** *n* : mystic

mitad *nf* **1** : half **2** MEDIO : middle

mítico, -ca *adj* : mythical, mythic

mitigar {52} *vt* : mitigate

mitin *nm, pl* **mítines** : (political) meeting

mito *nm* : myth — **mitología** *nm* : mythology — **mitológico, -ca** *adj* : mythological

mixto, -ta *adj* **1** : mixed, joint **2** : coeducational (of a school)

mnemónico, -ca *adj* : mnemonic

mobiliario *nm* : furniture

mocasín *nm, pl* **-sines** : moccasin

mochila *nf* : backpack, knapsack

moción *nf, pl* **-ciones** : motion

moco *nm* **1** : mucus **2 limpiarse los ~s** : wipe one's nose — **mocoso, -sa** *n fam* : kid, brat

moda *nf* **1** : fashion, style **2 a la ~** *or* **de ~** : in style, fashionable **3 ~ pasajera** : fad — **modal** *adj* : modal — **modales** *nmpl* : manners — **modalidad** *nf* : type, kind

modelar vt : model, mold — **modelo** adj : model — ~ nm : model, pattern — ~ nmf : model, mannequin

módem or **modem** ['moðɛm] nm : modem

moderar vt 1 : moderate 2 : reduce (speed, etc.) 3 PRESIDIR ⁴ chair (a meeting) — **moderarse** vr : restrain oneself — **moderación** nf, pl -ciones : moderation — **moderado, -da** adj & n : moderate — **moderador, -dora** n : moderator, chairperson

moderno, -na adj : modern — **modernismo** nm : modernism — **modernizar** {21} vt : modernize

modesto, -ta adj : modest — **modestia** nf : modesty

modificar {72} vt : modify, alter — **modificación** nf, pl -ciones : alteration

modismo nm : idiom

modista nmf 1 : dressmaker 2 : (fashion) designer

modo nm 1 : way, manner 2 : mood (in grammar) 3 : mode (in music) 4 a ~ de : by way of 5 de ~ que) : so (that) 6 de todos ~s : in any case, anyway

modorra nf : drowsiness

modular vt : modulate — **modulación** nf, pl -ciones : modulation

módulo nm : module, unit

mofa nf : ridicule, mockery — **mofarse** vr ~ de : make fun of

mofeta nf : skunk

moflete nm fam : fat cheek — **mofletudo, -da** adj fam : fat-cheeked, chubby

mohín nm, pl -hines : grimace — **mohíno, -na** adj : sulky

moho nm 1 : mold, mildew 2 ÓXIDO : rust — **mohoso, -sa** adj 1 : moldy 2 OXIDADO : rusty

moisés nm, pl -seses : bassinet, cradle

mojar vt 1 : wet, moisten 2 : dunk (food) — **mojarse** vr : get wet — **mojado, -da** adj : wet, damp

mojigato, -ta adj : prudish — ~ n : prude

mojón nm, pl -jones : boundary stone, marker

molar nm : molar

moldear vt : mold, shape — **molde** nm : mold, form — **moldura** nf : molding

mole[1] nf : mass, bulk

mole[2] nm 1 : Mexican chili sauce 2 : meat served with mole

molécula nf : molecule — **molecular** adj : molecular

moler {47} vt : grind, crush

molestar vt 1 : annoy, bother 2 no ~ : do not disturb — vi : be a nuisance — **molestarse** vr 1 : bother 2 OFENDERSE : take offense — **molestia** nf 1 : annoyance, nuisance 2 MALESTAR : discomfort — **molesto, -ta** adj 1 : annoyed 2 FASTIDIOSO : annoying 3 INCÓMODO : in discomfort — **molestoso, -sa** adj : bothersome, annoying

molido, -da adj 1 : ground (of meat, etc.) 2 fam : worn out, exhausted

molino nm 1 : mill 2 ~ de viento : windmill — **molinero, -ra** n : miller — **molinillo** nm : grinder, mill

mollera nf 1 : crown (of the head) 2 fam : brains pl

molusco nm : mollusk

momento nm 1 : moment, instant 2 : (period of) time 3 : momentum (in physics) 4 de ~ : for the moment 5 de un ~ a otro : any time now — **momentáneamente** adv : momentarily — **momentáneo, -nea** adj 1 : momentary 2 PASAJERO : temporary

momia nf : mummy

monaguillo nm : altar boy

monarca nmf : monarch — **monarquía** nf : monarchy

monasterio nm : monastery — **monástico, -ca** adj : monastic

mondadientes nms & pl : toothpick

mondar vt : peel

mondongo nm : innards pl, guts pl

moneda nf 1 : coin 2 : currency (of a country) — **monedero** nm : change purse

monetario, -ria adj : monetary

monitor nm : monitor

monja nf : nun — **monje** nm : monk

mono, -na n : monkey — ~ adj fam : lovely, cute

monogamia nf : monogamy — **monógamo -ma** adj : monogamous

monografía nf : monograph

monograma nm : monogram

monolingüe adj : monolingual

monólogo nm : monologue

monopatín nm, pl -tines : scooter, skateboard

monopolio nm : monopoly — **monopolizar** {21} vt : monopolize

monosílabo nm : monosyllable — **monosilábico, -ca** adj : monosyllabic

monoteísmo nm : monotheism — **monoteísta** adj : monotheistic

monotonía nf : monotony — **monótono, -na** adj : monotonous

monóxido nm ~ de carbono : carbon monoxide

monstruo nm : monster — **monstruosidad** nf : monstrosity — **monstruoso, -sa** adj : monstrous

monta *nf* : importance, value

montaje *nm* **1** : assembly **2** : staging (in theater), editing (of films)

montaña *nf* **1** : mountain **2** ~ **rusa** : roller coaster — **montañero, -ra** *n* : mountain climber — **montañoso, -sa** *adj* : mountainous

montar *vt* **1** : mount **2** ESTABLECER : establish **3** ENSAMBLAR : assemble, put together **4** : stage (a performance) **5** : cock (a gun) — *vi* **1** ~ **a caballo** : ride horseback **2** ~ **en bicicleta** : get on a bicycle

monte *nm* **1** : mountain **2** BOSQUE : woodland **3** *or* ~ **bajo** : scrubland **4** ~ **de piedad** : pawnshop

montés *adj, pl* **-teses** : wild (of animals or plants)

montículo *nm* : mound, hillock

montón *nm, pl* **-tones 1** : heap, pile **2** **un** ~ **de** *fam* : lots of

montura *nf* **1** : mount (horse) **2** SILLA : saddle **3** : frame (of glasses)

monumento *nm* : monument — **monumental** *adj fam* : monumental, huge

monzón *nm, pl* **-zones** : monsoon

moño *nm* **1** : bun (of hair) **2** *Lat* : bow (knot)

mora *nf* **1** : mulberry **2** ZARZAMORA : blackberry

morada *nf* : residence, dwelling

morado, -da *adj* : purple — **morado** *nm* : purple

moral *adj* : moral — ~ *nf* **1** : ethics, morals *pl* **2** ÁNIMO : morale — **moraleja** *nf* : moral (of a story) — **moralidad** *nf* : morality — **moralista** *adj* : moralistic — ~ *nmf* : moralist

morar *vi* : live, reside

morboso, -sa *adj* : morbid

mordaz *adj* : caustic, scathing — **mordacidad** *nf* : bite, sharpness

mordaza *nf* : gag

morder {47} *v* : bite — **mordedura** *nf* : bite (of an animal)

mordisquear *vt* : nibble (on) — **mordisco** *nm* : nibble, bite

moreno, -na *adj* **1** : dark-haired, brunette **2** : dark-skinned — ~ *n* **1** : brunette **2** : dark-skinned person

moretón *nm, pl* **-tones** : bruise

morfina *nf* : morphine

morir {46} *vi* **1** : die **2** APAGARSE : die out, go out — **morirse** *vr* **1** ~ **de** : die of **2** ~ **por** : be dying for — **moribundo, -da** *adj* : dying

moro, -ra *adj* : Moorish — ~ *n* : Moor

moroso, -sa *adj* : delinquent, in arrears — **morosidad** *nf* : delinquency (in payment)

morral *nm* : backpack

morriña *nf* : homesickness

morro *nm* : snout

morsa *nf* : walrus

morse *nm* : Morse code

mortaja *nf* : shroud

mortal *adj* **1** : mortal **2** : deadly (of a wound, an enemy, etc.) — ~ *nmf* : mortal — **mortalidad** *nf* : mortality — **mortandad** *nf* : death toll

mortero *nm* : mortar

mortífero, -ra *adj* : deadly, lethal

mortificar {72} *vt* **1** : mortify **2** ATORMENTAR : torment — **mortificarse** *vr* : be distressed

mosaico *nm* : mosaic

mosca *nf* : fly

moscada *adj* → **nuez**

mosquearse *vr fam* **1** : become suspicious **2** ENFADARSE : get annoyed

mosquito *nm* : mosquito — **mosquitero** *nm* **1** : (window) screen **2** : mosquito net

mostachón *nm, pl* **-chones** : macaroon

mostaza *nf* : mustard

mostrador *nm* : counter (in a store)

mostrar {19} *vt* : show — **mostrarse** *vr* : show oneself, appear

mota *nf* : spot, speck — **moteado, -da** *adj* : speckled, spotted

mote *nm* : nickname

motel *nm* : motel

motín *nm, pl* **-tines 1** : riot, uprising **2** : mutiny (of troops)

motivo *nm* **1** : motive, cause **2** : motif (in art, music, etc.) — **motivación** *nf, pl* **-ciones** : motivation — **motivar** *vt* **1** : cause **2** IMPULSAR : motivate

moto *nf* : motorcycle, motorbike — **motocicleta** *nf* : motorcycle — **motociclista** *nmf* : motorcyclist

motor, -triz *or* **-tora** *adj* : motor — **motor** *nm* : motor, engine — **motorista** *nmf* **1** : motorcyclist **2** *Lat* : motorist

mover {47} *vt* **1** : move, shift **2** : shake (the head) **3** PROVOCAR : provoke — **moverse** *vr* **1** : move (over) **2** APRESURARSE : get a move on — **movedizo, -za** *adj* : movable, shifting — **movible** *adj* : movable

móvil *adj* : mobile — ~ *nm* **1** MOTIVO : motive **2** : mobile — **movilidad** *nf* : mobility — **movilizar** {21} *vt* : mobilize

movimiento *nm* **1** : movement, motion **2** ~ **sindicalista** : labor movement

mozo, -za *adj* : young — ~ *n* **1** : young man *m*, young woman *f* **2** *Lat* : waiter *m*, waitress *f*

muchacho, -cha n : kid, boy m, girl f
muchedumbre nf : crowd
mucho adv 1 : very much, a lot 2 : long,
a long time — **mucho, -cha** adj 1 : a
lot of, many, much 2 **muchas veces**
: often — **~** pron : a lot, many, much
mucosidad nf : mucus
muda nf 1 : molting (of animals) 2
: change (of clothing) — **mudanza** nf
1 : change 2 TRASLADO : move, change
of residence — **mudar** v 1 : molt, shed
2 CAMBIAR : change — **mudarse** vr 1
: change (one's clothes) 2 TRASLA-
DARSE : move (one's residence)
mudo, -da adj 1 : mute 2 SILENCIOSO
: silent
mueble nm 1 : piece of furniture 2 **~s**
nmpl : furniture, furnishings
mueca nf 1 : grimace, face 2 **hacer ~s**
: makes faces
muela nf 1 : tooth, molar 2 **~ de juicio**
: wisdom tooth
muelle adj : soft — **~** nm 1 : wharf,
jetty 2 RESORTE : spring
muérdago nm : mistletoe
muerte nf : death — **muerto, -ta** adj 1
: dead 2 : dull (of colors, etc.) — **~**
nm : dead person, deceased
muesca nf : nick, notch
muestra nf 1 : sample 2 SEÑAL : sign,
show
mugir {35} vi : moo, bellow — **mugido**
nm : mooing, bellowing
mugre nf : grime, filth — **mugriento,
-ta** adj : filthy, grimy
muguete nm : lily of the valley
mujer nf 1 : woman 2 ESPOSA : wife 3
~ de negocios : businesswoman
mulato, -ta adj & n : mulatto
muleta nf 1 : crutch 2 APOYO : prop,
support
mullido, -da adj : soft, spongy
mulo, -la n : mule
multa nf : fine — **multar** vt : fine
multicolor adj : multicolored
multicultural adj : multicultural
multimedia adj : multimedia
multinacional adj : multinational
multiplicar {72} v : multiply — **multiplicarse** vr : multiply, reproduce —
múltiple adj : multiple — **multipli-**

cación nf, pl **-ciones** : multiplication
— **múltiplo** nm : multiple
multitud nf : crowd, multitude
mundo nm 1 : world 2 **todo el ~**
: everyone, everybody — **mundanal**
adj : worldly — **mundano, -na** adj 1
: worldly, earthly 2 **la vida mundana**
: high society — **mundial** adj : world,
worldwide
municiones nfpl : ammunition
municipal adj : municipal — **municipio** nm 1 : municipality 2 AYUN-
TAMIENTO : town council
muñeca nf 1 : doll 2 : wrist (in anatomy) — **muñeco** nm 1 : boy doll 2
MANIQUÍ : dummy, puppet
muñon nm, pl **-ñones** : stump (of an
arm or leg)
mural adj & nm : mural — **muralla** nf
: wall, rampart
murciélago nm : bat (animal)
murmullo nm 1 : murmur, murmuring 2
: rustling (of leaves, etc.)
murmurar vi 1 : murmur, whisper 2
CRITICAR : gossip
muro nm : wall
musa nf : muse
musaraña nf : shrew
músculo nm : muscle — **muscular** adj
: muscular — **musculatura** nf : muscles pl — **musculoso, -sa** adj : muscular
muselina nf : muslin
museo nm : museum
musgo nm : moss — **musgoso, -sa** adj
: mossy
música nf : music — **musical** adj : musical — **músico, -ca** adj : musical —
~ n : musician
musitar vt : mumble
muslo nm : thigh
musulmán, -mana adj & n, mpl
-manes : Muslim
mutar v : mutate — **mutación** nf, pl
-ciones : mutation — **mutante** adj &
nmf : mutant
mutilar vt : mutilate — **mutilación** nf,
pl **-ciones** : mutilation
mutuo, -tua adj : mutual
muy adv 1 : very, quite 2 DEMASIADO
: too

N

n *nf* : n, 14th letter of the Spanish alphabet
nabo *nm* : turnip
nácar *nm* : mother-of-pearl
nacer {48} *vi* **1** : be born **2** : hatch (of an egg), sprout (of a plant) **3** SURGIR : arise, spring up — **nacido, -da** *adj & n*
recién ~ : newborn — **naciente** *adj* **1** : new, growing **2** : rising (of the sun) — **nacimiento** *nm* **1** : birth **2** : source (of a river) **3** ORIGEN : beginning **4** BELÉN : Nativity scene
nación *nf, pl* **-ciones** : nation, country — **nacional** *adj* : national — ~ *nmf* : national, citizen — **nacionalidad** *nf* : nationality — **nacionalismo** *nm* : nationalism — **nacionalista** *adj & nmf* : nationalist — **nacionalizar** {21} *vt* **1** : nationalize **2** : naturalize (as a citizen) — **nacionalizarse** *vr* : become naturalized
nada *pron* **1** : nothing **2 de ~** : you're welcome **3 ~ más** : nothing else, nothing more — ~ *adv* : not at all — ~ *nf* **la ~** : nothingness
nadar *v* : swim — **nadador, -dora** *n* : swimmer
nadería *nf* : small thing, trifle
nadie *pron* : nobody, no one
nado: a ~ *adv phr* : swimming
nafta *nf Lat* : gasoline
naipe *nm* : playing card
nalgas *nfpl* : buttocks, bottom
nana *nf* : lullaby
naranja *adj & nm* : orange (color) — ~ *nf* : orange (fruit) — **naranjal** *nm* : orange grove — **naranjo** *nm* : orange tree
narciso *nm* : narcissus, daffodil
narcótico, -ca *adj* : narcotic — **narcótico** *nm* : narcotic — **narcotizar** {21} *vt* : drug — **narcotraficante** *nmf* : drug trafficker — **narcotráfico** *nm* : drug trafficking
nariz *nf, pl* **-rices 1** : nose **2** OLFATO : sense of smell **3 narices** *nfpl* : nostrils
narrar *vt* : narrate, tell — **narración** *nf, pl* **-ciones** : narration — **narrador, -dora** *n* : narrator — **narrativa** *nf* : narrative, storytelling
nasal *adj* : nasal
nata *nf Spain* : cream

natación *nf, pl* **-ciones** : swimming
natal *adj* : native, birth — **natalicio** *nm* : birthday — **natalidad** *nf* : birthrate
natillas *nfpl* : custard
natividad *nf* : birth, nativity
nativo, -va *adj & n* : native
natural *adj* **1** : natural **2** NORMAL : normal **3 ~ de** : native of, from — ~ *nm* **1** : temperament **2** NATIVO : native — **naturaleza** *nf* : nature — **naturalidad** *nf* : naturalness — **naturalista** *adj* : naturalistic — **naturalización** *nf, pl* **-ciones** : naturalization — **naturalizar** {21} *vt* : naturalize — **naturalizarse** *vr* : become naturalized — **naturalmente** *adv* **1** : naturally **2** POR SUPUESTO : of course
naufragar {52} *vi* **1** : be shipwrecked **2** FRACASAR : fail — **naufragio** *nm* : shipwreck — **náufrago, -ga** *adj* : shipwrecked — ~ *n* : castaway
náusea *nf* **1** : nausea **2 dar ~s** : nauseate **3 ~s matutinas** : morning sickness — **nauseabundo, -da** *adj* : nauseating
náutico, -ca *adj* : nautical
navaja *nf* : pocketknife, penknife
naval *adj* : naval
nave *nf* **1** : ship **2** : nave (of a church) **3 ~ espacial** : spaceship
navegar {52} *v* : navigate, sail — **navegable** *adj* : navigable — **navegación** *nf, pl* **-ciones** : navigation — **navegante** *adj* : sailing, seafaring — ~ *nmf* : navigator
Navidad *nf* **1** : Christmas **2 feliz ~** : Merry Christmas — **navideño, -ña** *adj* : Christmas
naviero, -ra *adj* : shipping
nazi *adj & nmf* : Nazi — **nazismo** *nm* : Nazism
neblina *nf* : mist
nebuloso, -sa *adj* **1** : hazy, misty, foggy **2** VAGO : vague, nebulous
necedad *nf* **1** : stupidity **2 decir ~es** : talk nonsense
necesario, -ria *adj* : necessary — **necesariamente** *adv* : necessarily — **necesidad** *nf* **1** : need, necessity **2** POBREZA : poverty **3 ~es** *nfpl* : hardships — **necesitado, -da** *adj* : needy — **necesitar** *vt* : need — *vi* **~ de** : have need of

necio, -cia *adj* : silly, dumb
necrología *nf* : obituary
néctar *nm* : nectar
nectarina *nf* : nectarine
neerlandés, -desa *adj, mpl* **-deses**
: Dutch — **neerlandés** *nm* : Dutch
(language)
nefasto, -ta *adj* **1** : ill-fated **2** *fam* : terrible, awful
negar {49} *vt* **1** : deny **2** REHUSAR : refuse **3** : disown (a person) — **negarse**
vr : refuse — **negable** *nf, pl* **-ciones**
1 : denial **2** : negative (in grammar) —
negativa *nf* **1** : denial **2** RECHAZO : refusal — **negativo, -va** *adj* : negative
— **negativo** *nm* : negative (of a photograph)
negligente *adj* : negligent — **negligencia** *nf* : negligence
negociar *vt* : negotiate — *vi* : deal, do
business — **negociable** *adj* : negotiable — **negociación** *nf, pl* **-ciones**
: negotiation — **negociante** *nmf*
: businessman *m*, businesswoman *f* —
negocio *nm* **1** : business **2** TRANSAC-
CIÓN : deal **3** **~s** : business, commerce
negro, -gra *adj* : black, dark — **~** *n*
: dark-skinned person — **negro** *nm*
: black (color) — **negrura** *nf* : black-
ness — **negruzco, -ca** *adj* : blackish
nene, -na *n fam* : baby, small child
nenúfar *nm* : water lily
neón *nm* : neon
neoyorquino, -na *adj* : of or from New
York
nepotismo *nm* : nepotism
Neptuno *nm* : Neptune
nervio *nm* **1** : nerve **2** : sinew (in meat)
3 VIGOR : vigor, energy **4 tener ~s**
: be nervous — **nerviosismo** *nf* : nervousness — **nervioso, -sa** *adj* **1**
: nervous, anxious **2 sistema nervioso** : nervous system
nervudo, -da *adj* : sinewy
neto, -ta *adj* **1** : clear, distinct **2** : net (of
weight, salaries, etc.)
neumático *nm* : tire
neumonía *nf* : pneumonia
neurología *nf* : neurology — **neu-
rológico, -ca** *adj* : neurological, neu-
rologic — **neurólogo, -ga** *n* : neurol-
ogist
neurosis *nfs & pl* : neurosis — **neurótico, -ca** *adj & n* : neurotic
neutral *adj* : neutral — **neutralidad** *nf*
: neutrality — **neutralizar** {21} *vt*
: neutralize — **neutro, -tra** *adj* **1** : neutral **2** : neuter (in biology and grammar)
neutrón *nm, pl* **-trones** : neutron
nevar {55} *v impers* : snow — **nevada**

nf : snowfall — **nevado, -da** *adj* **1**
: snow-covered, snowy **2** : snow-white
— **nevasca** *nf* : snowstorm
nevera *nf* : refrigerator
nevisca *nf* : light snowfall, flurry
nexo *nm* : link, connection
ni *conj* **1** : neither, nor **2 ~ que** : as if **3**
~ siquiera : not even
nicaragüense *adj* : Nicaraguan
nicho *nm* : niche
nicotina *nf* : nicotine
nidada *nf* : brood (of chicks, etc.)
nido *nm* **1** : nest **2** GUARIDA : hiding
place, den
niebla *nf* : fog, mist
nieto, -ta *n* **1** : grandson *m*, granddaughter *f* **2 nietos** *nmpl* : grandchil-
dren
nieve *nf* : snow
nigeriano, -na *adj* : Nigerian
nilón *or* **nilon** *nm, pl* **-lones** : nylon
nimio, -mia *adj* : insignificant, trivial —
nimiedad *nf* **1** : trifle **2** INSIGNIFICAN-
CIA : triviality
ninfa *nf* : nymph
ninguno, -na (**ningún** *before masculine singular nouns*) *adj* : no, not any
— **~** *pron* **1** : neither, none **2** : no one,
nobody
niña *nf* **1** : pupil (of the eye) **2 la ~ de
los ojos** : the apple of one's eye
niño, -ña *n* : child, boy *m*, girl *f* — **~**
adj **1** : young **2** INFANTIL : immature,
childish — **niñero, -ra** *n* : baby-sitter,
nanny — **niñez** *nf, pl* **-ñeces** : childhood
nipón, -pona *adj* : Japanese
níquel *nm* : nickel
nítido, -da *adj* : clear, sharp — **nitidez**
nf, pl **-deces** : clarity, sharpness
nitrato *nm* : nitrate
nitrógeno *nm* : nitrogen
nivel *nm* **1** : level, height **2 ~ de vida**
: standard of living — **nivelar** *vt*
: level (out)
no *adv* **1** : not **2** (*in answer to a question*) : no **3 ¡como ~!** : of course! **4**
~ bien : as soon as **5 ~ fumador**
: non-smoker — **~** *nm* : no
noble *adj & nmf* : noble — **nobleza** *nf*
: nobility
noche *nf* **1** : night, evening **2 buenas
~s** : good evening, good night **3 de
~** *or* **por la ~** : at night **4 hacerse de
~** : get dark — **Nochebuena** *nf*
: Christmas Eve — **nochecita** *nf* : dusk
— **Nochevieja** *nf* : New Year's Eve
noción *nf, pl* **-ciones** : notion, concept **2 nociones** *nfpl* : rudiments
nocivo, -va *adj* : harmful, noxious

nocturno, -na *adj* **1** : night **2** : nocturnal (of animals, etc.) — **nocturno** *nm* : nocturne

nogal *nm* **1** : walnut tree **2** ~ **americano** : hickory

nómada *nmf* : nomad — ~ *adj* : nomadic

nomás *adv Lat* : only, just

nombrar *vt* **1** : appoint **2** CITAR : mention — **nombrado, -da** *adj* : famous, well-known — **nombramiento** *nm* : appointment, nomination — **nombre** *nm* **1** : name **2** SUSTANTIVO : noun **3** FAMA : fame, renown **4** ~ **de pila** : first name

nómina *nf* : payroll

nominal *adj* : nominal

nominar *vt* : nominate — **nominación** *nf, pl* **-ciones** : nomination

nomo *nm* : gnome

non *adj* : odd, not even — ~ *nm* : odd number

nonagésimo, -ma *adj & n* : ninetieth

nopal *nm* : nopal, prickly pear

nordeste *or* **noreste** *adj* **1** : northeastern **2** : northeasterly (of wind, etc.) — ~ *nm* : northeast

nórdico, -ca *adj* : Scandinavian

noreste → **nordeste**

noria *nf* **1** : waterwheel **2** : Ferris wheel (at a fair, etc.)

norma *nf* : rule, norm, standard — **normal** *adj* **1** : normal **2 escuela** ~ : teacher-training college — **normalidad** *nf* : normality — **normalizar** {21} *vt* **1** : normalize **2** ESTANDARIZAR : standardize — **normalizarse** *vr* : return to normal — **normalmente** *adv* : ordinarily, generally

noroeste *adj* **1** : northwestern **2** : northwesterly (of wind, etc.) — ~ *nm* : northwest

norte *adj* : north, northern — ~ *nm* **1** : north **2** : north wind

norteamericano, -na *adj* : North American

norteño, -ña *adj* : northern

noruego, -ga *adj* : Norwegian — **noruego** *nm* : Norwegian (language)

nos *pron* **1** (*direct object*) : us **2** (*indirect object*) : to us, for us, from us **3** (*reflexive*) : ourselves **4** : each other, one another

nosotros, -tras *pron* **1** (*subject*) : we **2** (*object*) : us **3** *or* ~ **mismos** : ourselves

nostalgia *nf* **1** : nostalgia **2 sentir** ~ **por** : be homesick for — **nostálgico, -ca** *adj* : nostalgic

nota *nf* **1** : note **2** : grade, mark (in school) **3** CUENTA : bill, check — **notable** *adj* : noteworthy, notable — **notar** *vt* : notice — **notarse** *vr* : be evident, seem

notario, -ria *n* : notary (public)

noticia *nf* **1** : news item, piece of news **2** ~ **s** *nfpl* : news — **noticiario** *nm* : newscast — **noticiero** *nm Lat* : newscast

notificar {72} *vt* : notify — **notificación** *nf, pl* **-ciones** : notification

notorio, -ria *adj* **1** : obvious **2** CONOCIDO : well-known — **notoriedad** *nf* : fame, notoriety

novato, -ta *adj* : inexperienced — ~ *n* : beginner, novice

novecientos, -tas *adj* : nine hundred — **novecientos** *nms & pl* : nine hundred

novedad *nf* **1** : newness, innovation **2** NOTICIAS : news **3** ~ **es** : novelties, latest news — **novedoso, -sa** *adj* : original, novel

novela *nf* **1** : novel **2** : soap opera (on television) — **novelesco, -ca** *adj* **1** : fictional **2** FANTÁSTICO : fabulous — **novelista** *nmf* : novelist

noveno, -na *adj & nm* : ninth — **noveno** *nm* : ninth

noventa *adj & nm* : ninety — **noventavo, -va** *adj* : ninetieth — **noventavo** *nm* : ninetieth

novia → **novio**

noviazgo *nm* : engagement

novicio, -cia *n* : novice

noviembre *nm* : November

novillo, -lla *n* : young bull *m*, heifer *f*

novio, -via *n* **1** : boyfriend *m*, girlfriend *f* **2** PROMETIDO : fiancé *m*, fiancée *f* **3** : bridegroom *m*, bride *f* (at a wedding)

novocaína *nf* : novocaine

nube *nf* : cloud — **nubarrón** *nm, pl* **-rrones** : storm cloud — **nublado, -da** *adj* **1** : cloudy **2** ENTURBIADO : clouded, dim — **nublado** *nm* : storm cloud — **nublar** *vt* **1** : cloud **2** OSCURECER : obscure — **nublarse** *vr* : get cloudy — **nuboso, -sa** *adj* : cloudy

nuca *nf* : nape, back of the neck

núcleo *nm* **1** : nucleus **2** CENTRO : center, core — **nuclear** *adj* : nuclear

nudillo *nm* : knuckle

nudismo *nm* : nudism — **nudista** *adj & nmf* : nudist

nudo *nm* **1** : knot **2** : crux, heart (of a problem, etc.) — **nudoso, -sa** *adj* : knotty, gnarled

nuera *nf* : daughter-in-law

nuestro, -tra *adj* : our — ~ *pron* (*with definite article*) : ours, our own

nuevamente *adv* : again, anew

nueve *adj* & *nm* : nine
nuevo, -va *adj* **1** : new **2 de nuevo** : again, once more
nuez *nf, pl* **nueces 1** : nut **2** *or* ~ **de nogal** : walnut **3** ~ **de Adán** : Adam's apple **4** ~ **moscada** : nutmeg
nulo, -la *adj* **1** *or* ~ **y sin efecto** : null and void **2** INCAPAZ : useless, inept — **nulidad** *nf* **1** : nullity **2 es una** ~ *fam* : he's a total loss
numerar *vt* : number — **numeración** *nf, pl* **-ciones 1** : numbering **2** NÚMEROS : numbers *pl*, numerals *pl* — **numeral** *adj* : numeral — **número** *nm* **1** : number, numeral **2** : issue (of a

publication) **3 sin** ~ : countless — **numérico, -ca** *adj* : numerical — **numeroso, -sa** *adj* : numerous
nunca *adv* **1** : never, ever **2** ~ **más** : never again **3** ~ **jamás** : never ever
nupcial *adj* : nuptial, wedding — **nupcias** *nfpl* : nuptials, wedding
nutria *nf* : otter
nutrir *vt* **1** ALIMENTAR : feed, nourish **2** FOMENTAR : fuel, foster — **nutrición** *nf, pl* **-ciones** : nutrition — **nutrido, -da** *adj* **1** : nourished **2** ABUNDANTE : considerable, abundant — **nutriente** *nm* : nutrient — **nutritivo, -va** *adj* : nourishing, nutritious

O

o¹ *nf* : o, 16th letter of the Spanish alphabet
o² *conj* (**u** *before words beginning with* **o-** *or* **ho-**) **1** : or, either **2** ~ **sea** : in other words
oasis *nms* & *pl* : oasis
obcecar {72} *vt* : blind (by emotions) — **obcecarse** *vr* : become stubborn
obedecer {53} *vt* : obey — *vi* **1** : obey **2** ~ **a** : respond to **3** ~ **a** : be due to — **obediencia** *nf* : obedience — **obediente** *adj* : obedient
obertura *nf* : overture
obeso, -sa *adj* : obese — **obesidad** *nf* : obesity
obispo *nm* : bishop
objetar *v* : object — **objeción** *nf, pl* **-ciones** : objection
objeto *nm* : object — **objetivo, -va** *adj* : objective — **objetivo** *nm* **1** : objective, goal **2** : lens (in photography, etc.)
objetor, -tora *n* ~ **de conciencia** : conscientious objector
oblicuo, -cua *adj* : oblique
obligar {52} *vt* : require, oblige — **obligarse** *vr* : commit oneself (to do something) — **obligación** *nf, pl* **-ciones** : obligation — **obligado, -da** *adj* **1** : obligatory **2** FORZOSO : obligatory — **obligatorio, -ria** *adj* : mandatory
oblongo, -ga *adj* : oblong
oboe *nm* : oboe — *nmf* : oboist
obra *nf* **1** : work, deed **2** : work (of art, literature, etc.) **3** CONSTRUCCIÓN : construction work **4** ~ **maestra** : masterpiece **5** ~**s públicas** : public works — **obrar** *vt* : work, produce — *vi* : act, behave — **obrero, -ra** *adj* **la clase obrera** : the working class — ~ *n* : worker, laborer

obsceno, -na *adj* : obscene — **obscenidad** *nf* : obscenity
obsequiar *vt* : give, present — **obsequio** *nm* : gift, present
observar *vt* **1** : observe, watch **2** ADVERTIR : notice **3** ACATAR : observe, obey **4** COMENTAR : remark — **observación** *nf, pl* **-ciones** : observation — **observador, -dora** *adj* : observant — ~ *n* : observer — **observancia** *nf* : observance — **observatorio** *nm* : observatory
obsesionar *vt* : obsess — **obsesionarse** *vr* : be obsessed — **obsesión** *nf, pl* **-siones** : obsession — **obsesivo, -va** *adj* : obsessive — **obseso, -sa** *adj* : obsessed
obsoleto, -ta *adj* : obsolete
obstaculizar {21} *vt* : hinder — **obstáculo** *nm* : obstacle
obstante: no ~ *conj phr* : nevertheless, however — ~ *prep phr* : in spite of, despite
obstar {21} *vi* ~ **a** *or* ~ **para** : stop, prevent
obstetricia *nf* : obstetrics — **obstetra** *nmf* : obstetrician
obstinarse *vr* : be stubborn — **obstinado, -da** *adj* **1** : obstinate, stubborn **2** TENAZ : persistent
obstruir {41} *vt* : obstruct — **obstrucción** *nf, pl* **-ciones** : obstruction
obtener {80} *vt* : obtain, get
obtuso, -sa *adj* : obtuse
obviar *vt* : get around, avoid
obvio, -via *adj* : obvious — **obviamente** *adv* : obviously, clearly
oca *nf* : goose
ocasión *nf, pl* **-siones 1** : occasion **2** OPORTUNIDAD : opportunity **3** GANGA

: bargain — **ocasional** *adj* 1 : occasional 2 ACCIDENTAL : accidental, chance — **ocasionar** *vt* : cause

ocaso *nm* 1 : sunset 2 DECADENCIA : decline

occidente *nm* 1 : west 2 el Occidente : the West — **occidental** *adj* : western, Western

océano *nm* : ocean — **oceanografía** *nf* : oceanography

ochenta *adj & nm* : eighty

ocho *adj & nm* : eight — **ochocientos, -tas** *adj* : eight hundred — **ochocientos** *nms & pl* : eight hundred

ocio *nm* 1 : free time, leisure 2 INACTIVIDAD : idleness — **ociosidad** *nf* : idleness, inactivity — **ocioso, -sa** *adj* 1 : idle, inactive 2 INÚTIL : useless

ocre *adj & nm* : ocher

octágono *nm* : octagon — **octagonal** *adj* : octagonal

octava *nf* : octave

octavo, -va *adj & n* : eighth

octeto *nm* : byte

octogésimo, -ma *adj & n* : eightieth

octubre *nm* : October

ocular *adj* : ocular, eye — **oculista** *nmf* : ophthalmologist

ocultar *vt* : conceal, hide — **ocultarse** *vr* : hide — **oculto, -ta** *adj* : hidden, occult

ocupar *vt* 1 : occupy 2 : hold (a position, etc.) 3 : provide work for — **ocuparse** *vr* 1 ~ **de** : concern oneself with 2 ~ **de** : take care of (children, etc.) — **ocupación** *nf, pl* **-ciones** 1 : occupation 2 EMPLEO : job — **ocupado, -da** *adj* 1 : busy 2 : occupied (of a place) 3 señal de occupado : busy signal — **ocupante** *nmf* : occupant

ocurrir *vi* : occur, happen — **ocurrirse** *vr* ~ **a** : occur to — **ocurrencia** *nf* 1 : occurrence, event 2 SALIDA : witty remark, quip

oda *nf* : ode

odiar *vt* : hate — **odio** *nm* : hatred — **odioso, -sa** *adj* : hateful

odisea *nf* : odyssey

odontología *nf* : dentistry, dental surgery — **odontólogo, -ga** *n* : dentist, dental surgeon

oeste *nm* : west, western — ~ *nm* 1 : west 2 el Oeste : the West

ofender *v* : offend — **ofenderse** *vr* : take offense — **ofensa** *nf* : offense, insult — **ofensiva** *nf* : offensive — **ofensivo, -va** *adj* : offensive

oferta *nf* 1 : offer 2 **de** ~ : on sale 3 ~ **y demanda** : supply and demand

oficial *adj* : official — ~ *nmf* 1 : skilled worker 2 : officer (in the military)

oficina *nf* : office — **oficinista** *nmf* : office worker

oficio *nm* : trade, profession — **oficioso, -sa** *adj* : unofficial

ofrecer {53} *vt* 1 : offer 2 : provide, present (an opportunity, etc.) — **ofrecerse** *vr* : volunteer — **ofrecimiento** *nm* : offer

ofrenda *nf* : offering

oftalmología *nf* : ophthalmology — **oftalmólogo, -ga** *n* : ophthalmologist

ofuscar {72} *vt* 1 : blind, dazzle 2 CONFUNDIR : confuse — **ofuscarse** *vr* ~ **con** : be blinded by — **ofuscación** *nf, pl* **-ciones** 1 : blindness 2 CONFUSIÓN : confusion

ogro *nm* : ogre

oír {50} *vi* : hear — *vt* 1 : hear 2 ESCUCHAR : listen to 3 ¡oiga! *or* ¡oye! : excuse me!, listen! — **oídas: de** ~ *adv phr* : by hearsay — **oído** *nm* 1 : ear 2 : (sense of) hearing 3 duro de ~ : hard of hearing

ojal *nm* : buttonhole

ojalá *interj* : I hope so!, if only!

ojear *vt* : eye, look at — **ojeada** *nf* : glimpse, glance

ojeriza *nf* 1 : ill will 2 tener ~ **a** : have a grudge against

ojo *nm* 1 : eye 2 PERSPICACIA : shrewdness 3 : span (of a bridge) 4 ¡~! : look out!, pay attention!

ola *nf* : wave — **oleada** *nf* : wave, surge — **oleaje** *nm* : swell (of the sea)

olé *interj* : bravo!

oleada *nf* : wave, swell — **oleaje** *nm* : waves *pl*, surf

óleo *nm* 1 : oil 2 CUADRO : oil painting — **oleoducto** *nm* : oil pipeline

oler {51} *vt* : smell — *vi* 1 : smell 2 ~ **a** : smell of — **olerse** *vr fam* : have a hunch about

olfatear *vt* 1 : sniff 2 OLER : sense, sniff out — **olfato** *nm* 1 : sense of smell 2 PERSPICACIA : nose, instinct

Olimpíada *or* **Olimpíada** *nf* : Olympics *pl*, Olympic Games *pl* — **olímpico, -ca** *adj* : Olympic

oliva *nf* : olive — **olivo** *nm* : olive tree

olla *nf* 1 : pot 2 ~ **podrida** : (Spanish) stew

olmo *nm* : elm

olor *nm* : smell — **oloroso, -sa** *adj* : fragrant

olvidar *vt* 1 : forget 2 DEJAR : leave (behind) — **olvidarse** *vr* : forget — **olvidadizo, -za** *adj* : forgetful — **olvido** *nm* 1 : forgetfulness 2 DESCUIDO : oversight

ombligo *nm* : navel

omelette *nmf Lat* : omelet

ominoso, -sa *adj* : ominous

omitir *vt* : omit — **omisión** *nf, pl* -**siones** : omission

ómnibus *nm, pl* -**bus** *or* -**buses** : bus

omnipotente *adj* : omnipotent

omóplato *or* **omoplato** *nm* : shoulder blade

once *adj & nm* : eleven — **onceavo, -va** *adj & n* : eleventh

onda *nf* : wave — **ondear** *vi* : ripple — **ondulación** *nf, pl* -**ciones** : undulation — **ondulado, -da** *adj* : wavy — **ondular** *vt* : wave (hair) — *vi* : undulate, ripple

ónice *nmf or* **ónix** *nm* : onyx

onza *nf* : ounce

opaco, -ca *adj* 1 : opaque 2 DESLUSTRADO : dull

ópalo *nm* : opal

opción *nf, pl* -**ciones** : option — **opcional** *adj* : optional

ópera *nf* : opera

operar *vt* 1 : operate on 2 *Lat* : operate, run (a machine) — *vi* 1 : operate 2 NEGOCIAR : deal, do business — **operarse** *vr* 1 : have an operation 2 OCURRIR : take place — **operación** *nf, pl* -**ciones** 1 : operation 2 TRANSACCIÓN : transaction, deal — **operacional** *adj* : operational — **operador, -dora** *n* 1 : operator 2 : cameraman (for television, etc.)

opereta *nf* : operetta

opinar *vt* : think — *vi* : express an opinion — **opinión** *nf, pl* -**niones** : opinion

opio *nm* : opium

oponer {60} *vt* 1 : raise, put forward (arguments, etc.) 2 ~ **resistencia** : put up a fight — **oponerse** *vr* ~ **a** : oppose, be against — **oponente** *nmf* : opponent

oporto *nm* : port (wine)

oportunidad *nf* : opportunity — **oportunista** *nmf* : opportunist — **oportuno, -na** *adj* 1 : opportune, timely 2 APROPIADO : suitable

opositor, -tora *n* 1 : opponent 2 : candidate (for a position) — **oposición** *nf, pl* -**ciones** : opposition

oprimir *vt* 1 : press, squeeze 2 TIRANIZAR : oppress — **opresión** *nf, pl* -**siones** 1 : oppression 2 ~ **de pecho** : tightness in the chest — **opresivo, -va** *adj* : oppressive — **opresor, -sora** *n* : oppressor

optar *vi* 1 ~ **a** : apply for 2 ~ **por** : choose, opt for

óptica *nf* 1 : optics 2 : optician's (shop) — **óptico, -ca** *adj* : optical — ~ *n* : optician

optimismo *nm* : optimism — **optimista** *adj* : optimistic — ~ *nmf* : optimist

optometría *nf* : optometry — **optometrista** *nmf* : optometrist

opuesto *adj* 1 : opposite 2 CONTRADICTORIO : opposed, conflicting

opulencia *nf* : opulence — **opulento, -ta** *adj* : opulent

oración *nf, pl* -**ciones** 1 : prayer 2 FRASE : sentence, clause

oráculo *nm* : oracle

orador, -dora *n* : speaker

oral *adj* : oral

orar *vi* : pray

órbita *nf* 1 : orbit (in astronomy) 2 : eye socket — **orbitar** *vi* : orbit

orden *nm, pl* **órdenes** 1 : order 2 ~ **del día** : agenda (at a meeting) 3 ~ **público** : law and order — ~ *nf, pl* **órdenes** 1 : order (of food) 2 ~ **religiosa** : religious order 3 ~ **de compra** : purchase order

ordenador *nm Spain* : computer

ordenar *vt* 1 : order, command 2 ARREGLAR : put in order 3 : ordain (a priest) — **ordenanza** *nm* : orderly (in the armed forces) — ~ *nf* : ordinance, regulation

ordeñar *vt* : milk

ordinal *adj & nm* : ordinal

ordinario, -ria *adj* 1 : ordinary 2 GROSERO : common, vulgar

orear *vt* : air

orégano *nm* : oregano

oreja *nf* : ear

orfanato *or* **orfelinato** *nm* : orphanage

orfebre *nmf* : goldsmith, silversmith

orgánico, -ca *adj* : organic

organigrama *nm* : flowchart

organismo *nm* 1 : organism 2 ORGANIZACIÓN : agency, organization

organista *nmf* : organist

organizar {21} *vt* : organize — **organizarse** *vr* : get organized — **organización** *nf, pl* -**ciones** : organization — **organizador, -dora** *n* : organizer

órgano *nm* : organ

orgasmo *nm* : orgasm

orgía *nf* : orgy

orgullo *nm* : pride — **orgulloso, -sa** *adj* : proud

orientación *nf, pl* -**ciones** 1 : orientation 2 DIRECCIÓN : direction 3 CONSEJO : guidance

oriental *adj* 1 : eastern 2 : oriental — ~ *nmf* : Oriental

orientar *vt* 1 : orient, position 2 GUIAR : guide, direct — **orientarse** *vr* 1 : orient oneself 2 ~ **hacia** : turn towards

oriente *nm* **1** : east, East **2 el Oriente** : the Orient
orificio *nm* : orifice, opening
origen *nm, pl* **orígenes** : origin — **original** *adj & nm* : original — **originalidad** *nf* : originality — **originar** *vt* : give rise to — **originarse** *vr* : originate, arise — **originario, -ria** *adj* ~ **de** : native of
orilla *nf* **1** : border, edge **2** : bank (of a river), shore (of the sea)
orinar *vi* : urinate — **orina** *nf* : urine
oriol *nm* : oriole
oriundo, -da *adj* ~ **de** : native of
orla *nf* : border
ornamental *adj* : ornamental — **ornamento** *nm* : ornament
ornar *vt* : adorn
ornitología *nf* : ornithology
oro *nm* : gold
orquesta *nf* : orchestra — **orquestar** *vt* : orchestrate
orquídea *nf* : orchid
ortiga *nf* : nettle
ortodoxia *nf* : orthodoxy — **ortodoxo, -xa** *adj* : orthodox
ortografía *nf* : spelling
ortopedia *nf* : orthopedics — **ortopédico, -ca** *adj* : orthopedic
oruga *nf* : caterpillar
orzuelo *nm* : sty (in the eye)
os *pron pl Spain* **1** *(direct or indirect object)* : you, to you **2** *(reflexive)* : yourselves, to yourselves **3** : each other, to each other
osado, -da *adj* : bold, daring — **osadía** *nf* **1** : boldness, daring **2** DESCARO : audacity, nerve
osamenta *nf* : skeleton
osar *vi* : dare
oscilar *vi* **1** : swing, sway **2** FLUCTUAR : fluctuate — **oscilación** *nf, pl* **-ciones 1** : swinging **2** FLUCTUACIÓN : fluctuation
oscuro, -ra *adj* **1** : dark **2** : obscure (of ideas, persons, etc.) **3 a oscuras** : in the dark — **oscurecer** {53} *vt* **1** : darken **2** : confuse, cloud (the mind)

3 al ~ : at nightfall — *v impers* : get dark — **oscurecerse** *vr* : grow dark — **oscuridad** *nf* **1** : darkness **2** : obscurity (of ideas, persons, etc.)
óseo, ósea *adj* : skeletal, bony
oso, osa *n* **1** : bear **2** ~ **de peluche** *or* ~ **de felpa** : teddy bear
ostensible *adj* : evident, obvious
ostentar *vt* **1** : flaunt, display **2** POSEER : have, hold — **ostentación** *nf, pl* **-ciones** : ostentation — **ostentoso, -sa** *adj* : ostentatious, showy
osteopatía *n* : osteopathy — **osteópata** *nmf* : osteopath
osteoporosis *nf* : osteoporosis
ostra *nf* : oyster
ostracismo *nm* : ostracism
otear *vt* : scan, survey
otoño *nm* : autumn, fall — **otoñal** *adj* : autumn, fall
otorgar {52} *vt* **1** : grant, award **2** : draw up (a legal document)
otro, otra *adj* **1** : another, other **2 otra vez** : again — ~ *pron* **1** : another (one), other (one) **2 los otros, las otras** : the others, the rest
ovación *nf, pl* **-ciones** : ovation
óvalo *nm* : oval — **oval** *or* **ovalado, -da** *adj* : oval
ovario *nm* : ovary
oveja *nf* **1** : sheep, ewe **2** ~ **negra** : black sheep
overol *nm Lat* : overalls *pl*
ovillo *nm* **1** : ball (of yarn) **2 hacerse un** ~ : curl up (into a ball)
ovni *or* **OVNI** *nm (objeto volador no identificado)* : UFO
ovular *vi* : ovulate — **ovulación** *nf, pl* **-ciones** : ovulation
oxidar *vi* : rust — **oxidarse** *vr* : get rusty — **oxidación** *nf, pl* **-ciones** : rusting — **oxidado, -da** *adj* : rusty — **óxido** *nm* : rust
oxígeno *nm* : oxygen
oye → **oír**
oyente *nmf* **1** : listener **2** : auditor (student)
ozono *nm* : ozone

P

p *nf* : p, 17th letter of the Spanish alphabet
pabellón *nm, pl* **-llones 1** : pavilion **2** : block, building (in a hospital complex, etc.) **3** : summerhouse (in a garden, etc.) **4** BANDERA : flag

pabilo *nm* : wick
pacer {48} *v* : graze
paces → **paz**
paciencia *nf* : patience — **paciente** *adj & nmf* : patient
pacificar {72} *vt* : pacify, calm — **paci-**

ficarse *vr* : calm down — **pacífico, -ca** *adj* : peaceful, pacific — **pacifismo** *nm* : pacifism — **pacifista** *adj & nmf* : pacifist

pacotilla *nf de ~* : second-rate, trashy

pacto *nm* : pact, agreement — **pactar** *vt* : agree on — *vi* : come to an agreement

padecer {53} *vt* : suffer, endure — *vi ~ de* : suffer from — **padecimiento** *nm* : suffering

padre *nm* 1 : father 2 ~**s** *nmpl* : parents — ~ *adj Lat fam* : great, fantastic — **padrastro** *nm* : stepfather — **padrino** *nm* 1 : godfather 2 : best man (at a wedding)

padrón *nm, pl* -**drones** : register, roll

paella *nf* : paella

paga *nf* : pay, wages *pl* — **pagadero, -ra** *adj* : payable

pagano, -na *adj & n* : pagan, heathen

pagar {52} *vt* : pay, pay for — *vi* : pay — **pagaré** *nm* : IOU

página *nf* : page

pago *nm* : payment

país *nm* 1 : country, nation 2 REGIÓN : region, land — **paisaje** *nm* : scenery, landscape — **paisano, -na** *n* : compatriot

paja *nf* 1 : straw 2 *fam* : nonsense

pájaro *nm* 1 : bird 2 ~ **carpintero** : woodpecker — **pajarera** *nf* : aviary

pajita *nf* : (drinking) straw

pala *nf* 1 : shovel, spade 2 : blade (of an oar or a rotor) 3 : paddle, racket (in sports)

palabra *nf* 1 : word 2 HABLA : speech 3 **tener la** ~ : have the floor — **palabrota** *nf* : swearword

palacio *nm* 1 : palace, mansion 2 ~ **de justicia** : courthouse

paladar *nm* : palate — **paladear** *vt* : savor

palanca *nf* 1 : lever, crowbar 2 *fam* : leverage, influence 3 ~ **de cambio** *or* ~ **de velocidades** : gearshift

palangana *nf* : washbowl

palco *nm* : box (in a theater)

palestino, -na *adj* : Palestinian

paleta *nf* 1 : small shovel, trowel 2 : palette (in art) 3 : paddle (in sports, etc.)

paletilla *nf* : shoulder blade

paliar *vt* : alleviate, ease — **paliativo, -va** *adj* : palliative

pálido, -da *adj* : pale — **palidecer** {53} *vi* : turn pale — **palidez** *nf, pl* -**deces** : paleness, pallor

palillo *nm* 1 : small stick 2 *or* ~ **de dientes** : toothpick

paliza *nf* : beating

palma *nf* 1 : palm (of the hand) 2 : palm (tree or leaf) 3 **batir** ~**s** : clap, applaud — **palmada** *nf* 1 : pat, slap 2 ~**s** *nfpl* : clapping

palmera *nf* : palm tree

palmo *nm* 1 : span, small amount 2 ~ **a** ~ : bit by bit

palmotear *vi* : applaud — **palmoteo** *nm* : clapping, applause

palo *nm* 1 : stick 2 MANGO : shaft, handle 3 MÁSTIL : mast 4 POSTE : pole 5 GOLPE : blow 6 : suit (of cards)

paloma *nf* : pigeon, dove — **palomilla** *nf* : moth — **palomitas** *nfpl* : popcorn

palpar *vt* : feel, touch — **palpable** *adj* : palpable

palpitar *vi* : palpitate, throb — **palpitación** *nf, pl* -**ciones** : palpitation

palta *nf Lat* : avocado

paludismo *nm* : malaria

pampa *nf* : pampa

pan *nm* 1 : bread 2 : loaf (of bread, etc.) 3 ~ **tostado** : toast

pana *nf* : corduroy

panacea *nf* : panacea

panadería *nf* : bakery, bread shop — **panadero, -ra** *n* : baker

panal *nm* : honeycomb

panameño, -ña *adj* : Panamanian

pancarta *nf* : placard, banner

pancito *nm Lat* : (bread) roll

páncreas *nms & pl* : pancreas

panda *nmf* : panda

pandemonio *nm* : pandemonium

pandero *nm* : tambourine — **pandereta** *nf* : (small) tambourine

pandilla *nf* : gang

panecillo *nm Spain* : (bread) roll

panel *nm* : panel

panfleto *nm* : pamphlet

pánico *nm* : panic

panorama *nm* : panorama — **panorámico, -ca** *adj* : panoramic

panqueque *nm Lat* : pancake

pantaletas *nfpl Lat* : panties

pantalla *nf* 1 : screen 2 : lampshade

pantalón *nm, pl* -**lones** 1 *or* **pantalones** *nmpl* : pants *pl*, trousers *pl* 2 **pantalones vaqueros** : jeans

pantano *nm* 1 : swamp, marsh 2 EMBALSE : reservoir — **pantanoso, -sa** *adj* : marshy, swampy

pantera *nf* : panther

pantimedias *nfpl Lat* : panty hose

pantomima *nf* : pantomime

pantorrilla *nf* : calf (of the leg)

pantufla *nf* : slipper

panza *nf* : belly, paunch — **panzón, -zona** *adj, mpl* -**zones** : potbellied pañal *nm* : diaper

paño *nm* 1 : cloth 2 TRAPO : rag, dust cloth 3 ~ de cocina : dishcloth 4 ~ higiénico : sanitary napkin 5 ~s menores : underwear

pañuelo *nm* 1 : handkerchief 2 : scarf, kerchief

papa[1] *nm* : pope

papa[2] *nf Lat* 1 : potato 2 ~s fritas : potato chips, french fries

papá *nm fam* 1 : dad, pop 2 ~s *nmpl* : parents, folks

papada *nf* : double chin

papagayo *nm* : parrot

papal *adj* : papal

papalote *nm Lat* : kite

papanatas *nmfs & pl fam* : simpleton

papaya *nf* : papaya

papel *nm* 1 : paper, sheet of paper 2 : role, part (in theater, etc.) 3 ~ de aluminio : aluminum foil 4 ~ higiénico *or* ~ de baño : toilet paper 5 ~ de lija : sandpaper 6 ~ pintado : wallpaper — papeleo *nm* : paperwork, red tape — papelera *nf* : wastebasket — papelería *nf* : stationery store — papeleta *nf* 1 : ticket, slip 2 : ballot (paper)

paperas *nfpl* : mumps

papilla *nf* 1 : baby food, pap 2 hacer ~ : smash to bits

paquete *nm* 1 : package, parcel 2 : pack (of cigarettes, etc.)

paquistaní *adj* : Pakistani

par *nm* 1 : pair, couple 2 : par (in golf) 3 NOBLE : peer 4 abierto de ~ en ~ : wide open 5 sin ~ : without equal — ~ *adj* : even (in number) — ~ *nf* 1 : par 2 a la ~ que : at the same time as

para *prep* 1 : for 2 HACIA : towards 3 : (in order) to 4 : around, by (a time) 5 ~ adelante : forwards 6 ~ atrás : backwards 7 ~ que : so (that), in order that

parabienes *nmpl* : congratulations

parábola *nf* : parable

parabrisas *nms & pl* : windshield

paracaídas *nms & pl* : parachute — paracaidista *nmf* 1 : parachutist 2 : paratrooper (in the military)

parachoques *nms & pl* : bumper

parada *nf* 1 : stop 2 : (act of) stopping 3 DESFILE : parade — paradero *nm* 1 : whereabouts 2 *Lat* : bus stop — parado, -da *adj* 1 : idle, stopped 2 *Lat* : standing (up) 3 bien (mal) parado : in good (bad) shape

paradoja *nf* : paradox

parafernalia *nf* : paraphernalia

parafina *nf* : paraffin

parafrasear *vt* : paraphrase — paráfrasis *nfs & pl* : paraphrase

paraguas *nms & pl* : umbrella

paraguayo, -ya *adj* : Paraguayan

paraíso *nm* : paradise

paralelo, -la *adj* : parallel — paralelo *nm* : parallel — paralelismo *nm* : similarity

parálisis *nfs & pl* : paralysis — paralítico, -ca *adj* : paralytic — paralizar {21} *vt* : paralyze

parámetro *nm* : parameter

páramo *nm* : barren plateau

parangón *nm, pl* -gones 1 : comparison 2 sin ~ : matchless

paraninfo *nm* : auditorium, hall

paranoia *nf* : paranoia — paranoico, -ca *adj & n* : paranoid

parapeto *nm* : parapet, rampart

parapléjico, -ca *adj & n* : paraplegic

parar *vt* 1 : stop 2 *Lat* : stand, prop — *vi* 1 : stop 2 ir a ~ : end up, wind up — pararse *vr* 1 : stop 2 *Lat* : stand up

pararrayos *nms & pl* : lightning rod

parásito, -ta *adj* : parasitic — parásito *nm* : parasite

parasol *nm* : parasol

parcela *nf* : parcel, tract (of land) — parcelar *vt* : parcel (up)

parche *nm* : patch

parcial *adj* 1 : partial 2 a tiempo ~ : part-time — parcialidad *nf* : partiality, bias

parco, -ca *adj* : sparing, frugal

pardo, -da *adj* : brownish grey

parear *vt* : pair (up)

parecer {53} *vi* 1 : seem, look 2 ASEMEJARSE A : look like, seem like 3 me parece que : I think that, in my opinion 4 ¿qué te parece? : what do you think? 5 según parece : apparently — parecerse *vr* ~ a : resemble — ~ *nm* 1 : opinion 2 ASPECTO : appearance 3 al ~ : apparently — parecido, -da *adj* 1 : similar 2 bien parecido : good-looking — parecido *nm* : resemblance, similarity

pared *nf* : wall

parejo, -ja *adj* 1 : even, smooth 2 SEMEJANTE : similar — pareja *nf* 1 : couple, pair 2 : partner (dancing)

parentela *nf* : relatives *pl*, kin — parentesco *nm* : relationship, kinship

paréntesis *nms & pl* 1 : parenthesis 2 DIGRESIÓN : digression 3 entre ~ : by the way

paria *nmf* : outcast

paridad *nf* : equality

pariente *nmf* : relative, relation

parir *vi* : give birth, have a baby — *vt* : give birth to

parking *nm* : parking lot

parlamentar *vi* : discuss — **parlamentario, -ria** *adj* : parliamentary — ~ *n* : member of parliament — **parlamento** *nm* : parliament

parlanchín, -china *adj, mpl* **-chines** : talkative, chatty — ~ *n* : chatterbox

parlotear *vi fam* : chatter — **parloteo** *nm fam* : chatter

paro *nm* 1 : stoppage, shutdown 2 DESEMPLEO : unemployment 3 *Lat* : strike 4 ~ **cardíaco** : cardiac arrest

parodia *nf* : parody — **parodiar** *vt* : parody

párpado *nm* : eyelid — **parpadear** *vi* 1 : blink 2 : flicker (of light), twinkle (of stars) — **parpadeo** *nm* 1 : blink 2 : flicker (of light), twinkling (of stars)

parque *nm* 1 : park 2 ~ **de atracciones** : amusement park

parqué *nm* : parquet

parquear *vt Lat* : park

parquedad *nf* : frugality, moderation

parquímetro *nm* : parking meter

parra *nf* : grapevine

párrafo *nm* : paragraph

parranda *nf fam* : party, spree

parrilla *nf* 1 : broiler, grill 2 : grate (of a chimney, etc.) — **parrillada** *nf* : barbecue

párroco *nm* : parish priest — **parroquia** *nf* 1 : parish 2 : parish church — **parroquial** *adj* : parochial — **parroquiano, -na** *nm* 1 : parishioner 2 CLIENTE : customer

parsimonia *nf* 1 : calm 2 FRUGALIDAD : thrift — **parsimonioso, -sa** *adj* 1 : calm, unhurried 2 FRUGAL : thrifty

parte *nf* 1 : part 2 PORCIÓN : share 3 LADO : side 4 : party (in negotiations, etc.) 5 **de** ~ **de** : on behalf of 6 ¿**de** ~ **de quién?** : who is speaking? 7 **en alguna** ~ : somewhere 8 **en todas** ~**s** : everywhere 9 **tomar** ~ : take part — ~ *nm* 1 : report 2 ~ **meteorológico** : weather forecast

partero, -ra *n* : midwife

partición *nf, pl* **-ciones** : division, sharing

participar *vi* 1 : participate, take part 2 ~ **en** : have a share in — *vt* : notify — **participación** *nf, pl* **-ciones** 1 : participation 2 : share, interest (in a fund, etc.) 3 NOTICIA : notice — **participante** *adj* : participating — ~ *nmf* : participant — **participe** *nmf* : participant

participio *nm* : participle

partícula *nf* : particle

particular *adj* 1 : particular 2 PRIVADO : private — ~ *nm* 1 : matter 2 PERSONA : individual — **particularidad** *nf* : peculiarity — **particularizar** {21} *vt* : distinguish, characterize — *vi* : go into details

partir *vt* 1 : split, divide 2 ROMPER : break, crack 3 REPARTIR : share (out) — *vi* 1 : depart 2 ~ **de** : start from 3 **a** ~ **de** : as of, from — **partirse** *vr* 1 : split (open) 2 RAJARSE : crack — **partida** *nf* 1 : departure 2 : entry, item (in a register, etc.) 3 JUEGO : game 4 : group (of persons) 5 **mala** ~ : dirty trick 6 ~ **de nacimiento** : birth certificate — **partidario, -ria** *n* : follower, supporter — **partido** *nm* 1 : (political) party 2 : game, match (in sports) 3 PARTIDARIOS : following 4 **sacar** ~ **de** : make the most of

partitura *nf* : (musical) score

parto *nm* 1 : childbirth 2 **estar de** ~ : be in labor

parvulario *nm* : nursery school

pasa *nf* 1 : raisin 2 ~ **de Corinto** : currant

pasable *adj* : passable

pasada *nf* 1 : pass, wipe, coat (of paint, etc.) 2 **de** ~ : in passing 3 **mala** ~ : dirty trick — **pasadizo** *nm* : corridor — **pasado, -da** *adj* 1 : past 2 PODRIDO : bad, spoiled 3 ANTICUADO : out-of-date 4 **el año pasado** : last year — **pasado** *nm* : past

pasador *nm* 1 CERROJO : bolt 2 : barrette (for the hair)

pasaje *nm* 1 : passage 2 BILLETE : ticket, fare 3 PASILLO : passageway 4 PASAJEROS : passengers *pl* — **pasajero, -ra** *adj* : passing — ~ *n* : passenger

pasamanos *nms & pl* : handrail, banister

pasaporte *nm* : passport

pasar *vi* 1 : pass, go (by) 2 ENTRAR : come in 3 SUCEDER : happen 4 TERMINARSE : be over, end 5 ~ **de** : exceed 6 ¿**qué pasa?** : what's the matter? — *vt* 1 : pass 2 : spend (time) 3 CRUZAR : cross 4 TOLERAR : tolerate 5 SUFRIR : go through, suffer 6 : show (a movie, etc.) 7 **pasarlo bien** : have a good time 8 ~ **por alto** : overlook, omit — **pasarse** *vr* 1 : pass, go away 2 ESTROPEARSE : spoil, go bad 3 OLVIDARSE : slip one's mind 4 EXCEDERSE : go too far

pasarela *nf* 1 : footbridge 2 : gangway (on a ship)

pasatiempo *nm* : pastime, hobby

Pascua *nf* 1 : Easter (Christian feast) 2 : Passover (Jewish feast) 3 NAVIDAD : Christmas

pase *nm* : pass

pasear *vi* : take a walk, go for a ride — *vt* 1 : take for a walk 2 EXHIBIR : parade, show off — **pasearse** *vr* : go for a walk, go for a ride — **paseo** *nm* 1 : walk, ride 2 *Lat* : outing

pasillo *nm* : passage, corridor

pasión *nf*, *pl* **-siones** : passion

pasivo, -va *adj* : passive — **pasivo** *nm* : liabilities *pl*

pasmar *vt* : astonish, amaze — **pasmarse** *vr* : be astonished — **pasmado, -da** *adj* : stunned, flabbergasted — **pasmo** *nm* : astonishment — **pasmoso, -sa** *adj* : astonishing

paso¹, -sa *adj* : dried (of fruit)

paso² *nm* 1 : step 2 HUELLA : footprint 3 RITMO : pace 4 CRUCE : crossing 5 PASAJE : passage, way through 6 : (mountain) pass 7 **de ~** : in passing

pasta *nf* 1 : paste 2 MASA : dough 3 **or ~s** : pasta 4 **~ de dientes** *or* **~ dentífrica** : toothpaste

pastar *v* : graze

pastel *nm* 1 : cake 2 EMPANADA : pie 3 : pastel (crayon) — **pastelería** *nf* : pastry shop

pasteurizar {21} *vt* : pasteurize

pastilla *nf* 1 : pill, tablet 2 : bar (of chocolate, soap, etc.) 3 **~ para la tos** : lozenge, cough drop

pasto *nm* 1 : pasture 2 *Lat* : grass, lawn — **pastor, -tora** *n* 1 : shepherd 2 : pastor (in religion) — **pastoral** *adj* : pastoral

pata *nf* 1 : paw, leg (of an animal) 2 : foot, leg (of furniture) 3 **meter la ~** *fam* : put one's foot in it — **patada** *nf* 1 : kick 2 : stamp (of the foot) — **patalear** *vi* 1 : kick 2 : stamp (one's feet)

patata *nf* *Spain* : potato

patear *vt* : kick — *vi* 1 : kick 2 : stamp (one's feet)

patentar *vt* : patent — **patente** *adj* : obvious, patent — **~** *nf* : patent

paternal *adj* : fatherly, paternal — **paternidad** *nf* 1 : fatherhood 2 : paternity (in law) — **paterno, -na** *adj* : paternal

patético, -ca *adj* : pathetic, moving

patillas *nfpl* : sideburns

patinar *vi* 1 : skate 2 RESBALAR : slip, slide — **patín** *nm*, *pl* **-tines** : skate — **patinador, -dora** *n* : skater — **patinaje** *nm* : skating — **patinazo** *nm* 1 : skid 2 *fam* : blunder — **patinete** *nm* : scooter

patio *nm* 1 : courtyard, patio 2 *or* **~ de recreo** : playground

pato, -ta *n* 1 : duck 2 **pagar el pato** *fam* : take the blame — **patito, -ta** *n* : duckling

patología *nf* : pathology — **patológico, -ca** *adj* : pathological

patraña *nf* : hoax

patria *nf* : native land

patriarca *nm* : patriarch

patrimonio *nm* 1 : inheritance 2 : (historical or cultural) heritage

patriota *adj* : patriotic — **~** *nmf* : patriot — **patriótico, -ca** *adj* : patriotic — **patriotismo** *nm* : patriotism

patrocinador, -dora *n* : sponsor — **patrocinar** *vt* : sponsor — **patrocinio** *nm* : sponsorship

patrón, -trona *n*, *mpl* **-trones** 1 : patron 2 JEFE : boss 3 : landlord, landlady *f* (of a boarding house, etc.) — **patrón** *nm*, *pl* **-trones** : pattern (in sewing) — **patronato** *nm* 1 : patronage 2 FUNDACIÓN : foundation, trust

patrulla *nf* 1 : patrol 2 : (police) cruiser — **patrullar** *v* : patrol

paulatino, -na *adj* : gradual

pausa *nf* : pause, break — **pausado, -da** *adj* : slow, deliberate

pauta *nf* : guideline

pavimento *nm* : pavement — **pavimentar** *vt* : pave

pavo, -va *n* 1 : turkey 2 **pavo real** : peacock

pavonearse *vr* : strut, swagger

pavor *nm* : dread, terror — **pavoroso, -sa** *adj* : terrifying

payaso, -sa *n* : clown — **payasada** *nf* : antic, buffoonery — **payasear** *vi* *Lat* *fam* : clown (around)

paz *nf*, *pl* **paces** 1 : peace 2 **dejar en ~** : leave alone 3 **hacer las paces** : make up, reconcile

peaje *nm* : toll

peatón *nm*, *pl* **-tones** : pedestrian

peca *nf* : freckle

pecado *nm* : sin — **pecador, -dora** *adj* : sinful — **~** *n* : sinner — **pecaminoso, -sa** *adj* : sinful — **pecar** {72} *vi* : sin

pecera *nf* : fishbowl, fish tank

pecho *nm* 1 : chest 2 MAMA : breast 3 CORAZÓN : heart, courage 4 **dar el ~** : breast-feed 5 **tomar a ~** : take to heart — **pechuga** *nf* : breast (of fowl)

pecoso, -sa *adj* : freckled

pectoral *adj* : pectoral

peculiar *adj* 1 : particular 2 RARO : peculiar, odd — **peculiaridad** *nf* : peculiarity

pedagogía nf : education, pedagogy — **pedagogo, -ga** n : educator, teacher

pedal nm : pedal — **pedalear** vi : pedal

pedante adj : pedantic, pompous

pedazo nm 1 : piece, bit 2 **hacerse ~s** : fall to pieces

pedernal nm : flint

pedestal nm : pedestal

pediatra nmf : pediatrician

pedigrí nm : pedigree

pedir {54} vt 1 : ask for, request 2 : order (food, medicine, etc.) — vi 1 : ask 2 **~ prestado** : borrow — **pedido** nm 1 : order 2 **hacer un ~** : place an order

pedregoso, -sa adj : rocky, stony

pedrería nf : precious stones pl

pegar {52} vt 1 : stick, glue, paste 2 : sew on (a button, etc.) 3 JUNTAR : bring together 4 GOLPEAR : hit, strike 5 PROPINAR : deal (a blow, etc.) 6 : transmit (an illness) 7 **~ un grito** : let out a scream — vi 1 : adhere, stick 2 GOLPEAR : hit — **pegarse** vr 1 : hit oneself, hit each other 2 ADHERIRSE : stick, adhere 3 CONTAGIARSE : be transmitted — **pegadizo, -za** adj 1 : catchy 2 CONTAGIOSO : contagious — **pegajoso, -sa** adj 1 : sticky 2 Lat : catchy — **pegamento** nm : glue

peinar vt : comb — **peinarse** vr : comb one's hair — **peinado** nm : hairstyle, hairdo — **peine** nm : comb — **peineta** nf : ornamental comb

pelado, -da adj 1 : shorn, hairless 2 : peeled (of fruit, etc.) 3 fam : bare 4 fam : broke, penniless

pelaje nm : coat (of an animal), fur

pelar vt 1 : cut the hair of (a person) 2 MONDAR : peel (fruit) 3 : pluck (a chicken, etc.), skin (an animal) — **pelarse** vr 1 : peel 2 fam : get a haircut

peldaño nm 1 : step (of stairs) 2 : rung (of a ladder)

pelear vi 1 : fight 2 DISCUTIR : quarrel — **pelearse** vr : have a fight — **pelea** nf 1 : fight 2 DISCUSIÓN : quarrel

peletería nf : fur shop

peliagudo, -da adj : tricky, difficult

pelícano nm : pelican

película nf : movie, film

peligro nm 1 : danger 2 RIESGO : risk — **peligroso, -sa** adj : dangerous

pelirrojo, -ja adj : red-haired — **~** n : redhead

pellejo nm : skin, hide

pellizcar {72} vt : pinch — **pellizco** nm : pinch

pelo nm 1 : hair 2 : coat, fur (of an animal) 3 : pile, nap (of fabric) 4 **con ~s**

y **señales** : in great detail 5 **no tener ~ en la lengua** fam : not to mince words 6 **tomar el ~ a algn** fam : pull someone's leg — **pelón, -lona** adj fam, mpl **-lones** : bald

pelota nf : ball

pelotón nm, pl **-tones** : squad, detachment

peltre nm : pewter

peluca nf : wig

peluche nm 1 : plush 2 **oso de ~** : teddy bear

peludo, -da adj : hairy, furry

peluquería nf : hairdresser's, barber shop — **peluquero, -ra** n : barber, hairdresser

pelusa nf : fuzz, lint

pelvis nfs & pl : pelvis

pena nf 1 : penalty 2 TRISTEZA : sorrow 3 DOLOR : suffering, pain 4 Lat : embarrassment 5 **a duras ~s** : with great difficulty 6 **¡qué ~!** : what a shame! 7 **valer la ~** : be worthwhile

penacho nm 1 : crest, tuft 2 : plume (ornament)

penal adj : penal — **~** nm : prison, penitentiary — **penalidad** nf 1 : hardship 2 : penalty (in law) — **penalizar** {21} vt : penalize

penalty nm : penalty (in sports)

penar vt : punish — vi : suffer

pendenciero, -ra adj : quarrelsome

pender vi : hang — **pendiente** adj 1 : pending 2 **estar ~ de** : be watching out for — **~** nf : slope — **~** nm Spain : earring

pendón nm, pl **-dones** : banner

péndulo nm : pendulum

pene nm : penis

penetrar vi 1 : penetrate 2 **~ en** : go into — vt 1 : penetrate 2 : pierce (one's heart, etc.) 3 ENTENDER : fathom, grasp — **penetración** nf, pl **-ciones** 1 : penetration 2 PERSPICACIA : insight — **penetrante** adj 1 : penetrating 2 : sharp (of odors, etc.), piercing (of sounds) 3 : deep (of a wound, etc.)

penicilina nf : penicillin

península nf : peninsula — **peninsular** adj : peninsular

penitencia nf 1 : penitence 2 CASTIGO : penance — **penitenciaría** nf : penitentiary — **penitente** adj & nmf : penitent

penoso, -sa adj 1 : painful, distressing 2 TRABAJOSO : difficult 3 Lat : shy

pensar {55} vi 1 : think 2 **~ en** : think about — vt 1 : think 2 CONSIDERAR : think about 3 **~ hacer algo** : intend to do sth — **pensador, -dora** n

: thinker — **pensamiento** *nm* 1
: thought 2 : pansy (flower) — **pensativo, -va** *adj* : pensive, thoughtful
pensión *nf, pl* **-siones** 1 : boarding
house 2 : (retirement) pension 3 ∼ **alimenticia** : alimony — **pensionista**
nmf 1 : lodger 2 JUBILADO : retiree
pentágono *nm* : pentagon
pentagrama *nm* : staff (in music)
penúltimo, -ma *adj* : next to last, penul-
timate
penumbra *nf* : half-light
penuria *nf* : dearth, shortage
peña *nf* : rock, crag — **peñasco** *nm*
: crag, large rock — **peñón** *nm, pl*
-ñones : craggy rock
peón *nm, pl* **peones** 1 : laborer, peon 2
: pawn (in chess)
peonía *nf* : peony
peor *adv* 1 (*comparative of* **mal**)
: worse 2 (*superlative of* **mal**) : worst
— ∼ *adj* 1 (*comparative of* **malo**)
: worse 2 (*superlative of* **malo**) : worst
pepino *nm* : cucumber — **pepinillo** *nm*
: pickle, gherkin
pepita *nf* 1 : seed, pip 2 : nugget (of
gold, etc.)
pequeño, -ña *adj* : small, little — **pe-
queñez** *nf, pl* **-ñeces** 1 : smallness 2
NIMIEDAD : trifle
pera *nf* : pear — **peral** *nm* : pear tree
percance *nm* : mishap, setback
percatarse *vr* ∼ **de** : notice
percepción *nf, pl* **-ciones** : perception
— **perceptible** *adj* : perceptible
percha *nf* 1 : perch (for birds) 2 : (coat)
hanger 3 : coatrack (on a wall)
percibir *vt* 1 : perceive 2 : receive (a
salary, etc.)
percusión *nf, pl* **-siones** : percussion
perder {56} *vt* 1 : lose 2 : miss (an opportunity, etc.) 3 DESPERDICIAR : waste
(time) — *vi* 1 : lose — **perderse** *vr* 1
: get lost 2 DESAPARECER : disappear 3
DESPERDICIARSE : be wasted — **perdedor, -dora** *n* : loser — **pérdida** *nf* 1
: loss 2 ESCAPE : leak 3 ∼ **de tiempo**
: waste of time — **perdido, -da** *adj* 1
: lost 2 **un caso perdido** *fam* : a hopeless case
perdigón *nm, pl* **-gones** : shot, pellet
perdiz *nf, pl* **-dices** : partridge
perdón *nm, pl* **-dones** : forgiveness,
pardon — **perdón** *interj* : sorry! —
perdonar *vt* 1 DISCULPAR : forgive 2
: pardon (in law)
perdurar *vi* : last, endure — **per-
durable** *adj* : lasting
perecer {53} *vi* : perish, die — **perecedero, -ra** *adj* : perishable

peregrinación *nf, pl* **-ciones** *or* **pere-
grinaje** *nm* : pilgrimage — **peregrino, -na** *adj* 1 RARO : unusual, odd — ∼ *n* : pilgrim
perejil *nm* : parsley
perenne *adj* & *nm* : perennial
pereza *nf* : laziness — **perezoso, -sa**
adj : lazy
perfección *nf, pl* **-ciones** : perfection
— **perfeccionar** *vt* 1 : perfect 2 MEJO-
RAR : improve — **perfeccionista** *nmf*
: perfectionist — **perfecto, -ta** *adj*
: perfect
perfidia *nf* : treachery — **pérfido, -da**
adj : treacherous
perfil *nm* 1 : profile 2 CONTORNO : outline 3 ∼**es** *nmpl* RASGOS : features —
perfilar *vt* : outline — **perfilarse** *vr* 1
: be outlined 2 CONCRETARSE : take
shape
perforar *vt* 1 : perforate 2 : drill, bore (a
hole) — **perforación** *nf, pl* **-ciones**
: perforation — **perforadora** *nf*
: (paper) punch
perfume *nm* : perfume, scent — **per-
fumar** *vt* : perfume — **perfumarse** *vr*
: put perfume on
pergamino *nm* : parchment
pericia *nf* : skill
periferia *nf* : periphery, outskirts (of a
city, etc.) — **periférico, -ca** *adj* : peripheral
perilla *nf* 1 : goatee 2 *Lat* : knob 3 **venir
de** ∼**s** *fam* : come in handy
perímetro *nm* : perimeter
periódico, -ca *adj* : periodic — **periódico** *nm* : newspaper — **periodismo** *nm* : journalism — **periodista** *nmf*
: journalist
período *or* **periodo** *nm* : period
periquito *nm* : parakeet
periscopio *nm* : periscope
perito, -ta *adj* & *n* : expert
perjudicar {72} *vt* : harm, damage —
perjudicial *adj* : harmful — **perjuicio**
nm 1 : harm, damage 2 **en** ∼ **de** : to
the detriment of
perjurar *vi* : perjure oneself — **perjurio**
nm : perjury
perla *nf* 1 : pearl 2 **de** ∼**s** *fam* : great,
just fine
permanecer {53} *vi* : remain — **permanencia** *nf* 1 : permanence 2 : stay,
staying (in a place) — **permanente**
adj : permanent — ∼ *nf* : permanent
(wave)
permeable *adj* : permeable
permitir *vt* 1 : permit, allow 2 ¿**me per-
mite?** : may I? — **permitirse** *vr*
: allow oneself — **permisible** *adj*

: permissible, allowable — **permisivo, -va** *adj* : permissive — **permiso** *nm* **1** : permission **2** : permit, license (document) **3** : leave (in the military) **4 con ~** : excuse me

permuta *nf* : exchange

pernicioso, -sa *adj* : pernicious, destructive

pero *conj* : but — **~** *nm* **1** : fault **2** REPARO : objection

perorar *vi* : make a speech — **perorata** *nf* : (long-winded) speech

perpendicular *adj & nf* : perpendicular

perpetrar *vt* : perpetrate

perpetuar {3} *vt* : perpetuate — **perpetuo, -tua** *adj* : perpetual

perplejo, -ja *adj* : perplexed — **perplejidad** *nf* : perplexity

perro, -rra *n* **1** : dog, bitch *f* **2 perro caliente** : hot dog — **perrera** *nf* : kennel

perseguir {75} *vt* **1** : pursue, chase **2** ACOSAR : persecute — **persecución** *nf, pl* **-ciones 1** : pursuit, chase **2** ACOSO : persecution

perseverar *vi* : persevere — **perseverancia** *nf* : perseverance

persiana *nf* : (venetian) blind

persistir *vi* : persist — **persistencia** *nf* : persistence — **persistente** *adj* : persistent

persona *nf* : person — **personaje** *nm* **1** : character (in literature, etc.) **2** : important person, celebrity — **personal** *adj* : personal — **~** *nm* : personnel, staff — **personalidad** *nf* : personality — **personificar** {72} *vi* : personify

perspectiva *nf* **1** : perspective **2** VISTA : view **3** POSIBILIDAD : prospect, outlook

perspicacia *nf* : shrewdness, insight — **perspicaz** *adj, pl* **-caces** : shrewd, discerning

persuadir *vt* : persuade — **persuadirse** *vr* : become convinced — **persuasión** *nf, pl* **-siones** : persuasion — **persuasivo, -va** *adj* : persuasive

pertenecer {53} *vi* **~ a** : belong to — **perteneciente** *adj* **~ a** : belonging to — **pertenencia** *nf* **1** : ownership **2 ~s** *nfpl* : belongings

pertinaz *adj, pl* **-naces 1** OBSTINADO : obstinate **2** PERSISTENTE : persistent

pertinente *adj* : pertinent, relevant — **pertinencia** *nf* : relevance

perturbar *vt* : disturb — **perturbación** *nf, pl* **-ciones** : disturbance

peruano, -na *adj* : Peruvian

pervertir {76} *vt* : pervert — **perversión** *nf, pl* **-siones** : perversion —

perverso, -sa *adj* : perverse — **pervertido, -da** *adj* : perverted, depraved — **~** *n* : pervert

pesa *nf* **1** : weight **2 ~s** : weights (in sports) — **pesadez** *nf, pl* **-deces 1** : heaviness **2** *fam* : tediousness, drag

pesadilla *nf* : nightmare

pesado, -da *adj* **1** : heavy **2** LENTO : sluggish **3** MOLESTO : annoying **4** ABURRIDO : tedious **5** DURO : tough, difficult — **~** *n fam* : bore, pest — **pesadumbre** *nf* : grief, sorrow

pésame *nm* : condolences *pl*

pesar *vt* : weigh — *vi* **1** : weigh, be heavy **2** INFLUIR : carry weight **3 pese a** : despite — **~** *nm* **1** : sorrow, grief **2** REMORDIMIENTO : remorse **3 a ~ de** : in spite of

pescado *nm* : fish — **pesca** *nf* **1** : fishing **2** PECES : fish *pl*, catch **3 ir de ~** : go fishing — **pescadería** *nf* : fish market — **pescador, -dora** *n, mpl* **-dores** : fisherman — **pescar** {72} *vt* **1** : fish for **2** *fam* : catch (a cold, etc.) **3** *fam* : catch hold of, nab — *vi* : fish

pescuezo *nm* : neck (of an animal)

pese a → pesar

pesebre *nm* : manger

pesero *nm Lat* : minibus

peseta *nf* : peseta

pesimismo *nm* : pessimism — **pesimista** *adj* : pessimistic — **~** *nmf* : pessimist

pésimo, -ma *adj* : awful

peso *nm* **1** : weight **2** CARGA : burden **3** : peso (currency) **4 ~ pesado** : heavyweight

pesquero, -ra *adj* : fishing

pesquisa *nf* : inquiry

pestaña *nf* : eyelash — **pestañear** *vi* : blink — **pestañeo** *nm* : blink

peste *nm* **1** : plague **2** *fam* : stench, stink **3** *Lat fam* : cold, bug — **pesticida** *nm* : pesticide — **pestilencia** *nf* **1** : stench **2** PLAGA : pestilence

pestillo *nm* : bolt, latch

petaca *nf Lat* : suitcase

pétalo *nm* : petal

petardo *nm* : firecracker

petición *nf, pl* **-ciones** : petition, request

petirrojo *nm* : robin

petrificar {72} *vt* : petrify

petróleo *nm* : oil, petroleum — **petrolero, -ra** *adj* : oil — **petrolero** *nm* : oil tanker

petulante *adj* : insolent, arrogant

peyorativo, -va *adj* : pejorative

pez *nm, pl* **peces 1** : fish **2 ~ de col-**

ores : goldfish **3** ~ **espada** : swordfish **4** ~ **gordo** *fam* : big shot

pezón *nm, pl* **-zones** : nipple

pezuña *nf* : hoof

piadoso, -sa *adj* **1** : compassionate **2** DEVOTO : pious, devout

piano *nm* : piano — **pianista** *nmf* : pianist, piano player

piar {85} *vi* : chirp, tweet

pibe, -ba *n Lat fam* : kid, child

pica *nf* **1** : pike, lance **2** : spade (in playing cards)

picado, -da *adj* **1** : perforated **2** : minced, chopped (of meat, etc.) **3** : decayed (of teeth) **4** : choppy (of the sea) **5** *fam* : annoyed — **picada** *nf* **1** : bite, sting **2** *Lat* : sharp descent — **picadillo** *nm* : minced meat — **picadura** *nf* **1** : sting, bite **2** : (moth) hole

picante *adj* : hot, spicy

picaporte *nm* **1** : door handle **2** ALDABA : door knocker **3** PESTILLO : latch

picar {72} *vt* **1** : sting, bite **2** : peck at, nibble on (food) **3** PERFORAR : prick, puncture **4** TRITURAR : chop, mince — *vi* **1** : bite, take the bait **2** ESCOCER : sting, itch **3** COMER : nibble **4** : be spicy (of food) — **picarse** *vr* **1** : get a cavity **2** ENFADARSE : take offense

picardía *nf* **1** : craftiness **2** TRAVESURA : prank — **picaresco, -ca** *adj* **1** : picaresque **2** TRAVIESO : roguish — **pícaro, -ra** *adj* **1** : mischievous **2** MALICIOSO : villainous — ~ *n* : rascal, scoundrel

picazón *nf, pl* **-zones** : itch

pichón, -chona *n, mpl* **-chones** : (young) pigeon

picnic *nm, pl* **-nics** : picnic

pico *nm* **1** : beak **2** CIMA : peak **3** PUNTA : (sharp) point **4** : pick, pickax (tool) **5 las siete y** ~ : a little after seven — **picotazo** *nm* : peck — **picotear** *vt* : peck — *vi fam* : nibble, pick — **picudo, -da** *adj* : pointy

pie *nm* **1** : foot (in anatomy) **2** : base, bottom, stem **3 al** ~ **de la letra** : word for word **4 dar** ~ **a** : give rise to **5 de** ~ : standing (up) **6 de** ~**s a cabeza** : from top to bottom

piedad *nf* **1** : pity, mercy **2** DEVOCIÓN : piety

piedra *nf* **1** : stone **2** : flint (of a lighter) **3** GRANIZO : hailstone **4** ~ **angular** : cornerstone **5** → **pómez**

piel *nf* **1** : skin **2** CUERO : leather **3** PELO : fur, pelt

pienso *nm* : feed, fodder

pierna *nf* : leg

pieza *nf* **1** : piece, part **2** *or* ~ **de teatro** : play **3** HABITACIÓN : room

pigmento *nm* : pigment — **pigmentación** *nf, pl* **-ciones** : pigmentation

pigmeo, -mea *adj* : pygmy

pijama *nm* : pajamas *pl*

pila *nf* **1** : battery **2** MONTÓN : pile **3** FREGADERO : sink **4** : basin (of a fountain, etc.)

pilar *nm* : pillar

píldora *nf* : pill

pillar *vt* **1** : catch **2** : get (a joke, etc.) — **pillaje** *nm* : pillage — **pillo, -lla** *adj* : crafty — ~ *n* : rascal, scoundrel

piloto *nmf* : pilot — **pilotar** *vt* : pilot

pimienta *nf* : pepper (condiment) — **pimiento** *nm* : pepper (fruit) — **pimentero** *nm* : pepper shaker — **pimentón** *nm, pl* **-tones 1** : paprika **2** : cayenne pepper

pináculo *nm* : pinnacle

pincel *nm* : paintbrush

pinchar *vt* **1** : pierce, prick **2** : puncture (a tire, etc.) **3** INCITAR : goad — **pinchazo** *nm* **1** : prick **2** : puncture (of a tire, etc.)

pingüino *nm* : penguin

pino *nm* : pine (tree)

pintar *v* : paint — **pintarse** *vr* : put on makeup — **pinta** *nf* **1** : spot **2** : pint (measure) **3** *fam* : appearance — **pintada** *nf* : graffiti — **pinto, -ta** *adj* : speckled, spotted — **pintor, -tora** *n, mpl* **-tores** : painter — **pintoresco, -ca** *adj* : picturesque, quaint — **pintura** *nf* **1** : paint **2** CUADRO : painting

pinza *nf* **1** : clothespin **2** : claw, pincer (of a crab, etc.) **3** ~**s** *nfpl* : tweezers

pinzón *nm, pl* **-zones** : finch

piña *nf* **1** : pine cone **2** ANANÁS : pineapple

piñata *nf* : piñata

piñón *nm, pl* **-ñones** : pine nut

pío¹, pía *adj* **1** : pious **2** : piebald (of a horse)

pío² *nm* : peep, chirp

piojo *nm* : louse

pionero, -ra *n* : pioneer

pipa *nf* **1** : pipe (for smoking) **2** *Spain* : seed, pip

pique *nm* **1** : grudge **2** RIVALIDAD : rivalry **3 irse a** ~ : sink, founder

piqueta *nf* : pickax

piquete *nm* : picket (line) — **piquetear** *v* : picket

piragua *nf* : canoe

pirámide *nf* : pyramid

piraña *nf* : piranha

pirata *adj* : bootleg, pirated — ~ *nmf* : pirate — **piratear** *vt* **1** : bootleg, pirate **2** : hack into (a computer)

piropo *nm* : (flirtatious) compliment
pirueta *nf* : pirouette
pirulí *nm* : (cone-shaped) lollipop
pisada *nf* 1 : footstep 2 HUELLA : footprint
pisapapeles *nms & pl* : paperweight
pisar *vt* 1 : step on 2 HUMILLAR : walk all over, abuse — *vi* : step, tread
piscina *nf* 1 : swimming pool 2 : (fish) pond
piso *nm* 1 : floor, story 2 *Lat* : floor (of a room) 3 *Spain* : apartment
pisotear *vt* : trample (on)
pista *nf* 1 : trail, track 2 INDICIO : clue 3 ~ de aterrizaje : runway, airstrip 4 ~ de baile : dance floor 5 ~ de hielo : ice-skating rink
pistacho *nm* : pistachio
pistola *nf* 1 : pistol, gun 2 PULVER-IZADOR : spray gun — **pistolera** *nf* : holster — **pistolero** *nm* : gunman
pistón *nm, pl* **-tones** : piston
pito *nm* 1 SILBATO : whistle 2 CLAXON : horn — **pitar** *vi* 1 : blow a whistle 2 : beep, honk (of a horn) — *vt* : whistle at — **pitido** *nm* 1 : whistle, whistling 2 : beep (of a horn) — **pitillo** *nm fam* : cigarette
pitón *nm, pl* **-tones** *nm* : python
pitorro *nm* : spout
pivote *nm* : pivot
piyama *nmf Lat* : pajamas *pl*
pizarra *nf* 1 : slate 2 ENCERADO : blackboard — **pizarrón** *nm, pl* **-rrones** *Lat* : blackboard
pizca *nf* 1 : pinch (of salt) 2 ÁPICE : speck, tiny bit 3 *Lat* : harvest
pizza ['pitsa, 'pisa] *nf* : pizza — **pizzería** *nf* : pizzeria
placa *nf* 1 : sheet, plate 2 INSCRIPCIÓN : plaque 3 : (police) badge
placenta *nf* : placenta
placer {57} *vt* : please — ~ *nm* : pleasure — **placentero, -ra** *adj* : pleasant, agreeable
plácido, -da *adj* : placid, calm
plaga *nf* 1 : plague 2 CALAMIDAD : disaster — **plagar** {52} *vt* : plague, infest
plagiar *vt* : plagiarize — **plagio** *nm* : plagiarism
plan *nm* 1 : plan 2 **en ~ de** : as 3 **no te pongas en ese ~** *fam* : don't be that way
plana *nf* 1 : page 2 **en primera ~** : on the front page
plancha *nf* 1 : iron (for ironing) 2 : grill (for cooking) 3 LÁMINA : sheet, plate — **planchar** *v* : iron — **planchado** *nm* : ironing

planear *vt* : plan — *vi* : glide — **planeador** *nm* : glider
planeta *nm* : planet
planicie *nf* : plain
planificar {72} *vt* : plan — **planificación** *nf, pl* **-ciones** : planning
planilla *nf Lat* : list, roster
plano, -na *adj* : flat — **plano** *nm* 1 : map, plan 2 : plane (surface) 3 NIVEL : level 4 **de ~** : flatly, outright 5 **primer ~** : foreground, close-up (in photography)
planta *nf* 1 : plant 2 PISO : floor, story 3 : sole (of the foot) — **plantación** *nf, pl* **-ciones** 1 : plantation 2 : (action of) planting — **plantar** *vt* 1 : plant 2 *fam* : deal, land — **plantarse** *vr* : stand firm
plantear *vt* 1 : expound, set forth 2 : raise (a question) 3 CAUSAR : create, pose (a problem) — **plantearse** *vr* : think about, consider
plantel *nm* 1 : staff, team 2 *Lat* : educational institution
plantilla *nf* 1 : insole 2 PATRÓN : pattern, template 3 : staff (of a business, etc.)
plasma *nm* : plasma
plástico, -ca *adj* : plastic — **plástico** *nm* : plastic
plata *nf* 1 : silver 2 *Lat fam* : money 3 ~ **de ley** : sterling silver
plataforma *nf* 1 : platform 2 ~ **petrolífera** : oil rig 3 ~ **de lanzamiento** : launching pad
plátano *nm* 1 : banana 2 : plantain
platea *nf* : orchestra, pit (in a theater)
plateado, -da *adj* 1 : silver, silvery (color) 2 : silver-plated
platicar {72} *vi* : talk, chat — **plática** *nf* : chat, conversation
platija *nf* : flatfish, flounder
platillo *nm* 1 : saucer 2 CÍMBALO : cymbal 3 *Lat* : dish, course
platino *nm* : platinum
plato *nm* 1 : plate, dish 2 : course (of a meal) 3 ~ **principal** : entrée
platónico, -ca *adj* : platonic
playa *nf* 1 : beach, seashore 2 ~ **de estacionamiento** *Lat* : parking lot
plaza *nf* 1 : square, plaza 2 : seat (in transportation) 3 PUESTO : post, position 4 MERCADO : market, marketplace 5 ~ **de toros** : bullring
plazo *nm* 1 : period, term 2 PAGO : installment 3 **a largo ~** : long-term
plazoleta *or* **plazuela** *nf* : small square
pleamar *nf* : high tide
plebe *nf* : common people — **plebeyo, -ya** *adj & nm* : plebeian
plegar {49} *vt* : fold, bend — **plegarse** *vr* 1 : give in, yield 2 : jackknife (of a

truck) — **plegable** or **plegadizo, -za**
adj : folding, collapsible
plegaria *nf* : prayer
pleito *nm* 1 : lawsuit 2 *Lat* : dispute, fight
plenilunio *nm* : full moon
pleno, -na *adj* 1 : full, complete 2 **en
plena forma** : in top form 3 **en pleno
día** : in broad daylight — **plenitud** *nf*
: fullness, abundance
pleuresía *nf* : pleurisy
pliego *nm* 1 : sheet (of paper) — **pliegue**
nm 1 : crease, fold 2 : pleat (in fabric)
plisar *vt* : pleat
plomería *nf Lat* : plumbing — **plomero, -ra** *n Lat* : plumber
plomo *nm* 1 : lead 2 FUSIBLE : fuse
pluma *nf* 1 : feather 2 : (fountain) pen
— **plumaje** *nm* : plumage — **plumero**
nm : feather duster — **plumilla** *nf* : nib
— **plumón** *nm, pl* **-mones** : down
plural *adj & nm* : plural — **pluralidad**
nf : plurality
pluriempleo *nm* **hacer ~** : have more
than one job
plus *nm* : bonus
plusvalía *nf* : appreciation, capital gain
plutocracia *nf* : plutocracy
Plutón *nm* : Pluto
plutonio *nm* : plutonium
pluvial *adj* : rain
poblar {19} *vt* 1 : settle, colonize 2
HABITAR : inhabit — **poblarse** *vr* : become crowded — **población** *nf, pl*
-ciones 1 : city, town, village 2 HABI-
TANTES : population — **poblado, -da**
adj 1 : populated 2 : thick, bushy (of a
beard, eyebrows, etc.) — **poblado** *nm*
: village
pobre *adj* 1 : poor 2 **¡~ de mí!** : poor
me! — **~** *nmf* 1 : poor person 2 **los
~s** : the poor 3 **¡pobre!** : poor thing!
— **pobreza** *nf* : poverty
pocilga *nf* : pigsty
poción *nf, pl* **-ciones** or **pócima** *nf*
: potion
poco, -ca *adj* 1 : little, not much, (a)
few 2 **pocas veces** : rarely — **~**
pron 1 : little, few 2 **hace poco** : not
long ago 3 **poco a poco** : bit by bit,
gradually 4 **por poco** : nearly, just
about 5 **un poco** : a little, a bit —
poco *adv* : little, not much
podar *vt* : prune
poder {58} *v aux* 1 : be able to, can
2 (*expressing possibility*) : might, may
3 (*expressing permission*) : can, may
4 **¿cómo puede ser?** : how can it be?
5 **¿puedo pasar?** : may I come in? —
vi 1 : be possible 2 **~ con** : cope
with, manage 3 **no puedo más** : I've

had enough — **~** *nm* 1 : power 2 PO-
SESIÓN : possession — **poderío** *nm*
: power — **poderoso, -sa** *adj* : powerful
podólogo, -ga *n* : chiropodist
podrido, -da *adj* : rotten
poema *nm* : poem — **poesía** *nf* 1 : poetry 2 POEMA : poem — **poeta** *nmf*
: poet — **poético, -ca** *adj* : poetic
póker *nm → **póquer**
polaco, -ca *adj* : Polish
polar *adj* : polar — **polarizar** {21} *vt*
: polarize
polea *nf* : pulley
polémica *nf* : controversy — **polémico, -ca** *adj* : controversial — **polemi-
zar** *vt* : argue
polen *nm, pl* **pólenes** : pollen
policía *nf* : police — **~** *nmf* : police officer, policeman *m*, policewoman *f* —
policíaco, -ca *adj* 1 : police 2 **novela
policíaca** : detective story
poliéster *nm* : polyester
poligamia *nf* : polygamy — **polígamo,
-ma** *n* : polygamist
polígono *nm* : polygon
polilla *nf* : moth
polio or **poliomielitis** *nf* : polio, poliomyelitis
politécnico, -ca *adj* : polytechnic
política *nf* 1 : politics 2 POSTURA : policy — **político, -ca** *adj* 1 : political 2
hermano político : brother-in-law —
~ *n* : politician
póliza *nf* or **~ de seguros** : insurance
policy
polizón *nm, pl* **-zones** : stowaway
pollo, -lla *n* 1 : chicken, chick 2 : chick-
en (for cooking) — **pollera** *nf Lat*
: skirt — **pollería** *nf* : poultry shop —
pollito, -ta *n* : chick
polo *nm* 1 : pole 2 : polo (sport) 3 **~
norte** : North Pole
poltrona *nf* : easy chair
polución *nf, pl* **-ciones** : pollution
polvo *nm* 1 : powder 2 SUCIEDAD : dust
3 **~s** *nmpl* : face powder 4 **hacer ~**
fam : crush, shatter — **polvareda** *nf*
: cloud of dust — **polvera** *nf* : compact (for powder) — **pólvora** *nf* : gun-
powder — **polvoriento, -ta** *adj* : dusty
pomada *nf* : ointment
pomelo *nm* : grapefruit
pómez *nm* or **piedra ~** *nf* : pumice
pomo *nm* : knob, doorknob
pompa *nf* 1 : (soap) bubble 2 ESPLEN-
DOR : pomp 3 **~s fúnebres** : funeral
— **pomposo, -sa** *adj* 1 : pompous 2
ESPLÉNDIDO : splendid
pómulo *nm* : cheekbone

ponchar *vt Lat* : puncture — **poncha-**
dura *nf Lat* : puncture
ponche *nm* : punch (drink)
poncho *nm* : poncho
ponderar *vt* **1** : consider **2** ALABAR
: speak highly of
poner {60} *vt* **1** : put **2** AGREGAR : add **3**
CONTRIBUIR : contribute **4** SUPONER
: suppose **5** DISPONER : arrange, set out
6 : give (a name), call **7** ENCENDER
: turn on **8** ESTABLECER : set up, establish **9** : lay (eggs) — *vi* : lay eggs —
ponerse *vr* **1** : move (into a position)
2 : put on (clothing, etc.) **3** : set (of the
sun) **4 ~ furioso** : become angry
poniente *nm* **1** OCCIDENTE : west **2**
: west wind
pontífice *nm* : pontiff
pontón *nm, pl* **-tones** : pontoon
ponzoña *nf* : poison, venom
popa *nf* **1** : stern **2 a ~** : astern
popelín *nm, pl* **-lines** : poplin
popote *nm Lat* : (drinking) straw
populacho *nm* : rabble, masses *pl*
popular *adj* **1** : popular **2** : colloquial (of
language) — **popularidad** *nf* : popu-
larity — **popularizar** {21} *vt* : popularize — **populoso, -sa** *adj* : populous
póquer *nm* : poker (card game)
por *prep* **1** : for **2** (*indicating an ap-*
proximate time) : around, during **3** (*in-*
dicating an approximate place)
: around, about **4** A TRAVÉS DE
: through, along **5** A CAUSA DE : because of **6** (*indicating rate or ratio*)
: per **7** *or* **~ medio de** : by means of
8 : times (in mathematics) **9** SEGÚN
: as for, according to **10 estar ~** : be
about to **11 ~ ciento** : percent **12 ~**
favor : please **13 ~ lo tanto** : therefore **14 ¿por qué?** : why?
porcelana *nf* : porcelain, china
porcentaje *nm* : percentage
porción *nf, pl* **-ciones** : portion, piece
pordiosero, -ra *n* : beggar
porfiar {85} *vi* : insist — **porfiado, -da**
adj : obstinate, persistent
pormenor *nm* : detail
pornografía *nf* : pornography —
pornográfico, -ca *adj* : pornographic
poro *nm* : pore — **poroso, -sa** *adj*
: porous
poroto *nm Lat* : bean
porque *conj* **1** : because **2** *or* **por que**
: in order that — **porqué** *nm* : reason
porquería *nf* **1** SUCIEDAD : filth **2** : shoddy thing, junk
porra *nf* : nightstick, club — **porrazo**
nm : blow, whack

portaaviones *nms & pl* : aircraft carrier
portada *nf* **1** : facade **2** : title page (of a
book), cover (of a magazine)
portador, -dora *n* : bearer
portaequipajes *nms & pl* : luggage rack
portafolio *or* **portafolios** *nm, pl* **-lios 1**
: portfolio **2** MALETÍN : briefcase
portal *nm* **1** : doorway **2** VESTÍBULO
: hall, vestibule
portamonedas *nms & pl* : purse
portar *vt* : carry, bear — **portarse** *vr*
: behave
portátil *adj* : portable
portaviones *nm → **portaaviones**
portavoz *nmf, pl* **-voces** : spokesper-
son, spokesman *m*, spokeswoman *f*
portazo *nm* **dar un ~** : slam the door
porte *nm* **1** : transport, freight **2** ASPEC-
TO : bearing, appearance **3 ~ pagado**
: postage paid
portento *nm* : marvel, wonder — **por-**
tentoso, -sa *adj* : marvelous
porteño, -ña *adj* : of or from Buenos
Aires
portería *nf* **1** : superintendent's office **2**
: goal, goalposts *pl* (in sports) —
portero, -ra *n* **1** : goalkeeper, goalie **2**
CONSERJE : janitor, superintendent
portezuela *nf* : door (of an automobile)
pórtico *nm* : portico
portilla *nf* : porthole
portugués, -guesa *adj, mpl* **-gueses**
: Portuguese — **portugués** *nm* : Portuguese (language)
porvenir *nm* : future
pos: en ~ de *adv phr* : in pursuit of
posada *nf* : inn
posaderas *nfpl fam* : backside, bottom
posar *vi* : pose — *vt* : place, lay —
posarse *vr* : settle, rest
posavasos *nms & pl* : coaster
posdata *nf* : postscript
pose *nf* : pose
poseer {20} *vt* : possess, own —
poseedor, -dora *n* : possessor, owner
— **poseído, -da** *adj* : possessed —
posesión *nf, pl* **-siones** : possession
— **posesionarse** *vr* **~ de** : take possession of, take over — **posesivo, -va**
adj : possessive
posguerra *nf* : postwar period
posibilidad *nf* : possibility — **posibili-**
tar *vt* : make possible — **posible** *adj* **1**
: possible **2 de ser ~** : if possible
posición *nf, pl* **-ciones** : position —
posicionar *vt* : position — **posi-**
cionarse *vr* : take a stand
positivo, -va *adj* : positive
poso *nm* : sediment, (coffee) grounds

posponer {60} *vt* **1** : postpone **2** RELE-GAR : put behind, subordinate
postal *adj* : postal — ~ *nf* : postcard
postdata → **posdata**
poste *nm* : post, pole
póster *nm, pl* **-ters** : poster
postergar {52} *vt* **1** : pass over **2** APLAZAR : postpone
posteridad *nf* : posterity — **posterior** *adj* **1** : later, subsequent **2** TRASERO : back, rear — **posteriormente** *adv* : subsequently, later
postigo *nm* **1** : small door **2** CONTRA-VENTANA : shutter
postizo, -za *adj* : artificial, false
postrarse *vr* : prostrate oneself — **postrado, -da** *adj* : prostrate
postre *nm* : dessert
postular *vt* **1** : advance, propose **2** *Lat* : nominate — **postulado** *nm* : postulate
póstumo, -ma *adj* : posthumous
postura *nf* : position, stance
potable *adj* : drinkable, potable
potaje *nm* : thick vegetable soup
potasio *nm* : potassium
pote *nm* : jar
potencia *nf* : power — **potencial** *adj & nm* : potential — **potente** *adj* : powerful
potro, -tra *n* : colt *m*, filly *f* — **potro** *nm* : horse (in gymnastics)
pozo *nm* **1** : well **2** : shaft (in a mine)
práctica *nf* **1** : practice **2 en la ~** : in practice — **practicable** *adj* : practicable, feasible — **practicante** *adj* : practicing — ~ *nmf* : practitioner — **practicar** {72} *vt* **1** : practice **2** RE-ALIZAR : perform, carry out — *vi* : practice — **práctico, -ca** *adj* : practical
pradera *nf* : grassland, prairie — **prado** *nm* : meadow
pragmático, -ca *adj* : pragmatic
preámbulo *nm* : preamble
precario, -ria *adj* : precarious
precaución *nf, pl* **-ciones 1** : precaution **2** PRUDENCIA : caution, care **3 con ~** : cautiously
precaver *vt* : guard against — **precavido, -da** *adj* : prudent, cautious
preceder *v* : precede — **precedencia** *nf* : precedence, priority — **precedente** *adj* : preceding, previous — ~ *nm* : precedent
precepto *nm* : precept
preciado, -da *adj* : prized, valuable — **preciarse** *vr* ~ **de** : pride oneself on, boast about
precinto *nm* : seal

precio *nm* : price, cost — **preciosidad** *nf* **1** VALOR : value **2** : beautiful thing — **precioso, -sa** *adj* **1** HERMOSO : beautiful **2** VALIOSO : precious
precipicio *nm* : precipice
precipitar *vt* **1** : hasten, speed up **2** AR-ROJAR : hurl — **precipitarse** *vr* **1** APRESURARSE : rush **2** : act rashly **3** AR-ROJARSE : throw oneself — **precipitación** *nf, pl* **-ciones 1** : precipitation **2** PRISA : haste — **precipitadamente** *adv* : in a rush, hastily — **precipitado, -da** *adj* : hasty
preciso, -sa *adj* **1** : precise **2** NECESARIO : necessary — **precisamente** *adv* : precisely, exactly — **precisar** *vt* **1** : specify, determine **2** NECESITAR : require — **precisión** *nf, pl* **-siones 1** : precision **2** NECESIDAD : necessity
preconcebido *adj* : preconceived
precoz *adj, pl* **-coces 1** : early **2** : precocious (of children)
precursor, -sora *n* : forerunner
predecesor, -sora *n* : predecessor
predecir {11} *vt* : foretell, predict
predestinado, -da *adj* : predestined
predeterminar *vt* : predetermine
prédica *nf* : sermon
predicado *nm* : predicate
predicar {72} *v* : preach — **predicador, -dora** *n* : preacher
predicción *nf, pl* **-ciones 1** : prediction **2** PRONÓSTICO : forecast
predilección *nf, pl* **-ciones** : preference — **predilecto, -ta** *adj* : favorite
predisponer {60} *vt* : predispose — **predisposición** *nf, pl* **-ciones** : predisposition
predominar *vi* : predominate — **predominante** *adj* : predominant, prevailing — **predominio** *nm* : predominance
preeminente *adj* : preeminent
prefabricado, -da *adj* : prefabricated
prefacio *nm* : preface
preferir {76} *vt* : prefer — **preferencia** *nf* **1** : preference **2 de ~** : preferably — **preferente** *adj* : preferential — **preferible** *adj* : preferable — **preferido, -da** *adj* : favorite
prefijo *nm* **1** : prefix **2** *Spain* : area code
pregonar *vt* : proclaim, announce
pregunta *nf* **1** : question **2 hacer ~s** : ask questions — **preguntar** *v* : ask — **preguntarse** *vr* : wonder
prehistórico, -ca *adj* : prehistoric
prejuicio *nm* : prejudice
preliminar *adj & nm* : preliminary
preludio *nm* : prelude
prematrimonial *adj* : premarital

prematuro, -ra *adj* : premature

premeditar *vt* : premeditate — **premeditación** *nf, pl* **-ciones** : premeditation

premenstrual *adj* : premenstrual

premio *nm* 1 : prize 2 RECOMPENSA : reward 3 ~ **gordo** : jackpot — **premiado, -da** *adj* : prizewinning — **premiar** *vt* 1 : award a prize to 2 RECOMPENSAR : reward

premisa *nf* : premise

premonición *nf, pl* **-ciones** : premonition

premura *nf* : haste, urgency

prenatal *adj* : prenatal

prenda *nf* 1 : piece of clothing 2 GARANTÍA : pledge 3 : forfeit (in a game) — **prendar** *vt* : captivate — **prendarse** *vr* ~ **de** : fall in love with

prender *vt* 1 SUJETAR : pin, fasten 2 APRESAR : capture 3 : light (a match, etc.) 4 *Lat* : turn on (a light, etc.) — *vi* 1 : take root 2 ARDER : catch, burn (of fire) — **prenderse** *vr* : catch fire — **prendedor** *nm Lat* : brooch, pin

prensa *nf* : press — **prensar** *vt* : press

preñado, -da *adj* 1 : pregnant 2 ~ **de** : filled with

preocupar *vt* : worry — **preocuparse** *vr* 1 : worry 2 ~ **de** : take care of — **preocupación** *nf, pl* **-ciones** : worry

preparar *vt* : prepare — **prepararse** *vr* : get ready — **preparación** *nf, pl* **-ciones** : preparation — **preparado, -da** *adj* : prepared, ready — **preparado** *nm* : preparation — **preparativo, -va** *adj* : preparatory, preliminary — **preparativos** *nmpl* : preparations — **preparatorio, -ria** *adj* : preparatory

preposición *nf, pl* **-ciones** : preposition

prepotente *adj* : arrogant, domineering

prerrogativa *nf* : prerogative

presa *nf* 1 : catch, prey 2 DIQUE : dam 3 hacer ~ **en** : seize

presagiar *vt* : presage, forebode — **presagio** *nm* 1 : omen 2 PREMONICIÓN : premonition

presbítero *nm* : presbyter, priest

prescindir *vi* ~ **de** 1 : do without 2 OMITIR : dispense with

prescribir {33} *vt* : prescribe — **prescripción** *nf, pl* **-ciones** : prescription

presencia *nf* 1 : presence 2 ASPECTO : appearance — **presenciar** *vt* : be present at, witness

presentar *vt* 1 : present 2 OFRECER : offer, give 3 MOSTRAR : show 4 : introduce (persons) — **presentarse** *vr* 1 : show up 2 : arise, come up (of a problem, etc.) 3 : introduce oneself — **presentación** *nf, pl* **-ciones** 1 : presentation 2 : introduction (of persons) 3 ASPECTO : appearance — **presentador, -dora** *n* : presenter, host (of a television program, etc.)

presente *adj* 1 : present 2 **tener** ~ : keep in mind — ~ *nm* 1 : present 2 **entre los** ~**s** : among those present

presentir {76} *vt* : have a presentiment of — **presentimiento** *nm* : premonition

preservar *vt* : preserve, protect — **preservación** *nf, pl* **-ciones** : preservation — **preservativo** *nm* : condom

presidente, -ta *n* 1 : president 2 : chair, chairperson (of a meeting) — **presidencia** *nf* 1 : presidency 2 : chairmanship (of a meeting) — **presidencial** *adj* : presidential

presidio *nm* : prison — **presidiario, -ria** *n* : convict

presidir *vt* 1 : preside over, chair 2 PREDOMINAR : dominate

presión *nf, pl* **-siones** 1 : pressure 2 ~ **arterial** : blood pressure 3 **hacer** ~ : press — **presionar** *vt* 1 : press 2 COACCIONAR : put pressure on

preso, -sa *adj* : imprisoned — ~ *n* : prisoner

prestar *vt* 1 : lend, loan 2 : give (aid) 3 ~ **atención** : pay attention — **prestado, -da** *adj* 1 : borrowed, on loan 2 **pedir** ~ : borrow — **prestamista** *nmf* : moneylender — **préstamo** *nm* : loan

prestidigitación *nf, pl* **-ciones** : sleight of hand — **prestidigitador, -dora** *n* : magician

prestigio *nm* : prestige — **prestigioso, -sa** *adj* : prestigious

presto, -ta *adj* : prompt, ready — **presto** *adv* : promptly, right away

presumir *vt* : presume — *vi* : boast, show off — **presumido, -da** *adj* : conceited, vain — **presunción** *nf, pl* **-ciones** 1 : presumption 2 VANIDAD : vanity — **presunto, -ta** *adj* : presumed, alleged — **presuntuoso, -sa** *adj* : conceited

presuponer {60} *vt* : presuppose — **presupuesto** *nm* 1 : budget, estimate 2 SUPUESTO : assumption

presuroso, -sa *adj* : hasty, quick

pretender *vt* 1 : try to 2 AFIRMAR : claim 3 CORTEJAR : court, woo 4 ~ **que** : expect — **pretencioso, -sa** *adj* : pretentious — **pretendido** *adj* : supposed — **pretendiente** *nmf* 1 : candidate 2 : pretender (to a throne) — ~

nm : suitor — **pretensión** *nf, pl* **-siones** 1 INTENCIÓN : intention, aspiration 2 : claim (to a throne, etc.) 3 **pretensiones** *nfpl* : pretensions

pretérito *nm* : past (in grammar)

pretexto *nm* : pretext, excuse

prevalecer {53} *vi* : prevail — **prevaleciente** *adj* : prevailing, prevalent

prevenir {87} *vt* 1 : prevent 2 AVISAR : warn — **prevenirse** {87} *vr* ~ **contra** *or* ~ **de** : take precautions against — **prevención** *nf, pl* **-ciones** 1 : prevention 2 PRECAUCIÓN : precaution 3 PREJUICIO : prejudice — **prevenido, -da** *adj* 1 : prepared, ready 2 PRECAVIDO : cautious — **preventivo, -va** *adj* : preventive

prever {88} *vt* 1 : foresee 2 PLANEAR : plan

previo, -via *adj* : previous, prior

previsible *adj* : foreseeable — **previsión** *nf, pl* **-siones** 1 : foresight 2 PREDICCIÓN : prediction, forecast — **previsor, -sora** *adj* : farsighted, prudent

prieto, -ta *adj* 1 CEÑIDO : tight 2 *Lat fam* : dark-skinned

prima *nf* 1 : bonus 2 : (insurance) premium 3 → **primo**

primario, -ria *adj* 1 : primary 2 **escuela primaria** : elementary school

primate *nm* : primate

primavera *nf* 1 : spring (season) 2 : primrose (flower) — **primaveral** *adj* : spring

primero, -ra *adj* (**primer** *before masculine singular nouns*) 1 : first 2 MEJOR : top, leading 3 PRINCIPAL : main, basic 4 **de primera** : first-rate — ~ *n* : first (person or thing) — **primero** *adv* 1 : first 2 MÁS BIEN : rather, sooner

primitivo, -va *adj* : primitive

primo, -ma *n* : cousin

primogénito, -ta *adj & n* : firstborn

primor *nm* : beautiful thing

primordial *adj* : basic, fundamental

primoroso, -sa *adj* 1 : exquisite, fine 2 HÁBIL : skillful

princesa *nf* : princess

principado *nm* : principality

principal *adj* : main, principal

príncipe *nm* : prince

principio *nm* 1 : principle 2 COMIENZO : beginning, start 3 ORIGEN : origin 4 **al** ~ : at first 5 **a** ~**s de** : at the beginning of — **principiante** *nmf* : beginner

pringar {52} *vt* : spatter (with grease) — **pringoso, -sa** *adj* : greasy

prioridad *nf* : priority

prisa *nf* 1 : hurry, rush 2 **a** ~ *or* **de** ~

: quickly 3 **a toda** ~ : as fast as possible 4 **darse** ~ : hurry 5 **tener** ~ : be in a hurry

prisión *nf, pl* **-siones** 1 : prison 2 ENCARCELAMIENTO : imprisonment — **prisionero, -ra** *n* : prisoner

prisma *nm* : prism — **prismáticos** *nmpl* : binoculars

privar *vt* 1 : deprive 2 PROHIBIR : forbid 3 *Lat* : knock out — **privarse** *vr* : deprive oneself — **privación** *nf, pl* **-ciones** : deprivation — **privado, -da** *adj* : private — **privativo, -va** *adj* : exclusive

privilegio *nm* : privilege — **privilegiado, -da** *adj* : privileged

pro *prep* : for, in favor of — ~ *nm* 1 : pro, advantage 2 **en** ~ **de** : for, in support of 3 **los pros y los contras** : the pros and cons

proa *nf* : bow, prow

probabilidad *nf* : probability — **probable** *adj* : probable, likely — **probablemente** *adv* : probably

probar {19} *vt* 1 : try, test 2 : try on (clothing) 3 DEMOSTRAR : prove 4 DEGUSTAR : taste — *vi* : try — **probarse** *vr* : try on (clothing) — **probeta** *nf* : test tube

problema *nm* : problem — **problemático, -ca** *adj* : problematic

proceder *vi* 1 : proceed, act 2 : be appropriate 3 ~ **de** : come from — **procedencia** *nf* : origin — **procedente** *adj* ~ **de** : coming from, originating in — **procedimiento** *nm* 1 : procedure, method 2 : proceedings *pl* (in law)

procesar *vt* 1 : prosecute 2 : process (data) — **procesador** *nm* ~ **de textos** : word processor — **procesamiento** *nm* : processing — **procesión** *nf, pl* **-siones** : procession — **proceso** *nm* 1 : process 2 : trial, proceedings *pl* (in law)

proclamar *vt* : proclaim — **proclama** *nf* : proclamation — **proclamación** *nf, pl* **-ciones** : proclamation

procrear *vi* : procreate — **procreación** *nf, pl* **-ciones** : procreation

procurar *vt* 1 : try, endeavor 2 CONSEGUIR : obtain, procure — **procurador, -dora** *n* : attorney

prodigar {52} *vt* : lavish — **prodigio** *nm* : wonder, prodigy — **prodigioso, -sa** *adj* : prodigious

pródigo, -ga *adj* : extravagant, prodigal

producir {61} *vt* 1 : produce 2 CAUSAR : cause 3 : yield, bear (interest, fruit, etc.) — **producirse** *vr* : take place —

producción *nf, pl* **-ciones** : production — **productividad** *nf* : productivity — **productivo, -va** *adj* : productive — **producto** *nm* : product — **productor, -tora** *n* : producer
proeza *nf* : exploit
profanar *vt* : profane, desecrate — **profanación** *nf, pl* **-ciones** : desecration — **profano, -na** *adj* : profane
profecía *nf* : prophecy
proferir {76} *vt* **1** : utter **2** : hurl (insults)
profesar *vt* **1** : profess **2** : practice (a profession, etc.) — **profesión** *nf, pl* **-siones** : profession — **profesional** *adj & nmf* : professional — **profesor, -sora** *n* **1** : teacher **2** : professor (at a university, etc.) — **profesorado** *nm* **1** : teaching profession **2** PROFESORES : faculty
profeta *nm* : prophet — **profético, -ca** *adj* : prophetic — **profetisa** *nf* : (female) prophet — **profetizar** {21} *vt* : prophesy
prófugo, -ga *adj & n* : fugitive
profundo, -da *adj* **1** HONDO : deep **2** : profound (of thoughts, etc.) — **profundamente** *adv* : deeply, profoundly — **profundidad** *nf* : depth — **profundizar** {21} *vt* : study in depth
profuso, -sa *adj* : profuse — **profusión** *nf, pl* **-siones** : profusion
progenie *nf* : progeny, offspring
programa *nm* **1** : program **2** : curriculum (in education) — **programación** *nf, pl* **-ciones** : programming — **programador, -dora** *n* : programmer — **programar** *vt* **1** : schedule **2** : program (a computer, etc.)
progreso *nm* : progress — **progresar** *vi* : (make) progress — **progresión** *nf, pl* **-ciones** : progression — **progresista** *adj & nmf* : progressive — **progresivo, -va** *adj* : progressive, gradual
prohibir {62} *vt* : prohibit, forbid — **prohibición** *nf, pl* **-ciones** : ban, prohibition — **prohibido, -da** *adj* : forbidden — **prohibitivo, -va** *adj* : prohibitive
prójimo *nm* : neighbor, fellow man
prole *nf* : offspring
proletariado *nm* : proletariat — **proletario, -ria** *adj & n* : proletarian
proliferar *vi* : proliferate — **proliferación** *nf, pl* **-ciones** : proliferation — **prolífico, -ca** *adj* : prolific
prolijo, -ja *adj* : wordy, long-winded
prólogo *nm* : prologue, foreword
prolongar {52} *vt* **1** : prolong **2** ALARGAR : lengthen — **prolongarse** *vr* : last, continue — **prolongación** *nf, pl* **-ciones** : extension

promedio *nm* : average
promesa *nf* : promise — **prometedor, -dora** *adj* : promising, hopeful — **prometer** *vt* : promise — *vi* : show promise — **prometerse** *vr* : get engaged — **prometido, -da** *adj* : engaged — *~ n* : fiancé *m*, fiancée *f*
prominente *adj* : prominent — **prominencia** *nf* : prominence
promiscuo, -cua *adj* : promiscuous — **promiscuidad** *nf* : promiscuity
promocionar *vt* : promote — **promoción** *nf, pl* **-ciones** : promotion
promontorio *nm* : promontory
promover {47} *vt* **1** : promote **2** CAUSAR : cause — **promotor, -tora** *n* : promoter
promulgar {52} *vt* **1** : proclaim **2** : enact (a law)
pronombre *nm* : pronoun
pronosticar {72} *vt* : predict, forecast — **pronóstico** *nm* **1** : prediction, forecast **2** : (medical) prognosis
pronto, -ta *adj* **1** : quick, prompt **2** PREPARADO : ready — **pronto** *adv* **1** : soon **2** RAPIDAMENTE : quickly, promptly **3 de ~** : suddenly **4 por lo ~** : for the time being **5 tan ~ como** : as soon as
pronunciar *vt* **1** : pronounce **2** : give, deliver (a speech) — **pronunciarse** *vr* **1** : declare oneself **2** SUBLEVARSE : revolt — **pronunciación** *nf, pl* **-ciones** : pronunciation
propagación *nf, pl* **-ciones** : propagation
propaganda *nf* **1** : propaganda **2** PUBLICIDAD : advertising
propagar {52} *vt* : propagate, spread — **propagarse** *vr* : propagate
propano *nm* : propane
propasarse *vr* : go too far
propensión *nf, pl* **-siones** : inclination, propensity — **propenso, -sa** *adj* : prone, inclined
propiamente *adv* : exactly
propicio, -cia *adj* : favorable, propitious
propiedad *nf* **1** : property **2** PERTINENCIA : ownership, possession — **propietario, -ria** *n* : owner, proprietor
propina *nf* : tip
propinar *vt* : give, deal (a blow, etc.)
propio, -pia *adj* **1** : own **2** APROPIADO : proper, appropriate **3** CARACTERÍSTICO : characteristic, typical **4** MISMO : himself, herself, oneself
proponer {60} *vt* **1** : propose **2** : nominate (a person) — **proponerse** *vr* : propose, intend

proporción *nf, pl* **-ciones** : proportion — **proporcionado, -da** *adj* : proportionate — **proporcional** *adj* : proportional — **proporcionar** *vt* **1** : provide **2** AJUSTAR : adapt, proportion

proposición *nf, pl* **-ciones** : proposal, proposition

propósito *nm* **1** : purpose, intention **2 a ~** : incidentally, by the way **3 a ~** : on purpose, intentionally

propuesta *nf* **1** : proposal **2** : offer (of employment, etc.)

propulsar *vt* **1** : propel, drive **2** PROMOVER : promote — **propulsión** *nf, pl* **-siones** : propulsion

prorrogar {52} *vt* **1** : extend **2** APLAZAR : postpone — **prórroga** *nf* **1** : extension, deferment **2** : overtime (in sports)

prorrumpir *vi* : burst forth, break out

prosa *nf* : prose

proscribir {33} *vt* **1** : prohibit, ban **2** DESTERRAR : exile — **proscripción** *nf, pl* **-ciones** **1** : ban **2** DESTIERRO : banishment — **proscrito, -ta** *adj* : banned — **~** *n* : exile, outlaw

proseguir {75} *v* : continue — **prosecución** *nf, pl* **-ciones** : continuation

prospección *nf, pl* **-ciones** : prospecting, exploration

prospecto *nm* : prospectus

prosperar *vi* : prosper, thrive — **prosperidad** *nf* : prosperity — **próspero, -ra** *adj* : prosperous, flourishing

prostituir {41} *vt* : prostitute — **prostitución** *nf, pl* **-ciones** : prostitution — **prostituta** *nf* : prostitute

protagonista *nmf* : protagonist — **protagonizar** *vt* : star in

proteger {15} *vt* : protect — **protegerse** *vr* : protect oneself — **protección** *nf, pl* **-ciones** : protection — **protector, -tora** *adj* : protective — **~** *n* : protector — **protegido, -da** *n* : protégé

proteína *nf* : protein

protestar *v* : protest — **protesta** *nf* : protest — **protestante** *adj & nmf* : Protestant

protocolo *nm* : protocol

prototipo *nm* : prototype

protuberancia *nf* : protuberance — **protuberante** *adj* : protuberant

provecho *nm* **1** : benefit, advantage **2 ¡buen ~!** : enjoy your meal! — **provechoso, -sa** *adj* : profitable, beneficial

proveer {63} *vt* : provide, supply — **proveedor, -dora** *n* : supplier

provenir {87} *vi* **~ de** : come from

proverbio *nm* : proverb — **proverbial** *adj* : proverbial

providencia *nf* **1** : providence **2** PRE-

CAUCIÓN : precaution — **providencial** *adj* : providential

provincia *nf* : province — **provincial** *adj* : provincial — **provinciano, -na** *adj* : provincial, parochial

provisión *nf, pl* **-siones** : provision — **provisional** *adj* : provisional

provocar {72} *vt* **1** : provoke, cause **2** IRRITAR : irritate — **provocación** *nf, pl* **-ciones** : provocation — **provocativo, -va** *adj* : provocative

próximo, -ma *adj* **1** CERCANO : near **2** SIGUIENTE : next — **próximamente** *adv* : shortly, soon — **proximidad** *nf* **1** : proximity **2 ~es** *nfpl* : vicinity

proyectar *vt* **1** : plan **2** LANZAR : throw, hurl **3** : cast (light) **4** : show (a film) — **proyección** *nf, pl* **-ciones** : projection — **proyectil** *nm* : missile — **proyecto** *nm* : plan, project — **proyector** *nm* : projector

prudencia *nf* : prudence, care — **prudente** *adj* : prudent, sensible

prueba *nf* **1** : proof, evidence **2** : test (in education, medicine, etc.) **3** : event (in sports) **4 a ~ de agua** : waterproof

psicoanálisis *nm* : psychoanalysis — **psicoanalista** *nmf* : psychoanalyst — **psicoanalizar** {21} *vt* : psychoanalyze

psicología *nf* : psychology — **psicológico, -ca** *adj* : psychological — **psicólogo, -ga** *n* : psychologist

psicópata *nmf* : psychopath

psicosis *nfs & pl* : psychosis

psicoterapia *nf* : psychotherapy — **psicoterapeuta** *nmf* : psychotherapist

psicótico, -ca *adj & n* : psychotic

psiquiatría *nf* : psychiatry — **psiquiatra** *nmf* : psychiatrist — **psiquiátrico, -ca** *adj* : psychiatric

psíquico, -ca *adj* : psychic

púa *nf* **1** : sharp point **2** : tooth (of a comb) **3** : thorn (of a plant), quill (of a porcupine, etc.) **4** : (guitar) pick

pubertad *nf* : puberty

publicar {72} *vt* **1** : publish **2** DIVULGAR : divulge, disclose — **publicación** *nf, pl* **-ciones** : publication

publicidad *nf* **1** : publicity **2** : advertising (in marketing) — **publicista** *nmf* : publicist — **publicitar** *vt* **1** : publicize **2** : advertise (a product, etc.) — **publicitario, -ria** *adj* : advertising

público, -ca *adj* : public — **público** *nm* **1** : public **2** : audience (of theater, etc.), spectators *pl* (of sports)

puchero *nm* **1** : (cooking) pot **2** GUISADO : stew **3 hacer ~s** : pout

púdico, -ca *adj* : modest

pudiente *adj* : wealthy

pudín *nm, pl* **-dines** : pudding
pudor *nm* : modesty — **pudoroso, -sa** *adj* : modest
pudrir {59} *vt* 1 : rot 2 *fam* : annoy — **pudrirse** *vr* : rot
pueblo *nm* 1 : town, village 2 NACIÓN : people, nation
puente *nm* 1 : bridge 2 **hacer ~** : have a long weekend 3 **~ levadizo** : drawbridge
puerco, -ca *n* 1 : pig 2 **puerco espín** : porcupine — **~** *adj* : dirty, filthy
pueril *adj* : childish
puerro *nm* : leek
puerta *nf* 1 : door, gate 2 **a ~ cerrada** : behind closed doors
puerto *nm* 1 : port 2 : (mountain) pass 3 REFUGIO : haven
puertorriqueño, -ña *adj* : Puerto Rican
pues *conj* 1 : since, because 2 POR LO TANTO : so, therefore 3 (*used interjectionally*) : well, then
puesta *nf* 1 **~ a punto** : tune-up 2 **~ de sol** : sunset 3 **~ en marcha** : starting up — **puesto, -ta** *adj* 1 : put, set 2 VESTIDO : dressed — **puesto** *nm* 1 : place 2 EMPLEO : position, job 3 : stand, stall (in a market) 4 **~ avanzado** : outpost — **~ que** *conj* : since, given that
púgil *nm* : boxer
pugnar *vi* : fight — **pugna** *nf* : fight, battle
pulcro, -cra *adj* : tidy, neat
pulga *nf* 1 : flea 2 **tener malas ~s** : have a bad temper
pulgada *nf* : inch — **pulgar** *nm* 1 : thumb 2 : big toe
pulir *vt* 1 : polish 2 REFINAR : touch up, perfect
pulla *nf* : cutting remark, gibe
pulmón *nm, pl* **-mones** : lung — **pulmonar** *adj* : pulmonary — **pulmonía** *nf* : pneumonia
pulpa *nf* : pulp
pulpería *nf Lat* : grocery store
púlpito *nm* : pulpit
pulpo *nm* : octopus
pulsar *vt* 1 : press (a button), strike (a key) 2 : play (music) — **pulsación** *nf, pl* **-ciones** 1 : beat, throb 2 : keystroke (on a typewriter, etc.)
pulsera *nf* : bracelet
pulso *nm* 1 : pulse 2 : steadiness (of hand)
pulular *vi* : swarm
pulverizar {21} *vt* 1 : pulverize, crush 2 : spray (a liquid) — **pulverizador** *nm* : atomizer, spray
puma *nf* : puma
punitivo, -va *adj* : punitive
punta *nf* 1 : tip, end 2 : point (of a nee-

dle, etc.) 3 **~ del dedo** : fingertip 4 **sacar ~ a** : sharpen
puntada *nf* 1 : stitch 2 **~s** *nfpl* : seam
puntal *nm* : prop, support
puntapié *nm* : kick
puntear *vt* : pluck (a guitar)
puntería *nf* : aim, marksmanship
puntiagudo, -da *adj* : sharp, pointed
puntilla *nf* 1 : lace edging 2 **de ~s** : on tiptoe
punto *nm* 1 : dot, point 2 : period (in punctuation) 3 ASUNTO : item, question 4 LUGAR : spot, place 5 MOMENTO : moment 6 : point (in a score) 7 PUNTADA : stitch 8 **a las dos en ~** : at two o'clock sharp 9 **dos ~s** : colon 10 **hasta cierto ~** : up to a point 11 **~ de partida** : starting point 12 **~ muerto** : deadlock 13 **~ y coma** : semicolon
puntuación *nf, pl* **-ciones** 1 : punctuation 2 : scoring, score (in sports)
puntual *adj* 1 : prompt, punctual 2 EXACTO : accurate, detailed — **puntualidad** *nf* 1 : punctuality 2 EXACTITUD : accuracy
puntuar {3} *vt* : punctuate — *vi* : score (in sports)
punzar {21} *vt* : prick, puncture — **punzada** *nf* 1 PINCHAZO : prick 2 : sharp pain — **punzante** *adj* 1 : sharp 2 MORDAZ : biting, caustic
puñado *nm* 1 : handful 2 **a ~s** : by the handful
puñal *nm* : dagger — **puñalada** *nf* : stab
puño *nm* 1 : fist 2 : cuff (of a shirt) 3 : handle, hilt (of a sword, etc.) — **puñetazo** *nm* : punch (with the fist)
pupila *nf* : pupil (of the eye)
pupitre *nm* : desk
puré *nm* 1 : purée 2 **~ de papas** *or* **~ de patatas** *Spain* : mashed potatoes
pureza *nf* : purity
purga *nf* : purge — **purgar** {52} *vt* : purge — **purgatorio** *nm* : purgatory
purificar {72} *vt* : purify — **purificación** *nf, pl* **-ciones** : purification
puritano, -na *adj* : puritanical — **~** *n* : puritan
puro, -ra *adj* 1 : pure 2 SIMPLE : plain, simple 3 *Lat fam* : only, just — **puro** *nm* : cigar
púrpura *nf* : purple — **purpúreo, -rea** *adj* : purple
pus *nm* : pus
pusilánime *adj* : cowardly
puta *nf* : whore
putrefacción *nf, pl* **-ciones** : putrefaction, rot — **pútrido, -da** *adj* : putrid, rotten

Q

q *nf* : q, 18th letter of the Spanish alphabet

que *conj* **1** : that **2** (*in comparisons*) : than **3** (*introducing a reason or cause*) : so that, or else **4 es ~** : the thing is that **5 yo ~ tú** : if I were you — **~** *pron* **1** (*referring to persons*) : who, whom **2** (*referring to things*) : that, which **3 el (la, lo, las, los) ~** : he (she, it, they) who, whoever, the one(s) that

qué *adv* **1** : how, what **2 ¡~ lindo!** : how lovely! — **~** *adj* : what, which — **~** *pron* **1** : what **2 ¿~ crees?** : what do you think?

quebrar {55} *vt* : break — *vi* : go bankrupt — **quebrarse** *vr* : break — **quebrada** *nf* : ravine, gorge — **quebradizo, -za** *adj* : breakable, fragile — **quebrado, -da** *adj* **1** : bankrupt **2** : rough, uneven (of land, etc.) **3** ROTO : broken — **quebrado** *nm* : fraction — **quebradura** *nf* : crack, fissure — **quebrantar** *vt* **1** : break **2** DEBILITAR : weaken — **quebranto** *nm* **1** : harm, damage **2** AFLICCIÓN : grief, pain

queda *nf* → **toque**

quedar *vi* **1** PERMANECER : remain, stay **2** ESTAR : be **3** FALTAR : be left **4** : fit, look (of clothing, etc.) **5 no queda lejos** : it's not far **6 ~ en** : agree to, agree on — **quedarse** *vr* **1** : stay **2 ~ con** : keep

quedo, -da *adj* : quiet, still — **quedo** *adv* : softly, quietly

quehacer *nm* **1** : task **2 ~es** *nmpl* : chores

queja *nf* : complaint — **quejarse** *vr* **1** : complain **2** GEMIR : moan, groan — **quejido** *nm* : moan, whimper — **quejoso, -sa** *adj* : complaining, whining

quemar *vt* **1** : burn **2** MALGASTAR : squander — *vi* : burn — **quemarse** *vr* **1** : burn oneself **2** : burn (up) **3** : get sunburned — **quemado, -da** *adj* **1** : burned **2** AGOTADO : burned-out **3 estar ~** : be fed up — **quemador** *nm* : burner — **quemadura** *nf* : burn — **quemarropa: a ~** *adj & adv phr* : point-blank

querella *nf* **1** : dispute, quarrel **2** : charge (in law)

querer {64} *vt* **1** : want **2** AMAR : love **3**

~ decir : mean **4 ¿quieres pasarme la leche?** : please pass the milk **5 sin ~** : unintentionally — **~** *nm* : love — **querido, -da** *adj* : dear, beloved — **~** *n* **1** : darling **2** AMANTE : lover

queroseno *nm* : kerosene

querubín *nm, pl* **-bines** : cherub

queso *nm* : cheese — **quesadilla** *nf Lat* : quesadilla

quicio *nm* **1 estar fuera de ~** : be beside oneself **2 sacar de ~** : drive crazy

quiebra *nf* **1** : break **2** BANCARROTA : bankruptcy

quien *pron, pl* **quienes 1** (*subject*) : who **2** (*object*) : whom **3** (*indefinite*) : whoever, anyone, some people

quién *pron, pl* **quiénes 1** (*subject*) : who **2** (*object*) : whom **3 ¿de ~ es este lápiz?** : whose pencil is this?

quienquiera *pron, pl* **quienesquiera** : whoever, whomever

quieto, -ta *adj* **1** : calm, quiet **2** INMÓVIL : still — **quietud** *nf* : stillness

quijada *nf* : jaw, jawbone (of an animal)

quilate *nm* : carat, karat

quilla *nf* : keel

quimera *nf* : illusion — **quimérico, -ca** *adj* : fanciful

química *nf* : chemistry — **químico, -ca** *adj* : chemical — **~** *n* : chemist

quince *adj & nm* : fifteen — **quinceañero, -ra** *n* : fifteen-year-old, teenager — **quincena** *nf* : two-week period, fortnight — **quincenal** *adj* : semimonthly, twice a month

quincuagésimo, -ma *adj & n* : fiftieth

quinientos, -tas *adj* : five hundred — **quinientos** *nms & pl* : five hundred

quinina *nf* : quinine

quinqué *nm* : oil lamp

quinta *nf* : country house, villa

quintaesencia *nf* : quintessence

quinteto *nm* : quintet

quinto, -ta *adj & n* : fifth — **quinto** *nm* : fifth

quiosco *nm* : kiosk, newsstand

quiropráctico, -ca *n* : chiropractor

quirúrgico, -ca *adj* : surgical

quisquilloso, -sa *adj* : fastidious, fussy

quiste *nm* : cyst

quitar *vt* **1** : remove, take away **2** : take off (clothes) **3** : get rid of, relieve (pain, etc.) — **quitarse** *vr* **1** : withdraw, leave **2** : take off (one's clothes) **3** ~ **de** : give up (a habit) **4** ~ **de encima** : get rid of — **quitaesmalte** *nm* : nail-polish remover — **quita-**

manchas *nms & pl* : stain remover — **quitanieves** *nm* : snowplow — **quitasol** *nm* : parasol

quizá *or* **quizás** *adv* : maybe, perhaps

R

r *nf* : r, 19th letter of the Spanish alphabet

rábano *nm* **1** : radish **2** ~ **picante** : horseradish

rabí *nmf, pl* **-bíes** : rabbi

rabia *nf* **1** : rage, anger **2** : rabies (disease) — **rabiar** *vi* **1** : be furious **2** : be in great pain **3** ~ **por** : be dying for — **rabioso, -sa** *adj* **1** : enraged, furious **2** : rabid, having rabies

rabino, -na *n* : rabbi

rabo *nm* **1** : tail **2 el** ~ **del ojo** : the corner of one's eye

racha *nf* **1** : gust of wind **2** SERIE : series, string — **racheado, -da** *adj* : gusty

racial *adj* : racial

racimo *nm* : bunch, cluster

raciocinio *nm* : reason, reasoning

ración *nf, pl* **-ciones 1** : share, ration **2** : helping (of food)

racional *adj* : rational — **racionalizar** {21} *vt* : rationalize

racionar *vt* : ration — **racionamiento** *nm* : rationing

racismo *nm* : racism — **racista** *adj & nmf* : racist

radar *nm* : radar

radiación *nf, pl* **-ciones** : radiation

radiactivo, -va *adj* : radioactive — **radiactividad** *nf* : radioactivity

radiador *nm* : radiator

radiante *adj* : radiant

radical *adj & nmf* : radical

radicar {72} *vi* ~ **en** : lie in, be rooted in

radio *nm* **1** : radius **2** : spoke (of a wheel) **3** : radium (element) — ~ *nmf* : radio

radioactivo, -va *adj* : radioactive — **radioactividad** *nf* : radioactivity

radiodifusión *nf, pl* **-siones** : broadcasting — **radioemisora** *nf* : radio station — **radioescucha** *nmf* : listener — **radiofónico, -ca** *adj* : radio

radiografía *nf* : X ray — **radiografiar** {85} *vt* : x-ray

radiología *nf* : radiology — **radiólogo, -ga** *n* : radiologist

raer {65} *vt* : scrape off

ráfaga *nf* **1** : gust (of wind) **2** : flash (of light)

raído, -da *adj* : worn, shabby

raíz *nf, pl* **raíces 1** : root **2** ORIGEN : origin, source **3 echar raíces** : take root

raja *nf* **1** : crack, slit **2** RODAJA : slice — **rajar** *vt* : crack, split — **rajarse** *vr* **1** : crack, split open **2** *fam* : back out

rajatabla: a ~ *adv phr* : strictly, to the letter

ralea *nf* : sort, kind

ralentí *nm* : neutral (gear)

rallar *vt* : grate — **rallador** *nm* : grater

rama *nf* : branch — **ramaje** *nm* : branches *pl* — **ramal** *nm* : branch (of a railroad, etc.) — **ramificarse** {72} *vr* : branch (off) — **ramillete** *nm* **1** : bouquet **2** GRUPO : cluster, bunch — **ramo** *nm* **1** : branch **2** RAMILLETE : bouquet

rampa *nf* : ramp, incline

rana *nf* **1** : frog **2** ~ **toro** : bullfrog

rancho *nm* : ranch, farm — **ranchero, -ra** *n* : rancher, farmer

rancio, -cia *adj* **1** : rancid **2** : aged (of wine)

rango *nm* **1** : rank **2** : (social) standing

ranúnculo *nm* : buttercup

ranura *nf* : groove, slot

rapar *vt* **1** : shave **2** : crop (hair)

rapaz *adj, pl* **-paces** : rapacious, predatory

rápido, -da *adj* : rapid, quick — **rápidamente** *adv* : rapidly, fast — **rapidez** *nf* : speed — **rápido** *adv* : quickly, fast — ~ *nm* **1** : express train **2** ~ **s** *nmpl* : rapids

rapiña *nf* **1** : plunder **2 ave de** ~ : bird of prey

rapsodia *nf* : rhapsody

raptar *vt* : kidnap — **rapto** *nm* : kidnapping — **raptor, -tora** *n* : kidnapper

raqueta *nf* : racket (in sports)

raro, -ra *adj* **1** : rare **2** EXTRAÑO : odd, strange — **raramente** *adv* : rarely, infrequently — **rareza** *nf* : rarity

ras *nm* **a** ~ **de** : level with

rascacielos *nms & pl* : skyscraper

rascar {72} *vt* **1** : scratch **2** RASPAR : scrape — **rascarse** *vr* : scratch oneself

rasgar {52} *vt* : rip, tear — **rasgarse** *vr* : rip

rasgo *nm* **1** : stroke (of a pen) **2** CARAC-
TERÍSTICA : trait, characteristic **3** ~**s**
nmpl FACCIONES : features
rasguear *vt* : strum
rasguñar *vt* : scratch — **rasguño** *nm*
: scratch
raso, -sa *adj* **1** : level, flat **2** : low (of a
flight) **3 soldado raso** : private (in the
army) — **raso** *nm* : satin
raspar *vt* **1** : scrape **2** LIMAR : file down,
smooth — *vi* : be rough — **raspadura**
nf **1** : scratch **2** ~**s** *nfpl* : scrapings
rastra *nf* **1** : rake **2 a** ~**s** : unwillingly
— **rastrear** *vt* : track, trace — **ras-
trero, -ra** *adj* **1** : creeping **2** DESPRE-
CIABLE : despicable — **rastrillar** *vt*
: rake — **rastrillo** *nm* : rake — **rastro**
nm **1** : trail, track **2** SEÑAL : sign
rasurar *vt Lat* : shave — **rasurarse** *vr
Lat* : shave
rata *nf* : rat
ratear *vt* : steal — **ratero, -ra** *n* : thief
ratificar {72} *vt* : ratify — **ratificación**
nf, pl **-ciones** : ratification
rato *nm* **1** : while **2 al poco** ~ : shortly after **3 pasar el** ~ : pass the time
ratón *nm, pl* **-tones** : mouse — **ratonera** *nf* : mousetrap
raudal *nm* **1** : torrent **2 a** ~**es** : in
abundance — **raudo, -da** *adj* : swift
raya *nf* **1** : line **2** LISTA : stripe **3** : part
(in the hair) — **rayar** *vt* : scratch — *vi*
1 al ~ **el día** : at daybreak **2** ~ **en**
: border on — **rayarse** *vr* : get
scratched
rayo *nm* **1** : ray, beam **2** : bolt of lightning **3** ~**s X** : X rays
rayón *nm* : rayon
raza *nf* **1** : (human) race **2** : breed (of
animals) **3 de** ~ : thoroughbred,
pedigreed
razón *nf, pl* **-zones** **1** : reason **2 dar** ~
: inform **3 en** ~ **de** : because of **4**
tener ~ : be right — **razonable** *adj*
: reasonable — **razonamiento** *nm*
: reasoning — **razonar** *v* : reason,
think
reacción *nf, pl* **-ciones** : reaction —
reaccionar *vi* : react — **reaccionario,
-ria** *adj & n* : reactionary
reacio, -cia *adj* : resistant, stubborn
reactivar *vt* : reactivate, revive
reactor *nm* **1** : jet (airplane) **2** ~ **nuclear** : nuclear reactor
reajustar *vt* : readjust — **reajuste** *nm*
: readjustment
real *adj* **1** : royal **2** VERDADERO : real,
true
realce *nm* **1** : relief **2 dar** ~ : highlight
realeza *nf* : royalty

realidad *nf* **1** : reality **2 en** ~ : actually, in fact
realismo *nm* : realism — **realista** *adj*
: realistic — ~ *nmf* : realist
realizar {21} *vt* **1** : carry out **2** : achieve
(a goal) **3** : produce (a film or play) **4**
: realize (a profit) — **realizarse** *vr* **1**
: fulfill oneself **2** : come true (of a
dream, etc.) — **realización** *nf, pl*
-ciones : execution, realization
realmente *adv* : really, actually
realzar {21} *vt* : highlight, enhance
reanimar *vt* : revive
reanudar *vt* : resume, renew — **reanudarse** *vr* : resume
reaparecer {53} *vi* : reappear — **rea-
parición** *nf, pl* **-ciones** : reappearance
reavivar *vt* : revive
rebajar *vt* **1** : lower, reduce **2** HUMILLAR
: humiliate — **rebajarse** *vr* **1** : humble
oneself **2** ~ **a** : stoop to — **rebaja** *nf*
1 : reduction **2** DESCUENTO : discount **3**
~**s** *nfpl* : sales
rebanada *nf* : slice
rebaño *nm* **1** : herd **2** : flock (of sheep)
rebasar *vt* : surpass, exceed
rebatir *vt* : refute
rebelarse *vr* : rebel — **rebelde** *adj* : rebellious — ~ *nmf* : rebel — **rebeldía**
nf : rebelliousness — **rebelión** *nf, pl*
-liones : rebellion
reblandecer *vt* : soften
rebobinar *vt* : rewind
rebosar *vi* **1** : overflow **2** ~ **de** : be
bursting with — *vt* : overflow with
rebotar *vi* : bounce, rebound — **rebote**
nm **1** : bounce **2 de** ~ : on the rebound
rebozar {21} *vt* : coat in batter
rebuscado, -da *adj* : pretentious
rebuznar *vi* : bray
recabar *vt* **1** : obtain, collect **2** ~ **fondos** : raise money
recado *nm* **1** MENSAJE : message **2**
Spain : errand
recaer {13} *vi* **1** : relapse **2** ~ **sobre**
: fall on — **recaída** *nf* : relapse
recalcar {72} *vt* : emphasize, stress
recalcitrante *adj* : recalcitrant
recalentar {55} *vt* **1** : overheat **2** : re-
heat, warm up (food) — **recalentarse**
vr : overheat
recámara *nf* **1** : chamber (of a firearm)
2 *Lat* : bedroom
recambio *nm* **1** : spare part **2** : refill (for
a pen, etc.)
recapitular *vt* : recapitulate, sum up —
recapitulación *nf, pl* **-ciones** : reca-
pitulation
recargar {52} *vt* **1** : overload **2**

: recharge (a battery), reload (a firearm, etc.) — **recargado, -da** *adj* : overly elaborate — **recargo** *nm* : surcharge

recato *nm* : modesty — **recatado, -da** *adj* : modest, demure

recaudar *vt* : collect — **recaudación** *nf, pl* **-ciones** : collection — **recaudador, -dora** *n* ~ **de impuestos** : tax collector

recelar *vt* : distrust, fear — **recelo** *nm* : distrust, suspicion — **receloso, -sa** *adj* : distrustful, suspicious

recepción *nf, pl* **-ciones** : reception — **recepcionista** *nmf* : receptionist

receptáculo *nm* : receptacle

receptivo, -va *adj* : receptive — **receptor, -tora** *n* : recipient — **receptor** *nm* : receiver (of a radio, etc.)

recesión *nf, pl* **-siones** : recession

receso *nm Lat* : recess, adjournment

receta *nf* 1 : recipe 2 : prescription (in medicine)

rechazar {21} *vt* 1 : reject, refuse 2 REPELER : repel 3 : reflect (light) — **rechazo** *nm* 1 : rejection

rechinar *vi* 1 : squeak, creak 2 : grind, gnash (one's teeth)

rechoncho, -cha *adj fam* : chubby

recibir *vt* 1 : receive 2 ACOGER : welcome — *vi* : receive visitors — **recibidor** *nm* : vestibule, entrance hall — **recibimiento** *nm* : reception, welcome — **recibo** *nm* : receipt

reciclar *vt* 1 : recycle 2 : retrain (workers) — **reciclaje** *nm* : recycling

recién *adv* 1 : newly, recently 2 ~ **casados** : newlyweds — **reciente** *adj* : recent — **recientemente** *adv* : recently

recinto *nm* 1 : enclosure 2 ÁREA : area, site

recio, -cia *adj* : tough, strong

recipiente *nm* : container, receptacle — ~ *nmf* : recipient

recíproco, -ca *adj* : reciprocal, mutual

recitar *vt* : recite — **recital** *nm* : recital

reclamar *vt* : demand, ask for — *vi* : complain — **reclamación** *nf, pl* **-ciones** 1 : claim, demand 2 QUEJA : complaint — **reclamo** *nm* 1 : lure (in hunting) 2 *Lat* : inducement, attraction

reclinar *vt* : rest, lean — **reclinarse** *vr* : recline, lean back

recluir {41} *vt* : confine, lock up — **recluirse** *vr* : shut oneself away — **reclusión** *nf, pl* **-siones** : imprisonment — **recluso, -sa** *n* : prisoner

recluta *nmf* : recruit — **reclutamiento** *nm* : recruitment — **reclutar** *vt* : recruit, enlist

recobrar *vt* : recover, regain — **recobrarse** *vr* ~ **de** : recover from

recodo *nm* : bend

recoger {15} *vt* 1 : collect, gather 2 COGER : pick up 3 LIMPIAR, ORDENAR : clean up, tidy (up) — **recogerse** *vr* : retire, withdraw — **recogedor** *nm* : dustpan — **recogido, -da** *adj* : quiet, secluded

recolección *nf, pl* **-ciones** 1 : collection 2 COSECHA : harvest

recomendar {55} *vt* : recommend — **recomendación** *nf, pl* **-ciones** : recommendation

recompensar *vt* : reward — **recompensa** *nf* : reward

reconciliar *vt* : reconcile — **reconciliarse** *vr* : be reconciled — **reconciliación** *nf, pl* **-ciones** : reconciliation

recóndito, -ta *adj* : hidden

reconfortar *vt* : comfort

reconocer {18} *vt* 1 : recognize 2 ADMITIR : admit 3 EXAMINAR : examine — **reconocible** *adj* : recognizable — **reconocido, -da** *adj* 1 : recognized, accepted 2 AGRADECIDO : grateful — **reconocimiento** *nm* 1 : recognition 2 AGRADECIMIENTO : gratitude 3 : (medical) examination

reconsiderar *vt* : reconsider

reconstruir {41} *vt* : reconstruct — **reconstrucción** *nf, pl* **-ciones** : reconstruction

recopilar *vt* 1 RECOGER : collect, gather 2 : compile — **recopilación** *nf, pl* **-ciones** : collection, compilation

récord *nm, pl* **-cords** : record

recordar {19} *vt* 1 ACORDARSE DE : remember 2 : remind — *vi* : remember — **recordatorio** *nm* : reminder

recorrer *vt* 1 : travel through 2 : cover (a distance) — **recorrido** *nm* 1 : journey, trip 2 TRAYECTO : route, course

recortar *vt* 1 : reduce 2 CORTAR : cut (out) 3 : trim (hair) — **recortarse** *vr* : stand out — **recorte** *nm* 1 : cut, cutting 2 ~**s de periódicos** : newspaper clippings

recostar {19} *vt* : lean, rest — **recostarse** *vr* : lie down

recoveco *nm* 1 : bend 2 RINCÓN : nook, corner

recrear *vt* 1 : recreate 2 ENTRETENER : entertain — **recrearse** *vr* : to enjoy oneself — **recreativo, -va** *adj* : recreational — **recreo** *nm* 1 : recreation, amusement 2 : recess, break (at school)

recriminar *vt* : reproach
recrudecer {53} *vi* : worsen — **recrudecerse** *vr* : intensify, get worse
rectángulo *nm* : rectangle — **rectangular** *adj* : rectangular
rectificar {72} *vt* 1 : rectify, correct 2 AJUSTAR : straighten (out) — **rectitud** *nf* 1 : straightness 2 : (moral) rectitude — **recto, -ta** *adj* 1 : straight 2 ÍNTEGRO : upright, honorable — **recto** *nm* : rectum
rector, -tora *adj* : governing, managing — **~** *n* : rector — **rectoría** *nf* : rectory
recubrir {2} *vt* : cover, coat
recuento *nm* : count, recount
recuerdo *nm* 1 : memory 2 : souvenir, remembrance (of a journey, etc.) 3 **~s** *nmpl* SALUDOS : regards
recuperar *vt* 1 : recover, retrieve 2 **~ el tiempo perdido** : make up for lost time — **recuperarse** *vr* **~ de** : recover from — **recuperación** *nf, pl* **-ciones** 1 : recovery 2 **~ de datos** : data retrieval
recurrir *vi* **~ a** : turn to (a person), resort to (force, etc.) — **recurso** *nm* 1 : recourse, resort 2 : appeal (in law) 3 **~s** *nmpl* : resources
red *nf* 1 : net 2 SISTEMA : network, system 3 **la Red** : the Internet
redactar *vt* : write (up), draft — **redacción** *nf, pl* **-ciones** 1 : writing, drafting 2 : editing (of a newspaper, etc.) — **redactor, -tora** *n* : editor
redada *nf* 1 : (police) raid 2 : catch (in fishing)
redescubrir {2} *vt* : rediscover
redención *nf, pl* **-ciones** : redemption — **redentor, -tora** *adj* : redeeming
redil *nm* : fold, pen
rédito *nm* : interest, yield
redoblar *vt* : redouble
redomado, -da *adj* : out-and-out
redondear *vt* 1 : make round 2 : round off (a number, etc.) — **redonda** *nf* 1 : whole note (in music) 2 **a la ~** : in the surrounding area — **redondel** *nm* 1 : ring, circle 2 : bullring — **redondo, -da** *adj* 1 : round 2 PERFECTO : excellent
reducir {61} *vt* : reduce — **reducirse** *vr* **~ a** : come down to, amount to — **reducción** *nf, pl* **-ciones** : reduction — **reducido, -da** *adj* 1 : reduced, limited 2 PEQUEÑO : small
redundante *adj* : redundant — **redundancia** *nf* : reduncancy
reedición *nf, pl* **-ciones** : reprint
reembolsar *vt* : refund, reimburse,

repay — **reembolso** *nm* : refund, reimbursement
reemplazar {21} *vt* : replace — **reemplazo** *nm* : replacement
reencarnación *nf, pl* **-ciones** : reincarnation
reencuentro *nm* : reunion
reestructurar *vt* : restructure
refaccionar *vt Lat* : repair, renovate — **refacciones** *nfpl Lat* : repairs, renovations
referir {76} *vt* 1 : tell 2 REMITIR : refer — **referirse** *vr* **~ a** : refer to — **referencia** *nf* 1 : reference 2 **hacer ~ a** : refer to — **referéndum** *nm, pl* **-dums** : referendum — **referente** *adj* **~ a** : concerning
refinar *vt* : refine — **refinado, -da** *adj* : refined — **refinamiento** *nm* : refinement — **refinería** *nf* : refinery
reflector *nm* 1 : reflector 2 : spotlight, searchlight, floodlight
reflejar *vt* : reflect — **reflejarse** *vr* : be reflected — **reflejo** *nm* 1 : reflection 2 : (physical) reflex 3 **~s** *nmpl* : highlights (in hair)
reflexionar *vi* : reflect, think — **reflexión** *nf, pl* **-xiones** : reflection, thought — **reflexivo, -va** *adj* 1 : reflective, thoughtful 2 : reflexive (in grammar)
reflujo *nm* : ebb (tide)
reforma *nf* 1 : reform 2 **~s** *nfpl* : renovations — **reformador, -dora** *n* : reformer — **reformar** *vt* 1 : reform 2 : renovate, repair (a house, etc.) — **reformarse** *vr* : mend one's ways — **reformatorio** *nm* : reformatory
reforzar {36} *vt* : reinforce
refrán *nm, pl* **-franes** : proverb, saying
refregar {49} *vt* : scrub
refrenar *vt* 1 : rein in (a horse) 2 CONTENER : restrain — **refrenarse** *vr* : restrain oneself
refrendar *vt* : approve, endorse
refrescar {72} *vt* 1 : refresh, cool 2 : brush up on (knowledge) — *vi* : turn cooler — **refrescante** *adj* : refreshing — **refresco** *nm* : soft drink
refriega *nf* : scuffle, skirmish
refrigerar *vt* 1 : refrigerate 2 CLIMATIZAR : air-condition — **refrigeración** *nf, pl* **-ciones** 1 : refrigeration 2 AIRE ACONDICIONADO : air-conditioning — **refrigerador** *nmf Lat* : refrigerator — **refrigerio** *nm* : refreshments *pl*
refrito, -ta *adj* : refried — **refrito** *nm* : rehash
refuerzo *nm* : reinforcement
refugiar *vt* : shelter — **refugiarse** *vr* : take refuge — **refugiado, -da** *n*

: refugee — **refugio** *nm* : refuge, shelter
refulgir {35} *vi* : shine brightly
refunfuñar *vi* : grumble, groan
refutar *vt* : refute
regadera *nf* 1 : watering can 2 *Lat* : shower head, shower
regalar *vt* : give (as a gift) — **regalarse** *vr* ~ **con** : treat oneself to
regaliz *nm, pl* **-lices** : licorice
regalo *nm* 1 : gift, present 2 PLACER : pleasure, delight
regañadientes : a ~ *adv phr* : reluctantly, unwillingly
regañar *vt* : scold — *vi* 1 QUEJARSE : grumble 2 *Spain* : quarrel — **regañon, -ñona** *adj, mpl* **-ñones** *fam* : grumpy, irritable
regar {49} *vt* 1 : irrigate, water 2 ESPARCIR : scatter
regatear *vt* 1 : haggle over 2 ESCATIMAR : skimp on — *vi* : bargain, haggle
regazo *nm* : lap (of a person)
regenerar *vt* : regenerate
regentar *vt* : run, manage
régimen *nm, pl* **regímenes** 1 : regime 2 DIETA : diet 3 ~ **de vida** : lifestyle
regimiento *nm* : regiment
regio, -gia *adj* : royal, regal
región *nf, pl* **-giones** : region, area — **regional** *adj* : regional
regir {28} *vt* 1 : rule 2 ADMINISTRAR : manage, run 3 DETERMINAR : govern, determine — *vi* : apply, be in force — **regirse** *vr* ~ **por** : be guided by
registrar *vt* 1 : register 2 GRABAR : record, tape 3 : search (a house, etc.), frisk (a person) — **registrarse** *vr* 1 : register 2 : be recorded (of temperatures, etc.) — **registrador, -dora** *adj* **caja registradora** : cash register — ~ *n* : registrar — **registro** *nm* 1 : registration 2 : register (book) 3 : registry (office) 4 : range (of a voice, etc.) 5 INSPECCIÓN : search
regla *nf* 1 : rule, regulation 2 : ruler (for measuring) 3 MENSTRUACIÓN : period — **reglamentación** *nf, pl* **-ciones** 1 : regulation 2 REGLAS : rules *pl* — **reglamentar** *vt* : regulate — **reglamentario, -ria** *adj* : regulation, official — **reglamento** *nm* : regulations *pl*, rules *pl*
regocijar *vt* : gladden, delight — **regocijarse** *vr* : rejoice — **regocijo** *nm* : delight, rejoicing
regodearse *vr* : be delighted — **regodeo** *nm* : delight
regordete *adj fam* : chubby
regresar *vi* : return, come back, go

back — *vt Lat* : give back — **regresión** *nf, pl* **-siones** : regression — **regresivo, -va** *adj* : regressive — **regreso** *nm* 1 : return 2 **estar de** ~ : be back, be home again
reguero *nm* 1 : irrigation ditch 2 SEÑAL : trail, trace 3 **correr como un** ~ **de pólvora** : spread like wildfire
regular *adj* 1 : regular 2 MEDIANO : medium, average 3 **por lo** ~ : in general — ~ *vt* : regulate, control — **regulación** *nf, pl* **-ciones** : regulation, control — **regularidad** *nf* : regularity — **regularizar** {21} *vt* : normalize, make regular
rehabilitar *vt* 1 : rehabilitate 2 : reinstate (s.o. in a position) 3 : renovate (a building, etc.) — **rehabilitación** *nf* 1 : rehabilitation 2 : reinstatement (in a position) 3 : renovation (of a building, etc.)
rehacer {40} *vt* 1 : redo 2 REPARAR : repair — **rehacerse** *vr* 1 : recover 2 ~ **de** : get over
rehén *nm, pl* **-henes** : hostage
rehuir {41} *vt* : avoid, shun
rehusar {8} *v* : refuse
reimprimir *vt* : reprint — **reimpresión** *nf, pl* **-siones** : reprinting, reprint
reina *nf* : queen — **reinado** *nm* : reign — **reinante** *adj* : reigning — **reinar** *vi* 1 : reign 2 PREVALECER : prevail
reincidir *vi* : backslide, relapse
reino *nm* : kingdom, realm
reintegrar *vt* 1 : reinstate 2 : refund (money), reimburse (expenses, etc.) — **reintegrarse** *vr* ~ **a** : return to — **reintegro** *nm* : reimbursement
reír {66} *vi* : laugh — *vt* : laugh at — **reírse** *vr* : laugh
reiterar *vt* : repeat, reiterate
reivindicar {72} *vt* 1 : claim 2 RESTAURAR : restore
reja *nf* : grille, grating — **rejilla** *nf* : grille, grate, screen
rejuvenecer {53} *vt* : rejuvenate — **rejuvenecerse** *vr* : be rejuvenated
relación *nf, pl* **-ciones** 1 : relation, connection 2 COMUNICACIÓN : relationship, relations *pl* 3 RELATO : account 4 LISTA : list 5 **con** ~ **a** *or* **en** ~ **a** : in relation to — **relacionar** *vt* : relate, connect — **relacionarse** *vr* ~ **con** : be connected to, interact with
relajar *vt* : relax — **relajarse** *vr* : relax — **relajación** *nf, pl* **-ciones** : relaxation — **relajado, -da** *adj* 1 : relaxed 2 : dissolute, lax (in behavior)
relamerse *vr* : smack one's lips, lick its chops

relámpago *nm* : flash of lightning — **relampaguear** *vi* : flash

relatar *vt* : relate, tell

relativo, -va *adj* 1 : relative 2 **en lo relativo a** : with regard to — **relatividad** *nf* : relativity

relato *nm* 1 : account, report 2 CUENTO : story, tale

releer {20} *vt* : reread

relegar {52} *vt* : relegate

relevante *adj* : outstanding, important

relevar *vt* 1 : relieve, take over from 2 ~ **de** : exempt from — **relevo** *nm* 1 : relief, replacement 2 **carrera de** ~**s** : relay race

relieve *nm* 1 : relief (in art, etc.) 2 IMPORTANCIA : prominence, importance 3 **poner en** ~ : emphasize

religión *nf, pl* **-giones** : religion — **religioso, -sa** *adj* : religious — ~ *n* : monk *m*, nun *f*

relinchar *vi* : neigh, whinny — **relincho** *nm* : neigh, whinny

reliquia *nf* 1 : relic 2 ~ **de familia** : family heirloom

rellenar *vt* 1 : refill 2 : stuff, fill (in cooking) — **relleno, -na** *adj* : stuffed, filled — **relleno** *nm* : stuffing, filling

reloj *nm* 1 : clock 2 *or* ~ **de pulsera** : wristwatch 3 ~ **de arena** : hourglass 4 **como un** ~ : like clockwork

relucir {45} *vi* 1 : glitter, shine 2 **sacar a** ~ : bring up, mention — **reluciente** *adj* : brilliant, shining

relumbrar *vi* : shine brightly

remachar *vt* 1 : rivet 2 RECALCAR : stress, drive home — **remache** *nm* : rivet

remanente *nm* : remainder, surplus

remanso *nm* : pool

remar *vi* : row

rematar *vt* 1 : conclude, finish up 2 MATAR : finish off 3 LIQUIDAR : sell off cheaply 4 *Lat* : auction — *vi* 1 : shoot (in sports) 2 TERMINAR : end — **rematado, -da** *adj* : utter, complete — **remate** *nm* 1 : shot (in sports) 2 FIN : end

remedar *vt* : imitate, mimic

remediar *vt* 1 : remedy, repair 2 : solve (a problem) 3 EVITAR : avoid — **remedio** *nm* 1 : remedy, cure 2 SOLUCIÓN : solution 3 **sin** ~ : hopeless

rememorar *vi* : recall

remendar {55} *vt* : mend

remesa *nf* 1 : remittance 2 : shipment (of merchandise)

remezón *nm, pl* **-zones** *Lat* : mild earthquake, tremor

remiendo *nm* : mend, patch

remilgado, -da *adj* 1 : prudish 2 AFEC-

TADO : affected — **remilgo** *nm* : primness, affectation

reminiscencia *nf* : reminiscence

remisión *nf, pl* **-siones** : remission

remiso, -sa *adj* 1 : reluctant 2 NEGLIGENTE : remiss

remitir *vt* 1 : send, remit 2 ~ **a** : refer to, direct to — *vi* : subside, let up — **remite** *nm* : return address — **remitente** *nmf* : sender (of a letter, etc.)

remo *nm* : paddle, oar

remodelar *vt* 1 : remodel 2 : restructure (an organization)

remojar *vt* : soak, steep — **remojo** *nm* **poner en** ~ : soak

remolacha *nf* : beet

remolcar {72} *vt* : tow, tug — **remolcador** *nm* : tugboat

remolino *nm* 1 : whirlwind, whirlpool 2 : crowd (of people) 3 : cowlick (of hair)

remolque *nm* 1 : towing, tow 2 : trailer (vehicle)

remontar *vt* 1 : overcome 2 SUBIR : go up — **remontarse** *vr* 1 : soar 2 ~ **a** : date from, go back to

rémora *nf* : hindrance

remorder {47} *vt* : trouble, worry — **remordimiento** *nm* : remorse

remoto, -ta *adj* : remote — **remotamente** *adv* : remotely, slightly

remover {47} *vt* 1 : stir 2 : move around, turn over (earth, embers, etc.) 3 REAVIVAR : bring up again 4 DESPEDIR : fire, dismiss

remunerar *vt* : remunerate

renacer {48} *vi* : be reborn, revive — **renacimiento** *nm* 1 : rebirth, revival 2 **el Renacimiento** : the Renaissance

renacuajo *nm* : tadpole, pollywog

rencilla *nf* : quarrel

renco, -ca *adj Lat* : lame

rencor *nm* 1 : rancor, hostility 2 **guardar** ~ : hold a grudge — **rencoroso, -sa** *adj* : resentful

rendición *nf, pl* **-ciones** : surrender — **rendido, -da** *adj* 1 : submissive 2 AGOTADO : exhausted

rendija *nf* : crack, split

rendir {54} *vt* 1 : render, give 2 PRODUCIR : yield, produce 3 CANSAR : exhaust — *vi* : make progress, go a long way — **rendirse** *vr* : surrender, give up — **rendimiento** *nm* 1 : performance 2 : yield, return (in finance, etc.)

renegar {49} *vt* : deny — *vi* 1 QUEJARSE : grumble 2 ~ **de** ABJURAR : renounce, disown — **renegado, -da** *n* : renegade

renglón *nm, pl* **-glones 1** : line (of writing) **2** *Lat* : line (of products)

reno *nm* : reindeer

renombre *nm* : renown — **renombrado, -da** *adj* : famous, renowned

renovar {19} *vt* **1** : renew, restore **2** : renovate (a building, etc.) — **renovación** *nf, pl* **-ciones 1** : renewal **2** : renovation (of a building, etc.)

renquear *vi* : limp, hobble

rentar *vt* **1** : produce, yield **2** *Lat* : rent — **renta** *nf* **1** : income **2** ALQUILER : rent **3 impuesto sobre la ~** : income tax — **rentable** *adj* : profitable

renunciar *vi* **1** : resign **2 ~ a** : renounce, relinquish — **renuncia** *nf* **1** : renunciation **2** DIMISIÓN : resignation

reñir {67} *vi* **~ con** : argue with, fall out with — *vt* **1** : scold **2** DISPUTAR : fight — **reñido, -da** *adj* **1** : hard-fought **2 ~ con** : on bad terms with

reo, rea *n* **1** : accused, defendant **2** CULPABLE : culprit

reojo *nm* **de ~** : out of the corner of one's eye

reorganizar {21} *vt* : reorganize

repantigarse {52} *vr* : sprawl out

reparar *vt* **1** : repair, fix **2** : make amends for (an offense, etc.) — *vi* **1 ~ en** ADVERTIR : take notice of **2 ~ en** CONSIDERAR : consider — **reparación** *nf, pl* **-ciones 1** : reparation, amends **2** ARREGLO : repair — **reparo** *nm* **1** : reservation, objection **2 poner ~s a** : object to

repartir *vt* **1** : allocate **2** DISTRIBUIR : distribute **3** ESPARCIR : spread — **repartición** *nf, pl* **-ciones** : distribution — **repartidor, -dora** *n* : delivery person, distributor — **reparto** *nm* **1** : allocation **2** DISTRIBUCIÓN : delivery **3** : cast (of characters)

repasar *vt* **1** : review, go over **2** ZURCIR : mend — **repaso** *nm* **1** : review **2** : mending (of clothes)

repeler *vt* **1** : repel **2** REPUGNAR : disgust — **repelente** *adj* : repellent, repulsive

repente *nm* **1** : fit, outburst **2 de ~** : suddenly — **repentino, -na** *adj* : sudden

repercutir *vi* **1** : reverberate **2 ~ en** : have repercussions on — **repercusión** *nf, pl* **-siones** : repercussion

repertorio *nm* : repertoire

repetir {54} *vt* **1** : repeat **2** : have a second helping of (food) — **repetirse** *vr* **1** : repeat oneself **2** : recur (of an event, etc.) — **repetición** *nf, pl* **-ciones 1** : repetition **2** : rerun, repeat (of a program, etc.) — **repetido, -da**

adj **1** : repeated **2 repetidas veces** : repeatedly, time and again — **repetitivo, -va** *adj* : repetitive, repetitious

repicar {72} *vt* : ring — *vi* : ring out, peal — **repique** *nm* : ringing, pealing

repisa *nf* **1** : shelf, ledge **2 ~ de ventana** : windowsill

replegar {49} *vt* : fold — **replegarse** *vr* : retreat, withdraw

repleto, -ta *adj* **1** : replete, full **2 ~ de** : packed with

replicar {72} *vt* : reply, retort — *vi* : answer back — **réplica** *nf* **1** RESPUESTA : reply **2** COPIA : replica, reproduction

repliegue *nm* **1** : fold **2** : (military) withdrawal

repollo *nm* : cabbage

reponer {60} *vt* **1** : replace **2** REPLICAR : reply — **reponerse** *vr* : recover

reportar *vt* **1** : yield, bring **2** *Lat* : report — **reportaje** *nm* : article, (news) report — **reporte** *nm Lat* : report — **reportero, -ra** *n* : reporter

reposar *vi* **1** DESCANSAR : rest **2** : stand, settle (of liquids, dough, etc.) — **reposado, -da** *adj* : calm, relaxed — **reposición** *nf, pl* **-ciones 1** : replacement **2** : rerun, repeat (of a program, etc.) — **reposo** *nm* : rest

repostar *vi* **1** : stock up on **2** : refuel (an airplane, etc.) — *vi* : fill up, refuel

reprender *vt* : reprimand, scold — **reprensible** *adj* : reprehensible

represalia *nf* **1** : reprisal **2 tomar ~s** : retaliate

represar *vt* : dam

representar *vt* **1** : represent **2** : perform (a play, etc.) **3** APARENTAR : look, appear as — **representación** *nf, pl* **-ciones 1** : representation **2** : performance (of a play, etc.) **3 en ~ de** : on behalf of — **representante** *nmf* **1** : representative **2** ACTOR : performer — **representativo, -va** *adj* : representative

represión *nf, pl* **-siones** : repression

reprimenda *nf* : reprimand

reprimir *vt* **1** : repress **2** : suppress (a rebellion, etc.)

reprobar {19} *vt* **1** : reprove, condemn **2** *Lat* : fail (an exam, etc.)

reprochar *vt* : reproach — **reprocharse** *vr* : reproach oneself — **reproche** *nm* : reproach

reproducir {61} *vt* : reproduce — **reproducirse** *vr* **1** : breed, reproduce **2** : recur (of an event, etc.) — **reproducción** *nf, pl* **-ciones** : reproduction — **reproductor, -tora** *adj* : reproductive

reptil *nm* : reptile

república *nf* : republic — **republicano,
-na** *adj & n* : republican

repudiar *vt* : repudiate

repuesto *nm* : spare (auto) part

repugnar *vt* : disgust — **repugnancia**
nf : disgust — **repugnante** *adj* : disgusting

repujar *vt* : emboss

repulsivo, -va *adj* : repulsive

reputar *vt* : consider, deem — **reputación** *nf, pl* **-ciones** : reputation

requerir {76} *vt* 1 : require 2 : summon, send for (a person)

requesón *nm, pl* **-sones** : cottage
cheese

réquiem *nm* : requiem

requisito *nm* 1 : requirement 2 ~ **previo** : prerequisite

res *nf* 1 : beast, animal 2 *Lat or* **carne
de** ~ : beef

resabio *nm* 1 VICIO : bad habit, vice 2
DEJO : aftertaste

resaca *nf* 1 : undertow 2 **tener** ~
: have a hangover

resaltar *vi* 1 : stand out 2 **hacer** ~
: bring out, highlight — *vt* : emphasize

resarcir {83} *vt* : compensate, repay —
resarcirse *vr* ~ **de** : make up for

resbalar *vi* 1 : slip, slide 2 : skid (of an
automobile) — **resbalarse** *vr* : slip,
skid — **resbaladizo, -za** *adj* : slippery
— **resbalón** *nm, pl* **-lones** : slip —
resbaloso, -sa *adj Lat* : slippery

rescatar *vt* 1 : rescue, ransom 2 RECUPERAR : recover, get back — **rescate**
nm 1 : rescue 2 : ransom (money) 3
RECUPERACIÓN : recovery

rescindir *vt* : cancel — **rescisión** *nf, pl*
-siones : cancellation

rescoldo *nm* : embers *pl*

resecar {72} *vt* : dry (out) — **resecarse** *vr* : dry up — **reseco, -ca** *adj*
: dry, dried-up

resentirse {76} *vr* 1 : suffer, be weakened 2 OFENDERSE : be offended 3 ~
de : feel the effects of — **resentido,
-da** *adj* : resentful — **resentimiento**
nm : resentment

reseñar *vt* 1 : review 2 DESCRIBIR : describe — **reseña** *nf* 1 : review, report 2
DESCRIPCIÓN : description

reservar *vt* 1 : reserve 2 GUARDAR
: keep, save — **reservarse** *vr* 1 : save
oneself 2 : keep for oneself — **reserva**
nf 1 : reservation 2 PROVISIÓN : reserve
3 **de** ~ : spare, in reserve — **reservación** *nf, pl* **-ciones** : reservation —
reservado, -da *adj* 1 : reserved 2
: confidential (of a document, etc.)

resfriar {85} *vt* : cool — **resfriarse** *vr* 1

: cool off 2 CONSTIPARSE : catch a cold
— **resfriado** *nm* CATARRO : cold —
resfrío *nm Lat* : cold

resguardar *vt* : protect — **resguardarse** *vr* : protect oneself — **resguardo** *nm* 1 : protection 2 RECIBO
: receipt

residir *vi* 1 : reside, live 2 ~ **en** : lie in
— **residencia** *nf* 1 : residence 2 *or* ~
universitaria : dormitory — **residencial** *adj* : residential — **residente** *adj
& nmf* : resident

residuo *nm* 1 : residue 2 ~**s** *nmpl*
: waste — **residual** *adj* : residual

resignar *vt* : resign — **resignarse** *vr* ~
a : resign oneself to — **resignación** *nf,
pl* **-ciones** : resignation

resina *nf* 1 : resin 2 ~ **epoxídica**
: epoxy

resistir *vt* 1 AGUANTAR : stand, bear 2
: withstand (temptation, etc.) — *vi* : resist — **resistirse** *vr* ~ **a** : be resistant
to — **resistencia** *nf* 1 : resistance 2
AGUANTE : endurance, stamina — **resistente** *adj* : resistant, strong, tough

resma *nf* : ream

resollar {19} *vi* : breathe heavily, pant

resolver {89} *vt* 1 : resolve 2 DECIDIR
: decide — **resolverse** *vr* : make up
one's mind — **resolución** *nf, pl*
-ciones 1 : resolution 2 DECISIÓN : decision 3 FIRMEZA : determination, resolve

resonar {19} *vi* : resound — **resonancia** *nf* 1 : resonance 2 CONSECUENCIAS
: impact, repercussions *pl* — **resonante** *adj* : resonant, resounding

resoplar *vi* 1 : puff, pant 2 : snort (with
annoyance)

resorte *nm* 1 MUELLE : spring 2 **tocar**
~**s** : pull strings

respaldar *vt* : back, endorse — **respaldarse** *vr* : lean back — **respaldo** *nm* 1
: back (of a chair, etc.) 2 APOYO : support, backing

respectar *vt* : concern, relate to — **respectivo, -va** *adj* : respective — **respecto** *nm* 1 **al** ~ : in this respect 2
~ **a** : in regard to, concerning

respetar *vt* : respect — **respetable** *adj*
: respectable — **respeto** *nm* 1 : respect 2 **presentar sus** ~**s** : pay one's
respects — **respetuoso, -sa** *adj* : respectful

respingo *nm* : start, jump

respirar *v* : breathe — **respiración** *nf,
pl* **-ciones** : respiration, breathing —
respiratorio, -ria *adj* : respiratory —
respiro *nm* 1 : breath 2 DESCANSO
: respite, break

resplandecer {53} *vi* : shine — **resplandeciente** *adj* : shining, gleaming — **resplandor** *nm* **1** : brilliance, gleam **2** : flash (of lightning, etc.)

responder *vt* : answer, reply — *vi* **1** : answer **2** REPLICAR : answer back **3** ~ **a** : respond to **4** ~ **de** : answer for (something)

responsable *adj* : responsible — **responsabilidad** *nf* : responsibility

respuesta *nf* **1** : answer, reply **2** REACCIÓN : response

resquebrajar *vt* : split, crack — **resquebrajarse** *vr* : crack

resquicio *nm* **1** : crack, crevice **2** VESTIGIO : trace, glimmer

resta *nf* : subtraction

restablecer {53} *vt* : reestablish, restore — **restablecerse** *vr* : recover — **restablecimiento** *nm* : restoration, recovery

restallar *vi* : crack, crackle

restar *vt* **1** : deduct, subtract **2** DISMINUIR : minimize — *vi* : be left — **restante** *adj* **1** : remaining **2** lo ~ : the rest

restauración *nf*, *pl* **-ciones** : restoration

restaurante *nm* : restaurant

restaurar *vt* : restore

restituir {41} *vt* : return, restore — **restitución** *nf*, *pl* **-ciones** : restitution

resto *nm* **1** : rest, remainder **2** ~s *nmpl* : leftovers **3** *or* ~s **mortales** : mortal remains

restregar {49} *vt* : rub, scrub — **restregarse** *vr* : rub

restringir {35} *vt* : restrict, limit — **restricción** *nf*, *pl* **-ciones** : restriction, limitation — **restrictivo, -va** *adj* : restrictive

resucitar *vt* : resuscitate, revive — *vi* : come back to life

resuelto, -ta *adj* : determined, resolved

resuello *nm* : heavy breathing, panting

resultar *vi* **1** : succeed, work out **2** SALIR : turn out (to be) **3** ~ **de** : be the result of **4** ~ **en** : result in — **resultado** *nm* : result, outcome

resumir *v* : summarize, sum up — **resumen** *nm*, *pl* **-súmenes** **1** : summary **2** **en** ~ : in short

resurgir {35} *vi* : reappear, revive — **resurgimiento** *nm* : resurgence — **resurrección** *nf*, *pl* **-ciones** : resurrection

retahíla *nf* : string, series

retal *nm* : remnant

retardar *vt* **1** RETRASAR : delay **2** POSPONER : postpone

retazo *nm* **1** : remnant, scrap **2** : fragment (of a text, etc.)

retener {80} *vt* **1** : retain, keep **2** : withhold (funds, etc.) **3** DETENER : detain — **retención** *nf*, *pl* **-ciones** **1** : retention **2** : deduction, withholding (of funds)

reticente *adj* : reluctant — **reticencia** *nf* : reluctance

retina *nf* : retina

retintín *nm*, *pl* **-tines** **1** : tinkling, jingle **2** **con** ~ : sarcastically

retirar *vt* **1** : remove, take away **2** : withdraw (funds, statements, etc.) — **retirarse** *vr* **1** : retreat, withdraw **2** JUBILARSE : retire — **retirada** *nf* **1** : withdrawal **2** **batirse en** ~ : beat a retreat — **retirado, -da** *adj* **1** : remote, secluded **2** JUBILADO : retired — **retiro** *nm* **1** : retreat **2** JUBILACIÓN : retirement **3** *Lat* : withdrawal

reto *nm* : challenge, dare

retocar {72} *vt* : touch up

retoño *nm* : sprout, shoot

retoque *nm* **1** : retouching **2** **el último** ~ : the finishing touch

retorcer {14} *vt* **1** : twist, contort **2** : wring out (clothes, etc.) — **retorcerse** *vr* **1** : get twisted up **2** : squirm, writhe (in pain) — **retorcijón** *nm*, *pl* **-jones** : cramp, spasm — **retorcimiento** *nm* : twisting, wringing out

retórica *nf* : rhetoric — **retórico, -ca** *adj* : rhetorical

retornar *v* : return — **retorno** *nm* : return

retozar {21} *vi* : frolic, romp — **retozón, -zona** *adj* : playful, frisky

retractarse *vr* **1** : withdraw, back down **2** ~ **de** : take back, retract

retraer {81} *vt* : retract — **retraerse** *vr* : withdraw — **retraído, -da** *adj* : withdrawn, shy

retrasar *vt* **1** : delay, hold up **2** APLAZAR : postpone **3** : set back (a clock) — **retrasarse** *vr* **1** : be late **2** : fall behind (in work, etc.) — **retrasado, -da** *adj* **1** : retarded **2** : in arrears (of payments) **3** : backward (of a country) **4** : slow (of a clock) — **retraso** *nm* **1** : delay **2** SUBDESARROLLO : backwardness **3** ~ **mental** : mental retardation

retratar *vt* **1** : portray **2** FOTOGRAFIAR : photograph **3** DIBUJAR : paint a portrait of — **retrato** *nm* **1** : portrayal **2** DIBUJO : portrait **3** FOTOGRAFÍA : photograph

retrete *nm* : restroom, toilet

retribuir {41} *vt* **1** : pay **2** RECOMPENSAR : reward — **retribución** *nf*, *pl*

-ciones 1 : payment **2** RECOMPENSA : reward

retroactivo, -va *adj* : retroactive

retroceder *vi* **1** : go back, turn back **2** CEDER : back down — **retroceso** *nm* **1** : backward movement **2** : backing down

retrógrado, -da *adj & nmf* : reactionary

retrospectiva *nf* : hindsight — **retrospectivo, -va** *adj* : retrospective

retrovisor *nm* : rearview mirror

retumbar *vi* : resound, reverberate, rumble

reumatismo *nm* : rheumatism

reunir {68} *vt* **1** : unite, join **2** TENER : have, possess **3** RECOGER : gather, collect — **reunirse** *vr* : meet, gather — **reunión** *nf, pl* **-niones 1** : meeting **2** : (social) gathering, reunion

revalidar *vt* : confirm, ratify

revancha *nf* **1** : revenge **2** : rematch (in sports)

revelar *vt* **1** : reveal, disclose **2** : develop (film) — **revelación** *nf, pl* **-ciones** : revelation — **revelado** *nm* : developing (of film) — **revelador, -dora** *adj* : revealing

reventar {55} *v* : burst, blow up — **reventarse** *vr* : burst — **reventón** *nm, pl* **-tones** : blowout, flat tire

reverberar *vi* : reverberate — **reverberación** *nf, pl* **-ciones** : reverberation

reverenciar *vt* : revere — **reverencia** *nf* **1** : bow, curtsy **2** VENERACIÓN : reverence — **reverendo, -da** *adj & nmf* : reverend — **reverente** *adj* : reverent

reversa *nf Lat* : reverse (gear)

reverso *nm* **1** : back, reverse **2 el ~ de la medalla** : the complete opposite — **reversible** *adj* : reversible

revertir {76} *vi* **1** : revert **2 ~ en** : result in

revés *nm, pl* **-veses 1** : back, wrong side **2** CONTRATIEMPO : setback **3** BOFETADA : slap **4** : backhand (in sports) **5 al ~** : the other way around, upside down, inside out

revestir {54} *vt* **1** : coat, cover **2** ASUMIR : take on, assume — **revestimiento** *nm* : covering, coating

revisar *vt* **1** : examine, inspect **2** : check over, overhaul (machinery, etc.) **3** MODIFICAR : revise — **revisión** *nf, pl* **-siones 1** : revision **2** INSPECCIÓN : inspection, check — **revisor, -sora** *n* : inspector

revistar *vt* : review, inspect (troops, etc.) — **revista** *nf* **1** : magazine, jour-

nal **2** : revue (in theater) **3 pasar ~** : review, inspect

revivir *vi* : revive, come alive again — *vt* : relive

revocar {72} *vt* : revoke

revolcar {82} *vt* : knock over, knock down — **revolcarse** *vr* : roll around

revolotear *vi* : flutter, flit — **revoloteo** *nm* : fluttering, flitting

revoltijo *nm* : mess, jumble

revoltoso, -sa *adj* : rebellious

revolución *nf, pl* **-ciones** : revolution — **revolucionar** *vt* : revolutionize — **revolucionario, -ria** *adj & n* : revolutionary

revolver {89} *vt* **1** : mix, stir **2** : upset (one's stomach) **3** DESORGANIZAR : mess up — **revolverse** *vr* **1** : toss and turn **2** VOLVERSE : turn around

revólver *nm* : revolver

revuelo *nm* : commotion

revuelta *nf* : uprising, revolt — **revuelto, -ta** *adj* **1** : choppy, rough **2** DESORDENADO : messed up **3 huevos revueltos** : scrambled eggs

rey *nm* : king

reyerta *nf* : brawl, fight

rezagarse {52} *vr* : fall behind, lag

rezar {21} *vi* **1** : pray **2** DECIR : say — *vt* : say, recite — **rezo** *nm* : prayer

razongar {52} *vi* : gripe, grumble

rezumar *v* : ooze

ría *nf* : estuary

riachuelo *nm* : brook, stream

riada *nf* : flood

ribera *nf* : bank, shore

ribetear *vt* : border, trim — **ribete** *nm* **1** : border, trim **2** : embellishment

rico, -ca *adj* **1** : rich, wealthy **2** ABUNDANTE : abundant **3** SABROSO : rich, tasty — **~** *n* : rich person

ridiculizar {21} *vt* : ridicule — **ridículo, -la** *adj* : ridiculous — **ridículo** *nm* **1 hacer el ~** : make a fool of oneself **2 poner en ~** : ridicule

riego *nm* : irrigation

riel *nm* : rail

rienda *nf* **1** : rein **2 dar ~ suelta a** : give free rein to

riesgo *nm* : risk

rifa *nf* : raffle — **rifar** *vt* : raffle (off) — **rifarse** *vr fam* : fight over

rifle *nm* : rifle

rígido, -da *adj* **1** : rigid, stiff **2** SEVERO : harsh, strict — **rigidez** *nf, pl* **-deces 1** : rigidity, stiffness **2** SEVERIDAD : harshness, strictness

rigor *nm* **1** : rigor, harshness **2** EXACTITUD : precision **3 de ~** : essential, obligatory — **riguroso, -sa** *adj* : rigorous

rima *nf* 1 : rhyme 2 ~**s** *nfpl* : verse, poetry — **rimar** *vi* : rhyme

rimbombante *adj* : showy, pompous

rímel *nm* : mascara

rincón *nm, pl* -**cones** : corner, nook

rinoceronte *nm* : rhinoceros

riña *nf* 1 : fight, brawl 2 DISPUTA : dispute, quarrel

riñón *nm, pl* -**ñones** : kidney

río *nm* 1 : river 2 TORRENTE : torrent, stream

riqueza *nf* 1 : wealth 2 ABUNDANCIA : richness 3 ~**s naturales** : natural resources

risa *nf* 1 : laughter, laugh 2 **dar** ~ **a algn** : make s.o. laugh 3 **morirse de la** ~ *fam* : die laughing

risco *nm* : crag, cliff

risible *adj* : laughable

ristra *nf* : string, series

risueño, -ña *adj* : cheerful, smiling

ritmo *nm* 1 : rhythm 2 VELOCIDAD : pace, speed — **rítmico, -ca** *adj* : rhythmical

rito *nm* : rite, ritual — **ritual** *adj & nm* : ritual

rival *adj & nmf* : rival — **rivalidad** *nf* : rivalry, competition — **rivalizar** {21} *vi* ~ **con** : rival, compete with

rizar {21} *vt* 1 : curl 2 : ripple (a surface) — **rizarse** *vr* : curl — **rizado, -da** *adj* 1 : curly 2 : choppy (of water) — **rizo** *nm* 1 : curl 2 : ripple (in water) 3 : loop (in aviation)

róbalo *nm* : bass (fish)

robar *vt* 1 : steal 2 : burglarize (a house, etc.) 3 SECUESTRAR : kidnap — **robo** *nm* : robbery, theft

roble *nm* : oak

robot *nm, pl* -**bots** : robot — **robótica** *nf* : robotics

robustecer {53} *vt* : make stronger, strengthen — **robusto, -ta** *adj* : robust, sturdy

roca *nf* : rock, boulder

roce *nm* 1 : rubbing, chafing 2 RASGUÑO : graze, scratch 3 **tener un** ~ **con** : have a brush with

rociar {85} *vt* : spray, sprinkle — **rocío** *nm* : dew

rocoso, -sa *adj* : rocky

rodaja *nf* : slice

rodar {19} *vi* 1 : roll, roll down, roll along 2 GIRAR : turn, go around 3 : travel (of a vehicle) 4 : film (of movies, etc.) — *vt* 1 : film, shoot 2 : break in (a vehicle) — **rodaje** *nm* 1 : filming, shooting 2 : breaking in (of a vehicle)

rodear *vt* 1 : surround, encircle 2 *Lat* : round up (cattle) — **rodearse** *vr* ~ **de** : surround oneself with — **rodeo** *nm* 1 : rodeo, roundup 2 DESVÍO,: detour 3 **andar con** ~**s** : beat around the bush

rodilla *nf* : knee

rodillo *nm* 1 : roller 2 : rolling pin (for pastry)

roer {69} *vt* 1 : gnaw 2 ATORMENTAR : eat away at, torment — **roedor** *nm* : rodent

rogar {16} *vt* : beg, request — *vi* : pray

rojo, -ja *adj* 1 : red 2 **ponerse** ~ : blush — **rojo** *nm* : red — **rojez** *nf* : redness — **rojizo, -za** *adj* : reddish

rollizo, -za *adj* : plump, chubby

rollo *nm* 1 : roll, coil 2 *fam* : boring speech, lecture

romance *nm* 1 : romance 2 : Romance (language)

romano, -na *adj & n* : Roman

romántico, -ca *adj* : romantic — **romanticismo** *nm* : romanticism

romería *nf* : pilgrimage, procession

romero *nm* : rosemary

romo, -ma *adj* : blunt, dull

rompecabezas *nms & pl* : puzzle

romper {70} *vt* 1 : break 2 RASGAR : rip, tear 3 : break off (relations), break (a contract) — *vi* 1 : break (of the day, waves, etc.) 2 ~ **a** : begin to, burst out with 3 ~ **con** : break off with — **romperse** *vr* : break

ron *nm* : rum

roncar {72} *vi* : snore — **ronco, -ca** *adj* : hoarse

ronda *nf* 1 : rounds *pl*, patrol 2 : round (of drinks, etc.) — **rondar** *vt* 1 : patrol 2 : hang around (a place) 3 : be approximately (an age, a number, etc.) — *vi* 1 : be on patrol 2 MERODEAR : prowl about

ronquera *nf* : hoarseness

ronquido *nm* : snore

ronronear *vi* : purr — **ronroneo** *nm* : purr, purring

ronzar {21} *vt* : munch, crunch

roña *nf* 1 : mange 2 SUCIEDAD : dirt, filth — **roñoso, -sa** *adj* 1 : mangy 2 SUCIO : dirty 3 *fam* : stingy

ropa *nf* 1 : clothes *pl*, clothing 2 ~ **interior** : underwear — **ropaje** *nm* : robes *pl*, regalia — **ropero** *nm* : wardrobe, closet

rosa *nf* : rose (flower) — ~ *adj* : rose-colored — ~ *nm* : rose (color) — **rosado, -da** *adj* 1 : pink 2 **vino rosado** : rosé — **rosado** *nm* : pink (color) — **rosal** *nm* : rosebush

rosario *nm* : rosary
rosbif *nm* : roast beef
rosca *nf* 1 : thread (of a screw) 2 ESPI-RAL : ring, coil
roseta *nf* : rosette
rosquilla *nf* : doughnut
rostro *nm* : face
rotación *nf, pl* **-ciones** : rotation — **rotativo, -va** *adj* : rotary, revolving
roto, -ta *adj* : broken, torn
rotonda *nf* : traffic circle, rotary
rótula *nf* : kneecap
rótulo *nm* 1 : heading, title 2 ETIQUETA : label, sign
rotundo, -da *adj* : categorical, absolute
rotura *nf* : break, tear, fracture
rozar {21} *vt* 1 : graze, touch lightly 2 APROXIMARSE DE : touch on, border on — *vi* : scrape, rub — **rozarse** *vr* 1 : rub, chafe 2 — **con** *fam* : rub elbows with — **rozadura** *nf* : scratch
rubí *nm, pl* **rubíes** : ruby
rubicundo, -da *adj* : ruddy
rubio, -bia *adj & n* : blond
rubor *nm* : flush, blush — **ruborizarse** {21} *vr* : blush
rúbrica *nf* 1 : flourish (in writing) 2 TÍTULO : title, heading
rudeza *nf* : roughness, coarseness
rudimentos *nmpl* : rudiments, basics — **rudimentario, -ria** *adj* : rudimentary
rudo, -da *adj* 1 : rough, harsh 2 GROSERO : coarse, unpolished
rueda *nf* 1 : wheel 2 CORRO : circle, ring 3 RODAJA : (round) slice 4 **ir sobre ~s** : go smoothly — **ruedo** *nm* : bullring

ruego *nm* : request
rugir {35} *vi* : roar — **rugido** *nm* : roar
rugoso, -sa *adj* 1 : rough 2 ARRUGADO : wrinkled
ruibarbo *nm* : rhubarb
ruido *nm* : noise — **ruidoso, -sa** *adj* : loud, noisy
ruina *nf* 1 : ruin, destruction 2 COLAPSO : collapse 3 **~s** *nfpl* : ruins, remains — **ruinoso, -sa** *adj* : run-down, dilapidated
ruiseñor *nm* : nightingale
ruleta *nf* : roulette
rulo *nm* : curler, roller
rumano, -na *adj* : Romanian, Rumanian
rumba *nf* : rumba
rumbo *nm* 1 : direction, course 2 ESPLENDIDEZ : lavishness 3 **con ~ a** : bound for, heading for 4 **perder el ~** : go off course
rumiar *vt* : mull over — *vi* : chew the cud — **rumiante** *adj & nm* : ruminant
rumor *nm* 1 : rumor 2 MURMULLO : murmur — **rumorearse** *or* **rumorarse** *vr* : be rumored — **rumoroso, -sa** *adj* : murmuring, babbling
ruptura *nf* 1 : break, rupture 2 : breach (of a contract) 3 : breaking off (of relations)
rural *adj* : rural
ruso, -sa *adj* : Russian — **ruso** *nm* : Russian (language)
rústico, -ca *adj* 1 : rural, rustic 2 **en rústica** : in paperback
ruta *nf* : route
rutina *nf* : routine — **rutinario, -ria** *adj* : routine

S

s *nf* : s, 20th letter of the Spanish alphabet
sábado *nm* : Saturday
sábana *nf* : sheet
sabandija *nf* : bug
saber {71} *vt* 1 : know 2 SER CAPAZ DE : know how to, be able to 3 ENTERARSE : learn, find out 4 **a ~** : namely — *vi* 1 : taste 2 **~ de** : know about — **~** *nm* : knowledge — **sabelotodo** *nmf fam* : know-it-all — **sabido, -da** *adj* : well-known — **sabiduría** *nf* 1 : wisdom 2 CONOCIMIENTO : learning, knowledge — **sabiendas: a ~** *adv phr* : knowingly — **sabio, -bia** *adj* 1 : learned 2 PRUDENTE : wise, sensible

sabor *nm* : flavor, taste — **saborear** *vt* : savor
sabotaje *nm* : sabotage — **saboteador, -dora** *n* : saboteur — **sabotear** *vt* : sabotage
sabroso, -sa *adj* : delicious, tasty
sabueso *nm* 1 : bloodhound 2 *fam* : sleuth
sacacorchos *nms & pl* : corkscrew
sacapuntas *nms & pl* : pencil sharpener
sacar {72} *vt* 1 : take out 2 OBTENER : get, obtain 3 EXTRAER : extract, withdraw 4 : bring out (a book, a product, etc.) 5 : take (photos), make (copies) 6 QUITAR : remove 7 **~ adelante** : bring up (children), carry out (a project,

etc.) 8 ~ **la lengua** : stick out one's tongue — *vi* : serve (in sports)

sacarina *nf* : saccharin

sacerdote, -tisa *n* : priest *m*, priestess *f* — **sacerdocio** *nm* : priesthood — **sacerdotal** *adj* : priestly

saciar *vt* : satisfy

saco *nm* 1 : bag, sack 2 : sac (in anatomy) 3 *Lat* : jacket

sacramento *nm* : sacrament — **sacramental** *adj* : sacramental

sacrificar {72} *vt* : sacrifice — **sacrificarse** *vr* : sacrifice oneself — **sacrificio** *nm* : sacrifice

sacrilegio *nm* : sacrilege — **sacrílego, -ga** *adj* : sacrilegious

sacro, -cra *adj* : sacred — **sacrosanto, -ta** *adj* : sacrosanct

sacudir *vt* 1 : shake 2 GOLPEAR : beat 3 CONMOVER : shake up, shock — **sacudirse** *vr* : shake off — **sacudida** *nf* 1 : shaking 2 : jolt (of a train, etc.), tremor (of an earthquake) 3 : (emotional) shock

sádico, -ca *adj* : sadistic — ~ *n* : sadist — **sadismo** *nm* : sadism

saeta *nf* : arrow

safari *nm* : safari

sagaz *adj, pl* **-gaces** : shrewd, sagacious — **sagacidad** *nf* : shrewdness

sagrado, -da *adj* : sacred, holy

sal *nf* : salt

sala *nf* 1 : room, hall 2 : living room (of a house) 3 ~ **de espera** : waiting room

salar *vt* : salt — **salado, -da** *adj* 1 : salty 2 GRACIOSO : witty 3 **agua salada** : salt water

salario *nm* : salary, wage

salchicha *nf* : sausage — **salchichón** *nf, pl* **-chones** : salami-like cold cut

saldar *vt* 1 : settle, pay off 2 VENDER : sell off — **saldo** *nm* 1 : balance (of an account) 2 ~s *nmpl* : remainders, sale items

salero *nm* : saltshaker

salir {73} *vi* 1 : go out, come out 2 PARTIR : leave 3 APARECER : appear 4 RESULTAR : turn out 5 : rise (of the sun) 6 ~ **adelante** : get by 7 ~ **con** : go out with, date 8 ~ **de** : come from — **salirse** *vr* 1 : leave 2 ESCAPARSE : leak out, escape 3 SOLTARSE : come off 4 ~ **con la suya** : get one's own way — **salida** *nf* 1 : exit 2 : (action of) leaving, departure 3 SOLUCIÓN : way out 4 : leak (of gas, liquid, etc.) 5 OCURRENCIA : witty remark 6 ~ **de emergencia** : emergency exit 7 ~ **del sol** : sunrise — **saliente** *adj* 1 : departing, outgoing 2 DESTACADO : outstanding

saliva *nf* : saliva

salmo *nm* : psalm

salmón *nm, pl* **-mones** : salmon

salmuera *nf* : brine

salón *nm, pl* **-lones** 1 : lounge, sitting room 2 ~ **de belleza** : beauty salon 3 ~ **de clase** : classroom

salpicar {72} *vt* 1 : splash, spatter 2 ~ **de** : pepper with — **salpicadera** *nf* *Lat* : fender — **salpicadura** *nf* : splash

salsa *nf* 1 : sauce 2 : (meat) gravy 3 : salsa (music)

saltamontes *nms & pl* : grasshopper

saltar *vi* 1 : jump, leap 2 REBOTAR : bounce 3 : come off (of a button, etc.) 4 ROMPERSE : shatter 5 ESTALLAR : explode, blow up — *vt* 1 : jump (over) 2 OMITIR : skip, miss — **saltarse** *vr* 1 : come off 2 OMITIR : skip, miss

saltear *vt* : sauté

saltimbanqui *nmf* : acrobat

salto *nm* 1 : jump, leap 2 : dive (into water) 3 ~ **de agua** : waterfall — **saltón, -tona** *adj, mpl* **-tones** : bulging, protruding

salud *nf* 1 : health 2 **¡salud!** : here's to your health! 3 **¡salud!** *Lat* : bless you! (when someone sneezes) — **saludable** *adj* : healthy

saludar *vt* 1 : greet, say hello to 2 : salute (in the military) — **saludo** *nm* 1 : greeting 2 : (military) salute 3 ~s : best wishes, regards

salva *nf* ~ **de aplausos** : round of applause

salvación *nf, pl* **-ciones** : salvation

salvado *nm* : bran

salvador, -dora *n* : savior, rescuer

salvadoreño, -ña *adj* : (El) Salvadoran

salvaguardar *vt* : safeguard

salvaje *adj* 1 : wild 2 PRIMITIVO : savage, primitive — ~ *nmf* : savage

salvar *vt* 1 : save, rescue 2 RECORRER : cover, travel 3 SUPERAR : overcome — **salvarse** *vr* : save oneself — **salvavidas** *nms & pl* 1 : life preserver 2 ~ **bote** : lifeboat

salvia *nf* : sage (plant)

salvo, -va *adj* : safe — **salvo** *prep* 1 : except (for), save 2 ~ **que** : unless

samba *nf* : samba

San → santo

sanar *vt* : heal, cure — *vi* : recover — **sanatorio** *nm* 1 : sanatorium 2 HOSPITAL : clinic, hospital

sanción *nf, pl* **-ciones** : sanction — **sancionar** *vt* : sanction

sandalia *nf* : sandal

sándalo *nm* : sandalwood

sandía *nf* : watermelon

sandwich ['sandwitʃ, 'saŋgwitʃ] *nm, pl* -**wiches** [-dwitʃes, -gwi-] : sandwich
saneamiento *nm* : sanitation
sangrar *vt* 1 : bleed 2 : indent (a paragraph) — *vi* : bleed — **sangrante** *adj* : bleeding — **sangre** *nf* 1 : blood 2 a ~ **fría** : in cold blood — **sangriento,** -**ta** *adj* : bloody
sanguijuela *nf* : leech
sanguinario, -**ria** *adj* : bloodthirsty — **sanguíneo,** -**nea** *adj* : blood
sano, -**na** *adj* 1 : healthy 2 : (morally) wholesome 3 ENTERO : intact 4 **sano y salvo** : safe and sound — **sanidad** *nf* 1 : health 2 : public health, sanitation — **sanitario,** -**ria** *adj* : sanitary, health — **sanitario** *nm Lat* : toilet
santiamén *nm* **en un** ~ : in no time at all
santo, -**ta** *adj* 1 : holy 2 **Santo, Santa** (**San** *before masculine names except those beginning with D or T*) : Saint — ~ *n* : saint — **santo** *nm* 1 : saint's day 2 *Lat* : birthday — **santidad** *nf* : holiness, sanctity — **santiguarse** {10} *vr* : cross oneself — **santuario** *nm* : sanctuary
saña *nf* 1 : fury 2 BRUTALIDAD : viciousness
sapo *nm* : toad
saque *nm* : serve (in tennis, etc.), throw-in (in soccer)
saquear *vt* : sack, loot — **saqueador,** -**dora** *n* : looter — **saqueo** *nm* : sacking, looting
sarampión *nm* : measles *pl*
sarape *nm Lat* : serape
sarcasmo *nm* : sarcasm — **sarcástico,** -**ca** *adj* : sarcastic
sardina *nf* : sardine
sardónico, -**ca** *adj* : sardonic
sargento *nmf* : sergeant
sarpullido *nm* : rash
sartén *nmf, pl* -**tenes** : frying pan
sastre, -**tra** *n* : tailor — **sastrería** *nf* 1 : tailoring 2 : tailor's shop
Satanás *nm* : Satan — **satánico,** -**ca** *adj* : satanic
satélite *nm* : satellite
sátira *nf* : satire — **satírico,** -**ca** *adj* : satirical
satisfacer {74} *vt* 1 : satisfy 2 CUMPLIR : fulfill, meet 3 PAGAR : pay — **satisfacerse** *vr* 1 : be satisfied 2 VENGARSE : take revenge — **satisfacción** *nf, pl* -**ciones** : satisfaction — **satisfactorio,** -**ria** *adj* : satisfactory — **satisfecho,** -**cha** *adj* : satisfied
saturar *vt* : saturate — **saturación** *nf, pl* -**ciones** : saturation

Saturno *nm* : Saturn
sauce *nm* : willow
sauna *nmf* : sauna
savia *nf* : sap
saxofón *nm, pl* -**fones** : saxophone
sazón *nf, pl* -**zones** 1 : seasoning 2 MADUREZ : ripeness 3 **a la** ~ : at that time, then 4 **en** ~ : ripe, in season — **sazonar** *vt* : season
se *pron* 1 (*reflexive*) : himself, herself, itself, oneself, yourself, yourselves, themselves 2 (*indirect object*) : (to) him, (to) her, (to) you, (to) them 3 : each other, one another 4 ~ **dice que** : it is said that 5 ~ **habla inglés** : English spoken
sebo *nm* 1 : fat 2 : tallow (for candles, etc.) 3 : suet (for cooking)
secar {72} *v* : dry — **secarse** *vr* : dry (up) — **secador** *nm* : hair dryer — **secadora** *nf* : (clothes) dryer
sección *nf, pl* -**ciones** : section
seco, -**ca** *adj* 1 : dry 2 : dried (of fruits, etc.) 3 TAJANTE : sharp, brusque 4 *fam* : thin, skinny 5 **a secas** : simply, just 6 **en seco** : suddenly
secretar *vt* : secrete — **secreción** *nf, pl* -**ciones** : secretion
secretario, -**ria** *n* : secretary — **secretaría** *nf* : secretariat
secreto, -**ta** *adj* : secret — **secreto** *nm* 1 : secret 2 **en** ~ : in confidence
secta *nf* : sect
sector *nm* : sector
secuaz *nmf, pl* -**cuaces** : follower, henchman
secuela *nf* : consequence
secuencia *nf* : sequence
secuestrar *vt* 1 : kidnap 2 : hijack (an airplane, etc.) 3 EMBARGAR : confiscate, seize — **secuestrador,** -**dora** *n* 1 : kidnapper 2 : hijacker (of an airplane, etc.) — **secuestro** *nm* 1 : kidnapping 2 : hijacking (of an airplane, etc.) 3 : seizure (of goods)
secular *adj* : secular
secundar *vt* : support, second — **secundario,** -**ria** *adj* : secondary
sed *nf* 1 : thirst 2 **tener** ~ : be thirsty
seda *nf* : silk
sedal *nm* : fishing line
sedar *vt* : sedate — **sedante** *adj & nm* : sedative
sede *nf* 1 : seat, headquarters 2 **Santa Sede** : Holy See
sedentario, -**ria** *adj* : sedentary
sedición *nf, pl* -**ciones** : sedition — **sedicioso,** -**sa** *adj* : seditious
sediento, -**ta** *adj* : thirsty
sedimento *nm* : sediment

sedoso, -sa *adj* : silky, silken
seducir {61} *vt* **1** : seduce **2** ATRAER
: captivate, charm — **seducción** *nf, pl*
-ciones : seduction — **seductor,**
-tora *adj* **1** : seductive **2** ENCANTADOR
: charming — **~** *n* : seducer
segar {49} *vt* : reap — **segador, -dora**
n : reaper, harvester
seglar *adj* **1** : lay, secular — **~** *nm*
: layperson, layman *m*, laywoman *f*
segmento *nm* : segment
segregar {52} *vt* : segregate — **segre-**
gación *nf, pl* **-ciones** : segregation
seguir {75} *vt* : follow — *vi* : go on,
continue — **seguida**: **en ~** *adv phr*
: right away — **seguido** *adv* **1**
: straight (ahead) **2** *Lat* : often —
seguido, -da *adj* **1** : continuous **2**
CONSECUTIVO : consecutive — **segui-**
dor, -dora *n* : follower
según *prep* : according to — **~** *adv* : it
depends — **~** *conj* : as, just as
segundo, -da *adj* : second — **~** *n*
: second (one) — **segundo** *nm* : second (unit of time)
seguro, -ra *adj* **1** : safe **2** FIRME : secure
3 CIERTO : sure, certain **4** FIABLE : reliable — **seguramente** *adv* : for sure,
surely — **seguridad** *nf* **1** : safety **2**
GARANTÍA : security **3** CERTEZA : certainty **4** CONFIANZA : confidence —
seguro *adv* : certainly — **~** *nm* **1**
: insurance **2** : safety (device)
seis *adj & nm* : six — **seiscientos, -tas**
adj : six hundred — **seiscientos** *nms*
& *pl* : six hundred
seísmo *nm* : earthquake
selección *nf, pl* **-ciones** : selection —
seleccionar *vt* : select, choose — **se-**
lectivo, -va *adj* : selective — **selecto,**
-ta *adj* : choice, select
sellar *vt* **1** : seal **2** TIMBRAR : stamp —
sello *nm* **1** : seal **2** TIMBRE : stamp **3** *or*
~ distintivo : hallmark
selva *nf* **1** : jungle **2** BOSQUE : forest
semáforo *nm* : traffic light
semana *nf* : week — **semanal** *adj*
: weekly — **semanario** *nm* : weekly
semántica *nf* : semantics — **semánti-**
co, -ca *adj* : semantic
semblante *nm* **1** : countenance, face **2**
APARIENCIA : look
sembrar {55} *vt* **1** : sow **2 ~ de** : strew
with
semejar *vi* : resemble — **semejarse** *vr*
: look alike — **semejante** *adj* **1** : similar **2** TAL : such — **~** *nm* : fellowman
— **semejanza** *nf* : similarity
semen *nm* : semen — **semental** *nm* **1**
: stud **2 caballo ~** : stallion

semestre *nm* : semester
semiconductor *nm* : semiconductor
semifinal *nf* : semifinal
semilla *nf* : seed — **semillero** *nm* **1**
: nursery (for plants) **2** HERVIDERO
: hotbed, breeding ground
seminario *nm* **1** : seminary **2** CURSO
: seminar, course
sémola *nf* : semolina
senado *nm* : senate — **senador, -dora**
n : senator
sencillo, -lla *adj* **1** : simple **2** ÚNICO
: single — **sencillez** *nf* : simplicity
senda *nf or* **sendero** *nm* : path, way
sendos, -das *adj pl* : each, both
senil *adj* : senile
seno *nm* **1** : breast, bosom **2** : sinus (in
anatomy) **3 ~ materno** : womb
sensación *nf, pl* **-ciones** : feeling, sensation — **sensacional** *adj* : sensational — **sensacionalista** *adj* : sensation-
alistic, lurid
sensato, -ta *adj* : sensible — **sensatez**
nf : good sense
sensible *adj* **1** : sensitive **2** APRECIABLE
: considerable, significant — **sensi-**
bilidad *nf* : sensitivity — **sensitivo,**
-va *or* **sensorial** *adj* : sense, sensory
sensual *adj* : sensual, sensuous — **sen-**
sualidad *nf* : sensuality
sentar {55} *vt* **1** : seat, sit **2** ESTABLECER
: establish, set — *vi* **1** : suit **2 ~ bien**
a : agree with (of food or drink) —
sentarse *vr* : sit (down) — **sentado,**
-da *adj* **1** : sitting, seated **2 dar por**
sentado : take for granted
sentencia *nf* **1** FALLO : sentence, judgment **2** MÁXIMA : saying — **senten-**
ciar *vt* : sentence
sentido, -da *adj* **1** : heartfelt, sincere **2**
SENSIBLE : touchy, sensitive — **senti-**
do *nm* **1** : sense **2** CONOCIMIENTO
: consciousness **3** DIRECCIÓN : direction **4 doble ~** : double entendre **5**
~ común : common sense **6 ~ del**
humor : sense of humor **7 ~ único**
: one-way
sentimiento *nm* **1** : feeling, emotion **2**
PESAR : regret — **sentimental** *adj*
: sentimental — **sentimentalismo** *nm*
: sentimentality
sentir {76} *vt* **1** : feel **2** OÍR : hear **3**
LAMENTAR : be sorry for **4 lo siento**
: I'm sorry — *vi* : feel — **sentirse** *vr*
: feel
seña *nf* **1** : sign **2 ~s** *nfpl* DIRECCIÓN
: address **3 ~s particulares** : distin-
guishing marks
señal *nf* **1** : signal **2** AVISO, INDICIO
: sign **3** DEPÓSITO : deposit **4 dar ~es**

de : show signs of **5 en ~ de** : as a token of — **señalado, -da** adj : notable — **señalar** vt **1** INDICAR : indicate, point out **2** MARCAR : mark **3** FIJAR : fix, set — **señalarse** vr : distinguish oneself

señor, -ñora n **1** : gentleman m, man m, lady f, woman f **2** : Sir m, Madam f **3** : Mr. m, Mrs. f **4 señora** : wife f **5 el Señor** : the Lord — **señorial** adj : stately — **señorita** nf **1** : young lady, young woman **2** : Miss

señuelo nm **1** : decoy **2** TRAMPA : bait, lure

separar vt **1** : separate **2** QUITAR : detach, remove **3** APARTAR : move away **4** DESTITUIR : dismiss — **separarse** vr **1** APARTARSE : separate **2** : part company — **separación** nf, pl **-ciones** : separation — **separado, -da** adj **1** : separate **2** : separated (of persons) **3 por separado** : separately

septentrional adj : northern

séptico, -ca adj : septic

septiembre nm : September

séptimo, -ma adj : seventh — ~ n : seventh

sepulcro nm : tomb, sepulchre — **sepultar** vt : bury — **sepultura** nf **1** : burial **2** TUMBA : grave

sequedad nf : dryness — **sequía** nf : drought

séquito nm : retinue, entourage

ser {77} vi **1** : be **2 a no ~ que** : unless **3 ¿cuánto es?** : how much is it? **4 es más** : what's more **5 ~ de** : belong to **6 ~ de** : come from **7 son las diez** : it's ten o'clock — ~ nm **1** ENTE : being **2 ~ humano** : human being

serbio, -bia adj : Serb, Serbian

serenar vt : calm — **serenarse** vr : calm down — **serenata** nf : serenade — **serenidad** nf : serenity — **sereno, -na** adj **1** : serene, calm **2** : fair, clear (of weather) — **sereno** nm : night watchman

serie nf **1** : series **2 fabricación en ~** : mass production **3 fuera de ~** : extraordinary — **serial** nm : serial

serio, -ria adj **1** : serious **2** RESPONSABLE : reliable **3 en serio** : seriously — **seriedad** nf : seriousness

sermón nm, pl **-mones** : sermon — **sermonear** vt : lecture, reprimand

serpentear vi : twist, wind — **serpiente** nf **1** : serpent, snake **2 ~ de cascabel** : rattlesnake

serrado, -da adj : serrated

serrano, -na adj **1** : mountain **2 jamón serrano** : cured ham

serrar {55} vt : saw — **serrín** nm, pl **-rrines** : sawdust — **serrucho** nm : saw, handsaw

servicio nm **1** : service **2 ~s** nmpl : restroom — **servicial** adj : obliging, helpful — **servidor, -dora** n **1** : servant **2 su seguro servidor** : yours truly — **servidumbre** nf **1** : servitude **2** CRIADOS : help, servants pl — **servil** adj : servile

servilleta nf : napkin

servir {54} vt : serve — vi **1** : work, function **2** VALER : be of use — **servirse** vr **1** : help oneself **2 sírvase sentarse** : please have a seat

sesenta adj & nm : sixty

sesgo nm : bias, slant

sesión nf, pl **-siones** **1** : session **2** : showing (of a film), performance (of a play)

seso nm : brain — **sesudo, -da** adj **1** : sensible **2** fam : brainy

seta nf : mushroom

setecientos, -tas adj : seven hundred — **setecientos** nms & pl : seven hundred

setenta adj & nm : seventy

setiembre nm → **septiembre**

seto nm **1** : fence **2 ~ vivo** : hedge

seudónimo nm : pseudonym

severo, -ra adj **1** : harsh, severe **2** : strict (of a teacher, etc.) — **severidad** nf : severity

sexagésimo, -ma adj & n : sixtieth

sexo nm : sex — **sexismo** nm : sexism — **sexista** adj & nmf : sexist

sexteto nm : sextet

sexto, -ta adj & n : sixth

sexual adj : sexual — **sexualidad** nf : sexuality

sexy adj, pl **sexy** or **sexys** : sexy

si conj **1** : if **2** (in indirect questions) : whether **3 ~ bien** : although **4 ~ no** : otherwise, or else

sí¹ adv **1** : yes **2 creo que ~** : I think so **3 porque ~** fam : (just) because — ~ nm : consent

sí² pron **1 de por ~** or **en ~** : by itself, in itself, per se **2 fuera de ~** : beside oneself **3 para ~ (mismo)** : to himself, to herself, for himself, for herself **4 entre ~** : among themselves

sico- → **psico-**

SIDA or **sida** nm : AIDS

siderurgia nf : iron and steel industry

sidra nf : (hard) cider

siega nf **1** : harvesting **2** : harvest (time)

siembra nf **1** : sowing **2** : sowing season

siempre *adv* 1 : always 2 *Lat* : still 3
para ~ : forever, for good 4 **~ que**
: whenever, every time 5 **~ que** *or* **~
y cuando** : provided that
sien *nf* : temple
sierra *nf* 1 : saw CORDILLERA : mountain range 3 **la ~** : the mountains *pl*
siervo, -va *n* : slave
siesta *nf* : nap, siesta
siete *adj & nm* : seven
sífilis *nf* : syphilis
sifón *nm, pl* **-fones** : siphon
sigilo *nm* : secrecy
sigla *nf* : acronym, abbreviation
siglo *nm* 1 : century 2 **hace ~s** : for
ages
significar {72} *vt* 1 : mean, signify 2
EXPRESAR : express — **significación**
nf, pl **-ciones** 1 : significance, importance 2 : meaning (of a word, etc.) —
significado, -da *adj* : well-known —
significado *nm* : meaning — **significativo, -va** *adj* : significant
signo *nm* 1 : sign 2 **~ de admiración**
: exclamation point 3 **~ de interrogación** : question mark
siguiente *adj* : next, following
sílaba *nf* : syllable
silbar *v* 1 : whistle 2 ABUCHEAR : hiss,
boo — **silbato** *nm* : whistle — **silbido**
nm 1 : whistle, whistling 2 ABUCHEO
: hiss, booing
silenciar *vt* : silence — **silenciador** *nm*
: muffler — **silencio** *nm* : silence —
silencioso, -sa *adj* : silent, quiet
silicio *nm* : silicon
silla *nf* 1 : chair 2 *or* **~ de montar**
: saddle 3 **~ de ruedas** : wheelchair
— **sillón** *nm, pl* **-llones** : armchair,
easy chair
silo *nm* : silo
silueta *nf* 1 : silhouette 2 CONTORNO
: outline, shape
silvestre *adj* : wild
silvicultura *nf* : forestry
símbolo *nm* : symbol — **simbólico,
-ca** *adj* : symbolic — **simbolismo** *nm*
: symbolism — **simbolizar** {21} *vt*
: symbolize
simetría *nf* : symmetry — **simétrico,
-ca** *adj* : symmetrical, symmetric
simiente *nf* : seed
símil *nm* 1 : simile 2 COMPARACIÓN
: comparison — **similar** *adj* : similar,
alike
simio *nm* : ape
simpatía *nf* 1 : liking, affection 2 AMA-
BILIDAD : friendliness — **simpático,
-ca** *adj* 1 : nice, likeable 2 AMABLE
: pleasant, kind — **simpatizante** *nmf*

: sympathizer — **simpatizar** {21} *vi* 1
: get along, hit it off 2 **~ con** : sympathize with
simple *adj* 1 SENCILLO : simple 2 MERO
: pure, sheer 3 TONTO : simpleminded
— **~** *n* : fool, simpleton — **simpleza**
nf 1 : simpleness 2 TONTERÍA : silly
thing — **simplicidad** *nf* : simplicity —
simplificar {72} *vt* : simplify
simposio *or* **simposium** *nm* : symposium
simular *vt* 1 : simulate 2 FINGIR : feign
— **simulacro** *nm* : simulation, drill
simultáneo, -nea *adj* : simultaneous
sin *prep* 1 : without 2 **~ que** : without
sinagoga *nf* : synagogue
sincero, -ra *adj* : sincere — **sinceramente** *adv* : sincerely — **sinceridad**
nf : sincerity
síncopa *nf* : syncopation
sincronizar {21} *vt* : synchronize
sindicato *nm* : (labor) union — **sindi-
cal** *adj* : union, labor
síndrome *nm* : syndrome
sinfín *nm* 1 : endless number 2 **un ~
de** : no end of
sinfonía *nf* : symphony — **sinfónico,
-ca** *adj* : symphonic
singular *adj* 1 : exceptional, outstanding 2 PECULIAR : peculiar 3 : singular
(in grammar) — **~** *nm* : singular —
singularizar {21} *vt* : single out —
singularizarse *vr* : stand out
siniestro, -tra *adj* 1 : sinister 2 IZQUIER-
DO : left — **siniestro** *nm* : disaster
sinnúmero *nm* → **sinfín**
sino *conj* 1 : but, rather 2 EXCEPTO : except, save
sinónimo, -ma *adj* : synonymous —
sinónimo *nm* : synonym
sinopsis *nfs & pl* : synopsis
sinrazón *nf, pl* **-zones** : wrong
sintaxis *nfs & pl* : syntax
síntesis *nfs & pl* : synthesis — **sintético, -ca** *adj* : synthetic — **sintetizar**
{21} *vt* 1 : synthesize 2 RESUMIR
: summarize
síntoma *nm* : symptom — **sintomático, -ca** *adj* : symptomatic
sintonía *nf* 1 : tuning in (of a radio) 2
en ~ con : in tune with — **sintonizar**
{21} *vt* : tune (in) to
sinuoso, -sa *adj* : winding
sinvergüenza *nmf* : scoundrel
sionismo *nm* : Zionism
siquiera *adv* 1 : at least 2 **ni ~** : not
even — **~** *conj* : even if
sirena *nf* 1 : mermaid 2 : siren (of an
ambulance, etc.)
sirio, -ria *adj* : Syrian

sirviente, -ta n : servant, maid f
sisear vi : hiss — siseo nm : hiss
sismo nm : earthquake — sísmico, -ca adj : seismic
sistema nm 1 : system 2 por ~ : systematically — sistemático, -ca adj : systematic
sitiar vt : besiege
sitio nm 1 : place, site 2 ESPACIO : room, space 3 CERCO : siege 4 en cualquier ~ : anywhere
situar {3} vt : situate, place — situarse vr 1 : be located 2 ESTABLECERSE : get oneself established — situación nf, pl -ciones : situation, position — situado, -da adj : situated, placed
slip nm : briefs pl, underpants pl
smoking nm : tuxedo
so prep : under
sobaco nm : armpit
sobar vt 1 : finger, handle 2 : knead (dough) — sobado, -da adj : worn, shabby
soberanía nf : sovereignty — soberano, -na adj & n : sovereign
soberbia nf : pride, arrogance — soberbio, -bia adj : proud, arrogant
sobornar vt : bribe — soborno nm 1 : bribe 2 : (action of) bribery
sobrar vi 1 : be more than enough 2 RESTAR : be left over — sobra nf 1 : surplus 2 de ~ : to spare 3 ~s nfpl : leftovers — sobrado, -da adj : more than enough — sobrante adj : remaining
sobre¹ nm : envelope
sobre² prep 1 : on, on top of 2 POR ENCIMA DE : over, above 3 ACERCA DE : about 4 ~ todo : especially, above all
sobrecama nmf Lat : bedspread
sobrecargar {52} vt : overload, overburden
sobrecoger {15} vt : startle — sobrecogerse vr : be startled
sobrecubierta nf : dust jacket
sobredosis nfs & pl : overdose
sobreentender {56} vt : infer, understand — sobreentenderse vr : be understood
sobreestimar vt : overestimate
sobregiro nm : overdraft
sobrellevar vt : endure, bear
sobremesa nf de ~ : after-dinner
sobrenatural adj : supernatural
sobrenombre nm : nickname
sobrentender → sobreentender
sobrepasar vt : exceed
sobreponer {60} vt 1 : superimpose 2 ANTEPONER : put before — sobreponerse vr ~ a : overcome

sobresalir {73} vi 1 : protrude 2 DESTACARSE : stand out — sobresaliente adj : outstanding
sobresaltar vt : startle — sobresaltarse vr : start, jump up — sobresalto nm : fright
sobrestimar → sobreestimar
sobretodo nm : overcoat
sobrevenir {87} vi : happen, ensue
sobrevivencia nf → supervivencia
sobreviviente adj & nmf → superviviente
sobrevivir vi : survive — vt : outlive
sobrevolar {19} vt : fly over
sobriedad nf 1 : sobriety 2 MODERACIÓN : restraint
sobrino, -na n : nephew m, niece f
sobrio, -bria adj : sober
socarrón, -rrona adj, mpl -rrones : sarcastic
socavar vt : undermine
sociable adj : sociable — social adj : social — socialismo nm : socialism — socialista adj & nmf : socialist — sociedad nf 1 : society 2 EMPRESA : company 3 ~ anónima : incorporated company — socio, -cia n 1 : partner 2 MIEMBRO : member — sociología nf : sociology — sociólogo, -ga n : sociologist
socorrer vt : help — socorrista nmf : lifeguard — socorro nm : help
soda nf : soda (water)
sodio nf : sodium
sofá nm : couch, sofa
sofisticación nf, pl -ciones : sophistication — sofisticado, -da adj : sophisticated
sofocar {72} vt 1 : suffocate, smother 2 : put out (a fire), stifle (a rebellion, etc.) — sofocarse vr 1 : suffocate 2 fam : get upset — sofocante adj : suffocating, stifling
sofreír {66} vt : sauté
soga nf : rope
soja nf → soya
sojuzgar vt : subdue, subjugate
sol nm 1 : sun 2 hacer ~ : be sunny
solamente adv : only, just
solapa nf 1 : lapel (of a jacket) 2 : flap (of an envelope) — solapado, -da adj : secret, underhanded
solar¹ adj : solar, sun
solar² nm : lot, site
solariego, -ga adj : ancestral
solaz nm, pl -laces 1 : solace 2 DESCANSO : relaxation — solazarse {21} vr : relax
soldado nm 1 : soldier 2 ~ raso : private
soldar {19} vt : weld, solder — solda-

dor *nm* : soldering iron — **soldador, -dora** *n* : welder
soleado, -da *adj* : sunny
soledad *nf* : loneliness, solitude
solemne *adj* : solemn — **solemnidad** *nf* : solemnity
soler {78} *vi* **1** : be in the habit of **2 suele llegar tarde** : he usually arrives late
solicitar *vt* **1** : request, solicit **2** : apply for (a job, etc.) — **solicitante** *nmf* : applicant — **solícito, -ta** *adj* : solicitous, obliging — **solicitud** *nf* **1** : concern **2** PETICIÓN : request **3** : application (for a job, etc.)
solidaridad *nf* : solidarity
sólido, -da *adj* **1** : solid **2** : sound (of an argument, etc.) — **sólido** *nm* : solid — **solidez** *nf* : solidity — **solidificar** {72} *vt* : solidify — **solidificarse** *vr* : solidify, harden
soliloquio *nm* : soliloquy
solista *nmf* : soloist
solitario, -ria *adj* **1** : solitary **2** AISLADO : lonely, deserted — **~** *n* : recluse — **solitaria** *nf* : tapeworm — **solitario** *nm* : solitaire
sollozar {21} *vi* : sob — **sollozo** *nm* : sob
solo, -la *adj* **1** : alone **2** AISLADO : lonely **3 a solas** : alone, by oneself — **solo** *nm* : solo
sólo *adv* : just, only
solomillo *nm* : sirloin
solsticio *nm* : solstice
soltar {19} *vt* **1** : release **2** DEJAR CAER : let go of, drop **3** DESATAR : unfasten, undo — **soltarse** *vr* **1** : break free **2** DESATARSE : come undone
soltero, -ra *adj* : single, unmarried — **~** *n* **1** : bachelor *m*, single woman *f* **2 apellido de soltera** : maiden name
soltura *nf* **1** : looseness **2** : fluency (in language) **3** AGILIDAD : agility, ease
soluble *adj* : soluble
solución *nf, pl* **-ciones** : solution — **solucionar** *vt* : solve, resolve
solventar *vt* **1** : settle, pay **2** RESOLVER : resolve — **solvente** *adj & nm* : solvent
sombra *nf* **1** : shadow **2** : shade (of a tree, etc.) **3 ~s** *nfpl* : darkness, shadows — **sombreado, -da** *adj* : shady
sombrero *nm* : hat
sombrilla *nf* : parasol, umbrella
sombrío, -bría *adj* : dark, somber, gloomy
somero, -ra *adj* : superficial
someter *vt* **1** : subjugate **2** SUBORDINAR : subordinate **3** : subject (to treatment,

etc.) **4** PRESENTAR : submit, present — **someterse** *vr* **1** : submit, yield **2 ~ a** : undergo
somnífero, -ra *adj* : soporific — **somnífero** *nm* : sleeping pill — **somnoliento, -ta** *adj* : drowsy, sleepy
somos → **ser**
son¹ → **ser**
son² *nm* **1** : sound **2 en ~ de** : as, in the manner of
sonajero *nm* : (baby's) rattle
sonámbulo, -la *n* : sleepwalker
sonar {19} *vi* **1** : sound **2** : ring (as a bell) **3** : look or sound familiar **4 ~ a** : sound like — **sonarse** *vr or* **~ las narices** : blow one's nose
sonata *nf* : sonata
sondear *vt* **1** : sound, probe **2** : survey, sound out (opinions, etc.) — **sondeo** *nm* **1** : sounding, probing **2** ENCUESTA : survey, poll
soneto *nm* : sonnet
sónico, -ca *adj* : sonic
sonido *nm* : sound
sonoro, -ra *adj* **1** : resonant, sonorous **2** RUIDOSO : loud
sonreír {66} *vi* : smile — **sonreírse** *vr* : smile — **sonriente** *adj* : smiling — **sonrisa** *nf* : smile
sonrojar *vt* : cause to blush — **sonrojarse** *vr* : blush — **sonrojo** *nm* : blush
sonrosado, -da *adj* : rosy, pink
sonsacar {72} *vt* : wheedle (out)
soñar {19} *v* **1** : dream **2 ~ con** : dream about **3 ~ despierto** : daydream — **soñador, -dora** *adj* : dreamy — **~** *n* : dreamer — **soñoliento, -ta** *adj* : sleepy, drowsy
sopa *nf* : soup
sopesar *vt* : weigh, consider
soplar *vi* : blow — *vt* : blow out, blow off, blow up — **soplete** *nm* : blowtorch — **soplo** *nm* : puff, gust
soplón, -plona *n, pl* **-plones** *fam* : sneak
sopor *nm* : drowsiness — **soporífero, -ra** *adj* : soporific
soportar *vt* **1** SOSTENER : support **2** AGUANTAR : bear — **soporte** *nm* : support
soprano *nmf* : soprano
sor *nf* : Sister (in religion)
sorber *vt* **1** : sip **2** ABSORBER : absorb **3** CHUPAR : suck up — **sorbete** *nm* : sherbet — **sorbo** *nm* **1** : sip, swallow **2 beber a ~s** : sip
sordera *nf* : deafness
sórdido, -da *adj* : sordid, squalid
sordo, -da *adj* **1** : deaf **2** : muted (of a

sound) — **sordomudo, -da** *n* : deaf-mute

sorna *nf* : sarcasm

sorprender *vt* : surprise — **sorprenderse** *vr* : be surprised — **sorprendente** *adj* : surprising — **sorpresa** *nf* : surprise

sortear *vt* **1** : raffle off, draw lots for **2** ESQUIVAR : dodge — **sorteo** *nm* : drawing, raffle

sortija *nf* **1** : ring **2** : ringlet (of hair)

sortilegio *nm* **1** HECHIZO : spell **2** HECHICERÍA : sorcery

sosegar {49} *vt* : calm, pacify — **sosegarse** *vr* : calm down — **sosegado, -da** *adj* : calm, tranquil — **sosiego** *nm* : calm

soslayo : de ~ *adv phr* : obliquely, sideways

soso, -sa *adj* **1** : insipid, tasteless **2** ABURRIDO : dull

sospechar *vt* : suspect — **sospecha** *nf* : suspicion — **sospechoso, -sa** *adj* : suspicious — **~** *n* : suspect

sostener {80} *vt* **1** : support **2** SUJETAR : hold **3** MANTENER : sustain, maintain — **sostenerse** *vr* **1** : stand (up) **2** CONTINUAR : remain **3** SUSTENTARSE : support oneself — **sostén** *nm, pl* **-tenes 1** APOYO : support **2** SUSTENTO : sustenance **3** : brassiere, bra — **sostenido, -da** *adj* **1** : sustained **2** : sharp (in music) — **sostenido** *nm* : sharp

sótano *nm* : basement

soterrar {55} *vt* **1** : bury **2** ESCONDER : hide

soto *nm* : grove

soviético, -ca *adj* : Soviet

soy → ser

soya *nf* : soy

Sr. *nm* : Mr. — **Sra.** *nf* : Mrs., Ms. — **Srta.** *or* **Srita.** *nf* : Miss, Ms.

su *adj* **1** : his, her, its, their, one's **2** (*formal*) : your

suave *adj* **1** : soft **2** LISO : smooth **3** APACIBLE : gentle, mild — **suavidad** *nf* **1** : softness, smoothness **2** APACIBILIDAD : mildness, gentleness — **suavizar** {21} *vt* : soften, smooth

subalimentado, -da *adj* : undernourished, underfed

subalterno, -na *adj* **1** SUBORDINADO : subordinate **2** SECUNDARIO : secondary — **~** *n* : subordinate

subarrendar {55} *vt* : sublet

subasta *nf* : auction — **subastar** *vt* : auction (off)

subcampeón, -peona *n, mpl* **-peones** : runner-up

subcomité *nm* : subcommittee

subconsciente *adj & nm* : subconscious

subdesarrollado, -da *adj* : underdeveloped

subdirector, -tora *n* : assistant manager

súbdito, -ta *n* : subject

subdividir *vt* : subdivide — **subdivisión** *nf, pl* **-siones** : subdivision

subestimar *vt* : underestimate

subir *vt* **1** : climb, go up **2** LLEVAR : bring up, take up **3** AUMENTAR : raise — *vi* **1** : go up, come up **2 ~ a** : get in (a car), get on (a bus, etc.) — **subirse** *vr* **1** : climb (up) **2 ~ a** : get in (a car), get on (a bus, etc.) **3 ~ a la cabeza** : go to one's head — **subida** *nf* **1** : ascent, climb **2** AUMENTO : rise **3** PENDIENTE : slope — **subido, -da** *adj* **1** : bright, strong **2 ~ de tono** : risqué

súbito, -ta *adj* **1** : sudden **2 de súbito** : all of a sudden, suddenly

subjetivo, -va *adj* : subjective

subjuntivo, -va *adj* : subjunctive — **subjuntivo** *nm* : subjunctive (case)

sublevar *vt* : stir up, incite to rebellion — **sublevarse** *vr* : rebel — **sublevación** *nf, pl* **-ciones** : uprising, rebellion

sublime *adj* : sublime

submarino, -na *adj* : underwater — **submarino** *nm* : submarine — **submarinismo** *nm* : scuba diving

subordinar *vt* : subordinate — **subordinado, -da** *adj & n* : subordinate

subproducto *nm* : by-product

subrayar *vt* **1** : underline **2** ENFATIZAR : emphasize, stress

subrepticio, -cia *adj* : surreptitious

subsanar *vt* **1** : rectify, correct **2** : make up for (a deficiency), overcome (an obstacle)

subscribir → suscribir

subsidio *nm* : subsidy, benefit

subsiguiente *adj* : subsequent

subsistir *vi* **1** : live, subsist **2** SOBREVIVIR : survive — **subsistencia** *nf* : subsistence

substancia *nf → sustancia*

subterfugio *nm* : subterfuge

subterráneo, -nea *adj* : underground, subterranean — **subterráneo** *nm* : underground passage

subtítulo *nm* : subtitle

suburbio *nm* **1** : suburb **2** : slum (outside a city) — **suburbano, -na** *adj* : suburban

subvencionar *vt* : subsidize — **sub-**

vención *nf, pl* **-ciones** : subsidy, grant
subvertir {76} *vt* : subvert — **subversión** *nf, pl* **-siones** : subversion — **subversivo, -va** *adj & n* : subversive
subyacente *adj* : underlying
subyugar {52} *vt* : subjugate, subdue
succión *nf, pl* **-ciones** : suction — **succionar** *vt* : suck up, draw in
sucedáneo *nm* : substitute
suceder *vi* 1 : happen, occur 2 ~ a : follow 3 **suceda lo que suceda** : come what may — **sucesión** *nf, pl* **-siones** : succession — **sucesivo, -va** *adj* : successive — **suceso** *nm* 1 : event 2 INCIDENTE : incident — **sucesor, -sora** *n* : successor
suciedad *nf* 1 : dirtiness 2 MUGRE : dirt, filth
sucinto, -ta *adj* : succinct, concise
sucio, -cia *adj* : dirty, filthy
suculento, -ta *adj* : succulent
sucumbir *vi* : succumb
sucursal *nf* : branch (of a business)
sudadera *nf* : sweatshirt — **sudado, -da** *adj* : sweaty
sudafricano, -na *adj* : South African
sudamericano, -na *adj* : South American
sudar *vi* : sweat
sudeste → **sureste**
sudoeste → **suroeste**
sudor *nm* : sweat — **sudoroso, -sa** *adj* : sweaty
sueco, -ca *adj* : Swedish — **sueco** *nm* : Swedish (language)
suegro, -gra *n* 1 : father-in-law *m*, mother-in-law *f* 2 **suegros** *nmpl* : in-laws
suela *nf* : sole (of a shoe)
sueldo *nm* : salary, wage
suelo *nm* 1 : ground 2 : floor (in a house) 3 TIERRA : soil, land
suelto, -ta *adj* : loose, free — **suelto** *nm* : loose change
sueño *nm* 1 : dream 2 **coger el** ~ : get to sleep 3 **tener** ~ : be sleepy
suero *nm* 1 : whey 2 : serum (in medicine)
suerte *nf* 1 : luck, fortune 2 AZAR : chance 3 DESTINO : fate 4 CLASE : sort, kind 5 **por** ~ : luckily 6 **tener** ~ : be lucky
suéter *nm* : sweater
suficiencia *nf* 1 CAPACIDAD : competence, proficiency 2 PRESUNCIÓN : smugness — **suficiente** *adj* 1 : enough, sufficient 2 PRESUNTUOSO : smug — **suficientemente** *adv* : enough

sufijo *nm* : suffix
sufragio *nm* : suffrage, vote
sufrir *vt* 1 : suffer 2 SOPORTAR : bear, stand — *vi* : suffer — **sufrido, -da** *adj* 1 : long-suffering 2 : sturdy, serviceable (of clothing) — **sufrimiento** *nm* : suffering
sugerir {76} *vt* : suggest — **sugerencia** *nf* : suggestion — **sugestión** *nf, pl* **-tiones** : suggestion — **sugestionable** *adj* : impressionable — **sugestionar** *vt* : influence — **sugestivo, -va** *adj* 1 : suggestive 2 ESTIMULANTE : interesting, stimulating
suicidio *nm* : suicide — **suicida** *adj* : suicidal — ~ *nmf* : suicide (victim) — **suicidarse** *vr* : commit suicide
suite *nf* : suite
suizo, -za *adj* : Swiss
sujetar *vt* 1 : hold (on to) 2 FIJAR : fasten 3 DOMINAR : subdue — **sujetarse** *vr* 1 ~ a : hold on to, cling to 2 ~ a : abide by — **sujeción** *nf, pl* **-ciones** 1 : fastening 2 DOMINACIÓN : subjection — **sujetador** *nm Spain* : brassiere, bra — **sujetapapeles** *nms & pl* : paper clip — **sujeto, -ta** *adj* 1 : fastened 2 ~ a : subject to — **sujeto** *nm* 1 : individual 2 : subject (in grammar)
sulfuro *nm* : sulfur — **sulfúrico, -ca** *adj* : sulfuric
sultán *nm, pl* **-tanes** : sultan
suma *nf* 1 : sum, total 2 : addition (in mathematics) 3 **en** ~ : in short — **sumamente** *adv* : extremely — **sumar** *vt* 1 : add (up) 2 TOTALIZAR : add up to, total — *vi* : add up — **sumarse** *vr* ~ a : join
sumario, -ria *adj* : concise — **sumario** *nm* 1 : summary 2 : indictment (in law)
sumergir {35} *vt* : submerge, plunge — **sumergirse** *vr* : be submerged — **sumergible** *adj* : waterproof (of a watch, etc.)
sumidero *nm* : drain
suministrar *vt* : supply, provide — **suministro** *nm* : supply, provision
sumir *vt* : plunge, immerse — **sumirse** *vr* ~ **en** : sink into
sumisión *nf, pl* **-siones** : submission — **sumiso, -sa** *adj* : submissive
sumo, -ma *adj* 1 : highest, supreme 2 **de suma importancia** : of great importance
suntuoso, -sa *adj* : sumptuous, lavish
super *or* **súper** *nm fam* : supermarket
superabundancia *nf* : overabundance
superar *vt* 1 : surpass, outdo 2 VENCER : overcome — **superarse** *vr* : improve oneself

superávit *nm* : surplus
superestructura *nf* : superstructure
superficie *nf* **1** : surface **2** ÁREA : area
— **superficial** *adj* : superficial
superfluo, -flua *adj* : superfluous
superintendente *nmf* : supervisor, superintendent
superior *adj* **1** : superior **2** : upper (of a floor, etc.) **3** — **a** : above, higher than — ～ *nm* : superior — **superioridad** *nf* : superiority
superlativo, -va *adj* : superlative — **superlativo** *nm* : superlative
supermercado *nm* : supermarket
superpoblado, -da *adj* : overpopulated
supersónico, -ca *adj* : supersonic
superstición *nf, pl* **-ciones** : superstition — **supersticioso, -sa** *adj* : superstitious
supervisar *vt* : supervise, oversee — **supervisión** *nf, pl* **-siones** : supervision — **supervisor, -sora** *n* : supervisor
supervivencia *nf* : survival — **superviviente** *adj* : surviving — ～ *nmf* : survivor
suplantar *vt* : supplant, replace
suplemento *nm* : supplement — **suplementario, -ria** *adj* : supplementary
suplente *adj & nmf* : substitute
suplicar {72} *vt* : beg, entreat — **súplica** *nf* : plea, entreaty
suplicio *nm* : ordeal, torture
suplir *vt* **1** : make up for **2** REEMPLAZAR : replace
supo, etc. → **saber**
suponer {60} *vt* **1** : suppose, assume **2** SIGNIFICAR : mean **3** IMPLICAR : involve, entail — **suposición** *nf, pl* **-ciones** : supposition
supositorio *nm* : suppository
supremo, -ma *adj* : supreme — **supremacía** *nf* : supremacy
suprimir *vt* **1** : suppress, eliminate **2** : delete (text) — **supresión** *nf, pl* **-siones** **1** : suppression, elimination **2** : deletion (of text)
supuesto, -ta *adj* **1** : supposed, alleged **2 por supuesto** : of course — **supuesto** *nm* : assumption — **supuestamente** *adv* : allegedly
sur *nm* **1** : south, South **2** : south wind **3 del** ～ : south, southerly
surafricano, -na → **sudafricano**
suramericano, -na → **sudamericano**
surcar {72} *vt* **1** : plow (earth) **2** : cut through (air, water, etc.) — **surco** *nm* : groove, furrow, rut
sureño, -ña *adj* : southern, Southern — ～ *n* : Southerner

sureste *adj* **1** : southeast, southeastern **2** : southeasterly (of wind, etc.) — ～ *nm* : southeast, Southeast
surf *or* **surfing** *nm* : surfing
surgir {35} *vi* **1** : arise **2** APARECER : appear — **surgimiento** *nm* : rise, emergence
suroeste *adj* **1** : southwest, southwestern **2** : southwesterly (of wind, etc.) — ～ *nm* : southwest, Southwest
surtir *vt* **1** : supply, provide **2** ～ **efecto** : have an effect — **surtirse** *vr* ～ **de** : stock up on — **surtido, -da** *adj* **1** : assorted, varied **2** : stocked (with merchandise) — **surtido** *nm* : assortment, selection — **surtidor** *nm* : gas pump
susceptible *adj* **1** : susceptible, sensitive **2** ～ **de** : capable of — **susceptibilidad** *nf* : sensitivity
suscitar *vt* : provoke, arouse
suscribir {33} *vt* **1** : sign (a formal document) **2** RATIFICAR : endorse — **suscribirse** *vr* ～ **a** : subscribe to — **suscripción** *nf, pl* **-ciones** : subscription — **suscriptor, -tora** *n* : subscriber
susodicho, -cha *adj* : aforementioned
suspender *vt* **1** : suspend **2** COLGAR : hang **3** *Spain* : fail (an exam, etc.) — **suspensión** *nf, pl* **-siones** : suspension — **suspenso** *nm* **1** *Spain* : failure (in an exam, etc.) **2** *Lat* : suspense
suspicaz *adj, pl* **-caces** : suspicious
suspirar *vi* : sigh — **suspiro** *nm* : sigh
sustancia *nf* **1** : substance **2 sin** ～ : shallow, lacking substance — **sustancial** *adj* : substantial, significant — **sustancioso, -sa** *adj* : substantial, solid
sustantivo *nm* : noun
sustentar *vt* **1** : support **2** ALIMENTAR : sustain, nourish **3** MANTENER : maintain — **sustentarse** *vr* : support oneself — **sustentación** *nf, pl* **-ciones** : support — **sustento** *nm* **1** : means of support, livelihood **2** ALIMENTO : sustenance
sustituir {41} *vt* : replace, substitute — **sustitución** *nf, pl* **-ciones** : replacement, substitution — **sustituto, -ta** *n* : substitute
susto *nm* : fright, scare
sustraer {81} *vt* **1** : remove, take away **2** : subtract (in mathematics) — **sustraerse** *vr* ～ **a** : avoid, evade — **sustracción** *nf, pl* **-ciones** : subtraction
susurrar *vi* **1** : whisper **2** : murmur (of water) **3** : rustle (of leaves, etc.) — *vt* : whisper — **susurro** *nm* **1** : whisper **2**

: murmur (of water) **3** : rustle, rustling (of leaves, etc.)
sutil *adj* **1** : delicate, fine **2** : subtle (of fragrances, differences, etc.) — **sutileza** *nf* : subtlety
sutura *nf* : suture

suyo, -ya *adj* **1** : his, her, its, one's, theirs **2** (*formal*) : yours **3 un primo suyo** : a cousin of his/hers — **~** *pron* **1** : his, hers, its (own), one's own, theirs **2** (*formal*) : yours
switch *nm Lat* : switch

T

t *nf* : t, 21st letter of the Spanish alphabet
taba *nf* : anklebone
tabaco *nm* : tobacco — **tabacalero, -ra** *adj* : tobacco
tábano *nm* : horsefly
taberna *nf* : tavern
tabicar {72} *vt* : wall up — **tabique** *nm* : thin wall, partition
tabla *nf* **1** : board, plank **2** LISTA : table, list **3 ~ de planchar** : ironing board **4 ~s** *nfpl* : stage, boards *pl* — **tablado** *nm* **1** : flooring **2** PLATAFORMA : platform **3** : (theater) stage — **tablero** *nm* **1** : bulletin board **2** : board (in games) **3** PIZARRA : blackboard **4 ~ de instrumentos** : dashboard, instrument panel
tableta *nf* **1** : tablet, pill **2** : bar (of chocolate)
tablilla *nf* : slat — **tablón** *nm, pl* **-lones 1** : plank, beam **2 ~ de anuncios** : bulletin board
tabú *adj* : taboo — **tabú** *nm, pl* **-búes** or **-bús** : taboo
tabular *vt* : tabulate
taburete *nm* : stool
tacaño, -na *adj* : stingy, miserly
tacha *nf* **1** : flaw, defect **2 sin ~** : flawless
tachar *vt* **1** : cross out, delete **2 ~ de** : accuse of, label as
tachón *nm, pl* **-chones** : stud, hobnail — **tachuela** *nf* : tack, hobnail
tácito, -ta *adj* : tacit
taciturno, -na *adj* : taciturn
taco *nm* **1** : stopper, plug **2** *Lat* : heel (of a shoe) **3** : cue (in billiards) **4** : taco (in cooking)
tacón *nm, pl* **-cones 1** : heel (of a shoe) **2 de ~ alto** : high-heeled
táctica *nf* : tactic, tactics *pl* — **táctico, -ca** *adj* : tactical
tacto *nm* **1** : (sense of) touch, feel **2** DELICADEZA : tact
tafetán *nm, pl* **-tanes** : taffeta
tailandés, -desa *adj* : Thai
taimado, -da *adj* : crafty, sly
tajar *vt* : cut, slice — **tajada** *nf* **1** : slice **2 sacar ~** *fam* : get one's share — **ta-**

jante *adj* : categorical — **tajo** *nm* **1** : cut, gash **2** ESCARPA : steep cliff
tal *adv* **1** : so, in such a way **2 con ~ que** : provided that, as long as **3 ¿qué ~?** : how are you?, how's it going? — **~** *adj* **1** : such, such a **2 ~ vez** : maybe, perhaps — **~** *pron* **1** : such a one, such a thing **2 ~ para cual** : two of a kind
taladrar *vt* : drill — **taladro** *nm* : drill
talante *nm* **1** HUMOR : mood **2** VOLUNTAD : willingness
talar *vt* : cut down, fell
talco *nm* : talcum powder
talego *nm* : sack
talento *nm* : talent — **talentoso, -sa** *adj* : talented
talismán *nm, pl* **-manes** : talisman, charm
talla *nf* **1** : sculpture, carving **2** ESTATURA : height **3** : size (in clothing) — **tallar** *vt* **1** : sculpt, carve **2** : measure (someone's height)
tallarín *nf, pl* **-rines** : noodle
talle *nm* **1** : waist, waistline **2** FIGURA : figure **3** : measurements *pl* (of clothing)
taller *nm* **1** : workshop **2** : studio (of an artist)
tallo *nm* : stalk, stem
talón *nm, pl* **-lones 1** : heel (of the foot) **2** : stub (of a check) — **talonario** *nm* : checkbook
taltuza *nf* : gopher
tamal *nm* : tamale
tamaño, -ña *adj* : such a, such a big — **tamaño** *nm* **1** : size **2 de ~ natural** : life-size
tambalearse *vr* **1** : teeter, wobble **2** : stagger, totter (of persons)
también *adv* : too, as well, also
tambor *nm* : drum — **tamborilear** *vi* : drum
tamiz *nm* : sieve — **tamizar** {21} *vt* : sift
tampoco *adv* : neither, not either
tampón *nm, pl* **-pones 1** : tampon **2** : ink pad (for stamping)
tan *adv* **1** : so, so very **2 ~ pronto como** : as soon as **3 ~ sólo** : only, merely

tanda *nf* 1 TURNO : turn, shift 2 GRUPO : batch, lot, series

tangente *nf* : tangent

tangible *adj* : tangible

tango *nm* : tango

tanque *nm* : tank

tantear *vt* 1 : feel, grope 2 SOPESAR : size up, weigh — *vi* : feel one's way — **tanteador** *nm* : scoreboard — **tanteo** *nm* 1 : weighing, sizing up 2 PUNTUACIÓN : scoring (in sports)

tanto *adv* 1 : so much 2 (*in expressions of time*) : so long — ~ *nm* 1 : certain amount 2 : goal, point (in sports) 3 **un** ~ : somewhat, rather — **tanto, -ta** *adj* 1 : so much, so many 2 (*in comparisons*) : as much, as many 3 *fam* : however many — ~ *pron* 1 : so much, so many 2 **entre** ~ : meanwhile 3 **por lo** ~ : therefore

tañer {79} *vt* 1 : ring (a bell) 2 : play (a musical instrument)

tapa *nf* 1 : cover, top, lid 2 *Spain* : snack

tapacubos *nms & pl* : hubcap

tapar *vt* 1 : cover, put a lid on 2 OCULTAR : block out 3 ENCUBRIR : cover up — **tapadera** *nf* 1 : cover, lid 2 : front (to hide a deception)

tapete *nm* 1 : small rug, mat 2 : cover (for a table)

tapia *nf* : (adobe) wall, garden wall — **tapiar** *vt* 1 : wall in 2 : block off (a door, etc.)

tapicería *nf* 1 : upholstery 2 TAPIZ : tapestry — **tapicero, -ra** *n* : upholsterer

tapioca *nf* : tapioca

tapiz *nm, pl* **-pices** : tapestry — **tapizar** {21} *vt* : upholster

tapón *nm, pl* **-pones** 1 : cork 2 : cap (for a bottle, etc.) 3 : plug, stopper (for a sink)

tapujo *nm* **sin** ~**s** : openly, outright

taquigrafía *nf* : stenography, shorthand — **taquígrafo, -fa** *n* : stenographer

taquilla *nf* 1 : box office 2 RECAUDACIÓN : earnings *pl*, take — **taquillero, -ra** *adj* **un éxito taquillero** : a box-office hit

tarántula *nf* : tarantula

tararear *vt* : hum

tardar *vi* 1 : take a long time, be late 2 **a más** ~ : at the latest — *vt* : take (time) — **tardanza** *nf* : lateness, delay — **tarde** *adv* 1 : late 2 ~ **o temprano** : sooner or later — ~ *nf* 1 : afternoon, evening 2 **¡buenas** ~**s!** : good afternoon!, good evening! 3 **en la** ~ **or por la** ~ : in the afternoon, in the evening — **tardío, -día** *adj* : late, tardy — **tardo, -da** *adj* : slow

tarea *nf* 1 : task, job 2 : homework (in education)

tarifa *nf* 1 : fare, rate 2 LISTA : price list 3 ARANCEL : duty, tariff

tarima *nf* : platform, stage

tarjeta *nf* 1 : card 2 ~ **de crédito** : credit card 3 ~ **postal** : postcard

tarro *nm* : jar, pot

tarta *nf* 1 : cake 2 TORTA : tart

tartamudear *vi* : stammer, stutter — **tartamudeo** *nm* : stutter, stammer

tartán *nm, pl* **-tanes** : tartan, plaid

tártaro *nm* : tartar

tarugo *nm* 1 : block (of wood) 2 *fam* : blockhead, dunce

tasa *nf* 1 : rate 2 IMPUESTO : tax 3 VALORACIÓN : appraisal — **tasación** *nf, pl* **-ciones** : appraisal — **tasar** *vt* 1 : set the price of 2 VALORAR : appraise, value

tasca *nf* : cheap bar, dive

tatuar {3} *vt* : tattoo — **tatuaje** *nm* : tattoo, tattooing

taurino, -na *adj* : bull, bullfighting — **tauromaquia** *nf* : (art of) bullfighting

taxi *nm, pl* **taxis** : taxi, taxicab — **taxista** *nmf* : taxi driver

taza *nf* 1 : cup 2 : (toilet) bowl — **tazón** *nm, pl* **-zones** : bowl

te *pron* 1 (*direct object*) : you 2 (*indirect object*) : for you, to you, from you 3 (*reflexive*) : yourself, for yourself, to yourself, from yourself

té *nm* : tea

teatro *nm* : theater — **teatral** *adj* : theatrical

techo *nm* 1 : roof 2 : ceiling (of a room) 3 LÍMITE : upper limit, ceiling — **techumbre** *nf* : roofing

tecla *nf* : key (of a musical instrument or a machine) — **teclado** *nm* : keyboard — **teclear** *vt* : type in, enter

técnica *nf* 1 : technique, skill 2 TECNOLOGÍA : technology — **técnico, -ca** *adj* : technical — ~ *n* : technician

tecnología *nf* : technology — **tecnológico, -ca** *adj* : technological

tecolote *nm Lat* : owl

tedio *nm* : boredom — **tedioso, -sa** *adj* : tedious, boring

teja *nf* : tile — **tejado** *nm* : roof

tejer *v* 1 : knit, crochet 2 : weave (on a loom)

tejido *nm* 1 : fabric, cloth 2 : tissue (of the body)

tejón *nm, pl* **-jones** : badger

tela *nf* 1 : fabric, material 2 ~ **de araña** : spiderweb — **telar** *nm* : loom — **telaraña** *nf* : spiderweb, cobweb

tele *nf fam* : TV, television

telecomunicación *nf, pl* **-ciones** : telecommunication

teledifusión *nf, pl* **-siones** : television broadcasting

teledirigido, -da *adj* : remote-controlled

telefonear *v* : telephone, call — **telefónico, -ca** *adj* : telephone — **telefonista** *nmf* : telephone operator — **teléfono** *nm* **1** : telephone **2 llamar por** ~ : make a phone call

telegrafiar {85} *v* : telegraph — **telegráfico, -ca** *adj* : telegraphic — **telégrafo** *nm* : telegaph

telegrama *nm* : telegram

telenovela *nf* : soap opera

telepatía *nf* : telepathy — **telepático, -ca** *adj* : telepathic

telescopio *nm* : telescope — **telescópico, -ca** *adj* : telescopic

telespectador, -dora *n* : (television) viewer

telesquí *nm, pl* **-squís** : ski lift

televidente *nmf* : (television) viewer

televisión *nf, pl* **-siones** : television, TV — **televisar** *vt* : televise — **televisor** *nm* : television set

telón *nm, pl* **-lones 1** : curtain (in theater) **2** ~ **de fondo** : backdrop, background

tema *nm* : theme

temblar {55} *vi* **1** : tremble, shiver **2** : shake (of a building, the ground, etc.) — **temblor** *nm* **1** : shaking, trembling **2** *or* ~ **de tierra** : tremor, earthquake — **tembloroso, -sa** *adj* : trembling, shaky

temer *vt* : fear, dread — *vi* : be afraid — **temerario, -ria** *adj* : reckless — **temeridad** *nf* **1** : recklessness **2** : rash act — **temeroso, -sa** *adj* : fearful — **temor** *nm* : fear, dread

temperamento *nm* : temperament — **temperamental** *adj* : temperamental

temperatura *nf* : temperature

tempestad *nf* : storm — **tempestuoso, -sa** *adj* : stormy

templar *vt* **1** : temper (steel) **2** : moderate (temperature) **3** : tune (a musical instrument) — **templarse** *vr* : warm up, cool down — **templado, -da** *adj* **1** : temperate, mild **2** TIBIO : lukewarm **3** VALIENTE : courageous — **templanza** *nf* **1** : moderation **2** : mildness (of weather)

templo *nm* : temple, synagogue

tempo *nm* : tempo

temporada *nf* **1** : season, time **2** PERÍODO : period, spell — **temporal** *adj* **1** : temporal **2** PROVISIONAL : temporary — ~ *nm* : storm — **temporero, -ra** *n* : temporary or seasonal worker

temporizador *nm* : timer

temprano, -na *adj* : early — **temprano** *adv* : early

tenaz *adj, pl* **-naces** : tenacious — **tenaza** *nf or* **tenazas** *nfpl* **1** : pliers **2** : tongs (for the fireplace, etc.) **3** : claw (of a crustacean)

tendedero *nm* : clothesline

tendencia *nf* : tendency, trend

tender {56} *vt* **1** : spread out, stretch out **2** : hang out (clothes) **3** : lay (cables, etc.) **4** : set (a trap) — *vi* ~ **a** : have a tendency towards — **tenderse** *vr* : stretch out, lie down

tendero, -ra *n* : shopkeeper

tendido *nm* **1** : laying (of cables, etc.) **2** : seats *pl*, stand (at a bullfight)

tendón *nm, pl* **-dones** : tendon

tenebroso, -sa *adj* **1** : gloomy, dark **2** SINIESTRO : sinister

tenedor, -dora *n* **1** : holder **2** ~ **de libros** : bookkeeper — **tenedor** *nm* : table fork — **teneduría** *nf* ~ **de libros** : bookkeeping

tener {80} *vt* **1** : have, possess **2** SUJETAR : hold **3** TOMAR : take **4** ~ **frío (hambre, etc.)** : be cold (hungry, etc.) **5** ~ **... años** : be ... years old **6** ~ **por** : think, consider — *v aux* **1** ~ **que** : have to, ought to **2 tenía pensado escribirte** : I've been thinking of writing to you — **tenerse** *vr* **1** : stand up **2** ~ **por** : consider oneself

tenería *nf* : tannery

tengo → **tener**

tenia *nf* : tapeworm

teniente *nmf* : lieutenant

tenis *nms & pl* **1** : tennis **2** ~ *nmpl* : sneakers — **tenista** *nmf* : tennis player

tenor *nm* **1** : tenor **2** : tone, sense (in style)

tensar *vt* **1** : tense, make taut **2** : draw (a bow) — **tensarse** *vr* : become tense — **tensión** *nf, pl* **-siones 1** : tension **2** ~ **arterial** : blood pressure — **tenso, -sa** *adj* : tense

tentación *nf, pl* **-ciones** : temptation

tentáculo *nm* : tentacle

tentar {55} *vt* **1** : feel, touch **2** ATRAER : tempt — **tentador, -dora** *adj* : tempting

tentativa *nf* : attempt

tentempié *nm fam* : snack

tenue *adj* **1** : tenuous **2** : faint, weak (of sounds) **3** : light, fine (of thread, rain, etc.)

teñir {67} *vt* **1** : dye **2** ~ **de** : tinge with

teología *nf* : theology — **teólogo, -ga** *n* : theologian

teorema *nm* : theorem
teoría *nf* 1 : theory — **teórico, -ca** *adj* : theoretical
tequila *nm* : tequila
terapia *nf* 1 : therapy 2 ~ **ocupacional** : occupational therapy — **terapeuta** *nmf* : therapist — **terapéutico, -ca** *adj* : therapeutic
tercermundista *adj* : third-world
tercero, -ra *adj* (**tercer** *before masculine singular nouns*) 1 : third 2 **el Tercer Mundo** : the Third World — ~ *n* : third (in a series)
terciar *vt* : sling (sth over one's shoulders), tilt (a hat) — *vi* 1 : intervene 2 ~ **en** : take part in
tercio *nm* : third
terciopelo *nm* : velvet
terco, -ca *adj* : obstinate, stubborn
tergiversar *vt* : distort, twist
termal *adj* : thermal, hot — **termas** *nfpl* : hot springs
terminar *vt* : conclude, finish — *vi* 1 : finish 2 ACABARSE : come to an end — **terminarse** *vr* 1 : run out 2 ACABARSE : come to an end — **terminación** *nf, pl* **-ciones** : termination, conclusion — **terminal** *adj* : terminal, final — ~ *nm* (*in some regions f*) : (electric or electronic) terminal — ~ *nf* (*in some regions m*) : terminal, station — **término** *nm* 1 : end 2 PLAZO : period, term 3 ~ **medio** : happy medium 4 ~**s** *nmpl* : terms — **terminología** *nf* : terminology
termita *nf* : termite
termo *nm* : thermos
termómetro *nm* : thermometer
termóstato *nm* : thermostat
ternero, -ra *n* : calf — **ternera** *nf* : veal
ternura *nf* : tenderness
terquedad *nf* : obstinacy, stubbornness
terracota *nf* : terra-cotta
terraplén *nm, pl* **-plenes** : embankment
terráqueo, -quea *adj* : earth, terrestrial
terrateniente *nmf* : landowner
terraza *nf* 1 : terrace 2 BALCÓN : balcony
terremoto *nm* : earthquake
terreno *nm* 1 : terrain 2 SUELO : earth, ground 3 SOLAR : plot, tract of land — **terreno, -na** *adj* : earthly — **terrestre** *adj* : terrestrial
terrible *adj* : terrible
terrier *nmf* : terrier
territorio *nm* : territory — **territorial** *adj* : territorial
terrón *nm, pl* **-rones** 1 : clod (of earth) 2 ~ **de azúcar** : lump of sugar
terror *nm* : terror — **terrorífico, -ca** *adj*

: terrifying — **terrorismo** *nm* : terrorism — **terrorista** *adj & nmf* : terrorist
terroso, -sa *adj* : earthy
terso, -sa *adj* 1 : smooth 2 : polished, flowing (of a style) — **tersura** *nf* : smoothness
tertulia *nf* : gathering, group
tesis *nfs & pl* : thesis
tesón *nm* : persistence, tenacity
tesoro *nm* 1 : treasure 2 : thesaurus (book) 3 **el Tesoro** : the Treasury — **tesorero, -ra** *n* : treasurer
testaferro *nm* : figurehead
testamento *nm* : testament, will — **testamentario, -ria** *n* : executor, executrix *f* — **testar** *vi* : draw up a will
testarudo, -da *adj* : stubborn
testículo *nm* : testicle
testificar {72} *v* : testify — **testigo** *nmf* 1 : witness 2 ~ **ocular** : eyewitness — **testimoniar** *vi* : testify — **testimonio** *nm* : testimony
tétano *or* **tétanos** *nm* : tetanus
tetera *nf* : teapot
tetilla *nf* 1 : teat, nipple (of a man) 2 : nipple (of a baby bottle) — **tetina** *nf* : nipple (of a baby bottle)
tétrico, -ca *adj* : somber, gloomy
textil *adj & nm* : textile
texto *nm* : text — **textual** *adj* 1 : textual 2 EXACTO : literal, exact
textura *nf* : texture
tez *nf, pl* **teces** : complexion
ti *pron* 1 : you 2 ~ **mismo, ~ misma** : yourself
tía → **tío**
tianguis *nms & pl Lat* : open-air market
tibio, -bia *adj* : lukewarm
tiburón *nm, pl* **-rones** : shark
tic *nm* : tic
tiempo *nm* 1 : time 2 ÉPOCA : age, period 3 : weather (in meteorology) 4 : halftime (in sports) 5 : tempo (in music) 6 : tense (in grammar)
tienda *nf* 1 : store, shop 2 *or* ~ **de campaña** : tent
tiene → **tener**
tienta *nf* **andar a** ~**s** : feel one's way, grope around
tierno, -na *adj* 1 : tender, fresh, young 2 CARIÑOSO : affectionate
tierra *nf* 1 : land 2 SUELO : ground, earth 3 *or* ~ **natal** : native land 4 **la Tierra** : the Earth 5 **por** ~ : overland 6 ~ **adentro** : inland
tieso, -sa *adj* 1 : stiff, rigid 2 ERGUIDO : erect 3 ENGREÍDO : haughty
tiesto *nm* : flowerpot
tifoideo, -dea *adj* **fiebre tifoidea** : typhoid fever

tifón *nm, pl* **-fones** : typhoon
tifus *nm* : typhus
tigre, -gresa *n* 1 : tiger, tigress *f* 2 *Lat* : jaguar
tijera *nf or* **tijeras** *nfpl* : scissors — **tijeretada** *nf* : cut, snip
tildar *vt* ~ **de** : brand as, call
tilde *nf* 1 : tilde 2 ACENTO : accent mark
tilo *nm* : linden (tree)
timar *vt* : swindle, cheat
timbre *nm* 1 : bell 2 : tone, timbre (of a voice, etc.) 3 SELLO : seal, stamp 4 *Lat* : postage stamp — **timbrar** *vt* : stamp
tímido, -da *adj* : timid, shy — **timidez** *nf* : timidity, shyness
timo *nm fam* : swindle, hoax
timón *nm, pl* **-mones** 1 : rudder 2 **coger el** ~ : take the helm, take charge
tímpano *nm* 1 : eardrum 2 ~s *nmpl* : timpani, kettledrums
tina *nf* 1 : vat 2 BAÑERA : bathtub
tinieblas *nfpl* 1 : darkness 2 **estar en** ~ **sobre** : be in the dark about
tino *nm* 1 : good judgment, sense 2 TACTO : tact
tinta *nf* 1 : ink 2 **saberlo de buena** ~ : have it on good authority — **tinte** *nm* 1 : dye, coloring 2 MATIZ : overtone — **tintero** *nm* : inkwell
tintinear *vi* : jingle, tinkle, clink — **tintineo** *nm* : jingle, tinkle, clink
tinto, -ta *adj* 1 : dyed, stained 2 : red (of wine)
tintorería *nf* : dry cleaner (service)
tintura *nf* 1 : dye, tint 2 ~ **de yodo** : tincture of iodine
tiña *nf* : ringworm
tío, tía *n* : uncle *m*, aunt *f*
tiovivo *nm* : merry-go-round
típico, -ca *adj* : typical
tiple *nm* : soprano
tipo *nm* 1 : type, kind 2 FIGURA : figure (of a woman), build (of a man) 3 : rate (of interest, etc.) 4 : (printing) type, typeface — **tipo, -pa** *n fam* : guy *m*, gal *f*
tipografía *nf* : typography, printing — **tipográfico, -ca** *adj* : typographical — **tipógrafo, -fa** *n* : printer
tique *or* **tíquet** *nm* : ticket — **tiquete** *nm Lat* : ticket
tira *nf* 1 : strip, strap 2 ~ **cómica** : comic strip
tirabuzón *nf, pl* **-zones** 1 : corkscrew 2 RIZO : curl, coil
tirada *nf* 1 : throw 2 DISTANCIA : distance 3 IMPRESIÓN : printing, issue — **tirador** *nm* : handle, knob — **tirador, -dora** *n* : marksman *m*, markswoman *f*

tiranía *nf* : tyranny — **tiránico, -ca** *adj* : tyrannical — **tiranizar** {21} *vt* : tyrannize — **tirano, -na** *adj* : tyrannical — ~ *n* : tyrant
tirante *adj* 1 : taut, tight 2 : tense (of a situation, etc.) — ~ *nm* 1 : (shoulder) strap 2 ~s *nmpl* : suspenders
tirar *vt* 1 : throw 2 DESECHAR : throw away 3 DERRIBAR : knock down 4 DISPARAR : shoot, fire 5 IMPRIMIR : print — *vi* 1 : pull 2 DISPARAR : shoot 3 ATRAER : attract 4 *fam* : get by, manage 5 ~ **a** : tend towards — **tirarse** *vr* 1 : throw oneself 2 *fam* : spend (time)
tiritar *vi* : shiver
tiro *nm* 1 : shot, gunshot 2 : shot, kick (in sports) 3 : team (of horses, etc.) 4 **a** ~ : within range
tiroides *nmf* : thyroid (gland)
tirón *nm, pl* **-rones** 1 : pull, yank 2 **de un** ~ : in one go
tirotear *vt* : shoot at — **tiroteo** *nm* : shooting
tisis *nfs & pl* : tuberculosis
títere *nm* : puppet
titilar *vi* : flicker
titiritero, -ra *n* 1 : puppeteer 2 ACRÓBATA : acrobat
titubear *vi* 1 : hesitate 2 BALBUCEAR : stutter, stammer — **titubeante** *adj* : hesitant, faltering — **titubeo** *nm* : hesitation
titular *vt* : title, call — **titularse** *vr* 1 : be called, be titled 2 LICENCIARSE : receive a degree — ~ *adj* : titular, official — ~ *nm* : headline — ~ *nmf* : holder, incumbent — **título** *nm* 1 : title 2 : degree, qualification (in education)
tiza *nf* : chalk
tiznar *vt* : blacken (with soot, etc.) — **tizne** *nm* : soot
toalla *nf* : towel — **toallero** *nm* : towel rack
tobillo *nm* : ankle
tobogán *nm, pl* **-ganes** 1 : toboggan, sled 2 : slide (in a playground, etc.)
tocadiscos *nms & pl* : record player
tocado, -da *adj fam* : touched, not all there — **tocado** *nm* : headgear, headdress
tocador *nm* : dressing table
tocar {72} *vt* 1 : touch, feel 2 MENCIONAR : touch on, refer to 3 : play (a musical instrument) — *vi* 1 : knock, ring 2 ~ **en** : touch on, border on
tocayo, -ya *n* : namesake
tocino *nm* 1 : bacon 2 : salt pork (for cooking) — **tocineta** *nf Lat* : bacon
tocólogo, -ga *n* : obstetrician
tocón *nm, pl* **-cones** : stump (of a tree)

todavía *adv* **1** AÚN : still **2** (*in comparisons*) : even **3 ~ no** : not yet
todo, -da *adj* **1** : all **2** CADA, CUALQUIER : every, each **3 a toda velocidad** : at top speed **4 todo el mundo** : everyone, everybody — **~** *pron* **1** : everything, all **2 todos, -das** *pl* : everybody, everyone, all — **todo** *nm* : whole — **todopoderoso, -sa** *adj* : almighty, all-powerful
toga *nf* **1** : toga **2** : gown, robe (of a judge, etc.)
toldo *nm* : awning, canopy
tolerar *vt* : tolerate — **tolerancia** *nf* : tolerance — **tolerante** *adj* : tolerant
toma *nf* **1** : capture **2** DOSIS : dose **3** : take (in film) **4 ~ de corriente** : wall socket, outlet **5 ~ y daca** : give-and-take — **tomar** *vt* **1** : take **2** : have (food or drink) **3** CAPTURAR : capture, seize **4 ~ el sol** : sunbathe **5 ~ tierra** : land — *vi* : drink (alcohol) — **tomarse** *vr* **1** : take (time, etc.) **2** : drink, eat, have (food, drink)
tomate *nm* : tomato
tomillo *nm* : thyme
tomo *nm* : volume
ton *nm* **sin ~ ni son** : without rhyme or reason
tonada *nf* : tune
tonel *nm* : barrel, cask
tonelada *nf* : ton — **tonelaje** *nm* : tonnage
tónica *nf* **1** : tonic (water) **2** TENDENCIA : trend, tone — **tónico, -ca** *adj* : tonic — **tónico** *nm* : tonic (in medicine)
tono *nm* **1** : tone **2** : shade (of colors) **3** : key (in music)
tontería *nf* **1** : silly thing or remark **2** ESTUPIDEZ : foolishness **3 decir ~s** : talk nonsense — **tonto, -ta** *adj* **1** : stupid, silly **2 a tontas y a locas** : haphazardly — **~** *n* : fool, idiot
topacio *nm* : topaz
toparse *vr* **~ con** : run into, come across
tope *nm* **1** : limit, end **2** *or* **~ de puerta** : doorstop **3** *Lat* : bump — **~** *adj* : maximum
tópico, -ca *adj* **1** : topical, external **2** MANIDO : trite — **tópico** *nm* : cliché
topo *nm* : mole (animal)
toque *nm* **1** : (light) touch **2** : ringing, peal (of a bell) **3 ~ de queda** : curfew **4 ~ de diana** : reveille — **toquetear** *vt* : finger, handle
tórax *nms & pl* : thorax
torbellino *nm* : whirlwind
torcer {14} *vt* **1** : twist, bend **2** : turn (a corner) **3** : wring (out) — *vi* : turn —

torcerse *vr* **1** : twist, sprain **2** FRUSTRARSE : go wrong **3** DESVIARSE : go astray — **torcedura** *nf* **1** : twisting **2** ESGUINCE : sprain — **torcido, -da** *adj* : twisted, crooked
tordo, -da *adj* : dappled — **tordo** *nm* : thrush (bird)
torear *vt* **1** : fight (bulls) **2** ELUDIR : dodge, sidestep — *vi* : fight bulls — **toreo** *nm* : bullfighting — **torero, -ra** *n* : bullfighter
tormenta *nf* : storm — **tormento** *nm* **1** : torture **2** ANGUSTIA : torment, anguish — **tormentoso, -sa** *adj* : stormy
tornado *nm* : tornado
tornar *vt* CONVERTIR : render, turn — *vi* : go back, return — **tornarse** *vr* : become, turn into
torneo *nm* : tournament
tornillo *nm* : screw
torniquete *nm* **1** : turnstile **2** : tourniquet (in medicine)
torno *nm* **1** : winch **2** : (carpenter's) lathe **3 ~ de alfarero** : (potter's) wheel **4 ~ de banco** : vise **5 en ~ a** : around, about
toro *nm* **1** : bull **2 ~s** *nmpl* : bullfight
toronja *nf* : grapefruit
torpe *adj* **1** : clumsy, awkward **2** ESTÚPIDO : stupid, dull
torpedear *vt* : torpedo — **torpedo** *nm* : torpedo
torpeza *nf* **1** : clumsiness, awkwardness **2** ESTUPIDEZ : slowness, stupidity
torre *nf* **1** : tower **2** : turret (on a ship, etc.) **3** : rook, castle (in chess)
torrente *nm* **1** : torrent **2 ~ sanguíneo** : bloodstream — **torrencial** *adj* : torrential
tórrido, -da *adj* : torrid
torsión *nf, pl* **-siones** : twisting
torta *nf* **1** : torte, cake **2** *Lat* : sandwich
tortazo *nm fam* : blow, wallop
tortícolis *nfs & pl* : stiff neck
tortilla *nf* **1** : tortilla **2** *or* **~ de huevo** : omelet
tórtola *nf* : turtledove
tortuga *nf* **1** : turtle, tortoise **2 ~ de agua dulce** : terrapin
tortuoso, -sa *adj* : tortuous, winding
tortura *nf* : torture — **torturar** *vt* : torture
tos *nf* **1** : cough **2 ~ ferina** : whooping cough
tosco, -ca *adj* : rough, coarse
toser *vi* : cough
tosquedad *nf* : coarseness
tostar {19} *vt* **1** : toast **2** BRONCEAR : tan — **tostarse** *vr* : get a tan — **tostada**

nf **1** : piece of toast **2** *Lat* : tostada —
tostador *nm* : toaster

tostón *nm, pl* **-tones** *Lat* : fried plantain chip

total *adj & nm* : total — ~ *adv* : so,
after all — **totalidad** *nf* : whole — **totalitario, -ria** *adj & n* : totalitarian —
totalitarismo *nm* : totalitarianism —
totalizar {21} *vt* : total, add up to

tóxico, -ca *adj* : toxic, poisonous —
tóxico *nm* : poison — **toxicomanía** *nf*
: drug addiction — **toxicómano, -na** *n*
: drug addict — **toxina** *nf* : toxin

tozudo, -da *adj* : stubborn

traba *nf* : obstacle, hindrance

trabajar *vi* **1** : work **2** : act, perform (in
theater, etc.) — *vt* **1** : work (metal) **2**
: knead (dough) **3** MEJORAR : work on,
work at — **trabajador, -dora** *adj*
: hard-working — ~ *n* : worker —
trabajo *nm* **1** : work **2** EMPLEO : job **3**
TAREA : task **4** ESFUERZO : effort **5**
costar ~ : be difficult **6** ~ **en
equipo** : teamwork **7** ~s *nmpl*
: hardships, difficulties — **trabajoso,
-sa** *adj* : hard, laborious

trabalenguas *nms & pl* : tongue twister

trabar *vt* **1** : join, connect **2** OBSTAC-
ULIZAR : impede **3** : strike up (a conversation, etc.) **4** : thicken (sauces) —
trabarse *vr* **1** : jam **2** ENREDARSE : become entangled **3 se le traba la
lengua** : he gets tongue-tied

trabucar {72} *vt* : mix up

tracción *nf* : traction

tractor *nm* : tractor

tradición *nf, pl* **-ciones** : tradition —
tradicional *adj* : traditional

traducir {61} *vt* : translate — **traducción** *nf, pl* **-ciones** : translation — **traductor, -tora** *n* : translator

traer {81} *vt* **1** : bring **2** CAUSAR : cause,
bring about **3** CONTENER : carry, have **4**
LLEVAR : wear — **traerse** *vr* **1** : bring
along **2 traérselas** : be difficult

traficar {72} *vi* ~ **en** : traffic in —
traficante *nmf* : dealer, trafficker —
tráfico *nm* **1** : trade (of merchandise)
2 : traffic (of vehicles)

tragaluz *nf, pl* **-luces** : skylight

tragar {52} *vt* **1** : swallow **2** *fam* : put up
with — *vi* : swallow — **tragarse** *vr* **1**
: swallow **2** ABSORBER : absorb, swallow up

tragedia *nf* : tragedy — **trágico, -ca** *adj*
: tragic

trago *nm* **1** : swallow, swig **2** *fam*
: drink, liquor — **tragón, -gona** *adj*
fam : greedy — ~ *nmf fam* : glutton

traicionar *vt* : betray — **traición** *nf, pl*

-ciones 1 : betrayal **2** : treason (in
law) — **traidor, -dora** *adj* : traitorous,
treacherous — ~ *n* : traitor

trailer *nm* : trailer

traje *nm* **1** : dress, costume **2** : (man's)
suit **3** ~ **de baño** : bathing suit

trajinar *vi fam* : rush around — **trajín**
nm, pl **-jines** *fam* : hustle and bustle

trama *nf* **1** : plot **2** : weave, weft (of fabric) — **tramar** *vt* **1** : plot, plan **2**
: weave (fabric)

tramitar *vt* : negotiate — **trámite** *nm*
: procedure, step

tramo *nm* **1** : stretch, section **2** : flight
(of stairs)

trampa *nf* **1** : trap **2 hacer** ~s : cheat
— **trampear** *vi* : cheat

trampilla *nf* : trapdoor

trampolín *nm, pl* **-lines** : diving board
2 : trampoline (in a gymnasium, etc.)

tramposo, -sa *adj* : crooked, cheating
— ~ *n* : cheat, swindler

tranca *nf* **1** : cudgel, club **2** : bar (for a
door or window)

trance *nm* **1** : critical juncture **2** : (hypnotic) trance **3 en** ~ **de** : in the
process of

tranquilo, -la *adj* : calm, tranquil —
tranquilidad *nf* : tranquility, peace —
tranquilizante *nm* : tranquilizer —
tranquilizar {21} *vt* : calm, soothe —
tranquilizarse *vr* : calm down

trans- *see also* **tras-**

transacción *nf, pl* **-ciones** : transaction

transatlántico, -ca *adj* : transatlantic
— **transatlántico** *nm* : ocean liner

transbordador *nm* **1** : ferry **2** ~ **espacial** : space shuttle — **transbordar** *vt*
: transfer — *vi* : change (of trains, etc.)
— **transbordo** *nm* **hacer** ~ : change
(trains, etc.)

transcribir {33} *vt* : transcribe —
transcripción *nf, pl* **-ciones** : tran-
scription

transcurrir *vi* : elapse, pass — **trans-
curso** *nm* : course, progression

transeúnte *nmf* : passerby

transferir {76} *vt* : transfer — **transferencia** *nf* : transfer, transference

transformar *vt* **1** : transform, change **2**
CONVERTIR : convert — **transfor-
marse** *vr* : be transformed — **transformación** *nf, pl* **-ciones** : transformation — **transformador** *nm*
: transformer

transfusión *nf, pl* **-siones** : transfusion

transgredir {1} *vt* : transgress —
transgresión *nf* : transgression

transición *nf, pl* **-ciones** : transition

transido, -da *adj* : overcome, stricken

transigir {35} *vi* : give in, compromise
transistor *nm* : transistor
transitar *vi* : go, travel — **transitable** *adj* : passable
transitivo, -va *adj* : transitive
tránsito *nm* 1 : transit 2 TRÁFICO : traffic 3 **hora de máximo ~** : rush hour — **transitorio, -ria** *adj* : transitory
transmitir *vt* 1 : transmit 2 : broadcast (radio, TV, etc.) 3 CEDER : pass on — **transmisión** *nf, pl* **-siones** 1 : broadcast 2 TRANSFERENCIA : transfer 3 : transmission (of an automobile) — **transmisor** *nm* : transmitter
transparentarse *vr* : be transparent — **transparente** *adj* : transparent
transpirar *vi* : perspire, sweat — **transpiración** *nf, pl* **-ciones** : perspiration, sweat
transponer {60} *vt* : transpose, move — **transponerse** *vr* 1 : set (of the sun, etc.) 2 DORMITAR : doze off
transportar *vt* : transport, carry — **transportarse** *vr* : get carried away — **transporte** *nm* : transport, transportation
transversal *adj* **corte ~** : cross section
tranvía *nm* : streetcar, trolley
trapear *vt Lat* : mop
trapecio *nm* : trapeze
trapisonda *nf* : scheme, plot
trapo *nm* 1 : cloth, rag 2 **~s** *nmpl fam* : clothes
tráquea *nf* : trachea, windpipe
traquetear *vi* 1 : rattle around, shake — **traqueteo** *nm* : rattling
tras *prep* 1 DESPUÉS DE : after 2 DETRÁS DE : behind
tras- see also trans-
trascender {56} *vi* 1 : leak out, become known 2 EXTENDERSE : spread 3 **~ de** : transcend — **trascendencia** *nf* : importance — **trascendental** *adj* 1 : transcendental 2 IMPORTANTE : important
trasegar *vt* : move around
trasero, -ra *adj* : rear, back — **trasero** *nm* : buttocks *pl*
trasfondo *nm* 1 : background 2 : undercurrent (of suspicion, etc.)
trasladar *vt* 1 : transfer, move 2 POSPONER : postpone — **trasladarse** *vr* : move, relocate — **traslado** *nm* 1 : transfer, move 2 COPIA : copy
traslapar *vt* : overlap — **traslaparse** *vr* : overlap
traslucirse {45} *vr* 1 : be translucent 2 REVELARSE : be revealed — **traslúcido, -da** : translucent

trasnochar *vi* : stay up all night
traspasar *vt* 1 : pierce, go through 2 EXCEDER : go beyond 3 ATRAVESAR : cross, go across 4 : transfer (a business, etc.) — **traspaso** *nm* : transfer, sale
traspié *nm* 1 : stumble, trip 2 ERROR : blunder
trasplantar *vt* : transplant — **trasplante** *nm* : transplant
trasquilar *vt* : shear
traste *nm* 1 : fret (on a guitar, etc.) 2 *Lat* : (kitchen) utensil 3 **dar al ~ con** : ruin 4 **irse al ~** : fall through
trastos *nmpl fam* : pieces of junk, stuff
trastornar *vt* 1 : disturb, disrupt 2 VOLVER LOCO : drive crazy — **trastornarse** *vr* : go crazy — **trastornado, -da** *adj* : disturbed, deranged — **trastorno** *nm* 1 : disturbance, disruption 2 : (medical or psychological) disorder
trastrocar *vt* : change, switch around
tratable *adj* : friendly, sociable
tratar *vi* 1 **~ con** : deal with 2 **~ de** : try to 3 **~ de** *or* **~ sobre** : be about, concern 4 **~ en** : deal in — *vt* 1 : treat MANEJAR : deal with, handle — **tratarse** *vr* **~ de** : be about, concern — **tratado** *nm* 1 : treatise 2 CONVENIO : treaty — **tratamiento** *nm* : treatment — **trato** *nm* 1 : treatment 2 ACUERDO : deal, agreement 3 **~s** *nmpl* : dealings
trauma *nm* : trauma — **traumático, -ca** *adj* : traumatic
través *nm* 1 **a ~ de** : across, through 2 **de ~** : sideways
travesaño *nm* : crosspiece
travesía *nf* : voyage, crossing (of the sea)
travesura *nf* 1 : prank 2 **~s** *nfpl* : mischief — **travieso, -sa** *adj* : mischievous, naughty
trayecto *nm* 1 : trajectory, path 2 VIAJE : journey 3 RUTA : route — **trayectoria** *nf* : path, trajectory
traza *nf* 1 : design, plan 2 ASPECTO : appearance — **trazado** *nm* 1 : outline, sketch 2 DISEÑO : plan, layout — **trazar** {21} *vt* 1 : trace, outline 2 : draw up (a plan, etc.) — **trazo** *nm* : stroke, line
trébol *nm* 1 : clover, shamrock 2 **~es** *nmpl* : clubs (in playing cards)
trece *adj & nm* : thirteen — **treceavo, -va** *adj* : thirteenth — **treceavo** *nm* : thirteenth (fraction)
trecho *nm* 1 : stretch, period 2 DISTANCIA : distance 3 **de ~ a ~** : at intervals

tregua nf **1** : truce **2 sin ~** : without respite

treinta adj & nm : thirty — **treintavo, -va** adj : thirtieth — **treintavo** nm : thirtieth (fraction)

tremendo, -da adj : tremendous, enormous

trementina nf : turpentine

trémulo, -la adj : trembling, flickering

tren nm **1** : train **2 ~ de aterrizaje** : landing gear

trenza nf : braid, pigtail — **trenzar** {21} vt : braid — **trenzarse** vr Lat : get involved

trepar vi **1** : climb **2** : creep, spread (of a plant) — **treparse** vr : climb (up) — **trepador, -dora** adj : climbing — **trepadora** nf **1** : climbing plant **2** fam : social climber

trepidar vi : shake, vibrate

tres adj & nm : three — **trescientos, -tas** adj : three hundred — **trescientos** nms & pl : three hundred

treta nf : trick

triángulo nm : triangle — **triangular** adj : triangular

tribu nf : tribe — **tribal** adj : tribal

tribulación nf, pl **-ciones** : tribulation

tribuna nf **1** : dais, platform **2** : grandstand, bleachers pl (in a stadium)

tribunal nm : court, tribunal

tributar vt : pay, render — vi : pay taxes — **tributo** nm **1** : tribute **2** IMPUESTO : tax

triciclo nm : tricycle

tricolor adj : tricolored

tridimensional adj : three-dimensional

trigésimo, -ma adj & n : thirtieth

trigo nm : wheat

trigonometría nf : trigonometry

trillado, -da adj : trite

trillar vt : thresh — **trilladora** nf : threshing machine

trillizo, -za n : triplet

trilogía nf : trilogy

trimestral adj : quarterly

trinar vi : warble

trinchar vt : carve

trinchera nf **1** : trench, ditch **2** IMPERMEABLE : trench coat

trineo nm : sled, sleigh

trinidad nf : trinity

trino nm : trill, warble

trío nm : trio

tripa nf **1** : gut, intestine **2 ~s** nfpl fam : belly, tummy

triple adj & nm : triple — **triplicar** {72} vt : triple

trípode nm : tripod

tripular vt : man — **tripulación** nf, pl **-ciones** : crew — **tripulante** nmf : crew member

tris nm **estar en un ~ de** : be within an inch of

triste adj **1** : sad **2** SOMBRÍO : dismal, gloomy **3** MISERABLE : sorry, miserable — **tristeza** nf : sadness, grief

tritón nm, pl **-tones** : newt

triturar vt : crush, grind

triunfar vi : triumph, win — **triunfal** adj : triumphal — **triunfante** adj : triumphant — **triunfo** nm : triumph, victory

trivial adj : trivial

triza nf **1** : shred, bit **2 hacer ~s** : smash to pieces

trocar {82} vt **1** CONVERTIR : change **2** INTERCAMBIAR : exchange

trocha nf : path, trail

trofeo nm : trophy

trombón nm, pl **-bones 1** : trombone **2** : trombonist (musician)

trombosis nf : thrombosis

trompa nf **1** : trunk (of an elephant), snout **2** : horn (musical instrument) **3** : tube (in anatomy)

trompeta nf : trumpet — **trompetista** nmf : trumpet player

trompo nm : top (toy)

tronada nf : thunderstorm — **tronar** {19} vi : thunder, rage — vt Lat fam : shoot — v impers : thunder

tronchar vt **1** : snap **2** TRUNCAR : cut short

tronco nm **1** : trunk (of a tree) **2** : torso (of a person) **3 dormir como un ~** : sleep like a log

trono nm : throne

tropa nf : troops pl, soldiers pl

tropel nm : mob

tropezar {29} vi **1** : trip, stumble **2 ~ con** : come up against, run into — **tropezón** nm, pl **-zones 1** : stumble **2** EQUIVOCACIÓN : mistake, slip

trópico nm : tropic — **tropical** adj : tropical

tropiezo nm **1** CONTRATIEMPO : snag, setback **2** EQUIVOCACIÓN : mistake, slip

trotar vi **1** : trot **2** fam : rush about — **trote** nm **1** : trot **2** fam : rush, bustle **3 al ~** : at a trot, quickly

trozo nm : piece, bit, chunk

trucha nf : trout

truco nm **1** : knack **2** ARDID : trick

trueno nm : thunder

trueque nm : barter, exchange

trufa nf : truffle

truncar {72} vt **1** : cut short **2** : thwart, spoil (plans, etc.)

tu *adj* : your
tú *pron* : you
tuba *nf* : tuba
tuberculosis *nf* : tuberculosis
tubo *nm* **1** : tube, pipe **2** ~ **de escape**
: exhaust pipe (of a vehicle) **3** ~ **de**
desagüe : drainpipe — **tubería** *nf*
: pipes *pl*, tubing
tuerca *nf* : nut (for a screw)
tuerto, -ta *adj* : one-eyed, blind in one
eye
tuétano *nm* : marrow
tufo *nm* **1** : vapor **2** *fam* : stench, stink
tugurio *nm* : hovel
tulipán *nm, pl* **-panes** : tulip
tullido, -da *adj* : crippled, paralyzed
tumba *nf* : tomb, grave
tumbar *vt* : knock down, knock over —
tumbarse *vr* : lie down — **tumbo** *nm*
dar ~**s** : jolt, bump around
tumor *nm* : tumor
tumulto *nm* **1** : commotion, tumult **2**
MOTÍN : riot — **tumultuoso, -sa** *adj*
: tumultuous
tuna *nf* : prickly pear
túnel *nm* : tunnel
túnica *nf* : tunic
tupé *nm* : toupee
tupido, -da *adj* : dense, thick
turba *nf* **1** : peat **2** MUCHEDUMBRE
: mob, throng

turbación *nf, pl* **-clones 1** : disturbance
2 CONFUSIÓN : confusion
turbante *nm* : turban
turbar *vt* **1** : disturb, upset **2** CONFUNDIR
: confuse, bewilder
turbina *nf* : turbine
turbio, -bia *adj* **1** : cloudy, murky **2**
: blurred (of vision, etc.) — **turbión**
nm, pl **-blones** : squall
turbulencia *nf* : turbulence — **turbu-**
lento, -ta *adj* : turbulent
turco, -ca *adj* : Turkish — **turco** *nm*
: Turkish (language)
turista *nmf* : tourist — **turismo** *nm*
: tourism, tourist industry — **turísti-**
co, -ca *adj* : tourist, travel
turnarse *vr* : take turns, alternate —
turno *nm* **1** : turn **2** ~ **de noche**
: night shift
turquesa *nf* : turquoise
turrón *nm, pl* **-rrones** : nougat
tutear *vt* : address as *tú*
tutela *nf* **1** : guardianship (in law) **2**
bajo la ~ **de** : under the protection of
tuteo *nm* : addressing as *tú*
tutor, -tora *n* **1** : guardian **2** : tutor (in
education)
tuyo, -ya *adj* : yours, of yours — ~
pron **1 el tuyo, la tuya, lo tuyo, los**
tuyos, las tuyas : yours **2 los tuyos**
: your family, your friends

U

u¹ *nf* : u, 22d letter of the Spanish alphabet
u² *conj* (*used before words beginning*
with o- or ho-) : or
uapití *nm* : American elk, wapiti
ubicar {72} *vt Lat* **1** COLOCAR : place,
position **2** LOCALIZAR : find — **ubi-**
carse *vr* : be located
ubre *nf* : udder
Ud., Uds. → **usted**
ufanarse *vr* ~ **de** : boast about —
ufano, -na *adj* **1** : proud **2** ENGREÍDO
: self-satisfied
ujier *nm* : usher
úlcera *nf* : ulcer
ulterior *adj* : later, subsequent — **ulteri-**
ormente *adv* : subsequently
últimamente *adv* : lately, recently
ultimar *vt* **1** : complete, finish **2** *Lat*
: kill — **ultimátum** *nm, pl* **-tums** : ultimatum
último, -ma *adj* **1** : last **2** : latest, most

recent (in time) **3** : farthest (in space)
4 por último : finally
ultrajar *vt* : outrage, insult — **ultraje** *nm*
: outrage, insult
ultramar *nm* **de** ~ *or* **en** ~ : overseas
— **ultramarino, -na** *adj* : overseas —
ultramarinos *nmpl* **tienda de** ~
: grocery store
ultranza: a ~ *adv phr* : to the extreme
— **a** ~ *adj phr* : out-and-out, complete
ultrasonido *nm* : ultrasound
ultravioleta *adj* : ultraviolet
ulular *vi* **1** : hoot (of an owl) **2** : howl (of
a wolf, the wind, etc.) — **ululato** *nm*
: hoot (of an owl)
umbilical *adj* : umbilical
umbral *nm* : threshold
un, una *art, mpl* **unos 1** : a, an **2 unos**
or **unas** *pl* : some, a few **3 unos** *or*
unas *pl* : about, approximately — **un**
adj → **uno**

unánime *adj* : unanimous — **unanimidad** *nf* : unanimity
uncir {83} *vt* : yoke
undécimo, -ma *adj & n* : eleventh
ungir {35} *vt* : anoint — **ungüento** *nm* : ointment
único, -ca *adj* **1** : only, sole **2** EXCEPCIONAL : unique — **~** *n* : only one — **únicamente** *adv* : only
unicornio *nm* : unicorn
unidad *nf* **1** : unit **2** ARMONÍA : unity — **unido, -da** *adj* **1** : united **2** : close (of friends, etc.)
unificar {72} *vt* : unify — **unificación** *nf, pl* **-ciones** : unification
uniformar *vt* **1** : standardize **2** : put into uniform — **uniformado, -da** *adj* : uniformed — **uniforme** *adj & nm* : uniform — **uniformidad** *nf* : uniformity
unilateral *adj* : unilateral
unir *vt* **1** : unite, join **2** COMBINAR : combine, mix together — **unirse** *vr* **1** : join together **2 ~ a** : join — **unión** *nf, pl* **uniones 1** : union **2** JUNTURA : joint, coupling
unísono *nm* **al ~** : in unison
unitario, -ria *adj* : unitary
universal *adj* : universal
universidad *nf* : university, college — **universitario, -ria** *adj* : university, college
universo *nm* : universe
uno, una (**un** *before masculine singular nouns*) *adj* : one — **~** *pron* **1** : one **2 unos, unas** *pl* : some **3 uno(s) a otro(s)** : one another, each other **4 uno y otro** : both — **uno** *nm* : one (number)
untar *vt* **1** : smear, grease **2** *fam* : bribe — **untuoso, -sa** *adj* : greasy, sticky
uña *nf* **1** : nail, fingernail **2** : claw (of a cat, etc.), hoof (of a horse, etc.)
uranio *nm* : uranium

Urano *nm* : Uranus
urbano, -na *adj* : urban, city — **urbanidad** *nf* : politeness, courtesy — **urbanización** *nf, pl* **-ciones** : housing development — **urbanizar** *vt* : develop, urbanize — **urbe** *nf* : large city
urdir *vt* **1** : warp **2** PLANEAR : plot — **urdimbre** *nf* : warp (of a fabric)
urgir {35} *v impers* : be urgent, be pressing — **urgencia** *nf* **1** : urgency **2** EMERGENCIA : emergency — **urgente** *adj* : urgent
urinario, -ria *adj* : urinary — **urinario** *nm* : urinal (place)
urna *nf* **1** : urn **2** : ballot box (for voting)
urraca *nf* : magpie
uruguayo, -ya *adj* : Uruguayan
usar *vt* **1** : use **2** LLEVAR : wear — **usarse** **1** EMPLEARSE : be used **2** : be worn, be in fashion — **usado, -da** *adj* **1** : used **2** GASTADO : worn, worn-out — **usanza** *nf* : custom, usage — **uso** *nm* **1** : use **2** DESGASTE : wear and tear **3** USANZA : custom, usage
usted *pron* **1** (*used in formal address; often written as* **Ud.** *or* **Vd.**) : you **2 ~es** *pl* (*often written as* **Uds.** *or* **Vds.**) : you (all)
usual *adj* : usual
usuario, -ria *n* : user
usura *nf* : usury — **usurero, -ra** *n* : usurer
usurpar *vt* : usurp
utensilio *nm* : utensil, tool
útero *nm* : uterus, womb
utilizar {21} *vt* : use, utilize — **útil** *adj* : useful — **útiles** *nmpl* : implements, tools — **utilidad** *nf* : utility, usefulness — **utilitario, -ria** *adj* : utilitarian — **utilización** *nf, pl* **-ciones** : utilization, use
uva *nf* : grape

V

v *nf* : v, 23d letter of the Spanish alphabet
va → ir
vaca *nf* : cow
vacaciones *nfpl* **1** : vacation **2 estar de ~** : be on vacation **3 irse de ~** : go on vacation
vacante *adj* : vacant — **~** *nf* : vacancy
vaciar {85} *vt* **1** : empty (out) **2** AHUECAR : hollow out **3** : cast, mold (a statue, etc.)

vacilar *vi* **1** : hesitate, waver **2** : flicker (of light) **3** TAMBALEARSE : be unsteady, wobble **4** *fam* : joke, fool around — **vacilación** *nf, pl* **-ciones** : hesitation — **vacilante** *adj* **1** : hesitant **2** OSCILANTE : unsteady
vacío, -cía *adj* : empty — **vacío** *nm* **1** : void **2** : vacuum (in physics) **3** HUECO : space, gap
vacuna *nf* : vaccine — **vacunación** *nf,*

pl -**ciones** : vaccination — **vacunar** *vt* : vaccinate
vacuno, -na *adj* : bovine
vadear *vt* : ford — **vado** *nm* : ford
vagabundear *vi* : wander — **vagabundo, -da** *adj* **1** : vagrant **2** : stray (of a dog, etc.) — ~ *n* : hobo, bum — **vagancia** *nf* **1** : vagrancy **2** PEREZA : laziness, idleness — **vagar** {52} *vi* : roam, wander
vagina *nf* : vagina
vago, -ga *adj* **1** : vague **2** PEREZOSO : lazy, idle — ~ *n* : idler, loafer
vagón *nm, pl* -**gones** : car (of a train)
vahído *nm* : dizzy spell
vaho *nm* **1** : breath **2** VAPOR : vapor, steam
vaina *nf* **1** : sheath, scabbard **2** : pod (in botany) **3** *Lat fam* : bother, pain
vainilla *nf* : vanilla
vaivén *nm, pl* -**venes** **1** : swinging, swaying **2** : coming and going (of people, etc.) **3** **vaivenes** *nmpl* : ups and downs
vajilla *nf* : dishes *pl*
vale *nm* **1** : voucher **2** PAGARÉ : IOU — **valedero, -ra** *adj* : valid
valentía *nf* : courage, bravery
valer {84} *vt* **1** : be worth **2** COSTAR : cost **3** GANAR : gain, earn **4** EQUIVALER A : be equal to — *vi* **1** : have value, cost **2** SER VÁLIDO : be valid, count **3** SERVIR : be of use **4** **hacerse** ~ : assert oneself **5 más vale** : it's better — **valerse** *vr* **1** ~ **de** : take advantage of **2** ~ **solo** *or* ~ **por sí mismo** : look after oneself
valeroso, -sa *adj* : courageous
valga, etc. → **valer**
valía *nf* : worth
validar *vt* : validate — **validez** *nf* : validity — **válido, -da** *adj* : valid
valiente *adj* **1** : brave **2** (*used ironically*) : fine, great
valija *nf* : case, valise
valioso, -sa *adj* : valuable
valla *nf* **1** : fence **2** : hurdle (in sports) — **vallar** *vt* : put a fence around
valle *nm* : valley
valor *nm* **1** : value, worth **2** VALENTÍA : courage, valor **3** **objetos de** ~ : valuables **4 sin** ~ : worthless — ~**es** *nmpl* : values, principles **6** ~**es** *nmpl* : securities, bonds — **valoración** *nf, pl* -**ciones** : valuation — **valorar** *vt* : evaluate, assess
vals *nm* : waltz
válvula *nf* : valve
vamos → **ir**
vampiro *nm* : vampire

van → **ir**
vanagloriarse *vr* : boast, brag
vándalo *nm* : vandal — **vandalismo** : vandalism
vanguardia *nf* **1** : vanguard **2** : avantgarde (in art, music, etc.) **3 a la** ~ : at/in the forefront
vanidad *nf* : vanity — **vanidoso, -sa** *adj* : vain, conceited
vano, -na *adj* **1** INÚTIL : vain, useless **2** SUPERFICIAL : empty, hollow **3 en vano** : in vain
vapor *nm* **1** : steam, vapor **2 al** ~ : steamed — **vaporizador** *nm* : vaporizer — **vaporizar** {21} *vt* : vaporize
vaquero, -ra *n* : cowboy *m*, cowgirl *f* — **vaqueros** *nmpl* : jeans
vara *nf* **1** : stick, rod **2** : staff (of office)
varado, -da *adj* : stranded
variar {85} *vt* **1** : vary **2** CAMBIAR : change, alter — *vi* : vary, change — **variable** *adj & nf* : variable — **variación** *nf, pl* -**ciones** : variation — **variado, -da** *adj* : varied — **variante** *nf* : variant
varicela *nf* : chicken pox
varicoso, -sa *adj* : varicose
variedad *nf* : variety
varilla *nf* : rod, stick
vario, -ria *adj* **1** : varied **2** ~**s** *pl* : several
varita *nf* : wand
variz *nf, pl* -**rices** *or* **várices** : varicose vein
varón *nm, pl* -**rones** **1** : man, male **2** NIÑO : boy — **varonil** *adj* : manly
vas → **ir**
vasco, -ca *adj* : Basque — **vasco** *nm* : Basque (language)
vasija *nf* : container, vessel
vaso *nm* **1** : glass **2** : vessel (in anatomy)
vástago *nm* **1** : offspring, descendent **2** BROTE : shoot **3** VARILLA : rod
vasto, -ta *adj* : vast
vaticinar *vt* : prophesy, predict — **vaticinio** *nm* : prophecy
vatio *nm* : watt
vaya, etc. → **ir**
Vd., Vds. → **usted**
ve, etc. → **ir, ver**
vecinal *adj* : local
vecino, -na *n* **1** : neighbor **2** HABITANTE : resident, inhabitant — ~ *adj* : neighboring — **vecindad** *nf* : neighborhood, vicinity — **vecindario** *nm* **1** : neighborhood **2** VECINOS : community, residents *pl*
vedar *vt* : prohibit — **veda** *nf* **1** : prohibition, ban **2** : closed season (for hunt-

ing and fishing) — **vedado** *nm* : preserve (for game, etc.)

vega *nf* : fertile lowland

vegetal *nm* : vegetable, plant — ~ *adj* : vegetable — **vegetación** *nf, pl* **-ciones** : vegetation — **vegetar** *vi* : vegetate — **vegetariano, -na** *adj & n* : vegetarian

vehemente *adj* : vehement

vehículo *nm* : vehicle

veinte *adj & nm* : twenty — **veinteavo, -va** *adj* : twentieth — **veinteavo** *nm* : twentieth — **veintena** *nf* : group of twenty, score

vejar *vt* : mistreat, humiliate — **vejación** *nf, pl* **-ciones** : humiliation

vejez *nf* : old age

vejiga *nf* 1 : bladder 2 AMPOLLA : blister

vela *nf* 1 : candle 2 : sail (of a ship) 3 VIGILIA : vigil **4 pasar la noche en ~** : have a sleepless night

velada *nf* : evening (party)

velar *vt* 1 : hold a wake over 2 CUIDAR : watch over 3 : blur (a photograph) 4 OCULTAR : veil, mask — *vi* 1 : stay awake 2 **~ por** : watch over — **velado, -da** *adj* 1 : veiled, hidden 2 : blurred (of a photograph)

velero *nm* : sailing ship

veleta *nf* : weather vane

vello *nm* 1 : body hair 2 PELUSA : down, fuzz — **vellón** *nm, pl* **-llones** : fleece — **velloso, -sa** *adj* : downy, fluffy — **velludo, -da** *adj* : hairy

velo *nm* : veil

veloz *adj, pl* **-loces** : fast, quick — **velocidad** *nf* 1 : speed, velocity 2 MARCHA : gear (of an automobile) — **velocímetro** *nm* : speedometer

vena *nf* 1 : vein 2 : grain (of wood) 3 DISPOSICIÓN : mood **4 tener ~ de** : have a talent for

venado *nm* 1 : deer 2 : venison (in cooking)

vencer {86} *vt* 1 : beat, defeat 2 SUPERAR : overcome — *vi* 1 : win 2 CADUCAR : expire — **vencerse** *vr* : collapse, give way — **vencedor, -dora** *adj* : winning — ~ *n* : winner — **vencido, -da** *adj* 1 : beaten, defeated 2 CADUCADO : expired 3 : due, payable (in finance) **4 darse por ~** : give up — **vencimiento** *nm* 1 : expiration 2 : maturity (of a loan)

venda *nf* : bandage — **vendaje** *nm* : bandage, dressing — **vendar** *vt* 1 : bandage 2 **~ los ojos** : blindfold

vendaval *nm* : gale

vender *vt* : sell — **venderse** *vr* 1 : be sold 2 **se vende** : for sale — **vende-**

dor, -dora *n* 1 : seller 2 : salesman *m*, saleswoman *f* (in a store)

vendimia *nf* : grape harvest

vendrá, etc. → **venir**

veneno *nm* 1 : poison 2 : venom (of a snake, etc.) — **venenoso, -sa** *adj* : poisonous

venerar *vt* : venerate, revere — **venerable** *adj* : venerable — **veneración** *nf, pl* **-ciones** : veneration, reverence

venéreo, -rea *adj* : venereal

venezolano, -na *adj* : Venezuelan

venga → **venir**

vengar {52} *vt* : avenge — **vengarse** *vr* : get even, take revenge — **venganza** *nf* : vengeance, revenge — **vengativo, -va** *adj* : vindictive, vengeful

venia *nf* 1 : permission 2 : pardon (in law)

venial *adj* : venial, petty

venir {87} *vi* 1 : come 2 LLEGAR : arrive 3 HALLARSE : be, appear 4 QUEDAR : fit **5 que viene** : coming, next **6 ~ a ser** : turn out to be **7 ~ bien** : be suitable — **venirse** *vr* 1 : come **2 ~ abajo** : fall apart, collapse — **venida** *nf* 1 : arrival, coming 2 REGRESO : return — **venidero, -ra** *adj* : coming

venta *nf* 1 : sale, selling **2 en ~** : for sale

ventaja *nf* : advantage — **ventajoso, -sa** *adj* : advantageous

ventana *nf* 1 : window **2 ~ de la nariz** : nostril — **ventanilla** *nf* 1 : window (of a vehicle or airplane) 2 : ticket window, box office (of a theater, etc.)

ventilar *vt* : ventilate, air (out) — **ventilación** *nf, pl* **-ciones** : ventilation — **ventilador** *nm* : fan, ventilator

ventisca *nf* : blizzard — **ventisquero** *nm* : snowdrift

ventoso, -sa *adj* : windy — **ventosidad** *nf* : wind, flatulence

ventrílocuo, -cua *n* : ventriloquist

ventura *nf* 1 : fortune, luck 2 SATISFACCIÓN : happiness **3 a la ~** : at random — **venturoso, -sa** *adj* : fortunate, happy

ver {88} *vt* 1 : see 2 : watch (television, etc.) — *vi* 1 : see **2 a ~** *or* **vamos a ~** : let's see **3 no tener nada que ~ con** : have nothing to do with **4 ya veremos** : we'll see — **verse** *vr* 1 : see oneself 2 HALLARSE : find oneself 3 ENCONTRARSE : see each other, meet

vera *nf* 1 : side, edge 2 : bank (of a river)

veracidad *nf* : truthfulness

verano *nm* : summer — **veraneante** *nmf* : summer vacationer — **veranear**

vi : spend the summer — **veraniego,
-ga** *adj* : summer
veras *nfpl* **de ~** : really
veraz *adj, pl* **-races** : truthful
verbal *adj* : verbal
verbena *nf* : festival, fair
verbo *nm* : verb — **verboso, -sa** *adj*
: verbose
verdad *nf* 1 : truth 2 **de ~** : really, truly
3 **¿verdad?** : right?, isn't that so? —
verdaderamente *adv* : really, truly —
verdadero, -dera *adj* : true, real
verde *adj* 1 : green 2 : dirty, risqué (of a
joke, etc.) — **~** *nm* : green — **verdor**
nm : greenness
verdugo *nm* 1 : executioner, hangman 2
: cruel person, tyrant
verdura *nf* : vegetable(s), green(s)
vereda *nf* 1 : path, trail 2 *Lat* : sidewalk
veredicto *nm* : verdict
vergüenza *nf* 1 : shame 2 TIMIDEZ
: bashfulness, shyness — **vergonzoso, -sa** *adj* 1 : shameful 2 TÍMI-
DO : bashful, shy
verídico, -ca *adj* : true, truthful
verificar {72} *vt* 1 : verify, confirm 2
EXAMINAR : test, check out — **verifi-
carse** *vr* 1 : take place 2 : come true
(of a prophecy, etc.) — **verificación**
nf, pl **-ciones** : verification
verja *nf* 1 : (iron) gate 2 : rails *pl* (of a
fence) 3 ENREJADO : grating, grille
vermut *nm, pl* **-muts** : vermouth
vernáculo, -la *adj* : vernacular
verosímil *adj* 1 : probable, likely 2
CREÍBLE : credible
verraco *nm* : boar
verruga *nf* : wart
versar *vi* **~ sobre** : deal with, be
about — **versado, -da** *adj* **~ en**
: versed in
versátil *adj* 1 : versatile 2 VOLUBLE
: fickle
versión *nf, pl* **-siones** 1 : version 2
TRADUCCIÓN : translation
verso *nm* 1 : poem, verse 2 : line (of poetry)
vértebra *nf* : vertebra
verter {56} *vt* 1 : pour (out) 2 DERRA-
MAR : spill 3 TIRAR : dump — *vi* : flow
— **vertedero** *nm* 1 : dump, landfill 2
DESAGÜE : drain, outlet
vertical *adj & nf* : vertical
vértice *nm* : vertex, apex
vertiente *nf* : slope
vértigo *nm* : vertigo, dizziness — **vertiginoso, -sa** *adj* : dizzy
vesícula *nf* 1 : blister 2 **~ biliar** : gallbladder
vestíbulo *nm* : vestibule, hall, foyer

vestido *nm* 1 : dress 2 ROPA : clothing,
clothes *pl*
vestigio *nm* : vestige, trace
vestir {54} *vt* 1 : dress, clothe 2 LLEVAR
: wear — *vi* : dress — **vestirse** *vr* : get
dressed — **vestimenta** *nf* : clothing —
vestuario *nm* 1 : wardrobe, clothes *pl*
2 : dressing room (in a theater), locker
room (in sports)
veta *nf* 1 : vein, seam 2 : grain (of
wood)
vetar *vt* : veto
veteado, -da *adj* : streaked, veined
veterano, -na *adj & n* : veteran
veterinaria *nf* : veterinary medicine —
veterinario, -ria *adj* : veterinary — **~**
n : veterinarian
veto *nm* : veto
vetusto, -ta *adj* : ancient
vez *nf, pl* **veces** 1 : time 2 TURNO : turn
3 **a la ~** : at the same time 4 **a veces**
: sometimes 5 **de una ~** : all at once
6 **de una ~ para siempre** : once and
for all 7 **de ~ en cuando** : from time
to time 8 **dos veces** : twice 9 **en ~
de** : instead of 10 **una ~** : once
vía *nf* 1 : way, road, route 2 MEDIO
: means 3 : track, line (of a railroad) 4
: (anatomical) tract 5 **en ~ de** : in the
process of — **~** *prep* : via
viable *adj* : viable, feasible — **viabili-
dad** *nf* : viability
viaducto *nm* : viaduct
viajar *vi* : travel — **viajante** *nmf* : traveling salesperson — **viaje** *nm* : trip,
journey — **viajero, -ra** *adj* : traveling
— **~** *n* 1 : traveler 2 PASAJERO : passenger
vial *adj* : road, traffic
víbora *nf* : viper
vibrar *vi* : vibrate — **vibración** *nf, pl*
-ciones : vibration — **vibrante** *adj*
: vibrant
vicario, -ria *n* : vicar
vicepresidente, -ta *n* : vice president
viceversa *adv* : vice versa
vicio *nm* 1 : vice 2 MALA COSTUMBRE
: bad habit 3 DEFECTO : defect — **viciado, -da** *adj* 1 : corrupt 2 : stuffy, stale
(of air, etc.) — **viciar** *vt* 1 : corrupt 2
ESTROPEAR : spoil, pollute — **vicioso,
-sa** *adj* : depraved, corrupt
vicisitud *nf* : vicissitude
víctima *nf* : victim
victoria *nf* : victory — **victorioso, -sa**
adj : victorious
vid *nf* : vine, grapevine
vida *nf* 1 : life 2 DURACIÓN : lifetime 3
de por ~ : for life 4 **estar con ~**
: be alive

video *or* **vídeo** *nm* **1** : video **2** : VCR, videocassette recorder
vidrio *nm* : glass — **vidriado** *nm* : glaze — **vidriar** *vt* : glaze — **vidriera** *nf* **1** : stained-glass window **2** : glass door **3** *Lat* : shopwindow — **vidrioso, -sa** *adj* **1** : delicate (of a subject, etc.) **2 ojos vidriosos** : glassy eyes
vieira *nf* : scallop
viejo, -ja *adj* : old — ~ *n* **1** : old man *m*, old woman *f* **2 hacerse** ~ : get old
viene, etc. → **venir**
viento *nm* : wind
vientre *nm* **1** : abdomen, belly **2** MATRIZ : womb **3** INTESTINO : bowels *pl*
viernes *nms & pl* **1** : Friday **2 Viernes Santo** : Good Friday
vietnamita *adj & nm* : Vietnamese
viga *nf* : beam, girder
vigencia *nf* **1** : validity **2 entrar en** ~ : go into effect — **vigente** *adj* : valid, in force
vigésimo, -ma *adj & n* : twentieth
vigía *nmf* : lookout
vigilar *vt* : look after, watch over — *vi* : keep watch — **vigilancia** *nf* **1** : vigilance **2 bajo** ~ : under surveillance — **vigilante** *adj* : vigilant — ~ *nmf* : watchman, guard — **vigilia** *nf* **1** : wakefulness **2** : vigil (in religion)
vigor *nm* **1** : vigor **2 entrar en** ~ : go into effect — **vigorizante** *adj* : invigorating — **vigoroso, -sa** *adj* : vigorous
VIH *nm* : HIV
vil *adj* : vile, despicable — **vileza** *nf* **1** : vileness **2** : despicable act — **vilipendiar** *vt* : revile
villa *nf* **1** : town, village **2** : villa (house)
villancico *nm* : (Christmas) carol
villano, -na *n* : villain
vilo *nm* **en** ~ : suspended, in the air
vinagre *nm* : vinegar — **vinagrera** *nf* : cruet — **vinagreta** *nf* : vinaigrette
vincular *vt* : tie, link — **vínculo** *nm* : link, tie, bond
vindicar *vt* **1** : vindicate **2** VENGAR : avenge
vino¹, etc. → **venir**
vino² *nm* : wine
viña *nf or* **viñedo** *nm* : vineyard
vio, etc. → **ver**
viola *nf* : viola
violar *vt* **1** : violate (a law, etc.) **2** : rape (a person) — **violación** *nf, pl* **-ciones 1** : violation, offense **2** : rape (of a person)
violencia *nf* : violence, force — **violentar** *vt* **1** : force **2** : break into (a house, etc.) — **violentarse** *vr* **1** : force one-

self **2** AVERGONZARSE : be embarrassed — **violento, -ta** *adj* **1** : violent **2** INCÓMODO : awkward, embarrassing
violeta *adj & nm* : violet (color) — ~ *nf* : violet (flower)
violín *nm, pl* **-lines** : violin — **violinista** *nmf* : violinist — **violoncelista** *or* **violonchelista** *nmf* : cellist — **violoncelo** *or* **violonchelo** *nm* : cello, violoncello
virar *vi* : turn, change direction — **viraje** *nm* **1** : turn, swerve **2** CAMBIO : change
virgen *adj & nmf, pl* **vírgenes** : virgin — **virginal** *adj* : virginal — **virginidad** *nf* : virginity
viril *adj* : virile — **virilidad** *nf* : virility
virtual *adj* : virtual
virtud *nf* **1** : virtue **2 en** ~ **de** : by virtue of — **virtuoso, -sa** *adj* : virtuous — ~ *n* : virtuoso
viruela *nf* **1** : smallpox **2 picado de** ~**s** : pockmarked
virulento, -ta *adj* : virulent
virus *nms & pl* : virus
visa *nf Lat* : visa — **visado** *nm Spain* : visa
vísceras *nfpl* : entrails — **visceral** *adj* : visceral
viscoso, -sa *adj* : viscous — **viscosidad** *nf* : viscosity
visera *nf* : visor
visible *adj* : visible — **visibilidad** *nf* : visibility
visión *nf, pl* **-siones 1** : eyesight **2** APARICIÓN : vision, illusion **3** PUNTO DE VISTA : view, perspective — **visionario, -ria** *adj & n* : visionary
visitar *vt* : visit — **visita** *nf* **1** : visit **2 tener** ~ : have company — **visitante** *adj* : visiting — ~ *nmf* : visitor
vislumbrar *vt* : make out, discern — **vislumbre** *nf* **1** : glimpse, sign **2** RESPLANDOR : glimmer, gleam
viso *nm* **1** : sheen **2 tener** ~**s de** : seem, show signs of
visón *nm, pl* **-sones** : mink
víspera *nf* : eve, day before
vista *nf* **1** : vision, eyesight **2** MIRADA : look, gaze **3** PANORAMA : view, vista **4** : hearing (in court) **5 a primera** ~ *or* **a simple** ~ : at first sight **6 hacer la** ~ **gorda** : turn a blind eye **7 perder de** ~ : lose sight of — **vistazo** *nm* **1** : glance **2 echar un** ~ : have a look
visto, -ta *adj* **1** : clear, obvious **2** COMÚN : commonly seen **3 estar bien** ~ : be approved of **4 estar mal** ~ : be frowned upon **5 nunca** ~ : unheard-

of **6 por lo visto** : apparently **7 visto que** : since, given that — **visto** *nm* ~ **bueno** : approval — ~ *pp* → **ver**

vistoso, -sa *adj* : colorful, bright

visual *adj* : visual — **visualizar** {21} *vt* : visualize

vital *adj* : vital — **vitalicio, -cia** *adj* : life, for life — **vitalidad** *nf* : vitality

vitamina *nf* : vitamin

viticultor, -tora *n* : winegrower — **viticultura** *nf* : wine growing

vitorear *vt* : cheer, acclaim

vítreo, -trea *adj* : glassy

vitrina *nf* 1 : showcase, display case 2 *Lat* : shopwindow

vituperar *vt* : censure — **vituperio** *nm* : censure

viudo, -da *n* : widower *m*, widow *f* — ~ *adj* : widowed — **viudez** *nf* : widowerhood, widowhood

viva *nm* **dar** ~**s** : cheer

vivacidad *nf* : vivacity, liveliness

vivamente *adv* 1 : vividly 2 PROFUNDA-MENTE : deeply, acutely

vivaz *adj, pl* **-vaces** 1 : lively, vivacious 2 AGUDO : vivid, sharp

víveres *nmpl* : provisions, supplies

vivero *nm* 1 : nursery (for plants) 2 : (fish) hatchery, (oyster) bed

viveza *nf* 1 : liveliness 2 : vividness (of colors, descriptions, etc.) 3 ASTUCIA : sharpness (of mind) — **vívido, -da** *adj* : vivid

vividor, -dora *n* : freeloader

vivienda *nf* 1 : housing 2 MORADA : dwelling

viviente *adj* : living

vivificar {72} *vt* : enliven

vivir *vi* 1 : live, be alive 2 ~ **de** : live on — *vt* : experience, live (through) — ~ *nm* 1 : life, lifestyle 2 **de mal** ~ : disreputable — **vivo, -va** *adj* 1 : alive 2 INTENSO : intense, bright 3 ANIMADO : lively 4 ASTUTO : sharp, quick 5 **en vivo** : live

vocablo *nm* : word — **vocabulario** *nm* : vocabulary

vocación *nf, pl* **-ciones** : vocation — **vocacional** *adj* : vocational

vocal *adj* : vocal — ~ *nmf* : member (of a committee, etc.) — ~ *nf* : vowel — **vocalista** *nmf* : singer, vocalist

vocear *v* : shout — **vocerío** *nm* : shouting

vociferar *vi* : shout

vodka *nmf* : vodka

volar {19} *vi* 1 : fly 2 : blow away (of papers, etc.) 3 *fam* : disappear 4 **irse volando** : rush off — *vt* : blow up — **volador, -dora** *adj* : flying — **volan-**

das: en ~ *adv phr* : in the air —

volante *adj* : flying — ~ *nm* 1 : steering wheel 2 : shuttlecock (in badminton) 3 : flounce (of fabric) 4 *Lat* : flier, circular

volátil *adj* : volatile

volcán *nm, pl* **-canes** : volcano — **volcánico, -ca** *adj* : volcanic

volcar {82} *vt* 1 : upset, knock over 2 VACIAR : empty out — *vi* : overturn — **volcarse** *vr* 1 : overturn, tip over 2 ~ **en** : throw oneself into

voleibol *nm* : volleyball

voltaje *nm* : voltage

voltear *vt* : turn over, turn upside down — **voltearse** *vr Lat* : turn (around) — **voltereta** *nf* : somersault

voltio *nm* : volt

voluble *adj* : fickle

volumen *nm, pl* **-lúmenes** : volume — **voluminoso, -sa** *adj* : voluminous

voluntad *nf* 1 : will 2 DESEO : wish 3 IN-TENCIÓN : intention 4 **a** ~ : at will 5 **buena** ~ : goodwill 6 **mala** ~ : ill will 7 **fuerza de** ~ : willpower — **voluntario, -ria** *adj* : voluntary — ~ *n* : volunteer — **voluntarioso, -sa** *adj* 1 : willing 2 TERCO : stubborn, willful

voluptuoso, -sa *adj* : voluptuous

volver {89} *vi* 1 : return, come or go back 2 ~ **a** : return to, do again 3 ~ **en sí** : come to — *vt* 1 : turn, turn over, turn inside out 2 CONVERTIR EN : turn (into) 3 ~ **loco** : drive crazy — **volverse** *vr* 1 : turn (around) 2 HACERSE : become

vomitar *vi* : vomit — *vt* 1 : vomit 2 : spew (out) — **vómito** *nm* 1 : (action of) vomiting 2 : vomit

voraz *adj, pl* **-races** : voracious

vos *pron Lat* : you

vosotros, -tras *pron Spain* : you, yourselves

votar *vi* : vote — *vt* : vote for — **votación** *nf, pl* **-ciones** : vote, voting — **votante** *nmf* : voter — **voto** *nm* 1 : vote 2 : vow (in religion)

voy → **ir**

voz *nf, pl* **voces** 1 : voice 2 GRITO : shout, yell 3 VOCABLO : word, term 4 RUMOR : rumor 5 **dar voces** : shout 6 **en** ~ **alta** : loudly 7 **en** ~ **baja** : softly

vuelco *nm* : upset, overturning

vuelo *nm* 1 : flight 2 : (action of) flying 3 : flare (of clothing) 4 **al** ~ : on the wing

vuelta *nf* 1 : turn 2 REVOLUCIÓN : circle, revolution 3 CURVA : bend, curve 4 RE-GRESO : return 5 : round, lap (in sports)

6 PASEO : walk, drive, ride **7** REVÉS : back, other side **8** *Spain* : change **9** **dar** **~s** : spin **10 estar de ~** : be back — **vuelto** *nm Lat* : change
vuestro, -tra *adj Spain* : your, of yours — **~** *pron Spain* (*with definite article*) : yours

vulgar *adj* **1** : vulgar **2** CORRIENTE : common — **vulgaridad** *nf* **1** : vulgarity **2** BANALIDAD : banality — **vulgo** *nm* **el ~** : the masses, common people
vulnerable *adj* : vulnerable — **vulnerabilidad** *nf* : vulnerability

WXYZ

w *nf* : w, 24th letter of the Spanish alphabet
wáter *nm Spain* : toilet
whisky *nm, pl* **-skys** *or* **-skies** : whiskey
x *nf* : x, 25th letter of the Spanish alphabet
xenofobia *nf* : xenophobia
xilófono *nm* : xylophone
y[1] *nf* : y, 26th letter of the Spanish alphabet
y[2] *conj* : and
ya *adv* **1** : already **2** AHORA : (right) now **3** MÁS TARDE : later, soon **4 ~ no** : no longer **5 ~ que** : now that, since, inasmuch as
yacer {90} *vi* : lie (on or in the ground) — **yacimiento** *nm* : bed, deposit
yanqui *adj & nmf* : Yankee
yate *nm* : yacht
yegua *nf* : mare
yelmo *nm* : helmet
yema *nf* **1** : bud, shoot **2** : yolk (of an egg) **3** *or* **~ del dedo** : fingertip
yerba *nf* **1** *or* **~ mate** : maté **2 → hierba**
yermo, -ma *adj* : barren, deserted — **yermo** *nm* : wasteland
yerno *nm* : son-in-law
yerro *nm* : blunder, mistake
yerto, -ta *adj* : stiff
yesca *nf* : tinder
yeso *nm* **1** : gypsum **2** : plaster (for art, construction)
yo *pron* **1** (*subject*) : I **2** (*object*) : me **3 soy ~** : it is I, it's me — **~** *nm* : ego, self
yodo *nm* : iodine
yoga *nm* : yoga
yogurt *or* **yogur** *nm* : yogurt
yuca *nf* : yucca
yugo *nm* : yoke (of oxen)
yugoslavo, -va *adj* : Yugoslavian
yugular *adj* : jugular
yunque *nm* : anvil
yunta *nf* : yoke

yuxtaponer {60} *vt* : juxtapose — **yuxtaposición** *nf, pl* **-ciones** : juxtaposition
z *nf* : z, 27th letter of the Spanish alphabet
zacate *nm Lat* : grass
zafar *vt Lat* : loosen, untie — **zafarse** *vr* **1** : come undone **2** : get free of (an obligation, etc.)
zafio, -fia *adj* : coarse
zafiro *nm* : sapphire
zaga *nf* **a la ~** *or* **en ~** : behind, in the rear
zaguán *nm, pl* **-guanes** : (entrance) hall
zaherir {76} *vt* : hurt (s.o.'s feelings)
zaino, -na *adj* : chestnut (color)
zalamería *nf* : flattery — **zalamero, -ra** *adj* : flattering — **~** *n* : flatterer
zambullirse {38} *vr* : dive, plunge — **zambullida** *nf* : dive, plunge
zanahoria *nf* : carrot
zancada *nf* : stride, step — **zancadilla** *nf* **1** : trip, stumble **2 hacer una ~ a algn** : trip s.o. up
zancos *nmpl* : stilts
zancudo *nm Lat* : mosquito
zángano, -na *n fam* : lazy person, slacker — **zángano** *nm* : drone (bee)
zanja *nf* : ditch, trench — **zanjar** *vt* : settle, resolve
zapallo *nm Lat* : pumpkin — **zapallito** *nm Lat* : zucchini
zapapico *nm* : pickax
zapato *nm* : shoe — **zapatería** *nf* : shoe store — **zapatero, -ra** *n* : shoemaker, cobbler — **zapatilla** *nf* **1** : slipper **2** : sneaker (for sports, etc.)
zar *nm* : czar
zarandear *vt* **1** : sift **2** SACUDIR : shake
zarcillo *nm* : earring
zarpa *nf* : paw
zarpar *vi* : set sail, raise anchor
zarza *nf* : bramble — **zarzamora** *nf* : blackberry
zigzag *nm, pl* **-zags** *or* **-zagues** : zigzag — **zigzaguear** *vi* : zigzag

zinc *nm* : zinc
zíper *nm Lat* : zipper
zircón *nm, pl* **-cones** : zircon
zócalo *nm* **1** : base (of a column, etc.) **2** : baseboard (of a wall) **3** *Lat* : main square, plaza
zodíaco *nm* : zodiac
zona *nf* : zone, area
zoo *nm* : zoo — **zoología** *nf* : zoology — **zoológico, -ca** *adj* : zoological — **zoológico** *nm* : zoo — **zoólogo, -ga** *n* : zoologist
zopilote *nm Lat* : buzzard
zoquete *nmf fam* : oaf, blockhead

zorrillo *nm Lat* : skunk
zorro, -rra *n* : fox, vixen *f* — ~ *adj* : foxy, sly
zozobra *nf* : anxiety, worry — **zozobrar** *vi* : capsize
zueco *nm* : clog (shoe)
zumbar *vi* : buzz — *vt fam* : hit, beat — **zumbido** *nm* : buzzing
zumo *nf* : juice
zurcir {83} *vt* : darn, mend
zurdo, -da *adj* : left-handed — ~ *n* : left-handed person — **zurda** *nf* : left hand
zutano, -na → **fulano**

English-Spanish
Dictionary

A

a¹ ['eɪ] *n*, *pl* **a's** *or* **as** ['eɪz] : a *f*, primera letra del alfabeto inglés

a² [ə, 'eɪ] *art* (**an** [ən, æn] *before vowel or silent h*) **1** : un *m*, una *f* **2** PER : por, a la, al

aback [ə'bæk] *adv* **be taken ∼** : quedarse desconcertado

abacus ['æbəkəs] *n*, *pl* **abaci** ['æbəˌsaɪ, -ˌkiː] *or* **abacuses** : ábaco *m*

abandon [ə'bændən] *vt* **1** DESERT : abandonar **2** GIVE UP : renunciar a — **∼** *n* : desenfreno *m* — **abandonment** [ə'bændənmənt] *n* : abandono *m*

abashed [ə'bæʃt] *adj* : avergonzado

abate [ə'beɪt] *vi* **abated; abating** : amainar, disminuir

abattoir ['æbəˌtwɑr] *n* : matadero *m*

abbey ['æbi] *n*, *pl* **-beys** : abadía *f* — **abbot** ['æbət] *n* : abad *m*

abbreviate [ə'briːviˌeɪt] *vt* **-ated; -ating** : abreviar — **abbreviation** [əˌbriːvi'eɪʃən] *n* : abreviatura *f*, abreviación *f*

abdicate ['æbdɪˌkeɪt] *v* **-cated; -cating** : abdicar — **abdication** [ˌæbdɪ'keɪæən] *n* : abdicación *f*

abdomen ['æbdəmən, æb'doːmən] *n* : abdomen *m*, vientre *m* — **abdominal** [æb'dɑmənəl] *adj* : abdominal

abduct [æb'dʌkt] *vt* : secuestrar — **abduction** [æb'dʌkʃən] *n* : secuestro *m*

aberration [ˌæbə'reɪʃən] *n* : aberración *f*

abet [ə'bet] *vt* **abetted; abetting** *or* **aid and ∼** : ser cómplice de

abeyance [ə'beɪənts] *n* : desuso *m*

abhor [əb'hɔr, æb-] *vt* **-horred; -horring** : aborrecer

abide [ə'baɪd] *v* **abode** [ə'boːd] *or* **abided; abiding** *vt* : soportar, tolerar — *vi* **1** DWELL : morar **2 ∼ by** : atenerse a

ability [ə'bɪləṭi] *n*, *pl* **-ties 1** CAPABILITY : aptitud *f*, capacidad *f* **2** SKILL : habilidad *f*

abject ['æbˌdʒɛkt, æb'-] *adj* : miserable, desdichado

ablaze [ə'bleɪz] *adj* : en llamas

able ['eɪbəl] *adj* **abler; ablest 1** CAPABLE : capaz, hábil **2** COMPETENT : competente

abnormal [æb'nɔrməl] *adj* : anormal — **abnormality** [ˌæbnər'mæləṭi, -nɔr-] *n*, *pl* **-ties** : anormalidad *f*

aboard [ə'bord] *adv* : a bordo — **∼** *prep* : a bordo de

abode *n* : morada *f*, domicilio *m*

abolish [ə'bɑlɪʃ] *vt* : abolir, suprimir — **abolition** [ˌæbə'lɪʃən] *n* : abolición *f*

abominable [ə'bɑmənəbəl] *adj* : abominable, aborrecible, más o menos [ə'bɑmə'neɪʃən] : **abomination** [ə,bɑmə'neɪʃən] *n* : abominación *f*

aborigine [ˌæbə'rɪdʒəni] *n* : aborigen *mf*

abort [ə'bort] *vt* : abortar — **abortion** [ə'borʃən] *n* : aborto *m* — **abortive** [ə'borṭɪv] *adj* UNSUCCESSFUL : malogrado

abound [ə'baʊnd] *vi* **∼ in** : abundar en

about [ə'baʊt] *adv* **1** APPROXIMATELY : aproximadamente, más o menos **2** AROUND : alrededor **3 be ∼ to** : estar a punto de **4 be up and ∼** : estar levantado — **∼** *prep* **1** AROUND : alrededor de **2** CONCERNING : acerca de, sobre

above [ə'bʌv] *adv* : arriba — **∼** *prep* **1** : encima de **2 ∼ all** : sobre todo — **aboveboard** *adj* : honrado

abrasive [ə'breɪsɪv] *adj* **1** : abrasivo **2** BRUSQUE : brusco, mordaz

abreast [ə'brest] *adv* **1** : al lado **2 keep ∼ of** : mantenerse al corriente de

abridge [ə'brɪdʒ] *vt* **abridged; abridging** : abreviar

abroad [ə'brɔd] *adv* **1** : en el extranjero **2** WIDELY : por todas partes **3 go ∼** : ir al extranjero

abrupt [ə'brʌpt] *adj* **1** SUDDEN : repentino **2** BRUSQUE : brusco

abscess ['æbˌses] *n* : absceso *m*

absence ['æbsənts] *n* **1** : ausencia *f* **2** LACK : falta *f*, carencia *f* — **absent** ['æbsənt] *adj* : ausente — **absentee** [ˌæbsən'tiː] *n* : ausente *mf* — **absent-minded** [ˌæbsənt'maɪndəd] *adj* : distraído, despistado

absolute ['æbsəˌluːt, ˌæbsə'luːt] *adj* : absoluto — **absolutely** [ˌæbsə'luːtli] *adv* : absolutamente

absolve [əb'zɑlv, æb-, -'sɑlv] *vt* **-solved; -solving** : absolver

absorb [əb'zɔrb, æb-, -'sɔrb] *vt* : absorber — **absorbent** [əb'zɔrbənt, æb-, -'sor-] *adj* : absorbente — **absorption** [əb'zɔrpʃən, æb-, -'sɔrp-] *n* : absorción *f*

abstain [əb'steɪn, æb-] *vi* **∼ from** : abstenerse de — **abstinence** ['æbstənənts] *n* : abstinencia *f*

abstract [æb'strækt, 'æb-] *adj* : abstracto — ~ *vt* : extraer — ~ ['æb,strækt] *n* : resumen *m* — **abstraction** [æb-'strækʃən] *n* : abstracción *f*

absurd [əb'sərd, -'zərd] *adj* : absurdo — **absurdity** [əb'sərdəṭi, -'zərdəṭi] *n, pl* **-ties** : absurdo *m*

abundant [ə'bʌndənt] *adj* : abundante — **abundance** [ə'bʌndənts] *n* : abundancia *f*

abuse [ə'bjuːz] *vt* **abused; abusing 1** MISUSE : abusar de **2** MISTREAT : maltratar **3** REVILE : insultar — ~ [ə'bjuːs] *n* **1** : abuso *m* **2** INSULTS : insultos *mpl* — **abusive** [ə'bjuːsɪv] *adj* : injurioso

abut [ə'bʌt] *vi* **abutted; abutting** ~ **on** : colindar con

abyss [ə'bɪs, 'æbɪs] *n* : abismo *m* — **abysmal** [ə'bɪzməl] *adj* : atroz, pésimo

academy [ə'kædəmi] *n, pl* **-mies** : academia *f* — **academic** [,ækə'demɪk] *adj* **1** : académico **2** THEORETICAL : teórico

accelerate [ɪk'selə,reɪt, æk-] *v* **-ated; -ating** : acelerar — **acceleration** [ɪk-,selə'reɪʃən, æk-] *n* : aceleración *f*

accent [æk,sent, æk'sent] *vt* : acentuar — ~ ['æk,sent, sent] *n* : acento *m* — **accentuate** [ɪk'sentʃəʊ,eɪt, æk-] *vt* **-ated; -ating** : acentuar, subrayar

accept [ɪk'sept, æk-] *vt* : aceptar — **acceptable** [ɪk'septəbəl, æk-] *adj* : aceptable — **acceptance** [ɪk'septənts, æk-] *n* **1** : aceptación *f* **2** APPROVAL : aprobación *f*

access ['æk,ses] *n* : acceso *m* — **accessible** [ɪk'sesəbəl, æk-] *adj* : accesible, asequible

accessory *n, pl* **-ries 1** : accesorio *m* **2** ACCOMPLICE : cómplice *mf*

accident ['æksədənt] *n* **1** MISHAP : accidente *m* **2** CHANCE : casualidad *f* — **accidental** [,æksə'dentəl] *adj* : accidental — **accidentally** [,æksə'dentəli, -'dentli] *adv* **1** BY CHANCE : por casualidad **2** UNINTENTIONALLY : sin querer

acclaim [ə'kleɪm] *vt* : aclamar — ~ *n* : aclamación *f*

acclimatize [ə'klaɪmə,taɪz] *vt* **-tized; -tizing** : aclimatar

accommodate [ə'kamə,deɪt] *vt* **-dated; -dating 1** ADAPT : acomodar, adaptar **2** SATISFY : complacer, satisfacer **3** HOLD : tener cabida para — **accomodation** [ə,kamə'deɪʃən] *n* **1** : adaptación *f* **2** ~s *npl* LODGING : alojamiento *m*

accompany [ə'kʌmpəni, -'kam-] *vt* **-nied; -nying** : acompañar

accomplice [ə'kampləs, -'kʌm-] *n* : cómplice *mf*

accomplish [ə'kamplɪʃ, -'kʌm-] *vt* : realizar, llevar a cabo — **accomplishment** [ə'kamplɪʃmənt, -'kʌm-] *n* **1** COMPLETION : realización *f* **2** ACHIEVEMENT : logro *m*, éxito *m*

accord *n* **1** AGREEMENT : acuerdo *m* **2 of one's own** ~ : voluntariamente — **accordance** [ə'kordənts] *n* **in** ~ **with** : conforme a, de acuerdo con — **accordingly** [ə'kordɪŋli] *adv* : en consecuencia — **according to** [ə'kordɪŋ] *prep* : según

accordion [ə'kordiən] *n* : acordeón *m*

accost [ə'kost] *vt* : abordar

account [ə'kaʊnt] *n* **1** : cuenta *f* **2** REPORT : relato *m*, informe *m* **3** WORTH : importancia *f* **4 on** ~ **of** : a causa de, debido a **5 on no** ~ : de ninguna manera — ~ *vi* ~ **for** : dar cuenta de, explicar — **accountable** [ə'kaʊntəbəl] *adj* : responsable — **accountant** [ə'kaʊntənt] *n* : contador *m*, -dora *f Lat*; contable *mf Spain* — **accounting** [ə'kaʊntɪŋ] *n* : contabilidad *f*

accrue [ə'kruː] *vi* **-crued; -cruing** : acumularse

accumulate [ə'kjuːmjə,leɪt] *v* **-lated; -lating** *vt* : acumular — *vi* : acumularse — **accumulation** [ə,kjuːmjə-'leɪʃən] *n* : acumulación *f*

accurate ['ækjərət] *adj* : exacto, preciso — **accuracy** ['ækjərəsi] *n* : exactitud *f*, precisión *f*

accuse [ə'kjuːz] *vt* **-cused; -cusing** : acusar — **accusation** [,ækjə'zeɪʃən] *n* : acusación *f*

accustomed [ə'kʌstəmd] *adj* **1** : acostumbrado **2 become** ~ **to** : acostumbrarse a

ace ['eɪs] *n* : as *m*

ache ['eɪk] *vi* **ached; aching** : doler — ~ *n* : dolor *m*

achieve [ə'tʃiːv] *vt* **achieved; achieving** : lograr, realizar — **achievement** [ə'tʃiːvmənt] *n* : logro *m*, éxito *m*

acid ['æsəd] *adj* : ácido — ~ *n* : ácido *m*

acknowledge [ɪk'nalɪdʒ, æk-] *vt* **-edged; -edging 1** ADMIT : admitir **2** RECOGNIZE : reconocer **3** ~ **receipt of** : acusar recibo de — **acknowledgment** [ɪk'nalɪdʒmənt, æk-] *n* **1** : reconocimiento *m* **2** THANKS : agradecimiento *m* **3** ~ **of receipt** : acuse *m* de recibo

acne ['ækni] *n* : acné *m*

acorn ['eɪ,korn, -kərn] *n* : bellota *f*

acoustic [ə'kuːstɪk] *or* **acoustical** [-stɪkəl] *adj* : acústico — **acoustics** [ə'kuːstɪks] *ns & pl* : acústica *f*

acquaint [ə'kweɪnt] *vt* **1** ~ **s.o. with**

: poner a algn al corriente de **2 be ~ed with** : conocer a (una persona), saber (un hecho) — **acquaintance** [ə'kweintəns] n 1 : conocimiento m 2 : conocido m, -da f (persona)

acquire [ə'kwair] vt **-quired; -quiring** : adquirir — **acquisition** [,ækwə'zɪʃən] n : adquisición f

acquit [ə'kwɪt] vt **-quitted; -quitting** : absolver

acre ['eikər] n : acre m — **acreage** ['eikəridʒ] n : superficie f en acres

acrid ['ækrəd] adj : acre

acrobat ['ækrə,bæt] n : acróbata mf — **acrobatic** [,ækrə'bætɪk] adj : acrobático

acronym ['ækrə,nɪm] n : siglas fpl

across [ə'krɔs] adv **1** : de un lado a otro **2** CROSSWISE : a través **3 go ~** : atravesar — ~ prep **1** : a través de **2 ~ the street** : al otro lado de la calle

acrylic [ə'krɪlɪk] n : acrílico m

act ['ækt] vi **1** : actuar **2** PRETEND **3** FUNCTION : funcionar **4 ~ as** : servir de — vt : interpretar (un papel) — ~ n **1** ACTION : acto m, acción f **2** DECREE : ley f **3** : acto m (en una obra de teatro), número m (en un espectáculo) — **acting** adj : interino

action ['ækʃən] n **1** : acción f **2** LAWSUIT : demanda f **3 take ~** : tomar medidas

activate ['æktə,veit] vt **-vated; -vating** : activar

active ['æktɪv] adj **1** : activo **2** LIVELY : enérgico **3 ~ volcano** : volcán m en actividad — **activity** [æk'tɪvəṭi] n, pl **-ties** : actividad f

actor ['æktər] n : actor m — **actress** ['æktrəs] n : actriz f

actual ['æktʃuəl] adj : real, verdadero — **actually** ['æktʃuəli, -æəli] adv : realmente, en realidad

acupuncture ['ækju,pʌŋktʃər] n : acupuntura f

acute [ə'kjuːt] adj **acuter; acutest 1** : agudo **2** PERCEPTIVE : perspicaz

ad ['æd] → **advertisement**

adamant ['ædəmənt, -,mænt] adj : inflexible

adapt [ə'dæpt] vt : adaptar — vi : adaptarse — **adaptable** [ə'dæptəbəl] adj : adaptable — **adaptation** [,æ,dæp-'teiʃən, -dəp-] n : adaptación f — **adapter** [ə'dæptər] n : adaptador m

add ['æd] vt **1** : añadir **2 or ~ up** : sumar — vi : sumar

addict ['ædɪkt] n **1** : adicto m, -ta f **2 or drug ~** : drogadicto m, -ta f; toxicómano m, -na f — **addiction** [ə'dɪkʃən] n : dependencia f

addition [ə'dɪʃən] n **1** : suma f (en matemáticas) **2** ADDING : adición f **3 in ~** : además — **additional** [ə'dɪʃənəl] adj : adicional — **additive** ['ædəṭɪv] n : aditivo m

address [ə'drɛs] vt **1** : dirigirse a (una persona) **2** : ponerle la dirección a (una carta) **3** : tratar (un asunto) — ~ [ə'drɛs, 'æ,drɛs] n **1** : dirección f, domicilio m **2** SPEECH : discurso m

adept [ə'dɛpt] adj : experto, hábil

adequate ['ædɪkwət] adj : adecuado, suficiente

adhere [æd'hɪr, əd-] vi **-hered; -hering 1** STICK : adherirse **2 ~ to** : observar — **adherence** [æd'hɪrənts, əd-] n **1** : adhesión f **2** : observancia f (de una ley, etc.) — **adhesive** [æd'hiːsɪv, əd-, -zɪv] adj : adhesivo — ~ n : adhesivo m

adjacent [ə'dʒeisənt] adj : adyacente, contiguo

adjective ['ædʒɪktɪv] n : adjetivo m

adjoining [ə'dʒɔinɪŋ] adj : contiguo, vecino

adjourn [ə'dʒərn] vt : aplazar, suspender — vi : suspenderse

adjust [ə'dʒʌst] vt : ajustar, arreglar — vi : adaptarse — **adjustable** [ə'dʒʌstəbəl] adj : ajustable — **adjustment** [ə'dʒʌstmənt] n : ajuste m (a una máquina, etc.), adaptación f (de una persona)

ad-lib ['æd'lɪb] v **-libbed; -libbing** : improvisar

administer [æd'mɪnəstər, əd-] vt : administrar — **administration** [æd,mɪnə-'streiʃən, əd-] n : administración f — **administrative** [æd'mɪnə,streiṭɪv, əd-] adj : administrativo — **administrator** [æd'mɪnə,streiṭər, əd-] n : administrador m, -dora f

admirable ['ædmərəbəl] adj : admirable

admiral ['ædmərəl] n : almirante m

admire [æd'mair] vt **-mired; -miring** : admirar — **admiration** [,ædmə'reiʃən] n : admiración f — **admirer** [æd'mairər] n : admirador m, -dora f

admit [æd'mɪt, əd-] vt **-mitted; -mitting 1** : admitir, dejar entrar **2** ACKNOWLEDGE : reconocer — **admission** [æd'mɪʃən] n **1** ADMITTANCE : entrada f, admisión f **2** ACKNOWLEDGMENT : reconocimiento m — **admittance** [æd'mɪtənts, əd-] n : admisión f, entrada f

admonish [æd'mɑnɪʃ, əd-] vt : amonestar, reprender

ado [ə'duː] n **1** : alboroto m, bulla f **2 without further ~** : sin más (preámbulos)

adolescent [ˌædəlˈesənt] n : adolescente mf — **adolescence** [ˌædəlˈesənts] n : adolescencia f

adopt [əˈdɑpt] vt : adoptar — **adoption** [əˈdɑpʃən] n : adopción f

adore [əˈdor] vt **adored; adoring 1** : adorar **2** LIKE, LOVE : encantarle (algo a uno) — **adorable** [əˈdorəbəl] adj : adorable — **adoration** [ˌædəˈreɪæən] n : adoración f

adorn [əˈdorn] vt : adornar — **adornment** [əˈdornmənt] n : adorno m

adrift [əˈdrɪft] adj & adv : a la deriva

adroit [əˈdrɔɪt] adj : diestro, hábil

adult [əˈdʌlt, ˈæˌdʌlt] adj : adulto — ~ n : adulto m, -ta f

adultery [əˈdʌltəri] n, pl **-teries** : adulterio m

advance [ædˈvænts, əd-] v **-vanced; -vancing** vt : adelantar — vi : avanzar, adelantarse — ~ n 1 : avance m 2 PROGRESS : adelanto m 3 **in** ~ : por adelantado — **advancement** [ædˈvæntsmənt, əd-] n : adelanto m, progreso m

advantage [ədˈvæntɪdʒ, æd-] n 1 : ventaja f 2 **take** ~ **of** : aprovecharse de — **advantageous** [ˌædˌvænˈteɪdʒəs, -vən-] adj : ventajoso

advent [ˈædˌvent] n 1 ARRIVAL : llegada f 2 **Advent** : Adviento m

adventure [ədˈventʃər, əd-] n : aventura f — **adventurous** [ædˈventʃərəs, əd-] adj 1 : intrépido 2 RISKY : arriesgado

adverb [ˈædˌvərb] n : adverbio m

adversary [ˈædvərˌseri] n, pl **-saries** : adversario m, -ria f

adverse [ædˈvərs, ˈæd-] adj : adverso, desfavorable — **adversity** [ædˈvərsəti, əd-] n, pl **-ties** : adversidad f

advertise [ˈædvərˌtaɪz] v **-tised; -tising** vt : anunciar — vi : hacer publicidad — **advertisement** [ˈædvərˌtaɪzmənt] n : anuncio m — **advertiser** [ˈædvərˌtaɪzər] n : anunciante mf — **advertising** [ˈædvərˌtaɪzɪŋ] n : publicidad f

advice [ædˈvaɪs] n : consejo m

advise [ædˈvaɪz, əd-] vt **-vised; -vising** 1 COUNSEL : aconsejar, asesorar 2 RECOMMEND : recomendar 3 INFORM : informar — **advisable** [ædˈvaɪzəbəl, əd-] adj : aconsejable — **adviser** [ædˈvaɪzər, əd-] n : consejero m, -ra f; asesor m, -sora f — **advisory** [ædˈvaɪzəri, əd-] adj : consultivo

advocate [ˈædvəˌkeɪt] vt **-cated; -cating** : recomendar — ~ [ˈædvəkət] n : defensor m, -sora f

aerial [ˈæriəl] adj : aéreo — ~ n : antena f

aerobics [ˌærˈoːbɪks] ns & pl : aeróbic m

aerodynamic [ˌæroːdaɪˈnæmɪk] adj : aerodinámico

aerosol [ˈærəˌsɔl] n : aerosol m

aesthetic [esˈθeţɪk] adj : estético

afar [əˈfɑr] adv : lejos

affable [ˈæfəbəl] adj : afable

affair [əˈfær] n 1 : asunto m, cuestión f 2 **or love** — : amorío m, aventura f

affect [əˈfekt, æ-] vt 1 : afectar 2 FEIGN : fingir — **affection** [əˈfekʃən] n : afecto m, cariño m — **affectionate** [əˈfekʃənət] adj : afectuoso, cariñoso

affinity [əˈfɪnəţi] n, pl **-ties** : afinidad f

affirm [əˈfərm] vt : afirmar — **affirmative** [əˈfərməˌţɪv] adj : afirmativo

affix [əˈfɪks] vt : fijar, pegar

afflict [əˈflɪkt] vt : afligir — **affliction** [əˈflɪkʃən] n : aflicción f

affluent [ˈæˌfluənt; æˈflu-, ə-] adj : próspero, adinerado

afford [əˈford] vt 1 : tener los recursos para, permitirse (el lujo de) 2 PROVIDE : brindar

affront [əˈfrʌnt] n : afrenta f

afloat [əˈfloːt] adv & adj : a flote

afoot [əˈfʊt] adj : en marcha

afraid [əˈfreɪd] adj 1 **be** ~ : tener miedo 2 **I'm** ~ **not** : me temo que no

African [ˈæfrɪkən] adj : africano

after [ˈæftər] adv 1 AFTERWARD : después 2 BEHIND : detrás, atrás — ~ conj : después de (que) — ~ prep 1 : después de 2 ~ **all** : después de todo 3 **it's ten** ~ **five** : son las cinco y diez

aftereffect [ˈæftərəˌfekt] n : efecto m secundario

aftermath [ˈæftərˌmæθ] n : consecuencias fpl

afternoon [ˌæftərˈnuːn] n : tarde f

afterward [ˈæftərwərd] or **afterwards** [-wərdz] adv : después, más tarde

again [əˈgen, -ˈgɪn] adv 1 : otra vez, de nuevo 2 ~ **and** ~ : una y otra vez 3 **then** ~ : por otra parte

against [əˈgentst, -ˈgɪntst] prep : contra, en contra de

age [ˈeɪdʒ] n 1 : edad f 2 ERA : era f, época f 3 **be of** ~ : ser mayor de edad 4 **for** ~s : hace siglos 5 **old** ~ : vejez f — ~ vi **aged; aging** : envejecer — **aged** adj 1 [ˈeɪdʒd, ˈeɪdʒd] OLD : anciano, viejo 2 [ˈeɪdʒd] **children** ~ **10 to 17** : niños de 10 a 17 años

agency [ˈeɪdʒəntsi] n, pl **-cies** : agencia f

agenda [əˈdʒendə] n : orden m del día

agent [ˈeɪdʒənt] n : agente mf, representante mf

aggravate [ˈægrəˌveɪt] vt **-vated; -vating**

1 WORSEN : agravar, empeorar **2** AN-
NOY : irritar

aggregate ['ægrɪgət] *adj* : total, global
— ~ *n* : total *m*

aggression [ə'greʃən] *n* : agresión *f* —
aggressive [ə'gresɪv] *adj* : agresivo —
aggressor [ə'gresər] *n* : agresor *m*,
-sora *f*

aghast [ə'gæst] *adj* : horrorizado

agile ['ædʒəl] *adj* : ágil — **agility** [ə-
'dʒɪləʧi] *n*, *pl* **-ties** : agilidad *f*

agitate ['ædʒə,teɪt] *v* **-tated; -tating** *vt* **1**
SHAKE : agitar **2** TROUBLE : inquietar —
agitation [,ædʒə'teɪʃən] *n* : agitación *f*,
inquietud *f*

agnostic [æg'nɑstɪk] *n* : agnóstico *m*,
-ca *f*

ago [ə'goː] *adv* **1** : hace **2** long ~ : hace
mucho tiempo

agony ['ægəni] *n*, *pl* **-nies** **1** PAIN : dolor
m **2** ANGUISH : angustia *f* — **agonize**
['ægə,naɪz] *vi* **-nized; -nizing** : atormentarse — **agonizing** ['ægə,naɪzɪŋ]
adj : angustioso

agree [ə'griː] *v* **agreed; agreeing** *vt* **1**
: acordar **2** ~ **that** : estar de acuerdo
de que — *vi* **1** : estar de acuerdo **2**
CORRESPOND : concordar **3** ~ **to** : acceder a **4 this climate** ~**s with me**
: este clima me sienta bien — **agreeable** [ə'griːəbəl] *adj* **1** PLEASING
: agradable **2** WILLING : dispuesto —
agreement [ə'griːmənt] *n* : acuerdo *m*

agriculture ['ægrɪ,kʌltʃər] *n* : agricultura
f — **agricultural** [,ægrɪ'kʌltʃərəl] *adj*
: agrícola

aground [ə'graʊnd] *adv* run ~ : encallar

ahead [ə'hed] *adv* **1** IN FRONT : delante,
adelante **2** BEFOREHAND : por adelantado **3** LEADING : a la delantera **4 get** ~
: adelantar — **ahead of** *prep* **1** : delante de, antes de **2** get ~ **of** : adelantarse a

aid ['eɪd] *vt* : ayudar — ~ *n* : ayuda *f*,
asistencia *f*

AIDS ['eɪdz] *n* : SIDA *m*, sida *m*

ail ['eɪl] *vi* : estar enfermo — **ailment**
['eɪlmənt] *n* : enfermedad *f*

aim ['eɪm] *vt* : apuntar (un arma), dirigir
(una observación) — *vi* **1** : apuntar **2**
ASPIRE : aspirar — ~ *n* **1** : puntería *f* **2**
GOAL : propósito *m*, objetivo *m* —
aimless ['eɪmləs] *adj* : sin objetivo

air ['ær] *vt or* ~ **out** : airear **2** EXPRESS
: expresar **3** BROADCAST : emitir — ~
n **1** : aire *m* **2 be on the** ~ : estar en
el aire — **air–conditioning** ['ærkən-
'dɪʃənɪŋ] : aire *m* acondicionado —
air conditioned ['ærkən,dɪʃənd] *n*

: climatizado — **aircraft** ['ær,kræft] *ns
& pl* **1** : avión *m*, aeronave *f* **2** ~ **carrier** : portaaviones *m* — **air force** *n*
: fuerza *f* aérea — **airline** ['ær,laɪn] *n*
: aerolínea *f*, línea *f* aérea — **airliner**
['ær,laɪnər] *n* : avión *m* de pasajeros —
airmail *n* : correo *m* aéreo — **airplane**
['ær,pleɪn] *n* : avión *m* — **airport** ['ær-
,port] *n* : aeropuerto *m* — **airstrip** ['ær-
,strɪp] *n* : pista *f* de aterrizaje — **air-
tight** ['ær'taɪt] *adj* : hermético — **airy**
['æri] *adj* **airier** [-iər]; **-est** : aireado,
bien ventilado

aisle ['aɪl] *n* **1** : pasillo *m* **2** : nave *f* lateral (de una iglesia)

ajar [ə'dʒɑr] *adj* : entreabierto

akin [ə'kɪn] *adj* ~ **to** : semejante a

alarm [ə'lɑrm] *n* **1** : alarma *f* **2** ANXIETY
: inquietud *f* — *vt* : alarmar, asustar —
alarm clock *n* : despertador *m*

alas [ə'læs] *interj* : ¡ay!

album ['ælbəm] *n* : álbum *m*

alcohol ['ælkə,hɔl] *n* : alcohol *m* — **alcoholic** [,ælkə'hɔlɪk] *adj* : alcohólico
— ~ *n* : alcohólico *m*, -ca *f* — **alcoholism** ['ælkəhɔ,lɪzəm] *n* : alcoholismo *m*

alcove ['æl,koːv] *n* : nicho *m*, hueco *m*

ale ['eɪl] *n* : cerveza *f*

alert [ə'lərt] *adj* **1** WATCHFUL : alerta,
atento **2** LIVELY : vivo — ~ *n* : alerta *f*
— ~ *vt* : alertar, poner sobre aviso

alfalfa [æl'fælfə] *n* : alfalfa *f*

alga ['ælgə] *n*, *pl* **-gae** ['æl,dʒiː] : alga *f*

algebra ['ældʒəbrə] *n* : álgebra *f*

alias ['eɪliəs] *adv* : alias — ~ *n* : alias *m*

alibi ['ælə,baɪ] *n* : coartada *f*

alien ['eɪliən] *adj* : extranjero — ~ *n* **1**
FOREIGNER : extranjero *m*, -ra *f* **2** EX-
TRATERRESTRIAL : extraterrestre *mf* —
alienate ['eɪliə,neɪt] *vt* **-ated; -ating**
: enajenar — **alienation** [,eɪliə'neɪæən]
n : enajenación *f*

alight [ə'laɪt] *vi* **1** LAND : posarse **2** ~
from : apearse de

align [ə'laɪn] *vt* : alinear — **alignment**
[ə'laɪnmənt] *n* : alineación *f*

alike [ə'laɪk] *adv* : igual, del mismo
modo — ~ *adj* : parecido

alimony ['ælə,moːni] *n*, *pl* **-nies** : pensión *f* alimenticia

alive [ə'laɪv] *adj* **1** LIVING : vivo,
viviente **2** LIVELY : animado, activo

all ['ɔl] *adv* **1** COMPLETELY : todo, completamente **2** ~ **the better** : tanto
mejor **3** ~ **the more** : aún más, todavía más — ~ *adj* : todo — ~ *pron*
1 : todo, -da **2** ~ **in** ~ : en general **3**
not at ~ : de ninguna manera —

all–around [,ɔlə'raund] *adj* VERSATILE
: completo
allay [ə'leɪ] *vt* 1 ALLEVIATE : aliviar 2
CALM : aquietar
allege [ə'lɛdʒ] *vt* -**leged**; -**leging** : alegar
— **allegation** [,ælɪ'geɪʃən] *n* : alegato
m, acusación *f* — **alleged** [ə'lɛdʒd,
ə'lɛdʒəd] *adj* : presunto — **allegedly**
[ə'lɛdʒədli] *adv* : supuestamente
allegiance [ə'li:dʒənʦ] *n* : lealtad *f*
allegory ['æləgori] *n, pl* -**ries** : alegoría
f — **allegorical** [,ælə'gorɪkəl] *adj*
: alegórico
allergy ['ælərdʒi] *n, pl* -**gies** : alergia *f* —
allergic [ə'lərdʒɪk] *adj* : alérgico
alleviate [ə'li:vi,eɪt] *vt* -**ated**; -**ating**
: aliviar
alley ['æli] *n, pl* -**leys** : callejón *m*
alliance [ə'laɪənʦ] *n* : alianza *f*
alligator ['ælə,geɪtər] *n* : caimán *m*
allocate ['ælə,keɪt] *vt* -**cated**; -**cating**
: asignar — **allocation** [,ælə'keɪʃən] *n*
: asignación *f*, reparto *m*
allot [ə'lɑt] *vt* -**lotted**; -**lotting** : asignar
— **allotment** [ə'lɑtmənt] *n* : reparto *m*,
asignación *f*
allow [ə'laʊ] *vt* 1 PERMIT : permitir 2
GRANT : dar, conceder 3 ADMIT : admitir 4 CONCEDE : reconocer — *vi* —
for : tener en cuenta — **allowance**
[ə'laʊənʦ] *n* 1 : pensión *f*, subsidio *m*
2 **make ～s for** : tener en cuenta, disculpar
alloy ['æˌlɔɪ, ə'lɔɪ] *n* : aleación *f*
all right *adv* 1 YES : sí, de acuerdo 2
WELL : bien 3 DEFINITELY : bien, sin
duda — **～** *adj* : bien, bueno
allude [ə'lu:d] *vi* -**luded**; -**luding** : aludir
allure [ə'lʊr] *vt* -**lured**; -**luring** : atraer —
alluring [ə'lʊrɪŋ] *adj* : atrayente, seductor
allusion [ə'lu:ʒən] *n* : alusión *f*
ally [ə'laɪ, 'æˌlaɪ] *vi* -**lied**; -**lying ～ oneself with** : aliarse con — **～** ['æˌlaɪ,
ə'laɪ] *n* : aliado *m*, -da *f*
almanac ['ɔlmə,næk, 'æl-] *n* : almanaque
m
almighty [ɔl'maɪti] *adj* : omnipotente,
todopoderoso
almond ['ɑmənd, 'ɑl-, 'æ-, 'æl-] *n* : almendra *f*
almost ['ɔl,moːst, ɔl'moːst] *adv* : casi
alms ['ɑmz, 'ɑlmz, 'ælmz] *ns & pl*
: limosna *f*
alone [ə'lo:n] *adv* : sólo, solamente, únicamente — *adj* : solo
along [ə'lɔŋ] *adv* 1 FORWARD : adelante 2
～ with : con, junto con 3 **all ～**
: desde el principio — **～** *prep* : por, a
lo largo de — **alongside** [ə'lɔŋ'saɪd]

adv : al costado — **～** *or* **～ of** *prep*
: al lado de
aloof [ə'lu:f] *adj* : distante, reservado
aloud [ə'laʊd] *adv* : en voz alta
alphabet ['ælfə,bɛt] *n* : alfabeto *m* — **alphabetical** [,ælfə'bɛtɪkəl] *or* **alpha-
betic** [-'bɛtɪk] *adj* : alfabético
already [ɔl'rɛdi] *adv* : ya
also ['ɔl,so:] *adv* : también, además
altar ['ɔltər] *n* : altar *m*
alter ['ɔltər] *vt* : alterar, modificar — **alteration** [,ɔltə'reɪʃən] *n* : alteración *f*,
modificación *f*
alternate ['ɔltərnət] *adj* : alterno — **～**
['ɔltər,neɪt] *v* -**nated**; -**nating** : alternar
— **alternating current** *n* : corriente *f*
alterna — **alternative** [ɔl'tərnətɪv] *adj*
: alternativo — **～** *n* : alternativa *f*
although [ɔl'ðo:] *conj* : aunque
altitude ['æltə,tu:d, -,tju:d] *n* : altitud *f*
altogether [,ɔltə'gɛðər] *adv* 1 COMPLETE-
LY : completamente, del todo 2 ON THE
WHOLE : en suma, en general
aluminum [ə'lu:mənəm] *n* : aluminio *m*
always ['ɔlwɪz, -,weɪz] *adv* 1 : siempre 2
FOREVER : para siempre
am → be
amass [ə'mæs] *vt* : amasar, acumular
amateur ['æmət̬ər, -tər, -,tʊr, -,tjur] *adj*
: amateur — **～** *n* : amateur *mf*; aficionado *m*, -da *f*
amaze [ə'meɪz] *vt* **amazed**; **amazing**
: asombrar — **amazement** [ə'meɪz-
mənt] *n* : asombro *m* — **amazing**
[ə'meɪzɪŋ] *adj* : asombroso
ambassador [æm'bæsədər] *n* : embajador *m*, -dora *f*
amber ['æmbər] *n* : ámbar *m*
ambiguous [æm'bɪgjuəs] *adj* : ambiguo
— **ambiguity** [,æmbə'gju:ət̬i] *n, pl* -**ties**
: ambigüedad *f*
ambition [æm'bɪʃən] *n* : ambición *f* —
ambitious [æm'bɪʃəs] *adj* : ambicioso
ambivalence [æm'bɪvələnʦ] *n* : ambiva-
lencia *f* — **ambivalent** [æm'bɪvələnt]
adj : ambivalente
amble ['æmbəl] *vi* *or* **～ along** : andar
sin prisa
ambulance ['æmbjələnʦ] *n* : ambulancia *f*
ambush ['æm,bʊʃ] *vt* : emboscar — **～** *n*
: emboscada *f*
amen ['eɪ'mɛn, 'ɑ-] *interj* : amén
amenable [ə'mi:nəbəl, -'mɛ-] *adj* **～ to**
: receptivo a
amend [ə'mɛnd] *vt* : enmendar —
amendment [ə'mɛndmənt] *n* : enmienda *f* — **amends** [ə'mɛndz] *ns & pl*
make ～ for : reparar

amenities [ə'menəṭiz, -'miː-] *npl* : servicios *mpl*, comodidades *fpl*

American [ə'merɪkən] *adj* : americano

amethyst ['æməθəst] *n* : amatista *f*

amiable ['eɪmiːəbəl] *adj* : amable, agradable

amicable ['æmɪkəbəl] *adj* : amigable, amistoso

amid [ə'mɪd] *or* **amidst** [ə'mɪdst] *prep* : en medio de, entre

amiss [ə'mɪs] *adv* **1** : mal **2 take sth ~** : tomar algo a mal — **~** *adj* **1** WRONG : malo **2 something is ~** : algo anda mal

ammonia [ə'moːnjə] *n* : amoníaco *m*

ammunition [,æmjə'nɪʃən] *n* : municiones *fpl*

amnesia [æm'niːʒə] *n* : amnesia *f*

amnesty ['æmnəsti] *n*, *pl* **-ties** : amnistía *f*

among [ə'mʌŋ] *prep* : entre

amorous ['æmərəs] *adj* : amoroso

amount [ə'maʊnt] *vi* **1 ~ to** : equivaler a **2 ~ to** TOTAL : sumar, ascender a — **~** *n* : cantidad *f*

amphibian [æm'fɪbiən] *n* : anfibio *m* — **amphibious** [æm'fɪbiəs] *adj* : anfibio

amphitheater ['æmfə,θiːəṭər] *n* : anfiteatro *m*

ample ['æmpəl] *adj* **-pler; -plest 1** SPACIOUS : amplio, extenso **2** ABUNDANT : abundante

amplify ['æmpləˌfaɪ] *vt* **-fied; -fying** : amplificar — **amplifier** ['æmpləˌfaɪər] *n* : amplificador *m*

amputate ['æmpjəˌteɪt] *vt* **-tated; -tating** : amputar — **amputation** [,æmpjə'teɪʃən] *n* : amputación *f*

amuse [ə'mjuːz] *vt* **amused; amusing 1** : hacer reír, divertir **2** ENTERTAIN : entretener — **amusement** [ə'mjuːzmənt] *n* : diversión *f* — **amusing** *adj* : divertido

an → a²

analogy [ə'nælədʒi] *n*, *pl* **-gies** : analogía *f* — **analogous** [ə'næləgəs] *adj* : análogo

analysis [ə'næləsəs] *n*, *pl* **-yses** [-ˌsiːz] : análisis *m* — **analytic** [,ænə'lɪṭɪk] *or* **analytical** [-ˌṭɪkəl] *adj* : analítico — **analyze** ['ænəˌlaɪz] *vt* **-lyzed; -lyzing** : analizar

anarchy ['ænərki, -nɑr-] *n* : anarquía *f* — **anarchist** ['ænərkɪst] *n* : anarquista *mf*

anatomy [ə'næṭəmi] *n*, *pl* **-mies** : anatomía *f* — **anatomic** [,ænə'tɑmɪk] *or* **anatomical** [-mɪkəl] *adj* : anatómico

ancestor ['ænˌsestər] *n* : antepasado *m*, -da *f* — **ancestral** [æn'sestrəl] *adj* : ancestral — **ancestry** ['ænˌsestri] *n* **1** DESCENT : linaje *m*, abolengo *m* **2** ANCESTORS : antepasados *mpl*, -das *fpl*

anchor ['æŋkər] *n* **1** : ancla *f* **2** : presentador *m*, -dora *f* (en televisión) — **~** *vt* **1** : anclar **2** FASTEN : sujetar — *vi* : anclar

anchovy ['ænˌtʃoːvi, æn'tʃoː-] *n*, *pl* **-vies** *or* **-vy** : anchoa *f*

ancient ['eɪntʃənt] *adj* : antiguo, viejo

and ['ænd] *conj* **1** : y (e *before words beginning with i- or hi-*) **2 come ~ see** : ven a ver **3 more ~ more** : cada vez más **4 try ~ finish it soon** : trata de terminarlo pronto

anecdote ['ænɪkˌdoːt] *n* : anécdota *f*

anemia [ə'niːmiə] *n* : anemia *f* — **anemic** [ə'niːmɪk] *adj* : anémico

anesthesia [,ænəs'θiːʒə] *n* : anestesia *f* — **anesthetic** [,ænəs'θeṭɪk] *adj* : anestésico — **~** *n* : anestésico *m*

anew [ə'nuː, -'njuː] *adv* : de nuevo, nuevamente

angel ['eɪndʒəl] *n* : ángel *m* — **angelic** [æn'dʒelɪk] *or* **angelical** [-lɪkəl] *adj* : angélico

anger ['æŋgər] *vt* : enojar, enfadar — **~** *n* : ira *f*, enojo *m*, enfado *m*

angle *n* **1** : ángulo *m* **2** POINT OF VIEW : perspectiva *f*, punto *m* de vista — **angler** ['æŋglər] *n* : pescador *m*, -dora *f*

Anglo–Saxon [,æŋglo'sæksən] *adj* : anglosajón

angry ['æŋgri] *adj* **-grier; -est** : enojado, enfadado

anguish ['æŋgwɪʃ] *n* : angustia *f*

angular ['æŋgjələr] *adj* **1** : angular **2 ~ features** : rasgos *mpl* angulosos

animal ['ænəməl] *n* : animal *m*

animate ['ænəmət] *adj* : animado — **~** ['ænəˌmeɪt] *vt* **-mated; -mating** : animar — **animated** *adj* **1** : animado **2 ~ cartoon** : dibujos *mpl* animados — **animation** [,ænə'meɪʃən] *n* : animación *f*

animosity [,ænə'mɑsəṭi] *n*, *pl* **-ties** : animosidad *f*

anise ['ænəs] *n* : anís *m*

ankle ['æŋkəl] *n* : tobillo *m*

annals ['ænəlz] *npl* : anales *mpl*

annex [ə'neks, 'æˌneks] *vt* : anexar — **~** ['æˌneks, -nɪks] *n* : anexo *m*

annihilate [ə'naɪəˌleɪt] *vt* **-lated; -lating** : aniquilar — **annihilation** [ə,naɪə'leɪʃən] *n* : aniquilación *f*

anniversary [,ænə'vərsəri] *n*, *pl* **-ries** : aniversario *m*

annotate ['ænəˌteɪt] *vt* **-tated; -tating** : anotar — **annotation** [,ænə'teɪʃən] *n* : anotación *f*

announce [ə'naʊns] *vt* **-nounced;**

-nouncing : anunciar — **announce-ment** [ə'naʊntsmənt] n : anuncio m — **announcer** [ə'naʊntsər] n : locutor m, -tora f

annoy [ə'nɔɪ] vt : fastidiar, molestar — **annoyance** [ə'nɔɪənts] n : fastidio m, molestia f — **annoying** [ə'nɔɪɪŋ] adj : molesto, fastidioso

annual ['ænjʊəl] adj : anual — **~** n : anuario m

annuity [ə'nuːəṭi] n, pl -ties : anualidad f

annul [ə'nʌl] vt annulled; annulling : anular — **annulment** [ə'nʌlmənt] n : anulación f

anoint [ə'nɔɪnt] vt : ungir

anomaly [ə'nɑməli] n, pl -lies : anomalía f

anonymous [ə'nɑnəməs] adj : anónimo — **anonymity** [,ænə'nɪməṭi] n : anonimato m

another [ə'nʌðər] adj 1 : otro 2 in **~** minute : en un minuto más — **~** pron : otro, otra

answer ['æntsər] n 1 REPLY : respuesta f, contestación f 2 SOLUTION : solución f — **~** n 1 : contestar a, responder a 2 **~ the door** : abrir la puerta — vi : contestar, responder

ant ['ænt] n : hormiga f

antagonize [æn'tægənaɪz] vt -nized; -nizing : provocar la enemistad de — **antagonism** [æn'tægənɪzəm] n : antagonismo m

antarctic [ænt'ɑrktɪk, -'ɑrṭɪk] adj : antártico

antelope ['æntəloʊp] n, pl -lope or -lopes : antílope m

antenna [æn'tenə] n, pl -nae [-,niː, -,naɪ] or -nas : antena f

anthem ['ænθəm] n : himno m

anthology [æn'θɑlədʒi] n, pl -gies : antología f

anthropology [,ænθrə'pɑlədʒi] n : antropología f

antibiotic [,æntibar'ɑṭɪk, ,æntaɪ-, -bi-] adj : antibiótico — **~** n : antibiótico m

antibody ['ænti,bɑdi] n, pl -bodies : anticuerpo m

anticipate [æn'tɪsə,peɪt] vt -pated; -pating 1 FORESEE : anticipar, prever 2 EXPECT : esperar — **anticipation** [æn,tɪsə'peɪʃən] n : anticipación f, expectación f

antics ['æntɪks] npl : payasadas fpl

antidote ['ænti,doːt] n : antídoto m

antifreeze ['ænti,friːz] n : anticongelante m

antipathy [æn'tɪpəθi] n, pl -thies : antipatía f

antiquated ['æntə,kweɪṭəd] adj : anticuado

antique [æn'tiːk] adj : antiguo — **~** n : antigüedad f — **antiquity** [æn'tɪkwəṭi] n, pl -ties : antigüedad f

anti-Semitic [,æntisə'mɪṭɪk, ,æntaɪ-] adj : antisemita

antiseptic [,ænti'septɪk] adj : antiséptico — **~** n : antiséptico m

antisocial [,ænti'soːʃəl, ,æntaɪ-] adj 1 : antisocial 2 UNSOCIABLE : poco sociable

antithesis [æn'tɪθəsɪs] n, pl -eses [-,siːz] : antítesis f

antlers ['æntlərz] npl : cornamenta f

antonym ['æntə,nɪm] n : antónimo m

anus ['eɪnəs] n : ano m

anvil ['ænvəl, -vɪl] n : yunque m

anxiety [æŋk'zaɪəṭi] n, pl -eties 1 APPREHENSION : inquietud f, ansiedad f 2 EAGERNESS : anhelo m — **anxious** ['æŋkʃəs] adj 1 WORRIED : inquieto, preocupado 2 EAGER : ansioso — **anxiously** ['æŋkʃəsli] adv : con ansiedad

any ['eni] adv 1 SOMEWHAT : algo, un poco 2 **it's not ~ good** : no sirve para nada 3 **we can't wait ~ longer** : no podemos esperar más — **~** adj 1 : alguno 2 (in negative constructions) : ningún 3 WHATEVER : cualquier 4 in **~ case** : en todo caso — **~** pron 1 : alguno, -na 2 : ninguno, -na 3 **do you want ~ more rice?** : ¿quieres más arroz?

anybody ['eni,bʌdi, -bə-] → **anyone**

anyhow ['eni,haʊ] adv 1 : de todas formas 2 HAPHAZARDLY : de cualquier modo

anymore [,eni'mor] adv **not ~** : ya no

anyone ['eni,wʌn] pron 1 SOMEONE : alguien 2 WHOEVER : quienquiera 3 **I don't see ~** : no veo a nadie

anyplace ['eni,pleɪs] → **anywhere**

anything ['eni,θɪŋ] pron 1 SOMETHING : algo, alguna cosa 2 (in negative constructions) : nada 3 WHATEVER : cualquier cosa, lo que sea

anytime ['eni,taɪm] adv : en cualquier momento

anyway ['eni,weɪ] → **anyhow**

anywhere ['eni,ʰwer] adv 1 : en cualquier parte, dondequiera 2 (used in questions) : en algún sitio 3 **I can't find it ~** : no lo encuentro por ninguna parte

apart [ə'pɑrt] adv 1 : aparte 2 **~ from** : excepto, aparte de 3 **fall ~** : deshacerse, hacerse pedazos 4 **live ~** : vivir separados 5 **take ~** : desmontar, desmantelar apartment [ə'pɑrtmənt] *n* : apartamento *m*

apathy ['æpəθi] *n* : apatía *f* — **apathetic** [ˌæpə'θεtɪk] *adj* : apático, indiferente

ape *n* : simio *m*

aperture ['æpərtʃər, -ˌtʃʊr] *n* : abertura *f*

apex ['eɪˌpɛks] *n, pl* apexes *or* apices ['eɪpəˌsiːz, 'æ-] : ápice *m*, cumbre *f*

apiece [ə'piːs] *adv* : cada uno

aplomb [ə'plɑm, -'plʌm] *n* : aplomo *m*

apology [ə'pɑlədʒi] *n, pl* -gies : disculpa *f* — **apologetic** [əˌpɑlə'dʒεtɪk] *adj* : lleno de disculpas — **apologize** [ə'pɑləˌdʒaɪz] *vi* -gized; -gizing : disculparse, pedir perdón

apostle [ə'pɑsəl] *n* : apóstol *m*

apostrophe [ə'pɑstrəˌfiː] *n* : apóstrofo *m*

appall [ə'pɔl] *vt* : horrorizar — **appalling** [ə'pɔlɪŋ] *adj* : horroroso

apparatus [ˌæpə'ræt̬əs, -'reɪ-] *n, pl* -tuses *or* -tus : aparato *m*

apparel [ə'pærəl] *n* : ropa *f*

apparent [ə'pærənt] *adj* **1** OBVIOUS : claro, evidente **2** SEEMING : aparente — **apparently** [ə'pærəntli] *adv* : al parecer, por lo visto

apparition [ˌæpə'rɪʃən] *n* : aparición *f*

appeal [ə'piːl] *vi* **1** ~ **for** : solicitar **2** ~ **to** : apelar a (la bondad de algn, etc.) **3** ~ **to** ATTRACT : atraer a — ~ *n* **1** : apelación *f* (en derecho) **2** REQUEST : llamamiento *m* **3** ATTRACTION : atractivo *m* — **appealing** [ə'piːlɪŋ] *adj* : atractivo

appear [ə'pɪr] *vi* **1** : aparecer **2** : comparecer (ante un tribunal), actuar (en el teatro) **3** SEEM : parecer — **appearance** [ə'pɪrənts] *n* **1** : aparición *f* **2** LOOK : apariencia *f*, aspecto *m*

appease [ə'piːz] *vt* -peased; -peasing : apaciguar, aplacar

appendix [ə'pendɪks] *n, pl* -dixes *or* -dices [-dəˌsiːz] : apéndice *m* — **appendicitis** [əˌpendə'saɪt̬əs] *n* : apendicitis *f*

appetite ['æpəˌtaɪt] *n* : apetito *m* — **appetizer** ['æpəˌtaɪzər] *n* : aperitivo *m* — **appetizing** ['æpəˌtaɪzɪŋ] *adj* : apetitoso

applaud [ə'plɔd] *v* : aplaudir — **applause** [ə'plɔz] *n* : aplauso *m*

apple ['æpəl] *n* : manzana *f*

appliance [ə'plaɪənts] *n* : aparato *m*

apply [ə'plaɪ] *v* -plied; -plying *vt* **1** : aplicar **2** ~ **oneself** : aplicarse — *vi* **1** : aplicarse **2** ~ **for** : solicitar, pedir — **applicable** ['æplɪkəbəl, ə'plɪkə-] *adj* : aplicable — **applicant** ['æplɪkənt] *n* : solicitante *mf*; candidato *m*, -ta *f* — **application** [ˌæplə'keɪʃən] *n* **1** : apli-

cación *f* **2** : solicitud *f* (para un empleo, etc.)

appoint [ə'pɔɪnt] *vt* **1** NAME : nombrar **2** FIX, SET : fijar, señalar — **appointment** [ə'pɔɪntmənt] *n* **1** APPOINTING : nombramiento *m* **2** ENGAGEMENT : cita *f*

apportion [ə'pɔrʃən] *vt* : distribuir, repartir

appraise [ə'preɪz] *vt* -praised; -praising : evaluar, valorar — **appraisal** [ə'preɪzəl] *n* : evaluación *f*

appreciate [ə'priːʃiˌeɪt, -'prɪ-] *v* -ated; -ating *vt* **1** VALUE : apreciar **2** UNDERSTAND : darse cuenta de **3 I ~ your help** : te agradezco tu ayuda — *vi* : aumentar en valor — **appreciation** [əˌpriːʃi'eɪʃən, -ˌprɪ-] *n* **1** GRATITUDE : agradecimiento *m* **2** VALUING : apreciación *f*, valoración *f* — **appreciative** [ə'priːʃət̬ɪv, -'prɪ-; ə'priːʃiˌeɪ-] *adj* **1** : apreciativo **2** GRATEFUL : agradecido

apprehend [ˌæprɪ'hend] *vt* **1** ARREST : aprehender, detener **2** DREAD : temer **3** COMPREHEND : comprender — **apprehension** [ˌæprɪ'hentʃən] *n* **1** ARREST : detención *f*, aprehensión *f* **2** ANXIETY : aprensión *f*, temor *m* — **apprehensive** [ˌæprɪ'hentsɪv] *adj* : aprensivo, inquieto

apprentice [ə'prentis] *n* : aprendiz *m*, -diza *f*

approach [ə'proːtʃ] *vt* **1** NEAR : acercarse a **2** : dirigirse a (algn), abordar (un problema, etc.) — *vi* : acercarse — ~ *n* **1** NEARING : acercamiento *m* **2** POSITION : enfoque *m* **3** ACCESS : acceso *m* — **approachable** [ə'proːtʃəbəl] *adj* : accesible, asequible

appropriate [ə'proːpriˌeɪt] *vt* -ated; -ating : apropiarse de — ~ [ə'proːpriət] *adj* : apropiado

approve [ə'pruːv] *vt* -proved; -proving : aprobar — **approval** [ə'pruːvəl] *n* : aprobación *f*

approximate [ə'prɑksəmət] *adj* : aproximado — ~ [ə'prɑksəˌmeɪt] *vt* -mated; -mating : aproximarse a — **approximately** [ə'prɑksəmətli] *adv* : aproximadamente

apricot ['æprəˌkɑt, 'eɪ-] *n* : albaricoque *m*, chabacano *m Lat*

April ['eɪprəl] *n* : abril *m*

apron ['eɪprən] *n* : delantal *m*

apropos [ˌæprə'poː, 'æprəˌpoː] *adv* : a propósito

apt ['æpt] *adj* **1** FITTING : apto, apropiado **2** LIABLE : propenso — **aptitude** ['æptəˌtuːd, -ˌtjuːd] *n* : aptitud *f* aquarium [ə'kwæriəm] n, pl -iums or -ia [-iə] : acuario m

aquatic [ə'kwɑtɪk, -'kwæ-] adj : acuático

aqueduct ['ækwədʌkt] n : acueducto m

Arab ['ærəb] adj : árabe — Arabic ['ærəbɪk] adj : árabe — ~ n : árabe m (idioma)

arbitrary ['ɑrbə,treri] adj : arbitrario

arbitrate ['ɑrbə,treɪt] v -trated; -trating : arbitrar — arbitration [,ɑrbə'treɪʃən] n : arbitraje m

arc ['ɑrk] n : arco m

arcade [ɑr'keɪd] n 1 : arcada f 2 shopping ~ : galería f comercial

arch ['ɑrtʃ] n : arco m — ~ vt : arquear — vi : arquearse

archaeology or archeology [,ɑrki'ɑlədʒi] n : arqueología f — archaeological [,ɑrkiə'lɑdʒɪkəl] adj : arqueológico — archaeologist [,ɑrki'ɑlədʒɪst] n : arqueólogo m, -ga f

archaic [ɑr'keɪɪk] adj : arcaico

archbishop [ɑrtʃ'bɪʃəp] n : arzobispo m

archery ['ɑrtʃəri] n : tiro m al arco

archipelago [,ɑrkə'pelə,goː, ,ɑrtʃə-] n, pl -goes or -gos [-goːz] : archipiélago m

architecture ['ɑrkə,tektʃər] n : arquitectura f — architect ['ɑrkə,tekt] n : arquitecto m, -ta f — architectural [,ɑrkə'tektʃərəl] adj : arquitectónico

archives ['ɑr,kaɪvz] npl : archivo m

archway ['ɑrtʃ,weɪ] n : arco m (de entrada)

arctic ['ɑrktɪk, 'ɑrʃ-] adj : ártico

ardent ['ɑrdənt] adj : ardiente, fervoroso — ardor ['ɑrdər] n : ardor m, fervor m

arduous ['ɑrdʒʊəs] adj : arduo

are → be

area ['æriə] n 1 REGION : área f, zona f 2 FIELD : campo m 3 ~ code : código m de la zona Lat, prefijo m Spain

arena [ə'riːnə] n : arena f, ruedo m

aren't ['ɑrnt, 'ɑrənt] (contraction of are not) → be

Argentine ['ɑrdʒən,taɪn, -,tiːn] or Argentinean or Argentinian [,ɑrdʒən'tɪniən] adj : argentino

argue ['ɑr,gjuː] v -gued; -guing vi 1 QUARREL : discutir 2 ~ against : argumentar contra — vt : argumentar, sostener — argument ['ɑrgjəmənt] n 1 QUARREL : disputa f, discusión f 2 REASONING : argumentos mpl

arid ['ærəd] adj : árido — aridity [ə'rɪdə̯ti, æ-] n : aridez f

arise [ə'raɪz] vi arose [ə'roːz]; arisen [ə'rɪzən]; arising 1 : levantarse 2 ~ from : surgir de

aristocracy [,ærə'stɑkrəsi] n, pl -cies : aristocracia f — aristocrat [ə'rɪstə-

,kræt] n : aristócrata mf — aristocratic [ə,rɪstə'krætɪk] adj : aristocrático

arithmetic [ə'rɪθmətɪk] n : aritmética f

ark ['ɑrk] n : arca f

arm ['ɑrm] n 1 : brazo m 2 WEAPON : arma f — ~ vt : armar — armament ['ɑrməmənt] n : armamento m — armchair ['ɑrm,tʃer] n : sillón m — armed ['ɑrmd] adj 1 ~ forces : fuerzas fpl armadas 2 ~ robbery : robo m a mano armada

armistice ['ɑrməstɪs] n : armisticio m

armor or Brit armour ['ɑrmər] n : armadura f — armored or Brit armoured ['ɑrmərd] adj : blindado, acorazado — armory or Brit armoury ['ɑrmri, 'ɑrməri] : arsenal m

armpit ['ɑrm,pɪt] n : axila f, sobaco m

army ['ɑrmi] n, pl -mies : ejército m

aroma [ə'roːmə] n : aroma m — aromatic [,ærə'mætɪk] adj : aromático

around [ə'raʊnd] adv 1 : de circunferencia 2 NEARBY : por ahí 3 APPROXIMATELY : más o menos, aproximadamente 4 all ~ : por todos lados, todo alrededor 5 turn ~ : voltearse — ~ prep 1 SURROUNDING : alrededor de 2 THROUGHOUT : por 3 NEAR : cerca de 4 ~ the corner : a la vuelta de la esquina

arouse [ə'raʊz] vt aroused; arousing 1 AWAKE : despertar 2 EXCITE : excitar

arrange [ə'reɪndʒ] vt -ranged; -ranging : arreglar, poner en orden — arrangement [ə'reɪndʒmənt] n 1 ORDER : arreglo m 2 ~s npl : preparativos mpl

array [ə'reɪ] n : selección f, surtido m

arrears [ə'rɪrz] npl 1 : atrasos mpl 2 be in ~ : estar atrasado en pagos

arrest [ə'rest] vt : detener — ~ n 1 : arresto m, detención f 2 under ~ : detenido

arrive [ə'raɪv] vi -rived; -riving : llegar — arrival [ə'raɪvəl] n : llegada f

arrogance ['ærəgənts] n : arrogancia f — arrogant ['ærəgənt] adj : arrogante

arrow ['æroː] n : flecha f

arsenal ['ɑrsənəl] n : arsenal m

arsenic ['ɑrsənɪk] n : arsénico m

arson ['ɑrsən] n : incendio m premeditado

art ['ɑrt] n 1 : arte m 2 ~s npl : letras fpl (en educación) 3 fine ~s : bellas artes fpl

artefact Brit → artifact

artery ['ɑrtəri] n, pl -teries : arteria f

artful ['ɑrtfəl] adj : astuto, taimado

arthritis [ɑr'θraɪtəs] n, pl -tides [ɑr'θrɪtə,diːz] : artritis f — arthritic [ɑr'θrɪtɪk] adj : artrítico

artichoke ['ɑrtə‚tʃoːk] n : alcachofa f
article ['ɑrtıkəl] n : artículo m
articulate [ɑr'tıkjə‚leɪt] vt -lated; -lating
: articular — ~ [ɑr'tıkjələt] adj be ~
: expresarse bien
artifact or Brit **artefact** ['ɑrtə‚fækt] n
: artefacto m
artificial [‚ɑrtə'fıʃəl] adj : artificial
artillery [ɑr'tıləri] n, pl -leries : artillería
f
artisan ['ɑrtəzən, -sən] n : artesano m,
-na f
artist ['ɑrtıst] n : artista mf — **artistic**
[ɑr'tıstık] adj : artístico
as ['æz] adv 1 : tan, tanto 2 ~ **much**
: tanto como 3 ~ **tall** : tan alto
como 4 ~ **well** : también — ~ conj 1
WHILE : mientras 2 (referring to manner) : como 3 SINCE : ya que 4 THOUGH
: por más que — ~ prep 1 : de 2 LIKE
: como — ~ pron : que
asbestos [æz'bestəs, æs-] n : asbesto m,
amianto m
ascend [ə'send] vi : ascender, subir — vt
: subir (a) — **ascent** [ə'sent] n : ascensión f, subida f
ascertain [‚æsər'teɪn] vt : averiguar, determinar
ascribe [ə'skraɪb] vt -cribed; -cribing
: atribuir
as for prep : en cuanto a
ash[1] ['æʃ] n : ceniza f
ash[2] n : fresno m (árbol)
ashamed [ə'ʃeɪmd] adj : avergonzado,
apenado Lat
ashore [ə'ʃor] adv 1 : en tierra 2 **go** ~
: desembarcar
ashtray ['æʃ‚treɪ] n : cenicero m
Asian ['eɪʒən, -ʃən] adj : asiático
aside [ə'saɪd] adv 1 : a un lado 2 APART
: aparte 3 **set** ~ : guardar — **aside**
from prep 1 BESIDES : además de 2 EX-
CEPT : aparte de, menos
as if conj : como si
ask ['æsk] vt 1 : preguntar 2 REQUEST
: pedir 3 INVITE : invitar — vi : preguntar
askance [ə'skænts] adv **look** ~ : mirar
de soslayo
askew [ə'skjuː] adj : torcido, ladeado
asleep [ə'sliːp] adj 1 : dormido 2 **fall** ~
: dormirse, quedarse dormido
as of prep : desde, a partir de
asparagus [ə'spærəgəs] n : espárrago m
aspect ['æ‚spekt] n : aspecto m
asphalt ['æs‚fɔlt] n : asfalto m
asphyxiate [æs'fıksi‚eɪt] v -ated; -ating
vt : asfixiar — **asphyxiation** [æ‚sfıksi-
'eɪʃən] n : asfixia f
aspire [ə'spaɪr] vi -pired; -piring : aspi-

rar — **aspiration** [‚æspə'reɪʃən] n : aspiración f
aspirin ['æsprən, 'æspə-] n, pl aspirin or
aspirins : aspirina f
ass ['æs] n 1 : asno m 2 IDIOT : imbécil
mf, idiota mf
assail [ə'seɪl] vt : atacar, asaltar — **as-**
sailant [ə'seɪlənt] n : asaltante mf, atacante mf
assassin [ə'sæsən] n : asesino m, -na f
— **assassinate** [ə'sæsən‚eɪt] vt -nated;
-nating : asesinar — **assassination**
[ə‚sæsən'eɪʃən] n : asesinato m
assault [ə'sɔlt] n 1 : ataque m, asalto m
2 : agresión f (contra algn) — ~ vt
: atacar, asaltar
assemble [ə'sembəl] v -bled; -bling vt 1
GATHER : reunir, juntar 2 CONSTRUCT
: montar — vi : reunirse — **assembly**
[ə'sembli] n, pl -blies 1 MEETING : reunión f, asamblea f 2 CONSTRUCTING
: montaje m
assent [ə'sent] vi : asentir, consentir —
~ n : asentimiento m
assert [ə'sərt] vt 1 : afirmar 2 ~ **one-**
self : hacerse valer — **assertion**
[ə'sərʃən] n : afirmación f — **assertive**
[ə'sərtɪv] adj : firme, enérgico
assess [ə'ses] vt : evaluar, valorar —
assessment [ə'sesmənt] n : evaluación f, valoración f
asset ['æ‚set] n 1 : ventaja f, recurso m 2
~s npl : bienes mpl, activo m
assiduous [ə'sıdʒuəs] adj : asiduo
assign [ə'saɪn] vt 1 APPOINT : designar,
nombrar 2 ALLOT : asignar — **assign-**
ment [ə'saɪnmənt] n 1 TASK : misión f 2
HOMEWORK : tarea f 3 ASSIGNING : asignación f
assimilate [ə'sımə‚leɪt] vt -lated; -lating
: asimilar
assist [ə'sıst] vt : ayudar — **assistance**
[ə'sıstənts] n : ayuda f — **assistant**
[ə'sıstənt] n : ayudante mf
associate [ə'soːʃi‚eɪt, -si-] v -ated;
-ating vt : asociar — vi : asociarse —
~ [ə'soːʃiət, -siət] n : asociado m, -da f:
socio m, -cia f — **association** [ə‚soːʃi-
'eɪʃən, -si-] n : asociación f
as soon as conj : tan pronto como
assorted [ə'sortəd] adj : surtido — **as-**
sortment [ə'sortmənt] n : surtido m,
variedad f
assume [ə'suːm] vt -sumed; -suming 1
SUPPOSE : suponer 2 UNDERTAKE
: asumir 3 TAKE ON : adquirir, tomar —
assumption [ə'sʌmpʃən] n : suposición f
assure [ə'ʃur] vt -sured; -suring : asegurar — **assurance** [ə'ʃurənts] n 1

CERTAINTY : certeza *f*, garantía *f* **2** CON-FIDENCE : confianza *f*, seguridad *f* (de sí mismo)

asterisk ['æstə,rɪsk] *n* : asterisco *m*

asthma ['æzmə] *n* : asma *m*

as though → **as if**

as to *prep* : sobre, acerca de

astonish [ə'stɑnɪʃ] *vt* : asombrar — **astonishing** [ə'stɑnɪʃɪŋ] *adj* : asombroso — **astonishment** [ə'stɑnɪʃmənt] *n* : asombro *m*

astound [ə'staʊnd] *vt* : asombrar, pasmar — **astounding** [ə'staʊndɪŋ] *adj* : asombroso, pasmoso

astray [ə'streɪ] *adv* **1 go** ~ : extraviarse **2 lead** ~ : llevar por mal camino

astrology [ə'strɑlədʒi] *n* : astrología *f*

astronaut ['æstrə,nɔt] *n* : astronauta *mf*

astronomy [ə'strɑnəmi] *n, pl* **-mies** : astronomía *f* — **astronomer** [ə'strɑnəmər] *n* : astrónomo *m*, -ma *f* — **astronomical** [,æstrə'nɑmɪkəl] *adj* : astronómico

astute [ə'stuːt, -'stjuːt] *adj* : astuto, sagaz — **astuteness** [ə'stuːtnəs, -'stjuːt-] *n* : astucia *f*

as well as *conj* : tanto como — ~ *prep* : además de, aparte de

asylum [ə'saɪləm] *n* **1** : asilo *m* **2 insane** ~ : manicomio *m*

at ['æt] *prep* **1** : a **2** ~ **home** : en casa **3** ~ **night** : en la noche, por la noche **4** ~ **two o'clock** : a las dos **5 be angry** ~ : estar enojado con **6 laugh** ~ : reírse de — **at all** *adv* not ~ : en absoluto, nada

ate → **eat**

atheist ['eɪθiːɪst] *n* : ateo *m*, atea *f* — **atheism** [n 'eɪθi,ɪzəm] *n* : ateísmo *m*

athlete ['æθ,liːt] *n* : atleta *mf* — **athletic** [æθ'lɛtɪk] *adj* : atlético — **athletics** [æθ'lɛtɪks] *ns & pl* : atletismo *m*

atlas ['ætləs] *n* : atlas *m*

atmosphere ['ætməs,fɪr] *n* **1** : atmósfera *f* **2** AMBIENCE : ambiente *m* — **atmospheric** [,ætməs'fɪrɪk, -'sfɛr-] *adj* : atmosférico

atom ['ætəm] *n* : átomo *m* — **atomic** [ə'tɑmɪk] *adj* : atómico

atomizer ['ætə,maɪzər] *n* : atomizador *m*

atone [ə'tom] *vt* **atoned; atoning** ~ **for** : expiar

atrocity [ə'trɑsəti] *n, pl* **-ties** : atrocidad *f* — **atrocious** [ə'troːʃəs] *adj* : atroz

atrophy ['ætrəfi] *vi* **-phied; -phying** : atrofiarse

attach [ə'tætʃ] *vt* **1** : sujetar, atar **2** : adjuntar (un documento, etc.) **3** ~ **importance to** : atribuir importancia a **4 become** ~**ed to s.o.** : encariñarse

con algn — **attachment** [ə'tætʃmənt] *n* **1** ACCESSORY : accesorio *m* **2** FOND-NESS : cariño *m*

attack [ə'tæk] *v* : atacar — ~ *n* : ataque *m* — **attacker** [ə'tækər] *n* : agresor *m*, -sora *f*

attain [ə'teɪn] *vt* : lograr, alcanzar — **attainment** [ə'teɪnmənt] *n* : logro *m*

attempt [ə'tempt] *vt* : intentar — ~ *n* : intento *m*

attend [ə'tend] *vt* : asistir a — *vi* **1** : asistir **2** ~ **to** : ocuparse de — **attendance** [ə'tendənts] *n* **1** : asistencia *f* **2** TURNOUT : concurrencia *f* — **attendant** *n* : encargado *m*, -da *f*; asistente *mf*

attention [ə'tentʃən] *n* **1** : atención *f* **2 pay** ~ : prestar atención, hacer caso — **attentive** [ə'tentɪv] *adj* : atento

attest [ə'test] *vt* : atestiguar

attic ['ætɪk] *n* : desván *m*

attire [ə'taɪr] *n* : atavío *m*

attitude ['ætə,tuːd, -,tjuːd] *n* **1** : actitud *f* **2** POSTURE : postura *f*

attorney [ə'tɜrni] *n, pl* **-neys** : abogado *m*, -da *f*

attract [ə'trækt] *vt* : atraer — **attraction** [ə'trækʃən] *n* **1** : atracción *f* **2** APPEAL : atractivo *m* — **attractive** [ə'træktɪv] *adj* : atractivo, atrayente

attribute ['ætrə,bjuːt] *n* : atributo *m* — ~ [ə'trɪ,bjuːt] *vt* **-tributed; -tributing** : atribuir, imputar

auburn ['ɔbərn] *adj* : castaño rojizo

auction ['ɔkʃən] *n* : subasta *f* — ~ *vt or* ~ **off** : subastar

audacious [ɔ'deɪʃəs] *adj* : audaz — **audacity** [ɔ'dæsəti] *n, pl* **-ties** : audacia *f*, atrevimiento *m*

audible ['ɔdəbəl] *adj* : audible

audience ['ɔdiənts] *n* **1** INTERVIEW : audiencia *f* **2** PUBLIC : público *m*

audiovisual [,ɔdio'vɪʒuəl] *adj* : audiovisual

audition [ɔ'dɪʃən] *n* : audición *f*

auditor ['ɔdətər] *n* **1** : auditor *m*, -tora *f* (de finanzas) **2** STUDENT : oyente *mf*

auditorium [,ɔdə'toriəm] *n, pl* **-riums** *or* **-ria** [-riə] : auditorio *m*

augment [ɔg'ment] *vt* : aumentar

augur ['ɔgər] *vi* ~ **well** : ser de buen agüero

August ['ɔgəst] *n* : agosto *m*

aunt ['ænt, 'ant] *n* : tía *f*

aura ['ɔrə] *n* : aura *f*

auspices ['ɔspəsəz, -,siːz] *npl* : auspicios *mpl*

auspicious [ɔ'spɪʃəs] *adj* : propicio, prometedor

austere [ɔ'stɪr] *adj* : austero — **austeri-ty** [ɔ'sterəti] *n, pl* **-ties** : austeridad *f*
Australian [ɔ'streɪljən] *adj* : australiano
authentic [ə'θentɪk, ɔ-] *adj* : auténtico
author ['ɔθər] *n* : autor *m*, -tora *f*
authority [ə'θorəti, ɔ-] *n, pl* **-ties** : autoridad *f* — **authoritarian** [ə,θorə-'teriən, ə-] *adj* : autoritario — **authori-tative** [ə'θorə,teɪtɪv, ɔ-] *adj* **1** RELIABLE : autorizado **2** DICTATORIAL : autoritario — **authorization** [,ɔθərə'zeɪʃən] *n* : autorización *f* — **authorize** ['ɔθə,raɪz] *vt* **-rized; -rizing** : autorizar
autobiography [,ɔtəbaɪ'ɑgrəfi] *n, pl* **-phies** : autobiografía *f* — **autobio-graphical** [,ɔtə,baɪə'græfɪkəl] *adj* : autobiográfico
autograph ['ɔtə,græf] *n* : autógrafo *m* — ~ *vt* : autografiar
automatic [,ɔtə'mætɪk] *adj* : automático — **automate** ['ɔtə,meɪt] *vt* **-mated; -mating** : automatizar — **automation** [,ɔtə'meɪʃən] *n* : automatización *f*
automobile [,ɔtəmo'biːl, -'moː,biːl] *n* : automóvil *m*
autonomy [ɔ'tɑnəmi] *n, pl* **-mies** : autonomía *f* — **autonomous** [ɔ'tɑnəməs] *adj* : autónomo
autopsy ['ɔ,tɑpsi, -təp-] *n, pl* **-sies** : autopsia *f*
autumn ['ɔtəm] *n* : otoño *m*
auxiliary [ɔg'zɪljəri, -'zɪləri] *adj* : auxiliar — ~ *n, pl* **-ries** : auxiliar *mf*
avail [ə'veɪl] *vt* ~ **oneself of** : aprovecharse de — ~ *n* **to no** ~ : en vano — **available** [ə'veɪləbəl] *adj* : disponible — **availability** [ə,veɪlə-'bɪləti] *n, pl* **-ties** : disponibilidad *f*
avalanche ['ævə,læntʃ] *n* : avalancha *f*
avarice ['ævərəs] *n* : avaricia *f*
avenge [ə'vendʒ] *vt* **avenged; aveng-ing** : vengar
avenue ['ævə,nuː, -,njuː] *n* **1** : avenida *f* **2** MEANS : vía *f*
average ['ævrɪdʒ, 'ævə-] *n* : promedio *m* — ~ *adj* **1** MEAN : medio **2** ORDINARY : regular, ordinario — ~ *vt* **-aged; -aging 1** : hacer un promedio de **2** *or* ~ **out** : calcular el promedio de
averse [ə'vərs] *adj* **be** ~ **to** : sentir

aversión por — **aversion** [ə'vərʒən] *n* : aversión *f*
avert [ə'vərt] *vt* **1** AVOID : evitar, prevenir **2** ~ **one's eyes** : apartar los ojos
aviation [,eɪvi'eɪʃən] *n* : aviación *f* — **aviator** ['eɪvi,eɪtər] *n* : aviador *m*, -dora *f*
avid ['ævɪd] *adj* : ávido — **avidly** *adv* : con avidez
avocado [,ævə'kɑdo, ,ɑvə-] *n, pl* **-dos** : aguacate *m*
avoid [ə'vɔɪd] *vt* : evitar — **avoidable** [ə'vɔɪdəbəl] *adj* : evitable
await [ə'weɪt] *vt* : esperar
awake [ə'weɪk] *v* **awoke** [ə'woːk]; **awo-ken** [ə'woːkən] *or* **awaked; awaking** : despertar — ~ *adj* : despierto — **awaken** [ə'weɪkən] *v* → **awake**
award [ə'wɔrd] *vt* **1** : otorgar, conceder (un premio, etc.) **2** : adjudicar (daños y perjuicios) — ~ *n* **1** PRIZE : premio *m* **2** : adjudicación *f*
aware [ə'wær] *adj* **be** ~ **of** : estar consciente de — **awareness** [ə'wærnəs] *n* : conciencia *f*
away [ə'weɪ] *adv* **1** (*referring to dis-tance*) : de aquí, de distancia **2** **far** ~ : lejos **3 give** ~ : regalar **4 go** ~ : irse **5 right** ~ : en seguida **6 take** ~ : quitar — ~ *adj* **1** ABSENT : ausente **2** ~ **game** : partido *m* fuera de casa
awe [ɔ] *n* : temor *m* reverencial — **awe-some** ['ɔsəm] *adj* : imponente, formidable
awful ['ɔfəl] *adj* **1** : terrible, espantoso **2** **an** ~ **lot** : muchísimo — **awfully** ['ɔfəli] *adv* : terriblemente
awhile [ə'hwaɪl] *adv* : un rato
awkward ['ɔkwərd] *adj* **1** CLUMSY : torpe **2** EMBARRASSING : embarazoso, deli-cado **3** DIFFICULT : difícil — **awkward-ly** *adv* **1** : con dificultad **2** CLUMSILY : de manera torpe
awning ['ɔnɪŋ] *n* : toldo *m*
awry [ə'raɪ] *adj* **1** ASKEW : torcido **2 go** ~ : salir mal
ax *or* **axe** ['æks] *n* : hacha *f*
axiom ['æksiəm] *n* : axioma *m*
axis ['æksɪs] *n, pl* **axes** [-,siːz] : eje *m*
axle ['æksəl] *n* : eje *m*

B

b ['biː] *n*, *pl* b's *or* bs ['biːz] : b, segunda letra del alfabeto inglés

babble ['bæbəl] *vi* -bled; -bling 1 : balbucear 2 MURMUR : murmurar — ~ *n* : balbuceo *m* (de bebé), murmullo *m* (de voces, de un arroyo)

baboon [bæˈbuːn] *n* : babuino *m*

baby ['beɪbi] *n*, *pl* -bies : bebé *m;* niño *m*, -ña *f* — baby *vt* -bied; -bying : mimar, consentir — babyish ['beɪbiʃ] *adj* : infantil — baby-sit ['beɪbi,sɪt] *vi* -sat [-,sæt]; -sitting : cuidar a los niños

bachelor ['bætʃələr] *n* 1 : soltero *m* 2 GRADUATE : licenciado *m*, -da *f*

back ['bæk] *n* 1 : espalda *f* 2 REVERSE : reverso *m*, dorso *m*, revés *m* 3 REAR : fondo *m*, parte *f* trasera 4 : defensa *mf* (en deportes) — ~ *adv* 1 : atrás 2 be ~ : estar de vuelta 3 go ~ : volver 4 two years ~ : hace dos años — ~ *adj* 1 REAR : de atrás, trasero 2 OVERDUE : atrasado — ~ *vt* 1 SUPPORT : apoyar 2 *or* ~ up : darle marcha atrás a (un vehículo) — *vi* 1 ~ down : volverse atrás 2 ~ up : retroceder — backache ['bæk,eɪk] *n* : dolor *m* de espalda — backbone ['bæk,boːn] *n* : columna *f* vertebral — backfire ['bæk,faɪr] *vi* -fired; -firing : petardear — background ['bæk-,graʊnd] *n* 1 : fondo *m* (de un cuadro, etc.), antecedentes *mpl* (de una situación) 2 EXPERIENCE : formación *f* — backhand ['bæk,hænd] *adv* : de revés, con el revés — backhanded ['bæk,hændəd] *adj* : indirecto — backing ['bækɪŋ] *n* : apoyo *m*, respaldo *m* — backlash ['bæk,læʃ] *n* : reacción *f* violenta — backlog ['bæk,lɔɡ] *n* : atrasos *mpl* — backpack ['bæk,pæk] *n* : mochila *f* — backstage [,bæk'steɪdʒ, 'bæk,-] *adv & adj* : entre bastidores — backtrack ['bæk,træk] *vi* : dar marcha atrás — backup ['bæk,ʌp] *n* 1 SUPPORT : respaldo *m*, apoyo *m* 2 : copia *f* de seguridad (para computadoras) — backward ['bækwərd] *or* backwards [-wərdz] *adv* 1 : hacia atrás 2 do it ~ : hacerlo al revés 3 fall ~ : caer de espaldas 4 bend over ~s : hacer todo lo posible — backward *adj* 1 : hacia atrás 2 RETARDED : retrasado

3 SHY : tímido 4 UNDERDEVELOPED : atrasado

bacon ['beɪkən] *n* : tocino *m*, tocineta *f* *Lat*, bacon *m* *Spain*

bacteria [bæk'tɪriə] : bacterias *fpl*

bad ['bæd] *adj* worse ['wərs]; worst ['wərst] 1 : malo 2 ROTTEN : podrido 3 SEVERE : grave 4 from ~ to worse : de mal en peor 5 too ~! : ¡qué lástima! — ~ *adv* → badly

badge ['bædʒ] *n* : insignia *f*, chapa *f*

badger ['bædʒər] *n* : tejón *m* — ~ *vt* : acosar

badly ['bædli] *adv* 1 : mal 2 SEVERELY : gravemente 3 want ~ : desear mucho

baffle ['bæfəl] *vi* -fled; -fling : desconcertar

bag ['bæɡ] *n* 1 : bolsa *f*, saco *m* 2 HANDBAG : bolso *m*, cartera *f* *Lat* 3 SUITCASE : maleta *f* — ~ *vt* bagged; bagging : ensacar, poner en una bolsa

baggage ['bæɡɪdʒ] *n* : equipaje *m*

baggy ['bæɡi] *adj* -gier; -est : holgado

bail ['beɪl] *n* : fianza *f* — ~ *vt* 1 : achicar (agua de un bote) 2 ~ out RELEASE : poner en libertad bajo fianza 3 ~ out EXTRICATE : sacar de apuros

bailiff ['beɪləf] *n* : alguacil *mf*

bait ['beɪt] *vt* 1 : cebar 2 HARASS : acosar — ~ *n* : cebo *m*, carnada *f*

bake ['beɪk] *v* baked; baking *vt* : cocer al horno — *vi* : cocerse (al horno) — baker ['beɪkər] *n* : panadero *m*, -ra *f* — bakery ['beɪkəri] *n*, *pl* -ries : panadería *f*

balance ['bæləns] *n* 1 SCALES : balanza *f* 2 COUNTERBALANCE : contrapeso *m* 3 EQUILIBRIUM : equilibrio *m* 4 REMAINDER : resto *m* 5 *or* bank ~ : saldo *m* — ~ *v* -anced; -ancing *vt* 1 : hacer el balance de (una cuenta) 2 EQUALIZE : equilibrar 3 WEIGH : sopesar — *vi* 1 : sostenerse en equilibrio 2 : cuadrar (dícese de una cuenta)

balcony ['bælkəni] *n*, *pl* -nies 1 : balcón *m* 2 : galería *f* (de un teatro)

bald ['bɔld] *adj* 1 : calvo 2 WORN : pelado 3 the ~ truth : la pura verdad

bale *n* : bala *f*, fardo *m*

baleful ['beɪlfəl] *adj* : siniestro

balk ['bɔk] *vi* ~ at : resistarse a

ball ['bɔl] *n* 1 : pelota *f*, bola *f*, balón *m* 2 DANCE : baile *m* 3 ~ **of string** : ovillo *m* de cuerda

ballad ['bæləd] *n* : balada *f*

ballast *n* : lastre *m*

ball bearing *n* : cojinete *m* de bola

ballerina [,bælə'ri:nə] *n* : bailarina *f*

ballet [bæ'leɪ, 'bæ,leɪ] *n* : ballet *m*

ballistic [bə'lɪstɪk] *adj* : balístico

balloon *n* : globo *m*

ballot *n* 1 : papeleta *f* (de voto) 2 VOTING : votación *f*

ballpoint pen ['bɔl,pɔɪnt] *n* : bolígrafo *m*

ballroom ['bɔl,ru:m, -,rʊm] *n* : sala *f* de baile

balm ['bam, 'balm] *n* : bálsamo *m* — **balmy** ['bami, 'bal-] *adj* **balmier; -est** : templado, agradable

baloney [bə'lo:ni] *n* NONSENSE : tonterías *fpl*

bamboo [bæm'bu:] *n* : bambú *m*

bamboozle [bæm'bu:zəl] *vt* **-zled; -zling** : engañar, embaucar

ban ['bæn] *vt* **banned; banning** : prohibir — ~ *n* : prohibición *f*

banal [bə'nal, bə'næl, 'beɪnəl] *adj* : banal

banana [bə'nænə] *n* : plátano *m*, banana *f Lat*, banano *m Lat*

band ['bænd] *n* 1 STRIP : banda *f* 2 GROUP : banda *f*, grupo *m*, conjunto *m* — *vi* ~ **together** : unirse, juntarse

bandage ['bændɪdʒ] *n* : vendaje *m*, venda *f* — *vt* **-daged; -daging** : vendar

bandit ['bændət] *n* : bandido *m*, -da *f*

bandy ['bændi] *vt* **-died; -dying** ~ **about** : circular, repetir

bang ['bæŋ] *vt* 1 STRIKE : golpear 2 SLAM : cerrar de un golpe — *vi* 1 SLAM : cerrarse de un golpe 2 ~ **on** : golpear — ~ *n* 1 BLOW : golpe *m* 2 NOISE : estrépito *m* 3 SLAM : portazo *m*

bangle ['bæŋgəl] *n* : brazalete *m*, pulsera *f*

bangs ['bæŋz] *npl* : flequillo *m*

banish ['bænɪʃ] *vt* : desterrar

banister ['bænəstər] *n* : pasamanos *m*, barandal *m*

bank ['bæŋk] *n* 1 : banco *m* 2 : orilla *f*, ribera *f* (de un río) 3 EMBANKMENT : terraplén *m* — ~ *vt* : depositar — *vi* 1 : ladearse (dícese de un avión) 2 : tener una cuenta (en un banco) 3 ~ **on** : contar con — **banker** ['bæŋkər] *n* : banquero *m*, -ra *f* — **banking** ['bæŋkɪŋ] *n* : banca *f*

bankrupt ['bæŋ,krʌpt] *adj* : en bancarrota, en quiebra — **bankruptcy** ['bæŋ,krʌptsi] *n*, *pl* **-cies** : quiebra *f*, bancarrota *f*

banner ['bænər] *n* : bandera *f*, pancarta *f*

banquet ['bæŋkwət] *n* : banquete *m*

banter ['bæntər] *n* : bromas *fpl* — ~ *vi* : hacer bromas

baptize [bæp'taɪz, 'bæp,taɪz] *vt* **-tized; -tizing** : bautizar — **baptism** ['bæp,tɪzəm] *n* : bautismo *m*

bar ['bar] *n* 1 : barra *f* 2 BARRIER : barrera *f*, obstáculo *m* 3 COUNTER : mostrador *m*, barra *f* 4 TAVERN : bar *m* 5 **behind** ~**s** : entre rejas 6 ~ **of soap** : pastilla *f* de jabón — ~ *vt* **barred; barring** 1 OBSTRUCT : obstruir, bloquear 2 EXCLUDE : excluir 3 PROHIBIT : prohibir — ~ *prep* 1 : excepto 2 ~ **none** : sin excepción

barbarian [bar'bæriən] *n* : bárbaro *m*, -ra *f*

barbecue ['barbɪ,kju:] *vt* **-cued; -cuing** : asar a la parrilla — ~ *n* : barbacoa *f*

barbed wire ['barbd,waɪr] *n* : alambre *m* de púas

barber ['barbər] *n* : barbero *m*, -ra *f*

bare ['bær] *adj* 1 : desnudo 2 EMPTY : vacío 3 MINIMUM : mero, esencial — **barefaced** ['bær,feɪst] *adj* : descarado — **barefoot** ['bær,fʊt] *or* **barefooted** [-,fʊtəd] *adv & adj* : descalzo — **barely** ['bærli] *adv* : apenas, por poco

bargain ['bargən] *n* 1 AGREEMENT : acuerdo *m* 2 BUY : ganga *f* — ~ *vi* 1 : regatear, negociar 2 ~ **for** : contar con

barge ['bardʒ] *n* : barcaza *f* — ~ *vi* **barged; barging** ~ **in** : entrometerse, interrumpir

baritone ['bærə,to:n] *n* : barítono *m*

bark[1] ['bark] *vi* : ladrar — ~ *n* : ladrido *m* (de un perro)

bark[2] *n* : corteza *f* (de un árbol)

barley ['barli] *n* : cebada *f*

barn ['barn] *n* : granero *m* — **barnyard** ['barn,jard] *n* : corral *m*

barometer [bə'ramətər] *n* : barómetro *m*

baron ['bærən] *n* : barón *m* — **baroness** ['bærənis, -,nəs, -,nɛs] *n* : baronesa *f*

barracks ['bærəks] *ns & pl* : cuartel *m*

barrage [bə'raʒ, -radʒ] *n* 1 : descarga *f* (de artillería) 2 : aluvión *m* (de preguntas, etc.)

barrel ['bærəl] *n* 1 : barril *m*, tonel *m* 2 : cañón *m* (de un arma de fuego)

barren ['bærən] *adj* : estéril

barricade ['bærə,keɪd, ,bærə'-] *vt* **-caded; -cading** : cerrar con barricadas — ~ *n* : barricada *f*

barrier ['bæriər] *n* : barrera *f*

barring ['barɪŋ] *prep* : salvo

barrio ['bario, 'bær-] *n* : barrio *m*

bartender ['bɑr,tɛndər] *n* : camarero *m*, -ra *f*

barter ['bɑrtər] *vt* : cambiar, trocar — ~ *n* : trueque *m*

base ['beɪs] *n, pl* **bases** : base *f* — ~ *vt* **based; basing** : basar, fundamentar — ~ *adj* **baser; basest** : vil

baseball ['beɪs,bɔl] *n* : beisbol *m*, béisbol *m*

basement ['beɪsmənt] *n* : sótano *m*

bash ['bæʃ] *vt* : golpear violentamente — ~ *n* **1** BLOW : golpe *m* **2** PARTY : fiesta *f*

bashful ['bæʃfəl] *adj* : tímido, vergonzoso

basic ['beɪsɪk] *adj* : básico, fundamental — **basically** ['beɪsɪkli] *adv* : fundamentalmente

basil ['beɪzəl, 'bæzəl] *n* : albahaca *f*

basin ['beɪsən] *n* **1** WASHBOWL : palangana *f*, lavabo *m* **2** : cuenca *f* (de un río)

basis ['beɪsəs] *n, pl* **bases** [-,siːz] : base *f*

bask ['bæsk] *vi* ~ **in the sun** : tostarse al sol

basket ['bæskət] *n* : cesta *f*, cesto *m* — **basketball** ['bæskət,bɔl] *n* : baloncesto *m*, basquetbol *m Lat*

bass[1] ['bæs] *n, pl* **bass** *or* **basses** : róbalo *m* (pesca)

bass[2] ['beɪs] *n* : bajo *m* (tono, voz, instrumento)

bassoon [bə'suːn, bæ-] *n* : fagot *m*

bastard ['bæstərd] *n* : bastardo *m*, -da *f*

baste ['beɪst] *vt* **basted; basting 1** STITCH : hilvanar **2** : bañar (carne)

bat[1] ['bæt] *n* : murciélago *m* (animal)

bat[2] *n* : bate *m* — ~ *vt* **batted; batting** : batear

batch ['bætʃ] *n* : hornada *f* (de pasteles, etc.), lote *m* (de mercancías), montón *m* (de trabajo), grupo *m* (de personas)

bath ['bæθ, 'bɑθ] *n, pl* **baths** ['bæðz, 'bæθs, 'bɑðz, 'bɑθs] **1** : baño *m* **2** BATHROOM : baño *m*, cuarto *m* de baño **3 take a** ~ : bañarse — **bathe** ['beɪð] *v* **bathed; bathing** *vt* : bañar, lavar — *vi* : bañarse — **bathrobe** ['bæθ,roːb] *n* : bata *f* (de baño) — **bathroom** ['bæθ,ruːm, -,rʊm] *n* : baño *m*, cuarto *m* de baño — **bathtub** ['bæθ,tʌb] *n* : bañera *f*, tina *f* (de baño)

baton [bə'tɑn] *n* : batuta *f*

battalion [bə'tæljən] *n* : batallón *m*

batter ['bæțər] *vt* **1** BEAT : golpear **2** MISTREAT : maltratar — ~ *n* **1** : masa *f* para rebozar **2** HITTER : bateador *m*, -dora *f*

battery ['bæțəri] *n, pl* **-teries** : batería *f*, pila *f* (de electricidad)

battle ['bæțəl] *n* **1** : batalla *f* **2** STRUGGLE : lucha *f* — ~ *vi* **-tled; -tling** : luchar — **battlefield** ['bæțəl,fiːld] *n* : campo *m* de batalla — **battleship** ['bæțəl,ʃɪp] *n* : acorazado *m*

bawl ['bɔl] *vi* : llorar a gritos

bay[1] ['beɪ] *n* INLET : bahía *f*

bay[2] *n or* ~ **leaf** : laurel *m*

bay[3] *vi* : aullar — ~ *n* : aullido *m*

bayonet [,beɪə'nɛt, 'beɪə,nɛt] *n* : bayoneta *f*

bay window *n* : ventana *f* en saliente

bazaar [bə'zɑr] *n* **1** : bazar *m* **2** SALE : venta *f* benéfica

be ['biː] *v* was ['wɔz, 'wɑz], **were** ['wər], **been** ['bɪn]; **being; am** ['æm], **is** ['ɪz], **are** ['ɑr] *vi* **1** : ser **2** (*expressing location*) : estar **3** (*expressing existence*) : ser, existir **4** (*expressing a state of being*) : estar, tener — *v impers* **1** (*indicating time*) : ser **2** (*indicating a condition*) : hacer, estar — *v aux* **1** (*expressing occurrence*) : ser **2** (*expressing possibility*) : poderse **3** (*expressing obligation*) : deber **4** (*expressing progression*) : estar

beach ['biːtʃ] *n* : playa *f*

beacon ['biːkən] *n* : faro *m*

bead ['biːd] *n* **1** : cuenta *f* **2** DROP : gota *f* **3** ~**s** *npl* NECKLACE : collar *m*

beak ['biːk] *n* : pico *m*

beam ['biːm] *n* **1** : viga *f* (de madera, etc.) **2** RAY : rayo *m* — ~ *vi* SHINE : brillar — *vt* BROADCAST : transmitir, emitir

bean ['biːn] *n* **1** : habichuela *f*, frijol *m* **2 coffee** ~ : grano *m* **3 string** ~ : judía *f*

bear[1] ['bær] *n, pl* **bears** *or* **bear** : oso *m*, osa *f*

bear[2] *v* **bore** ['bor], **borne** ['born]; **bearing** *vt* **1** CARRY : portar **2** ENDURE : soportar — *vi* ~ **right/left** : doble a la derecha/a la izquierda — **bearable** ['bærəbəl] *adj* : soportable

beard ['bɪrd] *n* : barba *f*

bearer ['bærər] *n* : portador *m*, -dora *f*

bearing ['bærɪŋ] *n* **1** MANNER : comportamiento *m* **2** SIGNIFICANCE : relacíon *f*, importancia *f* **3 get one's** ~**s** : orientarse

beast ['biːst] *n* : bestia *f*

beat ['biːt] *v* **beat; beaten** ['biːtən] *or* **beat; beating** *vt* **1** HIT : golpear **2** : batir (huevos, etc.) **3** DEFEAT : derrotar — *vi* : latir (dícese del corazón) — ~ *n* **1** : golpe *m* **2** : latido *m* (del corazón) **3** RHYTHM : ritmo *m*, tiempo *m* — **beating** ['biːtɪŋ] *n* **1** : paliza *f* **2** DEFEAT : derrota *f*

beauty ['bjuːṭi] *n, pl* **-ties** : belleza *f* — **beautiful** ['bjuːṭɪfəl] *adj* : hermoso, lindo — **beautifully** ['bjuːṭɪfəli] *adv* WONDERFULLY : maravillosamente — **beautify** ['bjuːṭɪˌfaɪ] *vt* **-fied; -fying** : embellecer

beaver ['biːvər] *n* : castor *m*

because [bɪˈkʌz, -ˈkɒz] *conj* : porque — **because of** *prep* : por, a causa de, debido a

beckon ['bekən] *vt* : llamar, hacer señas a — *vi* : hacer una seña

become [bɪˈkʌm] *v* **-came** [-ˈkeɪm]; **-come; -coming** *vi* : hacerse, ponerse — *vt* SUIT : favorecer — **becoming** [bɪˈkʌmɪŋ] *adj* 1 SUITABLE : apropiado 2 FLATTERING : favorecedor

bed ['bed] *n* 1 : cama *f* 2 : cauce *m* (de un río), fondo *m* (del mar) 3 : macizo *m* (de flores) 4 **go to ~** : irse a la cama — **bedclothes** ['bedˌkloːz, -ˌkloːðz] *npl* : ropa *f* de cama

bedlam ['bedləm] *n* : confusión *f*, caos *m*

bedraggled [bɪˈdrægəld] *adj* : desaliñado, sucio

bedridden ['bedˌrɪdən] *adj* : postrado en cama

bedroom ['bedˌruːm, -ˌrʊm] *n* : dormitorio *m*, recámara *f Lat*

bedspread ['bedˌspred] *n* : colcha *f*

bedtime ['bedˌtaɪm] *n* : hora *f* de acostarse

bee ['biː] *n* : abeja *f*

beech ['biːtʃ] *n, pl* **beeches** *or* **beech** : haya *f*

beef ['biːf] *n* : carne *f* de vaca, carne *f* de res *Lat* — **beefsteak** ['biːfˌsteɪk] *n* : bistec *m*

beehive ['biːˌhaɪv] *n* : colmena *f*

beeline ['biːˌlaɪn] *n* **make a ~ for** : irse derecho a

beep ['biːp] *n* : pitido *m* — **~** *v* : pitar

beer ['bɪr] *n* : cerveza *f*

beet ['biːt] *n* : remolacha *f*

beetle ['biːṭəl] *n* : escarabajo *m*

before [bɪˈfor] *adv* 1 : antes 2 **the month ~** : el mes anterior — **~** *prep* 1 (*in space*) : delante de, ante 2 (*in time*) : antes de — **~** *conj* : antes de que — **beforehand** [bɪˈforˌhænd] *adv* : antes

befriend [bɪˈfrend] *vt* : hacerse amigo de

beg ['beg] *v* **begged; begging** *vt* 1 : pedir, mendigar 2 ENTREAT : suplicar — *vi* : mendigar, pedir limosna — **beggar** ['begər] *n* : mendigo *m*, -ga *f*

begin [bɪˈgɪn] *v* **-gan** [-ˈgæn]; **-gun** [-ˈgʌn]; **-ginning** : empezar, comenzar — **beginner** [bɪˈgɪnər] *n* : principiante

mf — **beginning** [bɪˈgɪnɪŋ] *n* : principio *m*, comienzo *m*

begrudge [bɪˈgrʌdʒ] *vt* **-grudged; -grudging** 1 : dar de mala gana 2 ENVY : envidiar

behalf [bɪˈhæf, -ˈhaf] *n* **on ~ of** : de parte de, en nombre de

behave [bɪˈheɪv] *vi* **-haved; -having** : comportarse, portarse — **behavior** [bɪˈheɪvjər] *n* : comportamiento *m*, conducta *f*

behind [bɪˈhaɪnd] *adv* 1 : detrás 2 **fall ~** : atrasarse — **~** *prep* 1 : atrás de, detrás de 2 **be ~ schedule** : ir retrasado 3 **her friends are ~ her** : tiene el apoyo de sus amigos

behold [bɪˈhoːld] *vt* **-held; -holding** : contemplar

beige ['beɪʒ] *adj & nm* : beige

being ['biːɪŋ] *n* 1 : ser *m* 2 **come into ~** : nacer

belated [bɪˈleɪṭəd] *adj* : tardío

belch ['beltʃ] *vi* : eructar — **~** *n* : eructo *m*

Belgian ['beldʒən] *adj* : belga

belie [bɪˈlaɪ] *vt* **-lied; -lying** : contradecir, desmentir

belief [bəˈliːf] *n* 1 TRUST : confianza *f* 2 CONVICTION : creencia *f*, convicción *f* 3 FAITH : fe *f* — **believable** [bəˈliːvəbəl] *adj* : creíble — **believe** [bəˈliːv] *v* **-lieved; -lieving** : creer — **believer** [bəˈliːvər] *n* : creyente *mf*

belittle [bɪˈlɪṭəl] *vt* **-littled; -littling** : menospreciar

Belizean [bəˈliːziən] *adj* : beliceño *m*, -ña *f*

bell ['bel] *n* 1 : campana *f* 2 : timbre *m* (de teléfono, de la puerta, etc.)

belligerent [bəˈlɪdʒərənt] *adj* : beligerante

bellow ['beˌloː] *vi* : bramar, mugir — *vt or* **~ out** : gritar

bellows ['beˌloːz] *ns & pl* : fuelle *m*

belly ['beli] *n, pl* **-lies** : vientre *m*

belong [bɪˈlɔŋ] *vi* 1 **~ to** : pertenecer a, ser propiedad de 2 **~ to** : ser miembro de (un club, etc.) 3 **where does it ~** : ¿dónde va? — **belongings** [bɪˈlɔŋɪŋz] *npl* : pertenencias *fpl*, efectos *mpl* personales

beloved [bɪˈlʌvəd, -ˈlʌvd] *adj* : querido, amado — **~** *n* : querido *m*, -da *f*

below [bɪˈloː] *adv* : abajo — **~** *prep* 1 : abajo de, debajo de 2 **~ average** : por debajo del promedio 3 **~ zero** : bajo cero

belt ['belt] *n* 1 : cinturón *m* 2 BAND, STRAP : cinta *f*, correa *f* 3 AREA : frente *m,* zona *f* — ~ *vt* **1** : ceñir con un cinturón **2** THRASH : darle una paliza a

bench ['bentʃ] *n* **1** : banco *m* **2** WORK-BENCH : mesa *f* de trabajo **3** COURT : tribunal *m*

bend ['bend] *v* **bent** ['bent]; **bending** *vt* : doblar, torcer — *vi* **1** : torcerse **2** ~ **over** : inclinarse — ~ *n* : curva *f,* ángulo *m*

beneath [br'ni:θ] *adv* : abajo, debajo — ~ *prep* : bajo, debajo de

benediction [,benə'dıkʃən] *n* : bendición *f*

benefactor ['benə,fæktər] *n* : benefactor *m,* -tora *f*

benefit ['benəfıt] *n* **1** ADVANTAGE : ventaja *f,* provecho *m* **2** AID : asistencia *f,* beneficio *m* — ~ *vt* : beneficiar — *vi* : beneficiarse — **beneficial** [,benə-'fıʃəl] *adj* : beneficioso — **beneficiary** [,benə'fıʃi,eri, -'fıʃəri] *n, pl* **-ries** : beneficiario *m,* -ria *f*

benevolent [bə'nevələnt] *adj* : benévolo

benign [br'naın] *adj* **1** KIND : benévolo, amable **2** : benigno (en medicina)

bent ['bent] *adj* **1** : encorvado **2 be** ~ **on** : estar empeñado en — ~ *n* : aptitud *f,* inclinación *f*

bequeath [br'kwi:θ, -'kwi:ð] *vt* : legar — **bequest** [br'kwest] *n* : legado *m*

berate [br'reıt] *vt* **-rated; -rating** : reprender, regañar

bereaved [br'ri:vd] *adj* : desconsolado, a luto

beret [bə'reı] *n* : boina *f*

berry ['beri] *n, pl* **-ries** : baya *f*

berserk [bər'sərk, -'zərk] *adj* **1** : enloquecido **2 go** ~ : volverse loco

berth ['bərθ] *n* **1** MOORING : atracadero *m* **2** BUNK : litera *f*

beseech [br'si:tʃ] *vt* **-sought** [-'sɔt] *or* **-seeched; -seeching** : suplicar, implorar

beset [br'set] *vt* **-set; -setting 1** HARASS : acosar **2** SURROUND : rodear

beside [br'saıd] *prep* **1** : al lado de, junto a **2 be** ~ **oneself** : estar fuera de sí — **besides** [br'saıdz] *adv* : además — ~ *prep* **1** : además de **2** EXCEPT : excepto

besiege [br'si:dʒ] *vt* **-sieged; -sieging** : asediar

best ['best] *adj (superlative of* **good***)* : mejor — ~ *adv (superlative of* **well***)* : mejor — ~ *n* **1 at** ~ : a lo más **2 do one's** ~ : hacer todo lo posible **3 the** ~ : lo mejor — **best man** *n* : padrino *m* (de boda)

bestow [br'sto:] *vt* : otorgar, conceder

bet ['bet] *n* : apuesta *f* — ~ *v* **bet; bet-**

ting *vt* : apostar — *vi* ~ **on sth** : apostarle a algo

betray [br'treı] *vt* : traicionar — **betrayal** [br'treıəl] *n* : traición *f*

better ['betər] *adj (comparative of* **good***)* **1** : mejor **2 get** ~ : mejorar — ~ *adv (comparative of* **well***)* **1** : mejor **2 all the** ~ : tanto mejor — ~ *n* **1 the** ~ : el mejor, la mejor **2 get the** ~ **of** : vencer a — ~ *vt* **1** IM-PROVE : mejorar **2** SURPASS : superar

between [br'twi:n] *prep* : entre — ~ *adv or* **in** ~ : en medio

beverage ['bevrıdʒ, 'bevə-] *n* : bebida *f*

beware [br'wær] *vi* ~ **of** : tener cuidado con

bewilder [br'wıldər] *vt* : desconcertar — **bewilderment** [br'wıldərmənt] *n* : desconcierto *m*

bewitch [br'wıtʃ] *vt* : hechizar, encantar

beyond [br'jand] *adv* : más allá, más lejos (en el espacio), más adelante (en el tiempo) — ~ *prep* : más allá de

bias ['baıəs] *n* **1** PREJUDICE : prejuicio *m* **2** TENDENCY : inclinación *f,* tendencia *f* — **biased** ['baıəst] *adj* : parcial

bib ['bıb] *n* : babero *m* (para niños)

Bible ['baıbəl] *n* : Biblia *f* — **biblical** ['bıblıkəl] *adj* : bíblico

bibliography [,bıbli'agrəfi] *n, pl* **-phies** : bibliografía *f*

bicarbonate of soda [,baı'karbənət, ,neıt] *n* : bicarbonato *m* de soda

biceps ['baı,seps] *ns & pl* : bíceps *m*

bicker ['bıkər] *vi* : reñir

bicycle ['baısıkəl, -sı-] *n* : bicicleta *f* — ~ *vi* **-cled; -cling** : ir en bicicleta

bid ['bıd] *vt* **bade** ['bæd, 'beıd] *or* **bid; bidden** ['bıdən] *or* **bid; bidding 1** OFFER : ofrecer **2** ~ **farewell** : decir adios — ~ *n* **1** OFFER : oferta *f* **2** AT-TEMPT : intento *m,* tentativa *f*

bide ['baıd] *vt* **bode** ['bo:d] *or* **bided; bided; biding** ~ **one's time** : esperar el momento oportuno

bifocals ['baı,fo:kəlz] *npl* : anteojos *mpl* bifocales

big ['bıg] *adj* **bigger; biggest** : grande

bigamy ['bıgəmi] *n* : bigamía *f*

bigot ['bıgət] *n* : intolerante *mf* — **bigotry** ['bıgətri] *n, pl* **-tries** : intolerancia *f,* fanatismo *m*

bike ['baık] *n* **1** BICYCLE : bici *f fam* **2** MOTORCYCLE : moto *f*

bikini [bə'ki:ni] *n* : bikini *m*

bile ['baıl] *n* : bilis *f*

bilingual [baı'lıŋgwəl] *adj* : bilingüe

bill ['bıl] *n* **1** BEAK : pico *m* **2** INVOICE : cuenta *f,* factura *f* **3** BANKNOTE : billete *m* **4** LAW : proyecto *m* de ley, ley *f*

— ~ vt : pasarle la cuenta a — **bill-board** ['bɪl,bɔrd] n : cartelera f — **bill-fold** ['bɪl,fo:ld] n : billetera f, cartera f

billiards ['bɪljərdz] n : billar m

billion ['bɪljən] n, pl **billions** or **billion** : mil millones mpl

billow ['bɪlo] vi : ondular, hincharse

billy goat ['bɪli,go:t] n : macho m cabrío

bin ['bɪn] n : cubo m, cajón m

binary ['baɪnəri, -,neri] adj : binario m

bind ['baɪnd] vt **bound** ['baʊnd]; **bind-ing 1** TIE : atar **2** OBLIGATE : obligar **3** UNITE : unir **4** BANDAGE : vendar **5** : encuadernar (un libro) — **binder** ['baɪndər] n FOLDER : carpeta f — **bind-ing** ['baɪndɪŋ] n : encuadernación f (de libros)

binge ['bɪndʒ] n : juerga f fam

bingo ['bɪŋgo:] n, pl **-gos** : bingo m

binoculars [bə'nɑkjələrz, baɪ-] npl : binoculares mpl, gemelos mpl

biochemistry [,baɪo'kemɪstri] n : bioquímica f

biography [baɪ'ɑgrəfi, bi:-] n, pl **-phies** : biografía f — **biographer** [baɪ-'ɑgrəfər] n : biógrafo m, -fa f — **bio-graphical** [,baɪə'græfɪkəl] adj : biográfico

biology [baɪ'ɑlədʒi] n : biología f — **bio-logical** [-dʒɪkəl] adj : biológico — **biologist** [baɪ'ɑlədʒɪst] n : biólogo m, -ga f

birch ['bərtʃ] n : abedul m

bird ['bərd] n : pájaro m (pequeño), ave f (grande)

birth ['bərθ] n **1** : nacimiento m, parto m **2** give ~ to : dar a luz a — **birthday** ['bərθ,deɪ] n : cumpleaños m — **birth-mark** ['bərθ,mɑrk] n : mancha f de nacimiento — **birthplace** ['bərθ,pleɪs] n : lugar m de nacimiento — **birthrate** ['bərθ,reɪt] n : índice m de natalidad

biscuit ['bɪskət] n : bizcocho m

bisect ['baɪ,sekt, ,baɪ-] vt : bisecar

bisexual [,baɪ'sekʃəwəl, -'sekʃəl] adj : bisexual

bishop ['bɪʃəp] n : obispo m

bison ['baɪzən, -sən] ns & pl : bisonte m

bit¹ ['bɪt] n : bocado m (de una brida)

bit² ['bɪt] n **1** : trozo m, pedazo m **2** : bit m (de información) **3 a** ~ : un poco

bitch ['bɪtʃ] n : perra f — ~ vi COMPLAIN : quejarse, reclamar

bite ['baɪt] v bit ['bɪt]; **bitten** ['bɪtən]; **bit-ing** vt **1** : morder **2** STING : picar — vi : morder — n **1** : picadura f (de un insecto), mordedura f (de un animal) **2** SNACK : bocado m — **biting** adj **1** PENE-TRATING : cortante, penetrante **2** CAUSTIC : mordaz

bitter ['bɪtər] adj **1** : amargo **2 it's** ~ **cold** : hace un frío glacial **3 to the** ~ **end** : hasta el final — **bitterness** ['bɪtərnəs] n : amargura f

bizarre [bə'zɑr] adj : extraño

black ['blæk] adj : negro — ~ n **1** : negro m (color) **2** : negro m, -gra f (persona) — **black–and–blue** [,blækən'blu:] adj : amoratado — **black-berry** ['blæk,beri] n, pl **-ries** : mora f — **blackbird** ['blæk,bərd] n : mirlo m — **blackboard** ['blæk,bɔrd] n : pizarra f, pizarrón m Lat — **blacken** ['blækən] vt : ennegrecer — **blackmail** ['blæk,meɪl] n : chantaje m — ~ vt : chantajear — **black market** n : mercado m negro — **blackout** ['blæk,aʊt] n **1** : apagón m (de poder eléctrico) **2** FAINT : desmayo m — **blacksmith** ['blæk,smɪθ] n : herrero m — **blacktop** ['blæk,tɑp] n : asfalto m

bladder ['blædər] n : vejiga f

blade ['bleɪd] n **1** : hoja f (de un cuchillo), cuchilla f (de un patín) **2** : pala f (de un remo, una hélice, etc.) **3** ~ **of grass** : brizna f (de hierba)

blame ['bleɪm] vt **blamed; blaming** : culpar, echar la culpa a — ~ n : culpa f — **blameless** ['bleɪmləs] adj : inocente

bland ['blænd] adj : soso, insulso

blank ['blæŋk] adj **1** : en blanco (dícese de un papel), liso (dícese de una pared) **2** EMPTY : vacío — ~ n : espacio m en blanco

blanket ['blæŋkət] n **1** : manta f, cobija f Lat **2** ~ **of snow** : manto m de nieve — ~ vt : cubrir

blare ['blær] vi **blared; blaring** : resonar

blasphemy ['blæsfəmi] n, pl **-mies** : blasfemia f

blast ['blæst] n **1** GUST : ráfaga f **2** EX-PLOSION : explosión f **3** : toque m (de trompeta, etc.) — ~ vt BLOW UP : volar — **blast-off** ['blæst,ɔf] n : despegue m

blatant ['bleɪtənt] adj : descarado

blaze ['bleɪz] n **1** FIRE : fuego m **2** BRIGHTNESS : resplandor m, brillantez f **3** ~ **of anger** : arranque m de cólera — ~ v **blazed; blazing** vi : arder, brillar — vt ~ **a trail** : abrir un camino

blazer ['bleɪzər] n : chaqueta f deportiva

bleach ['bli:tʃ] vt : blanquear, decolorar — ~ n : lejía f, blanqueador m Lat

bleachers ['bli:tʃərz] ns & pl : gradas fpl

bleak ['bli:k] adj **1** DESOLATE : desolado **2** GLOOMY : triste, sombrío

bleary–eyed ['blɪri,aɪd] adj : con los ojos nublados

bleat ['bli:t] vi : balar — ~ n : balido m

bleed ['bliːd] *v* **bled** ['blɛd]; **bleeding**
: sangrar
blemish ['blɛmɪʃ] *vt* : manchar, marcar
— ~ *n* : mancha *f*, marca *f*
blend ['blɛnd] *vt* : mezclar, combinar —
~ *n* : mezcla *f*, combinación *f* —
blender ['blɛndər] *n* : licuadora *f*
bless ['blɛs] *vt* **blessed** ['blɛst]; **blessing** : bendecir — **blessed** ['blɛsəd] *or*
blest ['blɛst] *adj* : bendito — **blessing**
['blɛsɪŋ] *n* : bendición *f*
blew → **blow**
blind ['blaɪnd] *adj* : ciego — ~ *vt* 1
: cegar, dejar ciego 2 DAZZLE : deslumbrar — ~ *n* 1 : persiana *f* (para una
ventana) 2 **the** ~ : los ciegos —
blindfold ['blaɪndˌfoːld] *vt* : vendar los
ojos — ~ *n* : venda *f* (para los ojos)
— **blindly** ['blaɪndli] *adv* : ciegamente
— **blindness** ['blaɪndnəs] *n* : ceguera *f*
blink ['blɪŋk] *vi* 1 : parpadear 2 FLICKER
: brillar intermitentemente — ~ *n*
: parpadeo *m* — **blinker** ['blɪŋkər] *n*
: intermitente *m*, direccional *f Lat*
bliss ['blɪs] *n* : dicha *f*, felicidad *f* (abso-
luta) — **blissful** ['blɪsfəl] *adj* : feliz
blister ['blɪstər] *n* : ampolla *f* — ~ *vi*
: ampollarse
blitz ['blɪts] *n* : bombardeo *m* aéreo
blizzard ['blɪzərd] *n* : ventisca *f* (de
nieve)
bloated ['bloːtəd] *adj* : hinchado
blob ['blɑb] *n* 1 DROP : gota *f* 2 SPOT
: mancha *f*
block ['blɑk] *n* 1 : bloque *m* 2 OBSTRUC-
TION : obstrucción *f* 3 : manzana *f*,
cuadra *f Lat* (de edificios) 4 *or* **building** ~ : cubo *m* de construcción — ~
vt : obstruir, bloquear — **blockade**
[blɑˈkeɪd] *n* : bloqueo *m* — **blockage**
['blɑkɪdʒ] *n* : obstrucción *f*
blond *or* **blonde** ['blɑnd] *adj* : rubio —
~ *n* : rubio *m*, -bia *f*
blood ['blʌd] *n* : sangre *f* — **bloodhound** ['blʌdˌhaʊnd] *n* : sabueso *m* —
blood pressure *n* : tensión *f* (arterial)
— **bloodshed** ['blʌdˌʃɛd] *n* : derramamiento *m* de sangre — **bloodshot**
['blʌdˌʃɑt] *adj* : inyectado de sangre —
bloodstained ['blʌdˌsteɪnd] *adj* : man-
chado de sangre — **bloodstream**
['blʌdˌstriːm] *n* : sangre *f*, torrente *m*
sanguíneo — **bloody** ['blʌdi] *adj*
bloodier; -est : ensangrentado, sangriento
bloom ['bluːm] *n* 1 : flor *f* 2 **in full** ~
: en plena floración — ~ *vi* : florecer
blossom ['blɑsəm] *n* : flor *f* — ~ *vi*
: florecer
blot ['blɑt] *n* 1 : borrón *m* (de tinta, etc.)

2 BLEMISH : mancha *f* — ~ *vt* **blotted;
blotting** 1 : emborronar 2 DRY : secar
blotch ['blɑtʃ] *n* : mancha *f*, borrón *m* —
blotchy ['blɑtʃi] *adj* **blotchier; -est**
: lleno de manchas
blouse ['blaʊs, 'blaʊz] *n* : blusa *f*
blow ['bloː] *v* **blew** ['bluː], **blown** ['bloːn];
blowing *vi* 1 : soplar 2 SOUND : sonar
3 *or* ~ **out** : fundirse (dícese de un
fusible eléctrico), reventarse (dícese
de una llanta) — *vt* 1 : soplar 2 SOUND
: tocar, sonar 3 BUNGLE : echar a
perder — ~ *n* : golpe *m* — **blowout**
['bloːˌaʊt] *n* : reventón *m* — **blow up** *vi*
: estallar, hacer explosión — *vt* 1 EX-
PLODE : volar 2 INFLATE : inflar
blubber ['blʌbər] *n* : esperma *f* de ballena
bludgeon ['blʌdʒən] *vt* : aporrear
blue ['bluː] *adj* **bluer; bluest** 1 : azul 2
MELANCHOLY : triste — ~ *n* : azul *m*
— **blueberry** ['bluːˌbɛri] *n, pl* **-ries**
: arándano *m* — **bluebird** ['bluːˌbərd] *n*
: azulejo *m* — **blue cheese** *n* : queso
m azul — **blueprint** ['bluːˌprɪnt] *n* PLAN
: proyecto *m* — **blues** ['bluːz] *npl* 1
SADNESS : tristeza *f* 2 : blues *m* (en
música)
bluff ['blʌf] *vi* : hacer un farol — ~ *n*
: farol *m*
blunder ['blʌndər] *vi* : meter la pata *fam*
— ~ *n* : metedura *f* de pata *fam*
blunt ['blʌnt] *adj* 1 DULL : desafilado 2
DIRECT : directo, franco
blur ['blər] *n* : imágen *f* borrosa — ~ *vt*
blurred; blurring : hacer borroso
blurb ['blərb] *n* : nota *f* publicitaria
blurt ['blərt] *vt or* ~ **out** : espetar
blush ['blʌʃ] *n* : rubor *m* — ~ *vi* : ruborizarse
blustery ['blʌstəri] *adj* : borrascoso,
tempestuoso
boar ['bor] *n* : cerdo *m* macho
board ['bord] *n* 1 PLANK : tabla *f*, tablón
m 2 COMMITTEE : junta *f*, consejo *m* 3
: tablero *m* (de juegos) 4 **room and** ~
: comida y alojamiento — ~ *vt* 1
: subir a bordo de (una nave, un avión,
etc.), subir a (un tren) 2 LODGE
: hospedar 3 ~ **up** : cerrar con tablas
— **boarder** ['bordər] *n* : huésped *mf*
boast ['boːst] *n* : jactancia *f* — ~ *vi*
: alardear, jactarse — **boastful**
['boːstfəl] *adj* : jactancioso
boat ['boːt] *n* : barco *m* (grande), barca *f*
(pequeña)
bob ['bɑb] *vi* **bobbed; bobbing** *or* ~
up and down : subir y bajar
bobbin ['bɑbən] *n* : bobina *f*, carrete *m*
bobby pin ['bɑbiˌpɪn] *n* : horquilla *f*

body ['bɑdi] *n, pl* **bodies 1** : cuerpo *m* **2**
CORPSE : cadáver *m* **3** : carrocería (de
un automóvil, etc.) **4** COLLECTION
: conjunto *m* **5** ~ **of water** : masa *f* de
agua — **bodily** *adj* : corporal — **body-**
guard ['bɑdi,gɑrd] *n* : guardaespaldas
mf

bog ['bɑg, 'bɔg] *n* : ciénaga *f* — ~ *vi*
bogged; bogging *or* ~ **down** : em-
pantanarse

bogus ['boːgəs] *adj* : falso

boil ['bɔɪl] *v* : hervir — **boiler** ['bɔɪlər] *n*
: caldera *f*

bold ['boːld] *adj* **1** DARING : audaz **2** IM-
PUDENT : descarado — **boldness**
['boːldnəs] *n* : audacia *f*

Bolivian [bə'lɪviən] *adj* : boliviano *m*,
-na *f*

bologna [bə'loːni] *n* : salchicha *f* ahuma-
da

bolster ['boːlstər] *vt* **-stered; -stering** *or*
~ **up** : reforzar

bolt ['boːlt] *n* **1** LOCK : cerrojo *m* **2** SCREW
: tornillo *m* **3** ~ **of lightning** : relámpago *m*, rayo *m* — ~ *vt* **1** FASTEN
: atornillar **2** LOCK : echar el cerrojo a
— *vi* FLEE : salir corriendo

bomb ['bɑm] *n* : bomba *f* — ~ *vt*
: bombardear — **bombard** [bɑm'bɑrd,
bəm-] *vt* : bombardear — **bombard-**
ment [bɑm'bɑrdmənt] *n* : bombardeo
m — **bomber** ['bɑmər] *n* : bombardero
m

bond ['bɑnd] *n* **1** TIE : vínculo *m*, lazo *m*
2 SURETY : fianza *f* **3** : bono *m* (en finanzas) — ~ *vi* STICK : adherirse

bondage ['bɑndɪʤ] *n* : esclavitud *f*

bone ['boːn] *n* : hueso *m* — ~ *vt*
boned; boning : deshuesar

bonfire ['bɑn,faɪr] *n* : hoguera *f*

bonus ['boːnəs] *n* **1** PAY : prima *f* **2** BEN-
EFIT : beneficio *m* adicional

bony ['boːni] *adj* **bonier; -est 1** : huesudo **2** : lleno de espinas (dícese de
pescados)

boo ['buː] *n, pl* **boos** : abucheo *m* — ~
vt : abuchear

book ['bʊk] *n* **1** : libro *m* **2** NOTEBOOK
: libreta *f*, cuaderno *m* — ~ *vt* : reservar — **bookcase** ['bʊk,keɪs] *n* : estantería *f* — **bookkeeping** ['bʊk,kiːpɪŋ] *n*
: teneduría *f* de libros, contabilidad *f*
— **booklet** ['bʊklət] *n* : folleto *m* —
bookmark ['bʊk,mɑrk] *n* : marcador *m*
de libros — **bookseller** ['bʊk,sɛlər] *n*
: librero *m*, -ra *f* — **bookshelf** ['bʊk-
,ʃɛlf] *n, pl* **-shelves** : estante *m* —
bookstore ['bʊk,stor] *n* : librería *f*

boom ['buːm] *vi* **1** : tronar, resonar **2**
PROSPER : estar en auge, prosperar —

~ *n* **1** : bramido *m*, estruendo *m* **2**
: auge *m* (económico)

boon ['buːn] *n* : ayuda *f*, beneficio *m*

boost ['buːst] *vt* **1** LIFT : levantar **2** IN-
CREASE : aumentar — ~ *n* **1** INCREASE
: aumento *m* **2** ENCOURAGEMENT : estímulo *m*

boot ['buːt] *n* : bota *f*, botín *m* — ~ *vt* **1**
: dar una patada a **2** *or* ~ **up** : cargar
(un ordenador)

booth ['buːθ] *n, pl* **booths** ['buːðz, 'buːθs]
: cabina *f* (de teléfono, de votar), caseta *f* (de información)

booty ['buːti] *n, pl* **-ties** : botín *m*

booze ['buːz] *n* : trago *m*, bebida *f* (alco-
hólica)

border ['bɔrdər] *n* **1** EDGE : borde *m*,
orilla *f* **2** TRIM : ribete *m* **3** FRONTIER
: frontera *f*

bore¹ ['bor] *vt* **bored; boring** DRILL : taladrar

bore² *vt* TIRE : aburrir — ~ *n* : pesado
m, -da *fam f* (persona), lata *f fam*
(cosa, situación) — **boredom** ['bor-
dəm] *n* : aburrimiento *m* — **boring**
['borɪŋ] *adj* : aburrido, pesado

born ['bɔrn] *adj* **1** : nacido **2 be** ~
: nacer

borough ['bəro] *n* : distrito *m* municipal

borrow ['bɑro] *vt* : pedir prestado, tomar
prestado

Bosnian ['bɑzniən, 'bɔz-] *adj* : bosnio *m*,
-nia *f*

bosom ['bʊzəm, 'buː-] *n* **1** BREAST : pecho
m, seno *m* — ~ *adj* ~ **friend** : amigo
m íntimo

boss ['bɔs] *n* : jefe *m*, -fa *f*; patrón *m*,
-trona *f* — ~ *vt* SUPERVISE : dirigir —
bossy ['bɔsi] *adj* **bossier; -est** : autoritario

botany ['bɑtəni] *n* : botánica *f* — **botan-**
ical [bə'tænɪkəl] *adj* : botánico

botch ['bɑtʃ] *vt* : hacer una chapuza de,
estropear

both ['boːθ] *adj* : ambos, los dos, las dos
— ~ *pron* : ambos *m*, -bas *f*; los dos,
las dos

bother ['bɑðər] *vt* **1** TROUBLE : preocupar
2 PESTER : molestar, fastidiar — *vi* ~
to : molestarse en — ~ *n* : molestia *f*

bottle ['bɑtəl] *n* **1** : botella *f*, frasco *m* **2**
or **baby** ~ : biberón *m* — ~ *vt* **bot-**
tled; bottling : embotellar — **bottle-**
neck ['bɑtəl,nɛk] *n* : embotellamiento
m

bottom ['bɑtəm] *n* **1** : fondo *m* (de una
caja, del mar, etc.), pie *m* (de una escalera, una montaña, etc.), final *m* (de
una lista) **2** BUTTOCKS : nalgas *fpl*,
trasero *m* — ~ *adj* : más bajo, inferi-

or, de abajo — **bottomless** ['bɑt̬əmləs]
adj : sin fondo
bough ['bau] *n* : rama *f*
bought → **buy**
bouillon ['buːjɑn; 'buljɑn, -jən] *n* : caldo
m
boulder ['boːldər] *n* : canto *m* rodado
boulevard ['buləˌvɑrd, 'buː-] *n* : bulevar *m*
bounce ['baunts] *v* **bounced; bouncing** *vt* : hacer rebotar — *vi* : rebotar —
~ *n* : rebote *m*
bound[1] ['baund] *adj* **be** ~ **for** : ir rumbo
a
bound[2] *adj* **1** OBLIGED : obligado **2** DETERMINED : decidido **3** **be** ~ **to** : tener que
bound[3] *n* **out of** ~**s** : (en) zona prohibida — **boundary** ['baundri, -dəri] *n*,
pl **-aries** : límite *m* — **boundless**
['baundləs] *adj* : sin límites
bouquet [boːˈkei, buː-] *n* : ramo *m*
bourgeois ['burˌʒwɑ, burˈʒwɑ] *adj* : burgués
bout ['baut] *n* **1** : combate *m* (en deportes) **2** : ataque *m* (de una enfermedad) **3** : período *m* (de actividad)
bow[1] ['bau] *vi* : inclinarse — *vt* ~
one's head : inclinar la cabeza — ~
['bau] *n* : reverencia *f*, inclinación *f*
bow[2] ['boː] *n* **1** : arco *m* **2** **tie a** ~
: hacer un lazo
bow[3] ['bau] *n* : proa *f* (de un barco)
bowels ['bauəlz] *npl* **1** : intestinos *mpl* **2**
DEPTHS : entrañas *fpl*
bowl[1] ['boːl] *n* : tazón *m*, cuenco *m*
bowl[2] *vi* : jugar a los bolos — **bowling**
['boːlɪŋ] *n* : bolos *mpl*
box[1] ['bɑks] *n* *vi* FIGHT : boxear — **boxer**
['bɑksər] *n* : boxeador *m*, -dora *f* —
boxing ['bɑksɪŋ] *n* : boxeo *m*
box[2] *n* **1** : caja *f*, cajón *m* **2** : palco *m* (en
el teatro) — ~ *vt* : empaquetar — **box
office** *n* : taquilla *f*, boletería *f* Lat
boy ['bɔi] *n* : niño *m*, chico *m*
boycott ['bɔiˌkɑt] *vt* : boicotear — ~ *n*
: boicot *m*
boyfriend ['bɔiˌfrend] *n* : novio *m*
bra ['brɑ] → **brassiere**
brace ['breis] *n* **1** SUPPORT : abrazadera *f*
2 ~**s** *npl* : aparatos *mpl* (para dientes)
— ~ *vi* ~ **oneself for** : prepararse
para
bracelet ['breis[l]ət] *n* : brazalete *m*
bracket ['brækət] *n* **1** SUPPORT : soporte
m **2** : corchete *m* (marca de puntuación) **3** CATEGORY : categoría *f* —
~ *vt* **1** : poner entre corchetes **2** CATEGORIZE : catalogar
brag ['bræg] *vi* **bragged; bragging**
: jactarse

braid ['breid] *vt* : trenzar — ~ *n* : trenza *f*
braille ['breil] *n* : braille *m*
brain ['brein] *n* **1** : cerebro *m* **2** ~**s** *npl*
: inteligencia *f* — **brainstorm** ['breinˌstɔrm] *n* : idea *f* genial — **brainwash**
['breinˌwɑʃ, -ˌwɔʃ] *vt* : lavar el cerebro
— **brainy** ['breini] *adj* **brainier; -est**
: inteligente, listo
brake ['breik] *n* : freno *m* — ~ *v*
braked; braking : frenar
bramble ['bræmbəl] *n* : zarza *f*
bran ['bræn] *n* : salvado *m*
branch ['bræntʃ] *n* **1** : rama *f* (de una
planta) **2** DIVISION : ramal *m* (de un
camino, etc.), sucursal *f* (de una empresa), agencia *f* (del gobierno) — ~
vi *or* ~ **off** : ramificarse, bifurcarse
brand ['brænd] *n* **1** : marca *f* (de ganado)
2 *or* ~ **name** : marca *f* de fábrica —
~ *vt* **1** : marcar (ganado) **2** LABEL
: tachar, tildar
brandish ['brændɪʃ] *vt* : blandir
brand–new ['brændˌnuː, -ˈnjuː] *adj* : flamante
brandy ['brændi] *n*, *pl* **-dies** : brandy *m*,
coñac *m*
brass ['bræs] *n* **1** : latón *m* **2** : metales
mpl (de una orquesta)
brassiere [brəˈzɪr, brɑ-] *n* : sostén *m*,
brasier *m* Lat
brat ['bræt] *n* : mocoso *m*, -sa *f* fam
bravado [brəˈvɑdo] *n*, *pl* **-does** *or* **-dos**
: bravuconadas *fpl*
brave ['breiv] *adj* **braver; bravest** : valiente, valeroso — ~ *vt* **braved;
braving** : afrontar, hacer frente a —
~ *n* : guerrero *m* indio — **bravery**
['breivəri] *n* : valor *m*, valentía *f*
brawl ['brɔl] *n* : pelea *f*, reyerta *f*
brawn ['brɔn] *n* : músculos *mpl* —
brawny ['brɔni] *adj* **brawnier; -est**
: musculoso
bray ['brei] *vi* : rebuznar
brazen ['breizən] *adj* : descarado
Brazilian [brəˈzɪljən] *adj* : brasileño *m*,
-ña *f*
breach ['briːtʃ] *n* **1** VIOLATION : infracción *f*, violación *f* **2** GAP : brecha *f*
bread ['bred] *n* **1** : pan *m* **2** ~ **crumbs**
: migajas *fpl*
breadth ['bretθ] *n* : anchura *f*
break ['breik] *v* **broke** ['broːk]; **broken**
['broːkən]; **breaking** *vt* **1** : romper,
quebrar **2** VIOLATE : infringir, violar **3**
INTERRUPT : interrumpir **4** SURPASS
: batir (un récord, etc.) **5** ~ **a habit**
: quitarse una costumbre **6** ~ **the
news** : dar la noticia — *vi* **1**
: romperse, quebrarse **2** ~ **away** : es

capar 3 ~ **down** : estropearse (dícese de una máquina), fallar (dícese de un sistema, etc.) 4 ~ **into** : entrar en 5 ~ **off** : interrumpirse 6 ~ **out of** : escaparse de 7 ~ **up** SEPARATE : separarse — ~ n 1 : ruptura f, fractura f 2 GAP : interrupción f, claro m (entre las nubes) 3 **lucky** ~ : golpe m de suerte 4 **take a** ~ : tomar(se) un descanso — **breakable** ['breɪkəbəl] adj : quebradizo, frágil — **breakdown** ['breɪk-ˌdaʊn] n 1 : avería f (de máquinas), interrupción f (de comunicaciones), fracaso m (de negociaciones) 2 or **nervous** ~ : crisis f nerviosa

breakfast ['brɛkfəst] n : desayuno m

breast ['brɛst] n 1 : seno m (de una mujer) 2 CHEST : pecho m — **breast–feed** ['brɛstˌfiːd] vt -fed [-ˌfɛd]; -feeding : amamantar

breath ['brɛθ] n : aliento m, respiración f — **breathe** ['briːð] v breathed; breathing : respirar — **breathless** ['brɛθləs] adj : sin aliento, jadeante — **breathtaking** ['brɛθˌteɪkɪŋ] adj : impresionante

breed ['briːd] v bred ['brɛd]; breeding vt 1 : criar (animales) 2 ENGENDER : engendrar, producir — vi : reproducirse — ~ n 1 : raza f 2 CLASS : clase f, tipo m

breeze ['briːz] n : brisa f — **breezy** ['briːzi] adj breezier; -est 1 WINDY : ventoso 2 NONCHALANT : despreocupado

brevity ['brɛvəti] n, pl -ties : brevedad f

brew ['bruː] vt : hacer (cerveza, etc.), preparar (té) — vi 1 : fabricar cerveza 2 : amenazar (dícese de una tormenta) — **brewery** ['bruːəri, 'bruri] n, pl -eries : cervecería f

bribe ['braɪb] n : soborno m — ~ vt bribed; bribing : sobornar — **bribery** ['braɪbəri] n, pl -eries : soborno m

brick ['brɪk] n : ladrillo m — **bricklayer** ['brɪkˌleɪər] n : albañil mf

bride ['braɪd] n : novia f — **bridal** ['braɪdəl] adj : nupcial, de novia — **bridegroom** ['braɪdˌgruːm] n : novio m — **bridesmaid** ['braɪdzˌmeɪd] n : dama f de honor

bridge ['brɪdʒ] n 1 : puente m 2 : caballete m (de la nariz) 3 : bridge m (juego de naipes) — ~ vt bridged; bridging 1 : tender un puente sobre 2 ~ **the gap** : salvar las diferencias

bridle ['braɪdəl] n : brida f — ~ vt -dled; -dling : embridar

brief ['briːf] adj : breve — ~ n 1 : resumen m, sumario m 2 ~**s** npl UN-

DERPANTS : calzoncillos mpl — ~ vt : dar órdenes a, instruir — **briefcase** ['briːfˌkeɪs] n : portafolio m, maletín m — **briefly** ['briːfli] adv : brevemente

bright ['braɪt] adj 1 : brillante, claro 2 CHEERFUL : alegre, animado 3 INTELLIGENT : listo, inteligente — **brighten** ['braɪtən] vi 1 : hacerse más brillante 2 or ~ **up** : animarse, alegrarse — ~ vt 1 ILLUMINATE : iluminar 2 ENLIVEN : alegrar, animar

brilliant ['brɪljənt] adj : brillante — **brilliance** ['brɪljənts] n 1 BRIGHTNESS : resplandor m, brillantez f 2 INTELLIGENCE : inteligencia f

brim ['brɪm] n 1 : borde m (de una taza, etc.) 2 : ala f (de un sombrero) — ~ vi brimmed; brimming or ~ **over** : desbordarse, rebosar

brine ['braɪn] n : salmuera f

bring ['brɪŋ] vt brought ['brɔt]; bringing 1 : traer 2 ~ **about** : ocasionar 3 ~ **around** PERSUADE : convencer 4 ~ **back** : devolver 5 ~ **down** : derribar 6 ~ **on** CAUSE : provocar 7 ~ **out** : sacar 8 ~ **to an end** : terminar (con) 9 ~ **up** REAR : criar 10 ~ **up** MENTION : sacar

brink ['brɪŋk] n : borde m

brisk ['brɪsk] adj 1 FAST : rápido 2 LIVELY : enérgico

bristle ['brɪsəl] n : cerda f (de un animal), pelo m (de una planta) — ~ vi -tled; -tling : erizarse

British ['brɪtɪʃ] adj : británico

brittle ['brɪtəl] adj -tler; -tlest : frágil, quebradizo

broach ['broːtʃ] vt : abordar

broad ['brɔd] adj 1 WIDE : ancho 2 GENERAL : general 3 **in** ~ **daylight** : en pleno día

broadcast ['brɔdˌkæst] vt -cast; -casting : emitir — ~ n : emisión f

broaden ['brɔdən] vt : ampliar, ensanchar — vi : ensancharse — **broadly** ['brɔdli] adv : en general — **broad–minded** ['brɔdˌmaɪndəd] adj : de miras amplias, tolerante

broccoli ['brɑkəli] n : brócoli m, brécol m

brochure [broˈʃʊr] n : folleto m

broil ['brɔɪl] vt : asar a la parrilla

broke ['broːk] → **break** — ~ adj : pelado fam — **broken** ['broːkən] adj : roto, quebrado — **brokenhearted** [ˌbroːkənˈhɑrtəd] adj : desconsolado, con el corazón destrozado

broker ['broːkər] n : corredor m, -dora f

bronchitis [brɑŋˈkaɪtəs, brɑŋ-] n : bronquitis f

bronze ['brɑnz] *n* : bronce *m*

brooch ['broːtʃ, 'bruːtʃ] *n* : broche *m*

brood ['bruːd] *n* : nidada *f* (de pájaros), camada *f* (de mamíferos) — ~ *vi* 1 INCUBATE : empollar 2 ~ **about** : dar vueltas a, pensar demasiado en

brook ['brʊk] *n* : arroyo *m*

broom ['bruːm, 'brʊm] *n* : escoba *f* — **broomstick** ['bruːmˌstɪk, 'brʊm-] *n* : palo *m* de escoba

broth ['brɔθ] *n, pl* **broths** ['brɔθs, 'brɔðz] : caldo *m*

brothel ['brɑθəl, 'brɔ-] *n* : burdel *m*

brother ['brʌðər] *n* : hermano *m* — **brotherhood** ['brʌðərˌhʊd] *n* : fraternidad *f* — **brother–in–law** ['brʌðərɪnˌlɔ] *n, pl* **brothers–in–law** : cuñado *m* — **brotherly** ['brʌðərli] *adj* : fraternal

brought → **bring**

brow ['braʊ] *n* 1 EYEBROW : ceja *f* 2 FOREHEAD : frente *f* 3 : cima *f* (de una colina)

brown ['braʊn] *adj* : marrón, castaño (dícese del pelo), moreno (dícese de la piel) — ~ *n* : marrón *m* — ~ *vt* : dorar (en cocinar)

browse ['braʊz] *vi* **browsed; browsing** : mirar, echar un vistazo

bruise ['bruːz] *vt* **bruised; bruising** 1 : contusionar, magullar (a una persona) 2 : machucar (frutas) — ~ *n* : cardenal *m*, magulladura *f*

brunch ['brʌntʃ] *n* : brunch *m*

brunet *or* **brunette** ['bruːˈnet] *adj* : moreno — ~ *n* : moreno *m*, -na *f*

brunt ['brʌnt] *n* **bear the ~ of** : aguantar el mayor impacto de

brush ['brʌʃ] *n* 1 : cepillo *m*, pincel *m* (de artista), brocha *f* (de pintor) 2 UNDERBRUSH : maleza *f* — ~ *vt* 1 : cepillar 2 GRAZE : rozar 3 ~ **aside** : rechazar 4 ~ **off** DISREGARD : hacer caso omiso de — *vi* ~ **up on** : repasar — **brush–off** ['brʌʃˌɔf] *n* **give the ~ to** : dar calabazas a

brusque ['brʌsk] *adj* : brusco

brutal ['bruːtəl] *adj* : brutal — **brutality** [bruːˈtæləti] *n, pl* **-ties** : brutalidad *f*

brute ['bruːt] *adj* : bruto — ~ *n* : bestia *f*; bruto *m*, -ta *f*

bubble ['bʌbəl] *n* : burbuja *f* — ~ *vi* **-bled; -bling** : burbujear

buck ['bʌk] *n, pl* **buck** *or* **bucks** 1 : animal *m* macho, ciervo *m* (macho) 2 DOLLAR : dólar *m* — ~ *vi* 1 : corcovear (dícese de un caballo) 2 ~ **up** : animarse, levantar el ánimo — *vt* OPPOSE : oponerse a, ir en contra de

bucket ['bʌkət] *n* : cubo *m*

buckle ['bʌkəl] *n* : hebilla *f* — ~ *v* **-led;**

-ling *vt* 1 FASTEN : abrochar 2 BEND : combar, torcer — *vi* 1 : combarse, torcerse 2 : doblarse (dícese de las rodillas)

bud ['bʌd] *n* 1 : brote *m* 2 *or* **flower ~** : capullo *m* — ~ *vi* **budded; budding** : brotar, hacer brotes

Buddhism ['buːˌdɪzəm, 'bʊ-] *n* : budismo *m* — **Buddhist** ['buːdɪst, 'bʊ-] *adj* : budista — ~ *n* : budista *mf*

buddy ['bʌdi] *n, pl* **-dies** : compañero *m*, -ra *f*

budge ['bʌdʒ] *vi* **budged; budging** 1 MOVE : moverse 2 YIELD : ceder

budget ['bʌdʒət] *n* : presupuesto *m* — ~ *vi* : presupuestar — **budgetary** ['bʌdʒəˌteri] *adj* : presupuestario

buff ['bʌf] *n* 1 : beige *m*, color *m* de ante 2 ENTHUSIAST : aficionado *m*, -da *f* — ~ *adj* : beige — ~ *vt* POLISH : pulir

buffalo ['bʌfəˌloː] *n, pl* **-lo** *or* **-loes** : búfalo *m*

buffet [ˌbʌˈfeɪ, ˌbuː-] *n* 1 : bufé *m* (comida) 2 SIDEBOARD : aparador *m*

bug ['bʌg] *n* 1 INSECT : bicho *m*, insecto *m* 2 FLAW : defecto *m* 3 GERM : microbio *m* 4 MICROPHONE : micrófono *m* (oculto) — ~ *vt* **bugged; bugging** 1 PESTER : fastidiar, molestar 2 : ocultar micrófonos en (una habitación, etc.)

buggy ['bʌgi] *n, pl* **-gies** 1 CARRIAGE : calesa *f* 2 *or* **baby ~** : cochecito *m* (para niños)

bugle ['bjuːgəl] *n* : clarín *m*, corneta *f*

build ['bɪld] *v* **built** ['bɪlt]; **building** *vt* 1 : construir 2 DEVELOP : desarrollar — *vi* 1 *or* ~ **up** INTENSIFY : aumentar, intensificar 2 *or* ~ **up** ACCUMULATE : acumularse — ~ *n* PHYSIQUE : físico *m*, complexión *f* — **builder** ['bɪldər] *n* : constructor *m*, -tora *f* — **building** ['bɪldɪŋ] *n* 1 STRUCTURE : edificio *m* 2 CONSTRUCTION : construcción *f* — **built–in** ['bɪltˈɪn] *adj* : empotrado

bulb ['bʌlb] *n* 1 : bulbo *m* (de una planta) 2 LIGHTBULB : bombilla *f*

bulge ['bʌldʒ] *vi* **bulged; bulging** : sobresalir — ~ *n* : bulto *m*, protuberancia *f*

bulk ['bʌlk] *n* 1 VOLUME : volumen *m*, bulto *m* 2 **in ~** : en grandes cantidades — **bulky** ['bʌlki] *adj* **bulkier; -est** : voluminoso

bull ['bʊl] *n* 1 : toro *m* 2 MALE : macho *m*

bulldog ['bʊlˌdɔg] *n* : buldog *m*

bulldozer ['bʊlˌdoːzər] *n* : bulldozer *m*

bullet ['bʊlət] *n* : bala *f*

bulletin ['bʊlətən, -lətən] *n* : boletín *m* — **bulletin board** *n* : tablón *m* de anuncios

bulletproof ['bʊlət,pruːf] *adj* : a prueba de balas

bullfight ['bʊl,faɪt] *n* : corrida *f* (de toros) — **bullfighter** ['bʊl,faɪtər] *n* : torero *m*, -ra *f*; matador *m*

bullion ['bʊljən] *n* : oro *m* en lingotes, plata *f* en lingotes

bull's-eye ['bʊlz,aɪ] *n, pl* **bull's-eyes** : diana *f*

bully ['bʊli] *n, pl* **-lies** : matón *m* — ~ *vt* **-lied; -lying** : intimidar

bum ['bʌm] *n* : vagabundo *m*, -da *f*

bumblebee ['bʌmbəl,biː] *n* : abejorro *m*

bump ['bʌmp] *n* **1** BULGE : bulto *m*, protuberancia *f* **2** IMPACT : golpe *m* **3** JOLT : sacudida *f* — ~ *vt* : chocar contra — *vi* ~ **into** MEET : encontrarse con — **bumper** ['bʌmpər] *n* : parachoques *mpl* — ~ *adj* : extraordinario, récord — **bumpy** ['bʌmpi] *adj* **bumpier; -est** **1** : desigual, lleno de baches (dícese de un camino) **2 a** ~ **flight** : un vuelo agitado

bun ['bʌn] *n* : bollo *m*

bunch ['bʌntʃ] *n* : grupo *m* (de personas), racimo *m* (de frutas, etc.), ramo *m* (de flores), manojo *m* (de llaves) — ~ *vi or* ~ **up** : amontonarse, agruparse

bundle ['bʌndəl] *n* **1** : lío *m*, bulto *m*, atado *m*, haz *m* (de palos) **2** PARCEL : paquete *m* **3** ~ **of nerves** : manojo *m* de nervios — ~ *vt* **-dled; -dling** *or* ~ **up** : liar, atar

bungalow ['bʌŋgə,loː] *n* : casa *f* de un solo piso

bungle ['bʌŋgəl] *vt* **-gled; -gling** : echar a perder

bunion ['bʌnjən] *n* : juanete *m*

bunk ['bʌŋk] *n or* **bunk bed** : litera *f*

bunny ['bʌni] *n, pl* **-nies** : conejo *m*, -ja *f*

buoy ['buːi, 'bɔɪ] *n* : boya *f* — ~ *vt or* ~ **up** HEARTEN : animar, levantar el ánimo a — **buoyant** ['bɔɪənt, 'buːjənt] *adj* **1** : boyante, flotante **2** LIGHTHEARTED : alegre, optimista

burden ['bərdən] *n* : carga *f* — ~ *vt* ~ **s.o. with** : cargar a algn con — **burdensome** ['bərdənsəm] *adj* : oneroso

bureau ['bjʊro] *n* **1** : cómoda *f* (mueble) **2** : departamento *m* (del gobierno) **3** AGENCY : agencia *f* — **bureaucracy** [bjʊ'rɑkrəsi] *n, pl* **-cies** : burocracia *f* — **bureaucrat** ['bjʊrə,kræt] *n* : burócrata *mf* — **bureaucratic** [bjʊrə'kræt̬ɪk] *adj* : burocrático

burglar ['bərglər] *n* : ladrón *m*, -drona *f* — **burglarize** ['bərglə,raɪz] *vt* **-ized; -izing** : robar — **burglary** ['bərgləri] *n, pl* **-glaries** : robo *m*

burgundy ['bərgəndi] *n, pl* **-dies** : borgoña *m*, vino *m* de Borgoña

burial ['beriəl] *n* : entierro *m*

burly ['bərli] *adj* **-lier; -liest** : fornido

burn ['bərn] *v* **burned** ['bərnd, 'bərnt] *or* **burnt** ['bərnt]; **burning** *vt* **1** : quemar **2** *or* ~ **down** : incendiar **3** ~ **up** : consumir — *vi* **1** : arder (dícese de un fuego), quemarse (dícese de la comida, etc.) **2** : estar encendido (dícese de una luz) **3** ~ **out** : apagarse — ~ *n* : quemadura *f* — **burner** ['bərnər] *n* : quemador *m*

burnish ['bərnɪʃ] *vt* : pulir

burp ['bərp] *vi* : eructar — ~ *n* : eructo *m*

burro ['bəro, 'bʊr-] *n, pl* **-os** : burro *m*

burrow ['bəro] *n* : madriguera *f* — ~ *vi* **1** : cavar **2** ~ **into** : hurgar en

bursar ['bərsər] *n* : tesorero *m*, -ra *f*

burst ['bərst] *v* **burst** *or* **bursted; bursting** *vi* : reventarse — *vt* : reventar — ~ *n* **1** EXPLOSION : estallido *m*, explosión *f* **2** OUTBURST : arranque *m*, arrebato *m* **3** ~ **of laughter** : carcajada *f*

bury ['beri] *vt* **buried; burying** **1** INTER : enterrar **2** HIDE : esconder

bus ['bʌs] *n, pl* **buses** *or* **busses** : autobús *m*, bus *m* — ~ *v* **bused** *or* **bussed** ['bʌst]; **busing** *or* **bussing** ['bʌsɪŋ] *vt* : transportar en autobús — *vi* : viajar en autobús

bush ['bʊʃ] *n* SHRUB : arbusto *m*, mata *f*

bushel ['bʊʃəl] *n* : medida *f* de áridos igual a 35.24 litros

bushy ['bʊʃi] *adj* **bushier; -est** : poblado, espeso

busily ['bɪzəli] *adv* : afanosamente

business ['bɪznəs, -nəz] *n* **1** COMMERCE : negocios *mpl*, comercio *m* **2** COMPANY : empresa *f*, negocio *m* **3 it's none of your** ~ : no es asunto tuyo — **businessman** ['bɪznəs,mæn, -nəz-] *n, pl* **-men** [-mən, -,men] : empresario *m*, hombre *m* de negocios — **businesswoman** ['bɪznəs,wʊmən, -nəz-] *n, pl* **-women** [-,wɪmən] : empresaria *f*, mujer *f* de negocios

bust¹ ['bʌst] *vt* BREAK : romper

bust² *n* **1** : busto *m* (en la escultura) **2** BREASTS : pecho *m*, senos *mpl*

bustle ['bʌsəl] *vi* **-tled; -tling** *or* ~ **about** : ir y venir, ajetrearse — ~ *n or* **hustle and** ~ : bullicio *m*, ajetreo *m*

busy ['bɪzi] *adj* **busier; -est** **1** : ocupado **2** BUSTLING : concurrido

but ['bʌt] *conj* **1** : pero **2 not one** ~ **two** : no uno sino dos — ~ *prep* : excepto, menos

butcher ['butʃər] *n* : carnicero *m*, -ra *f* — ~ *vt* **1** : matar **2** BOTCH : hacer una carnicería de

butler ['bʌtlər] *n* : mayordomo *m*

butt ['bʌt] *vt* : embestir (con los cuernos), darle un cabezazo a — *vi* — **in** : interrumpir — ~ *n* **1** BUTTING : embestida *f* (de cuernos) **2** TARGET : blanco *m* **3** : extremo *m*, culata *f* (de un rifle), colilla *f* (de un cigarillo)

butter ['bʌtər] *n* : mantequilla *f* — ~ *vt* : untar con mantequilla

buttercup ['bʌtər,kʌp] *n* : ranúnculo *m*

butterfly ['bʌtər,flaɪ] *n*, *pl* **-flies** : mariposa *f*

buttocks ['bʌtəks, -,tɑks] *npl* : nalgas *fpl*

button ['bʌtən] *n* : botón *m* — ~ *vt* : abotonar — *vi* **or** ~ **up** : abotonarse — **buttonhole** ['bʌtən,hoːl] *n* : ojal *m* — ~ *vt* **-holed; -holing** : acorralar

buy ['baɪ] *vt* **bought** ['bɔt]; **buying** : comprar — ~ *n* : compra *f* — **buyer** ['baɪər] *n* : comprador *m*, -dora *f*

buzz ['bʌz] *vi* : zumbar — ~ *n* : zumbido *m*

buzzard ['bʌzərd] *n* : buitre *m*

buzzer ['bʌzər] *n* : timbre *m*

by ['baɪ] *prep* **1** NEAR : cerca de **2** VIA : por **3** PAST : por, por delante de **4** DURING : de, durante **5** (*in expressions of time*) : para **6** (*indicating cause or agent*) : por, de, a — ~ *adv* **1** ~ **and** ~ : poco después **2** ~ **and large** : en general **3** **go** ~ : pasar **4** **stop** ~ : pasar por casa

bygone ['baɪ,gɔn] *adj* : pasado — ~ *n* **let** ~**s be** ~**s** : lo pasado, pasado está

bypass ['baɪ,pæs] *n* : carretera *f* de circunvalación — ~ *vt* : evitar

by-product ['baɪ,prɑdəkt] *n* : subproducto *m*

bystander ['baɪ,stændər] *n* : espectador *m*, -dora *f*

byte ['baɪt] *n* : byte *m*, octeto *m*

byword ['baɪ,wərd] *n* **be a** ~ **for** : estar sinónimo de

C

c ['siː] *n*, *pl* **c's** *or* **cs** : c, tercera letra del alfabeto inglés

cab ['kæb] *n* **1** : taxi *m* **2** : cabina *f* (de un camión, etc.)

cabbage ['kæbɪdʒ] *n* : col *f*, repollo *m*

cabin ['kæbən] *n* **1** : cabaña *f* **2** : cabina *f* (de un avión, etc.), camarote *m* (de un barco)

cabinet ['kæbnət] *n* **1** CUPBOARD : armario *m* **2** : gabinete *m* (del gobierno) **3** *or* **medicine** ~ : botiquín *m*

cable ['keɪbəl] *n* : cable *m* — **cable television** *n* : televisión *f* por cable

cackle ['kækəl] *vi* **-led; -ling 1** CLUCK : cacarear **2** LAUGH : reírse a carcajadas

cactus ['kæktəs] *n*, *pl* **cacti** [-,taɪ] *or* **-tuses** : cactus *m*

cadence ['keɪdənts] *n* : cadencia *f*, ritmo *m*

cadet [kə'dɛt] *n* : cadete *mf*

café [kæ'feɪ, kə-] *n* : café *m*, cafetería *f* — **cafeteria** [,kæfə'tɪriə] *n* : restaurante *m* autoservicio, cantina *f*

caffeine [kæ'fiːn] *n* : cafeína *f*

cage ['keɪdʒ] *n* : jaula *f* — ~ *vt* **caged; caging** : enjaular

cajole [kə'dʒoːl] *vt* **-joled; -joling** : engatusar

cake ['keɪk] *n* **1** : pastel *m*, torta *f* **2** : pastilla *f* (de jabón) **3** **take the** ~ : ser el colmo — **caked** ['keɪkt] *adj* ~ **with** : cubierto de

calamity [kə'læmətɪ] *n*, *pl* **-ties** : calamidad *f*

calcium ['kælsiəm] *n* : calcio *m*

calculate ['kælkjə,leɪt] *v* **-lated; -lating** : calcular — **calculating** ['kælkjə,leɪtɪŋ] *adj* : calculador — **calculation** [,kælkjə'leɪʃən] *n* : cálculo *m* — **calculator** ['kælkjə,leɪtər] *n* : calculadora *f*

calendar ['kæləndər] *n* : calendario *m*

calf[1] ['kæf, 'kɑf] *n*, *pl* **calves** ['kævz, 'kɑvz] **1** : becerro *m*, -rra *f*; ternero *m*, -ra *f* (de vacunos) **2** : cría *f* (de otros mamíferos)

calf[2] *n*, *pl* **calves** : pantorrilla *f* (de la pierna)

caliber *or* **calibre** ['kæləbər] *n* : calibre *m*

call ['kɔl] *vi* **1** : llamar **2** VISIT : pasar, hacer (una) visita **3** ~ **for** : requerir — *vt* **1** : llamar **2** ~ **off** : cancelar — ~ *n* **1** : llamada *f* **2** SHOUT : grito *m* **3** VISIT : visita *f* **4** DEMAND : petición *f* — **calling** ['kɔlɪŋ] *n* : vocación *f*

callous ['kæləs] *adj* : insensible, cruel

calm ['kɑm, 'kɑlm] *n* : calma *f*, tranquilidad *f* — ~ *vt* : calmar — *vi* **or** ~ **down** : calmarse — ~ *adj* : tranquilo, en calma — **calmly** ['kɑmli, 'kɑlm-] *adv* : con calma

calorie ['kæləri] *n* : caloría *f*
came → **come**
camel ['kæməl] *n* : camello *m*
camera ['kæmrə, 'kæmərə] *n* : cámara *f*
camouflage ['kæmə,flɑʒ, -,flɑdʒ] *n* : camuflaje *m* — ~ *vt* **-flaged; -flaging** : camuflar
camp ['kæmp] *n* **1** : campamento *m* **2** FACTION : bando *m* — ~ *vi* : acampar, ir de camping
campaign [kæm'peɪn] *n* : campaña *f* — ~ *vi* : hacer (una) campaña
camping ['kæmpɪŋ] *n* : camping *m*
campus ['kæmpəs] *n* : ciudad *f* universitaria
can[1] ['kæn] *v aux, past* **could** ['kʊd]; *present s & pl* **can 1** (*expressing possibility or permission*) : poder **2** (*expressing knowledge or ability*) : saber **3 that cannot be!** : ¡no puede ser!
can[2] ['kæn] *n* : lata *f* — ~ *vt* **canned; canning** : enlatar
Canadian [kə'neɪdiən] *adj* : canadiense
canal [kə'næl] *n* : canal *m*
canary [kə'neri] *n, pl* **-naries** : canario *m*
cancel ['kæntsəl] *vt* **-celed** *or* **-celled; -celing** *or* **-celling** : cancelar — **cancellation** [,kæntsə'leɪʃən] *n* : cancelación *f*
cancer ['kæntsər] *n* : cáncer *m* — **cancerous** ['kæntsərəs] *adj* : canceroso
candelabra [,kændə'lɑbrə, -'læ-] *n, pl* **-bra** *or* **-bras** : candelabro *m*
candid ['kændɪd] *adj* : franco
candidate ['kændə,deɪt, -dət] *n* : candidato *m*, -ta *f* — **candidacy** ['kændədəsi] *n, pl* **-cies** : candidatura *f*
candle ['kændəl] *n* : vela *f* — **candlestick** ['kændəl,stɪk] *n* : candelero *m*
candor *or Brit* **candour** ['kændər] *n* : franqueza *f*
candy ['kændi] *n, pl* **-dies** : dulce *m*, caramelo *m*
cane ['keɪn] *n* **1** : bastón *m* (para andar), vara *f* (para castigar) **2** REED : caña *f*, mimbre *m* — ~ *vt* **caned; caning 1** : tapizar con mimbre **2** FLOG : azotar
canine ['keɪ,naɪn] *n or* ~ **tooth** : colmillo *m*, diente *m* canino — ~ *adj* : canino
canister ['kænəstər] *n* : lata *f*, bote *m* Spain
cannibal ['kænəbəl] *n* : caníbal *mf*
cannon ['kænən] *n, pl* **-nons** *or* **-non** : cañón *m*
cannot (can not) ['kæn,ɑt, kæ'nɑt] → **can**[1]
canny ['kæni] *adj* **cannier; -est** : astuto
canoe [kə'nu:] *n* : canoa *f*, piragua *f* — ~ *vt* **-noed; -noeing** : ir en canoa

canon ['kænən] *n* : canon *m* — **canonize** ['kænə,naɪz] *vt* **-ized; -izing** : canonizar
can opener *n* : abrelatas *m*
canopy ['kænəpi] *n, pl* **-pies** : dosel *m*
can't ['kænt, 'kant] (*contraction of* **can not**) → **can**[1]
cantaloupe ['kæntəl,oʊp] *n* : melón *m*, cantalupo *m*
cantankerous [kæn'tæŋkərəs] *adj* : irritable, irascible
canteen [kæn'tin] *n* **1** FLASK : cantimplora *f* **2** CAFETERIA : cantina *f*
canter ['kæntər] *vi* : ir a medio galope — ~ *n* : medio galope *m*
canvas ['kænvəs] *n* **1** : lona *f* (tela) **2** : lienzo *m* (de pintar)
canvass ['kænvəs] *vt* **1** : solicitar votos de, hacer campaña entre **2** POLL : sondear — ~ *n* **1** : solicitación *f* (de votos) **2** POLL : sondeo *m*
canyon ['kænjən] *n* : cañón *m*
cap *n* **1** : gorra *f*, gorro *m* **2** TOP : tapa *f*, tapón *m* (de botellas) **3** LIMIT : tope *m* — ~ ['kæp] *vt* **capped; capping 1** COVER : tapar, cubrir **2** OUTDO : superar
capable ['keɪpəbəl] *adj* : capaz, competente — **capability** [,keɪpə'bɪləti] *n, pl* **-ties** : capacidad *f*
capacity [kə'pæsəti] *n, pl* **-ties 1** : capacidad *f* **2** ROLE : calidad *f*
cape[1] ['keɪp] *n* : cabo *m* (en geografía)
cape[2] *n* CLOAK : capa *f*
caper[1] ['keɪpər] *n* : alcaparra *f*
caper[2] *n* PRANK : broma *f*, travesura *f*
capital ['kæpətəl] *adj* **1** : capital **2** : mayúsculo (dícese de las letras) — ~ *n* **1** *or* ~ **city** : capital *f* **2** WEALTH : capital *m* **3** *or* ~ **letter** : mayúscula *f* — **capitalism** ['kæpəţəl,ɪzəm] *n* : capitalismo *m* — **capitalist** ['kæpəţəlɪst] *or* **capitalistic** [,kæpəţəl'ɪstɪk] *adj* : capitalista — **capitalize** ['kæpəţəl,aɪz] *vt* **-ized; -izing 1** FINANCE : capitalizar **2** : escribir con mayúscula — *vi* ~ **on** : sacar partido de
capitol ['kæpəţəl] *n* : capitolio *m*
capitulate [kə'pɪtʃə,leɪt] *vi* **-lated; -lating** : capitular
capsize ['kæp,saɪz, kæp'saɪz] *v* **-sized; -sizing** *vt* : hacer volcar — *vi* : zozobrar, volcar(se)
capsule ['kæpsəl, -,su:l] *n* : cápsula *f*
captain ['kæptən] *n* : capitán *m*, -tana *f*
caption ['kæpʃən] *n* **1** : leyenda *f* (al pie de una ilustración) **2** SUBTITLE : subtítulo *m*
captivate ['kæptə,veɪt] *vt* **-vated; -vating** : cautivar, encantar

captive ['kæptɪv] *adj* : cautivo — **~** *n* : cautivo *m*, -va *f* — **captivity** [kæp-'tɪvəṭi] *n* : cautiverio *m*

capture ['kæpʃər] *n* : captura *f*, apresamiento *m* — **~** *vt* **-tured; -turing 1** SEIZE : capturar, apresar **2 ~ one's interest** : captar el interés de uno

car ['kɑr] *n* **1** : automóvil *m*, coche *m*, carro *m Lat* **2** *or* **railroad ~** : vagón *m*

carafe [kə'ræf, -'rɑf] *n* : garrafa *f*

caramel ['kɑrməl; 'kærəməl, -,mel] *n* : caramelo *m*, azúcar *f* quemada

carat ['kærət] *n* : quilate *m*

caravan ['kærə,væn] *n* : caravana *f*

carbohydrate [,kɑrbo'haɪ,dreɪt, -drət] *n* : carbohidrato *m*, hidrato *m* de carbono

carbon ['kɑrbən] *n* : carbono *m* — **carbon copy** *n* : copia *f*, duplicado *m*

carburetor ['kɑrbə,reɪṭər, -bjə-] *n* : carburador *m*

carcass ['kɑrkəs] *n* : cuerpo *m* (de un animal muerto)

card ['kɑrd] *n* **1** : tarjeta *f* **2** *or* **playing ~** : carta *f*, naipe *m* — **cardboard** ['kɑrd,bord] *n* : cartón *m*

cardiac ['kɑrdi,æk] *adj* : cardíaco

cardigan ['kɑrdɪgən] *n* : cárdigan *m*

cardinal ['kɑrdənəl] *n* : cardenal *m* — **~** *adj* : cardinal, fundamental

care ['kær] *n* **1** : cuidado *m* **2** WORRY : preocupación *f* **3 take ~ of** : cuidar (de) — **~** *vi* **cared; caring 1** : preocuparse, inquietarse **2 ~ for** TEND : cuidar (de), atender **3 ~ for** LIKE : querer **4 I don't ~** : no me importa

career [kə'rɪr] *n* : carrera *f* — **~** *vi* : ir a toda velocidad

carefree ['kær,fri:, 'kær-] *adj* : despreocupado

careful ['kærfəl] *adj* : cuidadoso — **carefully** ['kærfəli] *adv* : con cuidado, cuidadosamente — **careless** ['kærləs] *adj* : descuidado — **carelessness** ['kærləsnəs] *n* : descuido *m*

caress [kə'res] *n* : caricia *f* — **~** *vt* : acariciar

cargo ['kɑr,go:] *n*, *pl* **-goes** *or* **-gos** : cargamento *m*, carga *f*

caricature ['kærɪkə,tʃur] *n* : caricatura *f* — **~** *vt* **-tured; -turing** : caricaturizar

caring ['kærɪŋ] *adj* : solícito, afectuoso

carnage ['kɑrnɪdʒ] *n* : matanza *f*, carnicería *f*

carnal ['kɑrnəl] *adj* : carnal

carnation [kɑr'neɪʃən] *n* : clavel *m*

carnival ['kɑrnəvəl] *n* : carnaval *m*

carol ['kærəl] *n* : villancico *m*

carp ['kɑrp] *vi* **~ at** : quejarse de

carpenter ['kɑrpəntər] *n* : carpintero *m*,

-ra *f* — **carpentry** ['kɑrpəntri] *n* : carpintería *f*

carpet ['kɑrpət] *n* : alfombra *f*

carriage ['kærɪdʒ] *n* **1** : transporte *m* (de mercancías) **2** BEARING : porte *m* **3** *or* **baby ~** : cochecito *m* **4** *or* **horse-drawn ~** : carruaje *m*, coche *m*

carrier ['kæriər] *n* **1** : transportista *mf*, empresa *f* de transportes **2** : portador *m*, -dora *f* (de una enfermedad)

carrot ['kærət] *n* : zanahoria *f*

carry ['kæri] *v* **-ried; -rying** *vt* **1** : llevar **2** TRANSPORT : transportar **3** STOCK : vender **4** ENTAIL : acarrear, implicar **5 ~ oneself** : portarse — *vi* : oírse (dícese de sonidos) — **carry away** *vt* **get carried away** : exaltarse, entusiasmarse — **carry on** *vt* CONDUCT : realizar — *vi* **1** : portarse inapropiadamente **2** CONTINUE : seguir, continuar — **carry out** *vt* **1** PERFORM : llevar a cabo, realizar **2** FULFILL : cumplir

cart ['kɑrt] *n* : carreta *f*, carro *m* — **~** *vt* *or* **~ around** : acarrear

cartilage ['kɑrṭəlɪdʒ] *n* : cartílago *m*

carton ['kɑrtən] *n* : caja *f* (de cartón)

cartoon [kɑr'tu:n] *n* **1** : caricatura *f* **2** COMIC STRIP : historieta *f* **3** *or* **animated ~** : dibujos *mpl* animados

cartridge ['kɑrtrɪdʒ] *n* : cartucho *m*

carve ['kɑrv] *vt* **carved; carving 1** : tallar, esculpir **2** : trinchar (carne)

case *n* **1** : caso *m* **2** BOX : caja *f* **3 in any ~** : en todo caso **4 in ~ of** : en caso de **5 just in ~** : por si acaso

cash ['kæʃ] *n* : efectivo *m*, dinero *m* en efectivo — **~** *vt* : convertir en efectivo, cobrar

cashew ['kæ,ʃu:, kə'ʃu:] *n* : anacardo *m*

cashier [kæ'ʃɪr] *n* : cajero *m*, -ra *f*

cashmere ['kæʒ,mɪr, 'kæʃ-] *n* : cachemira *f*

cash register *n* : caja *f* registradora

casino [kə'si:no:] *n*, *pl* **-nos** : casino *m*

cask ['kæsk] *n* : barril *m*

casket ['kæskət] *n* : ataúd *m*

casserole ['kæsə,ro:l] *n* **1** *or* **~ dish** : cazuela *f* **2** : guiso *m* (comida)

cassette [kə'set, kæ-] *n* : cassette *mf*

cast ['kæst] *vt* **cast; casting 1** THROW : arrojar, lanzar **2** : depositar (un voto) **3** : repartir (papeles dramáticos) **4** MOLD : fundir — **~** *n* **1** : elenco *m*, reparto *m* (de actores) **2** *or* **plaster ~** : molde *m* de yeso, escayola *f*

castanets [,kæstə'nets] *npl* : castañuelas *fpl*

castaway ['kæstə,weɪ] *n* : náufrago *m*, -ga *f*

cast iron *n* : hierro *m* fundido

castle ['kæsəl] *n* 1 : castillo *m* 2 : torre *f* (en ajedrez)

castrate ['kæs,treɪt] *vt* **-trated; -trating** : castrar

casual ['kæʒuəl] *adj* 1 CHANCE : casual, fortuito 2 INDIFFERENT : despreocupado 3 INFORMAL : informal — **casually** ['kæʒuəli, 'kæʒəli] *adv* 1 : de manera despreocupada 2 INFORMALLY : informalmente

casualty ['kæʒuəlti, 'kæʒəl-] *n, pl* **-ties** 1 : accidente *m* 2 VICTIM : víctima *f*; herido *m*, -da *f* 3 **casualties** *npl* : bajas *fpl* (militares)

cat ['kæt] *n* : gato *m*, -ta *f*

catalog *or* **catalogue** ['kætə,lɔg] *n* : catálogo *m* — ~ *vt* **-loged** *or* **-logued; -loging** *or* **-loguing** : catalogar

catapult ['kætə,pʌlt, -,pʊlt] *n* : catapulta *f*

cataract ['kætə,rækt] *n* : catarata *f*

catastrophe [kə'tæstrə,fi:] *n* : catástrofe *f* — **catastrophic** [,kætə'strɑfɪk] *adj* : catastrófico

catch ['kætʃ, 'ketʃ] *v* **caught** ['kɔt]; **catching** *vt* 1 CAPTURE, TRAP : capturar, atrapar 2 SURPRISE : sorprender 3 GRASP : agarrar, captar 4 SNAG : enganchar 5 : tomar (un tren, etc.) 6 ~ **a cold** : resfriarse — *vi* 1 SNAG : engancharse 2 ~ **fire** : prender fuego — **catching** ['kætʃɪŋ, 'kɛ-] *adj* : contagioso — **catchy** ['kætʃi, 'kɛ-] *adj* **catchier; -est** : pegadizo, pegajoso *Lat*

category ['kætə,gori] *n, pl* **-ries** : categoría *f* — **categorical** [,kætə'gorɪkəl] *adj* : categórico

cater ['keɪtər] *vi* 1 : proveer comida 2 ~ **to** : atender a — **caterer** ['keɪtərər] *n* : proveedor *m*, -dora *f* de comida

caterpillar ['kætər,pɪlər] *n* : oruga *f*

catfish ['kæt,fɪʃ] *n* : bagre *m*

cathedral [kə'θi:drəl] *n* : catedral *f*

catholic ['kæθəlɪk] *adj* 1 : universal 2 **Catholic** : católico — **catholicism** [kə'θɑlə,sɪzəm] *n* : catolicismo *m*

cattle ['kætəl] *npl* : ganado *m* (vacuno)

caught → **catch**

cauldron ['kɔldrən] *n* : caldera *f*

cauliflower ['kɑlɪ,flaʊər, 'kɔ-] *n* : coliflor *f*

cause ['kɔz] *n* 1 : causa *f* 2 REASON : motivo *m* — ~ *vt* **caused; causing** : causar

caustic ['kɔstɪk] *adj* : cáustico

caution ['kɔʃən] *n* 1 WARNING : advertencia *f* 2 CARE : precaución *f*, cautela *f* — ~ *vt* : advertir — **cautious** ['kɔʃəs] *adj* : cauteloso, precavido —

cautiously ['kɔʃəsli] *adv* : con precaución

cavalier [,kævə'lɪr] *adj* : arrogante, desdeñoso

cavalry ['kævəlri] *n, pl* **-ries** : caballería *f*

cave ['keɪv] *n* : cueva *f* — ~ *vi* **caved; caving** *or* ~ **in** : hundirse

cavern ['kævərn] *n* : caverna *f*

cavity ['kævəti] *n, pl* **-ties** 1 : cavidad *f* 2 : caries *f* (dental)

cavort [kə'vɔrt] *vi* : brincar

CD [,si:'di:] *n* : CD *m*, disco *m* compacto

cease ['si:s] *v* **ceased; ceasing** *vt* : dejar de — *vi* : cesar — **cease-fire** ['si:s,faɪr] *n* : alto *m* el fuego — **ceaseless** ['si:sləs] *adj* : incesante

cedar ['si:dər] *n* : cedro *m*

ceiling ['si:lɪŋ] *n* : techo *m*

celebrate ['selə,breɪt] *v* **-brated; -brating** *vt* : celebrar — *vi* : divertirse — **celebrated** ['selə,breɪtəd] *adj* : célebre — **celebration** [,selə'breɪʃən] *n* 1 : celebración *f* 2 FESTIVITY : fiesta *f* — **celebrity** [sə'lebrəti] *n, pl* **-ties** : celebridad *f*

celery ['seləri] *n, pl* **-eries** : apio *m*

cell ['sel] *n* 1 : célula *f* 2 : celda *f* (en una cárcel, etc.)

cellar ['selər] *n* 1 BASEMENT : sótano *m* 2 : bodega *f* (de vinos)

cello ['tʃe,loʊ] *n, pl* **-los** : violoncelo *m*

cellular ['seljələr] *adj* : celular

cement [sɪ'ment] *n* : cemento *m* — ~ *vt* : cementar

cemetery ['semə,teri] *n, pl* **-teries** : cementerio *m*

censor ['sensər] *vt* : censurar — **censorship** ['sensər,ʃɪp] *n* : censura *f* — **censure** ['sentʃər] *n* : censura *f* — ~ *vt* **-sured; -suring** : censurar, criticar

census ['sensəs] *n* : censo *m*

cent ['sent] *n* : centavo *m*

centennial [sen'teniəl] *n* : centenario *m*

center *or Brit* **centre** ['sentər] *n* : centro *m* — ~ *v* **centered** *or Brit* **centred; centering** *or Brit* **centring** *vt* : centrar — *vi* ~ **on** : centrarse en

centigrade ['sentə,greɪd, 'san-] *adj* : centígrado

centimeter ['sentə,mi:tər, 'san-] *n* : centímetro *m*

centipede ['sentə,pi:d] *n* : ciempiés *m*

central ['sentrəl] *adj* 1 : central 2 **a** ~ **location** : un lugar céntrico — **centralize** ['sentrə,laɪz] *vt* **-ized; -izing** : centralizar

centre ['sentər] → **center**

century ['sentʃəri] *n, pl* **-ries** : siglo *m*

ceramics [sə'ræmɪks] *npl* : cerámica *f*

cereal ['sɪriəl] n : cereal m

ceremony ['serə,moni] n, pl -nies : ceremonia f — ceremonial [ˌserə'moniəl] adj : ceremonial

certain ['sərtən] adj 1 : cierto 2 be ~ of : estar seguro de 3 for ~ : seguro, con toda seguridad 4 make ~ of : asegurarse de — certainly ['sərtənli] adv : desde luego, por supuesto — certainty ['sərtənti] n, pl -ties : certeza f, seguridad f

certify ['sərtə,faɪ] vt -fied; -fying : certificar — certificate [sər'tɪfɪkət] n : certificado m, partida f, acta f

chafe ['tʃeɪf] v chafed; chafing vi : rozarse — vt : rozar

chain ['tʃeɪn] n 1 : cadena f 2 ~ of events : serie f de acontecimientos — ~ vt : encadenar

chair ['tʃer] n 1 : silla f 2 : cátedra f (en una universidad) — ~ vt : presidir — chairman ['tʃermən] n, pl -men [-mən, -ˌmen] : presidente m — chairperson ['tʃer,pərsən] n : presidente m, -ta f

chalk ['tʃɔk] n : tiza f, gis m Lat

challenge ['tʃælɪndʒ] vt -lenged; -lenging 1 DISPUTE : disputar, poner en duda 2 DARE : desafiar — ~ n : reto m, desafío m — challenging ['tʃælɪndʒɪŋ] adj : estimulante

chamber ['tʃeɪmbər] n : cámara f — chambermaid ['tʃeɪmbər,meɪd] n : camarera f

champagne [ʃæm'peɪn] n : champaña m, champán m

champion ['tʃæmpiən] n : campeón m, -peona f — ~ vt : defender — championship ['tʃæmpiən,ʃɪp] n : campeonato m

chance ['tʃænts] n 1 LUCK : azar m, suerte f 2 OPPORTUNITY : oportunidad f 3 LIKELIHOOD : probabilidad f 4 by ~ : por casualidad 5 take a ~ : arriesgarse — ~ vt chanced; chancing RISK : arriesgar — ~ adj : fortuito

chandelier [ˌʃændə'lɪr] n : araña f (de luces)

change ['tʃeɪndʒ] v changed; changing vt 1 : cambiar 2 SWITCH : cambiar de — vi 1 : cambiar 2 or ~ clothes : cambiarse (de ropa) — ~ n : cambio m — changeable ['tʃeɪndʒəbəl] adj : cambiable

channel ['tʃænəl] n 1 : canal m 2 : cauce m (de un río) 3 MEANS : vía f, medio m

chant ['tʃænt] v : cantar — ~ n : canto m

chaos ['keɪˌas] n : caos m — chaotic [keɪ'atɪk] adj : caótico

chap[1] ['tʃæp] vi chapped; chapping : agrietarse

chap[2] n : tipo m fam

chapel ['tʃæpəl] n : capilla f

chaperon or chaperone ['ʃæpə,roːn] n : acompañante mf

chaplain ['tʃæplɪn] n : capellán m

chapter ['tʃæptər] n : capítulo m

char ['tʃar] vt charred; charring : carbonizar

character ['kærɪktər] n 1 : carácter m 2 : personaje m (en una novela, etc.) — characteristic [ˌkærɪktə'rɪstɪk] adj : característico — ~ n : característica f — characterize ['kærɪktə,raɪz] vt -ized; -izing : caracterizar

charcoal ['tʃar,koːl] n : carbón m

charge ['tʃardʒ] n 1 : carga f (eléctrica) 2 COST : precio m 3 BURDEN : carga f, peso m 4 ACCUSATION : cargo m, acusación f 5 in ~ of : encargado de 6 take ~ of : hacerse cargo de — ~ v charged; charging vt 1 : cargar 2 ENTRUST : encargar 3 COMMAND : ordenar, mandar 4 ACCUSE : acusar — vi 1 : cargar 2 ~ too much : cobrar demasiado

charisma [kə'rɪzmə] n : carisma m — charismatic [ˌkærəz'mætɪk] adj : carismático

charity ['tʃærəti] n, pl -ties 1 : organización f benéfica 2 GOODWILL : caridad f

charlatan ['ʃarlətən] n : charlatán m, -tana f

charm ['tʃarm] n 1 : encanto m 2 SPELL : hechizo m — ~ vt : encantar, cautivar — charming ['tʃarmɪŋ] adj : encantador

chart ['tʃart] n 1 MAP : carta f 2 DIAGRAM : gráfico m, tabla f — ~ vt : trazar un mapa de

charter ['tʃartər] n : carta f — ~ vt : alquilar, fletar

chase ['tʃeɪs] n : persecución f — ~ vt chased; chasing 1 PURSUE : perseguir 2 or ~ away : ahuyentar

chasm ['kæzəm] n : abismo m

chaste ['tʃeɪst] adj chaster; -est : casto — chastity ['tʃæstəti] n : castidad f

chat ['tʃæt] vi chatted; chatting : charlar — ~ n : charla f — chatter ['tʃætər] vi 1 : parlotear fam 2 : castañetear (dícese de los dientes) — ~ n : parloteo m, cháchara f — chatterbox ['tʃætər,baks] n : parlanchín m, -china f — chatty ['tʃæti] adj chattier; chattiest 1 : parlanchín 2 INFORMAL : familiar

chauffeur ['ʃoːfər, ʃo'fər] n : chofer mf

chauvinist ['ʃoːvənɪst] or chauvinistic

[ˌʃoːvənɪstɪk] *adj* : chauvinista, patriotero

cheap ['tʃiːp] *adj* **1** INEXPENSIVE : barato **2** SHODDY : de baja calidad — **∼** *adv* : barato — **cheapen** ['tʃiːpən] *vt* : rebajar — **cheaply** ['tʃiːpli] *adv* : barato, a precio bajo

cheat ['tʃiːt] *vt* : defraudar, estafar — *vi* **1** : hacer trampa(s) **2 ∼ on s.o.** : engañar a algn — **∼** *or* **cheater** ['tʃiːtər] *n* : tramposo *m*, -sa *f*

check ['tʃɛk] *n* **1** RESTRAINT : freno *m* **2** INSPECTION : inspección *f*, comprobación *f* **3** DRAFT : cheque *m* **4** BILL : cuenta *f* **5** : jaque *m* (en ajedrez) **6** : tela *f* a cuadros — **∼** *vt* **1** RESTRAIN : frenar, contener **2** INSPECT : revisar **3** VERIFY : comprobar **4** : dar jaque (en ajedrez) **5 ∼ in** : enregistrarse (en un hotel) **6 ∼ out** : irse (de un hotel) **7 ∼ out** VERIFY : comprobar

checkers ['tʃɛkərz] *n* : damas *fpl*

checkmate ['tʃɛkˌmeɪt] *n* : jaque *m* mate

checkpoint ['tʃɛkˌpɔɪnt] *n* : puesto *m* de control

checkup ['tʃɛkˌʌp] *n* : chequeo *m*, examen *m* médico

cheek ['tʃiːk] *n* : mejilla *f*

cheer ['tʃɪr] *n* **1** CHEERFULNESS : alegría *f* **2** APPLAUSE : aclamación *f* **3 ∼s!** : ¡salud! — **∼** *vt* **1** GLADDEN : alegrar **2** APPLAUD, SHOUT : aclamar, aplaudir — **cheerful** ['tʃɪrfəl] *adj* : alegre

cheese ['tʃiːz] *n* : queso *m*

cheetah ['tʃiːtə] *n* : guepardo *m*

chef ['ʃɛf] *n* : chef *m*

chemical ['kɛmɪkəl] *adj* : químico — **∼** *n* : sustancia *f* química — **chemist** ['kɛmɪst] *n* : químico *m*, -ca *f* — **chemistry** ['kɛmɪstri] *n, pl* **-tries** : química *f*

cheque ['tʃɛk] *Brit* → **check**

cherish ['tʃɛrɪʃ] *vt* **1** : querer, apreciar **2** HARBOR : abrigar (un recuerdo, una esperanza, etc.)

cherry ['tʃɛri] *n, pl* **-ries** : cereza *f*

chess ['tʃɛs] *n* : ajedrez *m*

chest ['tʃɛst] *n* **1** BOX : cofre *m* **2** : pecho *m* (del cuerpo) **3** *or* **∼ of drawers** : cómoda *f*

chestnut ['tʃɛstˌnʌt] *n* : castaña *f*

chew ['tʃuː] *vt* : masticar, mascar — **chewing gum** *n* : chicle *m*

chic ['ʃiːk] *adj* : elegante

chick ['tʃɪk] *n* : polluelo *m*, -la *f* — **chicken** ['tʃɪkən] *n* : pollo *m* — **chicken pox** *n* : varicela *f*

chicory ['tʃɪkəri] *n, pl* **-ries 1** : endivia *f* (para ensaladas) **2** : achicoria *f* (aditivo de café)

chief ['tʃiːf] *adj* : principal — **∼** *n* : jefe

m, -fa *f* — **chiefly** ['tʃiːfli] *adv* : principalmente

child ['tʃaɪld] *n, pl* **children** ['tʃɪldrən] **1** : niño *m*, -ña *f* **2** OFFSPRING : hijo *m*, -ja *f* — **childbirth** ['tʃaɪldˌbərθ] *n* : parto *m* — **childhood** ['tʃaɪldˌhʊd] *n* : infancia *f*, niñez *f* — **childish** ['tʃaɪldɪʃ] *adj* : infantil — **childlike** ['tʃaɪldˌlaɪk] *adj* : infantil, inocente — **childproof** ['tʃaɪldˌpruːf] *adj* : a prueba de niños

Chilean ['tʃɪliən, tʃɪ'leɪən] *adj* : chileno

chili *or* **chile** *or* **chilli** ['tʃɪli] *n, pl* **chilies** *or* **chiles** *or* **chillies 1** *or* **∼ pepper** : chile *m* **2** : chile *m* con carne

chill ['tʃɪl] *n* **1** CHILLINESS : frío *m* **2** **catch a ∼** : resfriarse **3 there's a ∼ in the air** : hace fresco — **∼** *adj* : frío — **∼** *vi* : enfriar — **chilly** ['tʃɪli] *adj* **chillier; -est** : fresco, frío

chime ['tʃaɪm] *vi* **chimed; chiming** : repicar, sonar — **∼** *n* : carillón *m*

chimney ['tʃɪmni] *n, pl* **-neys** : chimenea *f*

chimpanzee [ˌtʃɪmˌpæn'ziː, ˌʃɪm-; tʃɪm'pænzi, ʃɪm-] *n* : chimpancé *m*

chin ['tʃɪn] *n* : barbilla *f*

china ['tʃaɪnə] *n* : porcelana *f*, loza *f*

Chinese ['tʃaɪˈniːz, -ˈniːs] *adj* : chino — **∼** *n* : chino *m* (idioma)

chink ['tʃɪŋk] *n* : grieta *f*

chip ['tʃɪp] *n* **1** : astilla *f* (de madera o vidrio), lasca *f* (de piedra) **2** : ficha *f* (de póker, etc.) **3** NICK : desportilladura *f* **4** *or* **computer ∼** : chip *m* **5 → potato chips** — **∼** *v* **chipped; chipping** *vt* : desportillar — *vi* **1** : desportillarse **2 ∼ in** : contribuir

chipmunk ['tʃɪpˌmʌŋk] *n* : ardilla *f* listada

chiropodist [kə'rɑpədɪst, ʃə-] *n* : podólogo *m*, -ga *f*

chiropractor ['kaɪrəˌpræktər] *n* : quiropráctico *m*, -ca *f*

chirp ['tʃərp] *vi* : piar, gorjear

chisel ['tʃɪzəl] *n* : cincel *m* (para piedras, etc.), formón *m*, escoplo *m* (para madera) — **∼** *vt* **-eled** *or* **-elled; -eling** *or* **-elling** : cincelar, tallar

chit ['tʃɪt] *n* : nota *f*

chitchat ['tʃɪtˌtʃæt] *n* : cháchara *f fam*

chivalrous ['ʃɪvəlrəs] *adj* : caballeroso — **chivalry** ['ʃɪvəlri] *n, pl* **-ries** : caballerosidad *f*

chive ['tʃaɪv] *n* : cebollino *m*

chlorine ['klorˌiːn] *n* : cloro *m*

chock-full ['tʃɑk'fʊl, 'tʃʌk-] *adj* : repleto, atestado

chocolate ['tʃɑkələt, 'tʃɔk-] *n* : chocolate *m*

choice ['tʃɔɪs] *n* **1** : elección *f*, selección

f **2** PREFERENCE : preferencia *f* — ~
adj **choicer; -est** : selecto
choir ['kwaɪr] *n* : coro *m*
choke ['tʃoːk] *v* **choked; choking** *vt* **1**
: asfixiar, estrangular **2** BLOCK : atascar — *vi* : asfixiarse, atragantarse (con
comida) — ~ *n* : estárter *m* (de un
motor)
choose ['tʃuːz] *v* **chose** ['tʃoːz]; **chosen**
['tʃoːzən]; **choosing** *vt* **1** SELECT : escoger, elegir **2** DECIDE : decidir — *vi*
: escoger — **choosy** *or* **choosey**
['tʃuːzi] *adj* **choosier; -est** : exigente
chop ['tʃɑp] *vt* **chopped; chopping 1**
: cortar, picar (carne, etc.) **2** ~ **down**
: talar — ~ *n* : chuleta *f* (de cerdo,
etc.) — **choppy** ['tʃɑpi] *adj* **-pier; -est**
: picado, agitado
chopsticks ['tʃɑpˌstɪks] *npl* : palillos
mpl
chord ['kɔrd] *n* : acorde *m* (en música)
chore ['tʃor] *n* **1** : tarea *f* **2 household**
~**s** : faenas *fpl* domésticas
choreography [ˌkori'ɑɡrəfi] *n, pl* **-phies**
: coreografía *f*
chortle ['tʃɔrtəl] *vi* **-tled; -tling** : reírse
(con satisfacción o júbilo)
chorus ['korəs] **1** : coro *m* (grupo de
personas) **2** REFRAIN : estribillo *m*
chose, chosen → **choose**
christen ['krɪsən] *vt* : bautizar — **christening** ['krɪsənɪŋ] *n* : bautizo *m*
Christian ['krɪstʃən] *n* : cristiano *m*, -na *f*
— ~ *adj* : cristiano — **Christianity**
[ˌkrɪstʃi'ænəti, ˌkrɪs'tʃæ-] *n* : cristianismo *m*
Christmas ['krɪsməs] *n* : Navidad *f*
chrome ['kroːm] *n* : cromo *m*
chronic ['krɑnɪk] *adj* : crónico
chronicle ['krɑnɪkəl] *n* : crónica *f*
chronology [krə'nɑlədʒi] *n, pl* **-gies**
: cronología *f* — **chronological**
[ˌkrɑnəl'ɑdʒɪkəl] *adj* : cronológico
chrysanthemum [krɪ'sænθəməm] *n*
: crisantemo *m*
chubby ['tʃʌbi] *adj* **-bier; -est** : regordete *fam*, rechoncho *fam*
chuck ['tʃʌk] *vt* : tirar, arrojar
chuckle ['tʃʌkəl] *vi* **-led; -ling** : reírse
(entre dientes) — ~ *n* : risa *f* ahogada
chum ['tʃʌm] *n* : amigo *m*, -ga *f*; compinche *mf fam* — **chummy** ['tʃʌmi] *adj*
-mier; -est : muy amigable
chunk ['tʃʌŋk] *n* : trozo *m*, pedazo *m*
church ['tʃɔrtʃ] *n* : iglesia *f*
churn ['tʃɔrn] *n* : mantequera *f* — ~ *vt*
1 : agitar **2** ~ **out** : producir en
grandes cantidades
chute ['ʃuːt] *n* **1** : vertedor *m* **2** SLIDE : tobogán *m*

cider ['saɪdər] *n* : sidra *f*
cigar [sɪ'ɡɑr] *n* : puro *m* — **cigarette**
[ˌsɪɡə'ret, 'sɪɡəˌret] *n* : cigarrillo *m*, cigarro *m*
cinch ['sɪntʃ] *n* **it's a** ~ : es pan comido
cinema ['sɪnəmə] *n* : cine *m*
cinnamon ['sɪnəmən] *n* : canela *f*
cipher ['saɪfər] *n* **1** ZERO : cero *m* **2** CODE
: cifra *f*
circa ['sərkə] *prep* : hacia
circle ['sərkəl] *n* : círculo *m* — ~ *v*
-cled; -cling *vt* **1** : dar vueltas alrededor de **2** : trazar un círculo alrededor
de (un número, etc.) — *vi* : dar vueltas
circuit ['sərkət] *n* : circuito *m* — **cir-
cuitous** [sər'kjuːətəs] *adj* : tortuoso
circular ['sərkjələr] *adj* : circular — ~ *n*
LEAFLET : circular *f*
circulate ['sərkjəˌleɪt] *v* **-lated; -lating** *vt*
: hacer circular — *vi* : circular — **circulation** [ˌsərkjə'leɪʃən] *n* **1** : circulación *f* **2** : tirada *f* (de una publicación)
circumcise ['sərkəmˌsaɪz] *vt* **-cised;
-cising** : circuncidar — **circumcision**
[ˌsərkəm'sɪʒən, 'sərkəm-] *n* : circuncisión *f*
circumference [sər'kʌmfrənts] *n* : circunferencia *f*
circumspect ['sərkəmˌspekt] *adj* : circunspecto, prudente
circumstance ['sərkəmˌstænts] *n* **1** : circunstancia *f* **2 under no** ~**s** : bajo
ningún concepto
circus ['sərkəs] *n* : circo *m*
cistern ['sɪstərn] *n* : cisterna *f*
cite ['saɪt] *vt* **cited; citing** : citar — **cita-
tion** [saɪ'teɪʃən] *n* : citación *f*
citizen ['sɪtəzən] *n* : ciudadano *m*, -na *f*
— **citizenship** ['sɪtəzənˌʃɪp] *n* : ciudadanía *f*
citrus ['sɪtrəs] *n, pl* **-rus** *or* **-ruses** *or* ~
fruit : cítrico *m*
city ['sɪti] *n, pl* **cities** : ciudad *f*
civic ['sɪvɪk] *adj* : cívico — **civics**
['sɪvɪks] *ns & pl* : civismo *m*
civil ['sɪvəl] *adj* : civil — **civilian** [sə-
'vɪljən] *n* : civil *mf* — **civility** [sə'vɪləti]
n, pl **-ties** : cortesía *f* — **civilization**
[ˌsɪvələ'zeɪʃən] *n* : civilización *f* — **civilize** ['sɪvəˌlaɪz] *vt* **-lized; -lizing** : civilizar
clad ['klæd] *adj* ~ **in** : vestido de
claim ['kleɪm] *vt* **1** DEMAND : reclamar **2**
MAINTAIN : afirmar, sostener **3** ~ **responsibility** : atribuirse la responsabilidad — ~ *n* **1** DEMAND : demanda
f, reclamación *f* **2** ASSERTION : afirmación *f*
clam ['klæm] *n* : almeja *f*

clamber ['klæmbər] *vi* : trepar (con torpeza)

clammy ['klæmi] *adj* **-mier; -est** : húmedo y algo frío

clamor ['klæmər] *n* : clamor *m* — **~** *vi* : clamar

clamp ['klæmp] *n* : abrazadera *f* — **~** *vt* : sujetar con abrazaderas — *vi* **~ down on** : reprimir

clan ['klæn] *n* : clan *m*

clandestine [klæn'dɛstɪn] *adj* : clandestino

clang ['klæŋ] *n* : ruido *m* metálico

clap ['klæp] *v* **clapped; clapping** *vt* **1** : aplaudir **2 ~ one's hands** : dar palmadas — *vi* : aplaudir — **~** *n* : palmada *f*

clarify ['klærəˌfaɪ] *vt* **-fied; -fying** : aclarar — **clarification** [ˌklærəfə-'keɪʃən] *n* : clarificación *f*

clarinet [ˌklærə'nɛt] *n* : clarinete *m*

clarity ['klærəti] *n* : claridad *f*

clash ['klæʃ] *vi* **1** : chocar, enfrentarse **2** CONFLICT : estar en conflicto — **~** *n* **1** CRASH : choque *m* **2** CONFLICT : conflicto *m*

clasp ['klæsp] *n* : broche *m*, cierre *m* — **~** *vt* **1** : abrazar (a una persona), agarrar (una cosa) **2** FASTEN : abrochar

class ['klæs] *n* : clase *f*

classic ['klæsɪk] *or* **classical** ['klæsɪkəl] *adj* : clásico — **classic** *n* : clásico *m*

classify ['klæsəˌfaɪ] *vt* **-fied; -fying** : clasificar — **classification** [ˌklæsəfə-'keɪʃən] *n* : clasificación *f* — **classified** ['klæsəˌfaɪd] *adj* RESTRICTED : secreto

classmate ['klæsˌmeɪt] *n* : compañero *m*, -ra *f* de clase

classroom ['klæsˌruːm] *n* : aula *f*, salón *m* de clase

clatter ['klætər] *vi* : hacer ruido — **~** *n* : estrépito *m*

clause ['klɔz] *n* : cláusula *f*

claustrophobia [ˌklɔstrə'foːbiə] *n* : claustrofobia *f*

claw ['klɔ] *n* : garra *f*, uña *f* (de un gato), pinza *f* (de un crustáceo) — **~** *v* : arañar

clay ['kleɪ] *n* : arcilla *f*

clean ['kliːn] *adj* **1** : limpio **2** UNADULTERATED : puro **3** SPOTLESS : impecable — **~** *vt* : limpiar — **~** *adv* : limpio — **cleaner** ['kliːnər] *n* **1** : limpiador *m*, -dora *f* **2** DRY CLEANER : tintorería *f* — **cleanliness** ['klɛnlinəs] *n* : limpieza *f* — **cleanse** ['klɛnz] *vt* **cleansed; cleansing** : limpiar, purificar

clear ['klɪr] *adj* **1** : claro **2** TRANSPARENT : transparente **3** UNOBSTRUCTED : despejado, libre — **~** *vt* **1** : despejar (una superficie), desatascar (un tubo, etc.) **2** EXONERATE : absolver **3** : saltar por encima de (un obstáculo) **4 ~ the table** : levantar la mesa **5 ~ up** RESOLVE : aclarar, resolver — *vi* **1 ~ up** BRIGHTEN : despejarse (dícese del tiempo, etc.) **2 ~ up** VANISH : desaparecer (dícese de una infección, etc.) — **~** *adv* **1 make oneself ~** : explicarse **2 stand ~ !** : ¡aléjate! — **clearance** ['klɪrənts] *n* **1** SPACE : espacio *m* (libre) **2** AUTHORIZATION : autorización *f* **3 ~ sale** : liquidación *f* — **clearing** ['klɪrɪŋ] *n* : claro *m* — **clearly** ['klɪrli] *adv* **1** DISTINCTLY : claramente **2** OBVIOUSLY : obviamente

cleaver ['kliːvər] *n* : cuchillo *m* de carnicero

clef ['klɛf] *n* : clave *f*

cleft ['klɛft] *n* : hendidura *f*, grieta *f*

clement ['klɛmənt] *adj* : clemente — **clemency** ['klɛməntsi] *n* : clemencia *f*

clench ['klɛntʃ] *vt* : apretar

clergy ['klɜrdʒi] *n, pl* **-gies** : clero *m* — **clergyman** ['klɜrdʒimən] *n, pl* **-men** [-mən, -ˌmɛn] : clérigo *m* — **clerical** ['klɛrɪkəl] *adj* **1** : clerical **2 ~ work** : trabajo *m* de oficina

clerk ['klɜrk, *Brit* 'klɑrk] *n* **1** : oficinista *mf*; empleado *m*, -da *f* de oficina **2** SALESPERSON : dependiente *m*, -ta *f*

clever ['klɛvər] *adj* **1** SKILLFUL : ingenioso, hábil **2** SMART : listo, inteligente — **cleverly** ['klɛvərli] *adv* : ingeniosamente — **cleverness** ['klɛvərnəs] *n* **1** SKILL : ingenio *m* **2** INTELLIGENCE : inteligencia *f*

cliché [kli'ʃeɪ] *n* : cliché *m*

click ['klɪk] *vt* : chasquear — *vi* **1** : chasquear **2** GET ALONG : llevarse bien — **~** *n* : chasquido *m*

client ['klaɪənt] *n* : cliente *m*, -ta *f* — **clientele** [ˌklaɪən'tɛl, ˌkli-] *n* : clientela *f*

cliff ['klɪf] *n* : acantilado *m*

climate ['klaɪmət] *n* : clima *m*

climax ['klaɪˌmæks] *n* : clímax *m*, punto *m* culminante

climb ['klaɪm] *vt* : escalar, subir a, trepar a — *vi* **1** RISE : subir **2** *or* **~ up** : subirse, treparse — **~** *n* : subida *f*

clinch ['klɪntʃ] *vt* : cerrar (un acuerdo, etc.)

cling ['klɪŋ] *vi* **clung** ['klʌŋ]; **clinging** : adherirse, pegarse

clinic ['klɪnɪk] *n* : clínica *f* — **clinical** ['klɪnɪkəl] *adj* : clínico

clink ['klɪŋk] *vi* : tintinear

clip ['klɪp] *vt* **clipped; clipping 1** CUT

: cortar, recortar **2** FASTEN : sujetar (con un clip) — **~** *n* **1** FASTENER : clip *m* **2 at a good ~** : a buen trote **3** — **paper clip** — **clippers** ['klɪpərz] *npl* **1** : maquinilla *f* para cortar el pelo **2** *or* **nail ~** : cortauñas *m*

cloak ['kloːk] *n* : capa *f*

clock ['klɑk] **1** : reloj *m* (de pared) **2 around the ~** : las veinticuatro horas — **clockwise** ['klɑk,waɪz] *adv & adj* : en el sentido de las agujas del reloj — **clockwork** ['klɑk,wərk] *n* **1** : mecanismo *m* de relojería **2 like ~** : con precisión

clog ['klɑg] *n* : zueco *m* — **~** *v* **clogged; clogging** *vt* : atascar, obstruir — *vi or* **~ up** : atascarse

cloister ['klɔɪstər] *n* : claustro *m*

close¹ ['kloːz] *v* **closed; closing** *vt* **1** : cerrar — *vi* **1** : cerrarse **2** TERMINATE : terminar **3 ~ in** : acercarse — **~** *n* : final *m*

close² ['kloːs] *adj* **closer; closest 1** NEAR : cercano, próximo **2** INTIMATE : íntimo **3** STRICT : estricto **4** STUFFY : sofocante **5 a ~ game** : un juego reñido — **~** *adv* : cerca, de cerca — **closely** ['kloːsli] *adv* : cerca, de cerca — **closeness** ['kloːsnəs] *n* **1** NEARNESS : cercanía *f* **2** INTIMACY : intimidad *f*

closet ['klɑzət] *n* : armario *m*, clóset *m* Lat

closure ['kloːʒər] *n* : cierre *m*

clot ['klɑt] *n* : coágulo *m* — **~** *v* **clotted; clotting** *vt* : coagular, cuajar — *vi* : coagularse

cloth ['klɔθ] *n, pl* **cloths** ['klɔðz, 'klɔθs] **1** FABRIC : tela *f* **2** RAG : trapo *m*

clothe ['kloːð] *vt* **clothed** *or* **clad** ['klæd]; **clothing** : vestir — **clothes** ['kloːz, 'kloːðz] *npl* **1** : ropa *f* **2 put on one's ~** : vestirse — **clothespin** ['kloːz,pɪn] *n* : pinza *f* (para la ropa) — **clothing** ['kloːðɪŋ] *n* : ropa *f*

cloud ['klaʊd] *n* : nube *f* — **~** *vt* : nublar — *vi or* **~ over** : nublarse — **cloudy** ['klaʊdi] *adj* **cloudier; -est** : nublado

clout ['klaʊt] *n* **1** BLOW : golpe *m*, tortazo *m* fam **2** INFLUENCE : influencia *f*

clove ['kloːv] *n* **1** : clavo *m* **2** : diente *m* (de ajo)

clover ['kloːvər] *n* : trébol *m*

clown ['klaʊn] *n* : payaso *m*, -sa *f* — **~** *or* **~ around** *vi* : payasear

cloying ['klɔɪɪŋ] *adj* : empalagoso

club ['klʌb] *n* **1** : garrote *m*, porra *f* **2** ASSOCIATION : club *m* **3 ~s** *mpl* : tréboles *mpl* (en los naipes) — **~** *vt* **clubbed; clubbing** : aporrear

cluck ['klʌk] *vi* : cloquear

clue ['kluː] *n* **1** : pista *f*, indicio *m* **2 I haven't got a ~** : no tengo la menor idea

clump ['klʌmp] *n* : grupo *m* (de arbustos)

clumsy ['klʌmzi] *adj* **-sier; -est** : torpe — **clumsiness** ['klʌmzinəs] *n* : torpeza *f*

cluster ['klʌstər] *n* : grupo *m*, racimo *m* (de uvas, etc.) — **~** *vi* : agruparse

clutch ['klʌtʃ] *vt* : agarrar, asir — *vi* **~ at** : tratar de agarrarse de — **~** *n* : embrague *m*, clutch *m* Lat (de un automóvil)

clutter ['klʌtər] *vt* : llenar desordenadamente — **~** *n* : desorden *m*, revoltijo *m*

coach ['koːtʃ] *n* **1** CARRIAGE : carruaje *m*, carroza *f* **2** : vagón *m* de pasajeros (de un tren) **3** BUS : autobús *m* **4** : pasaje *m* aéreo de segunda clase **5** TRAINER : entrenador *m*, -dora *f* — *vt* : entrenar (un atleta), dar clases particulares a (un alumno)

coagulate [koˈægjə,leɪt] *v* **-lated; -lating** *vt* : coagular — *vi* : coagularse

coal ['koːl] *n* : carbón *m*

coalition [,koːəˈlɪʃən] *n* : coalición *f*

coarse ['kɔrs] *adj* **coarser; -est 1** : tosco, basto **2** CRUDE, VULGAR : grosero, ordinario — **coarseness** ['kɔrsnəs] *n* : aspereza *f*, tosquedad *f*

coast ['koːst] *n* : costa *f* — *vi* : ir en punto muerto (dícese de un automóvil), deslizarse (dícese de una bicicleta) — **coastal** ['koːstəl] *adj* : costero

coaster ['koːstər] *n* : posavasos *m*

coast guard *n* : guardacostas *mpl*

coastline ['koːst,laɪn] *n* : litoral *m*

coat ['koːt] *n* **1** : abrigo *m* **2** : pelaje *m* (de un animal) **3** : mano *f* (de pintura) — **~** *vt* : cubrir, revestir — **coating** ['koːtɪŋ] *n* : capa *f* — **coat of arms** *n* : escudo *m* de armas

coax ['koːks] *vt* : engatusar

cob ['kɑb] → **corncob**

cobblestone ['kɑbəl,stoːn] *n* : adoquín *m*

cobweb ['kɑb,wɛb] *n* : telaraña *f*

cocaine [koˈkeɪn, 'koː,keɪn] *n* : cocaína *f*

cock ['kɑk] *n* **1** ROOSTER : gallo *m* **2** FAUCET : grifo *m* **3** : martillo *m* (de un arma de fuego) — *vt* **1** : amartillar (un arma de fuego) **2 ~ one's head** : ladear la cabeza — **cockeyed** ['kɑk,aɪd] *adj* **1** ASKEW : ladeado **2** ABSURD : absurdo

cockpit ['kɑk,pɪt] *n* : cabina *f*

cockroach ['kɑk,roːtʃ] *n* : cucaracha *f*

cocktail ['kɑk,teɪl] *n* : coctel *m*, cóctel *m*

cocky ['kɑki] *adj* **cockier; -est** : engreído, arrogante

cocoa ['koː,koː] *n* **1** : cacao *m* **2** : chocolate *m* (bebida)

coconut ['koːkə,nʌt] *n* : coco *m*

cocoon [kəˈkuːn] *n* : capullo *m*

cod ['kɑd] *ns & pl* : bacalao *m*

coddle ['kɑdəl] *vt* **-dled; -dling** : mimar

code ['koːd] *n* : código *m*

coeducational [,koːˌedʒəˈkeɪʃənəl] *adj* : mixto

coerce [koˈərs] *vt* **-erced; -ercing** : coaccionar, forzar — **coercion** [koˈərʒən, -ʃən] *n* : coacción *f*

coffee ['kɔfi] *n* : café *m* — **coffeepot** ['kɔfi,pɑt] *n* : cafetera *f*

coffer ['kɔfər] *n* : cofre *m*

coffin ['kɔfən] *n* : ataúd *m*, féretro *m*

cog ['kɑg] *n* : diente *m* (de una rueda)

cogent ['koːdʒənt] *adj* : convincente, persuasivo

cognac ['koːn,jæk] *n* : coñac *m*

cogwheel ['kɑg,hwiːl] *n* : rueda *f* dentada

coherent [koˈhɪrənt] *adj* : coherente

coil ['kɔɪl] *vt* : enrollar — *vi* : enrollarse — **~** *n* **1** ROLL : rollo *m* **2** : tirabuzón *m* (de pelo), espiral *f* (de humo)

coin ['kɔɪn] *n* : moneda *f* — **~** *vt* : acuñar

coincide [,koːənˈsaɪd, 'koːən,saɪd] *vi* **-cided; -ciding** : coincidir — **coincidence** [koˈɪnsədənts] *n* : coincidencia *f*, casualidad *f* — **coincidental** [koˌɪntsəˈdɛntəl] *adj* : casual, fortuito

coke ['koːk] *n* : coque *m* (combustible)

colander ['kɑləndər, 'kʌ-] *n* : colador *m*

cold ['koːld] *adj* **1** : frío **2 to be ~** : tener frío **3 it's ~ today** : hace frío hoy — **~** *n* **1** : frío *m* **2** : resfriado *m* (en medicina) **3 catch a ~** : resfriarse

coleslaw ['koːl,slɔ] *n* : ensalada *f* de col

colic ['kɑlɪk] *n* : cólico *m*

collaborate [kəˈlæbə,reɪt] *vi* **-rated; -rating** : colaborar — **collaboration** [kəˌlæbəˈreɪʃən] *n* : colaboración *f* — **collaborator** [kəˈlæbə,reɪtər] *n* : colaborador *m*, -dora *f*

collapse [kəˈlæps] *vi* **-lapsed; -lapsing** **1** : derrumbarse, hundirse **2** : sufrir un colapso (físico o mental) — **~** *n* **1** FALL : derrumbamiento *m* **2** BREAKDOWN : colapso *m* — **collapsible** [kəˈlæpsəbəl] *adj* : plegable

collar ['kɑlər] *n* : cuello *m* (de camisa, etc.), collar *m* (para animales) — **collarbone** ['kɑlər,boːn] *n* : clavícula *f*

colleague ['kɑ,liːg] *n* : colega *mf*

collect [kəˈlɛkt] *vt* **1** GATHER : reunir **2** : coleccionar, juntar (timbres, etc.) **3** : recaudar (fondos, etc.) — *vi* **1** ACCUMULATE : acumularse, juntarse **2** CONGREGATE : congregarse, reunirse — **~** *adv* **call ~** : llamar a cobro revertido, llamar por cobrar *Lat* — **collection** [kəˈlɛkʃən] *n* **1** : colección *f* **2** : colecta *f* (de contribuciones) — **collective** [kəˈlɛktɪv] *adj* : colectivo — **collector** [kəˈlɛktər] *n* **1** : coleccionista *mf* **2** : cobrador *m*, -dora *f* (de deudas)

college ['kɑlɪdʒ] *n* **1** : instituto *m* (a nivel universitario) **2** : colegio *m* (electoral, etc.)

collide [kəˈlaɪd] *vi* **-lided; -liding** : chocar, colisionar — **collision** [kəˈlɪʒən] *n* : choque *m*, colisión *f*

colloquial [kəˈloːkwiəl] *adj* : coloquial, familiar

cologne [kəˈloːn] *n* : colonia *f*

Colombian [kəˈlʌmbiən] *adj* : colombiano

colon[1] ['koːlən] *n, pl* **colons** *or* **cola** [-lə] : colon *m* (en anatomía)

colon[2] *n, pl* **colons** : dos puntos *mpl* (signo de puntuación)

colonel ['kərnəl] *n* : coronel *m*

colony ['kɑləni] *n, pl* **-nies** : colonia *f* — **colonial** [kəˈloːniəl] *adj* : colonial — **colonize** ['kɑlə,naɪz] *vt* **-nized; -nizing** : colonizar

color *or Brit* **colour** ['kʌlər] *n* : color *m* — **~** *vt* : colorear, pintar — *vi* BLUSH : sonrojarse — **color–blind** *or Brit* **colour–blind** ['kʌlər,blaɪnd] *adj* : daltónico — **colored** *or Brit* **coloured** ['kʌlərd] *adj* : de color — **colorful** *or Brit* **colourful** ['kʌlərfəl] *adj* **1** : de vivos colores **2** PICTURESQUE : pintoresco — **colorless** *or Brit* **colourless** ['kʌlərləs] *adj* : incoloro

colossal [kəˈlɑsəl] *adj* : colosal

colt ['koːlt] *n* : potro *m*

column ['kɑləm] *n* : columna *f* — **columnist** ['kɑləm,nɪst, -ləmɪst] *n* : columnista *mf*

coma ['koːmə] *n* : coma *m*

comb ['koːm] *n* **1** : peine *m* **2** : cresta *f* (de un gallo) — **~** *vt* : peinar

combat ['kɑm,bæt] *n* : combate *m* — **~** [kəmˈbæt, 'kɑm,bæt] *vt* **-bated** *or* **-batted; -bating** *or* **-batting** : combatir — **combatant** [kəmˈbætənt] *n* : combatiente *mf*

combine [kəmˈbaɪn] *v* **-bined; -bining** *vt* : combinar — *vi* : combinarse — **~** ['kɑm,baɪn] *n* HARVESTER : cosechadora *f* — **combination** [kɑmbəˈneɪʃən] *n* : combinación *f*

combustion [kəmˈbʌstʃən] *n* : combustión *f*

come ['kʌm] vi came ['keɪm]; come;
coming 1 : venir 2 ARRIVE : llegar 3
~ about : suceder 4 ~ back : regresar, volver 5 ~ from : venir de,
provenir de 6 ~ in : entrar 7 ~ out
: salir 8 ~ to REVIVE : volver en sí 9
~ on! : ¡ándale! 10 ~ up OCCUR
: surgir 11 how ~? : ¿por qué? —
comeback ['kʌm,bæk] n 1 RETURN : retorno m 2 RETORT : réplica f
comedy ['kamədi] n, pl -dies : comedia
f — comedian [kə'mi:diən] n : cómico
m, -ca f
comet ['kamət] n : cometa m
comfort ['kʌmpfərt] vt : consolar — ~
n 1 : comodidad f 2 SOLACE : consuelo
m — comfortable ['kʌmpfərtəbəl,
'kʌmpftə-] adj : cómodo
comic ['kamik] or comical ['kamikəl]
adj : cómico — ~ n 1 COMEDIAN
: cómico m, -ca f 2 or ~ book : revista
f de historietas, cómic m — comic
strip n : tira f cómica, historieta f
coming ['kʌmiŋ] adj : próximo, que
viene
comma ['kamə] n : coma f
command [kə'mænd] vt 1 ORDER : ordenar, mandar 2 : estar al mando de
(un barco, etc.) 3 ~ respect : inspirar
(el) respeto — vi : dar órdenes — ~ n
1 ORDER : orden f 2 LEADERSHIP
: mando m 3 MASTERY : maestría f, dominio m — commander [kə'mændər]
n : comandante mf — commandment
[kə'mændmənt] n : mandamiento m
commemorate [kə'mɛmə,reɪt] vt -rated;
-rating : conmemorar — commemoration [kəmɛmə'reɪʃən] n : conmemoración f
commence [kə'mɛnts] v -menced;
-mencing : comenzar, empezar —
commencement [kə'mɛntsmənt] n 1
BEGINNING : comienzo m 2 GRADUA-
TION : ceremonia f de graduación
commend [kə'mɛnd] vt 1 ENTRUST : encomendar 2 PRAISE : alabar — com-
mendable [kə'mɛndəbəl] adj : loable
comment ['kament] n : comentario m,
observación f — ~ vi : hacer comen-
tarios — commentary ['kamən,teri] n,
pl -taries : comentario m — commentator ['kamən,teɪtər] n : comentarista mf
commerce ['kamərs] n : comercio m —
commercial [kə'mərʃəl] adj : comercial — ~ n : anuncio m, aviso m Lat
— commercialize [kə'mərʃə,laɪz] vt
-ized; -izing : comercializar
commiserate [kə'mɪzə,reɪt] vi -ated;
-ating : compadecerse

commission [kə'mɪʃən] n : comisión f
— ~ vt : encargar (una obra de arte)
— commissioner [kə'mɪʃənər] n
: comisario m, -ria f
commit [kə'mɪt] vt -mitted; -mitting 1
ENTRUST : confiar 2 : cometer (un
crimen) 3 : internar (a algn en un hospital) 4 ~ oneself : comprometerse 5
~ to memory : aprender de memoria
— commitment [kə'mɪtmənt] n : compromiso m
committee [kə'mɪti] n : comité m, comisión f
commodity [kə'madəti] n, pl -ties
: artículo m de comercio, producto m
common ['kamən] adj 1 : común 2 OR-
DINARY : ordinario, común y corriente
— ~ n in : en común — commonly ['kamənli] adv : comúnmente
— commonplace ['kamən,pleɪs] adj
: común, banal — common sense n
: sentido m común
commotion [kə'mo:ʃən] n : alboroto m,
jaleo m
commune¹ ['ka,mjuːn, kə'mjuːn] n : comuna f — communal [kə'mjuːnəl] adj
: comunal
commune² [kə'mjuːn] vi -muned;
-muning ~ with : comunicarse con
communicate [kə'mjuːnə,keɪt] v -cated;
-cating vt : comunicar — vi : comunicarse — communicable [kə-
'mjuːnɪkəbəl] adj : transmisible —
communication [kəmjuːnə'keɪʃən] n
: comunicación f — communicative
[kə'mjuːnɪ,keɪtɪv, -kətɪv] adj : comunicativo
communion [kə'mjuːnjən] n : comunión
f
Communism ['kamjə,nɪzəm] n : comunismo m — Communist ['kamjə,nɪst]
adj : comunista — ~ n : comunista
mf
community [kə'mjuːnəti] n, pl -ties : comunidad f
commute [kə'mjuːt] v -muted; -muting
vt : conmutar, reducir (una sentencia)
— vi : viajar de la residencia al trabajo
compact [kəm'pækt, 'kam,pækt] adj
: compacto — ~ ['kam,pækt] n 1 or ~
car : auto m compacto 2 or powder
~ : polvera f — compact disc ['kam-
,pækt'dɪsk] n : disco m compacto
companion [kəm'pænjən] n : compañero m, -ra f — companionship
[kəm'pænjən,ʃɪp] n : compañerismo m
company ['kʌmpəni] n, pl -nies
: compañía f 2 GUESTS : visita f
compare [kəm'pær] v -pared; -paring

vt : comparar — *vi* ~ **with** : poderse comparar con — **comparable** ['kampərəbəl] *adj* : comparable — **comparative** [kəm'pærəṭiv] *adj* : comparativo, relativo — **comparison** [kəm'pærəsən] *n* : comparación *f*

compartment [kəm'partmənt] *n* : compartimento *m*

compass ['kʌmpəs, 'kam-] *n* **1** : compás *m* **2 points of the** ~ : puntos *mpl* cardinales

compassion [kəm'pæʃən] *n* : compasión *f* — **compassionate** [kəm'pæʃənət] *adj* : compasivo

compatible [kəm'pæṭəbəl] *adj* : compatible, afín — **compatibility** [kəm,pæṭə-'bɪləṭi] *n* : compatibilidad *f*

compel [kəm'pɛl] *vt* **-pelled; -pelling** : obligar — **compelling** [kəm'pɛlɪŋ] *adj* : convincente

compensate ['kampən,seɪt] *v* **-sated; -sating** *vi* ~ **for** : compensar — *vt* : indemnizar, compensar — **compensation** [kampən'seɪʃən] *n* : compensación *f*, indemnización *f*

compete [kəm'piːt] *vi* **-peted; -peting** : competir — **competent** ['kampəṭənt] *adj* : competente — **competition** [,kampə'tɪʃən] *n* **1** : competencia *f* **2** CONTEST : concurso *m* — **competitor** [kəm'pɛṭəṭər] *n* : competidor *m*, -dora *f*

compile [kəm'paɪl] *vt* **-piled; -piling** : compilar, recopilar

complacency [kəm'pleɪsənʦi] *n* : satisfacción *f* consigo mismo — **complacent** [kəm'pleɪsənt] *adj* : satisfecho de sí mismo

complain [kəm'pleɪn] *vi* : quejarse — **complaint** [kəm'pleɪnt] *n* **1** : queja *f* **2** AILMENT : enfermedad *f*

complement ['kampləmənt] *n* : complemento *m* — ~ ['kamplə,mɛnt] *vt* : complementar — **complementary** [kamplə'mɛntəri] *adj* : complementario

complete [kəm'pliːt] *adj* **-pleter; -est 1** WHOLE : completo, entero **2** FINISHED : terminado **3** TOTAL : total — ~ *vt* **-pleted; -pleting** : completar — **completion** [kəm'pliːʃən] *n* : conclusión *f*

complex [kam'plɛks, kəm-; 'kam,plɛks] *adj* : complejo — ~ ['kam,plɛks] *n* : complejo *m*

complexion [kəm'plɛkʃən] *n* : cutis *m*, tez *f*

complexity [kəm'plɛksəṭi, kam-] *n, pl* **-ties** : complejidad *f*

compliance [kəm'plaɪənʦ] *n* **1** : acatamiento *m* **2 in** ~ **with** : conforme a — **compliant** [kəm'plaɪənt] *adj* : sumiso

complicate ['kamplə,keɪt] *vt* **-cated; -cating** : complicar — **complicated** ['kamplə,keɪṭəd] *adj* : complicado — **complication** [,kamplə'keɪʃən] *n* : complicación *f*

compliment ['kampləmənt] *n* **1** : cumplido *m* **2** ~**s** *npl* : saludos *mpl* — ~ ['kamplə,mɛnt] *vt* : felicitar — **complimentary** [,kamplə'mɛntəri] *adj* **1** FLATTERING : halagador, halagüeño **2** FREE : de cortesía, gratis

comply [kəm'plaɪ] *vi* **-plied; -plying** ~ **with** : cumplir, obedecer

component [kəm'poːmənt, 'kampoː-] *n* : componente *m*

compose [kəm'poːz] *vt* **-posed; -posing 1** : componer **2** ~ **oneself** : serenarse — **composer** [kəm'poːzər] *n* : compositor *m*, -tora *f* — **composition** [,kampə'zɪʃən] *n* **1** : composición *f* **2** ESSAY : ensayo *m* — **composure** [kəm'poːʒər] *n* : calma *f*

compound[1] ['kam,paʊnd, kəm-; 'kam,paʊnd] *vt* **1** COMPOSE : componer **2** : agravar (un problema, etc.) — ~ ['kam,paʊnd; kam'paʊnd, kəm-] *adj* : compuesto — ~ ['kam,paʊnd] *n* : compuesto *m*

compound[2] ['kam,paʊnd] *n* ENCLOSURE : recinto *m*

comprehend [,kamprɪ'hɛnd] *vt* : comprender — **comprehension** [,kamprɪ'hɛntʃən] *n* : comprensión *f* — **comprehensive** [,kamprɪ'hɛnsɪv] *adj* **1** INCLUSIVE : inclusivo **2** BROAD : amplio

compress [kəm'prɛs] *vt* : comprimir — **compression** [kəm'prɛʃən] *n* : compresión *f*

comprise [kəm'praɪz] *vt* **-prised; -prising** : comprender

compromise ['kamprə,maɪz] *n* : acuerdo *m*, arreglo *m* — ~ *v* **-mised; -mising** *vi* : llegar a un acuerdo — *vt* : comprometer

compulsion [kəm'pʌlʃən] *n* **1** COERCION : coacción *f* **2** URGE : impulso *m* — **compulsive** [kəm'pʌlsɪv] *adj* : compulsivo — **compulsory** [kəm'pʌlsəri] *adj* : obligatorio

compute [kəm'pjuːt] *vt* **-puted; -puting** : computar — **computer** [kəm'pjuːṭər] *n* : computadora *f*, computador *m*, ordenador *m* *Spain* — **computerize** [kəm'pjuːṭə,raɪz] *vt* **-ized; -izing** : informatizar

comrade ['kam,ræd] *n* : camarada *mf*

con ['kan] *vt* **conned; conning** : estafar — ~ *n* **1** SWINDLE : estafa *f* **2 the pros and** ~**s** : los pros y los contras

concave [kan'keɪv, 'kan,keɪv] *adj* : cóncavo

conceal [kən'si:l] vt : ocultar

concede [kən'si:d] vt -ceded; -ceding : conceder, admitir

conceit [kən'si:t] n : vanidad f — conceited [kən'si:təd] adj : engreído

conceive [kən'si:v] v -ceived; -ceiving vt : concebir — vi ~ of : concebir — conceivable [kən'si:vəbəl] adj : concebible

concentrate ['kɑntsən,treɪt] v -trated; -trating vt : concentrar — vi : concentrarse — concentration [,kɑntsən-'treɪʃən] n : concentración f

concept ['kɑn,sept] n : concepto m — conception [kən'sepʃən] n : concepción f

concern [kən'sərn] vt 1 : concernir 2 ~ oneself about : preocuparse por — ~ n 1 AFFAIR : asunto m 2 WORRY : preocupación f 3 BUSINESS : negocio m — concerned [kən'sərnd] adj 1 ANXIOUS : ansioso 2 as far as I'm ~ : en cuanto a mí — concerning [kən'sərnɪŋ] prep : con respecto a

concert ['kɑn,sərt] n : concierto m — concerted [kən'sərtəd] adj : concertado

concession [kən'seʃən] n : concesión f

concise [kən'saɪs] adj : conciso

conclude [kən'klu:d] v -cluded; -cluding : concluir — conclusion [kən'klu:ʒən] n : conclusión f — conclusive [kən'klu:sɪv] adj : concluyente

concoct [kən'kɑkt, kɑn-] vt 1 PREPARE : confeccionar 2 DEVISE : inventarse, tramar — concoction [kən'kɑkʃən] n : mezcla f, brebaje m

concourse ['kɑn,kors] n : vestíbulo m, salón m

concrete [kɑn'kri:t, 'kɑn,kri:t] adj : concreto — ~ ['kɑn,kri:t, kɑn'kri:t] n : hormigón m, concreto m Lat

concur [kən'kər] vi concurred; concurring AGREE : estar de acuerdo

concussion [kən'kʌʒən] n : conmoción f cerebral

condemn [kən'dem] vt : condenar — condemnation [,kɑn,dem'neɪʃən] n : condenación f

condense [kən'dens] v -densed; -densing vt : condensar — vi : condensarse — condensation [,kɑn,den-'seɪʃən, -dən-] n : condensación f

condescending [,kɑndɪ'sendɪŋ] adj : condescendiente

condiment ['kɑndəmənt] n : condimento m

condition [kən'dɪʃən] n 1 : condición f 2 in good ~ : en buen estado — conditional [kən'dɪʃənəl] adj : condicional

condolences [kən'do:ləntsəz] npl : pésame m

condom ['kɑndəm] n : condón m

condominium [,kɑndə'mɪniəm] n, pl -ums : condominio m Lat

condone [kən'do:n] vt -doned; -doning : aprobar

conducive [kən'du:sɪv, -'dju:-] adj : propicio, favorable

conduct ['kɑn,dʌkt] n : conducta f — ~ [kən'dʌkt] vt 1 DIRECT, GUIDE : conducir, dirigir 2 CARRY OUT : llevar a cabo 3 ~ oneself : conducirse, comportarse — conductor [kən'dʌktər] n : revisor m, -sora f (en un tren); cobrador m, -dora f (en un autobús); director m, -tora f (de una orquesta)

cone ['ko:n] n 1 : cono m 2 or ice-cream ~ : cucurucho m, barquillo m Lat

confection [kən'fekʃən] n : dulce m

confederation [kənfedə'reɪʃən] n : confederación f

confer [kən'fər] v -ferred; -ferring vt : conferir, otorgar — vi ~ with : consultar — conference ['kɑnfrənts, -fərənts] n : conferencia f

confess [kən'fes] vt : confesar — vi 1 : confesarse 2 ~ to : confesar, admitir — confession [kən'feʃən] n : confesión f

confetti [kən'feʈi] n : confeti m

confide [kən'faɪd] v -fided; -fiding : confiar — confidence ['kɑnfədənts] n 1 TRUST : confianza f 2 SELF-ASSURANCE : confianza f en sí mismo 3 SECRET : confidencia f — confident ['kɑnfədənt] adj 1 SURE : seguro 2 SELF-ASSURED : confiado, seguro de sí mismo — confidential [,kɑnfə'dentʃəl] adj : confidencial

confine [kən'faɪn] vt -fined; -fining 1 LIMIT : confinar, limitar 2 IMPRISON : encerrar — confines ['kɑn,faɪnz] npl : confines mpl

confirm [kən'fərm] vt : confirmar — confirmation [,kɑnfər'meɪʃən] n : confirmación f — confirmed adj : inveterado

confiscate ['kɑnfə,skeɪt] vt -cated; -cating : confiscar

conflict ['kɑn,flɪkt] n : conflicto m — ~ [kən'flɪkt] vi : estar en conflicto, oponerse

conform [kən'fɔrm] vi 1 COMPLY : ajustarse 2 ~ with : corresponder a — conformity [kən'fɔrməʈi] n, pl -ties : conformidad f

confound [kən'faʊnd, kɑn-] vt : confundir, desconcertar

confront [kən'frʌnt] *vt* : afrontar, encarar — **confrontation** [ˌkɑnfrən'teɪʃən] *n* : confrontación *f*

confuse [kən'fjuːz] *vt* **-fused; -fusing** : confundir — **confusing** [kən'fjuːzɪŋ] *adj* : confuso, desconcertante — **confusion** [kən'fjuːʒən] *n* : confusión *f*, desconcierto *m*

congeal [kən'dʒiːl] *vi* : coagularse

congenial [kən'dʒiːniəl] *adj* : agradable

congested [kən'dʒɛstəd] *adj* : congestionado — **congestion** [kən'dʒɛstʃən] *n* : congestión *f*

congratulate [kən'grædʒəˌleɪt, -'grætʃə-] *vt* **-lated; -lating** : felicitar — **congratulations** [kənˌgrædʒə'leɪʃən, -ˌgrætʃə-] *npl* : felicitaciones *fpl*

congregate ['kɑŋgrɪˌgeɪt] *vi* **-gated; -gating** : congregarse — **congregation** [ˌkɑŋgrɪ'geɪʃən] *n* : feligreses *mpl* (en religión)

congress ['kɑŋgrəs] *n* : congreso *m* — **congressional** [kən'grɛʃənəl, kɑn-] *adj* : del congreso — **congressman** ['kɑŋgrəsmən] *n, pl* **-men** [-mən, -ˌmɛn] : congresista *mf*

conjecture [kən'dʒɛktʃər] *n* : conjetura *f*, presunción *f* — ~ *v* **-tured; -turing** *vt* : conjeturar — *vi* : hacer conjeturas

conjugal ['kɑndʒɪgəl, kən'dʒuː-] *adj* : conyugal

conjugate ['kɑndʒəˌgeɪt] *vt* **-gated; -gating** : conjugar — **conjugation** [ˌkɑndʒə'geɪʃən] *n* : conjugación *f*

conjunction [kən'dʒʌŋkʃən] *n* **1** : conjunción *f* **2 in ~ with** : en combinación con

conjure ['kɑndʒər, 'kʌn-] *v* **-jured; -juring** *vi* : hacer juegos de manos — ~ *vt or* ~ **up** : evocar

connect [kə'nɛkt] *vi* : conectarse — *vt* **1** JOIN : conectar, juntar **2** ASSOCIATE : asociar — **connection** [kə'nɛkʃən] *n* **1** : conexión *f* **2** : enlace *m* (con un tren, etc.) **3 ~s** *npl* : relaciones *fpl* (personas)

connoisseur [ˌkɑnə'sər, -'sʊr] *n* : conocedor *m*, -dora *f*

connote [kə'noːt] *vt* **-noted; -noting** : connotar, implicar

conquer ['kɑŋkər] *vt* : conquistar — **conqueror** ['kɑŋkərər] *n* : conquistador *m*, -dora *f* — **conquest** ['kɑnˌkwɛst, 'kɑŋ-] *n* : conquista *f*

conscience ['kɑntʃənts] *n* : conciencia *f* — **conscientious** [ˌkɑntʃi'ɛntʃəs] *adj* : concienzudo

conscious ['kɑntʃəs] *adj* **1** AWARE : consciente **2** INTENTIONAL : intencional — **consciously** *adv* : deliberadamente

— **consciousness** ['kɑntʃəsnəs] *n* **1** AWARENESS : consciencia *f* **2 lose ~** : perder el conocimiento

consecrate ['kɑntsəˌkreɪt] *vt* **-crated; -crating** : consagrar — **consecration** [ˌkɑntsə'kreɪʃən] *n* : consagración *f*

consecutive [kən'sɛkjətɪv] *adj* : consecutivo, sucesivo

consensus [kən'sɛntsəs] *n* : consenso *m*

consent [kən'sɛnt] *vi* : consentir — ~ *n* : consentimiento *m*

consequence ['kɑntsəˌkwɛnts, -kwənts] *n* **1** : consecuencia *f* **2 of no ~** : sin importancia — **consequent** ['kɑntsəˌkwənt, -ˌkwɛnt] *adj* : consiguiente — **consequently** ['kɑntsəˌkwəntli, -ˌkwɛnt-] *adv* : por consiguiente

conserve [kən'sərv] *vt* **-served; -serving** : conservar, preservar — **conservation** [ˌkɑntsər'veɪʃən] *n* : conservación *f* — **conservative** [kən'sərvətɪv] *adj* **1** : conservador **2** CAUTIOUS : moderado, prudente — ~ *n* : conservador *m*, -dora *f* — **conservatory** [kən'sərvəˌtori] *n, pl* **-ries** : conservatorio *m*

consider [kən'sɪdər] *vt* **1** : considerar **2 all things considered** : teniéndolo todo en cuenta — **considerable** [kən'sɪdərəbəl] *adj* : considerable — **considerate** [kən'sɪdərət] *adj* : considerado — **consideration** [kənˌsɪdə'reɪʃən] *n* **1** : consideración *f* **2 take into ~** : tener en cuenta — **considering** [kən'sɪdərɪŋ] *prep* : teniendo en cuenta

consign [kən'saɪn] *vt* **1** : relegar **2** SEND : enviar — **consignment** [kən'saɪnmənt] *n* : envío *m*

consist [kən'sɪst] *vi* **1 ~ in** : consistir en **2 ~ of** : constar de, componerse de — **consistency** [kən'sɪstəntsi] *n, pl* **-cies 1** TEXTURE : consistencia *f* **2** COHERENCE : coherencia *f* **3** UNIFORMITY : regularidad *f* — **consistent** [kən'sɪstənt] *adj* **1** UNCHANGING : constante, regular **2 ~ with** : consecuente con

console [kən'soːl] *vt* **-soled; -soling** : consolar — **consolation** [ˌkɑntsə'leɪʃən] *n* **1** : consuelo *m* **2 ~ prize** : premio *m* de consolación

consolidate [kən'sɑləˌdeɪt] *vt* **-dated; -dating** : consolidar — **consolidation** [kənˌsɑlə'deɪʃən] *n* : consolidación *f*

consonant ['kɑntsənənt] *n* : consonante *f*

conspicuous [kən'spɪkjuəs] *adj* **1** OBVIOUS : visible, evidente **2** STRIKING : llamativo — **conspicuously** [kən'spɪkjuəsli] *adv* : de manera llamativa

conspire [kən'spaɪr] *vi* **-spired;**
-spiring : conspirar — **conspiracy**
[kən'spɪrəsi] *n, pl* **-cies** : conspiración *f*
constant ['kɑnstənt] *adj* : constante —
constantly ['kɑnstəntli] *adv* : constantemente
constellation [ˌkɑnstə'leɪʃən] *n* : constelación *f*
constipated ['kɑnstəˌpeɪtəd] *adj* : estre-
ñido — **constipation** [ˌkɑnstə'peɪʃən]
n : estreñimiento *m*
constituent [kən'stɪtʃuənt] *n* **1** COMPO-
NENT : componente *m* **2** VOTER : elector *m*, -tora *f;* votante *mf*
constitute ['kɑnstəˌtuːt, -ˌtjuːt] *vt* **-tuted;**
-tuting : constituir — **constitution**
[ˌkɑnstə'tuːʃən, -'tjuː-] *n* : constitución
f — **constitutional** [ˌkɑnstə'tuːʃənəl,
-'tjuː-] *adj* : constitucional
constraint [kən'streɪnt] *n* : restricción *f,*
limitación *f*
construct [kən'strʌkt] *vt* : construir —
construction [kən'strʌkʃən] *n* : construcción *f* — **constructive** [kən-
'strʌktɪv] *adj* : constructivo
construe [kən'struː] *vt* **-strued; -struing**
: interpretar
consul ['kɑnsəl] *n* : cónsul *mf* — **consulate** ['kɑnsələt] *n* : consulado *m*
consult [kən'sʌlt] *v* : consultar — **consultant** [kən'sʌltənt] *n* : asesor *m*, -sora
f; consultor *m*, -tora *f* — **consultation**
[ˌkɑnsəl'teɪʃən] *n* : consulta *f*
consume [kən'suːm] *vt* **-sumed;**
-suming : consumir — **consumer**
[kən'suːmər] *n* : consumidor *m*, -dora *f*
— **consumption** [kən'sʌmpʃən] *n*
: consumo *m*
contact ['kɑnˌtækt] *n* : contacto *m* — **~**
['kɑnˌtækt, kən'-] *vt* : ponerse en contacto con — **contact lens** ['kɑnˌtækt'lenz]
n : lente *mf* (de contacto)
contagious [kən'teɪdʒəs] *adj* : contagioso
contain [kən'teɪn] *vt* **1** : contener **2** ~
oneself : contenerse — **container**
[kən'teɪnər] *n* : recipiente *m*, envase *m*
contaminate [kən'tæməˌneɪt] *vt* **-nated;**
-nating : contaminar — **contamination** [kən'tæmə'neɪʃən] *n* : contaminación *f*
contemplate ['kɑntəmˌpleɪt] *v* **-plated;**
-plating *vt* **1** : contemplar **2** CONSIDER
: considerar, pensar en — *vi* : reflexionar — **contemplation** [ˌkɑntəm-
'pleɪʃən] *n* : contemplación *f*
contemporary [kən'tempəˌreri] *adj*
: contemporáneo — **~** *n, pl* **-raries**
: contemporáneo *m*, -nea *f*
contempt [kən'tempt] *n* : desprecio *m* —

contemptible [kən'temptəbəl] *adj*
: despreciable — **contemptuous** [kən-
'temptʃuəs] *adj* : desdeñoso
contend [kən'tend] *vi* **1** COMPETE : contender, competir **2** ~ **with** : enfrentarse a — *vt* : sostener, afirmar —
contender [kən'tendər] *n* : contendiente *mf*
content[1] ['kɑnˌtent] *n* **1** : contenido *m* **2**
table of ~**s** : índice *m* de materias
content[2] [kən'tent] *adj* : contento — ~
vt ~ **oneself with** : contentarse con
— **contented** [kən'tentəd] *adj* : satisfecho, contento
contention [kən'tentʃən] *n* **1** DISPUTE
: disputa *f* **2** OPINION : argumento *m*,
opinión *f*
contentment [kən'tentmənt] *n* : satisfacción *f*
contest [kən'test] *vt* : disputar — ~
['kɑnˌtest] *n* **1** STRUGGLE : contienda *f* **2**
COMPETITION : concurso *m*, competen-
cia *f* — **contestant** [kən'testənt] *n*
: concursante *mf*, contendiente *mf*
context ['kɑnˌtekst] *n* : contexto *m*
continent ['kɑntənənt] *n* : continente *m*
— **continental** [ˌkɑntən'entəl] *adj*
: continental
contingency [kən'tɪndʒəntsi] *n, pl* **-cies**
: contingencia *f*
continue [kən'tɪnjuː] *v* **-tinued; -tinuing**
: continuar — **continual** [kən'tɪnjuəl]
adj : continuo, constante — **continuation** [kən'tɪnjuˈeɪʃən] *n* : continuación *f*
— **continuity** [ˌkɑntən'uːəti, -juː-] *n, pl*
-ties : continuidad *f* — **continuous**
[kən'tɪnjuəs] *adj* : continuo
contort [kən'tɔrt] *vt* : retorcer — **contortion** [kən'tɔrʃən] *n* : contorsión *f*
contour ['kɑnˌtur] *n* **1** : contorno *m* **2** *or*
~ **line** : curva *f* de nivel
contraband ['kɑntrəˌbænd] *n* : contrabando *m*
contraception [ˌkɑntrə'sepʃən] *n* : anticoncepción *f* — **contraceptive** [ˌkɑn-
trə'septɪv] *adj* : anticonceptivo — ~ *n*
: anticonceptivo *m*
contract ['kɑnˌtrækt] *n* : contrato *m* —
~ [kən'trækt] *vt* : contraer — *vi* : contraerse — **contraction** [kən'trækʃən] *n*
: contracción *f* — **contractor** ['kɑn-
ˌtræktər, kən'træk-] *n* : contratista *mf*
contradiction [ˌkɑntrə'dɪkʃən] *n* : contradicción *f* — **contradict** [ˌkɑntrə'dɪkt]
vt : contradecir — **contradictory**
[ˌkɑntrə'dɪktəri] *adj* : contradictorio
contraption [kən'træpʃən] *n* : artilugio
m, artefacto *m*
contrary ['kɑnˌtreri] *n, pl* **-traries 1**
: contrario **2 on the** ~ : al contrario

— ~ ['kɑn,treri] *adj* **1** : contrario, opuesto **2** ~ **to** : en contra de

contrast [kən'træst] *v* : contrastar — ~ ['kɑn,træst] *n* : contraste *m*

contribute [kən'trɪbjət] *v* **-uted; -uting** : contribuir — **contribution** [,kɑntrə'bju:ʃən] *n* : contribución *f* — **contributor** [kən'trɪbjəʧər] *n* **1** : contribuyente *mf* **2** : colaborador *m*, -dora *f* (en periodismo)

contrite ['kɑn,traɪt, kən'traɪt] *adj* : arrepentido

contrive [kən'traɪv] *vt* **-trived; -triving 1** DEVISE : idear **2** ~ **to do sth** : lograr hacer algo

control [kən'tro:l] *vt* **-trolled; -trolling** : controlar — ~ *n* **1** : control *m* **2** ~**s** *npl* : mandos *mpl*

controversy ['kɑntrə,vərsi] *n, pl* **-sies** : controversia *f* — **controversial** [,kɑntrə'vərʃəl, -siəl] *adj* : polémico

convalescence [,kɑnvə'lesənts] *n* : convalecencia *f* — **convalescent** [,kɑnvə'lesənt] *adj* : convaleciente — ~ *n* : convaleciente *mf*

convene [kən'vi:n] *v* **-vened; -vening** *vt* : convocar — *vi* : reunirse

convenience [kən'vi:njənts] *n* : conveniencia *f*, comodidad *f* — **convenient** [kən'vi:njənt] *adj* : conveniente

convent ['kɑnvənt, -,vɛnt] *n* : convento *m*

convention [kən'vɛntʃən] *n* : convención *f* — **conventional** [kən'vɛntʃənəl] *adj* : convencional

converge [kən'vərdʒ] *vi* **-verged; -verging** : converger, convergir

converse¹ [kən'vərs] *vi* **-versed; -versing** : conversar — **conversation** [,kɑnvər'seɪʃən] *n* : conversación *f* — **conversational** [,kɑnvər'seɪʃənəl] *adj* : familiar

converse² [kən'vərs, 'kɑn,vərs] *adj* : contrario, opuesto — **conversely** [kən'vərsli, 'kɑn,vərs-] *adv* : a la inversa

conversion [kən'vərʒən] *n* : conversión *f* — **convert** [kən'vərt] *vt* : convertir — *vi* : convertirse — **convertible** [kən'vərt̬əbəl] *adj* : convertible — ~ *n* : descapotable *m*, convertible *m Lat*

convex [kɑn'veks, 'kɑn,-, kən'-] *adj* : convexo

convey [kən'veɪ] *vt* **1** TRANSPORT : llevar, transportar **2** TRANSMIT : comunicar

convict [kən'vɪkt] *vt* : declarar culpable a — ~ ['kɑn,vɪkt] *n* : presidiario *m*, -ria *f* — **conviction** [kən'vɪkʃən] *n* **1** : condena *f* (de un acusado) **2** BELIEF : convicción *f*

convince [kən'vɪnts] *vt* **-vinced; -vincing** : convencer — **convincing** [kən'vɪnsɪŋ] *adj* : convincente

convoke [kən'vo:k] *vt* **-voked; -voking** : convocar

convoluted ['kɑnvə,lu:t̬əd] *adj* : complicado

convulsion [kən'vʌlʃən] *n* : convulsión *f* — **convulsive** [kən'vʌlsɪv] *adj* : convulsivo

cook ['kʊk] *n* : cocinero *m*, -ra *f* — ~ *vi* : cocinar, guisar — *vt* : preparar (comida) — **cookbook** ['kʊk,bʊk] *n* : libro *m* de cocina

cookie *or* **cooky** ['kʊki] *n, pl* **-ies** : galleta *f* (dulce)

cooking *n* : cocina *f*

cool ['ku:l] *adj* **1** : fresco **2** CALM : tranquilo **3** UNFRIENDLY : frío — ~ *vt* : enfriar — *vi* : enfriarse — ~ *n* **1** : fresco *m* **2** COMPOSURE : calma *f* — **cooler** ['ku:lər] *n* : nevera *f* portátil — **coolness** ['ku:lnəs] *n* : frescura *f*

coop ['ku:p, 'kʊp] *n* : gallinero *m* — ~ *vt or* ~ **up** : encerrar

cooperate [ko'ɑpə,reɪt] *vi* **-ated; -ating** : cooperar — **cooperation** [ko,ɑpə'reɪʃən] *n* : cooperación *f* — **cooperative** [ko'ɑpərət̬ɪv, -,ɑpə,reɪt̬ɪv] *adj* : cooperativo

coordinate [ko'ɔrdən,eɪt] *v* **-nated; -nating** *vt* : coordinar — **coordination** [ko,ɔrdən'eɪʃən] *n* : coordinación *f*

cop ['kɑp] *n* **1** : poli *mf fam* **2 the** ~**s** : la poli *fam*

cope ['ko:p] *vi* **coped; coping 1** : arreglárselas **2** ~ **with** : hacer frente a, poder con

copier ['kɑpiər] *n* : fotocopiadora *f*

copious ['ko:piəs] *adj* : copioso

copper ['kɑpər] *n* : cobre *m*

copy ['kɑpi] *n, pl* **copies 1** : copia *f* **2** : ejemplar *m* (de un libro), número *m* (de una revista) — ~ *vt* **copied; copying 1** DUPLICATE : hacer una copia de **2** IMITATE : copiar — **copyright** ['kɑpi,raɪt] *n* : derechos *mpl* de autor

coral ['kɔrəl] *n* : coral *m*

cord ['kɔrd] *n* **1** : cuerda *f* **2** *or* **electric** ~ : cable *m* (eléctrico)

cordial ['kɔrdʒəl] *adj* : cordial

corduroy ['kɔrdə,rɔɪ] *n* : pana *f*

core ['kor] *n* **1** : corazón *m* (de una fruta) **2** CENTER : núcleo *m*, centro *m*

cork ['kɔrk] *n* : corcho *m* — **corkscrew** ['kɔrk,skru:] *n* : sacacorchos *m*

corn ['kɔrn] *n* **1** : grano *m* **2** *or* **Indian** ~ : maíz *m* **3** : callo *m* (del pie) — **corncob** ['kɔrn,kɑb] *n* : mazorca *f*

corner ['kɔrnər] *n* : ángulo *m*, rincón *m* (en una habitación), esquina *f* (de una intersección) — ~ *vt* **1** TRAP : acorralar **2** MONOPOLIZE : acaparar (un mercado) — **cornerstone** ['kɔrnər,stoːn] *n* : piedra *f* angular

cornmeal ['kɔrn,miːl] *n* : harina *f* de maíz — **cornstarch** ['kɔrn,stɑrtʃ] *n* : maicena *f*

corny ['kɔrni] *adj* : cursi, sentimental

coronary ['kɔrə,neri] *n*, *pl* **-naries** : trombosis *f* coronaria

coronation [,kɔrə'neiʃən] *n* : coronación *f*

corporal ['kɔrpərəl] *n* : cabo *m*

corporation [,kɔrpə'reiʃən] *n* : sociedad *f* anónima, compañía *f* — **corporate** ['kɔrpərət] *adj* : corporativo

corps ['kor], *pl* **corps** ['korz] : cuerpo *m*

corpse ['kɔrps] *n* : cadáver *m*

corpulent ['kɔrpjələnt] *adj* : obeso, gordo

corpuscle ['kɔr,pʌsəl] *n* : glóbulo *m*

corral [kə'ræl] *n* : corral *m* — ~ *vt* **-ralled; -ralling** : acorralar

correct [kə'rekt] *vt* : corregir — ~ *adj* : correcto — **correction** [kə'rekʃən] *n* : corrección *f*

correlation [,kɔrə'leiʃən] *n* : correlación *f*

correspond [,kɔrə'spɑnd] *vi* **1** WRITE : corresponderse **2** ~ **to** : corresponder a — **correspondence** [,kɔrə'spɑndənts] *n* : correspondencia *f*

corridor ['kɔrədər, -,dɔr] *n* : pasillo *m*

corroborate [kə'rɑbə,reit] *vt* **-rated; -rating** : corroborar

corrode [kə'roːd] *v* **-roded; -roding** *vt* : corroer — *vi* : corroerse — **corrosion** [kə'roːʒən] *n* : corrosión *f* — **corrosive** [kə'roːsiv] *adj* : corrosivo

corrugated ['kɔrə,geitəd] *adj* : ondulado

corrupt [kə'rʌpt] *vt* : corromper — ~ *adj* : corrupto, corrompido — **corruption** [kə'rʌpʃən] *n* : corrupción *f*

corset ['kɔrsət] *n* : corsé *m*

cosmetic [kɑz'metik] *n* : cosmético *m* — ~ *adj* : cosmético

cosmic ['kɑzmik] *adj* : cósmico

cosmopolitan [,kɑzmə'pɑlətən] *adj* : cosmopolita

cosmos ['kɑzməs, -,moːs, -,mɑs] *n* : cosmos *m*

cost ['kɔst] *n* : costo *m*, coste *m* — ~ *vi* **cost; costing 1** : costar **2 how much does it** ~**?** : ¿cuánto cuesta?, ¿cuánto vale?

Costa Rican [,kɔstə'riːkən] *adj* : costarricense

costly ['kɔstli] *adj* : costoso

costume ['kɑs,tuːm, -,tjuːm] *n* **1** OUTFIT : traje *m* **2** DISGUISE : disfraz *m*

cot ['kɑt] *n* : catre *m*

cottage ['kɑtidʒ] *n* : casita *f* (de campo) — **cottage cheese** *n* : requesón *m*

cotton ['kɑtən] *n* : algodón *m*

couch ['kautʃ] *n* : sofá *m*

cough ['kɔf] *vi* : toser — ~ *n* : tos *f*

could ['kud] → **can¹**

council ['kauntsəl] *n* **1** : concejo *m* **2** *or* **city** ~ : ayuntamiento *m* — **councilor** *or* **councillor** ['kauntsələr] *n* : concejal *m*, -jala *f*

counsel *n* **1** ADVICE : consejo *m* **2** LAWYER : abogado *m*, -da *f* — ~ ['kauntsəl] *vt* **-seled** *or* **-selled; -seling** *or* **-selling** : aconsejar — **counselor** *or* **counsellor** ['kauntsələr] *n* : consejero *m*, -ra *f*

count¹ ['kaunt] *vt* : contar — *vi* **1** : contar **2** ~ **on** : contar con **3 that doesn't** ~ : eso no vale — ~ *n* **1** : recuento *m* **2 keep** ~ **of** : llevar la cuenta de

count² *n* : conde *m* (noble)

counter¹ ['kauntər] *n* **1** : mostrador *m* (de un negocio) **2** TOKEN : ficha *f* (de un juego)

counter² *vt* : oponerse a — *vi* : contraatacar — ~ *adv* ~ **to** : contrario a — **counteract** [,kauntər'ækt] *vt* : contrarrestar — **counterattack** ['kauntərə,tæk] *n* : contraataque *m* — **counterbalance** [,kauntər'bæləns] *n* : contrapeso *m* — **counterclockwise** [,kauntər'klɑk,waiz] *adv & adj* : en sentido opuesto a las agujas del reloj — **counterfeit** ['kauntər,fit] *vt* : falsificar — ~ *adj* : falsificado — *n* : falsificación *f* — **counterpart** ['kauntər,pɑrt] *n* : homólogo *m* (de una persona), equivalente *m* (de una cosa) — **counterproductive** [,kauntərprə'dʌktiv] *adj* : contraproducente

countess ['kauntis] *n* : condesa *f*

countless ['kauntləs] *adj* : incontable, innumerable

country ['kʌntri] *n*, *pl* **-tries 1** NATION : país *m* **2** COUNTRYSIDE : campo *m* — ~ *adj* : campestre, rural — **countryman** ['kʌntrimən] *n*, *pl* **-men** [-mən, -,men] *or* **fellow** ~ : compatriota *mf* — **countryside** ['kʌntri,said] *n* : campo *m*, campiña *f*

county ['kaunti] *n*, *pl* **-ties** : condado *m*

coup ['kuː] *n*, *pl* **coups** ['kuːz] *or* ~ **d'etat** : golpe *m* (de estado)

couple ['kʌpəl] *n* **1** : pareja *f* (de per-

sonas) **2 a ~ of** : un par de — **~** vt
-pled; -pling : acoplar, unir
coupon ['ku:ɹɑn, 'kju:-] n : cupón m
courage ['kərɪdʒ] n : valor m — **courageous** [kə'reɪdʒəs] adj : valiente
courier ['kuriər, 'kəriər] n : mensajero m,
-ra f
course ['kors] n 1 : curso m 2 : plato m
(de una cena) 3 or **golf ~** : campo m
de golf 4 **in the ~ of** : en el transcur-
so de 5 **of ~** : desde luego, por
supuesto
court ['kort] n 1 : corte f (de un rey, etc.)
2 : cancha f, pista f (en deportes) 3 TRI-
BUNAL : corte f, tribunal m — **~** vt
: cortejar
courteous ['kərtiəs] adj : cortés —
courtesy ['kərtəsi] n, pl **-sies** : cortesía f
courthouse ['kort,haus] n : palacio m de
justicia, juzgado m — **courtroom**
['kort,ruːm] n : sala f (de un tribunal)
courtship ['kort,ʃɪp] n : cortejo m, noviazgo m
courtyard ['kort,jɑrd] n : patio m
cousin ['kʌzən] n : primo m, -ma f
cove ['koːv] n : ensenada f, cala f
covenant ['kʌvənənt] n : pacto m, convenio m
cover ['kʌvər] vt 1 : cubrir 2 or **~ up**
: encubrir, ocultar 3 TREAT : tratar —
~ n 1 : cubierta f 2 SHELTER : abrigo
m, refugio m 3 LID : tapa f 4 : cubierta
f (de un libro), portada f (de una revista) 5 **~s** npl BEDCLOTHES : mantas
fpl, cobijas fpl Lat 6 **take ~** : ponerse
a cubierto 7 **under ~ of** : al amparo
de — **coverage** ['kʌvərɪdʒ] n : cobertura f — **covert** ['koːvərt, 'kʌvərt] adj
: encubierto — **cover–up** ['kʌvərˌʌp] n
: encubrimiento m
covet ['kʌvət] vt : codiciar — **covetous**
['kʌvətəs] adj : codicioso
cow ['kau] n : vaca f — **~** vt : intimidar,
acobardar
coward ['kauərd] n : cobarde mf —
cowardice ['kauərdɪs] n : cobardía f —
cowardly ['kauərdli] adj : cobarde
cowboy ['kau,bɔɪ] n : vaquero m
cower ['kauər] vi : encogerse (de miedo)
coy ['kɔɪ] adj : tímido y coqueto
coyote [kaɪ'oːti, 'kaɪˌoːt] n, pl **coyotes**
or **coyote** : coyote m
cozy ['koːzi] adj **-zier; -est** : acogedor
crab ['kræb] n : cangrejo m, jaiba f Lat
crack ['kræk] v 1 SPLIT : rajar, partir
2 : cascar (nueces, huevos) 3 : chasquear (un látigo, etc.) 4 **~ down on**
: tomar medidas enérgicas contra —
vi 1 SPLIT : rajarse, agrietarse 2

: chasquear (dícese de un látigo) 3 **~
up** : sufrir una crisis nerviosa — **~** n
1 CRACKING : chasquido m, crujido m 2
CREVICE : raja f, grieta f 3 **have a ~ at**
: intentar
cracker ['krækər] n : galleta f (de soda,
etc.)
crackle ['krækəl] vi **-led; -ling** : crepitar,
chisporrotear — **~** n : crujido m,
chisporroteo m
cradle ['kreɪdəl] n : cuna f — **~** vt
-dled; -dling : acunar
craft ['kræft] n 1 TRADE : oficio m 2 CUN-
NING : astucia f 3 → **craftsmanship** 4
pl usually **craft** BOAT : embarcación f
— **craftsman** ['kræftsmən] n, pl **-men**
[-mən, -ˌmen] : artesano m, -na f —
craftsmanship ['kræftsmənˌʃɪp]
: artesanía f, destreza f — **crafty**
['kræfti] adj **craftier; -est** : astuto,
taimado
crag ['kræg] n : peñasco m
cram ['kræm] v **crammed; cramming**
vt 1 STUFF : embutir 2 **~ with** : atiborrar de — vi : estudiar a última hora
cramp ['kræmp] n 1 : calambre m, espasmo m (de los músculos) 2 **~s** npl
: retorcijones mpl
cranberry ['krænˌberi] n, pl **-berries**
: arándano m (rojo y agrio)
crane ['kreɪn] n 1 : grulla f (ave) 2 : grúa
f (máquina) — **~** vt **craned; craning**
: estirar (el cuello)
crank ['kræŋk] n 1 : manivela f 2 ECCEN-
TRIC : excéntrico m, -ca f — **cranky**
['kræŋki] adj **crankier; -est** : malhumorado
crash ['kræʃ] vi 1 : caerse con estrépito
2 COLLIDE : estrellarse, chocar — vt
: estrellar — **~** n 1 DIN : estrépito m 2
COLLISION : choque m
crass ['kræs] adj : burdo, grosero
crate ['kreɪt] n : cajón m (de madera)
crater ['kreɪtər] n : cráter m
crave ['kreɪv] vt **craved; craving** : ansiar — **craving** ['kreɪvɪŋ] n : ansia f
crawl ['krɔl] vi : arrastrarse, gatear
(dícese de un bebé) — **~** n **at a ~** : a
paso lento
crayon ['kreɪˌɑn, -ən] n : lápiz m de cera
craze ['kreɪz] n : moda f pasajera, manía
f
crazy ['kreɪzi] adj **-zier; -est** 1 : loco 2
go ~ : volverse loco — **craziness**
['kreɪzinəs] n : locura f
creak ['kriːk] vi : chirriar, crujir — **~** n
: chirrido m, crujido m
cream ['kriːm] n : crema f, nata f Spain
— **cream cheese** n : queso m crema

— **creamy** ['kri:mi] *adj* **creamier; -est** : cremoso

crease ['kri:s] *n* : pliegue *m*, raya *f* (del pantalón) — ~ *vt* **creased; creasing** : plegar, poner una raya en (el pantalón)

create [kri'eɪt] *vt* **-ated; -ating** : crear — **creation** [kri'eɪʃən] *n* : creación *f* — **creative** [kri'eɪtɪv] *adj* : creativo — **creator** [kri'eɪtər] *n* : creador *m*, -dora *f*

creature ['kri:tʃər] *n* : criatura *f*, animal *m*

credence ['kri:dənts] *n* **lend ~ to** : dar crédito a

credentials [kri'dentʃəlz] *npl* : credenciales *fpl*

credible ['kredəbəl] *adj* : creíble — **credibility** [,kredə'bɪləti] *n* : credibilidad *f*

credit ['kredɪt] *n* **1** : crédito *m* **2** RECOGNITION : reconocimiento *m* **3 be a ~ to** : ser el orgullo de — ~ *vt* **1** BELIEVE : creer **2** : abonar (en una cuenta) **3 ~ s.o. with sth** : atribuir algo a algn — **credit card** *n* : tarjeta *f* de crédito

credulous ['kredʒələs] *adj* : crédulo

creed ['kri:d] *n* : credo *m*

creek ['kri:k, 'krɪk] *n* : arroyo *m*, riachuelo *m*

creep ['kri:p] *vi* **crept** ['krept]; **creeping** **1** CRAWL : arrastrarse **2** SLINK : ir a hurtadillas — ~ *n* **1** CRAWL : paso *m* lento **2 the ~s** : escalofríos *mpl* — **creeping** *adj* ~ **plant** : planta *f* trepadora

cremate ['kri:meɪt] *vt* **-mated; -mating** : incinerar

crescent ['kresənt] *n* : media luna *f*

cress ['kres] *n* : berro *m*

crest ['krest] *n* : cresta *f* — **crestfallen** ['krest,fɔlən] *adj* : alicaído

crevice ['krevɪs] *n* : grieta *f*

crew ['kru:] *n* **1** : tripulación *f* (de una nave) **2** TEAM : equipo *m*

crib ['krɪb] *n* : cuna *f* (de un bebé)

cricket ['krɪkət] *n* **1** : grillo *m* (insecto) **2** : críquet *m* (juego)

crime ['kraɪm] *n* : crimen *m* — **criminal** ['krɪmənəl] *adj* : criminal — ~ *n* : criminal *mf*

crimp ['krɪmp] *vt* : rizar

crimson ['krɪmzən] *n* : carmesí *m*

cringe ['krɪndʒ] *vi* **cringed; cringing** : encogerse

crinkle ['krɪŋkəl] *vt* **-kled; -kling** : arrugar

cripple ['krɪpəl] *vt* **-pled; -pling 1** DISABLE : lisiar, dejar inválido **2** INCAPACITATE : inutilizar, paralizar

crisis ['kraɪsɪs] *n, pl* **crises** [-,si:z] : crisis *f*

crisp ['krɪsp] *adj* **1** CRUNCHY : crujiente **2** : frío y vigorizante (dícese del aire) — **crispy** ['krɪspi] *adj* **crispier; -est** : crujiente

crisscross ['krɪs,krɔs] *vt* : entrecruzar

criterion [krɑɪ'tɪriən] *n, pl* **-ria** [-iə] : criterio *m*

critic ['krɪtɪk] *n* : crítico *m*, -ca *f* — **critical** ['krɪtɪkəl] *adj* : crítico — **criticism** ['krɪtə,sɪzəm] *n* : crítica *f* — **criticize** ['krɪtə,saɪz] *vt* **-cized; -cizing** : criticar

croak ['kro:k] *vi* : croar

crock ['krɑk] *n* : vasija *f* de barro — **crockery** ['krɑkəri] *n* : vajilla *f*, loza *f*

crocodile ['krɑkə,daɪl] *n* : cocodrilo *m*

crony ['kro:ni] *n, pl* **-nies** : amigote *m* *fam*

crook ['krʊk] *n* **1** STAFF : cayado *m* **2** THIEF : ratero *m*, -ra *f*; ladrón *m*, -drona *f* **3** BEND : pliegue *m* — **crooked** ['krʊkəd] *adj* **1** BENT : torcido, chueco *Lat* **2** DISHONEST : deshonesto

crop ['krɑp] *n* **1** WHIP : fusta *f* **2** HARVEST : cosecha *f* **3** : cultivo *m* (de maíz, tabaco, etc.) — ~ *v* **cropped; cropping** *vt* TRIM : recortar, cortar — *vi* ~ **up** : surgir

cross ['krɔs] *n* **1** : cruz *f* **2** HYBRID : cruce *m* — ~ *vt* **1** : cruzar, atravesar **2** CROSSBREED : cruzar **3** *or* ~ **out** : tachar — ~ *adj* **1** : que atraviesa **2** ANGRY : enojado — **crossbreed** ['krɔs,bri:d] *vt* **-bred** [-bred]; **-breeding** : cruzar — **cross–examine** *vt* : interrogar — **cross–eyed** ['krɔs,aɪd] *adj* : bizco — **cross fire** *n* : fuego *m* cruzado — **crossing** ['krɔsɪŋ] *n* **1** INTERSECTION : cruce *m*, paso *m* **2** VOYAGE : travesía *f* (del mar) — **cross–reference** [,krɔs'refrənts, -'rɛfərənts] *n* : referencia *f* — **crossroads** ['krɔs,ro:dz] *n* : cruce *m* — **cross section** *n* **1** : corte *m* transversal **2** SAMPLE : muestra *f* representativa — **crosswalk** ['krɔs,wɔk] *n* : cruce *m* peatonal, paso *m* de peatones — **crossword puzzle** ['krɔs,wərd] *n* : crucigrama *m*

crotch ['krɑtʃ] *n* : entrepierna *f*

crouch ['kraʊtʃ] *vi* : agacharse

crouton ['kru:,tɑn] *n* : crutón *m*

crow ['kro:] *n* **1** : cuervo *m* — ~ *vi* **crowed** *or Brit* **crew; crowing** : cacarear

crowbar ['kro:,bɑr] *n* : palanca *f*

crowd ['kraʊd] *vi* : amontonarse — *vt* : atestar, llenar — ~ *n* : multitud *f*, muchedumbre *f*

crown ['kraʊn] n 1 : corona f 2 : cima f (de una colina) — ~ vt : coronar

crucial ['kruːʃəl] adj : crucial

crucify ['kruːsəˌfaɪ] vt -fied; -fying : crucificar — **crucifix** ['kruːsəˌfɪks] n : crucifijo m — **crucifixion** [ˌkruːsəˈfɪkʃən] n : crucifixión f

crude ['kruːd] adj cruder; -est 1 RAW : crudo 2 VULGAR : grosero 3 ROUGH : tosco, rudo

cruel ['kruːəl] adj -eler or -eller; -elest or -ellest : cruel — **cruelty** ['kruːəlti] n, pl -ties : crueldad f

cruet ['kruːɪt] n : vinagrera f

cruise ['kruːz] v cruised; cruising 1 : hacer un crucero 2 : ir a velocidad de crucero — ~ n : crucero m — **cruiser** ['kruːzər] n 1 WARSHIP : crucero m 2 : patrulla f (de policía)

crumb ['krʌm] n : miga f, migaja f

crumble ['krʌmbəl] v -bled; -bling vt : desmenuzar — vi : desmenuzarse, desmoronarse

crumple ['krʌmpəl] vt -pled; -pling : arrugar

crunch ['krʌntʃ] vt : ronzar (con los dientes), hacer crujir (con los pies, etc.) — **crunchy** ['krʌntʃi] adj crunchier; -est : crujiente

crusade [kruːˈseɪd] n : cruzada f

crush ['krʌʃ] vt : aplastar, apachurrar Lat — ~ n have a ~ on : estar chiflado por

crust ['krʌst] n : corteza f

crutch ['krʌtʃ] n : muleta f

crux ['krʌks, 'kruks] n : quid m

cry ['kraɪ] vi cried; crying 1 SHOUT : gritar 2 WEEP : llorar — ~ n, pl cries : grito m

crypt ['krɪpt] n : cripta f

crystal ['krɪstəl] n : cristal m

cub ['kʌb] n : cachorro m, -rra f

Cuban ['kjuːbən] adj : cubano

cube ['kjuːb] n : cubo m — **cubic** ['kjuːbɪk] adj : cúbico

cubicle ['kjuːbɪkəl] n : cubículo m

cuckoo ['kuˌkuː, 'ku-] n : cuco m, cuclillo m

cucumber ['kjuːˌkʌmbər] n : pepino m

cuddle ['kʌdəl] v -dled; -dling vi : acurrucarse, abrazarse — vt : abrazar

cudgel ['kʌdʒəl] n : porra f — ~ vt -geled or -gelled; -geling or -gelling : aporrear

cue[1] ['kjuː] n SIGNAL : señal f

cue[2] n : taco m (de billar)

cuff[1] ['kʌf] 1 : puño m (de una camisa) 2 ~s npl → **handcuffs**

cuff[2] vt : bofetear — ~ n SLAP : bofetada f

cuisine [kwɪˈziːn] n : cocina f

culinary ['kʌləˌneri, 'kjuːlə-] adj : culinario

cull ['kʌl] vt : seleccionar, entresacar

culminate ['kʌlməˌneɪt] vi -nated; -nating : culminar — **culmination** [ˌkʌlməˈneɪʃən] n : culminación f

culprit ['kʌlprɪt] n : culpable mf

cult ['kʌlt] n : culto m

cultivate ['kʌltəˌveɪt] vt -vated; -vating : cultivar — **cultivation** [ˌkʌltəˈveɪʃən] n : cultivo m

culture ['kʌltʃər] n 1 : cultura f 2 : cultivo m (en biología) — **cultural** ['kʌltʃərəl] adj : cultural — **cultured** ['kʌltʃərd] adj : culto

cumbersome ['kʌmbərsəm] adj : torpe (y pesado), difícil de manejar

cumulative ['kjuːmjələˌtɪv, -ˌleɪtɪv] adj : acumulativo

cunning ['kʌnɪŋ] adj : astuto, taimado — ~ n : astucia f

cup ['kʌp] n 1 : taza f 2 TROPHY : copa f

cupboard ['kʌbərd] n : alacena f, armario m

curator ['kjʊrˌeɪtər, kjʊˈreɪtər] n : conservador m, -dora f; director m, -tora f

curb ['kərb] n 1 RESTRAINT : freno m 2 : borde m de la acera — ~ vt : refrenar

curdle ['kərdəl] v -dled; -dling vi : cuajarse — vt : cuajar

cure ['kjʊr] n : cura f, remedio m — ~ vt cured; curing : curar

curfew ['kərˌfjuː] n : toque m de queda

curious ['kjʊriəs] adj : curioso — **curio** ['kjʊriˌoː] n, pl -rios : curiosidad f — **curiosity** [ˌkjʊriˈɑsəti] n, pl -ties : curiosidad f

curl ['kərl] vt 1 : rizar 2 COIL : enrollar, enroscar — vi 1 : rizarse 2 ~ up : acurrucarse — ~ n : rizo m — **curler** ['kərlər] n : rulo m — **curly** ['kərli] adj curlier; -est : rizado

currant ['kərənt] n 1 : grosella f (fruta) 2 RAISIN : pasa f de Corinto

currency ['kərəntsi] n, pl -cies MONEY : moneda f 2 gain ~ : ganar aceptación

current ['kərənt] adj 1 PRESENT : actual 2 PREVALENT : corriente — ~ n : corriente f

curriculum [kəˈrɪkjələm] n, pl -la [-lə] : plan m de estudios

curry ['kəri] n, pl -ries : curry m

curse ['kərs] n : maldición f — ~ v cursed; cursing : maldecir

cursor ['kərsər] n : cursor m

cursory ['kərsəri] adj : superficial

curt ['kərt] adj : corto, seco

curtail [kərˈteɪl] *vt* : acortar

curtain [ˈkərtən] *n* : cortina *f* (de una ventana), telón *m* (en un teatro)

curtsy [ˈkərtsi] *vi* **-sied** *or* **-seyed; -sying** *or* **-seying** : hacer una reverencia — ~ *n* : reverencia *f*

curve [ˈkərv] *v* **curved; curving** *vi* : hacer una curva — *vt* : encorvar — ~ *n* : curva *f*

cushion [ˈkʊʃən] *n* : cojín *m* — ~ *vt* : amortiguar

custard [ˈkʌstərd] *n* : natillas *fpl*

custody [ˈkʌstədi] *n, pl* **-dies 1** : custodia *f* **2 be in ~** : estar detenido — **custodian** [kʌˈstoːdiən] *n* : custodio *m*, -dia *f*; guardián, -diana *f*

custom [ˈkʌstəm] *n* : costumbre *f* — **customary** [ˈkʌstəˌmeri] *adj* : habitual, acostumbrado — **customer** [ˈkʌstəmər] *n* : cliente *m*, -ta *f* — **customs** [ˈkʌstəmz] *npl* : aduana *f*

cut [ˈkʌt] *v* **cut; cutting** *vt* **1** : cortar **2** REDUCE : reducir, rebajar **3 ~ oneself** : cortarse **4 ~ up** : cortar en pedazos — *vi* **1** : cortar **2 ~ in** : interrumpir —

~ *n* **1** : corte *m* **2** REDUCTION : rebaja *f*, reducción *f*

cute [ˈkjuːt] *adj* **cuter; -est** : mono *fam*, lindo

cutlery [ˈkʌtləri] *n* : cubiertos *mpl*

cutlet [ˈkʌtlət] *n* : chuleta *f*

cutting [ˈkʌtɪŋ] *adj* : cortante, mordaz

cyanide [ˈsaɪəˌnaɪd, -nɪd] *n* : cianuro *m*

cycle [ˈsaɪkəl] *n* **1** : ciclo *m* **2** BICYCLE : bicicleta *f* — ~ *vi* **-cled; -cling** : ir en bicicleta — **cyclic** [ˈsaɪklɪk, ˈsɪ-] *or* **cyclical** [-klɪkəl] *adj* : cíclico — **cyclist** [ˈsaɪklɪst] *n* : ciclista *mf*

cyclone [ˈsaɪkloːn] *n* : ciclón *m*

cylinder [ˈsɪləndər] *n* : cilindro *m* — **cylindrical** [səˈlɪndrɪkəl] *adj* : cilíndrico

cymbal [ˈsɪmbəl] *n* : platillo *m*, címbalo *m*

cynic [ˈsɪnɪk] *n* : cínico *m*, -ca *f* — **cynical** [ˈsɪnɪkəl] *adj* : cínico — **cynicism** [ˈsɪnəˌsɪzəm] *n* : cinismo *m*

cypress [ˈsaɪprəs] *n* : ciprés *m*

cyst [ˈsɪst] *n* : quiste *m*

czar [ˈzɑr, ˈsɑr] *n* : zar *m*

Czech [ˈtʃɛk] *adj* : checo — ~ *n* : checo *m* (idioma)

D

d [ˈdiː] *n, pl* **d's** *or* **ds** [ˈdiːz] : d *f*, cuarta letra del alfabeto inglés

dab [ˈdæb] *n* : toque *m* — ~ *vt* **dabbed; dabbing** : dar toques ligeros a, aplicar suavemente

dabble [ˈdæbəl] *vi* **-bled; -bling ~ in** : interesarse superficialmente en — **dabbler** *n* : aficionado *m*, -da *f*

dad [ˈdæd] *n* : papá *m fam* — **daddy** [ˈdædi] *n, pl* **-dies** : papá *m fam*

daffodil [ˈdæfəˌdɪl] *n* : narciso *m*

dagger [ˈdæɡər] *n* : daga *f*, puñal *m*

daily [ˈdeɪli] *adj* : diario — ~ *adv* : diariamente

dainty [ˈdeɪnti] *adj* **-tier; -est** : delicado

dairy [ˈdæri] *n, pl* **-ies 1** : lechería *f* (tienda) **2** *or* **~ farm** : granja *f* lechera

daisy [ˈdeɪzi] *n, pl* **-sies** : margarita *f*

dam [ˈdæm] *n* : presa *f* — ~ *vt* **dammed; damming** : represar

damage [ˈdæmɪdʒ] *n* **1** : daño *m*, perjuicio *m* **2 ~s** *npl* : daños y perjuicios *mpl* — ~ *vt* **-aged; -aging** : dañar

damn [ˈdæm] *vt* **1** CONDEMN : condenar **2** CURSE : maldecir — ~ *n* **not give a ~** : no importarse un comino *fam* — ~ *or* **damned** [ˈdæmd] *adj* : maldito *fam*

damp [ˈdæmp] *adj* : húmedo — **dampen** [ˈdæmpən] *vt* **1** MOISTEN : humede-

cer **2** DISCOURAGE : desalentar, desanimar — **dampness** [ˈdæmpnəs] *n* : humedad *f*

dance [ˈdænts] *v* **danced; dancing** : bailar — ~ *n* : baile *m* — **dancer** [ˈdæntsər] *n* : bailarín *m*, -rina *f*

dandelion [ˈdændəˌlaɪən] *n* : diente *m* de león

dandruff [ˈdændrəf] *n* : caspa *f*

dandy [ˈdændi] *adj* **-dier; -est** : de primera, excelente

danger [ˈdeɪndʒər] *n* : peligro *m* — **dangerous** [ˈdeɪndʒərəs] *adj* : peligroso

dangle [ˈdæŋɡəl] *v* **-gled; -gling** *vi* HANG : colgar, pender — *vt* : hacer oscilar

Danish [ˈdeɪnɪʃ] *adj* : danés — ~ *n* : danés *m* (idioma)

dank [ˈdæŋk] *adj* : frío y húmedo

dare [ˈdær] *v* **dared; daring** *vt* : desafiar — *vi* : osar — ~ *n* : desafío *m* — **daredevil** [ˈdærˌdɛvəl] *n* : persona *f* temeraria — **daring** [ˈdærɪŋ] *adj* : atrevido, audaz — ~ *n* : audacia *f*

dark [ˈdɑrk] *adj* **1** : oscuro **2** : moreno (dícese del pelo o de la piel) **3** GLOOMY : sombrío **4 get ~** : hacerse de noche — **darken** [ˈdɑrkən] *vt* : oscurecer — *vi* : oscurecerse — **darkness** [ˈdɑrknəs] *n* : oscuridad *f*

darling ['dɑrlɪŋ] n BELOVED : querido m, -da f — ~ adj : querido

darn ['dɑrn] vt : zurcir — ~ adj : maldito fam

dart ['dɑrt] n 1 : dardo m 2 ~s npl : juego m de dardos — ~ vi : precipitarse

dash ['dæʃ] vt 1 SMASH : romper 2 HURL : lanzar 3 ~ off : hacer (algo) rápidamente — vi : irse corriendo — ~ n 1 : guión m largo (signo de puntuación) 2 PINCH : poquito m, pizca f 3 RACE : carrera f — **dashboard** ['dæʃ,bord] n : tablero m de instrumentos — **dashing** ['dæʃɪŋ] adj : gallardo, apuesto

data ['deɪtə, 'dæ-, 'dɑ-] ns & pl : datos mpl — **database** ['deɪtə,beɪs, 'dæ-, 'dɑ-] n : base f de datos

date[1] ['deɪt] n : dátil m (fruta)

date[2] n 1 : fecha f 2 APPOINTMENT : cita f — ~ v dated; dating vt 1 : fechar (una carta, etc.) 2 : salir con (algn) — vi ~ from : datar de — **dated** ['deɪtəd] adj : pasado de moda

daub ['dɑb] vt : embadurnar

daughter ['dɔtər] n : hija f — **daughter-in-law** ['dɔtərɪnˌlɔ] n, pl **daughters-in-law** : nuera f

daunt ['dɔnt] vt : intimidar

dawdle ['dɑdəl] vi -dled; -dling : entretenerse, perder tiempo

dawn ['dɔn] vi 1 : amanecer 2 it ~ed on him that : cayó en la cuenta de que — ~ n : amanecer m

day ['deɪ] n 1 : día m 2 or working ~ : jornada f 3 the ~ before : el día anterior 4 the ~ before yesterday : anteayer 5 the ~ after : el día siguiente 6 the ~ after tomorrow : pasada mañana — **daybreak** ['deɪˌbreɪk] n : amanecer m — **daydream** ['deɪˌdriːm] n : ensueño m — ~ vi : soñar despierto — **daylight** ['deɪˌlaɪt] n : luz f del día — **daytime** ['deɪˌtaɪm] n : día m

daze ['deɪz] vt dazed; dazing : aturdir — ~ n in a ~ : aturdido

dazzle ['dæzəl] vt -zled; -zling : deslumbrar

dead ['dɛd] adj 1 LIFELESS : muerto 2 NUMB : entumecido — ~ n 1 in the ~ of night : en plena noche 2 the ~ : los muertos — ~ adv ABSOLUTELY : absolutamente — **deaden** ['dɛdən] vt 1 : atenuar (dolores) 2 MUFFLE : amortiguar — **dead end** ['dɛdˌɛnd] n : callejón m sin salida — **deadline** ['dɛdˌlaɪn] n : fecha f límite — **deadlock** ['dɛdˌlɑk] n : punto m muerto — **deadly**

['dɛdli] adj -lier; -est 1 : mortal, letal 2 ACCURATE : certero, preciso

deaf ['dɛf] adj : sordo — **deafen** ['dɛfən] vt : ensordecer — **deafness** ['dɛfnəs] n : sordera f

deal ['diːl] n 1 TRANSACTION : trato m, transacción f 2 : reparto m (de naipes) 3 a good ~ : mucho — ~ v dealt; dealing vt 1 : dar 2 : repartir, dar (naipes) 3 ~ a blow : asestar un golpe — vi 1 : dar, repartir (en juegos de naipes) 2 ~ in : comerciar en 3 ~ with CONCERN : tratar de 4 ~ with s.o. : tratar con algn — **dealer** ['diːlər] n : comerciante mf — **dealings** npl : trato m, relaciones fpl

dean ['diːn] n : decano m, -na f

dear ['dɪr] adj : querido — ~ n : querido m, -da f — **dearly** ['dɪrli] adv 1 : mucho 2 pay ~ : pagar caro

death ['dɛθ] n : muerte f

debar [dɪ'bɑr] vt : excluir

debate [dɪ'beɪt] n : debate m, discusión f — ~ vt -bated; -bating : debatir, discutir

debit ['dɛbɪt] vt : adeudar, cargar — ~ n : débito m, debe m

debris [də'briː, deɪ-; 'deɪˌbriː] n, pl -bris [-'briːz, -ˌbriːz] : escombros mpl

debt ['dɛt] n : deuda f — **debtor** ['dɛtər] n : deudor m, -dora f

debunk [dɪ'bʌŋk] vt : desmentir

debut [deɪ'bjuː, 'deɪˌbjuː] n : debut m — ~ vi : debutar

decade ['dɛˌkeɪd, dɛ'keɪd] n : década f

decadence ['dɛkədəns] n : decadencia f — **decadent** ['dɛkədənt] adj : decadente

decal ['diːˌkæl, dɪ'kæl] n : calcomanía f

decanter [dɪ'kæntər] n : licorera f

decapitate [dɪ'kæpəˌteɪt] vt -tated; -tating : decapitar

decay [dɪ'keɪ] vi 1 DECOMPOSE : descomponerse 2 DETERIORATE : deteriorarse 3 : cariarse (dícese de los dientes) — ~ n 1 : descomposición f 2 : deterioro m (de un edificio, etc.) 3 : caries f (de los dientes)

deceased [dɪ'siːst] adj : difunto — ~ n the ~ : el difunto, la difunta

deceive [dɪ'siːv] vt -ceived; -ceiving : engañar — **deceit** [dɪ'siːt] n : engaño m — **deceitful** [dɪ'siːtfəl] adj : engañoso

December [dɪ'sɛmbər] n : diciembre m

decent [dɪ'sɪnt] adj 1 : decente 2 KIND : bueno, amable — **decency** ['diːsəntsi] n, pl -cies : decencia f

deception [dɪ'sɛpʃən] n : engaño m — **deceptive** [dɪ'sɛptɪv] adj : engañoso

decide [dɪ'saɪd] v **-cided; -ciding** vt : decidir — vi : decidirse — **decided** [dɪ'saɪdəd] adj **1** UNQUESTIONABLE : indudable **2** RESOLUTE : decidido — **decidedly** [dɪ'saɪdədli] adv **1** DEFINITELY : decididamente **2** RESOLUTELY : con decisión

decimal ['dɛsəməl] adj : decimal — ∼ n : número m decimal — **decimal point** n : coma f decimal

decipher [dɪ'saɪfər] vt : descifrar

decision [dɪ'sɪʒən] n : decisión f — **decisive** [dɪ'saɪsɪv] adj **1** RESOLUTE : decidido **2** CONCLUSIVE : decisivo

deck ['dɛk] n **1** : cubierta f (de un barco) **2** or ∼ **of cards** : baraja f (de naipes) **3** TERRACE : entarimado m

declare [dɪ'klær] vt **-clared; -claring** : declarar — **declaration** [ˌdɛklə'reɪʃən] n : declaración f

decline [dɪ'klaɪn] v **-clined; -clining** vt REFUSE : declinar, rehusar — vi DECREASE : disminuir — ∼ n **1** DETERIORATION : decadencia f, deterioro m **2** DECREASE : disminución f

decode [dɪ'koːd] vt **-coded; -coding** : descodificar

decompose [ˌdiːkəm'poːz] vt **-posed; -posing** : descomponer — vi : descomponerse

decongestant [ˌdiːkən'dʒɛstənt] n : descongestionante m

decorate ['dɛkəˌreɪt] vt **-rated; -rating** : decorar — **decor** or **décor** [deɪˈkor, 'deɪˌkor] n : decoración f — **decoration** [ˌdɛkə'reɪʃən] n : decoración f — **decorator** ['dɛkəˌreɪtər] n : decorador m, -dora f

decoy ['diːˌkɔɪ, dɪ'-] n : señuelo m

decrease [dɪ'kriːs] v **-creased; -creasing** : disminuir — ∼ ['diːˌkriːs] n : disminución f

decree [dɪ'kriː] n : decreto m — ∼ vt **-creed; -creeing** : decretar

decrepit [dɪ'krɛpɪt] adj **1** FEEBLE : decrépito **2** DILAPIDATED : ruinoso

dedicate ['dɛdɪˌkeɪt] vt **-cated; -cating 1** : dedicar **2** ∼ **oneself to** : consagrarse a — **dedication** [ˌdɛdɪ'keɪʃən] n **1** DEVOTION : dedicación f **2** INSCRIPTION : dedicatoria f

deduce [dɪ'duːs, -'djuːs] vt **-duced; -ducing** : deducir — **deduct** [dɪ'dʌkt] vt : deducir — **deduction** [dɪ'dʌkʃən] n : deducción f

deed ['diːd] n : acción f, hecho m

deem ['diːm] vt : considerar, juzgar

deep ['diːp] adj : hondo, profundo — ∼ adv **1** DEEPLY : profundamente **2** ∼ **down** : en el fondo **3** **dig** ∼ : cavar hondo — **deepen** ['diːpən] vt : ahondar — vi : hacerse más profundo — **deeply** ['diːpli] adv : hondo, profundamente

deer ['dɪr] ns & pl : ciervo m

deface [dɪ'feɪs] vt **-faced; -facing** : desfigurar

default [dɪ'fɔlt, 'diːˌfɔlt] n **by** ∼ : en rebeldía — ∼ vi **1** ∼ **on** : no pagar (una deuda) **2** : no presentarse (en deportes)

defeat [dɪ'fiːt] vt **1** BEAT : vencer, derrotar **2** FRUSTRATE : frustrar — ∼ n : derrota f

defect ['diːˌfɛkt, dɪ'fɛkt] n : defecto m — ∼ [dɪ'fɛkt] vi : desertar — **defective** [dɪ'fɛktɪv] adj : defectuoso

defend [dɪ'fɛnd] vt : defender — **defendant** [dɪ'fɛndənt] n : acusado m, -da f — **defense** or Brit **defence** [dɪ'fɛns, 'diːˌfɛns] n : defensa f — **defenseless** or Brit **defenceless** adj : indefenso — **defensive** [dɪ'fɛnsɪv] adj : defensivo — ∼ n **on the** ∼ : a la defensiva

defer [dɪ'fər] v **-ferred; -ferring** vt : diferir, aplazar — vi ∼ **to** : deferir a — **deference** ['dɛfərənts] n : deferencia f — **deferential** [ˌdɛfə'rɛntʃəl] adj : deferente

defiance [dɪ'faɪənts] n **1** : desafío m **2** **in** ∼ **of** : a despecho de — **defiant** [dɪ'faɪənt] adj : desafiante

deficiency [dɪ'fɪʃəntsi] n, pl **-cies** : deficiencia f — **deficient** [dɪ'fɪʃənt] adj : deficiente

deficit ['dɛfəsɪt] n : déficit m

defile [dɪ'faɪl] vt **-filed; -filing 1** DIRTY : ensuciar **2** DESECRATE : profanar

define [dɪ'faɪn] v **-fined; -fining** : definir — **definite** ['dɛfənɪt] adj **1** : definido **2** CERTAIN : seguro, incuestionable — **definition** [ˌdɛfə'nɪʃən] n : definición f — **definitive** [dɪ'fɪnətɪv] adj : definitivo

deflate [dɪ'fleɪt] v **-flated; -flating** vt : desinflar (una llanta, etc.) — vi : desinflarse

deflect [dɪ'flɛkt] vt : desviar — vi : desviarse

deform [dɪ'fɔrm] vt : deformar — **deformity** [dɪ'fɔrməti] n, pl **-ties** : deformidad f

defraud [dɪ'frɔd] vt : defraudar

defrost [dɪ'frɔst] vt : descongelar — vi : descongelarse

deft ['dɛft] adj : hábil, diestro

defy [dɪ'faɪ] vt **-fied; -fying 1** CHALLENGE : desafiar **2** RESIST : resistir

degenerate [dɪ'dʒɛnəˌreɪt] vi : degenerar — ∼ [dɪ'dʒɛnərət] adj : degenerado

degrade [dɪ'greɪd] *vt* **-graded; -grading** : degradar — **degrading** *adj* : degradante

degree [dɪ'griː] *n* 1 : grado *m* 2 *or* academic ~ : título *m*

dehydrate [diː'haɪˌdreɪt] *vt* **-drated; -drating** : deshidratar

deign ['deɪn] *vi* ~ **to** : dignarse (a)

deity ['diːəti, 'deɪ-] *n, pl* **-ties** : deidad *f*

dejected [dɪ'dʒɛktəd] *adj* : abatido — **dejection** [dɪ'dʒɛkʃən] *n* : abatimiento *m*

delay [dɪ'leɪ] *n* : retraso *m* — ~ *vt* 1 POSTPONE : aplazar 2 HOLD UP : retrasar — *vi* : demorar

delectable [dɪ'lɛktəbəl] *adj* : delicioso

delegate ['dɛlɪgət, -geɪt] *n* : delegado *m*, -da *f* — ['dɛlɪˌgeɪt] *v* **-gated; -gating** : delegar — **delegation** [ˌdɛlɪ'geɪʃən] *n* : delegación *f*

delete [dɪ'liːt] *vt* **-leted; -leting** : borrar

deliberate [dɪ'lɪbəˌreɪt] *v* **-ated; -ating** *vt* : deliberar sobre — *vi* : deliberar — [dɪ'lɪbərət] *adj* : deliberado — **deliberately** [dɪ'lɪbərətli] *adv* INTENTIONALLY : a propósito — **deliberation** [dɪˌlɪbə'reɪʃən] *n* : deliberación *f*

delicacy ['dɛlɪkəsi] *n, pl* **-cies** 1 : delicadeza *f* 2 FOOD : manjar *m*, exquisitez *f* — **delicate** ['dɛlɪkət] *adj* : delicado

delicatessen [ˌdɛlɪkə'tɛsən] *n* : charcutería *f*

delicious [dɪ'lɪʃəs] *adj* : delicioso

delight [dɪ'laɪt] *n* : placer *m*, deleite *m* — ~ *vt* : deleitar, encantar — *vi* ~ **in** : deleitarse con — **delightful** [dɪ'laɪtfəl] *adj* : delicioso, encantador

delinquent [dɪ'lɪŋkwənt] *adj* : delincuente — ~ *n* : delincuente *mf*

delirious [dɪ'lɪriəs] *adj* : delirante — **delirium** [dɪ'lɪriəm] *n* : delirio *m*

deliver [dɪ'lɪvər] *vt* 1 DISTRIBUTE : entregar, repartir 2 FREE : liberar 3 : asistir en el parto de (un niño) 4 : pronunciar (un discurso, etc.) 5 DEAL : asestar (un golpe, etc.) — **delivery** [dɪ'lɪvəri] *n, pl* **-eries** 1 DISTRIBUTION : entrega *f*, reparto *m* 2 LIBERATION : liberación *f* 3 CHILDBIRTH : parto *m*, alumbramiento *m*

delude [dɪ'luːd] *vt* **-luded; -luding** 1 : engañar 2 ~ **oneself** : engañarse

deluge ['dɛlˌjuːdʒ, -ˌjuːʒ] *n* : diluvio *m*

delusion [dɪ'luːʒən] *n* : ilusión *f*

deluxe [dɪ'lʌks, -'luːks] *adj* : de lujo

delve ['dɛlv] *vi* **delved; delving** 1 : escarbar 2 ~ **into** PROBE : investigar

demand [dɪ'mænd] *n* 1 REQUEST : petición *f* 2 CLAIM : reclamación *f*, exigencia *f* 3 → supply — ~ *vt* : exigir — **demanding** *adj* : exigente

demean [dɪ'miːn] *vt* ~ **oneself** : rebajarse

demeanor [dɪ'miːnər] *n* : comportamiento *m*

demented [dɪ'mɛntəd] *adj* : demente, loco

demise [dɪ'maɪz] *n* : fallecimiento *m*

democracy [dɪ'mɑːkrəsi] *n, pl* **-cies** : democracia *f* — **democrat** ['dɛmə-ˌkræt] *n* : demócrata *mf* — **democratic** [ˌdɛmə'krætɪk] *adj* : democrático

demolish [dɪ'mɑːlɪʃ] *vt* : demoler — **demolition** [ˌdɛmə'lɪʃən, ˌdiː-] *n* : demolición *f*

demon ['diːmən] *n* : demonio *m*

demonstrate ['dɛmənˌstreɪt] *v* **-strated; -strating** *vt* : demostrar — *vi* RALLY : manifestarse — **demonstration** [ˌdɛmən'streɪʃən] *n* 1 : demostración *f* 2 RALLY : manifestación *f*

demoralize [dɪ'mɔːrəˌlaɪz] *vt* **-ized; -izing** : desmoralizar

demote [dɪ'moːt] *vt* **-moted; -moting** : bajar de categoría

demure [dɪ'mjʊr] *adj* : recatado

den ['dɛn] *n* LAIR : guarida *f*

denial [dɪ'naɪəl] *n* 1 : negación *f*, rechazo *m* 2 REFUSAL : denegación *f*

denim ['dɛnəm] *n* : tela *f* vaquera, mezclilla *f Lat*

denomination [dɪˌnɑːmə'neɪʃən] *n* 1 : confesión *f* (religiosa) 2 : valor *m* (de una moneda)

denounce [dɪ'naʊnts] *vt* **-nounced; -nouncing** : denunciar

dense ['dɛnts] *adj* **denser; -est** 1 THICK : denso 2 STUPID : estúpido — **density** ['dɛntsəti] *n, pl* **-ties** : densidad *f*

dent ['dɛnt] *vt* : abollar — ~ *n* : abolladura *f*

dental ['dɛntəl] *adj* : dental — **dental floss** *n* : hilo *m* dental — **dentist** ['dɛntɪst] *n* : dentista *mf* — **dentures** ['dɛntʃərz] *npl* : dentadura *f* postiza

deny [dɪ'naɪ] *vt* **-nied; -nying** 1 : negar 2 REFUSE : denegar

deodorant [diː'oːdərənt] *n* : desodorante *m*

depart [dɪ'pɑrt] *vi* 1 : salir 2 ~ **from** : apartarse de (la verdad, etc.)

department [dɪ'pɑrtmənt] *n* : sección *f* (de una tienda, etc.), departamento *m* (de una empresa, etc.), ministerio *m* (del gobierno) — **department store** *n* : grandes almacenes *mpl*

departure [dɪ'pɑrtʃər] *n* 1 : salida *f* 2 DEVIATION : desviación *f*

depend [dɪ'pɛnd] *vi* 1 ~ **on** : depender

de 2 ~ on s.o. : contar con algn 3
that ~s : eso depende — **dependable** [dɪ'pliːtɪ] *adj* : digno de confianza — **dependence** [dɪ'pendənts]
n : dependencia *f* — **dependent** [dɪ-
'pendənt] *adj* : dependiente

depict [dɪ'pɪkt] *vt* 1 PORTRAY : representar 2 DESCRIBE : describir

deplete [dɪ'pliːt] *vt* **-pleted; -pleting**
: agotar, reducir

deplore [dɪ'plor] *vt* **-plored; -ploring**
: deplorar, lamentar — **deplorable**
[dɪ'plorəbəl] *adj* : lamentable

deploy [dɪ'plɔɪ] *vt* : desplegar

deport [dɪ'port] *vt* : deportar, expulsar
(de un país) — **deportation** [ˌdiˌpor-
'teɪʃən] *n* : deportación *f*

depose [dɪ'poːz] *vt* **-posed; -posing**
: deponer

deposit [dɪ'pazət] *vt* **-ited; -iting** : depositar — ~ *n* 1 : depósito *m* 2 DOWN
PAYMENT : entrega *f* inicial

depot [*in sense 1 usu* 'dɛˌpoː, 2 *usu* 'diː-]
n 1 WAREHOUSE : almacén *m*, depósito
m 2 STATION : terminal *mf*

depreciate [dɪ'priːʃiˌeɪt] *vi* **-ated; -ating**
: depreciarse — **depreciation** [dɪ-
ˌpriːʃi'eɪʃən] *n* : depreciación *f*

depress [dɪ'pres] *vt* 1 : deprimir 2 PRESS
: apretar — **depressed** [dɪ'prest] *adj*
: abatido, deprimido — **depressing**
[dɪ'presɪŋ] *adj* : deprimente — **depression** [dɪ'preʃən] *n* : depresión *f*

deprive [dɪ'praɪv] *vt* **-prived; -priving**
: privar

depth ['depθ] *n, pl* **depths** ['depθs,
'deps] 1 : profundidad *f* 2 **in the ~s of
night** : en lo más profundo de la noche

deputy ['depjuti] *n, pl* **-ties** : suplente
mf; sustituto *m*, -ta *f*

derail [dɪ'reɪl] *vt* : hacer descarrilar

deranged [dɪ'reɪndʒd] *adj* : trastornado

derelict ['derəlɪkt] *adj* : abandonado

deride [dɪ'raɪd] *vt* **-rided; -riding** : burlarse de — **derision** [dɪ'rɪʒən] *n* : mofa
f

derive [dɪ'raɪv] *vi* **-rived; -riving** : derivar — **derivation** [ˌderə'veɪʃən] *n* : derivación *f*

derogatory [dɪ'rɑgəˌtori] *adj* : despectivo

descend [dɪ'send] *v* : descender, bajar
— **descendant** [dɪ'sendənt] *n* : descendiente *mf* —**descent** [dɪ'sent] *n* 1
: descenso *m* 2 LINEAGE : descendencia *f*

describe [dɪ'skraɪb] *vt* **-scribed; -scrib-
ing** : describir — **description** [dɪ-
'skrɪpʃən] *n* : descripción *f* — **descriptive** [dɪ'skrɪptɪv] *adj* : descriptivo

desecrate ['desɪˌkreɪt] *vt* **-crated;
-crating** : profanar

desert ['dezərt] *n* : desierto *m* — ~ *adj*
~ **island** : isla *f* desierta — ~ [dɪ-
'zərt] *vt* : abandonar — *vi* : desertar —
deserter [dɪ'zərtər] *n* : desertor *m*,
-tora *f*

deserve [dɪ'zərv] *vt* **-served; -serving**
: merecer

design [dɪ'zaɪn] *vt* 1 DEVISE : diseñar 2
PLAN : proyectar — ~ *n* 1 : diseño *m*
2 PLAN : plan *m*, proyecto *m*

designate ['dezɪɡˌneɪt] *vt* **-nated;
-nating** : nombrar, designar

designer [dɪ'zaɪnər] *n* : diseñador *m*,
-dora *f*

desire [dɪ'zaɪr] *vt* **-sired; -siring** : desear — ~ *n* : deseo *m* — **desirable** [dɪ-
'zaɪrəbəl] *adj* : deseable

desk ['desk] *n* : escritorio *m*, pupitre *m*
(en la escuela)

desolate ['desələt, -zə-] *adj* : desolado

despair [dɪ'spær] *vi* : desesperar — ~ *n*
: desesperación *f*

desperate ['despərət] *adj* : desesperado
— **desperation** [ˌdespə'reɪʃən] *n* : desesperación *f*

despise [dɪ'spaɪz] *vt* **-spised; -spising**
: despreciar — **despicable** [dɪ-
'spɪkəbəl, 'despɪ-] *adj* : despreciable

despite [dɪ'spaɪt] *prep* : a pesar de

despondent [dɪ'spandənt] *adj* : desanimado

dessert [dɪ'zərt] *n* : postre *m*

destination [ˌdestə'neɪʃən] *n* : destino *m*
— **destined** ['destənd] *adj* 1 : destinado 2 ~ **for** : con destino a — **destiny**
['destəni] *n, pl* **-nies** : destino *m*

destitute ['destəˌtuːt, -ˌtjuːt] *adj* : indigente

destroy [dɪ'strɔɪ] *vt* : destruir — **destruction** [dɪ'strʌkʃən] *n* : destrucción *f*
— **destructive** [dɪ'strʌktɪv] *adj* : destructivo

detach [dɪ'tætʃ] *vt* : separar — **de-
tached** [dɪ'tætʃt] *adj* 1 : separado 2 IM-
PARTIAL : objetivo

detail [dɪ'teɪl, 'diːˌteɪl] *n* 1 : detalle *m* 2 **go
into** ~ : entrar en detalles — ~ *vt*
: detallar — **detailed** *adj* : detallado

detain [dɪ'teɪn] *vt* 1 : detener (un prisionero) 2 DELAY : entretener

detect [dɪ'tekt] *vt* : detectar — **detec-
tion** [dɪ'tekʃən] *n* : detección *f*, descubrimiento *m* — **detective** [dɪ'tektɪv]
n : detective *mf*

detention [dɪ'tentʃən] *n* : detención *m*

deter [dɪ'tər] *vt* **-terred; -terring** : disuadir

detergent [dɪ'tərdʒənt] *n* : detergente *m*

deteriorate [di'tiriə,reit] vi -**rated;** -**rating** : deteriorarse — **deterioration** [di,tiriə'reiʃən] n : deterioro m

determine [di'tərmən] vt -**mined;** -**mining** : determinar — **determined** [di'tərmənd] adj RESOLUTE : decidido — **determination** [di,tərmə'neiʃən] n : determinación f

deterrent [di'tərənt] n : medida f disuasiva

detest [di'test] vt : detestar — **detestable** [di'testəbəl] adj : odioso

detonate ['detən,eit] v -**nated;** -**nating** vt : hacer detonar — vi EXPLODE : detonar, estallar — **detonation** [,detə'neiʃən, deta -] n : detonación f

detour ['di:,tur, di'tur] n 1 : desviación f 2 **make a ~** : dar un rodeo — ~ vi : desviarse

detract [di'trækt] vi ~ **from** : aminorar, restar importancia a

detrimental [,detrə'mentəl] adj : perjudicial

devalue [di'væl,ju:] vt -**ued;** -**uing** : devaluar

devastate ['devə,steit] vt -**tated;** -**tating** : devastar — **devastating** adj : devastador — **devastation** [,devə'steiʃən] n : devastación f

develop [di'veləp] vt 1 : desarrollar 2 ~ **an illness** : contraer una enfermedad — vi 1 GROW : desarrollarse 2 HAPPEN : aparecer — **development** [di'veləpmənt] n : desarrollo m

deviate ['di:vi,eit] v -**ated;** -**ating** vi : desviarse — **deviation** [,di:vi'eiʃən] n : desviación f

device [di'vais] n : dispositivo m, mecanismo m

devil ['devəl] n : diablo m, demonio m — **devilish** ['devəliʃ] adj : diabólico

devious ['di:viəs] adj 1 CRAFTY : taimado 2 WINDING : tortuoso

devise [di'vaiz] v -**vised;** -**vising** : idear, concebir

devoid [di'vɔid] adj ~ **of** : desprovisto de

devote [di'vot] vt -**voted;** -**voting** : consagrar, dedicar — **devoted** [di'votəd] adj : leal — **devotee** [,devə'ti:, -'tei] n : devoto m, -ta f — **devotion** [di'voːʃən] n 1 : devoción f, dedicación f 2 : oración f (en religión)

devour [di'vauər] vt : devorar

devout [di'vaut] adj : devoto

dew ['du:, 'dju:] n : rocío m

dexterity [dek'sterəti] n, pl -**ties** : destreza f

diabetes [,daiə'bi:ti:z] n : diabetes f —

diabetic [,daiə'betik] adj : diabético — ~ n : diabético m, -ca f

diabolic [,daiə'balik] or **diabolical** [-likəl] adj : diabólico

diagnosis [,daing'noːsis] n, pl -**noses** [-'noː,si:z] : diagnóstico m — **diagnose** ['daing,noːs, ,daing'noːs] vt -**nosed;** -**nosing** : diagnosticar — **diagnostic** [,daing'nastik] adj : diagnóstico

diagonal [dai'ægənəl] adj : diagonal, en diagonal — ~ n : diagonal f

diagram ['daiə,græm] n : diagrama m

dial ['dail] n : esfera f (de un reloj), dial m (de un radio, etc.) — ~ v **dialed** or **dialled; dialing** or **dialling** : marcar

dialect ['daiə,lekt] n : dialecto m

dialogue ['daiə,lɔg] n : diálogo m

diameter [dai'æmətər] n : diámetro m

diamond ['daimənd, 'daiə-] n 1 : diamante m 2 : rombo m (forma) 3 or **baseball ~** : cuadro m, diamante m

diaper ['daipər, 'daiə-] n : pañal m

diaphragm ['daiə,fræm] n : diafragma m

diarrhea [,daiə'riːə] n : diarrea f

diary ['daiəri] n, pl -**ries** : diario m

dice ['dais] ns & pl : dados mpl (juego)

dictate ['dik,teit, dik'teit] vt -**tated;** -**tating** : dictar — **dictation** [dik'teiʃən] n : dictado m — **dictator** ['dik,teitər] n : dictador m, -dora f — **dictatorship** [dik'teitər,ʃip, 'dik,-] n : dictadura f

dictionary ['dikʃə,neri] n, pl -**naries** : diccionario m

did → do

die¹ ['dai] vi **died** ['daid]; **dying** ['daiiŋ] 1 : morir 2 ~ **down** : amainar, disminuir 3 ~ **out** : extinguirse 4 **be dying for** : morirse por

die² ['dai] n 1 pl **dice** ['dais] : dado m (para jugar) 2 pl **dies** ['daiz] MOLD : molde m

diesel ['diːzəl, -səl] n : diesel m

diet ['daiət] n 1 FOOD : alimentación f 2 **go on a ~** : ponerse a régimen — ~ vi : estar a régimen

differ ['difər] vi -**ferred;** -**ferring** 1 : diferir, ser distinto 2 DISAGREE : no estar de acuerdo — **difference** ['difrənts, 'difərənts] n : diferencia f — **different** ['difrənt, 'difərənt] adj : distinto, diferente — **differentiate** [,difə'rentʃi,eit] v -**ated;** -**ating** vt : diferenciar — vi : distinguir — **differently** ['difrəntli, 'difərənt-] adv : de otra manera

difficult ['difi,kʌlt] adj : difícil — **difficulty** ['difi,kʌlti] n, pl -**ties** : dificultad f

diffident ['difədənt] adj : tímido, que falta confianza

dig ['dɪg] v **dug** ['dʌg]; **digging** vt 1 : cavar 2 ~ **up** : desenterrar — vi : cavar — ~ n 1 GIBE : pulla f 2 EXCAVATION : excavación f

digest ['daɪˌdʒest] n : resumen m — ~ [daɪ'dʒest] vt 1 : digerir 2 SUMMARIZE : resumir — **digestible** [daɪ'dʒestəbəl, dɪ-] adj : digerible — **digestion** [daɪ'dʒestʃən, dɪ-] n : digestión f — **digestive** [daɪ'dʒestɪv, dɪ-] adj : digestivo

digit ['dɪdʒət] n 1 NUMERAL : dígito m, número m 2 FINGER, TOE : dedo m — **digital** ['dɪdʒətəl] adj : digital

dignity ['dɪgnəti] n, pl **-ties** : dignidad f — **dignified** ['dɪgnəˌfaɪd] adj : digno, decoroso

digress [daɪ'gres, də-] vi : desviarse del tema, divagar — **digression** [daɪ'greʃən, də-] n : digresión f

dike ['daɪk] n : dique m

dilapidated [də'læpəˌdeɪtəd] adj : ruinoso

dilate [daɪ'leɪt, 'daɪˌleɪt] v **-lated; -lating** vt : dilatar — vi : dilatarse

dilemma [dɪ'lemə] n : dilema m

diligence ['dɪlədʒənts] n : diligencia f — **diligent** ['dɪlədʒənt] adj : diligente

dilute [daɪ'luːt, də-] vt **-luted; -luting** : diluir

dim ['dɪm] v **dimmed; dimming** vt : atenuar — vi : irse atenuando — ~ adj **dimmer; dimmest** 1 DARK : oscuro 2 FAINT : débil, tenue

dime ['daɪm] n : moneda f de diez centavos

dimension [də'mentʃən, daɪ-] n : dimensión f

diminish [də'mɪnɪʃ] v : disminuir

diminutive [də'mɪnjətɪv] adj : diminuto

dimple ['dɪmpəl] n : hoyuelo m

din ['dɪn] n : estrépito m

dine ['daɪn] vi **dined; dining** : cenar — **diner** ['daɪnər] n 1 : comensal mf (persona) 2 : cafetería f (restaurante)

dingy ['dɪndʒi] adj **-gier; -est** : sucio, deslucido

dinner ['dɪnər] n : cena f, comida f

dinosaur ['daɪnəˌsɔr] n : dinosaurio m

dint ['dɪnt] n **by ~ of** : a fuerza de

dip ['dɪp] v **dipped; dipping** vt : mojar — vi : bajar, descender — ~ n 1 DROP : descenso m, caída f 2 SWIM : chapuzón m 3 SAUCE : salsa f

diploma [də'ploːmə] n, pl **-mas** : diploma m

diplomacy [də'ploːməsi] n : diplomacia f — **diplomat** ['dɪpləˌmæt] n : diplomático m, -ca f — **diplomatic** [ˌdɪplə'mætɪk] adj : diplomático

dire ['daɪr] adj **direr; direst** 1 : grave, terrible 2 EXTREME : extremo

direct [də'rekt, daɪ-] vt 1 : dirigir 2 ORDER : mandar — ~ adj 1 STRAIGHT : directo 2 FRANK : franco — ~ adv : directamente — **direct current** n : corriente f continua — **direction** [də'rekʃən, daɪ-] n 1 : dirección f 2 ask ~s : pedir indicaciones — **directly** [də'rektli, daɪ-] adv 1 STRAIGHT : directamente 2 IMMEDIATELY : en seguida — **director** [də'rektər, daɪ-] n : director m, -tora f 2 **board of ~s** : directorio m — **directory** [də'rektəri, daɪ-] n, pl **-ries** : guía f (telefónica)

dirt ['dərt] n 1 : suciedad f 2 SOIL : tierra f — **dirty** ['dərti] adj **dirtier; -est** 1 : sucio 2 INDECENT : obsceno, cochino fam

disability [ˌdɪsə'bɪləti] n, pl **-ties** : minusvalía f, invalidez f — **disable** [dɪs'eɪbəl] vt **-abled; -abling** : incapacitar — **disabled** [dɪs'eɪbəld] adj : minusválido

disadvantage [ˌdɪsədˈvæntɪdʒ] n : desventaja f

disagree [ˌdɪsə'griː] vi 1 : no estar de acuerdo (con algn) 2 CONFLICT : no coincidir — **disagreeable** [ˌdɪsə'griːəbəl] adj : desagradable — **disagreement** [ˌdɪsə'griːmənt] n 1 : desacuerdo m 2 ARGUMENT : discusión f

disappear [ˌdɪsə'pɪr] vi : desaparecer — **disappearance** [ˌdɪsə'pɪrənts] n : desaparición f

disappoint [ˌdɪsə'pɔɪnt] vt : decepcionar, desilusionar — **disappointment** [ˌdɪsə'pɔɪntmənt] n : decepción f, desilusión f

disapprove [ˌdɪsə'pruːv] vi **-proved; -proving ~ of** : desaprobar — **disapproval** [ˌdɪsə'pruːvəl] n : desaprobación f

disarm [dɪs'ɑrm] vt : desarmar — **disarmament** [dɪs'ɑrməmənt] n : desarme m

disarray [ˌdɪsə'reɪ] n : desorden m

disaster [dɪ'zæstər] n : desastre m — **disastrous** [dɪ'zæstrəs] adj : desastroso

disbelief [ˌdɪsbrˈliːf] n : incredulidad f

disc → disk

discard [dɪs'kɑrd, 'dɪsˌkɑrd] vt : desechar, deshacerse de

discern [dɪ'sərn, -'zərn] vt : percibir, discernir — **discernible** [dɪ'sərnəbəl, -'zər-] adj : perceptible

discharge [dɪs'tʃɑrdʒ, 'dɪs-] vt **-charged; -charging** 1 UNLOAD : descargar 2 RELEASE : liberar, poner en libertad 3 DISMISS : despedir 4

CARRY OUT : cumplir con (una obligación) — **~** ['dɪs,tʃɑrdʒ, dɪs-] *n* 1 : descarga *f* (de electricidad), emisión *f* (de humo, etc.) 2 DISMISSAL : despido *m* 3 RELEASE : alta *f* (de un paciente), puesta *f* en libertad (de un preso) 4 : supuración *f* (en medicina)

disciple [dɪ'saɪpəl] *n* : discípulo *m*, -la *f*

discipline ['dɪsəplən] *n* 1 : disciplina *f* 2 PUNISHMENT : castigo *m* — **~** *vt* -**plined; -plining** 1 CONTROL : disciplinar 2 PUNISH : castigar

disclaim [dɪs'kleɪm] *vt* : negar

disclose [dɪs'kloːz] *vt* -**closed; -closing** : revelar — **disclosure** [dɪs'kloːʒər] *n* : revelación *f*

discomfort [dɪs'kʌmfərt] *n* 1 : incomodidad *f* 2 PAIN : malestar *m* 3 UNEASINESS : inquietud *f*

disconcert [,dɪskən'sərt] *vt* : desconcertar

disconnect [,dɪskə'nekt] *vt* : desconectar

disconsolate [dɪs'kɑntsələt] *adj* : desconsolado

discontented [,dɪskən'tentəd] *adj* : descontento

discontinue [,dɪskən'tɪnjuː] *vt* -**ued; -uing** : suspender, descontinuar

discount ['dɪs,kaʊnt, dɪs-] *n* : descuento *m*, rebaja *f* — **~** *vt* 1 : descontar (precios) 2 DISREGARD : descartar

discourage [dɪs'kərɪdʒ] *vt* -**aged; -aging** : desalentar, desanimar — **discouragement** [dɪs'kərɪdʒmənt] *n* : desánimo *m*, desaliento *m*

discover [dɪs'kʌvər] *vt* : descubrir — **discovery** [dɪs'kʌvəri] *n, pl* -**ries** : descubrimiento *m*

discredit [dɪs'krɛdət] *vt* : desacreditar — **~** *n* : descrédito *m*

discreet [dɪs'kriːt] *adj* : discreto

discrepancy [dɪs'krepəntsi] *n, pl* -**cies** : discrepancia *f*

discretion [dɪs'kreʃən] *n* : discreción *f*

discriminate [dɪs'krɪmə,neɪt] *vi* -**nated; -nating** 1 **~ against** : discriminar 2 **~ between** : distinguir entre — **discrimination** [dɪs,krɪmə'neɪʃən] *n* 1 PREJUDICE : discriminación *f* 2 DISCERNMENT : discernimiento *m*

discuss [dɪs'kʌs] *vt* : hablar de, discutir — **discussion** [dɪs'kʌʃən] *n* : discusión *f*

disdain [dɪs'deɪn] *n* : desdén *m* — **~** *vt* : desdeñar

disease [dɪ'ziːz] *n* : enfermedad *f* — **diseased** [dɪ'ziːzd] *adj* : enfermo

disembark [,dɪsɪm'bɑrk] *vi* : desembarcar

disengage [,dɪsɪn'geɪdʒ] *vt* -**gaged;**

-**gaging** 1 RELEASE : soltar 2 **~ the clutch** : desembragar

disentangle [,dɪsɪn'tæŋgəl] *vt* -**gled; -gling** : desenredar

disfavor [dɪs'feɪvər] *n* : desaprobación *f*

disfigure [dɪs'fɪgjər] *vt* -**ured; -uring** : desfigurar

disgrace [dɪs'kreɪs] *vt* -**graced; -gracing** : deshonrar — **~** *n* 1 DISHONOR : deshonra *f* 2 SHAME : vergüenza *f* — **disgraceful** [dɪs'kreɪsfəl] *adj* : vergonzoso, deshonroso

disgruntled [dɪs'grʌntəld] *adj* : descontento

disguise [dɪs'kaɪz] *vt* -**guised; -guising** : disfrazar — **~** *n* : disfraz *m*

disgust [dɪs'kʌst] *n* : asco *m*, repugnancia *f* — **~** *vt* : asquear — **disgusting** [dɪs'kʌstɪŋ] *adj* : asqueroso

dish ['dɪʃ] *n* 1 : plato *m* 2 *or* **serving ~** : fuente *f* 3 **wash the ~es** : lavar los platos — **~** *vt or* **~ up** : servir — **dishcloth** ['dɪʃ,kloθ] *n* : paño *m* de cocina (para secar), trapo *m* de fregar (para lavar)

dishearten [dɪs'hɑrtən] *vt* : desanimar

disheveled *or* **dishevelled** [dɪ'ʃevəld] *adj* : desaliñado, despeinado (dícese del pelo)

dishonest [dɪs'ɑnəst] *adj* : deshonesto — **dishonesty** [dɪs'ɑnəsti] *n, pl* -**ties** : falta *f* de honradez

dishonor [dɪs'ɑnər] *n* : deshonra *f* — **~** *vt* : deshonrar — **dishonorable** [dɪs'ɑnərəbəl] *adj* : deshonroso

dishwasher ['dɪʃ,wɔʃər] *n* : lavaplatos *m*, lavavajillas *m*

disillusion [,dɪsə'luːʒən] *vt* : desilusionar — **disillusionment** [,dɪsə'luːʒənmənt] *n* : desilusión *f*

disinfect [,dɪsɪn'fekt] *vt* : desinfectar — **disinfectant** [,dɪsɪn'fektənt] *n* : desinfectante *m*

disintegrate [dɪs'ɪntə,greɪt] *vi* -**grated; -grating** : desintegrarse

disinterested [dɪs'ɪntərəstəd, -,res-] *adj* : desinteresado

disk *or* **disc** ['dɪsk] *n* : disco *m*

dislike [dɪs'laɪk] *n* : aversión *f*, antipatía *f* — **~** *vt* -**liked; -liking** 1 : tener aversión a 2 I **~ dancing** : no me gusta bailar

dislocate ['dɪslo,keɪt, dɪs'loː-] *vt* -**cated; -cating** : dislocar

dislodge [dɪs'lɑdʒ] *vt* -**lodged; -lodging** : sacar, desalojar

disloyal [dɪs'lɔɪəl] *adj* : desleal — **disloyalty** [dɪs'lɔɪəlti] *n, pl* -**ties** : deslealtad *f*

dismal ['dɪzməl] *adj* : sombrío, deprimente

dismantle [dɪs'mæntəl] *vt* **-tled; -tling** : desmontar, desarmar

dismay [dɪs'meɪ] *vt* : consternar — ∼ *n* : consternación *f*

dismiss [dɪs'mɪs] *vt* **1** DISCHARGE : despedir, destituir **2** REJECT : descartar, rechazar — **dismissal** [dɪs'mɪsəl] *n* **1** : despido *m* (de un empleado), destitución *f* (de un funcionario) **2** REJECTION : rechazo *m*

dismount [dɪs'maunt] *vi* : desmontar

disobey [ˌdɪsə'beɪ] *v* : desobedecer — **disobedience** [ˌdɪsə'biːdiənts] *n* : desobediencia *f* — **disobedient** [-ənt] *adj* : desobediente

disorder [dɪs'ɔrdər] *n* **1** : desorden *m* **2** AILMENT : afección *f*, problema *m* — **disorderly** [dɪs'ɔrdərli] *adj* : desordenado

disorganize [dɪs'ɔrgənaɪz] *vt* **-nized; -nizing** : desorganizar

disown [dɪs'on] *vt* : renegar de

dispassionate [dɪs'pæʃənət] *adj* : desapasionado

dispatch [dɪs'pætʃ] *vt* : despachar, enviar

dispel [dɪs'pɛl] *vt* **-pelled; -pelling** : disipar

dispensation [ˌdɪspən'seɪʃən] *n* EXEMPTION : exención *m*, dispensa *f*

dispense [dɪs'pɛns] *v* **-pensed; -pensing** *vt* : repartir, distribuir — *vi* **with** : prescindir de

disperse [dɪs'pərs] *v* **-persed; -persing** *vt* : dispersar — *vi* : dispersarse

displace [dɪs'pleɪs] *vt* **-placed; -placing** **1** : desplazar **2** REPLACE : reemplazar

display [dɪs'pleɪ] *vt* **1** EXHIBIT : exponer, exhibir **2** ∼ **anger** : manifestar la ira — ∼ *n* : muestra *f*, exposición *f*

displease [dɪs'pliz] *vt* **-pleased; -pleasing** : desagradar — **displeasure** [dɪs'plɛʒər] *n* : desagrado *m*

dispose [dɪs'poz] *v* **-posed; -posing** *vt* : disponer — *vi* **of** : deshacerse de — **disposable** [dɪs'pozəbəl] *adj* : desechable — **disposal** [dɪs'pozəl] *n* **1** REMOVAL : eliminación *f* **2 have at one's** ∼ : tener a su disposición — **disposition** [dɪspə'zɪʃən] *n* **1** ARRANGEMENT : disposición *f* **2** TEMPERAMENT : temperamento *m*, carácter *m*

disprove [dɪs'pruv] *vt* **-proved; -proving** : refutar

dispute [dɪs'pjuːt] *v* **-puted; -putting** *vt* QUESTION : cuestionar — *vi* ARGUE : discutir — ∼ *n* : disputa *f*, conflicto *m*

disqualification [dɪsˌkwɑləfə'keɪʃən] *n* : descalificación *f* — **disqualify** [dɪs'kwɑləˌfaɪ] *vt* **-fied; -fying** : descalificar

disregard [ˌdɪsrɪ'gɑrd] *vt* : ignorar, hacer caso omiso de — ∼ *n* : indiferencia *f*

disrepair [ˌdɪsrɪ'pær] *n* : mal estado *m*

disreputable [dɪs'rɛpjʊtəbəl] *adj* : de mala fama

disrespect [ˌdɪsrɪ'spɛkt] *n* : falta *f* de respeto — **disrespectful** [ˌdɪsrɪ'spɛktfəl] *adj* : irrespetuoso

disrupt [dɪs'rʌpt] *vt* : trastornar, perturbar — **disruption** [dɪs'rʌpʃən] *n* : trastorno *m*

dissatisfaction [dɪsˌsætəs'fækʃən] *n* : descontento *m* — **dissatisfied** [dɪs'sætəsˌfaɪd] *adj* : descontento

dissect [dɪ'sɛkt] *vt* : disecar

disseminate [dɪ'semə,neɪt] *vt* **-nated; -nating** : diseminar, difundir

dissent [dɪ'sɛnt] *vi* : disentir — ∼ *n* : disentimiento *m*

dissertation [ˌdɪsər'teɪʃən] THESIS : tesis *f*

disservice [dɪs'sərvɪs] *n* **do a** ∼ **to** : no hacer justicia a

dissident ['dɪsədənt] *n* : disidente *mf*

dissimilar [dɪ'sɪmələr] *adj* : distinto

dissipate ['dɪsə,peɪt] *vt* **-pated; -pating** **1** DISPEL : disipar **2** SQUANDER : desperdiciar

dissolve [dɪ'zɑlv] *v* **-solved; -solving** *vt* : disolver — *vi* : disolverse

dissuade [dɪ'sweɪd] *vt* **-suaded; -suading** : disuadir

distance ['dɪstənts] *n* **1** : distancia *f* **2 in the** ∼ : a lo lejos — **distant** ['dɪstənt] *adj* : distante

distaste [dɪs'teɪst] *n* : desagrado *m* — **distasteful** [dɪs'teɪstfəl] *adj* : desagradable

distend [dɪs'tɛnd] *vt* : dilatar — *vi* : dilatarse

distill [dɪs'tɪl] *or Brit* **distil** *vt* **-tilled; -tilling** : destilar

distinct [dɪs'tɪŋkt] *adj* **1** DIFFERENT : distinto **2** CLEAR : claro — **distinction** [dɪs'tɪŋkʃən] *n* : distinción *f* — **distinctive** [dɪs'tɪŋktɪv] *adj* : distintivo

distinguish [dɪs'tɪŋgwɪʃ] *vt* : distinguir — **distinguished** [dɪs'tɪŋgwɪʃt] *adj* : distinguido

distort [dɪs'tɔrt] *vt* : deformar, distorsionar — **distortion** [dɪs'tɔrʃən] *n* : deformación *f*

distract [dɪs'strækt] *vt* : distraer — **distraction** [dɪs'strækʃən] *n* : distracción *f*

distraught [dɪs'rɔt] *adj* : muy afligido

distress [dɪs'træs] *n* **1** : angustia *f*, aflicción *f* **2 in** ∼ : en peligro — *vt*

: afligir — **distressing** [dɪ'strɛsɪŋ] adj
: penoso

distribute [dɪ'strɪˌbjuːt, -bjʊt] vt **-uted;
-uting** : distribuir, repartir — **distribution** [ˌdɪstrəˈbjuːʃən] n : distribución f —
distributor [dɪ'strɪbjuɾər] n : distribuidor m, -dora f

district ['dɪstrɪkt] n **1** REGION : región f,
zona f, barrio m (de una ciudad) **2**
: distrito m (zona política)

distrust [dɪs'trʌst] n : desconfianza f —
~ vt : desconfiar de

disturb [dɪ'stərb] vt **1** BOTHER : molestar,
perturbar **2** WORRY : inquietar — **disturbance** [dɪ'stərbəns] n **1** COMMOTION
: alboroto m, disturbio m **2** INTERRUPTION : interrupción f

disuse [dɪs'juːs] n **fall into** ~ : caer en
desuso

ditch ['dɪtʃ] n : zanja f, cuneta f — ~ vt
DISCARD : deshacerse de, botar

ditto ['dɪˌtoː] n, pl **-tos 1** : ídem m **2** ~
marks : comillas fpl

dive ['daɪv] vi **dived** or **dove** ['doːv];
dived; diving 1 : zambullirse, tirarse
al agua **2** DESCEND : bajar en picada
(dícese de un avión, etc.) — ~ n **1**
: zambullida f, clavado m Lat **2** DESCENT : descenso m en picada — **diver**
['daɪvər] n : saltador m, -dora f

diverge [də'vərdʒ, daɪ-] vi **-verged;
-verging** : divergir

diverse [daɪ'vərs, də-, 'daɪˌvərs] adj : diverso — **diversify** [daɪ'vərsəˌfaɪ, də-] v
-fied; -fying vt : diversificar — vi : diversificarse

diversion [daɪ'vərʒən, də-] n **1**
: desviación f **2** AMUSEMENT : diversión f, distracción f

diversity [daɪ'vərsəti, də-] n, pl **-ties**
: diversidad f

divert [də'vərt, daɪ-] vt **1** : desviar **2** DISTRACT : distraer **3** AMUSE : divertir

divide [də'vaɪd] v **-vided; -viding** vt : dividir — vi : dividirse

dividend ['dɪvəˌdɛnd, -dənd] n : dividendo m

divine [də'vaɪn] adj **-viner; -est** : divino
— **divinity** [də'vɪnəti] n, pl **-ties** : divinidad f

division [dɪ'vɪʒən] n : división f

divorce [də'vors] n : divorcio m — ~ v
-vorced; -vorcing vt : divorciar — vi
: divorciarse — **divorcée** [dɪˌvorˈseɪ,
-ˈsiː; -ˈvor-] n : divorciada f

divulge [də'vʌldʒ, daɪ-] vt **-vulged;
-vulging** : revelar, divulgar

dizzy ['dɪzi] adj **dizzier; -est 1** : mareado **2 a** ~ **speed** : una velocidad vertiginosa — **dizziness** ['dɪzinəs] n
: mareo m, vértigo m

DNA [ˌdiˌɛn'eɪ] n : AND m

do ['duː] v **did** ['dɪd]; **done** ['dʌn]; **doing;
does** ['dʌz] vt **1** : hacer **2** PREPARE
: preparar — vi **1** BEHAVE : hacer **2**
FARE : estar, ir, andar **3** SUFFICE : ser
suficiente **4** ~ **away with** : abolir,
eliminar **5 how are you doing?**
: ¿cómo estás? — v aux **1** (used in interrogative sentences) **do you know
her?** : ¿la conoces? **2** (used in negative statements) **I don't know** : yo no
sé **3** (used as a substitute verb to
avoid repetition) **do you speak English? yes, I do** : ¿habla inglés? sí

dock ['dak] n : muelle m — ~ vt : descontar dinero de (un sueldo) — vi
ANCHOR : fondear, atracar

doctor ['daktər] n **1** : doctor m, -tora f
(en derecho, etc.) **2** PHYSICIAN : médico m, -ca; doctor m, -tora f — vt
ALTER : alterar, falsificar

doctrine ['daktrɪn] n : doctrina f

document ['dakjumənt] n : documento
m — ~ ['dakjuˌment] vt : documentar
— **documentary** [ˌdakjuˈmɛntəri] n, pl
-ries : documental m

dodge ['dadʒ] n : artimaña f, truco m —
~ v **dodged; dodging** vt : esquivar,
eludir — vi : echarse a un lado

doe ['doː] n, pl **does** or **doe** : gama f,
cierva f

does → do

dog ['dɔɡ, 'dɑɡ] n : perro m, -rra f — ~
vt **dogged; dogging** : perseguir —
dogged ['dɔɡəd] adj : tenaz

dogma ['dɔɡmə] n : dogma m — **dogmatic** [dɔɡ'mætɪk] adj : dogmático

doily ['dɔɪli] n, pl **-lies** : tapete m

doings ['duːɪŋz] npl : actividades fpl

doldrums ['doːldrəmz, 'dɑl-] npl **be in
the** ~ : estar abatido

dole ['doːl] n : subsidio m de desempleo
— ~ vt **doled; doling** or ~ **out**
: repartir

doleful ['doːlfəl] adj : triste, lúgubre

doll ['dɑl, 'dɔl] n : muñeco m, -ca f

dollar ['dɑlər] n : dólar m

dolphin ['dɑlfən, 'dɔl-] n : delfín m

domain [doːˈmeɪn, də-] n **1** TERRITORY
: dominio m **2** FIELD : campo m, esfera
f

dome ['doːm] n : cúpula f

domestic [dəˈmɛstɪk] adj **1** : doméstico
2 INTERNAL : nacional — ~ n SERVANT
: empleado m doméstico, empleada f
doméstica — **domesticate** [dəˈmɛstɪˌkeɪt] vt **-cated; -cating** : domesticar

domination [ˌdɑməˈneɪʃən] n : dominación *f* — **dominant** ['dɑmənənt] *adj* : dominante — **dominate** ['dɑmə,neɪt] *v* -**nated; -nating** : dominar — **domineer** [,dɑmə'nɪr] *vi* : dominar, tiranizar

dominos ['dɑmə,noːz] *n* : dominó *m* (juego)

donate ['doː,neɪt, doː'-] *vt* -**nated; -nating** : donar, hacer un donativo de — **donation** [doː'neɪʃən] *n* : donativo *m*

done ['dʌn] → **do** — **~** *adj* **1** FINISHED : terminado, hecho **2** COOKED : cocido

donkey ['dɑŋki, 'dʌŋ-] *n, pl* -**keys** : burro *m*

donor ['doːnər] *n* : donante *mf*

don't ['doːnt] (*contraction of* **do not**) → **do**

doodle ['duːdəl] *v* -**dled; -dling** : garabatear — **~** *n* : garabato *m*

doom ['duːm] *n* : perdición *f*, fatalidad *f* — **~** *vt* : condenar

door ['doːr] *n* **1** : puerta *f* **2** ENTRANCE : entrada *f* — **doorbell** ['dor,bel] *n* : timbre *m* — **doorknob** ['dor,nɑb] *n* : pomo *m* — **doorman** ['dorman] *n, pl* -**men** [-mən, -,men] : portero *m* — **doormat** ['dor,mæt] *n* : felpudo *m* — **doorstep** ['dor,step] *n* : umbral *m* — **doorway** ['dor,weɪ] *n* : entrada *f*, portal *m*

dope ['doːp] *n* **1** DRUG : droga *f* **2** IDIOT : idiota *mf* — **~** *vt* **doped; doping** : drogar

dormant ['dormənt] *adj* : inactivo, latente

dormitory ['dormə,tori] *n, pl* -**ries** : dormitorio *m*

dose ['doːs] *n* : dosis *f* — **dosage** ['doː,sɪdʒ] *n* : dosis *f*

dot ['dɑt] *n* **1** : punto *m* **2 on the ~** : en punto

dote ['doːt] *vi* **doted; doting ~ on** : adorar

double ['dʌbəl] *adj* : doble — **~** *v* -**bled; -bling** *vt* : doblar — *vi* : doblarse — **~** *adv* : (el) doble — **~** *n* : doble *mf* — **double bass** *n* : contrabajo *m* — **double-cross** [,dʌbəl-'krɔs] *vt* : traicionar — **doubly** ['dʌbli] *adv* : doblemente

doubt ['daʊt] *vt* **1** : dudar **2** DISTRUST : desconfiar de, dudar de — **~** *n* : duda *f* — **doubtful** ['daʊtfəl] *adj* : dudoso — **doubtless** ['daʊtləs] *adv* : sin duda

dough ['doː] *n* : masa *f* — **doughnut** ['doː,nʌt] *n* : rosquilla *f*, dona *f Lat*

douse ['daʊs, 'daʊz] *vt* **doused; dousing 1** DRENCH : empapar, mojar **2** EXTINGUISH : apagar

dove[1] ['dʌv] → **dive**

dove[2] ['dʌv] *n* : paloma *f*

dowdy ['daʊdi] *adj* **dowdier; -est** : poco elegante

down ['daʊn] *adv* **1** DOWNWARD : hacia abajo **2 come/go ~** : bajar **3 ~ here** : aquí abajo **4 fall ~** : caer **5 ~ lie ~** : acostarse **6 sit ~** : sentarse — **~** *prep* **1** ALONG : a lo largo de **2** THROUGH : a través de **3 ~ the hill** : cuesta abajo — **~** *adj* **1** DESCENDING : de bajada **2** DOWNCAST : abatido — **~** *n* **1** : plumón *m* — **downcast** ['daʊn,kæst] *adj* : triste, abatido — **downfall** ['daʊn,fɔl] *n* : ruina *f* — **downhearted** ['daʊn,hɑrtəd] *adj* : desanimado — **downhill** ['daʊn,hɪl] *adv & adj* : cuesta abajo — **down payment** *n* : entrega *f* inicial — **downpour** ['daʊn,por] *n* : chaparrón *m* — **downright** ['daʊn,raɪt] *adv* : absolutamente — **~** *adj* : absoluto, categórico — **downstairs** ['daʊn,stærz] *adv* : abajo — **~** ['daʊn,stærz] *adj* : de abajo — **downstream** ['daʊn,strim] *adv* : río abajo — **down-to-earth** [,daʊntu'ərth] *adj* : realista — **downtown** [,daʊn'taʊn, 'daʊn,taʊn] *n* : centro *m* (de la ciudad) — **~** [,daʊn'taʊn] *adv* : al centro, en el centro — **~** *adj* : del centro — **downward** ['daʊnwərd] *or* **downwards** [-wərdz] *adv & adj* : hacia abajo

dowry ['daʊri] *n, pl* -**ries** : dote *f*

doze ['doːz] *vi* **dozed; dozing** : dormitar

dozen ['dʌzən] *n, pl* **dozens** *or* **dozen** : docena *f*

drab ['dræb] *adj* **drabber; drabbest** : monótono, apagado

draft ['dræft, 'draft] *n* **1** : corriente *f* de aire **2** *or* **rough ~** : borrador *m* **3** : conscripción *f* (militar) **4** *or* **~ beer** : cerveza *f* de barril — **~** *vt* **1** SKETCH : hacer el borrador de **2** CONSCRIPT : reclutar — **drafty** ['dræfti] *adj* **draftier; -est** : con corrientes de aire

drag ['dræg] *v* **dragged; dragging** *vt* **1** : arrastrar **2** DREDGE : dragar — *vi* : arrastrar(se) — **~** *n* **1** RESISTANCE : resistencia *f* (aerodinámica) **2** BORE : pesadez *f*, plomo *m fam*

dragon ['drægən] *n* : dragón *m* — **dragonfly** ['drægən,flaɪ] *n, pl* -**flies** : libélula *f*

drain ['dreɪn] *vt* **1** EMPTY : vaciar, drenar **2** EXHAUST : agotar — *vi* **1** : escurrir(se) (se dice de los platos) **2** *or* **~ away** : desaparecer poco a poco — **~** *n* **1** : desagüe *m* **2** SEWER : alcantarilla *f* **3** DEPLETION : agotamiento *m* — **drainage** ['dreɪnɪdʒ] *n* : drenaje *m* — **drainpipe** ['dreɪn,paɪp] *n* : tubo *m* de desagüe

drama ['drɑmə, 'dræ-] *n* : drama *m* —

dramatic [drə'mætɪk] *adj* : dramático — **dramatist** ['dræmətɪst, 'drɑ-] *n* : dramaturgo *m*, -ga *f* — **dramatize** ['dræmə,taɪz, 'drɑ-] *vt* **-tized; -tizing** : dramatizar

drank → **drink**

drape ['dreɪp] *v* **draped; draping** 1 COVER : cubrir (con tela) 2 HANG : drapear — **drapes** *npl* CURTAINS : cortinas *fpl*

drastic ['dræstɪk] *adj* : drástico

draught ['dræft, 'draft] → **draft**

draw ['drɔ] *v* **drew** ['dru:]; **drawn** ['drɔn]; **drawing** *vt* 1 PULL : tirar de 2 ATTRACT : atraer 3 SKETCH : dibujar, trazar 4 : sacar (una espada, etc.) 5 ~ **a conclusion** : llegar a una conclusión 6 ~ **up** DRAFT : redactar — *vi* 1 SKETCH : dibujar 2 ~ **near** : acercarse — ~ *n* 1 DRAWING : sorteo *m* 2 TIE : empate *m* 3 ATTRACTION : atracción *f* — **drawback** ['drɔ,bæk] *n* : desventaja *f* — **drawer** ['drɔr, 'drɔər] *n* : gaveta *f*, cajón *m* (en un mueble) — **drawing** ['drɔɪŋ] *n* 1 LOTTERY : sorteo *m* 2 SKETCH : dibujo *m*

drawl ['drɔl] *n* : habla *f* lenta y con vocales prolongadas

dread ['drɛd] *vt* : temer — ~ *n* : pavor *m*, temor *m* — **dreadful** ['drɛdfəl] *adj* : espantoso, terrible

dream ['dri:m] *n* : sueño *m* — ~ *v* **dreamed** ['drɛmpt, 'dri:md] *or* **dreamt** ['drɛmpt]; **dreaming** *vi* : soñar — *vt* 1 : soñar 2 ~ **up** : idear — **dreamer** ['dri:mər] *n* : soñador *m*, -dora *f* — **dreamy** ['dri:mi] *adj* **dreamier; -est** : soñador

dreary ['drɪri] *adj* **-rier; -est** : sombrío, deprimente

dredge ['drɛdʒ] *vt* **dredged; dredging** : dragar — ~ *n* : draga *f*

dregs ['drɛgz] *npl* : heces *fpl*

drench ['drɛntʃ] *vt* : empapar

dress ['drɛs] *vt* 1 : vestir 2 : preparar (pollo o pescado), aliñar (ensalada) — *vi* 1 : vestirse 2 ~ **up** : ponerse elegante — ~ *n* 1 CLOTHING : ropa *f* 2 : vestido *m* (de mujer) — **dresser** ['drɛsər] *n* : cómoda *f* con espejo — **dressing** ['drɛsɪŋ] *n* 1 : aliño *m* (de ensalada), relleno *m* (de pollo) 2 BANDAGE : vendaje *m* — **dressmaker** ['drɛs,meɪkər] *n* : modista *mf* — **dressy** ['drɛsi] *adj* **dressier; -est** : elegante

drew → **draw**

dribble ['drɪbəl] *vi* **-bled; -bling** 1 DRIP : gotear 2 DROOL : babear 3 : driblar (en basquetbol) — ~ *n* 1 TRICKLE : goteo *m*, hilo *m* 2 DROOL : baba *f*

drier, driest → **dry**

drift ['drɪft] *n* 1 MOVEMENT : movimiento *m* 2 HEAP : montón *m* (de arena, etc.), ventisquero *m* (de nieve) 3 MEANING : sentido *m* — ~ *vi* 1 : ir a la deriva 2 ACCUMULATE : amontonarse

drill ['drɪl] *n* 1 : taladro *m* 2 : ejercicio *m* (en educación), simulacro *m* (de incendio, etc.) — ~ *vt* 1 : perforar, taladrar 2 TRAIN : instruir por repetición — *vi* ~ **for** : perforar en busca de

drink ['drɪŋk] *v* **drank** ['dræŋk]; **drunk** ['drʌŋk] *or* **drank; drinking** : beber — ~ *n* : bebida *f*

drip ['drɪp] *vi* **dripped; dripping** : gotear — ~ *n* 1 DROP : gota *f* 2 DRIPPING : goteo *m*

drive ['draɪv] *v* **drove** ['dro:v]; **driven** ['drɪvən]; **driving** *vt* 1 : manejar 2 IMPEL : impulsar 3 ~ **crazy** : volver loco 4 ~ **s.o. to (do sth)** : llevar a algn a (hacer algo) — *vi* : manejar, conducir — ~ *n* 1 : paseo *m* (en coche) 2 CAMPAIGN : campaña *f* 3 VIGOR : energía *f* 4 NEED : instinto *m*

drivel ['drɪvəl] *n* : tonterías *fpl*

driver ['draɪvər] *n* : conductor *m*, -tora *f*; chofer *m*

driveway ['draɪv,weɪ] *n* : camino *m* de entrada

drizzle ['drɪzəl] *n* : llovizna *f* — ~ *vi* **-zled; -zling** : lloviznar

drone ['dro:n] *n* 1 BEE : zángano *m* 2 HUM : zumbido *m* — ~ *vi* **droned; droning** 1 BUZZ : zumbar 2 *or* ~ **on** : hablar con monotonía

drool ['dru:l] *vi* : babear — ~ *n* : baba *f*

droop ['dru:p] *vi* : inclinarse (dícese de la cabeza), encorvarse (dícese de los escombros), marchitarse (dícese de las flores)

drop ['drɑp] *n* 1 : gota *f* (de líquido) 2 DECLINE, FALL : caída *f* — ~ *v* **dropped; dropping** *vt* 1 : dejar caer 2 LOWER : bajar 3 ABANDON : abandonar, dejar 4 ~ **off** LEAVE : dejar — *vi* 1 FALL : caer(se) 2 DECREASE : bajar, descender 3 ~ **by** *or* ~ **in** : pasar

drought ['draʊt] *n* : sequía *f*

drove → **drive**

droves ['dro:vz] *n* **in** ~ : en manada

drown ['draʊn] *vt* : ahogar — *vi* : ahogarse

drowsy ['draʊzi] *adj* **drowsier; -est** : somnoliento

drudgery ['drʌdʒəri] *n*, *pl* **-eries** : trabajo *m* pesado

drug ['drʌg] *n* 1 MEDICATION : medicamento *m* 2 NARCOTIC : droga *f*, estupefaciente *m* — ~ *vt* **drugged; drugging** : drogar — **drugstore** ['drʌg,stor] *n* : farmacia *f*

drum ['drʌm] *n* **1** : tambor *m* **2** *or oil* ~
: bidón *m* (de petróleo) — ~ *v*
drummed; drumming *vi* : tocar el
tambor — *vt* : tamborilear con (los
dedos, etc.) — **drumstick** ['drʌm,stɪk]
n **1** : palillo *m* (de tambor) **2** : muslo *m*
(de pollo)

drunk ['drʌŋk] → **drink** — ~ *adj* : borracho — ~ *or* **drunkard** ['drʌŋkərd] *n*
: borracho *m*, -cha *f* — **drunken**
['drʌŋkən] *adj* : borracho, ebrio

dry ['draɪ] *adj* **drier; driest** : seco — ~
v **dried; drying** *vt* : secar — *vi* : secarse — **dry-clean** ['draɪ,klin] *vt*
: limpiar en seco — **dry cleaner** *n*
: tintorería *f* (servicio) — **dry cleaning** *n* : limpieza *f* en seco — **dryer**
['draɪər] *n* : secadora *f* — **dryness**
['draɪnəs] *n* : sequedad *f*, aridez *f*

dual ['duːəl, 'djuː-] *adj* : doble

dub ['dʌb] *vt* **dubbed; dubbing 1** CALL
: apodar **2** : doblar (una película)

dubious ['duːbiəs, 'djuː-] *adj* **1** UNCER-
TAIN : dudoso **2** QUESTIONABLE : sospechoso

duchess ['dʌtʃəs] *n* : duquesa *f*

duck ['dʌk] *n, pl* **duck** *or* **ducks** : pato
m, -ta *f* — ~ *vt* **1** LOWER : agachar,
bajar **2** EVADE : eludir, esquivar — *vi*
: agacharse — **duckling** ['dʌklɪŋ] *n*
: patito *m*, -ta *f*

duct ['dʌkt] *n* : conducto *m*

due ['duː, 'djuː] *adj* PAYABLE : pagadero
2 APPROPRIATE : debido, apropiado **3**
EXPECTED : esperado **4** ~ **to** : debido
a — ~ *n* **1** **give s.o. their** ~ : hacer
justicia a algn **2** ~**s** *npl* : cuota *f* —
~ *adv* ~ **east** : justo al este

duel ['duːəl, 'djuː-] *n* : duelo *m*

duet ['duːet, djuː-] *n* : dúo *m*

dug → **dig**

duke ['duːk, 'djuːk] *n* : duque *m*

dull ['dʌl] *adj* **1** STUPID : torpe **2** BLUNT
: desafilado **3** BORING : aburrido **4**
LACKLUSTER : apagado — ~ *vt* : entorpecer (los sentidos), aliviar (el dolor)

dumb ['dʌm] *adj* **1** MUTE : mudo **2** STU-
PID : estúpido

dumbfound *or* **dumfound** [,dʌm'faʊnd]
vt : dejar sin habla

dummy ['dʌmi] *n, pl* **-mies 1** SHAM
: imitación *f* **2** MANNEQUIN : maniquí
m **3** IDIOT : tonto *m*, -ta *f*

dump ['dʌmp] *vt* : descargar, verter —
~ *n* **1** : vertedero *m*, tiradero *m Lat* **2**
down in the ~**s** : triste, deprimido

dumpling ['dʌmplɪŋ] *n* : bola *f* de masa
hervida

dumpy ['dʌmpi] *adj* **dumpier; -est** : regordete

dunce ['dʌnts] *n* : burro *m*, -rra *f fam*

dune ['duːn, 'djuːn] *n* : duna *f*

dung ['dʌŋ] *n* **1** : excrementos *mpl* **2** MA-
NURE : estiércol *m*

dungarees [,dʌŋɡə'riː] *npl* JEANS : vaqueros *mpl*, jeans *mpl*

dungeon ['dʌndʒən] *n* : calabozo *m*

dunk ['dʌŋk] *vt* : mojar

duo ['duːoː, 'djuː-] *n, pl* **duos** : dúo *m*

dupe ['duːp, djuːp] *vt* **duped; duping**
: engañar — ~ *n* : inocentón *m*, -tona
f

duplex ['duː,plɛks, 'djuː-] *n* : casa *f* de dos
viviendas, dúplex *m*

duplicate ['duːplɪkət, 'djuː-] *adj* : duplicado — ~ ['duːplɪkeɪt, 'djuː-] *vt*
-cated; -cating : duplicar, hacer
copias de — ~ ['duːplɪkət, 'djuː-] *n*
: duplicado *m*, copia *f*

durable ['dʊrəbəl, 'djʊr-] *adj* : duradero

duration [dʊ'reɪʃən, djʊ-] *n* : duración *f*

duress [dʊ'res, djʊ-] *n* : coacción *f*

during ['dʊrɪŋ, 'djʊr-] *prep* : durante

dusk ['dʌsk] *n* : anochecer *m*, crepúsculo *m*

dust ['dʌst] *n* : polvo *m* — ~ *vt* **1**
: quitar el polvo a **2** SPRINKLE : espolvorear — **dustpan** ['dʌst,pæn] *n*
: recogedor *m* — **dusty** ['dʌsti] *adj*
dustier; -est : polvoriento

Dutch ['dʌtʃ] *adj* : holandés — ~ *n* **1**
: holandés *m* (idioma) **2** **the** ~ : los
holandeses

duty ['duːti, 'djuː-] *n, pl* **-ties 1** OBLIGA-
TION : deber *m* **2** TAX : impuesto *m* **3**
on ~ : de servicio — **dutiful** ['duːtɪfəl,
'djuː-] *adj* : obediente

dwarf ['dwɔrf] *n, pl* **dwarfs** ['dwɔrfs] *or*
dwarves ['dwɔrvz] : enano *m*, -na *f* —
~ *vt* : hacer parecer pequeño

dwell ['dwel] *vi* **dwelled** *or* **dwelt**
['dwelt]; **dwelling 1** RESIDE : morar,
vivir **2** ~ **on** : pensar demasiado en
— **dweller** ['dwelər] *n* : habitante *mf* —
dwelling ['dwelɪŋ] *n* : morada *f*,
vivienda *f*

dwindle ['dwɪndəl] *vi* **-dled; -dling** : disminuir

dye ['daɪ] *n* : tinte *m* — ~ *vt* **dyed; dye-
ing** : teñir

dying → **die**[1]

dynamic [daɪ'næmɪk] *adj* : dinámico

dynamite ['daɪnə,maɪt] *n* : dinamita *f*

dynamo ['daɪnə,moː] *n, pl* **-mos** : dínamo *m*

dynasty ['daɪnəsti, -,næs-] *n, pl* **-ties** : dinastía *f*

dysentery ['dɪsən,teri] *n, pl* **-teries** : disentería *f*

E

e ['iː] *n, pl* **e's** *or* **es** ['iːz] : e *f*, quinta letra del alfabeto inglés

each ['iːtʃ] *adj* : cada — ~ *pron* **1** : cada uno *m*, cada una *f* **2** ~ **other** : el uno al otro **3 they hate** ~ **other** : se odian — ~ *adv* : cada uno, por persona

eager ['iːgər] *adj* **1** ENTHUSIASTIC : entusiasta **2** IMPATIENT : impaciente — **eagerness** ['iːgərnəs] *n* : entusiasmo *m*, impaciencia *f*

eagle ['iːgəl] *n* : águila *f*

ear ['ɪr] *n* **1** : oreja *f* **2** ~ **of corn** : mazorca *f*, choclo *m* Lat — **eardrum** ['ɪr-drʌm] *n* : tímpano *m*

earl ['ərl] *n* : conde *m*

earlobe ['ɪr,loːb] *n* : lóbulo *m* de la oreja

early ['ərli] *adv* **earlier; -est 1** : temprano **2 as** ~ **as possible** : lo más pronto posible **3 ten minutes** ~ : diez minutos de adelanto — ~ *adj* **earlier; -est 1** FIRST : primero **2** ANCIENT : primitivo, antiguo **3 an** ~ **death** : una muerte prematura **4 be** ~ : llegar temprano **5 in the** ~ **spring** : a principios de la primavera

earmark ['ɪr,mɑrk] *vt* : destinar

earn ['ərn] *vt* **1** : ganar **2** DESERVE : merecer

earnest ['ərnəst] *adj* : serio — ~ *n* **in** ~ : en serio

earnings ['ərnɪŋz] *npl* **1** WAGES : ingresos *mpl* **2** PROFITS : ganancias *fpl*

earphone ['ɪr,foːn] *n* : audífono *m*

earring ['ɪr,rɪŋ] *n* : pendiente *m*, arete *m* Lat

earshot ['ɪr,ʃɑt] *n* **within** ~ : al alcance del oído

earth ['ərθ] *n* : tierra *f* — **earthenware** ['ərθən,wær, -ðən-] *n* : loza *f* — **earthly** ['ərθli] *adj* : terrenal — **earthquake** ['ərθ,kweɪk] *n* : terremoto *m* — **earthworm** ['ərθ,wərm] *n* : lombriz *f* (de tierra) — **earthy** ['ərθi] *adj* **earthier; -est 1** : terroso **2** COARSE, CRUDE : grosero

ease ['iːz] *n* **1** FACILITY : facilidad *f* **2** COMFORT : comodidad *f* **feel at** ~ : sentir cómodo — ~ *v* **eased; easing** *vt* **1** ALLEVIATE : aliviar, calmar **2** FACILITATE : facilitar — *vi* **1** : calmarse **2** ~ **up** : disminuir

easel ['iːzəl] *n* : caballete *m*

easily ['iːzəli] *adv* **1** : fácilmente, con facilidad **2** UNQUESTIONABLY : con mucho, de lejos Lat

east ['iːst] *adv* : al este — ~ *adj* : este, del este — ~ *n* **1** : este *m* **2 the East** : el Oriente

Easter ['iːstər] *n* : Pascua *f*

easterly ['iːstərli] *adv & adj* : del este

eastern ['iːstərn] *adj* **1** : del este **2 Eastern** : oriental, del este

easy ['iːzi] *adj* **easier; -est 1** : fácil **2** RELAXED : relajado — **easygoing** [,iːzi'goːɪŋ] *adj* : tolerante, relajado

eat ['iːt] *v* **ate** ['eɪt]; **eaten** ['iːtən]; **eating** *vt* : comer — *vi* **1** : comer **2** ~ **into** CORRODE : corroer **3** ~ **into** DEPLETE : comerse — **eatable** ['iːtəbəl] *adj* : comestible

eaves ['iːvz] *npl* : alero *m* — **eavesdrop** ['iːvz,drɑp] *vi* **-dropped; -dropping** : escuchar a escondidas

ebb ['eb] *n* : reflujo *m* — ~ *vi* **1** : bajar (dícese de la marea) **2** DECLINE : decaer

ebony ['ebəni] *n, pl* **-nies** : ébano *m*

eccentric [ɪk'sɛntrɪk] *adj* : excéntrico — ~ *n* : excéntrico *m*, -ca *f* — **eccentricity** [,ɛksen'trɪsəṭi] *n, pl* **-ties** : excentricidad *f*

echo ['ɛ,koː] *n, pl* **echoes** : eco *m* — ~ *v* **echoed; echoing** *vt* : repetir — *vi* : hacer eco, resonar

eclipse [ɪ'klɪps] *n* : eclipse *m* — ~ *vt* **eclipsed; eclipsing** : eclipsar

ecology [iˈkɑlədʒi, ɛ-] *n, pl* **-gies** : ecología *f* — **ecological** [,iːkə-'lɑdʒɪkəl, ,ɛkə-] *adj* : ecológico

economy [iˈkɑnəmi] *n, pl* **-mies** : economía *f* — **economic** [,iːkəˈnɑmɪk, ,ɛkə-] *or* **economical** [,iːkəˈnɑmɪkəl, ,ɛkə-] *adj* : económico — **economics** [,iːkəˈnɑmɪks, ,ɛkə-] *n* : economía *f* — **economist** [iˈkɑnəmɪst] *n* : economista *mf* — **economize** [iˈkɑnəˌmaɪz] *v* **-mized; -mizing** : economizar

ecstasy ['ɛkstəsi] *n, pl* **-sies** : éxtasis *m* — **ecstatic** [ɛk'stætɪk, ɪk-] *adj* : extático

Ecuadoran [,ɛkwəˈdorən] *or* **Ecuadorean** *or* **Ecuadorian** [,ɛkwəˈdoriən] *adj* : ecuatoriano

edge ['ɛdʒ] *n* **1** BORDER : borde *m* **2** : filo *m* (de un cuchillo) **3** ADVANTAGE : ventaja *f* — ~ *v* **edged; edging** *vt* : bordear, ribetear — *vi* : avanzar poco a poco — **edgewise** ['ɛdʒ,waɪz] *adv* : de lado — **edgy** ['ɛdʒi] *adj* **edgier; -est** : nervioso

edible ['ɛdəbəl] *adj* : comestible

edit ['ɛdɪt] *vt* **1** : editar, reḍactar, corregir **2 ~ out** : suprimir, cortar — **edition** ['rdɪʃən] *n* : edición *f* — **editor** ['ɛdɪtər] *n* : director *m*, -tora *f* (de un periódico); redactor *m*, -tora *f* (de un libro) — **editorial** [,ɛdɪ'toriəl] *n* : editorial *m*

educate ['ɛdʒə,keɪt] *vt* **-cated; -cating 1** TEACH : educar, instruir **2** INFORM : informar — **education** [,ɛdʒə'keɪʃən] *n* : educación *f* — **educational** [,ɛdʒə-'keɪʃənəl] *adj* **1** : educativo, instructivo **2** TEACHING : docente — **educator** ['ɛdʒə,keɪtər] *n* : educador *m*, -dora *f*

eel ['iːl] *n* : anguila *f*

eerie ['ɪri] *adj* **-rier; -est** : extraño e inquietante, misterioso

effect [ɪ'fɛkt] *n* **1** : efecto *m* **2 go into ~** : entrar en vigor — *vt* : efectuar, llevar a cabo — **effective** [rfɛktɪv] *adj* **1** : eficaz **2** ACTUAL : efectivo, vigente — **effectiveness** [rfɛktɪvnəs] *n* : eficacia *f*

effeminate [ə'fɛmənət] *adj* : afeminado

effervescent [,ɛfər'vɛsənt] *adj* : efervescente

efficient [ɪ'fɪʃənt] *adj* : eficiente — **efficiency** [ɪ'fɪʃənsi] *n, pl* **-cies** : eficiencia *f*

effort ['ɛfərt] *n* **1** : esfuerzo *m* **2 it's not worth the ~** : no vale la pena — **effortless** ['ɛfərtləs] *adj* : fácil, sin esfuerzo

egg ['ɛg] *n* : huevo *m* — *vt* ~ **on** : incitar — **eggplant** ['ɛg,plænt] *n* : berenjena *f* — **eggshell** ['ɛg,ʃɛl] *n* : cascarón *m*

ego ['iː,goː] *n, pl* **egos 1** SELF : ego *m*, yo *m* **2** SELF-ESTEEM : amor *m* propio — **egotism** ['iːgə,tɪzəm] *n* : egotismo *m* — **egotist** ['iːgətɪst] *n* : egotista *mf* — **egotistic** [,iːgə'tɪstɪk] *or* **egotistical** [-'tɪstɪkəl] *adj* : egotista

eiderdown ['aɪdər,daʊn] *n* **1** DOWN : plumón *m* **2** COMFORTER : edredón *m*

eight ['eɪt] *n* : ocho *m* — *adj* : ocho — **eight hundred** : ochocientos *m*

eighteen [eɪt'tiːn] *n* : dieciocho *m* — *adj* : dieciocho — **eighteenth** [eɪt-'tiːnθ] *adj* : decimoctavo — ~ *n* **1** : decimoctavo *m*, -va *f* (en una serie) **2** : dieciochoavo *m*, dieciochoava parte *f*

eighth ['eɪtθ] *n* **1** : octavo *m*, -va *f* (en una serie) **2** : octavo *m*, octava parte *f* — ~ *adj* : octavo

eighty ['eɪti] *n, pl* **eighties** : ochenta *m* — ~ *adj* : ochenta

either ['iːðər, 'aɪ-] *adj* **1** : cualquiera (de los dos) **2** (*in negative constructions*) : ninguno (de los dos) **3** EACH : cada — ~ *pron* **1** : cualquiera *mf* (de los dos) **2** (*in negative constructions*) : ninguno *m*, -na *f* (de los dos) **3** *or* ~ **one** : algún *m*, alguna *f* — ~ *conj* **1** : o **2** (*in negative constructions*) : ni

eject [i'dʒɛkt] *vt* : expulsar, expeler

eke ['iːk] *vt* **eked; eking** *or* ~ **out** : ganar a duras penas

elaborate [i'læbərət] *adj* **1** DETAILED : detallado **2** COMPLEX : complicado — ~ [i'læbə,reɪt] *vt* **-rated; -rating** : elaborar — *vi* : entrar en detalles

elapse [i'læps] *vi* **elapsed; elapsing** : transcurrir

elastic [i'læstɪk] *adj* : elástico — ~ *n* **1** : elástico *m* **2** RUBBER BAND : goma *f* (elástica) — **elasticity** [i,læs'tɪsəti, i,læs-] *n, pl* **-ties** : elasticidad *f*

elated [i'leɪtəd] *adj* : regocijado

elbow ['ɛl,boː] *n* : codo *m*

elder ['ɛldər] *adj* : mayor — ~ *n* **1** : mayor *mf* **2** : anciano *m*, -na *f* (de una tribu, etc.) — **elderly** ['ɛldərli] *adj* : mayor, anciano

elect [i'lɛkt] *vt* : elegir — ~ *adj* : electo — **election** [i'lɛkʃən] *n* : elección *f* — **electoral** [i'lɛktərəl] *adj* : electoral — **electorate** [i'lɛktərət] *n* : electorado *m*

electricity [i,lɛk'trɪsəti] *n, pl* **-ties** : electricidad *f* — **electric** [i'lɛktrɪk] *or* **electrical** [-trɪkəl] *adj* : eléctrico — **electrician** [i,lɛk'trɪʃən] *n* : electricista *mf* — **electrify** [i'lɛktrə,faɪ] *vt* **-fied; -fying** : electrificar — **electrocute** [i'lɛktrə,kjuːt] *vt* **-cuted; -cuting** : electrocutar

electron [i'lɛk,trɑn] *n* : electrón *m* — **electronic** [i,lɛk'trɑnɪk] *adj* : electrónico — **electronic mail** *n* : correo *m* electrónico — **electronics** [i,lɛk'trɑnɪks] *n* : electrónica *f*

elegant ['ɛligənt] *adj* : elegante — **elegance** ['ɛligənts] *n* : elegancia *f*

element ['ɛləmənt] *n* **1** : elemento *m* **2 ~s** *npl* BASICS : elementos *mpl*, rudimentos *mpl* — **elementary** [,ɛlə-'mɛntri] *adj* : elemental — **elementary school** *n* : escuela *f* primaria

elephant ['ɛləfənt] *n* : elefante *m*, -ta *f*

elevate ['ɛlə,veɪt] *vt* **-vated; -vating** : elevar — **elevator** ['ɛlə,veɪtər] *n* : ascensor *m*

eleven [i'lɛvən] *n* : once *m* — ~ *adj* : once — **eleventh** [i'lɛvənθ] *adj* : undécimo — ~ *n* **1** : undécimo *m*, -ma *f* (en una serie) 2 : onceavo m, onceava parte f

elf ['elf] n, pl **elves** ['elvz] : duende m

elicit [ɪ'lɪsət] vt : provocar

eligible ['elədʒəbəl] adj : elegible

eliminate [ɪ'lɪmə,neɪt] vt **-nated; -nating** : eliminar — **elimination** [ɪ,lɪmə'neɪʃən] n : eliminación f

elite [eɪ'liːt, i-] n : elite f

elk ['elk] n : alce m (de Europa), uapití m (de América)

elliptical [ɪ'lɪptɪkəl, ɛ-] or **elliptic** [-tɪk] adj : elíptico

elm ['elm] n : olmo m

elongate [i'lɔŋˌɡeɪt] vt **-gated; -gating** : alargar

elope [i'loːp] vi **eloped; eloping** : fugarse — **elopement** [i'loːpmənt] n : fuga f

eloquence ['eləkwənts] n : elocuencia f — **eloquent** ['eləkwənt] adj : elocuente

else ['els] adv **1 how ~ ?** : ¿de qué otro modo? **2 where ~ ?** : ¿en qué otro sitio? **3 or ~** : si no, de lo contrario — **~** adj **1 everyone ~** : todos los demás **2 nobody ~** : ningún otro, nadie más **3 nothing ~** : nada más **4 what ~ ?** : ¿qué más? — **elsewhere** ['els,hwer] adv : en otra parte

elude [i'luːd] vt **eluded; eluding** : eludir, esquivar — **elusive** [i'luːsɪv] adj : esquivo

elves → **elf**

emaciated [j'meɪʃiˌeɪtd] adj : esquálido, demacrado

E-mail ['iːˌmeɪl] → **electronic mail**

emanate ['eməˌneɪt] vi **-nated; -nating** : emanar

emancipate [i'mæntsəˌpeɪt] vt **-pated; -pating** : emancipar — **emancipation** [i,mæntsə'peɪʃən] n : emancipación f

embalm [ɪm'bɑm, ɛm-, -'bɑlm] vt : embalsamar

embankment [ɪm'bæŋkmənt, ɛm-] n : terraplén m, dique m (de un río)

embargo [ɪm'bɑrɡo, ɛm-] n, pl **-goes** : embargo m

embark [ɪm'bɑrk, ɛm-] vt : embarcar — vi **1** : embarcarse **2 ~ upon** : emprender — **embarkation** [ɛmˌbɑr'keɪʃən] n : embarque m, embarco m

embarrass [ɪm'bærəs, ɛm-] vt : avergonzar — **embarrassing** [ɪm'bærəsɪŋ, ɛm-] adj : embarazoso — **embarrassment** [ɪm'bærəsmənt, ɛm-] n : vergüenza f

embassy ['embəsi] n, pl **-sies** : embajada f

embed [ɪm'bed, ɛm-] vt **-bedded; -bedding** : incrustar, enterrar

embellish [ɪm'belɪʃ, ɛm-] vt : adornar, embellecer — **embellishment** [ɪm'belɪʃmənt, ɛm-] n : adorno m

embers ['embəz] npl : ascuas fpl

embezzle [ɪm'bezəl, ɛm-] vt **-zled; -zling** : desfalcar, malversar — **embezzlement** [ɪm'bezəlmənt, ɛm-] n : desfalco m, malversación f

emblem ['embləm] n : emblema m

embody [ɪm'bɑdi, ɛm-] vt **-bodied; -bodying** : encarnar, personificar

emboss [ɪm'bɑs, ɛm-, -'bɔs] vt : repujar, grabar en relieve

embrace [ɪm'breɪs, ɛm-] v **-braced; -bracing** vt : abrazar — vi : abrazarse — **~** n : abrazo m

embroider [ɪm'brɔɪdər, ɛm-] vt : bordar — **embroidery** [ɪm'brɔɪdəri, ɛm-] n, pl **-deries** : bordado m

embryo ['embriˌoː] n, pl **embryos** : embrión m

emerald ['emrəld, 'emə-] n : esmeralda f

emerge [i'mərdʒ] vi **emerged; emerging** : salir, aparecer — **emergence** [i'mərdʒənts] n : aparición f

emergency [i'mərdʒəntsi] n, pl **-cies 1** : emergencia f **2 ~ exit** : salida f de emergencia **3 ~ room** : sala f de urgencias, sala f de guardia

emery ['eməri] n, pl **-eries 1** : esmeril m **2 ~ board** : lima f de uñas

emigrant ['emɪɡrənt] n : emigrante mf — **emigrate** ['emɪˌɡreɪt] vi **-grated; -grating** : emigrar — **emigration** [ˌemə'ɡreɪʃən] n : emigración f

eminence ['emənənts] n : eminencia f — **eminent** ['emənənt] adj : eminente

emission [i'mɪʃən] n : emisión f — **emit** [i'mɪt] vt **emitted; emitting** : emitir

emotion [i'moːʃən] n : emoción f — **emotional** [i'moːʃənəl] adj **1** : emocional **2** MOVING : emotivo

emperor ['empərər] n : emperador m

emphasis ['emfəsɪs] n, pl **-phases** [-ˌsiːz] : énfasis m — **emphasize** ['emfəˌsaɪz] vt **-sized; -sizing** : subrayar, hacer hincapié en — **emphatic** [ɪm'fætɪk, ɛm-] adj : enérgico, categórico

empire ['emˌpaɪr] n : imperio m

employ [ɪm'plɔɪ, ɛm-] vt : emplear — **employee** [ɪmˌplɔɪˈiː, ɛm-, -'plɔɪˌiː] n : empleado m, -da f — **employer** [ɪm'plɔɪər, ɛm-] n : patrón m, -trona f; empleador m, -dora f — **employment** [ɪm'plɔɪmənt, ɛm-] n : trabajo m, empleo m

empower [ɪm'paʊər, ɛm-] vt : autorizar

empress ['emprəs] n : emperatriz f

empty ['empti] adj **emptier; -est 1** : vacío **2** MEANINGLESS : vano — **~** v

-tied; -tying vt : vaciar — vi : vaciarse
— **emptiness** ['emptinəs] n : vacío m
emulate ['emjəˌleɪt] vt **-lated; -lating**
: emular
enable [ɪˈneɪbəl, ɛ-] vt **-abled; -abling**
: hacer posible, permitar
enact [ɪˈnækt, ɛ-] vt 1 : promulgar (un
ley o un decreto) 2 PERFORM : representar
enamel [ɪˈnæməl] n : esmalte m
encampment [ɪnˈkæmpmənt, ɛn-] n
: campamento m
encase [ɪnˈkeɪs, ɛn-] vt **-cased; -casing**
: encerrar, revestir
enchant [ɪnˈtʃænt, ɛn-] vt : encantar —
enchanting [ɪnˈtʃæntɪŋ, ɛn-] adj : encantador — **enchantment** [ɪnˈtʃænt-
mənt, ɛn-] n : encanto m
encircle [ɪnˈsərkəl, ɛn-] vt **-cled; -cling**
: rodear
enclose [ɪnˈkloːz, ɛn-] vt **-closed;**
-closing 1 SURROUND : encerrar, cercar 2 INCLUDE : adjuntar (a una carta)
— **enclosure** [ɪnˈkloːʒər, ɛn-] n 1 AREA
: recinto m 2 : anexo m (con una
carta)
encompass [ɪnˈkʌmpəs, ɛn-, -ˈkɑm-] vt 1
ENCIRCLE : cercar 2 INCLUDE : abarcar
encore ['ɑnˌkor] n : bis m
encounter [ɪnˈkaʊntər, ɛn-] vt : encontrar — n : encuentro m
encourage [ɪnˈkərɪdʒ, ɛn-] vt **-aged;**
-aging 1 : animar, alentar 2 FOSTER
: promover, fomentar — **encourage-**
ment [ɪnˈkərɪdʒmənt, ɛn-] n 1 : aliento
m 2 PROMOTION : fomento m
encroach [ɪnˈkroːtʃ, ɛn-] vi ~ on : invadir, usurpar, quitar (el tiempo)
encyclopedia [ɪnˌsaɪkləˈpiːdiə, ɛn-] n
: enciclopedia f
end ['ɛnd] n 1 : fin 2 EXTREMITY : extremo m, punta f 3 come to an ~
: llegar a su fin 4 in the ~ : por fin —
~ vt : terminar, poner fin a — vi : ter-
minar(se)
endanger [ɪnˈdeɪndʒər, ɛn-] vt : poner en
peligro
endearing [ɪnˈdɪrɪŋ, ɛn-] adj : simpático
endeavor or Brit **endeavour** [ɪnˈdɛvər,
ɛn-] vt ~ to : esforzarse por — ~ n
: esfuerzo m
ending ['ɛndɪŋ] n : final m, desenlace m
endive ['ɛnˌdaɪv, ˌɑnˈdiːv] n : endibia f,
endivia f
endless ['ɛndləs] adj 1 INTERMINABLE
: interminable 2 INNUMERABLE : innumerable 3 ~ possibilities : posibilidades fpl infinitas
endorse [ɪnˈdɔrs, ɛn-] vt **-dorsed;**
-dorsing 1 SIGN : endosar 2 APPROVE

: aprobar — **endorsement** [ɪnˈdɔrs-
mənt, ɛn-] n APPROVAL : aprobación f
endow [ɪnˈdaʊ, ɛn-] vt : dotar
endure [ɪnˈdʊr, ɛn-, -ˈdjur] v **-dured;**
-during vt : soportar, aguantar — vi
LAST : durar — **endurance** [ɪnˈdʊrəns,
ɛn-, -ˈdjur-] n : resistencia f
enemy ['ɛnəmi] n, pl **-mies** : enemigo
m, -ga f
energy ['ɛnərdʒi] n, pl **-gies** : energía f
— **energetic** [ˌɛnərˈdʒɛtɪk] adj : enérgico
enforce [ɪnˈfors, ɛn-] vt **-forced;**
-forcing 1 : hacer cumplir (un ley,
etc.) 2 IMPOSE : imponer — **enforced**
adj : forzoso — **enforcement** [ɪn-
ˈforsmənt, ɛn-] n : imposición f del
cumplimiento
engage [ɪnˈɡeɪdʒ, ɛn-] v **-gaged;**
-gaging vt 1 : captar, atraer (la atención, etc.) 2 ~ the clutch : embragar
— vi ~ in : dedicarse a, entrar en —
engagement [ɪnˈɡeɪdʒmənt, ɛn-] n 1
APPOINTMENT : cita f, hora f 2 BE-
TROTHAL : compromiso m — **engag-**
ing [ɪnˈɡeɪdʒɪŋ, ɛn-] adj : atractivo
engine ['ɛndʒən] n 1 : motor m 2 LOCO-
MOTIVE : locomotora f — **engineer**
[ˌɛndʒəˈnɪr] n 1 : ingeniero m, -ra f 2
: maquinista mf (de locomotoras) —
~ vt 1 CONSTRUCT : construir 2 CON-
TRIVE : tramar — **engineering** [ˌɛndʒə-
ˈnɪrɪŋ] n : ingeniería f
English ['ɪŋɡlɪʃ, 'ɪŋlɪʃ] adj : inglés — ~
n : inglés m (idioma) — **Englishman**
['ɪŋɡlɪʃmən, 'ɪŋlɪʃ-] n : inglés m — **Eng-**
lishwoman ['ɪŋɡlɪʃˌwʊmən, 'ɪŋlɪʃ-] n
: inglesa f
engrave [ɪnˈɡreɪv, ɛn-] vt **-graved;**
-graving : grabar — **engraving** [ɪn-
ˈɡreɪvɪŋ, ɛn-] n : grabado m
engross [ɪnˈɡroːs, ɛn-] vt : absorber
engulf [ɪnˈɡʌlf, ɛn-] vt : envolver
enhance [ɪnˈhænts, ɛn-] vt **-hanced;**
-hancing : aumentar, mejorar
enjoy [ɪnˈdʒɔɪ, ɛn-] vt 1 : disfrutar, gozar
de 2 ~ oneself : divertirse — **enjoy-**
able [ɪnˈdʒɔɪəbəl, ɛn-] adj : agradable
— **enjoyment** [ɪnˈdʒɔɪmənt, ɛn-] n
: placer m
enlarge [ɪnˈlɑrdʒ, ɛn-] v **-larged;**
-larging vt : agrandar, ampliar — vi 1
: agrandarse 2 ~ upon : extenderse
sobre — **enlargement** [ɪnˈlɑrdʒmənt,
ɛn-] n : ampliación f
enlighten [ɪnˈlaɪtən, ɛn-] vt : aclarar, iluminar
enlist [ɪnˈlɪst, ɛn-] vt 1 ENROLL : alistar 2
OBTAIN : conseguir — vi : alistarse
enliven [ɪnˈlaɪvən, ɛn-] vt : animar

enmity ['ɛnmətɪ] *n, pl* **-ties** : enemistad *f*

enormous ['rnɔrməs] *adj* : enorme

enough [ɪ'nʌf] *adj* : bastante, suficiente — ~ *adv* : bastante — ~ *pron* **1** : (lo) suficiente, (lo) bastante **2 it's not ~** : no basta **3 I've had ~!** : ¡estoy harto!

enquire [ɪn'kwaɪr, ɛn-], **enquiry** ['ɪn-,kwaɪrɪ, 'ɛn-, -kwərɪ; ɪn'kwaɪrɪ, ɛn'-] → **inquire, inquiry**

enrage [ɪn'reɪdʒ, ɛn-] *vt* **-raged; -raging** : enfurecer

enrich [ɪn'rɪtʃ, ɛn-] *vt* : enriquecer

enroll *or* **enrol** [ɪn'roːl, ɛn-] *v* **-rolled; -rolling** *vt* : matricular, inscribir — *vi* : matricularse, inscribirse

ensemble [ɑn'sɑmbəl] *n* : conjunto *m*

ensign ['ɛnsən, 'ɛn,saɪn] *n* **1** FLAG : enseña *f* **2** : alférez *mf* (de fragata)

enslave [ɪn'sleɪv, ɛn-] *vt* **-slaved; -slaving** : esclavizar

ensue [ɪn'suː, ɛn-] *vi* **-sued; -suing** : seguir, resultar

ensure [ɪn'ʃʊr, ɛn-] *vt* **-sured; -suring** : asegurar

entail [ɪn'teɪl, ɛn-] *vt* : suponer, conllevar

entangle [ɪn'tæŋgəl, ɛn-] *vt* **-gled; -gling** : enredar — **entanglement** [ɪn'tæŋgəlmənt, ɛn-] *n* : enredo *m*

enter ['ɛntər] *vt* **1** : entrar en **2** RECORD : inscribir — *vi* **1** : entrar **2** ~ **into** : firmar (un acuerdo), entablar (negociaciones, etc.)

enterprise ['ɛntər,praɪz] *n* **1** : empresa *f* **2** INITIATIVE : iniciativa *f* — **enterprising** ['ɛntər,praɪzɪŋ] *adj* : emprendedor

entertain [,ɛntər'teɪn] *vt* **1** AMUSE : entretener, divertir **2** CONSIDER : considerar **3** ~ **guests** : recibir invitados — **entertainment** [,ɛntər'teɪnmənt] *n* : entretenimiento *m*, diversión *f*

enthrall *or* **enthral** [ɪn'θrɔl, ɛn-] *vt* **-thralled; -thralling** : cautivar, embelesar

enthusiasm [ɪn'θuːzi,æzəm, ɛn-, -θjuː-] *n* : entusiasmo *m* — **enthusiast** [ɪn'θuːzi,æst, ɛn-, -θjuː-, -əst] *n* : entusiasta *mf* — **enthusiastic** [ɪn,θuːzi'æstɪk, ɛn-, -θjuː-] *adj* : entusiasta

entice [ɪn'taɪs, ɛn-] *vt* **-ticed; -ticing** : atraer, tentar

entire [ɪn'taɪr, ɛn-] *adj* : entero, completo — **entirely** [ɪn'taɪrli, ɛn-] *adv* : completamente — **entirety** [ɪn'taɪrtɪ, ɛn-, -'taɪrətɪ] *n, pl* **-ties** : totalidad *f*

entitle [ɪn'taɪtəl, ɛn-] *vt* **-tled; -tling 1** NAME : titular **2** AUTHORIZE : dar derecho a — **entitlement** [ɪn'taɪtəlmənt, ɛn-] *n* : derecho *m*

entity ['ɛntətɪ] *n, pl* **-ties** : entidad *f*

entrails ['ɛn,treɪlz, -trəlz] *npl* : entrañas *fpl*, vísceras *fpl*

entrance¹ [ɪn'træns, ɛn-] *vt* **-tranced; -trancing** : encantar, fascinar

entrance² ['ɛntrəns] *n* : entrada *f* — **entrant** ['ɛntrənt] *n* : participante *mf*

entreat [ɪn'triːt, ɛn-] *vt* : suplicar

entrée *or* **entree** ['ɑn,treɪ, 'ɑn-] *n* : plato *m* principal

entrepreneur [,ɑntrəprə'nər, -'njʊr] *n* : empresario *m*, -ria *f*

entrust [ɪn'trʌst, ɛn-] *vt* : confiar

entry ['ɛntrɪ] *n, pl* **-tries 1** ENTRANCE : entrada *f* **2** NOTATION : entrada *f*, anotación *f*

enumerate [ɪ'nuːmə,reɪt, ɛ-, -'njuː-] *vt* **-ated; -ating** : enumerar

enunciate [ɪ'nʌnsi,eɪt, ɛ-] *vt* **-ated; -ating 1** STATE : enunciar **2** PRONOUNCE : articular

envelop [ɪn'vɛləp, ɛn-] *vt* : envolver — **envelope** ['ɛnvə,loːp, 'ɑn-] *n* : sobre *m*

envious ['ɛnviəs] *adj* : envidioso — **enviously** *adv* : con envidia

environment [ɪn'vaɪrənmənt, ɛn-, -'vaɪəm-] *n* : medio *m* ambiente — **environmental** [ɪn,vaɪrən'mɛntəl, ɛn-, -'vaɪəm-] *adj* : ambiental — **environmentalist** [ɪn,vaɪrən'mɛntəlɪst, ɛn-, -,vaɪəm-] *n* : ecologista *mf*

envision [ɪn'vɪʒən, ɛn-] *vt* : prever, imaginar

envoy ['ɛn,vɔɪ, 'ɑn-] *n* : enviado *m*, -da *f*

envy ['ɛnvi] *n, pl* **envies** : envidia *f* — ~ *vt* **-vied; -vying** : envidiar

enzyme ['ɛn,zaɪm] *n* : enzima *f*

epic ['ɛpɪk] *adj* : épico — ~ *n* : epopeya *f*

epidemic [,ɛpə'dɛmɪk] *n* : epidemia *f* — ~ *adj* : epidémico

epilepsy ['ɛpə,lɛpsɪ] *n, pl* **-sies** : epilepsia *f* — **epileptic** [,ɛpə'lɛptɪk] *adj* : epiléptico — ~ *n* : epiléptico *m*, -ca *f*

episode ['ɛpə,soːd] *n* : episodio *m*

epitaph ['ɛpə,tæf] *n* : epitafio *m*

epitome [ɪ'pɪtəmi] *n* : personificación *f* — **epitomize** [ɪ'pɪtə,maɪz] *vt* **-mized; -mizing** : ser la personificación de, personificar

epoch ['ɛpək, 'ɛ,pɑk, 'iː,pɑk] *n* : época *f*

equal ['iːkwəl] *adj* **1** SAME : igual **2 be ~ to** : estar a la altura de (una tarea, etc.) — ~ *n* : igual *mf* — ~ *vt* **equaled** *or* **equalled; equaling** *or* **equalling 1** : igualar **2** : ser igual a (en matemáticas) — **equality** [ɪ'kwɑlətɪ] *n, pl* **-ties** : igualdad *f* — **equalize** ['iːkwə,laɪz] *vt* **-ized; -izing** : igualar — **equally** ['iːkwəli] *adv* **1** : igualmente **2 ~ important** : igual de importante

equate [ɪ'kweɪt] *vt* **equated; equating ~ with** : equiparar con — **equation** [ɪ'kweɪʒən] *n* : ecuación *f*

equator [ɪ'kweɪtər] *n* : ecuador *m*

equilibrium [ˌiːkwə'lɪbriəm, ˌɛ-] *n*, *pl* **-riums** *or* **-ria** [-briə] : equilibrio *m*

equinox [ˈiːkwəˌnɑks, ˈɛ-] *n* : equinoccio *m*

equip [ɪ'kwɪp] *vt* **equipped; equipping** : equipar — **equipment** [ɪ'kwɪpmənt] *n* : equipo *m*

equity [ˈɛkwəṭi] *n*, *pl* **-ties 1** FAIRNESS : equidad *f* **2 equities** *npl* STOCKS : acciones *fpl* ordinarias

equivalent [ɪ'kwɪvələnt] *adj* : equivalente — **~** *n* : equivalente *m*

era [ˈɪrə, ˈɛrə, ˈiːrə] *n* : era *f*, época *f*

eradicate [ɪ'rædəˌkeɪt] *vt* **-cated; -cating** : erradicar

erase [ɪ'reɪs] *vt* **erased; erasing** : borrar — **eraser** [ɪ'reɪsər] *n* : goma *f* de borrar, borrador *m*

erect [ɪ'rɛkt] *adj* : erguido — **~** *vt* : erigir, levantar — **erection** [ɪ'rɛkʃən] *n* **1** BUILDING : construcción *f* **2** : erección *f* (en fisiología)

erode [ɪ'roːd] *vt* **eroded; eroding** : erosionar (el suelo), corroer (metales) — **erosion** [ɪ'roːʒən] *n* : erosión *f*, corrosión *f*

erotic [ɪ'rɑṭɪk] *adj* : erótico

err [ˈɛr, ˈər] *vi* : equivocarse, errar

errand [ˈɛrənd] *n* : mandado *m*, recado *m Spain*

erratic [ɪ'ræṭɪk] *adj* : errático, irregular

error [ˈɛrər] *n* : error *m* — **erroneous** [ɪ'roːniəs, ɛ-] *adj* : erróneo

erupt [ɪ'rʌpt] *vi* **1** : hacer erupción (dícese de un volcán) **2** : estallar (dícese de la cólera, la violencia, etc.) — **eruption** [ɪ'rʌpʃən] *n* : erupción *f*

escalate [ˈɛskəˌleɪt] *vi* **-lated; -lating** : intensificarse

escalator [ˈɛskəˌleɪtər] *n* : escalera *f* mecánica

escapade [ˈɛskəˌpeɪd] *n* : aventura *f*

escape [ɪ'skeɪp, ɛ-] *v* **-caped; -caping** *vt* : escapar a, evitar — *vi* : escaparse, fugarse — **~** *n* **1** : fuga *f* **2 ~ from reality** : evasión *f* de la realidad — **escapee** [ɪˌskeˈpiː, ɛ-] *n* : fugitivo *m*, -va *f*

escort [ˈɛsˌkɔrt] *n* **1** GUARD : escolta *f* **2** COMPANION : acompañante *mf* — **~** [ɪ'skɔrt, ɛ-] *vt* **1** : escoltar **2** ACCOMPANY : acompañar

Eskimo [ˈɛskəˌmoː] *adj* : esquimal

especially [ɪ'spɛʃəli] *adv* : especialmente

espionage [ˈɛspiəˌnɑʒ, -ˌnɑdʒ] *n* : espionaje *m*

espresso [ɛ'sprɛˌsoː] *n*, *pl* **-sos** : café *m* exprés

essay [ˈɛˌseɪ] *n* : ensayo *m* (literario), composición *f* (académica)

essence [ˈɛsənts] *n* : esencia *f* — **essential** [ɪ'sɛntʃəl] *adj* : esencial — **~** *n* **1** : elemento *m* esencial **2 the ~s** : lo indispensable

establish [ɪ'stæblɪʃ, ɛ-] *vt* : establecer — **establishment** [ɪ'stæblɪʃmənt, ɛ-] *n* : establecimiento *m*

estate [ɪ'steɪt, ɛ-] *n* **1** POSSESSIONS : bienes *mpl* **2** LAND, PROPERTY : finca *f*

esteem [ɪ'stiːm, ɛ-] *n* : estima *f* — **~** *vt* : estimar

esthetic [ɛs'θɛṭɪk] → **aesthetic**

estimate [ˈɛstəˌmeɪt] *vt* **-mated; -mating** : calcular, estimar — **~** [ˈɛstəmət] *n* **1** : cálculo *m* (aproximado) **2** *or* **~ of costs** : presupuesto *m* — **estimation** [ˌɛstəˈmeɪʃən] *n* **1** JUDGMENT : juicio *m* **2** ESTEEM : estima *f*

estuary [ˈɛstʃuˌweri] *n*, *pl* **-aries** : estuario *m*, ría *f*

eternal [ɪ'tərnəl, iː-] *adj* : eterno — **eternity** [ɪ'tərnəṭi, iː-] *n*, *pl* **-ties** : eternidad *f*

ether [ˈiːθər] *n* : éter *m*

ethical [ˈɛθɪkəl] *adj* : ético — **ethics** [ˈɛθɪks] *ns & pl* : ética *f*, moralidad *f*

ethnic [ˈɛθnɪk] *adj* : étnico

etiquette [ˈɛṭɪkət, -ˌkɛt] *n* : etiqueta *f*

Eucharist [ˈjuːkərɪst] *n* : Eucaristía *f*

eulogy [ˈjuːlədʒi] *n*, *pl* **-gies** : elogio *m*, panegírico *m*

euphemism [ˈjuːfəˌmɪzəm] *n* : eufemismo *m*

euphoria [juˈforiə] *n* : euforia *f*

European [ˌjurə'piːən, -ˌpiːn] *adj* : europeo

evacuate [ɪ'vækjuˌeɪt] *vt* **-ated; -ating** : evacuar — **evacuation** [ɪˌvækjuˈeɪʃən] *n* : evacuación *f*

evade [ɪ'veɪd] *vt* **evaded; evading** : evadir, eludir

evaluate [ɪ'væljuˌeɪt] *vt* **-ated; -ating** : evaluar

evaporate [ɪ'væpəˌreɪt] *vi* **-rated; -rating** : evaporarse

evasion [ɪ'veɪʒən] *n* : evasión *f* — **evasive** [ɪ'veɪsɪv] *adj* : evasivo

eve [ˈiːv] *n* : víspera *f*

even [ˈiːvən] *adj* **1** REGULAR, STEADY : regular, constante **2** LEVEL : plano, llano **3** SMOOTH : liso **4** EQUAL : igual **5 ~ number** : número *m* par **6 get ~ with** : desquitarse con — **~** *adv* **1** : hasta, incluso **2 ~ better** : aún

mejor, todavía mejor 3 ~ **if** : aunque
4 ~ **so** : aun así — ~ *vt* : igualar —
vi or ~ **out** : nivelarse

evening ['i:vnɪŋ] *n* : tarde *f*, noche *f*

event [ɪ'vɛnt] *n* **1** : acontecimiento *m*,
suceso *m* **2** : prueba *f* (en deportes) **3**
in the ~ **of** : en caso de — **eventful**
[ɪ'vɛntfəl] *adj* : lleno de incidentes

eventual [ɪ'vɛntʃʊəl] *adj* : final — **even-**
tuality [ɪ,vɛntʃʊ'æləti] *n, pl* **-ties**
: eventualidad *f* — **eventually** [ɪ-
'vɛntʃʊəli] *adv* : al fin, finalmente

ever ['ɛvər] *adv* **1** ALWAYS : siempre **2** ~
since : desde entonces **3** **hardly** ~
: casi nunca **4 have you** ~ **done it?**
: ¿lo has hecho alguna vez?

evergreen ['ɛvər,gri:n] *n* : planta *f* de
hoja perenne

everlasting [,ɛvər'læstɪŋ] *adj* : eterno

every ['ɛvri] *adj* **1** EACH : cada **2** ~
month : todos los meses **3** ~ **other**
day : cada dos días — **everybody**
['ɛvri,bʌdi, -,ba-] *pron* : todos *mpl*, -das
fpl; todo el mundo — **everyday** [,ɛvri-
'deɪ, 'ɛvri,-] *adj* : cotidiano, de todos los
días — **everyone** ['ɛvri,wʌn] → **every-**
body — **everything** ['ɛvri,θɪŋ] *pron*
: todo — **everywhere** ['ɛvri,hwɛr] *adv*
: en todas partes, por todas partes

evict [ɪ'vɪkt] *vt* : desahuciar, desalojar —
eviction [ɪ'vɪkʃən] *n* : desahucio *m*

evidence ['ɛvədənts] *n* **1** PROOF : prue-
bas *fpl* **2** TESTIMONY : testimonio *m*,
declaración *f* — **evident** ['ɛvədənt] *adj*
: evidente — **evidently** ['ɛvidəntli, ,ɛvi-
'dɛntli] *adv* **1** OBVIOUSLY : obviamente
2 APPARENTLY : evidentemente, al
parecer

evil ['i:vəl, -vɪl] *adj* **eviler** *or* **eviller;**
evilest *or* **evillest** : malvado, malo —
~ *n* : mal *m*, maldad *f*

evoke [i'voːk] *vt* **evoked; evoking**
: evocar

evolution [,ɛvə'lu:ʃən, ,i:-] *n* : evolución
f, desarrollo *m* — **evolve** [i'vɑlv] *vi*
evolved; evolving : evolucionar, desarrollarse

exact [ɪg'zækt, ɛg-] *adj* : exacto, preciso
— ~ *vt* : exigir — **exacting** [ɪg-
'zæktɪŋ, ɛg-] *adj* : exigente — **exactly**
[ɪg'zæktli, ɛg-] *adv* : exactamente

exaggerate [ɪg'zædʒə,reɪt, ɛg-] *v* **-ated;**
-ating : exagerar — **exaggeration** [ɪg-
,zædʒə'reɪʃən, ɛg-] *n* : exageración *f*

examine [ɪg'zæmən, ɛg-] *vt* **-ined;**
-ining 1 : examinar **2** INSPECT : revisar
3 QUESTION : interrogar — **exam** [ɪg-
'zæm, ɛg-] *n* : examen *m* — **examina-**
tion [ɪg,zæmə'neɪʃən, ɛg-] *n* : examen
m

example [ɪg'zæmpəl, ɛg-] *n* : ejemplo *m*

exasperate [ɪg'zæspə,reɪt, ɛg-] *v* **-ated;**
-ating : exasperar — **exasperation**
[ɪg,zæspə'reɪʃən, ɛg-] *n* : exasperación *f*

excavate ['ɛkskə,veɪt] *vt* **-vated; -vating**
: excavar — **excavation** [,ɛkskə'veɪʃən]
n : excavación *f*

exceed [ɪk'si:d, ɛk-] *vt* : exceder, sobrepasar — **exceedingly** [ɪk'si:dɪŋli,
ɛk-] *adv* : extremadamente

excel [ɪk'sɛl, ɛk-] *v* **-celled; -celling** *vi*
: sobresalir — *vt* SURPASS : superar —
excellence ['ɛksələnts] *n* : excelencia *f*
— **excellent** ['ɛksələnt] *adj* : excelente

except [ɪk'sɛpt] *prep or* ~ **for** : excepto, menos, salvo — ~ *vt* : exceptuar
— **exception** [ɪk'sɛpʃən] *n* : excepción
f — **exceptional** [ɪk'sɛpʃənəl] *adj* : excepcional

excerpt ['ɛk,sərpt, 'ɛg,zərpt] *n* : extracto
m

excess [ɪk'sɛs, 'ɛk,sɛs] *n* : exceso *m* —
~ ['ɛk,sɛs, ɪk'sɛs] *adj* : excesivo, de
sobra — **excessive** [ɪk'sɛsɪv, ɛk-] *adj*
: excesivo

exchange [ɪks'tʃeɪndʒ, ɛks-; 'ɛks,tʃeɪndʒ]
n **1** : intercambio *m* **2** : cambio *m* (en
finanzas) — ~ *vt* **-changed; -chang-**
ing : cambiar, intercambiar

excise [ɪk'saɪz, ɛk-] *n* ~ **tax** : impuesto
m interno, impuesto *m* sobre el consumo

excite [ɪk'saɪt, ɛk-] *vt* **-cited; -citing**
: excitar, emocionar — **excited** [ɪk-
'saɪtəd, ɛk-] *adj* : excitado, entusias-
mado — **excitement** [ɪk'saɪtmənt, ɛk-]
n : entusiasmo *m*, emoción *f*

exclaim [ɪks'kleɪm, ɛk-] *v* : exclamar —
exclamation [,ɛksklə'meɪʃən] *n* : exclamación *f* — **exclamation point** *n*
: signo *m* de admiración

exclude [ɪks'klu:d, ɛks-] *vt* **-cluded;**
-cluding : excluir — **excluding** [ɪks-
'klu:dɪŋ, ɛks-] *prep* : excepto, con excepción de — **exclusion** [ɪks'klu:ʒən,
ɛks-] *n* : exclusión *f* — **exclusive** [ɪks-
'klu:sɪv, ɛks-] *adj* : exclusivo

excrement ['ɛkskrəmənt] *n* : excremento *m*

excruciating [ɪk'skru:ʃi,eɪtɪŋ, ɛk-] *adj*
: insoportable, atroz

excursion [ɪk'skərʒən, ɛk-] *n* : excursión *f*

excuse [ɪk'skju:z, ɛk-] *vt* **-cused;**
-cusing 1 : perdonar **2** ~ **me**
: perdóne, perdón — ~ [ɪk'skju:s, ɛk-]
n : excusa *f*

execute ['ɛksɪ,kju:t] *vt* **-cuted; -cuting**
: ejecutar — **execution** [,ɛksɪ'kju:ʃən] *n*
: ejecución *f* — **executioner** [,ɛksɪ-
'kju:ʃənər] *n* : verdugo *m*

executive [ɪg'zɛkjət̬ɪv, ɛg-] *adj* : ejecutivo — **~** *n* **1** MANAGER : ejecutivo *m*, -va *f* **2** *or* **~ branch** : poder *m* ejecutivo

exemplify [ɪg'zɛmplə,faɪ, ɛg-] *vt* **-fied; -fying** : ejemplificar — **exemplary** [ɪg'zɛmpləri, ɛg-] *adj* : ejemplar

exempt [ɪg'zɛmpt, ɛg-] *adj* : exento — **~** *vt* : dispensar — **exemption** [ɪg'zɛmpʃən, ɛg-] *n* : exención *f*

exercise ['ɛksər,saɪz] *n* : ejercicio *m* — **~** *v* **-cised; -cising** *vt* USE : ejercer, hacer uso de — *vi* : hacer ejercicio

exert [ɪg'zərt, ɛg-] *vt* **1** : ejercer **2** **~ oneself** : esforzarse — **exertion** [ɪg'zərʃən, ɛg-] *n* : esfuerzo *m*

exhale [ɛks'heɪl] *v* **-haled; -haling** : exhalar

exhaust [ɪg'zɔst, ɛg-] *vt* : agotar — **~** *n* **1** *or* **~ fumes** : gases *mpl* de escape **2** *or* **~ pipe** : tubo *m* de escape — **exhaustion** [ɪg'zɔstʃən, ɛg-] *n* : agotamiento *m* — **exhaustive** [ɪg'zɔstɪv, ɛg-] *adj* : exhaustivo

exhibit [ɪg'zɪbət, ɛg-] *vt* **1** DISPLAY : exponer **2** SHOW : mostrar — **~** *n* **1** : objeto *m* expuesto **2** EXHIBITION : exposición *f* — **exhibition** [ˌɛksə'bɪʃən] *n* : exposición *f*

exhilarate [ɪg'zɪlə,reɪt, ɛg-] *vt* **-rated; -rating** : alegrar — **exhilaration** [ɪgˌzɪlə'reɪʃən, ɛg-] *n* : regocijo *m*

exile ['ɛg,zaɪl, 'ɛk,saɪl] *n* **1** : exilio *m* **2** OUTCAST : exiliado *m*, -da *f* — **~** *vt* **exiled; exiling** : exiliar

exist [ɪg'zɪst, ɛg-] *vi* : existir — **existence** [ɪg'zɪstənts, ɛg-] *n* : existencia *f* — **existing** *adj* : existente

exit ['ɛg,zət, 'ɛk,sət] *n* : salida *f* — **~** *vi* : salir

exodus ['ɛksədəs] *n* : éxodo *m*

exonerate [ɪg'zɑnə,reɪt, ɛg-] *vt* **-ated; -ating** : exonerar, disculpar

exorbitant [ɪg'zɔrbət̬ənt, ɛg-] *adj* : exorbitante, excesivo

exotic [ɪg'zɑtɪk, ɛg-] *adj* : exótico

expand [ɪk'spænd, ɛk-] *vt* **1** : ampliar, extender **2** : dilatar (metales, etc.) — *vi* **1** : ampliarse, extenderse **2** : dilatarse (dícese de metales, etc.) — **expanse** [ɪk'spænts, ɛk-] *n* : extensión *f* — **expansion** [ɪk'spæntʃən, ɛk-] *n* : expansión *f*

expatriate [ɛks'peɪtriət, -,eɪt] *n* : expatriado *m*, -da *f* — **~** *adj* : expatriado

expect [ɪk'spɛkt, ɛk-] *vt* **1** : esperar **2** REQUIRE : contar con — *vi* **be expecting** : estar embarazada — **expectancy** [ɪk'spɛktəntsi, ɛk-] *n*, *pl* **-cies** : esperanza *f* — **expectant** [ɪk'spɛktənt, ɛk-] *adj* **1**

: expectante **2** **~ mother** : futura madre *f* — **expectation** [ˌɛk,spɛk'teɪʃən] *n* : esperanza *f*

expedient [ɪk'spiːdiənt, ɛk-] *adj* : conveniente — **~** *n* : expediente *m*, recurso *m*

expedition [ˌɛkspə'dɪʃən] *n* : expedición *f*

expel [ɪk'spɛl, ɛk-] *vt* **-pelled; -pelling** : expulsar (a una persona), expeler (humo, etc.)

expend [ɪk'spɛnd, ɛk-] *vt* : gastar — **expendable** [ɪk'spɛndəbəl, ɛk-] *adj* : prescindible — **expenditure** [ɪk'spɛndɪtʃər, ɛk-, -,tʃʊr] *n* : gasto *m* — **expense** [ɪk'spɛnts, ɛk-] *n* **1** : gasto *m* **2** **~s** *npl* : gastos *mpl*, expensas *fpl* **3** **at the ~ of** : a expensas de — **expensive** [ɪk'spɛntsɪv, ɛk-] *adj* : caro

experience [ɪk'spɪriənts, ɛk-] *n* : experiencia *f* — **~** *vt* **-enced; -encing** : experimentar — **experienced** [ɪk'spɪriəntst, ɛk-] *adj* : experimentado

experiment [ɪk'spɛrəmənt, ɛk-, -'spɪr-] *n* : experimento *m* — **~** *vi* : experimentar — **experimental** [ɪkˌspɛrə'mɛntəl, ɛk-, -spɪr-] *adj* : experimental

expert ['ɛk,spərt, ɪk'spərt] *adj* : experto — **~** ['ɛk,spərt] *n* : experto *m*, -ta *f* — **expertise** [ˌɛkspər'tiːz] *n* : pericia *f*, competencia *f*

expire [ɪk'spaɪr, ɛk-] *vi* **-pired; -piring 1** : caducar, vencer **2** DIE : expirar, morir — **expiration** [ˌɛkspə'reɪʃən] *n* : vencimiento *m*, caducidad *f*

explain [ɪk'spleɪn, ɛk-] *vt* : explicar — **explanation** [ˌɛksplə'neɪʃən] *n* : explicación *f* — **explanatory** [ɪk'splænə,tori, ɛk-] *adj* : explicativo

explicit [ɪk'splɪsət, ɛk-] *adj* : explícito

explode [ɪk'sploːd, ɛk-] *v* **-ploded; -ploding** *vt* : hacer explotar — *vi* : explotar, estallar

exploit ['ɛk,sploɪt] *n* : hazaña *f*, proeza *f* — **~** [ɪk'sploɪt, ɛk-] *vt* : explotar — **exploitation** [ˌɛksploɪ'teɪʃən] *n* : explotación *f*

exploration [ˌɛksplə'reɪʃən] *n* : exploración *f* — **explore** [ɪk'splor, ɛk-] *vt* **-plored; -ploring** : explorar — **explorer** [ɪk'splorər, ɛk-] *n* : explorador *m*, -dora *f*

explosion [ɪk'sploːʒən, ɛk-] *n* : explosión *f* — **explosive** [ɪk'sploːsɪv, ɛk-] *adj* : explosivo — **~** *n* : explosivo *m*

export [ɛk'sport, 'ɛk,sport] *vt* : exportar — **~** ['ɛk,sport] *n* : exportación *f*

expose [ɪk'spoːz, ɛk-] *vt* **-posed; -posing 1** : exponer **2** REVEAL : descubrir, revelar — **exposed** [ɪk'spoːzd, ɛk-] *adj*

: expuesto, al descubierto — **exposure** [ɪk'spoʒər, ɛk-] *n* : exposición *f*
express [ɪk'sprɛs, ɛk-] *adj* **1** SPECIFIC : expreso, específico **2** FAST : expreso, rápido — ∼ *adv* : por correo urgente — ∼ *n or* — **train** : expreso *m* — ∼ *vt* : expresar — **expression** [ɪk'sprɛʃən, ɛk-] *n* **1** : expresión *f* — **expressive** [ɪk'sprɛsɪv, ɛk-] *adj* : expresivo — **expressly** [ɪk'sprɛsli, ɛk-] *adv* : expresamente — **expressway** [ɪk'sprɛs,weɪ, ɛk-] *n* : autopista *f*
expulsion [ɪk'spʌlʃən, ɛk-] *n* : expulsión *f*
exquisite [ɛk'skwɪzət, 'ɛk,skwɪ-] *adj* : exquisito
extend [ɪk'stɛnd, ɛk-] *vt* **1** STRETCH : extender **2** LENGTHEN : prolongar **3** ENLARGE : ampliar **4** ∼ **one's hand** : tender la mano — *vi* : extenderse — **extension** [ɪk'stɛntʃən, ɛk-] *n* **1** : tensión *f* **2** LENGTHENING : prolongación *f* **3** ANNEX : ampliación *f*, anexo *m* **4** ∼ **cord** : alargador *m* — **extensive** [ɪk'stɛntsɪv, ɛk-] *adj* : extenso — **extent** [ɪk'stɛnt, ɛk-] *n* **1** SIZE : extensión *f* **2** DEGREE : alcance *m*, grado *m* **3 to a certain** ∼ : hasta cierto punto
extenuating [ɪk'stɛnjə,weɪtɪŋ, ɛk-] *adj* ∼ **circumstances** : circunstancias *fpl* atenuantes
exterior [ɛk'stɪriər] *adj* : exterior — ∼ *n* : exterior *m*
exterminate [ɪk'stərmə,neɪt, ɛk-] *vt* **-nated; -nating** : exterminar — **extermination** [ɪk,stərmə'neɪʃən, ɛk-] *n* : exterminación *f*
external [ɪk'stərnəl, ɛk-] *adj* : externo — **externally** [ɪk'stərnəli, ɛk-] *adv* : exteriormente
extinct [ɪk'stɪŋkt, ɛk-] *adj* : extinto — **extinction** [ɪk'stɪŋkʃən, ɛk-] *n* : extinción *f*
extinguish [ɪk'stɪŋgwɪʃ, ɛk-] *vt* : extinguir, apagar — **extinguisher** [ɪk'stɪŋgwɪʃər, ɛk-] *n* : extintor *m*
extol [ɪk'stoːl, ɛk-] *vt* **-tolled; -tolling** : ensalzar, alabar
extort [ɪk'stɔrt, ɛk-] *vt* : arrancar (algo a algn) por la fuerza — **extortion** [ɪk'stɔrʃən, ɛk-] *n* : extorsión *f*
extra ['ɛkstrə] *adj* : suplementario, de

más — ∼ *n* : extra *m* — ∼ *adv* **1** : extra, más **2** ∼ **special** : super especial
extract [ɪk'strækt, ɛk-] *vt* : extraer, sacar — ∼ ['ɛkstrækt] *n* : extracto *m* — **extraction** [ɪk'strækʃən, ɛk-] *n* : extracción *f*
extracurricular [,ɛkstrəkə'rɪkjələr] *adj* : extracurricular
extradite ['ɛkstrə,daɪt] *vt* **-dited; -diting** : extraditar
extraordinary [ɪk'strɔrdən,ɛri, ,ɛkstrə-'ɔrd-] *adj* : extraordinario
extraterrestrial [,ɛkstrətə'rɛstriəl] *adj* : extraterrestre — ∼ *n* : extraterrestre *mf*
extravagant [ɪk'strævɪgənt, ɛk-] *adj* **1** WASTEFUL : despilfarrador, derrochador **2** EXAGGERATED : extravagante, exagerado — **extravagance** [ɪk'strævɪgənts, ɛk-] *n* **1** WASTEFULNESS : derroche *m*, despilfarro *m* **2** LUXURY : lujo *m* **3** EXAGGERATION : extravagancia *f*
extreme [ɪk'striːm, ɛk-] *adj* : extremo — ∼ *n* : extremo *m* — **extremely** [ɪk'striːmli, ɛk-] *adv* : extremadamente — **extremity** [ɪk'strɛməti, ɛk-] *n, pl* **-ties** : extremidad *f*
extricate ['ɛkstrə,keɪt] *vt* **-cated; -cating** : librar, (lograr) sacar
extrovert ['ɛkstrə,vərt] *n* : extrovertido *m*, **-da** *f* — **extroverted** ['ɛkstrə,vərtəd] *adj* : extrovertido
exuberant [ɪg'zuːbərənt, ɛg-] *adj* **1** JOYOUS : eufórico **2** LUSH : exuberante — **exuberance** [ɪg'zuːbərənts, ɛg-] *n* **1** JOYOUSNESS : euforia *f* **2** VIGOR : exuberancia *f*
exult [ɪg'zʌlt, ɛg-] *vi* : exultar
eye ['aɪ] *n* **1** : ojo *m* **2** VISION : visión *f*, vista *f* **3** GLANCE : mirada *f* — ∼ *vt* **eyed; eyeing** *or* **eying** : mirar — **eyeball** ['aɪ,bɔl] *n* : globo *m* ocular — **eyebrow** ['aɪ,braʊ] *n* : ceja *f* — **eyeglasses** ['aɪ,glæsəz] *npl* : anteojos *mpl*, lentes *mpl* — **eyelash** ['aɪ,læʃ] *n* : pestaña *f* — **eyelid** ['aɪ,lɪd] *n* : párpado *m* — **eyesight** ['aɪ,saɪt] *n* : vista *f*, visión *f* — **eyesore** ['aɪ,sor] *n* : monstruosidad *f* — **eyewitness** ['aɪ'wɪtnəs] *n* : testigo *mf* ocular

F

f ['ef] *n*, *pl* **f's** *or* **fs** ['efs] : f, sexta letra del alfabeto inglés

fable ['feɪbəl] *n* : fábula *f*

fabric ['fæbrɪk] *n* : tela *f*, tejido *m*

fabulous ['fæbjələs] *adj* : fabuloso

facade [fə'sɑd] *n* : fachada *f*

face ['feɪs] *n* **1** : cara *f*, rostro *m* (de una persona) **2** APPEARANCE : fisonomía *f*, aspecto *m* **3** : cara *f* (de una moneda), fachada *f* (de un edificio) **4** ~ **value** : valor *m* nominal **5 in the** ~ **of** : en medio de, ante **6 lose** ~ : desprestigiarse **7 make** ~**s** : hacer muecas — ~ **faced; facing** *vt* **1** : estar frente a **2** CONFRONT : enfrentarse a **3** OVERLOOK : dar a — *vi* ~ **to the north** : mirar hacia el norte — **facedown** ['feɪs,daʊn] *adv* : boca abajo — **faceless** ['feɪsləs] *adj* : anónimo — **face–lift** ['feɪs,lɪft] *n* : estiramiento *m* facial

facet ['fæsət] *n* : faceta *f*

face–to–face *adv* & *adj* : cara a cara

facial ['feɪʃəl] *adj* : de la cara, facial — ~ *n* : limpieza *f* de cutis

facetious [fə'si:ʃəs] *adj* : gracioso, burlón

facility [fə'sɪləti] *n*, *pl* -**ties 1** EASE : facilidad *f* **2** CENTER : centro *m* **3 facilities** *npl* : comodidades *fpl*, servicios *mpl*

facsimile [fæk'sɪməli] *n* : facsímile *m*, facsímil *m*

fact ['fækt] *n* **1** : hecho *m* **2 in** ~ : en realidad, de hecho

faction ['fækʃən] *n* : facción *m*, bando *m*

factor ['fæktər] *n* : factor *m*

factory ['fæktəri] *n*, *pl* -**ries** : fábrica *f*

factual ['fæktʃʊəl] *adj* : basado en hechos

faculty ['fækəlti] *n*, *pl* -**ties** : facultad *f*

fad ['fæd] *n* : moda *f* pasajera, manía *f*

fade ['feɪd] *v* **faded; fading** *vi* **1** WITHER : marchitarse **2** DISCOLOR : desteñirse, decolorarse **3** DIM : apagarse **4** VANISH : desvanecerse — *vt* : desteñir

fail ['feɪl] *vi* **1** : fracasar (dícese de una empresa, un matrimonio, etc.) **2** BREAK DOWN : fallar **3** ~ **in** : faltar a, no cumplir con **4** FLUNK : suspender *Spain*, ser reprobado *Lat* **5** ~ **to do sth** : no hacer algo — *vt* **1** DISAPPOINT : fallar **2** FLUNK : suspender *Spain*, reprobar *Lat* — ~ *n* **without** ~ : sin

falta — **failing** ['feɪlɪŋ] *n* : defecto *m* — **failure** ['feɪljər] *n* **1** : fracaso *m* **2** BREAKDOWN : falla *f*

faint ['feɪnt] *adj* **1** WEAK : débil **2** INDISTINCT : tenue, indistinto **3 feel** ~ : estar mareado — ~ *vi* : desmayarse — ~ *n* : desmayo *m* — **fainthearted** ['feɪnt'hɑrtəd] *adj* : cobarde, pusilánime — **faintly** ['feɪntli] *adv* **1** WEAKLY : débilmente **2** SLIGHTLY : ligeramente, levemente

fair[1] ['fær] *n* : feria *f*

fair[2] *adj* **1** BEAUTIFUL : bello, hermoso **2** : bueno (dícese del tiempo) **3** JUST : justo **4** : rubio (dícese del pelo), blanco (dícese de la tez) **5** ADEQUATE : adecuado — ~ *adv* **play** ~ : jugar limpio — **fairly** ['færli] *adv* **1** JUSTLY : justamente **2** QUITE : bastante — **fairness** ['færnəs] *n* : justicia *f*

fairy ['færi] *n*, *pl* **fairies 1** : hada *f* **2** ~ **tale** : cuento *m* de hadas

faith ['feɪθ] *n*, *pl* **faiths** ['feɪθs, 'feɪðz] : fe *f* — **faithful** ['feɪθfəl] *adj* : fiel — **faithfully** *adv* : fielmente — **faithfulness** ['feɪθfəlnəs] *n* : fidelidad *f*

fake ['feɪk] *v* **faked; faking** *vt* **1** FALSIFY : falsificar, falsear **2** FEIGN : fingir — *vi* PRETEND : fingir — ~ *adj* : falso — ~ *n* **1** IMITATION : falsificación *f* **2** IMPOSTOR : impostor *m*, -tora *f*

falcon ['fælkən, 'fɔl-] *n* : halcón *m*

fall ['fɔl] *vi* **fell** ['fɛl]; **fallen** ['fɔlən]; **falling 1** : caer, bajar (dícese de los precios), descender (dícese de la temperatura) **2** ~ **asleep** : dormirse **3** ~ **back** : retirarse **4** ~ **back on** : recurrir a **5** ~ **down** : caerse **6** ~ **in love** : enamorarse **7** ~ **out** QUARREL : pelearse **8** ~ **through** : fracasar — ~ *n* **1** : caída *f*, bajada *f* (de precios), descenso *m* (de temperatura) **2** AUTUMN : otoño *m* **3** ~**s** *npl* WATERFALL : cascada *f*, catarata *f*

fallacy ['fæləsi] *n*, *pl* -**cies** : concepto *m* erróneo

fallible ['fæləbəl] *adj* : falible

fallow ['fælo] *adj* **lie** ~ : estar en barbecho

false ['fɔls] *adj* **falser; falsest 1** : falso **2** ~ **alarm** : falsa alarma *f* **3** ~ **teeth** : dentadura *f* postiza — **falsehood** ['fɔls,hʊd] *n* : mentira *f* — **falseness**

['fɔlsnəs] n : falsedad f — **falsify**
['fɔlsə,faɪ] vt **-fied; fying** : falsificar,
falsear

falter ['fɔltər] vi **-tered; -tering 1** STUM-
BLE : tambalearse **2** WAVER : vacilar

fame ['feɪm] n : fama f

familiar [fə'mɪljər] adj **1** : familiar **2 be**
~ with : estar familiarizado con —
familiarity [fə,mɪl'ærəti, -,mɪl'jær-] n,
pl **-ties** : familiaridad f — **familiarize**
[fə'mɪljə,raɪz] vt **-ized; -izing ~ one-**
self : familiarizarse

family ['fæmli, 'fæmə-] n, pl **-lies** : familia f

famine ['fæmən] n : hambre f, hambruna
f

famished ['fæmɪʃt] adj : famélico

famous ['feɪməs] adj : famoso

fan ['fæn] n **1** : ventilador m, abanico m
2 : aficionado m, -da f (a un pasatiempo); admirador m, -dora f (de una persona) — **~** vt **fanned; fanning**
: abanicar (a una persona), avivar (un
fuego)

fanatic [fə'næt̬ɪk] or **fanatical** [-t̬ɪkəl]
adj : fanático — **~** n : fanático m, -ca
f — **fanaticism** [fə'næt̬ə,sɪzəm] n : fanatismo m

fancy ['fæntsi] vt **-cied; -cying 1** IMAG-
INE : imaginarse **2** DESIRE : apetecerle
(algo a uno) — **~** adj **-cier; -est 1**
ELABORATE : elaborado **2** LUXURIOUS
: lujoso, elegante — **~** n, pl **-cies 1**
WHIM : capricho m **2** IMAGINATION
: imaginación f **3 take a ~ to** : aficionarse a (una cosa), tomar cariño a
(una persona) — **fanciful** ['fæntsɪfəl]
adj **1** CAPRICIOUS : caprichoso **2** IMAG-
INATIVE : imaginativo

fanfare ['fæn,fær] n : fanfarria f

fang ['fæŋ] n : colmillo m (de un animal), diente m (de una serpiente)

fantasy ['fæntəsi] n, pl **-sies** : fantasía f
— **fantasize** ['fæntə,saɪz] vt **-sized;**
-sizing : fantasear — **fantastic** ['fæn-
'tæstɪk] adj : fantástico

far ['fɑr] adv **farther** ['fɑrðər] or **further**
['fər-]; **farthest** or **furthest** [-ðəst] adv
1 : lejos **2** MUCH : muy, mucho **3 as ~**
as : hasta (un lugar), con respecto a
(un tema) **4 by ~** : con mucho **5 ~**
and wide : por todas partes **6 ~ away**
: a lo lejos **7 ~ from it!** : ¡todo lo contrario! **8 so ~** : hasta ahora, todavía
— **~** adj **farther** or **further; farthest**
or **furthest 1** REMOTE : lejano **2** EX-
TREME : extremo — **faraway** ['fɑrə,weɪ]
adj : remoto, lejano

farce ['fɑrs] n : farsa f

fare ['fær] vi **fared; faring** : irle a uno —

~ n **1** : precio m del pasaje **2** FOOD
: comida f

farewell [fær'wel] n : despedida f — **~**
adj : de despedida

far–fetched ['fɑr'fetʃt] adj : improbable,
exagerado

farm ['fɑrm] n : granja f, hacienda f —
~ vt : cultivar (la tierra), criar (animales) — vi : ser agricultor — **farmer**
['fɑrmər] n : agricultor m, -tora f;
granjero m, -jera f — **farmhand**
['fɑrm,hænd] n : peón m — **farmhouse**
['fɑrm,haʊs] n : granja f, casa f de hacienda — **farming** ['fɑrmɪŋ] n : agricultura f, cultivo m (de plantas), crianza f (de animales) — **farmyard**
['fɑrm,jɑrd] n : corral m

far–off ['fɑr,ɔf, -ˈɔf] adj : lejano

far–reaching ['fɑr'riːtʃɪŋ] adj : de gran
alcance

farsighted ['fɑr,saɪt̬əd] adj **1** : hiper-
métrope **2** PRUDENT : previsor

farther ['fɑrðər] adv **1** : más lejos **2**
MORE : más — adj : más lejano — **far-**
thest adv **1** : lo más lejos **2** MOST
: más — adj : más lejano

fascinate ['fæsən,eɪt] vt **-nated; -nating**
: fascinar — **fascination** [,fæsən'eɪʃən]
n : fascinación f

fascism ['fæʃ,ɪzəm] n : fascismo m —
fascist ['fæʃɪst] adj : fascista — **~** n
: fascista mf

fashion ['fæʃən] n **1** MANNER : manera f
2 STYLE : moda f **3 out of ~** : pasada
de moda — **fashionable** ['fæʃənəbəl]
adj : de moda

fast¹ ['fæst] vi : ayunar — **~** n : ayuno
m

fast² adj **1** SWIFT : rápido **2** SECURE
: firme, seguro **3** : adelantado (dícese
de un reloj) **4 ~ friends** : amigos mpl
leales — **~** adv **1** SECURELY : firmemente **2** SWIFTLY : rápidamente **3 ~**
asleep : profundamente dormido

fasten ['fæsən] vt : sujetar (papeles,
etc.), abrochar (una blusa, etc.), cerrar
(una maleta, etc.) — vi : abrocharse,
cerrar — **fastener** ['fæsənər] n : cierre
m

fat ['fæt] adj **fatter; fattest 1** : gordo **2**
THICK : grueso — **~** n : grasa f

fatal ['feɪt̬əl] adj **1** : mortal **2** FATEFUL
: fatal, fatídico — **fatality** [feɪ'tæləti,
fə-] n, pl **-ties** : víctima f mortal

fate ['feɪt] n **1** : destino m **2** LOT : suerte
f — **fateful** ['feɪtfəl] adj : fatídico

father ['fɑðər] n : padre m — **~** vt : engendrar — **fatherhood** ['fɑðər,hʊd] n
: paternidad f — **father–in–law**
['fɑðərɪn,lɔ] n, pl **fathers–in–law** : sue-

gro *m* — **fatherly** ['foðərli] *adj* : paternal

fathom ['fæðəm] *vt* : comprender

fatigue [fə'tiːg] *n* : fatiga *f* — ~ *vt* **-tigued; -tiguing** : fatigar

fatten ['fætən] *vt* : engordar — **fattening** *adj* : que engorda

fatty ['fæti] *adj* **fattier; -est** : graso

faucet ['fɔsət] *n* : llave *f Lat*, grifo *m Spain*

fault ['fɔlt] *n* **1** FLAW : defecto *m* **2** RESPONSIBILITY : culpa *f* **3** : falla *f* (geológica) — *vt* : encontrar defectos a — **faultless** ['fɔltləs] *adj* : impecable — **faulty** ['fɔlti] *adj* **faultier; -est** : defectuoso

fauna ['fɔnə] *n* : fauna *f*

favor *or Brit* **favour** ['feɪvər] *n* **1** : favor *m* **2 in ~ of** : a favor de — ~ *vt* **1** : favorecer **2** SUPPORT : estar a favor de **3** PREFER : preferir — **favorable** *or Brit* **favourable** ['feɪvərəbəl] *adj* : favorable — **favorite** *or Brit* **favourite** ['feɪvərət] *n* : favorito *m*, -ta *f* — ~ *adj* : favorito — **favoritism** *or Brit* **favouritism** ['feɪvərə,tɪzəm] *n* : favoritismo *m*

fawn[1] ['fɔn] *vi* ~ **over** : adular

fawn[2] *n* : cervato *m*

fax ['fæks] *n* : fax *m* — ~ *vt* : faxear, enviar por fax

fear ['fɪr] *v* : temer — ~ *n* **1** : miedo *m*, temor *m* **2 for ~ of** : por temor a — **fearful** ['fɪrfəl] *adj* **1** FRIGHTENING : espantoso **2** AFRAID : temeroso

feasible ['fiːzəbəl] *adj* : viable, factible

feast ['fiːst] *n* **1** BANQUET : banquete *m*, festín *m* **2** FESTIVAL : fiesta *f* — ~ *vi* **1** : banquetear **2 ~ upon** : darse un festín de

feat ['fiːt] *n* : hazaña *f*

feather ['feðər] *n* : pluma *f*

feature ['fiːtʃər] *n* **1** : rasgo *m* (de la cara) **2** CHARACTERISTIC : característica *f* **3** : artículo *m* (en un periódico) **4** ~ **film** : largometraje *m* — *v* **-tured; -turing** *vt* **1** PRESENT : presentar **2** EMPHASIZE : destacar — *vi* : figurar

February ['febju,eri, 'febu-, 'febru-] *n* : febrero *m*

feces ['fiː,siːz] *npl* : excremento *mpl*

federal ['fedrəl, -dərəl] *adj* : federal — **federation** [,fedə'reɪʃən] *n* : federación *f*

fed up *adj* : harto

fee ['fiː] *n* **1** : honorarios *mpl* **2 entrance ~** : entrada *f*

feeble ['fiːbəl] *adj* **-bler; -blest 1** : débil **2 a ~ excuse** : una pobre excusa

feed ['fiːd] *v* **fed** ['fed]; **feeding** *vt* **1** : dar

de comer a, alimentar **2** SUPPLY : alimentar — *vi* : comer, alimentarse — ~ *n* : pienso *m*

feel ['fiːl] *v* **felt** ['felt]; **feeling** *vt* **1** : sentir (una sensación, etc.) **2** TOUCH : tocar, palpar **3** BELIEVE : creer — *vi* **1** : sentirse (bien, cansado, etc.) **2** SEEM : parecer **3 ~ hot/thirsty** : tener calor/sed **4 ~ like doing** : tener ganas de hacer — ~ *n* : tacto *m*, sensación *f* — **feeling** ['fiːlɪŋ] *n* **1** SENSATION : sensación *f* **2** EMOTION : sentimiento *m* **3** OPINION : opinión *f* **4 hurt s.o.'s ~s** : herir los sentimientos de algn

feet → **foot**

feign ['feɪn] *vt* : fingir

feline ['fiːlaɪn] *adj* : felino — ~ *n* : felino *m*, -na *f*

fell[1] → **fall**

fell[2] ['fel] *vt* : talar (un árbol)

fellow ['fe,loː] *n* **1** COMPANION : compañero *m*, -ra *f* **2** MEMBER : socio *m*, -cia *f* **3** MAN : tipo *m* — **fellowship** ['felo,ʃɪp] *n* **1** : compañerismo *m* **2** ASSOCIATION : fraternidad *f* **3** GRANT : beca *f*

felon ['felən] *n* : criminal *mf* — **felony** ['feləni] *n, pl* **-nies** : delito *m* grave

felt[1] → **feel**

felt[2] ['felt] *n* : fieltro *m*

female ['fiː,meɪl] *adj* : femenino — ~ *n* **1** : hembra *f* (animal) **2** WOMAN : mujer *f*

feminine ['femənən] *adj* : femenino — **femininity** [,femɪ'nɪnəti] *n* : femineidad *f* — **feminism** ['femə,nɪzəm] *n* : feminismo *m* — **feminist** ['femənɪst] *adj* : feminista — ~ *n* : feminista *mf*

fence ['fens] *n* : cerca *f*, valla *f*, cerco *m Lat* — ~ *v* **fenced; fencing** *vt* or ~ **in** : vallar, cercar — *vi* : hacer esgrima — **fencing** ['fensɪŋ] *n* : esgrima *m* (deporte)

fend ['fend] *vt* ~ **off** : rechazar (un enemigo), eludir (una pregunta) — *vi* ~ **for oneself** : valerse por sí mismo

fender ['fendər] *n* : guardabarros *mpl*

fennel ['fenəl] *n* : hinojo *m*

ferment ['fərmənt] *v* : fermentar — **fermentation** [,fərmən'teɪʃən, -,men-] *n* : fermentación *f*

fern ['fərn] *n* : helecho *m*

ferocious [fə'roːʃəs] *adj* : feroz — **ferocity** [fə'rɑsəti] *n* : ferocidad *f*

ferret ['ferət] *n* : hurón *m* — ~ *vt* ~ **out** : descubrir

Ferris wheel ['ferɪs] *n* : noria *f*

ferry ['feri] *vt* **-ried; -rying** : transportar — ~ *n, pl* **-ries** : ferry *m*

fertile ['fərṭəl] *adj* : fértil — **fertility** [fər-'tɪləṭi] *n* : fertilidad *f* — **fertilize** ['fərṭəl‚aɪz] *vt* **-ized; -izing** : fecundar (un huevo), abonar (el suelo) — **fertilizer** ['fərṭəl‚aɪzər] *n* : fertilizante *m*, abono *m*

fervent ['fərvənt] *adj* : ferviente — **fervor** *or Brit* **fervour** ['fərvər] *n* : fervor *m*

fester ['fɛstər] *vi* : enconarse

festival ['fɛstəvəl] *n* 1 : fiesta *f* 2 **film** ~ : festival *m* de cine — **festive** ['fɛstɪv] *adj* : festivo — **festivity** [fɛs'tɪvəṭi] *n, pl* **-ties** : festividad *f*

fetch ['fɛtʃ] *vt* 1 : ir a buscar 2 : venderse por (un precio)

fête ['feɪt, 'fɛt] *n* : fiesta *f*

fetid ['fɛṭəd] *adj* : fétido

fetish ['fɛṭɪʃ] *n* : fetiche *f*

fetters ['fɛṭərz] *npl* : grillos *mpl* — **fetter** ['fɛṭər] *vt* : encadenar

fetus ['fiːṭəs] *n* : feto *m*

feud ['fjuːd] *n* : enemistad *f* (entre familiares) — ~ *vi* : pelear

feudal ['fjuːdəl] *adj* : feudal — **feudalism** ['fjuːdəl‚ɪzəm] *n* : feudalismo *m*

fever ['fiːvər] *n* : fiebre *f* — **feverish** ['fiːvərɪʃ] *adj* : febril

few ['fjuː] *adj* 1 : pocos 2 a ~ **times** : varias veces — ~ *pron* 1 : pocos 2 a ~ : algunos, unos cuantos 3 **quite a** ~ : muchos — **fewer** ['fjuːər] *adj & pron* : menos

fiancé, fiancée [‚fiːɑnˈseɪ, ‚fiːɑnˈseɪ] *n* : prometido *m*, -da *f*; novio *m*, -via *f*

fiasco [fiˈæsˌkoː] *n, pl* **-coes** : fiasco *m*

fib ['fɪb] *n* : mentirilla *f* — ~ *vi* **fibbed; fibbing** : decir mentirillas

fiber *or* **fibre** ['faɪbər] *n* : fibra *f* — **fiberglass** ['faɪbər‚glæs] *n* : fibra *f* de vidrio — **fibrous** ['faɪbrəs] *adj* : fibroso

fickle ['fɪkəl] *adj* : inconstante

fiction ['fɪkʃən] *n* : ficción *f* — **fictional** ['fɪkʃənəl] *or* **fictitious** [fɪkˈtɪʃəs] *adj* : ficticio

fiddle ['fɪdəl] *n* : violín *m* — ~ *vi* **-dled; -dling** 1 : tocar el violín 2 ~ **with** : juguetear con

fidelity [fəˈdɛləṭi, faɪ-] *n, pl* **-ties** : fidelidad *f*

fidget ['fɪdʒət] *vi* 1 : estarse inquieto, moverse 2 ~ **with** : juguetear con — **fidgety** ['fɪdʒəṭi] *adj* : inquieto, nervioso

field ['fiːld] *n* : campo *m* — ~ *vt* : interceptar (una pelota), sortear (una pregunta) — **field glasses** *npl* : binoculares *mpl*, gemelos *mpl* — **field trip** *n* : viaje *m* de estudio

fiend ['fiːnd] *n* 1 : demonio *m* 2 FANATIC : fanático *m*, -ca *f* — **fiendish** ['fiːndɪʃ] *adj* : diabólico

fierce ['fɪrs] *adj* **fiercer; -est** 1 : feroz 2 INTENSE : fuerte (dícese del viento), acalorado (dícese de un debate) — **fierceness** ['fɪrsnəs] *n* : ferocidad *f*

fiery ['faɪəri] *adj* **fierier; -est** 1 BURNING : llameante 2 SPIRITED : ardiente, fogoso — **fieriness** ['faɪərinəs] *n* : pasión *f*, ardor *m*

fifteen [fɪfˈtiːn] *n* : quince *m* — ~ *adj* : quince — **fifteenth** [fɪfˈtiːnθ] *adj* : decimoquinto — ~ *n* 1 : decimoquinto *m*, -ta *f* (en una serie) 2 : quinceavo *m* (en matemáticas)

fifth ['fɪfθ] *n* 1 : quinto *m*, -ta *f* (en una serie) 2 : quinto *m* (en matemáticas) — ~ *adj* : quinto

fiftieth ['fɪftiəθ] *adj* : quincuagésimo — ~ *n* 1 : quincuagésimo *m*, -ma *f* (en una serie) 2 : cincuentavo *m* (en matemáticas)

fifty ['fɪfti] *n, pl* **-ties** : cincuenta *m* — ~ *adj* : cincuenta — **fifty-fifty** [‚fɪfti-ˈfɪfti] *adv* : a medias, mitad y mitad — ~ *adj* a ~ **chance** : un cincuenta por ciento de posibilidades

fig ['fɪg] *n* : higo *m*

fight ['faɪt] *v* **fought** ['fɔt]; **fighting** *vi* 1 BATTLE : luchar 2 QUARREL : pelear 3 ~ **back** : defenderse — *vt* : luchar contra — ~ *n* 1 STRUGGLE : lucha *f* 2 QUARREL : pelea *f* — **fighter** ['faɪṭər] *n* 1 : luchador *m*, -dora *f* 2 *or* ~ **plane** : avión *m* de caza

figment ['fɪgmənt] *n* ~ **of the imagination** : producto *m* de la imaginación

figurative ['fɪgjərəṭɪv, -gə-] *adj* : figurado

figure ['fɪgjər, -gər] *n* 1 NUMBER : número *m*, cifra *f* 2 PERSON, SHAPE : figura *f* 3 ~ **of speech** : figura *f* retórica 4 **watch one's** ~ : cuidar la línea — ~ *v* **-ured; -uring** *vt* : calcular — *vi* 1 : figurar 2 **that** ~**s!** : ¡no me extraña! — **figurehead** ['fɪgjər‚hɛd, -gər] *n* : testaferro *m* — **figure out** *vt* 1 UNDERSTAND : entender 2 RESOLVE : resolver

file¹ ['faɪl] *n* : lima *f* (instrumento) — ~ *vt* **filed; filing** : limar

file² *vt* **filed; filing** 1 : archivar (documentos) 2 ~ **charges** : presentar cargos — ~ *n* : archivo *m*

file³ *n* IN LINE : fila *f* — ~ *vi* ~ **in/out** : entrar/salir en fila

fill ['fɪl] *vt* 1 : llenar, rellenar 2 : cumplir con (un requisito) 3 : tapar (un agujero), empastar (un diente) — *vi* 1 ~ **in for** : reemplazar 2 *or* ~ **up**

: llenarse — ~ n 1 eat one's ~
: comer lo suficiente 2 have one's ~
of : estar harto de
fillet ['fɪlət, frɪeɪ, 'fɪleɪ] n : filete m
filling ['fɪlɪŋ] n 1 : relleno m 2 : empaste
m (de dientes) 3 ~ **station** → **service
station**
filly ['fɪli] n, pl -**lies** : potra f
film ['fɪlm] n : película f — ~ vt : filmar
filter ['fɪltər] n : filtro m — ~ vt : filtrar
filth ['fɪlθ] n : mugre f — **filthy** ['fɪlθi] adj
filthier; -est 1 OBSCENE
: obsceno 2 obsceno
fin ['fɪn] n : aleta f
final ['faɪnəl] adj 1 LAST : último 2 DE-
FINITIVE : definitivo 3 ULTIMATE : final
— ~ n 1 : final f (en deportes) 2 ~**s**
npl : exámenes mpl finales — **finalist**
['faɪnəlɪst] n : finalista mf — **finalize**
['faɪnəlˌaɪz] vt -**ized; -izing** ['faɪnəli] adj
— **finally** ['faɪnəli] adv : finalmente
finance [fə'næns, 'faɪˌnænts] n 1 : finanzas fpl 2 ~**s** npl : recursos mpl fi-
nancieros — ~ vt -**nanced; -nancing**
: financiar — **financial** [fə'næntʃəl,
faɪ-] adj : financiero — **financially** [fə-
'næntʃəli, faɪ-] adv : económicamente
find ['faɪnd] vt **found** ['faʊnd]; **finding** 1
LOCATE : encontrar 2 REALIZE : darse
cuenta de 3 ~ **guilty** : declarar culpable 4 or ~ **out** : descubrir — vi ~
out : enterarse — ~ n : hallazgo m —
finding ['faɪndɪŋ] n 1 FIND : hallazgo m
2 ~**s** npl : conclusiones fpl
fine[1] ['faɪn] n : multa f — ~ vt **fined;
fining** : multar
fine[2] adj **finer; -est 1** DELICATE : fino 2
EXCELLENT : excelente 3 SUBTLE : sutil
4 : bueno (dícese del tiempo) 5 ~
print : letra f menuda 6 **it's ~ with
me** : me parece bien — ~ adv OK
: bien — **fine arts** npl : bellas artes fpl
— **finely** ['faɪnli] adv 1 EXCELLENTLY
: excelentemente 2 PRECISELY : con
precisión 3 MINUTELY : fino, menudo
finger ['fɪŋgər] n : dedo m — ~ vt
: tocar, toquetear — **fingernail** ['fɪŋ-
gərˌneɪl] n : uña f — **fingerprint** ['fɪŋ-
gərˌprɪnt] n : huella f digital — **fingertip** ['fɪŋgərˌtɪp] n : punta f del dedo
finicky ['fɪnɪki] adj : maniático, mañoso
Lat
finish ['fɪnɪʃ] v : acabar, terminar — ~
n 1 END : fin m, final m 2 or ~ **line**
: meta f 3 SURFACE : acabado m
finite ['faɪˌnaɪt] adj : finito
fir ['fər] n : abeto m
fire ['faɪr] n 1 : fuego m 2 CONFLAGRA-
TION : incendio m 3 **catch ~** : incendiarse (dícese de bosques, etc.), pren-

derse (dícese de fósforos, etc.) 4 **on
~** : en llamas 5 **open ~ on** : abrir
fuego sobre — ~ vt **fired; firing** 1
DISMISS : despedir 2 SHOOT : disparar
— vi : disparar — **fire alarm** n : alarma f contra incendios — **firearm** ['faɪr-
ˌɑrm] n : arma f de fuego — **firecracker** ['faɪrˌkrækər] n : petardo m — **fire
engine** n : carro m de bomberos Lat,
coche m de bomberos Spain — **fire
escape** n : escalera f de incendios —
fire extinguisher n : extintor m (de
incendios) — **firefighter** ['faɪrˌfaɪtər] n
: bombero m, -ra f — **firefly** ['faɪrˌflaɪ]
n, pl -**flies** : luciérnaga f — **firehouse**
→ **fire station** — **fireman** ['faɪrmən] n,
pl -**men** [-mən, -ˌmen] → **firefighter** —
fireplace ['faɪrˌpleɪs] n : hogar m,
chimenea f — **fireproof** ['faɪrˌpruːf] adj
: ignífugo — **fireside** ['faɪrˌsaɪd] n
: hogar m — **fire station** n : estación f
de bomberos Lat, parque m de
bomberos Spain — **firewood** ['faɪr-
ˌwʊd] n : leña f — **fireworks** ['faɪrˌwərk]
npl : fuegos mpl artificiales
firm[1] ['fərm] n : empresa f
firm[2] adj : firme — **firmly** ['fərmli] adv
: firmemente — **firmness** ['fərmnəs] n
: firmeza f
first ['fərst] adj 1 : primero 2 **at ~ sight**
: a primera vista 3 **for the ~ time**
: por primera vez — ~ adv 1
: primero 2 ~ **and foremost** : ante
todo 3 ~ **of all** : en primer lugar —
~ n 1 : primero m, -ra f 2 **at ~** : al
principio — **first aid** n : primeros aux-
ilios mpl — **first-class** ['fərst'klæs]
adv : en primera — ~ adj : de
primera f — **firsthand** ['fərst'hænd] adv
: directamente — ~ adj : de primera
mano — **firstly** ['fərstli] adv : en
primer lugar — **first name** n : nombre
m de pila — **first-rate** ['fərst'reɪt] adj
→ **first-class**
fiscal ['fɪskəl] adj : fiscal
fish ['fɪʃ] n, pl **fish** or **fishes** : pez m
(vivo), pescado m (para comer) — ~
vi 1 : pescar 2 ~ **for** SEEK : buscar 3
go ~ing : ir de pesca — **fisherman**
['fɪʃərmən] n, pl -**men** [-mən, -ˌmen]
: pescador m, -dora f — **fishhook** ['fɪʃ-
ˌhʊk] n : anzuelo m — **fishing** ['fɪʃɪŋ] n
: pesca f — **fishing pole** n : caña f de
pescar — **fish market** n : pescadería f
— **fishy** ['fɪʃi] adj **fishier; -est 1** : a
pescado (dícese de sabores, etc.) 2
SUSPICIOUS : sospechoso
fist ['fɪst] n : puño m
fit[1] ['fɪt] n 1 : ataque m 2 **he had a ~**
: le dio un ataque

fit² *adj* **fitter; fittest 1** SUITABLE : apropiado **2** HEALTHY : en forma **3 be ~ for** : ser apto para — *v* **fitted; fitting** *vt* **1** : encajar en (un hueco, etc.) **2** *(relating to clothing)* : quedar bien a **3** SUIT : ser apropiado para **4** MATCH : coincidir con **5** *or* **~ out** : equipar — *vi* **1** : caber (en una caja, etc.), encajar (en un hueco, etc.) **2** *or* **~ in** BELONG : encajar **3 this dress doesn't ~** : este vestido no me queda bien — **~** *n* **it's a good fit** : me queda bien — **fitful** ['fɪtfəl] *adj* : irregular — **fitness** ['fɪtnəs] *n* **1** HEALTH : salud *f* **2** SUITABILITY : idoneidad *f* — **fitting** ['fɪtɪŋ] *adj* : apropiado

five ['faɪv] *n* : cinco *m* — **~** *adj* : cinco — **five hundred** *n* : quinientos *m* — **~** *adj* : quinientos

fix ['fɪks] *vt* **1** ATTACH : fijar, sujetar **2** REPAIR : arreglar **3** PREPARE : preparar — **~** *n* PREDICAMENT : aprieto *m*, apuro *m* — **fixed** ['fɪkst] *adj* : fijo — **fixture** ['fɪkstʃər] *n* : instalación *f*

fizz ['fɪz] *vi* : burbujear — **~** *n* : efervescencia *f*

fizzle ['fɪzəl] *vi* **-zled; -zling** *or* **~ out** : quedar en nada

flabbergasted ['flæbərˌgæstəd] *adj* : estupefacto, pasmado

flabby ['flæbi] *adj* **-bier; -est** : fofo

flaccid ['flæksəd, 'flæsəd] *adj* : fláccido

flag¹ ['flæg] *vi* WEAKEN : flaquear

flag² *n* : bandera *f* — **~** *vt* **flagged; flagging** *or* **~ down** : hacer señales de parada a — **flagpole** ['flægˌpoːl] *n* : asta *f*

flagrant ['fleɪgrənt] *adj* : flagrante

flair ['flær] *n* : don *m*, facilidad *f*

flake ['fleɪk] *n* : copo *m* (de nieve), escama *f* (de pintura, de la piel) — **~** *vi* **flaked; flaking** : pelarse

flamboyant [flæm'bɔɪənt] *adj* : extravagante

flame ['fleɪm] *n* **1** : llama *f* **2 burst into ~s** : estallar en llamas **3 go up in ~s** : incendiarse

flamingo [flə'mɪŋgo] *n*, *pl* **-gos** : flamenco *m*

flammable ['flæməbəl] *adj* : inflamable

flank ['flæŋk] *n* : ijada *m* (de un animal), flanco *m* (militar) — **~** *vt* : flanquear

flannel ['flænəl] *n* : franela *f*

flap ['flæp] *n* : solapa *f* (de un sobre, un libro, etc.), tapa *f* (de un recipiente) — **~** *v* **flapped; flapping** *vi* : agitarse — *vt* : batir, agitar

flapjack ['flæpˌdʒæk] → **pancake**

flare ['flær] *vi* **flared; flaring 1 ~ up** BLAZE : llamear **2 ~ up** EXPLODE,

ERUPT : estallar, explotar — **~** *n* **1** BLAZE : llamarada *f* **2** SIGNAL : (luz *f* de) bengala *f*

flash ['flæʃ] *vi* **1** : brillar, destellar **2 ~ past** : pasar como un rayo — *vt* **1** : dirigir (una luz) **2** SHOW : mostrar **3 ~ a smile** : sonreír — **~** *n* **1** : destello *m* **2 ~ of lightning** : relámpago *m* **3 in a ~** : de repente — **flashlight** ['flæʃˌlaɪt] *n* : linterna *f* — **flashy** ['flæʃi] *adj* **flashier; -est** : ostentoso

flask ['flæsk] *n* : frasco *m*

flat ['flæt] *adj* **flatter; flattest 1** LEVEL : plano, llano **2** DOWNRIGHT : categórico **3** FIXED : fijo **4** MONOTONOUS : monótono **5** : bemol (en la música) **6 ~ tire** : neumático *m* desinflado — **~** *n* **1** : bemol *m* (en la música) **2** *Brit* APARTMENT : apartamento *m*, departamento *m* *Lat* **3** PUNCTURE : pinchazo *m* — **~** *adv* **1 ~ broke** : pelado **2 in one hour ~** : en una hora justa — **flatly** ['flætli] *adv* : categóricamente — **flat-out** ['flætˌaʊt] *adj* **1** : frenético **2** DOWNRIGHT : categórico — **flatten** ['flætən] *vt* **1** LEVEL : aplanar, allanar **2** KNOCK DOWN : arrasar

flatter ['flætər] *vt* **1** : halagar **2** BECOME : favorecer — **flatterer** ['flætərər] *n* : adulador *m*, -dora *f* — **flattering** ['flætərɪŋ] *adj* **1** : halagador **2** BECOMING : favorecedor — **flattery** ['flætəri] *n*, *pl* **-ries** : halagos *mpl*

flaunt ['flɔnt] *vt* : hacer alarde de

flavor *or Brit* **flavour** ['fleɪvər] *n* : gusto *m*, sabor *m* — **~** *vt* : sazonar — **flavorful** *or Brit* **flavourful** ['fleɪvərfəl] *adj* : sabroso — **flavoring** *or Brit* **flavouring** ['fleɪvərɪŋ] *n* : condimento *m*, sazón *f*

flaw ['flɔ] *n* : defecto *m* — **flawless** ['flɔləs] *adj* : perfecto

flax ['flæks] *n* : lino *m*

flea ['fliː] *n* : pulga *f*

fleck ['flɛk] *n* **1** PARTICLE : mota *f* **2** SPOT : pinta *f*

flee ['fliː] *v* **fled** ['flɛd]; **fleeing** *vi* : huir — *vt* : huir de

fleece ['fliːs] *n* : vellón *m* — **~** *vt* **fleeced; fleecing 1** SHEAR : esquilar **2** DEFRAUD : desplumar

fleet ['fliːt] *n* : flota *f*

fleeting ['fliːtɪŋ] *adj* : fugaz

Flemish ['flɛmɪʃ] *adj* : flamenco

flesh ['flɛʃ] *n* **1** : carne *f* **2** PULP : pulpa *f* **3 in the ~** : en persona — **fleshy** ['flɛʃi] *adj* **fleshier; -est 1** : gordo **2** PULPY : carnoso

flew → fly

flex ['flɛks] *vt* : flexionar — **flexibility**

[fleksə'bıləti] *n, pl* **-ties** : flexibilidad *f*
— **flexible** ['fleksəbəl] *adj* : flexible

flick ['flık] *n* : golpecito *m* — ~ *vt* : dar un golpecito a — *vi* ~ **through** : hojear

flicker ['flıkər] *vi* : parpadear — ~ *n* **1** : parpadeo *m* **2 a** ~ **of hope** : un rayo de esperanza

flier ['flaıər] *n* **1** AVIATOR : aviador *m*, -dora *f* **2** *or* **flyer** LEAFLET : folleto *m*, volante *m Lat*

flight[1] ['flaıt] *n* **1** : vuelo *m* **2** TRAJECTORY : trayectoria *f* **3** ~ **of stairs** : tramo *m*

flight[2] *n* ESCAPE : huida *f*

flimsy ['flımzi] *adj* **flimsier; -est 1** LIGHT : ligero **2** SHAKY : poco sólido **3 a** ~ **excuse** : una excusa floja

flinch ['flıntʃ] *vi* ~ **from** : encogerse ante

fling ['flıŋ] *vt* **flung** ['flʌŋ]; **flinging 1** : arrojar **2** ~ **open** : abrir de un golpe — ~ *n* **1** AFFAIR : aventura *f* **2 have a** ~ **at** : intentar

flint ['flınt] *n* : pedernal *m*

flip ['flıp] *v* **flipped; flipping** *vt* **1** *or* ~ **over** : dar la vuelta a **2** ~ **a coin** : echarlo a cara o cruz — *vi* **1** *or* ~ **over** : volcarse **2** ~ **through** : hojear — ~ *n* SOMERSAULT : voltereta *f*

flippant ['flıpənt] *adj* : ligero, frívolo

flipper ['flıpər] *n* : aleta *f*

flirt ['flərt] *vi* : coquetear — ~ *n* : coqueto *m*, -ta *f* — **flirtatious** [flər'teıʃəs] *adj* : coqueto

flit ['flıt] *vi* **flitted; flitting** : revolotear

float ['flot] *n* **1** : flotador *m* **2** : carroza *f* (en un desfile) — ~ *vi* : flotar — *vt* : hacer flotar

flock ['flɑk] *n* : rebaño *m* (de ovejas), bandada *f* (de pájaros) — ~ *vi* : congregarse

flog ['flɑg] *vt* **flogged; flogging** : azotar

flood ['flʌd] *n* **1** : inundación *f* **2** : torrente *m* (de palabras, de lágrimas, etc.) — ~ *vt* : inundar — **floodlight** ['flʌd-,laıt] *n* : foco *m*

floor ['flor] *n* **1** : suelo *m*, piso *m Lat* **2** STORY : piso *m* **3 dance** ~ : pista *f* de baile **4 ground** ~ : planta *f* baja — *vt* **1** KNOCK DOWN : derribar **2** NONPLUS : desconcertar — **floorboard** ['flor-,bord] *n* : tabla *f* del suelo

flop ['flɑp] *vi* **flopped; flopping 1** FLAP : agitarse **2** COLLAPSE : dejarse caer **3** FAIL : fracasar — ~ *n* FAILURE : fracaso *m* — **floppy** ['flɑpi] *adj* **-pier; -est** : flojo, flexible — **floppy disk** *n* : diskette *m*, disquete *m*

flora ['florə] *n* : flora *f* — **floral** ['florəl]

adj : floral — **florid** ['florıd] *adj* **1** FLOWERY : florido **2** RUDDY : rojizo — **florist** ['florıst] *n* : florista *mf*

floss ['flɔs] *n* → **dental floss**

flounder[1] ['flaundər] *n, pl* **flounder** *or* **flounders** : platija *f*

flounder[2] *vi* **1** *or* ~ **about** : resbalarse, revolcarse **2** : titubear (en un discurso)

flour ['flaur] *n* : harina *f*

flourish ['flərıʃ] *vi* : florecer — *vt* BRANDISH : blandir — ~ *n* : floritura *f* — **flourishing** ['flərıʃıŋ] *adj* : floreciente

flout ['flaut] *vt* : desacatar, burlarse de

flow ['flo] *vi* : fluir, correr — ~ *n* **1** : flujo *m*, circulación *f* **2** : corriente *f* (de información, etc.)

flower ['flauər] *n* : flor *f* — ~ *vi* : florecer — **flowered** [flauərd] *adj* : floreado — **flowerpot** ['flauər,pɑt] *n* : maceta *f* — **flowery** ['flauəri] *adj* : florido

flown → **fly**

flu ['flu] *n* : gripe *f*

fluctuate ['flʌktʃu̯eıt] *vi* **-ated; -ating** : fluctuar — **fluctuation** [,flʌktʃu̯'eıʃən] *n* : fluctuación *f*

fluency ['flu̯əntsi] *n* : fluidez *f* — **fluent** ['flu̯ənt] *adj* **1** : fluido **2 be** ~ **in** : hablar con fluidez — **fluently** ['flu̯əntli] *adv* : con fluidez

fluff ['flʌf] *n* : pelusa *f* — **fluffy** ['flʌfi] *adj* **fluffier; -est** : de pelusa, velloso

fluid ['flu̯ıd] *adj* : fluido — ~ *n* : fluido *m*

flung → **fling**

flunk ['flʌŋk] *vt* : reprobar *Lat*, suspender *Spain* — *vi* : ser reprobado *Lat*, suspender *Spain*

fluorescence [,flu̯r'esənts, ,flor-] *n* : fluorescencia *f* — **fluorescent** [,flu̯r'esənt, ,flor-] *adj* : fluorescente

flurry ['fləri] *n, pl* **-ries 1** GUST : ráfaga *f* **2** *or* **snow** ~ : nevisca *f* **3** ~ **of questions** : aluvión *m* de preguntas

flush ['flʌʃ] *vi* BLUSH : ruborizarse, sonrojarse — *vt* ~ **the toilet** : tirar de la cadena, jalarle a la cadena *Lat* — ~ *n* BLUSH : rubor *m*, sonrojo *m* — ~ *adj* ~ **with** : a nivel con, a ras de — ~ *adv* : al mismo nivel, a ras

fluster ['flʌstər] *vt* : poner nervioso

flute ['flut] *n* : flauta *f*

flutter ['flʌtər] *vi* **1** FLIT : revolotear **2** WAVE : ondear **3** *or* ~ **about** : ir y venir — ~ *n* **1** : revoloteo *m* (de alas) **2** STIR : revuelo *m*

flux ['flʌks] *n* **be in a state of** ~ : cambiar continuamente

fly[1] ['flaı] *v* **flew** ['flu]; **flown** ['flon]; **flying** *vi* **1** : volar **2** TRAVEL : ir en avión **3** WAVE : ondear **4** RUSH : correr **5** ~

by : pasar volando — *vt* **1** PILOT : pilotar **2** : hacer volar (una cometa), enarbolar (una bandera) — **~** *n, pl* **flies** : bragueta *f* (de un pantalón)

fly³ *n, pl* **flies** : mosca *f* (insecto)

flyer → **flier**

flying saucer *n* : platillo *m* volador *Lat*, platillo *m* volante *Spain*

flyswatter ['flaɪ,swɑt̬ər] *n* : matamoscas *m*

foal ['foːl] *n* : potro *m*, -tra *f*

foam ['foːm] *n* : espuma *f* — *vi* : hacer espuma — **foamy** ['foːmi] *adj* **foamier; -est** : espumoso

focus ['foːkəs] *n, pl* **-ci** ['foːˌsaɪ, -ˌkaɪ] **1** : foco *m* **2 be in ~** : estar enfocado **3** **~ of attention** : centro *m* de atención — **~** *v* **-cused** *or* **-cussed; -cusing** *or* **-cussing** *vt* **1** : enfocar **2** : centrar (la atención, etc.) — *vi* **~ on** : enfocar (con los ojos), concentrarse en (con la mente)

fodder ['fɑd̬ər] *n* : forraje *m*

foe ['foː] *n* : enemigo *m*, -ga *f*

fog ['fɔg, 'fɑg] *n* : niebla *f* — **~** *v* **fogged; fogging** *vt* : empañar — *vi or* **~ up** : empañarse — **foggy** ['fɔgi, 'fɑ-] *adj* **foggier; -est** : nebuloso — **foghorn** ['fɔg,hɔrn, 'fɑg-] *n* : sirena *f* de niebla

foil¹ ['fɔɪl] *vt* : frustrar

foil² *n or* **aluminum ~** : papel *m* de aluminio

fold¹ ['foːld] *n* **1** : redil *m* (para ovejas) **2 return to the ~** : volver al redil

fold² *vt* **1** : doblar, plegar **2 ~ one's arms** : cruzar los brazos — *vi* **1** *or* **~ up** : doblarse, plegarse **2** FAIL : fracasar — **~** *n* : pliegue *m* — **folder** ['foːldər] *n* : carpeta *f*

foliage ['foːliˌɪdʒ, -lɪdʒ] *n* : follaje *m*

folk ['foːk] *n, pl* **folk** *or* **folks 1** : gente *f* **2 ~s** *npl* PARENTS : padres *mpl* — **~** *adj* **1** : popular **2 ~ dance** : danza *f* folklórica — **folklore** ['foːk,lor] *n* : folklore *m*

follow ['fɑlo] *vt* **1** : seguir **2** UNDERSTAND : entender **3 ~ up** : seguir — *vi* **1** : seguir **2** UNDERSTAND : entender **3 ~ up on** : seguir con — **follower** ['fɑloər] *n* : seguidor *m*, -dora *f* — **following** ['fɑloɪŋ] *adj* : siguiente — **~** *n* : seguidores *mpl* — **~** *prep* : después de

folly ['fɑli] *n, pl* **-lies** : locura *f*

fond ['fɑnd] *adj* **1** : cariñoso **2 be ~ of sth** : ser aficionado a algo **3 be ~ of s.o.** : tener cariño a algn

fondle ['fɑndəl] *vt* **-dled; -dling** : acariciar

fondness ['fɑndnəs] *n* **1** LOVE : cariño *m* **2** LIKING : afición *f*

food ['fuːd] *n* : comida *f*, alimento *m* — **foodstuffs** ['fuːd,stʌfs] *npl* : comestibles *mpl*

fool ['fuːl] *n* **1** : idiota *mf* **2** JESTER : bufón *m*, -fona *f* — *vi* **1** JOKE : bromear **2 ~ around** : perder el tiempo — *vt* TRICK : engañar — **foolhardy** ['fuːl,hɑrdi] *adj* : temerario — **foolish** ['fuːlɪʃ] *adj* : tonto — **foolishness** ['fuːlɪʃnəs] *n* : tontería *f* — **foolproof** ['fuːl,pruːf] *adj* : infalible

foot ['fʊt] *n, pl* **feet** ['fiːt] : pie *m* — **footage** ['fʊt̬ɪdʒ] *n* : secuencias *fpl* (cinemáticas) — **football** ['fʊt,bɔl] *n* : fútbol *m* americano — **footbridge** ['fʊt,brɪdʒ] *n* : pasarela *f*, puente *m* peatonal — **foothills** ['fʊt,hɪlz] *npl* : estribaciones *fpl* — **foothold** ['fʊt,hoːld] *n* : punto *m* de apoyo — **footing** ['fʊt̬ɪŋ] *n* **1** BALANCE : equilibrio *m* **2 on equal ~** : en igualdad — **footlights** ['fʊt,laɪts] *npl* : candilejas *fpl* — **footnote** ['fʊt,noːt] *n* : nota *f* al pie de la página — **footpath** ['fʊt,pæθ] *n* : sendero *m* — **footprint** ['fʊt,prɪnt] *n* : huella *f* — **footstep** ['fʊt,stɛp] *n* : paso *m* — **footstool** ['fʊt,stuːl] *n* : escabel *m* — **footwear** ['fʊt,wær] *n* : calzado *m*

for ['fɔr] *prep* **1** (*indicating purpose, etc.*) : para **2** (*indicating motivation, etc.*) : por **3** (*indicating duration*) : durante **4 we walked ~ 3 miles** : andamos 3 millas **5** AS FOR : con respecto a — **~** *conj* : puesto que, porque

forage ['fɔrɪdʒ] *n* : forraje *m* — *vi* **-aged; -aging 1** : forrajear **2 ~ for** : buscar

foray ['fɔr,eɪ] *n* : incursión *f*

forbid ['fərˈbɪd] *vt* **-bade** [-ˈbæd, -ˈbeɪd] *or* **-bad** [-ˈbæd]; **-bidden** [-ˈbɪdən]; **-bidding** : prohibir — **forbidding** [fərˈbɪdɪŋ] *adj* : intimidante, severo

force ['fɔrs] *n* **1** : fuerza *f* **2 by ~** : por la fuerza **3 in ~** : en vigor, en vigencia **4 armed ~s** : fuerzas *fpl* armadas — **~** *vt* **forced; forcing 1** : forzar **2** OBLIGATE : obligar — **forced** ['fɔrst] *adj* : forzado, forzoso — **forceful** ['fɔrsfəl] *adj* : fuerte, enérgico

forceps ['fɔrsəps, -ˌsɛps] *ns & pl* : fórceps *m*

forcibly [-bli] *adv* : por la fuerza

ford ['fɔrd] *n* : vado *m* — *vt* : vadear

fore ['fɔr] *n* **come to the ~** : empezar a destacarse

forearm ['fɔr,ɑrm] *n* : antebrazo *m*

foreboding [fɔrˈboːdɪŋ] *n* : premonición *f*, presentimiento *m*

forecast ['fɔr,kæst] *vt* **-cast; -casting** : predecir, pronosticar — ~ *n* : predicción *f*, pronóstico *m*

forefathers ['fɔr,faðərz] *n* : antepasados *mpl*

forefinger ['fɔr,fɪŋgər] *n* : índice *m*, dedo *m* índice

forefront ['fɔr,frʌnt] *n* **at/in the** ~ : a la vanguardia

forego [fɔr'goː] → **forgo**

foregone [fɔr'gɔn] *adj* ~ **conclusion** : resultado *m* inevitable

foreground ['fɔr,graund] *n* : primer plano *m*

forehead ['fɔrəd, 'fɔr,hed] *n* : frente *f*

foreign ['fɔrən] *adj* **1** : extranjero **2** ~ **trade** : comercio *m* exterior — **foreigner** ['fɔrənər] *n* : extranjero *m*, -ra *f*

foreman ['fɔrmən] *n, pl* **-men** [-mən, -,men] : capataz *mf*

foremost ['fɔr,moːst] *adj* : principal — *adv* **first and** ~ : ante todo

forensic [fə'rɛntsɪk] *adj* : forense

forerunner ['fɔr,rʌnər] *n* : precursor *m*, -sora *f*

foresee [fɔr'siː] *vt* **-saw; -seen; -seeing** : prever — **foreseeable** [fɔr'siːəbəl] *adj* : previsible

foreshadow [fɔr'ʃædoː] *vt* : presagiar

foresight ['fɔr,saɪt] *n* : previsión *f*

forest ['fɔrəst] *n* : bosque *m* — **forestry** ['fɔrəstri] *n* : silvicultura *f*

foretaste ['fɔr,teɪst] *n* : anticipo *m*

foretell [fɔr'tel] *vt* **-told; -telling** : predecir

forethought ['fɔr,θɔt] *n* : reflexión *f* previa

forever [fɔr'evər] *adv* **1** ETERNALLY : para siempre **2** CONTINUALLY : siempre, constantemente

forewarn [fɔr'wɔrn] *vt* : advertir, prevenir

foreword ['fɔrwərd] *n* : prólogo *m*

forfeit ['fɔrfət] *n* **1** PENALTY : pena *f* **2** : prenda *f* (en un juego) — ~ *vt* : perder

forge ['fɔrdʒ] *n* : forja *f* — ~ *v* **forged; forging** *vt* **1** : forjar (metal, etc.) **2** COUNTERFEIT : falsificar — *vi* ~ **ahead** : avanzar, seguir adelante — **forger** ['fɔrdʒər] *n* : falsificador *m*, -dora *f* — **forgery** ['fɔrdʒəri] *n, pl* **-eries** : falsificación *f*

forget [fər'get] *v* **-got** [-'gɑt]; **-gotten** [-'gɑtən] *or* **-got; -getting** *vt* **1** : olvidar, olvidarse de — *vi* **1** : olvidarse **2 I forgot** : se me olvidó — **forgetful** [fər'getfəl] *adj* : olvidadizo

forgive [fər'gɪv] *vt* **-gave; -given**
[-'gɪvən]; **-giving** : perdonar — **forgiveness** [fər'gɪvnəs] *n* : perdón *m*

forgo *or* **forego** [fɔr'goː] *vt* **-went; -gone; -going** : privarse de, renunciar a

fork ['fɔrk] *n* **1** : tenedor *m* **2** PITCHFORK : horca *f* **3** : bifurcación *f* (de un camino, etc.) — *vi* : ramificarse, bifurcarse — *vt* ~ **over** : desembolsar

forlorn [fɔr'lɔrn] *adj* : triste

form ['fɔrm] *n* **1** : forma *f* **2** DOCUMENT : formulario *m* **3** KIND : tipo *m* — ~ *vt* **1** : formar **2** ~ **a habit** : adquirir un hábito — *vi* : formarse

formal ['fɔrməl] *adj* : formal — ~ *n* **1** BALL : baile *m* (formal) **2** *or* ~ **dress** : traje *m* de etiqueta — **formality** [fɔr'mæləti] *n, pl* **-ties** : formalidad *f*

format ['fɔr,mæt] *n* : formato *m* — ~ *vt* **-matted; -matting** : formatear

formation [fɔr'meɪʃən] *n* **1** : formación *f* **2** SHAPE : forma *f*

former ['fɔrmər] *adj* **1** PREVIOUS : antiguo, anterior **2** : primero (de dos) — **formerly** ['fɔrmərli] *adv* : anteriormente, antes

formidable ['fɔrmədəbəl, fɔr'mɪdə-] *adj* : formidable

formula ['fɔrmjələ] *n, pl* **-las** *or* **-lae** [-,liː, -,laɪ] **1** : fórmula *f* **2** *or* **baby** ~ : preparado *m* para biberón

forsake [fər'seɪk] *vt* **-sook** [-'sʊk]; **-saken** [-'seɪkən]; **-saking** : abandonar

fort ['fɔrt] *n* : fuerte *m*

forth ['fɔrθ] *adv* **1 and so** ~ : etcétera **2 back and** ~ → **back 3 from this day** ~ : de hoy en adelante — **forthcoming** [fɔrθ'kʌmɪŋ, 'fɔrθ-] *adj* **1** COMING : próximo **2** OPEN : comunicativo — **forthright** ['fɔrθ,raɪt] *adj* : directo, franco

fortieth ['fɔrtiəθ] *adj* : cuadragésimo — ~ *n* **1** : cuadragésimo *m*, -ma *f* (en una serie) **2** : cuarentavo *m*, cuarentava parte *f*

fortify ['fɔrtə,faɪ] *vt* **-fied; -fying** : fortificar — **fortification** [,fɔrtəfə'keɪʃən] *n* : fortificación *f*

fortitude ['fɔrtə,tuːd, -,tjuːd] *n* : fortaleza *f*

fortnight ['fɔrt,naɪt] *n* : quince días *mpl*, quincena *f*

fortress ['fɔrtrəs] *n* : fortaleza *f*

fortunate ['fɔrtʃənət] *adj* : afortunado — **fortunately** ['fɔrtʃənətli] *adv* : afortunadamente — **fortune** ['fɔrtʃən] *n* : fortuna *f* — **fortune-teller** ['fɔrtʃən,telər] *n* : adivino *m*, -na *f*

forty ['fɔrti] *n, pl* **forties** : cuarenta *m* — ~ *adj* : cuarenta

forum ['forəm] *n*, *pl* **-rums** : foro *m*
forward ['forwərd] *adj* **1** : hacia adelante (en dirección), delantero (en posición) **2** BRASH : descarado — ~ *adv* **1** : (hacia) adelante **2 from this day** ~ : de aquí en adelante — ~ *vt* : remitir, enviar — ~ *n* : delantero *m*, -ra *f* (en deportes) — **forwards** ['forwərdz] *adv* → **forward**
fossil ['fasəl] *n* : fósil *m*
foster ['fostər] *adj* : adoptivo — ~ *vt* : promover, fomentar
fought → **fight**
foul ['faul] *adj* **1** REPULSIVE : asqueroso **2** ~ **language** : palabrotas *fpl* **3** ~ **play** : actos *mpl* criminales **4** ~ **weather** : mal tiempo *m* — ~ *n* : falta *f* (en deportes) — ~ *vi* : cometer faltas (en deportes) — ~ *vt* : ensuciar
found¹ ['faund] → **find**
found² *vt* : fundar, establecer — **foundation** [faun'deɪʃən] *n* **1** : fundación *f* **2** BASIS : fundamento *m* **3** : cimientos *mpl* (de un edificio)
founder¹ ['faundər] *n* : fundador *m*, -dora *f*
founder² *vi* SINK : hundirse
fountain ['fauntən] *n* : fuente *f*
four ['for] *n* : cuatro *m* — ~ *adj* : cuatro — **fourfold** ['for,fold, -'fold] *adj* : cuadruple — **four hundred** *adj* : cuatrocientos — ~ *n* : cuatrocientos *m*
fourteen [for'tin] *n* : catorce *m* — ~ *adj* : catorce — **fourteenth** [for'tinθ] *adj* : decimocuarto — ~ *n* **1** : decimocuarto *m*, -ta *f* (en una serie) **2** : catorceavo *m*, catorceava parte *f*
fourth ['forθ] *n* **1** : cuarto *m*, -ta *f* (en una serie) **2** : cuarto *m*, cuarta parte *f* — ~ *adj* : cuarto
fowl ['faul] *n*, *pl* **fowl** *or* **fowls** : ave *f*
fox ['faks] *n*, *pl* **foxes** : zorro *m*, -ra *f* — ~ *vt* TRICK : engañar — **foxy** ['faksi] *adj* **foxier; -est** SHREWD : astuto
foyer ['foɪər, 'foɪjer] *n* : vestíbulo *m*
fraction ['frækʃən] *n* : fracción *f*
fracture ['fræktʃər] *n* : fractura *f* — ~ *vt* **-tured; -turing** : fracturar
fragile ['frædʒəl, -,dʒaɪl] *adj* : frágil
fragment ['frægmənt] *n* : fragmento *m*
fragrant ['freɪgrənt] *adj* : fragante — **fragrance** ['freɪgrənts] *n* : fragancia *f*, aroma *m*
frail ['freɪl] *adj* : débil, delicado
frame ['freɪm] *vt* **framed; framing 1** ENCLOSE : enmarcar **2** COMPOSE, DRAFT : formular **3** INCRIMINATE : incriminar — ~ *n* **1** : armazón *mf* (de un edificio, etc.) **2** : marco *m* (de un cuadro, una puerta, etc.) **3** *or* ~**s** *npl* : montura *f*

(para anteojos) **4** ~ **of mind** : estado *m* de ánimo — **framework** ['freɪm,wərk] *n* : armazón *f*
franc ['fræŋk] *n* : franco *m*
frank ['fræŋk] *adj* : franco — **frankly** *adv* : francamente — **frankness** ['fræŋknəs] *n* : franqueza *f*
frantic ['fræntɪk] *adj* : frenético
fraternal [frə'tərnəl] *adj* : fraterno, fraternal — **fraternity** [frə'tərnəṭi] *n*, *pl* **-ties** : fraternidad *f* — **fraternize** ['fræṭər,naɪz] *vi* **-nized; -nizing** : confraternizar
fraud ['frod] *n* **1** DECEIT : fraude *m* **2** IMPOSTOR : impostor *m*, -tora *f* — **fraudulent** ['frodʒələnt] *adj* : fraudulento
fraught ['frot] *adj* ~ **with** : lleno de, cargado de
fray¹ ['freɪ] *n* **1 join the** ~ : salir a la palestra **2 return to the** ~ : volver a la carga
fray² *vt* : crispar (los nervios) — *vi* : deshilacharse
freak ['frik] *n* **1** ODDITY : fenómeno *m* **2** ENTHUSIAST : entusiasta *mf* — **freakish** ['frikɪʃ] *adj* : anormal
freckle ['frekəl] *n* : peca *f*
free ['fri] *adj* **freer; freest 1** : libre **2** *or* ~ **of charge** : gratuito, gratis **3** LOOSE : suelto — ~ *vt* **freed; freeing 1** : liberar, poner en libertad **2** RELEASE, UNFASTEN : soltar, desatar — ~ *adv* *or* **for** ~ : gratis — **freedom** ['fridəm] *n* : libertad *f* — **freelance** ['fri,lænts] *adj* : por cuenta propia — **freely** ['fri:li] *adv* **1** : libremente **2** LAVISHLY : con generosidad — **freeway** ['fri:,weɪ] *n* : autopista *f* — **free will** *n* **1** : libre albedrío *m* **2 of one's own** ~ : por su propia voluntad
freeze ['friz] *v* **froze** ['froz]; **frozen** ['frozən]; **freezing** *vi* **1** : congelarse, helarse **2** STOP : quedarse inmóvil — *vt* : helar (agua, etc.), congelar (alimentos, precios, etc.) — **freeze-dry** ['fri:z-'draɪ] *vt* **-dried; -drying** : liofilizar — **freezer** ['frizər] *n* : congelador *m* — **freezing** ['fri:zɪŋ] *adj* **1** CHILLY : helado **2 it's freezing!** : ¡hace un frío espantoso!
freight ['freɪt] *n* **1** SHIPPING : porte *m*, flete *m* *Lat* **2** CARGO : carga *f*
French ['frentʃ] *adj* : francés — ~ *n* **1** : francés *m* (idioma) **2 the** ~ *npl* : los franceses — **Frenchman** ['frentʃmən] *n* : francés *m* — **Frenchwoman** ['frentʃ,wumən] *n* : francesa *f* — **french fries** ['frentʃ,fraɪz] *npl* : papas *fpl* fritas
frenetic [frɪ'neṭɪk] *adj* : frenético

frenzy ['frenzi] *n, pl* **-zies** : frenesí *m* —
frenzied ['frenzid] *adj* : frenético
frequent [fri'kwent, 'fri:kwənt] *vt* : frecuentar — ~ ['fri:kwənt] *adj* : frecuente — **frequency** ['fri:kwəntsi] *n, pl*
-cies : frecuencia *f* — **frequently** *adv*
: a menudo, frecuentemente
fresco ['fres,ko:] *n, pl* **-coes** : fresco *m*
fresh ['frɛʃ] *adj* **1** : fresco **2** IMPUDENT
: descarado **3** CLEAN : limpio **4** NEW
: nuevo **5** ~ **water** : agua *m* dulce —
freshen ['frɛʃən] *vt* : refrescar — *vi* ~
up : arreglarse — **freshly** ['frɛʃli] *adv*
: recién — **freshman** ['frɛʃmən] *n, pl*
-men [-mən, -,mɛn] : estudiante *mf* de
primer año — **freshness** ['frɛʃnəs] *n*
: frescura *f*
fret ['frɛt] *vi* **fretted; fretting** : preocuparse — **fretful** ['frɛtfəl] *adj* : nervioso,
irritable
friar ['fraɪər] *n* : fraile *m*
friction ['frɪkʃən] *n* : fricción *f*
Friday ['fraɪ,deɪ, -di] *n* : viernes *m*
friend ['frɛnd] *n* : amigo *m*, -ga *f* —
friendliness ['frɛndlinəs] *n* : simpatía *f*
— **friendly** ['frɛndli] *adj* **-lier; -est**
: simpático, amable — **friendship**
['frɛnd,ʃɪp] *n* : amistad *f*
frigate ['frɪgət] *n* : fragata *f*
fright ['fraɪt] *n* : miedo *m*, susto *m* —
frighten ['fraɪtən] *vt* : asustar, espantar
— **frightened** ['fraɪtənd] *adj* **1** : asustado, temeroso **2 be** ~ **of** : tener miedo
de — **frightening** ['fraɪtənɪŋ] *adj* : espantoso — **frightful** ['fraɪtfəl] *adj* : espantoso, terrible
frigid ['frɪdʒɪd] *adj* : frío, glacial
frill ['frɪl] *n* **1** RUFFLE : volante *m* **2** LUX-
URY : lujo *m*
fringe ['frɪndʒ] *n* **1** : fleco *m* **2** EDGE
: periferia *f*, margen *m* **3** ~ **benefits**
: incentivos *mpl*, extras *mpl*
frisk ['frɪsk] *vt* SEARCH : cachear, registrar — **frisky** ['frɪski] *adj* **friskier; -est**
: retozón, juguetón
fritter ['frɪtər] *n* : buñuelo *m* — ~ *vt or*
~ **away** : malgastar (dinero), desperdiciar (tiempo)
frivolous ['frɪvələs] *adj* : frívolo — **frivolity** [frɪ'vɑləti] *n, pl* **-ties** : frivolidad
f
frizzy ['frɪzi] *adj* **frizzier; -est** : rizado,
crespo
fro ['fro:] *adv* **to and** ~ → **to**
frock ['frɑk] *n* : vestido *m*
frog ['frɔg, 'frɑg] *n* **1** : rana *f* **2 have a** ~
in one's throat : tener carraspera
frolic ['frɑlɪk] *vi* **-icked; -icking** : retozar
from ['frʌm, 'frɑm] *prep* **1** : de **2** (*indicating a starting point*) : desde **3** (*in-*

dicating a cause) : de, por **4** ~ **now
on** : a partir de ahora
front ['frʌnt] *n* **1** : parte *f* delantera **2**
: delantera *f* (de un vestido, etc.),
fachada *f* (de un edificio), frente *m*
(militar) **3 cold** ~ : frente *m* frío **4 in**
~ **of** : delante de, adelante de *Lat* —
~ *vi or* ~ **on** : dar a, estar orientado
a — ~ *adj* **1** : delantero, de adelante **2
the** ~ **row** : la primera fila
frontier [,frʌn'tɪr] *n* : frontera *f*
frost ['frɔst] *n* **1** : helada *f* **2** : escarcha *f*
(en una superficie) — ~ *vt* ICE : bañar
(pasteles) — **frostbite** ['frɔst,baɪt] *n*
: congelación *f* — **frosting** ['frɔstɪŋ] *n*
ICING : baño *m* — **frosty** ['frɔsti] *adj*
frostier; -est 1 : cubierto de escarcha
2 CHILLY : helado, frío
froth ['frɔθ] *n, pl* **froths** ['frɔθs, 'frɔðz]
: espuma *f* — **frothy** ['frɔθi] *adj* **froth-
ier; -est** : espumoso
frown ['fraʊn] *vi* **1** : fruncir el ceño,
fruncir el entrecejo **2** ~ **at** : mirar con
ceño **3** ~ **upon** : desaprobar — ~ *n*
: ceño *m* (fruncido)
froze, frozen → **freeze**
frugal ['fru:gəl] *adj* : frugal
fruit ['fru:t] *n* **1** : fruta *f* **2** PRODUCT, RE-
SULT : fruto *m* — **fruitcake** ['fru:t,keɪk]
n : pastel *m* de frutas — **fruitful**
['fru:tfəl] *adj* : fructífero — **fruition**
[fru'ɪʃən] *n* **come to** ~ : realizarse —
fruitless ['fru:tləs] *adj* : infructuoso —
fruity ['fru:ti] *adj* **fruitier; -est** : (con
sabor) a fruta
frustrate ['frʌs,treɪt] *vt* **-trated; -trating**
: frustrar — **frustrating** ['frʌs,treɪtɪŋ]
adj : frustrante — **frustration** [,frʌs-
'treɪʃən] *n* : frustración *f*
fry ['fraɪ] *vt* **fried; frying** : freír — ~ *n,
pl* **fries 1 small** ~ : gente *f* de poca
monta **2 fries** *npl* → **french fries** —
frying pan *n* : sartén *mf*
fudge ['fʌdʒ] *n* : dulce *m* blando de
chocolate y leche
fuel ['fju:əl] *n* : combustible *m* — ~ *vt*
-eled *or* **-elled; -eling** *or* **-elling 1**
: alimentar (un horno), abastecer de
combustible (un avión) **2** STIMULATE
: estimular
fugitive ['fju:dʒətɪv] *n* : fugitivo *m*, -va *f*
fulfill *or* **fulfil** [fʊl'fɪl] *vt* **-filled; -filling 1**
: cumplir con (una obligación), desar-
rollar (potencial) **2** FILL, MEET
: cumplir — **fulfillment** [fʊl'fɪlmənt] *n*
1 ACCOMPLISHMENT : cumplimiento *m*
2 SATISFACTION : satisfacción *f*
full ['fʊl, 'fʌl] *adj* **1** FILLED : lleno **2** COM-
PLETE : completo, detallado **3** : redon-
do (dícese de la cara), amplio (dícese

de ropa) **4 at ~ speed** : a toda velocidad **5 in ~ bloom** : en plena flor — **~** adv **1** DIRECTLY : de lleno **2 know ~ well** : saber muy bien — **~** n **1 pay in ~** : pagar en su totalidad **2 to the ~** : al máximo — **full-fledged** ['ful'fledʒd] adj : hecho y derecho — **fully** ['fuli] adv **1** COMPLETELY : completamente **2** AT LEAST : al menos, por lo menos

fumble ['fʌmbəl] vi **-bled; -bling 1** RUMMAGE : hurgar **2 ~ with** : manejar con torpeza

fume ['fju:m] vi **fumed; fuming 1** SMOKE : echar humo, humear **2** RAGE : estar furioso — **fumes** npl : gases mpl

fumigate ['fju:məgeɪt] vt **-gated; -gating** : fumigar

fun ['fʌn] n **1** AMUSEMENT : diversión f **2 have ~** : divertirse **3 make ~ of** : reírse de, burlarse de — **~** adj : divertido

function ['fʌŋkʃən] n **1** : función f **2** GATHERING : recepción f, reunión f social — **~** vi : funcionar — **functional** ['fʌŋkʃənəl] adj : funcional

fund ['fʌnd] n **1** : fondo m **2 ~s** npl RESOURCES : fondos mpl — **~** vt : financiar

fundamental [ˌfʌndəˈmentəl] adj : fundamental — **fundamentals** npl : fundamentos mpl

funeral ['fju:nərəl] adj : funeral, fúnebre — **~** n : funeral m, funerales mpl — **funeral home** or **funeral parlor** n : funeraria f

fungus ['fʌŋgəs] n, pl **fungi** ['fʌnˌdʒaɪ, 'fʌŋˌgaɪ] : hongo m

funnel ['fʌnəl] n **1** : embudo m **2** SMOKESTACK : chimenea f

funny ['fʌni] adj **funnier; -est 1** : divertido, gracioso **2** STRANGE : extraño, raro — **funnies** ['fʌniz] npl : tiras fpl cómicas

fur ['fər] n **1** : pelaje m, pelo m (de un animal) **2** or **~ coat** : (prenda f de) piel f — **~** adj : de piel

furious ['fjuriəs] adj : furioso

furnace ['fərnəs] n : horno m

furnish ['fərnɪʃ] vt **1** SUPPLY : proveer **2** : amueblar (una casa, etc.) — **furnishings** ['fərnɪʃɪŋz] npl : muebles mpl, mobiliario m — **furniture** ['fərnɪtʃər] n : muebles mpl, mobiliario m

furrow ['fəroː] n : surco m

furry ['fəri] adj **furrier; -est** : peludo (dícese de un animal), de peluche (dícese de un juguete, etc.)

further ['fərðər] adv **1** FARTHER : más lejos **2** MOREOVER : además **3** MORE : más — **~** vt : promover, fomentar — **~** adj **1** FARTHER : más lejano **2** ADDITIONAL : adicional, más **3 until ~ notice** : hasta nuevo aviso — **furthermore** ['fərðərˌmor] adv : además — **furthest** ['fərðəst] → **farthest**

furtive ['fərtɪv] adj : furtivo

fury ['fjuri] n, pl **-ries** : furia f

fuse[1] or **fuze** ['fju:z] n : mecha f (de una bomba, etc.)

fuse[2] v **fused; fusing** vt **1** MELT : fundir **2** UNITE : fusionar — vi : fundirse, fusionarse — **~** n **1** : fusible m **2 blow a ~** : fundir un fusible — **fusion** ['fju:ʒən] n : fusión f

fuss ['fʌs] n **1** : jaleo m, alboroto m **2 make a ~** : armar un escándalo — **~** vi **1** WORRY : preocuparse **2** COMPLAIN : quejarse — **fussy** ['fʌsi] adj **fussier; -est 1** IRRITABLE : irritable **2** ELABORATE : recargado **3** FINICKY : quisquilloso

futile ['fju:təl, 'fju:taɪl] adj : inútil, vano — **futility** [fju:'tɪləti] n, pl **-ties** : inutilidad f

future ['fju:tʃər] adj : futuro — **~** n : futuro m

fuze → **fuse**[1]

fuzz ['fʌz] n : pelusa f — **fuzzy** ['fʌzi] adj **fuzzier; -est 1** FURRY : con pelusa, peludo **2** BLURRY : borroso **3** VAGUE : confuso

G

g ['dʒi:] n, pl **g's** or **gs** ['dʒi:z] : g f, séptima letra del alfabeto inglés

gab ['gæb] vi **gabbed; gabbing** : charlar, cotorrear fam — **~** n CHATTER : charla f

gable ['geɪbəl] n : aguilón m

gadget ['gædʒət] n : artilugio m

gag ['gæg] v **gagged; gagging** vt : amordazar — vi CHOKE : atragantarse — **~** n **1** : mordaza f **2** JOKE : chiste m

gage → **gauge**

gaiety ['geɪəti] n, pl **-eties** : alegría f — **gaily** ['geɪli] adv : alegremente

gain ['geɪn] n **1** PROFIT : ganancia f **2** INCREASE : aumento m — **~** vt **1** OBTAIN : ganar, adquirir **2 ~ weight** : aumentar de peso — *vi* **1** PROFIT : beneficiarse **2** : adelantar(se) (dícese de un reloj) — **gainful** ['geɪnfəl] *adj* : lucrativo

gait ['geɪt] *n* : modo *m* de andar

gala ['geɪlə, 'gæ-, 'gɑ-] *n* : fiesta *f*

galaxy ['gæləksi] *n, pl* **-axies** : galaxia *f*

gale ['geɪl] *n* **1** : vendaval *f* **2** ~**s of laughter** : carcajadas *fpl*

gall ['gɔl] *n* **have the** ~ **to** : tener el descaro de

gallant ['gælənt] *adj* **1** BRAVE : valiente **2** CHIVALROUS : galante

gallbladder ['gɔl,blædər] *n* : vesícula *f* biliar

gallery ['gæləri] *n, pl* **-leries** : galería *f*

gallon ['gælən] *n* : galón *m*

gallop ['gæləp] *vi* : galopar — ~ *n* : galope *m*

gallows ['gæˌloːz] *n, pl* **-lows** *or* **-lowses** [-ˌloːzəz] : horca *f*

gallstone ['gɔlˌstoʊn] *n* : cálculo *m* biliar

galore [gə'lor] *adj* : en abundancia

galoshes [gə'lɑʃ] *n* : galochas *fpl*, chanclos *mpl*

galvanize ['gælvənˌaɪz] *vt* **-nized; -nizing** : galvanizar

gamble ['gæmbəl] *v* **-bled; -bling** *vi* : jugar — *vt* : jugarse — ~ *n* **1** BET : apuesta *f* **2** RISK : riesga *f* — **gambler** ['gæmblər] *n* : jugador *m*, -dora *f*

game ['geɪm] *n* **1** : juego *m* **2** MATCH : partido *m* **3** *or* ~ **animals** : caza *f* — ~ *adj* READY : listo, dispuesto

gamut ['gæmət] *n* : gama *f*

gang ['gæŋ] *n* : banda *f*, pandilla *f* — ~ *vi* ~ **up on** : unirse contra

gangplank ['gæŋˌplæŋk] *n* : pasarela *f*

gangrene ['gæŋˌgriːn, 'gæn-; 'gæŋ'-, gæn'-] *n* : gangrena *f*

gangster ['gæŋstər] *n* : gángster *mf*

gangway ['gæŋˌweɪ] *n* → **gangplank**

gap ['gæp] *n* **1** OPENING : espacio *m* **2** INTERVAL : intervalo *m* **3** DISPARITY : brecha *f*, distancia *f* **4** DEFICIENCY : laguna *f*

gape ['geɪp] *vi* **gaped; gaping 1** OPEN : estar abierto **2** STARE : mirar boquiabierto

garage [gə'rɑʒ, -'rɑdʒ] *n* : garaje *m* — ~ *vt* **-raged; -raging** : dejar en un garaje

garb ['gɑrb] *n* : vestido *m*

garbage ['gɑrbɪdʒ] *n* : basura *f* — **garbage can** *n* : cubo *m* de la basura

garble ['gɑrbəl] *v* **-bled; -bling** : tergiversar — **garbled** ['gɑrbəld] *adj* : confuso, incomprensible

garden ['gɑrdən] *n* : jardín *m* — ~ *vi* : trabajar en el jardín — **gardener** ['gɑrdənər] *n* : jardinero *m*, -ra *f* — **gardening** ['gɑrdənɪŋ] *n* : jardinería *f*

gargle ['gɑrgəl] *vi* **-gled; -gling** : hacer gárgaras

garish ['gærɪʃ] *adj* : chillón

garland ['gɑrlənd] *n* : guirnalda *f*

garlic ['gɑrlɪk] *n* : ajo *m*

garment ['gɑrmənt] *n* : prenda *f*

garnish ['gɑrnɪʃ] *vt* : guarnecer — ~ *n* : adorno *m*, guarnición *f*

garret ['gærət] *n* : buhardilla *f*

garrison ['gærəsən] *n* : guarnición *f*

garrulous ['gærələs] *adj* : charlatán, parlanchín

garter ['gɑrtər] *n* : liga *f*

gas ['gæs] *n, pl* **gases** ['gæsəz] **1** : gas *m* **2** GASOLINE : gasolina *f* — ~ *v* **gassed; gassing** *vt* : asfixiar con gas — *vi* ~ **up** : llenar el tanque con gasolina

gash ['gæʃ] *n* : tajo *m* — ~ *vt* : hacer un tajo en, cortar

gasket ['gæskət] *n* : junta *f*

gasoline ['gæsəˌliːn, ˌgæsə'-] *n* : gasolina *f*

gasp ['gæsp] *vi* **1** : dar un grito ahogado **2** PANT : jadear — ~ *n* : grito *m* ahogado

gas station *n* : gasolinera *f*

gastric ['gæstrɪk] *adj* : gástrico

gastronomy [gæs'trɑnəmi] *n* : gastronomía *f*

gate ['geɪt] *n* **1** DOOR : puerta *f* **2** BARRIER : barrera *f* — **gateway** ['geɪtˌweɪ] *n* : puerta *f*

gather ['gæðər] *vt* **1** ASSEMBLE : reunir **2** COLLECT : recoger **3** CONCLUDE : deducir **4** : fruncir (una tela) **5** ~ **speed** : acelerar — *vi* : reunirse (dícese de personas), acumularse (dícese de cosas) — **gathering** ['gæðərɪŋ] *n* : reunión *f*

gaudy ['gɔdi] *adj* **gaudier; -est** : chillón, llamativo

gauge ['geɪdʒ] *n* **1** INDICATOR : indicador *m* **2** CALIBER : calibre *m* — ~ *vt* **gauged; gauging 1** MEASURE : medir **2** ESTIMATE : calcular, evaluar

gaunt ['gɔnt] *adj* : demacrado, descarnado

gauze ['gɔz] *n* : gasa *f*

gave → **give**

gawky ['gɔki] *adj* **gawkier; -est** : desgarbado

gay ['geɪ] *adj* **1** : alegre **2** HOMOSEXUAL : gay, homosexual

gaze ['geɪz] *vi* **gazed; gazing** : mirar (fijamente) — ~ *n* : mirada *f*

gazelle [gə'zel] *n* : gacela *f*

gazette [gə'zet] *n* : gaceta *f*

gear ['gɪr] *n* **1** EQUIPMENT : equipo *m* **2** POSSESSIONS : efectos *mpl* personales

3 : marcha *f* (de un vehículo) **4** *or* ～
wheel : rueda *f* dentada — ～ *vt* : orientar, adaptar — *vi* ～ **up** : prepararse
— **gearshift** ['gɪr,ʃɪft] *n* : palanca *f* de
cambio, palanca *f* de velocidades *Lat*
geese → **goose**
gelatin ['dʒelətən] *n* : gelatina *f*
gem ['dʒɛm] *n* : gema *f*, piedra *f* preciosa
— **gemstone** ['dʒɛm,stoɪn] *n* : piedra *f*
preciosa
gender ['dʒɛndər] *n* **1** SEX ; sexo *m* **2**
: género *m* (en la gramática)
gene ['dʒiːn] *n* : gen *m*, gene *m*
genealogy [,dʒiːni'alədʒi, ,dʒe-, -'æ-] *n*, *pl*
-**gies** : genealogía *f*
general ['dʒenrəl, 'dʒenə-] *adj* : general
— ～ *n* **1** : general *mf* (militar) **2** **in** ～
: en general, por lo general — **generalize** ['dʒenrə,laɪz, 'dʒenərə-] *v* -**ized**;
-**izing** : generalizar — **generally**
['dʒenrəli, 'dʒenərə-] *adv* : generalmente, en general — **general practitioner** *n* : médico *m*, -ca *f* de cabecera
generate ['dʒenə,reɪt] *vt* -**ated**; -**ating**
: generar — **generation** [,dʒenə'reɪʃən]
n : generación *f* — **generator** ['dʒenə-
,reɪtər] *n* : generador *m*
generous ['dʒenərəs] *adj* **1** : generoso **2**
AMPLE : abundante — **generosity**
[,dʒenə'rasəti] *n*, *pl* -**ties** : generosidad *f*
genetic [dʒə'nɛtɪk] *adj* : genético — **genetics** [dʒə'nɛtɪks] *n* : genética *f*
genial ['dʒiːniəl] *adj* : afable, simpático
genital ['dʒenətəl] *adj* : genital — **genitals** ['dʒenət̬əlz] *npl* : genitales *mpl*
genius ['dʒiːnjəs] *n* : genio *m*
genocide ['dʒenə,saɪd] *n* : genocidio *m*
genteel [dʒen'tiːl] *adj* : refinado
gentle ['dʒentəl] *adj* -**tler**; -**tlest 1** MILD
: suave, dulce **2** LIGHT : ligero **3 a** ～
hint : una indirecta discreta — **gentleman** ['dʒentəlmən] *n*, *pl* -**men** [-mən,
-,mɛn] **1** MAN : caballero *m*, señor *m* **2**
a perfect ～ : un perfecto caballero —
gentleness ['dʒentəlnəs] *n* : delicadeza *f*, ternura *f*
genuine ['dʒenjuwən] *adj* **1** AUTHENTIC
: verdadero, auténtico **2** SINCERE : sincero
geography [dʒi'agrəfi] *n*, *pl* -**phies** : geografía *f* — **geographic** [,dʒiːə'græfɪk]
or **geographical** [-fɪkəl] *adj* : geográ-
fico
geology [dʒi'alədʒi] *n* : geología *f* — **geologic** [,dʒiːə'lodʒɪk] *or* **geological**
[-dʒkəl] *adj* : geológico
geometry [dʒi'amətri] *n*, *pl* -**tries**
: geometría *f* — **geometric** [,dʒiːə-
'metrɪk] *or* **geometrical** [-trɪkəl] *adj*
: geométrico

geranium [dʒə'reɪniəm] *n* : geranio *m*
geriatric [,dʒeri'ætrɪk] *adj* : geriátrico —
geriatrics [,dʒeri'ætrɪks] *n* : geriatría
f
germ ['dʒərm] *n* **1** : germen *m* **2** MICROBE
: microbio *m*
German ['dʒərmən] *adj* : alemán — ～ *n*
: alemán *m* (idioma)
germinate ['dʒərmə,neɪt] *v* -**nated**;
-**nating** *vi* : germinar — *vt* : hacer germinar
gestation [dʒe'steɪʃən] *n* : gestación *f*
gesture ['dʒestʃər] *n* : gesto *m* — ～ *vi*
-**tured**; -**turing 1** : hacer gestos **2** ～
to : hacer señas a
get ['gɛt] *v* **got** ['gɑt]; **got** *or* **gotten**
['gɑtən]; **getting** *vt* **1** OBTAIN : conseguir, obtener **2** RECEIVE : recibir **3**
EARN : ganar **4** FETCH : traer **5** CATCH
: coger, agarrar *Lat* **6** UNDERSTAND
: entender **7** PREPARE : preparar **8** ～
one's hair cut : cortarse el pelo **9** ～
s.o. to do sth : lograr que uno haga
algo **10 have got** : tener **11 have got
to** : tener que — *vi* **1** BECOME : ponerse, hacerse **2** GO, MOVE : ir **3**
PROGRESS : avanzar **4** ～ **ahead** : progresar **5** ～ **at** MEAN : querer decir **6**
～ **away** : escaparse **7** ～ **away with**
: salir impune de **8** ～ **back at**
: desquitarse con **9** ～ **by** : arreglárselas **10** ～ **home** : llegar a casa **11** ～
out : salir **12** ～ **over** : reponerse de,
consolarse de **13** ～ **together** : reunirse **14** ～ **up** : levantarse — **get-
away** ['gɛt̬ə,weɪ] *n* : fuga *f*, huida *f* —
get-together *n* : reunión *f*
geyser ['gaɪzər] *n* : géiser *m*
ghastly ['gæstli] *adj* -**lier**; -**est** : horrible, espantoso
ghetto ['gɛt̬oɪ] *n*, *pl* -**tos** *or* -**toes**
: gueto *m*
ghost ['goɪst] *n* : fantasma *f*, espectro *m*
— **ghostly** ['goɪstli] *adv* : fantasmal
giant ['dʒaɪənt] *n* : gigante *m*, -ta *f* — ～
adj : gigantesco
gibberish ['dʒɪbərɪʃ] *n* : galimatías *m*,
jerigonza *f*
gibe ['dʒaɪb] *vi* **gibed**; **gibing** ～ **at**
: mofarse de — ～ *n* : pulla *f*, mofa *f*
giblets ['dʒɪbləts] *npl* : menudillos *mpl*
giddy ['gɪdi] *adj* -**dier**; -**est** : mareado,
vertiginoso — **giddiness** ['gɪdinəs] *n*
: vértigo *m*
gift ['gɪft] *n* **1** PRESENT : regalo *m* **2** TAL-
ENT : don *m* — **gifted** ['gɪftəd] *adj* : talentoso, de talento
gigantic [dʒaɪ'gæntɪk] *adj* : gigantesco
giggle ['gɪgəl] *vi* -**gled**; -**gling** : reírse
tontamente — ～ *n* : risa *f* tonta

gild ['gɪld] *vt* **gilded** ['gɪldəd] *or* **gilt** ['gɪlt]; **gilding** : dorar

gill ['gɪl] *n* : agalla *f*, branquia *f*

gilt ['gɪlt] *adj* : dorado

gimmick ['gɪmɪk] *n* : truco *m*, ardid *m*

gin ['dʒɪn] *n* : ginebra *f*

ginger ['dʒɪndʒər] *n* : jengibre *m* — **ginger ale** *n* : refresco *m* de jengibre — **gingerbread** ['dʒɪndʒər,brɛd] *n* : pan *m* de jengibre — **gingerly** ['dʒɪndʒərli] *adv* : con cuidado, cautelosamente

giraffe ['dʒəˈræf] *n* : jirafa *f*

girder ['gərdər] *n* : viga *f*

girdle ['gərdəl] *n* CORSET : faja *f*

girl ['gərl] *n* 1 : niña *f*, muchacha *f*, chica *f* — **girlfriend** ['gərl,frɛnd] *n* : novia *f*, amiga *f*

girth ['gərθ] *n* : circunferencia *f*

gist ['dʒɪst] *n* **get the ~ of** : comprender lo esencial de

give ['gɪv] *v* **gave** ['geɪv]; **given** ['gɪvən]; **giving** *vt* 1 : dar 2 INDICATE : señalar 3 PRESENT : presentar 4 **~ away** : regalar 5 **~ back** : devolver 6 **~ out** : repartir 7 **~ up smoking** : dejar de fumar — *vi* 1 YIELD : ceder 2 COLLAPSE : romperse 3 **~ out** : agotarse 4 **~ up** : rendirse — **~** *n* : elasticidad *f* — **given** ['gɪvən] *adj* 1 SPECIFIED : determinado 2 INCLINED : dado, inclinado — **given name** *n* : nombre *m* de pila

glacier ['gleɪʃər] *n* : glaciar *m*

glad ['glæd] *adj* **gladder**; **gladdest** 1 : alegre, contento 2 **be ~** : alegrarse 3 **~ to meet you!** : ¡mucho gusto! : — **gladden** ['glædən] *vt* : alegrar — **gladly** ['glædli] *adv* : con mucho gusto — **gladness** ['glædnəs] *n* : alegría *f*, gozo *m*

glade ['gleɪd] *n* : claro *m*

glamor *or* **glamour** ['glæmər] *n* : atractivo *m*, encanto *m* — **glamorous** ['glæmərəs] *adj* : atractivo

glance ['glænts] *vi* **glanced**; **glancing** 1 **~ at** : mirar, dar un vistazo a 2 **~ off** : rebotar en — **~** *n* : mirada *f*, vistazo *m*

gland ['glænd] *n* : glándula *f*

glare ['glær] *vi* **glared**; **glaring** 1 : brillar, relumbrar 2 **~ at** : lanzar una mirada feroz a — **~** *n* 1 : luz *f* deslumbrante 2 STARE : mirada *f* feroz — **glaring** ['glærɪŋ] *adj* 1 BRIGHT : deslumbrante 2 FLAGRANT : flagrante

glass ['glæs] *n* 1 : vidrio *m*, cristal *m* 2 **a ~ of milk** : un vaso de leche 3 **~es** *npl* SPECTACLES : anteojos *mpl*, lentes *fpl* — **~** *adj* : de vidrio — **glassware** ['glæs,wær] *n* : cristalería *f* — **glassy**

['glæsi] *adj* **glassier**; **-est** 1 : vítreo 2 **~ eyes** : ojos *mpl* vidriosos

glaze ['gleɪz] *vt* **glazed**; **glazing** 1 : poner vidrios a (una ventana, etc.) 2 : vidriar (cerámica) 3 ICE : glasear — **~** *n* 1 : vidriado *m*, barniz *m* (de cerámica) 2 ICING : glaseado *m*

gleam ['gliːm] *n* 1 : destello *m* 2 **a ~ of hope** : un rayo de esperanza — **~** *vi* : destellar, relucir

glee ['gliː] *n* : alegría *f* — **gleeful** ['gliːfəl] *adj* : lleno de alegría

glib ['glɪb] *adj* **glibber**; **glibbest** 1 : de mucha labia 2 **~ reply** : una respuesta simplista — **glibly** ['glɪbli] *adv* : con mucha labia

glide ['glaɪd] *vi* **glided**; **gliding** : deslizarse (en una superficie), planear (en el aire) — **glider** ['glaɪdər] *n* : planeador *m*

glimmer ['glɪmər] *vi* : brillar con luz trémula — **~** *n* : luz *f* trémula, luz *f* tenue

glimpse ['glɪmps] *vt* **glimpsed**; **glimpsing** : vislumbrar — **~** *n* : vislumbre *f*

glint ['glɪnt] *vi* : destellar — **~** *n* : destello *m*

glisten ['glɪsən] *vi* : brillar

glitter ['glɪtər] *vi* : relucir, brillar

gloat ['gloːt] *vi* **~ over** : regodearse con

globe ['gloːb] *n* : globo *m* — **global** ['gloːbəl] *adj* : global, mundial

gloom ['gluːm] *n* 1 DARKNESS : oscuridad *f* 2 SADNESS : tristeza *f* — **gloomy** ['gluːmi] *adj* **gloomier**; **-est** 1 DARK : sombrío, tenebroso 2 DISMAL : deprimente, lúgubre 3 PESSIMISTIC : pesimista

glory ['gloːri] *n*, *pl* **-ries** : gloria *f* — **glorify** ['gloːrəˌfaɪ] *vt* **-fied**; **-fying** : glorificar — **glorious** ['gloːriəs] *adj* : glorioso, espléndido

gloss ['gloːs, 'glɑs] *n* : lustre *m*, brillo *m* — **~** *vt* **~ over** : minimizar (la importancia de algo)

glossary ['gloːsəri, 'glɑ-] *n*, *pl* **-ries** : glosario *m*

glossy ['gloːsi, 'glɑ-] *adj* **glossier**; **-est** : lustroso, brillante

glove ['glʌv] *n* : guante *m*

glow ['gloː] *vi* 1 : brillar, resplandecer 2 **~ with health** : rebosar de salud — **~** *n* : resplandor *m*, brillo *m*

glue ['gluː] *n* : pegamento *m*, cola *f* — **~** *vt* **glued**; **gluing** *or* **glueing** : pegar

glum ['glʌm] *adj* **glummer**; **glummest** : sombrío, triste

glut ['glʌt] *n* : superabundancia *f*, exceso *m*

glutton ['glʌtən] *n* : glotón *m*, -tona *f* — **gluttonous** ['glʌtənəs] *adj* : glotón — **gluttony** ['glʌtəni] *n, pl* **-tonies** : glotonería *f*

gnarled ['nɑrld] *adj* : nudoso

gnash ['næʃ] *vt* ~ **one's teeth** : hacer rechinar los dientes

gnat ['næt] *n* : jején *m*

gnaw ['nɔ] *vt* : roer

go ['goː] *v* **went** ['wɛnt]; **gone** ['gɔn, 'gɑn]; **going**; **goes** ['goːz] *vi* **1** : ir **2** LEAVE : irse, salir **3** EXTEND : ir, extenderse **4** SELL : venderse **5** FUNCTION : funcionar, marchar **6** DISAPPEAR : desaparecer **7** ~ **back on one's word** : faltar a su palabra **8** ~ **crazy** : volverse loco **9** ~ **for** LIKE : gustar **10** ~ **off** EXPLODE : estallar **11** ~ **with** MATCH : armonizar con **12** ~ **without** : pasar sin — *v aux* **be going to** : ir a — ~ *n, pl* **goes 1 be on the** ~ : no parar **2 have a** ~ **at** : intentar

goad ['goːd] *vt* : aguijonear (un animal), incitar (a una persona)

goal ['goːl] *n* **1** AIM : meta *m*, objetivo *m* **2** : gol *m* (en deportes) — **goalkeeper** ['goːlˌkiːpər] *or* **goalie** ['goːli] *n* : portero *m*, -ra *f*; arquero *m*, -ra *f*

goat ['goːt] *n* : cabra *f*

goatee [goˈtiː] *n* : barbita *f* de chivo

gobble ['gɑbəl] *vt* **-bled; -bling** *or* ~ **up** : engullir

goblet ['gɑblət] *n* : copa *f*

goblin ['gɑblən] *n* : duende *m*

god ['gɑd, 'gɔd] *n* **1** : dios *m* **2 God** : Dios *m* — **goddess** ['gɑdəs, 'gɔ-] *n* : diosa *f* — **godchild** ['gɑdˌtʃaɪld, 'gɔd-] *n, pl* **-children** : ahijado *m*, -da *f* — **godfather** ['gɑdˌfɑðər, 'gɔd-] *n* : padrino *m* — **godmother** ['gɑdˌmʌðər, 'gɔd-] *n* : madrina *f* — **godparents** ['gɑdˌpærənt, 'gɔd-] *npl* : padrinos *mpl* — **godsend** ['gɑdˌsend, 'gɔd-] *n* : bendición *f* (del cielo)

goes → **go**

goggles ['gɑgəlz] *npl* : gafas *fpl* (protectoras), anteojos *mpl*

goings-on [ˌgoːɪŋzˈɑn, -ˈɔn] *npl* : sucesos *mpl*

gold ['goːld] *n* : oro *m* — **golden** ['goːldən] *adj* **1** : (hecho) de oro **2** : dorado, de color oro — **goldfish** ['goːldˌfiʃ] *n* : pez *m* de colores — **goldsmith** ['goːld ˌsmɪθ] *n* : orfebre *mf*

golf ['gɑlf, 'goːlf] *n* : golf *m* — ~ *vi* : jugar (al) golf — **golf ball** *n* : pelota *f* de golf — **golf course** *n* : campo *m* de golf — **golfer** ['gɑlfər, 'goːl-] *n* : golfista *mf*

gone ['gɔn] *adj* **1** : ido, pasado **2** DEAD : muerto **3** LOST : desaparecido

good ['gʊd] *adj* **better** ['bɛtər]; **best** ['bɛst] **1** : bueno **2** KIND : amable **3** ~ **afternoon (evening)** : buenas tardes **4 be** ~ **at** : tener facilidad para **5 feel** ~ : sentirse bien **6** ~ **for a cold** : beneficioso para los resfriados **7 have a** ~ **time** : divertirse **8** ~ **morning** : buenos días **9** ~ **night** : buenas noches — ~ *n* **1** : bien *m* **2** GOODNESS : bondad *f* **3** ~**s** *npl* PROPERTY : bienes *mpl* **4** ~**s** *npl* WARES : mercancías *fpl*, mercaderías *fpl* **5 for** ~ : para siempre — ~ *adv* : bien — **good-bye** *or* **good-by** ['gʊdˈbaɪ] *n* : adiós *m* — **Good Friday** *n* : Viernes *m* Santo — **good-looking** ['gʊdˈlʊkɪŋ] *adj* : bello, guapo — **goodness** ['gʊdnəs] *n* **1** : bondad *f* **2 thank** ~ **!** : ¡gracias a Dios!, ¡menos mal! — **goodwill** [ˌgʊdˈwɪl] *n* : buena voluntad *f* — **goody** ['gʊdi] *n, pl* **goodies** : golosina *f*

gooey ['guːi] *adj* **gooier; gooiest** : pegajoso

goof *n* ['guːf] : pifia *f fam* — ~ *vi* **1** *or* ~ **up** : cometer un error **2** ~ **around** : hacer tonterías

goose ['guːs] *n, pl* **geese** ['giːs] : ganso *m*, -sa *f*; oca *f* — **goose bumps** *or* **goose pimples** *npl* : carne *f* de gallina

gopher ['goːfər] *n* : taltuza *f*

gore[1] ['gor] *n* BLOOD : sangre *f*

gore[2] *vt* **gored;** : cornear

gorge ['gɔrdʒ] *n* RAVINE : cañon *m* — ~ *vt* **gorged; gorging** ~ **oneself** : hartarse

gorgeous ['gɔrdʒəs] *adj* : magnífico, espléndido

gorilla [gəˈrɪlə] *n* : gorila *m*

gory ['gori] *adj* **gorier; -est** : sangriento

gospel ['gɑspəl] *n* **1** : evangelio *m* **2 the Gospel** : el Evangelio

gossip ['gɑsɪp] *n* **1** : chismoso *m*, -sa *f* (persona) **2** RUMOR : chisme *m* — ~ *vi* : chismear, contar chismes — **gossipy** ['gɑsɪpi] *adj* : chismoso

got → **get**

Gothic ['gɑθɪk] *adj* : gótico

gotten → **get**

gourmet ['gʊrˌmeɪ, gʊrˈmeɪ] *n* : gastrónomo *m*, -ma *f*

gout ['gaʊt] *n* : gota *f*

govern ['gʌvərn] *v* : gobernar — **governess** ['gʌvərnəs] *n* : institutriz *f* — **government** ['gʌvərmənt] *n* : gobierno *m* — **governor** ['gʌvənər, 'gʌvərnər] *n* : gobernador *m*, -dora *f*

gown ['gaun] n 1 : vestido m 2 : toga f (de magistrados, etc.)

grab ['græb] v **grabbed; grabbing** vt : agarrar, arrebatar

grace ['greɪs] n 1 : gracia f 2 **say** ~ : bendecir la mesa — ~ vt **graced; gracing** 1 HONOR : honrar 2 ADORN : adornar — **graceful** ['greɪsfəl] adj : lleno de gracia, grácil — **gracious** ['greɪʃəs] adj : cortés, gentil

grade ['greɪd] n 1 QUALITY : calidad f 2 RANK : grado m, rango m (militar) 3 YEAR : grado m, año m (a la escuela) 4 MARK : nota f 5 SLOPE : cuesta f — ~ vt **graded; grading** 1 CLASSIFY : clasificar 2 MARK : calificar (exámenes, etc.) — **grade school** → **elementary school**

gradual ['grædʒuəl] adj : gradual — **gradually** ['grædʒuəli, 'grædʒəli] adv : gradualmente, poco a poco

graduate ['grædʒuət] n : licenciado m, -da f (de la universidad), bachiller mf (de la escuela secundaria) — ~ ['grædʒuˌeɪt] v **-ated; -ating** vi : graduarse, licenciarse — vt CALIBRATE : graduar — **graduation** [ˌgrædʒu-ˈeɪʃən] n : graduación f

graffiti [grəˈfiːti, græ-] npl : graffiti mpl

graft ['græft] n : injerto m — ~ vt : injertar

grain ['greɪn] n 1 : grano m 2 CEREALS : cereales mpl 3 : veta f, vena f (de madera)

gram ['græm] n : gramo m

grammar ['græmər] n : gramática f — **grammar school** → **elementary school**

grand ['grænd] adj 1 : magnífico, espléndido 2 FABULOUS, GREAT : fabuloso, estupendo — **grandchild** ['grænd,tʃaɪld] n, pl **-children** : nieto m, -ta f — **granddaughter** ['grænd,dɔtər] n : nieta f — **grandeur** ['grændʒər] n : grandiosidad f — **grandfather** ['grænd,faðər] n : abuelo m — **grandiose** ['grændiˌos, ˌgrændi-] adj : grandioso — **grandmother** ['grænd,mʌðər] n : abuela f — **grandparents** ['grænd-ˌpærənt] npl : abuelos mpl — **grandson** ['grænd,sʌn] n : nieto m — **grandstand** ['grænd,stænd] n : tribuna f

granite ['grænɪt] n : granito m

grant ['grænt] vt 1 : conceder 2 ADMIT : reconocer, admitir 3 take for granted : dar (algo) por sentado — ~ n 1 SUBSIDY : subvención f 2 SCHOLARSHIP : beca f

grape ['greɪp] n : uva f

grapefruit ['greɪp,fruːt] n : toronja f, pomelo m

grapevine ['greɪp,vaɪn] n 1 : vid f, parra f 2 **I heard it through the** ~ : me lo dijo un pajarito fam

graph ['græf] n : gráfica f, gráfico m — **graphic** ['græfɪk] adj : gráfico

grapple ['græpəl] vi **-pled; -pling** ~ **with** : forcejear con (una persona), luchar con (un problema)

grasp ['græsp] vt 1 : agarrar 2 UNDERSTAND : comprender, captar — ~ n 1 : agarre m 2 UNDERSTANDING : comprensión f 3 REACH : alcance m

grass ['græs] n 1 : hierba f (planta) 2 LAWN : césped m, pasto m Lat — **grasshopper** ['græs,hɑpər] n : saltamontes m — **grassy** ['græsi] adj **grassier; -est** : cubierto de hierba

grate[1] ['greɪt] v **grated; -ing** vt 1 : rallar (en cocina) 2 ~ **one's teeth** : hacer rechinar los dientes — vi RASP : chirriar

grate[2] n GRATING : reja f, rejilla f

grateful ['greɪtfəl] adj : agradecido — **gratefully** ['greɪtfəli] adv : con agradecimiento — **gratefulness** ['greɪtfəlnəs] n : gratitud f, agradecimiento m

grater ['greɪtər] n : rallador m

gratify ['grætəˌfaɪ] vt **-fied; -fying** 1 PLEASE : complacer 2 SATISFY : satisfacer

grating ['greɪtɪŋ] n : reja f, rejilla f

gratitude ['grætəˌtuːd, -ˌtjuːd] n : gratitud f

gratuitous [grəˈtuːətəs] adj : gratuito

grave[1] ['greɪv] n : tumba f, sepultura f

grave[2] adj **graver; -est** : grave

gravel ['grævəl] n : grava f, gravilla f

gravestone ['greɪv,ston] n : lápida f — **graveyard** ['greɪv,jard] n : cementerio m

gravity ['grævəti] n, pl **-ties** : gravedad f

gravy ['greɪvi] n, pl **-vies** : salsa f (preparada con jugo de carne)

gray ['greɪ] adj 1 : gris 2 **hair** : pelo m canoso — ~ n : gris m — ~ vi or **turn** ~ : encanecer, ponerse gris

graze[1] ['greɪz] vi **grazed; grazing** : pastar, pacer

graze[2] vt 1 TOUCH : rozar 2 SCRATCH : rasguñarse

grease ['griːs] n : grasa f — ~ ['griːs, 'griːz] vt **greased; greasing** : engrasar — **greasy** ['griːsi, -zi] adj **greasier; -est** 1 : grasiento 2 OILY : graso, grasoso

great ['greɪt] adj 1 : grande 2 FANTASTIC : estupendo, fabuloso — **great-grandchild** [ˌgreɪtˈgrænd,tʃaɪld] n, pl

-children [-ˌʧɪldrən] : bisnieto *m*, -ta *f* — great—grandfather [ˌgreɪtˈgrænd-ˌfaðər] *n* : bisabuelo *m* — great—grandmother [ˌgreɪtˈgrændˌmʌðər] *n* : bisabuela *f* — greatly [ˈgreɪtli] *adv* 1 MUCH : mucho 2 VERY : muy — greatness [ˈgreɪtnəs] *n* : grandeza *f*

greed [ˈgriːd] *n* 1 : codicia *f*, avaricia *f* 2 GLUTTONY : glotonería *f* — greedily [ˈgriːdəli] *adv* : con avaricia — greedy [ˈgriːdi] *adj* greedier; -est 1 : codicioso, avaro 2 GLUTTONOUS : glotón

Greek [ˈgriːk] *adj* : griego — ~ *n* : griego *m* (idioma)

green [ˈgriːn] *adj* 1 : verde 2 INEXPERIENCED : novato — ~ *n* 1 : verde *m* (color) 2 ~s *npl* : verduras *fpl* — greenery [ˈgriːnəri] *n*, *pl* -eries : vegetación *f* — greenhouse [ˈgriːnˌhaʊs] *n* : invernadero *m*

greet [ˈgriːt] *vt* 1 : saludar 2 WELCOME : recibir — greeting [ˈgriːtɪŋ] *n* 1 : saludo *m* 2 ~s *npl* REGARDS : saludos *mpl*, recuerdos *mpl*

gregarious [grɪˈgæriəs] *adj* : sociable

grenade [grəˈneɪd] *n* : granada *f*

grew → grow

grey → gray

greyhound [ˈgreɪˌhaʊnd] *n* : galgo *m*

grid [ˈgrɪd] *n* 1 GRATING : rejilla *f* 2 NETWORK : red *f* 3 : cuadriculado *m* (de un mapa)

griddle [ˈgrɪdəl] *n* : plancha *f*

grief [ˈgriːf] *n* : dolor *m*, pesar *m* — grievance [ˈgriːvəns] *n* : queja *f* — grieve [ˈgriːv] *v* grieved; grieving *vt* : entristecer — *vi* ~ for : llorar (a), lamentar — grievous [ˈgriːvəs] *adj* : grave, doloroso

grill [ˈgrɪl] *vt* 1 : asar a la parrilla 2 INTERROGATE : interrogar — ~ *n* : parrilla *f* (para cocinar) — grille *or* grill [ˈgrɪl] GRATING : reja *f*, rejilla *f*

grim [ˈgrɪm] *adj* grimmer; grimmest 1 STERN : severo 2 GLOOMY : sombrío

grimace [ˈgrɪməs, grɪˈmeɪs] *n* : mueca *f* — ~ *vi* -maced; -macing : hacer muecas

grime [ˈgraɪm] *n* : mugre *f*, suciedad *f* — grimy [ˈgraɪmi] *adj* grimier; -est : mugriento, sucio

grin [ˈgrɪn] *vi* grinned; grinning : sonreír (abiertamente) — ~ *n* : sonrisa *f* (abierta)

grind [ˈgraɪnd] *v* ground [ˈgraʊnd]; grinding *vt* 1 : moler (el café, etc.) 2 SHARPEN : afilar 3 ~ one's teeth : rechinar los dientes — *vi* : rechinar — ~ *n* the daily ~ : la rutina diaria — grinder [ˈgraɪndər] *n* : molinillo *m*

grip [ˈgrɪp] *vt* gripped; gripping 1 : agarrar, asir 2 INTEREST : captar el interés de — ~ *n* 1 GRASP : agarre *m* 2 CONTROL : control *m*, dominio *m* 3 HANDLE : empuñadura *f* 4 come to ~s with : llegar a entender de

gripe [ˈgraɪp] *vi* griped; griping : quejarse — ~ *n* : queja *f*

grisly [ˈgrɪzli] *adj* -lier; -est : espeluznante, horrible

gristle [ˈgrɪsəl] *n* : cartílago *m*

grit [ˈgrɪt] *n* 1 : arena *f*, grava *f* 2 GUTS : agallas *fpl fam* 3 ~s *npl* : sémola *f* de maíz — ~ *vt* gritted; gritting ~ one's teeth : acorazarse

groan [ˈgroːn] *vi* : gemir — ~ *n* : gemido *m*

grocery [ˈgroːsəri, -ʃəri] *n*, *pl* -ceries 1 *or* ~ store : tienda *f* de comestibles, tienda *f* de abarrotes *Lat* 2 groceries *npl* : comestibles *mpl*, abarrotes *mpl Lat* — grocer [ˈgroːsər] *n* : tendero *m*, -ra *f*

groggy [ˈgrɑgi] *adj* -gier; -est : atontado, grogui *fam*

groin [ˈgroɪn] *n* : ingle *f*

groom [ˈgruːm, ˈgrʊm] *n* BRIDEGROOM : novio *m* — ~ *vt* 1 : almohazar (un animal) 2 PREPARE : preparar

groove [ˈgruːv] *n* : ranura *f*, surco *m*

grope [ˈgroːp] *vi* groped; groping : andar a tientas 2 ~ for: buscar a tientas

gross [ˈgroːs] *adj* 1 SERIOUS : grave 2 OBESE : obeso 3 TOTAL : bruto 4 VULGAR : grosero, basto — ~ *n* 1 *or* ~ income : ingresos *mpl* brutos 2 *pl* ~ : gruesa *f* (12 docenas) — grossly [ˈgroːsli] *adv* 1 EXTREMELY : enormemente 2 CRUDELY : groseramente

grotesque [groːˈtesk] *adj* : grotesco

grouch [ˈgraʊʧ] *n* : gruñón *m*, -ñona *f fam* — grouchy [ˈgraʊʧi] *adj* grouchier; -est : gruñón *fam*

ground¹ [ˈgraʊnd] → grind

ground² *n* 1 : suelo *m*, tierra *f* 2 *or* ~s LAND : terreno *m* 3 ~s REASON : razón *f*, motivos *mpl* 4 ~s DREGS : pozo *m* (de café) — ~ *vt* 1 BASE : fundar, basar 2 : conectar a tierra (un aparato eléctrico) 3 : restringir (un avión o un piloto) a la tierra — groundhog [ˈgraʊndˌhɔg] *n* : marmota *f* (de América) — groundless [ˈgraʊndləs] *adj* : infundado — groundwork [ˈgraʊndˌwərk] *n* : trabajo *m* preparatorio

group [ˈgruːp] *n* : grupo *m* — ~ *vt* : agrupar — *vi or* ~ together : agruparse

grove [ˈgroːv] *n* : arboleda *f*

grovel ['grɑvəl, 'grʌ-] *vi* **-eled** *or* **-elled;**
-eling *or* **-elling** : arrastrarse, humillarse
grow ['groː] *v* **grew** ['gruː]; **grown**
['groːn]; **growing** *vi* 1 : crecer 2 IN-
CREASE : aumentar 3 BECOME : volverse, ponerse 4 ~ **dark** : oscurecerse
5 ~ **up** : hacerse mayor — *vt* 1 CULTI-
VATE : cultivar 2 : dejarse crecer (el
pelo, etc.) — **grower** ['groːər] *n* : culti-
vador *m*, -dora *f*
growl ['graul] *vi* : gruñir — ~ *n* : gruñido *m*
grown–up ['groːnʌp] *adj* : mayor — ~
n : persona *f* mayor
growth ['groːθ] *n* 1 : crecimiento *m* 2 IN-
CREASE : aumento *m* 3 DEVELOPMENT
: desarrollo *m* 4 TUMOR : tumor *m*
grub ['grʌb] *n* 1 LARVA : larva *f* 2 FOOD
: comida *f*
grubby ['grʌbi] *adj* **grubbier; -est** : mugriento, sucio
grudge ['grʌdʒ] *vt* **grudged; grudging**
: dar de mala gana — ~ *n* **hold a** ~
: guardar rencor
grueling *or* **gruelling** ['gruːlɪŋ, 'gruːə-]
adj : extenuante, agotador
gruesome ['gruːsəm] *adj* : horripilante
gruff ['grʌf] *adj* 1 BRUSQUE : brusco 2
HOARSE : bronco
grumble ['grʌmbəl] *vi* **-bled; -bling** : refunfuñar, rezongar
grumpy ['grʌmpi] *adj* **grumpier; -est**
: malhumorado, gruñón *fam*
grunt ['grʌnt] *vi* : gruñir — ~ *n* : gruñido *m*
guarantee [ˌgærən'tiː] *n* : garantía *f* —
~ *vt* **-teed; -teeing** : garantizar
guard ['gɑrd] *n* 1 : guardia *f* 2 PRECAU-
TION : protección *f* — *vt* : proteger,
vigilar — *vi* ~ **against** : protegerse
contra — **guardian** ['gɑrdiən] *n* 1
: tutor *m*, -tora *f* (de niños) 2 PROTEC-
TOR : guardián *m*, -diana *f*
guava ['gwɑvə] *n* : guayaba *f*
guerrilla *or* **guerilla** [gə'rɪlə] *n* 1 : guerrillero *m*, -ra *f* 2 ~ **warfare** : guerra *f*
de guerrillas
guess ['ges] *vt* 1 : adivinar 2 SUPPOSE
: suponer, creer — *vi* ~ **at** : adivinar
— ~ *n* : conjetura *f*, suposición *f*
guest ['gest] *n* 1 : invitado *m*, -da *f* 2
: huésped *mf* (a un hotel)
guide ['gaɪd] *n* : guía *mf* (persona), guía
f (libro, etc.) — ~ *vt* **guided; guid-
ing** : guiar — **guidance** ['gaɪdənts] *n*
: orientación *f* — **guidebook** ['gaɪd-
ˌbʊk] *n* : guía *f* — **guideline** ['gaɪdˌlaɪn]
n : pauta *f*, directriz *f*
guild ['gɪld] *n* : gremio *m*

guile ['gaɪl] *n* : astucia *f*
guilt ['gɪlt] *n* : culpa *f*, culpabilidad *f* —
guilty ['gɪlti] *adj* **guiltier; -est** : culpable
guinea pig ['gɪni-] *n* : conejillo *m* de In-
dias, cobaya *f*
guise ['gaɪz] *n* : apariencia *f*
guitar [gə'tɑr, gɪ-] *n* : guitarra *f*
gulf ['gʌlf] *n* 1 : golfo *m* 2 ABYSS : abismo *m*
gull ['gʌl] *n* : gaviota *f*
gullet ['gʌlət] *n* 1 THROAT : garganta *f* 2
ESOPHAGUS : esófago *m*
gullible ['gʌləbəl] *adj* : crédulo
gully ['gʌli] *n, pl* **-lies** : barranco *m*
gulp ['gʌlp] *vt or* ~ **down** : tragarse,
engullir — *vi* : tragar saliva — ~ *n*
: trago *m*
gum[1] ['gʌm] *n* : encía *f* (de la boca)
gum[2] *n* 1 : resina *f* (de plantas) 2 CHEW-
ING GUM : goma *f* de mascar, chicle *m*
gumption ['gʌmpʃən] *n* : iniciativa *f*,
agallas *fpl fam*
gun ['gʌn] *n* 1 FIREARM : arma *f* de fuego
2 *or* **spray** ~ : pistola *f* 3 → **cannon,
pistol, revolver, rifle** — ~ *vt*
gunned; gunning 1 *or* ~ **down**
: matar a tiros, asesinar 2 ~ **the engine** : acelerar (el motor) — **gunboat**
['gʌnˌboːt] *n* : cañonero *m* — **gunfire**
['gʌnˌfaɪr] *n* : disparos *mpl* — **gunman**
['gʌnmən] *n, pl* **-men** [-mən, -ˌmen]
: pistolero *m*, gatillero *m Lat* — **gun-
powder** ['gʌnˌpaʊdər] *n* : pólvora *f* —
gunshot ['gʌnˌʃɑt] *n* : disparo *m*, tiro *m*
gurgle ['gərgəl] *vi* **-gled; -gling** 1 : borbotar, gorgotear 2 : gorjear (dícese de
un niño)
gush ['gʌʃ] *vi* 1 SPOUT : salir a chorros 2
~ **with praise** : deshacerse en elo-
gios
gust ['gʌst] *n* : ráfaga *f*
gusto ['gʌsˌtoː] *n, pl* **gustoes** : entusiasmo *m*
gusty ['gʌsti] *adj* **gustier; -est** : racheado, ventoso
gut ['gʌt] *n* 1 : intestino *m* 2 ~**s** *npl* IN-
NARDS : tripas *fpl* 3 ~**s** *npl* COURAGE
: agallas *fpl fam* — ~ *vt* **gutted; gut-
ting** 1 EVISCERATE : destripar (un
pollo, etc.), limpiar (un pescado) 2
: destruir el interior de (un edificio)
gutter ['gʌtər] *n* : canaleta *f* (de un
techo), cuneta *f* (de una calle)
guy ['gaɪ] *n* : tipo *m fam*
guzzle ['gʌzəl] *vt* **-zled; -zling** : chupar
fam, tragar
gym ['dʒɪm] *or* **gymnasium** [dʒɪm-
'neɪziəm, -ʒəm] *n, pl* **-siums** *or* **-sia**
[-ziə, -ʒə] : gimnasio *m* — **gymnast**

H

h ['eɪtʃ] n, pl h's or hs ['eɪtʃəz] : h f, octava letra del alfabeto inglés

habit ['hæbɪt] n 1 CUSTOM : hábito m, costumbre f 2 : hábito m (religioso)

habitat ['hæbɪˌtæt] n : hábitat m

habitual [həˈbɪtʃʊəl] adj 1 CUSTOMARY : habitual 2 INVETERATE : empedernido

hack¹ ['hæk] n 1 : caballo m de alquiler 2 or ~ writer : escritorzuelo m, -la f

hack² vt : cortar — vi or ~ into : piratear (un sistema informático)

hackneyed ['hæknid] adj : manido, trillado

hacksaw ['hækˌsɔ] n : sierra f para metales

had → have

haddock ['hædək] ns & pl : eglefino m

hadn't ['hædənt] (contraction of had not) → have

hag ['hæg] n : bruja f

haggard ['hægərd] adj : demacrado

haggle ['hægəl] vi -gled; -gling : regatear

hail¹ ['heɪl] vt 1 GREET : saludar 2 : llamar (un taxi)

hail² n : granizo m (en meteorología) — ~ vi : granizar — hailstone ['heɪlˌstoːn] n : piedra f de granizo

hair ['hær] n 1 : pelo m, cabello m 2 : vello m (en las piernas, etc.) — hairbrush ['hærˌbrʌʃ] n : cepillo m (para el pelo) — haircut ['hærˌkʌt] n 1 : corte m de pelo 2 get a ~ : cortarse el pelo — hairdo ['hærˌduː] n, pl -dos : peinado m — hairdresser ['hærˌdrɛsər] n : peluquero m, -ra f — hairless ['hærləs] adj : sin pelo, calvo — hairpin ['hærˌpɪn] n : horquilla f — hair-raising ['hærˌreɪzɪŋ] adj : espeluznante — hairstyle ['hærˌstaɪl] n : hairdo — hair spray n : laca f (para el pelo) — hairy ['hæri] adj hairier; -est : peludo, velludo

hale ['heɪl] adj : saludable, robusto

half ['hæf, 'haf] n, pl halves ['hævz, 'havz] 1 : mitad f 2 or halftime : tiempo m (en deportes) 3 in ~ : por la mitad — ~ adj 1 : medio 2 ~ an hour : una media hora — ~ adv : medio — half brother n : medio hermano m, hermanastro m — halfhearted ['hæfˈhɑrtəd] adj : sin ánimo, poco entusiasta — half sister n : media her-

mana f, hermanastra f — halfway ['hæfˈweɪ] adv : a medio camino — ~ adj : medio

halibut ['hælɪbət] ns & pl : halibut m

hall ['hɔl] n 1 HALLWAY : corredor m, pasillo m 2 AUDITORIUM : sala f 3 LOBBY : vestíbulo m 4 DORMITORY : residencia f universitaria

hallmark ['hɔlˌmɑrk] n : sello m (distintivo)

Halloween [ˌhælə'wiːn, ˌhɑ-] n : víspera f de Todos los Santos

hallucination [həˌluːsənˈeɪʃən] n : alucinación f

hallway ['hɔlˌweɪ] n 1 ENTRANCE : entrada f 2 CORRIDOR : corredor m, pasillo m

halo ['heɪˌloː] n, pl -los or -loes : aureola f, halo m

halt ['hɔlt] n 1 call a ~ to : poner fin a 2 come to a ~ : pararse — ~ vi : pararse — vt : parar

halve ['hæv, 'hav] vt halved; halving 1 DIVIDE : partir por la mitad 2 REDUCE : reducir a la mitad — halves → half

ham ['hæm] n : jamón m

hamburger ['hæmˌbərɡər] or hamburg [-ˌbərɡ] n 1 : carne f molida 2 or ~ patty : hamburguesa f

hammer ['hæmər] n : martillo m — ~ v : martillar, martillear

hammock ['hæmək] n : hamaca f

hamper¹ ['hæmpər] vt : obstaculizar, dificultar

hamper² n : cesto m, canasta f (para ropa sucia)

hamster ['hæmpstər] n : hámster m

hand ['hænd] n 1 : mano f 2 : manecilla f, aguja f (de un reloj, etc.) 3 HANDWRITING : letra f, escritura f 4 WORKER : obrero m, -ra f 5 by ~ : a mano 6 lend a ~ : echar una mano 7 on ~ : a mano, disponible 8 on the other ~ : por otro lado — ~ vt 1 : pasar, dar 2 ~ out : distribuir 3 ~ over : entregar — handbag ['hændˌbæg] n : cartera f Lat, bolso m Spain — handbook ['hændˌbʊk] n : manual m — handcuffs ['hændˌkʌfs] npl : esposas fpl — handful ['hændˌfʊl] n : puñado m — handgun ['hændˌɡʌn] n : pistola f, revólver m

handicap ['hændiˌkæp] n 1 : minusvalía f

(física) **2** : hándicap *m* (en deportes) — ~ *vt* **-capped; -capping 1** : asignar un handicap a (en deportes) **2** HAMPER : obstaculizar — **handicapped** ['hændɪ,kæpt] *adj* : minusválido

handicrafts ['hændɪ,kræfts] *npl* : artesanía(s) *f(pl)*

handiwork ['hændɪ,wərk] *n* : trabajo *m* (manual)

handkerchief ['hæŋkərtʃəf, -,tʃiːf] *n, pl* **-chiefs** : pañuelo *m*

handle ['hændəl] *n* : asa *m* (de una taza, etc.), mango *m* (de un utensilio), pomo *m* (de una puerta), tirador *m* (de un cajón) — ~ *vt* **-dled; -dling 1** TOUCH : tocar **2** MANAGE : tratar, manejar — **handlebars** ['hændəl,barz] *npl* : manillar *m*, manubrio *m* *Lat*

handmade ['hænd,meɪd] *adj* : hecho a mano

handout ['hænd,aʊt] *n* **1** ALMS : dádiva *f*, limosna *f* **2** LEAFLET : folleto *m*

handrail ['hænd,reɪl] *n* : pasamanos *m*

handshake ['hænd,ʃeɪk] *n* : apretón *m* de manos

handsome ['hænʦəm] *adj* **-somer; -est 1** ATTRACTIVE : apuesto, guapo **2** GENEROUS : generoso **3** SIZABLE : considerable

handwriting ['hænd,raɪtɪŋ] *n* : letra *f*, escritura *f* — **handwritten** ['hænd,rɪtən] *adj* : escrito a mano

handy ['hændi] *adj* **handier; -est 1** NEARBY : a mano **2** USEFUL : práctico, útil **3** DEFT : habilidoso — **handyman** ['hændɪmən] *n, pl* **-men** [-mən, -,mɛn] : hombre *m* habilidoso

hang ['hæŋ] *v* **hung** ['hʌŋ]; **hanging** *vt* **1** : colgar **2** (*past tense often* **hanged**) EXECUTE : ahorcar **3** ~ **one's head** : bajar la cabeza — *vi* **1** : colgar, pender **2** : caer (dícese de la ropa, etc.) **3** ~ **up on s.o.** : colgar a algn — ~ *n* **1** DRAPE : caída *f* **2** **get the** ~ **of** : agarrar la onda de

hangar ['hæŋər, 'hæŋgər] *n* : hangar *m*

hanger ['hæŋər] *n* : percha *f*, gancho *m* (para ropa) *Lat*

hangover ['hæŋ,oːvər] *n* : resaca *f*

hanker ['hæŋkər] *vi* ~ **for** : tener ansias de — **hankering** ['hæŋkərɪŋ] *n* : ansia *f*, anhelo *m*

haphazard [hæp'hæzərd] *adj* : casual, fortuito

happen ['hæpən] *vi* **1** : pasar, suceder, ocurrir **2** ~ **to do sth** : hacer algo por casualidad **3 it so happens that...** : da la casualidad de que... — **happening** ['hæpənɪŋ] *n* : suceso *m*, acontecimiento *m*

happy ['hæpi] *adj* **-pier; -est 1** : feliz **2 be** ~ : alegrarse **3 be** ~ **with** : estar contento con **4 be** ~ **to do sth** : hacer algo con mucho gusto — **happily** ['hæpəli] *adv* : alegremente — **happiness** ['hæpinəs] *n* : felicidad *f* — **happy–go–lucky** ['hæpigoː'lʌki] *adj* : despreocupado

harass [hə'ræs, 'hærəs] *vt* : acosar — **harassment** [hə'ræsmənt, 'hærəsmənt] *n* : acoso *m*

harbor *or Brit* **harbour** ['harbər] *n* : puerto *m* — ~ *vt* **1** SHELTER : albergar **2** ~ **a grudge against** : guardar rencor a

hard ['hard] *adj* **1** : duro **2** DIFFICULT : difícil **3 be a** ~ **worker** : ser muy trabajador **4** ~ **liquor** : bebidas *fpl* fuertes **5** ~ **water** : agua *f* dura — ~ *adv* **1** FORCEFULLY : fuerte **2 work** ~ : trabajar duro **3 take sth** ~ : tomarse algo muy mal — **harden** ['hardən] *vt* : endurecer — **hardheaded** [,hard-'hedəd] *adj* : testarudo, terco — **hard–hearted** [,hard'hartəd] *adj* : duro de corazón — **hardly** ['hardli] *adv* **1** : apenas **2** ~ **ever** : casi nunca — **hardness** ['hardnəs] *n* **1** : dureza *f* **2** DIFFICULTY : dificultad *f* — **hardship** ['hard,ʃɪp] *n* : dificultad *f* — **hardware** ['hard,wær] *n* **1** : ferretería *f* **2** : hardware *m* (en informática) — **hardworking** ['hard'wərkɪŋ] *adj* : trabajador

hardy ['hardi] *adj* **-dier; -est** : fuerte (dícese de personas), resistente (dícese de las plantas)

hare ['hær] *n, pl* **hare** *or* **hares** : liebre *f*

harm ['harm] *n* : daño *m* — ~ *vt* : hacer daño a (una persona), dañar (una cosa), perjudicar (la reputación de algn, etc.) — **harmful** ['harmfəl] *adj* : perjudicial — **harmless** ['harmləs] *adj* : inofensivo

harmonica [har'manɪkə] *n* : armónica *f*

harmony ['harmoni] *n, pl* **-nies** : armonía *f* — **harmonious** [har'moːniəs] *adj* : armonioso — **harmonize** ['harmə,naɪz] *v* **-nized; -nizing** : armonizar

harness ['harnəs] *n* : arnés *m* — ~ *vt* **1** : enjaezar **2** UTILIZE : utilizar

harp ['harp] *n* : arpa *m* — ~ *vi* ~ **on** : insistir sobre

harpoon [har'puːn] *n* : arpón *m*

harpsichord ['harpsɪ,kord] *n* : clavicémbalo *m*

harsh ['harʃ] *adj* **1** ROUGH : áspero **2** SEVERE : duro, severo **3** : fuerte (dícese de una luz), discordante (dícese de sonidos) — **harshness** ['harʃnəs] *n* : severidad *f*

harvest ['hɑrvəst] n : cosecha f — ~ v : cosechar

has → **have**

hash ['hæʃ] vt 1 CHOP : picar 2 ~ **over** DISCUSS : discutir — ~ n : picadillo m (comida)

hasn't ['hæzənt] (contraction of **has not**) → **has**

hassle ['hæsəl] n : problemas mpl, lío m — ~ vt **-sled; -sling** : fastidiar

haste ['heɪst] n 1 : prisa f, apuro m Lat 2 **make** ~ : darse prisa, apurarse Lat — **hasten** ['heɪsən] vt : acelerar — vi : apresurarse, apurarse Lat — **hasty** ['heɪsti] adj **hastier; -est** : precipitado

hat ['hæt] n : sombrero m

hatch ['hætʃ] n : escotilla f — ~ vt 1 : empollar (huevos) 2 CONCOCT : tramar — vi : salir del cascarón

hatchet ['hætʃət] n : hacha f

hate ['heɪt] n : odio m — ~ vt **hated; hating** : odiar, aborrecer — **hateful** ['heɪtfəl] adj : odioso, aborrecible — **hatred** ['heɪtrəd] n : odio m

haughty ['hɔti] adj **-tier; -est** : altanero, altivo

haul ['hɔl] vt : arrastrar, jalar Lat — ~ n 1 CATCH : redada f (de peces) 2 LOOT : botín m 3 **a long** ~ : un trayecto largo

haunch ['hɔntʃ] n : cadera f (de una persona), anca f (de un animal)

haunt ['hɔnt] vt 1 : frecuentar, rondar 2 TROUBLE : inquietar — ~ n : sitio m predilecto — **haunted** ['hɔntəd] adj : embrujado

have ['hæv, in sense 3 as an auxiliary verb usu 'hæf] v **had** ['hæd]; **having; has** ['hæz, in sense 3 as an auxiliary verb usu 'hæs] vt 1 : tener 2 CONSUME : comer, tomar 3 ALLOW : permitir 4 : dar (una fiesta, etc.), convocar (una reunión) 5 ~ **one's hair cut** : cortarse el pelo 6 ~ **sth done** : mandar hacer algo — v aux 1 : haber 2 ~ **just done sth** : acabar de hacer algo 4 **you've finished, haven't you?** : has terminado, ¿no?

haven ['heɪvən] n : refugio m

havoc ['hævək] n : estragos mpl

hawk¹ ['hɔk] n : halcón m

hawk² vt : pregonar (mercancías)

hay ['heɪ] n : heno m — **hay fever** n : fiebre f del heno — **haystack** ['heɪ-,stæk] n : almiar m — **haywire** ['heɪ-,waɪr] adj go ~ : estropearse

hazard ['hæzərd] n : peligro m, riesgo m — ~ vt : arriesgar, aventurar — **hazardous** ['hæzərdəs] adj : arriesgado, peligroso

haze ['heɪz] n : bruma f, neblina f

hazel ['heɪzəl] n : color m avellana — **hazelnut** ['heɪzəl,nʌt] n : avellana f

hazy ['heɪzi] adj **hazier; -est** : nebuloso

he ['hiː] pron : él

head ['hɛd] n 1 : cabeza f 2 END, TOP : cabeza f (de un clavo, etc.), cabecera f (de una mesa) 3 LEADER : jefe m, -fa f 4 **be out of one's** ~ : estar loco 5 **come to a** ~ : llegar a un punto crítico 6 ~**s or tails** : cara o cruz 7 **per** ~ : por cabeza — ~ adj MAIN : principal — vt : encabezar — vi : dirigirse — **headache** ['hɛd,eɪk] n : dolor m de cabeza — **headband** ['hɛd,bænd] n : cinta f del pelo — **headdress** ['hɛd-,drɛs] n : tocado m — **headfirst** ['hɛd-'fərst] adv : de cabeza — **heading** ['hɛdɪŋ] n : encabezamiento m, título m — **headland** ['hɛdlənd, -,lænd] n : cabo m — **headlight** ['hɛd,laɪt] n : faro m — **headline** ['hɛd,laɪn] n : titular m — **headlong** ['hɛd,lɔŋ] adv 1 HEADFIRST : de cabeza 2 HASTILY : precipitadamente — **headmaster** ['hɛd,mæstər] n : director m — **headmistress** ['hɛd-,mɪstrəs, -'mɪs-] n : directora f — **head-on** ['hɛd'ɑn, -'ɔn] adv & adj : de frente — **headphones** ['hɛd,fonz] npl : auriculares mpl, audífonos mpl Lat — **headquarters** ['hɛd,kwɔrtərz] ns & pl : oficina f central (de una compañía), cuartel m general (de los militares) — **head start** n : ventaja f — **headstrong** ['hɛd,strɔŋ] adj : testarudo, obstinado — **headwaiter** ['hɛd-'weɪtər] n : jefe m, -fa f de comedor — **headway** ['hɛd,weɪ] n 1 : progreso m 2 **make** ~ : avanzar — **heady** ['hɛdi] adj **headier; -est** : embriagador

heal ['hiːl] vt : curar — vi : cicatrizar

health ['hɛlθ] n : salud f — **healthy** ['hɛlθi] adj **healthier; -est** : sano, saludable

heap ['hiːp] n : montón m — ~ vt : amontonar

hear ['hɪr] v **heard** ['hərd]; **hearing** vt : oír — vi 1 : oír 2 ~ **about** : enterarse de 3 ~ **from** : tener noticias de — **hearing** ['hɪrɪŋ] n 1 : oído m 2 : vista f (en un tribunal) — **hearing aid** n : audífono m — **hearsay** ['hɪr,seɪ] n : rumores mpl

hearse ['hərs] n : coche m fúnebre

heart ['hɑrt] n 1 : corazón m 2 **at** ~ : en el fondo 3 **by** ~ : de memoria 4 **lose** ~ : descorazonarse 5 **take** ~ : animarse — **heartache** ['hɑrt,eɪk] n : pena f, dolor m — **heart attack** n : infarto m, ataque m al corazón — **heartbeat**

['hɑrt,bi:t] *n* : latido *m* (del corazón) —
heartbreak ['hɑrt,breɪk] *n* : congoja *f*,
angustia *f* — **heartbroken** ['hɑrt-
,bro:kən] *adj* : desconsolado — **heart-
burn** ['hɑrt,bərn] *n* : acidez *f* estomacal
hearth ['hɑrθ] *n* : hogar *m*
heartily ['hɑrt̬əli] *adv* : de buena gana
heartless ['hɑrt̬ləs] *adj* : de mal corazón, cruel
hearty ['hɑrt̬i] *adj* **heartier; -est 1** : cordial, caluroso **2** : abundante (dícese de
una comida)
heat ['hi:t] *vt* : calentar — *vi or* ~ **up**
: calentarse — ~ *n* **1** : calor *m* **2** HEAT-
ING : calefacción *f* — **heated** ['hi:t̬əd]
adj : acalorado — **heater** ['hi:t̬ər] *n*
: calentador *m*
heath ['hi:θ] *n* : brezal *m*
heathen ['hi:ðən] *adj* : pagano — ~ *n*,
pl **-thens** *or* **-then** : pagano *m*, -na *f*
heather ['hɛðər] *n* : brezo *m*
heave ['hi:v] *v* **heaved** *or* **hove** ['ho:v];
heaving *vt* **1** LIFT : levantar (con esfuerzo) **2** HURL : lanzar, tirar **3** ~ **a
sigh** : suspirar — ~ *vi or* ~ **up** : levantarse
heaven ['hɛvən] *n* : cielo *m* — **heavenly** ['hɛvənli] *adj* **1** : celestial **2** ~ **body**
: cuerpo *m* celeste
heavy ['hɛvi] *adj* **heavier; -est 1** : pesado **2** INTENSE : fuerte **3** ~ **sigh** : suspiro *m* profundo **4** ~ **traffic** : tráfico
m denso — **heavily** ['hɛvəli] *adv* **1**
: pesadamente **2** EXCESSIVELY : mucho
— **heaviness** ['hɛvinəs] *n* : peso *m*,
pesadez *f* — **heavyweight** ['hɛvi,weɪt]
n : peso *m* pesado
Hebrew ['hi:,bru:] *adj* : hebreo — ~ *n*
: hebreo *m* (idioma)
heckle ['hɛkəl] *vt* **-led; -ling** : interrumpir (a un orador) con preguntas mo-
lestas
hectic ['hɛktɪk] *adj* : agitado, ajetreado
he'd ['hi:d] (*contraction of* **he had** *or* **he
would**) → **have, would**
hedge ['hɛdʒ] *n* : seto *m* vivo — ~ *v*
hedged; hedging *vt* ~ **one's bets**
: cubrirse — *vi* : contestar con evasi-
vas — **hedgehog** ['hɛdʒ,hɔɡ, -,hɑɡ] *n*
: erizo *m*
heed ['hi:d] *vt* : prestar atención a, hacer
caso de — ~ *n* **take** ~ : tener cuidado — **heedless** ['hi:dləs] *adj* **be** ~ **of**
: hacer caso omiso de
heel ['hi:l] *n* : talón *m* (del pie), tacón *m*
(de un zapato)
hefty ['hɛfti] *adj* **heftier; -est** : robusto y
pesado
heifer ['hɛfər] *n* : novilla *f*
height ['haɪt] *n* **1** : estatura *f* (de una per-

sona), altura *f* (de un objeto) **2** PEAK
: cumbre *f* **3 the** ~ **of folly** : el colmo
de la locura **4 what is your** ~ **?**
: ¿cuánto mides? — **heighten** ['haɪt̬ən]
vt : aumentar, intensificar
heir ['ær] *n* : heredero *m*, -ra *f* —
heiress ['ærəs] *n* : heredera *f* — **heirloom** ['ær,lu:m] *n* : reliquia *f* de familia
held → **hold**
helicopter ['hɛlə,kɑptər] *n* : helicóptero
m
hell ['hɛl] *n* : infierno *m* — **hellish**
['hɛlɪʃ] *adj* : infernal
he'll ['hi:l, 'hɪl] (*contraction of* **he shall**
or **he will**) → **shall, will**
hello [hə'lo:, hɛ-] *interj* : ¡hola!
helm ['hɛlm] *n* : timón *m*
helmet ['hɛlmət] *n* : casco *m*
help ['hɛlp] *vt* **1** : ayudar **2** ~ **oneself**
: servirse **3 I can't** ~ **it** : no lo puedo
remediar — ~ *n* **1** : ayuda *f* **2** STAFF
: personal *m* **3 help!** : ¡socorro!, ¡auxilio! — **helper** ['hɛlpər] *n* : ayudante
mf — **helpful** ['hɛlpfəl] *adj* **1** OBLIGING
: servicial, amable **2** USEFUL : útil —
helping ['hɛlpɪŋ] *n* : porción *f* — **helpless** ['hɛlpləs] *adj* **1** POWERLESS : incapaz **2** DEFENSELESS : indefenso
hem ['hɛm] *n* : dobladillo *m* — ~ *vt*
hemmed; hemming ~ **in** : encerrar
hemisphere ['hɛmə,sfɪr] *n* : hemisferio
m
hemorrhage ['hɛmərɪdʒ] *n* : hemorragia
f
hemorrhoids ['hɛmə,rɔɪdz, 'hɛm,rɔɪdz]
npl : hemorroides *fpl*, almorranas *fpl*
hemp ['hɛmp] *n* : cáñamo *m*
hen ['hɛn] *n* : gallina *f*
hence ['hɛnts] *adv* **1** : de aquí, de ahí **2**
THEREFORE : por lo tanto **3 ten years**
~ : de aquí a 10 años — **henceforth**
['hɛnts,fɔrθ, ,hɛnts'-] *adv* : de ahora en
adelante
henpeck ['hɛn,pɛk] *vt* : dominar (al
marido)
hepatitis [,hɛpə'taɪt̬əs] *n*, *pl* **-titides**
[-'tɪt̬ə,di:z] : hepatitis *f*
her ['hər] *adj* : su, sus — ~ ['hər, ər]
pron **1** (*used as direct object*) : la **2**
(*used as indirect object*) : le, se **3**
(*used as object of a preposition*) : ella
herald ['hɛrəld] *vt* : anunciar
herb ['ərb, 'hərb] *n* : hierba *f*
herd ['hərd] *n* : manada *f* — ~ *vt* : conducir (en manada) — *vi or* ~ **together** : reunir
here ['hɪr] *adv* **1** : aquí, acá **2** ~ **you
are!** : ¡toma! — **hereabouts** ['hɪrə-
,baʊts] *or* **hereabout** [-,baʊt] *adv* : por
aquí (cerca) — **hereafter** [hɪr'æftər]

adv : en el futuro — **hereby** [hɪr'baɪ]
adv : por este medio
hereditary [həˈrɛdəˌteri] *adj* : hereditario
— **heredity** [həˈrɛdəti] *n* : herencia *f*
heresy [ˈhɛrəsi] *n, pl* **-sies** : herejía *f*
herewith [hɪrˈwɪθ] *adv* : adjunto
heritage [ˈhɛrəˌtɪdʒ] *n* **1** : herencia *f* **2**
: patrimonio *m* (nacional)
hermit [ˈhərmət] *n* : ermitaño *m*, -ña *f*
hernia [ˈhərniə] *n, pl* **-nias** *or* **-niae**
[-niˌiː, -niˌaɪ] : hernia *f*
hero [ˈhiːˌroː, ˈhɪˌroː] *n, pl* **-roes** : héroe *m*
— **heroic** [hɪˈroːɪk] *adj* : heroico —
heroine [ˈheroːən] *n* : heroína *f* —
heroism [ˈheroːˌɪzəm] *n* : heroísmo *m*
heron [ˈherən] *n* : garza *f*
herring [ˈhɛrɪŋ] *n, pl* **-ring** *or* **-rings**
: arenque *m*
hers [ˈhərz] *pron* **1** : (el) suyo, (la) suya,
(los) suyos, (las) suyas **2 some
friends of** ~ : unos amigos suyos,
unos amigos de ella — **herself** [hərˈsɛlf] *pron* **1** (*used reflexively*) : se **2**
(*used emphatically*) : ella misma
he's [ˈhiːz] (*contraction of* **he is** *or* **he
has**) → **be, have**
hesitant [ˈhɛzətənt] *adj* : titubeante,
vacilante — **hesitate** [ˈhɛzəˌteɪt] *vi*
-tated; -tating : vacilar, titubear —
hesitation [ˌhɛzəˈteɪʃən] *n* : vacilación
f, titubeo *m*
heterosexual [ˌhɛtəroˈsɛkʃ(ʊ)əl] *adj* : heterosexual — ~ *n* : heterosexual *mf*
hexagon [ˈhɛksəˌgən] *n* : hexágono *m*
hey [ˈheɪ] *interj* : ¡eh!, ¡oye!
heyday [ˈheɪˌdeɪ] *n* : auge *m*, apogeo *m*
hi [ˈhaɪ] *interj* : ¡hola!
hibernate [ˈhaɪbərˌneɪt] *vi* **-nated; -nating** : hibernar
hiccup [ˈhɪkəp] *n* **have the** ~**s** : tener
hipo — ~ *vi* **-cuped; -cuping** : tener
hipo
hide¹ [ˈhaɪd] *n* : piel *f*, cuero *m*
hide² *v* **hid** [ˈhɪd]; **hidden** [ˈhɪdən] *or*
hid; hiding *vt* **1** : esconder **2** : ocultar
(motivos, etc.) — *vi* : esconderse —
hide-and-seek [ˈhaɪdənˌdsiːk] *n* : escondite *m*, escondidas *fpl Lat*
hideous [ˈhɪdiəs] *adj* : horrible, espantoso
hideout [ˈhaɪdˌaʊt] *n* : escondite *m*, guarida *f*
hierarchy [ˈhaɪəˌrɑrki] *n, pl* **-chies** : jerarquía *f* — **hierarchical** [ˌhaɪəˈrɑrkɪkəl]
adj : jerárquico
high [ˈhaɪ] *adj* **1** : alto **2** INTOXICATED
: borracho, drogado **3** a ~ **voice** : una
voz aguda **4 it's two feet** ~ : tiene
dos pies de alto **5** ~ **winds** : fuertes
vientos *mpl* — ~ *adv* : alto — ~ *n*

: récord *m*, máximo *m* — **higher**
[ˈhaɪər] *adj* **1** : superior **2** ~ **education** : enseñanza *f* superior — **highlight** [ˈhaɪˌlaɪt] *n* : punto *m* culminante
— **highly** [ˈhaɪli] *adv* **1** VERY : muy,
sumamente **2 think** ~ **of** : tener en
mucho a — **Highness** [ˈhaɪnəs] *n*
His/Her ~ : Su Alteza *f* — **high
school** *n* : escuela *f* superior, escuela *f*
secundaria — **high-strung** [ˈhaɪˈstrʌŋ]
adj : nervioso, excitable — **highway**
[ˈhaɪˌweɪ] *n* : carretera *f*
hijack [ˈhaɪˌdʒæk] *vt* : secuestrar — **hijacker** [ˈhaɪˌdʒækər] *n* : secuestrador
m, -dora *f* — **hijacking** *n* : secuestro
m
hike [ˈhaɪk] *v* **hiked; hiking** *vi* : ir de
caminata — *vt or* ~ **up** RAISE : subir
— ~ *n* : caminata *f*, excursión *f* —
hiker [ˈhaɪkər] *n* : excursionista *mf*
hilarious [hɪˈlæriəs, haɪ-] *adj* : muy divertido — **hilarity** [hɪˈlærəti, haɪ-] *n*
: hilaridad *f*
hill [ˈhɪl] *n* **1** : colina *f*, cerro *m* **2** SLOPE
: cuesta *f* — **hillside** [ˈhɪlˌsaɪd] *n*
: ladera *f*, cuesta *f* — **hilly** [ˈhɪli] *adj*
hillier; -est : accidentado
hilt [ˈhɪlt] *n* : puño *m*
him [ˈhɪm, əm] *pron* **1** (*used as direct object*) : lo **2** (*used as indirect object*)
: le, se **3** (*used as object of a preposition*) : él — **himself** [hɪmˈsɛlf] *pron* **1**
(*used reflexively*) : se **2** (*used emphatically*) : él mismo
hind [ˈhaɪnd] *adj* : trasero, posterior
hinder [ˈhɪndər] *vt* : dificultar, estorbar
— **hindrance** [ˈhɪndrəns] *n* : obstáculo
m
hindsight [ˈhaɪndˌsaɪt] *n* **in** ~ : en retrospectiva
Hindu [ˈhɪnˌduː] *adj* : hindú
hinge [ˈhɪndʒ] *n* **1** : bisagra *f*, gozne *m* —
~ *vi* **hinged; hinging** ~ **on** : depender de
hint [ˈhɪnt] *n* **1** : indirecta *f* **2** TIP : consejo *m* **3** TRACE : asomo *m*, toque *m* —
~ *vt* : dar a entender — *vi* ~ **at** : insinuar
hip [ˈhɪp] *n* : cadera *f*
hippopotamus [ˌhɪpəˈpɑtəməs] *n, pl*
-muses *or* **-mi** [-ˌmaɪ] : hipopótamo *m*
hire [ˈhaɪr] *n* **1** : alquiler *m* **2 for** ~ : se
alquila — ~ *vt* **hired; hiring 1** EMPLOY : contratar, emplear **2** RENT
: alquilar
his [ˈhɪz, ɪz] *adj* : su, sus, de él — ~
pron **1** : (el) suyo, (la) suya, (los)
suyos, (las) suyas **2 some friends of**
~ : unos amigos suyos, unos amigos
de él

Hispanic [hɪ'spænɪk] *adj* : hispano, hispánico

hiss ['hɪs] *vi* : silbar — *n* : silbido *m*

history ['hɪstəri] *n, pl* **-ries 1** : historia *f* **2** BACKGROUND : historial *m* — **historian** [hɪ'storiən] *n* : historiador *m*, -dora *f* — **historic** [hɪ'storɪk] *or* **historical** [-ɪkəl] *adj* : histórico

hit ['hɪt] *v* **hit**; **hitting** *vt* **1** : golpear, pegar **2** : dar (con un proyectil) **3** AFFECT : afectar **4** REACH : alcanzar **5 the car ~ a tree** : el coche chocó contra un árbol — *vi* : pegar — *~ n* **1** : golpe *m* **2** SUCCESS : éxito *m*

hitch ['hɪtʃ] *vt* **1** ATTACH : enganchar **2** *or* **~ up** RAISE : subirse **3 ~ a ride** : hacer autostop — *~ n* PROBLEM : problema *m* — **hitchhike** ['hɪtʃ,haɪk] *vi* **-hiked**; **-hiking** : hacer autostop — **hitchhiker** ['hɪtʃ,haɪkər] *n* : autostopista *mf*

hitherto ['hɪðər,tu:, ,hɪðər'-] *adv* : hasta ahora

HIV [,eɪtʃ,ar'vi:] *n* : VIH *m*, virus *m* del sida

hive ['haɪv] *n* : colmena *f*

hives ['haɪvz] *ns & pl* : urticaria *f*

hoard ['hord] *n* : tesoro *m* (de dinero), reserva *f* (de provisiones) — *~ vt* : acumular

hoarse ['hors] *adj* **hoarser**; **-est** : ronco

hoax ['ho:ks] *n* : engaño *m*

hobble ['habəl] *vi* **-bled**; **-bling** : cojear

hobby ['habi] *n, pl* **-bies** : pasatiempo *m*

hobo ['ho:,bo:] *n, pl* **-boes** : vagabundo *m*, -da *f*

hockey ['haki] *n* : hockey *m*

hoe ['ho:] *n* : azada *f* — *~ vt* **hoed**; **hoeing** : azadonar

hog ['hɔg, 'hag] *n* : cerdo *m* — *~ vt* **hogged**; **hogging** MONOPOLIZE : acaparar

hoist ['hɔɪst] *vt* **1** : izar (una vela, etc.) **2** LIFT : levantar — *~ n* : grúa *f*

hold[1] ['ho:ld] *n* : bodega *f* (en un barco o un avión)

hold[2] *v* **held** ['held]; **holding** *vt* **1** GRIP : agarrar **2** POSSESS : tener **3** SUPPORT : sostener **4** : celebrar (una reunión, etc.), mantener (una conversación) **5** CONTAIN : contener **6** CONSIDER : considerar **7** *or* **~ back** : detener **8 ~ hands** : agarrarse de la mano **9 ~ up** ROB : atracar **10 ~ up** DELAY : retrasar — *vi* **1** LAST : durar, continuar **2** APPLY : ser válido — *~ n* **1** GRIP : agarre *m* **2 get ~ of** : conseguir **3 get ~ of oneself** : controlarse — **holder** ['ho:ldər] *n* : tenedor *m*, -dora *f* — **holdup** ['ho:ld-

,ʌp] *n* **1** ROBBERY : atraco *m* **2** DELAY : retraso *m*, demora *f*

hole ['ho:l] *n* : agujero *m*, hoyo *m*

holiday ['halə,deɪ] *n* **1** : día *m* feriado, fiesta *f* **2** *Brit* VACATION : vacaciones *fpl*

holiness ['ho:linəs] *n* : santidad *f*

holler ['halər] *vi* : gritar — *~ n* : grito *m*

hollow ['ha,lo:] *n* **1** : hueco *m* **2** VALLEY : hondonada *f* — *~ adj* **-lower**; **-est 1** : hueco **2** FALSE : vacío, falso — *~ vt or ~ out* : ahuecar

holly ['hali] *n, pl* **-lies** : acebo *m*

holocaust ['halə,kɔst, 'ho:-, 'hɔ-] *n* : holocausto *m*

holster ['ho:lstər] *n* : pistolera *f*

holy ['ho:li] *adj* **-lier**; **-est** : santo, sagrado

homage ['amɪdʒ, 'ha-] *n* : homenaje *m*

home ['ho:m] *n* **1** : casa *f* **2** FAMILY : hogar *m* **3** INSTITUTION : residencia *f*, asilo *m* **4 at ~ and abroad** : dentro y fuera del país — *~ adv* **go ~** : ir a casa — **homeland** ['ho:m,lænd] *n* : patria *f* — **homeless** ['ho:mləs] *adj* : sin hogar — **homely** ['ho:mli] *adj* **-lier**; **-est 1** DOMESTIC : casero **2** UGLY : feo — **homemade** ['ho:m'meɪd] *adj* : casero, hecho en casa — **homemaker** ['ho:m,meɪkər] *n* : ama *f* de casa — **home run** *n* : jonrón *m* — **homesick** ['ho:m,sɪk] *adj* **be ~** : echar de menos a la familia — **homeward** ['ho:mwərd] *adj* : de vuelta, de regreso — **homework** ['ho:m,wərk] *n* : tarea *f*, deberes *mpl* — **homey** ['ho:mi] *adj* **homier**; **-est** : hogareño, acogedor

homicide ['hamə,saɪd, 'ho:-] *n* : homicidio *m*

homogeneous [,ho:mə'dʒi:niəs, -njəs] *adj* : homogéneo

homosexual [,ho:mə'sekʃuəl] *adj* : homosexual — *~ n* : homosexual *mf* — **homosexuality** [,ho:mə,sekʃu'æləti] *n* : homosexualidad *f*

honest ['anəst] *adj* **1** : honrado **2** FRANK : sincero — **honestly** *adv* : sinceramente — **honesty** ['anəsti] *n, pl* **-ties** : honradez *f*

honey ['hʌni] *n, pl* **-eys** : miel *f* — **honeycomb** ['hʌni,ko:m] *n* : panal *m* — **honeymoon** ['hʌni,mu:n] *n* : luna *f* de miel

honk ['hɑŋk, 'hɔŋk] *vi* : tocar la bocina — *~ n* : bocinazo *m*

honor *or Brit* **honour** ['anər] *n* : honor *m* — *~ vt* **1** : honrar **2** : aceptar (un cheque, etc.), cumplir con (una promesa) — **honorable** *or Brit* **honourable** ['anərəbəl] *adj* : honorable, honroso — **honorary** ['anə,reri] *adj* : honorario

hood ['hʊd] *n* **1** : capucha *f* (de un abrigo, etc.) **2** : capó *m* (de un automóvil)

hoodlum ['hʊdləm, 'huːd-] *n* : matón *m*

hoodwink ['hʊd,wɪŋk] *vt* : engañar

hoof ['hʊf, 'huːf] *n, pl* **hooves** ['hʊvz, 'huːvz] *or* **hoofs** : pezuña *f* (de una vaca, etc.), casco *m* (de un caballo)

hook ['hʊk] *n* **1** : gancho *m* **2** *or* ~ **and eye** : corchete *m* **3** → **fishhook 4 off the** ~ : descolgado — ~ *vt* : enganchar — *vi* : engancharse

hoop ['huːp] *n* : aro *m*

hooray [hʊˈreɪ] → **hurrah**

hoot ['huːt] *vi* **1** : ulular (dícese de un búho) **2** ~ **with laughter** : reírse a carcajadas — ~ *n* **1** : ululato *m* (de un búho) **2 I don't give a** ~ : me importa un comino

hop[1] ['hɑp] *vi* **hopped; hopping** : saltar a la pata coja — ~ *n* : salto *m* a la pata coja

hop[2] *n* ~**s** : lúpulo *m* (planta)

hope ['hoːp] *v* **hoped; hoping** *vi* : esperar — *vt* : esperar que — ~ *n* : esperanza *f* — **hopeful** ['hoːpfəl] *adj* : esperanzado — **hopefully** *adv* **1** : con esperanza **2** ~ **it will help** : se espera que ayude — **hopeless** ['hoːpləs] *adj* : desesperado — **hopelessly** ['hoːpləsli] *adv* : desesperadamente

horde ['hord] *n* : horda *f*

horizon [həˈraɪzən] *n* : horizonte *m* — **horizontal** [ˌhorəˈzɑntəl] *adj* : horizontal

hormone ['hor,moːn] *n* : hormona *f*

horn ['horn] *n* **1** : cuerno *m* (de un animal) **2** : trompa *f* (instrumento musical) **3** : bocina *f*, claxon *m* (de un vehículo)

hornet ['hornət] *n* : avispón *m*

horoscope ['horə,skoːp] *n* : horóscopo *m*

horror ['horər] *n* : horror *m* — **horrendous** [hoˈrendəs] *adj* : horrendo — **horrible** ['horəbəl] *adj* : horrible — **horrid** ['horɪd] *adj* : horroroso, horrible — **horrify** ['horə,faɪ] *vt* **-fied; -fying** : horrorizar

hors d'oeuvre [orˈdərv] *n, pl* **hors d'oeuvres** [-ˈdərvz] : entremés *m*

horse ['hors] *n* : caballo *m* — **horseback** ['hors,bæk] *n* **on** ~ : a caballo — **horsefly** ['hors,flaɪ] *n, pl* **-flies** : tábano *m* — **horseman** ['horsmən] *n, pl* **-men** [-mən, -ˌmen] : jinete *m* — **horseplay** ['hors,pleɪ] *n* : payasadas *fpl* — **horsepower** ['hors,paʊər] *n* : caballo *m* de fuerza — **horseradish** ['hors,rædɪʃ] *n* : rábano *m* picante — **horseshoe** ['horsʃuː] *n* : herradura *f* — **horse-**

woman ['hors,wʊmən] *n, pl* **-women** [-,wɪmən] : jinete *f*

horticulture ['hortəˌkʌltʃər] *n* : horticultura *f*

hose ['hoːz] *n* **1** *pl* **hoses** : manguera *f*, manga *f* **2 hose** *pl* STOCKINGS : medias *fpl* — ~ *vt* **hosed; hosing** : regar (con manguera) — **hosiery** ['hoːʒəri, 'hoːʒə-] *n* : calcetería *f*

hospice ['hɑspəs] *n* : hospicio *m*

hospital ['hɑs,pɪtəl] *n* : hospital *m* — **hospitable** [hɑˈspɪtəbəl, 'hɑs,pɪ-] *adj* : hospitalario — **hospitality** [ˌhɑspəˈtæləti] *n, pl* **-ties** : hospitalidad *f* — **hospitalize** ['hɑs,pɪtəl,aɪz] *vt* **-ized; -izing** : hospitalizar

host[1] ['hoːst] *n* **a** ~ **of** : toda una serie de

host[2] *n* **1** : anfitrión *m*, -triona *f* **2** : presentador *m*, -dora *f* (de televisión, etc.) — ~ *vt* : presentar (un programa de televisión, etc.)

host[3] *n* EUCHARIST : hostia *f*, Eucaristía *f*

hostage ['hɑstɪdʒ] *n* : rehén *m*

hostel ['hɑstəl] *n* *or* **youth** ~ : albergue *m* juvenil

hostess ['hoːstɪs] *n* : anfitriona *f*

hostile ['hɑstəl, -,taɪl] *adj* : hostil — **hostility** [hɑsˈtɪləti] *n, pl* **-ties** : hostilidad *f*

hot ['hɑt] *adj* **hotter; hottest 1** : caliente, caluroso (dícese del tiempo), cálido (dícese del clima) **2** SPICY : picante **3 feel** ~ : tener calor **4 have a** ~ **temper** : tener mal genio **5** ~ **news** : noticias *fpl* de última hora **6 it's** ~ **today** : hace calor

hot dog *n* : perro *m* caliente

hotel [hoːˈtel] *n* : hotel *m*

hotheaded ['hɑt,hedəd] *adj* : exaltado

hound ['haʊnd] *n* : perro *m* (de caza) — ~ *vt* : acosar, perseguir

hour ['aʊər] *n* : hora *f* — **hourglass** ['aʊər,glæs] *n* : reloj *m* de arena — **hourly** ['aʊərli] *adv* & *adj* : cada hora, por hora

house ['haʊs] *n, pl* **houses** ['haʊzəz, -səz] **1** : casa *f* **2** : cámara *f* (del gobierno) **3 publishing** ~ : editorial *f* — ~ ['haʊz] *vt* **housed; housing** : albergar — **houseboat** ['haʊs,boːt] *n* : casa *f* flotante — **housefly** ['haʊs,flaɪ] *n, pl* **-flies** : mosca *f* común — **household** ['haʊs,hoːld] *adj* **1** : doméstico **2** ~ **name** : nombre *m* muy conocido — ~ *n* : casa *f* — **housekeeper** ['haʊs,kiːpər] *n* : ama *f* de llaves — **housekeeping** ['haʊs,kiːpɪŋ] *n* : gobierno *m* de la casa — **housewarming** ['haʊs,wormɪŋ] *n* : fiesta *f* de estreno de

una casa — **housewife** ['haus,waɪf] n,
pl **-wives** : ama f de casa — **housework** ['haus,wərk] n : faenas fpl domésticas — **housing** ['hauzɪŋ] n 1 : viviendas fpl 2 CASE : caja f protectora
hove → heave
hovel ['hʌvəl, 'hɑ-] n : casucha f, tugurio
m
hover ['hʌvər, 'hɑ-] vi 1 : cernerse 2 ~
about : rondar
how ['hau] adv 1 : cómo 2 (used in exclamations) : qué 3 ~ **are you?**
: ¿cómo está Ud.? 4 ~ **come** : por
qué 5 ~ **much** : cuánto 6 ~ **do you
do?** : mucho gusto 7 ~ **old are you?**
: ¿cuántos años tienes? — ~ conj
: como
however [hau'ɛvər] conj 1 : de cualquier
manera que 2 ~ **you like** : como
quieras — ~ adv 1 NEVERTHELESS
: sin embargo, no obstante 2 ~ **difficult it is** : por difícil que sea 3 ~
hard I try : por más que me esfuerce
howl ['haul] vi : aullar — ~ n : aullido
m
hub ['hʌb] n 1 CENTER : centro m 2
: cubo m (de una rueda)
hubbub ['hʌ,bʌb] n : alboroto m, jaleo m
hubcap ['hʌb,kæp] n : tapacubos m
huddle ['hʌdəl] vi **-dled; -dling** or ~
together : apiñarse
hue ['hju:] n : color m, tono m
huff ['hʌf] n **be in a** ~ : estar enojado
hug ['hʌg] vt **hugged; hugging** : abrazar — ~ n : abrazo m
huge ['hju:dʒ] adj **huger; hugest** : inmenso, enorme
hull ['hʌl] n : casco m (de un barco, etc.)
hum ['hʌm] v **hummed; humming** vi 1
: tararear 2 BUZZ : zumbar — vt
: tararear (una melodía) — ~ n
: zumbido m
human ['hju:mən, 'ju:-] adj : humano —
~ n : (ser m) humano m — **humane**
[hju:'meɪn, ju:-] adj : humano, humanitario — **humanitarian** [hju:,mænə-
'teriən, ju:-] adj : humanitario — **humanity** [hju:'mænəti, ju:-] n, pl **-ties**
: humanidad f
humble ['hʌmbəl] vt **-bled; -bling 1**
: humillar 2 ~ **oneself** : humillarse
— ~ adj **-bler; -blest** : humilde
humdrum ['hʌm,drʌm] adj : monótono,
rutinario
humid ['hju:məd, 'ju:-] adj : húmedo —
humidity [hju:'mɪdəti, ju:-] n, pl **-ties**
: humedad f
humiliate [hju:'mɪli,eɪt, ju:-] vt **-ated;
-ating** : humillar — **humiliating** [hju:-
'mɪli,eɪtɪŋ, ju:-] adj : humillante — **hu-**

miliation [hju:,mɪli'eɪʃən, ju:-] n : humillación f — **humility** [hju:'mɪləti,
ju:-] n : humildad f
humor or Brit **humour** ['hju:mər, 'ju:-] n
: humor m — ~ vt : seguir la corriente
a, complacer — **humorous** ['hju:mərəs,
'ju:-] adj : humorístico, cómico
hump ['hʌmp] n : joroba f
hunch ['hʌntʃ] vi or ~ **over** : encorvarse — ~ n : presentimiento m
hundred ['hʌndrəd] adj : cien, ciento —
~ n, pl **-dreds** or **-dred** : ciento m —
hundredth ['hʌndrədθ] adj : centésimo
— ~ n 1 : centésimo m, -ma f (en una
serie) 2 : centésimo m (en matemáticas)
hung → hang
Hungarian [hʌŋ'gæriən] adj : húngaro
— ~ n : húngaro m (idioma)
hunger ['hʌŋgər] n : hambre m — ~ vi
1 : tener hambre 2 ~ **for** : ansiar, anhelar — **hungry** ['hʌŋgri] adj **-grier;
-est 1** : hambriento 2 **be** ~ : tener
hambre
hunk ['hʌŋk] n : pedazo m (grande)
hunt ['hʌnt] vt 1 : cazar 2 ~ **for** : buscar
— ~ n 1 : caza f, cacería f 2 SEARCH
: búsqueda f, busca f — **hunter**
['hʌntər] n : cazador m, -dora f — **hunting** ['hʌntɪŋ] n 1 : caza f 2 **go** ~ : ir de
caza
hurdle ['hərdəl] n 1 : valla f (en deportes) 2 OBSTACLE : obstáculo m
hurl ['hərl] vt : lanzar, arrojar
hurrah [hu'rɑ, -'rɔ] interj : ¡hurra!
hurricane ['hərə,keɪn] n : huracán m
hurry ['həri] n : prisa f, apuro m Lat — v
-ried; -rying vi : darse prisa, apurarse
Lat — vt : apurar, dar prisa a — **hur-
ried** ['hərid] adj : apresurado — **hurriedly** ['həridli] adv : apresuradamente, de prisa
hurt ['hərt] v **hurt; hurting** vt 1 INJURE
: hacer daño a, lastimar 2 OFFEND
: ofender, herir — vi 1 : doler 2 **my
foot** ~**s** : me duele el pie — ~ n 1
INJURY : herida f 2 DISTRESS : dolor m,
pena f — **hurtful** ['hərtfəl] adj : hiriente, doloroso
hurtle ['hərtəl] vi **-tled; -tling** : lanzarse,
precipitarse
husband ['hʌzbənd] n : esposo m, marido m
hush ['hʌʃ] vt : hacer callar, acallar —
~ n : silencio m
husk ['hʌsk] n : cáscara f
husky[1] ['hʌski] adj **-kier; -est** HOARSE
: ronco
husky[2] n, pl **-kies** : perro m, -rra f esquimal

husky³ *adj* BURLY : fornido
hustle ['həsəl] *v* **-tled; -tling** *vt* : dar prisa a, apurar *Lat* — *vi* : darse prisa, apurarse *Lat* — ~ *n* ~ **and bustle** : ajetreo *m*, bullicio *m*
hut ['hʌt] *n* : cabaña *f*
hutch ['hʌtʃ] *n or* **rabbit** ~ : conejera *f*
hyacinth ['haɪəˌsɪnθ] *n* : jacinto *m*
hybrid ['haɪbrɪd] *n* : híbrido *m* — ~ *adj* : híbrido
hydrant ['haɪdrənt] *n or* **fire** ~ : boca *f* de incendios
hydraulic [haɪ'drɔlɪk] *adj* : hidráulico
hydroelectric [ˌhaɪdroʊˈlɛktrɪk] *adj* : hidroeléctrico
hydrogen ['haɪdrədʒən] *n* : hidrógeno *m*
hyena [haɪˈinə] *n* : hiena *f*
hygiene ['haɪˌdʒin] *n* : higiene *f* — **hygienic** [haɪˈdʒɛnɪk, -ˈdʒi-; ˌhaɪdʒiˈɛnɪk] *adj* : higiénico
hymn ['hɪm] *n* : himno *m*

hyperactive [ˌhaɪpərˈæktɪv] *adj* : hiperactivo
hyphen ['haɪfən] *n* : guión *m*
hypnosis [hɪpˈnoːsɪs] *n, pl* **-noses** [-ˌsiːz] : hipnosis *f* — **hypnotic** [hɪpˈnɑˌtɪk] *adj* : hipnótico — **hypnotism** ['hɪpnəˌtɪzəm] *n* : hipnotismo *m* — **hypnotize** ['hɪpnəˌtaɪz] *vt* **-tized; -tizing** : hipnotizar
hypochondriac [ˌhaɪpəˈkɑndriˌæk] *n* : hipocondríaco *m*, -ca *f*
hypocrisy [hɪˈpɑkrəsi] *n, pl* **-sies** : hipocresía *f* — **hypocrite** ['hɪpəˌkrɪt] *n* : hipócrita *mf* — **hypocritical** [ˌhɪpəˈkrɪtɪkəl] *adj* : hipócrita
hypothesis [haɪˈpɑθəsɪs] *n, pl* **-eses** [-ˌsiːz] : hipótesis *f* — **hypothetical** [ˌhaɪpəˈθɛtɪkəl] *adj* : hipotético
hysteria [hɪsˈtɛriə, -ˈtɪr-] *n* : histeria *f*, histerismo *m* — **hysterical** [hɪsˈtɛrɪkəl] *adj* : histérico

I

i ['aɪ] *n, pl* **i's** *or* **is** ['aɪz] : i *f*, novena letra del alfabeto inglés
I ['aɪ] *pron* : yo
ice ['aɪs] *n* : hielo *m* — ~ *v* **iced; icing** *vt* **1** FREEZE : congelar **2** CHILL : enfriar **3** : bañar (pasteles, etc.) — ~ *vi or* ~ **up** : helarse, congelarse — **iceberg** ['aɪsˌbərg] *n* : iceberg *m* — **icebox** ['aɪs-ˌbɑks] ~ : **refrigerator** — **ice-cold** ['aɪs'koːld] *adj* : helado — **ice cream** *n* : helado *m* — **ice cube** *n* : cubito *m* de hielo — **ice-skate** ['aɪsˌskeɪt] *vi* **-skated; -skating** : patinar — **ice skate** *n* : patín *m* de cuchilla — **icicle** ['aɪsɪkəl] *n* : carámbano *m* — **icing** ['aɪsɪŋ] *n* : baño *m*
icon ['aɪˌkɑn, -kən] *n* : icono *m*
icy ['aɪsi] *adj* **icier; -est 1** : cubierto de hielo (dícese de pavimento, etc.) **2** FREEZING : helado
I'd ['aɪd] (*contraction of* **I should** *or* **I would**) → **should, would**
idea [aɪˈdiə] *n* : idea *f*
ideal [aɪˈdiəl] *adj* : ideal — ~ *n* : ideal *m* — **idealist** [aɪˈdiːəlɪst] *n* : idealista *mf* — **idealistic** [aɪˌdiːəˈlɪstɪk] *adj* : idealista — **idealize** [aɪˈdiːəˌlaɪz] *vt* **-ized; -izing** : idealizar
identity [aɪˈdɛntəˌti] *n, pl* **-ties** : identidad *f* — **identical** [aɪˈdɛntɪkəl] *adj* : idéntico — **identify** [aɪˈdɛntəˌfaɪ] *v* **-fied; -fying** *vt* : identificar — *vi* ~ **with** : identificarse con — **identifica-**

tion [aɪˌdɛntəfəˈkeɪʃən] *n* **1** : identificación *f* **2** ~ **card** : carnet *m*, carné *m*
ideology [hɪpˈnoːsɪs, ˌɪ-] *n, pl* **-gies** : ideología *f* — **ideological** [ˌaɪdiə-ˈlɑdʒɪkəl, ˌɪ-] *adj* : ideológico
idiocy ['ɪdiəsi] *n, pl* **-cies** : idiotez *f*
idiom ['ɪdiəm] *n* EXPRESSION : modismo *m* — **idiomatic** [ˌɪdiəˈmætɪk] *adj* : idiomático
idiosyncrasy [ˌɪdioʊˈsɪŋkrəsi] *n, pl* **-sies** : idiosincrasia *f*
idiot ['ɪdiət] *n* : idiota *mf* — **idiotic** [ˌɪdiˈɑtɪk] *adj* : idiota
idle ['aɪdəl] *adj* **idler; idlest 1** LAZY : haragán, holgazán **2** INACTIVE : parado (dícese de una máquina) **3** UNEMPLOYED : desocupado **4** VAIN : frívolo, vano **5 out of** ~ **curiosity** : por pura curiosidad — ~ *v* **idled; idling** *vi* : andar al ralentí (dícese de un motor) — *vt* ~ **away the hours** : pasar el rato — **idleness** ['aɪdəlnəs] *n* : ociosidad *f*
idol ['aɪdəl] *n* : ídolo *m* — **idolize** ['aɪdəˌlaɪz] *vt* **-ized; -izing** : idolatrar
idyllic [aɪˈdɪlɪk] *adj* : idílico
if ['ɪf] *conj* **1** : si **2** THOUGH : aunque, si bien **3** ~ **so** : si es así
igloo ['ɪglu] *n, pl* **-loos** : iglú *m*
ignite [ɪgˈnaɪt] *v* **-nited; -niting** *vt* : encender — *vi* : encenderse — **ignition** [ɪgˈnɪʃən] *n* **1** : ignición *f* **2** *or* ~ **switch** : encendido *m*

ignore [ɪg'nor] vt **-nored; -noring** : ignorar, no hacer caso de — **ignorance** [ˈɪgnərənts] n : ignorancia f — **ignorant** [ˈɪgnərənt] adj 1 : ignorante 2 **be — of** : desconocer, ignorar

ilk [ˈɪlk] n : tipo m, clase f

ill [ˈɪl] adj **worse** [ˈwərs]; **worst** [ˈwərst] 1 SICK : enfermo 2 BAD : malo — adv **worse; worst** : mal — **ill-advised** [ˌɪlæd'vaɪzd, -əd-] adj : imprudente — **ill at ease** adj : incómodo

I'll [ˈaɪl] (contraction of **I shall** or **I will**) → **shall, will**

illegal [ɪl'liːgəl] adj : ilegal

illegible [ɪl'ledʒəbəl] adj : ilegible

illegitimate [ˌɪlɪ'dʒɪtəmət] adj : ilegítimo — **illegitimacy** [ˌɪlɪ'dʒɪtəməsi] n : ilegitimidad f

illicit [ɪl'lɪsət] adj : ilícito

illiterate [ɪl'lɪtərət] adj : analfabeto — **illiteracy** [ɪl'lɪtərəsi] n, pl **-cies** : analfabetismo m

ill-mannered [ˌɪl'mænərd] adj : descortés, maleducado

ill-natured [ˌɪl'neɪtʃərd] adj : de mal genio

illness [ˈɪlnəs] n : enfermedad f

illogical [ɪl'lɑdʒɪkəl] adj : ilógico

ill-treat [ˌɪl'triːt] vt : maltratar

illuminate [ɪ'luːmənˌeɪt] vt **-nated; -nating** : iluminar — **illumination** [ɪˌluːmə'neɪʃən] n : iluminación f

illusion [ɪ'luːʒən] n : ilusión f — **illusory** [ɪ'luːsəri, -zəri] adj : ilusorio

illustrate [ˈɪləsˌtreɪt] v **-trated; -trating** : ilustrar — **illustration** [ˌɪlə'streɪʃən] n 1 : ilustración f 2 EXAMPLE : ejemplo m — **illustrative** [ɪ'lʌstrətɪv, 'ɪləˌstreɪtɪv] adj : ilustrativo

illustrious [ɪ'lʌstriəs] adj : ilustre, glorioso

ill will n : animadversión f, mala voluntad f

I'm [ˈaɪm] (contraction of **I am**) → **be**

image [ˈɪmɪdʒ] n : imagen f — **imaginary** [ɪ'mædʒəˌneri] adj : imaginario — **imagination** [ɪˌmædʒə'neɪʃən] n : imaginación f — **imaginative** [ɪ'mædʒəˌnətɪv, -əneɪˌtɪv] adj : imaginativo — **imagine** [ɪ'mædʒən] vt **-ined; -ining** : imaginar(se)

imbalance [ɪm'bælənts] n : desequilibrio m

imbecile [ˈɪmbəsəl, -ˌsɪl] n : imbécil mf

imbue [ɪm'bjuː] vt **-bued; -buing** : imbuir

imitation [ˌɪmə'teɪʃən] n : imitación f — **~** adj : de imitación, artificial — **imitate** [ˈɪməˌteɪt] vt **-tated; -tating** : imitar, remedar — **imitator** [ˈɪməˌteɪtər] n : imitador m, -dora f

immaculate [ɪ'mækjələt] adj : inmaculado

immaterial [ˌɪmə'tɪriəl] adj : irrelevante, sin importancia

immature [ˌɪmə'tʃʊr, -'tjʊr, -'tʊr] adj : inmaduro — **immaturity** [ˌɪmə'tʃʊrəti, -'tjʊr-, -'tʊr-] n, pl **-ties** : inmadurez f

immediate [ɪ'miːdiət] adj : inmediato — **immediately** [ɪ'miːdiətli] adv : inmediatamente

immense [ɪ'mɛnts] adj : inmenso — **immensity** [ɪ'mɛntsəti] n, pl **-ties** : inmensidad f

immerse [ɪ'mərs] vt **-mersed; -mersing** : sumergir — **immersion** [ɪ'mərʒən] n : inmersión f

immigrate [ˈɪməˌgreɪt] vi **-grated; -grating** : inmigrar — **immigrant** [ˈɪmɪgrənt] n : inmigrante mf — **immigration** [ˌɪmə'greɪʃən] n : inmigración f

imminent [ˈɪmənənt] adj : inminente — **imminence** [ˈɪmənənts] n : inminencia f

immobile [ɪm'oːbəl] adj : inmóvil — **immobilize** [ɪm'oːbəˌlaɪz] vt **-lized; -lizing** : inmovilizar

immoral [ɪm'mɔrəl] adj : inmoral — **immorality** [ˌɪmɔ'ræləti, ˌɪmə-] n, pl **-ties** : inmoralidad f

immortal [ɪm'mɔrtəl] adj : inmortal — **~** n : inmortal mf — **immortality** [ˌɪˌmɔr'tæləti] n : inmortalidad f

immune [ɪ'mjuːn] adj : inmune — **immunity** [ɪ'mjuːnəti] n, pl **-ties** : inmunidad f — **immunization** [ˌɪmjunə'zeɪʃən] n : inmunización f — **immunize** [ˈɪmjuˌnaɪz] vt **-nized; -nizing** : inmunizar

imp [ˈɪmp] n RASCAL : diablillo m

impact [ˈɪmˌpækt] n : impacto m

impair [ɪm'pær] vt : dañar, perjudicar

impart [ɪm'pɑrt] vt : impartir (información), conferir (una calidad, etc.)

impartial [ɪm'pɑrʃəl] adj : imparcial — **impartiality** [ɪmˌpɑrʃi'æləti] n, pl **-ties** : imparcialidad f

impassable [ɪm'pæsəbəl] adj : intransitable

impasse [ˈɪmˌpæs] n : impasse m

impassioned [ɪm'pæʃənd] adj : apasionado

impassive [ɪm'pæsɪv] adj : impasible

impatience [ɪm'peɪʃənts] n : impaciencia f — **impatient** [ɪm'peɪʃənt] adj : impaciente — **impatiently** [ɪm'peɪʃəntli] adv : con impaciencia

impeccable [ɪm'pekəbəl] adj : impecable

impede [ɪm'piːd] *vt* **-peded; -peding** : dificultar — **impediment** [ɪm-'pɛdəmənt] *n* : impedimento *m*, obstáculo *m*

impel [ɪm'pɛl] *vt* **-pelled; -pelling** : impeler

impending [ɪm'pɛndɪŋ] *adj* : inminente

impenetrable [ɪm'pɛnətrəbəl] *adj* : impenetrable.

imperative [ɪm'pɛrətɪv] *adj* **1** COMMANDING : imperativo **2** NECESSARY : imprescindible — **~** *n* : imperativo *m*

imperceptible [ˌɪmpər'sɛptəbəl] *adj* : imperceptible

imperfection [ɪm,pərfɛkʃən] *n* : imperfección *f* — **imperfect** [ɪm'pərfɪkt] *adj* : imperfecto — **~** *n or* **~ tense** : imperfecto *m*

imperial [ɪm'pɪriəl] *adj* : imperial — **imperialism** [ɪm'pɪriəˌlɪzəm] *n* : imperialismo *m* — **imperious** [ɪm'pɪriəs] *adj* : imperioso

impersonal [ɪm'pərsənəl] *adj* : impersonal

impersonate [ɪm'pərsənˌeɪt] *vt* **-ated; -ating** : hacerse pasar por, imitar — **impersonation** [ɪm,pərsən'eɪʃən] *n* : imitación *f* — **impersonator** [ɪm-'pərsənˌeɪtər] *n* : imitador *m*, -dora *f*

impertinent [ɪm'pərtənənt] *adj* : impertinente — **impertinence** [ɪm'pərtənənts] *n* : impertinencia *f*

impervious [ɪm'pərviəs] *adj* **~ to** : impermeable a

impetuous [ɪm'pɛtʃuəs] *adj* : impetuoso, impulsivo

impetus ['ɪmpətəs] *n* : ímpetu *m*, impulso *m*

impinge [ɪm'pɪndʒ] *vi* **-pinged; -pinging ~ on** : afectar, incidir en

impish ['ɪmpɪʃ] *adj* : pícaro, travieso

implant [ɪm'plænt] *vt* : implantar

implausible [ɪm'plɔːzəbəl] *adj* : inverosímil

implement ['ɪmpləmənt] *n* : instrumento *m*, implemento *m* *Lat* — **~** ['ɪmplə-ˌmɛnt] *vt* : poner en práctica

implicate ['ɪmpləˌkeɪt] *vt* **-cated; -cating** : implicar — **implication** [ɪmplə'keɪ-ʃən] *n* **1** INVOLVEMENT : implicación *f* **2** CONSEQUENCE : consecuencia *f* **3** by **~** : de forma indirecta

implicit [ɪm'plɪsɪt] *adj* **1** : implícito **2** UNQUESTIONING : absoluto, incondicional

implore [ɪm'plor] *vt* **-plored; -ploring** : implorar, suplicar

imply [ɪm'plaɪ] *vt* **-plied; -plying 1** HINT : insinuar **2** ENTAIL : implicar

impolite [ɪmpə'laɪt] *adj* : descortés, maleducado

import [ɪm'port] *vt* : importar (mercancías). — **important** [ɪm'portənt] *adj* : importante — **importance** [ɪm-'portənts] *n* : importancia *f* — **importation** [ˌɪmpor'teɪʃən] *n* : importación *f* — **importer** [ɪm'portər] *n* : importador *m*, -dora *f*

impose [ɪm'poːz] *v* **-posed; -posing** *vt* : imponer — *vi* **~ on** : importunar, molestar — **imposing** [ɪm'poːzɪŋ] *adj* : imponente — **imposition** [ˌɪmpə-'zɪʃən] *n* **1** ENFORCEMENT : imposición *f* **2 be an ~ on** : molestar

impossible [ɪm'pasəbəl] *adj* : imposible — **impossibility** [ɪm,pasə'bɪləti] *n, pl* **-ties** : imposibilidad *f*

impostor *or* **imposter** [ɪm'pastər] *n* : impostor *m*, -tora *f*

impotent ['ɪmpətənt] *adj* : impotente — **impotence** ['ɪmpətənts] *n* : impotencia *f*

impound [ɪm'paʊnd] *vt* : incautar, embargar

impoverished [ɪm'pavərɪʃt] *adj* : empobrecido

impracticable [ɪm'præktɪkəbəl] *adj* : impracticable

impractical [ɪm'præktɪkəl] *adj* : poco práctico

imprecise [ˌɪmprɪ'saɪs] *adj* : impreciso — **imprecision** [ˌɪmprɪ'sɪʒən] *n* : imprecisión *f*

impregnable [ɪm'prɛgnəbəl] *adj* : impenetrable

impregnate [ɪm'prɛgˌneɪt] *vt* **-nated; -nating 1** : impregnar **2** FERTILIZE : fecundar

impress [ɪm'prɛs] *vt* **1** : causar una buena impresión a **2** AFFECT : impresionar **3 ~ sth on s.o.** : recalcar algo a algn — *vi* : impresionar — **impression** [ɪm'prɛʃən] *n* : impresión *f* — **impressionable** [ɪm'prɛʃənəbəl] *adj* : impresionable — **impressive** [ɪm'prɛsɪv] *adj* : impresionante

imprint [ɪm'prɪnt, 'ɪm,-] *vt* : imprimir — **~** ['ɪm,prɪnt] *n* MARK : impresión *f*, huella *f*

imprison [ɪm'prɪzən] *vt* : encarcelar — **imprisonment** [ɪm'prɪzənmənt] *n* : encarcelamiento *m*

improbable [ɪm'prabəbəl] *adj* : improbable — **improbability** [ɪm,prabə'bɪləti] *n, pl* **-ties** : improbabilidad *f*

impromptu [ɪm'prampˌtuː, -ˌtjuː] *adj* : improvisado

improper [ɪm'prapər] *adj* **1** UNSEEMLY : indecoroso **2** INCORRECT : impropio

— **impropriety** [ˌɪmprəˈpraɪəti] *n, pl*
-eties : inconveniencia *f*

improve [ɪmˈpruːv] *v* **-proved; -proving**
: mejorar — **improvement** [ɪm-
ˈpruːvmənt] *n* : mejora *f*

improvise [ˈɪmprəˌvaɪz] *v* **-vised;
-vising** : improvisar — **improvisation** [ˌɪmprəvəˈzeɪʃən, ˌɪmprəvə-] *n* : improvisación *f*

impudent [ˈɪmpjədənt] *adj* : insolente —
impudence [ˈɪmpjədənts] *n* : insolencia *f*

impulse [ˈɪmˌpʌls] *n* **1** : impulso *m* **2 on
~** : sin reflexionar — **impulsive** [ɪm-
ˈpʌlsɪv] *adj* : impulsivo — **impulsiveness** [ɪmˈpʌlsɪvnəs] *n* : impulsividad *f*

impunity [ɪmˈpjunəti] *n* **1** : impunidad *f*
2 with ~ : impunemente

impure [ɪmˈpjʊr] *adj* : impuro — **impurity** [ɪmˈpjʊrəti] *n, pl* **-ties** : impureza *f*

in [ˈɪn] *prep* **1** : en **2** DURING : por, en *Lat*
3 WITHIN : dentro de **4 dressed ~ red**
: vestido de rojo **5 ~ the rain** : bajo la
lluvia **6 ~ the sun** : al sol **7 ~ this
way** : de esta manera **8 the best ~
the world** : el mejor del mundo **9 written ~ ink/French** : escrito con
tinta/en francés — *adv* **1** INSIDE : dentro, adentro **2 be ~** : estar (en casa) **3
be ~ on** : participar en **4 come in!**
: ¡entre!, ¡pase! **5 he's ~ for a shock**
: se va a llevar un shock — **~** *adj* : de
moda

inability [ˌɪnəˈbɪləti] *n, pl* **-ties** : incapacidad *f*

inaccessible [ˌɪnɪkˈsesəbəl] *adj* : inaccesible

inaccurate [ɪnˈækjərət] *n* : inexacto

inactive [ɪnˈæktɪv] *n* : inactivo — **inactivity** [ˌɪnˌækˈtɪvəti] *n, pl* **-ties** : inactividad *f*

inadequate [ɪnˈædɪkwət] *adj* : insuficiente

inadvertently [ˌɪnədˈvərtəntli] *adv* : sin
querer

inadvisable [ˌɪnədˈvaɪzəbəl] *adj* : desaconsejable

inane [ɪˈneɪn] *adj* **inaner; -est** : estúpido, tonto

inanimate [ɪnˈænəmət] *adj* : inanimado

inapplicable [ɪnˈæplɪkəbəl, ˌɪnəˈplɪkəbəl]
adj : inaplicable

inappropriate [ˌɪnəˈproːpriət] *adj* : impropio, inoportuno

inarticulate [ˌɪnɑrˈtɪkjələt] *adj* : incapaz
de expresarse

inasmuch as [ˌɪnəzˈmʌtʃˌæz] *conj* : ya
que, puesto que

inattentive [ˌɪnəˈtentɪv] *adj* : poco atento

inaudible [ɪnˈodəbəl] *adj* : inaudible

inaugural [ɪˈnɔɡjərəl, -ɡərəl] *adj* **1** : inaugural **2 ~ address** : discurso *m* de
investidura — **inaugurate** [ɪˈnɔɡjəˌreɪt,
-ɡə-] *vt* **-rated; -rating 1** : investir (a
un presidente, etc.) **2** BEGIN : inaugurar — **inauguration** [ɪˌnɔɡjəˈreɪʃən,
-ɡə-] *n* : investidura *f* (de una persona), inauguración *f* (de un edificio,
etc.)

inborn [ˈɪnˌbɔrn] *adj* : innato

inbred [ˈɪnˌbred] *adj* INNATE : innato

incalculable [ɪnˈkælkjələbəl] *adj* : incalculable

incapable [ɪnˈkeɪpəbəl] *adj* : incapaz —
incapacitate [ˌɪnkəˈpæsəˌteɪt] *vt* **-tated;
-tating** : incapacitar — **incapacity**
[ˌɪnkəˈpæsəti] *n, pl* **-ties** : incapacidad *f*

incarcerate [ɪnˈkɑrsəˌreɪt] *vt* **-ated;
-ating** : encarcelar

incarnate [ɪnˈkɑrnət, -ˌneɪt] *adj* : encarnado — **incarnation** [ˌɪnˌkɑrˈneɪʃən] *n*
: encarnación *f*

incendiary [ɪnˈsendiˌeri] *adj* : incendiario

incense¹ [ˈɪnˌsents] *n* : incienso *m*

incense² [ˈɪnsents] *vt* **-censed;
-censing** : indignar, enfurecer

incentive [ɪnˈsentɪv] *n* : incentivo *m*

inception [ɪnˈsepʃən] *n* : comienzo *m*,
principio *m*

incessant [ɪnˈsesənt] *adj* : incesante

incest [ˈɪnˌsest] *n* : incesto *m* — **incestuous** [ɪnˈsestʃuəs] *adj* : incestuoso

inch [ˈɪntʃ] *n* : pulgada *f* — **~** *v* : avanzar poco a poco

incident [ˈɪnsədənt] *n* : incidente *m* —
incidence [ˈɪnsədənts] *n* : índice *m* (de
crímenes, etc.) — **incidental** [ˌɪnsə-
ˈdentəl] *adj* **1** MINOR : incidental **2**
CHANCE : casual — **incidentally**
[ˌɪnsəˈdentəli, -ˈdentli] *adv* : a propósito

incinerate [ɪnˈsɪnəˌreɪt] *vt* **-ated; -ating**
: incinerar — **incinerator** [ɪnˈsɪnə-
ˌreɪtər] *n* : incinerador *m*

incision [ɪnˈsɪʒən] *n* : incisión *f*

incite [ɪnˈsaɪt] *vt* **-cited; -citing** : incitar,
instigar

incline [ɪnˈklaɪn] *v* **-clined; -clining** *vt* **1**
BEND : inclinar **2 be ~ed to** : incli-
narse a, tender a — **~** *vi* : inclinarse
— **~** [ˈɪnˌklaɪn] *n* : pendiente *f* — **inclination** [ˌɪnkləˈneɪʃən] *n* **1** : inclinación *f*
2 DESIRE : deseo *m*, ganas *fpl*

include [ɪnˈkluːd] *vt* **-cluded; -cluding**
: incluir — **inclusion** [ɪnˈkluːʒən] *n*
: inclusión *f* — **inclusive** [ɪnˈkluːsɪv]
adj : inclusivo

incognito [ˌɪnkɑɡˈniːto, ɪnˈkɑɡnəˌtoː] *adv*
& *adj* : de incógnito

incoherent [ˌɪnkoˈhɪrənt, -ˈher-] *adj* : incoherente — **Incoherence** [ˌɪnko-ˈhɪrənts, -ˈher-] n : incoherencia f

income [ˈɪnˌkʌm] n : ingresos mpl — **income tax** n : impuesto m sobre la renta

incomparable [ɪnˈkɑmpərəbəl] adj : incomparable

incompatible [ˌɪnkəmˈpætəbəl] adj : incompatible

incompetent [ɪnˈkɑmpətənt] adj : incompetente — **incompetence** [ɪnˈkɑmpətənts] n : incompetencia f

incomplete [ˌɪnkəmˈpliːt] adj : incompleto

incomprehensible [ˌɪnˌkɑmprɪˈhentsəbəl] adj : incomprensible

inconceivable [ˌɪnkənˈsiːvəbəl] adj : inconcebible

inconclusive [ˌɪnkənˈkluːsɪv] adj : no concluyente

incongruous [ɪnˈkɑŋgruəs] adj : incongruente

inconsiderate [ˌɪnkənˈsɪdərət] adj : desconsiderado

inconsistent [ˌɪnkənˈsɪstənt] adj 1 : inconsecuente 2 be ~ with : no concordar con — **inconsistency** [ˌɪnkənˈsɪstəntsi] n, pl -cies : inconsecuencia f

inconspicuous [ˌɪnkənˈspɪkjuəs] adj : que no llama la atención

inconvenient [ˌɪnkənˈvinjənt] adj : incómodo, inconveniente — **inconvenience** [ˌɪnkənˈvinjənts] n 1 BOTHER : incomodidad f, molestia f 2 DRAWBACK : inconveniente m — ~ vt -nienced; -niencing vt : importunar, molestar

incorporate [ɪnˈkɔrpəˌreɪt] vt -rated; -rating : incorporar

incorrect [ˌɪnkəˈrekt] adj : incorrecto

increase [ˈɪnˌkriːs, ɪnˈkriːs] n : aumento m — ~ [ɪnˈkriːs, ˈɪnˌkriːs] v -creased; -creasing : aumentar — **increasingly** [ɪnˈkriːsɪŋli] adv : cada vez más

incredible [ɪnˈkredəbəl] adj : increíble

incredulous [ɪnˈkredʒələs] adj : incrédulo

incriminate [ɪnˈkrɪməˌneɪt] vt -nated; -nating : incriminar

incubator [ˈɪŋkjuˌbeɪtər, ˈɪn-] n : incubadora f

incumbent [ɪnˈkʌmbənt] n : titular mf

incur [ɪnˈkər] vt **incurred; incurring** : provocar (al enojo, etc.), incurrir en (gastos)

incurable [ɪnˈkjurəbəl] adj : incurable

indebted [ɪnˈdeṭəd] adj 1 : endeudado 2 be ~ to s.o. : estar en deuda con algn

indecent [ɪnˈdiːsənt] adj : indecente — **indecency** [ɪnˈdiːsəntsi] n, pl -cies : indecencia f

indecisive [ˌɪndɪˈsaɪsɪv] adj : indeciso

indeed [ɪnˈdiːd] adv 1 TRULY : verdaderamente, sin duda 2 IN FACT : en efecto 3 ~? : ¿de veras?

indefinite [ɪnˈdefənət] adj 1 : indefinido 2 VAGUE : impreciso — **indefinitely** [ɪnˈdefənətli] adv : indefinidamente

indelible [ɪnˈdeləbəl] adj : indeleble

indent [ɪnˈdent] vt : sangrar (un párrafo) — **indentation** [ˌɪnˌdenˈteɪʃən] n DENT, NOTCH : mella f

independent [ˌɪndəˈpendənt] adj : independiente — **Independence** [ˌɪndəˈpendənts] n : independencia f

indescribable [ˌɪndɪˈskraɪbəbəl] adj : indescriptible

indestructible [ˌɪndɪˈstrʌktəbəl] adj : indestructible

index [ˈɪnˌdeks] n, pl **-dexes** or **-dices** [ˈɪndəˌsiːz] : índice m — ~ vt : incluir en un índice — **index finger** n : dedo m índice

Indian [ˈɪndiən] adj : indio m, -dia f

indication [ˌɪndəˈkeɪʃən] n : indicio m, señal f — **indicate** [ˈɪndəˌkeɪt] vt **-cated; -cating** : indicar — **indicative** [ɪnˈdɪkəˌtɪv] adj : indicativo — **indicator** [ˈɪndəˌkeɪtər] n : indicador m

indict [ɪnˈdaɪt] vt : acusar (de un crimen) — **indictment** [ɪnˈdaɪtmənt] n : acusación f

indifferent [ɪnˈdɪfrənt, -ˈdɪfə-] adj 1 : indiferente 2 MEDIOCRE : mediocre — **indifference** [ɪnˈdɪfrənts, -ˈdɪfə-] n : indiferencia f

indigenous [ɪnˈdɪdʒənəs] adj : indígena

indigestion [ˌɪndarˈdʒestʃən, -dɪ-] n : indigestión f — **indigestible** [ˌɪndarˈdʒestəbəl, -dɪ-] adj : indigesto

indignation [ˌɪndɪgˈneɪʃən] n : indignación f — **indignant** [ɪnˈdɪgnənt] adj : indignado — **indignity** [ɪnˈdɪgnəṭi] n, pl -ties : indignidad f

indigo [ˈɪndɪˌgoʊ] n, pl -gos or -goes : añil m

indirect [ˌɪndəˈrekt, -dar-] adj : indirecto

indiscreet [ˌɪndɪˈskriːt] adj : indiscreto — **indiscretion** [ˌɪndɪˈskreʃən] n : indiscreción f

indiscriminate [ˌɪndɪˈskrɪmənət] adj : indiscriminado

indispensable [ˌɪndɪˈspentsəbəl] adj : indispensable, imprescindible

indisputable [ˌɪndɪˈspjuːtəbəl, ɪnˈdɪspjuːtə-] adj : indiscutible

indistinct [ˌɪndɪˈstɪŋkt] adj : indistinto

individual [ˌɪndəˈvɪdʒuəl] adj 1 : individual 2 PARTICULAR : particular — ~ n : individuo m — **Individuality** [ˌɪndəˌvɪdʒuˈæləṭi] n, pl -ties : individualidad *f* — **individually** [,ɪndə'vɪdʒʊəli, -dʒəli] *adv* : individualmente

indoctrinate [ɪn'dɑktrə,neɪt] *vt* **-nated; -nating** : adoctrinar — **indoctrination** [ɪn,dɑktrə'neɪʃən] *n* : adoctrinamiento *m*

indoor ['ɪn'dor] *adj* 1 : (de) interior 2 ~ **plant** : planta *f* de interior 3 ~ **pool** : piscina *f* cubierta 4 ~ **sports** : deportes *mpl* bajo techo — **indoors** ['ɪn'dorz] *adv* : adentro, dentro

induce [ɪn'duːs, -'djuːs] *vt* **-duced; -ducing** 1 : inducir 2 CAUSE : provocar — **inducement** [ɪn'duːsmənt, -'djuːs-] *n* : incentivo *m*

indulge [ɪn'dʌldʒ] *v* **-dulged; -dulging** *vt* 1 GRATIFY : satisfacer 2 PAMPER : consentir — *vi* ~ **in** : permitirse — **indulgence** [ɪn'dʌldʒənts] *n* 1 : indulgencia *f* 2 SATISFYING : satisfacción *f* — **indulgent** [ɪn'dʌldʒənt] *adj* : indulgente

industry ['ɪndəstri] *n, pl* **-tries** 1 : industria *f* 2 DILIGENCE : diligencia *f* — **industrial** [ɪn'dʌstriəl] *adj* : industrial — **industrialize** [ɪn'dʌstriə,laɪz] *vt* **-ized; -izing** : industrializar — **industrious** [ɪn'dʌstriəs] *adj* : diligente, trabajador

inebriated [ɪ'niːbri,eɪtəd] *adj* : ebrio, embriagado

inedible [ɪ'nedəbəl] *adj* : no comestible

ineffective [,ɪnɪ'fɛktɪv] *adj* 1 : ineficaz 2 INCOMPETENT : incompetente — **ineffectual** [,ɪnɪ'fɛktʃʊəl] *adj* : inútil, ineficaz

inefficient [,ɪnɪ'fɪʃənt] *adj* 1 : ineficiente 2 INCOMPETENT : incompetente — **inefficiency** [,ɪnɪ'fɪʃəntsi] *n, pl* **-cies** : ineficiencia *f*

ineligible [ɪ'nelədʒəbəl] *adj* : ineligible

inept [ɪ'nept] *adj* 1 : inepto 2 ~ **at** : incapaz para

inequality [,ɪnɪ'kwɑləti] *n, pl* **-ties** : desigualdad *f*

inert [ɪ'nərt] *adj* : inerte — **inertia** [ɪ'nərʃə] *n* : inercia *f*

inescapable [,ɪnɪ'skeɪpəbəl] *adj* : ineludible

inevitable [ɪ'nevətəbəl] *adj* : inevitable — **inevitably** [-bli] *adv* : inevitablemente

inexcusable [,ɪnɪk'skjuːzəbəl] *adj* : inexcusable

inexpensive [,ɪnɪk'spentsɪv] *adj* : barato, económico

inexperienced [,ɪnɪk'spɪriəntst] *adj* : inexperto

inexplicable [,ɪnɪk'splɪkəbəl] *adj* : inexplicable

infallible [ɪn'fæləbəl] *adj* : infalible

infamous ['ɪnfəməs] *adj* : infame

infancy ['ɪnfəntsi] *n, pl* **-cies** : infancia *f* — **infant** ['ɪnfənt] *n* : bebé *m*; niño *m*, -ña *f* — **infantile** ['ɪnfən,taɪl, -təl, -,tiːl] *adj* : infantil

infantry ['ɪnfəntri] *n, pl* **-tries** : infantería *f*

infatuated [ɪn'fætʃʊeɪtəd] *adj* **be ~ with** : estar encaprichado con — **infatuation** [ɪn,fætʃʊ'eɪʃən] *n* : encaprichamiento *m*

infect [ɪn'fɛkt] *vt* : infectar — **infection** [ɪn'fɛkʃən] *n* : infección *f* — **infectious** [ɪn'fɛkʃəs] *adj* : contagioso

infer [ɪn'fər] *vt* **inferred; inferring** : deducir, inferir — **inference** ['ɪnfərənts] *n* : deducción *f*

inferior [ɪn'fɪriər] *adj* : inferior — ~ *n* : inferior *mf* — **inferiority** [ɪn,fɪri'orəti] *n, pl* **-ties** : inferioridad *f*

infernal [ɪn'fərnəl] *adj* : infernal — **inferno** [ɪn'fər,noː] *n, pl* **-nos** : infierno *m*

infertile [ɪn'fərtəl, -,taɪl] *adj* : estéril — **infertility** [,ɪnfər'tɪləti] *n* : esterilidad *f*

infest [ɪn'fest] *vt* : infestar

infidelity [,ɪnfə'deləti, -faɪ-] *n, pl* **-ties** : infidelidad *f*

infiltrate [ɪn'fɪl,treɪt, 'ɪnfɪl-] *v* **-trated; -trating** *vt* : infiltrar — *vi* : infiltrarse

infinite ['ɪnfənət] *adj* : infinito

infinitive [ɪn'fɪnətɪv] *n* : infinitivo *m*

infinity [ɪn'fɪnəti] *n, pl* **-ties** 1 : infinito *m* 2 **an ~ of** : una infinidad de

infirm [ɪn'fərm] *adj* : enfermizo, endeble — **infirmary** [ɪn'fərməri] *n, pl* **-ries** : enfermería *f* — **infirmity** [ɪn'fərməti] *n, pl* **-ties** 1 FRAILTY : endeblez *f* 2 AILMENT : enfermedad *f*

inflame [ɪn'fleɪm] *vt* **-flamed; -flaming** : inflamar — **inflammable** [ɪn'flæməbəl] *adj* : inflamable — **inflammation** [,ɪnflə'meɪʃən] *n* : inflamación *f* — **inflammatory** [ɪn'flæmə,tori] *adj* : inflamatorio

inflate [ɪn'fleɪt] *vt* **-flated; -flating** : inflar — **inflation** [ɪn'fleɪʃən] *n* : inflación *f* — **inflationary** [ɪn'fleɪʃə,neri] *adj* : inflacionario, inflacionista

inflexible [ɪn'fleksəbəl] *adj* : inflexible

inflict [ɪn'flɪkt] *vt* : infligir

influence ['ɪn,fluːənts, ɪn'fluːənts] *n* 1 : influencia *f* 2 **under the ~** : embriagado — ~ *vt* **-enced; -encing** : influir en, influenciar — **influential** [,ɪnflu'entʃəl] *adj* : influyente

influenza [,ɪnflu'enzə] *n* : gripe *f*, influenza *f*

influx ['ɪn,flʌks] *n* : afluencia *f*

inform [ɪn'form] *vt* 1 : informar 2 **keep me ~ed** : manténme al corriente — *vi* ~ **on** : delatar, denunciar

informal [ɪnˈforməl] *adj* 1 : informal 2 : familiar (dícese del lenguaje) — **informality** [ˌɪnforˈmæləṭi, -fər-] *n, pl* **-ties** : falta *f* de ceremonia — **informally** [ɪnˈforməli] *adv* : de manera informal

information [ˌɪnfərˈmeɪʃən] *n* : información *f* — **informative** [ɪnˈforməṭɪv] *adj* : informativo — **informer** [ɪnˈformər] *n* : informante *mf*

infrared [ˌɪnfrəˈrɛd] *adj* : infrarrojo

infrastructure [ˈɪnfrəˌstrʌktʃər] *n* : infraestructura *f*

infrequent [ɪnˈfriːkwənt] *adj* : infrecuente — **infrequently** [ɪnˈfriːkwəntli] *adv* : raramente

infringe [ɪnˈfrɪndʒ] *v* **-fringed; -fringing** *vt* : infringir — *vi* ~ **on** : violar — **infringement** [ɪnˈfrɪndʒmənt] *n* : violación *f*

infuriate [ɪnˈfjʊriˌeɪt] *vt* **-ated; -ating** : enfurecer, poner furioso — **infuriating** [ɪnˈfjʊriˌeɪṭɪŋ] *adj* : exasperante

infuse [ɪnˈfjuːz] *vt* **-fused; -fusing** : infundir — **infusion** [ɪnˈfjuːʒən] *n* : infusión *f*

ingenious [ɪnˈdʒiːnjəs] *adj* : ingenioso — **ingenuity** [ˌɪndʒəˈnuːəṭi, -ˈnjuː-] *n, pl* **-ities** : ingenio

ingenuous [ɪnˈdʒɛnjuəs] *adj* : ingenuo

ingest [ɪnˈdʒɛst] *vt* : ingerir

ingot [ˈɪŋgət] *n* : lingote *m*

ingrained [ɪnˈgreɪnd] *adj* : arraigado

ingratiate [ɪnˈgreɪʃiˌeɪt] *vt* **-ated; -ating** ~ **oneself with** : congraciarse con

ingratitude [ɪnˈgræṭəˌtuːd, -ˌtjuːd] *n* : ingratitud *f*

ingredient [ɪnˈgriːdiənt] *n* : ingrediente *m*

ingrown [ˈɪnˌgroʊn] *adj* ~ **nail** : uña *f* encarnada

inhabit [ɪnˈhæbət] *vt* : habitar — **inhabitant** [ɪnˈhæbətənt] *n* : habitante *mf*

inhale [ɪnˈheɪl] *v* **-haled; -haling** *vt* : inhalar, aspirar — *vi* : inspirar

inherent [ɪnˈhɪrənt, -ˈher-] *adj* : inherente — **inherently** [ɪnˈhɪrəntli, -ˈher-] *adv* : intrínsecamente

inherit [ɪnˈherət] *vt* : heredar — **inheritance** [ɪnˈherəṭənts] *n* : herencia *f*

inhibit [ɪnˈhɪbət] *vt* IMPEDE : inhibir — **inhibition** [ˌɪnhəˈbɪʃən, ˌɪnə-] *n* : inhibición *f*

inhuman [ɪnˈhjuːmən, -ˈjuː-] *adj* : inhumano — **inhumane** [ˌɪnhjuˈmeɪn, -juˈ-] *adj* : inhumano — **inhumanity** [ˌɪnhjuˈmænəṭi, -juˈ-] *n, pl* **-ties** : inhumanidad *f*

initial [ɪˈnɪʃəl] *adj* : inicial — *n* : inicial *f* — *vt* **-tialed** *or* **-tialled; -tialing** *or* **-tialling** : poner las iniciales a

initiate [ɪˈnɪʃiˌeɪt] *vt* **-ated; -ating** 1 BEGIN : iniciar 2 ~ **s.o. into sth** : iniciar a algn en algo — **initiation** [ɪˌnɪʃiˈeɪʃən] *n* : iniciación *f* — **initiative** [ɪˈnɪʃəṭɪv] *n* : iniciativa *f*

inject [ɪnˈdʒɛkt] *vt* : inyectar — **injection** [ɪnˈdʒɛkʃən] *n* : inyección *f*

injure [ˈɪndʒər] *vt* **-jured; -juring** 1 : herir 2 ~ **oneself** : hacerse daño — **injurious** [ɪnˈdʒʊriəs] *adj* : perjudicial — **injury** [ˈɪndʒəri] *n, pl* **-ries** 1 : herida *f* 2 HARM : perjuicio *m*

injustice [ɪnˈdʒʌstəs] *n* : injusticia *f*

ink [ˈɪŋk] *n* : tinta *f* — **inkwell** [ˈɪŋkˌwel] *n* : tintero *m*

inland [ˈɪnˌlænd, -lənd] *adj* : interior — ~ *adv* : hacia el interior, tierra adentro

in-laws [ˈɪnˌloz] *npl* : suegros *mpl*

inlet [ˈɪnˌlet, -lət] *n* : ensenada *f*, cala *f*

inmate [ˈɪnˌmeɪt] *n* 1 PATIENT : paciente *mf* 2 PRISONER : preso *m*, -sa *f*

inn [ˈɪn] *n* : posada *f*, hostería *f*

innards [ˈɪnərdz] *npl* : entrañas *fpl*, tripas *fpl fam*

innate [ɪˈneɪt] *adj* : innato

inner [ˈɪnər] *adj* : interior, interno — **innermost** [ˈɪnərˌmoʊst] *adj* : más íntimo, más profundo

inning [ˈɪnɪŋ] *n* : entrada *f*

innocent [ˈɪnəsənt] *adj* : inocente — ~ *n* : inocente *mf* — **innocence** [ˈɪnəsənts] *n* : inocencia *f*

innocuous [ɪˈnɑkjəwəs] *adj* : inocuo

innovate [ˈɪnəˌveɪt] *vi* **-vated; -vating** : innovar — **innovation** [ˌɪnəˈveɪʃən] *n* : innovación *f* — **innovative** [ˈɪnəˌveɪṭɪv] *adj* : innovador — **innovator** [ˈɪnəˌveɪṭər] *n* : innovador *m*, -dora *f*

innuendo [ˌɪnjuˈendo] *n, pl* **-dos** *or* **-does** : insinuación *f*, indirecta *f*

innumerable [ɪˈnuːmərəbəl, -ˈnjuː-] *adj* : innumerable

inoculate [ɪˈnɑkjəˌleɪt] *vt* **-lated; -lating** : inocular — **inoculation** [ɪˌnɑkjəˈleɪʃən] *n* : inoculación *f*

inoffensive [ˌɪnəˈfensɪv] *adj* : inofensivo

inpatient [ˈɪnˌpeɪʃənt] *n* : paciente *mf* hospitalizado

input [ˈɪnˌpʊt] *n* 1 : contribución *f* 2 : entrada *f* (de datos) — ~ *vt* **-putted** *or* **-put; -putting** : entrar (datos, etc.)

inquire [ɪnˈkwaɪr] *v* **-quired; -quiring** *vt* : preguntar — *vi* 1 ~ **about** : informarse sobre 2 ~ **into** : investigar — **inquiry** [ˈɪnˌkwaɪri, ɪnˈkwaɪri; ˈɪnkwəri, ˈɪŋ-] *n, pl* **-ries** 1 QUESTION : pregunta *f* 2 INVESTIGATION : investigación *f* — **inquisition** [ˌɪnkwəˈzɪʃən, ˌɪŋ-] *n* : in-

quisición f — **inquisitive** [ɪnˈkwɪzət̬ɪv]
adj : curioso

insane [ɪnˈseɪn] *adj* : loco — **insanity**
[ɪnˈsænət̬i] *n, pl* **-ties** : locura f

insatiable [ɪnˈseɪʃəbəl] *adj* : insaciable

inscribe [ɪnˈskraɪb] *vt* **-scribed;**
-scribing : inscribir — **inscription**
[ɪnˈskrɪpʃən] *n* : inscripción f

inscrutable [ɪnˈskruːt̬əbəl] *adj* : inescru-
table

insect [ˈɪnˌsɛkt] *n* : insecto m — **insecti-**
cide [ɪnˈsɛkt̬əˌsaɪd] *n* : insecticida m

insecure [ˌɪnsɪˈkjʊr] *adj* : inseguro, poco
seguro — **insecurity** [ˌɪnsɪˈkjʊrət̬i] *n, pl*
-ties : inseguridad f

insensitive [ɪnˈsɛnsət̬ɪv] *adj* : insensible — **insensitivity** [ˌɪnˌsɛnsəˈt̬ɪvət̬i] *n,*
pl **-ties** : insensibilidad f

inseparable [ɪnˈsɛpərəbəl] *adj* : inseparable

insert [ɪnˈsərt] *vt* : insertar (texto), introducir (una moneda, etc.)

inside [ɪnˈsaɪd, ˈɪnˌsaɪd] *n* **1** : interior m **2**
~ **out** : al revés — *adv* : dentro, aden-
tro — ~ *adj* : interior — ~ *prep* **1** *or*
~ **of** : dentro de **2** ~ **an hour** : en
menos de una hora

insidious [ɪnˈsɪdiəs] *adj* : insidioso

insight [ˈɪnˌsaɪt] *n* : perspicacia f

insignia [ɪnˈsɪɡniə] *or* **insigne** [-niː] *n,*
pl **-nia** *or* **-nias** : insignia f, enseña f

insignificant [ˌɪnsɪɡˈnɪfɪkənt] *adj* : insignificante

insincere [ˌɪnsɪnˈsɪr] *adj* : insincero

insinuate [ɪnˈsɪnjuˌeɪt] *vt* **-ated; -ating**
: insinuar — **insinuation** [ɪnˌsɪnju-
ˈeɪʃən] *n* : insinuación f

insipid [ɪnˈsɪpəd] *adj* : insípido

insist [ɪnˈsɪst] *v* : insistir — **insistent**
[ɪnˈsɪstənt] *adj* : insistente

insofar as [ˌɪnsəˈfɑːræz] *conj* : en la medida en que

insole [ˈɪnˌsoʊl] *n* : plantilla f

insolent [ˈɪnsələnt] *adj* : insolente — **in-**
solence [ˈɪnsələnts] *n* : insolencia f

insolvent [ɪnˈsɑːlvənt] *adj* : insolvente

insomnia [ɪnˈsɑːmniə] *n* : insomnio m

inspect [ɪnˈspɛkt] *vt* : inspeccionar, revisar — **inspection** [ɪnˈspɛkʃən] *n* : inspección f — **inspector** [ɪnˈspɛktər] *n*
: inspector m, -tora f

inspire [ɪnˈspaɪr] *vt* **-spired; -spiring**
: inspirar — **inspiration** [ˌɪnspəˈreɪʃən]
n : inspiración f — **inspirational**
[ˌɪnspəˈreɪʃənəl] *adj* : inspirador

instability [ˌɪnstəˈbɪlət̬i] *n, pl* **-ties** : inestabilidad f

install [ɪnˈstɔːl] *vt* **-stalled; -stalling** : instalar — **installation** [ˌɪnstəˈleɪʃən] *n*
: instalación f — **installment** [ɪn-

instolment *n* **1** PAYMENT : plazo m, cuota
f **2** : entrega f (de una publicación o telenovela)

instance [ˈɪnstənts] *n* **1** : ejemplo m **2**
for ~ : por ejemplo **3 in this** ~ : en
este caso

instant [ˈɪnstənt] *n* : instante m — ~
adj **1** IMMEDIATE : inmediato **2** ~ **cof-**
fee : café m instantáneo — **instanta-**
neous [ˌɪnstənˈteɪniəs] *adj* : instantáneo — **instantly** [ˈɪnstəntli] *adv* : al
instante, instantáneamente

instead [ɪnˈstɛd] *adv* **1** : en cambio **2 I**
went ~ : fui en su lugar — **instead**
of *prep* : en vez de, en lugar de

instep [ˈɪnˌstɛp] *n* : empeine m

instigate [ˈɪnstəˌɡeɪt] *vt* **-gated; -gating**
: instigar a — **instigation** [ˌɪnstə-
ˈɡeɪʃən] *n* : instigación f — **instigator**
[ˈɪnstəˌɡeɪt̬ər] *n* : instigador m, -dora f

instill [ɪnˈstɪl] *or Brit* **instil** [ɪnˈstrəmɛntl]
-stilling : inculcar, infundir

instinct [ˈɪnˌstɪŋkt] *n* : instinto m — **in-**
stinctive [ɪnˈstɪŋktɪv] *or* **instinctual**
[ɪnˈstɪŋktʃuəl] *adj* : instintivo

institute [ˈɪnstəˌtut, -ˌtjut] *vt* **-tuted;**
-tuting 1 : instituir **2** INITIATE : iniciar
— ~ *n* : instituto m — **institution**
[ˌɪnstəˈtuːʃən, -ˌtju-] *n* : institución f

instruct [ɪnˈstrʌkt] *vt* **1** : instruir **2** COM-
MAND : mandar — **instruction** [ɪn-
ˈstrʌkʃən] *n* : instrucción f — **instruc-**
tor [ɪnˈstrʌktər] *n* : instructor m, -tora f

instrument [ˈɪnstrəmənt] *n* : instrumento m — **instrumental** [ˌɪnstrəˈmɛntəl]
adj **1** : instrumental **2 be** ~ **in** : jugar
un papel fundamental en

insubordinate [ˌɪnsəˈbɔrdənət] *adj* : insubordinado — **insubordination**
[ˌɪnsəˌbɔrdənˈeɪʃən] *n* : insubordinación
f

insufferable [ɪnˈsʌfərəbəl] *adj* : insoportable

insufficient [ˌɪnsəˈfɪʃənt] *adj* : insuficiente

insular [ˈɪnsələr, -sju-] *adj* **1** : insular **2**
NARROW-MINDED : estrecho de miras

insulate [ˈɪnsəˌleɪt] *vt* **-lated; -lating**
: aislar — **insulation** [ˌɪnsəˈleɪʃən] *n*
: aislamiento m

insulin [ˈɪnsələn] *n* : insulina f

insult [ɪnˈsʌlt] *vt* : insultar — ~ [ˈɪnˌsʌlt]
n : insulto m — **insulting** [ɪnˈsʌltɪŋ] *adj*
: insultante, ofensivo

insure [ɪnˈʃʊr] *vt* **-sured; -suring** : asegurar — **insurance** [ɪnˈʃʊrənts, ˈɪnˌʃʊr-]
n : seguro m

insurmountable [ˌɪnsərˈmaʊntəbəl] *adj*
: insuperable

intact [ɪnˈtækt] *adj* : intacto

intake ['ɪn,teɪk] n : consumo m (de alimentos), entrada f (de aire, etc.)

intangible [ɪn'tændʒəbəl] adj : intangible

integral ['ɪntɪgrəl] adj : integral

integrate ['ɪntə,greɪt] v -grated; -grating vt : integrar — vi : integrarse

integrity [ɪn'tegrəti] n : integridad f

intellect ['ɪntəl,ekt] n : intelecto m — **intellectual** [,ɪntə'lektʃuəl] adj : intelectual — ~ n : intelectual mf — **intelligence** [ɪn'telədʒənts] n : inteligencia f — **intelligent** [ɪn'telədʒənt] adj : inteligente — **intelligible** [ɪn'telədʒəbəl] adj : inteligible

intend [ɪn'tend] vt 1 be ~ed for : ser para 2 ~ to do : pensar hacer, tener la intención de hacer — **intended** [ɪn'tendəd] adj : intencionado, deliberado

intense [ɪn'tents] adj : intenso — **intensely** [ɪn'tentsli] adv : sumamente, profundamente — **intensify** [ɪn'tentsə,faɪ] v -fied; -fying vt : intensificar — vi : intensificarse — **intensity** [ɪn'tentsəti] n, pl -ties : intensidad f — **intensive** [ɪn'tentsɪv] adj : intensivo

intent [ɪn'tent] n : intención f — ~ adj 1 : atento, concentrado 2 ~ on doing : resuelto a hacer — **intention** [ɪn'tentʃən] n : intención f — **intentional** [ɪn'tentʃənəl] adj : intencional, deliberado — **intently** [ɪn'tentli] adv : atentamente, fijamente

interact [,ɪntər'ækt] vi 1 : interactuar 2 ~ with : relacionarse con — **interaction** [,ɪntər'ækʃən] n : interacción f — **interactive** [,ɪntər'æktɪv] adj : interactivo

intercede [,ɪntər'siːd] vi -ceded; -ceding : interceder

intercept [,ɪntər'sept] vt : interceptar

interchange [,ɪntər'tʃeɪndʒ] vt -changed; -changing : intercambiar — ~ ['ɪntər,tʃeɪndʒ] n 1 : intercambio m 2 JUNCTION : enlace m — **interchangeable** [,ɪntər'tʃeɪndʒəbəl] adj : intercambiable

intercourse ['ɪntər,kors] n : relaciones fpl (sexuales)

interest ['ɪntrəst, -tə,rest] n : interés m — ~ vt : interesar — **interested** [-əd] adj : interesado — **interesting** ['ɪntrəstɪŋ, -tə,restɪŋ] adj : interesante

interface ['ɪntər,feɪs] n : interfaz mf (de una computadora)

interfere [,ɪntər'fɪr] vi -fered; -fering 1 ~ in : entrometerse en, interferir en 2 ~ with DISRUPT : afectar (una actividad, etc.) — **interference** [,ɪntər-'fɪrənts] n 1 : interferencia f 2 : intromisión f (en el radio, etc.)

interim ['ɪntərəm] n 1 : interín m 2 in the ~ : mientras tanto — ~ adj : interino, provisional

interior [ɪn'tɪriər] adj : interior — ~ n : interior m

interjection [,ɪntər'dʒekʃən] n : interjección f

interlock [,ɪntər'lɑk] vt : engranar

interloper [,ɪntər'lo:pər] n : intruso m, -sa f

interlude ['ɪntər,luːd] n 1 : intervalo m 2 : interludio m (en música, etc.)

intermediate [,ɪntər'miːdiət] adj : intermedio — **intermediary** [,ɪntər'miːdi,eri] n, pl -aries : intermediario m, -ria f

interminable [ɪn'tərmənəbəl] adj : interminable

intermission [,ɪntər'mɪʃən] n : intervalo m, intermedio m

intermittent [,ɪntər'mɪtənt] adj : intermitente

intern¹ ['ɪn,tərn, ɪn'tərn] vt : confinar

intern² ['ɪn,tərn] vi : hacer las prácticas — ~ n : interno m, -na f

internal [ɪn'tərnəl] adj : interno

international [,ɪntər'næʃənəl] adj : internacional

interpret [ɪn'tərprət] vt : interpretar — **interpretation** [ɪn,tərprə'teɪʃən] n : interpretación f — **interpreter** [ɪn'tərprə-tər] n : intérprete mf

interrogate [ɪn'terə,geɪt] vt -gated; -gating : interrogar — **interrogation** [ɪn,terə'geɪʃən] n QUESTIONING : interrogatorio m — **interrogative** [,ɪntə-'rɑgətɪv] adj : interrogativo

interrupt [,ɪntə'rʌpt] v : interrumpir — **interruption** [,ɪntə'rʌpʃən] n : interrupción f

intersect [,ɪntər'sekt] vt : cruzar (dícese de calles), cortar (dícese de líneas) — vi : cruzarse, cortarse — **intersection** [,ɪntər'sekʃən] n : cruce m, intersección f

intersperse [,ɪntər'spərs] vt -spersed; -spersing : intercalar

interstate [,ɪntər'steɪt] n or ~ highway : carretera f interestatal

intertwine [,ɪntər'twaɪn] vi -twined; -twining : entrelazarse

interval ['ɪntərvəl] n : intervalo m

intervene [,ɪntər'viːn] vi -vened; -vening 1 : intervenir 2 ELAPSE : transcurrir, pasar — **intervention** [,ɪntər'ven-tʃən] n : intervención f

interview ['ɪntər,vjuː] n : entrevista f — ~ vt : entrevistar — **interviewer** ['ɪntər,vjuːər] n : entrevistador m, -dora f

intestine [ɪn'tɛstən] *n* : intestino *m* — **intestinal** [ɪn'tɛstənəl] *adj* : intestinal
intimate[1] ['ɪntə,meɪt] *vt* -**mated; -mating** : insinuar, dar a entender
intimate[2] ['ɪntəmət] *adj* : íntimo — **intimacy** ['ɪntəməsi] *n, pl* -**cies** : intimidad *f*
intimidate [ɪn'tɪmə,deɪt] *vt* -**dated; -dating** : intimidar — **intimidation** [ɪn,tɪmə'deɪʃən] *n* : intimidación *f*
into ['ɪn,tu:] *prep* **1** : en, a **2 bump** ~ : darse contra **3** (*used in mathematics*) **3** ~ **12** : 12 dividido por 3
intolerable [ɪn'tɑlərəbəl] *adj* : intolerable — **intolerance** [ɪn'tɑlərənts] *n* : intolerancia *f* — **intolerant** [ɪn'tɑlərənt] *adj* : intolerante
intoxicate [ɪn'tɑksə,keɪt] *vt* -**cated; -cating** : embriagar — **intoxicated** [ɪn'tɑksə,keɪtəd] *adj* **1** : embriagado **2** ~ **with** : ebrio de
intransitive [ɪn'træntsəʔɪv, -'trænzə-] *adj* : intransitivo
intravenous [,ɪntrə'vi:məs] *adj* : intravenoso
intrepid [ɪn'trɛpəd] *adj* : intrépido
intricate ['ɪntrɪkət] *adj* : complicado, intrincado — **intricacy** ['ɪntrɪkəsi] *n, pl* -**cies** : complejidad *f*
intrigue ['ɪn,tri:g, ɪn'tri:g] *n* : intriga *f* — ~ [ɪn'tri:g] *v* -**trigued; -triguing** : intrigar — **intriguing** [ɪn'tri:gɪŋli] *adj* : intrigante
intrinsic [ɪn'trɪnzɪk, -'trɪntsɪk] *adj* : intrínseco
introduce [,ɪntrə'du:s, -'dju:s] *vt* -**duced; -ducing 1** : introducir **2** : presentar (a una persona) — **introduction** [,ɪntrə'dʌkʃən] *n* **1** : introducción *f* **2** : presentación *f* (de una persona) — **introductory** [,ɪntrə'dʌktəri] *adj* : introductorio
introvert ['ɪntrə,vərt] *n* : introvertido *m*, -da *f* — **introverted** ['ɪntrə,vərtəd] *adj* : introvertido
intrude [ɪn'tru:d] *vi* -**truded; -truding 1** : entrometerse **2** ~ **on s.o.** : molestar a algn — **intruder** [ɪn'tru:dər] *n* : intruso *m*, -sa *f* — **intrusion** [ɪn'tru:ʒən] *n* : intrusión *f* — **intrusive** [ɪn'tru:sɪv] *adj* : intruso
intuition [,ɪntu'ɪʃən, -tju-] *n* : intuición *f* — **intuitive** [ɪn'tu:əʔɪv, -'tju:-] *adj* : intuitivo
inundate ['ɪnən,deɪt] *vt* -**dated; -dating** : inundar
invade [ɪn'veɪd] *vt* -**vaded; -vading** : invadir
invalid[1] [ɪn'væləd] *adj* : inválido
invalid[2] ['ɪnvələd] *n* : inválido *m*, -da *f*

invaluable [ɪn'væljəbəl, -'vælju-] *adj* : inestimable, invalorable *Lat*
invariable [ɪn'væriəbəl] *adj* : invariable
invasion [ɪn'veɪʒən] *n* : invasión *f*
invent [ɪn'vɛnt] *vt* : inventar — **invention** [ɪn'vɛntʃən] *n* : invención *f* — **inventive** [ɪn'vɛntɪv] *adj* : inventivo — **inventor** [ɪn'vɛntər] *n* : inventor *m*, -tora *f*
inventory ['ɪnvən,tori] *n, pl* -**ries** : inventario *m*
invert [ɪn'vərt] *vt* : invertir
invertebrate [ɪn'vərtəbrət, -,breɪt] *adj* : invertebrado — ~ *n* : invertebrado *m*
invest [ɪn'vɛst] *vt* : invertir
investigate [ɪn'vɛstə,geɪt] *v* -**gated; -gating** : investigar — **investigation** [ɪn,vɛstə'geɪʃən] *n* : investigación *f* — **investigator** [ɪn'vɛstə,geɪtər] *n* : investigador *m*, -dora *f*
investment [ɪn'vɛstmənt] *n* : inversión *f* — **investor** [ɪn'vɛstər] *n* : inversor *m*, -sora *f*
inveterate [ɪn'vɛʔərət] *adj* : inveterado
invigorating [ɪn'vɪgə,reɪʔɪŋ] *adj* : vigorizante
invincible [ɪn'vɪntsəbəl] *adj* : invencible
invisible [ɪn'vɪzəbəl] *adj* : invisible
invitation [,ɪnvə'teɪʃən] *n* : invitación *f* — **invite** [ɪn'vaɪt] *vt* -**vited; -viting 1** : invitar **2** SEEK : buscar (problemas, etc.) — **inviting** [ɪn'vaɪʔɪŋ] *adj* : atrayente
invoice ['ɪn,vɔɪs] *n* : factura *f*
invoke [ɪn'vo:k] *vt* -**voked; -voking** : invocar
involuntary [ɪn'vɑlən,teri] *adj* : involuntario
involve [ɪn'vɑlv] *vt* -**volved; -volving 1** CONCERN : concernir, afectar **2** ENTAIL : suponer — **involved** [ɪn'vɑlvd] *adj* **1** COMPLEX : complicado **2** CONCERNED : afectado — **involvement** [ɪn'vɑlvmənt] *n* : participación *f*
invulnerable [ɪn'vʌlnərəbəl] *adj* : invulnerable
inward ['ɪnwərd] *adj* INNER : interior, interno — ~ *or* **inwards** [-wərdz] *adv* : hacia adentro, hacia el interior
iodine ['aɪə,daɪn, -dən] *n* : yodo *m*, tintura *f* de yodo
ion ['aɪən, 'aɪ,ɑn] *n* : ion *m*
iota [aɪ'oːʔə] *n* : pizca *f*, ápice *m*
IOU [,aɪ,oː'ju:] *n* : pagaré *m*, vale *m*
Iranian [i'reɪniən, -'ræ-, -'rɑ-; aɪ'-] *adj* : iraní
Iraqi [i'rɑki, -'ræk-] *adj* : iraquí
ire ['aɪr] *n* : ira *f* — **irate** [aɪ'reɪt] *adj* : furioso
iris ['aɪrəs] *n, pl* **irises** *or* **irides** ['aɪrə-

ˌdiːz, 'ɪr-] **1** : iris *m* (del ojo) **2** : lirio *m* (planta)

Irish ['aɪrɪʃ] *adj* : irlandés

irksome ['ərksəm] *adj* : irritante, fastidioso

iron ['aɪərn] *n* **1** : hierro *m*, fierro *m* Lat (metal) **2** : plancha *f* (para la ropa) — ~ *v* : planchar

ironic [aɪ'rɑnɪk] *or* **ironical** [-nɪkəl] *adj* : irónico

ironing board *n* : tabla *f* (de planchar)

irony ['aɪrəni] *n, pl* **-nies** : ironía *f*

irrational [ɪ'ræʃənəl] *adj* : irracional

irreconcilable [ɪˌrekən'saɪləbəl] *adj* : irreconciliable

irrefutable [ɪrɪ'fjuːtəbəl, ɪ'refjə-] *adj* : irrefutable

irregular [ɪ'regjələr] *adj* : irregular — **irregularity** [ɪˌregjə'lærəti] *n, pl* **-ties** : irregularidad *f*

irrelevant [ɪ'reləvənt] *adj* : irrelevante

irreparable [ɪ'repərəbəl] *adj* : irreparable

irreplaceable [ˌɪrɪ'pleɪsəbəl] *adj* : irreemplazable

irresistible [ˌɪrɪ'zɪstəbəl] *adj* : irresistible

irresolute [ɪ'rezəˌluːt] *adj* : irresoluto

irrespective of [ˌɪrɪ'spektɪvəv] *prep* : sin tener en cuenta

irresponsible [ˌɪrɪ'spɑntsəbəl] *adj* : irresponsable — **irresponsibility** [ˌɪrɪˌspɑntsəˈbɪləti] *n, pl* **-ties** : irresponsabilidad *f*

irreverent [ɪ'revərənt] *adj* : irreverente

irreversible [ˌɪrɪ'vərsəbəl] *adj* : irreversible, irrevocable

irrigate ['ɪrəˌgeɪt] *vt* **-gated; -gating** : irrigar, regar — **irrigation** [ˌɪrə'geɪʃən] *n* : irrigación *f*, riego *m*

irritate ['ɪrəˌteɪt] *vt* **-tated; -tating** : irritar — **irritable** ['ɪrəṭəbəl] *adj* : irritable — **irritably** ['ɪrəṭəbli] *adv* : con irritación — **irritating** ['ɪrəˌteɪṭɪŋ] *adj* : irritante — **irritation** [ˌɪrə'teɪʃən] *n* : irritación *f*

is → **be**

Islam [ɪs'lɑm, ɪz-, -'læm; 'ɪsˌlɑm, 'ɪz-, -ˌlæm] *n* : el Islam — **Islamic** [ɪs'lɑmɪk, ɪz-, -'læ-] *adj* : islámico

island ['aɪlənd] *n* : isla *f* — **isle** ['aɪl] *n* : isla *f*

isolate ['aɪsəˌleɪt] *vt* **-lated; -lating** : aislar — **isolation** [ˌaɪsə'leɪʃən] *n* : aislamiento *m*

Israeli [ɪz'reɪli] *adj* : israelí

issue ['ɪˌʃuː] *n* **1** MATTER : asunto *m*, cuestión *f* **2** : número *m* (de una revista, etc.) **3 make an ~ of** : insistir demasiado sobre **4 take ~ with** : disentir de — ~ *v* **-sued; -suing** *vi* ~ **from** : surgir de — *vt* **1** : emitir (sellos, etc.), distribuir (provisiones, etc.) **2** PUBLISH : publicar

isthmus ['ɪsməs] *n* : istmo *m*

it ['ɪt] *pron* **1** (*as subject*) : él, ella **2** (*as indirect object*) : le, se **3** (*as direct object*) : lo, la **4** (*as object of a preposition*) : él, ella **5 it's raining** : está lloviendo **6 it's 8 o'clock** : son las ocho **7 it's hot out** : hace calor **8 ~ is necessary** : es necesario **9 who is ~?** : ¿quién es? **10 it's me** : soy yo

Italian [ɪ'tæliən, aɪ-] *adj* : italiano — ~ *n* : italiano *m* (idioma)

italics ['ɪtælɪks, aɪ-] *n* : cursiva *f*

itch ['ɪtʃ] *vi* **1** : picar **2 be ~ing to** : morirse por — ~ *n* : picazón *f* — **itchy** ['ɪtʃi] *adj* **itchier; -est** : que pica

it'd ['ɪṭəd] (*contraction of* **it had** *or* **it would**) → **have, would**

item ['aɪṭəm] *n* **1** : artículo *m* **2** : punto *m* (en una agenda) **3 ~ of clothing** : prenda *f* de vestir **4 news ~** : noticia *f* — **itemize** ['aɪṭəˌmaɪz] *vt* **-ized; -izing** : detallar, enumerar

itinerant [aɪ'tɪnərənt] *adj* : ambulante

itinerary [aɪ'tɪnəˌreri] *n, pl* **-aries** : itinerario *m*

it'll ['ɪṭəl] (*contraction of* **it shall** *or* **it will**) → **shall, will**

its ['ɪts] *adj* : su, sus

it's ['ɪts] (*contraction of* **it is** *or* **it has**) → **be, have**

itself [ɪt'sɛlf] *pron* **1** (*used reflexively*) : se **2** (*used for emphasis*) : (él) mismo, (ella) misma, sí (mismo) **3 by ~** : solo

I've ['aɪv] (*contraction of* **I have**) → **have**

ivory ['aɪvəri] *n, pl* **-ries** : marfil *m*

ivy ['aɪvi] *n, pl* **ivies** : hiedra *f*

J

j ['dʒeɪ] *n*, *pl* **j's** *or* **js** ['dʒeɪz] : j *f*, décima letra del alfabeto inglés

jab ['dʒæb] *vt* **jabbed; jabbing 1** PIERCE : pinchar **2** POKE : golpear (con la punta de algo) — ∼ *n* **1** PRICK : pinchazo *m* **2** POKE : golpe *m* abrupto

jabber ['dʒæbər] *vi* : farfullar

jack ['dʒæk] *n* **1** : gato *m* (mecanismo) **2** : sota *f* (de naipes) — ∼ *vt or* ∼ **up 1** : levantar (con un gato) **2** INCREASE : subir

jackal ['dʒækəl] *n* : chacal *m*

jackass ['dʒæk,æs] *n* : asno *m*, burro *m*

jacket ['dʒækət] *n* **1** : chaqueta *f* **2** : sobrecubierta *f* (de un libro), carátula *f* (de un disco)

jackhammer ['dʒæk,hæmər] *n* : martillo *m* neumático

jackknife ['dʒæk,naɪf] *n* : navaja *f* — ∼ *vi* **-knifed; -knifing** : plegarse (dícese de un camión)

jack-o'-lantern ['dʒækə,læntərn] *n* : linterna *f* hecha de una calabaza

jackpot ['dʒæk,pat] *n* : premio *m* gordo

jaded ['dʒeɪdəd] *adj* **1** TIRED : agotado **2** BORED : hastiado

jagged ['dʒægəd] *adj* : dentado

jail ['dʒeɪl] *n* : cárcel *f* — ∼ *vt* : encarcelar — **jailer** *or* **jailor** ['dʒeɪlər] *n* : carcelero *m*, -ra *f*

jalapeño [,halə'peɪnjo, ,hæ-, -'piːno] *n* : jalapeño *m* Lat

jam¹ ['dʒæm] *v* **jammed; jamming** *vt* **1** CRAM : apiñar, embutir **2** BLOCK : atascar, atorar — *vi* : atascarse, atrancarse — ∼ *n* **1** *or* **traffic** ∼ : embotellamiento *m* (de tráfico) **2** FIX : lío *m*, aprieto *m*

jam² *n* PRESERVES : mermelada *f*

jangle ['dʒæŋgəl] *v* **-gled; -gling** *vi* : hacer un ruido metálico — *vt* : hacer sonar — ∼ *n* : ruido *m* metálico

janitor ['dʒænətər] *n* : portero *m*, -ra *f*; conserje *mf*

January ['dʒænju,ɛri] *n* : enero *m*

Japanese [,dʒæpə'niːz, -'niːs] *adj* : japonés — ∼ *n* : japonés *m* (idioma)

jar¹ ['dʒar] *v* **jarred; jarring** *vi* **1** GRATE : chirriar **2** CLASH : desentonar **3** ∼ **on** IRRITATE : crispar, enervar (a algn) — *vt* JOLT : sacudir — ∼ *n* : sacudida *f*

jar² *n* : tarro *m*

jargon ['dʒargən] *n* : jerga *f*

jaundice ['dʒɔndɪs] *n* : ictericia *f*

jaunt ['dʒɔnt] *n* : excursión *f*

jaunty ['dʒɔnti] *adj* **-tier; -est** : garboso, desenvuelto

jaw ['dʒɔ] *n* : mandíbula *f* (de una persona), quijada *f* (de un animal) — **jawbone** ['dʒɔ,boːn] *n* : mandíbula *f*, quijada *f*

jay ['dʒeɪ] *n* : arrendajo *m*

jazz ['dʒæz] *n* : jazz *m* — ∼ *vt or* ∼ **up** : animar, alegrar — **jazzy** ['dʒæzi] *adj* **jazzier; -est** FLASHY : llamativo

jealous ['dʒɛləs] *adj* : celoso — **jealousy** ['dʒɛləsi] *n* : celos *mpl*, envidia *f*

jeans ['dʒiːnz] *npl* : jeans *mpl*, vaqueros *mpl*

jeer ['dʒɪr] *vt* **1** BOO : abuchear **2** MOCK : mofarse de — *vi* ∼ **at** : mofarse de — ∼ *n* : mofa *f*

jell ['dʒɛl] *vi* : cuajar

jelly ['dʒɛli] *n*, *pl* **-lies** : jalea *f* — **jellyfish** ['dʒɛli,fɪʃ] *n* : medusa *f*

jeopardy ['dʒɛpərdi] *n* : peligro *m*, riesgo *m* — **jeopardize** ['dʒɛpər,daɪz] *vt* **-dized; -dizing** : arriesgar, poner en peligro

jerk ['dʒərk] *n* **1** JOLT : sacudida *f* brusca **2** FOOL : idiota *mf* — ∼ *vt* : sacudir — *vi* JOLT : dar sacudidas

jersey ['dʒərzi] *n*, *pl* **-seys** : jersey *m*

jest ['dʒɛst] *n* : broma *f* — ∼ *vi* : bromear — **jester** ['dʒɛstər] *n* : bufón *m*

Jesus ['dʒiːzəs, -zəz] *n* : Jesús *m*

jet ['dʒɛt] *n* **1** STREAM : chorro *m* **2** *or* ∼ **airplane** : avión *m* a reacción, reactor *m* — **jet-propelled** *adj* : a reacción

jettison ['dʒɛtəsən] *vt* **1** : echar al mar **2** DISCARD : deshacerse de

jetty ['dʒɛti] *n*, *pl* **-ties** : desembarcadero *m*, muelle *m*

jewel ['dʒuːəl] *n* **1** : joya *f* **2** GEM : piedra *f* preciosa — **jeweler** *or* **jeweller** ['dʒuːələr] *n* : joyero *m*, -ra *f* — **jewelry** ['dʒuːəlri] *n* : joyas *fpl*, alhajas *fpl*

Jewish ['dʒuːɪʃ] *adj* : judío

jibe ['dʒaɪb] *vi* **jibed; jibing** AGREE : concordar

jiffy ['dʒɪfi] *n*, *pl* **-fies** : santiamén *m*, segundo *m*

jig ['dʒɪg] *n* : giga *f*

jiggle ['dʒɪgəl] *vt* **-gled; -gling** : sacudir, zarandear — ∼ *n* : sacudida *f*

jigsaw ['dʒɪgˌsɔ] n 1 : sierra f de vaivén 2 or ~ **puzzle** : rompecabezas m

jilt ['dʒɪlt] vt : dejar plantado

jingle ['dʒɪŋgəl] v **-gled; -gling** vi : tintinear — vt : hacer sonar — ~ n TINKLE : tintineo m

jinx ['dʒɪŋks] n CURSE : maldición f

jitters ['dʒɪt̬ərz] npl have the ~ : estar nervioso — **jittery** ['dʒɪt̬əri] adj : nervioso

job ['dʒɑb] n 1 EMPLOYMENT : empleo m, trabajo m 2 TASK : trabajo m

jockey ['dʒɑki] n, pl **-eys** : jockey mf

jog ['dʒɑg] v **jogged; jogging** vt — s.o.'s memory : refrescar la memoria a algn — vi : hacer footing — **jogging** n : footing m

join ['dʒɔɪn] vt 1 UNITE : unir, juntar 2 MEET : reunirse con 3 : hacerse socio de (una organización, etc.) — vi 1 or ~ **together** : unirse 2 : hacerse socio (de una organización, etc.)

joint ['dʒɔɪnt] n 1 : articulación f (en anatomía) 2 JUNCTURE : juntura f, unión f — adj : conjunto — **jointly** ['dʒɔɪntli] adv : conjuntamente

joke ['dʒoːk] n : chiste m, broma f — vi joked; joking : bromear — **joker** ['dʒoːkər] n 1 : bromista mf 2 : comodín m (en los naipes)

jolly ['dʒɑli] adj **-lier; -est** : alegre, jovial

jolt ['dʒoːlt] vt : sacudir — ~ n 1 : sacudida f brusca 2 SHOCK : golpe m (emocional)

jostle ['dʒɑsəl] v **-tled; -tling** vt : empujar, dar empujones — vi : empujarse

jot ['dʒɑt] vt jotted; jotting or ~ down : anotar, apuntar

journal ['dʒərnəl] n 1 DIARY : diario m 2 PERIODICAL : revista f — **journalism** ['dʒərnəlˌɪzəm] n : periodismo m — **journalist** ['dʒərnəlɪst] n : periodista mf

journey ['dʒərni] n, pl **-neys** : viaje m — ~ vi -neyed; -neying : viajar

jovial ['dʒoːviəl] adj : jovial

joy ['dʒɔɪ] n : alegría f — **joyful** ['dʒɔɪfəl] adj : alegre, feliz — **joyous** ['dʒɔɪəs] adj : jubiloso, alegre

jubilant ['dʒuːbələnt] adj : jubiloso — **jubilee** ['dʒuːbəˌliː] n : aniversario m especial

Judaism ['dʒuːdəˌɪzəm, 'dʒuːdi-, 'dʒuːˌdeɪ-] n : judaísmo m

judge ['dʒʌdʒ] vt judged; judging : juzgar — ~ n : juez mf — **judgment** or **judgement** ['dʒʌdʒmənt] n 1 RULING : fallo m, sentencia f 2 VIEW : juicio m

judicial [dʒuˈdɪʃəl] adj : judicial — **judicious** [dʒuˈdɪʃəs] adj : juicioso

jug ['dʒʌg] n : jarra f

juggle ['dʒʌgəl] vi **-gled; -gling** : hacer juegos malabares — **juggler** ['dʒʌgələr] n : malabarista mf

jugular vein ['dʒʌgjʊlər-] n : vena f yugular

juice ['dʒuːs] n : jugo m — **juicy** ['dʒuːsi] adj **juicier; -est** : jugoso

jukebox ['dʒuːkˌbɑks] n : máquina f de discos

July [dʒuˈlaɪ] n : julio m

jumble ['dʒʌmbəl] vt **-bled; -bling** : mezclar — ~ n : revoltijo m

jumbo ['dʒʌmˌboː] adj : gigante

jump ['dʒʌmp] vi 1 LEAP : saltar 2 START : sobresaltarse 3 RISE : subir de un golpe 4 ~ at : no dejar escapar (una oportunidad, etc.) — vt : saltar — ~ n 1 LEAP : salto m 2 INCREASE : aumento m — **jumper** ['dʒʌmpər] n 1 : saltador m, -dora f (en deportes) 2 : jumper m (vestido) — **jumpy** ['dʒʌmpi] adj jumpier; -est : nervioso

junction ['dʒʌŋkʃən] n 1 JOINING : unión f 2 : cruce m (de calles), empalme m (de un ferrocarril) — **juncture** ['dʒʌŋktʃər] n : coyuntura f

June ['dʒuːn] n : junio m

jungle ['dʒʌŋgəl] n : selva f

junior ['dʒuːnjər] adj 1 YOUNGER : más joven 2 SUBORDINATE : subalterno — ~ n 1 : persona f de menor edad 2 SUBORDINATE : subalterno m, -na f 3 : estudiante mf de penúltimo año

junk ['dʒʌŋk] n : trastos mpl (viejos) — ~ vt : echar a la basura

junta ['huntə, 'dʒʌn-, 'hʌn-] n : junta f (militar)

jurisdiction [ˌdʒʊrəsˈdɪkʃən] n : jurisdicción f

jury ['dʒʊri] n, pl **-ries** : jurado m — **juror** ['dʒʊrər] n : jurado mf

just ['dʒʌst] adj : justo — ~ adv 1 BARELY : apenas 2 EXACTLY : exactamente 3 ONLY : sólo, solamente 4 ~ now : ahora mismo 5 she has ~ left : acaba de salir 6 we were ~ leaving : justo íbamos a salir

justice ['dʒʌstɪs] n 1 : justicia f 2 JUDGE : juez mf

justify ['dʒʌstəˌfaɪ] vt **-fied; -fying** : justificar — **justification** [ˌdʒʌstəfəˈkeɪʃən] n : justificación f

jut ['dʒʌt] vi jutted; jutting or ~ out : sobresalir

juvenile ['dʒuːvəˌnaɪl, -vənəl] adj 1 YOUNG : juvenil 2 CHILDISH : infantil — ~ n : menor mf

juxtapose ['dʒʌkstəˌpoːz] vt **-posed; -posing** : yuxtaponer

K

k ['keɪ] *n, pl* **k's** *or* **ks** ['keɪz] : **k** *f*, undécima letra del alfabeto inglés

kaleidoscope [kə'laɪdəˌskop] *n* : calidoscopio *m*

kangaroo [ˌkæŋɡə'ru:] *n, pl* **-roos** : canguro *m*

karat ['kærət] *n* : quilate *m*

karate [kə'rɑti] *n* : karate *m*

keel ['ki:l] *n* : quilla *f* — ~ *vi or* ~ **over** : volcarse (dícese de un barco), desplomarse (dícese de una persona)

keen ['ki:n] *adj* **1** SHARP : afilado **2** PENETRATING : cortante, penetrante **3** ENTHUSIASTIC : entusiasta **4** ~ **eyesight** : visión *f* aguda

keep ['ki:p] *v* **kept** ['kɛpt]; **keeping** *vt* **1** : guardar **2** : cumplir (una promesa), acudir a (una cita) **3** DETAIN : hacer quedar, detener **4** PREVENT : impedir **5** ~ **up** : mantener — *vi* **1** REMAIN : mantenerse **2** LAST : conservarse **3** *or* ~ **on** CONTINUE : no dejar — ~ *n* **1** **earn one's** ~ : ganarse el pan **2 for** ~**s** : para siempre — **keeper** ['ki:pər] *n* : guarda *mf* — **keeping** ['ki:pɪŋ] *n* **1** CARE : cuidado *m* **2 in** ~ **with** : de acuerdo con — **keepsake** ['ki:pˌseɪk] *n* : recuerdo *m*

keg ['kɛg] *n* : barril *m*

kennel ['kɛnəl] *n* : caseta *f* para perros, perrera *f*

kept → **keep**

kerchief ['kərtʃəf, -ˌtʃi:f] *n* : pañuelo *m*

kernel ['kərnəl] *n* **1** : almendra *f* **2** CORE : meollo *m*

kerosene *or* **kerosine** ['kɛrəˌsi:n, ˌkɛrə'-] *n* : queroseno *m*

ketchup ['kɛtʃəp, 'kæ-] *n* : salsa *f* de tomate

kettle ['kɛtəl] *n* : hervidor *m*, tetera *f* (para hervir)

key ['ki:] *n* **1** : llave *f* **2** : tecla *f* (de un piano o una máquina) — ~ *vt* ~ **up** : estar nervioso — ~ *adj* : clave — **keyboard** ['ki:ˌbord] *n* : teclado *m* — **keyhole** ['ki:ˌho:l] *n* : ojo *m* (de la cerradura) — **keynote** ['ki:ˌno:t] *n* : tónica *f* — **key ring** *n* : llavero *m*

khaki ['kæki, 'kɑ-] *adj* : caqui

kick ['kɪk] *vt* **1** : dar una patada a **2** ~ **out** : echar a patadas — *vi* **1** : dar patadas (dícese de una persona), co-

cear (dícese de un animal) **2** RECOIL : dar un culatazo — ~ *n* **1** : patada *f*, coz *f* (de un animal) **2** RECOIL : culatazo *m* **3** PLEASURE, THRILL : placer *m*

kid ['kɪd] *n* **1** GOAT : chivo *m*, -va *f*; cabrito *m* **2** CHILD : niño *m*, -ña *f* — ~ *v* **kidded; kidding** *vi or* ~ **around** : bromear — *vt* TEASE : tomar el pelo a — **kidnap** ['kɪdˌnæp] *vt* **-napped** *or* **-naped** [-ˌnæpt]; **-napping** *or* **-naping** [-ˌnæpɪŋ] : secuestrar, raptar

kidney ['kɪdni] *n, pl* **-neys** : riñón *m*

kidney bean *n* : frijol *m*

kill ['kɪl] *vt* **1** SLAY, DESTROY : acabar con **3** ~ **time** : matar el tiempo — ~ *n* **1** KILLING : matanza *f* **2** PREY : presa *f* — **killer** ['kɪlər] *n* : asesino *m*, -na *f* — **killing** ['kɪlɪŋ] *n* **1** : matanza *f* **2** MURDER : asesinato *m*

kiln ['kɪl, 'kɪln] *n* : horno *m*

kilo ['ki:lo:] *n, pl* **-los** : kilo *m* — **kilogram** ['kɪləˌɡræm, 'ki:-] *n* : kilogramo *m* — **kilometer** [kɪ'lɑmətər, 'kɪləˌmi:-] *n* : kilómetro *m* — **kilowatt** ['kɪləˌwɑt] *n* : kilovatio *m*

kin ['kɪn] *n* : parientes *mpl*

kind ['kaɪnd] *n* : tipo *m*, clase *f* — ~ *adj* : amable

kindergarten ['kɪndərˌɡɑrtən, -dən] *n* : jardín *m* infantil, jardín *m* de niños *Lat*

kindhearted [ˌkaɪnd'hɑrtəd] *adj* : de buen corazón

kindle ['kɪndəl] *vt* **-dled; -dling** **1** : encender (un fuego) **2** AROUSE : despertar

kindly ['kaɪndli] *adj* **-lier; -est** : bondadoso, amable — ~ *adv* **1** : amablemente **2 take** ~ **to** : aceptar de buena gana **3 we** ~ **ask you not smoke** : les rogamos que no fumen — **kindness** ['kaɪndnəs] *n* : bondad *f* — **kind of** *adv* SOMEWHAT : un tanto, algo

kindred ['kɪndrəd] *adj* **1** : emparentado **2** ~ **spirit** : alma *f* gemela

king ['kɪŋ] *n* : rey *m* — **kingdom** ['kɪŋdəm] *n* : reino *m*

kink ['kɪŋk] *n* **1** TWIST : vuelta *f*, curva *f* **2** FLAW : problema *m*

kinship ['kɪnˌʃɪp] *n* : parentesco *m*

kiss ['kɪs] *vt* : besar — *vi* : besarse — ~ *n* : beso *m*

kit ['kɪt] *n* **1** : juego *m*, kit *m* **2 first-aid**

~ : botiquín m 3 tool ~ : caja f de herramientas

kitchen ['kɪtʃən] n : cocina f

kite ['kaɪt] n : cometa f, papalote m Lat

kitten ['kɪtən] n : gatito m, -ta f — **kitty** ['kɪt̬i] n, pl **-ties** FUND : fondo m común

knack ['næk] n : maña f, facilidad f

knapsack ['næp,sæk] n : mochila f

knead ['niːd] vt 1 : amasar, sobar 2 MASSAGE : masajear

knee ['niː] n : rodilla f — **kneecap** ['niː,kæp] n : rótula f

kneel ['niːl] vi **knelt** ['nɛlt] or **kneeled** ['niːld]; **kneeling** : arrodillarse

knew → **know**

knickknack ['nɪk,næk] n : chuchería f

knife ['naɪf] n, pl **knives** ['naɪvz] : cuchillo m — ~ vt **knifed** ['naɪft]; **knifing** : acuchillar

knight ['naɪt] n 1 : caballero m 2 : caballo m (en ajedrez) — **knighthood** ['naɪt,hud] n : título m de Sir

knit ['nɪt] v **knit** or **knitted** ['nɪt̬əd]; **knitting** v : tejer — ~ n : prenda f tejida

knob ['nɑb] n : tirador m, botón m, perilla f Lat

knock ['nɑk] vt 1 : golpear 2 CRITICIZE : criticar 3 ~ **down** : derribar, echar

al suelo — vi 1 : dar un golpe, llamar (a la puerta) 2 COLLIDE : darse, chocar — ~ n : golpe m, llamada f (a la puerta)

knot ['nɑt] n : nudo m — ~ vt **knotted**; **knotting** : anudar — **knotty** ['nɑt̬i] adj **-tier; -est** 1 : nudoso 2 : enredado (dícese de un problema)

know ['noː] v **knew** ['nuː, 'njuː]; **known** ['noːn]; **knowing** vt 1 : saber 2 : conocer (a una persona, un lugar) 3 ~ **how to** : saber — vi : saber — **knowing** ['noːɪŋ] adj : cómplice — **knowingly** ['noːɪŋli] adv 1 : de manera cómplice 2 DELIBERATELY : a sabiendas — **know-it-all** ['noːɪt̬,ɔl] n : sabelotodo mf fam — **knowledge** ['nɑlɪdʒ] n 1 : conocimiento m 2 LEARNING : conocimientos mpl, saber m — **knowledgeable** ['nɑlɪdʒəbəl] adj : informado, entendido

knuckle ['nʌkəl] n : nudillo m

Koran [kə'rɑn, -'ræn] n the Koran : el Corán m

Korean [kə'riːən] adj : coreano m, -na f — ~ n : coreano m (idioma)

kosher ['koːʃər] adj : aprobado por la ley judía

L

l ['ɛl] n, pl **l's** or **ls** ['ɛlz] : l f, duodécima letra del alfabeto inglés

lab ['læb] → **laboratory**

label ['leɪbəl] n 1 TAG : etiqueta f 2 BRAND : marca f — ~ vt **-beled** or **-belled; -beling** or **-belling** : etiquetar

labor ['leɪbər] n 1 : trabajo m 2 WORKERS : mano f de obra 3 in ~ : de parto — ~ vi 1 : trabajar 2 STRUGGLE : avanzar penosamente — vt BELABOR : insistir en (un punto)

laboratory ['læbrə,tori, lə'bɔrə-] n, pl **-ries** : laboratorio m

laborer ['leɪbərər] n : trabajador m, -dora f

laborious [lə'boriəs] adj : laborioso

lace ['leɪs] n 1 : encaje m 2 SHOELACE : cordón m (de zapatos), agujeta f Lat — ~ vt **laced; lacing** 1 TIE : atar 2 be **laced with** : echar licor a (una bebida, etc.)

lacerate ['læsə,reɪt] vt **-ated; -ating** : lacerar

lack ['læk] vt : carecer de, no tener — vi **be lacking** : faltar — ~ n : falta f, carencia f

lackadaisical [,lækə'deɪzɪkəl] adj : apático, indolente

lackluster ['læk,lʌstər] adj : sin brillo, apagado

laconic [lə'kɑnɪk] adj : lacónico

lacquer ['lækər] n : laca f

lacrosse [lə'krɔs] n : lacrosse f

lacy ['leɪsi] adj **lacier; -est** : como de encaje

lad ['læd] n : muchacho m, niño m

ladder ['lædər] n : escalera f

laden ['leɪdən] adj : cargado

ladle ['leɪdəl] n : cucharón m — ~ vt **-dled; -dling** : servir con cucharón

lady ['leɪdi] n, pl **-dies** : señora f, dama f — **ladybug** ['leɪdi,bʌg] n : mariquita f — **ladylike** ['leɪdi,laɪk] adj : elegante, como señora

lag ['læg] n 1 DELAY : retraso m 2 INTERVAL : intervalo m — ~ vi **lagged; lagging** : quedarse atrás, rezagarse

lager ['lɑgər] n : cerveza f rubia

lagoon [lə'guːn] n : laguna f

laid pp → **lay**[1]

lain pp → **lie**[1]

lair ['lær] n : guarida f

lake ['leɪk] *n* : lago *m*

lamb ['læm] *n* : cordero *m*

lame ['leɪm] *adj* **lamer; lamest 1** : cojo, renco **2 a ~ excuse** : una excusa poco convincente

lament [lə'ment] *vt* **1** MOURN : llorar **2** DEPLORE : lamentar — ~ *n* : lamento *m* — **lamentable** ['læməntəbəl, lə-'mentə-] *adj* : lamentable

laminate ['læmə,neɪt] *vt* **-nated; -nating** : laminar

lamp ['læmp] *n* : lámpara *f* — **lamppost** ['læmp,poːst] *n* : farol *m* — **lampshade** ['læmp,ʃeɪd] *n* : pantalla *f*

lance ['lænʧ] *n* : lanza *f* — ~ *vt* **lanced; lancing** : abrir con lanceta (en medicina)

land ['lænd] *n* **1** : tierra *f* **2** COUNTRY : país *m* **3** *or* **plot of ~** : terreno *m* — ~ *vt* **1** : desembarcar (pasajeros de un barco), hacer aterrizar (un avión) **2** CATCH : sacar (un pez) del agua **3** SECURE : conseguir (empleo, etc.) — *vi* **1** : aterrizar (dícese de un avión) **2** FALL : caer — **landing** ['lændɪŋ] *n* **1** : aterrizaje *m* (de aviones) **2** : desembarco *m* (de barcos) **3** : descanso *m* (de una escalera) — **landlady** ['lænd,leɪdi] *n, pl* **-dies** : casera *f* — **landlord** ['lænd,lɔrd] *n* : casero *m* — **landmark** ['lænd,mɑrk] *n* **1** : punto *m* de referencia **2** MONUMENT : monumento *m* histórico — **landowner** ['lænd,oːnər] *n* : hacendado *m*, -da *f*; terrateniente *mf* — **landscape** ['lænd,skeɪp] *n* : paisaje *m* — ~ *vt* **-scaped; -scaping** : ajardinar — **landslide** ['lænd,slaɪd] *n* **1** : desprendimiento *m* de tierras **2** *or* **~ victory** : victoria *f* arrolladora

lane ['leɪn] *n* **1** : carril *m* (de una carretera) **2** PATH, ROAD : camino *m*

language ['læŋgwɪʤ] *n* **1** : idioma *m*, lengua *f* **2** SPEECH : lenguaje *m*

languid ['læŋgwɪd] *adj* : lánguido — **languish** ['læŋgwɪʃ] *vi* : languidecer

lanky ['læŋki] *adj* **lankier; -est** : delgado, larguirucho *fam*

lantern ['læntərn] *n* : linterna *f*

lap ['læp] *n* **1** : regazo *m* (de una persona) **2** : vuelta *f* (en deportes) — ~ *v* **lapped; lapping** *vt or* **~ up** : beber a lengüetadas — *vi* **~ against** : lamer

lapel [lə'pel] *n* : solapa *f*

lapse ['læps] *n* **1** : lapsus *m*, falla *f* (de memoria, etc.) **2** INTERVAL : lapso *m*, intervalo *m* — ~ *vi* **lapsed; lapsing 1** EXPIRE : caducar **2** ELAPSE : transcurrir, pasar **3 ~ into** : caer en

laptop ['læp,tɑp] *adj* : portátil

larceny ['lɑrsəni] *n, pl* **-nies** : robo *m*

lard ['lɑrd] *n* : manteca *f* de cerdo

large ['lɑrʤ] *adj* **larger; largest 1** : grande **2 at ~** : en libertad **3 by and ~** : por lo general — **largely** ['lɑrʤli] *adv* : en gran parte

lark ['lɑrk] *n* **1** : alondra *f* (pájaro) **2 for a ~** : por divertirse

larva ['lɑrvə] *n, pl* **-vae** [-,viː, -,vaɪ] : larva *f*

larynx ['lærɪŋks] *n, pl* **-rynges** [lə'rɪn-dʒiːz] *or* **-ynxes** ['lærɪŋksəz] : laringe *f* — **laryngitis** [,lærən'dʒaɪtəs] *n* : laringitis *f*

lasagna [lə'zɑnjə] *n* : lasaña *f*

laser ['leɪzər] *n* : láser *m*

lash ['læʃ] *vt* **1** WHIP : azotar **2** BIND : amarrar — *vi* **~ out at** : arremeter contra — ~ *n* **1** BLOW : latigazo *m* (con un látigo) **2** EYELASH : pestaña *f*

lass ['læs] *or* **lassie** ['læsi] *n* : muchacha *f*, chica *f*

lasso ['læ,soː, læ'suː] *n, pl* **-sos** *or* **-soes** : lazo *m*

last ['læst] *vi* : durar — ~ *n* **1** : último *m*, -ma *f* **2 at ~** : por fin, finalmente — ~ *adv* **1** : por última vez, en último lugar **2 arrive ~** : llegar el último — ~ *adj* **1** : último **2 ~ year** : el año pasado — **lastly** ['læstli] *adv* : por último, finalmente

latch ['læʧ] *n* : picaporte *m*, pestillo *m*

late ['leɪt] *adj* **later; latest 1** : tarde **2** : avanzado (dícese de la hora) **3** DECEASED : difunto **4** RECENT : reciente — ~ *adv* **later; latest** : tarde — **lately** ['leɪtli] *adv* : recientemente, últimamente — **lateness** ['leɪtnəs] *n* **1** : retraso *m* **2** : lo avanzado (de la hora)

latent ['leɪtənt] *adj* : latente

lateral ['læʈərəl] *adj* : lateral

latest ['leɪtəst] *n* **at the ~** : a más tardar

lathe ['leɪð] *n* : torno *m*

lather ['læðər] *n* : espuma *f* — ~ *vt* : enjabonar — *vi* : hacer espuma

Latin-American [,lætənə'merɪkən] *adj* : latinoamericano

latitude ['lætə,tuːd, -,tjuːd] *n* : latitud *f*

latter ['læʈər] *adj* **1** : último **2** SECOND : segundo — ~ *pron* **the ~** : éste, ésta, éstos *pl*, éstas *pl*

lattice ['lætəs] *n* : enrejado *m*

laugh ['læf] *vi* : reír(se) — ~ *n* : risa *f* — **laughable** ['læfəbəl] *adj* : risible, ridículo — **laughter** ['læftər] *n* : risa *f*, risas *fpl*

launch ['lɔnʧ] *vt* : lanzar — ~ *n* : lanzamiento *m*

launder ['lɔndər] *vt* **1** : lavar y planchar (ropa) **2** : blanquear, lavar (dinero) — **laundry** ['lɔndri] *n, pl* **-dries 1** : ropa *f* sucia **2** : lavandería *f* (servicio) **3 do the ~** : lavar la ropa

lava ['lɑvə, 'læ-] *n* : lava *f*

lavatory ['lævə,tori] *n, pl* **-ries** BATH-ROOM : baño *m*, cuarto *m* de baño

lavender ['lævəndər] *n* : lavanda *f*

lavish ['lævɪʃ] *adj* **1** EXTRAVAGANT : pródigo **2** ABUNDANT : abundante **3** LUXURIOUS : lujoso — **~** *vt* : prodigar

law ['lɔ] *n* **1** : ley *f* **2** : derecho *m* (profesión, etc.) **3 practice ~** : ejercer la abogacía — **lawful** ['lɔfəl] *adj* : legal, legítimo

lawn ['lɔn] *n* : césped *m* — **lawn mower** *n* : cortadora *f* de césped

lawsuit ['lɔ,su:t] *n* : pleito *m*

lawyer ['lɔɪər, 'lɔjər] *n* : abogado *m*, -da *f*

lax ['læks] *adj* : poco estricto, relajado

laxative ['læksətɪv] *n* : laxante *m*

lay¹ ['leɪ] *vt* **laid** ['leɪd]; **laying 1** PLACE, PUT : poner, colocar **2 ~ eggs** : poner huevos **3 ~ off** : despedir (a un empleado) **4 ~ out** PRESENT : presentar, exponer **5 ~ out** DESIGN : diseñar (el trazado de)

lay² *pp* → **lie¹**

lay³ *adj* **1** SECULAR : laico **2** NONPROFESSIONAL : lego, profano

layer ['leɪər] *n* : capa *f*

layman ['leɪmən] *n, pl* **-men** : lego *m*, laico *m* (en religión)

layout ['leɪ,aʊt] *n* ARRANGEMENT : disposición *f*

lazy ['leɪzi] *adj* **-zier; -est** : perezoso — **laziness** ['leɪzinəs] *n* : pereza *f*

lead¹ ['li:d] *vt* **led** ['led]; **leading 1** GUIDE : conducir **2** DIRECT : dirigir **3** HEAD : encabezar, ir al frente de — *vi* : llevar, conducir (a algo) — **~** *n* **1** : delantera *f* **2 follow s.o.'s ~** : seguir el ejemplo de algn

lead² ['led] *n* **1** : plomo *m* (metal) **2** GRAPHITE : mina *f* — **leaden** ['ledən] *adj* **1** : de plomo **2** HEAVY : pesado

leader ['li:dər] *n* : jefe *m*, -fa *f* — **leadership** ['li:dər,ʃɪp] *n* : mando *m*, dirección *f*

leaf ['li:f] *n, pl* **leaves** ['li:vz] **1** : hoja *f* **2 turn over a new ~** : hacer borrón y cuenta nueva — *vi* **~ through** : hojear (un libro, etc.) — **leaflet** ['li:flət] *n* : folleto *m*

league ['li:g] *n* **1** : liga *f* **2 be in ~ with** : estar confabulado con

leak ['li:k] *vt* **1** : dejar escapar (un líquido o un gas) **2** : filtrar (información) — *vi* **1** : gotear, escaparse (dícese de un líquido o un gas) **2** : filtrarse (dícese de información) — **~** *n* **1** : agujero *m* (de un cubo, etc.), gotera *f*

(de un techo) **2** : fuga *f*, escape *m* (de un líquido o un gas) **3** : filtración *f* (de información) — **leaky** ['li:ki] *adj* **leakier; -est** : que hace agua

lean¹ ['li:n] *v* **leaned** *or Brit* **leant** ['lent]; **leaning** *vi* **1** BEND : inclinarse **2 ~ against** : apoyarse contra — *vt* : apoyar

lean² *adj* **1** THIN : delgado **2** : sin grasa (dícese de la carne)

leaning ['li:nɪŋ] *n* : inclinación *f*

leanness ['li:nnəs] *n* : delgadez *f* (de una persona), lo magro (de la carne)

leap ['li:p] *vi* **leapt** *or* **leaped** ['li:pt, 'lept]; **leaping** : saltar, brincar — **~** *n* : salto *m*, brinco *m* — **leap year** *n* : año *m* bisiesto

learn ['lərn] *v* **learned** ['lərnd, 'lərnt]; **learning** : aprender — **learned** ['lərnəd] *adj* : sabio, erudito — **learner** ['lərnər] *n* : principiante *mf*, estudiante *mf* — **learning** ['lərnɪŋ] *n* : erudición *f*, saber *m*

lease ['li:s] *n* : contrato *m* de arrendamiento — **~** *vt* **leased; leasing** : arrendar

leash ['li:ʃ] *n* : correa *f*

least ['li:st] *adj* **1** : menor **2** SLIGHTEST : más mínimo — **~ 1 at ~** : por lo menos **2 the ~** : lo menos **3 to say the ~** : por no decir más — **~** *adv* : menos

leather ['leðər] *n* : cuero *m*

leave ['li:v] *v* **left** ['left]; **leaving** *vt* **1** : dejar **2** : salir(se) de (un lugar) **3 ~ out** : omitir — *vi* DEPART : irse — **~** *n* **1** *or* **~ of absence** : permiso *m*, licencia *f* **2 take one's ~** : despedirse

leaves → **leaf**

lecture ['lektʃər] *n* **1** TALK : conferencia *f* **2** REPRIMAND : sermón *m*, reprimenda *f* — *v* **~ -tured; -turing** *vt* : sermonear — *vi* : dar clase, dar una conferencia

led *pp* → **lead¹**

ledge ['ledʒ] *n* : antepecho *m* (de una ventana), saliente *m* (de una montaña)

leech ['li:tʃ] *n* : sanguijuela *f*

leek ['li:k] *n* : puerro *m*

leer ['lɪr] *vi* : lanzar una mirada lasciva — **~** *n* : mirada *f* lasciva

leery ['lɪri] *adj* : receloso

leeway ['li:,weɪ] *n* : libertad *f* de acción, margen *m*

left¹ → **leave**

left² ['left] *adj* : izquierdo — **~** *adv* : a la izquierda — **~** *n* : izquierda *f* — **left–handed** ['left'handəd] *adj* : zurdo

leftovers ['left,o:vərz] *npl* : restos *mpl*, sobras *fpl*

leg ['lɛg] *n* **1** : pierna *f* (de una persona, de ropa), pata *f* (de un animal, de muebles) **2** : etapa *f* (de un viaje)

legacy ['lɛgəsi] *n, pl* **-cies** : legado *m*

legal ['li:gəl] *adj* **1** LAWFUL : legítimo, legal **2** JUDICIAL : legal, jurídico — **legality** [li'gæləṭi] *n, pl* **-ties** : legalidad *f* — **legalize** ['li:gə,laɪz] *vt* **-ized; -izing** : legalizar

legend ['lɛdʒənd] *n* : leyenda *f* — **legendary** ['lɛdʒən,deri] *adj* : lengendario

legible ['lɛdʒəbəl] *adj* : legible

legion ['li:dʒən] *n* : legión *f*

legislate ['lɛdʒəs,leɪt] *vi* **-lated; -lating** : legislar — **legislation** [,lɛdʒəs'leɪʃən] *n* : legislación *f* — **legislative** ['lɛdʒəs,leɪṭɪv] *adj* : legislativo, legislador — **legislature** ['lɛdʒəs,leɪtʃər] *n* : asamblea *f* legislativa

legitimate [lɪ'dʒɪṭəmət] *adj* : legítimo — **legitimacy** [lɪ'dʒɪṭəməsi] *n* : legitimidad *f*

leisure ['li:ʒər, 'lɛ-] *n* **1** : ocio *m*, tiempo *m* libre **2 at your ~** : cuando te venga bien — **leisurely** ['li:ʒərli, 'lɛ-] *adj & adv* : lento, sin prisas

lemon ['lɛmən] *n* : limón *m* — **lemonade** ['lɛmə'neɪd] *n* : limonada *f*

lend ['lɛnd] *vt* **lent** ['lɛnt]; **lending** : prestar

length ['lɛŋkθ] *n* **1** : largo *m* **2** DURATION : duración *f* **3 at ~** FINALLY : por fin **4 at ~** : EXTENSIVELY : extensamente **5 go to any ~s** : hacer todo lo posible — **lengthen** ['lɛŋkθən] *vt* **1** : alargar **2** PROLONG : prolongar — *vi* : alargarse — **lengthways** ['lɛŋkθ,weɪz] *or* **lengthwise** ['lɛŋkθ,waɪz] *adv* : a lo largo — **lengthy** ['lɛŋkθi] *adj* **lengthier; -est** : largo

lenient ['li:niənt] *adj* : indulgente — **leniency** ['li:niənsi] *n, pl* **-cies** : indulgencia *f*

lens ['lɛnz] *n* **1** : cristalino *m* (del ojo) **2** : lente *mf* (de un instrumento) **3** → **contact lens**

Lent ['lɛnt] *n* : Cuaresma *f*

lentil ['lɛntəl] *n* : lenteja *f*

leopard ['lɛpərd] *n* : leopardo *m*

leotard ['li:ə,tɑrd] *n* : leotardo *m*, malla *f*

lesbian ['lɛzbiən] *n* : lesbiana *f*

less ['lɛs] *adv* (*comparative of* **little**) : menos — *~ adj* (*comparative of* **little**) : menos — *~ pron* : menos — *~ prep* MINUS : menos — **lessen** ['lɛsən] *v* : disminuir — **lesser** ['lɛsər] *adj* : menor

lesson ['lɛsən] *n* **1** CLASS : clase *f*, curso *m* **2 learn one's ~** : aprender la lección

lest ['lɛst] *conj* **~ we forget** : para que no olvidemos

let ['lɛt] *vt* **let; letting 1** ALLOW : dejar, permitir **2** RENT : alquilar **3 ~'s go!** : ¡vamos!, ¡vámonos! **4 ~ down** DISAPPOINT : fallar **5 ~ in** : dejar entrar **6 ~ off** FORGIVE : perdonar **7 ~ up** ABATE : amainar, disminuir

letdown ['lɛt,daʊn] *n* : chasco *m*, decepción *f*

lethal ['li:θəl] *adj* : letal

lethargic [lɪ'θɑrdʒɪk] *adj* : letárgico

let's ['lɛts] (*contraction of* **let us**) → **let**

letter ['lɛṭər] *n* **1** : carta *f* **2** : letra *f* (del alfabeto)

lettuce ['lɛṭəs] *n* : lechuga *f*

letup ['lɛtəp] *n* : pausa *f*, descanso *m*

leukemia [lu:'ki:miə] *n* : leucemia *f*

level ['lɛvəl] *n* **1** : nivel *m* **2 be on the ~** : ser honrado — *~ vt* **-eled** *or* **-elled; -eling** *or* **-elling 1** : nivelar **2** AIM : apuntar **3** RAZE : arrasar — *~ adj* **1** FLAT : llano, plano **2** : nivel (de altura) — **levelheaded** ['lɛvəl'hɛdəd] *adj* : sensato, equilibrado

lever ['lɛvər, 'li:-] *n* : palanca *f* — **leverage** ['lɛvərɪdʒ, 'li:-] *n* **1** : apalancamiento *m* (en física) **2** INFLUENCE : influencia *f*

levity ['lɛvəṭi] *n* : ligereza *f*

levy ['lɛvi] *n, pl* **levies** : impuesto *m* — *~ vt* **levied; levying** : imponer, exigir (un impuesto)

lewd ['lu:d] *adj* : lascivo

lexicon ['lɛksɪ,kɑn] *n, pl* **-ica** [-kə] *or* **-icons** : léxico *m*, lexicón *m*

liable ['laɪəbəl] *adj* **1** : responsable **2** LIKELY : probable **3** SUSCEPTIBLE : propenso — **liability** [,laɪə'bɪləṭi] *n, pl* **-ties 1** RESPONSIBILITY : responsabilidad *f* **2** DRAWBACK : desventaja *f* **3 liabilities** *npl* DEBTS : deudas *fpl*, pasivo *m*

liaison ['li:ə,zɑn, li'eɪ-] *n* **1** : enlace *m* **2** AFFAIR : amorío *m*

liar ['laɪər] *n* : mentiroso *m*, -sa *f*

libel ['laɪbəl] *n* : libelo *m*, difamación *f* — *~ vt* **-beled** *or* **-belled; -beling** *or* **-belling** : difamar

liberal ['lɪbrəl, 'lɪbərəl] *adj* : liberal — *~ n* : liberal *mf*

liberate ['lɪbə,reɪt] *vt* **-ated; -ating** : liberar — **liberation** [,lɪbə'reɪʃən] *n* : liberación *f*

liberty ['lɪbərṭi] *n, pl* **-ties** : libertad *f*

library ['laɪ,breri] *n, pl* **-braries** : biblioteca *f* — **librarian** [laɪ'breriən] *n* : bibliotecario *m*, -ria *f*

lice → **louse**

license *or* **licence** ['laɪsənts] *n* **1** PERMIT

: licencia f 2 FREEDOM : libertad f 3 AUTHORIZATION : permiso m — ~ vt **licensed; licensing** : autorizar

lick ['lɪk] vt 1 : lamer 2 DEFEAT : dar una paliza a fam — ~ n : lamida f

licorice ['lɪkərɪʃ, -rəs] n : regaliz m

lid ['lɪd] n 1 : tapa f 2 EYELID : párpado m

lie[1] ['laɪ] vi **lay** ['leɪ]; **lain** ['leɪn]; **lying** ['laɪŋ] **1** or ~ **down** : acostarse, echarse **2** BE : estar, encontrarse

lie[2] vi **lied; lying** ['laɪŋ] : mentir — ~ n : mentira f

lieutenant [luˈtɛnənt] n : teniente mf

life ['laɪf] n, pl **lives** ['laɪvz] : vida f — **lifeboat** ['laɪf,boːt] n : bote m salvavidas — **lifeguard** ['laɪf,ɡɑrd] n : socorrista mf — **lifeless** ['laɪfləs] adj : sin vida — **lifelike** ['laɪf,laɪk] adj : natural, realista — **lifelong** ['laɪf,lɒŋ] adj : de toda la vida — **life preserver** n : salvavidas m — **lifestyle** ['laɪf,staɪl] n : estilo m de vida — **lifetime** ['laɪf,taɪm] n : vida f

lift ['lɪft] vt 1 RAISE : levantar 2 STEAL : robar — vi 1 CLEAR UP : despejarse 2 or ~ **off** : despegar (dícese de un avión, etc.) — ~ n 1 LIFTING : levantamiento m 2 **give s.o. a ~** : llevar en coche a algn — **liftoff** ['lɪft,ɔf] n : despegue m

light[1] ['laɪt] n 1 : luz f 2 LAMP : lámpara f 3 HEADLIGHT : faro m 4 **do you have a ~?** : ¿tienes fuego? — ~ adj 1 BRIGHT : bien iluminado 2 : claro (dícese de los colores), rubio (dícese del pelo) — ~ v **lit** ['lɪt] or **lighted; lighting** vt 1 : encender (un fuego) 2 ILLUMINATE : iluminar — vi or ~ **up** : iluminarse — **lightbulb** ['laɪt,bʌlb] n : bombilla f, bombillo m Lat — **lighten** ['laɪtən] vt BRIGHTEN : iluminar — **lighter** ['laɪtər] n : encendedor m — **lighthouse** ['laɪt,haʊs] n : faro m — **lighting** ['laɪtɪŋ] n : alumbrado m — **lightning** ['laɪtnɪŋ] n : relámpago m, rayo m — **light-year** ['laɪt,jɪr] n : año m luz

light[2] adj : ligero — **lighten** ['laɪtən] vt : aligerar — **lightly** ['laɪtli] adv 1 : suavemente 2 **let off ~** : tratar con indulgencia — **lightness** ['laɪtnəs] n : ligereza f — **lightweight** ['laɪt,weɪt] adj : ligero

like[1] ['laɪk] v **liked; liking** vt 1 : gustarle (a uno) 2 WANT : querer — vi **if you ~** : si quieres — **likes** npl : preferencias fpl, gustos mpl — **likable** or **likeable** ['laɪkəbəl] adj : simpático

like[2] adj SIMILAR : parecido — ~ prep : como — ~ conj 1 AS : como 2 AS IF : como si — **likelihood** ['laɪkli,hʊd] n : probabilidad f — **likely** ['laɪkli] adj **-lier; -est** : probable — **liken** ['laɪkən] vt : comparar — **likeness** ['laɪknəs] n : semejanza f, parecido m — **likewise** ['laɪk,waɪz] adv 1 : lo mismo 2 ALSO : también

liking ['laɪkɪŋ] n : afición f (por una cosa), simpatía f (por una persona)

lilac ['laɪlək, -læk, -lɑk] n : lila f

lily ['lɪli] n, pl **lilies** : lirio m, azucena f — **lily of the valley** : lirio m de los valles

lima bean ['laɪmə] n : frijol m de media luna

limb ['lɪm] n 1 : miembro m (en anatomía) 2 : rama f (de un árbol)

limber ['lɪmbər] vi or ~ **up** : calentarse, hacer ejercicios preliminares — ~ adj : ágil

limbo ['lɪm,boː] n, pl **-bos** : limbo m

lime ['laɪm] n : lima f, limón m verde Lat

limelight ['laɪm,laɪt] n **be in the ~** : estar en el candelero

limerick ['lɪmərɪk] n : poema m jocoso de cinco versos

limestone ['laɪm,stoːn] n : (piedra f) caliza f

limit ['lɪmət] n : límite m — ~ vt : limitar, restringir — **limitation** [ˌlɪmə-ˈteɪʃən] n : limitación f, restricción f — **limited** ['lɪmətəd] adj : limitado

limousine ['lɪmə,ziːn, ˌlɪmə-'] n : limusina f

limp[1] ['lɪmp] vi : cojear — ~ n : cojera f

limp[2] adj : flojo, fláccido

line ['laɪn] n 1 : línea f 2 ROPE : cuerda f 3 ROW : fila f 4 QUEUE : cola f 5 WRINKLE : arruga f 6 **drop a ~** : mándar unas líneas — ~ v **lined; lining** vt 1 : forrar (un vestido, etc.), cubrir (las paredes, etc.) 2 MARK : rayar, trazar líneas en 3 BORDER : bordear — vi ~ **up** : ponerse en fila, hacer cola

lineage ['lɪniɪdʒ] n : linaje m

linear ['lɪniər] adj : lineal

linen ['lɪnən] n : lino m

liner ['laɪnər] n 1 LINING : forro m 2 SHIP : buque m, transatlántico m

lineup ['laɪn,əp] n 1 or **police ~** : fila f de sospechosos 2 : alineación f (en deportes)

linger ['lɪŋɡər] vi 1 : quedarse, entretenerse 2 PERSIST : persistir

lingerie [ˌlɑndʒəˈreɪ, ˌlænʒəˈriː] n : ropa f íntima femenina, lencería f

lingo ['lɪŋɡoː] n, pl **-goes** JARGON : jerga f

linguistics [lɪŋˈɡwɪstɪks] n : lingüística f — **linguist** ['lɪŋɡwɪst] n : lingüista mf

— **linguistic** [lɪŋ'gwɪstɪk] *adj* : lingüístico

lining ['laɪnɪŋ] *n* : forro *m*

link ['lɪŋk] *n* **1** : eslabón *m* (de una cadena) **2** BOND : lazo *m* **3** CONNECTION : conexión *f* — ~ *vt* : enlazar, conectar — *vi* ~ **up** : unirse, conectar

linoleum [lə'no:liəm] *n* : linóleo *m*

lint ['lɪnt] *n* : pelusa *f*

lion ['laɪən] *n* : león *m* — **lioness** ['laɪənɪs] *n* : leona *f*

lip ['lɪp] *n* **1** : labio *m* **2** EDGE : borde *m* — **lipstick** ['lɪp,stɪk] *n* : lápiz *m* de labios

liqueur [lɪ'kʊr, -'kər, -'kjʊr] *n* : licor *m*

liquid ['lɪkwəd] *adj* : líquido — ~ *n* : líquido *m* — **liquidate** ['lɪkwə,deɪt] *vt* **-dated; -dating** : liquidar — **liquidation** [,lɪkwə'deɪʃən] *n* : liquidación *f*

liquor ['lɪkər] *n* : bebidas *fpl* alcohólicas

lisp ['lɪsp] *vi* : cecear — ~ *n* : ceceo *m*

list[1] ['lɪst] *n* : lista *f* — ~ *vt* **1** ENUMERATE : hacer una lista de, enumerar **2** INCLUDE : incluir (en una lista)

list[2] *vi* : escorar (dícese de un barco)

listen ['lɪsən] *vi* **1** : escuchar **2** ~ **to** HEED : hacer caso de **3** ~ **to reason** : atender a razones — **listener** ['lɪsənər] *n* : oyente *mf*

listless ['lɪstləs] *adj* : apático

lit ['lɪt] *pp* → **light**

litany ['lɪtəni] *n*, *pl* **-nies** : letanía *f*

liter ['liːtər] *n* : litro *m*

literacy ['lɪtərəsi] *n* : alfabetismo *m*

literal ['lɪtərəl] *adj* : literal — **literally** *adv* : literalmente, al pie de la letra

literate ['lɪtərət] *adj* : alfabetizado

literature ['lɪtərə,tʃʊr, -tʃər] *n* : literatura *f* — **literary** ['lɪtəˌreri] *adj* : literario

lithe ['laɪð, 'laɪθ] *adj* : ágil y grácil

litigation [,lɪtə'geɪʃən] *n* : litigio *m*

litre → **liter**

litter ['lɪtər] *n* **1** RUBBISH : basura *f* **2** : camada *f* (de animales) **3** *or* **kitty** ~ : arena *f* higiénica — ~ *vt* : tirar basura en, ensuciar — *vi* : tirar basura

little ['lɪtəl] *adj* **littler** *or* **less** ['lɛs] *or* **lesser** ['lɛsər]; **littlest** *or* **least** ['liːst] **1** SMALL : pequeño **2 a** ~ SOME : un poco de **3 he speaks** ~ **English** : habla poco inglés — ~ *adv* **less** ['lɛs]; **least** ['liːst] : poco — ~ *pron* **1** : poco *m*, -ca *f* **2** ~ **by** ~ : poco a poco

liturgy ['lɪtərdʒi] *n*, *pl* **-gies** : liturgia *f* — **liturgical** [lə'tərdʒɪkəl] *adj* : litúrgico

live ['lɪv] *vi* **lived; living 1** : vivir **2** RESIDE : residir **3** ~ **on** : vivir de — *vt* : vivir, llevar (una vida) — ~ ['laɪv] *adj* **1** : vivo **2** : con corriente (dícese de cables eléctricos) **3** : en vivo, en directo (dícese de programas de televisión, etc.) — **livelihood** ['laɪvli,hʊd] *n* : sustento *m*, medio *m* de vida — **lively** ['laɪvli] *adj* **-lier; -est** : animado, alegre — **liven** ['laɪvən] *vt or* ~ **up** : animar — *vi* : animarse

liver ['lɪvər] *n* : hígado *m*

livestock ['laɪv,stɑk] *n* : ganado *m*

livid ['lɪvəd] *adj* **1** : lívido **2** ENRAGED : furioso

living ['lɪvɪŋ] *adj* : vivo — ~ *n* **make a** ~ : ganarse la vida — **living room** *n* : living *m*, sala *f* (de estar)

lizard ['lɪzərd] *n* : lagarto *m*

llama ['lɑmə, 'jɑ-] *n* : llama *f*

load ['loːd] *n* **1** CARGO : carga *f* **2** BURDEN : carga *f*, peso *m* **3** ~**s of** : un montón de — ~ *vt* : cargar

loaf[1] ['loːf] *n*, *pl* **loaves** ['loːvz] : pan *m*, barra *f* (de pan)

loaf[2] *vi* : holgazanear — **loafer** ['loːfər] *n* **1** : holgazán *m*, -zana *f* **2** : mocasín *m* (zapato)

loan ['loːn] *n* : préstamo *m* — ~ *vt* : prestar

loathe ['loːð] *vt* **loathed; loathing** : odiar — **loathsome** ['loːθsəm, 'loːð-] *adj* : odioso

lobby ['lɑbi] *n*, *pl* **-bies 1** : vestíbulo *m* **2** *or* **political** ~ : grupo *m* de presión, lobby *m* — ~ *v* **-bied; -bying** *vt* : ejercer presión sobre

lobe ['loːb] *n* : lóbulo *m*

lobster ['lɑbstər] *n* : langosta *f*

local ['loːkəl] *adj* : local — ~ *n* **the** ~**s** : los vecinos del lugar — **locale** [loː'kæl] *n* : escenario *m* — **locality** [loː'kæləti] *n*, *pl* **-ties** : localidad *f*

locate ['loː,keɪt, loː'keɪt] *vt* **-cated; -cating 1** SITUATE : situar, ubicar **2** FIND : localizar — **location** [loː'keɪʃən] *n* : situación *f*, lugar *m*

lock[1] ['lɑk] *n* : mechón *m* (de pelo)

lock[2] *n* **1** : cerradura *f* (de una puerta, etc.) **2** : esclusa *f* (de un canal) — ~ *vt* **1** : cerrar (con llave) **2** *or* ~ **up** CONFINE : encerrar — *vi* **1** : cerrarse con llave **2** : bloquearse (dícese de una rueda, etc.) — **locker** ['lɑkər] *n* **1** : armario *m* — **locket** ['lɑkət] *n* : medallón *m* — **locksmith** ['lɑk,smɪθ] *n* : cerrajero *m*, -ra *f*

locomotive [,loːkə'moːtɪv] *n* : locomotora *f*

locust ['loːkəst] *n* : langosta *f*, chapulín *m Lat*

lodge ['lɑdʒ] *v* **lodged; lodging** *vt* **1** HOUSE : hospedar, alojar **2** FILE : presentar — *vi* : hospedarse, alojarse — ~ *n* : pabellón *m* — **lodger** ['lɑdʒər] *n*

: huésped *m*, -peda *f* — **lodging**
['lɑdʒɪŋ] *n* 1 : alojamiento *m* 2 ~s *npl*
: habitaciones *fpl*

loft ['lɔft] *n* 1 : desván *m* (en una casa) 2
HAYLOFT : pajar *m* — **lofty** ['lɔfti] *adj*
loftier; -est 1 : noble, elevado 2
HAUGHTY : altanero

log ['lɔg, 'lɑg] *n* 1 : tronco *m*, leño *m* 2
RECORD : diario *m* — ~ *vi* **logged;
logging** 1 : talar (árboles) 2 RECORD
: registrar, anotar 3 ~ **on** : entrar (en
el sistema) 4 ~ **off** : salir (del sistema) — **logger** ['lɔgər, 'lɑ-] *n*
: leñador *m*, -dora *f*

logic ['lɑdʒɪk] *n* : lógica *f* — **logical**
['lɑdʒɪkəl] *adj* : lógico — **logistics** [lə-
'dʒɪstɪks, lo-] *ns & pl* : logística *f*

logo ['loːgoː] *n, pl* **logos** [-goːz] : logotipo *m*

loin ['lɔɪn] *n* : lomo *m*

loiter ['lɔɪtər] *vi* : vagar, holgazanear

lollipop *or* **lollypop** ['lɑli,pɑp] *n* : pirulí
m, chupete *m* Lat

lone ['loːn] *adj* : solitario — **loneliness**
['loːnlinəs] *n* : soledad *f* — **lonely** ['loːn-
li] *adj* **-lier; -est** : solitario, solo —
loner ['loːnər] *n* : solitario *m*, -ria *f* —
lonesome ['loːnsəm] *adj* : solo, solitario

long¹ ['lɔŋ] *adj* **longer** ['lɔŋgər];
longest ['lɔŋgəst] : largo — ~ *adv* 1
: mucho tiempo 2 **all day** ~ : todo el
día 3 **as** ~ **as** : mientras 4 **no** ~ **er**
: ya no 5 **so** ~! : ¡hasta luego!,
¡adiós! — ~ *n* 1 **before** ~ : dentro
de poco 2 **the** ~ **and the short** : lo
esencial

long² *vi* ~ **for** : anhelar, desear

longevity [lɑn'dʒevəti] *n* : longevidad *f*

longing ['lɔŋɪŋ] *n* : ansia *f*, anhelo *m*

longitude ['lɑndʒə,tuːd, -,tjuːd] *n* : longitud *f*

look ['lʊk] *vi* 1 : mirar 2 SEEM : parecer 3
~ **after** : cuidar (de) 4 ~ **for** EXPECT
: esperar 5 ~ **for** SEEK : buscar 6 ~
into : investigar 7 ~ **out** : tener
cuidado 8 ~ **over** EXAMINE : revisar 9
~ **up to** : respetar — *vt* : mirar — ~
n 1 : mirada *f* 2 APPEARANCE : aspecto
m, aire *m* — **lookout** ['lʊk,aʊt] *n* 1
: puesto *m* de observación 2 WATCH-
MAN : vigía *mf* 3 **be on the** ~ **for**
: estar al acecho de

loom¹ ['luːm] *n* : telar *m*

loom² *vi* 1 APPEAR : aparecer, surgir 2
APPROACH : ser inminente

loop ['luːp] *n* : lazada *f*, lazo *m* — ~ *vt*
: hacer lazadas con — **loophole** ['luːp-
,hoːl] *n* : escapatoria *f*

loose ['luːs] *adj* **looser; -est** 1 MOVABLE

: flojo, suelto 2 SLACK : flojo 3 ROOMY
: holgado 4 APPROXIMATE : libre,
aproximado 5 FREE : suelto 6 IMMORAL
: relajado — **loosely** ['luːsli] *adv* 1 : sin
apretar 2 ROUGHLY : aproximadamente
— **loosen** ['luːsən] *vt* : aflojar

loot ['luːt] *n* — ~ *vt* : saquear,
robar — **looter** ['luːtər] *n* : saqueador
m, -dora *f* — **looting** ['luːtɪŋ] *n* : saqueo
m

lop ['lɑp] *vt* **lopped; lopping** : cortar,
podar

lopsided ['lɑp,saɪdəd] *adj* : torcido,
chueco Lat

lord ['lɔrd] *n* 1 : señor *m*, noble *m* 2 **the
Lord** : el Señor

lore ['lɔr] *n* : saber *m* popular, tradición *f*

lose ['luːz] *v* **lost** ['lɔst]; **losing** ['luːzɪŋ]
vt 1 : perder 2 ~ **one's way** : perder-
se 3 ~ **time** : atrasarse (dícese de un
reloj) — *vi* : perder — **loser** ['luːzər] *n*
: perdedor *m*, -dora *f* — **loss** ['lɔs] *n* 1
: pérdida *f* 2 DEFEAT : derrota *f* 3 **be at
a** ~ **for words** : no encontrar palabras — **lost** ['lɔst] *adj* 1 : perdido 2
get ~ : perderse

lot ['lɑt] *n* 1 FATE : suerte *f* 2 PLOT : solar
m 3 **a** ~ **of** *or* ~**s of** : mucho, un
montón de

lotion ['loːʃən] *n* : loción *f*

lottery ['lɑtəri] *n, pl* **-teries** : lotería *f*

loud ['laʊd] *adj* 1 : alto, fuerte 2 NOISY
: ruidoso 3 FLASHY : llamativo — ~
adv 1 : fuerte 2 **out** ~ : en voz alta —
loudly ['laʊdli] *adv* : en voz alta —
loudspeaker ['laʊd,spiːkər] *n* : altavoz
m

lounge ['laʊndʒ] *vi* **lounged; lounging**
1 : repantigarse 2 *or* ~ **about** : holgazanear — ~ *n* : salón *m*

louse ['laʊs] *n, pl* **lice** ['laɪs] : piojo *m* —
lousy ['laʊzi] *adj* **lousier; -est** 1 : pio-
joso 2 BAD : pésimo, muy malo

love ['lʌv] *n* 1 : amor *m* 2 **fall in** ~ : enamorarse — ~ *v* **loved; loving**
: querer, amar — **lovable** ['lʌvəbəl] *adj*
: adorable, amoroso Lat — **lovely**
['lʌvli] *adj* **-lier; -est** : lindo, precioso
— **lover** ['lʌvər] *n* : amante *mf* — **loving** ['lʌvɪŋ] *adj* : cariñoso

low ['loː] *adj* **lower** ['loːər]; **-est** 1 : bajo
2 SCARCE : escaso 3 DEPRESSED : de-
primido — ~ *adv* 1 : bajo 2 **turn the
lights down** ~ : bajar las luces — ~
n 1 : punto *m* bajo 2 *or* ~ **gear**
: primera velocidad *f* — **lower** ['loːər]
adj : inferior, más bajo — ~ *vt* : bajar
— **lowly** ['loːli] *adj* **-lier; -est** : humilde

loyal ['lɔɪəl] *adj* : leal, fiel — **loyalty**
['lɔɪəlti] *n, pl* **-ties** : lealtad *f*

lozenge ['lɑzəndʒ] *n* : pastilla *f*
lubricate ['lu:brɪˌkeɪt] *vt* -**cated; -cating** : lubricar — **lubricant** ['lu:brɪkənt] *n* : lubricante *m* — **lubrication** [ˌlu:brɪˈkeɪʃən] *n* : lubricación *f*
lucid ['lu:səd] *adj* : lúcido — **lucidity** [luˈsɪdət̬i] *n* : lucidez *f*
luck ['lʌk] *n* **1** : suerte *f* **2 good ~!** : ¡buena suerte! — **luckily** ['lʌkəli] *adv* : afortunadamente — **lucky** ['lʌki] *adj* **luckier; -est 1** : afortunado **2 ~ charm** : amuleto *m* (de la suerte)
lucrative ['lu:krət̬ɪv] *adj* : lucrativo
ludicrous ['lu:dəkrəs] *adj* : ridículo, absurdo
lug ['lʌg] *vt* **lugged; lugging** : arrastrar
luggage ['lʌgɪdʒ] *n* : equipaje *m*
lukewarm ['lu:k'wɔrm] *adj* : tibio
lull ['lʌl] *vt* **1** CALM : calmar **2 ~ to sleep** : adormecer — **~** *n* : período *m* de calma, pausa *f*
lullaby ['lʌləˌbaɪ] *n*, *pl* -**bies** : canción *f* de cuna, nana *f*
lumber ['lʌmbər] *n* : madera *f* — **lumberjack** ['lʌmbərˌdʒæk] *n* : leñador *m*, -dora *f*
luminous ['lu:mənəs] *adj* : luminoso
lump ['lʌmp] *n* **1** CHUNK, PIECE : pedazo *m*, trozo *m* **2** SWELLING : bulto *m* **3** : grumo *m* (en un líquido) — **~** *vt or* **~ together** : juntar, agrupar — **lumpy** ['lʌmpi] *adj* **lumpier; -est** : grumoso (dícese de una salsa), lleno de bultos (dícese de un colchón)
lunacy ['lu:nəsi] *n*, *pl* -**cies** : locura *f*
lunar ['lu:nər] *adj* : lunar
lunatic ['lu:nəˌtɪk] *n* : loco *m*, -ca *f*

lunch ['lʌntʃ] *n* : almuerzo *m*, comida *f* — **~** *vi* : almorzar, comer — **luncheon** ['lʌntʃən] *n* : comida *f*, almuerzo *m*
lung ['lʌŋ] *n* : pulmón *m*
lunge ['lʌndʒ] *vi* **lunged; lunging 1** : lanzarse **2 ~ at** : arremeter contra
lurch[1] ['lərtʃ] *vi* **1** STAGGER : tambalearse **2** : dar bandazos (dícese de un vehículo)
lurch[2] *n* **leave in a ~** : dejar en la estacada
lure ['lʊr] *n* **1** BAIT : señuelo *m* **2** ATTRACTION : atractivo *m* — **~** *vt* **lured; luring** : atraer
lurid ['lʊrəd] *adj* **1** GRUESOME : espeluznante **2** SENSATIONAL : sensacionalista **3** GAUDY : chillón
lurk ['lərk] *vi* : estar al acecho
luscious ['lʌʃəs] *adj* : delicioso, exquisito
lush ['lʌʃ] *adj* : exuberante, suntuoso
lust ['lʌst] *n* **1** : lujuria *f* **2** CRAVING : ansia *f*, anhelo *m* — **~** *vi* **after** : desear (a una persona), codiciar (riquezas, etc.)
luster *or* **lustre** ['lʌstər] *n* : lustre *m*
lusty ['lʌsti] *adj* **lustier; -est** : fuerte, vigoroso
luxurious [ˌlʌgˈʒʊriəs, ˌlʌkˈʃʊr-] *adj* : lujoso — **luxury** ['lʌkʃəri, 'lʌgʒə-] *n*, *pl* -**ries** : lujo *m*
lye ['laɪ] *n* : lejía *f*
lying → lie
lynch ['lɪntʃ] *vt* : linchar
lynx ['lɪŋks] *n* : lince *m*
lyric ['lɪrɪk] *or* **lyrical** ['lɪrɪkəl] *adj* : lírico — **lyrics** *npl* : letra *f* (de una canción)

M

m ['em] *n*, *pl* **m's** *or* **ms** ['emz] : m *f*, decimotercera letra del alfabeto inglés
ma'am ['mæm] → **madam**
macabre [məˈkɑb, -ˈkɑbər, -ˈkɑbrə] *adj* : macabro
macaroni [ˌmækəˈroːni] *n* : macarrones *mpl*
mace ['meɪs] *n* **1** : maza *f* (arma o símbolo) **2** : macis *f* (especia)
machete [məˈʃet̬i] *n* : machete *m*
machine [məˈʃiːn] *n* : máquina *f* — **machinery** [məˈʃiːnəri] *n*, *pl* -**eries 1** : maquinaria *f* **2** WORKS : mecanismo *m* — **machine gun** *n* : ametralladora *f*
mad ['mæd] *adj* **madder; maddest 1** INSANE : loco **2** FOOLISH : insensato **3** ANGRY : furioso

madam ['mædəm] *n*, *pl* **mesdames** [meɪˈdam] : señora *f*
madden ['mædən] *vt* : enfurecer
made → make
madly ['mædli] *adv* : como un loco, locamente — **madman** ['mædˌmæn, -mən] *n*, *pl* -**men** [-mən, -ˌmen] : loco *m* — **madness** ['mædnəs] *n* : locura *f*
Mafia ['mɑfiə] *n* : Mafia *f*
magazine ['mægəˌziːn] *n* **1** PERIODICAL : revista *f* **2** : recámara *f* (de un arma de fuego)
maggot ['mægət] *n* : gusano *m*
magic ['mædʒɪk] *n* : magia *f* — **~** *or* **magical** ['mædʒɪkəl] *adj* : mágico — **magician** [məˈdʒɪʃən] *n* : mago *m*, -ga *f*

magistrate ['mædʒə‚streɪt] *n* : magistrado *m*, -da *f*
magnanimous [mæg'nænəməs] *adj* : magnánimo
magnate ['mæg‚neɪt, -nət] *n* : magnate *mf*
magnet ['mægnət] *n* : imán *m* — **magnetic** [mæg'nɛʈɪk] *adj* : magnético — **magnetism** ['mægnə‚tɪzəm] *n* : magnetismo *m* — **magnetize** ['mægnə‚taɪz] *vt* **-tized; -tizing** : magnetizar
magnificent [mæg'nɪfəsənt] *adj* : magnífico — **magnificence** [mæg'nɪfəsənts] *n* : magnificencia *f*
magnify ['mægnə‚faɪ] *vt* **-fied; -fying 1** ENLARGE : ampliar **2** EXAGGERATE : exagerar — **magnifying glass** *n* : lupa *f*
magnitude ['mægnə‚tuːd, -‚tjuːd] *n* : magnitud *f*
magnolia [mæg'noːljə] *n* : magnolia *f*
mahogany [mə'hagəni] *n*, *pl* **-nies** : caoba *f*
maid ['meɪd] *n* : sirvienta *f*, criada *f*, muchacha *f* — **maiden** ['meɪdən] *adj* FIRST : inaugural — **maiden name** *n* : nombre *m* de soltera
mail ['meɪl] *n* **1** : correo *m* **2** LETTERS : correspondencia *f* — ~ *vt* : enviar por correo — **mailbox** ['meɪl‚baks] *n* : buzón *m* — **mailman** ['meɪl‚mæn, -mən] *n*, *pl* **-men** [-mən, -‚mɛn] : cartero *m*
maim ['meɪm] *vt* : mutilar
main ['meɪn] *n* : tubería *f* principal (de agua o gas), cable *m* principal (de un circuito) — ~ *adj* : principal — **mainframe** ['meɪn‚freɪm] *n* : computadora *f* central — **mainland** ['meɪn‚lænd, -lənd] *n* : continente *m* — **mainly** ['meɪnli] *adv* : principalmente — **mainstay** ['meɪn‚steɪ] *n* : sostén *m* (principal) — **mainstream** ['meɪn‚striːm] *n* : corriente *f* principal — ~ *adj* : dominante, convencional
maintain [meɪn'teɪn] *vt* : mantener — **maintenance** ['meɪntənənts] *n* : mantenimiento *m*
maize ['meɪz] *n* : maíz *m*
majestic [mə'dʒɛstɪk] *adj* : majestuoso — **majesty** ['mædʒəsti] *n*, *pl* **-ties** : majestad *f*
major ['meɪdʒər] *adj* **1** : muy importante, principal **2** : mayor (en música) — ~ *n* **1** : mayor *mf*, comandante *mf* (en las fuerzas armadas) **2** : especialidad *f* (universitaria) — ~ *vi* **-jored; -joring** : especializarse — **majority** [mə'dʒɔrəʈi] *n*, *pl* **-ties** : mayoría *f*
make ['meɪk] *v* **made** ['meɪd]; **making** *vt* **1** : hacer **2** MANUFACTURE : fabricar **3**

CONSTITUTE : constituir **4** PREPARE : preparar **5** RENDER : poner **6** COMPEL : obligar **7** ~ **a decision** : tomar una decisión **8** ~ **a living** : ganar la vida — *vi* **1** ~ **do** : arreglárselas **2** ~ **for** : dirigirse a **3** ~ **good** SUCCEED : tener éxito — ~ *n* BRAND : marca *f* — **make-believe** [‚meɪkbə'liːv] *n* : fantasía *f* — ~ *adj* : imaginario — **make out** *vt* **1** : hacer (un cheque, etc.) **2** DISCERN : distinguir **3** UNDERSTAND : comprender — *vi* **how did you** ~? : ¿qué tal te fue? — **maker** ['meɪkər] *n* MANUFACTURER : fabricante *mf* — **makeshift** ['meɪk‚ʃɪft] *adj* : improvisado — **makeup** ['meɪk‚ʌp] *n* **1** COMPOSITION : composición *f* **2** COSMETICS : maquillaje *m* — **make up** *vt* **1** PREPARE : preparar **2** INVENT : inventar **3** CONSTITUTE : formar — *vi* RECONCILE : hacer las paces
maladjusted [‚mælə'dʒʌstəd] *adj* : inadaptado
malaria [mə'lɛriə] *n* : malaria *f*, paludismo *m*
male ['meɪl] *n* : macho *m* (de animales o plantas), varón *m* (de personas) — ~ *adj* **1** : macho **2** MASCULINE : masculino
malevolent [mə'lɛvələnt] *adj* : malévolo
malfunction [mæl'fʌŋkʃən] *vi* : funcionar mal — ~ *n* : mal funcionamiento *m*
malice ['mælɪs] *n* : mala intención *f*, rencor *m* — **malicious** [mə'lɪʃəs] *adj* : malicioso
malign [mə'laɪn] *adj* : maligno — ~ *vt* : calumniar
malignant [mə'lɪgnənt] *adj* : maligno
mall ['mɔl] *n or* **shopping** ~ : centro *m* comercial
malleable ['mæliəbəl] *adj* : maleable
mallet ['mælət] *n* : mazo *m*
malnutrition [‚mælnu'trɪʃən, -nju-] *n* : desnutrición *f*
malpractice [‚mæl'præktəs] *n* : mala práctica *f*, negligencia *f*
malt ['mɔlt] *n* : malta *f*
mama *or* **mamma** ['mɑmə] *n* : mamá *f*
mammal ['mæməl] *n* : mamífero *m*
mammogram ['mæmə‚græm] *n* : mamografía *f*
mammoth ['mæməθ] *adj* : gigantesco
man ['mæn] *n*, *pl* **men** ['mɛn] : hombre *m* — ~ *vt* **manned; manning** : tripular (un barco o avión), encargarse de (un servicio)
manage ['mænɪdʒ] *v* **-aged; -aging** *vt* **1** HANDLE : manejar **2** DIRECT : administrar, dirigir — *vi* COPE : arreglárselas

— **manageable** ['mænɪdʒəbəl] *adj* : manejable — **management** ['mænɪdʒmənt] *n* : dirección *f* — **manager** ['mænɪdʒər] *n* : director *m*, -tora *f*; gerente *mf* — **managerial** [,mænə'dʒɪriəl] *adj* : directivo

mandarin ['mændərən] *n or* ~ **orange** : mandarina *f*

mandate ['mæn,deɪt] *n* : mandato *m* — **mandatory** ['mændə,tori] *adj* : obligatorio

mane ['meɪn] *n* : crin *f* (de un caballo), melena *f* (de un león)

maneuver [mə'nu:vər, -'nju:-] *n* : maniobra *f* — ~ *v* -**vered; -vering** : maniobrar

mangle ['mæŋgəl] *vt* -**gled; -gling** : destrozar

mango ['mæŋgo:] *n, pl* -**goes** : mango *m*

mangy ['meɪndʒi] *adj* **mangier; -est** : sarnoso

manhandle ['mæn,hændəl] *vi* -**dled; -dling** : maltratar

manhole ['mæn,ho:l] *n* : boca *f* de alcantarilla

manhood ['mæn,hʊd] *n* **1** : madurez *f* (de un hombre) **2** VIRILITY : virilidad *f*

mania ['meɪniə, -njə] *n* : manía *f* — **maniac** ['meɪni,æk] *n* : maníaco *m*, -ca *f*

manicure ['mænə,kjʊr] *n* : manicura *f* — ~ *vt* -**cured; -curing** : hacer la manicura a

manifest ['mænə,fest] *adj* : manifiesto, patente — ~ *vt* : manifestar — **manifesto** [,mænə'fes,to:] *n, pl* -**tos** *or* -**toes** : manifiesto *m*

manipulate [mə'nɪpjə,leɪt] *vt* -**lated; -lating** : manipular — **manipulation** [mə,nɪpjə'leɪʃən] *n* : manipulación *f*

mankind ['mæn'kaɪnd, -,kaɪnd] *n* : género *m* humano, humanidad *f*

manly ['mænli] *adj* -**lier; -est** : viril — **manliness** ['mænlinəs] *n* : virilidad *f*

man-made ['mæn'meɪd] *adj* : artificial

mannequin ['mænɪkən] *n* : maniquí *m*

manner ['mænər] *n* **1** : manera *f* **2** KIND : clase *f* **3** ~**s** *npl* ETIQUETTE : modales *mpl*, educación *f* — **mannerism** ['mænə,rɪzəm] *n* : peculiaridad *f* (de una persona)

manoeuvre *Brit* → **maneuver**

manor ['mænər] *n* : casa *f* solariega

manpower ['mæn,paʊər] *n* : mano *f* de obra

mansion ['mæntʃən] *n* : mansión *f*

manslaughter ['mæn,slɔtər] *n* : homicidio *m* sin premeditación

mantel ['mæntəl] *or* **mantelpiece** ['mæntəl,pi:s] *n* : repisa *f* de la chimenea

manual ['mænjʊəl] *adj* : manual — ~ *n* : manual *m*

manufacture [,mænjə'fæktʃər] *n* : fabricación *f* — ~ *vt* -**tured; -turing** : fabricar — **manufacturer** [,mænjə'fæktʃərər] *n* : fabricante *mf*

manure [mə'nʊr, -'njʊr] *n* : estiércol *m*

manuscript ['mænjə,skrɪpt] *n* : manuscrito *m*

many ['meni] *adj* **more** ['mor]; **most** ['mo:st] **1** : muchos **2** as ~ : tantos **3** how ~ : cuántos **4** too ~ : demasiados — ~ *pron* : muchos *pl*, -chas *pl*

map ['mæp] *n* : mapa *m* — ~ *vt* **mapped; mapping 1** : trazar el mapa de **2** ~ **out** : planear, proyectar

maple ['meɪpəl] *n* : arce *m*

mar ['mar] *vt* **marred; marring** : estropear

marathon ['mærə,θan] *n* : maratón *m*

marble ['marbəl] *n* **1** : mármol *m* **2** ~**s** *npl* : canicas *fpl* (para jugar)

march ['martʃ] *n* : marcha *f* — ~ *vi* : marchar, desfilar

March ['martʃ] *n* : marzo *m*

mare ['mær] *n* : yegua *f*

margarine ['mardʒərən] *n* : margarina *f*

margin ['mardʒən] *n* : margen *m* — **marginal** ['mardʒənəl] *adj* : marginal

marigold ['mærə,go:ld] *n* : caléndula *f*

marijuana [,mærə'hwanə] *n* : marihuana *f*

marinate ['mærə,neɪt] *vt* -**nated; -nating** : marinar

marine [mə'ri:n] *adj* : marino — ~ *n* : soldado *m* de marina

marionette [,mæriə'net] *n* : marioneta *f*

marital ['mærətəl] *adj* **1** : matrimonial **2** ~ **status** : estado *m* civil

maritime ['mærə,taɪm] *adj* : marítimo

mark ['mark] *n* **1** : marca *f* **2** STAIN : mancha *f* **3** IMPRINT : huella *f* **4** TARGET : blanco *m* **5** GRADE : nota *f* — ~ *vt* **1** : marcar **2** STAIN : manchar **3** POINT OUT : señalar **4** : calificar (un examen, etc.) **5** COMMEMORATE : conmemorar **6** CARACTERIZE : caracterizar **7** ~ **off** : delimitar — **marked** ['markt] *adj* : marcado, notable — **markedly** ['markədli] *adv* : notablemente — **marker** ['markər] *n* : marcador *m*

market ['markət] *n* : mercado *m* — ~ *vt* : vender, comercializar — **marketable** ['markətəbəl] *adj* : vendible — **marketplace** ['markət,pleɪs] *n* : mercado *m*

marksman ['marksmən] *n, pl* -**men** [-mən, -,men] : tirador *m* — **marksmanship** ['marksmən,ʃɪp] *n* : puntería *f*

marmalade ['marmə,leɪd] *n* : mermelada *f*

maroon¹ [mə'ruːn] *vt* : abandonar, aislar
maroon² *n* : rojo *m* oscuro
marquee [mar'kiː] *n* CANOPY : marquesina *f*
marriage ['mærɪdʒ] *n* **1** : matrimonio *m* **2** WEDDING : casamiento *m*, boda *f* — **married** ['mærid] *adj* **1** : casado **2 get ～** : casarse
marrow ['mæroː] *n* : médula *f*, tuétano *m*
marry ['mæri] *v* **-ried; -rying** *vt* **1** : casar **2** WED : casarse con — *vi* : casarse
Mars ['mɑrz] *n* : Marte *m*
marsh ['mɑrʃ] *n* **1** : pantano *m* **2** *or* **salt ～** : marisma *f*
marshal ['mɑrʃəl] *n* : mariscal *m* (en el ejército); jefe *m*, -fa *f* (de policía, de bomberos, etc.) — *vt* **-shaled** *or* **-shalled; -shaling** *or* **-shalling** : poner en orden (los pensamientos, etc.), reunir (las tropas)
marshmallow ['mɑrʃˌmeloː, -ˌmæloː] *n* : malvavisco *m*
marshy ['mɑrʃi] *adj* **marshier; -est** : pantanoso
mart ['mɑrt] *n* : mercado *m*
martial ['mɑrʃəl] *adj* : marcial
martyr ['mɑrtər] *n* : mártir *mf* — *vt* : martirizar
marvel ['mɑrvəl] *n* : maravilla *f* — *vi* **-veled** *or* **-velled; -veling** *or* **-velling** : maravillarse — **marvelous** ['mɑrvələs] *or* **marvellous** *adj* : maravilloso
mascara [mæs'kærə] *n* : rímel *m*
mascot ['mæsˌkɑt, -kət] *n* : mascota *f*
masculine ['mæskjələn] *adj* : masculino — **masculinity** [ˌmæskjə'linəti] *n* : masculinidad *f*
mash ['mæʃ] *vt* **1** CRUSH : aplastar, majar **2** PUREE : hacer puré de — **mashed potatoes** *npl* : puré *m* de patatas, puré *m* de papas *Lat*
mask ['mæsk] *n* : máscara *f* — *vt* : enmascarar
masochism ['mæsəˌkɪzəm, 'mæzə-] *n* : masoquismo *m* — **masochist** ['mæsəˌkɪst, 'mæzə-] *n* : masoquista *mf* — **masochistic** [ˌmæsə'kɪstɪk, ˌmæzə-] *adj* : masoquista
mason ['meɪsən] *n* : albañil *mf* — **masonry** ['meɪsənri] *n*, *pl* **-ries** : albañilería *f*
masquerade [ˌmæskə'reɪd] *n* : mascarada *f* — *vi* **-aded; -ading ～ as** : disfrazarse de, hacerse pasar por
mass ['mæs] *n* **1** : masa *f* **2** MULTITUDE : cantidad *f* **3 the ～es** : las masas
Mass ['mæs] *n* : misa *f*
massacre ['mæsɪkər] *n* : masacre *f* — *vt* **-cred; -cring** : masacrar

massage [mə'sɑʒ, -'sɑdʒ] *n* : masaje *m* — *vt* **-saged; -saging** : dar masaje a, masajear — **masseur** [mæ'sər] *n* : masajista *m* — **masseuse** [mæ'səz, -'sərz, -'suːz] *n* : masajista *f*
massive ['mæsɪv] *adj* **1** BULKY, SOLID : macizo **2** HUGE : enorme, masivo
mast ['mæst] *n* : mástil *m*
master ['mæstər] *n* **1** : amo *m*, señor *m* (de la casa) **2** EXPERT : maestro *m*, -tra *f* **3 ～'s degree** : maestría *f* — *vt* : dominar — **masterful** ['mæstərfəl] *adj* : magistral — **masterpiece** ['mæstərˌpiːs] *n* : obra *f* maestra — **mastery** ['mæstəri] *n* : maestría *f*
masturbate ['mæstərˌbeɪt] *v* **-bated; -bating** : masturbarse — **masturbation** [ˌmæstər'beɪʃən] *n* : masturbación *f*
mat ['mæt] *n* **1** DOORMAT : felpudo *m* **2** RUG : estera *f*
matador ['mætəˌdɔr] *n* : matador *m*
match ['mætʃ] *n* **1** EQUAL : igual *mf* **2** : fósforo *m*, cerilla *f* (para encender) **3** GAME : partido *m*, combate *m* (en boxeo) **4 be a good ～** : hacer buena pareja — *vt* **1** *or* **～ up** : emparejar **2** EQUAL : igualar **3** : combinar con, hacer juego con (ropa, colores, etc.) — *vi* : concordar, coincidir
mate ['meɪt] *n* **1** COMPANION : compañero *m*, -ra *f*; amigo *m*, -ga *f* **2** : macho *m*, hembra *f* (de animales) — *vi* **mated; mating** : aparearse
material [mə'tɪriəl] *adj* **1** : material — **2** IMPORTANT : importante — *n* **1** : material *m* **2** CLOTH : tela *f*, tejido *m* — **materialistic** [məˌtɪriə'lɪstɪk] *adj* : materialista — **materialize** [mə'tɪriəˌlaɪz] *vi* **-ized; -izing** : aparecer
maternal [mə'tərnəl] *adj* : maternal — **maternity** [mə'tərnəti] *n*, *pl* **-ties** : maternidad *f* — *adj* **1** : de maternidad **2 ～ clothes** : ropa *f* de futura mamá
math ['mæθ] → **mathematics**
mathematics [ˌmæθə'mætɪks] *ns* & *pl* : matemáticas *fpl* — **mathematical** [ˌmæθə'mætɪkəl] *adj* : matemático — **mathematician** [ˌmæθəmə'tɪʃən] *n* : matemático *m*, -ca *f*
matinee *or* **matinée** [ˌmætən'eɪ] *n* : matiné(e) *f*, función *f* de tarde
matrimony ['mætrəˌmoːni] *n* : matrimonio *m* — **matrimonial** [ˌmætrə'moːniəl] *adj* : matrimonial
matrix ['meɪtrɪks] *n*, *pl* **-trices** ['meɪtrəˌsiːz, 'mæ-] *or* **-trixes** ['meɪtrɪksəz] : matriz *f*
matte ['mæt] *adj* : mate
matter ['mætər] *n* **1** SUBSTANCE : materia

f **2** QUESTION : asunto *m*, cuestión *f* **3**
as a ~ of fact : en efecto, en realidad
4 for that ~ : de hecho **5 to make
~s worse** : para colmo de males **6
what's the ~?** : ¿qué pasa? — **~** *vi*
: importar

mattress ['mætrəs] *n* : colchón *m*

mature [mə'tʊr, -'tjʊr, -'tʃʊr] *adj* **-turer;
-est** : maduro — *vi* **-tured; -turing**
: madurar — **maturity** [mə'tʊrəti, -'tjʊr-
, -'tʃʊr-] *n* : madurez *f*

maul ['mɔl] *vt* : maltratar, aporrear

mauve ['moːv, 'mɔv] *n* : malva *m*

maxim ['mæksəm] *n* : máxima *f*

maximum ['mæksəməm] *n, pl* **-ma**
['mæksəmə] *or* **-mums** : máximo *m*
— *adj* : máximo — **maximize**
['mæksə,maɪz] *vt* **-mized; -mizing** : llevar al máximo

may ['meɪ] *v aux, past* **might** ['maɪt];
present s & pl **may 1** : poder **2 come
what ~** : pase lo que pase **3 it ~
happen** : puede pasar **4 ~ the best
man win** : que gane el mejor

May ['meɪ] *n* : mayo *m*

maybe ['meɪbi] *adv* : quizás, tal vez

mayhem ['meɪ,hɛm, 'meɪəm] *n* : alboroto
m

mayonnaise ['meɪə,neɪz] *n* : mayonesa *f*

mayor ['meɪər, 'mɛr] *n* : alcalde *m*, -desa
f

maze ['meɪz] *n* : laberinto *m*

me ['miː] *pron* **1** : me **2 for ~** : para mí
3 give it to ~! : ¡dámelo! **4 it's ~**
: soy yo **5 with ~** : conmigo

meadow ['mɛdoː] *n* : prado *m*, pradera *f*

meager ['miːgər] *or* **meagre** *adj* : escaso

meal ['miːl] *n* **1** : comida *f* **2** : harina *f* (de
maíz, etc.) — **mealtime** ['miːl,taɪm] *n*
: hora *f* de comer

mean[1] ['miːn] *vt* **meant** ['mɛnt]; **meaning 1** SIGNIFY : querer decir **2** INTEND
: querer, tener la intención de **3 be
meant for** : estar destinado a **4 he
didn't ~ it** : no lo dijo en serio

mean[2] *adj* **1** UNKIND : malo **2** STINGY
: mezquino, tacaño **3** HUMBLE : humilde

mean[3] *adj* AVERAGE : medio — **~** *n*
: promedio *m*

meander [mi'ændər] *vi* **-dered; -dering
1** WIND : serpentear **2** WANDER : vagar

meaning *m* ['miːnɪŋ] *n* : significado *m*,
sentido *m* — **meaningful** ['miːnɪŋfəl]
adj : significativo — **meaningless**
['miːnɪŋləs] *adj* : sin sentido

meanness ['miːnnəs] *n* **1** UNKINDNESS
: maldad *f* **2** STINGINESS : mezquinidad
f

means ['miːnz] *n* **1** : medio *m* **2 by all
~** : por supuesto **3 by ~ of** : por
medio de **4 by no ~** : de ninguna
manera

meantime ['miːn,taɪm] *n* **1** : ínterin *m* **2
in the ~** : mientras tanto — *adv* →
meanwhile

meanwhile ['miːn,hwaɪl] *adv* : mientras
tanto — *n* → **meantime**

measles ['miːzəlz] *npl* : sarampión *m*

measly ['miːzli] *adj* **-slier; -est** : miserable, misero

measure ['mɛʒər, 'meɪ-] *n* : medida *f* —
v **-sured; -suring** : medir — **measurable** ['mɛʒərəbəl, 'meɪ-] *adj* : mensurable — **measurement** ['mɛʒərmənt,
'meɪ-] *n* : medida *f* — **measure up** *vi*
~ to : estar a la altura de

meat ['miːt] *n* : carne *f* — **meatball**
['miːt,bɔl] *n* : albóndiga *f* — **meaty**
['miːti] *adj* **meatier; -est 1** : carnoso **2**
SUBSTANTIAL : sustancioso

mechanic [mɪ'kænɪk] *n* : mecánico *m*,
-ca *f* — **mechanical** [mɪ'kænɪkəl] *adj*
: mecánico — **mechanics** [mɪ'kænɪks]
ns & pl **1** : mecánica *f* **2** WORKINGS
: mecanismo *m* — **mechanism**
['mɛkə,nɪzəm] *n* : mecanismo *m* —
mechanize ['mɛkə,naɪz] *vt* **-nized;
-nizing** : mecanizar

medal ['mɛdəl] *n* : medalla *f* — **medallion** [mə'dæljən] *n* : medallón *m*

meddle ['mɛdəl] *vi* **-dled; -dling** : entrometerse

media ['miːdiə] *or* **mass ~** *npl* : me-
dios *mpl* de comunicación

median ['miːdiən] *adj* : medio

mediate ['miːdi,eɪt] *vi* **-ated; -ating**
: mediar — **mediation** [,miːdi'eɪʃən] *n*
: mediación *f* — **mediator** ['miːdi,eɪtər]
n : mediador *m*, -dora *f*

medical ['mɛdɪkəl] *adj* : médico —
medicated ['mɛdə,keɪtəd] *adj* : medicinal — **medication** [,mɛdə'keɪʃən] *n*
: medicamento *m* — **medicinal** [mə-
'dɪsənəl] *adj* : medicinal — **medicine**
['mɛdəsən] *n* **1** : medicina *f* **2** MEDICA-
TION : medicina *f*, medicamento *m*

medieval *or* **mediaeval** [mɪ'diːvəl, ,miː-,
,mɛ-, -di'iːvəl] *adj* : medieval

mediocre [,miːdi'oːkər] *adj* : mediocre —
mediocrity [,miːdi'ɑkrəti] *n, pl* **-ties**
: mediocridad *f*

meditate ['mɛdə,teɪt] *vi* **-tated; -tating**
: meditar — **meditation** [,mɛdə'teɪʃən]
n : meditación *f*

medium ['miːdiəm] *n, pl* **-diums** *or* **-dia**
['miːdiə] **1** MEANS : medio *m* **2** MIDDLE
: punto *m* medio, término *m* medio **3**
→ **media** — **~** *adj* : mediano

medley ['mɛdli] *n, pl* **-leys 1** : mezcla *f*
2 : popurrí *m* (de canciones)

meek ['miːk] *adj* : dócil

meet ['miːt] *v* **met** ['mɛt]; **meeting** *vt* **1**
ENCOUNTER : encontrarse con **2** SATIS-
FY : satisfacer **3 pleased to** ~ **you**
: encantado de conocerlo — *vi* **1** : encontrarse **2** ASSEMBLE : reunirse **3** BE
INTRODUCED : conocerse — ~ *n* : encuentro *m* — **meeting** ['miːtɪŋ] *n* : reunión *f*

megabyte ['mɛgəˌbaɪt] *n* : megabyte *m*

megaphone ['mɛgəˌfoːn] *n* : megáfono
m

melancholy ['mɛlənˌkɑli] *n, pl* **-cholies**
: melancolía *f* — ~ *adj* : melancólico,
triste

mellow ['mɛloː] *adj* **1** : suave, dulce **2**
CALM : apacible **3** : maduro (dícese de
frutas), añejo (dícese de vinos) — ~
vt : suavizar, endulzar — *vi* : suavizarse

melody ['mɛlədi] *n, pl* **-dies** : melodía *f*

melon ['mɛlən] *n* : melón *m*

melt ['mɛlt] *vi* : derretirse, fundirse — *vt*
: derretir

member ['mɛmbər] *n* : miembro *m* —
membership ['mɛmbərˌʃɪp] *n* **1** : calidad *f* de miembro **2** MEMBERS : miem-
bros *mpl*

membrane ['mɛmˌbreɪn] *n* : membrana *f*

memory ['mɛmri, 'mɛmə-] *n, pl* **-ries 1**
: memoria *f* **2** RECOLLECTION : recuerdo *m* — **memento** [mɪˈmɛnˌtoː] *n, pl*
-tos *or* **-toes** : recuerdo *m* — **memo**
['mɛmoː] *n, pl* **memos** *or* **memorandum** [ˌmɛməˈrændəm] *n, pl* **-dums** *or*
-da [-də] : memorándum *m* — **memoirs** ['mɛmˌwɑrz] *npl* : memorias *fpl* —
memorable ['mɛmərəbəl] *adj* : memorable — **memorial** [məˈmoːriəl] *adj*
: conmemorativo — ~ *n* : monumento *m* (conmemorativo) — **memorize**
['mɛməˌraɪz] *vt* **-rized; -rizing** : aprender de memoria

men → **man**

menace ['mɛnəs] *n* : amenaza *f* — ~ *vt*
-aced; -acing : amenazar — **menac-
ing** ['mɛnəsɪŋ] *adj* : amenazador

mend ['mɛnd] *vt* **1** : reparar, arreglar **2**
DARN : zurcir — *vi* HEAL : curarse

menial ['miːniəl] *adj* : servil, bajo

meningitis [ˌmɛnənˈdʒaɪtəs] *n, pl*
-gitides [-ˈdʒɪtəˌdiːz] : meningitis *f*

menopause ['mɛnəˌpɔz] *n* : menopausia
f

menstruate ['mɛnˌstruˌeɪt] *vi* **-ated;
-ating** : menstruar — **menstruation**
[ˌmɛnstruˈeɪʃən] *n* : menstruación *f*

mental ['mɛntəl] *adj* : mental — **men-**

tality [mɛnˈtæləti] *n, pl* **-ties** : mentalidad *f*

mention ['mɛntʃən] *n* : mención *f* —
mention *vt* **1** : mencionar **2 don't** ~
it! : ¡de nada!, ¡no hay de qué!

menu ['mɛnˌjuː] *n* : menú *m*

meow [miˈaʊ] *n* : maullido *m*, miau *m*
— ~ *vi* : maullar

mercenary ['mərsənˌɛri] *n, pl* **-naries**
: mercenario *m*, -ria *f* — ~ *adj* : mercenario

merchant ['mərtʃənt] *n* : comerciante *mf*
— **merchandise** ['mərtʃənˌdaɪz, -ˌdaɪs]
n : mercancía *f*, mercadería *f*

merciful ['mərsɪfəl] *adj* : misericordioso, compasivo — **merciless** ['mər-
sɪləs] *adj* : despiadado

mercury ['mərkjəri] *n, pl* **-ries** : mercurio *m*

Mercury *n* : Mercurio *m*

mercy ['mərsi] *n, pl* **-cies 1** : misericordia *f*, compasión *f* **2 at the** ~ **of** : a
merced de

mere ['mɪr] *adj, superlative* **merest**
: mero, simple — **merely** ['mɪrli] *adv*
: simplemente

merge ['mərdʒ] *v* **merged; merging** *vi*
: unirse, fusionarse (dícese de las
compañías), confluir (dícese de los
ríos, las calles, etc.) — *vt* : unir, fusionar, combinar — **merger** ['mərdʒər]
n : unión *f*, fusión *f*

merit ['mɛrət] *n* : mérito *m* — ~ *vt*
: merecer

mermaid ['mərˌmeɪd] *n* : sirena *f*

merry ['mɛri] *adj* **-rier; -est** : alegre —
merry–go–round ['mɛriɡoˌraʊnd] *n*
: tiovivo *m*

mesa ['meɪsə] *n* : mesa *f*

mesh ['mɛʃ] *n* : malla *f*

mesmerize ['mɛzməˌraɪz] *vt* **-ized;
-izing** : hipnotizar

mess ['mɛs] *n* **1** : desorden *m* **2** MUDDLE
: lío *m* **3** : rancho *m* (militar) — ~ *vt*
1 *or* ~ **up** SOIL : ensuciar **2** ~ **up** DIS-
ARRANGE : desordenar **3** ~ **up** BUN-
GLE : echar a perder — *vi* **1** ~ **around**
PUTTER : entretenerse **2** ~ **with** PRO-
VOKE : meterse con

message ['mɛsɪdʒ] *n* : mensaje *m* —
messenger ['mɛsəndʒər] *n* : mensajero
m, -ra *f*

messy ['mɛsi] *adj* **messier; -est** : desordenado, sucio

met → **meet**

metabolism [məˈtæbəˌlɪzəm] *n* : metabolismo *m*

metal ['mɛṯəl] *n* : metal *m* — **metallic**
[məˈtælɪk] *adj* : metálico

metamorphosis [ˌmɛtəˈmɔrfəsɪs] *n, pl* **-phoses** [-ˌsiːz] : metamorfosis *f*
metaphor [ˈmɛtəˌfɔr, -fər] *n* : metáfora *f*
meteor [ˈmiːtiər, -ˌtiːˌɔr] *n* : meteoro *m* — **meteorological** [ˌmiːtiˌɔrəˈlɑdʒɪkəl] *adj* : meteorológico — **meteorologist** [ˌmiːtiəˈrɑlədʒɪst] *n* : meteorólogo *m*, -ga *f* — **meteorology** [ˌmiːtiəˈrɑlədʒi] *n* : meteorología *f*
meter *or Brit* **metre** [ˈmiːtər] *n* **1** : metro *m* **2** : contador *m* (de electricidad, etc.)
method [ˈmɛθəd] *n* : método *m* — **methodical** [məˈθɑdɪkəl] *adj* : metódico
meticulous [məˈtɪkjələs] *adj* : meticuloso
metric [ˈmɛtrɪk] *or* **metrical** [-trɪkəl] *adj* : métrico
metropolis [məˈtrɑpələs] *n* : metrópoli *f* — **metropolitan** [ˌmɛtrəˈpɑlətən] *adj* : metropolitano
Mexican [ˈmɛksɪkən] *adj* : mexicano
mice → **mouse**
microbe [ˈmaɪˌkroːb] *n* : microbio *m*
microfilm [ˈmaɪkroˌfɪlm] *n* : microfilm *m*
microphone [ˈmaɪkrəˌfoːn] *n* : micrófono *m*
microscope [ˈmaɪkrəˌskoːp] *n* : microscopio *m* — **microscopic** [ˌmaɪkrəˈskɑpɪk] *adj* : microscópico
microwave [ˈmaɪkrəˌweɪv] *n or* ~ **oven** : microondas *m*
mid [ˈmɪd] *adj* **1** ~ **morning** : a media mañana **2** in ~-**August** : a mediados de agosto **3** **she is in her mid thirties** : tiene alrededor de 35 años — **midair** [ˈmɪdˌæɾ] *n* in ~ : en el aire — **midday** [ˈmɪdˌdeɪ] *n* : mediodía *m*
middle [ˈmɪdəl] *adj* : de en medio, del medio — ~ *n* **1** : medio *m*, centro *m* **2** in the ~ of : en medio de (un espacio), a mitad de (una actividad) **3** in the ~ of the month : a mediados del mes — **middle-aged** [ˌmɪdəlˈeɪdʒd] *adj* : de mediana edad — **Middle Ages** *npl* : Edad *f* Media — **middle class** *n* : clase *f* media — **middleman** [ˈmɪdəlˌmæn] *n, pl* **-men** [-mən, -ˌmɛn] : intermediario *m*, -ria *f*
midget [ˈmɪdʒət] *n* : enano *m*, -na *f*
midnight [ˈmɪdˌnaɪt] *n* : medianoche *f*
midriff [ˈmɪdˌrɪf] *n* : diafragma *m*
midst [ˈmɪdst] *n* **1** in the ~ of : en medio de **2** in our ~ : entre nosotros
midsummer [ˈmɪdˌsʌmər, -ˌsʌ-] *n* : pleno verano *m*
midway [ˈmɪdˌweɪ] *adv* : a mitad de camino, a medio camino
midwife [ˈmɪdˌwaɪf] *n, pl* **-wives** [-ˌwaɪvz] : comadrona *f*

midwinter [ˈmɪdˌwɪntər, -ˌwɪn-] *n* : pleno invierno *m*
miff [ˈmɪf] *vt* : ofender
might[1] [ˈmaɪt] (*used to express permission or possibility or as a polite alternative to* **may**) → **may**
might[2] *n* : fuerza *f*, poder *m* — **mighty** [ˈmaɪti] *adj* **mightier, -est 1** : fuerte, poderoso **2** GREAT : enorme — ~ *adv* : muy
migraine [ˈmaɪˌgreɪn] *n* : jaqueca *f*, migraña *f*
migrate [ˈmaɪˌgreɪt] *vi* **-grated; -grating** : emigrar — **migrant** [ˈmaɪgrənt] *n* : trabajador *m*, -dora *f* ambulante
mild [ˈmaɪld] *adj* **1** GENTLE : suave **2** LIGHT : leve **3** a ~ **climate** : una clima templada
mildew [ˈmɪlˌduː, -ˌdjuː] *n* : moho *m*
mildly [ˈmaɪldli] *adv* : ligeramente, suavemente — **mildness** [ˈmaɪldnəs] *n* : apacibilidad *f* (de personas), suavedad *f* (de sabores, etc.)
mile [ˈmaɪl] *n* : milla *f* — **mileage** [ˈmaɪlɪdʒ] *n* : distancia *f* recorrida (en millas), kilometraje *m* — **milestone** [ˈmaɪlˌstoːn] *n* : hito *m*
military [ˈmɪləˌteri] *adj* : militar — ~ *n* the ~ : las fuerzas armadas — **militant** [ˈmɪlətənt] *adj* : militante — ~ *n* : militante *mf* — **militia** [məˈlɪʃə] *n* : milicia *f*
milk [ˈmɪlk] *n* : leche *f* — ~ *vt* **1** : ordeñar (una vaca, etc.) **2** EXPLOIT : explotar — **milky** [ˈmɪlki] *adj* **milkier, -est** : lechoso — **Milky Way** *n* the ~ : la Vía Láctea
mill [ˈmɪl] *n* **1** : molino *m* **2** FACTORY : fábrica *f* **3** GRINDER : molinillo *m* — ~ *vt* : moler — *vi or* ~ **about** : arremolinarse
millennium [məˈleniəm] *n, pl* **-nia** [-niə] *or* **-niums** : milenio *m*
miller [ˈmɪlər] *n* : molinero *m*, -ra *f*
milligram [ˈmɪləˌgræm] *n* : miligramo *m* — **millimeter** *or Brit* **millimetre** [ˈmɪləˌmiːtər] *n* : milímetro *m*
million [ˈmɪljən] *n, pl* **millions** *or* **million 1** : millón *m* **2** a ~ **people** : un millón de personas — ~ *adj* a ~ : un millón de — **millionaire** [ˌmɪljəˈnær, ˈmɪljəˌnær] *n* : millonario *m*, -ria *f* — **millionth** [ˈmɪljənθ] *adj* : millonésimo
mime [ˈmaɪm] *n* **1** : mimo *mf* **2** PANTOMIME : pantomima *f* — ~ *v* **mimed; miming** *vt* : imitar — *vi* : hacer la mímica — **mimic** [ˈmɪmɪk] *vt* **-icked; -icking** : imitar, remedar — ~ *n* : imitador *m*, -dora *f* — **mimicry** [ˈmɪmɪkri] *n, pl* **-ries** : imitación *f*

mince ['mɪnts] v **minced; mincing** vt 1
: picar, moler 2 **not to ~ one's
words** : no tener pelos en la lengua
mind ['maɪnd] n 1 : mente f 2 INTELLECT
: capacidad f intelectual 3 OPINION
: opinión f 4 REASON : razón f 5 **have a
~ to** : tener intención de — ~ vt 1
TEND : cuidar 2 OBEY : obedecer 3
WATCH : tener cuidado con 4 **I don't ~
the heat** : no me molesta el calor — vi
1 OBEY : obedecer 2 **I don't ~** : no me
importa, me es igual — **mindful**
['maɪndfəl] adj : atento — **mindless**
['maɪndləs] adj 1 SENSELESS : estúpido,
sin sentido 2 DULL : aburrido
mine¹ ['maɪn] pron 1 : (el) mío, (la) mía,
(los) míos, (las) mías 2 **a friend of ~**
: un amigo mío
mine² n : mina f — ~ vt **mined; mining** 1 : extraer (oro, etc.) 2 : minar
(con artefactos explosivos) — **mine-
field** ['maɪn.fiːld] n : campo m de minas
— **miner** ['maɪnər] n : minero m, -ra f
mineral ['mɪnərəl] n : mineral m
mingle ['mɪŋgəl] v **-gled; -gling** vt
: mezclar — vi 1 : mezclarse 2 : circular (a una fiesta, etc.)
miniature ['mɪniə.tʃʊr, 'mɪnɪ.tʃʊr, -tʃər] n
: miniatura f — ~ adj : en miniatura
minimal ['mɪnəməl] adj : mínimo —
minimize ['mɪnə.maɪz] vt **-mized;
-mizing** : minimizar — **minimum**
['mɪnəməm] adj : mínimo — ~ n, pl
-ma ['mɪnəmə] or **-mums** : mínimo m
mining ['maɪnɪŋ] n : minería f
minister ['mɪnəstər] n 1 : pastor m, -tora
f (de una iglesia) 2 : ministro m, -tra f
(en política) — ~ vi ~ **to** : cuidar
(de), atender a — **ministerial** [.mɪnə-
'strɪriəl] adj : ministerial — **ministry**
['mɪnəstri] n, pl **-tries** : ministerio m
mink ['mɪŋk] n, pl **mink** or **minks**
: visón m
minnow ['mɪnoː] n, pl **-nows** : pececillo
m de agua dulce
minor ['maɪnər] adj 1 : menor 2 IN-
SIGNIFICANT : sin importancia — ~ n
1 : menor mf (de edad) 2 : asignatura f
secundaria (de estudios) — **minority**
[mə'nɔrəti, maɪ-] n, pl **-ties** : minoría f
mint¹ ['mɪnt] n 1 : menta f (planta) 2
: pastilla f de menta (dulce)
mint² n 1 **the U.S. Mint** : la casa de la
moneda de los EE.UU. 2 **be worth a
~** : valer un dineral — ~ vt : acuñar
— ~ adj **in ~ condition** : como
nuevo
minus ['maɪnəs] prep 1 : menos 2 WITH-
OUT : sin — ~ n or ~ **sign** : signo m
de menos

minuscule ['mɪnəs.kjuːl, mɪ'nʌs-] adj
: minúsculo
minute¹ [mar'nuːt, mɪ-, -'njuːt] n 1 : minuto m 2 MOMENT : momento m 3 **~s**
npl : actas fpl (de una reunión)
minute² ['mɪnət] adj **-nuter; -est** 1 TINY
: diminuto, minúsculo 2 DETAILED
: minucioso
miracle ['mɪrɪkəl] n : milagro m — **miraculous** [mə'rækjələs] adj : milagroso
mirage [mɪ'rɑʒ, 'mɪr.ɑʒ] n : espejismo m
mire ['maɪr] n : lodo m, fango m
mirror ['mɪrər] n : espejo m — ~ vt : reflejar
mirth ['mərθ] n : alegría f, risas fpl
misapprehension [.mɪs.æprə'hentʃən] n
: malentendido m
misbehave [.mɪsbɪ'heɪv] vi **-haved;
-having** : portarse mal — **misbehav-
ior** [.mɪsbɪ'heɪvjər] n : mala conducta f
miscalculate [mɪs'kælkjə.leɪt] v **-lated;
-lating** : calcular mal
miscarriage [.mɪs'kærɪdʒ, 'mɪs.kærɪdʒ] n
1 : aborto m 2 ~ **of justice** : error m
judicial
miscellaneous [.mɪsə'leɪniəs] adj : diverso, vario
mischief ['mɪstʃəf] n : travesuras fpl —
mischievous ['mɪstʃəvəs] adj : travieso
misconception [.mɪskən'sepʃən] n : concepto m erróneo
misconduct [mɪs'kɑndəkt] n : mala conducta f
misdeed [mɪs'diːd] n : fechoría f
misdemeanor [.mɪsdɪ'miːnər] n : delito
m menor
miser ['maɪzər] n : avaro m, -ra f; tacaño
m, -ña f
miserable ['mɪzərəbəl] adj 1 UNHAPPY
: triste 2 WRETCHED : miserable 3 **~
weather** : tiempo m malo
miserly ['maɪzərli] adj : mezquino
misery ['mɪzəri] n, pl **-eries** 1 : sufrimiento m 2 WRETCHEDNESS : miseria f
misfire [mɪs'faɪr] vi **-fired; -firing** : fallar
misfit ['mɪs.fɪt, mɪs'fɪt] n : inadaptado m,
-da f
misfortune [mɪs'fɔrtʃən] n : desgracia f
misgiving [mɪs'gɪvɪŋ] n : duda f
misguided [mɪs'gaɪdəd] adj : descami-
nado, equivocado
mishap ['mɪs.hæp] n : contratiempo m
misinform [.mɪsɪn'fɔrm] vt : informar
mal
misinterpret [.mɪsɪn'tərprət] vt : interpretar mal
misjudge [mɪs'dʒʌdʒ] vt **-judged;
-judging** : juzgar mal

mislay ['mɪsˌleɪ] *vt* **-laid** [-ˌleɪd]; **-laying** : extraviar, perder

mislead [mɪsˈliːd] *vt* **-led** [-ˈled]; **-leading** : engañar — **misleading** [mɪsˈliːdɪŋ] *adj* : engañoso

misnomer [mɪsˈnoːmər] *n* : nombre *m* inapropiado

misplace [mɪsˈpleɪs] *vt* **-placed**; **-placing** : extraviar, perder

misprint [ˈmɪsˌprɪnt, mɪsˈ-] *n* : errata *f*, error *m* de imprenta

miss [ˈmɪs] *vt* **1** : errar, faltar **2** OVERLOOK : pasar por alto **3** : perder (una oportunidad, un vuelo, etc.) **4** AVOID : evitar **5** OMIT : saltarse **6** I ~ **you** : te echo de menos — ~ *n* **1** : fallo *m* (de un tiro, etc.) **2** FAILURE : fracaso *m*

Miss [ˈmɪs] *n* : señorita *f*

missile [ˈmɪsəl] *n* **1** : misil *m* **2** PROJECTILE : proyectil *m*

missing [ˈmɪsɪŋ] *adj* : perdido, desaparecido

mission [ˈmɪʃən] *n* : misión *f* — **missionary** [ˈmɪʃəˌneri] *n, pl* **-aries** : misionero *m*, -ra *f*

misspell [mɪsˈspel] *vt* : escribir mal

mist [ˈmɪst] *n* : neblina *f*, bruma *f*

mistake [mɪˈsteɪk] *vt* **mistook** [-ˈstʊk]; **mistaken** [-ˈsteɪkən]; **-taking** **1** MISINTERPRET : entender mal **2** CONFUSE : confundir — ~ *n* **1** : error *m* **2** **make a** ~ : equivocarse — **mistaken** [mɪˈsteɪkən] *adj* : equivocado

mister [ˈmɪstər] *n* : señor *m*

mistletoe [ˈmɪsəlˌtoː] *n* : muérdago *m*

mistreat [mɪsˈtriːt] *vt* : maltratar

mistress [ˈmɪstrəs] *n* **1** : dueña *f*, señora *f* (de una casa) **2** LOVER : amante *f*

mistrust [mɪsˈtrʌst] *n* : desconfianza *f* — ~ *vt* : desconfiar de

misty [ˈmɪsti] *adj* **mistier; -est** : neblinoso, nebuloso

misunderstand [ˌmɪsˌʌndərˈstænd] *vt* **-stood; -standing** : entender mal — **misunderstanding** [ˌmɪsˌʌndərˈstændɪŋ] *n* : malentendido *m*

misuse [mɪsˈjuːz] *vt* **-used; -using** **1** : emplear mal **2** MISTREAT : maltratar — ~ [mɪsˈjuːs] *n* : mal empleo *m*, abuso *m*

mitigate [ˈmɪtəˌgeɪt] *vt* **-gated; -gating** : mitigar

mitt [ˈmɪt] *n* : manopla *f*, guante *m* (de béisbol) — **mitten** [ˈmɪtən] *n* : manopla *f*, mitón *m*

mix [ˈmɪks] *vt* **1** : mezclar **2** ~ **up** : confundir — *vi* : mezclarse — ~ *n* : mezcla *f* — **mixture** [ˈmɪkstʃər] *n* : mezcla *f* — **mix-up** [ˈmɪksˌʌp] *n* : confusión *f*, lío *m fam*

moan [ˈmoːn] *n* : gemido *m* — ~ *vi* : gemir

mob [ˈmab] *n* : muchedumbre *f* — ~ *vt* **mobbed; mobbing** : acosar

mobile [ˈmoːbəl, -ˌbiːl, -ˌbaɪl] *adj* : móvil — ~ [ˈmoːbiːl] *n* : móvil *m* — **mobile home** *n* : caravana *f* — **mobility** [moːˈbɪləti] *n* : movilidad *f* — **mobilize** [ˈmoːbəˌlaɪz] *vt* **-lized; -lizing** : movilizar

moccasin [ˈmakəsən] *n* : mocasín *m*

mock [ˈmak, ˈmɔk] *vt* : burlarse de, mofarse de — ~ *adj* : falso — **mockery** [ˈmakəri, ˈmɔ-] *n, pl* **-eries** : burla *f* — **mock-up** [ˈmakˌʌp] *n* : maqueta *f*

mode [ˈmoːd] *n* **1** : modo *m* **2** FASHION : moda *f*

model [ˈmadəl] *n* **1** : modelo *m* **2** MOCK-UP : maqueta *f* **3** : modelo *mf* (persona) — ~ *v* **-eled** *or* **-elled; -eling** *or* **-elling** *vt* **1** SHAPE : modelar **2** WEAR : lucir — *vi* : trabajar de modelo — ~ *adj* : modelo

modem [ˈmoːdəm, -ˌdem] *n* : módem *m*

moderate [ˈmadərət] *adj* : moderado — ~ *n* : moderado *m*, -da *f* — ~ [ˈmadəˌreɪt] *v* **-ated; -ating** *vt* : moderar — *vi* : moderarse — **moderation** [ˌmadəˈreɪʃən] *n* : moderación *f* — **moderator** [ˈmadəˌreɪtər] *n* : moderador *m*, -dora *f*

modern [ˈmadərn] *adj* : moderno — **modernize** [ˈmadərˌnaɪz] *vt* **-ized; -izing** : modernizar

modest [ˈmadəst] *adj* : modesto — **modesty** [ˈmadəsti] *n* : modestia *f*

modify [ˈmadəˌfaɪ] *vt* **-fied; -fying** : modificar

moist [ˈmɔɪst] *adj* : húmedo — **moisten** [ˈmɔɪsən] *vt* : humedecer — **moisture** [ˈmɔɪstʃər] *n* : humedad *f* — **moisturizer** [ˈmɔɪstʃəˌraɪzər] *n* : crema *f* hidratante

molar [ˈmoːlər] *n* : muela *f*

molasses [məˈlæsəz] *n* : melaza *f*

mold[1] [ˈmoːld] *n* FORM : molde *m* — ~ *vt* : moldear, formar

mold[2] *n* FUNGUS : moho *m* — **moldy** [ˈmoːldi] *adj* **moldier; -est** : mohoso

mole[1] [ˈmoːl] *n* : lunar *m* (en la piel)

mole[2] *n* : topo *m* (animal)

molecule [ˈmalɪˌkjuːl] *n* : molécula *f*

molest [məˈlest] *vt* **1** HARASS : importunar **2** : abusar (sexualmente)

molten [ˈmoːltən] *adj* : fundido

mom [ˈmam, ˈmʌm] *n* : mamá *f*

moment [ˈmoːmənt] *n* : momento *m* — **momentarily** [ˌmoːmənˈterəli] *adv* **1** : momentáneamente **2** SOON : dentro de poco, pronto — **momentary** [ˈmoːmənˌteri] *adj* : momentáneo

momentous [moˈmentəs] *adj* : muy importante

momentum [moˈmentəm] *n, pl* **-ta** [-tə] *or* **-tums 1** : momento *m* (en física) **2** IMPETUS : ímpetu *m*

monarch [ˈmɑ,nɑrk, -nərk] *n* : monarca *mf* — **monarchy** [ˈmɑ,nɑrki, -nər-] *n, pl* **-chies** : monarquía *f*

monastery [ˈmɑnəˌsteri] *n, pl* **-teries** : monasterio *m*

Monday [ˈmʌn,dei, -di] *n* : lunes *m*

money [ˈmʌni] *n, pl* **-eys** *or* **-ies** [ˈmʌniz] : dinero *m* — **monetary** [ˈmɑnə,teri, ˈmʌnə-] *adj* : monetario — **money order** *n* : giro *m* postal

mongrel [ˈmʌŋgrəl, ˈmɑŋ-] *n* : perro *m* mestizo

monitor [ˈmɑnətər] *n* : monitor *m* (de una computadora, etc.) — ~ *vt* : controlar

monk [ˈmʌŋk] *n* : monje *m*

monkey [ˈmʌŋki] *n, pl* **-keys** : mono *m*, -na *f* — **monkey wrench** *n* : llave *f* inglesa

monogram [ˈmɑnəˌgræm] *n* : monograma *m*

monologue [ˈmɑnəˌlɔg] *n* : monólogo *m*

monopoly [məˈnɑpəli] *n, pl* **-lies** : monopolio *m* — **monopolize** [məˈnɑpəˌlaɪz] *vt* **-lized; -lizing** : monopolizar

monotonous [məˈnɑtənəs] *adj* : monótono — **monotony** [məˈnɑtəni] *n* : monotonía *f*

monster [ˈmɑnstər] *n* : monstruo *m* — **monstrosity** [mɑnˈstrɑsəti] *n, pl* **-ties** : monstruosidad *f* — **monstrous** [ˈmɑnstrəs] *adj* **1** : monstruoso **2** HUGE : gigantesco

month [ˈmʌnθ] *n* : mes *m* — **monthly** [ˈmʌnθli] *adv* : mensualmente — ~ *adj* : mensual

monument [ˈmɑnjəmənt] *n* : monumento *m* — **monumental** [ˌmɑnjəˈmentəl] *adj* : monumental

moo [ˈmuː] *vi* : mugir — ~ *n* : mugido *m*

mood [ˈmuːd] *n* : humor *m* — **moody** [ˈmuːdi] *adj* **moodier; -est 1** GLOOMY : melancólico, deprimido **2** IRRITABLE : malhumorado **3** TEMPERAMENTAL : de humor variable

moon [ˈmuːn] *n* : luna *f* — **moonlight** [ˈmuːnˌlaɪt] *n* : luz *f* de la luna

moor[1] [ˈmʊr, ˈmɔr] *n* : brezal *m*, páramo *m*

moor[2] *vt* : amarrar — **mooring** [ˈmʊrɪŋ, ˈmɔr-] *n* DOCK : atracadero *m*

moose [ˈmuːs] *ns & pl* : alce *m*

moot [ˈmuːt] *adj* : discutible

mop [ˈmɑp] *n* **1** : trapeador *m* Lat, fregona *f* Spain **2** *or* ~ **of hair** : pelambrera *f* — ~ *vt* **mopped; mopping** : trapear Lat, pasar la fregona a Spain

mope [ˈmoːp] *vi* **moped; moping** : andar deprimido

moped [ˈmoːped] *n* : ciclomotor *m*

moral [ˈmɔrəl] *adj* : moral — ~ *n* **1** : moraleja *f* (de un cuento, etc.) **2** ~**s** *npl* : moral *f*, moralidad *f* — **morale** [məˈræl] *n* : moral *f* — **morality** [məˈræləti] *n, pl* **-ties** : moralidad *f*

morbid [ˈmɔrbɪd] *adj* : morboso

more [ˈmor] *adj* : más — ~ *adv* **1** : más **2** ~ **and** ~ : cada vez más **3** ~ **or less** : más o menos **4 once** ~ : una vez más — ~ *n* : más *m* — ~ *pron* : más — **moreover** [morˈoːvər] *adv* : además

morgue [ˈmɔrg] *n* : depósito *m* de cadáveres

morning [ˈmɔrnɪŋ] *n* **1** : mañana *f* **2 good** ~! : ¡buenos días! **3 in the** ~ : por la mañana

moron [ˈmorˌɑn] *n* : estúpido *m*, -da *f*; imbécil *mf*

morose [məˈroːs] *adj* : malhumorado

morphine [ˈmɔrˌfiːn] *n* : morfina *f*

morsel [ˈmɔrsəl] *n* **1** BITE : bocado *m* **2** FRAGMENT : pedazo *m*

mortal [ˈmɔrtəl] *adj* : mortal — ~ *n* : mortal *mf* — **mortality** [mɔrˈtæləti] *n* : mortalidad *f*

mortar [ˈmɔrtər] *n* : mortero *m*

mortgage [ˈmɔrgɪdʒ] *n* : hipoteca *f* — ~ *vt* **-gaged; -gaging** : hipotecar

mortify [ˈmɔrtəˌfaɪ] *vt* **-fied; -fying 1** : mortificar **2** HUMILIATE : avergonzar

mosaic [moˈzeɪk] *n* : mosaico *m*

Moslem [ˈmɑzləm] → **Muslim**

mosque [ˈmɑsk] *n* : mezquita *f*

mosquito [məˈskiːˌto] *n, pl* **-toes** : mosquito *m*, zancudo *m* Lat

moss [ˈmɔs] *n* : musgo *m*

most [ˈmoːst] *adj* **1** : la mayoría de, la mayor parte de **2 (the)** ~ : más — ~ *adv* : más — ~ *n* : más *m*, máximo *m* — ~ *pron* : la mayoría, la mayor parte — **mostly** [ˈmoːstli] *adv* **1** MAINLY : en su mayor parte, principalmente **2** USUALLY : normalmente

motel [moˈtel] *n* : motel *m*

moth [ˈmɔθ] *n* : palomilla *f*, polilla *f*

mother [ˈmʌðər] *n* : madre *f* — ~ *vt* **1** : cuidar de **2** SPOIL : mimar — **motherhood** [ˈmʌðərˌhʊd] *n* : maternidad *f* — **mother-in-law** [ˈmʌðərˌɪnˌlɔ] *n, pl* **mothers-in-law** : suegra *f* — **motherly** [ˈmʌðərli] *adj* : maternal — **mother-of-pearl** [ˌmʌðərəvˈpərl] *n* : nácar *m*

motif [moˈtiːf] *n* : motivo *m*

motion ['moːʃən] *n* **1** : movimiento *m* **2** PROPOSAL : moción *f* **3 set in ~** : poner en marcha — **~** *vi* **~ to s.o.** : hacer una señal a algn — **motionless** ['moːʃənləs] *adj* : inmóvil — **motion picture** *n* : película *f*

motive ['moːtɪv] *n* : motivo *m* — **motivate** ['moːtəˌveɪt] *vt* **-vated; -vating** : motivar — **motivation** [ˌmoːtəˈveɪʃən] *n* : motivación *f*

motor ['moːtər] *n* : motor *m* — **motorbike** ['moːtərˌbaɪk] *n* : motocicleta *f* (pequeña), moto *f* — **motorboat** ['moːtərˌboːt] *n* : lancha *f* motora — **motorcycle** ['moːtərˌsaɪkəl] *n* : motocicleta *f* — **motorcyclist** ['moːtərˌsaɪkəlɪst] *n* : motociclista *mf* — **motorist** ['moːtərɪst] *n* : automovilista *mf*, motorista *mf Lat*

motto ['moːtoː] *n, pl* **-toes** : lema *m*

mould ['moːld] → **mold**

mound ['maʊnd] *n* **1** PILE : montón *m* **2** HILL : montículo *m*

mount¹ ['maʊnt] *n* **1** HORSE : montura *f* **2** SUPPORT : soporte *m* — **~** *vt* : montar (un caballo, etc.), subir (una escalera) — *vi* INCREASE : aumentar

mount² *n* HILL : monte *m* — **mountain** ['maʊntən] *n* : montaña *f* — **mountainous** ['maʊntənəs] *adj* : montañoso

mourn ['morn] *vt* : llorar (por) — *vi* : lamentarse — **mourner** ['mornər] *n* : doliente *mf* — **mournful** ['mornfəl] *adj* : triste — **mourning** ['mornɪŋ] *n* : luto *m*

mouse ['maʊs] *n, pl* **mice** ['maɪs] : ratón *m* — **mousetrap** ['maʊsˌtræp] *n* : ratonera *f*

moustache ['mʌˌstæʃ, məˈstæʃ] → **mustache**

mouth ['maʊθ] *n* : boca *f* (de una persona o un animal), desembocadura *f* (de un río) — **mouthful** ['maʊθˌfʊl] *n* : bocado *m* — **mouthpiece** ['maʊθˌpiːs] *n* : boquilla *f* (de un instrumento musical)

move ['muːv] *v* **moved; moving** *vi* **1** GO : ir **2** RELOCATE : mudarse **3** STIR : moverse **4** ACT : tomar medidas — *vt* **1** : mover **2** AFFECT : conmover **3** TRANSPORT : transportar, trasladar **4** PROPOSE : proponer — **~** *n* **1** MOVEMENT : movimiento *m* **2** RELOCATION : mudanza *f* **3** STEP : medida *f* — **movable** ['muːvəbəl] *or* **moveable** *adj* : movible, móvil — **movement** ['muːvmənt] *n* : movimiento *m*

movie ['muːvi] *n* **1** : película *f* **2 ~s** *npl* : cine *m*

mow ['moː] *vt* **mowed; mowed** *or* **mown** ['moːn]; **mowing** : cortar (la hierba) — **mower** ['moːər] → **lawn mower**

Mr. ['mɪstər] *n, pl* **Messrs.** ['mesərz] : señor *m*

Mrs. ['mɪsəz, -səs, *esp South* 'mɪzəz, -zəs] *n, pl* **Mesdames** [merˈdeɪm, -ˈdæm] : señora *f*

Ms. ['mɪz] *n* : señora *f*, señorita *f*

much ['mʌtʃ] *adj* **more; most** : mucho — **~** *adv* **more** ['mor]; **most** ['moːst] **1** : mucho **2 as ~ as** : tanto como **3 how ~?** : ¿cuánto? **4 too ~** : demasiado — **~** *pron* : mucho, -cha

muck ['mʌk] *n* **1** DIRT : mugre *f*, suciedad *f* **2** MANURE : estiércol *m*

mucus ['mjuːkəs] *n* : mucosidad *f*

mud ['mʌd] *n* : barro *m*, lodo *m*

muddle ['mʌdəl] *v* **-dled; -dling** *vt* **1** CONFUSE : confundir **2** JUMBLE : desordenar — *vi* **~ through** : arreglárselas — **~** *n* : confusión *f*, lío *m fam*

muddy ['mʌdi] *adj* **-dier; -est** : fangoso, lleno de barro

muffin ['mʌfən] *n* : mollete *m*

muffle ['mʌfəl] *vt* **-fled; -fling** : amortiguar (un sonido) — **muffler** ['mʌflər] *n* **1** SCARF : bufanda *f* **2** : silenciador *m*, mofle *m Lat* (de un automóvil)

mug ['mʌg] *n* CUP : tazón *m* — **~** *vt* : asaltar, atracar — **mugger** ['mʌgər] *n* : atracador *m*, -dora *f*

muggy ['mʌgi] *adj* **-gier; -est** : bochornoso

mule ['mjuːl] *n* : mula *f*

mull ['mʌl] *vt or* **~ over** : reflexionar sobre

multicolored [ˌmʌltiˈkʌlərd, ˌmʌltaɪ-] *adj* : multicolor

multimedia [ˌmʌltiˈmiːdiə, ˌmʌltaɪ-] *adj* : multimedia

multinational [ˌmʌltiˈnæʃənəl, ˌmʌltaɪ-] *adj* : multinacional

multiple ['mʌltəpəl] *adj* : múltiple — **~** *n* : múltiplo *m* — **multiplication** [ˌmʌltəpləˈkeɪʃən] *n* : multiplicación *f* — **multiply** ['mʌltəplaɪ] *v* **-plied; -plying** *vt* : multiplicar — *vi* : multiplicarse

multitude ['mʌltəˌtuːd, -ˌtjuːd] *n* : multitud *f*

mum ['mʌm] *adj* **keep ~** : guardar silencio

mumble ['mʌmbəl] *v* **-bled; -bling** *vt* : mascullar — *vi* : hablar entre dientes

mummy ['mʌmi] *n, pl* **-mies** : momia *f*

mumps ['mʌmps] *ns & pl* : paperas *fpl*

munch ['mʌntʃ] *v* : mascar, masticar

mundane [ˌmʌnˈdeɪn, 'mʌn-] *adj* : rutinario, ordinario

municipal [mjʊˈnɪsəpəl] *adj* : municipal — **municipality** [mjʊ͵nɪsəˈpæləţi] *n, pl* **-ties** : municipio *m*

munitions [mjʊˈnɪʃənz] *npl* : municiónes *fpl*

mural [ˈmjʊrəl] *n* : mural *m*

murder [ˈmərdər] *n* : asesinato *m*, homicidio *m* — *vt* : asesinar, matar — *vi* : matar — **murderer** [ˈmərdərər] *n* : asesino *m*, -na *f*; homicida *mf* — **murderous** [ˈmərdərəs] *adj* : asesino, homicida

murky [ˈmərki] *adj* **-kier; -est** : turbio, oscuro

murmur [ˈmərmər] *n* : murmullo *m* — **murmur** *v* : mumurar

muscle [ˈmʌsəl] *n* : músculo *m* — *vi* **-cled; -cling** *or* ~ **in** : meterse por la fuerza en — **muscular** [ˈmʌskjələr] *adj* **1** : muscular **2** STRONG : musculoso

muse[1] [ˈmjuːz] *n* : musa *f*

muse[2] *vi* **mused; musing** : meditar

museum [mjʊˈziːəm] *n* : museo *m*

mushroom [ˈmʌʃ͵ruːm, -͵rʊm] *n* **1** : hongo *m*, seta *f* **2** : champiñón *m* (en la cocina) — ~ *vi* GROW : crecer rápidamente, multiplicarse

mushy [ˈmʌʃi] *adj* **mushier; -est 1** SOFT : blando **2** MAWKISH : sensiblero

music [ˈmjuːzɪk] *n* : música *f* — **musical** [ˈmjuːzɪkəl] *adj* : musical — ~ *n* : comedia *f* musical — **musician** [mjʊˈzɪʃən] *n* : músico *m*, -ca *f*

Muslim [ˈmʌzləm, ˈmʊs-, ˈmʊz-] *adj* : musulmán — ~ *n* : musulmán *m*, -mana *f*

muslin [ˈmʌzlən] *n* : muselina *f*

mussel [ˈmʌsəl] *n* : mejillón *m*

must [ˈmʌst] *v aux* **1** : deber, tener que **2 you** ~ **come** : tienes que venir **3 you**

~ **be tired** : debes (de) estar cansado — ~ *n* : necesidad *f*

mustache [ˈmʌ͵stæʃ, mʌˈstæʃ] *n* : bigote *m*, bigotes *mpl*

mustang [ˈmʌ͵stæŋ] *n* : mustang *m*

mustard [ˈmʌstərd] *n* : mostaza *f*

muster [ˈmʌstər] *vt* **1** : reunir **2** *or* ~ **up** : armarse de, cobrar (valor, fuerzas, etc.)

musty [ˈmʌsti] *adj* **mustier; -est** : que huele a cerrado

mute [ˈmjuːt] *adj* **muter; mutest** : mudo — ~ *n* : mudo *m*, -da *f*

mutilate [ˈmjuːţə͵leɪt] *vt* **-lated; -lating** : mutilar

mutiny [ˈmjuːţəni] *n, pl* **-nies** : motín *m* — ~ *vi* **-nied; -nying** : amotinarse

mutter [ˈmʌţər] *vi* : murmurar

mutton [ˈmʌţən] *n* : carne *f* de carnero

mutual [ˈmjuːtʃʊəl] *adj* **1** : mutuo **2** COMMON : común — **mutually** [ˈmjuːtʃʊəli, -tʃəli] *adv* : mutuamente

muzzle [ˈmʌzəl] *n* **1** SNOUT : hocico *m* **2** : bozal *m* (para un perro, etc.) **3** : boca *f* (de un arma de fuego) — ~ *vt* **-zled; -zling** : poner un bozal a (un animal)

my [ˈmaɪ] *adj* : mi

myopia [maɪˈoːpiə] *n* : miopía *f* — **myopic** [maɪˈoːpɪk, -ˈɑ-] *adj* : miope

myself [maɪˈself] *pron* **1** (*reflexive*) : me **2** (*emphatic*) : yo mismo **3 by** ~ : solo

mystery [ˈmɪstəri] *n, pl* **-teries** : misterio *m* — **mysterious** [mɪˈstɪriəs] *adj* : misterioso

mystic [ˈmɪstɪk] *adj or* **mystical** [ˈmɪstɪkəl] : místico

mystify [ˈmɪstə͵faɪ] *vt* **-fied; -fying** : dejar perplejo, confundir

mystique [mɪˈstiːk] *n* : aura *f* de misterio

myth [ˈmɪθ] *n* : mito *m* — **mythical** [ˈmɪθɪkəl] *adj* : mítico

N

n [ˈɛn] *n, pl* **n's** *or* **ns** [ˈɛnz] : n *f*, decimocuarta letra del alfabeto inglés

nab [ˈnæb] *vt* **nabbed; nabbing 1** ARREST : pescar *fam* **2** GRAB : agarrar

nag [ˈnæg] *v* **nagged; nagging** *vi* COMPLAIN : quejarse — *vt* **1** ANNOY : fastidiar, dar la lata a **2** SCOLD : regañar — **nagging** *adj* : persistente

nail [ˈneɪl] *n* **1** : clavo *m* **2** : uña *f* (de un dedo) — ~ *vt or* ~ **down** : clavar — **nail file** *n* : lima *f* de uñas

naive *or* **naïve** [nɑˈiːv] *adj* **-iver; -est** : ingenuo — **naïveté** [͵nɑ͵iːvəˈteɪ, nɑˈiːvə-] *n* : ingenuidad *f*

naked [ˈneɪkəd] *adj* **1** : desnudo **2 the** ~ **truth** : la pura verdad **3 to the** ~ **eye** : a simple vista

name [ˈneɪm] *n* **1** : nombre *m* **2** REPUTATION : fama *f* **3 what is your** ~? : ¿cómo se llama? **4** → **first name, surname** — ~ *vt* **named; naming 1** : poner nombre a **2** APPOINT : nombrar **3** ~ **a price** : fijar un precio — **nameless** [ˈneɪmləs] *adj* : anónimo — **namely** [ˈneɪmli] *adv* : a saber — **namesake** [ˈneɪm͵seɪk] *n* : tocayo *m*, -ya *f*

nap[1] [ˈnæp] *vi* **napped; napping** : echarse una siesta — ~ *n* : siesta *f*

nap² *n* : pelo *m* (de una tela)
nape ['neɪp, 'næp] *n or* ~ **of the neck** : nuca *f*
napkin ['næpkən] *n* 1 : servilleta *f* 2 → **sanitary napkin**
narcotic [nɑrˈkɑtɪk] *n* : narcótico *m*, estupefaciente *m*
narrate ['nær,eɪt] *vt* **-rated; -rating** : narrar — **narration** [næˈreɪʃən] *n* : narración *f* — **narrative** ['nærətɪv] *n* : narración *f* — **narrator** ['nær,eɪtər] *n* : narrador *m*, -dora *f*
narrow ['nær,oː] *adj* 1 : estrecho, angosto 2 RESTRICTED : limitado — ~ *vi* : estrecharse — *vt* 1 : estrechar 2 or ~ **down** : limitar — **narrowly** ['næroli] *adv* : por poco — **narrow–minded** [næroˈmaɪndəd] *adj* : de miras estrechas
nasal ['neɪzəl] *adj* : nasal
nasty ['næsti] *adj* **-tier; -est** 1 MEAN : malo, cruel 2 UNPLEASANT : desagradable 3 REPUGNANT : asqueroso — **nastiness** ['næstinəs] *n* : maldad *f*
nation ['neɪʃən] *n* : nación *f* — **national** ['næʃənəl] *adj* : nacional — **nationalism** ['næʃənəˌlɪzəm] *n* : nacionalismo *m* — **nationality** [næʃəˈnæləti] *n, pl* **-ties** : nacionalidad *f* — **nationalize** ['næʃənəˌlaɪz] *vt* **-ized; -izing** : nacionalizar — **nationwide** ['neɪʃənˈwaɪd] *adj* : por todo el país
native ['neɪtɪv] *adj* 1 : natal (dícese de un país, etc.) 2 INNATE : innato 3 ~ **language** : lengua *f* materna — ~ *n* 1 : nativo *m*, -va *f* 2 be a ~ **of** : ser natural de — **Native American** : indio *m* americano, india *f* americana — **nativity** [nəˈtɪvəti, neɪ-] *n, pl* **-ties the Nativity** : la Navidad
nature ['neɪtʃər] *n* 1 : naturaleza *f* 2 KIND : índole *f*, clase *f* 3 DISPOSITION : carácter *m*, natural *m* — **natural** ['nætʃərəl] *adj* : natural — **naturalize** ['nætʃərəˌlaɪz] *vt* **-ized; -izing** : naturalizar — **naturally** ['nætʃərəli] *adv* : naturalmente
naught ['nɔt] *n* 1 NOTHING : nada *f* 2 ZERO : cero *m*
naughty ['nɔti] *adj* **-tier; -est** 1 : travieso, pícaro 2 RISQUÉ : picante
nausea ['nɔziə, 'nɔʃə] *n* : náuseas *fpl* — **nauseating** *adj* : nauseabundo — **nauseous** ['nɔʃəs, -ziəs] *adj* 1 feel ~ : sentir náuseas 2 SICKENING : nauseabundo
nautical ['nɔtɪkəl] *adj* : náutico
naval ['neɪvəl] *adj* : naval
nave ['neɪv] *n* : nave *f* (de una iglesia)
navel ['neɪvəl] *n* : ombligo *m*

navigate ['nævəˌgeɪt] *v* **-gated; -gating** *vi* : navegar — *vt* 1 : gobernar (un barco), pilotar (un avión) 2 : navegar por (un río, etc.) — **navigable** ['nævɪgəbəl] *adj* : navegable — **navigation** [nævəˈgeɪʃən] *n* : navegación *f* — **navigator** ['nævəˌgeɪtər] *n* : navegante *mf*
navy ['neɪvi] *n, pl* **-vies** 1 : marina *f* de guerra 2 or ~ **blue** : azul *m* marino
near ['nɪr] *adv* : cerca — ~ *prep* : cerca de — ~ *adj* : cercano, próximo — ~ *vt* : acercarse a — **nearby** [nɪrˈbaɪ, 'nɪr,baɪ] *adv* : cerca — ~ *adj* : cercano — **nearly** ['nɪrli] *adv* : casi — **nearsighted** ['nɪrˌsaɪtəd] *adj* : miope, corto de vista
neat ['niːt] *adj* 1 TIDY : muy arreglado 2 CLEVER : hábil, ingenioso — **neatly** ['niːtli] *adv* 1 : ordenadamente 2 CLEVERLY : hábilmente — **neatness** ['niːtnəs] *n* : pulcritud *f*, orden *m*
nebulous ['nɛbjʊləs] *adj* : nebuloso
necessary ['nɛsəˌseri] *adj* : necesario — **necessarily** [nɛsəˈserəli] *adv* : necesariamente — **necessitate** [nɪˈsesəˌteɪt] *vt* **-tated; -tating** : exigir, requerir — **necessity** [nɪˈsesəti] *n, pl* **-ties** 1 : necesidad *f* 2 **necessities** *npl* : cosas *fpl* indispensables
neck ['nɛk] *n* 1 : cuello *m* (de una persona o una botella), pescuezo *m* (de un animal) 2 COLLAR : cuello *m* — **necklace** ['nɛkləs] *n* : collar *m* — **necktie** ['nɛk,taɪ] *n* : corbata *f*
nectar ['nɛktər] *n* : néctar *m*
nectarine [nɛktəˈriːn] *n* : nectarina *f*
need ['niːd] *n* 1 : necesidad *f* 2 if ~ **be** : si hace falta — ~ *vt* 1 : necesitar, exigir 2 ~ **to** : tener que — *v aux* : tener que
needle ['niːdəl] *n* : aguja *f* — ~ *vt* **-dled; -dling** : pinchar
needless ['niːdləs] *adj* 1 : innecesario 2 ~ **to say** : de más está decir
needlework ['niːdəlˌwərk] *n* : bordado *m*
needn't ['niːdənt] (*contraction of* **need not**) → **need**
needy ['niːdi] *adj* **needier; -est** *adj* : necesitado
negative ['nɛgətɪv] *adj* : negativo — ~ *n* 1 : negación *f* (en gramática) 2 : negativo *m* (en fotografía)
neglect [nɪˈglɛkt] *vt* : descuidar — ~ *n* : descuido *m*, abandono *m*
negligee [nɛgləˈʒeɪ] *n* : negligé *m*
negligence ['nɛglɪdʒənts] *n* : negligencia *f*, descuido *m* — **negligent** ['nɛglɪdʒənt] *adj* : negligente, descuidado
negligible ['nɛglɪdʒəbəl] *adj* : insignificante

negotiate [nɪ'goːʃiˌeɪt] v **-ated; -ating** : negociar — **negotiable** [nɪ'goːʃəbəl, -ʃiə-] adj : negociable — **negotiation** [nɪˌgoːʃiˈeɪʃən, -siˈeɪ-] n : negociación f — **negotiator** [nɪˈgoːʃiˌeɪtər, -siˌeɪ-] n : negociador m, -dora f

Negro ['niːˌgroː] n, pl **-groes** sometimes considered offensive : negro m, -gra f

neigh ['neɪ] vi : relinchar — ~ n : relincho m

neighbor or Brit **neighbour** ['neɪbər] n : vecino m, -na f — **neighborhood** or Brit **neighbourhood** ['neɪbərˌhʊd] n 1 : barrio m, vecindario m 2 **in the ~ of** : alrededor de — **neighborly** or Brit **neighbourly** ['neɪbərli] adv : amable

neither ['niːðər, 'naɪ-] conj 1 ~...**nor** : ni...ni 2 ~ **am/do I** : yo tampoco — ~ pron : ninguno, -na — ~ adj : ninguno (de los dos)

neon ['niːˌɑn] n : neón m

nephew ['neˌfjuː, chiefly British 'neˌvjuː] n : sobrino m

Neptune ['nepˌtuːn, -ˌtjuːn] n : Neptuno m

nerve ['nərv] n 1 : nervio m 2 COURAGE : coraje m 3 GALL : descaro m 4 ~**s** npl JITTERS : nervios mpl — **nervous** ['nərvəs] adj : nervioso — **nervousness** ['nərvəsnəs] n : nerviosismo m — **nervy** ['nərvi] adj **nervier; -est** : descarado

nest ['nest] n : nido m — ~ vi : anidar

nestle ['nesəl] vi **-tled; -tling** : acurrucarse

net[1] ['net] n : red f — ~ vt **netted; netting** : pescar, atrapar (con una red)

net[2] adj : neto — ~ vt **netted; netting** YIELD : producir neto

nettle ['netəl] n : ortiga f

network ['netˌwərk] n : red f

neurology [nʊˈrɑlədʒi, njʊ-] n : neurología f

neurosis [nʊˈroːsɪs, njʊ-] n, pl **-roses** [-ˌsiːz] : neurosis f — **neurotic** [nʊˈrɑtɪk, njʊ-] adj : neurótico

neuter ['nuːtər, 'njuː-] adj : neutro — ~ vt : castrar

neutral ['nuːtrəl, 'njuː-] n : punto m muerto (de un automóvil) — ~ adj 1 : neutral 2 : neutro (en electrotecnia o química) — **neutrality** [nuːˈtrælət̬i, njuː-] n : neutralidad f — **neutralize** ['nuːtrəˌlaɪz, 'njuː-] vt **-ized; -izing** : neutralizar

neutron ['nuːˌtrɑn, 'njuː-] n : neutrón m

never ['nevər] adv 1 : nunca, jamás 2 NOT : no 3 ~ **again** : nunca más 4 ~ **mind** : no importa — **nevermore** [ˌnevərˈmor] adv : nunca jamás — **nev-**

ertheless [ˌnevərðəˈles] adv : sin embargo, no obstante

new ['nuː, 'njuː] adj : nuevo — **newborn** ['nuːˌbɔrn, 'njuː-] adj : recién nacido — **newcomer** ['nuːˌkʌmər, 'njuː-] n : recién llegado m, -da f — **newly** ['nuːli, 'njuː-] adv : recién, recientemente — **newlywed** ['nuːliˌwed, 'njuː-] n : recién casado m, -da f — **news** ['nuːz, 'njuːz] n : noticias fpl — **newscast** ['nuːzˌkæst, 'njuːz-] n : noticiario m, noticiero m Lat — **newscaster** ['nuːzˌkæstər, 'njuːz-] n : presentador m, -dora f (de un noticiario) — **newsletter** ['nuːzˌlet̬ər, 'njuːz-] n : boletín m informativo — **newspaper** ['nuːzˌpeɪpər, 'njuːz-] n : periódico m, diario m — **newsstand** ['nuːzˌstænd, 'njuːz-] n : puesto m de periódicos

newt ['nuːt, 'njuːt] n : tritón m

New Year's Day n : día m del Año Nuevo

next ['nekst] adj 1 : próximo 2 FOLLOWING : siguiente — ~ adv 1 : la próxima vez 2 AFTERWARD : después, luego 3 NOW : ahora — **next-door** ['nekst-'dor] adj : de al lado — **next to** adv ALMOST : casi — ~ prep BESIDE : al lado de

nib ['nɪb] n : plumilla f

nibble ['nɪbəl] vt **-bled; -bling** : mordisquear

Nicaraguan [ˌnɪkəˈrɑgwən] adj : nicaragüense

nice ['naɪs] adj **nicer; nicest** 1 PLEASANT : agradable, bueno 2 KIND : amable — **nicely** ['naɪsli] adv 1 WELL : bien 2 KINDLY : amablemente — **niceness** ['naɪsnəs] n : amabilidad f — **niceties** ['naɪsət̬iz] npl : detalles mpl, sutilezas fpl

niche ['nɪtʃ] n 1 : nicho m 2 **find one's ~** : hacerse su hueco

nick ['nɪk] n 1 : corte m pequeño, muesca f 2 **in the ~ of time** : justo a tiempo — ~ vt : hacer una muesca en

nickel ['nɪkəl] n 1 : níquel m (metal) 2 : moneda f de cinco centavos

nickname ['nɪkˌneɪm] n : apodo m, sobrenombre m — ~ vt **-named; -naming** : apodar

nicotine ['nɪkəˌtiːn] n : nicotina f

niece ['niːs] n : sobrina f

niggling ['nɪgəlɪŋ] adj 1 PETTY : insignificante 2 PERSISTENT : constante

night ['naɪt] n 1 : noche f 2 **at ~** : de noche 3 **last ~** : anoche 4 **tomorrow ~** : mañana por la noche — **nightclub** ['naɪtˌklʌb] n : club m nocturno — **nightfall** ['naɪtˌfɔl] n : anochecer m — **nightgown** ['naɪtˌgaʊn] n : camisón m (de noche) — **nightly** ['naɪt] *adj* : de todas las noches — ~ *adv* : cada noche — **nightmare** ['naɪt,mær] *n* : pesadilla *f* — **nighttime** ['naɪt,taɪm] *n* : noche *f*

nil ['nɪl] *n* NOTHING : nada *f*

nimble ['nɪmbəl] *adj* **-bler; -blest** : ágil

nine ['naɪn] *adj* : nueve — ~ *n* : nueve *m* — **nine hundred** *adj* : novecientos — ~ *n* : novecientos *m* — **nineteen** [naɪn'tiːn] *adj* : diecinueve — ~ *n* : diecinueve *m* — **nineteenth** [naɪn-'tiːnθ] *adj* : decimonoveno, decimonono — ~ *n* **1** : decimonoveno *m*, -na *f*; decimonono *m*, -na *f* (en una serie) **2** : diecinueveavo *m* (en matemáticas) — **ninetieth** ['naɪntiəθ] *adj* : nonagésimo — ~ *n* **1** : nonagésimo *m*, -ma *f* (en una serie) **2** : noventavo *m* (en matemáticas) — **ninety** ['naɪnt̬i] *adj* : noventa — ~ *n*, *pl* **-ties** : noventa *m* — **ninth** ['naɪnθ] *adj* : noveno — ~ *n* **1** : noveno *m*, -na *f* (en una serie) **2** : noveno *m* (en matemáticas)

nip ['nɪp] *vt* **nipped; nipping 1** PINCH : pellizcar **2** BITE : mordisquear **3** ~ **in the bud** : cortar de raíz — ~ *n* **1** PINCH : pellizco *m* **2** NIBBLE : mordisco *m*

nipple ['nɪpəl] *n* **1** : pezón *m* (de una mujer) **2** : tetilla *f* (de un hombre o un biberón)

nitrogen ['naɪtrədʒən] *n* : nitrógen *m*

nitwit ['nɪt,wɪt] *n* : idiota *mf*

no ['noː] *adv* : no — ~ *adj* **1** : ninguno **2 I have** ~ **money** : no tengo dinero **3 it's** ~ **trouble** : no es ningún problema **4** ~ **smoking** : prohibido fumar — ~ *n*, *pl* **noes** *or* **nos** ['noːz] : no *m*

noble ['noːbəl] *adj* **-bler; -blest** : noble — ~ *n* : noble *mf* — **nobility** [noˈbɪlət̬i] *n* : nobleza *f*

nobody ['noːbədi, -,bɑdi] *pron* : nadie

nocturnal [nɑkˈtərnəl] *adj* : nocturno

nod ['nɑd] *v* **nodded; nodding** *vi* **1** *or* ~ **yes** : asentir con la cabeza **2** ~ **off** : dormirse — *vt* ~ **one's head** : asentir con la cabeza — ~ *n* : señal *m* con la cabeza

noes → **no**

noise ['nɔɪz] *n* : ruido *m* — **noisily** ['nɔɪzəli] *adv* : ruidosamente — **noisy** ['nɔɪzi] *adj* **noisier; -est** : ruidoso

nomad ['noː,mæd] *n* : nómada *mf* — **nomadic** [noˈmædɪk] *adj* : nómada

nominal ['nɑmənəl] *adj* : nominal

nominate ['nɑmə,neɪt] *vt* **-nated; -nating 1** : proponer, postular *Lat* **2** APPOINT : nombrar — **nomination**

[,nɑməˈneɪʃən] *n* **1** : propuesta *f*, postulación *f Lat* **2** APPOINTMENT : nombramiento *m*

nonalcoholic [,nɑn,ælkəˈhɔlɪk] *adj* : no alcohólico

nonchalant [,nɑnʃəˈlɑnt] *adj* : despreocupado

noncommissioned officer [,nɑnkə-ˈmɪʃənd] *n* : suboficial *mf*

noncommittal [,nɑnkəˈmɪt̬əl] *adj* : evasivo

nondescript [,nɑndrˈskrɪpt] *adj* : anodino, soso

none ['nʌn] *pron* **1** : ninguno, ninguna — **there are** ~ **left** : no hay más — ~ *adv* **1 be** ~ **the worse** : no sufrir daño alguno **2** ~ **too happy** : nada contento **3** ~ **too soon** : a buena hora

nonentity [,nɑnˈent̬ət̬i] *n*, *pl* **-ties** : persona *f* insignificante

nonetheless [,nʌnðəˈles] *adv* : sin embargo, no obstante

nonexistent [,nɑnɪgˈzɪstənt] *adj* : inexistente

nonfat [,nɑnˈfæt] *adj* : sin grasa

nonfiction [,nɑnˈfɪkʃən] *n* : no ficción *f*

nonprofit [,nɑnˈprɑfət] *adj* : sin fines lucrativos

nonsense ['nɑn,sens, 'nɑnt,sənts] *n* : tonterías *fpl*, disparates *mpl* — **nonsensical** [nɑnˈsentsɪkəl] *adj* : absurdo

nonsmoker [,nɑnˈsmoːkər] *n* : no fumador *m*, -dora *f*

nonstop [,nɑnˈstɑp] *adj* : directo — ~ *adv* : sin parar

noodle ['nuːdəl] *n* : fideo *m*

nook ['nʊk] *n* : rincón *m*

noon ['nuːn] *n* : mediodía *m*

no one *pron* : nadie

noose ['nuːs] *n* **1** : dogal *m*, soga *f* **2** LASSO : lazo *m*

nor ['nɔr] *conj* **1 neither...~** : ni...ni **2** ~ **I** : yo tampoco

norm ['nɔrm] *n* **1** : norma *f* **2 the** ~ : lo normal — **normal** ['nɔrməl] *adj* : normal — **normality** [nɔrˈmælət̬i] *n* : normalidad *f* — **normally** *adv* : normalmente

north ['nɔrθ] *adv* : al norte — ~ *adj* : norte, del norte — ~ *n* **1** : norte *m* **2 the North** : el Norte — **North American** *adj* : norteamericano — **northeast** [nɔrˈθiːst] *adv* : hacia el nordeste — ~ *adj* : nordeste, del nordeste — ~ *n* : nordeste *m*, noreste *m* — **northeastern** [nɔrˈθiːstərn] *adj* : nordeste, del nordeste — **northerly** ['nɔrðərli] *adj* : del norte — **northern** ['nɔrðərn] *adj* : del norte, norteño — **northwest** [nɔrˈθwest] *adv* : hacia el noroeste —

~ *adj* : noroeste, del noroeste — ~ *n* : noroeste *m* — **northwestern** [nɔrθ-ˈwɛstərn] *adj* : noroeste, del noroeste

Norwegian [nɔrˈwiːdʒən] *adj* : noruego

nose [ˈnoːz] *n* **1** : nariz *f* (de una persona), hocico *m* (de un animal) **2 blow one's ~** : sonarse las narices — ~ *vi* **nosed; nosing** *or* ~ **around** : meter las narices — **nosebleed** [ˈnoːzˌbliːd] *n* : hemorragia *f* nasal — **nosedive** [ˈnoːzˌdaɪv] *n* : descenso *m* en picada

nostalgia [nɑˈstældʒə, nə-] *n* : nostalgia *f* — **nostalgic** [nɑˈstældʒɪk, nə-] *adj* : nostálgico

nostril [ˈnɑstrəl] *n* : ventana *f* de la nariz

nosy *or* **nosey** [ˈnoːzi] *adj* **nosier; -est** : entrometido

not [ˈnɑt] *adv* **1** : no **2 he's ~ tired** : no esta cansado **3 I hope ~** : espero que no **4 ~ ... anything** : no...nada

notable [ˈnoːtəbəl] *adj* : notable — ~ *n* : personaje *m* — **notably** [ˈnoːtəbli] *adv* : notablemente

notary public [ˈnoːtəri-] *n, pl* **notaries public** *or* **notary publics** : notario *m*, -ria *f*

notation [noˈteɪʃən] *n* : anotación *f*

notch [ˈnɑtʃ] *n* : muesca *f*, corte *m* — ~ *vt* : hacer un corte en

note [ˈnoːt] *vt* **noted; noting 1** NOTICE : observar, notar **2** RECORD : anotar — ~ *n* **1** : nota *f* **2 of ~** : destacado **3 take ~ of** : prestar atención a **4 take ~s** : apuntar — **notebook** [ˈnoːtˌbʊk] *n* : libreta *f*, cuaderno *m* — **noted** [ˈnoːtəd] *adj* : renombrado, célebre — **noteworthy** [ˈnoːtˌwərði] *adj* : notable

nothing [ˈnʌθɪŋ] *pron* **1** : nada **2 be ~ but** : no ser más que **3 for ~ FREE** : gratis — ~ *n* **1** ZERO : zero *m* **2** TRIFLE : nimiedad *f*

notice [ˈnoːtɪs] *n* **1** SIGN : letrero *m*, aviso *m* **2 at a moment's ~** : sin previo aviso **3 be given one's ~** : ser despedido **4 take ~ of** : prestar atención a — ~ *vt* **-ticed; -ticing** : notar — **noticeable** [ˈnoːtɪsəbəl] *adj* : perceptible, evidente

notify [ˈnoːtəˌfaɪ] *vt* **-fied; -fying** : notificar, avisar — **notification** [ˌnoːtəfə-ˈkeɪʃən] *n* : notificación *f*, aviso *m*

notion [ˈnoːʃən] *n* **1** : noción *f*, idea *f* **2 ~s** *npl* : artículos *mpl* de mercería

notorious [noˈtoːriəs] *adj* : de mala fama — **notoriety** [ˌnoːtəˈraɪəti] *n* : mala fama *f*, notoriedad *f*

notwithstanding [ˌnɑtwɪθˈstændɪŋ, -wɪð-] *prep* : a pesar de, no obstante — ~ *adv* : sin embargo — ~ *conj* : a pesar de que

nougat [ˈnuːgət] *n* : turrón *m*

nought [ˈnɔt, ˈnɑt] → **naught**

noun [ˈnaʊn] *n* : nombre *m*, sustantivo *m*

nourish [ˈnərɪʃ] *vt* : nutrir — **nourishing** [ˈnərɪʃɪŋ] *adj* : nutritivo — **nourishment** [ˈnərɪʃmənt] *n* : alimento *m*

novel [ˈnɑvəl] *adj* : original, novedoso — ~ *n* : novela *f* — **novelist** [ˈnɑvəlɪst] *n* : novelista *mf* — **novelty** [ˈnɑvəlti] *n, pl* **-ties** : novedad *f*

November [noˈvembər] *n* : noviembre *m*

novice [ˈnɑvɪs] *n* : novato *m*, -ta *f*; principiante *mf*

now [ˈnaʊ] *adv* **1** : ahora **2** THEN : entonces **3 from ~ on** : de ahora en adelante **4 ~ and then** : de vez en cuando **5 right ~** : ahora mismo — ~ *conj or* ~ **that** : ahora que, ya que — ~ *n* **1 a year from ~** : dentro de un año **2 by ~** : ya **3 until ~** : hasta ahora — **nowadays** [ˈnaʊəˌdeɪz] *adv* : hoy en día

nowhere [ˈnoːˌhwer] *adv* **1** (*indicating location*) : por ninguna parte, por ningún lado **2** (*indicating motion*) : a ninguna parte, a ningún lado **3 I'm ~ near finished** : aún me falta mucho para terminar **4 it's ~ near here** : queda bastante lejos de aquí — ~ *n* : ninguna parte *f*

nozzle [ˈnɑzəl] *n* : boca *f* (de una manguera, etc.)

nuance [ˈnuːˌɑns, ˈnjuː-] *n* : matiz *m*

nucleus [ˈnuːkliəs, ˈnjuː-] *n, pl* **-clei** [-kliˌaɪ] : núcleo *m* — **nuclear** [ˈnuːkliər, ˈnjuː-] *adj* : nuclear

nude [ˈnuːd, ˈnjuːd] *adj* **nuder; nudest** : desnudo — ~ *n* : desnudo *m*

nudge [ˈnʌdʒ] *vt* **nudged; nudging** : dar un codazo a — ~ *n* : toque *m* (con el codo)

nudity [ˈnuːdəti, ˈnjuː-] *n* : desnudez *f*

nugget [ˈnʌgət] *n* : pepita *f* (de oro, etc.)

nuisance [ˈnuːsəns, ˈnjuː-] *n* **1** ANNOYANCE : fastidio *m*, molestia *f* **2** PEST : pesado *m*, -da *f* fam

null [ˈnʌl] *adj* **~ and void** : nulo y sin efecto

numb [ˈnʌm] *adj* **1** : entumecido, dormido **2 ~ with fear** : paralizado de miedo — ~ *vt* : entumecer, adormecer

number [ˈnʌmbər] *n* **1** : número *m* **2 a ~ of** : varios — ~ *vt* **1** : numerar **2** INCLUDE : contar, incluir **3** TOTAL : ascender a

numeral [ˈnuːmərəl, ˈnjuː-] *n* : número *m* — **numeric** [nʊˈmɛrɪk, njuː-] *or* **numerical** [nʊˈmɛrɪkəl, njuː-] *adj* : numérico — **numerous** [ˈnuːmərəs, ˈnjuː-] *adj* : numeroso

nun ['nʌn] *n* : monja *f*
nuptial ['nʌpʃəl] *adj* : nupcial
nurse ['nərs] *n* **1** : enfermero *m*, -ra *f* **2** → **nursemaid** — ∼ *vt* **nursed; nursing 1** : cuidar (de), atender **2** SUCKLE : amamantar — **nursemaid** ['nərs‚meɪd] *n* : niñera *f* — **nursery** ['nərsəri] *n, pl* **-eries 1** : cuarto *m* de los niños **2** *or* **day** ∼ : guardería *f* **3** : vivero *m* (de plantas) — **nursing home** *n* : asilo *m* de ancianos
nurture ['nərtʃər] *vt* **-tured; -turing 1** NOURISH : nutrir **2** EDUCATE : criar, educar **3** FOSTER : alimentar
nut ['nʌt] *n* **1** : nuez *f* **2** LUNATIC : loco *m*, -ca *f* **3** ENTHUSIAST : fanático *m*, -ca *f* **4** ∼**s and bolts** : tuercas y tornillos —

nutcracker ['nʌt‚krækər] *n* : cascanueces *m*
nutmeg ['nʌt‚meg] *n* : nuez *f* moscada
nutrient ['nu:triənt, 'nju:-] *n* : nutriente *m*
nutrition [nʊ'trɪʃən, nju-] *n* : nutrición *f* — **nutritional** [nʊ'trɪʃənəl, nju-] *adj* : nutritivo — **nutritious** [nʊ'trɪʃəs, nju-] *adj* : nutritivo
nuts ['nʌts] *adj* : loco
nutshell ['nʌt‚ʃɛl] *n* **1** : cáscara *f* de nuez **2 in a** ∼ : en pocas palabras
nutty ['nʌt̬i] *adj* **-tier; -tiest** : loco
nuzzle ['nʌzəl] *v* **-zled; -zling** *vi* : acurrucarse — *vt* : acariciar con el hocico
nylon ['naɪ‚lɑn] *n* **1** : nilón *m* **2** ∼**s** *npl* : medias *fpl* de nilón
nymph ['nɪmpf] *n* : ninfa *f*

O

o ['oː] *n, pl* **o's** *or* **os** ['oːz] **1** : o *f*, decimoquinta letra del alfabeto inglés **2** ZERO : cero *m*
O ['oː] → **oh**
oaf ['oːf] *n* : zoquete *m*
oak ['oːk] *n, pl* **oaks** *or* **oak** : roble *m*
oar ['oːr] *n* : remo *m*
oasis [o'eɪsɪs] *n, pl* **oases** [-‚siːz] : oasis *m*
oath ['oːθ] *n, pl* **oaths** ['oːðz, 'oːθs] **1** : juramento *m* **2** SWEARWORD : palabrota *f*
oats ['oːts] *npl* : avena *f* — **oatmeal** ['oːt‚miːl] *n* : harina *f* de avena
obedient [o'biːdiənt] *adj* : obediente — **obedience** [o'biːdiənts] *n* : obediencia *f*
obese [o'biːs] *adj* : obeso — **obesity** [o'biːsət̬i] *n* : obesidad *f*
obey [o'beɪ] *v* **obeyed; obeying** : obedecer
obituary [ə'bɪtʃu‚ɛri] *n, pl* **-aries** : obituario *m*
object ['ɑbdʒɪkt] *n* **1** : objeto *m* **2** AIM : objetivo *m* **3** : complemento *m* (en gramática) — ∼ [əb'dʒɛkt] *vt* : objetar — *vi* ∼ **to** : oponerse a — **objection** [əb'dʒɛkʃən] *n* : objeción *f* — **objectionable** [əb'dʒɛkʃənəbəl] *adj* : desagradable — **objective** [əb'dʒɛktɪv] *adj* : objetivo — *n* : objetivo *m*
oblige [ə'blaɪdʒ] *vt* **obliged; obliging 1** : obligar **2 be much** ∼**d** : estar muy agradecido **3** — **s.o.** : hacer un favor a algn — **obligation** [‚ɑblə'geɪʃən] *n* : obligación *f* — **obligatory** [ə'blɪgə‚tori] *adj* : obligatorio — **obliging** [ə'blaɪdʒɪŋ] *adj* : atento, servicial

oblique [o'bliːk] *adj* **1** SLANTING : oblicuo **2** INDIRECT : indirecto
obliterate [ə'blɪt̬ə‚reɪt] *vt* **-ated; -ating 1** ERASE : borrar **2** DESTROY : arrasar
oblivion [ə'blɪviən] *n* : olvido *m* — **oblivious** [ə'blɪviəs] *adj* : inconsciente
oblong ['ɑ‚blɔŋ] *adj* : oblongo — ∼ *n* : rectángulo *m*
obnoxious [ɑb'nɑkʃəs, əb-] *adj* : odioso
oboe ['oː‚boː] *n* : oboe *m*
obscene [ɑb'siːn, əb-] *adj* : obsceno — **obscenity** [ɑb'sɛnət̬i, əb-] *n, pl* **-ties** : obscenidad *f*
obscurity [ɑb'skjʊrət̬i, əb-] *n, pl* **-ties** : oscuridad *f* — **obscure** [ɑb'skjʊr, əb-] *adj* : oscuro — ∼ *vt* **-scured; -scuring 1** DARKEN : oscurecer **2** HIDE : ocultar
observe [əb'zərv] *v* **-served; -serving** *vt* : observar — *vi* WATCH : mirar — **observance** [əb'zərvənts] *n* **1** : observancia *f* **2 religious** ∼**s** : prácticas *fpl* religiosas — **observant** [əb'zərvənt] *adj* : observador — **observation** [‚ɑbsər'veɪʃən, -zər-] *n* : observación *f* — **observatory** [əb'zərvə‚tori] *n, pl* **-ries** : observatorio *m*
obsess [əb'sɛs] *vt* : obsesionar — **obsession** [ɑb'sɛʃən, əb-] *n* : obsesión *f* — **obsessive** [ɑb'sɛsɪv, əb-] *adj* : obsesivo
obsolete [‚ɑbsə'liːt, 'ɑbsə-] *adj* : obsoleto, desusado
obstacle ['ɑbstɪkəl] *n* : obstáculo *m*
obstetrics [əb'stɛtrɪks] *n* : obstetricia *f*
obstinate ['ɑbstənət] *adj* : obstinado
obstruct [əb'strʌkt] *vt* **1** BLOCK : obstru-

ir **2** HINDER : obstaculizar — **obstruction** [əb'strʌkʃən] *n* : obstrucción *f*

obtain [əb'teɪn] *vt* : obtener, conseguir — **obtainable** [əb'teɪnəbəl] *adj* : asequible

obtrusive [əb'truːsɪv] *adj* : entrometido (dícese de las personas), demasiado prominente (dícese de las cosas)

obtuse [ab'tuːs, əb-, -'tjuːs] *adj* : obtuso

obvious ['abviəs] *adj* : obvio, evidente — **obviously** ['abviəsli] *adv* **1** CLEARLY : obviamente **2** OF COURSE : claro, por supuesto

occasion [ə'keɪʒən] *n* **1** : ocasión *f* **2 on ~** : de vez en cuando — **~** *vt* : ocasionar — **occasional** [ə'keɪʒənəl] *adj* : poco frecuente, ocasional — **occasionally** [ə'keɪʒənəli] *adv* : de vez en cuando

occult [ə'kʌlt, 'a,kʌlt] *adj* : oculto

occupy ['akjə,paɪ] *vt* **-pied; -pying 1** : ocupar **2 ~ oneself** : entretenerse — **occupancy** ['akjəpənsi] *n, pl* **-cies** : ocupación *f* — **occupant** ['akjəpənt] *n* : ocupante *mf* — **occupation** [,akjə'peɪʃən] *n* : ocupación *f* — **occupational** [,akjə'peɪʃənəl] *adj* : profesional

occur [ə'kər] *vi* **occurred; occurring 1** : ocurrir **2** APPEAR : encontrarse **3 ~ to s.o.** : occurírse a algn — **occurrence** [ə'kərənts] *n* **1** EVENT : acontecimiento *m*, suceso *m* **2** INCIDENCE : incidencia *f*

ocean ['oːʃən] *n* : océano *m*

ocher *or* **ochre** ['oːkər] *n* : ocre *m*

o'clock [ə'klak] *adv* **1 at 6 ~** : a las seis **2 it's one ~** : es la una **3 it's ten ~** : son las diez

octagon ['aktə,gan] *n* : octágono *m* — **octagonal** [ak'tægənəl] *adj* : octagonal

octave ['aktɪv] *n* : octava *f*

October [ak'toːbər] *n* : octubre *m*

octopus ['aktə,pus, -pəs] *n, pl* **-puses** *or* **-pi** [-,paɪ] : pulpo *m*

oculist ['akjəlɪst] *n* : oculista *mf*

odd ['ad] *adj* **1** STRANGE : extraño, raro **2** : sin pareja (dícese de un calcetín, etc.) **3 forty ~ years** : cuarenta y tantos años **4 ~ jobs** : algunos trabajos *mpl* **5 ~ number** : número *m* impar — **oddity** ['adəti] *n, pl* **-ties** : rareza *f* — **oddly** ['adli] *adv* : de manera extraña — **odds** ['adz] *npl* **1** CHANCES : probabilidades *fpl* **2 at ~** : en desacuerdo **3 five to one ~** : cinco contra uno (en apuestas) — **odds and ends** *npl* : cosas *fpl* sueltas

ode ['oːd] *n* : oda *f*

odious ['oːdiəs] *adj* : odioso

odor *or Brit* **odour** ['oːdər] *n* : olor *m* —

odorless *or Brit* **odourless** ['oːdərləs] *adj* : inodoro

of ['ʌv, 'əv] *prep* **1** : de **2 five minutes ~ ten** : las diez menos cinco **3 the eighth ~ April** : el ocho de abril

off ['of] *adv* **1 be ~** LEAVE : irse **2 cut ~** : cortar **3 day ~** : día *m* de descanso **4 fall ~** : caerse **5 doze ~** : dormirse **6 far ~** : lejos **7 ~ and on** : de vez en cuando **8 shut ~** : apagar **9 ten miles ~** : a diez millas de aquí — **~** *prep* **1** : de **2 be ~ duty** : estar libre **3 ~ center** : descentrado — **~** *adj* **1** CANCELED : cancelado **2** OUT : apagado **3 an ~ chance** : una posibilidad remota

offend [ə'fend] *vt* : ofender — **offender** [ə'fendər] *n* : delincuente *mf* — **offense** *or* **offence** [ə'fents, 'ɔ,fents] *n* **1** AFFRONT : afrenta *f* **2** ASSAULT : ataque *m* **3** : ofensiva *f* (en deportes) **4** CRIME : delito *m* **5 take ~** : ofenderse — **offensive** [ə'fentsɪv,'ɔ,fent-] *adj* : ofensivo — **~** *n* : ofensiva *f*

offer ['ofər] *vt* : ofrecer — **~** *n* : oferta *f* — **offering** ['ofərɪŋ] *n* : ofrenda *f*

offhand [of'hænd] *adv* : de improviso, en este momento — **~** *adj* : improvisado

office ['ofəs] *n* **1** : oficina *f* **2** POSITION : cargo *m* **3 run for ~** : presentarse como candidato — **officer** ['ofəsər] *n* **1** : oficial *mf* **2** *or* **police ~** : agente *mf* (de policía) — **official** [ə'fɪʃəl] *n* : funcionario *m*, -ria *f* — **~** *adj* : oficial

offing ['ofɪŋ] *n* **in the ~** : en perspectiva

offset ['of,set] *vt* **-set; -setting** : compensar

offshore ['of,ʃor] *adv* : a una distancia de la costa

offspring ['of,sprɪŋ] *ns & pl* : prole *f*, progenie *f*

often ['ofən, 'oftən] *adv* **1** : muchas veces, a menudo, con frecuencia **2 every so ~** : de vez en cuando

ogle ['oːgəl] *vt* **ogled; ogling** : comerse con los ojos

ogre ['oːgər] *n* : ogro *m*

oh ['oː] *interj* **1** : ¡oh!, ¡ah! **2 ~ no!** : ¡ay no! **3 ~ really?** : ¿de veras?

oil ['ɔɪl] *n* **1** : aceite *m* **2** PETROLEUM : petróleo *m* **3** *or* **~ painting** : óleo *m* — **~** *vt* : lubricar — **oilskin** ['ɔɪl,skɪn] *n* : hule *m* — **oily** ['ɔɪli] *adj* **oilier; -est** : aceitoso, grasiento

ointment ['ɔɪntmənt] *n* : ungüento *m*, pomada *f*

OK *or* **okay** ['oː,keɪ] *adv* **1** : muy bien **2 ~!** : ¡de acuerdo!, ¡bueno! — **~** *adj* **1**

ALL RIGHT : bien **2 it's ~ with me** : por mí no hay problema — **~** *n* : visto *m* bueno — **~** [ˌoːˈkeɪ] *vt* **OK'd** *or* **okayed** [ˌoːˈkeɪd]; **OK'ing** *or* **okaying** : dar el visto bueno a

okra [ˈoːkrə, *South also* -kri] *n* : quingombó *m*

old [ˈoːld] *adj* **1** : viejo **2** FORMER : antiguo **3 any ~** : cualquier **4 be ten years ~** : tener diez años (de edad) **5 ~ age** : vejez *f* **6 ~ man** : anciano *m* **7 ~ woman** : anciana *f* — **~** *n* **the ~** : los viejos, los ancianos — **old-fashioned** [ˈoːldˈfæʃənd] *adj* : anticuado

olive [ˈɑlɪv, -ləv] *n* **1** : aceituna *f* (fruta) **2** *or* **~ green** : verde *m* oliva

Olympic [oˈlɪmpɪk] *adj* : olímpico — **Olympics** [oˈlɪmpɪks] *npl* **the ~** : las Olimpiadas, las Olimpíadas

omelet *or* **omelette** [ˈɑmlət, ˈɑmə-] *n* : omelette *mf Lat*, tortilla *f* francesa *Spain*

omen [ˈoːmən] *n* : agüero *m* — **ominous** [ˈɑmənəs] *adj* : ominoso, de mal agüero

omit [oˈmɪt] *vt* **omitted; omitting** : omitir — **omission** [oˈmɪʃən] *n* : omisión *f*

omnipotent [ɑmˈnɪpətənt] *adj* : omnipotente

on [ˈɑn, ˈɔn] *prep* **1** : en **2** ABOUT : sobre **3 ~ foot** : a pie **4 ~ Monday** : el lunes **5 ~ the right** : a la derecha **6 ~ vacation** : de vacaciones **7 talk ~ the phone** : hablar por teléfono — **~** *adv* **1 and so ~** : etcétera **2 from that moment ~** : a partir de ese momento **3 keep ~** : seguir **4 later ~** : más tarde **5 ~ and ~** : sin parar **6 put ~** : ponerse (ropa), poner (música, etc.) **7 turn ~** : encender (una luz, etc.), abrir (una llave) — *adj* **1** : encendido (dícese de luces, etc.), abierto (dícese de llaves) **2 be ~ to** : estar enterado de

once [ˈwʌns] *adv* **1** : una vez **2** FORMERLY : antes — **~** *n* **1 at ~** TOGETHER : al mismo tiempo **2 at ~** IMMEDIATELY : inmediatamente — **~** *conj* : una vez que

oncoming [ˈɑnˌkʌmɪŋ, ˈɔn-] *adj* : que viene

one [ˈwʌn] *adj* **1** : un, uno **2** ONLY : único **3** *or* **~ and the same** : el mismo — **~** *n* **1** : uno *m* (número) **2 ~ by ~** : uno a uno — **~** *pron* **1** : uno **2 ~ another** : el uno al otro **3 ~ never knows** : nunca se sabe **4 that ~** : aquél, aquella **5 which ~?** : ¿cuál? — **oneself** [ˌwʌnˈsɛlf] *pron* **1** (*used re-*

flexively) : se **2** (*used after prepositions*) : sí mismo, sí misma **3** (*used emphatically*) : uno mismo, una misma **4 by ~** : solo — **one-sided** [ˈwʌnˈsaɪdəd] *adj* **1** UNEQUAL : desigual **2** BIASED : parcial — **one-way** [ˈwʌnˈweɪ] *adj* **1** : de sentido único (dícese de una calle) **2 ~ ticket** : boleto *m* de ida

ongoing [ˈɑnˌɡoːɪŋ] *adj* : en curso, corriente

onion [ˈʌnjən] *n* : cebolla *f*

only [ˈoːnli] *adj* : único — *adv* **1** : sólo, solamente **2 if ~** : ojalá, por lo menos — **~** *conj* BUT : pero

onset [ˈɑnˌsɛt] *n* : comienzo *m*, llegada *f*

onslaught [ˈɑnˌslɔt, ˈɔn-] *n* : ataque *m*, arremetida *f*

onto [ˈɑntuː, ˈɔn-] *prep* : sobre

onus [ˈoːnəs] *n* : responsabilidad *f*

onward [ˈɑnwərd, ˈɔn-] *adv & adj* : hacia adelante

onyx [ˈɑnɪks] *n* : ónix *m*

ooze [ˈuːz] *v* **oozed; oozing** : rezumar

opal [ˈoːpəl] *n* : ópalo *m*

opaque [oˈpeɪk] *adj* : opaco

open [ˈoːpən] *adj* **1** : abierto **2** AVAILABLE : vacante, libre **3 an ~ question** : una cuestión pendiente — *vt* : abrir — *vi* **1** : abrirse **2** BEGIN : comenzar — **~** *n* **in the ~** OUTDOORS : al aire libre **2** KNOWN : sacado a la luz — **open-air** [ˈoːpənˌær] *adj* : al aire libre — **opener** [ˈoːpənər] *n* **1** : abridor *m* **2** *or* **bottle ~** : abrebotellas *m* **3** *or* **can ~** : abrelatas *m* — **opening** [ˈoːpənɪŋ] *n* **1** : abertura *f* **2** BEGINNING : comienzo *m*, apertura *f* **3** OPPORTUNITY : oportunidad *f* — **openly** [ˈoːpənli] *adv* : abiertamente

opera [ˈɑprə, ˈɑpərə] *n* : ópera *f*

operate [ˈɑpəˌreɪt] *v* **-ated; -ating** *vi* **1** FUNCTION : funcionar **2 ~ on s.o.** : operar a algn — *vt* **1** : hacer funcionar (una máquina) **2** MANAGE : dirigir, manejar — **operation** [ˌɑpəˈreɪʃən] *n* **1** : operación *f* **2** FUNCTIONING : funcionamiento *m* — **operational** [ˌɑpəˈreɪʃənəl] *adj* : operacional — **operative** [ˈɑpərətɪv, -ˌreɪ-] *adj* : en vigor — **operator** [ˈɑpəˌreɪtər] *n* **1** : operador *m*, -dora *f* **2** *or* **machine ~** : operario *m*, -ria *f*

opinion [əˈpɪnjən] *n* : opinión *f* — **opinionated** [əˈpɪnjəˌneɪtəd] *adj* : dogmático

opium [ˈoːpiəm] *n* : opio *m*

opossum [əˈpɑsəm] *n* : zarigüeya *f*, oposum *m*

opponent [əˈpoːnənt] *n* : adversario *m*, -ria *f*; contrincante *mf* (en deportes)

opportunity [ˌapər'tuːnət̬i, -'tjuː-] *n*, *pl* **-ties** : oportunidad *f* — **opportune** [ˌapər'tuːn, -'tjuːn] *adj* : oportuno — **opportunist** [ˌapər'tuːnɪst, -'tjuː-] *n* : oportunista *mf*

oppose [ə'poːz] *vt* **-posed; -posing** : oponerse a — **opposed** *adj* ~ **to** : en contra de

opposite ['apəzət] *adj* **1** FACING : de enfrente **2** CONTRARY : opuesto — ~ *n* **the** ~ : lo contrario, lo opuesto — ~ *adv* : enfrente — ~ *prep* : enfrente de, frente a — **opposition** [ˌapə'zɪʃən] *n* **1** : oposición *f* **2 in** ~ **to** : en contra de

oppress [ə'pres] *vt* : oprimir — **oppression** [ə'preʃən] *n* : opresión *f* — **oppressive** [ə'presɪv] *adj* **1** : opresivo **2** STIFLING : agobiante — **oppressor** [ə'presər] *n* : opresor *m*, -sora *f*

opt ['apt] *vi* ~ **for** : optar por

optic ['aptɪk] *or* **optical** [-tɪkəl] *adj* : óptico — **optician** [ap'tɪʃən] *n* : óptico *m*, -ca *f*

optimism ['aptəˌmɪzəm] *n* : optimismo *m* — **optimist** ['aptəmɪst] *n* : optimista *mf* — **optimistic** [ˌaptə'mɪstɪk] *adj* : optimista

optimum ['aptəməm] *n*, *pl* **-ma** [-'mə] : lo óptimo, lo ideal

option ['apʃən] *n* **1** : opción *f* **2 have no** ~ : no tener más remedio — **optional** ['apʃənəl] *adj* : facultativo, opcional

opulence ['apjələns] *n* : opulencia *f* — **opulent** ['apjələnt] *adj* : opulento

or ['or] *conj* **1** (*indicating an alternative*) : o (u *before u- or ho-*) **2** (*following a negative*) : ni **3** ~ **else** : si no

oracle ['orəkəl] *n* : oráculo *m*

oral ['orəl] *adj* : oral

orange ['orɪndʒ] *n* **1** : naranja *f* (fruta) **2** : naranja *m* (color)

orator ['orət̬ər] *n* : orador *m*, -dora *f*

orbit ['orbət] *n* : órbita *f* — ~ *vt* : girar alrededor de — *vi* : orbitar

orchard ['ortʃərd] *n* : huerto *m*

orchestra ['orkəstrə] *n* : orquesta *f*

orchid ['orkɪd] *n* : orquídea *f*

ordain [or'deɪn] *vt* **1** : ordenar (un sacerdote, etc.) **2** DECREE : decretar

ordeal [or'diːl, 'or,diːl] *n* : prueba *f* dura

order ['ordər] *vt* : ordenar **2** : pedir (mercancías, etc.) — *vi* : hacer un pedido — ~ *n* **1** ARRANGEMENT : orden *m* **2** COMMAND : orden *f* **3** REQUEST : pedido *m* **4** : orden *f* (religiosa) **5 in** ~ **that** : para que **6 in** ~ **to** : para **7 out of** ~ : averiado, descompuesto *Lat* — **orderly** ['ordərli] *adj* : ordenado — ~ *n*, *pl* **-lies 1** : ordenanza *m* (en el

ejército) **2** : camillero *m* (en un hospital)

ordinary ['ordənˌeri] *adj* **1** : normal, corriente **2** MEDIOCRE : ordinario — **ordinarily** [ˌordən'erəli] *adv* : generalmente

ore ['or] *n* : mena *f*

oregano [ə'regəˌnoː] *n* : orégano *m*

organ ['orgən] *n* : órgano *m* — **organic** [or'gænɪk] *adj* : orgánico — **organism** ['orgəˌnɪzəm] *n* : organismo *m* — **organist** ['orgənɪst] *n* : organista *mf* — **organize** ['orgəˌnaɪz] *vt* **-nized; -nizing** : organizar — **organization** [ˌorgənə'zeɪʃən] *n* : organización *f* — **organizer** ['orgəˌnaɪzər] *n* : organizador *m*, -dora *f*

orgasm ['orˌgæzəm] *n* : orgasmo *m*

orgy ['ordʒi] *n*, *pl* **-gies** : orgía *f*

Orient ['oriˌent] *n* **the** ~ : el Oriente — **orient** *vt* : orientar — **oriental** [ˌori'ent̬əl] *adj* : del Oriente, oriental — **orientation** [ˌorien'teɪʃən] *n* : orientación *f*

orifice ['orəfəs] *n* : orificio *m*

origin ['orədʒən] *n* : origen *m* — **original** [ə'rɪdʒənəl] *n* : original *m* — ~ *adj* : original — **originality** [əˌrɪdʒə'næləti] *n* : originalidad *f* — **originally** [ə'rɪdʒənəli] *adv* : originariamente — **originate** [ə'rɪdʒəˌneɪt] *v* **-nated; -nating** *vt* : originar — *vi* **1** : originarse **2** ~ **from** : provenir de — **originator** [ə'rɪdʒəˌneɪt̬ər] *n* : creador *m*, -dora *f*

ornament ['ornəmənt] *n* : adorno *m* — ~ *vt* : adornar — **ornamental** [ˌornə'ment̬əl] *adj* : ornamental, de adorno — **ornate** [or'neɪt] *adj* : elaborado, adornado

ornithology [ˌornə'θaːlədʒi] *n*, *pl* **-gies** : ornitología *f*

orphan ['orfən] *n* : huérfano *m*, -na *f* — ~ *vt* : dejar huérfano — **orphanage** ['orfənɪdʒ] *n* : orfelinato *m*, orfanato *m*

orthodox ['orθəˌdaks] *adj* : ortodoxo — **orthodoxy** ['orθəˌdaksi] *n*, *pl* **-doxies** : ortodoxia *f*

orthopedic [ˌorθə'piːdɪk] *adj* : ortopédico

oscillation [ˌasə'leɪʃən] *n* : oscilación *f* — **oscillate** ['asəˌleɪt] *vi* **-lated; -lating** : oscilar

ostensible [a'stentsəbəl] *adj* : aparente, ostensible

ostentation [ˌastən'teɪʃən] *n* : ostentación *f* — **ostentatious** [ˌastən'teɪʃəs] *adj* : ostentoso

osteopath ['astiəˌpæθ] *n* : osteópata *f*

ostracism ['astrəˌsɪzəm] *n* : ostracismo *m* — **ostracize** ['astrəˌsaɪz] *vt* **-cized; -cizing** : aislar

ostrich ['astrɪtʃ, 'os-] *n* : avestruz *m*

other ['ʌðər] *adj* **1** : otro **2 every ~ day** : cada dos días **3 on the ~ hand** : por otra parte, por otro lado — *~ pron* **1** : otro, otra **2 the ~s** : los otros, las otras, los demás, las demás — **other than** *prep* : aparte de, fuera de — **otherwise** ['ʌðər,waɪz] *adv* **1** : eso aparte, por lo demás **2** DIFFERENTLY : de otro modo **3** OR ELSE : si no

otter ['ɑtər] *n* : nutria *f*

ought ['ɔt] *v aux* **1** : deber **2 you ~ to have done it** : deberías haberlo hecho

ounce ['aʊnts] *n* : onza *f*

our ['ar, 'aʊr] *adj* : nuestro — **ours** ['aʊrz, 'arz] *pron* **1** : (el) nuestro, (la) nuestra, (los) nuestros, (las) nuestras **2 a friend of ~** : un amigo nuestro — **ourselves** [ɑr'selvz, aʊr-] *pron* **1** (*used reflexively*) : nos **2** (*used after prepositions*) : nosotros, nosotras **3** (*used for emphasis*) : nosotros mismos, nosotras mismas

oust ['aʊst] *vt* : desbancar

out ['aʊt] *adv* **1** OUTSIDE : fuera, afuera **2 cry ~** : gritar **3 eat ~** : comer afuera **4 go ~** : salir **5 look ~** : mirar para afuera **6 run ~ of** : agotar **7 turn ~** : apagar (una luz) **8 take ~** REMOVE : sacar — *~ prep* → **out of** — *~ adj* **1** ABSENT : ausente **2** UNFASHIONABLE : fuera de moda **3** EXTINGUISHED : apagado **4 the sun is ~** : hace sol

outboard motor ['aʊt,bord] *n* : motor *m* fuera de borde

outbreak ['aʊt,breɪk] *n* : brote *m* (de una enfermedad), comienzo *m* (de guerra)

outburst ['aʊt,bərst] *n* : arranque *m*, arrebato *m*

outcast ['aʊt,kæst] *n* : paria *mf*

outcome ['aʊt,kʌm] *n* : resultado *m*

outcry ['aʊt,kraɪ] *n, pl* **-cries** : protesta *f*

outdated [,aʊt'deɪtəd] *adj* : anticuado

outdo [aʊt'du:] *vt* **-did** [-'dɪd]; **-done** [-'dʌn]; **-doing**; **-does** [-'dʌz] : superar

outdoor ['aʊt,dor] *adj* : al aire libre — **outdoors** ['aʊt'dorz] *adv* : al aire libre

outer ['aʊtər] *adj* : exterior — **outer space** *n* : espacio *m* exterior

outfit ['aʊt,fɪt] *n* **1** EQUIPMENT : equipo *m* **2** CLOTHES : conjunto *m* — *~ vt* **-fitted**; **-fitting** EQUIP : equipar

outgoing ['aʊt,goɪŋ] *adj* **1** SOCIABLE : extrovertido **2 ~ mail** : correo *m* (para enviar) **3 ~ president** : presidente *m*, -ta *f* saliente

outgrow [aʊt'groʊ] *vt* **-grew** [-'gru:]; **-grown** [-'groʊn]; **-growing** : crecer más que

outing ['aʊtɪŋ] *n* : excursión *f*

outlandish [aʊt'lændɪʃ] *adj* : estrafalario

outlast [,aʊt'læst] *vt* : durar más que

outlaw ['aʊt,lɔ] *n* : forajido *m*, -da *f* — *~ vt* : declarar ilegal

outlay ['aʊt,leɪ] *n* : desembolso *m*

outlet ['aʊt,let, -lət] *n* **1** EXIT : salida *f* **2** RELEASE : desahogo *m* **3** *or* **electrical ~** : toma *f* de corriente **4** *or* **retail ~** : tienda *f* al por menor

outline ['aʊt,laɪn] *n* **1** CONTOUR : contorno *m* **2** SKETCH : bosquejo *m*, boceto *m* **3** SUMMARY : esquema *m* — *~ vt* **-lined**; **-lining** **1** SKETCH : bosquejar **2** EXPLAIN : delinear, esbozar

outlive [,aʊt'lɪv] *vt* **-lived**; **-living** : sobrevivir a

outlook ['aʊt,lʊk] *n* **1** PROSPECTS : perspectivas *fpl* **2** VIEWPOINT : punto *m* de vista

outlying ['aʊt,laɪŋ] *adj* : alejado, distante

outmoded [,aʊt'moːdəd] *adj* : pasado de moda, anticuado

outnumber [,aʊt'nʌmbər] *vt* : superar en número a

out of *prep* **1** FROM : de **2** THROUGH : por **3** WITHOUT : sin **4 ~ curiosity** : por curiosidad **5 ~ control** : fuera de control **6 one ~ four** : uno de cada cuatro — **out-of-date** [aʊtəv'deɪt] *adj* : anticuado — **out-of-door** [aʊtəv'dor] *or* **out-of-doors** [-'dorz] *adj* → **outdoor**

outpatient ['aʊt,peɪʃənt] *n* : paciente *m* externo

outpost ['aʊt,poːst] *n* : puesto *m* avanzado

output ['aʊt,pʊt] *n* **1** : producción *f*, rendimiento *m* **2** : salida *f* (informática) — *~ vt* **-putted** *or* **-put**; **-putting** : producir

outrage ['aʊt,reɪdʒ] *n* **1** : atrocidad *f*, escándalo *m* **2** ANGER : ira *f*, indignación *f* — *~ vt* **-raged**; **-raging** : ultrajar — **outrageous** [,aʊt'reɪdʒəs] *adj* : escandaloso

outright [,aʊt'raɪt] *adv* **1** COMPLETELY : por completo **2** INSTANTLY : en el acto — *~* ['aʊt,raɪt] *adj* : completo, absoluto

outset ['aʊt,set] *n* : comienzo *m*, principio *m*

outside [,aʊt'saɪd, 'aʊt,-] *n* **1** : exterior *m* **2 from the ~** : desde fuera, desde afuera — *~ adj* **1** : exterior, externo **2 an ~ chance** : una posibilidad remota — *~ adv* : fuera, afuera — *~ prep* *or* *~* **of** : fuera de — **outsider** [,aʊt'saɪdər] *n* : forastero *m*, -ra *f*

outskirts ['aʊt,skərts] *npl* : afueras *fpl*, alrededores *mpl*

outspoken [,aʊt'spoːkən] *adj* : franco, directo

outstanding [,aʊt'stændɪŋ] *adj* 1 UNPAID : pendiente 2 EXCELLENT : excepcional

outstretched [,aʊt'stretʃt] *adj* : extendido

outstrip [aʊt'strɪp] *vt* **-stripped** *or* **-stript** [-'strɪpt]; **-stripping** : aventajar

outward ['aʊtwərd] *adj* 1 : hacia afuera 2 EXTERNAL : externo, external — ~ *or* **outwards** [-wərdz] *adv* : hacia afuera — **outwardly** ['aʊtwərdli] *adv* APPARENTLY : aparentemente

outweigh [aʊt'weɪ] *vt* : pesar más que

outwit [aʊt'wɪt] *vt* **-witted; -witting** : ser más listo que

oval ['oːvəl] *n* : óvalo *m* — ~ *adj* : ovalado

ovary ['oːvəri] *n, pl* **-ries** : ovario *m*

ovation [oː'veɪʃən] *n* : ovación *f*

oven ['ʌvən] *n* : horno *m*

over ['oːvər] *adv* 1 ABOVE : por encima 2 AGAIN : otra vez, de nuevo 3 MORE : más 4 **all** ~ : por todas partes 5 **ask** ~ : invitar 6 **cross** ~ : cruzar 7 **fall** ~ : caerse 8 ~ **and** ~ : una y otra vez 9 ~ **here** : aquí 10 ~ **there** : allí — ~ *prep* 1 ABOVE, UPON : encima de, sobre 2 ACROSS : por encima de, sobre 3 DURING : en, durante 4 **fight** ~ : pelearse por 5 ~ $5 : más de $5 6 ~ **the phone** : por teléfono — ~ *adj* : terminado, acabado

overall [,oːvər'ɔl] *adv* GENERALLY : en general — *adj* : total, en conjunto — **overalls** ['oːvər,ɔlz] *npl* : overol *m Lat*

overbearing [,oːvər'bærɪŋ] *adj* : dominante, imperioso

overboard ['oːvər,bord] *adv* **fall** ~ : caer al agua

overburden [,oːvər'bərdən] *vt* : sobrecargar

overcast [,oːvər,kæst] *adj* : nublado

overcharge [,oːvər'tʃɑrdʒ] *vt* **-charged; -charging** : cobrar demasiado

overcoat ['oːvər,koːt] *n* : abrigo *m*

overcome [,oːvər'kʌm] *v* **-came** [-'keɪm]; **-come; -coming** *vt* 1 CONQUER : vencer 2 OVERWHELM : agobiar — *vi* : vencer

overcook [,oːvər'kʊk] *vt* : cocer demasiado

overcrowded [,oːvər'kraʊdəd] *adj* : abarrotado de gente

overdo [,oːvər'duː] *vt* **-did** [-'dɪd]; **-done** [-'dʌn]; **-doing; -does** [-'dʌz] 1 : hacer demasiado 2 EXAGGERATE : exagerar 3 → **overcook**

overdose ['oːvər,doːs] *n* : sobredosis *f*

overdraw [,oːvər'drɔ] *vt* **-drew** [-'druː]; **-drawn** [-'drɔn]; **-drawing** : girar en descubierto — **overdraft** ['oːvər,dræft] *n* : sobregiro *m*, descubierto *m*

overdue [,oːvər'duː] *adj* : fuera de plazo (dícese de pagos, libros, etc.)

overeat [,oːvər'iːt] *vi* **-ate** [-'eɪt]; **-eaten** [-'eɪtən]; **-eating** : comer demasiado

overestimate [,oːvər'estə,meɪt] *vt* **-mated; -mating** : sobreestimar

overflow [,oːvər'floː] *vt* : desbordar — *vi* : desbordarse — ~ ['oːvər,floː] *n* : desbordamiento *m* (de un río)

overgrown [,oːvər'groːn] *adj* : cubierto (de malas hierbas, etc.)

overhand [,oːvər,hænd] *adv* : por encima de la cabeza

overhang [,oːvər'hæŋ] *v* **-hung** [-'hʌŋ]; **-hanging** : sobresalir

overhaul [,oːvər'hɔl] *vt* : revisar (un motor, etc.)

overhead [,oːvər'hed] *adv* : por encima — ~ ['oːvər,hed] *adj* : de arriba — ~ ['oːvər,hed] *n* : gastos *mpl* generales

overhear [,oːvər'hɪr] *vt* **-heard; -hearing** : oír por casualidad

overheat [,oːvər'hiːt] *vt* : calentar demasiado — *vi* : recalentarse

overjoyed [,oːvər'dʒɔɪd] *adj* : encantado

overland ['oːvər,lænd, -lənd] *adv & adj* : por tierra

overlap [,oːvər'læp] *v* **-lapped; -lapping** *vt* : traslapar — *vi* : traslaparse

overload [,oːvər'loːd] *vt* : sobrecargar

overlook [,oːvər'lʊk] *vt* 1 : dar a (un jardín, el mar, etc.) 2 MISS : pasar por alto

overly ['oːvərli] *adv* : demasiado

overnight [,oːvər'naɪt] *adv* 1 : por la noche 2 SUDDENLY : de la noche a la mañana — ~ ['oːvər,naɪt] *adj* 1 : de noche 2 SUDDEN : repentino

overpass ['oːvər,pæs] *n* : paso *m* elevado

overpopulated [,oːvər'pɑpjə,leɪtəd] *adj* : superpoblado

overpower [,oːvər'paʊər] *vt* 1 SUBDUE : dominar 2 OVERWHELM : agobiar, abrumar

overrated [,oːvər'reɪtəd] *adj* : sobreestimado

override [,oːvər'raɪd] *vt* **-rode** [-'roːd]; **-ridden** [-'rɪdən]; **-riding** 1 : predominar sobre 2 : anular (una decisión, etc.)

overrule [,oːvər'ruːl] *vt* **-ruled; -ruling** : anular (una decisión), rechazar (una protesta)

overrun [,oːvər'rʌn] *vt* **-ran** [-'ræn]; **-running** 1 INVADE : invadir 2 EXCEED : exceder

overseas [,o:vər'si:z] *adv* : en el extranjero — ['o:vər,si:z] *adj* : extranjero, exterior
oversee [,o:vər'si:] *vt* **-saw** [-'sɔ]; **-seen** [-'si:n]; **-seeing** : supervisar
overshadow [,o:vər'ʃædo:] *vt* : eclipsar
oversight ['o:vər,saɪt] *n* : descuido *m*
oversleep [,o:vər'sli:p] *vi* **-slept** [-'slept]; **-sleeping** : quedarse dormido
overstep [,o:vər'step] *vt* **-stepped**; **-stepping** : sobrepasar
overt ['o:vərt, 'o:,vərt] *adj* : manifiesto
overtake [,o:vər'teɪk] *vt* **-took** [-'tʊk], **-taken** [-'teɪkən]; **-taking** **1** PASS : adelantar **2** SURPASS : superar
overthrow [,o:vər'θro:] *vt* **-threw** [-'θru:]; **-thrown** [-'θro:n]; **-throwing** : derrocar
overtime ['o:vər,taɪm] *n* **1** : horas *fpl* extras (de trabajo) **2** : prórroga *f* (en deportes)
overtone ['o:vər,to:n] *n* SUGGESTION : tinte *m*, insinuación *f*
overture ['o:vər,tʃʊr, -tʃər] *n* : obertura *f* (en música)
overturn [,o:vər'tərn] *vt* **1** : dar la vuelta a **2** NULLIFY : anular — *vi* : volcar

overweight [,o:vər'weɪt] *adj* : demasiado gordo
overwhelm [,o:vər'hwelm] *vt* **1** : abrumar, agobiar **2** : aplastar (a un enemigo) — **overwhelming** [,o:vər'hwelmɪŋ] *adj* : abrumador, apabullante
overwork [,o:vər'wərk] *vt* : hacer trabajar demasiado — *vi* : trabajar demasiado
overwrought [,o:vər'rɔt] *adj* : alterado, sobreexcitado
owe ['o:] *vt* **owed; owing** : deber — **owing to** *prep* : debido a
owl ['aʊl] *n* : búho *m*
own ['o:n] *adj* : propio — ~ *vt* : poseer, tener — *vi* ~ **up** : confesar — ~ *pron* **1 my (your, his/her/their, our)** ~ : el mío, la mía; el tuyo, la tuya; el suyo, la suya; el nuestro, la nuestra **2 be on one's** ~ : estar solo **3 to each his** ~ : cada uno a lo suyo — **owner** ['o:nər] *n* : propietario *m*, -ria *f* — **ownership** ['o:nər,ʃɪp] *n* : propiedad *f*
ox ['ɑks] *n*, *pl* **oxen** ['ɑksən] : buey *m*
oxygen ['ɑksɪdʒən] *n* : oxígeno *m*
oyster ['ɔɪstər] *n* : ostra *f*
ozone ['o:,zo:n] *n* : ozono *m*

P

p ['pi:] *n*, *pl* **p's** *or* **ps** ['pi:z] : p *f*, decimosexta letra del alfabeto inglés
pace ['peɪs] *n* **1** STEP : paso *m* **2** RATE : ritmo *m* **3 keep** ~ **with** : andar al mismo paso que — ~ *vi* **paced; pacing** *or* ~ **up and down** : caminar de arriba para abajo
pacify ['pæsə,faɪ] *vt* **-fied; -fying** : apaciguar — **pacifier** ['pæsə,faɪər] *n* : chupete *m* — **pacifist** ['pæsəfɪst] *n* : pacifista *mf*
pack ['pæk] *n* **1** BUNDLE : fardo *m* **2** BACKPACK : mochila *f* **3** PACKAGE : paquete *m* **4** : baraja *f* (de naipes) **5** : manada *f* (de lobos, etc.), jauría *f* (de perros) — ~ *vt* **1** PACKAGE : empaquetar **2** FILL : llenar **3** : hacer (una maleta) — *vi* : hacer las maletas — **package** ['pækɪdʒ] *vt* **-aged; -aging** : empaquetar — ~ *n* : paquete *m* — **packet** ['pækət] *n* : paquete *m*
pact ['pækt] *n* : pacto *m*, acuerdo *m*
pad ['pæd] *n* **1** CUSHION : almohadilla *f* **2** TABLET : bloc *m* (de papel) **3** *or* **ink** ~ : tampón *m* **4 launching** ~ : plataforma *f* (de lanzamiento) — ~ *vt* **padded; padding** : rellenar — **pad-**

ding ['pædɪŋ] *n* **1** : relleno *m* **2** : paja *f* (en un discurso, etc.)
paddle ['pædəl] *n* **1** : canalete *m* (de una canoa) **2** : pala *f*, paleta *f* (en deportes) — ~ *vt* **-dled; -dling** : hacer avanzar (una canoa) con canalete
padlock ['pæd,lɑk] *n* : candado *m* — ~ *vt* : cerrar con candado
pagan ['peɪgən] *n* : pagano *m*, -na *f* — ~ *adj* : pagano
page[1] ['peɪdʒ] *vt* **paged; paging** : llamar por altavoz
page[2] *n* : página *f* (de un libro, etc.)
pageant ['pædʒənt] *n* : espectáculo *m* — **pageantry** ['pædʒəntri] *n* : pompa *f*, boato *m*
paid → **pay**
pail ['peɪl] *n* : cubo *m* *Spain*, cubeta *f* *Lat*
pain ['peɪn] *n* **1** : dolor *m* **2** : pena *f* (mental) **3** ~**s** *npl* EFFORT : esfuerzos *mpl* — ~ *vt* : doler — **painful** ['peɪnfəl] *adj* : doloroso — **painkiller** ['peɪn,kɪlər] *n* : analgésico *m* — **painless** ['peɪnləs] *adj* : indoloro, sin dolor — **painstaking** ['peɪn,steɪkɪŋ] *adj* : meticuloso, esmerado
paint ['peɪnt] *v* : pintar — ~ *n* : pintura

f — **paintbrush** ['peɪntˌbrʌʃ] *n* : pincel *m* (de un artista), brocha *f* (para pintar casas, etc.) — **painter** ['peɪntər] *n* : pintor *m*, -tora *f* — **painting** ['peɪntɪŋ] *n* : pintura *f*

pair ['pær] *n* **1** : par *m* **2** COUPLE : pareja *f* — ~ *vt* : emparejar

pajamas [pə'dʒɑməz, -'dʒæ-] *npl* : pijama *m*, piyama *mf Lat*

Pakistani [ˌpækɪ'stæni, ˌpɑkɪ'stɑni] *adj* : paquistaní

pal ['pæl] *n* : amigo *m*, -ga *f*

palace ['pæləs] *n* : palacio *m*

palate ['pælət] *n* : paladar *m* — **palatable** ['pælətəbəl] *adj* : sabroso

pale ['peɪl] *adj* **paler; palest 1** PALLID : pálido **2** : claro (dícese de los colores, etc.) — ~ *vi* **paled; paling** : palidecer — **paleness** ['peɪlnəs] *n* : palidez *f*

Palestinian [ˌpælə'stɪniən] *adj* : palestino

palette ['pælət] *n* : paleta *f*

pallbearer ['pɔlˌberər] *n* : portador *m*, -dora *f* del féretro

pallid ['pæləd] *adj* : pálido — **pallor** ['pælər] *n* : palidez *f*

palm¹ ['pɑm, 'pɑlm] *n* : palma *f* (de la mano)

palm² *or* ~ **tree** : palmera *f* — **Palm Sunday** *n* : Domingo *m* de Ramos

palpitate ['pælpəˌteɪt] *vi* **-tated; -tating** : palpitar — **palpitation** [ˌpælpə'teɪʃən] *n* : palpitación *f*

paltry ['pɔltri] *adj* **-trier; -est** : mísero, mezquino

pamper ['pæmpər] *vt* : mimar

pamphlet ['pæmpflət] *n* : panfleto *m*, folleto *m*

pan ['pæn] *n* **1** SAUCEPAN : cacerola *f* **2** FRYING PAN : sartén *mf* — ~ *vt* **panned; panning** CRITICIZE : poner por los suelos

pancake ['pænˌkeɪk] *n* : crepe *mf*, panqueque *m Lat*

panda ['pændə] *n* : panda *mf*

pandemonium [ˌpændə'moːniəm] *n* : pandemonio *m*

pander ['pændər] *vi* ~ **to** : complacer a

pane ['peɪn] *n* : cristal *m*, vidrio *m*

panel ['pænəl] *n* **1** : panel *m* **2** GROUP : jurado *m* **3** *or* **instrument** ~ : tablero *m* (de instrumentos) — ~ *vt* **-eled** *or* **-elled; -eling** *or* **-elling** : adornar con paneles — **paneling** ['pænəlɪŋ] *n* : paneles *mpl*

pang ['pæŋ] *n* : punzada *f*

panic ['pænɪk] *n* : pánico *m* — ~ *v* **-icked; -icking** *vt* : llenar del pánico — *vi* : ser presa del pánico — **panicky** ['pænɪki] *adj* : presa de pánico

panorama [ˌpænə'ræmə, -'rɑ-] *n* : panorama *m* — **panoramic** [ˌpænə'ræmɪk, -'rɑ-] *adj* : panorámico

pansy ['pænzi] *n*, *pl* **-sies** : pensamiento *m*

pant ['pænt] *vi* : jadear, resoplar

panther ['pænθər] *n* : pantera *f*

panties ['pæntiz] *npl* : bragas *fpl Spain*, calzones *mpl Lat*

pantomime ['pæntəˌmaɪm] *n* : pantomima *f*

pantry ['pæntri] *n*, *pl* **-tries** : despensa *f*

pants ['pænts] *npl* TROUSERS : pantalón *m*, pantalones *mpl*

papa ['pɑpə] *n* : papá *m fam*

papal ['peɪpəl] *adj* : papal

papaya [pə'paɪə] *n* : papaya *f*

paper ['peɪpər] *n* **1** : papel *m* **2** DOCUMENT : documento *m* **3** NEWSPAPER : periódico *m* — ~ *vt* WALLPAPER : empapelar — ~ *adj* : de papel — **paperback** ['peɪpərˌbæk] *n* : libro *m* en rústica — **paper clip** *n* : clip *m*, sujetapapeles *m* — **paperweight** ['peɪpərˌweɪt] *n* : pisapapeles *m* — **paperwork** ['peɪpərˌwɔrk] *n* : papeleo *m*

paprika [pə'priːkə, pæ-] *n* : pimentón *m*

par ['pɑr] *n* **1** : par *m* (en golf) **2** below ~ : debajo de la par **3** on a ~ with ~ : al nivel de

parable ['pærəbəl] *n* : parábola *f*

parachute ['pærəˌʃuːt] *n* : paracaídas *m* — ~ *vi* **-chuted; -chuting** : lanzarse en paracaídas

parade [pə'reɪd] *n* **1** : desfile *m* **2** DISPLAY : alarde *m* — ~ *v* **-raded; -rading** *vi* MARCH : desfilar — *vt* DISPLAY : hacer alarde de

paradise ['pærəˌdaɪs, -ˌdaɪz] *n* : paraíso *m*

paradox ['pærəˌdɑks] *n* : paradoja *f* — **paradoxical** [ˌpærə'dɑksɪkəl] *adj* : paradójico

paraffin ['pærəfən] *n* : parafina *f*

paragraph ['pærəˌgræf] *n* : párrafo *m*

Paraguayan [ˌpærə'gwaɪən, -'gweɪ-] *adj* : paraguayo

parakeet ['pærəˌkiːt] *n* : periquito *m*

parallel ['pærəˌlel, -ləl] *adj* : paralelo — ~ *n* **1** : paralelo *m* (en geografía) **2** SIMILARITY : paralelismo *m*, semejanza *f* — ~ *vt* : ser paralelo a

paralysis [pə'ræləsɪs] *n*, *pl* **-yses** [-ˌsiːz] : parálisis *f* — **paralyze** *or Brit* **-alise** ['pærəˌlaɪz] *vt* **-lyzed** *or Brit* **-lised; -lyzing** *or Brit* **-lising** : paralizar

parameter [pə'ræmətər] *n* : parámetro *m*

paramount ['pærəˌmaʊnt] *adj* **of** ~ **importance** : de suma importancia

paranoia [ˌpærəˈnɔɪə] n : paranoia f — **paranoid** [ˈpærəˌnɔɪd] adj : paranoico

paraphernalia [ˌpærəfəˈneɪljə, -fər-] ns & pl : parafernalia f

paraphrase [ˈpærəˌfreɪz] n : paráfrasis f — ~ vt **-phrased; -phrasing** : parafrasear

paraplegic [ˌpærəˈpliːdʒɪk] n : parapléjico m, -ca f

parasite [ˈpærəˌsaɪt] n : parásito m

paratrooper [ˈpærəˌtruːpər] n : paracaidista mf (militar)

parcel [ˈpɑrsəl] n : paquete m

parch [ˈpɑrtʃ] vt : resecar

parchment [ˈpɑrtʃmənt] n : pergamino m

pardon [ˈpɑrdən] n 1 : perdón m 2 RE-PRIEVE : indulto m 3 **I beg your ~** : perdone Ud., disculpe Ud. Lat — ~ vt 1 : perdonar 2 REPRIEVE : indultar (a un delincuente)

parent [ˈpærənt] n 1 : madre f, padre m 2 **~s** npl : padres mpl — **parental** [pəˈrentəl] adj : de los padres

parenthesis [pəˈrenθəsɪs] n, pl **-theses** [-ˌsiːz] : paréntesis m

parish [ˈpærɪʃ] n : parroquia f — **parishioner** [pəˈrɪʃənər] n : feligrés m, -gresa f

parity [ˈpærəti] n, pl **-ties** : igualdad f

park [ˈpɑrk] n : parque m — ~ v : estacionar, parquear Lat

parka [ˈpɑrkə] n : parka f

parking [ˈpɑrkɪŋ] n : estacionamiento m

parliament [ˈpɑrləmənt, ˈpɑrljə-] n : parlamento m — **parliamentary** [ˌpɑrləˈmentəri, ˌpɑrljə-] adj : parlamentario

parlor or Brit **parlour** [ˈpɑrlər] n : salón m

parochial [pəˈroːkiəl] adj 1 : parroquial 2 PROVINCIAL : de miras estrechas

parody [ˈpærədi] n, pl **-dies** : parodia f — ~ vt **-died; -dying** : parodiar

parole [pəˈroːl] n : libertad f condicional

parrot [ˈpærət] n : loro m, papagayo m

parry [ˈpæri] vt **-ried; -rying** 1 : parar (un golpe) 2 EVADE : eludir (una pregunta, etc.)

parsley [ˈpɑrsli] n : perejil m

parsnip [ˈpɑrsnɪp] n : chirivía f

parson [ˈpɑrsən] n : clérigo m

part [ˈpɑrt] n 1 : parte f 2 PIECE : pieza f 3 ROLE : papel m 4 : raya f (del pelo) — ~ vi 1 or **~ company** : separarse 2 **~ with** : deshacerse de — vt SEPARATE : separar

partake [pɑrˈteɪk, pər-] vi **-took; -taken; -taking ~ in** : participar en

partial [ˈpɑrʃəl] adj 1 : parcial 2 **be ~ to** : ser aficionado a

participate [pɑrˈtɪsəˌpeɪt, pər-] vi **-pated; -pating** : participar — **participant** [pɑrˈtɪsəpənt, pər-] n : participante mf

participle [ˈpɑrtəˌsɪpəl] n : participio m

particle [ˈpɑrtɪkəl] n : partícula f

particular [pɑrˈtɪkjələr] adj 1 : particular 2 FUSSY : exigente — ~ n 1 **in ~** : en particular, en especial 2 **~s** npl DE-TAILS : detalles mpl — **particularly** [pɑrˈtɪkjələrli] adv : especialmente

partisan [ˈpɑrtəzən, -sən] n : partidario m, -ria f

partition [pərˈtɪʃən, pɑr-] n 1 DISTRIBU-TION : partición f 2 DIVIDER : tabique m — ~ vt : dividir

partly [ˈpɑrtli] adv : en parte

partner [ˈpɑrtnər] n 1 : pareja f (en un juego, etc.) 2 or **business ~** : socio m, -cia f — **partnership** [ˈpɑrtnərˌʃɪp] n : asociación f

party [ˈpɑrti] n, pl **-ties** 1 : partido m (político) 2 GATHERING : fiesta f 3 GROUP : grupo m

pass [ˈpæs] vi 1 : pasar 2 CEASE : pasarse 3 : aprobar (en un examen) 4 or **~ away** DIE : morir 5 **~ for** : pasar por 6 **~ out** FAINT : desmayarse — vt 1 : pasar 2 or **~ in front of** : pasar por 3 OVERTAKE : adelantar 4 : aprobar (un examen, una ley, etc.) 5 **~ down** : transmitir — ~ n 1 PERMIT : pase m, permiso m 2 : pase m (en deportes) 3 or **mountain ~** : paso m de montaña — **passable** [ˈpæsəbəl] adj 1 ADE-QUATE : adecuado 2 : transitable (dícese de un camino, etc.) — **passage** [ˈpæsɪdʒ] n 1 : paso m 2 CORRI-DOR : pasillo m (dentro de un edificio), pasaje m (entre edificios) 3 VOYAGE : travesía f (por el mar) — **passageway** [ˈpæsɪdʒˌweɪ] n : pasillo m, corredor m

passenger [ˈpæsəndʒər] n : pasajero m, -ra f

passerby [ˌpæsərˈbaɪ, ˈpæsər-] n, pl **passersby** : transeúnte mf

passion [ˈpæʃən] n : pasión f — **passionate** [ˈpæʃənət] adj : apasionado

passive [ˈpæsɪv] adj : pasivo

Passover [ˈpæsˌoːvər] n : Pascua f (en el judaísmo)

passport [ˈpæsˌpɔrt] n : pasaporte m

password [ˈpæsˌwərd] n : contraseña f

past [ˈpæst] adj 1 : pasado 2 FORMER : anterior 3 **the ~ few months** : los últimos meses — ~ prep 1 IN FRONT OF : por delante de 2 BEYOND : más allá de 3 **half ~ two** : las dos y media — ~ n : pasado m — ~ adv : por delante

pasta ['pɑstə, 'pæs-] n : pasta f

paste ['peɪst] n 1 : pasta f 2 GLUE : engrudo m — ~ vt **pasted; pasting** : pegar

pastel [pæ'stɛl] n : pastel m — ~ adj : pastel

pasteurize ['pæstʃəˌraɪz, 'pæstjə-] vt **-ized; -izing** : pasteurizar

pastime ['pæsˌtaɪm] n : pasatiempo m

pastor ['pæstər] n : pastor m, -tora f

pastry ['peɪstri] n, pl **-ries** : pasteles mpl

pasture ['pæstʃər] n : pasto m

pasty ['peɪsti] adj **pastier; -est** 1 DOUGHY : pastoso 2 PALLID : pálido

pat ['pæt] n 1 : palmadita f 2 a ~ of butter : una porción de mantequilla — ~ vt **patted; patting** : dar palmaditas a — ~ adv **have down** ~ : saberse de memoria — ~ adj GLIB : fácil

patch ['pætʃ] n 1 : parche m, remiendo m (para la ropa) 2 SPOT : mancha f, trozo m 3 PLOT : parcela f (de tierra) — ~ vt 1 MEND : remendar 2 ~ up : arreglar — **patchy** ['pætʃi] adj **patchier; -est** 1 : desigual 2 INCOMPLETE : parcial, incompleto

patent adj ['peɪtənt] 1 or **patented** ['pætəntəd] : patentado 2 ['pætənt, 'peɪt-] OBVIOUS : patente, evidente — ~ ['pætənt] n : patente f — ~ ['pætənt] vt : patentar

paternal [pə'tərnəl] adj FATHERLY : paternal 2 ~ **grandmother** : abuela f paterna — **paternity** [pə'tərnəti] n : paternidad f

path ['pæθ, 'pɑθ] n 1 TRACK, TRAIL : camino m, sendero m 2 COURSE : trayectoria f

pathetic [pə'θɛtɪk] adj : patético

pathology [pə'θɑlədʒi] n, pl **-gies** : patología f

pathway ['pæθˌweɪ] n : camino m, sendero m

patience ['peɪʃənts] n : paciencia f — **patient** ['peɪʃənt] adj : paciente — ~ n : paciente mf — **patiently** adv : con paciencia

patio ['pæṭiˌo] n, pl **-tios** : patio m

patriot ['peɪtriət] n : patriota mf — **patriotic** [peɪtri'ɑtɪk] adj : patriótico

patrol [pə'troːl] n : patrulla f — ~ v **-trolled; -trolling** : patrullar

patron ['peɪtrən] n 1 SPONSOR : patrocinador m, -dora f 2 CUSTOMER : cliente m, -ta f — **patronage** ['peɪtrənɪdʒ, 'pæ-] n 1 SPONSORSHIP : patrocinio m 2 CLIENTELE : clientela f — **patronize** ['peɪtrəˌnaɪz, 'pæ-] vt **-ized; -izing** 1 : ser cliente de (una tienda, etc.) 2 : tratar (a algn) con condescencia

patter ['pæṭər] n : tamborileo m (de la lluvia), correteo m (de los pies)

pattern ['pæṭərn] n 1 MODEL : modelo m 2 DESIGN : diseño m 3 STANDARD : pauta f, modo m 4 : patrón m (en costura) — ~ vt : basar (en un modelo)

paunch ['pɔntʃ] n : panza f

pause ['pɔz] n : pausa f — ~ vi **paused; pausing** : hacer una pausa

pave ['peɪv] vt **paved; paving** : pavimentar — **pavement** ['peɪvmənt] n : pavimento m

pavilion [pə'vɪljən] n : pabellón m

paw ['pɔ] n 1 : pata f 2 : garra f (de un gato) — ~ vt : tocar con la pata

pawn[1] ['pɔn] n : peón m (en ajedrez)

pawn[2] vt : empeñar — **pawnbroker** ['pɔnˌbroːkər] n : prestamista mf — **pawnshop** ['pɔnˌʃɑp] n : casa f de empeños

pay ['peɪ] v **paid** ['peɪd]; **paying** vt 1 : pagar 2 ~ **attention** : prestar atención 3 ~ **back** : devolver 4 ~ **one's respects** : presentar uno sus respetos 5 ~ **a visit** : hacer una visita — vi 1 : pagar 2 **crime doesn't** ~ : no hay crimen sin castigo — ~ n : paga f — **payable** ['peɪəbəl] adj : pagadero — **paycheck** ['peɪˌtʃɛk] n : cheque m del sueldo — **payment** ['peɪmənt] n 1 : pago m 2 INSTALLMENT : plazo m, cuota f Lat — **payroll** : nómina f

PC [piˈsiː] n, pl **PCs** or **PC's** : PC mf, computadora f personal

pea ['piː] n : guisante m, arveja f Lat

peace ['piːs] n : paz f — **peaceful** ['piːsfəl] adj 1 : pacífico 2 CALM : tranquilo

peach ['piːtʃ] n : melocotón m, durazno m Lat

peacock ['piːˌkɑk] n : pavo m real

peak ['piːk] n 1 SUMMIT : cumbre f, cima f, pico m (de una montaña) 2 APEX : nivel m máximo — ~ adj : máximo — ~ vi : alcanzar su nivel máximo

peal ['piːl] n 1 : repique m 2 ~**s of laughter** : carcajadas fpl

peanut ['piːˌnʌt] n : cacajuete m, maní m Lat

pear ['pær] n : pera f

pearl ['pərl] n : perla f

peasant ['pɛzənt] n : campesino m, -na f

peat ['piːt] n : turba f

pebble ['pɛbəl] n : guijarro m

pecan [pɪ'kɑn, -'kæn, 'piːˌkæn] n : pacana f, nuez f Lat

peck ['pɛk] vt : picar, picotear — ~ n 1 : picotazo m (de un pájaro) 2 KISS : besito

peculiar [pɪ'kjuːljər] adj 1 DISTINCTIVE

: peculiar, característico **2** STRANGE
: extraño, raro — **peculiarity** [pɪˌkjuːl-
ˈjærəti, -kjuˈlɪ'ær-] *n, pl* **-ties 1** : peculiaridad *f* **2** ODDITY : rareza *f*
pedal ['pedəl] *n* : pedal *m* — ~ *vi* **-aled**
or **-alled; -aling** *or* **-alling** : pedalear
pedantic [pɪ'dæntɪk] *adj* : pedante
peddle ['pedəl] *vt* **-dled; -dling** : vender
en las calles — **peddler** ['pedlər] *n*
: vendedor *m*, -dora *f* ambulante
pedestal ['pedəstəl] *n* : pedestal *m*
pedestrian [pə'destriən] *n* : peatón *m*,
-tona *f* — ~ *adj* ~ **crossing** : paso *m*
de peatones
pediatrics [ˌpiːdiˈætrɪks] *ns & pl* : pedi-
atría *f* — **pediatrician** [ˌpiːdiə'trɪʃən] *n*
: pediatra *mf*
pedigree ['pedəˌgriː] *n* : pedigrí *m* (de un
animal), linaje *m* (de una persona)
peek ['piːk] *vi* : mirar a hurtadillas — ~
n : miradita *f* (furtiva)
peel ['piːl] *vt* : pelar (fruta, etc.) — *vi*
: pelarse (dícese de la piel), descon-
charse (dícese de la pintura) — ~ *n*
: piel *f*, cáscara *f*
peep¹ ['piːp] *vi* CHEEP : piar — ~ *n* : pío
m (de un pajarito)
peep² *vi* **1** PEEK : mirar a hurtadillas **2**
or ~ **out** : asomar — ~ *n* GLANCE
: mirada *f* (furtiva)
peer¹ ['pɪr] *n* : par *mf*
peer² *vi* : mirar (con atención)
peeve ['piːv] *vt* : irritar — **peevish**
['piːvɪʃ] *adj* : malhumorado
peg ['peg] *n* **1** : clavija *f* **2** HOOK : gancho
m
pelican ['pelɪkən] *n* : pelícano *m*
pellet ['pelət] *n* **1** : bolita *f* **2** SHOT
: perdigón *m*
pelt¹ ['pelt] *n* : piel *f* (de un animal)
pelt² *vt* : lanzar (algo a algn)
pelvis ['pelvɪs] *n, pl* **-vises** *or* **-ves** ['pel-
ˌviːz] : pelvis *f* — **pelvic** ['pelvɪk] *adj*
: pélvico
pen¹ ['pen] *vt* **penned; penning** EN-
CLOSE : encerrar — ~ *n* : corral *m*,
redil *m*
pen² *n* **1** *or* **ballpoint** ~ : bolígrafo *m* **2**
or **fountain** ~ : pluma *f*
penal ['piːnəl] *adj* : penal — **penalize**
['piːnəlˌaɪz, 'pen-] *vt* **-ized; -izing** : penalizar — **penalty** ['penəlti] *n, pl* **-ties**
1 : pena *f*, castigo *m* **2** : penalty *m* (en
deportes)
penance ['penənts] *n* : penitencia *f*
pencil ['pentsəl] *n* : lápiz *m* — **pencil
sharpener** ~ : sacapuntas *m*
pendant ['pendənt] *n* : colgante *m*
pending ['pendɪŋ] *adj* : pendiente — ~
prep : en espera de

penetrate ['penəˌtreɪt] *v* **-trated; -trating**
: penetrar — **penetrating** ['penəˌtreɪ-
tɪŋ] *adj* : penetrante — **penetration**
[ˌpenə'treɪʃən] *n* : penetración *f*
penguin ['peŋgwɪn, 'pen-] *n* : pingüino
m
penicillin [ˌpenə'sɪlən] *n* : penicilina *f*
peninsula [pə'nɪntsələ, -'nɪntʃulə] *n* : península *f*
penis ['piːnəs] *n, pl* **-nes** [-ˌniːz] *or*
-nises : pene *m*
penitentiary [ˌpenə'tentʃəri] *n, pl* **-ries**
: penitenciaría *f*
pen name *n* : seudónimo *m*
pennant ['penənt] *n* : banderín *m*
penny ['peni] *n, pl* **-nies** *or* **pence**
['pents] : centavo *m* (de los Estados
Unidos), penique *m* (del Reino Unido)
— **penniless** ['peniləs] *adj* : sin un
centavo
pension ['pentʃən] *n* : pensión *m*, jubilación *f*
pensive ['pentsɪv] *adj* : pensativo
pentagon ['pentəˌgɑn] *n* : pentágono *m*
penthouse ['penthaʊs] *n* : ático *m*
pent–up ['pent'ʌp] *adj* : reprimido
people ['piːpəl] *ns & pl* **1** people *npl*
: gente *f*, personas *fpl* **2** *pl* ~**s**
: pueblo *m*
pep ['pep] *n* : energía *f*, vigor *m* — ~ *vt*
or ~ **up** : animar
pepper ['pepər] *n* **1** : pimienta *f* (condimento) **2** : pimiento *m* (fruta) — **peppermint** ['pepərˌmɪnt] *n* : menta *f*
per ['pər] *prep* **1** : por **2** ACCORDING TO
: según **3** ~ **day** : al día **4** miles ~
hour : millas *fpl* por hora
perceive [pər'siːv] *vt* **-ceived; -ceiving**
: percibir
percent [pər'sent] *adv* : por ciento —
percentage [pər'sentɪdʒ] *n* : porcentaje *m*
perception [pər'sepʃən] *n* : percepción *f*
— **perceptive** [pər'septɪv] *adj* : perspicaz
perch¹ ['pərtʃ] *n* : percha *f* (para los pájaros) — ~ *vi* : posarse
perch² *n* : perca *f* (pez)
percolate ['pərkəˌleɪt] *vi* **-lated; -lating**
: filtrarse — **percolator** ['pərkəˌleɪtər]
n : cafetera *f* de filtro
percussion [pər'kʌʃən] *n* : percusión *f*
perennial [pə'reniəl] *adj* : perenne — ~
n : planta *f* perenne
perfect ['pərfɪkt] *adj* : perfecto — ~
[pər'fekt] *vt* : perfeccionar — **perfection** [pər'fekʃən] *n* : perfección *f* —
perfectionist [pər'fekʃənɪst] *n* : perfeccionista *mf*

perforate ['pərfə,reɪt] *vt* **-rated; -rating** : perforar

perform [pər'fɔrm] *vt* **1** CARRY OUT : realizar, hacer **2** : representar (una obra teatral), interpretar (una obra musical) — *vi* **1** FUNCTION : funcionar **2** ACT : actuar — **performance** [pər'fɔrmənts] *n* **1** : realización *f* **2** INTERPRETATION : interpretación *f* **3** PRESENTATION : representación *f* — **performer** [pər'fɔrmər] *n* : actor *m*, -triz *f*; intérprete *mf* (de música)

perfume ['pər,fju:m, pər-] *n* : perfume *m*

perhaps [pər'hæps] *adv* : tal vez, quizá, quizás

peril ['pərəl] *n* : peligro *m* — **perilous** ['pərələs] *adj* : peligroso

perimeter [pə'rɪmətər] *n* : perímetro *m*

period ['pɪriəd] *n* **1** : período *m* (de tiempo) **2** : punto *m* (en puntuación) **3** ERA : época *f* — **periodic** [,pɪri'ɑdɪk] *adj* : periódico — **periodical** [,pɪri'ɑdɪkəl] *n* : revista *f*

peripheral [pə'rɪfərəl] *adj* : periférico

perish ['pərɪʃ] *vi* : perecer — **perishable** ['pərɪʃəbəl] *adj* : perecedero — **perishables** ['pərɪʃəbəlz] *npl* : productos *mpl* perecederos

perjury ['pərdʒəri] *n* : perjurio *m*

perk ['pərk] *vi* ~ **up** : animarse, reanimarse — ~ *n* : extra *m* — **perky** ['pərki] *adj* **perkier; -est** : alegre

permanence ['pərmənənts] *n* : permanencia *f* — **permanent** ['pərmənənt] *adj* : permanente — ~ *n* : permanente *f*

permeate ['pərmi,eɪt] *v* **-ated; -ating** : penetrar

permission [pər'mɪʃən] *n* : permiso *m* — **permissible** [pər'mɪsəbəl] *adj* : permisible — **permissive** [pər'mɪsɪv] *adj* : permisivo — **permit** [pər'mɪt] *vt* **-mitted; -mitting** : permitir — ~ ['pər,mɪt, pər-] *n* : permiso *m*

peroxide [pə'rɑk,saɪd] *n* : peróxido *m*

perpendicular [,pərpən'dɪkjələr] *adj* : perpendicular

perpetrate ['pərpə,treɪt] *vt* **-trated; -trating** : cometer — **perpetrator** ['pərpə,treɪtər] *n* : autor *m*, -tora *f* (de un delito)

perpetual [pər'pɛtʃuəl] *adj* : perpetuo

perplex [pər'plɛks] *vt* : dejar perplejo — **perplexing** [pər'plɛksɪŋ] *adj* : desconcertante — **perplexity** [pər'plɛksəti] *n*, *pl* **-ties** : perplejidad *f*

persecute ['pərsɪ,kju:t] *vt* **-cuted; -cuting** : perseguir — **persecution** [,pərsɪ'kju:ʃən] *n* : persecución *f*

persevere [,pərsə'vɪr] *vi* **-vered; -vering**

: perseverar — **perseverance** [,pərsə-'vɪrənts] *n* : perseverancia *f*

persist [pər'sɪst] *vi* : persistir — **persistence** [pər'sɪstənts] *n* : persistencia *f* — **persistent** [pər'sɪstənt] *adj* : persistente

person ['pərsən] *n* : persona *f* — **personal** ['pərsənəl] *adj* : personal — **personality** [,pərsən'æləti] *n*, *pl* **-ties** : personalidad *f* — **personally** ['pərsənəli] *adv* : personalmente, en persona — **personnel** [,pərsən'el] *n* : personal *m*

perspective [pər'spɛktɪv] *n* : perspectiva *f*

perspiration [,pərspə'reɪʃən] *n* : transpiración *f* — **perspire** [pər'spaɪr] *vi* **-spired; -spiring** : transpirar

persuade [pər'sweɪd] *vt* **-suaded; -suading** : persuadir — **persuasion** [pər'sweɪʒən] *n* : persuasión *f*

pertain [pər'teɪn] *vi* ~ **to** : estar relacionado con — **pertinent** ['pərtənənt] *adj* : pertinente

perturb [pər'tərb] *vt* : perturbar

Peruvian [pə'ru:viən] *adj* : peruano

pervade [pər'veɪd] *vt* **-vaded; -vading** : penetrar — **pervasive** [pər'veɪsɪv, -zɪv] *adj* : penetrante

perverse [pər'vərs] *adj* **1** CORRUPT : perverso **2** STUBBORN : obstinado — **pervert** ['pər,vərt] *n* : pervertido *m*, -da *f*

peso ['peɪ,soɪ] *n*, *pl* **-sos** : peso *m*

pessimism ['pɛsə,mɪzəm] *n* : pesimismo *m* — **pessimist** ['pɛsəmɪst] *n* : pesimista *mf* — **pessimistic** [,pɛsə'mɪstɪk] *adj* : pesimista

pest ['pɛst] *n* **1** : insecto *m* nocivo, animal *m* nocivo **2** : peste *f fam* (persona) — **pester** ['pɛstər] *vt* **-tered; -tering** : molestar

pesticide ['pɛstə,saɪd] *n* : pesticida *m*

pet ['pɛt] *n* **1** : animal *m* doméstico **2** FAVORITE : favorito *m*, -ta *f* — ~ *vt* **petted; petting** : acariciar

petal ['pɛtəl] *n* : pétalo *m*

petite [pə'ti:t] *adj* : chiquita

petition [pə'tɪʃən] *n* : petición *f* — ~ *vt* : dirigir una petición a

petrify ['pɛtrə,faɪ] *vt* **-fied; -fying** : petrificar

petroleum [pə'tro:liəm] *n* : petróleo *m*

petticoat ['pɛti,ko:t] *n* : enagua *f*, fondo *m Lat*

petty ['pɛti] *adj* **-tier; -est 1** UNIMPORTANT : insignificante, nimio **2** MEAN : mezquino — **pettiness** ['pɛtinəs] *n* : mezquindad *f*

petulant ['pɛtʃələnt] *adj* : irritable, de mal genio

pew ['pju:] *n* : banco *m* (de iglesia)

pewter ['pjuːtər] n : peltre m

phallic ['fælɪk] adj : fálico

phantom ['fæntəm] n : fantasma m

pharmacy ['farməsi] n, pl -cies : farmacia f — pharmacist ['farməsɪst] n : farmacéutico m, -ca f

phase ['feɪz] n : fase f — ~ vt phased; phasing 1 — in : introducir progresivamente 2 ~ out : retirar progresivamente

phenomenon [fɪ'namənan, -nən] n, pl -na [-nə] or -nons : fenómeno m — phenomenal [fɪ'namənəl] adj : fenomenal

philanthropy [fə'lænθrəpi] n, pl -pies : filantropía f — philanthropist [fə'lænθrəpɪst] n : filántropo m, -pa f

philosophy [fə'lasəfi] n, pl -phies : filosofía f — philosopher [fə'lasəfər] n : filósofo m, -fa f

phlegm ['flem] n : flema f

phobia ['foːbiə] n : fobia f

phone ['foːn] → telephone

phonetic [fə'nɛtɪk] adj : fonético

phony or phoney ['foːni] adj -nier; -est : falso — ~ n, pl -nies : farsante mf

phosphorus ['fasfərəs] n : fósforo m

photo ['foːtoː] n, pl -tos : foto f — photocopier ['foːtoˌkapiər] n : fotocopiadora f — photocopy ['foːtoˌkapi] n, pl -copies : fotocopia f — ~ vt -copied; -copying : fotocopiar — photograph ['foːtəˌgræf] n : fotografía f, foto f — ~ vt : fotografiar — photographer [fə'tagrəfər] n : fotógrafo m, -fa f — photographic [ˌfoːtə'græfɪk] adj : fotográfico — photography [fə'tagrəfi] n : fotografía f

phrase ['freɪz] n : frase f — ~ vt phrased; phrasing : expresar

physical ['fɪzɪkəl] adj : físico — ~ n : reconocimiento m médico

physician [fə'zɪʃən] n : médico m, -ca f

physics ['fɪzɪks] ns & pl : física f — physicist ['fɪzəsɪst] n : físico m, -ca f

physiology [ˌfɪzi'alədʒi] n : fisiología f

physique [fə'ziːk] n : físico m

piano [pi'ænoː] n, pl -anos : piano m — pianist [pi'ænɪst, 'piːənɪst] n : pianista mf

pick ['pɪk] vt 1 CHOOSE : escoger 2 GATHER : recoger 3 REMOVE : quitar (poco a poco) 4 ~ a fight : buscar camorra — vi 1 ~ and choose : ser exigente 2 ~ on : meterse con — ~ n 1 CHOICE : selección f 2 or pickax ['pɪkˌæks] : pico m 3 the ~ of : lo mejor de

picket ['pɪkət] n 1 STAKE : estaca f 2 or ~ line : piquete m — ~ v : piquetear

pickle ['pɪkəl] n 1 : pepinillo m (encur-

tido) 2 JAM : lío m fam, apuro m — ~ vt -led; -ling : encurtir

pickpocket ['pɪkˌpakət] n : carterista mf

pickup ['pɪkˌəp] n 1 IMPROVEMENT : mejora f 2 or ~ truck : camioneta f — pick up vt 1 LIFT : levantar 2 TIDY : arreglar, ordenar — vi IMPROVE : mejorar

picnic ['pɪkˌnɪk] n : picnic m — ~ vi -nicked; -nicking : ir de picnic

picture ['pɪktʃər] n 1 PAINTING : cuadro m 2 DRAWING : dibujo m 3 PHOTO : fotografía f 4 IMAGE : imagen f 5 MOVIE : película f — ~ vt -tured; -turing 1 DEPICT : representar 2 IMAGINE : imaginarse — picturesque [ˌpɪktʃə'resk] adj : pintoresco

pie ['paɪ] n : pastel m (con fruta o carne), empanada f (con carne)

piece ['piːs] n 1 : pieza f 2 FRAGMENT : trozo m, pedazo m 3 a ~ of advice : un consejo — ~ vt pieced; piecing or ~ together : juntar, componer — piecemeal ['piːsˌmiːl] adv : poco a poco — ~ adj : poco sistemático

pier ['pɪr] n : muelle m

pierce ['pɪrs] vt pierced; piercing : perforar — piercing adj : penetrante

piety ['paɪəti] n, pl -eties : piedad f

pig ['pɪg] n : cerdo m, -da f; puerco m, -ca f

pigeon ['pɪdʒən] n : paloma f — pigeonhole ['pɪdʒənˌhoːl] n : casilla f

piggyback ['pɪgiˌbæk] adv & adj : a cuestas

pigment ['pɪgmənt] n : pigmento m

pigpen ['pɪgˌpen] n : pocilga f

pigtail ['pɪgˌteɪl] n : coleta f, trenza f

pile¹ ['paɪl] n HEAP : montón m, pila f — ~ v piled; piling vt : amontonar, apilar — vi ~ up : amontonarse, acumularse

pile² n NAP : pelo m (de telas)

pilfer ['pɪlfər] vt : robar, hurtar

pilgrim ['pɪlgrəm] n : peregrino m, -na f — pilgrimage ['pɪlgrəmɪdʒ] n : peregrinación f

pill ['pɪl] n : pastilla f, píldora f

pillage ['pɪlɪdʒ] n : saqueo m — ~ vt -laged; -laging : saquear

pillar ['pɪlər] n : pilar m, columna f

pillow ['pɪˌloː] n : almohada f — pillowcase ['pɪˌloːˌkeɪs] n : funda f (de almohada)

pilot ['paɪlət] n : piloto mf — ~ vt : pilotar, pilotear — pilot light n : piloto m

pimp ['pɪmp] n : proxeneta m

pimple ['pɪmpəl] n : grano m

pin ['pɪn] n 1 : alfiler m 2 BROOCH

: broche *m* **3** *or* **bowling ~** : bolo *m*
— **~** *vt* **pinned; pinning 1** FASTEN
: prender, sujetar (con alfileres) **2** *or*
~ down : inmovilizar

pincers ['pɪntsərz] *npl* : tenazas *fpl*

pinch ['pɪntʃ] *vt* **1** : pellizcar **2** STEAL
: robar — *vi* : apretar — **~** *n* **1** : pellizco *m* **2** BIT : pizca *f* **3 in a ~** : en
caso necesario

pine[1] ['paɪn] *n* : pino *m* (árbol)

pine[2] *vi* **pined; pining 1** LANGUISH
: languidecer **2 ~ for** : suspirar por

pineapple ['paɪnˌæpəl] *n* : piña *f*, ananás
m

pink ['pɪŋk] *n* : rosa *m*, rosado *m* — **~**
adj : rosa, rosado

pinnacle ['pɪnɪkəl] *n* : pináculo *m*

pinpoint ['pɪnˌpɔɪnt] *vt* : localizar, precisar

pint ['paɪnt] *n* : pinta *f*

pioneer [ˌpaɪəˈnɪr] *n* : pionero *m*, -ra *f*

pious ['paɪəs] *adj* : piadoso

pipe ['paɪp] *n* **1** : tubo *m*, caño *m* **2** : pipa
f (para fumar) — **pipeline** ['paɪpˌlaɪn] *n*
1 : conducto *m*, oleoducto *m* (para
petróleo)

piquant ['pi:kənt, 'pɪkwənt] *adj* : picante

pique ['pi:k] *n* : resentimiento *m*

pirate ['paɪrət] *n* : pirata *m*

pistachio [pəˈstæʃiˌoː, -stə-] *n, pl* **-chios**
: pistacho *m*

pistol ['pɪstəl] *n* : pistola *f*

piston ['pɪstən] *n* : pistón *m*

pit ['pɪt] *n* **1** HOLE : hoyo *m*, fosa *f* **2** MINE
: mina *f* **3** : hueso *m* (de una fruta) **4 ~
of the stomach** : boca *f* del estómago
— **~** *vt* **pitted; pitting 1** : marcar de
hoyos **2** : deshuesar (una fruta) **3 ~
against** : enfrentar a

pitch ['pɪtʃ] *vt* **1** : armar (una tienda) **2**
THROW : lanzar — *vi* **1** *or* **~ forward**
: caerse **2** LURCH : cabecear (dícese de
un barco o un avión) — **~** *n* **1** DE-
GREE, LEVEL : grado *m*, punto *m* **2**
TONE : tono *m* **3** THROW : lanzamiento
m **4** *or* **sales ~** : presentación *f* (de
un vendedor)

pitcher ['pɪtʃər] *n* **1** JUG : jarro *m* **2** : lan-
zador *m*, -dora *f* (en béisbol, etc.)

pitchfork ['pɪtʃˌfɔrk] *n* : horquilla *f*,
horca *f*

pitfall ['pɪtˌfɔl] *n* : riesgo *m*, dificultad *f*

pith ['pɪθ] *n* **1** : médula *f* (de un hueso,
etc.) **2** CORE : meollo *m* — **pithy** ['pɪθi]
adj **pithier; -est** : conciso y sustancioso

pity ['pɪti] *n, pl* **pities 1** COMPASSION
: compasión *f* **2 what a ~!** : ¡qué lástima! — **~** *vt* **pitied; pitying** : compadecerse de — **pitiful** ['pɪtɪfəl] *adj*

: lastimoso — **pitiless** ['pɪtɪləs] *adj*
: despiadado

pivot ['pɪvət] *n* : pivote *m* — **~** *vi* **1**
: girar sobre un eje **2 ~ on** : depender
de

pizza ['pi:tsə] *n* : pizza *f*

placard ['plækərd, -ˌkɑrd] *n* POSTER : cartel *m*, póster *m*

placate ['pleɪˌkeɪt, 'plæ-] *vt* **-cated;
-cating** : apaciguar

place ['pleɪs] *n* **1** : sitio *m*, lugar *m* **2**
SEAT : asiento *m* **3** POSITION : puesto *m*
4 ROLE : papel *m* **5 take ~** : tener
lugar **6 take the ~ of** : sustituir a —
~ *vt* **placed; placing 1** PUT, SET
: poner, colocar **2** IDENTIFY : identificar, recordar **3 ~ an order** : hacer
un pedido — **placement** ['pleɪsmənt] *n*
: colocación *f*

placid ['plæsəd] *adj* : plácido, tranquilo

plagiarism ['pleɪdʒəˌrɪzəm] *n* : plagio *m*
— **plagiarize** ['pleɪdʒəˌraɪz] *vt* **-rized;
-rizing** : plagiar

plague ['pleɪg] *n* **1** : plaga *f* (de insectos,
etc.) **2** : peste *f* (en medicina)

plaid ['plæd] *n* : tela *f* escocesa — **~** *adj*
: escocés

plain ['pleɪn] *adj* **1** SIMPLE : sencillo **2**
CLEAR : claro, evidente **3** CANDID
: franco **4** HOMELY : poco atractivo **5 in
~ sight** : a la vista (de todos) — **~** *n*
: llanura *f*, planicie *f* — **plainly** ['pleɪn-
li] *adv* **1** CLEARLY : claramente **2**
FRANKLY : francamente **3** SIMPLY : sencillamente

plaintiff ['pleɪntɪf] *n* : demandante *mf*

plan ['plæn] *n* **1** : plan *m*, proyecto *m* **2**
DIAGRAM : plano *m* — *v* **planned;
planning** *vt* **1** : planear, proyectar **2**
INTEND : tener planeado — *vi* : hacer
planes

plane[1] ['pleɪn] *n* **1** LEVEL : plano *m*,
nivel *m* **2** AIRPLANE : avión *m*

plane[2] *n* *or* **carpenter's ~** : cepillo *m*

planet ['plænət] *n* : planeta *f*

plank ['plæŋk] *n* : tabla *f*

planning ['plænɪŋ] *n* : planificación *f*

plant ['plænt] *vt* : plantar (flores, árboles), sembrar (semillas) — **~** *n* **1**
: planta *f* **2** FACTORY : fábrica *f*

plantain ['plæntən] *n* : plátano *m* (grande)

plantation [plænˈteɪʃən] *n* : plantación *f*

plaque ['plæk] *n* : placa *f*

plaster ['plæstər] *n* : yeso *m* — **~** *vt* **1**
: enyesar **2** COVER : cubrir — **plaster
cast** *n* : escayola *f*

plastic ['plæstɪk] *adj* **1** : de plástico **2**
FLEXIBLE : plástico, flexible **3 ~ sur-
gery** : cirugía *f* plástica — **~** *n* : plástico *m*

plate 334 pneumatic

plate ['pleɪt] *n* **1** SHEET : placa *f* **2** DISH : plato *m* **3** ILLUSTRATION : lámina *f* — ~ *vt* **plated; plating** : chapar (en metal)

plateau [plæˈtoː] *n, pl* **-teaus** *or* **-teaux** [-ˈtoːz] : meseta *f*

platform ['plætˌfɔrm] *n* **1** : plataforma *f* **2** : andén *m* (de una estación de ferrocarril) **3** *or* **political** ~ : programa *m* electoral

platinum ['plætənəm] *n* : platino *m*

platitude ['plætəˌtuːd, -ˌtjuːd] *n* : lugar *m* común

platoon [pləˈtuːn] *n* : sección *f* (en el ejército)

platter ['plætər] *n* : fuente *f*

plausible ['plɔzəbəl] *adj* : creíble, verosímil

play ['pleɪ] *n* **1** : juego *m* **2** DRAMA : obra *f* de teatro — *vi* **1** : jugar **2** ~ **in a band** : tocar en un grupo — *vt* **1** : jugar (deportes, etc.), jugar a (juegos) **2** : tocar (música o un instrumento) **3** ~ **the role of** : representar el papel de — **player** ['pleɪər] *n* **1** : jugador *m*, -dora *f* **2** ACTOR : actor *m*, actriz *f* **3** MUSICIAN : músico *m*, -ca *f* — **playful** ['pleɪfəl] *adj* : juguetón — **playground** ['pleɪˌgraʊnd] *n* : patio *m* de recreo — **playing card** : naipe *m*, carta *f* — **playmate** ['pleɪˌmeɪt] *n* : compañero *m*, -ra *f* de juego — **play–off** ['pleɪˌɔf] *n* : desempate *m* — **playpen** ['pleɪˌpɛn] *n* : corral *m* (para niños) — **plaything** ['pleɪˌθɪŋ] *n* : juguete *m* — **playwright** ['pleɪˌraɪt] *n* : dramaturgo *m*, -ga *f*

plea ['pliː] *n* **1** : acto *m* de declararse (en derecho) **2** APPEAL : ruego *m*, súplica *f* — **plead** ['pliːd] *v* **pleaded** *or* **pled** ['plɛd]; **pleading** *vi* **1** ~ **for** : suplicar **2** ~ **guilty** : declararse culpable **3** ~ **not guilty** : negar la acusación — *vt* **1** : alegar, pretextar **2** ~ **a case** : defender un caso

pleasant ['plɛzənt] *adj* : agradable, grato — **please** ['pliːz] *v* **pleased; pleasing** *vt* **1** GRATIFY : complacer **2** SATISFY : satisfacer — *vi* **1** : agradar **2** **do as you** ~ : haz lo que quieras — ~ *adv* : por favor — **pleased** ['pliːzd] *adj* : contento — **pleasing** ['pliːzɪŋ] *adj* : agradable — **pleasure** ['plɛʒər] *n* : placer *m*, gusto *m*

pleat ['pliːt] *vt* : plisar — ~ *n* : pliegue *m*

pledge ['plɛdʒ] *n* **1** SECURITY : prenda *f* **2** PROMISE : promesa *f* — ~ *vt* **pledged; pledging 1** PAWN : empeñar **2** PROMISE : prometer

plenty ['plɛnti] *n* **1** : abundancia *f* **2** ~ **of time** : tiempo *m* de sobra — **plentiful** ['plɛntɪfəl] *adj* : abundante

pliable ['plaɪəbəl] *adj* : flexible

pliers ['plaɪərz] *npl* : alicates *mpl*

plight ['plaɪt] *n* : situación *f* difícil

plod ['plɑd] *vi* **plodded; plodding 1** : caminar con paso pesado **2** DRUDGE : trabajar laboriosamente

plot ['plɑt] *n* **1** LOT : parcela *f* **2** : argumento *m* (de una novela, etc.) **3** CONSPIRACY : complot *m*, intriga *f* — *v* **plotted; plotting** *vt* : tramar (un plan), trazar (una gráfica, etc.) — *vi* CONSPIRE : conspirar

plow *or* **plough** ['plaʊ] *n* **1** : arado *m* **2** → **snowplow** — ~ *v* : arar

ploy ['plɔɪ] *n* : estratagema *f*

pluck ['plʌk] *vt* **1** : arrancar **2** : desplumar (un pollo, etc.) **3** : recoger (flores) **4** ~ **one's eyebrows** : depilarse las cejas

plug ['plʌg] *n* **1** STOPPER : tapón *m* **2** : enchufe *m* (eléctrico) — ~ *vt* **plugged; plugging 1** BLOCK : tapar **2** ADVERTISE : dar publicidad a **3** ~ **in** : enchufar

plum ['plʌm] *n* : ciruela *f*

plumb ['plʌm] *adj* : a plomo, vertical — **plumber** ['plʌmər] *n* : fontanero *m*, -ra *f*; plomero *m*, -ra *f* *Lat* — **plumbing** ['plʌmɪŋ] *n* **1** : fontanería *f*, plomería *f* *Lat* **2** PIPES : cañerías *fpl*

plume ['pluːm] *n* : pluma *f*

plummet ['plʌmət] *vi* : caer en picado

plump ['plʌmp] *adj* : rechoncho *fam*

plunder ['plʌndər] *vi* : saquear, robar — ~ *n* : botín *m*

plunge ['plʌndʒ] *v* **plunged; plunging** *vt* **1** IMMERSE : sumergir **2** THRUST : hundir — *vi* **1** : zambullirse (en el agua) **2** DESCEND : descender en picada — ~ *n* **1** DIVE : zambullida *f* **2** DROP : descenso *m* abrupto

plural ['plʊrəl] *adj* : plural — ~ *n* : plural *m*

plus ['plʌs] *adj* : positivo — ~ *n* **1** *or* ~ **sign** : signo *m* (de) más **2** ADVANTAGE : ventaja *f* — ~ *prep* : más — ~ *conj* : y, además

plush ['plʌʃ] *n* : felpa *f* — ~ *adj* **1** : de felpa **2** LUXURIOUS : lujoso

plutonium [pluːˈtoːniəm] *n* : plutonio *m*

ply ['plaɪ] *vt* **plied; plying 1** : ejercer (un oficio) **2** ~ **with questions** : acosar con preguntas

plywood ['plaɪˌwʊd] *n* : contrachapado *m*

pneumatic [nʊˈmætɪk, njʊ-] *adj* : neumático

pneumonia [nuˈmoːnjə, njʊ-] *n* : pulmonía *f*

poach[1] [ˈpoːtʃ] *vt* : cocer a fuego lento

poach[2] *vt or* **~ game** : cazar ilegalmente **— poacher** [ˈpoːtʃər] *n* : cazador *m* furtivo, cazadora *f* furtiva

pocket [ˈpakət] *n* : bolsillo *m* **—** *vt* : meterse en el bolsillo **— pocketbook** [ˈpakət,bʊk] *n* : cartera *f*, bolsa *f* *Lat* **— pocketknife** [ˈpakət,naɪf] *n, pl* **-knives** : navaja *f*

pod [ˈpad] *n* : vaina *f*

poem [ˈpoːəm] *n* : poema *m* **— poet** [ˈpoːət] *n* : poeta *mf* **— poetic** [poˈeʈɪk] *or* **poetical** [-ʈɪkəl] *adj* : poético **— poetry** [ˈpoːətri] *n* : poesía *f*

poignant [ˈpɔɪnjənt] *adj* : conmovedor

point [ˈpɔɪnt] *n* **1** : punto *m* **2** PURPOSE : sentido *m* **3** TIP : punta *f* **4** FEATURE : cualidad *f* **5 be beside the ~** : no venir al caso **6 there's no ~ ...** : no sirve de nada... **— ~** *vt* **1** AIM : apuntar **2** *or* **~ out** : señalar, indicar **—** *vi* **~ at** : señalar (con el dedo) **— point–blank** [ˈpɔɪntˈblæŋk] *adv* : a quemarropa **— pointer** [ˈpɔɪntər] *n* **1** NEEDLE : aguja *f* **2** : perro *m* de muestra **3** TIP : consejo *m* **— pointless** [ˈpɔɪntləs] *adj* : inútil **— point of view** *n* : perspectiva *f*, punto *m* de vista

poise [ˈpɔɪz] *n* **1** : elegancia *f* **2** COMPOSURE : aplomo *m*

poison [ˈpɔɪzən] *n* : veneno *m* **— ~** *vt* : envenenar **— poisonous** [ˈpɔɪzənəs] *adj* : venenoso (dícese de una culebra, etc.), tóxico (dícese de una sustancia)

poke [ˈpoːk] *vt* **poked; poking 1** JAB : golpear (con la punta de algo), dar **2** THRUST : introducir, asomar **— ~** *n* : golpe *m* abrupto (con la punta de algo)

poker[1] [ˈpoːkər] *n* : atizador *m* (para el fuego)

poker[2] *n* : póquer *m* (juego de naipes)

polar [ˈpoːlər] *adj* : polar **— polar bear** *n* : oso *m* blanco **— polarize** [ˈpoːlə,raɪz] *vt* **-ized; -izing** : polarizar

pole[1] [ˈpoːl] *n* : palo *m*, poste *m*

pole[2] *n* : polo *m* (en geografía)

police [pəˈliːs] *vt* **-liced; -licing** : mantener el orden en **— ~** *ns & pl* **the ~** : la policía **— policeman** [pəˈliːsmən] *n, pl* **-men** [-mən, -ˌmen] : policía *m* **— police officer** *n* : policía *mf*, agente *mf* de policía **— policewoman** [pəˈliːs,wʊmən] *n, pl* **-women** [-ˌwɪmən] : (mujer *f*) policía *f*

policy [ˈpaləsi] *n, pl* **-cies 1** : política *f* **2** *or* **insurance ~** : póliza *f* de seguros

polio [ˈpoːliˌoː] *or* **poliomyelitis** [ˌpoːliˌoːˌmaɪəˈlaɪtəs] *n* : polio *f*, poliomielitis *f*

polish [ˈpalɪʃ] *vt* **1** : pulir **2** : limpiar (zapatos), encerar (un suelo) **— ~** *n* **1** LUSTER : brillo *m*, lustre *m* **2** : betún *m* (para zapatos), cera *f* (para suelos y muebles), esmalte *m* (para las uñas)

Polish [ˈpoːlɪʃ] *adj* : polaco **— ~** *n* : polaco *m* (idioma)

polite [pəˈlaɪt] *adj* **-liter; -est** : cortés **— politeness** [pəˈlaɪtnəs] *n* : cortesía *f*

political [pəˈlɪʈɪkəl] *adj* : político **— politician** [ˌpaləˈtɪʃən] *n* : político *m*, -ca *f* **— politics** [ˈpaləˌtɪks] *ns & pl* : política *f*

polka [ˈpoːlkə, ˈpoːkə] *n* : polka *f* **— polka dot** [ˈpoːkəˌdat] *n* : lunar *m*

poll [ˈpoːl] *n* **1** : encuesta *f*, sondeo *m* **2 the ~s** : las urnas **— ~** *vt* **1** : obtener (votos) **2** CANVASS : encuestar, sondear

pollen [ˈpalən] *n* : polen *m*

pollute [pəˈluːt] *vt* **-luted; -luting** : contaminar **— pollution** [pəˈluːʃən] *n* : contaminación *f*

polyester [ˈpaliˌestər, ˌpali'-] *n* : poliéster *m*

polygon [ˈpaliˌgan] *n* : polígono *m*

pomegranate [ˈpaməˌgrænət, ˈpamˌgrænət] *n* : granada *f*

pomp [ˈpamp] *n* : pompa *f* **— pompous** [ˈpampəs] *adj* : pomposo

pond [ˈpand] *n* : charca *f* (natural), estanque *m* (artificial)

ponder [ˈpandər] *vt* : considerar **—** *vi* **~ over** : reflexionar sobre

pony [ˈpoːni] *n, pl* **-nies** : poni *m* **— ponytail** [ˈpoːniˌteɪl] *n* : cola *f* de caballo

poodle [ˈpuːdəl] *n* : caniche *m*

pool [ˈpuːl] *n* **1** PUDDLE : charco *m* **2** : fondo *m* común (de recursos) **3** BILLIARDS : billar *m* **4** *or* **swimming ~** : piscina *f* **— ~** *vt* : hacer un fondo común de

poor [ˈpʊr, ˈpor] *adj* **1** : pobre **2** INFERIOR : malo **3 the ~** : los pobres **— poorly** [ˈpʊrli, ˈpor-] *adv* : mal

pop[1] [ˈpap] *v* **popped; popping** *vt* **1** : hacer reventar **2 ~ sth into** : meter algo en **—** *vi* **1** BURST : reventarse, estallar **2 ~ in** : entrar (un momento) **3 ~ out** : saltar (dícese de los ojos) **4 ~ up** APPEAR : aparecer **— ~** *n* **1** : ruido *m* seco **2 ~ soda pop**

pop[2] *n or* **~ music** : música *f* popular

popcorn [ˈpapˌkorn] *n* : palomitas *fpl*

pope [ˈpoːp] *n* : papa *m*

poplar [ˈpaplər] *n* : álamo *m*

poppy [ˈpapi] *n, pl* **-pies** : amapola *f*

popular [ˈpapjələr] *adj* : popular **— pop-**

ularity [ˌpɑpjəˈlærəti] n : popularidad f
— **popularize** [ˈpɑpjələˌraɪz] vt **-ized**;
-izing : popularizar
populate [ˈpɑpjəˌleɪt] vt **-lated**; **-lating**
: poblar — **population** [ˌpɑpjəˈleɪʃən] n
: población f
porcelain [ˈpɔrsələn] n : porcelana f
porch [ˈpɔrtʃ] n : porche m
porcupine [ˈpɔrkjəˌpaɪn] n : puerco m
espín
pore[1] [ˈpor] vi **pored**; **poring** ~ **over**
: estudiar esmeradamente
pore[2] n : poro m
pork [ˈpork] n : carne f de cerdo
pornography [pɔrˈnɑgrəfi] n : pornografía f — **pornographic** [ˌpɔrnə-
ˈgræfɪk] adj : pornográfico
porous [ˈporəs] adj : poroso
porpoise [ˈpɔrpəs] n : marsopa f
porridge [ˈpɔrɪdʒ] n : avena f (cocida),
gachas fpl (de avena)
port[1] [ˈport] n HARBOR : puerto m
port[2] n or ~ **side** : babor m
port[3] n : oporto m (vino)
portable [ˈpɔrtəbəl] adj : portátil
portent [ˈpɔrˌtent] n : presagio m
porter [ˈpɔrtər] n : maletero m, mozo m
(de estación)
portfolio [pɔrtˈfoˌli̩o] n, pl **-lios** : cartera
f
porthole [ˈpɔrtˌhoːl] n : portilla f
portion [ˈpɔrʃən] n : porción f
portrait [ˈpɔrtrət, -ˌtreɪt] n : retrato m
portray [pɔrˈtreɪ] vt 1 : representar, retratar 2 : interpretar (un personaje)
Portuguese [ˌpɔrtʃəˈgiːz, -ˈgiːs] adj : portugués — n : portugués m (idioma)
pose [ˈpoːz] v **posed**; **posing** vt
: plantear (una pregunta, etc.), representar (una amenaza) — vi 1 : posar 2
~ **as** : hacerse pasar por — ~ n
: pose f
posh [ˈpɑʃ] adj : elegante, de lujo
position [pəˈzɪʃən] n 1 : posición f 2 JOB
: puesto m — ~ vt : colocar, situar
positive [ˈpɑzət̬ɪv] adj 1 : positivo 2
CERTAIN : seguro
possess [pəˈzes] vt : poseer — **possession** [pəˈzeʃən] n 1 : posesión f 2 ~s
npl BELONGINGS : bienes mpl — **possessive** [pəˈzesɪv] adj : posesivo
possible [ˈpɑsəbəl] adj : posible — **possibility** [ˌpɑsəˈbɪlət̬i] n, pl **-ties** : posibilidad f — **possibly** [ˈpɑsəbli] adv
: posiblemente
post[1] [ˈpoːst] n POLE : poste m, palo m
post[2] n POSITION : puesto m
post[3] n MAIL : cartas fpl — ~ vt 1
: echar al correo 2 **keep** ~**ed** : tener
al corriente — **postage** [ˈpoːstɪdʒ] n

: franqueo m — **postal** [ˈpoːstəl] adj
: postal — **postcard** [ˈpoːstˌkɑrd] n
: tarjeta f postal
poster [ˈpoːstər] n : cartel m
posterity [pɑˈsterət̬i] n : posteridad f
posthumous [ˈpɑstʃəməs] adj : póstumo
postman [ˈpoːstmən, -ˌmæn] → **mailman**
— **post office** n : oficina f de correos
postpone [ˌpoːstˈpoːn] vt **-poned**;
-poning : aplazar — **postponement**
[ˌpoːstˈpoːnmənt] n : aplazamiento m
postscript [ˈpoːstˌskrɪpt] n : posdata f
posture [ˈpɑstʃər] n : postura f
postwar [ˌpoːstˈwɔr] adj : de (la) posguerra
pot [ˈpɑt] n 1 : olla f (de cocina) 2 FLOW-
ERPOT : maceta f 3 ~s **and pans**
: cacharros mpl
potassium [pəˈtæsiəm] n : potasio m
potato [pəˈteɪt̬o] n, pl **-toes** : patata f,
papa f Lat
potent [ˈpoːtənt] adj 1 POWERFUL : poderoso 2 EFFECTIVE : eficaz
potential [pəˈtentʃəl] adj : potencial —
~ n : potencial m
pothole [ˈpɑtˌhoːl] n : bache m
potion [ˈpoːʃən] n : poción f
pottery [ˈpɑt̬əri] n, pl **-teries** : cerámica f
pouch [ˈpaʊtʃ] n 1 BAG : bolsa f pequeña
2 : bolsa f (de un animal)
poultry [ˈpoːltri] n : aves fpl de corral
pounce [ˈpaʊns] vi **pounced**; **pounc-
ing** : abalanzarse
pound[1] [ˈpaʊnd] n : libra f (unidad de
dinero o de peso)
pound[2] n or **dog** ~ : perrera f
pound[3] vt 1 CRUSH : machacar 2 HIT
: golpear — vi : palpitar (dícese del
corazón)
pour [ˈpor] vt : verter — vi 1 FLOW : fluir,
salir 2 **it's** ~**ing** : está lloviendo a
cántaros
pout [ˈpaʊt] vi : hacer pucheros — ~ n
: puchero m
poverty [ˈpɑvərt̬i] n : pobreza f
powder [ˈpaʊdər] vt 1 : empolvar 2
CRUSH : pulverizar — ~ n 1 : polvo m
2 or **face** ~ : polvos mpl — **pow-
dery** [ˈpaʊdəri] adj : polvoriento
power [ˈpaʊər] n 1 CONTROL : poder m 2
ABILITY : capacidad f 3 STRENGTH
: fuerza f 4 : potencia f (política) 5 EN-
ERGY : energía f 6 ELECTRICITY : electricidad f — vt : impulsar — **powerful** [ˈpaʊərfəl] adj : poderoso —
powerless [ˈpaʊərləs] adj : impotente
practical [ˈpræktɪkəl] adj : práctico —
practically [ˈpræktɪkli] adv : casi,
prácticamente
practice or **practise** [ˈpræktəs] v **-ticed**

or -**tised**; -**ticing** *or* -**tising** *vt* **1** : practicar **2** : ejercer (una profesión) — *vi* : practicar — **practice** *n* **1** : práctica *f* **2** CUSTOM : costumbre *f* **3** : ejercicio *m* (de una profesión) **4 be out of ~** : no estar en forma — **practitioner** [præk-'tɪʃənər] *n* **1** : profesional *mf* **2 general ~** : médico *m*, -ca *f* de medicina general

pragmatic [præg'mæt̬ɪk] *adj* : pragmático

prairie ['præri] *n* : pradera *f*

praise ['preɪz] *vt* **praised; praising** : elogiar, alabar — **~** *n* : elogio *m*, alabanza *f* — **praiseworthy** ['preɪz,wərði] *adj* : loable

prance ['prænts] *vi* **pranced; prancing** : hacer cabriolas

prank ['præŋk] *n* : travesura *f*

prawn ['prɔn] *n* : gamba *f*

pray ['preɪ] *vi* **1** : rezar **2 ~ for** : rogar — **prayer** ['prɛr] *n* : oración *f*

preach ['priːtʃ] *v* : predicar — **preacher** ['priːtʃər] *n* MINISTER : pastor *m*, -tora *f*

precarious [prɪ'kæriəs] *adj* : precario

precaution [prɪ'kɔʃən] *n* : precaución *f*

precede [prɪ'siːd] *vt* -**ceded; -ceding** : preceder a — **precedence** ['presədənts, prɪ'siːdənts] *n* : precedencia *f* — **precedent** ['presədənt] *n* : precedente *m*

precinct ['priː,sɪŋkt] *n* **1** DISTRICT : distrito *m* **2 ~s** *npl* : recinto *m*

precious ['preʃəs] *adj* : precioso

precipice ['presəpəs] *n* : precipicio *m*

precipitate [prɪ'sɪpə,teɪt] *vt* -**tated; -tating** : precipitar — **precipitation** [prɪ,sɪpə'teɪʃən] *n* **1** HASTE : precipitación *f* **2** : precipitaciones *fpl* (en meteorología)

precise [prɪ'saɪs] *adj* : preciso — **precisely** *adv* : precisamente — **precision** [prɪ'sɪʒən] *n* : precisión *f*

preclude [prɪ'kluːd] *vt* -**cluded; -cluding 1** PREVENT : impedir **2** EXCLUDE : excluir

precocious [prɪ'koːʃəs] *adj* : precoz

preconceived [,priːkən'siːv] *adj* : preconcebido

predator ['predət̬ər] *n* : depredador *m*

predecessor ['predə,sesər, 'priː-] *n* : antecesor *m*, -sora *f*; predecesor *m*, -sora *f*

predicament [prɪ'dɪkəmənt] *n* : apuro *m*

predict [prɪ'dɪkt] *vt* : pronosticar, predecir — **predictable** [prɪ'dɪktəbəl] *adj* : previsible — **prediction** [prɪ'dɪkʃən] *n* : pronóstico *m*, predicción *f*

predispose [,priːdɪ'spoːz] *vt* -**posed; -posing** : predisponer

predominant [prɪ'dɑmənənt] *adj* : predominante

preeminent [prɪ'emənənt] *adj* : preeminente

preempt [prɪ'empt] *vt* : adelantarse a (un ataque, etc.)

preen ['priːn] *vt* **1** : arreglarse (las plumas) **2 ~ oneself** : acicalarse

prefabricated [,priː'fæbrə,keɪt̬əd] *adj* : prefabricado

preface ['prefəs] *n* : prefacio *m*, prólogo *m*

prefer [prɪ'fər] *vt* -**ferred; -ferring** : preferir — **preferable** ['prefərəbəl] *adj* : preferible — **preference** ['prefrənts, 'prefər-] *n* : preferencia *f* — **preferential** [,prefə'rentʃəl] *adj* : preferente

prefix ['priː,fɪks] *n* : prefijo *m*

pregnancy ['pregnəntsi] *n*, *pl* -**cies** : embarazo *m* — **pregnant** ['pregnənt] *adj* : embarazada

prehistoric [,priːhɪs'tɔrɪk] *or* **prehistorical** [-ɪkəl] *adj* : prehistórico

prejudice ['predʒədəs] *n* **1** BIAS : prejuicio *m* **2** HARM : perjuicio *m* — **~** *vt* -**diced; -dicing 1** BIAS : predisponer **2** HARM : perjudicar — **prejudiced** ['predʒədəst] *adj* : parcial

preliminary [prɪ'lɪmə,neri] *adj* : preliminar

prelude ['prɛ,luːd, 'prɛl,juːd; 'preɪ,luːd, 'prɪ-] *n* : preludio *m*

premarital [,priː'mærət̬əl] *adj* : prematrimonial

premature [,priːmə'tʊr, -'tjʊr, -'tʃʊr] *adj* : prematuro

premeditated [prɪ'medə,teɪt̬əd] *adj* : premeditado

premier [prɪ'mɪr, -'mjɪr; 'priː,mɪər] *adj* : principal — **~** *n* PRIME MINISTER : primer ministro *m*, primera ministra *f*

premiere [prɪ'mjɛr, -'mɪr] *n* : estreno *m*

premise ['premɪs] *n* **1** : premisa *f* (de un argumento) **2 ~s** *npl* : recinto *m*, local *m*

premium ['priːmiəm] *n* **1** : premio *m* **2** *or* **insurance ~** : prima *f* (de seguro)

preoccupied [prɪ'ɑkjə,paɪd] *adj* : preocupado

prepare [prɪ'pær] *v* -**pared; -paring** *vt* : preparar — *vi* : prepararse — **preparation** [,prepə'reɪʃən] *n* **1** : preparación *f* **2 ~s** *npl* ARRANGEMENTS : preparativos *mpl* — **preparatory** [prɪ'pærə,tori] *adj* : preparatorio

prepay [,priː'peɪ] *vt* -**paid; -paying** : pagar por adelantado

preposition [,prepə'zɪʃən] *n* : preposición *f*

preposterous [pri'pɑstərəs] *adj* : absurdo, ridículo

prerequisite [pri'rɛkwəzət] *n* : requisito *m* previo

prerogative [pri'ragətɪv] *n* : prerrogativa *f*

prescribe [pri'skraɪb] *vt* **-scribed; -scribing** 1 : prescribir 2 : recetar (en medicina) — **prescription** [pri'skrɪpʃən] *n* : receta *f*

presence ['prɛzənts] *n* : presencia *f*

present[1] ['prɛzənt] *adj* 1 CURRENT : actual 2 **be ~ at** : estar presente en — **~** *n* 1 : presente *m* 2 **at ~** : actualmente

present[2] ['prɛzənt] *n* GIFT : regalo *m* — **~** [pri'zɛnt] *vt* 1 INTRODUCE : presentar 2 GIVE : entregar — **presentation** [,priːzən'teɪʃən, ,prɛzən-] *n* 1 : presentación *f* 2 *or* **~ ceremony** : ceremonia *f* de entrega

presently ['prɛzəntli] *adv* 1 SOON : dentro de poco 2 NOW : actualmente

preserve [pri'zərv] *vt* **-served; -serving** 1 : conservar 2 MAINTAIN : mantener — **~** *n* 1 JAM : confitura *f* 2 *or* **game ~** : coto *m* de caza — **preservation** [,prɛzər'veɪʃən] *n* : preservación *f*, conservación *f* — **preservative** [pri'zərvətɪv] *n* : conservante *m*

president ['prɛzədənt] *n* : presidente *m*, -ta *f* — **presidency** ['prɛzədəntsi] *n*, *pl* **-cies** : presidencia *f* — **presidential** [,prɛzə'dɛntʃəl] *adj* : presidencial

press ['prɛs] *n* : prensa *f* — **~** *vt* 1 : prensar 2 IRON : planchar — *vi* 1 : apretar 2 URGE : presionar — **pressing** ['prɛsɪŋ] *adj* : urgente — **pressure** ['prɛʃər] *n* : presión *f* — **~** *vt* **-sured; -suring** : presionar, apremiar

prestige [prɛ'stiːʒ, -'stiːdʒ] *n* : prestigio *m* — **prestigious** [prɛ'stɪdʒəs] *adj* : prestigioso

presume [pri'zuːm] *vt* **-sumed; -suming** : presumir — **presumably** [pri'zuːməbli] *adv* : es de suponer, supuestamente — **presumption** [pri'zʌmpʃən] *n* : presunción *f* — **presumptuous** [pri'zʌmptʃuəs] *adj* : presuntuoso

pretend [pri'tɛnd] *vt* 1 CLAIM : pretender 2 FEIGN : fingir — *vi* : fingir — **pretense** *or* **pretence** ['priːtɛnts, pri'tɛnts] *n* 1 CLAIM : pretensión *f* 2 **under false ~s** : con pretextos falsos — **pretentious** [pri'tɛntʃəs] *adj* : pretencioso

pretext ['priːtɛkst] *n* : pretexto *m*

pretty ['prɪti] *adj* **-tier; -est** : lindo, bonito — **~** *adv* FAIRLY : bastante

pretzel ['prɛtsəl] *n* : galleta *f* salada

prevail [pri'veɪl] *vi* 1 TRIUMPH : prevalecer 2 PREDOMINATE : predominar 3 **~ upon** : persuadir — **prevalent** ['prɛvələnt] *adj* : extendido

prevent [pri'vɛnt] *vt* : impedir — **prevention** [pri'vɛntʃən] *n* : prevención *f* — **preventive** [pri'vɛntɪv] *adj* : preventivo

preview ['priː,vjuː] *n* : preestreno *m*

previous ['priːviəs] *adj* : previo, anterior — **previously** ['priːviəsli] *adv* : anteriormente

prey ['preɪ] *n*, *pl* **preys** : presa *f* — **prey on** *vt* 1 : alimentarse de 2 **~ on one's mind** : atormentar a algn

price ['praɪs] *n* : precio *m* — **~** *vt* **priced; pricing** : poner un precio a — **priceless** ['praɪsləs] *adj* : inestimable

prick ['prɪk] *n* : pinchazo *m* — **~** *vt* 1 : pinchar 2 **~ up one's ears** : levantar las orejas — **prickly** ['prɪkəli] *adj* : espinoso

pride ['praɪd] *n* : orgullo *m* — **~** *vt* **prided; priding ~ oneself on** : enorgullecerse de

priest ['priːst] *n* : sacerdote *m* — **priesthood** ['priːsthʊd] *n* : sacerdocio *m*

prim ['prɪm] *adj* **primmer; primmest** : remilgado

primary ['praɪ,mɛri, 'praɪməri] *adj* 1 FIRST : primario 2 PRINCIPAL : principal — **primarily** [praɪ'mɛrəli] *adv* : principalmente

prime[1] ['praɪm] *vt* **primed; priming** 1 : cebar (un arma de fuego, etc.) 2 PREPARE : preparar

prime[2] *n* **the ~ of one's life** : la flor de la vida — **~** *adj* 1 MAIN : principal, primero 2 EXCELLENT : excelente — **prime minister** *n* : primero ministro *m*, primera ministra *f*

primer[1] ['praɪmər] *n* : base *f* (de pintura)

primer[2] ['prɪmər] *n* READER : cartilla *f*

primitive ['prɪmətɪv] *adj* : primitivo

primrose ['prɪm,roːz] *n* : primavera *f*

prince ['prɪnts] *n* : príncipe *m* — **princess** ['prɪntsəs, 'prɪn,sɛs] *n* : princesa *f*

principal ['prɪntsəpəl] *adj* : principal — **~** *n* : director *m*, -tora *f* (de un colegio)

principle ['prɪntsəpəl] *n* : principio *m*

print ['prɪnt] *n* 1 MARK : huella *f* 2 LETTERING : letra *f* 3 ENGRAVING : grabado *m* 4 : estampado *m* (de tela) 5 : copia *f* (en fotografía) 6 **out of ~** : agotado — **~** *vt* : imprimir (libros, etc.) — *vi* : escribir con letra de molde — **printer** ['prɪntər] *n* 1 : impresor *m*, -sora *f* (persona) 2 : impresora *f* (máquina) — **printing** ['prɪntɪŋ] *n* 1 : impresión *f* 2

prodigy ['pradədʒi] *n*, *pl* **-gies** : prodigio *m*

produce [prə'du:s, -'dju:s] *vt* **-duced;**
-ducing 1 : producir **2** CAUSE : causar
3 SHOW : presentar, mostrar **4** : poner
en escena (una obra de teatro) — ~
['pra,du:s, 'pro:-, -,dju:s] *n* : productos
mpl agrícolas — **producer** [prə'du:sər,
-'dju:-] *n* : productor *m*, -tora *f* — **product** ['pra,dʌkt] *n* : producto *m* — **productive** [prə'dʌktɪv] *adj* : productivo

profane [pro'feɪn] *adj* **1** : profano **2** IR-
REVERENT : blasfemo — **profanity**
[pro'fænəti] *n*, *pl* **-ties** : blasfemia *f*

profess [prə'fɛs] *vt* : profesar — **profession** [prə'fɛʃən] *n* : profesión *f* —
professional [prə'fɛʃənəl] *adj* : profesional — ~ *n* : profesional *mf* —
professor [prə'fɛsər] *n* : profesor *m*,
-sora *f*

proficiency [prə'fɪʃənsi] *n* : competencia *f* — **proficient** [prə'fɪʃənt] *adj*
: competente

profile ['pro:,faɪl] *n* **1** : perfil *m* **2** keep a
low ~ : no llamar la atención

profit ['prafət] *n* : beneficio *m*, ganancia
f — ~ *vi* : sacar provecho (de), beneficiarse (de) — **profitable** ['prafətəbəl]
adj : provechoso

profound [prə'faʊnd] *adj* : profundo

profuse [prə'fju:s] *adj* : profuso — **profusion** [prə'fju:ʒən] *n* : profusión *f*

prognosis [prag'no:sɪs] *n*, *pl* **-noses**
[-,si:z] : pronóstico *m*

program ['pro:,græm, -grəm] *n* : programa *m* — ~ *vt* **-grammed** *or*
-gramed; -gramming *or* **-graming**
: programar

progress ['pragrəs, -,gres] *n* **1** : progreso
m **2** ADVANCE : avance *m* — ~ [prə-
'gres] *vi* : progresar, avanzar — **progressive** [prə'gresɪv] *adj* **1** : progresista (dícese de la política, etc.) **2**
INCREASING : progresiva

prohibit [pro'hibət] *vt* : prohibir — **prohibition** [,pro:ə'bɪʃən, ,pro:hə-] *n* : prohibición *f*

project ['pradʒɛkt, -dʒɪkt] *n* : proyecto *m*
— ~ [prə'dʒɛkt] *vt* : proyectar — *vi*
PROTRUDE : sobresalir — **projectile**
[prə'dʒɛktəl, -,taɪl] *n* : proyectil *m* —
projection [prə'dʒɛkʃən] *n* **1** : proyección *f* **2** PROTRUSION : saliente *m* —
projector [prə'dʒɛktər] *n* : proyector *m*

proliferate [pro'lɪfə,reɪt] *vi* **-ated; -ating**
: proliferar — **proliferation** [prə,lɪfə-
'reɪʃən] *n* : proliferación *f* — **prolific**
[prə'lɪfɪk] *adj* : prolífico

prologue ['pro:,lɔg] *n* : prólogo *m*

prolong [prə'lɔŋ] *vt* : prolongar

prior ['praɪər] *adj* **1** : previo **2** ~ to
: antes de — **priority** [praɪ'ɔrəti] *n*, *pl*
-ties : prioridad *f*

prison ['prɪzən] *n* : prisión *f*, cárcel *f* —
prisoner ['prɪzənər] *n* **1** : preso *m*, -sa *f*
2 ~ **of war** : prisionero *m*, -ra *f* de
guerra

privacy ['praɪvəsi] *n*, *pl* **-cies** : intimidad
f — **private** ['praɪvət] *adj* **1** : privado **2**
SECRET : secreto — ~ *n* : soldado *m*
raso — **privately** ['praɪvətli] *adv* : en
privado

privilege ['prɪvlɪdʒ, 'prɪvə-] *n* : privilegio
m — **privileged** ['prɪvlɪdʒd, 'prɪvə-] *adj*
: privilegiado

prize ['praɪz] *n* : premio *m* — ~ *adj*
: premiado — ~ *vt* **prized; prizing**
: valorar, apreciar — **prizefighter**
['praɪz,faɪtər] *n* : boxeador *m*, -dora *f*
profesional — **prizewinning** ['praɪz-
,wɪnɪŋ] *adj* : premiado

pro ['pro:] *n* **1** → **professional 2** the ~s
and cons : los pros y los contras

probability [,prabə'bɪləti] *n*, *pl* **-ties**
: probabilidad *f* — **probable** ['prabə-
bəl] *adj* : probable — **probably** [-bli]
adv : probablemente

probation [pro'beɪʃən] *n* **1** : período *m*
de prueba (de un empleado, etc.) **2**
: libertad *f* condicional (de un preso)

probe ['pro:b] *n* **1** : sonda *f* (en medicina, etc.) **2** INVESTIGATION : investigación *f* — ~ *vt* **probed; probing 1**
: sondar **2** INVESTIGATE : investigar

problem ['prabləm] *n* : problema *m*

procedure [prə'si:dʒər] *n* : procedimiento *m*

proceed [pro'si:d] *vi* **1** ACT : proceder **2**
CONTINUE : continuar **3** ADVANCE
: avanzar — **proceedings** [pro'si:dɪŋz]
npl **1** EVENTS : actos *mpl* **2** : proceso *m*
(en derecho) — **proceeds** ['pro:,si:dz]
npl : ganancias *fpl*

process ['pra,ses, 'pro:-] *n*, *pl* **-cesses**
['pra,sesəz, 'pro:-, -səsəz, -sə,si:z] **1** : proceso *m* **2 in the** ~ **of** : en vías de —
~ *vt* : procesar — **procession** [prə-
'sɛʃən] *n* : desfile *m*

proclaim [pro'kleɪm] *vt* : proclamar —
proclamation [,praklə'meɪʃən] *n* : proclamación *f*

procrastinate [prə'kræstə,neɪt] *vi* **-nated;**
-nating : demorar, aplazar

procure [prə'kjʊr] *vt* **-cured; -curing**
: obtener

prod ['prad] *vt* **prodded; prodding**
: pinchar, aguijonear

prodigal ['pradɪgəl] *adj* : pródigo

prom ['prɑm] n : baile m formal (en un colegio)
prominent ['prɑmənənt] adj : prominente — **prominence** ['prɑmənənts] n 1 : prominencia f 2 IMPORTANCE : eminencia f
promiscuous [prə'mɪskjuəs] adj : promiscuo
promise ['prɑməs] n : promesa f — ~ v -ised; -ising : prometer — **promising** ['prɑməsɪŋ] adj : prometedor
promote [prə'moːt] vt -moted; -moting 1 : ascender (a un alumno o un empleado) 2 FURTHER : promover, fomentar 3 ADVERTISE : promocionar — **promoter** [prə'moːtər] n : promotor m, -tora f; empresario m, -ria f (en deportes) — **promotion** [prə'moːʃən] n 1 : ascenso m (de un alumno o un empleado) 2 ADVERTISING : publicidad f, propaganda f
prompt ['prɑmpt] vt 1 INCITE : provocar (una cosa), inducir (a una persona) 2 : apuntar (a un actor, etc.) — ~ adj 1 : rápido 2 PUNCTUAL : puntual
prone ['proːn] adj 1 : boca abajo, decúbito prono 2 be ~ to : ser propenso a
prong ['prɔŋ] n : punta f, diente m
pronoun ['proːnaʊn] n : pronombre m
pronounce [prə'naʊnts] vt -nounced; -nouncing : pronunciar — **pronouncement** [prə'naʊntsmənt] n : declaración f — **pronunciation** [prə-,nʌntsi'eɪʃən] n : pronunciación f
proof ['pruːf] n : prueba f — ~ adj ~ **against** : a prueba de — **proofread** ['pruːf,riːd] vt -read; -reading : corregir
prop ['prɑp] n 1 SUPPORT : puntal m, apoyo m 2 : accesorio m (en teatro) — ~ vt propped; propping 1 — **against** : apoyar contra 2 ~ up SUPPORT : apoyar
propaganda [,prɑpə'gændə, ,proː-] n : propaganda f
propagate ['prɑpə,geɪt] v -gated; -gating vt : propagar — vi : propagarse
propel [prə'pɛl] vt -pelled; -pelling : propulsar — **propeller** [prə'pɛlər] n : hélice f
propensity [prə'pɛntsəti] n, pl -ties : propensión f
proper ['prɑpər] adj 1 SUITABLE : apropiado 2 REAL : verdadero 3 CORRECT : correcto 4 GENTEEL : cortés 5 ~ **name** : nombre m propio — **properly** ['prɑpərli] adv : correctamente
property ['prɑpərti] n, pl -ties 1 : propiedad f 2 BUILDING : inmueble m 3 LAND, LOT : parcela f

prophet ['prɑfət] n : profeta m, profetisa f — **prophecy** ['prɑfəsi] n, pl -cies : profecía f — **prophesy** ['prɑfə,saɪ] v -sied; -sying vt : profetizar — vi : hacer profecías — **prophetic** [prə-'fɛtɪk] adj : profético
proportion [prə'porʃən] n 1 : proporción f 2 SHARE : parte f — **proportional** [prə'porʃənəl] adj : proporcional — **proportionate** [prə'porʃənət] adj : proporcional
proposal [prə'poːzəl] n : propuesta f
propose [prə'poːz] v -posed; -posing vt 1 SUGGEST : proponer 2 ~ **to do sth** : pensar hacer algo — vi : proponer matrimonio — **proposition** [,prɑpə-'zɪʃən] n : proposición f
proprietor [prə'praɪətər] n : propietario m, -ria f
propriety [prə'praɪəti] n, pl -eties : decencia f, decoro m
propulsion [prə'pʌlʃən] n : propulsión f
prose ['proːz] n : prosa f
prosecute ['prɑsɪ,kjuːt] vt -cuted; -cuting : procesar — **prosecution** [,prɑsɪ'kjuːʃən] n 1 : procesamiento m 2 **the ~** : la acusación — **prosecutor** ['prɑsɪ,kjuːtər] n : acusador m, -dora f
prospect ['prɑ,spɛkt] n 1 : perspectiva f 2 POSSIBILITY : posibilidad f — **prospective** [prə'spɛktɪv, 'prɑ,spɛk-] adj : futuro, posible
prosper ['prɑspər] vi : prosperar — **prosperity** [prɑ'spɛrəti] n : prosperidad f — **prosperous** ['prɑspərəs] adj : próspero
prostitute ['prɑstə,tuːt, -,tjuːt] n : prostituta f — **prostitution** [,prɑstə'tuːʃən, -'tjuː-] n : prostitución f
prostrate ['prɑ,streɪt] adj : postrado
protagonist [proː'tægənɪst] n : protagonista mf
protect [prə'tɛkt] vt : proteger — **protection** [prə'tɛkʃən] n : protección f — **protective** [prə'tɛktɪv] adj : protector — **protector** [prə'tɛktər] n : protector m, -tora f
protégé ['proːtə,ʒeɪ] n : protegido m, -da f
protein ['proː,tiːn] n : proteína f
protest ['proː,tɛst] n : protesta f — ~ [proː'tɛst] vt : protestar — vi ~ **against** : protestar contra — **Protestant** ['prɑtəstənt] n : protestante mf — **protester** or **protestor** ['proː,tɛstər, prə'-] n : manifestante mf
protocol ['proːtə,kɔl] n : protocolo m
prototype ['proːtə,taɪp] n : prototipo m
protract [proː'trækt] vt : prolongar
protrude [proː'truːd] vi -truded; -truding : sobresalir

proud ['praʊd] *adj* : orgulloso
prove ['pruːv] *v* **proved; proved** *or* **proven** ['pruːvən]; **proving** *vt* : probar — *vi* : resultar
proverb ['prɑˌvərb] *n* : proverbio *m*, refrán *m* — **proverbial** [prə'vərbiəl] *adj* : proverbial
provide [prə'vaɪd] *v* **-vided; -viding** : proveer — *vi* ~ **for** SUPPORT : mantener — **provided** [prə'vaɪdəd] *or* ~ **that** *conj* : con tal (de) que, siempre que — **providence** ['prɑvədəns] *n* : providencia *f*
province ['prɑvɪnts] *n* **1** : provincia *f* **2** SPHERE : campo *m*, competencia *f* — **provincial** [prə'vɪntʃəl] *adj* : provinciano
provision [prə'vɪʒən] *n* **1** : provisión *f*, suministro *m* **2** STIPULATION : condición *f* **3** ~**s** *npl* : víveres *mpl* — **provisional** [prə'vɪʒənəl] *adj* : provisional — **proviso** [prə'vaɪˌzoː] *n, pl* **-sos** *or* **-soes** : condición *f*
provoke [prə'voːk] *vt* **-voked; -voking** : provocar — **provocation** [ˌprɑvə'keɪʃən] *n* : provocación *f* — **provocative** [prə'vɑkətɪv] *adj* : provocador, provocativo
prow ['praʊ] *n* : proa *f*
prowess ['praʊəs] *n* **1** BRAVERY : valor *m* **2** SKILL : habilidad *f*
prowl ['praʊl] *vi* : merodear, rondar — *vt* : merodear por — **prowler** ['praʊlər] *n* : merodeador *m*, -dora *f*
proximity [prɑk'sɪməti] *n* : proximidad *f* — **proxy** ['prɑksi] *n, pl* **proxies by** ~ : por poder
prude ['pruːd] *n* : mojigato *m*, -ta *f*
prudence ['pruːdənts] *n* : prudencia *f* — **prudent** ['pruːdənt] *adj* : prudente
prune[1] ['pruːn] *n* : ciruela *f* pasa
prune[2] *vt* **pruned; pruning** : podar (arbustos, etc.)
pry ['praɪ] *v* **pried; prying** *vi* ~ **into** : entrometerse en — *vt* *or* ~ **open** : abrir (a la fuerza)
psalm ['sɑm, 'sɑlm] *n* : salmo *m*
pseudonym ['suːdəˌnɪm] *n* : seudónimo *m*
psychiatry [sə'kaɪətri, saɪ-] *n* : psiquiatría *f* — **psychiatric** [ˌsaɪki'ætrɪk] *adj* : psiquiátrico — **psychiatrist** [sə'kaɪətrɪst, saɪ-] *n* : psiquiatra *mf*
psychic ['saɪkɪk] *adj* : psíquico
psychoanalysis [ˌsaɪkoə'næləsɪs] *n, pl* **-yses** : psicoanálisis *m* — **psychoanalyst** [ˌsaɪko'ænəlɪst] *n* : psicoanalista *mf* — **psychoanalyze** [ˌsaɪko'ænəlˌaɪz] *vt* **-lyzed; -lyzing** : psicoanalizar
psychology [saɪ'kɑlədʒi] *n, pl* **-gies**

: psicología *f* — **psychological** [ˌsaɪkə'lɑdʒɪkəl] *adj* : psicológico — **psychologist** [saɪ'kɑlədʒɪst] *n* : psicólogo *m*, -ga *f*
psychopath ['saɪkəˌpæθ] *n* : psicópata *mf*
psychotherapy [ˌsaɪko'θerəpi] *n, pl* **-pies** : psicoterapia *f*
psychotic [saɪ'kɑtɪk] *adj* : psicótico
puberty ['pjuːbərti] *n* : pubertad *f*
pubic ['pjuːbɪk] *adj* : púbico
public ['pʌblɪk] *adj* : público — ~ *n* : público *m* — **publication** [ˌpʌblə'keɪʃən] *n* : publicación *f* — **publicity** [pə'blɪsəti] *n* : publicidad *f* — **publicize** ['pʌblə'saɪz] *vt* **-cized; -cizing** : publicitar, divulgar
publish ['pʌblɪʃ] *vt* : publicar — **publisher** ['pʌblɪʃər] *n* **1** : editor *m*, -tora *f* (persona) **2** : casa *f* editorial (negocio)
pucker ['pʌkər] *vt* : fruncir, arrugar — *vi* : arrugarse
pudding ['pʊdɪŋ] *n* : budín *m*, pudín *m*
puddle ['pʌdəl] *n* : charco *m*
pudgy ['pʌdʒi] *adj* **pudgier; -est** : rechoncho *fam*
Puerto Rican [ˌpwertə'riːkən, ˌportə-] *adj* : puertorriqueño
puff ['pʌf] *vi* **1** BLOW : soplar **2** PANT : resoplar **3** ~ **up** SWELL : hincharse — *vt* ~ **out** : hinchar — ~ *n* **1** : bocanada *f* (de humo) **2** : chupada *f* (a un cigarrillo) **3** *or* **cream** ~ : pastelito *m* de crema **4** *or* **powder** ~ : borla *f* — **puffy** ['pʌfi] *adj* **puffier; -est** : hinchado
pull ['pʊl, 'pʌl] *vt* **1** : tirar de **2** EXTRACT : sacar **3** TEAR : desgarrarse (un músculo, etc.) **4** ~ **off** REMOVE : quitar **5** ~ **oneself together** : calmarse **6** ~ **up** : levantar, subir — *vi* **1** : tirar **2** ~ **through** RECOVER : reponerse **3** ~ **together** COOPERATE : reunir **4** ~ **up** STOP : parar — ~ *n* **1** : tirón *m* **2** INFLUENCE : influencia *f* — **pulley** ['pʊli] *n, pl* **-leys** : polea *f* — **pullover** ['pʊlˌoːvər] *n* : suéter *m*
pulp ['pʌlp] *n* **1** : pulpa *f* (de frutas, etc.) **2** *or* **wood** ~ : pasta *f* de papel
pulpit ['pʊlˌpɪt] *n* : púlpito *m*
pulsate ['pʌlˌseɪt] *vi* **-sated; -sating** : palpitar — **pulse** ['pʌls] *n* : pulso *m*
pulverize ['pʌlvəˌraɪz] *vt* **-ized; -izing** : pulverizar
pummel ['pʌməl] *vt* **-meled; -meling** : aporrear
pump[1] ['pʌmp] *n* : bomba *f* — ~ *vt* **1** : bombear **2** ~ **up** : inflar
pump[2] *n* SHOE : zapato *m* de tacón
pumpernickel ['pʌmpərˌnɪkəl] *n* : pan *m* negro de centeno

pumpkin ['pʌmpkɪn, 'pʌŋkən] *n* : calabaza *f*, zapallo *m Lat*

pun ['pʌn] *n* : juego *m* de palabras — ~ *vi* **punned; punning** : hacer juegos de palabras

punch[1] ['pʌntʃ] *vt* 1 : dar un puñetazo a 2 PERFORATE : perforar (papeles, etc.), picar (un boleto) — ~ *n* 1 : golpe *m*, puñetazo *m* 2 *or* **paper** ~ : perforadora *f*

punch[2] *n* : ponche *m* (bebida)

punctual ['pʌŋktʃʊəl] *adj* : puntual — **punctuality** [ˌpʌŋktʃʊ'æləti] *n* : puntualidad *f*

punctuate ['pʌŋktʃʊˌeɪt] *vt* **-ated; -ating** : puntuar — **punctuation** [ˌpʌŋktʃʊ'eɪʃən] *n* : puntuación *f*

puncture ['pʌŋktʃər] *n* : pinchazo *m*, ponchadura *f Lat* — ~ *vt* **-tured; -turing** : pinchar, ponchar *Lat*

pungent ['pʌndʒənt] *adj* : acre

punish ['pʌnɪʃ] *vt* : castigar — **punishment** ['pʌnɪʃmənt] *n* : castigo *m* — **punitive** ['pjuːnəṭɪv] *adj* : punitivo

puny ['pjuːni] *adj* **-nier; -est** : enclenque

pup ['pʌp] *n* : cachorro *m*, -rra *f* (de un perro); cría *f* (de otros animales)

pupil[1] ['pjuːpəl] *n* : alumno *m*, -na *f* (de colegio)

pupil[2] *n* : pupila *f* (del ojo)

puppet ['pʌpət] *n* : títere *m*

puppy ['pʌpi] *n, pl* **-pies** : cachorro *m*, -rra *f*

purchase ['pərtʃəs] *vt* **-chased; -chasing** : comprar — ~ *n* : compra *f*

pure ['pjʊr] *adj* **purer; purest** : puro

puree [pjʊ'reɪ, -'riː] *n* : puré *m*

purely ['pjʊrli] *adv* : puramente

purgatory ['pərgəˌtori] *n, pl* **-ries** : purgatorio *m* — **purge** ['pərdʒ] *vt* **purged; purging** : purgar — ~ *n* : purga *f*

purify ['pjʊrəˌfaɪ] *vt* **-fied; -fying** : purificar — **purification** [ˌpjʊrəfə'keɪʃən] *n* : purificación *f*

puritanical [ˌpjʊrə'tænɪkəl] *adj* : puritano

purity ['pjʊrəti] *n* : pureza *f*

purple ['pərpəl] *n* : morado *m*

purport [pər'port] *vt* ~ **to be** : pretender ser

purpose ['pərpəs] *n* 1 : propósito *m* 2 RESOLUTION : determinación *f* 3 **on** ~ : a propósito — **purposeful** ['pərpəsfəl] *adj* : resuelto — **purposely** ['pərpəsli] *adv* : a propósito

purr ['pər] *n* : ronroneo *m* — ~ *vi* : ronronear

purse ['pərs] *n* 1 *or* **change** ~ : monedero *m* 2 HANDBAG : cartera *f*, bolso *m Spain*, bolsa *f Lat* — ~ *vt* **pursed; pursing** : fruncir

pursue [pər'suː] *vt* **-sued; -suing** 1 CHASE : perseguir 2 SEEK : buscar — **pursuer** [pər'suːər] *n* : perseguidor *m*, -dora *f* — **pursuit** [pər'suːt] *n* 1 CHASE : persecución *f* 2 SEARCH : búsqueda *f* 3 OCCUPATION : actividad *f*

pus ['pʌs] *n* : pus *m*

push ['pʊʃ] *vt* 1 SHOVE : empujar 2 PRESS : apretar 3 URGE : presionar 4 ~ **around** BULLY : mangonear — *vi* 1 : empujar 2 ~ **for** : presionar para — ~ *n* 1 SHOVE : empujón *m* 2 DRIVE : dinamismo *m* 3 EFFORT : esfuerzo *m* — **pushy** ['pʊʃi] *adj* **pushier; -est** : mandón, prepotente

pussy ['pʊsi] *n, pl* **pussies** : gatito *m*, -ta *f*; minino *m*, -na *f*

put ['pʊt] *v* **put; putting** *vt* 1 : poner 2 INSERT : meter 3 EXPRESS : decir 4 ~ **one's mind to sth** : proponerse hacer algo — *vi* ~ **up with** : aguantar — **put away** *vt* 1 STORE : guardar 2 *or* ~ **aside** : dejar a un lado — **put down** *vt* 1 SUPPRESS : aplastar, sofocar 2 ATTRIBUTE : atribuir — **put off** *vt* DEFER : aplazar, posponer — **put on** *vt* 1 ASSUME : adoptar 2 PRESENT : presentar (una obra de teatro, etc.) 3 WEAR : ponerse — **put out** *vt* INCONVENIENCE : incomodar — **put up** *vt* 1 BUILD : construir 2 LODGE : alojar 3 PROVIDE : poner (dinero)

putrefy ['pjuːtrəˌfaɪ] *vi* **-fied; -fying** : pudrirse

putty ['pʌti] *n, pl* **-ties** : masilla *f*

puzzle ['pʌzəl] *v* **-zled; -zling** *vt* : confundir, dejar perplejo — *vi* ~ **over** : tratar de descifrar — ~ *n* 1 : rompecabezas *m* 2 MYSTERY : enigma *m*

pylon ['paɪlɑn, -lən] *n* : pilón *m*

pyramid ['pɪrəmɪd] *n* : pirámide *f*

python ['paɪθɑn, -θən] *n* : pitón *f*

Q

q ['kjuː] *n, pl* **q's** *or* **qs** ['kjuːz] : q *f*, decimoséptima letra del alfabeto inglés

quack¹ ['kwæk] *vi* : graznar (dícese del pato) — ∼ *n* : graznido *m*

quack² *n* CHARLATAN : charlatán *m*, -tana *f*

quadruple [kwɑ'druːpəl, -'drʌ-; 'kwɑdrə-] *v* **-pled; -pling** *vt* : cuadruplicar — *vi* : cuadruplicarse

quagmire ['kwæg,maɪr, 'kwɑg-] *n* : atolladero *m*

quail ['kweɪl] *n, pl* **quail** *or* **quails** : codorniz *f*

quaint ['kweɪnt] *adj* **1** ODD : curioso **2** PICTURESQUE : pintoresco

quake ['kweɪk] *vi* **quaked; quaking** : temblar — ∼ *n* → **earthquake**

qualify ['kwɑlə,faɪ] *v* **-fied; -fying** *vt* **1** LIMIT : matizar **2** : calificar (en gramática) **3** EQUIP : habilitar — *vi* **1** : titularse (de abogado, etc.) **2** : clasificarse (en deportes) — **qualification** [,kwɑləfə'keɪʃən] *n* **1** REQUIREMENT : requisito *m* **2** ∼**s** *npl* ABILITY : capacidad *f* **3** without ∼ : sin reservas — **qualified** ['kwɑlə,faɪd] *adj* : capacitado

quality ['kwɑləti] *n, pl* **-ties 1** : calidad *f* **2** PROPERTY : cualidad *f*

qualm ['kwɑm, 'kwɑlm, 'kwɔm] *n* **1** DOUBT : duda *f* **2** have no ∼s about : no tener ningún escrúpulo en

quandary ['kwɑndri] *n, pl* **-ries** : dilema *m*

quantity ['kwɑntəti] *n, pl* **-ties** : cantidad *f*

quarantine ['kwɔrən,tiːn] *n* : cuarentena *f* — ∼ *vt* **-tined; -tining** : poner en cuarentena

quarrel ['kwɔrəl] *n* : pelea *f*, riña *f* — ∼ *vi* **-reled** *or* **-relled; -reling** *or* **-relling** : pelearse, reñir — **quarrelsome** ['kwɔrəlsəm] *adj* : pendenciero

quarry¹ ['kwɔri] *n, pl* **quarries** PREY : presa *f*

quarry² *n, pl* **quarries** EXCAVATION : cantera *f*

quart ['kwɔrt] *n* : cuarto *m* de galón

quarter ['kwɔrtər] *n* **1** : cuarto *m* (en matemáticas) **2** : moneda *f* de 25 centavos **3** DISTRICT : barrio *m* **4** ∼ after three : las tres y cuarto **5** ∼**s** *npl* LODGING : alojamiento *m* — ∼ *vt* **1**

: dividir en cuatro partes **2** : acuartelar (tropas) — **quarterly** ['kwɔrtərli] *adv* : cada tres meses — ∼ *adj* : trimestral — ∼ *n, pl* **-lies** : publicación *f* trimestral

quartet [kwɔr'tɛt] *n* : cuarteto *m*

quartz ['kwɔrts] *n* : cuarzo *m*

quash ['kwɑʃ, 'kwɔʃ] *vt* **1** ANNUL : anular **2** SUPPRESS : aplastar, sofocar

quaver ['kweɪvər] *vi* : temblar

quay ['kiː, 'keɪ, 'kweɪ] *n* : muelle *m*

queasy ['kwiːzi] *adj* **-sier; -est** : mareado

queen ['kwiːn] *n* : reina *f*

queer ['kwɪr] *adj* ODD : extraño

quell ['kwɛl] *vt* SUPPRESS : sofocar, aplastar

quench ['kwɛntʃ] *vt* **1** EXTINGUISH : apagar **2** ∼ one's thirst : quitar la sed

query ['kwɪri, 'kwɛr-] *n, pl* **-ries** : pregunta *f* — ∼ *vt* **-ried; -rying 1** ASK : preguntar **2** QUESTION : cuestionar

quest ['kwɛst] *n* : búsqueda *f*

question ['kwɛstʃən] *n* **1** QUERY : pregunta *f* **2** ISSUE : cuestión *f* **3** be out of the ∼ : ser indiscutible **4** call into ∼ : poner en duda **5** without ∼ : sin duda — ∼ *vt* **1** ASK : preguntar **2** DOUBT : cuestionar **3** INTERROGATE : interrogar — *vi* : preguntar — **questionable** ['kwɛstʃənəbəl] *adj* : discutible — **question mark** *n* : signo *m* de interrogación — **questionnaire** [kwɛstʃə'nær] *n* : cuestionario *m*

queue ['kjuː] *n* : cola *f* — ∼ *vi* **queued; queuing** *or* **queueing** : hacer cola

quibble ['kwɪbəl] *vi* **-bled; -bling** : discutir, quejarse por nimiedades

quick ['kwɪk] *adj* **1** : rápido **2** CLEVER : agudo — ∼ *n* to the ∼ : en lo vivo — ∼ *adv* : rápidamente — **quicken** ['kwɪkən] *vt* : acelerar — **quickly** ['kwɪkli] *adv* : rápidamente — **quicksand** ['kwɪk,sænd] *n* : arena *f* movediza — **quick–tempered** ['kwɪk'tɛmpərd] *adj* : irascible — **quick–witted** ['kwɪk-'wɪtəd] *adj* : agudo

quiet ['kwaɪət] *n* **1** : silencio *m* **2** CALM : tranquilidad *f* — ∼ *adj* **1** : silencioso **2** CALM : tranquilo **3** RESERVED : callado **4** : discreto (dícese de colores, etc.) — ∼ *vt* **1** SILENCE : hacer callar **2** CALM : calmar — *vi or* ∼ down : cal-

marse — **quietly** *adv* 1 : silenciosa-
mente 2 CALMLY : tranquilamente
quilt ['kwɪlt] *n* : edredón *m*
quintet [kwɪn'tɛt] *n* : quinteto *m*
quip ['kwɪp] *n* : ocurrencia *f*, salida *f* —
~ *vt* **quipped; quipping** : decir bro-
meando
quirk ['kwərk] *n* : peculiaridad *f*
quit ['kwɪt] *v* **quit; quitting** *vt* 1 LEAVE
: dejar, abandonar 2 ~ **doing** : dejar
de hacer — *vi* 1 STOP : parar 2 RESIGN
: dimitir, renunciar
quite ['kwaɪt] *adv* 1 COMPLETELY : completamente 2 RATHER : bastante

quits ['kwɪts] *adj* **call it** ~ : quedar en
paz
quiver ['kwɪvər] *vi* : temblar
quiz ['kwɪz] *n, pl* **quizzes** TEST : prueba
f — ~ *vt* **quizzed; quizzing** : interrogar
quota ['kwoːtə] *n* : cuota *f*, cupo *m*
quotation [kwoʊ'teɪʃən] *n* 1 : cita *f* 2 ESTI-
MATE : presupuesto *m* — **quotation
marks** *npl* : comillas *fpl* — **quote**
['kwoːt] *vt* **quoted; quoting** 1 CITE
: citar 2 : cotizar (en finanzas) — ~ *n*
1 → **quotation** 2 ~s *npl* → **quotation
marks**
quotient ['kwoːʃənt] *n* : cociente *m*

R

r ['ɑr] *n, pl* **r's** *or* **rs** ['ɑrz] : r *f*, decimoc-
tava letra del alfabeto inglés
rabbi ['ræbaɪ] *n* : rabino *m*, -na *f*
rabbit ['ræbət] *n, pl* **-bit** *or* **-bits** : conejo *m*, -ja *f*
rabble ['ræbəl] *n* : chusma *f*, populacho
m
rabies ['reɪbiːz] *ns & pl* : rabia *f* — **rabid**
['ræbɪd] *adj* 1 : rabioso 2 FANATIC
: fanático
raccoon [ræ'kuːn] *n, pl* **-coon** *or*
-coons : mapache *m*
race[1] ['reɪs] *n* 1 : raza *f* 2 **human** ~
: género *m* humano
race[2] *n* : carrera *f* (competitiva) — *vi*
raced; racing 1 : correr (en una carrera) 2 RUSH : ir corriendo — **race-
horse** ['reɪs,hɔrs] *n* : caballo *m* de carreras — **racetrack** ['reɪs,træk] *n* : pista
f (de carreras)
racial ['reɪʃəl] *adj* : racial — **racism**
['reɪ,sɪzəm] *n* : racismo *m* — **racist**
['reɪsɪst] *n* : racista *mf*
rack ['ræk] *n* 1 SHELF : estante *m* 2 **luggage** ~ : portaequipajes *m* — *vt* 1
~**ed with** : atormentado por 2 ~
one's brains : devanarse los sesos
racket[1] ['rækət] *n* : raqueta *f* (en deportes)
racket[2] *n* 1 DIN : alboroto *m*, bulla *f* 2
SWINDLE : estafa *f*
racy ['reɪsi] *adj* **racier; -est** : subido de
tono, picante
radar ['reɪ,dɑr] *n* : radar *m*
radiant ['reɪdiənt] *adj* : radiante — **radi-
ance** ['reɪdiəns] *n* : resplandor *m* —
radiate ['reɪdi,eɪt] *v* **-ated; -ating** *vt*
: irradiar — *vi* 1 : irradiar 2 *or* ~ **out**
: extenderse (desde un centro) — **radi-**

ation [,reɪdi'eɪʃən] *n* : radiación *f* —
radiator ['reɪdi,eɪtər] *n* : radiador *m*
radical ['rædɪkəl] *adj* : radical — ~ *n*
: radical *m*
radii → **radius**
radio ['reɪdi,oː] *n, pl* **-dios** : radio *mf*
(aparato), radio *f* (medio) — ~ *vt*
: transmitir por radio — **radioactive**
['reɪdio'æktɪv] *adj* : radioactivo, radiactivo
radish ['rædɪʃ] *n* : rábano *m*
radius ['reɪdiəs] *n, pl* **radii** [-di,aɪ] : radio
m
raffle ['ræfəl] *vt* **-fled; -fling** : rifar — ~
n : rifa *f*
raft ['ræft] *n* : balsa *f*
rafter ['ræftər] *n* : cabrio *m*
rag ['ræg] *n* 1 : trapo *m* 2 ~s *npl* TAT-
TERS : harapos *mpl*, andrajos *mpl*
rage ['reɪdʒ] *n* 1 : cólera *f*, rabia *f* 2 **be
all the** ~ : hacer furor — ~ *vi*
raged; raging 1 : estar furioso 2 : bramar (dícese del viento, etc.)
ragged ['rægəd] *adj* 1 UNEVEN : irregular 2 TATTERED : andrajoso, harapiento
raid ['reɪd] *n* 1 : invasión *f* (militar) 2
: asalto *m* (por delincuentes), redada *f*
(por la policía) — ~ *vt* 1 INVADE : invadir 2 ROB : asaltar 3 : hacer una
redada en (dícese de la policía) —
raider ['reɪdər] *n* ATTACKER : asaltante
mf
rail[1] ['reɪl] *vi* ~ **at s.o.** : recriminar a
algn
rail[2] *n* 1 BAR : barra *f* 2 HANDRAIL
: pasamanos *m* 3 TRACK : riel *m* 4 **by**
~ : por ferrocarril — **railing** ['reɪlɪŋ] *n*
1 : baranda *f* (de un balcón),
pasamanos *m* (de una escalera) 2

RAILS : reja *f* — **railroad** ['reɪlˌroːd] *n* : ferrocarril *m* — **railway** ['reɪlˌweɪ] → **railroad**

rain ['reɪn] *n* : lluvia *f* — ~ *vi* : llover — **rainbow** ['reɪnˌboː] *n* : arco *m* iris — **raincoat** ['reɪnˌkoːt] *n* : impermeable *m* — **rainfall** ['reɪnˌfɔl] *n* : precipitación *f* — **rainy** ['reɪni] *adj* **rainier; -est** : lluvioso

raise ['reɪz] *vt* **raised; raising** 1 : levantar 2 COLLECT : recaudar 3 REAR : criar 4 GROW : cultivar 5 INCREASE : aumentar 6 : sacar (objeciones, etc.) — ~ *n* : aumento *m*

raisin ['reɪzən] *n* : pasa *f*

rake ['reɪk] *n* : rastrillo *m* — ~ *vt* **raked; raking** : rastrillar

rally ['ræli] *v* **-lied; -lying** *vi* 1 : unirse, reunirse 2 RECOVER : recuperarse — *vt* : conseguir (apoyo), unir a (la gente) — ~ *n, pl* **-lies** : reunión *f*, mitin *m*

ram *n* ['ræm] : carnero *m* (animal) — *vt* **rammed; ramming** 1 CRAM : meter con fuerza 2 *or* ~ **into** : chocar contra

RAM ['ræm] *n* : RAM *f*

ramble ['ræmbəl] *vi* **-bled; -bling** 1 WANDER : pasear 2 *or* ~ **on** : divagar — ~ *n* : paseo *m*, excursión *f*

ramp ['ræmp] *n* : rampa *f*

rampage ['ræmˌpeɪdʒ, ræmˈpeɪdʒ] *vi* **-paged; -paging** : andar arrasando todo — ~ ['ræmˌpeɪdʒ] *n* : frenesí *m* (de violencia)

rampant ['ræmpənt] *adj* : desenfrenado

rampart ['ræmˌpɑrt] *n* : muralla *f*

ramshackle ['ræmˌʃækəl] *adj* : destartalado

ran → **run**

ranch ['ræntʃ] *n* : hacienda *f* — **rancher** ['ræntʃər] *n* : hacendado *m*, -da *f*

rancid ['rænsɪd] *adj* : rancio

rancor ['ræŋkər] *n* : rencor *m*

random ['rændəm] *adj* 1 : aleatorio 2 **at** ~ : al azar

rang → **ring**

range ['reɪndʒ] *n* 1 GRASSLAND : pradera *f* 2 STOVE : cocina *f* 3 VARIETY : gama *f* 4 SCOPE : amplitud *f* 5 *or* **mountain** ~ : cordillera *f* — ~ *vi* **ranged; ranging** 1 EXTEND : extenderse 2 ~ **from...to...** : variar entre...y... — **ranger** ['reɪndʒər] *n or* **forest** ~ : guardabosque *mf*

rank¹ ['ræŋk] *adj* 1 SMELLY : fétido 2 OUTRIGHT : completo

rank² *n* 1 ROW : fila *f* 2 : rango *m* (militar) 3 ~**s** *npl* : soldados *mpl* rasos 4 **the** ~ **and file** : las bases — ~ *vt* RATE : clasificar — *vi* : clasificarse

rankle ['ræŋkəl] *vi* **-kled; -kling** : causar rencor, doler

ransack ['rænˌsæk] *vt* 1 SEARCH : registrar 2 LOOT : saquear

ransom ['rænsəm] *n* : rescate *m* — ~ *vt* : rescatar

rant ['rænt] *vi or* ~ **and rave** : despotricar

rap¹ ['ræp] *n* KNOCK : golpecito *m* — ~ *v* **rapped; rapping** : golpear

rap² *n or* ~ **music** : rap *m*

rapacious [rəˈpeɪʃəs] *adj* : rapaz

rape ['reɪp] *vt* **raped; raping** : violar — ~ *n* : violación *f*

rapid ['ræpɪd] *adj* : rápido — **rapids** ['ræpɪdz] *npl* : rápidos *mpl*

rapist ['reɪpɪst] *n* : violador *m*, -dora *f*

rapport [ræˈpor] *n* **have a good** ~ : entenderse bien

rapt ['ræpt] *adj* : absorto, embelesado

rapture ['ræptʃər] *n* : éxtasis *m*

rare ['rær] *adj* **rarer; rarest** 1 FINE : excepcional 2 UNCOMMON : raro 3 : poco cocido (dícese de la carne) — **rarely** ['rærli] *adv* : raramente — **rarity** ['rærəˌti] *n, pl* **-ties** : rareza *f*

rascal ['ræskəl] *n* : pillo *m*, -lla *f*; pícaro *m*, -ra *f*

rash¹ ['ræʃ] *adj* : imprudente, precipitado

rash² *n* : sarpullido *m*, erupción *f*

rasp ['ræsp] *vt* SCRAPE : raspar — ~ *n* : escofina *f*

raspberry ['ræzˌberi] *n, pl* **-ries** : frambuesa *f*

rat ['ræt] *n* : rata *f*

rate ['reɪt] *n* 1 PACE : velocidad *f*, ritmo *m* 2 : tipo *m*, tasa *m* (de interés, etc.) 3 PRICE : tarifa *f* 4 **at any** ~ : de todos modos 5 **birth** ~ : índice *m* de natalidad — ~ *vt* **rated; rating** 1 REGARD : considerar 2 DESERVE : merecer

rather ['ræðər, 'rɑ-, 'rɑ-] *adv* 1 FAIRLY : bastante 2 **I'd** ~**...** : prefiero... 3 **or** ~ : o mejor dicho

ratify ['ræṭəˌfaɪ] *vt* **-fied; -fying** : ratificar — **ratification** [ˌræṭəfəˈkeɪʃən] *n* : ratificación *f*

rating ['reɪṭɪŋ] *n* 1 : clasificación *f* 2 ~**s** *npl* : índice *m* de audiencia

ratio ['reɪʃio] *n, pl* **-tios** : proporción *f*

ration ['ræʃən, 'reɪʃən] *n* 1 : ración *f* 2 ~**s** *npl* PROVISIONS : víveres *mpl* — ~ *vt* **rationed; rationing** : racionar

rational ['ræʃənəl] *adj* : racional — **rationale** [ˌræʃəˈnæl] *n* : lógica *f*, razones *fpl* — **rationalize** ['ræʃənəˌlaɪz] *vt* **-ized; -izing** : racionalizar

rattle ['ræṭəl] *v* **-tled; -tling** *vi* : traquetear — *vt* 1 SHAKE : agitar 2 UPSET : de-

sconcertar 3 ~ **off** : decir de corrido
— ~ *n* 1 : traqueteo *m* 2 *or* baby's ~
: sonajero *m* — **rattlesnake** ['ræt̮əl-
,sneɪk] *n* : serpiente *f* de cascabel

raucous ['rɔkəs] *adj* 1 HOARSE : ronco 2
BOISTEROUS : bullicioso

ravage ['rævɪdʒ] *vt* -**aged; -aging** : estragar, asolar — **ravages** ['rævɪdʒəz]
npl : estragos *mpl*

rave ['reɪv] *vi* **raved; raving** 1 : delirar 2
~ **about** : hablar con entusiasmo
sobre

raven ['reɪvən] *n* : cuervo *m*

ravenous ['rævənəs] *adj* 1 HUNGRY
: hambriento 2 VORACIOUS : voraz

ravine [rə'viːn] *n* : barranco *m*

ravishing ['rævɪʃɪŋ] *adj* : encantador

raw ['rɔ] *adj* **rawer; rawest** 1 UNCOOKED
: crudo 2 INEXPERIENCED : inexperto 3
CHAFED : en carne viva 4 : frío y
húmedo (dícese del tiempo) 5 ~ **deal**
: trato *m* injusto 6 ~ **materials** : materias *fpl* primas

ray ['reɪ] *n* : rayo *m*

rayon ['reɪˌɑn] *n* : rayón *m*

raze ['reɪz] *vt* **razed; razing** : arrasar

razor ['reɪzər] *n* : maquinilla *f* de afeitar
— **razor blade** *n* : hoja *f* de afeitar

reach ['riːtʃ] *vt* 1 : alcanzar 2 *or* ~ **out**
: extender 3 : llegar a (un acuerdo, un
límite, etc.) 4 CONTACT : contactar —
vi 1 : extenderse 2 ~ **for** : tratar de
agarrar — ~ *n* 1 : alcance *m* 2 **within**
~ : al alcance

react [ri'ækt] *vi* : reaccionar — **reaction**
[ri'ækʃən] *n* : reacción *f* — **reactionary**
[ri'ækʃəˌneri] *adj* : reaccionario — ~
n, pl -**ries** : reaccionario *m*, -ria *f* — **reactor** [ri'æktər] *n* : reactor *m*

read ['riːd] *v* **read** ['rɛd]; **reading** *vt* 1
: leer 2 INTERPRET : interpretar 3 SAY
: decir 4 INDICATE : marcar — *vi* 1
: leer 2 **it** ~**s as follows** : dice lo
siguiente — **readable** ['riːdəbəl] *adj*
: legible — **reader** ['riːdər] *n* : lector *m*,
-tora *f*

readily ['rɛdəli] *adv* 1 WILLINGLY : de
buena gana 2 EASILY : fácilmente

reading ['riːdɪŋ] *n* : lectura *f*

readjust [ˌriːə'dʒʌst] *vt* : reajustar — *vi*
: volverse a adaptar

ready ['rɛdi] *adj* **readier; -est** 1 : listo,
preparado 2 WILLING : dispuesto 3
AVAILABLE : disponible 4 **get** ~
: prepararse — ~ *vt* **readied; readying** : preparar

real ['riːl] *adj* 1 : verdadero, real 2 GENUINE : auténtico — ~ *adv* VERY : muy
— **real estate** *n* : propiedad *f* inmobiliaria, bienes *mpl* raíces — **realism**

['riːəˌlɪzəm] *n* : realismo *m* — **realist**
['riːəlɪst] *n* : realista *mf* — **realistic**
[ˌriːə'lɪstɪk] *adj* : realista — **reality** [ri-
'ælət̮i] *n, pl* -**ties** : realidad *f*

realize ['riːəˌlaɪz] *vt* -**ized; -izing** 1
: darse cuenta de 2 ACHIEVE : realizar
— **realization** [ˌriːələ'zeɪʃən] *n* 1 : comprensión *f* 2 FULFILLMENT : realización
f

really ['rɪli, 'riː-] *adv* : verdaderamente

realm ['rɛlm] *n* 1 KINGDOM : reino *m* 2
SPHERE : esfera *f*

ream ['riːm] *n* : resma *f* (de papel)

reap ['riːp] *v* : cosechar

reappear [ˌriːə'pɪr] *vi* : reaparecer

rear¹ ['rɪr] *vt* 1 RAISE : levantar 2 : criar
(niños, etc.) — *vi or* ~ **up** : encabritarse

rear² *n* 1 BACK : parte *f* de atrás 2 BUTTOCKS : trasero *m fam* — ~ *adj*
: trasero, posterior

rearrange [ˌriːə'reɪndʒ] *vt* -**ranged;
-ranging** : reorganizar, cambiar

reason ['riːzən] *n* : razón *f* — ~ *vt*
THINK : pensar — *vi* : razonar — **reasonable** ['riːzənəbəl] *adj* : razonable — **reasoning** ['riːzənɪŋ] *n* : razonamiento *m*

reassure [ˌriːə'ʃʊr] *vt* -**sured; -suring**
: tranquilizar — **reassurance** [ˌriːə-
'ʃʊrənts] *n* : (palabras *fpl* de) consuelo
m

rebate ['riːˌbeɪt] *n* : reembolso *m*

rebel ['rɛbəl] *n* : rebelde *mf* — ~ [rɪ'bɛl]
vi -**belled; -belling** : rebelarse — **rebellion** [rɪ'bɛljən] *n* : rebelión *f* — **rebellious** [rɪ'bɛljəs] *adj* : rebelde

rebirth [ˌriː'bərθ] *n* : renacimiento *m*

rebound [rɪ'baʊnd, ˌriː'baʊnd] *vi* : rebotar — ~ ['riːˌbaʊnd] *n* : rebote *m*

rebuff [rɪ'bʌf] *vt* : rechazar — ~ *n* : desaire *m*

rebuild [ˌriː'bɪld] *vt* -**built; -building** : reconstruir

rebuke [rɪ'bjuːk] *vt* -**buked; -buking**
: reprender — ~ *n* : reprimenda *f*

rebut [rɪ'bʌt] *vt* -**butted; -butting** : rebatir — **rebuttal** [rɪ'bʌt̮əl] *n* : refutación *f*

recall [rɪ'kɔl] *vt* 1 : llamar (al servicio,
etc.) 2 REMEMBER : recordar 3 REVOKE
: revocar — ~ [rɪ'kɔl, 'riːˌkɔl] *n* 1 : retirada *f* 2 MEMORY : memoria *f*

recant [rɪ'kænt] *vi* : retractarse

recapitulate [ˌriːkə'pɪtʃəˌleɪt] *v* -**lated;
-lating** : recapitular

recapture [ˌriː'kæptʃər] *vt* -**tured; -turing** 1 : recobrar 2 RELIVE : revivir

recede [rɪ'siːd] *vi* -**ceded; -ceding** : retirarse

receipt [ri'si:t] n 1 : recibo m 2 ~s npl : ingresos mpl

receive [ri'si:v] vt -ceived; -ceiving : recibir — **receiver** [ri'si:vər] n 1 : receptor m (de radio, etc.) 2 or **telephone** ~ : auricular m

recent ['ri:sənt] adj : reciente — **recently** [-li] adv : recientemente

receptacle [ri'septikəl] n : receptáculo m, recipiente m

reception [ri'sepʃən] n : recepción f — **receptionist** [ri'sepʃənɪst] n : recepcionista mf — **receptive** [ri'septɪv] adj : receptivo

recess ['ri:,ses, ri'ses] n 1 ALCOVE : hueco m 2 : recreo m (escolar) 3 ADJOURNMENT : suspensión f de actividades Spain, receso m Lat — **recession** [ri'seʃən] n : recesión f

recharge [,ri:'tʃɑrdʒ] vt -charged; -charging : recargar — **rechargeable** [,ri:'tʃɑrdʒəbəl] adj : recargable

recipe ['resəpi:] n : receta f

recipient [ri'sipiənt] n : recipiente mf

reciprocal [ri'siprəkəl] adj : recíproco

recite [ri'saɪt] vt -cited; -citing 1 : recitar (un poema, etc.) 2 LIST : enumerar — **recital** [ri'saɪtəl] n : recital m

reckless ['rekləs] adj : imprudente — **recklessness** ['rekləsnəs] n : imprudencia f

reckon ['rekən] vt 1 COMPUTE : calcular 2 CONSIDER : considerar — **reckoning** ['rekənɪŋ] n : cálculos mpl

reclaim [ri'kleɪm] vt 1 : reclamar 2 RECOVER : recuperar

recline [ri'klaɪn] vi -clined; -clining : reclinarse — **reclining** adj : reclinable (dícese de un asiento, etc.)

recluse ['re,klu:s, ri'klu:s] n : solitario m, -ria f

recognition [,rekɪg'nɪʃən] n : reconocimiento m — **recognizable** ['rekɪg,naɪzəbəl] adj : reconocible — **recognize** ['rekɪg,naɪz] vt -nized; -nizing : reconocer

recoil [ri'kɔɪl] vi : retroceder — ~ ['ri:,kɔɪl, ri'-] n : culatazo m (de un arma de fuego)

recollect [,rekə'lekt] v : recordar — **recollection** [,rekə'lekʃən] n : recuerdo m

recommend [,rekə'mend] vt : recomendar — **recommendation** [,rekəmən'deɪʃən] n : recomendación f

reconcile ['rekən,saɪl] v -ciled; -ciling vt 1 : reconciliar (personas), conciliar (datos, etc.) 2 ~ **oneself to** : resignarse a — vi MAKE UP : reconciliarse — **reconciliation** [,rekən,sɪli'eɪʃən] n : reconciliación f

reconnaissance [ri'kɑnəzənts, -sənts] n : reconocimiento m (militar)

reconsider [,ri:kən'sɪdər] vt : reconsiderar

reconstruct [,ri:kən'strʌkt] vt : reconstruir

record [ri'kɔrd] vt 1 WRITE DOWN : anotar, apuntar 2 REGISTER : registrar 3 : grabar (música, etc.) — ~ ['rekərd] n 1 DOCUMENT : documento m 2 REGISTER : registro m 3 HISTORY : historial m 4 : disco m (de música, etc.) 5 **criminal** ~ : antecedentes mpl penales 6 **world** ~ : récord m mundial — **recorder** [ri'kɔrdər] n 1 : flauta f dulce 2 or **tape** ~ : grabadora f — **recording** [-ɪŋ] n : disco m — **record player** n : tocadiscos m

recount[1] [ri'kaunt] vt NARRATE : narrar, relatar

recount[2] [,ri:'kaunt, ,ri'-] vt : volver a contar (votos, etc.) — ~ n : recuento m

recourse ['ri:,kors, ri'-] n 1 : recurso m 2 **have** ~ **to** : recurrir a

recover [ri'kʌvər] vt : recobrar — vi RECUPERATE : recuperarse — **recovery** [ri'kʌvəri] n, pl -eries : recuperación f

recreation [,rekri'eɪʃən] n : recreo m — **recreational** [,rekri'eɪʃənəl] adj : de recreo

recruit [ri'kru:t] vt : reclutar — ~ n : recluta mf — **recruitment** [ri'kru:tmənt] n : reclutamiento m

rectangle ['rek,tæŋgəl] n : rectángulo m — **rectangular** [rek'tæŋgjələr] adj : rectangular

rectify ['rektə,faɪ] vt -fied; -fying : rectificar

rector ['rektər] n 1 : parroco m (clérigo) 2 : rector m, -tora f (de una universidad) — **rectory** ['rektəri] n, pl -ries : rectoría f

rectum ['rektəm] n, pl -tums or -ta [-tə] : recto m

recuperate [ri'ku:pə,reɪt, -'kju:-] v -ated; -ating vt : recuperar — vi : recuperarse — **recuperation** [ri,ku:pə'reɪʃən, -,kju:-] n : recuperación f

recur [ri'kər] vi -curred; -curring : repetirse — **recurrence** [ri'kərənts] n : repetición f — **recurrent** [ri'kərənt] adj : que se repite

recycle [ri'saɪkəl] vt -cled; -cling : reciclar

red ['red] adj : rojo — ~ n : rojo m — **redden** ['redən] vt : enrojecer — vi : enrojecerse — **reddish** ['redɪʃ] adj : rojizo

redecorate [ri'dekə,reɪt] vt -rated; -rating : pintar de nuevo

redeem [ri'di:m] vt 1 SAVE : salvar,

rescatar **2** : desempeñar (de un monte de piedad) **3** : canjear (cupones, etc.) — **redemption** [rɪˈdɛmpʃən] n : redención f

red–handed [ˈrɛdˈhændəd] adv or adj : con las manos en la masa

redhead [ˈrɛdˌhɛd] n : pelirrojo m, -ja f

red–hot [ˈrɛdˌhɑt] adj : al rojo vivo

redness [ˈrɛdnəs] n : rojez f

redo [ˌriˈduː] vt **-did** [-ˈdɪd]; **-done** [-ˈdʌn]; **-doing** : hacer de nuevo

redouble [riˈdʌbəl] vt **-bled; -bling** : redoblar

red tape n : papeleo m

reduce [rɪˈduːs, -ˈdjuːs] v **-duced; -ducing** vt : reducir — vi SLIM : adelgazar — **reduction** [rɪˈdʌkʃən] n : reducción f

redundant [rɪˈdʌndənt] adj : redundante

reed [ˈriːd] n **1** : caña f **2** : lengüeta f (de un instrumento)

reef [ˈriːf] n : arrecife m

reek [ˈriːk] vi : apestar

reel [ˈriːl] n **1** : carrete m (de hilo, etc.) — ~ vt **1** ~ **in** : enrollar (un sedal), sacar (un pez) del agua **2** ~ **off** : enumerar — vi **1** SPIN : dar vueltas **2** STAGGER : tambalearse

reestablish [ˌriːɪˈstæblɪʃ] vt : restablecer

refer [rɪˈfər] v **-ferred; -ferring** vt **1** DIRECT : enviar, mandar **2** SUBMIT : remitir — vi ~ **to 1** MENTION : referirse a **2** CONSULT : consultar

referee [ˌrɛfəˈriː] n : árbitro m, -tra f — ~ v **-eed; -eeing** : arbitrar

reference [ˈrɛfrəns, ˈrɛfə-] n **1** : referencia f **2** CONSULTATION : consulta f **3** or ~ **book** : libro m de consulta **4 in** ~ **to** : con referencia a

refill [ˌriːˈfɪl] vt : rellenar — ~ [ˈriːˌfɪl] n : recambio m

refine [rɪˈfaɪn] vt **-fined; -fining** : refinar — **refined** [rɪˈfaɪnd] adj : refinado — **refinement** [rɪˈfaɪnmənt] n : refinamiento m — **refinery** [rɪˈfaɪnəri] n, pl **-eries** : refinería f

reflect [rɪˈflɛkt] vt : reflejar — vi **1** : reflejarse **2** ~ **badly on** : desacreditar **3** ~ **upon** : reflexionar sobre — **reflection** [rɪˈflɛkʃən] n **1** : reflexión f **2** IMAGE : reflejo m — **reflector** [rɪˈflɛktər] n : reflector m

reflex [ˈriːˌflɛks] n : reflejo m

reflexive [rɪˈflɛksɪv] adj : reflexivo

reform [rɪˈfɔrm] vt : reformar — vi : reformarse — ~ n : reforma f — **reformer** [rɪˈfɔrmər] n : reformador m, -dora f

refrain[1] [rɪˈfreɪn] vi ~ **from** : abstenerse de

refrain[2] n : estribillo m (en música)

refresh [rɪˈfrɛʃ] vt : refrescar — **refreshments** [rɪˈfrɛʃmənts] npl : refrigerio m

refrigerate [rɪˈfrɪdʒəˌreɪt] vt **-ated; -ating** : refrigerar — **refrigeration** [rɪˌfrɪdʒəˈreɪʃən] n : refrigeración f — **refrigerator** [rɪˈfrɪdʒəˌreɪtər] n : nevera f, refrigerador m Lat, frigorífico m Spain

refuel [riːˈfjuːəl] v **-eled** or **-elled; -eling** or **-elling** vt : llenar de carburante — vi : repostar

refuge [ˈrɛˌfjuːdʒ] n : refugio m — **refugee** [ˌrɛfjʊˈdʒiː] n : refugiado m, -da f

refund [rɪˈfʌnd, ˈriːˌfʌnd] vt : reembolsar — ~ [ˈriːˌfʌnd] n : reembolso m

refurbish [rɪˈfərbɪʃ] vt : renovar, restaurar

refuse[1] [rɪˈfjuːz] v **-fused; -fusing** vt **1** : rehusar, rechazar **2** ~ **to do sth** : negarse a hacer algo — vi : negarse — **refusal** [rɪˈfjuːzəl] n : negativa f

refuse[2] [ˈrɛfjuːs, -fjuːz] n : residuos mpl, desperdicios mpl

refute [rɪˈfjuːt] vt **-futed; -futing** : refutar

regain [riˈgeɪn] vt : recuperar, recobrar

regal [ˈriːgəl] adj : regio, majestuoso — **regalia** [rɪˈgeɪljə] n : ropaje m, insignias fpl

regard [rɪˈgɑrd] n **1** : consideración f **2** ESTEEM : estima f **3 in this** ~ : en este sentido **4** ~**s** npl : saludos mpl **5 with** ~ **to** : respecto a — ~ vt **1** : mirar (con recelo, etc.) **2** HEED : tener en cuenta **3** ESTEEM : estimar **4 as** ~**s** : en lo que se refiere a **5** ~ **as** : considerar — **regarding** [rɪˈgɑrdɪŋ] prep : respecto a — **regardless** [rɪˈgɑrdləs] adv : a pesar de todo — **regardless of** prep **1** : sin tener en cuenta **2** IN SPITE OF : a pesar de

regent [ˈriːdʒənt] n : regente mf

regime [reɪˈʒiːm, rɪ-] n : régimen m — **regimen** [ˈrɛdʒəmən] n : régimen m

regiment [ˈrɛdʒəmənt] n : regimiento m

region [ˈriːdʒən] n : región f — **regional** [ˈriːdʒənəl] adj : regional

register [ˈrɛdʒəstər] n : registro m — ~ vt **1** : registrar (a personas), matricular (vehículos) **2** SHOW : marcar, manifestar **3** : certificar (correo) — vi ENROLL : inscribirse, matricularse — **registrar** [ˈrɛdʒəˌstrɑr] n : registrador m, -dora f oficial — **registration** [ˌrɛdʒəˈstreɪʃən] n **1** : inscripción f, matriculación f **2** or ~ **number** : número m de matrícula — **registry** [ˈrɛdʒəstri] n, pl **-tries** : registro m

regret [rɪˈgrɛt] vt **-gretted; -gretting** : lamentar — ~ n **1** REMORSE : arrepentimiento m **2** SORROW : pesar m

— **regrettable** [rɪ'grɛʈəbəl] *adj* : lamentable

regular ['rɛgjələr] *adj* **1** : regular **2** CUSTOMARY : habitual — ∼ *n* : cliente *mf* habitual — **regularity** [ˌrɛgjə'lærəʈi] *n, pl* **-ties** : regularidad *f* — **regularly** ['rɛgjələrli] *adv* : regularmente — **regulate** ['rɛgjəˌleɪt] *vt* **-lated; -lating** : regular — **regulation** [ˌrɛgjə'leɪʃən] *n* **1** CONTROL : regulación *f* **2** RULE : regla *f*

rehabilitate [ˌriːhə'bɪləˌteɪt, ˌriːə-] *vt* **-tated; -tating** : rehabilitar — **rehabilitation** [ˌriːhəˌbɪlə'teɪʃən, ˌriːə-] *n* : rehabilitación *f*

rehearse [rɪ'hərs] *v* **-hearsed; -hearsing** : ensayar — **rehearsal** [rɪ'hərsəl] *n* : ensayo *m*

reign ['reɪn] *n* : reinado *m* — ∼ *vi* : reinar

reimburse [ˌriːəm'bərs] *vt* **-bursed; -bursing** : reembolsar — **reimbursement** [ˌriːəm'bərsmənt] *n* : reembolso *m*

rein ['reɪn] *n* : rienda *f*

reincarnation [ˌriːɪnkɑr'neɪʃən] *n* : reencarnación *f*

reindeer ['reɪnˌdɪr] *n* : reno *m*

reinforce [ˌriːən'fors] *vt* **-forced; -forcing** : reforzar — **reinforcement** [ˌriːən'forsmənt] *n* : refuerzo *m*

reinstate [ˌriːən'steɪt] *vt* **-stated; -stating** **1** : restablecer **2** : restituir (a algn en su cargo)

reiterate [rɪ'ɪʈəˌreɪt] *vt* **-ated; -ating** : reiterar

reject [rɪ'dʒɛkt] *vt* : rechazar — **rejection** [rɪ'dʒɛkʃən] *n* : rechazo *m*

rejoice [rɪ'dʒɔɪs] *vi* **-joiced; -joicing** : regocijarse

rejuvenate [rɪ'dʒuːvəˌneɪt] *vt* **-nated; -nating** : rejuvenecer

rekindle [ˌriː'kɪndəl] *vt* **-dled; -dling** : reavivar

relapse ['riːˌlæps, rɪ'læps] *n* : recaída *f* — ∼ [rɪ'læps] *vi* **-lapsed; -lapsing** : recaer

relate [rɪ'leɪt] *v* **-lated; -lating** *vt* **1** TELL : relatar **2** ASSOCIATE : relacionar — *vi* ∼ **to 1** CONCERN : estar relacionado con **2** UNDERSTAND : identificarse con **3** : relacionarse con (socialmente) — **related** [rɪ'leɪʈəd] *adj* ∼ **to** : emparentado con — **relation** [rɪ'leɪʃən] *n* **1** CONNECTION : relación *f* **2** RELATIVE : pariente *mf* **3 in** ∼ **to** : en relación con **4** ∼**s** *npl* : relaciones *fpl* — **relationship** [rɪ'leɪʃənˌʃɪp] *n* **1** : relación *f* **2** KINSHIP : parentesco *m* — **relative** ['rɛləʈɪv] *n* : pariente *mf* — ∼ *adj* : relativo — **relatively** *adv* : relativamente

relax [rɪ'læks] *vt* : relajar — *vi* : relajarse — **relaxation** [ˌriːˌlæk'seɪʃən] *n* **1** : relajación *f* **2** RECREATION : esparcimiento *m*

relay ['riːˌleɪ] *n* **1** : relevo *m* **2** *or* ∼ **race** : carrera *f* de relevos — ∼ ['riːˌleɪ, rɪ'leɪ] *vt* **-layed; -laying** : transmitir

release [rɪ'liːs] *vt* **-leased; -leasing 1** FREE : liberar, poner en libertad **2** : soltar (un freno, etc.) **3** EMIT : despedir **4** : sacar (un libro, etc.), estrenar (una película) — ∼ *n* **1** : liberación *f* **2** : estreno *m* (de una película), publicación *f* (de un libro) **3** : fuga *f* (de gases)

relegate ['rɛləˌgeɪt] *vt* **-gated; -gating** : relegar

relent [rɪ'lɛnt] *vi* : ceder — **relentless** [rɪ'lɛntləs] *adj* : implacable

relevant ['rɛləvənt] *adj* : pertinente — **relevance** ['rɛləvənts] *n* : pertinencia *f*

reliable [rɪ'laɪəbəl] *adj* : fiable (dícese de personas), fidedigno (dícese de información, etc.) — **reliability** [rɪˌlaɪə'bɪlə-ʈi] *n, pl* **-ties** : fiabilidad *f* (de una cosa), responsabilidad *f* (de una persona) — **reliance** [rɪ'laɪənts] *n* **1** : dependencia *f* **2** TRUST : confianza *f* — **reliant** [rɪ'laɪənt] *adj* : dependiente

relic ['rɛlɪk] *n* : reliquia *f*

relief [rɪ'liːf] *n* **1** : alivio *m* **2** AID : ayuda *f* **3** : relieve *m* (en la escultura) **4** REPLACEMENT : relevo *m* — **relieve** [rɪ'liːv] *vt* **-lieved; -lieving 1** : aliviar **2** REPLACE : relevar (a algn) **3** ∼ **s.o. of** : liberar a algn de

religion [rɪ'lɪdʒən] *n* : religión *f* — **religious** [rɪ'lɪdʒəs] *adj* : religioso

relinquish [rɪ'lɪŋkwɪʃ, -lɪn-] *vt* : renunciar a, abandonar

relish ['rɛlɪʃ] *n* **1** : salsa *f* (condimento) **2 with** ∼ : con gusto — ∼ *vt* : saborear

relocate [ˌriːˌloʊˌkeɪt, ˌriːloʊ'keɪt] *vt* **-cated; -cating** : trasladar — *vi* : trasladarse — **relocation** [ˌriːloʊˈkeɪʃən] *n* : traslado *m*

reluctance [rɪ'lʌktənts] *n* : reticencia *f*, desgana *f* — **reluctant** [rɪ'lʌktənt] *adj* : reacio, reticente — **reluctantly** [rɪ'lʌktəntli] *adv* : a regañadientes

rely [rɪ'laɪ] *vi* **-lied; -lying** ∼ **on 1** DEPEND ON : depender de **2** TRUST : confiar (en)

remain [rɪ'meɪn] *vi* **1** : quedar **2** STAY : quedarse **3** CONTINUE : seguir, continuar — **remainder** [rɪ'meɪndər] *n* : resto *m* — **remains** [rɪ'meɪnz] *npl* : restos *mpl*

remark [rɪ'mɑrk] *n* : comentario *m*, observación *f* — ∼ *vt* : observar — *vi* ∼

on : observar — **remarkable** [ri-'markəbəl] *adj* : extraordinario, notable
remedy ['remədi] *n, pl* **-dies** : remedio *m* — ~ *vt* **-died; -dying** : remediar — **remedial** [ri'mi:diəl] *adj* : correctivo
remember [ri'membər] *vt* 1 : acordarse de, recordar 2 ~ **to** : acordarse de — *vi* : acordarse, recordar — **remembrance** [ri'membrənts] *n* : recuerdo *m*
remind [ri'maind] *vt* : recordar — **reminder** [ri'maindər] *n* : recordatorio *m*
reminiscence [,remə'nisənts] *n* : recuerdo *m*, reminiscencia *f* — **reminisce** [,remə'nis] *vi* **-nisced; -niscing** : rememorar los viejos tiempos — **reminiscent** [,remə'nisənt] *adj* **be ~ of** : recordar
remiss [ri'mis] *adj* : negligente, remiso
remit [ri'mit] *vt* **-mitted; -mitting** 1 PARDON : perdonar 2 : enviar (dinero) — **remission** [ri'miʃən] *n* : remisión *f*
remnant ['remnənt] *n* 1 : resto *m* 2 TRACE : vestigio *m*
remorse [ri'mors] *n* : remordimiento *m* — **remorseful** [ri'morsfəl] *adj* : arrepentido
remote [ri'mo:t] *adj* **-moter; -est** 1 : remoto 2 ALOOF : distante 3 ~ **from** : apartado de, alejado de — **remote control** *n* : control *m* remoto — **remotely** [ri'mo:tli] *adv* SLIGHTLY : remotamente
remove [ri'mu:v] *vt* **-moved; -moving** 1 : quitar (una tapa, etc.), quitarse (ropa) 2 EXTRACT : sacar 3 DISMISS : destituir 4 ELIMINATE : eliminar — **removable** [ri'mu:vəbəl] *adj* : separable, de quita y pon — **removal** [ri'mu:vəl] *n* 1 : eliminación *f* 2 EXTRACTION : extracción *f*
remunerate [ri'mju:nə,reit] *vt* **-ated; -ating** : remunerar
render ['rendər] *vt* 1 : rendir (homenaje), prestar (ayuda) 2 MAKE : hacer 3 TRANSLATE : traducir
rendezvous ['randi,vu:, -dei-] *ns & pl* : cita *f*
rendition [ren'diʃən] *n* : interpretación *f*
renegade ['reni,geid] *n* : renegado *m*, -da *f*
renew [ri'nu:, -'nju:] *vt* 1 : renovar 2 RESUME : reanudar — **renewal** [ri'nu:əl, -'nju:-] *n* : renovación *f*
renounce [ri'naunts] *vt* **-nounced; -nouncing** : renunciar a
renovate ['renə,veit] *vt* **-vated; -vating** : renovar — **renovation** [,renə'veiʃən] *n* : renovación *f*
renown [ri'naun] *n* : renombre *m* — **renowned** [ri'naund] *adj* : célebre, renombrado

rent ['rent] *n* 1 : alquiler *m*, arrendamiento *m*, renta *f* 2 **for ~** : se alquila — ~ *vt* : alquilar — **rental** ['rentəl] *n* : alquiler *m* — ~ *adj* : de alquiler — **renter** ['rentər] *n* : arrendatario *m*, -ria *f*
renunciation [ri,nʌntsi'eiʃən] *n* : renuncia *f*
reopen [,ri:'o:pən] *vt* : volver a abrir
reorganize [,ri:'orgə,naiz] *vt* **-nized; -nizing** : reorganizar — **reorganization** [,ri:,orgənə'zeiʃən] *n* : reorganización *f*
repair [ri'pær] *vt* : reparar, arreglar — ~ *n* 1 : reparación *f*, arreglo *m* 2 **in bad ~** : en mal estado
repay [ri'pei] *vt* **-paid; -paying** 1 : devolver (dinero), pagar (una deuda) 2 : corresponder a (un favor, etc.)
repeal [ri'pi:l] *vt* : abrogar, revocar — ~ *n* : abrogación *f*, revocación *f*
repeat [ri'pi:t] *vt* : repetir — ~ *n* : repetición *f* — **repeatedly** [ri'pi:tədli] *adv* : repetidas veces
repel [ri'pel] *vt* **-pelled; -pelling** : repeler — **repellent** [ri'pelənt] *n* : repelente *m*
repent [ri'pent] *vi* : arrepentirse — **repentance** [ri'pentənts] *n* : arrepentimiento *m*
repercussion [,ri:pər'kʌʃən, ,repər-] *n* : repercusión *f*
repertoire ['repər,twar] *n* : repertorio *m*
repetition [,repə'tiʃən] *n* : repetición *f* — **repetitious** [,repə'tiʃəs] *adj* : repetitivo — **repetitive** [ri'petətiv] *adj* : repetitivo
replace [ri'pleis] *vt* **-placed; -placing** 1 : reponer 2 SUBSTITUTE : reemplazar, sustituir 3 EXCHANGE : cambiar — **replacement** [ri'pleismənt] *n* 1 : sustitución *f* 2 : sustituto *m*, -ta *f* (persona) *or* ~ **part** : repuesto *m*
replenish [ri'pleniʃ] *vt* 1 : reponer 2 REFILL : rellenar
replete [ri'pli:t] *adj* ~ **with** : repleto de
replica ['replikə] *n* : réplica *f*
reply [ri'plai] *vi* **-plied; -plying** : contestar, responder — ~ *n, pl* **-plies** : respuesta *f*
report [ri'port] *n* 1 : informe *m* 2 RUMOR : rumor *m* 3 *or* **news ~** : reportaje *m* 4 **weather ~** : boletín *m* meteorológico — ~ *vt* 1 RELATE : anunciar 2 ~ **a crime** : denunciar un delito 3 *or* ~ **on** : informar sobre — *vi* 1 : informar 2 ~ **for duty** : presentarse — **report card** *n* : boletín *m* de calificaciones — **reportedly** [ri'portədli] *adv*

: según se dice — **reporter** [rɪ'pɔrtər]
n : periodista mf; reportero m, -ra f
repose [rɪ'poːz] vi **-posed; -posing** : reposar — ~ n : reposo m
reprehensible [ˌreprɪ'hentsəbəl] adj
: reprensible
represent [ˌreprɪ'zent] vt **1** : representar
2 PORTRAY : presentar — **representation** [ˌreprɪzen'teɪʃən, -zən-] n : representación f — **representative** [ˌreprɪ-
'zentəṭɪv] adj : representativo — ~ n
: representante mf
repress [rɪ'pres] vt : reprimir — **repression** [rɪ'preʃən] n : represión f
reprieve [rɪ'priːv] n : indulto m
reprimand [ˈreprəˌmænd] n : reprimenda
f — ~ vt : reprender
reprint [rɪ'prɪnt] vt : reimprimir — ~
['riːˌprɪnt, rɪ'prɪnt] n : reedición f
reprisal [rɪ'praɪzəl] n : represalia f
reproach [rɪ'proːtʃ] n **1** : reproche m **2**
beyond ~ : irreprochable — ~ vt
: reprochar — **reproachful** [rɪ'proːtʃfəl]
adj : de reproche
reproduce [ˌriːprə'duːs, -'djuːs] v **-duced;
-ducing** vt : reproducir — vi : reproducirse — **reproduction** [ˌriːprə'dʌk-
ʃən] n : reproducción f — **reproductive** [ˌriːprə'dʌktɪv] adj : reproductor
reproof [rɪ'pruːf] n : reprobación f
reptile ['reptaɪl] n : reptil m
republic [rɪ'pʌblɪk] n : república f — **republican** [rɪ'pʌblɪkən] n : republicano
m, -na f — ~ adj : republicano
repudiate [rɪ'pjuːdiˌeɪt] vt **-ated; -ating**
: repudiar
repugnant [rɪ'pʌgnənt] adj : repugnante,
asqueroso — **repugnance** [rɪ-
'pʌgnənts] n : repugnancia f
repulse [rɪ'pʌls] vt **-pulsed; -pulsing**
: repeler, rechazar — **repulsive** [rɪ-
'pʌlsɪv] adj : repulsivo
reputation [ˌrepjə'teɪʃən] n : reputación f
— **reputable** ['repjəṭəbəl] adj : de confianza, acreditado — **reputed** [rɪ'pjuː-
ṭəd] adj : supuesto
request [rɪ'kwest] n : petición f — ~ vt
: pedir
requiem ['rekwiəm, 'reɪ-] n : réquiem m
require [rɪ'kwaɪr] vt **-quired; -quiring 1**
CALL FOR : requerir **2** NEED : necesitar
— **requirement** [rɪ'kwaɪrmənt] n **1**
NEED : necesidad f **2** DEMAND : requisito m — **requisite** ['rekwəzɪt] adj
: necesario
resale ['riːˌseɪl, ˌriːˈseɪl] n : reventa f
rescind [rɪ'sɪnd] vt : rescindir (un contrato), revocar (una ley, etc.)
rescue ['reskjuː] vt **-cued; -cuing**
: rescatar, salvar — ~ n : rescate m —

rescuer ['reskjuər] n : salvador m,
-dora f
research [rɪ'sərtʃ, 'riːˌsərtʃ] n : investigación f — ~ vt : investigar — **researcher** [rɪ'sərtʃər, 'riː-] n : investigador m, -dora f
resemble [rɪ'zembəl] vt **-sembled;
-sembling** : parecerse a — **resemblance** [rɪ'zembləns] n : parecido m
resent [rɪ'zent] vt : resentirse de, ofenderse por — **resentful** [rɪ'zentfəl] adj
: resentido — **resentment** [rɪ-
'zentmənt] n : resentimiento m
reserve [rɪ'zərv] vt **-served; -serving**
: reservar — ~ n **1** : reserva f **2** ~**s**
npl : reservas fpl (militares) — **reservation** [ˌrezər'veɪʃən] n : reserva f —
reserved [rɪ'zərvd] adj : reservado —
reservoir ['rezərˌvwɑr, -ˌvwɔr, -ˌvɔr] n
: embalse m
reset [ˌriːˈset] vt **-set; -setting** : volver a
poner (un reloj, etc.)
residence ['rezədənts] n : residencia f —
reside [rɪ'zaɪd] vi **-sided; -siding** : residir — **resident** ['rezədənt] adj : residente — ~ n : residente mf — **residential** [ˌrezə'dentʃəl] adj : residencial
residue ['rezəˌduː, -ˌdjuː] n : residuo m
resign [rɪ'zaɪn] vt **1** QUIT : dimitir **2** ~
oneself to : resignarse a — **resigna-
tion** [ˌrezɪg'neɪʃən] n **1** : dimisión f **2**
ACCEPTANCE : resignación f
resilient [rɪ'zɪljənt] adj **1** : resistente
(dícese de personas) **2** ELASTIC : elástico — **resilience** [rɪ'zɪljənts] n **1** : resistencia f **2** ELASTICITY : elasticidad f
resin ['rezən] n : resina f
resist [rɪ'zɪst] vt : resistir — vi : resistirse — **resistance** [rɪ'zɪstənts] n : resistencia f — **resistant** [rɪ'zɪstənt] adj
: resistente
resolve [rɪ'zɑlv] vt **-solved; -solving**
: resolver — ~ n : resolución f —
resolution [ˌrezə'luːʃən] n **1** : resolución f **2** DECISION, INTENTION : propósito m — **resolute** ['rezəˌluːt] adj : resuelto
resonance ['rezənənts] n : resonancia f
— **resonant** ['rezənənt] adj : resonante
resort [rɪ'zɔrt] n **1** RECOURSE : recurso m
2 or **tourist** ~ : centro m turístico —
~ vi ~ to : recurrir a
resounding [rɪ'zaʊndɪŋ] adj **1** RESONANT
: resonante **2** ABSOLUTE : rotundo
resource ['riːˌsɔrs, rɪ'sɔrs] n : recurso m
— **resourceful** [rɪ'sɔrsfəl, -'zɔrs-] adj
: ingenioso
respect [rɪ'spekt] n **1** ESTEEM : respeto m
2 in some ~**s** : en algún sentido **3**
pay one's ~**s** : presentar uno sus re-

spetos **4 with ~ to :** (con) respecto a
— **~** *vt* : respetar — **respectable** [ri-
'spektəbəl] *adj* : respetable — **respect-**
ful [ri'spektfəl] *adj* : respetuoso — **re-**
spective [ri'spektiv] *adj* : respectivo
— **respectively** *adv* : respectivamente

respiration [respə'reiʃən] *n* : respiración *f* — **respiratory** ['respərə,tori, ri-
'spaire-] *adj* : respiratorio

respite ['respit, ri'spait] *n* : respiro *m*

response [ri'spants] *n* : respuesta *f* —
respond [ri'spand] *vi* : responder —
responsibility [ri,spantsə'biləţi] *n, pl*
-ties : responsabilidad *f* — **responsi-**
ble [ri'spantsəbəl] *adj* : responsable —
responsive [ri'spantsiv] *adj* : sensible,
receptivo

rest[1] ['rest] *n* **1 :** descanso *m* **2** SUPPORT
: apoyo *m* **3 :** silencio *m* (en música)
— **~** *vi* **1 :** descansar **2** LEAN : apoyarse **3 ~ on** DEPEND ON : depender
de — *vt* **1** RELAX : descansar **2** LEAN
: apoyar

rest[2] *n* REMAINDER : resto *m*

restaurant ['restə,rant, -rənt] *n* : restaurante *m*

restful ['restfəl] *adj* : tranquilo, apacible

restitution [,restə'tu:ʃən, -'tju:-] *n* : restitución *f*

restless ['restləs] *adj* : inquieto, agitado

restore [ri'stor] *vt* **-stored; -storing 1**
RETURN : devolver **2** REESTABLISH
: restablecer **3** REPAIR : restaurar —
restoration [,restə'reiʃən] *n* **1 :** restablecimiento *m* **2** REPAIR : restauración *f*

restrain [ri'strein] *vt* **1 :** contener **2 ~**
oneself : contenerse — **restrained**
[ri'streind] *adj* : comedido, moderado
— **restraint** [ri'streint] *n* **1 :** restricción
f **2** SELF-CONTROL : moderación *f*, control *m* de sí mismo

restriction [ri'strikʃən] *n* : restricción *f*
— **restrict** [ri'strikt] *vt* : restringir —
restricted [ri'striktəd] *adj* : restringido
— **restrictive** [ri'striktiv] *adj* : restrictivo

result [ri'zʌlt] *vi* : resultar — **~** *n* **1 :** resultado *m* **2 as a ~ of :** como conse-
cuencia de

resume [ri'zu:m] *v* **-sumed; -suming** *vt*
: reanudar — *vi* : reanudarse

résumé *or* **resume** *or* **resumé** ['rezə-
,mei, ,rezə'-] *n* : currículum *m* (vitae)

resumption [ri'zʌmpʃən] *n* : reanuda-
ción *f*

resurgence [ri'sərdʒənts] *n* : resurgimiento *m*

resurrection [,rezə'rekʃən] *n* : resurrección *f* — **resurrect** [,rezə'rekt] *vt* : resucitar

resuscitate [ri'sʌsə,teit] *vt* **-tated; -tat-**
ing : resucitar

retail ['ri:,teil] *vt* : vender al por menor
— **~** *n* : venta *f* al por menor — **~**
adj : detallista, minorista — **~** *adv*
: al detalle, al por menor — **retailer**
['ri:,teilər] *n* : detallista *mf*, minorista
mf

retain [ri'tein] *vt* : retener

retaliate [ri'tæli,eit] *vi* **-ated; -ating :** tomar represalias — **retaliation** [ri,tæli-
'eiʃən] *n* : represalias *fpl*

retard [ri'tard] *vt* : retardar, retrasar —
retarded [ri'tardəd] *adj* : retrasado

retention [ri'tentʃən] *n* : retención *f*

reticence ['reţəsənts] *n* : reticencia *f* —
reticent ['reţəsənt] *adj* : reticente

retina ['retənə] *n, pl* **-nas** *or* **-nae** [-əni,
-ən,ai] : retina *f*

retinue ['retən,u, -,ju:] *n* : séquito *m*

retire [ri'tair] *vi* **-tired; -tiring 1** WITH-
DRAW : retirarse **2 :** jubilarse, retirarse
(de un trabajo) **3 :** acostarse (en la
cama) — **retirement** [ri'tairmənt] *n*
: jubilación *f* — **retiring** [ri'tairiŋ] *adj*
SHY : retraído

retort [ri'tort] *vt* : replicar — **~** *n* : réplica *f*

retrace [,ri:'treis] *vt* **-traced; -tracing ~**
one's steps : volver sobre sus pasos

retract [ri'trækt] *vt* **1** WITHDRAW : retirar
2 : retraer (garras, etc.) — *vi* : retractarse

retrain [,ri:'trein] *vt* : reciclar

retreat [ri'tri:t] *n* **1 :** retirada *f* **2** REFUGE
: refugio *m* — **~** *vi* : retirarse

retribution [,retrə'bju:ʃən] *n* : castigo *m*

retrieve [ri'tri:v] *vt* **-trieved; -trieving 1**
: cobrar, recuperar **2** RESCUE : salvar
— **retrieval** [ri'tri:vəl] *n* : recuperación
f — **retriever** [ri'tri:vər] *n* : perro *m* cobrador

retroactive [,retro'æktiv] *adj* : retroactivo

retrospect ['retrə,spekt] *n* **in ~ :** miran-
do hacia atrás — **retrospective** [,retrə-
'spektiv] *adj* : retrospectivo

return [ri'tərn] *vi* **1 :** volver, regresar **2**
REAPPEAR : reaparecer — *vt* **1 :** devolver **2** YIELD : producir — **~** *n* **1**
: regreso *m*, vuelta *f* **2 :** devolución *f*
(de algo prestado) **3** YIELD
: rendimiento *m* **4 in ~ for :** a cambio
de **5** *or* **tax ~ :** declaración *f* de impuestos — **~** *adj* : de vuelta

reunite [,ri:ju'nait] *vt* **-nited; -niting** : reunir — **reunion** [ri'ju:njən] *n* : reunión *f*

revamp [,ri'væmp] *vt* : renovar

reveal [ri'vi:l] *vt* **1 :** revelar **2** SHOW
: dejar ver

revel ['revəl] *vi* **-eled** *or* **-elled; -eling** *or* **-elling** ~ **in** : deleitarse en

revelation [,revəˈleɪʃən] *n* : revelación *f*

revelry ['revəlri] *n, pl* **-ries** : jolgorio *m*, regocijos *mpl*

revenge [rɪˈvendʒ] *vt* **-venged; -venging** : vengar — ~ *n* 1 : venganza *f* 2 **take** ~ **on** : vengarse de

revenue ['revə,nuː, -,njuː] *n* : ingresos *mpl*

reverberate [rɪˈvərbəreɪt] *vi* **-ated; -ating** : retumbar, resonar

reverence ['revərənts] *n* : reverencia *f*, veneración *f* — **revere** [rɪˈvɪr] *vt* **-vered; -vering** : venerar — **reverend** ['revərənd] *adj* : reverendo — **reverent** ['revərənt] *adj* : reverente

reverie ['revəri] *n, pl* **-eries** : ensueño *m*

reverse [rɪˈvərs] *adj* : inverso, contrario — ~ *v* **-versed; -versing** *vt* 1 : invertir 2 : cambiar (una política), revocar (una decisión) 3 : dar marcha atrás a (un automóvil) — *vi* : invertirse — ~ *n* 1 BACK : dorso *m*, revés *m* 2 *or* ~ **gear** : marcha *f* atrás 3 **the** ~ : lo contrario — **reversible** [rɪˈvərsəbəl] *adj* : reversible — **reversal** ['revərsəl] *n* 1 : inversión *f* 2 CHANGE : cambio *m* total 3 SETBACK : revés *m* — **revert** [rɪˈvərt] *vi* : revertir

review [rɪˈvjuː] *n* 1 : revisión *f* 2 OVERVIEW : resumen *m* 3 CRITIQUE : reseña *f*, crítica *f* 4 : repaso *m* (para un examen) — ~ *vt* 1 EXAMINE : examinar 2 : repasar (una lección) 3 CRITIQUE : reseñar — **reviewer** [rɪˈvjuːər] *n* : crítico *m*, -ca *f*

revile [rɪˈvaɪl] *vt* **-viled; -viling** : injuriar

revise [rɪˈvaɪz] *vt* **-vised; -vising** 1 : modificar (una política, etc.) 2 : revisar, corregir (una publicación) — **revision** [rɪˈvɪʒən] *n* : corrección *f*, modificación *f*

revive [rɪˈvaɪv] *v* **-vived; -viving** *vt* 1 : reanimar, reactivar 2 : resucitar (a una persona) 3 RESTORE : restablecer — *vi* 1 : reanimarse, reactivarse 2 COME TO : volver en sí — **revival** [rɪˈvaɪvəl] *n* : reanimación *f*, reactivación *f*

revoke [rɪˈvoːk] *vt* **-voked; -voking** : revocar

revolt [rɪˈvoːlt] *vi* : rebelarse, sublevarse — *vt* : dar asco a — ~ *n* : revuelta *f*, sublevación *f* — **revolting** [rɪˈvoːltɪŋ] *adj* : asqueroso

revolution [,revəˈluːʃən] *n* : revolución *f* — **revolutionary** [,revəˈluːʃənˌeri] *adj* : revolucionario — ~ *n, pl* **-aries** : revolucionario *m*, -ria *f* — **revolutionize** [,revəˈluːʃənˌaɪz] *vt* **-ized; -izing** : revolucionar

revolve [rɪˈvɑlv] *v* **-volved; -volving** *vt* : hacer girar — *vi* : girar

revolver [rɪˈvɑlvər] *n* : revólver *m*

revue [rɪˈvjuː] *n* : revista *f* (teatral)

revulsion [rɪˈvʌlʃən] *n* : repugnancia *f*

reward [rɪˈword] *vt* : recompensar — ~ *n* : recompensa *f*

rewrite [,riːˈraɪt] *vt* **-wrote; -written; -writing** : volver a escribir

rhetoric ['retərɪk] *n* : retórica *f* — **rhetorical** [rɪˈtorɪkəl] *adj* : retórico

rheumatism ['ruːməˌtɪzəm, 'ru-] *n* : reumatismo *m* — **rheumatic** [rʊˈmætɪk] *adj* : reumático

rhino ['raɪ,noː] *n, pl* **-no** *or* **-nos** → **rhinoceros** — **rhinoceros** [raɪˈnɑsərəs] *n, pl* **-noceroses** *or* **-noceros** *or* **-noceri** [-,raɪ] : rinoceronte *m*

rhubarb ['ruː,bɑrb] *n* : ruibarbo *m*

rhyme ['raɪm] *n* 1 : rima *f* 2 VERSE : verso *m* (en rima) — ~ *vi* **rhymed; rhyming** : rimar

rhythm ['rɪðəm] *n* : ritmo *m* — **rhythmic** ['rɪðmɪk] *or* **rhythmical** [-mɪkəl] *adj* : rítmico

rib ['rɪb] *n* : costilla *f* — ~ *vt* TEASE : tomar el pelo a

ribbon ['rɪbən] *n* : cinta *f*

rice ['raɪs] *n* : arroz *m*

rich ['rɪtʃ] *adj* 1 : rico 2 ~ **foods** : comidas *fpl* pesadas — **riches** ['rɪtʃəz] *npl* : riquezas *fpl* — **richness** ['rɪtʃnəs] *n* : riqueza *f*

rickety ['rɪkəti] *adj* : desvencijado, destartalado

ricochet ['rɪkəˌʃeɪ, -ˌʃet] *n* : rebote *m* — ~ *vi* **-cheted** [-ˌʃeɪd] *or* **-chetted** [-ˌʃetəd]; **-cheting** [-ˌʃeɪŋ] *or* **-chetting** [-ˌʃetɪŋ] : rebotar

rid ['rɪd] *vt* **rid; ridding** 1 : librar 2 **get** ~ **of** : deshacerse de — **riddance** ['rɪdənts] *n* **good** ~! : ¡adiós y buen viaje!

riddle¹ ['rɪdəl] *n* : acertijo *m*, adivinanza *f*

riddle² *vt* **-dled; -dling** 1 : acribillar 2 **riddled with** : lleno de

ride ['raɪd] *v* **rode** ['roːd]; **ridden** ['rɪdən]; **riding** *vt* 1 : montar (a caballo, en bicicleta), ir (en autobús, etc.) 2 TRAVERSE : recorrer — *vi* 1 *or* ~ **horseback** : montar a caballo 2 : ir (en auto, etc.) — ~ *n* 1 : paseo *m*, vuelta *f* 2 : aparato *m* (en un parque de diversiones) — **rider** ['raɪdər] *n* 1 : jinete *mf* (a caballo) 2 CYCLIST : ciclista *mf*, motociclista *mf*

ridge ['rɪdʒ] *n* : cadena *f* (de montañas)

ridiculous [rəˈdɪkjələs] *adj* : ridículo — **ridicule** ['rɪdəˌkjuːl] *n* : burlas *fpl* — ~ *vt* **-culed; -culing** : ridiculizar

rife ['raɪf] *adj* **1** : extendido **2 be ~ with** : estar plagado de

rifle[1] ['raɪfəl] *vi* **-fled; -fling ~ through** : revolver

rifle[2] *n* : rifle *m*, fusil *m*

rift ['rɪft] *n* **1** : grieta *f* **2** : ruptura *f* (entre personas)

rig[1] ['rɪg] *vt* : amañar (una elección)

rig[2] *vt* **rigged; rigging 1** : aparejar (un barco) **2** EQUIP : equipar **3** *or* ~ **out** DRESS : vestir **4** *or* ~ **up** CONSTRUCT : construir — ~ *n* **1** : aparejo *m* (de un barco) **2** *or* **oil** ~ : plataforma *f* petrolífera — **rigging** ['rɪgɪŋ, -gən] *n* : aparejo *m*

right ['raɪt] *adj* **1** JUST : bueno, justo **2** CORRECT : correcto **3** APPROPRIATE : apropiado, adecuado **4** STRAIGHT : recto **5 be ~** : tener razón **6** → **right–hand** — ~ *n* **1** GOOD : bien *m* **2** ENTITLEMENT : derecho *m* **3 on the ~** : a la derecha **4** *or* ~ **side** : derecha *f* — ~ *adv* **1** WELL : bien **2** PRECISELY : justo **3** DIRECTLY : derecho **4** IMMEDI-ATELY : inmediatamente **5** COMPLETELY : completamente **6** *or* **to the ~** : a la derecha — ~ *vt* **1** STRAIGHTEN : ende-rezar **2** ~ **a wrong** : reparar un daño — **right angle** *n* : ángulo *m* recto — **righteous** ['raɪtʃəs] *adj* : recto, hon-rado — **rightful** ['raɪtfəl] *adj* : legítimo — **right–hand** ['raɪt'hænd] *adj* : dere-cho — **right–handed** ['raɪt'hændəd] *adj* : diestro — **rightly** ['raɪtli] *adv* **1** : justamente **2** CORRECTLY : correcta-mente — **right–wing** ['raɪt'wɪŋ] *adj* : derechista

rigid ['rɪdʒɪd] *adj* : rígido

rigor *or Brit* **rigour** ['rɪgər] *n* : rigor *m* — **rigorous** ['rɪgərəs] *adj* : riguroso

rim ['rɪm] *n* **1** EDGE : borde *m* **2** : llanta *f* (de una rueda) **3** : montura *f* (de ante-ojos)

rind ['raɪnd] *n* : corteza *f*

ring[1] ['rɪŋ] *v* **rang** ['ræŋ]; **rung** ['rʌŋ]; **ringing** *vi* **1** : sonar (dícese de un tim-bre, etc.) **2** RESOUND : resonar — *vt* **1** : tocar (un timbre, etc.) — ~ *n* **1** : toque *m* (de un timbre, etc.) **2** CALL : llamada *f* (por teléfono)

ring[2] *n* **1** : anillo *m*, sortija *f* **2** BAND, HOOP : aro *m* **3** CIRCLE : círculo *m* **4** *or* **boxing ~** : cuadrilátero *m* **5** NET-WORK : red *f* — ~ *vt* **1** : cercar, rodear — **ringleader** ['rɪŋ,li:dər] *n* : cabecilla *mf*

ringlet ['rɪŋlət] *n* : rizo *m*, bucle *m*

rink ['rɪŋk] *n* : pista *f* (de patinaje)

rinse ['rɪns] *vt* **rinsed; rinsing** : enjua-gar — ~ *n* : enjuague *m*

riot ['raɪət] *n* : disturbio *m* — ~ *vi* : causar disturbios — **rioter** ['raɪətər] *n* : alborotador *m*, -dora *f*

rip ['rɪp] *v* **ripped; ripping** *vt* **1** : rasgar, desgarrar **2** ~ **off** : arrancar — *vi* : rasgarse — ~ *n* : rasgón *m*, desgar-rón *m*

ripe ['raɪp] *adj* **riper; ripest 1** : maduro **2** ~ **for** : listo por — **ripen** ['raɪpən] *v* : madurar — **ripeness** ['raɪpnəs] *n* : madurez *f*

rip–off ['rɪp,ɔf] *n* : timo *m fam*

ripple ['rɪpəl] *v* **-pled; -pling** *vi* : rizarse (dícese de agua) — *vt* : rizar — ~ *n* : onda *f*, rizo *m*

rise ['raɪz] *vi* **rose** ['ro:z]; **risen** ['rɪzən]; **rising 1** GET UP : levantarse **2** : salir (dícese del sol, etc.) **3** ASCEND : subir **4** INCREASE : aumentar **5** ~ **up** REBEL : sublevarse — ~ *n* **1** ASCENT : subida *f* **2** INCREASE : aumento *m* **3** SLOPE : cuesta *f* — **riser** ['raɪzər] *n* **1 early ~** : madrugador *m*, -dora *f* **2 late ~** : dormilón *m*, -lona *f*

risk ['rɪsk] *n* : riesgo *m* — ~ *vt* : arries-gar — **risky** ['rɪski] *adj* **riskier; -est** : arriesgado, riesgoso *Lat*

rite ['raɪt] *n* : rito *m* — **ritual** ['rɪtʃuəl] *adj* : ritual — ~ *n* : ritual *m*

rival ['raɪvəl] *n* : rival *mf* — ~ *adj* : rival — ~ *vt* **-valed** *or* **-valled; -valing** *or* **-valling** : rivalizar con — **rivalry** ['raɪvəlri] *n, pl* **-ries** : rivalidad *f*

river ['rɪvər] *n* : río *m*

rivet ['rɪvət] *n* : remache *m* — ~ *vt* **1** : remachar **2** FIX : fijar (los ojos, etc.) **3 be ~ed by** : estar fascinado con

roach ['ro:tʃ] → **cockroach**

road ['ro:d] *n* **1** : carretera *f* **2** STREET : calle *f* **3** PATH : camino *m* — **road-block** ['ro:d,blak] *n* : control *m* — **roadside** ['ro:d,saɪd] *n* : borde *m* de la carretera — **roadway** ['ro:d,weɪ] *n* : carretera *f*

roam ['ro:m] *vi* : vagar — *vt* : vagar por

roar ['ror] *vi* **1** : rugir **2** ~ **with laugh-ter** : reírse a carcajadas — *vt* : decir a gritos — ~ *n* **1** : rugido *m* (de un ani-mal), estruendo *m* (de un avión, etc.)

roast ['ro:st] *vt* : asar (carne, etc.), tostar (café, etc.) — *vi* : asarse — ~ *n* : asado *m* — ~ *adj* : asado — **roast beef** *n* : rosbif *m*

rob ['rab] *v* **robbed; robbing** *vt* **1** : robar **2** ~ **of** : privar de — *vi* : robar — **rob-ber** ['rabər] *n* : ladrón *m*, -drona *f* — **robbery** ['rabəri] *n, pl* **-beries** : robo *m*

robe ['ro:b] *n* **1** : toga *f* (de un magistra-do, etc.) **2** → **bathrobe**

robin ['rabən] *n* : petirrojo *m*

robot ['roːˌbɑt, -bət] *n* : robot *m*

robust [roˈbʌst, 'roːˌbʌst] *adj* : robusto

rock[1] ['rɑk] *vt* 1 : acunar (a un niño), mecer (una cuna) 2 SHAKE : sacudir — *vi* : mecerse — **∼** *n or* **∼ music** : música *f* rock

rock[2] *n* 1 : roca *f* (sustancia) 2 BOULDER : peña *f*, peñasco *m* 3 STONE : piedra *f*

rocket ['rɑkət] *n* : cohete *m*

rocking chair *n* : mecedora *f*

rocky ['rɑki] *adj* **rockier; -est** 1 : rocoso 2 SHAKY : tambaleante

rod ['rɑd] *n* 1 : varilla *f* 2 *or* **fishing ∼** : caña *f* de pescar

rode → **ride**

rodent ['roːdənt] *n* : roedor *m*

rodeo ['roːdiˌoː, roˈdeɪoː] *n*, *pl* **-deos** : rodeo *m*

roe ['roː] *n* : hueva *f*

rogue ['roːg] *n* : pícaro *m*, -ra *f*

role ['roːl] *n* : papel *m*

roll ['roːl] *n* 1 : rollo *m* (de película, etc.) 2 LIST : lista *f* 3 : redoble *m* (de un tambor) 4 SWAYING : balanceo *m* 5 BUN : pancito *m Lat*, panecillo *m Spain* — **∼** *vt* 1 : hacer rodar 2 *or* **∼ out** : estirar (masa) 3 **∼ up** : enrollar (papel, etc.), arremangar (una manga) — *vi* 1 : rodar 2 SWAY : balancearse 3 **∼ around** : revolcarse 4 **∼ over** : darse la vuelta — **roller** ['roːlər] *n* 1 : rodillo *m* 2 CURLER : rulo *m* — **roller coaster** ['roːlərˌkoːstər] *n* : montaña *f* rusa — **roller-skate** ['roːlərˌskeɪt] *vi* **-skated; -skating** : patinar (sobre ruedas) — **roller skate** *n* : patín *m* (de ruedas)

Roman ['roːmən] *adj* : romano — **Roman Catholic** *adj* : católico

romance [roˈmænts, 'roːˌmænts] *n* 1 : novela *f* romántica 2 AFFAIR : romance *m*

Romanian [ruˈmeɪniən, ro-] *adj* : rumano — **∼** *n* : rumano *m* (idioma)

romantic [roˈmæntɪk] *adj* : romántico

romp ['rɑmp] *n* : retozo *m* — **∼** *vi* : retozar

roof ['ruːf, 'rʊf] *n*, *pl* **roofs** ['ruːfs, 'rʊfs; 'ruːvz, 'ʊvz] 1 : tejado *m*, techo *m* 2 **∼ of the mouth** : paladar *m* — **roofing** ['ruːfɪŋ, 'rʊfɪŋ] *n* : techumbre *f* — **rooftop** ['ruːfˌtɑp, 'rʊf-] *n* : tejado *m*, techo *m*

rook[1] ['rʊk] *n* : grajo *m* (ave)

rook[2] *n* : torre *f* (en ajedrez)

rookie ['rʊki] *n* : novato *m*, -ta *f*

room ['ruːm, 'rʊm] *n* 1 : cuarto *m*, habitación *f* 2 BEDROOM : dormitorio *m* 3 SPACE : espacio *m* 4 OPPORTUNITY : posibilidad *f* — **roommate** ['ruːmˌmeɪt, 'rʊm-] *n* : compañero *m*, -ra *f* de

cuarto — **roomy** ['ruːmi, 'rʊmi] *adj* **roomier; -est** : espacioso

roost ['ruːst] *n* : percha *f* — **∼** *vi* : posarse — **rooster** ['ruːstər, 'rʊs-] *n* : gallo *m*

root[1] ['ruːt, 'rʊt] *n* : raíz *f* — **∼** *vt* **∼ out** : extirpar

root[2] *vi* **∼ around in** : hurgar en

root[3] *vi* **∼ for** SUPPORT : alentar

rope ['roːp] *n* : cuerda *f* — **∼** *vt* **roped; roping** 1 : atar (con cuerda) 2 **∼ off** : acordonar

rosary ['roːzəri] *n*, *pl* **-ries** : rosario *m*

rose[1] → **rise**

rose[2] ['roːz] *n* : rosa *f* (flor), rosa *m* (color) — **∼** *adj* : rosa — **rosebush** ['roːzˌbʊʃ] *n* : rosal *m*

rosemary ['roːzˌmeri] *n*, *pl* **-maries** : romero *m*

Rosh Hashanah [ˌrɑʃhɑˈʃɑnə, ˌroːʃ-] *n* : el Año Nuevo judío

roster ['rɑstər] *n* : lista *f*

rostrum ['rɑstrəm] *n*, *pl* **-tra** *or* **-trums** [-trə] : tribuna *f*

rosy ['roːzi] *adj* **rosier; -est** 1 : sonrosado 2 PROMISING : halagüeño

rot ['rɑt] *v* **rotted; rotting** *vi* : pudrirse — *vt* : pudrir — **∼** *n* : putrefacción *f*

rotary ['roːtəri] *adj* : rotativo — **∼** *n* : rotonda *f*, glorieta *f Spain*

rotate ['roːˌteɪt] *v* **-tated; -tating** *vi* : girar — *vt* 1 : girar 2 ALTERNATE : alternar — **rotation** [roˈteɪʃən] *n* : rotación *f*

rote ['roːt] *n* **by ∼** : de memoria

rotor ['roːtər] *n* : rotor *m*

rotten ['rɑtən] *adj* 1 : podrido 2 BAD : malo

rouge ['ruːʒ, 'ruːdʒ] *n* : colorete *m*

rough ['rʌf] *adj* 1 COARSE : áspero 2 RUGGED : accidentado 3 CHOPPY : agitado 4 DIFFICULT : duro 5 FORCEFUL : brusco 6 APPROXIMATE : aproximado 7 UNREFINED : tosco 8 **∼ draft** : borrador *m* — **∼** *vt* 1 **∼ roughen** 2 **∼ up** BEAT : dar una paliza a — **roughage** ['rʌfɪdʒ] *n* : fibra *f* — **roughen** ['rʌfən] *vt* : poner áspero — *vi* : ponerse áspero — **roughly** ['rʌfli] *adv* 1 : bruscamente 2 ABOUT : aproximadamente — **roughness** ['rʌfnəs] *n* COARSENESS : aspereza *f*

roulette [ruːˈlet] *n* : ruleta *f*

round ['raʊnd] *adj* : redondo — **∼** *adv* → **around** — **∼** *n* 1 : círculo *m* 2 : ronda *f* (de bebidas, negociaciones, etc.) 3 : asalto *m* (en boxeo), vuelta *f* (en juegos) 4 **∼ of applause** : aplauso *m* 5 **∼s** *npl* : visitas *fpl* (de un médico), rondas *fpl* (de un policía, etc.) — **∼** *vt* 1 TURN : doblar 2 **∼ off**

: redondear **3 ~ off** or **~ out** COMPLETE : rematar **4 ~ up** GATHER : reunir (personas), rodear (ganado) — **~ prep → around — roundabout** ['raʊndə,baʊt] *adj* : indirecto — **round–trip** ['raʊnd'trɪp] *n* : viaje *m* de ida y vuelta — **roundup** ['raʊndˌʌp] *n* : rodeo *m* (de animales), redada *f* (de delincuentes, etc.)

rouse ['raʊz] *vt* **roused; rousing 1** AWAKEN : despertar **2** EXCITE : excitar

rout ['raʊt] *n* : derrota *f* aplastante — **~** *vt* : derrotar

route ['ruːt, 'raʊt] *n* **1** : ruta *f* **2** or **delivery ~** : recorrido *m*

routine [ruː'tiːn] *n* : rutina *f* — **~** *adj* : rutinario

rove ['roːv] *v* **roved; roving** *vi* : errar, vagar — *vt* : errar por

row[1] ['roː] *vt* **1** : llevar a remo **2 ~ a boat** : remar — *vi* : remar

row[2] *n* **1** : fila *f* (de gente o asientos), hilera *f* (de casas, etc.) **2 in a ~** SUCCESSIVELY : seguido

row[3] ['raʊ] *n* **1** RACKET : bulla *f* **2** QUARREL : pelea *f*

rowboat ['roːˌboːt] *n* : bote *m* de remos

rowdy ['raʊdi] *adj* **-dier; -est** : escandaloso, alborotador — **~** *n, pl* **-dies** : alborotador *m*, -dora *f*

royal ['rɔɪəl] *adj* : real — **royalty** ['rɔɪəlti] *n, pl* **-ties 1** : realeza *f* **2 royalties** *npl* : derechos *mpl* de autor

rub ['rʌb] *v* **rubbed; rubbing** *vt* **1** : frotar **2** CHAFE : rozar **3 ~ in** : aplicar frotando — *vi* **1 ~ against** : rozar **2 ~ off** : salir (al frotar) — **~** *n* : frotamiento *m*

rubber ['rʌbər] *n* **1** : goma *f*, caucho *m* **2 ~s** *npl* : chanclos *mpl* — **rubber band** *n* : goma *f* (elástica) — **rubber stamp** *n* : sello *m* (de goma) — **rubbery** ['rʌbəri] *adj* : gomoso

rubbish ['rʌbɪʃ] *n* **1** : basura *f* **2** NONSENSE : tonterías *fpl*

rubble ['rʌbəl] *n* : escombros *mpl*

ruby ['ruːbi] *n, pl* **-bies** : rubí *m*

rudder ['rʌdər] *n* : timón *m*

ruddy ['rʌdi] *adj* **-dier; -est** : rubicundo

rude ['ruːd] *adj* **ruder; rudest 1** IMPOLITE : grosero, mal educado **2** ABRUPT : brusco — **rudely** ['ruːdli] *adv* : groseramente — **rudeness** ['ruːdnəs] *n* : mala educación *f*

rudiment ['ruːdəmənt] *n* : rudimento *m* — **rudimentary** [ˌruːdə'mentəri] *adj* : rudimentario

rue ['ruː] *vt* **rued; ruing** : lamentar — **rueful** ['ruːfəl] *adj* : triste, arrepentido

ruffle ['rʌfəl] *vt* **-fled; -fling 1** : des-

peinar (pelo), erizar (plumas) **2** VEX : alterar, contrariar — **~** *n* : volante *m* (de un vestido, etc.)

rug ['rʌg] *n* : alfombra *f*, tapete *m*

rugged ['rʌgəd] *adj* **1** : escabroso (dícese del terreno), escarpado (dícese de montañas) **2** HARSH : duro **3** STURDY : fuerte

ruin ['ruːən] *n* : ruina *f* — *vt* : arruinar

rule ['ruːl] *n* **1** : regla *f* **2** CONTROL : dominio *m* **3 as a ~** : por lo general — **~** *v* **ruled; ruling** *vt* **1** GOVERN : gobernar **2** : fallar (dícese de un juez) **3 ~ out** : descartar — *vi* : gobernar, reinar — **ruler** ['ruːlər] *n* **1** : gobernante *mf*; soberano *m*, -na *f* **2** : regla *f* (para medir) — **ruling** ['ruːlɪŋ] *n* VERDICT : fallo *m*

rum ['rʌm] *n* : ron *m*

Rumanian [ru'meɪniən] → **Romanian**

rumble ['rʌmbəl] *vi* **-bled; -bling 1** : retumbar **2** : hacer ruidos (dícese del estómago) — **~** *n* : retumbo *m*, estruendo *m*

rummage ['rʌmɪdʒ] *vi* **-maged; -maging** : hurgar

rumor ['ruːmər] *n* : rumor *m* — **~** *vt* **be ~ed** : rumorearse

rump ['rʌmp] *n* **1** : grupa *f* (de un animal) **2 ~ steak** : filete *m* de cadera

rumpus ['rʌmpəs] *n* : lío *m*, jaleo *m fam*

run ['rʌn] *v* **ran** ['ræn]; **run; running** *vi* **1** : correr **2** FUNCTION : funcionar **3** LAST : durar **4** : desteñir (dícese de colores) **5** EXTEND : correr, extenderse **6** : presentarse (como candidato) **7 ~ away** : huir **8 ~ into** ENCOUNTER : tropezar con **9 ~ into** HIT : chocar contra **10 ~ late** : ir retrasado **11 ~ out of** : quedarse sin **12 ~ over** : atropellar — *vt* **1** : correr **2** OPERATE : hacer funcionar **3** : hacer correr (agua) **4** MANAGE : dirigir **5 ~ a fever** : tener fiebre — **~** *n* **1** : carrera *f* **2** TRIP : viaje *m*, paseo *m* (en coche) **3** SERIES : serie *f* **4 in the long ~** : a la larga **5 in the short ~** : a corto plazo — **runaway** ['rʌnəˌweɪ] *n* : fugitivo *m*, -va *f* — **~** *adj* : fugitivo — **rundown** ['rʌnˌdaʊn] *n* : resumen *m* — **run–down** ['rʌn'daʊn] *adj* **1** : destartalado **2** EXHAUSTED : agotado

rung[1] → **ring**[1]

rung[2] ['rʌŋ] *n* : peldaño *m* (de una escalera, etc.)

runner ['rʌnər] *n* **1** : corredor *m*, -dora *f* **2** : patín *m* (de un trineo), riel *m* (de un cajón, etc.) — **runner–up** ['rʌnərˌʌp] *n, pl* **runners–up** : subcampeón *m*, -peona *f* — **running** ['rʌnɪŋ] *adj* **1**

FLOWING : corriente **2** CONTINUOUS : continuo **3** CONSECUTIVE : seguido
runt ['rʌnt] *n* : animal *m* más pequeño (de una camada)
runway ['rʌn,weɪ] *n* : pista *f* de aterrizaje
rupture ['rʌptʃər] *n* : ruptura *f* — ~ *v* **-tured; -turing** *vt* : romper — *vi* : reventar
rural ['rʊrəl] *adj* : rural
ruse ['ruːs, 'ruːz] *n* : ardid *m*
rush¹ ['rʌʃ] *n* : junco *m* (planta)
rush² *vi* : ir de prisa — *vt* **1** : apresurar, apurar **2** ATTACK : asaltar **3** : llevar rápidamente (al hospital, etc.) — ~ *n* **1** : prisa *f*, apuro *m* **2** : ráfaga *f* (de aire), torrente *m* (de agua) — ~ *adj* : ur-

gente — **rush hour** *n* : hora *f* punta
russet ['rʌsət] *n* : color *m* rojizo
Russian ['rʌʃən] *adj* : ruso — ~ *n* : ruso *m* (idioma)
rust ['rʌst] *n* : herrumbre *f*, óxido *m* — ~ *vi* : oxidarse — *vt* : oxidar
rustic ['rʌstɪk] *adj* : rústico
rustle ['rʌsəl] *v* **-tled; -tling** *vt* **1** : hacer susurrar **2** : robar (ganado) — *vi* : susurrar — ~ *n* : susurro *m*
rusty ['rʌsti] *adj* **rustier, -est** : oxidado
rut ['rʌt] *n* **1** : surco *m* **2 be in a** ~ : ser esclavo de la rutina
ruthless ['ruːθləs] *adj* : despiadado, cruel
rye ['raɪ] *n* : centeno *m*

S

s ['ɛs] *n*, *pl* **s's** *or* **ss** ['ɛsəz] : s *f*, decimonovena letra del alfabeto inglés
Sabbath ['sæbəθ] *n* **1** : sábado *m* (día santo judío) **2** : domingo *m* (día santo cristiano)
sabotage ['sæbə,tɑʒ] *n* : sabotaje *m* — ~ *vt* **-taged; -taging** : sabotear
saccharin ['sækərən] *n* : sacarina *f*
sack ['sæk] *n* : saco *m* — ~ *vt* **1** FIRE : despedir **2** PLUNDER : saquear
sacrament ['sækrəmənt] *n* : sacramento *m*
sacred ['seɪkrəd] *adj* : sagrado
sacrifice ['sækrə,faɪs] *n* : sacrificio *m* — ~ *vt* **-ficed; -ficing** : sacrificar
sacrilege ['sækrəlɪdʒ] *n* : sacrilegio *m* — **sacrilegious** [,sækrə'lɪdʒəs, -'liː-] *adj* : sacrílego
sad ['sæd] *adj* **sadder; saddest** : triste — **sadden** ['sædən] *vt* : entristecer
saddle ['sædəl] *n* : silla *f* (de montar) — ~ *vt* **-dled; -dling 1** : ensillar (un caballo, etc.) **2** ~ **s.o. with sth** : cargar a algn con algo
sadistic [sə'dɪstɪk] *adj* : sádico
sadness ['sædnəs] *n* : tristeza *f*
safari [sə'fɑri, -'fær-] *n* : safari *m*
safe ['seɪf] *adj* **safer; safest 1** : seguro **2** UNHARMED : ileso **3** CAREFUL : prudente **4** ~ **and sound** : sano y salvo — ~ *n* : caja *f* fuerte — **safeguard** ['seɪf,gɑrd] *n* : salvaguarda *f* — ~ *vt* : salvaguardar — **safely** ['seɪfli] *adv* **1** : sin peligro **2 arrive** ~ : llegar sin novedad — **safety** ['seɪfti] *n*, *pl* **-ties** : seguridad *f* — **safety belt** *n* : cinturón *m* de seguridad — **safety pin** *n* : imperdible *m*

saffron ['sæfrən] *n* : azafrán *m*
sag ['sæg] *vi* **sagged; sagging 1** : combarse **2** GIVE : aflojarse **3** FLAG : flaquear
saga ['sɑgə, 'sæ-] *n* : saga *f*
sage¹ ['seɪdʒ] *n* : salvia *f* (planta)
sage² *adj* **sager; -est** : sabio — ~ *n* : sabio *m*, -bia *f*
said → **say**
sail ['seɪl] *n* **1** : vela *f* (de un barco) **2 go for a** ~ : salir a navegar **3 set** ~ : zarpar — ~ *vi* : navegar — *vt* : gobernar (un barco), navegar (el mar) — **sailboat** ['seɪl,boːt] *n* : velero *m* — **sailor** ['seɪlər] *n* : marinero *m*
saint ['seɪnt, *before a name* ,seɪnt *or* sənt] *n* : santo *m*, -ta *f* — **saintly** ['seɪntli] *adj* **saintlier, -est** : santo
sake ['seɪk] *n* **1 for goodness'** ~! : ¡por Dios! **2 for the** ~ **of** : por (el bien de)
salad ['sæləd] *n* : ensalada *f*
salamander ['sælə,mændər] *n* : salamandra *f*
salami [sə'lɑmi] *n* : salami *m*
salary ['sæləri] *n*, *pl* **-ries** : sueldo *m*
sale ['seɪl] *n* **1** : venta *f* **2 for** ~ : se vende **3 on** ~ : de rebaja — **salesman** ['seɪlzmən] *n*, *pl* **-men** [-mən, -,mɛn] : vendedor *m*, dependiente *m* — **saleswoman** ['seɪlz,wʊmən] *n*, *pl* **-women** [-,wɪmən] : vendedora *f*, dependienta *f*
salient ['seɪljənt] *adj* : saliente
saliva [sə'laɪvə] *n* : saliva *f*
sallow ['sæloː] *adj* : amarillento, cetrino
salmon ['sæmən] *ns* & *pl* : salmón *m*
salon [sə'lɑn, 'sæ,lɑn] *n* → **beauty salon**

saloon [sə'lu:n] *n* : bar *m*

salsa ['sɔlsə, 'sɑl-] *n* : salsa *f* mexicana, salsa *f* picante

salt ['sɔlt] *n* : sal *f* — ~ *vt* : salar — **saltwater** ['sɔlt,wɔtər, -,wɑ-] *adj* : de agua salada — **salty** ['sɔlti] *adj* **saltier; -est** : salado

salute [sə'lu:t] *v* **-luted; -luting** *vt* : saludar — *vi* : hacer un saludo — ~ *n* : saludo *m*

salvage ['sælvɪdʒ] *n* : salvamento *m* — ~ *vt* **-vaged; -vaging** : salvar

salvation [sæl'veɪʃən] *n* : salvación *f*

salve ['sæv, 'sav] *n* : ungüento *m*

same ['seɪm] *adj* **1** : mismo **2 be the ~ (as)** : ser igual (que) **3 the ~ thing (as)** : la misma cosa (que) — ~ *pron* **1 all the ~** : igual **2 the ~** : lo mismo — ~ *adv* **the ~** : igual

sample ['sæmpəl] *n* : muestra *f* — ~ *vt* **-pled; -pling** : probar

sanatorium [,sænə'toriəm] *n, pl* **-riums** *or* **-ria** [-iə] : sanatorio *m*

sanctify ['sæŋktə,faɪ] *vt* **-fied; -fying** : santificar

sanction *n* ['sæŋkʃən] : sanción *f* — ~ *vt* : sancionar

sanctity ['sæŋktəti] *n, pl* **-ties** : santidad *f*

sanctuary ['sæŋktʃu,eri] *n, pl* **-aries** : santuario *m*

sand ['sænd] *n* : arena *f* — ~ *vt* : lijar (madera)

sandal ['sændəl] *n* : sandalia *f*

sandpaper ['sænd,peɪpər] *n* : papel *m* de lija — ~ *vt* : lijar

sandwich ['sænd,wɪtʃ] *n* : sandwich *m*, bocadillo *m* Spain — ~ *vt* ~ **between** : meter entre

sandy ['sændi] *adj* **sandier; -est** : arenoso

sane ['seɪn] *adj* **saner; sanest 1** : cuerdo **2** SENSIBLE : sensato

sang → **sing**

sanitarium [,sænə'teriəm] *n, pl* **-iums** *or* **-ia** [-iə] → **sanatorium**

sanitary ['sænəteri] *adj* **1** : sanitario **2** HYGIENIC : higiénico — **sanitary napkin** *n* : compresa *f* (higiénica) — **sanitation** [,sænə'teɪʃən] *n* : sanidad *f*

sanity ['sænəti] *n* : cordura *f*

sank → **sink**

Santa Claus ['sæntə,klɔz] *n* : Papá *m* Noel

sap¹ ['sæp] *n* **1** : savia *f* (de una planta) **2** SUCKER : inocentón *m*, -tona *f*

sap² *vt* **sapped; sapping** : minar (la fuerza, etc.)

sapphire ['sæ,faɪr] *n* : zafiro *m*

sarcasm ['sɑr,kæzəm] *n* : sarcasmo *m* — **sarcastic** [sɑr'kæstɪk] *adj* : sarcástico

sardine [sɑr'di:n] *n* : sardina *f*

sash ['sæʃ] *n* : faja *f* (de un vestido), fajín *m* (de un uniforme)

sat → **sit**

satanic [sə'tænɪk, seɪ-] *adj* : satánico

satchel ['sætʃəl] *n* : cartera *f*

satellite ['sætə,laɪt] *n* : satélite *m*

satin ['sætən] *n* : raso *m*

satire ['sæ,taɪr] *n* : sátira *f* — **satiric** [sə-'tɪrɪk] *or* **satirical** [-ɪkəl] *adj* : satírico

satisfaction [,sætəs'fækʃən] *n* : satisfacción *f* — **satisfactory** [,sætəs'fæktəri] *adj* : satisfactorio — **satisfy** ['sætəs,faɪ] *v* **-fied; -fying** *vt* **1** : satisfacer **2** CONVINCE : convencer — **satisfying** *adj* : satisfactorio

saturate ['sætʃə,reɪt] *vt* **-rated; -rating 1** : saturar **2** DRENCH : empapar — **saturation** [,sætʃə'reɪʃən] *n* : saturación *f*

Saturday ['sætər,deɪ, -di] *n* : sábado *m*

Saturn ['sætərn] *n* : Saturno *m*

sauce ['sɔs] *n* : salsa *f* — **saucepan** ['sɔs,pæn] *n* : cacerola *f* — **saucer** ['sɔsər] *n* : platillo *m* — **saucy** ['sɔsi] *adj* **saucier; -est** IMPUDENT : descarado

sauna ['sɔnə, 'saunə] *n* : sauna *mf*

saunter ['sɔntər, 'san-] *vi* : pasear

sausage ['sɔsɪdʒ] *n* : salchicha *f*

sauté [sɔ'teɪ, so:-] *vt* **-téed** *or* **-téd; -téing** : saltear, sofreír

savage ['sævɪdʒ] *adj* : salvaje, feroz — ~ *n* : salvaje *mf* — **savagery** ['sævɪdʒri, -dʒəri] *n, pl* **-ries** : ferocidad *f*

save ['seɪv] *vt* **saved; saving 1** RESCUE : salvar **2** RESERVE : guardar **3** : ahorrar (dinero, tiempo, etc.) — ~ *prep* EXCEPT : salvo

savior ['seɪvjər] *n* : salvador *m*, -dora *f*

savor ['seɪvər] *vt* : saborear — **savory** ['seɪvəri] *adj* : sabroso

saw¹ → **see**

saw² ['sɔ] *n* : sierra *f* — ~ *vt* **sawed; sawed** *or* **sawn; sawing** : serrar — **sawdust** ['sɔ,dʌst] *n* : serrín *m*, aserrín *m*

saxophone ['sæksə,foɪn] *n* : saxofón *m*

say ['seɪ] *v* **said** ['sed]; **saying; says** ['sez] *vt* **1** : decir **2** INDICATE : marcar (dícese de relojes, etc.) — *vi* **1** : decir **2 that is to ~** : es decir — ~ *n, pl* **says** ['seɪz] **1 have no ~** : no tener ni voz ni voto **2 have one's ~** : dar su opinión — **saying** ['seɪŋ] *n* : refrán *m*

scab ['skæb] *n* **1** : costra *f* (en una herida) **2** STRIKEBREAKER : esquirol *mf*

scaffold ['skæfəld, -,foːld] *n* : andamio *m* (en construcción)

scald ['skɔld] *vt* : escaldar

scale[1] ['skeɪl] n : balanza f (para pesar)

scale[2] n : escama f (de un pez, etc.) — ~ vt **scaled; scaling** : escamar

scale[3] vt **scaled; scaling 1** CLIMB : escalar **2 ~ down** : reducir — ~ n : escala f (musical, salarial, etc.)

scallion ['skæljən] n : cebolleta f

scallop ['skɑləp, 'skæ-] n : vieira f

scalp ['skælp] n : cuero m cabelludo

scam ['skæm] n : estafa f, timo m fam

scamper ['skæmpər] vi ~ **away** : irse corriendo

scan ['skæn] vt **scanned; scanning 1** : escandir (versos) **2** EXAMINE : escudriñar **3** SKIM : echar un vistazo a **4** : escanear (en informática)

scandal ['skændəl] n **1** : escándalo m **2** GOSSIP : habladurías fpl — **scandalous** ['skændələs] adj : escandaloso

Scandinavian [,skændəˈneɪviən] adj : escandinavo

scant ['skænt] adj : escaso

scapegoat ['skeɪp,goːt] n : chivo m expiatorio

scar ['skɑr] n : cicatriz f — ~ v **scarred; scarring** vt : dejar una cicatriz en — vi : cicatrizar

scarce ['skers] adj **scarcer, -est** : escaso — **scarcely** ['skersli] adv : apenas — **scarcity** ['skersəti] n, pl **-ties** : escasez f

scare ['sker] vt **scared; scaring 1** : asustar **2 be ~d of** : tener miedo a — ~ n **1** FRIGHT : susto m **2** ALARM : pánico m — **scarecrow** ['sker,kroː] n : espantapájaros m, espantajo m

scarf ['skɑrf] n, pl **scarves** ['skɑrvz] or **scarfs 1** : bufanda f **2** KERCHIEF : pañuelo m

scarlet ['skɑrlət] adj : escarlata — **scarlet fever** n : escarlatina f

scary ['skeri] adj **scarier; -est** : que da miedo

scathing ['skeɪðɪŋ] adj : mordaz

scatter ['skætər] vt **1** STREW : esparcir **2** DISPERSE : dispersar — vi : dispersarse

scavenger ['skævəndʒər] n : carroñero m, -ra f (animal)

scenario [səˈnæri,oː, -ˈnɑr-] n, pl **-ios 1** : guión m (cinemático) **2 the worst-case ~** : el peor de los casos

scene ['siːn] n **1** : escena f **2 behind the ~s** : entre bastidores **3 make a ~** : armar un escándalo — **scenery** ['siːnəri] n, pl **-eries 1** : decorado m **2** LANDSCAPE : paisaje m — **scenic** ['siːnɪk] adj : pintoresco

scent ['sent] n **1** : aroma m **2** PERFUME : perfume m **3** TRAIL : rastro m — **scented** ['sentəd] adj : perfumado

sceptic ['skeptɪk] → **skeptic**

schedule ['ske,dʒuːl, -dʒəl, esp Brit 'ʃed-juːl] n **1** : programa m **2** TIMETABLE : horario m **3 behind ~** : atrasado, con retraso **4 on ~** : según lo previsto — ~ vt **-uled; -uling** : planear, programar

scheme ['skiːm] n **1** PLAN : plan m **2** PLOT : intriga f **3** DESIGN : esquema f — ~ vi **schemed; scheming** : intrigar

schism ['sɪzəm, 'skɪ-] n : cisma m

schizophrenia [,skɪtsəˈfriːniə, ,skɪzə-, -ˈfre-] n : esquizofrenia f — **schizophrenic** [,skɪtsəˈfrenɪk, ,skɪzə-] adj : esquizofrénico

scholar ['skɑlər] n : erudito m, -ta f — **scholarly** ['skɑlərli] adj : erudito — **scholarship** ['skɑlər,ʃɪp] n **1** : erudición f **2** GRANT : beca f

school[1] ['skuːl] n : banco m (de peces)

school[2] n **1** : escuela f **2** COLLEGE : universidad f **3** DEPARTMENT : facultad f — ~ vt : instruir — **schoolboy** ['skuːl,bɔɪ] n : colegial m — **schoolgirl** ['skuːl,gərl] n : colegiala f — **schoolteacher** ['skuːl,tiːtʃər] n → **teacher**

science ['saɪənts] n : ciencia f — **scientific** [,saɪənˈtɪfɪk] adj : científico — **scientist** ['saɪəntɪst] n : científico m, -ca f

scissors ['sɪzərz] npl : tijeras fpl

scoff ['skɑf] vi ~ **at** : burlarse de, mofarse de

scold ['skoːld] vt : regañar

scoop ['skuːp] n **1** : pala f **2** : noticia f exclusiva (en periodismo) — ~ vt **1** : sacar (con pala) **2 ~ out** : ahuecar **3 ~ up** : recoger

scoot ['skuːt] vi : ir rápidamente — **scooter** ['skuːtər] n **1** : patinete m **2 or motor ~** : escúter m

scope ['skoːp] n **1** RANGE : alcance m **2** OPPORTUNITY : posibilidades fpl

scorch ['skɔrtʃ] vt : chamuscar

score ['skor] n, pl **scores 1** : tanteo m (en deportes) **2** RATING : puntuación f **3** : partitura f (musical) **4 or ~** score TWENTY : veintena f **5 keep ~** : llevar la cuenta **6 on that ~** : en ese sentido — ~ v **scored; scoring** vt **1** : marcar, anotarse Lat (un tanto) **2** : sacar (una nota) — vi : marcar (en deportes)

scorn ['skɔrn] n : desdén m — ~ vt : desdeñar — **scornful** ['skɔrnfəl] adj : desdeñoso

scorpion ['skɔrpiən] n : alacrán m, escorpión m

Scot ['skɑt] n : escocés m, -cesa f — **Scotch** ['skɑtʃ] adj → **Scottish** — ~ n or ~ **whiskey** : whisky m escocés — **Scottish** ['skɑtɪʃ] adj : escocés

scoundrel ['skaʊndrəl] *n* : sinvergüenza *mf*

scour ['skaʊər] *vt* **1** SCRUB : fregar **2** SEARCH : registrar

scourge ['skərdʒ] *n* : azote *m*

scout ['skaʊt] *n* : explorador *m*, -dora *f*

scowl ['skaʊl] *vi* : fruncir el ceño — ~ *n* : ceño *m* fruncido

scram ['skræm] *vi* scrammed; scramming : largarse

scramble ['skræmbəl] *v* -bled; -bling *vi* **1** CLAMBER : trepar **2** ~ **for** : pelearse por — *vt* : mezclar — ~ *n* : rebatiña *f*, pelea *f* — **scrambled eggs** *npl* : huevos *mpl* revueltos

scrap[1] ['skræp] *n* **1** PIECE : pedazo *m* **2** *or* ~ **metal** : chatarra *f* **3** ~**s** *npl* : sobras — ~ *vt* scrapped; scrapping : desechar

scrap[2] *n* FIGHT : pelea *f*

scrapbook ['skræp,bʊk] *n* : álbum *m* de recortes

scrape ['skreɪp] *v* scraped; scraping *vt* **1** : rascar **2** : rasparse (la rodilla, etc.) **3** *or* ~ **off** : raspar **4** ~ **together** : reunir — *vi* **1** RUB : rozar **2** ~ **by** : arreglárselas — ~ *n* **1** : rasguño *m* **2** PREDICAMENT : apuro *m*

scratch ['skrætʃ] *vt* **1** CLAW : arañar **2** MARK : rayar **3** : rascarse (la cabeza, etc.) **4** ~ **out** : tachar — ~ *n* **1** : arañazo *m* **2** MARK : rayón *m* **3** **start from** ~ : empezar desde cero

scrawl ['skrɔl] *v* : garabatear — ~ *n* : garabato *m*

scrawny ['skrɔni] *adj* scrawnier; -est : escuálido

scream ['skriːm] *vi* : gritar, chillar — ~ *n* : grito *m*, chillido *m*

screech ['skriːtʃ] *n* **1** : chillido *m* (de personas) **2** : chirrido *m* (de frenos, etc.) — ~ *vi* **1** : chillar **2** : chirriar (dícese de los frenos, etc.)

screen ['skriːn] *n* **1** : pantalla *f* **2** PARTITION : mampara *f* **3** *or* **window** ~ : mosquitero *m* — ~ *vt* **1** SHIELD : proteger **2** HIDE : ocultar **3** : seleccionar (candidatos, etc.)

screw ['skruː] *n* : tornillo *m* — ~ *vt* **1** : atornillar **2** ~ **up** RUIN : fastidiar — **screwdriver** ['skruː,draɪvər] *n* : destornillador *m*

scribble ['skrɪbəl] *v* -bled; -bling : garabatear — ~ *n* : garabato *m*

script ['skrɪpt] *n* **1** HANDWRITING : escritura *f* **2** : guión *m* (de cine, etc.) — **scripture** ['skrɪptʃər] *n* **1** : escritos *mpl* sagrados **2 the Scriptures** *npl* : las Escrituras *fpl*

scroll ['skroːl] *n* : rollo *m* (de pergamino, etc.)

scrounge ['skraʊndʒ] *v* scrounged; scrounging *vt* : gorrear *fam* — *vi* ~ **around for sth** : andar buscando algo

scrub[1] ['skrʌb] *n* UNDERBRUSH : maleza *f*

scrub[2] *vt* scrubbed; scrubbing SCOUR : fregar — ~ *n* : fregado *m*

scruff ['skrʌf] *n* **by the** ~ **of the neck** : por el pescuezo

scruple ['skruːpəl] *n* : escrúpulo *m* — **scrupulous** ['skruːpjələs] *adj* : escrupuloso

scrutiny ['skruːtəni] *n*, *pl* -nies : análisis *m* cuidadoso — **scrutinize** ['skruːtən̩,aɪz] *vt* -nized; -nizing : escudriñar

scuff ['skʌf] *vt* : raspar, rayar

scuffle ['skʌfəl] *n* : refriega *f*

sculpture ['skʌlptʃər] *n* : escultura *f* — **sculpt** ['skʌlpt] *v* : esculpir — **sculptor** ['skʌlptər] *n* : escultor *m*, -tora *f*

scum ['skʌm] *n* **1** FROTH : espuma *f* **2** : escoria *f* (dícese de personas)

scurry ['skəri] *vi* -ried; -rying : corretear

scuttle[1] ['skʌtəl] *n* : cubo *m* (para carbón)

scuttle[2] *vt* -tled; -tling : hundir (un barco)

scuttle[3] *vi* SCAMPER : corretear

sea ['siː] *n* **1** : mar *mf* **2 at** ~ : en el mar — ~ *adj* : del mar — **seafarer** ['siː,færər] *n* : marinero *m* — **seafood** ['siː,fuːd] *n* : mariscos *mpl* — **seagull** ['siː,gʌl] *n* : gaviota *f*

seal[1] ['siːl] *n* : foca *f* (animal)

seal[2] *n* **1** STAMP : sello *m* **2** CLOSURE : cierre *m* (hermético) — ~ *vt* : sellar

seam ['siːm] *n* **1** : costura *f* **2** VEIN : veta *f*

seaman ['siːmən] *n*, *pl* -men [-mən, -ˌmɛn] : marinero *m*

seamy ['siːmi] *adj* seamier; -est : sórdido

seaplane ['siː,pleɪn] *n* : hidroavión *m*

seaport ['siː,pɔrt] *n* : puerto *m* marítimo

search ['sərtʃ] *vt* : registrar — *vi* ~ **for** : buscar — ~ *n* **1** : registro *m* **2** HUNT : búsqueda *f* — **searchlight** ['sərtʃ,laɪt] *n* : reflector *m*

seashell ['siː,ʃɛl] *n* : concha *f* (marina) — **seashore** ['siː,ʃor] *n* : orilla *f* del mar — **seasick** ['siː,sɪk] *adj* **1** : mareado **2 be** ~ : marearse — **seasickness** ['siː,sɪknəs] *n* : mareo *m*

season ['siːzən] *n* **1** : estación *f* (del año) **2** : temporada *f* (en deportes, etc.) — ~ *vt* **1** FLAVOR : sazonar **2** : secar (madera) — **seasonal** ['siːzənəl] *adj*

: estacional — **seasoned** *adj* EXPERI-
ENCED : veterano — **seasoning**
['si:zənɪŋ] *n* : condimento *m*
seat ['si:t] *n* **1** : asiento *m* **2** : fondillos
mpl (de un pantalón) **3** BUTTOCKS
: trasero *m* **4** CENTER : sede *f* — ~ *vt* **1**
be ~ed : sentarse **2 the bus** ~s **30**
: el autobús tiene cabida para 30 —
seat belt *n* : cinturón *m* de seguridad
seaweed ['si:ˌwiːd] *n* : alga *f* marina
secede [srsi:d] *vi* **-ceded; -ceding**
: separarse (de una nación, etc.)
secluded [srklu:dəd] *adj* : aislado —
seclusion [srklu:ʒən] *n* : aislamiento
m
second ['sekənd] *adj* : segundo — ~ *or*
secondly ['sekəndli] *adv* : en segundo
lugar — ~ *n* **1** : segundo *m*, -da *f* **2**
MOMENT : segundo *m* **3** have ~s
: repetir (en una comida) — ~ *vt* : secundar — **secondary** ['sekənˌderi] *adj*
: secundario — **secondhand** ['sekənd-
'hænd] *adj* : de segunda mano — **second-rate** ['sekəndˈreit] *adj* : mediocre
secret ['si:krət] *adj* : secreto — ~ *n*
: secreto *m* — **secrecy** ['si:krəsi] *n*, *pl*
-cies : secreto *m*
secretary ['sekrəˌteri] *n*, *pl* **-taries 1**
: secretario *m*, -ria *f* **2** : ministro *m*, -tra
f (del gobierno)
secretion [srkri:ʃən] *n* : secreción *f* —
secrete [srkri:t] *vt* **-creted; -creting**
: secretar
secretive ['si:krətɪv, srkri:tɪv] *adj*
: reservado — **secretly** ['si:krətli] *adv*
: en secreto
sect ['sekt] *n* : secta *f*
section ['sekʃən] *n* : sección *f*, parte *f*
sector ['sektər] *n* : sector *m*
secular ['sekjələr] *adj* : secular
security [srkjurəti] *n*, *pl* **-ties 1** : seguridad *f* **2** GUARANTEE : garantía *f* **3** secu-
rities *npl* : valores *mpl* — **secure** [sr-
'kjur] *adj* **-curer; -est** : seguro — ~ *vt*
-cured; -curing 1 FASTEN : asegurar **2**
GET : conseguir
sedan [srdæn] *n* : sedán *m*
sedate [srdeit] *adj* : sosegado —
sedative ['sedətɪv] *adj* : sedante — ~ *n*
: sedante *m*
sedentary ['sedənˌteri] *adj* : sedentario
sediment ['sedəmənt] *n* : sedimento *m*
seduce [srduːs, -'djuːs] *vt* **-duced; -duc-
ing** : seducir — **seduction** [srdʌkʃən]
n : seducción *f* — **seductive** [srdʌktɪv]
adj : seductor
see ['si:] *v* **saw** ['sɔ]; **seen** ['si:n]; **seeing**
vt **1** : ver **2** UNDERSTAND : entender **3**
ESCORT : acompañar **4** ~ **s.o. off** : despedirse de algn **5** ~ **sth through** : ll-

evar algo a cabo **6** ~ **you later!**
: ¡hasta luego! — *vi* **1** : ver **2** UNDER-
STAND : entender **3 let's** ~ : vamos a
ver **4** ~ **to** : ocuparse de
seed ['si:d] *n*, *pl* **seed** *or* **seeds 1**
: semilla *f* **2** SOURCE : germen *m* —
seedy ['si:di] *adj* **seedier; -est**
SQUALID : sórdido
seek ['si:k] *v* **sought** ['sɔt]; **seeking** *vt* **1**
or ~ **out** : buscar **2** REQUEST : pedir **3**
~ **to** : tratar de — *vi* SEARCH : buscar
seem ['si:m] *vi* : parecer
seep ['si:p] *vi* : filtrarse
seesaw ['si:ˌsɔ] *n* : balancín *m*
seethe ['si:ð] *vi* **seethed; seething** : rabiar, estar furioso
segment ['segmənt] *n* : segmento *m*
segregate ['segrɪˌgeit] *vt* **-gated;
-gating** : segregar — **segregation**
[ˌsegrɪˈgeiʃən] *n* : segregación *f*
seize ['si:z] *v* **seized; seizing** *vt* **1**
GRASP : agarrar **2** CAPTURE : tomar **3**
: aprovechar (una oportunidad) — *vi*
or ~ **up** : agarrotarse — **seizure**
['si:ʒər] *n* **1** CAPTURE : toma *f* **2** : ataque
m (en medicina)
seldom ['seldəm] *adv* : pocas veces,
raramente
select [səlekt] *adj* : selecto — ~ *vt*
: seleccionar — **selection** [səlekʃən] *n*
: selección *f* — **selective** [səlektɪv]
adj : selectivo
self ['self] *n*, *pl* **selves** ['selvz] **1** : ser *m*
2 her better ~ : su lado bueno —
self-addressed [ˌselfəˈdrest] *adj* : con
la dirección del remitente — **self-assured** [ˌselfəˈʃurd] *adj* : seguro de sí
mismo — **self-centered** [ˌselfˈsentərd]
adj : egocéntrico — **self-confidence**
[ˌselfˈkanfədənts] *n* : confianza *f* en sí
mismo — **self-confident** [ˌselfˈkan-
fədənt] *adj* : seguro de sí mismo —
self-conscious [ˌselfˈkantʃəs] *adj*
: cohibido — **self-control** [ˌselfkən-
'troːl] *n* : dominio *m* de sí mismo —
self-defense [ˌselfdrˈfents] *n* : defensa
f propia — **self-employed** [ˌselfɪm-
'plɔid] *adj* : que trabaja por cuenta
propia — **self-esteem** [ˌselfɪˈstiːm] *n*
: amor *m* propio — **self-evident** [ˌself-
'evədənt] *adj* : evidente — **self-help**
[ˌselfhelp] *n* : autoayuda *f* — **self-
important** [ˌselfɪmˈpɔrtənt] *adj* : presumido — **self-interest** [ˌselfˈɪntrəst,
-tərest] *n* : interés *m* personal — **selfish** ['selfɪʃ] *adj* : egoísta — **selfish-
ness** ['selfɪʃnəs] *n* : egoísmo *m* — **self-
less** ['selfləs] *adj* : desinteresado —
self-pity [ˌselfˈpɪti] *n*, *pl* **-ties** : autocompasión *f* — **self-portrait** [ˌself-

'pɔrtrət] *n* : autorretrato *m* — **self-respect** [ˌsɛlfri'spɛkt] *n* : amor *m* propio — **self-righteous** [ˌsɛlf'raɪtʃəs] *adj* : santurrón — **self-service** [ˌsɛlf-'sərvɪs] *adj* : de autoservicio — **self-sufficient** [ˌsɛlfsə'fɪʃənt] *adj* : autosuficiente — **self-taught** [ˌsɛlf'tɔt] *adj* : autodidacta

sell ['sɛl] *v* **sold** ['soːld]; **selling** *vt* : vender — *vi* : venderse — **seller** ['sɛlər] *n* : vendedor *m*, -dora *f*

selves → **self**

semantics [sɪ'mæntɪks] *ns & pl* : semántica *f*

semblance ['sɛmblənts] *n* : apariencia *f*

semester [sə'mɛstər] *n* : semestre *m*

semicolon ['sɛmiˌkoːlən, 'sɛˌmaɪ-] *n* : punto y coma *m*

semifinal ['sɛmiˌfaɪnəl, 'sɛˌmaɪ-] *n* : semifinal *f*

seminary ['sɛmə̩nɛri] *n*, *pl* **-naries** : seminario *m* — **seminar** ['sɛmə̩nɑr] *n* : seminario *m*

senate ['sɛnət] *n* : senado *m* — **senator** ['sɛnə̩tər] *n* : senador *m*, -dora *f*

send ['sɛnd] *vt* **sent** ['sɛnt]; **sending** **1** : mandar, enviar **2** ~ **away for** : pedir **3** ~ **back** : devolver (mercancías, etc.) **4** ~ **for** : mandar a buscar — **sender** ['sɛndər] *n* : remitente *mf*

senile ['siːˌnaɪl] *adj* : senil — **senility** [sɪ'nɪlə̩ti] *n* : senilidad *f*

senior ['siːnjər] *n* **1** SUPERIOR : superior *m* **2** : estudiante *mf* de último año (en educación) **3** *or* ~ **citizen** : persona *f* mayor **4 be s.o.'s** ~ : ser mayor que algn — ~ *adj* **1** : superior (en rango) **2** ELDER : mayor — **seniority** [ˌsiː-'njɔrə̩ti] *n* : antigüedad *f*

sensation [sɛn'seɪʃən] *n* : sensación *f* — **sensational** [sɛn'seɪʃənəl] *adj* : sensacional

sense ['sɛnts] *n* **1** : sentido *m* **2** FEELING : sensación *f* **3** COMMON SENSE : sentido *m* común **4 make** ~ : tener sentido — ~ *vt* **sensed; sensing** : sentir — **senseless** ['sɛntsləs] *adj* **1** : sin sentido **2** UNCONSCIOUS : inconsciente — **sensible** ['sɛntsəbəl] *adj* : sensato, práctico — **sensibility** [ˌsɛntsə'bɪlə̩ti] *n*, *pl* **-ties** : sensibilidad *f* — **sensitive** ['sɛntsə̩tɪv] *adj* **1** : sensible **2** TOUCHY : susceptible — **sensitivity** [ˌsɛntsə-'tɪvə̩ti] *n*, *pl* **-ties** : sensibilidad *f* — **sensual** ['sɛntʃʊəl] *adj* : sensual — **sensuous** ['sɛntʃʊəs] *adj* : sensual

sent → **send**

sentence ['sɛntənts, -ənz] *n* **1** : frase *f* **2** JUDGMENT : sentencia *f* — ~ *vt* **-tenced; -tencing** : sentenciar

sentiment ['sɛntəmənt] *n* **1** : sentimiento *m* **2** BELIEF : opinión *f* — **sentimental** [ˌsɛntə'mɛntəl] *adj* : sentimental — **sentimentality** [ˌsɛntə̩mɛn'tælə̩ti] *n*, *pl* **-ties** : sentimentalismo *m*

sentry ['sɛntri] *n*, *pl* **-tries** : centinela *m*

separation [ˌsɛpə'reɪʃən] *n* : separación *f* — **separate** ['sɛpə̩reɪt] *v* **-rated; -rating** *vt* **1** : separar **2** DISTINGUISH : distinguir — *vi* : separarse — ~ ['sɛprət, 'sɛpə-] *adj* **1** : separado **2** DE-TACHED : aparte **3** DISTINCT : distinto — **separately** ['sɛprə̩tli, 'sɛpə-] *adv* : por separado

September [sɛp'tɛmbər] *n* : septiembre *m*, setiembre *m*

sequel ['siːkwəl] *n* **1** : continuación *f* **2** CONSEQUENCE : secuela *f*

sequence ['siːkwənts] *n* **1** ORDER : orden *m* **2** : secuencia *f* (de números o escenas)

Serb ['sərb] *or* **Serbian** ['sərbiən] *adj* : serbio

serene [sə'riːn] *adj* : sereno — **serenity** [sə'rɛnə̩ti] *n* : serenidad *f*

sergeant ['sɑrdʒənt] *n* : sargento *mf*

serial ['sɪriəl] *adj* : seriado — ~ *n* : serial *m* — **series** ['sɪrˌiːz] *n*, *pl* **series** : serie *f*

serious ['sɪriəs] *adj* : serio — **seriously** ['sɪriəsli] *adv* **1** : seriamente **2** GRAVELY : gravemente **3 take** ~ : tomar en serio

sermon ['sərmən] *n* : sermón *m*

serpent ['sərpənt] *n* : serpiente *f*

servant ['sərvənt] *n* : criado *m*, -da *f*

serve ['sərv] *v* **served; serving** *vi* **1** : servir **2** : sacar (en deportes) **3** ~ **as** : servir de — *vt* **1** : servir **2** ~ **time** : cumplir una condena — **server** ['sərvər] *n* **1** WAITER : camarero *m*, -ra *f* **2** : servidor *m* (en informática)

service ['sərvəs] *n* **1** : servicio *m* **2** CER-EMONY : oficio *m* **3** MAINTENANCE : revisión *f* **4 armed** ~**s** : fuerzas *fpl* armadas — ~ *vt* **-viced; -vicing** : revisar (un vehículo, etc.) — **serviceman** ['sərvəsˌmæn, -mən] *n*, *pl* **-men** [-mən, -ˌmɛn] : militar *m* — **service station** *n* : estación *f* de servicio — **serving** ['sərvɪŋ] *n* : porción *f*, ración *f*

session ['sɛʃən] *n* : sesión *f*

set ['sɛt] *n* **1** : juego *m* (de platos, etc.) **2** : set *m* (en tenis, etc.) **3** *or* **stage** ~ : decorado *m* **4 television** ~ : aparato *m* de televisión — ~ *v* **set; setting** *vt* **1** *or* ~ **down** : poner **2** : poner en hora (un reloj) **3** FIX : fijar (una fecha, etc.) **4** ~ **fire to** : prender fuego a **5** ~ **free** : poner en libertad **6** ~ **off**

: hacer sonar (una alarma), hacer estallar (una bomba) 7 ~ out to (do sth) : proponerse (hacer algo) 8 ~ up ASSEMBLE : montar, armar 9 ~ up ESTABLISH : establecer — vi 1 : cuajarse (dícese de la gelatina, etc.), fraguar (dícese del cemento) 2 : ponerse (dícese del sol, etc.) 3 ~ in BEGIN : empezar 4 ~ off or ~ out : salir (de viaje) — ~ adj 1 FIXED : fijo 2 READY : listo, preparado — setback ['sɛt̬bæk] n : revés m — setting ['sɛt̬ɪŋ] n 1 : posición f (de un control) 2 MOUNTING : engaste m (de joyas) 3 SCENE : escenario m

settle ['sɛt̬əl] v settled; settling vi 1 : asentarse (dícese de polvo, colonos, etc.) 2 ~ down RELAX : calmarse 3 ~ for : conformarse con 4 ~ in : instalarse — vt 1 DECIDE : fijar, decidir 2 RESOLVE : resolver 3 PAY : pagar 4 CALM : calmar 5 COLONIZE : colonizar — settlement ['sɛt̬əlmənt] n 1 PAYMENT : pago m 2 COLONY : colonia f, poblado m 3 AGREEMENT : acuerdo m — settler ['sɛt̬lər] n : colono m, -na f

seven ['sɛvən] adj : siete — ~ n : siete m — seven hundred adj : setecientos — ~ n : setecientos m — seventeen [ˌsɛvənˈtiːn] adj : diecisiete — ~ n : diecisiete m — seventeenth [ˌsɛvənˈtiːnθ] adj : decimoséptimo — ~ n 1 : decimoséptimo m, -ma f (en una serie) 2 : diecisieteavo m (en matemáticas) — seventh ['sɛvənθ] adj : séptimo — ~ n 1 : séptimo m, -ma f (en una serie) 2 : séptimo m (en matemáticas) — seventieth ['sɛvəntiəθ] adj : septuagésimo — ~ n 1 : septuagésimo m, -ma f (en una serie) 2 : setentavo m (en matemáticas) — seventy ['sɛvənt̬i] adj : setenta — ~ n, pl -ties : setenta m

sever ['sɛvər] vt -ered; -ering : cortar, romper

several ['sɛvrəl, 'sɛvə-] adj : varios — ~ pron : varios, varias

severance ['sɛvrənts, 'sɛvə-] n : ruptura f

severe [səˈvɪr] adj severer; -est 1 : severo 2 SERIOUS : grave — severely adv 1 : severamente 2 SERIOUSLY : gravemente — severity [səˈvɛrət̬i] n 1 : severidad f 2 SERIOUSNESS : gravedad f

sew ['soː] v sewed; sewn ['soːn] or sewed; sewing : coser

sewer ['suːər] n : cloaca f — sewage ['suːɪdʒ] n : aguas fpl negras

sewing ['soːɪŋ] n : costura f

sex ['sɛks] n 1 : sexo m 2 INTERCOURSE : relaciones fpl sexuales — sexism ['sɛkˌsɪzəm] n : sexismo m — sexist ['sɛksɪst] adj : sexista — sexual ['sɛkʃʊəl] adj : sexual — sexuality [ˌsɛkʃʊˈælət̬i] n : sexualidad f — sexy ['sɛksi] adj sexier; -est : sexy

shabby ['ʃæbi] adj shabbier; -est 1 WORN : gastado 2 UNFAIR : malo, injusto

shack ['ʃæk] n : choza f

shackle ['ʃækəl] n : grillete m

shade ['ʃeɪd] n 1 : sombra f 2 : tono m (de un color) 3 NUANCE : matiz m 4 or lampshade : pantalla f 5 or window ~ : persiana f — ~ vt shaded; shading : proteger de la luz — shadow ['ʃædoː] n : sombra f — shadowy ['ʃædowi] adj INDISTINCT : vago — shady ['ʃeɪdi] adj shadier; -est 1 : sombreado 2 DISREPUTABLE : sospechoso

shaft ['ʃæft] n 1 : asta f (de una flecha, etc.) 2 HANDLE : mango m 3 AXLE : eje m 4 : rayo m (de luz) 5 or mine ~ : pozo m

shaggy ['ʃægi] adj shaggier; -est : peludo

shake ['ʃeɪk] v shook ['ʃʊk]; shaken ['ʃeɪkən]; shaking vt 1 : sacudir 2 MIX : agitar 3 ~ hands with s.o. : dar la mano a algn 4 ~ one's head : negar con la cabeza 5 ~ up UPSET : afectar — vi : temblar — ~ n 1 : sacudida f 2 → handshake — shaker ['ʃeɪkər] n 1 salt ~ : salero m 2 pepper ~ : pimentero m — shaky ['ʃeɪki] adj shakier; -est 1 : tembloroso 2 UNSTABLE : poco firme

shall ['ʃæl] v aux, past should ['ʃʊd]; pres sing & pl shall 1 (expressing volition or futurity) → will 2 (expressing possibility or obligation) → should 3 ~ we go? : ¿nos vamos?

shallow ['ʃæloː] adj 1 : poco profundo 2 SUPERFICIAL : superficial

sham ['ʃæm] n : farsa f — ~ v shammed; shamming : fingir

shambles ['ʃæmbəlz] ns & pl : caos m, desorden m

shame ['ʃeɪm] n 1 : vergüenza f 2 what a ~! : ¡qué lástima! — ~ vt shamed; shaming : avergonzar — shameful ['ʃeɪmfəl] adj : vergonzoso — shameless ['ʃeɪmləs] adj : desvergonzado

shampoo [ʃæmˈpuː] vt : lavar (el pelo) — ~ n, pl -poos : champú m

shamrock ['ʃæmˌrɑk] n : trébol m

shan't ['ʃænt] (contraction of shall not) → shall

shape ['ʃeɪp] v **shaped; shaping** vt 1 : formar 2 DETERMINE : determinar 3 **be ~d like** : tener forma de — vi or **~ up** : tomar forma — **~** n 1 : forma f 2 **get in ~** : ponerse en forma — **shapeless** ['ʃeɪpləs] adj : informe

share ['ʃer] n 1 : porción f 2 : acción f (en una compañía) — **~** v **shared; sharing** vt 1 : compartir 2 DIVIDE : dividir — vi : compartir — **shareholder** ['ʃer,hoːldər] n : accionista mf

shark ['ʃɑrk] n : tiburón m

sharp ['ʃɑrp] adj 1 : afilado 2 POINTY : puntiagudo 3 ACUTE : agudo 4 HARSH : duro, severo 5 CLEAR : nítido 6 : sostenido (en música) 7 **a ~ curve** : una curva cerrada — **~** adv **at two o'clock ~** : a las dos en punto — **~** n : sostenido (en música) — **sharpen** ['ʃɑrpən] vt : afilar (un cuchillo, etc.), sacar punta a (un lápiz) — **sharpener** ['ʃɑrpənər] n 1 or **knife ~** : afilador m 2 or **pencil ~** : sacapuntas m — **sharply** ['ʃɑrpli] adv : bruscamente

shatter ['ʃætər] vt 1 : hacer añicos 2 DEVASTATE : destrozar — vi : hacerse añicos

shave ['ʃeɪv] v **shaved; shaved** or **shaven** ['ʃeɪvən]; **shaving** vt 1 : afeitar 2 SLICE : cortar — vi : afeitarse — **~** n : afeitada f — **shaver** ['ʃeɪvər] n : máquina f de afeitar

shawl ['ʃɔl] n : chal m

she ['ʃiː] pron : ella

sheaf ['ʃiːf] n, pl **sheaves** ['ʃiːvz] 1 : gavilla f 2 : fajo m (de papeles)

shear ['ʃɪr] vt **sheared; sheared** or **shorn** ['ʃorn]; **shearing** : esquilar — **shears** ['ʃɪrz] npl : tijeras fpl (grandes)

sheath ['ʃiːθ] n, pl **sheaths** ['ʃiːðz, 'ʃiːθs] : funda f, vaina f

shed[1] ['ʃed] v **shed; shedding** vt 1 : derramar (lágrimas, etc.) 2 : mudar (de piel, etc.), quitarse (ropa) 3 **~ light on** : aclarar

shed[2] n : cobertizo m

she'd ['ʃid] (contraction of **she had** or **she would**) → **have, would**

sheen ['ʃin] n : brillo m, lustre m

sheep ['ʃiːp] n, pl **sheep** : oveja f — **sheepish** ['ʃiːpɪʃ] adj : avergonzado

sheer ['ʃɪr] adj 1 THIN : transparente 2 PURE : puro 3 STEEP : escarpado

sheet ['ʃiːt] n 1 : sábana f (de la cama) 2 : hoja f (de papel) 3 : capa f (de hielo, etc.) 4 PLATE : placa f, lámina f

shelf ['ʃelf] n, pl **shelves** ['ʃelvz] : estante m

shell ['ʃel] n 1 : concha f 2 : caparazón m (de un crustáceo, etc.) 3 : cáscara f

(de un huevo, etc.) 4 : armazón mf (de un edificio, etc.) 5 POD : vaina f 6 MISSILE : proyectil m — **~** vt 1 : pelar (nueces, etc.) 2 BOMBARD : bombardear

she'll ['ʃiːl, 'ʃil] (contraction of **she shall** or **she will**) → **shall, will**

shellfish ['ʃel,fɪʃ] n : marisco m

shelter ['ʃeltər] n 1 : refugio m 2 **take ~** : refugiarse — **~** vt 1 PROTECT : proteger 2 HARBOR : albergar

shelve ['ʃelv] vt **shelved; shelving** DEFER : dar carpetazo a

shepherd ['ʃepərd] n : pastor m — **~** vt GUIDE : conducir, guiar

sherbet ['ʃərbət] n : sorbete m

sheriff ['ʃerɪf] n : sheriff m

sherry ['ʃeri] n, pl **-ries** : jerez m

she's ['ʃiːz] (contraction of **she is** or **she has**) → **be, have**

shield ['ʃiːld] n : escudo m — **~** vt : proteger

shier, shiest → **shy**

shift ['ʃɪft] vt 1 MOVE : mover 2 SWITCH : transferir — vi 1 CHANGE : cambiar 2 MOVE : moverse 3 or **~ gears** : cambiar de velocidad — **~** n 1 CHANGE : cambio m 2 : turno m (de trabajo) — **shiftless** ['ʃɪftləs] adj : holgazán — **shifty** ['ʃɪfti] adj **shiftier; -est** : sospechoso

shimmer ['ʃɪmər] vi : brillar, relucir

shin ['ʃɪn] n : espinilla f

shine ['ʃaɪn] v **shone** ['ʃoːn] or **shined; shining** vi : brillar — vt 1 : alumbrar (una luz) 2 POLISH : sacar brillo a — **~** n : brillo m

shingle ['ʃɪŋgəl] n : teja f plana y delgada (en construcción) — **~** vt **-gled; -gling** : techar — **shingles** ['ʃɪŋgəlz] npl : herpes m

shiny ['ʃaɪni] adj **shinier; -est** : brillante

ship ['ʃɪp] n 1 : barco m, buque m 2 → **spaceship** — **~** vt **shipped; shipping** : transportar, enviar (por barco) — **shipbuilding** ['ʃɪp,bɪldɪŋ] n : construcción f naval — **shipment** ['ʃɪpmənt] n : envío m — **shipping** ['ʃɪpɪŋ] n 1 : transporte m 2 SHIPS : barcos mpl — **shipshape** ['ʃɪp,ʃeɪp] adj : ordenado — **shipwreck** ['ʃɪp,rek] n : naufragio m — **~** vt **be ~ed** : naufragar — **shipyard** ['ʃɪp,jɑrd] n : astillero m

shirk ['ʃərk] vt : esquivar

shirt ['ʃərt] n : camisa f

shiver ['ʃɪvər] vi : temblar (del frío, etc.) — **~** n : escalofrío m

shoal ['ʃoːl] n : banco m

shock ['ʃɑk] n **1** IMPACT : choque m **2** SURPRISE, UPSET : golpe m emocional **3** : shock m (en medicina) **4** or **electric** ~ : descarga f (eléctrica) — ~ vt : escandalizar — **shock absorber** n : amortiguador m — **shocking** ['ʃɑkɪŋ] adj : escandaloso

shoddy ['ʃɑdi] adj **shoddier; -est** : de mala calidad

shoe ['ʃuː] n **1** : zapato m — ~ vt **shod** ['ʃɑd]; **shoeing** : herrar (un caballo) — **shoelace** ['ʃuːˌleɪs] n : cordón m (de zapato) — **shoemaker** ['ʃuːˌmeɪkər] n : zapatero m, -ra f

shone → **shine**

shook → **shake**

shoot ['ʃuːt] v **shot** ['ʃɑt]; **shooting** vt **1** : disparar **2** : echar (una mirada) **3** PHOTOGRAPH : fotografiar **4** FILM : rodar — vi **1** : disparar **2** ~ **by** : pasar como una bala — ~ n : brote m, retoño m (de una planta) — **shooting star** n : estrella f fugaz

shop ['ʃɑp] n **1** : tienda f **2** WORKSHOP : taller m — ~ vi **shopped; shopping 1** : hacer compras **2 go shopping** : ir de compras — **shopkeeper** ['ʃɑpˌkiːpər] n : tendero m, -ra f — **shoplift** ['ʃɑpˌlɪft] vi : hurtar mercancía (en tiendas) — **shoplifter** ['ʃɑpˌlɪftər] n : ladrón m, -drona f (que roba en tiendas) — **shopper** ['ʃɑpər] n : comprador m, -dora f

shore ['ʃoːr] n : orilla f

shorn → **shear**

short ['ʃɔrt] adj **1** : corto **2** : bajo (de estatura) **3** CURT : brusco **4 a** ~ **time ago** : hace poco **5 be** ~ **of** : estar corto de — ~ adv **1 stop** ~ : parar en seco **2 fall** ~ : quedarse corto — **shortage** ['ʃɔrtɪdʒ] n : escasez f, carencia f — **shortcake** ['ʃɔrtˌkeɪk] n : tarta f de fruta — **shortcoming** ['ʃɔrtˌkʌmɪŋ] n : defecto m — **shortcut** ['ʃɔrtˌkʌt] n : atajo m — **shorten** ['ʃɔrtən] vt : acortar — **shorthand** ['ʃɔrtˌhænd] n : taquigrafía f — **short-lived** ['ʃɔrt-ˈlɪvd, -ˈlaɪvd] adj : efímero — **shortly** ['ʃɔrtli] adv : dentro de poco — **shortness** ['ʃɔrtnəs] n **1** : lo corto (de una cosa), baja estatura f (de una persona) **2** ~ **of breath** : falta f de aliento — **shorts** npl : shorts mpl, pantalones mpl cortos — **shortsighted** ['ʃɔrtˌsaɪtəd] → **nearsighted**

shot ['ʃɑt] n **1** : disparo m, tiro m **2** : tiro m (en deportes) **3** ATTEMPT : intento m **4** PHOTOGRAPH : foto f **5** INJECTION : inyección f **6** : trago m (de licor) — **shotgun** ['ʃɑtˌgʌn] n : escopeta f

should ['ʃud] past of **shall 1 if she** ~ **call** : si llama **2 I** ~ **have gone** : debería haber ido **3 they** ~ **arrive soon** : deben llegar pronto **4 what** ~ **we do?** : ¿qué hacemos?

shoulder ['ʃoːldər] n **1** : hombro m **2** : arcén m (de una carretera) — ~ vt : cargar con (la responsabilidad, etc.) — **shoulder blade** n : omóplato m

shouldn't ['ʃudənt] (contraction of **should not**) → **should**

shout ['ʃaʊt] v : gritar — ~ n : grito m

shove ['ʃʌv] v **shoved; shoving** : empujar — ~ n : empujón m

shovel ['ʃʌvəl] n : pala f — ~ vt **-veled** or **-velled; -veling** or **-velling 1** : mover (tierra, etc.) con una pala **2** DIG : cavar (con una pala)

show ['ʃoː] v **showed; shown** ['ʃoːn] or **showed; showing** vt **1** : mostrar **2** TEACH : enseñar **3** PROVE : demostrar **4** ESCORT : acompañar **5** : proyectar (una película), dar (un programa de televisión) **6** ~ **off** : hacer alarde de — vi **1** : notarse, verse **2** ~ **off** : lucirse **3** ~ **up** ARRIVE : aparecer — ~ n **1** : demostración f **2** EXHIBITION : exposición f **3** PARTY : espectáculo m (teatral), programa m (de televisión, etc.) — **showdown** ['ʃoːˌdaʊn] n : confrontación f

shower ['ʃaʊər] n **1** : ducha f **2** : chaparrón m (en meteorología) **3** PARTY : fiesta f — ~ vt **1** SPRAY : regar **2** ~ **s.o. with** : colmar a algn de — vi **1** : ducharse **2** RAIN : llover

showy ['ʃoːi] adj **showier; -est** : llamativo, ostentoso

shrank → **shrink**

shrapnel ['ʃræpnəl] ns & pl : metralla f

shred ['ʃred] n **1** : tira f (de tela, etc.) **2** IOTA : pizca f — ~ vt **shredded; shredding 1** : hacer tiras **2** GRATE : rallar

shrewd ['ʃruːd] adj : astuto

shriek ['ʃriːk] vi : chillar — ~ n : chillido m, alarido m

shrill ['ʃrɪl] adj : agudo, estridente

shrimp ['ʃrɪmp] n : camarón m

shrine ['ʃraɪn] n **1** TOMB : sepulcro m **2** SANCTUARY : santuario m

shrink ['ʃrɪŋk] v **shrank** ['ʃræŋk]; **shrunk** ['ʃrʌŋk] or **shrunken** ['ʃrʌŋkən]; **shrinking** vi : encoger — vi **1** : encogerse (dícese de ropa), reducirse (dícese de números, etc.) **2** or ~ **back** : retroceder

shrivel ['ʃrɪvəl] vi **-veled** or **-velled; -veling** or **-velling** or ~ **up** : arrugarse, marchitarse

shroud ['ʃraʊd] *n* **1** : sudario *m*, mortaja *f* **2** VEIL : velo *m* — ~ *vt* : envolver

shrub ['ʃrʌb] *n* : arbusto *m*, mata *f*

shrug ['ʃrʌg] *vi* **shrugged; shrugging** : encogerse de hombros

shrunk → shrink

shudder ['ʃʌdər] *vi* : estremecerse — ~ *n* : estremecimiento *m*

shuffle ['ʃʌfəl] *v* **-fled; -fling** *vt* : barajar (naipes), revolver (papeles, etc.) — *vi* : caminar arrastrando los pies

shun ['ʃʌn] *vi* **shunned; shunning** : evitar, esquivar

shut ['ʃʌt] *v* **shut; shutting** *vt* **1** CLOSE : cerrar **2** ~ **off → turn off 3** ~ **up** CONFINE : encerrar — *vi* **1** *or* ~ **down** : cerrarse **2** ~ **up!** : ¡cállate! — **shutter** ['ʃʌtər] *n* **1** *or* **window** ~ : contraventana *f* **2** : obturador *m* (de una cámara)

shuttle ['ʃʌtəl] *n* **1** : lanzadera *f* (para tejer) **2** *or* ~ **bus** : autobús *m* (de corto recorrido) **3 → space shuttle** — ~ *v* **-tled; -tling** *vt* : transportar — *vi* : ir y venir

shy ['ʃaɪ] *adj* **shier** *or* **shyer** ['ʃaɪər]; **shiest** *or* **shyest** ['ʃaɪəst] : tímido — ~ *vi* **shied; shying** *or* ~ **away** : retroceder — **shyness** ['ʃaɪnəs] *n* : timidez *f*

sibling ['sɪblɪŋ] *n* : hermano *m*, hermana *f*

sick ['sɪk] *adj* **1** : enfermo **2** **be** ~ VOMIT : vomitar **3** **be** ~ **of** : estar harto de **4** **feel** ~ : tener náuseas — **sicken** ['sɪkən] *vt* DISGUST : dar asco a — **sickening** ['sɪkənɪŋ] *adj* : nauseabundo

sickle ['sɪkəl] *n* : hoz *f*

sickly ['sɪkli] *adj* **sicklier; -est 1** UNHEALTHY : enfermizo **2 → sickening** — **sickness** ['sɪknəs] *n* : enfermedad *f*

side ['saɪd] *n* **1** : lado *m* **2** : costado *m* (de una persona), ijada *f* (de un animal) **3** : parte *f* (en una disputa, etc.) **4** ~ **by** ~ : uno al lado de otro **5** **take** ~**s** : tomar partido — ~ *vi* ~ **with** : ponerse de parte de — **sideboard** ['saɪd,bord] *n* : aparador *m* — **sideburns** ['saɪd,bərnz] *npl* : patillas *fpl* — **side effect** *n* : efecto *m* secundario — **sideline** ['saɪd,laɪn] *n* : línea *f* de banda (en deportes) — **sidestep** ['saɪd,stɛp] *vt* **-stepped; -stepping** : eludir, esquivar — **sidetrack** ['saɪd,træk] *vt* **get** ~**ed** : distraerse — **sidewalk** ['saɪd,wɔk] *n* : acera *f* — **sideways** ['saɪd,weɪz] *adj & adv* : de lado — **siding** ['saɪdɪŋ] *n* : revestimiento *m* exterior

siege ['siːdʒ, 'siːʒ] *n* : sitio *m*

sieve ['sɪv] *n* : tamiz *m*, cedazo *m*

sift ['sɪft] *vt* **1** : cerner, tamizar **2** *or* ~ **through** : pasar por el tamiz

sigh ['saɪ] *vi* : suspirar — ~ *n* : suspiro *m*

sight ['saɪt] *n* **1** : vista *f* **2** SPECTACLE : espectáculo *m* **3** : lugar *m* de interés (turístico) **4** **catch** ~ **of** : avistar — ~ *vt* : avistar — **sightseer** ['saɪt,siːər] *n* : turista *mf*

sign ['saɪn] *n* **1** : signo *m* **2** NOTICE : letrero *m* **3** GESTURE : seña *f*, señal *f* — ~ *vt* : firmar (un cheque, etc.) — *vi* **1** : firmar **2** ~ **up** ENROLL : inscribirse

signal ['sɪgnəl] *n* : señal *f* — ~ *v* **-naled** *or* **-nalled; -naling** *or* **-nalling** *vt* **1** : hacer señas a **2** INDICATE : señalar — *vi* **1** : hacer señas **2** : señalizar (en un vehículo)

signature ['sɪgnətʃur] *n* : firma *f*

significance [sɪg'nɪfɪkənts] *n* **1** : significado *m* **2** IMPORTANCE : importancia *f* — **significant** [sɪg'nɪfɪkənt] *adj* : importante — **signify** ['sɪgnə,faɪ] *vt* **-fied; -fying** : significar

sign language *n* : lenguaje *m* gestual — **signpost** ['saɪn,post] *n* : poste *m* indicador

silence ['saɪlənts] *n* : silencio *m* — ~ *vt* **-lenced; -lencing** : silenciar — **silent** ['saɪlənt] *adj* **1** : silencioso **2** MUM : callado **3** : mudo (dícese de películas y letras)

silhouette [,sɪlə'wɛt] *n* : silueta *f* — ~ *vt* **-etted; -etting** **be** ~**d against** : perfilarse contra

silicon ['sɪlɪkən, -,kɑn] *n* : silicio *m*

silk ['sɪlk] *n* : seda *f* — **silky** ['sɪlki] *adj* **silkier; -est** : sedoso

sill ['sɪl] *n* : alféizar *m* (de una ventana), umbral *m* (de una puerta)

silly ['sɪli] *adj* **sillier; -est** : tonto, estúpido

silt ['sɪlt] *n* : cieno *m*

silver ['sɪlvər] *n* **1** : plata *f* **2 → silverware** — ~ *adj* : de plata — **silverware** ['sɪlvər,wær] *n* : plata *f* — **silvery** ['sɪlvəri] *adj* : plateado

similar ['sɪmələr] *adj* : similar, parecido — **similarity** [,sɪmə'lærəṭi] *n, pl* **-ties** : semejanza *f*, parecido *m*

simmer ['sɪmər] *v* : hervir a fuego lento

simple ['sɪmpəl] *adj* **simpler; -plest 1** : simple **2** EASY : sencillo — **simplicity** [sɪm'plɪsəṭi] *n* : simplicidad *f*, sencillez *f* — **simplify** ['sɪmplə,faɪ] *vt* **-fied; -fying** : simplificar — **simply** ['sɪmpli] *adv* **1** : sencillamente **2** ABSOLUTELY : realmente

simulate ['sɪmjə,leɪt] *vt* **-lated; -lating** : simular

simultaneous [,saɪməl'teɪniəs] *adj* : simultáneo

sin ['sɪn] *n* : pecado *m* — ~ *vi* **sinned; sinning** : pecar

since ['sɪns] *adv* 1 *or* ~ **then** : desde entonces 2 **long** ~ : hace mucho — ~ *conj* 1 : desde que 2 BECAUSE : ya que, como 3 **it's been years** ~... : hace años que... — ~ *prep* : desde

sincere [sɪn'sɪr] *adj* **-cerer; -est** : sincero — **sincerely** *adv* : sinceramente — **sincerity** [sɪn'serəti] *n* : sinceridad *f*

sinful ['sɪnfəl] *adj* : pecador (dícese de las personas), pecaminoso (dícese de las acciones)

sing ['sɪŋ] *v* **sang** ['sæŋ] *or* **sung** ['sʌŋ]; **sung; singing** : cantar

singe ['sɪndʒ] *vt* **singed; singeing** : chamuscar

singer ['sɪŋər] *n* : cantante *mf*

single ['sɪŋgəl] *adj* 1 : solo, único 2 UN- MARRIED : soltero 3 **every** ~ **day** : cada día, todos los días — ~ *n* 1 : soltero *m*, -ra *f* 2 *or* ~ **room** : habitación *f* individual — ~ *vt* **-gled; -gling** ~ **out** SELECT : escoger 2 DISTINGUISH : señalar — **single–handed** ['sɪŋgəl'hændəd] *adj* : sin ayuda, solo

singular ['sɪŋgjələr] *adj* : singular — ~ *n* : singular *m*

sinister ['sɪnəstər] *adj* : siniestro

sink ['sɪŋk] *v* **sank** ['sæŋk] *or* **sunk** ['sʌŋk]; **sunk; sinking** *vi* 1 : hundirse (en un líquido) 2 DROP : bajar, caer — *vt* 1 : hundir 2 ~ **sth into** : clavar algo en — ~ *n* 1 *or* **kitchen** ~ : fregadero *m* 2 *or* **bathroom** ~ : lavabo *m*, lavamanos *m*

sinner ['sɪnər] *n* : pecador *m*, -dora *f*

sip ['sɪp] *v* **sipped; sipping** *vt* : sorber — *vi* : beber a sorbos — ~ *n* : sorbo *m*

siphon ['saɪfən] *n* : sifón *m* — ~ *vt* : sacar con sifón

sir ['sər] *n* 1 (*in titles*) : sir *m* 2 (*as a form of address*) : señor *m* 3 **Dear Sir** : Estimado señor

siren ['saɪrən] *n* : sirena *f*

sirloin ['sər,lɔɪn] *n* : solomillo *m*

sissy ['sɪsi] *n*, *pl* **-sies** : mariquita *mf* *fam*

sister ['sɪstər] *n* : hermana *f* — **sister–in–law** ['sɪstərɪn,lɔ] *n*, *pl* **sisters–in–law** : cuñada *f*

sit ['sɪt] *v* **sat** ['sæt]; **sitting** *vi* 1 *or* ~ **down** : sentarse 2 LIE : estar (ubicado) 3 MEET : estar en sesión 4 *or* ~ **up** : incorporarse — *vt* : sentar

site ['saɪt] *n* 1 : sitio *m*, lugar *m* 2 LOT : solar *m*

sitting room → **living room**

sitter ['sɪtər] → **baby–sitter**

situated ['sɪtʃə,weɪtəd] *adj* : ubicado, situado — **situation** [,sɪtʃu'eɪʃən] *n* : situación *f*

six ['sɪks] *adj* : seis — ~ *n* : seis *m* — **six hundred** *adj* : seiscientos — ~ *n* : seiscientos *m* — **sixteen** [sɪks'ti:n] *adj* : dieciséis — ~ *n* : dieciséis *m* — **sixteenth** [sɪks'ti:nθ] *adj* : decimosexto — ~ *n* 1 : decimosexto *m*, -ta *f* (en una serie) 2 : dieciseisavo *m*, dieciseisava parte *f* — **sixth** ['sɪksθ, 'sɪkst] *adj* : sexto — ~ *n* 1 : sexto *m*, -ta *f* (en una serie) 2 : sexto *m* (en matemáticas) — **sixtieth** ['sɪkstiəθ] *adj* : sexagésimo — ~ *n* 1 : sexagésimo *m*, -ma *f* (en una serie) 2 : sesentavo *m* (en matemáticas) — **sixty** ['sɪksti] *adj* : sesenta — ~ *n*, *pl* **-ties** : sesenta *m*

size ['saɪz] *n* 1 : tamaño *m*, talla *f* (de ropa), número *m* (de zapatos) 2 EX- TENT : magnitud *f* — ~ *vt* **sized; sizing** ~ **up** : evaluar — **sizable** *or* **sizeable** ['saɪzəbəl] *adj* : considerable

sizzle ['sɪzəl] *vi* **-zled; -zling** : chisporrotear

skate¹ ['skeɪt] *n* : raya *f* (pez)

skate² *n* : patín *m* — ~ *vi* **skated; skating** : patinar — **skateboard** ['skeɪt,bord] *n* : monopatín *m* — **skater** ['skeɪtər] *n* : patinador *m*, -dora *f*

skeleton ['skelətən] *n* : esqueleto *m*

skeptic ['skeptɪk] *n* : escéptico *m*, -ca *f* — **skeptical** ['skeptɪkəl] *adj* : escéptico — **skepticism** ['skeptə,sɪzəm] *n* : escepticismo *m*

sketch ['sketʃ] *n* 1 : esbozo *m*, bosquejo *m* 2 SKIT : sketch *m* — ~ *vt* : bosquejar — *vi* : hacer bosquejos — **sketchy** ['sketʃi] *adj* **sketchier; -est** : incompleto

skewer ['skjuːər] *n* : brocheta *f*, broqueta *f*

ski ['ski:] *n*, *pl* **skis** : esquí *m* — ~ *vi* **skied; skiing** : esquiar

skid ['skɪd] *n* : derrape *m*, patinazo *m* — ~ *vi* **skidded; skidding** : derrapar, patinar

skier ['ski:ər] *n* : esquiador *m*, -dora *f*

skill ['skɪl] *n* 1 : habilidad *f*, destreza *f* 2 TECHNIQUE : técnica *f* — **skilled** ['skɪld] *adj* : hábil

skillet ['skɪlət] *n* : sartén *mf*

skillful ['skɪlfəl] *adj* : hábil, diestro

skim ['skɪm] *vt* **skimmed; skimming** 1 : espumar (sopa, etc.), descremar (leche) 2 : pasar rozando (una superfi-

cie) **3** *or* ~ **through** : echar un vistazo a — ~ *adj* : descremado

skimp ['skɪmp] *vi* ~ **on** : escatimar —
skimpy ['skɪmpi] *adj* **skimpier; -est 1**
: exiguo, escaso **2** : brevísimo (dícese
de ropa)

skin ['skɪn] *n* : piel *f* — ~ *vt* **skinned;
skinning** : despellejar — **skin diving**
n : buceo *m*, submarinismo *m* — **skinny** ['skɪni] *adj* **skinnier; -est** : flaco

skip ['skɪp] *v* **skipped; skipping** *vi* : ir
brincando — *vt* OMIT : saltarse — ~ *n*
: brinco *m*, salto *m*

skipper ['skɪpər] *n* : capitán *m*, -tana *f*

skirmish ['skərmɪʃ] *n* : escaramuza *f*

skirt ['skərt] *n* : falda *f* — ~ *vt* **1** BORDER
: bordear **2** EVADE : eludir

skull ['skʌl] *n* : cráneo *m* (de una persona
viva), calavera *f* (de un esqueleto)

skunk ['skʌŋk] *n* : mofeta *f*, zorrillo *m*
Lat

sky ['skaɪ] *n, pl* **skies** : cielo *m* — **skylight** ['skaɪˌlaɪt] *n* : claraboya *f*, tragaluz
m — **skyline** ['skaɪˌlaɪn] *n* : horizonte
m — **skyscraper** ['skaɪˌskreɪpər] *n*
: rascacielos *m*

slab ['slæb] *n* : bloque *m* (de piedra,
etc.)

slack ['slæk] *adj* **1** LOOSE : flojo **2** CARE-
LESS : descuidado — ~ *n* **1 take up
the** ~ : tensar (una cuerda, etc.) **2**
~**s** *npl* : pantalones *mpl* — **slacken**
['slækən] *vt* : aflojar — *vi* : aflojarse

slain → **slay**

slam ['slæm] *n* : golpe *m*, portazo *m* (de
una puerta) — ~ *v* **slammed; slam-
ming 1** *or* ~ **down** : tirar, plantar **2**
or ~ **shut** : cerrar de golpe **3** ~ **the
door** : dar un portazo — *vi* **1** : cerrarse
de golpe **2** ~ **into** : chocar contra

slander ['slændər] *vt* : calumniar, difamar — ~ *n* : calumnia *f*, difamación *f*

slang ['slæŋ] *n* : argot *m*

slant ['slænt] *n* : inclinación *f* — ~ *vi*
: inclinarse

slap ['slæp] *vt* **slapped; slapping 1**
: dar una bofetada a **2** ~ **s.o. on the
back** : dar una palmada en la espalda
a algn — ~ *n* : bofetada *f*, cachetada *f*
Lat

slash ['slæʃ] *vt* **1** : hacer un tajo en **2**
: rebajar (precios) drásticamente —
~ *n* : tajo *m*

slat ['slæt] *n* : tablilla *f*

slate ['sleɪt] *n* : pizarra *f*

slaughter ['slɔtər] *n* : matanza *f* — ~ *vt*
1 : matar (animales) **2** MASSACRE
: masacrar — **slaughterhouse** ['slɔ-
tərˌhaus] *n* : matadero *m*

slave ['sleɪv] *n* : esclavo *m*, -va *f* — ~ *vi*

slaved; slaving : trabajar como un
burro — **slavery** ['sleɪvəri] *n* : esclavitud *f*

Slavic ['slɑvɪk, 'slæ-] *adj* : eslavo

slay ['sleɪ] *vt* **slew** ['slu:]; **slain** ['sleɪn];
slaying : asesinar

sleazy ['sli:zi] *adj* **sleazier; -est** : sórdido

sled ['sled] *n* : trineo *m*

sledgehammer ['sledʒˌhæmər] *n* : almádena *f*

sleek ['sli:k] *adj* : liso y brillante

sleep ['sli:p] *n* **1** : sueño *m* **2 go to** ~
: dormirse — ~ *vi* **slept** ['slept];
sleeping : dormir — **sleeper** ['sli:pər]
n **be a light** ~ : tener el sueño ligero
— **sleepless** ['sli:pləs] *adj* **have a** ~
night : pasar la noche en blanco —
sleepwalker ['sli:pˌwɔkər] *n* : sonámbulo *m*, -la *f* — **sleepy** ['sli:pi] *adj*
sleepier; -est 1 : somnoliento,
soñoliento **2 be** ~ : tener sueño

sleet ['sli:t] *n* : aguanieve *f* — ~ *vi*
: caer aguanieve

sleeve ['sli:v] *n* : manga *f* — **sleeveless**
['sli:vləs] *adj* : sin mangas

sleigh ['sleɪ] *n* : trineo *m*

slender ['slendər] *adj* : delgado

slew ['slu:] → **slay**

slice ['slaɪs] *vt* **sliced; slicing** : cortar
— ~ *n* : trozo *m*, rebanada *f* (de pan,
etc.), tajada *f* (de carne)

slick ['slɪk] *adj* SLIPPERY : resbaladizo,
resbaloso *Lat*

slide ['slaɪd] *v* **slid** ['slɪd]; **sliding**
['slaɪdɪŋ] *vi* : deslizarse — *vt* : deslizar
— ~ *n* **1** : deslizamiento *m* **2** : tobogán *m* (para niños) **3** : diapositiva *f*
(fotográfica) **4** DECLINE : descenso *m*

slier, sliest → **sly**

slight ['slaɪt] *adj* **1** : ligero, leve **2** SLEN-
DER : delgado — ~ *vt* : desairar —
slightly ['slaɪtli] *adv* : ligeramente, un
poco

slim ['slɪm] *adj* **slimmer; slimmest 1**
: delgado **2 a** ~ **chance** : escasas
posibilidades *fpl* — ~ *v* **slimmed;
slimming** : adelgazar

slime ['slaɪm] *n* **1** : baba *f* (de un caracol,
etc.) **2** MUD : limo *m* — **slimy** ['slaɪmi]
adj **slimier; -est** : viscoso

sling ['slɪŋ] *vt* **slung** ['slʌŋ]; **slinging 1**
THROW : lanzar **2** HANG : colgar — ~
n **1** : honda *f* **2** : cabestrillo *m* (en medicina) — **slingshot** ['slɪŋˌʃɑt] *n*
: tirachinas *m*

slink ['slɪŋk] *vi* **slunk** ['slʌŋk]; **slinking**
: andar furtivamente

slip[1] ['slɪp] *v* **slipped; slipping** *vi* **1**
SLIDE : resbalarse **2 let sth** ~ : dejar

escapar algo **3** ~ **away** : escabullirse
4 ~ **up** : equivocarse — *vt* **1** : deslizar
2 ~ **into** : ponerse (una prenda) **3** it
slipped my mind : se me olvidó — ~
n **1** MISTAKE : error *m*, desliz *m* **2** ~ **of
the tongue** : lapsus *m* **3** PETTICOAT
: enagua *f*

slip² *n* ~ **of paper** : papelito *m*

slipper ['slɪpər] *n* : zapatilla *f*, pantufla *f*

slippery ['slɪpəri] *adj* **slipperier; -est**
: resbaladizo, resbaloso *Lat*

slit ['slɪt] *n* **1** OPENING : rendija *f* **2** CUT
: corte *m*, raja *f* — ~ *vt* **slit; slitting**
: cortar

slither ['slɪðər] *vi* : deslizarse

sliver ['slɪvər] *n* : astilla *f*

slogan ['sloːgən] *n* : eslogan *m*

slop ['slɑp] *v* **slopped; slopping** *vt*
: derramar — *vi* : derramarse

slope ['sloːp] *vi* **sloped; sloping** : inclinarse — ~ *n* : pendiente *f*, declive *m*

sloppy ['slɑpi] *adj* **sloppier; -est 1**
CARELESS : descuidado **2** UNKEMPT
: desaliñado

slot ['slɑt] *n* : ranura *f*

sloth ['sloːθ, 'sloːθ] *n* : pereza *f*

slouch ['slaʊtʃ] *vi* : andar con los hombros caídos (en una silla)

slovenly ['slʌvənli, 'slʌv-] *adj* : desaliñado

slow ['sloː] *adj* **1** : lento **2 be** ~ : estar
atrasado (dícese de un reloj) — ~ *adv*
→ **slowly** — ~ *vt* : retrasar, retardar
— *vi* or ~ **down** : ir más despacio —
slowly ['sloːli] *adv* : lentamente, despacio — **slowness** ['sloːnəs] *n* : lentitud *f*

sludge ['slʌdʒ] *n* SEWAGE : aguas *fpl* negras

slug¹ ['slʌg] *n* **1** : babosa *f* (molusco) **2**
BULLET : bala *f* **3** TOKEN : ficha *f*

slug² *vt* **slugged; slugging** : pegar un
porrazo a

sluggish ['slʌgɪʃ] *adj* : lento

slum ['slʌm] *n* : barrio *m* bajo

slumber ['slʌmbər] *vi* : dormir — ~ *n*
: sueño *m*

slump ['slʌmp] *vi* **1** DROP : bajar **2** COL-
LAPSE : dejarse caer **3** → **slouch** — ~
n : bajón *m*

slung → **sling**

slunk → **slink**

slur¹ ['slər] *n* ASPERSION : calumnia *f*,
difamación *f*

slur² *vt* **slurred; slurring** : arrastrar (las
palabras)

slurp ['slərp] *v* : beber haciendo ruido —
~ *n* : sorbo *m* (ruidoso)

slush ['slʌʃ] *n* : nieve *f* medio derretida

sly ['slaɪ] *adj* **slier** ['slaɪər]; **sliest**

['slaɪəst] **1** : astuto, taimado **2 on the**
~ : a escondidas

smack¹ ['smæk] *vi* ~ **of** : oler a

smack² *vt* **1** : pegar una bofetada a **2**
KISS : besar **3** ~ **one's lips** : relamerse — ~ *n* : **1** SLAP : bofetada *f* **2**
KISS : beso *m* — ~ *adv* : justo, exactamente

small ['smɔl] *adj* : pequeño, chico —
smallpox ['smɔl͵pɑks] *n* : viruela *f*

smart ['smɑrt] *adj* **1** : listo, inteligente **2**
STYLISH : elegante — ~ *vi* STING : es-
cocer — **smartly** ['smɑrtli] *adv* : ele-
gantemente

smash ['smæʃ] *n* **1** BLOW : golpe *m* **2**
COLLISION : choque *m* **3** BANG, CRASH
: estrépito *m* — ~ *vt* **1** BREAK
: romper **2** DESTROY : aplastar — *vi* **1**
SHATTER : hacerse pedazos **2** ~ **into**
: estrellarse contra

smattering ['smætərɪŋ] *n* : nociones *fpl*

smear ['smɪr] *n* : mancha *f* — ~ *vt* **1**
: embadurnar (de pinta, etc.), untar (de
aceite, etc.) **2** SMUDGE : manchar

smell ['smel] *v* **smelled** or **smelt**
['smelt] **smelling** : oler — ~ *n* **1**
: (sentido *m* del) olfato *m* **2** ODOR
: olor *m* — **smelly** ['smeli] *adj* **smelli-
er; -est** : maloliente

smelt ['smelt] *vt* : fundir

smile ['smaɪl] *vi* **smiled; smiling** : sonreír — ~ *n* : sonrisa *f*

smirk ['smərk] *vi* : sonreír con suficiencia — ~ *n* : sonrisa *f* satisfecha

smitten ['smɪtən] *adj* **be** ~ **with** : estar
enamorado de

smith ['smɪθ] → **blacksmith**

smock ['smɑk] *n* : blusón *m*, bata *f*

smog ['smɑg, 'smɔg] *n* : smog *m*

smoke ['smoːk] *n* : humo *m* — ~ *v*
smoked; smoking *vi* **1** : humear
(dícese de fuegos, etc.) **2** : fumar
(dícese de personas) — *vt* **1** : ahumar
(carne, etc.) **2** : fumar (cigarillos) —
smoker ['smoːkər] *n* : fumador *m*,
-dora *f* — **smokestack** ['smoːk͵stæk] *n*
: chimenea *f* — **smoky** ['smoːki] *adj*
smokier; -est 1 : lleno de humo **2** ~ : a
humo (dícese de sabores, etc.)

smolder ['smoːldər] *vi* : arder (sin llama)

smooth ['smuːð] *adj* **1** : liso (dícese de
superficies), suave (dícese de
movimientos), tranquilo (dícese del
mar) **2** : sin grumos (dícese de salsas,
etc.) — ~ *vt* : alisar — **smoothly**
['smuːðli] *adv* : suavemente —
smoothness ['smuːðnəs] *n* : suavidad *f*

smother ['smʌðər] *vt* : asfixiar (a algn),
sofocar (llamas, etc.)

smudge ['smʌdʒ] *v* **smudged; smudg-**

ing *vt* : emborronar — *vi* : correrse — ~ *n* : mancha *f*, borrón *m*

smug ['smʌg] *adj* **smugger; smuggest** : suficiente

smuggle ['smʌgəl] *vt* **-gled; -gling** : pasar de contrabando — **smuggler** ['smʌgələr] *n* : contrabandista *mf*

snack ['snæk] *n* : refrigerio *m*, tentempié *m fam*

snag ['snæg] *n* : problema *m* — ~ *v* **snagged; snagging** *vt* : enganchar — *vi* : engancharse

snail ['sneɪl] *n* : caracol *m*

snake ['sneɪk] *n* : culebra *f*, serpiente *f*

snap ['snæp] *v* **snapped; snapping** *vi* **1** BREAK : romperse **2** TIGHT : ajustado (dícese de un perro, etc.) **3** ~ **at** : contestar bruscamente a — *vt* **1** BREAK : romper **2** ~ **one's fingers** : chasquear los dedos **3** ~ **open/shut** : abrir/cerrar de golpe — ~ *n* **1** : chasquido *m* **2** FASTENER : broche *m* (de presión) **3 be a** ~ : ser facilísimo — **snappy** ['snæpi] *adj* **snappier; -est 1** FAST : rápido **2** STYLISH : elegante — **snapshot** ['snæp‚ʃɑt] *n* : instantánea *f*

snare ['snær] *n* : trampa *f* — ~ *vt* **snared; snaring** : atrapar

snarl[1] ['snɑrl] *vi* TANGLE : enmarañar, enredar — ~ *n* : enredo *m*, maraña *f*

snarl[2] *vi* GROWL : gruñir — ~ *n* : gruñido *m*

snatch ['snætʃ] *vt* : arrebatar

sneak ['sniːk] *vi* : ir a hurtadillas — *vt* : hacer furtivamente — ~ *n* : soplón *m*, -plona *f fam* — **sneakers** ['sniːkərz] *npl* : tenis *mpl*, zapatillas *fpl* — **sneaky** ['sniːki] *adj* **sneakier; -est** : solapado

sneer ['snɪr] *vi* : sonreír con desprecio — ~ *n* : sonrisa *f* de desprecio

sneeze ['sniːz] *vi* **sneezed; sneezing** : estornudar — ~ *n* : estornudo *m*

snide ['snaɪd] *adj* : sarcástico

sniff ['snɪf] *vi* : oler — *vt* **1** : oler **2** → **sniffle** — ~ *n* : aspiración *f* por la nariz — **sniffle** ['snɪfəl] *vi* **-fled; -fling** : sorberse la nariz — **sniffles** ['snɪfəlz] *npl* **have the** ~ : estar resfriado

snip ['snɪp] *n* : tijeretada *f* — ~ *vt* **snipped; snipping** : cortar (con tijeras)

snivel ['snɪvəl] *vi* **-veled** *or* **-velled; -veling** *or* **-velling** : lloriquear

snob ['snɑb] *n* : esnob *mf* — **snobbish** ['snɑbɪʃ] *adj* : esnob

snoop ['snuːp] *vi* : husmear — ~ *n* : fisgón *m*, -gona *f*

snooze ['snuːz] *vi* **snoozed; snoozing** : dormitar — ~ *n* : siestecita *f*, siesta *f*

snore ['snor] *vi* **snored; snoring** : roncar — ~ *n* : ronquido *m*

snort ['snort] *vi* : bufar — ~ *n* : bufido *m*

snout ['snaʊt] *n* : hocico *m*, morro *m*

snow ['snoː] *n* : nieve *f* — ~ *vi* : nevar — **snowfall** ['snoː‚fɔl] *n* : nevada *f* — **snowflake** ['snoː‚fleɪk] *n* : copo *m* de nieve — **snowman** ['snoː‚mæn] *n* : muñeco *m* de nieve — **snowplow** ['snoː‚plaʊ] *n* : quitanieves *m* — **snowshoe** ['snoː‚ʃuː] *n* : raqueta *f* (para nieve) — **snowstorm** ['snoː‚storm] *n* : tormenta *f* de nieve — **snowy** ['snoːi] *adj* **snowier; -est 1 a** ~ **day** : un día nevoso **2** ~ **mountains** : montañas *fpl* nevadas

snub ['snʌb] *vt* **snubbed; snubbing** : desairar — ~ *n* : desaire *m*

snuff ['snʌf] *vt or* ~ **out** : apagar

snug ['snʌg] *adj* **snugger; snuggest 1** : cómodo **2** TIGHT : ajustado — **snuggle** ['snʌgəl] *vi* **-gled; -gling** : acurrucarse

so ['soː] *adv* **1** LIKEWISE : también **2** THUS : así **3** THEREFORE : por lo tanto **4** *or* ~ **much** : tanto **5** *or* ~ **very** : tan **6 and** ~ **on** : etcétera **7 I think** ~ : creo que sí **8 I told you** ~ : te lo dije — ~ *conj* **1** THEREFORE : así que **2** *or* ~ **that** : para que **3** ~ **what?** : ¿y qué? — ~ *adj* TRUE : cierto — ~ *pron* **or** ~ : más o menos

soak ['soːk] *vi* : estar en remojo — *vt* **1** : poner en remojo **2** ~ **up** : absorber — ~ *n* : remojo *m*

soap ['soːp] *n* : jabón *m* — ~ *vt or* ~ **up** : enjabonar — **soapy** ['soːpi] **soapier; -est** *adj* : jabonoso

soar ['sor] *vi* **1** : planear **2** SKYROCKET : dispararse

sob ['sɑb] *vi* **sobbed; sobbing** : sollozar — ~ *n* : sollozo *m*

sober ['soːbər] *adj* **1** : sobrio **2** SERIOUS : serio — **sobriety** [səˈbraɪəti, so-] *n* **1** : sobriedad *f* **2** SERIOUSNESS : seriedad *f*

so-called ['soːˈkold] *adj* : supuesto, presunto

soccer ['sɑkər] *n* : futbol *m*, fútbol *m*

social ['soːʃəl] *adj* : social — ~ *n* : reunión *f* social — **sociable** ['soːʃəbəl] *adj* : sociable — **socialism** ['soːʃə‚lɪzəm] *n* : socialismo *m* — **socialist** ['soːʃəlɪst] *n* : socialista *mf* — ~ *adj* : socialista — **socialize** ['soːʃə‚laɪz] *v* **-ized; -izing** *vt* : socializar — *vi* ~ **with** : alternar con — **society** [səˈsaɪəti] *n, pl* **-eties** : sociedad *f* — **sociology** [‚soːsiˈɑlədʒi] *n* : sociología *f*

sock¹ ['sak] *n, pl* **socks** *or* **sox** ['saks] : calcetín *m*

sock² *vt* : pegar, golpear — ~ *n* PUNCH : puñetazo *m*

socket ['sakət] *n* 1 *or* **electric** ~ : enchufe *m*, toma *f* de corriente 2 *or* **eye** ~ : órbita *f*, cuenca *f* 3 : glena *f* (de una articulación)

soda ['so:də] *n* 1 *or* ~ **pop** : refresco *m*, gaseosa *f* 2 *or* ~ **water** : soda *f*

sodium ['so:diəm] *n* : sodio *m*

sofa ['so:fə] *n* : sofá *m*

soft ['sɔft] *adj* 1 : blando 2 SMOOTH : suave — **softball** ['sɔft,bɔl] *n* : softbol *m* — **soft drink** *n* : refresco *m* — **soften** ['sɔfən] *vt* 1 : ablandar 2 EASE, SMOOTH : suavizar — *vi* 1 : ablandarse 2 EASE : suavizarse — **softly** ['sɔftli] *adv* : suavemente — **software** ['sɔft,wær] *n* : software *m*

soggy ['sagi] *adj* **soggier; -est** : empapado

soil ['sɔil] *vt* : ensuciar — ~ *n* DIRT : tierra *f*

solace ['saləs] *n* : consuelo *m*

solar ['so:lər] *adj* : solar

sold → **sell**

solder ['sadər, 'sɔ-] *n* : soldadura *f* — ~ *vt* : soldar

soldier ['so:ldʒər] *n* : soldado *mf*

sole¹ ['so:l] *n* : lenguado *m* (pez)

sole² *n* : planta *f* (del pie), suela *f* (de un zapato)

sole³ *adj* 1 : único — **solely** ['so:li] *adv* : únicamente, sólo

solemn ['saləm] *adj* : solemne — **solemnity** [sə'lɛmnəti] *n, pl* **-ties** : solemnidad *f*

solicit [sə'lɪsət] *vt* : solicitar

solid ['saləd] *adj* 1 : sólido 2 UNBROKEN : continuo 3 ~ **gold** : oro *m* macizo 4 **two** ~ **hours** : dos horas seguidas — ~ *n* : sólido *m* — **solidarity** [,salə'dærəti] *n* : solidaridad *f* — **solidify** [sə'lɪdə,faɪ] *v* **-fied; -fying** *vt* : solidificar — *vi* : solidificarse — **solidity** [sə'lɪdəti] *n, pl* **-ties** : solidez *f*

solitary ['salə,tɛri] *adj* : solitario — **solitude** ['salə,tu:d, -,tju:d] *n* : soledad *f*

solo ['so:lo:] *n, pl* **solos** : solo *m* — **soloist** ['so:lo:ɪst] *n* : solista *mf*

solution [sə'lu:ʃən] *n* : solución *f* — **soluble** ['saljəbəl] *adj* : soluble — **solve** ['salv] *vt* **solved; solving** : resolver — **solvent** ['salvənt] *n* : solvente *m*

somber ['sambər] *adj* : sombrío

some ['sʌm] *adj* 1 (*of unspecified identity*) : un 2 (*of an unspecified amount*) : algo de, un poco de 3 (*of an unspecified number*) : unos 4 CERTAIN : al-

gunos 5 **that was** ~ **game!** : ¡fue un partidazo! — ~ *pron* 1 SEVERAL : algunos, unos 2 PART : un poco, algo — ~ *adv* ~ **twenty people** : unas veinte personas — **somebody** ['sʌm,badi, -,bədi] *pron* : alguien — **someday** ['sʌm,deɪ] *adv* : algún día — **somehow** ['sʌm,haʊ] *adv* 1 : de algún modo 2 ~ **or other** : de alguna manera u otra — **someone** ['sʌm,wʌn] *pron* : alguien

somersault ['sʌmər,sɔlt] *n* : voltereta *f*, salto *m* mortal

something ['sʌmθɪŋ] *pron* 1 : algo 2 ~ **else** : otra cosa — **sometime** ['sʌm,taɪm] *adv* 1 : algún día, en algún momento 2 ~ **next month** : (durante) el mes que viene — **sometimes** ['sʌm,taɪmz] *adv* : a veces — **somewhat** ['sʌm,hwʌt, -,hwat] *adv* : algo — **somewhere** ['sʌm,hwɛr] *adv* 1 : en alguna parte, en algún lado 2 ~ **around** : alrededor de 3 ~ **else** → **elsewhere**

son ['sʌn] *n* : hijo *m*

song ['sɔŋ] *n* : canción *f*

son–in–law ['sʌnɪn,lɔ] *n, pl* **sons–in–law** : yerno *m*

sonnet ['sanət] *n* : soneto *m*

soon ['su:n] *adv* 1 : pronto 2 SHORTLY : dentro de poco 3 **as** ~ **as** : en cuanto 4 **as** ~ **as possible** : lo más pronto posible 5 ~ **after** : poco después 6 ~**er or later** : tarde o temprano 7 **the** ~**er the better** : cuanto antes mejor

soot ['sʊt, 'su:t, 'sʌt] *n* : hollín *m*

soothe ['su:ð] *vt* **soothed; soothing** 1 CALM : calmar 2 RELIEVE : aliviar

sop ['sap] *vt* **sopped; sopping** ~ **up** : absorber

sophistication [sə,fɪstə'keɪʃən] *n* : sofisticación *f* — **sophisticated** [sə'fɪstə-,keɪtəd] *adj* : sofisticado

sophomore ['saf,mor, 'safə,mor] *n* : estudiante *mf* de segundo año

soprano [sə'præno:] *n, pl* **-nos** : soprano *mf*

sorcerer ['sɔrsərər] *n* : hechicero *m*, brujo *m* — **sorcery** ['sɔrsəri] *n* : hechicería *f*, brujería *f*

sordid ['sɔrdɪd] *adj* : sórdido

sore ['sor] *adj* **sorer; sorest** 1 : dolorido 2 ANGRY : enfadado 3 ~ **throat** : dolor *m* de garganta 4 **I have a** ~ **throat** : me duele la garganta — ~ *n* : llaga *f* — **sorely** ['sorli] *adv* : muchísimo — **soreness** ['sornəs] *n* : dolor *m*

sorrow ['saro:] *n* : pesar *m*, pena *f* — **sorry** ['sari] *adj* **sorrier; -est** 1 PITIFUL : lamentable 2 **feel** ~ **for** : compadecer 3 **I'm** ~ : lo siento

sort ['sɔrt] *n* **1** : tipo *m*, clase *f* **2 a ~ of** : una especie de — ~ *vt* : clasificar — **sort of** *adv* **1** SOMEWHAT : algo **2** MORE OR LESS : más o menos

SOS [ˌesˌoːˈes] *n* : SOS *m*

so-so ['soːˌsoː] *adj & adv* : así así *fam*

soufflé [suːˈfleɪ] *n* : suflé *m*

sought → **seek**

soul ['soːl] *n* : alma *f*

sound[1] ['saʊnd] *adj* **1** HEALTHY : sano **2** FIRM : sólido **3** SENSIBLE : lógico **4 a ~ sleep** : un sueño profundo **5 safe and ~** : sano y salvo

sound[2] *n* : sonido *m* — *vt* : hacer sonar, tocar (una trompeta, etc.) — *vi* **1** : sonar **2** SEEM : parecer

sound[3] *n* CHANNEL : brazo *m* de mar — ~ *vt* **1** : sondar (en navegación) **2 or ~ out** : sondear

soundly ['saʊndli] *adv* **1** SOLIDLY : sólidamente **2** DEEPLY : profundamente

soundproof ['saʊndˌpruːf] *adj* : insonorizado

soup ['suːp] *n* : sopa *f*

sour ['saʊər] *adj* **1** : agrio **2 ~ milk** : leche *f* cortada — ~ *vt* : agriar

source ['sɔrs] *n* : fuente *f*, origen *m*

south ['saʊθ] *adv* **1** : al sur — ~ *adj* : (del) sur — ~ *n* : sur *m* — **South African** *adj* : sudafricano — **South American** *adj* : sudamericano — **southeast** [saʊˈθiːst] *adv* : hacia el sureste — ~ *adj* : (del) sureste — ~ *n* : sureste *m*, sudeste *m* — **southeastern** [saʊˈθiːstərn] *adj* → **southeast** — **southerly** ['sʌðərli] *adv & adj* : del sur — **southern** ['sʌðərn] *adj* : del sur, meridional — **southwest** [saʊθˈwest] *adv* : hacia el suroeste — ~ *adj* : (del) suroeste — ~ *n* : suroeste *m*, sudoeste *m* — **southwestern** [saʊθˈwestərn] *adj* → **southwest**

souvenir [ˌsuːvəˈnɪr, ˈsuːvəˌ-] *n* : recuerdo *m*

sovereign ['sʌvərən] *n* : soberano *m*, -na *f* — ~ *adj* : soberano — **sovereignty** ['sʌvərənti] *n, pl* **-ties** : soberanía *f*

Soviet ['soːviˌet, 'sɑ-, -viət] *adj* : soviético

sow[1] ['saʊ] *n* : cerda *f*

sow[2] ['soː] *vt* **sowed; sown** ['soːn] *or* **sowed; sowing** : sembrar

sox → **sock**

soybean ['sɔɪˌbiːn] *n* : soya *f*, soja *f*

spa ['spɑ] *n* : balneario *m*

space ['speɪs] *n* **1** : espacio *m* **2** ROOM, SPOT : sitio *m*, lugar *m* — ~ *vt* **spaced; spacing** : espaciar — **spaceship** ['speɪsˌʃɪp] *n* : nave *f* espacial — **space shuttle** *n* : transbordador *m* espacial — **spacious** ['speɪʃəs] *adj* : espacioso, amplio

spade[1] ['speɪd] *n* SHOVEL : pala *f*

spade[2] *n* : pica *f* (naipe)

spaghetti [spəˈgeti] *n* : espaguetis *mpl*

span ['spæn] *n* **1** PERIOD : espacio *m* **2** : luz *f* (entre dos soportes) — ~ *vt* **spanned; spanning 1** : abarcar (un período) **2** CROSS : extenderse sobre

Spaniard ['spænjərd] *n* : español *m*, -ñola *f*

spaniel ['spænjəl] *n* : spaniel *m*

Spanish ['spænɪʃ] *adj* : español — ~ *n* : español *m* (idioma)

spank ['spæŋk] *vt* : dar palmadas a (en las nalgas)

spar ['spɑr] *vi* **sparred; sparring** : entrenarse (en boxeo)

spare ['spær] *vt* **spared; sparing 1** PARDON : perdonar **2** SAVE : ahorrar **3 can you ~ a dollar?** : ¿me das un dólar? **4 I can't ~ the time** : no tengo tiempo **5 ~ no expense** : no reparar en gastos **6 to ~** : de sobra — ~ *adj* **1** : de repuesto **2** EXCESS : de más **3** LEAN : delgado — ~ *n or* **~ part** : repuesto *m* — **spare time** *n* : tiempo *m* libre — **sparing** ['spærɪŋ] *adj* : parco, económico

spark ['spɑrk] *n* : chispa *f* — ~ *vi* : chispear, echar chispas — ~ *vt* : despertar (interés), provocar (crítica) — **sparkle** ['spɑrkəl] *vi* **-kled; -kling** : destellar, centellear — ~ *n* : destello *m*, centelleo *m* — **spark plug** *n* : bujía *f*

sparrow ['spæroː] *n* : gorrión *m*

sparse ['spɑrs] *adj* **sparser; -est** : escaso

spasm ['spæzəm] *n* : espasmo *m*

spat[1] → **spit**

spat[2] *n* QUARREL : disputa *f*, pelea *f*

spatter ['spætər] *vt* : salpicar

spawn ['spɔn] *vi* : desovar — *vt* : engendrar, producir — ~ *n* : hueva *f*

speak ['spiːk] *v* **spoke** ['spoːk]; **spoken** ['spoːkən]; **speaking** *vi* **1** : hablar **2 ~ out against** : denunciar **3 ~ up** : hablar más alto **4 ~ up for** : defender — *vt* **1** : decir **2** : hablar (un idioma) — **speaker** ['spiːkər] *n* **1** ORATOR : orador *m*, -dora *f* **2** : hablante *mf* (de un idioma) **3** LOUDSPEAKER : altavoz *m*

spear ['spɪr] *n* : lanza *f* — **spearhead** ['spɪrˌhed] *n* : punta *f* de lanza — ~ *vt* : encabezar — **spearmint** ['spɪrmɪnt] *n* : menta *f* verde

special ['speʃəl] *adj* : especial — **specialist** ['speʃəlɪst] *n* : especialista *mf* — **specialization** [ˌspeʃələˈzeɪʃən] *n* : especialización *f* — **specialize** ['speʃə-

‚laɪz] *vi* **-ized; -izing** : especializarse — **specially** *adv* : especialmente — **specialty** ['spɛʃəlti] *n*, *pl* **-ties** : especialidad *f*

species ['spi:ʃiːz, -ˌsiːz] *ns & pl* : especie *f*

specify ['spɛsəˌfaɪ] *vt* **-fied; -fying** : especificar — **specific** [sprˈsɪfɪk] *adj* : específico — **specifically** [sprˈsɪfɪkli] *adv* 1 : específicamente 2 EXPLICITLY : expresamente — **specification** [ˌspɛsəfəˈkeɪʃən] *n* : especificación *f*

specimen ['spɛsəmən] *n* : espécimen *m*

speck ['spɛk] *n* 1 SPOT : mancha *f* 2 BIT : mota *f* — **speckled** ['spɛkəld] *adj* : moteado

spectacle ['spɛktɪkəl] *n* 1 : espectáculo *m* 2 **~s** *npl* GLASSES : gafas *fpl*, lentes *fpl*, anteojos *mpl* — **spectacular** [spɛkˈtækjələr] *adj* : espectacular — **spectator** ['spɛkˌteɪtər] *n* : espectador *m*, -dora *f*

specter *or* **spectre** ['spɛktər] *n* : espectro *m*

spectrum ['spɛktrəm] *n*, *pl* **-tra** [-trə] *or* **-trums** 1 : espectro *m* 2 RANGE : gama *f*

speculation [ˌspɛkjəˈleɪʃən] *n* : especulación *f*

speech ['spiːtʃ] *n* 1 : habla *f* 2 ADDRESS : discurso *m* — **speechless** ['spiːtʃləs] *adj* : mudo

speed ['spiːd] *n* 1 : rapidez *f* 2 VELOCITY : velocidad *f* — *v* **sped** ['spɛd] *or* **speeded; speeding** *vi* 1 : conducir a exceso de velocidad 2 **~ off** : irse a toda velocidad 3 **~ up** : acelerarse — *vt or* **~ up** : acelerar — **speed limit** : velocidad *f* máxima — **speedometer** [sprˈdɑmətər] *n* : velocímetro *m* — **speedy** ['spiːdi] *adj* **speedier, -est** : rápido

spell[1] ['spɛl] *vt* 1 : escribir (las letras de) 2 *or* **~ out** : deletrear 3 MEAN : significar

spell[2] *n* ENCHANTMENT : hechizo *m*

spell[3] *n* : período *m* (de tiempo)

spellbound ['spɛlˌbaʊnd] *adj* : embelesado

spelling ['spɛlɪŋ] *n* : ortografía *f*

spend ['spɛnd] *vt* **spent** ['spɛnt]; **spending** 1 : gastar (dinero) 2 : pasar (las vacaciones, etc.) 3 **~ time on** : dedicar tiempo a

sperm ['spərm] *n*, *pl* **sperm** *or* **sperms** : esperma *mf*

spew ['spjuː] *vt* : vomitar, arrojar (lava, etc.)

sphere ['sfɪr] *n* : esfera *f* — **spherical** ['sfɪrɪkəl, 'sfɛr-] *adj* : esférico

spice ['spaɪs] *n* : especia *f* — **~** *vt* **spiced; spicing** : condimentar, sazonar — **spicy** ['spaɪsi] *adj* **spicier; -est** : picante

spider ['spaɪdər] *n* : araña *f*

spigot ['spɪgət, -kət] *n* : grifo *m* *Spain*, llave *f* *Lat*

spike ['spaɪk] *n* 1 : clavo *m* (grande) 2 POINT : punta *f* — **spiky** ['spaɪki] *adj* : puntiagudo

spill ['spɪl] *vt* : derramar — *vi* : derramarse

spin ['spɪn] *v* **spun** ['spʌn]; **spinning** *vi* : girar — *vt* 1 : hilar (lana, etc.) 2 TWIRL : hacer girar — *~ n* 1 : vuelta *f*, giro *m* 2 **go for a ~** : dar una vuelta (en auto)

spinach ['spɪnɪtʃ] *n* : espinacas *fpl*

spinal cord ['spaɪnəl] *n* : médula *f* espinal

spindle ['spɪndəl] *n* : huso *m* (para hilar) — **spindly** ['spɪndli] *adj* : larguirucho *fam*

spine ['spaɪn] *n* 1 : columna *f* vertebral 2 QUILL : púa *f* 3 THORN : espina *f* 4 : lomo *m* (de un libro)

spinster ['spɪnstər] *n* : soltera *f*

spiral ['spaɪrəl] *adj* : de espiral, en espiral — **~** *n* : espiral *f* — **~** *vi* **-raled** *or* **-ralled; -raling** *or* **-ralling** : ir en espiral

spire ['spaɪr] *n* : aguja *f*

spirit ['spɪrət] *n* 1 : espíritu *m* 2 **in good ~s** : animado 3 **~s** *npl* : licores *mpl* — **spirited** ['spɪrətəd] *adj* : animado — **spiritual** ['spɪrɪtʃuəl, -tʃəl] *adj* : espiritual — **spirituality** [ˌspɪrɪtʃuˈæləti] *n*, *pl* **-ties** : espiritualidad *f*

spit[1] ['spɪt] *n* ROTISSERIE : asador *m*

spit[2] *v* **spit** *or* **spat** ['spæt]; **spitting** : escupir — *n* SALIVA : saliva *f*

spite ['spaɪt] *n* 1 : rencor *m* 2 **in ~ of** : a pesar de — *vt* **spited; spiting** : fastidiar — **spiteful** ['spaɪtfəl] *adj* : rencoroso

spittle ['spɪtəl] *n* : saliva *f*

splash ['splæʃ] *vt* : salpicar — *vi* 1 : salpicar 2 *or* **~** : chapotear — **~** *n* 1 : salpicadura *f* 2 : mancha *f* (de color, etc.)

splatter ['splætər] → **spatter**

spleen ['spliːn] *n* : bazo *m* (órgano)

splendor ['splɛndər] *n* : esplendor *m* — **splendid** ['splɛndəd] *adj* : espléndido

splint ['splɪnt] *n* : tablilla *f*

splinter ['splɪntər] *n* : astilla *f* — *vi* : astillarse

split ['splɪt] *v* **split; splitting** *vt* 1 : partir 2 BURST : reventar 3 *or* **~ up** : dividir — *vi* 1 : partirse, rajarse 2 *or* **~ up**

: dividirse — **~** *n* 1 CRACK : rajadura *f*
2 *or* **~ seam** : descosido *m* 3 DIVI-
SION : división *f*

splurge ['splərdʒ] *vi* **splurged; splurg-
ing** : derrochar dinero

spoil ['spɔɪl] *vt* **spoiled** *or* **spoilt**
['spɔɪlt]; **spoiling** 1 RUIN : estropear 2
PAMPER : consentir, mimar — **spoils**
npl : botín *m*

spoke¹ ['spoːk] → **speak**

spoke² *n* : rayo *m* (de una rueda)

spoken → **speak**

spokesman ['spoːksmən] *n, pl* **-men**
[-mən, -ˌmɛn] : portavoz *mf* — **spokeswoman** ['spoːksˌwʊmən] *n, pl* **-women**
[-ˌwɪmən] : portavoz *f*

sponge ['spʌndʒ] *n* : esponja *f* — **~** *vt*
sponged; sponging : limpiar con
una esponja — **spongy** ['spʌndʒi] *adj*
spongier; -est : esponjoso

sponsor ['spɑntsər] *n* : patrocinador *m*,
-dora *f* — **~** *vt* : patrocinar — **sponsorship** ['spɑntsərˌʃɪp] *n* : patrocinio *m*

spontaneity [ˌspɑntən'iːəti, -'neɪ-] *n*
: espontaneidad *f* — **spontaneous**
[spɑn'teɪniəs] *adj* : espontáneo

spooky ['spuːki] *adj* **spookier; -est** : es-
peluzante

spool ['spuːl] *n* : carrete *m*

spoon ['spuːn] *n* : cuchara *f* — **spoonful**
['spuːnˌfʊl] *n* : cucharada *f*

sporadic [spə'rædɪk] *adj* : esporádico

spore ['spɔr] *n* : espora *f*

sport ['spɔrt] *n* 1 : deporte *m* 2 **be a
good ~** : tener espíritu deportivo —
sportsman ['spɔrtsmən] *n, pl* **-men**
[-mən, -ˌmɛn] : deportista *m* — **sportswoman** ['spɔrtsˌwʊmən] *n, pl* **-women**
[-ˌwɪmən] : deportista *f* — **sporty**
['spɔrti] *adj* **sportier; -est** : deportivo

spot ['spɑt] *n* 1 : mancha *f* 2 DOT : punto
m 3 PLACE : lugar *m*, sitio *m* 4 **in a
tight ~** : en apuros 5 **on the ~** IN-
STANTLY : en ese mismo momento —
~ *vt* **spotted; spotting** 1 STAIN
: manchar 2 DETECT, NOTICE : ver, descubrir — **spotless** ['spɑtləs] *adj* : impecable — **spotlight** ['spɑtˌlaɪt] *n* 1
: foco *m*, reflector *m* 2 **be in the ~**
: ser el centro de atención — **spotty**
['spɑti] *adj* **spottier; -est** : irregular

spouse ['spaʊs] *n* : cónyuge *mf*

spout ['spaʊt] *vi* : salir a chorros — **~** *n*
1 : pico *m* (de una jarra, etc.) 2 STREAM
: chorro *m*

sprain ['spreɪn] *n* : esguince *m* — **~** *vt*
: sufrir un esguince en

sprawl ['sprɔl] *vi* 1 : repantigarse (en un
sillón, etc.) 2 EXTEND : extenderse —
~ *n* : extensión *f*

spray¹ ['spreɪ] *n* BOUQUET : ramillete *m*

spray² *n* 1 MIST : rocío *m* 2 *or* **aerosol
~** : spray *m* 3 *or* **~ bottle** : atomizador *m* — **~** *vt* : rociar (una superficie), pulverizar (un líquido)

spread ['sprɛd] *v* **spread; spreading** *vt*
1 : propagar (enfermedades), difundir
(noticias, etc.) 2 *or* **~ out** : extender 3
: untar (con mantequilla, etc.) — *vi* 1
: propagarse, difundirse 2 *or* **~ out**
: extenderse — **~** *n* 1 : propagación *f*,
difusión *f* 2 PASTE : pasta *f* (para untar)
— **spreadsheet** ['sprɛdˌʃiːt] *n* : hoja *f*
de cálculo

spree ['spri] *n* **go on a ~** : ir de juerga
fam

sprig ['sprɪg] *n* : ramito *m*

sprightly ['spraɪtli] *adj* **sprightlier; -est**
: vivo

spring ['sprɪŋ] *v* **sprang** ['spræŋ] *or*
sprung ['sprʌŋ]; **sprung; springing**
vi 1 : saltar 2 **~ from** : surgir de 3 **~
up** : surgir — *vt* 1 ACTIVATE : accionar
2 **~ a leak** : hacer agua 3 **~ sth on
s.o.** : sorprender a algn con algo — **~**
n 1 : manantial *m* (de aguas) 2 : primavera *f* (estación) 3 LEAP : salto *m* 4
RESILIENCE : elasticidad *f* 5 : resorte *m*
(mecanismo) 6 *or* **bedspring** : muelle
m — **springboard** ['sprɪŋˌbord] *n*
: trampolín *m* — **springtime** ['sprɪŋ-
ˌtaɪm] *n* : primavera *f* — **springy** ['sprɪ-
ŋi] *adj* **springier; -est** : mullido

sprinkle ['sprɪŋkəl] *vt* **-kled; -kling** 1
: salpicar, rociar 2 DUST : espolvorear
— **~** *n* : llovizna *f* — **sprinkler**
['sprɪŋkələr] *n* : aspersor *m*

sprint ['sprɪnt] *vi* 1 : correr 2 : esprintar
(en deportes) — **~** *n* : esprint *m* (en
deportes)

sprout ['spraʊt] *vi* : brotar — **~** *n* : brote
m

spruce¹ ['spruːs] *vt* **spruced; sprucing
~ up** : arreglar

spruce² *n* : picea *f* (árbol)

spry ['spraɪ] *adj* **sprier** *or* **spryer**
['spraɪər]; **spriest** *or* **spryest** ['spraɪəst]
: ágil, activo

spun → **spin**

spur ['spər] *n* 1 : espuela *f* 2 STIMULUS
: acicate *m* 3 **on the ~ of the moment** : sin pensarlo — **~** *vt* **spurred;
spurring** *or* **~ on** 1 : espolear (un caballo) 2 MOTIVATE : motivar

spurn ['spərn] *vt* : desdeñar, rechazar

spurt¹ ['spərt] *vi* : salir a chorros — **~** *n*
: chorro *m*

spurt² *n* 1 : arranque *m* (de energía,
etc.) 2 **work in ~s** : trabajar por
rachas

spy ['spaɪ] v **spied; spying** vt : ver, divisar — vi ~ **on s.o.** : espiar a algn — ~ n : espía mf

squabble ['skwɑbəl] n : riña f, pelea f — vi **-bled; -bling** : reñir, pelearse

squad ['skwɑd] n : pelotón m (militar), brigada f (de policías)

squadron ['skwɑdrən] n : escuadrón m (de soldados), escuadra f (de aviones o naves)

squalid ['skwɑlɪd] adj : miserable

squall ['skwɔl] n : turbión m

squalor ['skwɑlər] n : miseria f

squander ['skwɑndər] vt : derrochar (dinero, etc.), desperdiciar (oportunidades, etc.)

square ['skwær] n 1 : cuadrado m 2 : plaza f (de una ciudad) — ~ adj **squarer; -est** 1 : cuadrado 2 HONEST : justo 3 EVEN : en paz 4 a ~ **meal** : una comida decente — ~ vt **squared; squaring** 1 : elevar al cuadrado (un número) 2 : saldar (una cuenta) — **square root** n : raíz f cuadrada

squash[1] ['skwɑʃ, 'skwɔʃ] vt 1 : aplastar 2 : acallar (protestas, etc.) — ~ n : squash m (deporte)

squash[2] n, pl **squashes** or **squash** : calabaza f (vegetal)

squat ['skwɑt] vi **squatted; squatting** 1 or ~ **down** : ponerse en cuclillas 2 : ocupar un lugar sin derecho — ~ adj **squatter; squattest** : achaparrado

squawk ['skwɔk] n : graznido m — vi : graznar

squeak ['skwiːk] vi 1 : chillar 2 CREAK : chirriar — ~ n 1 : chillido m 2 CREAK : chirrido m — **squeaky** ['skwiːki] adj **squeakier; -est** : chirriante

squeal ['skwiːl] vi 1 : chillar (dícese de personas, etc.), chirriar (dícese de frenos, etc.) 2 PROTEST : quejarse — ~ n : chillido m (de una persona), chirrido m (de frenos, etc.)

squeamish ['skwiːmɪʃ] adj : impresionable, delicado

squeeze ['skwiːz] vt **squeezed; squeezing** 1 : apretar 2 : exprimir (frutas, etc.) 3 : extraer (jugo, etc.) — ~ n : apretón m

squid ['skwɪd] n, pl **squid** or **squids** : calamar m

squint ['skwɪnt] vi : entrecerrar los ojos — ~ n : estrabismo m

squirm ['skwərm] vi : retorcerse

squirrel ['skwərəl] n : ardilla f

squirt ['skwərt] vt : lanzar un chorro de — vi : salir a chorros — ~ n : chorrito m

stab ['stæb] n 1 : puñalada f 2 ~ **of pain** : pinchazo m 3 **take a** ~ **at** : intentar — ~ vt **stabbed; stabbing** 1 KNIFE : apuñalar 2 STICK : clavar

stable[1] ['steɪbəl] n 1 : establo m (para ganado), 2 or **horse** ~ : caballeriza f — ~ adj **-bler; -blest** : estable — **stability** [stə'bɪləti] n, pl **-ties** : estabilidad f — **stabilize** ['steɪbəˌlaɪz] vt **-lized; -lizing** : estabilizar

stack ['stæk] n : montón m, pila f — ~ vt : amontonar, apilar

stadium ['steɪdiəm] n, pl **-dia** or **-diums** : estadio m

staff ['stæfs, 'stævz] n, pl **staffs** or **staves** ['stævz, 'steɪvz] 1 : bastón m 2 pl **staffs** PERSONNEL : personal m 3 pl **staffs** : pentagrama m (en música) — ~ ['stæf] vt : proveer de personal

stag ['stæg] n, pl **stags** or **stag** : ciervo m, venado m — ~ adj : sólo para hombres — ~ adv **go** ~ : ir solo

stage ['steɪdʒ] n 1 : escenario m (de un teatro) 2 PHASE : etapa f 3 **the** ~ : el teatro — ~ vt **staged; staging** 1 : poner en escena 2 ARRANGE : montar — **stagecoach** ['steɪdʒˌkotʃ] n : diligencia f

stagger ['stægər] vi : tambalearse — vt 1 : escalonar (turnos, etc.) 2 **be** ~ **ed by** : quedarse estupefacto por — ~ n : tambaleo m — **staggering** ['stægərɪŋ] adj : asombroso

stagnant ['stægnənt] adj : estancado — **stagnate** ['stægˌneɪt] vi **-nated; -nating** : estancarse

stain ['steɪn] vt 1 : manchar 2 : teñir (madera) — ~ n 1 : mancha f 2 DYE : tinte m, tintura f — **stainless steel** ['steɪnləs-] n : acero m inoxidable

stair ['stær] n 1 STEP : escalón m, peldaño m 2 ~ **s** npl : escalera(s) f(pl) — **staircase** ['stærˌkeɪs] n : escalera(s) f(pl) — **stairway** ['stærˌweɪ] n : escalera(s) f(pl)

stake ['steɪk] n 1 POST : estaca f 2 BET : apuesta f 3 INTEREST : intereses mpl 4 **be at** ~ : estar en juego — ~ vt **staked; staking** 1 : estacar 2 BET : jugarse 3 ~ **a claim to** : reclamar

stale ['steɪl] adj **staler; stalest** 1 : duro (dícese del pan) 2 OLD : viejo 3 STUFFY : viciado

stalk[1] ['stɔk] n : tallo m (de una planta)

stalk[2] vt : acechar — vi or ~ **off** : irse con altivez

stall[1] ['stɔl] n 1 : compartimiento m (de un establo) 2 STAND : puesto m — ~ vt : parar (un motor) — vi : pararse

stall[2] *vt* DELAY : entretener — *vi* : andar con rodeos

stallion ['stæljən] *n* : caballo *m* semental

stalwart ['stɔlwərt] *adj* 1 STRONG : fornido 2 ~ **supporter** : partidario *m* leal

stamina ['stæmənə] *n* : resistencia *f*

stammer ['stæmər] *vi* : tartamudear — ~ *n* : tartamudeo *m*

stamp ['stæmp] *n* 1 SEAL : sello *m* 2 DIE : cuño *m* 3 *or* **postage** ~ : sello *m*, estampilla *f Lat*, timbre *m Lat* — ~ *vt* 1 : franquear (una carta) 2 IMPRINT : sellar 3 MINT : acuñar 4 ~ **one's foot** : dar una patada (en el suelo)

stampede [stæm'piːd] *n* : estampida *f* — ~ *vi* **-peded; -peding** : salir en estampida

stance ['stænʦ] *n* : postura *f*

stand ['stænd] *v* **stood** ['stʊd]; **standing** *vi* 1 : estar de pie, estar parado *Lat* 2 BE : estar 3 CONTINUE : seguir vigente 4 LIE, REST : reposar 5 ~ **aside** *or* ~ **back** : apartarse 6 ~ **out** : sobresalir 7 *or* ~ **up** : ponerse de pie, pararse *Lat* — *vt* 1 PLACE : poner, colocar 2 ENDURE : soportar 3 ~ **a chance** : tener una posibilidad — **stand by** *vt* 1 : mantener (una promesa, etc.) 2 SUPPORT : apoyar — **stand for** *vt* 1 MEAN : significar 2 PERMIT : permitir — **stand up** *vi* 1 ~ **for** : defender 2 ~ **up to** : resistir a — ~ *n* 1 RESISTANCE : resistencia *f* 2 STALL : puesto *m* 3 BASE : base *f* 4 POSITION : posición *f* 5 ~**s** *npl* : tribuna *f*

standard ['stændərd] *n* 1 : norma *f* 2 BANNER : estandarte *m* 3 CRITERION : criterio *m* 4 ~ **of living** : nivel *m* de vida — ~ *adj* : estándar — **standardize** ['stændər,daɪz] *vt* **-ized; -izing** : estandarizar

standing ['stændɪŋ] *n* 1 RANK : posición *f* 2 DURATION : duración *f*

standpoint ['stænd,pɔɪnt] *n* : punto *m* de vista

standstill ['stænd,stɪl] *n* 1 **be at a** ~ : estar paralizado 2 **come to a** ~ : pararse

stank → **stink**

stanza ['stænzə] *n* : estrofa *f*

staple[1] ['steɪpəl] *n* : producto *m* principal — ~ *adj* : principal, básico

staple[2] *n* : grapa *f* (para papeles) — ~ *vt* **-pled; -pling** : grapar, engrapar *Lat* — **stapler** ['steɪplər] *n* : grapadora *f*, engrapadora *f Lat*

star ['stɑr] *n* : estrella *f* — ~ *v* **starred; starring** *vt* FEATURE : estar protagonizado por — *vi* ~ **in** : protagonizar

starboard ['stɑrbərd] *n* : estribor *m*

starch ['stɑrʧ] *vt* : almidonar — ~ *n* 1 : almidón *m* 2 : fécula *f* (comida)

stardom ['stɑrdəm] *n* : estrellato *m*

stare ['stær] *vi* **stared; staring** : mirar fijamente — ~ *n* : mirada *f* fija

starfish ['stɑr,fɪʃ] *n* : estrella *f* de mar

stark ['stɑrk] *adj* 1 PLAIN : austero 2 HARSH : severo, duro 3 SHARP : marcado — ~ *adv* 1 : completamente 2 ~ **naked** : en cueros (vivos)

starlight ['stɑr,laɪt] *n* : luz *f* de las estrellas

starling ['stɑrlɪŋ] *n* : estornino *m*

starry ['stɑri] *adj* **starrier; -est** : estrellado

start ['stɑrt] *vi* 1 : empezar, comenzar 2 SET OUT : salir 3 JUMP : sobresaltarse 4 *or* ~ **up** : arrancar — *vt* 1 : empezar, comenzar 2 CAUSE : provocar 3 *or* ~ **up** ESTABLISH : montar 4 *or* ~ **up** : arrancar (un motor, etc.) — ~ *n* 1 : principio *m* 2 **get an early** ~ : salir temprano 3 **give s.o. a** ~ : asustar a algn — **starter** ['stɑrtər] *n* : motor *m* de arranque (de un vehículo)

startle ['stɑrtəl] *vt* **-tled; -tling** : asustar

starve ['stɑrv] *v* **starved; starving** *vi* : morirse de hambre — *vt* : privar de comida — **starvation** [stɑr'veɪʃən] *n* : inanición *f*, hambre *f*

stash ['stæʃ] *vt* : esconder

state ['steɪt] *n* 1 : estado *m* 2 **the States** : los Estados Unidos — ~ *vt* **stated; stating** 1 SAY : decir 2 REPORT : exponer — **stately** ['steɪtli] *adj* **statelier; -est** : majestuoso — **statement** ['steɪtmənt] *n* 1 : declaración *f* 2 *or* **bank** ~ : estado *m* de cuenta — **statesman** ['steɪtsmən] *n, pl* **-men** [-mən, -,mɛn] : estadista *mf*

static ['stætɪk] *adj* : estático — ~ *n* : estática *f*

station ['steɪʃən] *n* 1 : estación *f* (de trenes, etc.) 2 RANK : condición *f* (social) 3 : canal *m* (de televisión), emisora *f* (de radio) 4 → **fire station**, **police station** — *vt* : apostar, estacionar — **stationary** ['steɪʃəˌneri] *adj* : estacionario

stationery ['steɪʃəˌneri] *n* : papel *m* y sobres *mpl* (para cartas)

station wagon *n* : camioneta *f* (familiar)

statistic [stə'tɪstɪk] *n* : estadística *f* — **statistical** [stə'tɪstɪkəl] *adj* : estadístico

statue ['stætʃuː] *n* : estatua *f*

stature ['stætʃər] *n* : estatura *f*, talla *f*

status ['steɪʧəs, 'stæ-] *n* 1 : situación *f* 2 *or* **social** ~ : estatus *m* 3 **marital** ~ : estado *m* civil

statute ['stæ,tʃuːt] *n* : estatuto *m*
staunch ['stɔntʃ] *adj* : leal
stave ['steɪv] *vt* **staved** *or* **stove** ['stoːv];
  staving 1 ~ **in** : romper 2 ~ **off**
  : evitar
staves → **staff**
stay¹ ['steɪ] *vi* 1 REMAIN : quedarse, permanecer 2 LODGE : alojarse 3 ~
  awake : mantenerse despierto 4 ~ **in**
  : quedarse en casa — *vt* : suspender
  (una ejecución, etc.) — ~ *n* 1 : estancia *f*, estadía *f Lat* 2 SUSPENSION
  : suspensión *f*
stay² *n* SUPPORT : soporte *m*
stead ['sted] *n* 1 **in s.o.'s** ~ : en lugar
  de algn 2 **stand s.o. in good** ~ : ser
  muy útil a algn — **steadfast** ['sted-
  ,fæst] *adj* 1 FIRM : firme 2 LOYAL : leal,
  fiel — **steadily** ['stedəli] *adv* 1 : progresivamente 2 INCESSANTLY : sin
  parar 3 FIXEDLY : fijamente — **steady**
  ['stedi] *adj* **steadier; -est** 1 FIRM, SURE
  : firme, seguro 2 FIXED : fijo 3 DE-
  PENDABLE : responsable 4 CONSTANT
  : constante — *vt* **steadied; steady-
  ing** 1 : mantener firme 2 : calmar (los
  nervios)
steak ['steɪk] *n* : bistec *m*, filete *m*
steal ['stiːl] *v* **stole** ['stoːl]; **stolen**
  ['stoːlən]; **stealing** *vt* : robar — *vi* 1
  : robar 2 ~ **away** : escabullirse
stealth ['stelθ] *n* : sigilo *m* — **stealthy**
  ['stelθi] *adj* **stealthier; -est** : furtivo,
  sigiloso
steam ['stiːm] *n* 1 : vapor *m* 2 **let off** ~
  : desahogarse — *vi* : echar vapor —
  vt 1 : cocer al vapor 2 ~ **up** : empañar
  — **steam engine** *n* : motor *m* de vapor
  — **steamship** ['stiːm,ʃɪp] *n* : (barco *m*
  de) vapor *m* — **steamy** ['stiːmi] *adj*
  steamier; -est 1 : lleno de vapor 2
  PASSIONATE : tórrido
steel ['stiːl] *n* : acero *m* — *vt* ~ **oneself** : armarse de valor — ~ *adj* : de
  acero
steep¹ ['stiːp] *adj* 1 : empinado 2 CON-
  SIDERABLE : considerable 3 : muy alto
  (dícese de precios)
steep² *vt* : dejar (té, etc.) en infusión
steeple ['stiːpəl] *n* : aguja *f*, campanario
  m
steer¹ ['stɪr] *n* : buey *m*
steer² *vt* : dirigir (un auto, etc.), pilotear
  (un barco) — **steering wheel** *n*
  : volante
stem¹ ['stem] *n* : tallo *m* (de una planta),
  pie *m* (de una copa) — ~ *vi* ~ **from**
  : provenir de
stem² *vt* **stemmed; stemming** : contener, detener

stench ['stentʃ] *n* : hedor *m*, mal olor *m*
stencil ['stentsəl] *n* : plantilla *f* (para
  marcar)
step ['step] *n* 1 : paso *m* 2 RUNG, STAIR
  : escalón *m* 3 ~ **by** ~ : paso por paso
  4 **take** ~**s** : tomar medidas 5 **watch
  your** ~ : mira por dónde caminas —
  ~ *vi* **stepped; stepping** 1 : dar un
  paso 2 ~ **back** : retoceder 3 ~ **down**
  RESIGN : retirarse 4 ~ **in** : intervenir 5
  ~ **out** : salir (por un momento) 6 ~
  this way : pase por aquí — **step up** *vt*
  INCREASE : aumentar
stepbrother ['step,brʌðər] *n* : hermanastro *m* — **stepdaughter** ['step,dɔtər] *n*
  : hijastra *f* — **stepfather** ['step,faðər,
  -fa-] *n* : padrastro *m*
stepladder ['step,lædər] *n* : escalera *f* de
  tijera
stepmother ['step,mʌðər] *n* : madrastra *f*
  — **stepsister** ['step,sɪstər] *n* : hermanastra *f* — **stepson** ['step,sʌn] *n*
  : hijastro *m*
stereo ['sterioː, 'stɪr-] *n, pl* **stereos** : estéreo *m* — ~ *adj* : estéreo
stereotype ['sterio,taɪp, 'stɪr-] *vt* **-typed;
  -typing** : estereotipar — ~ *n* : estereotipo *m*
sterile ['sterəl] *adj* : estéril — **sterility**
  [stə'rɪləti] *n* : esterilidad *f* — **steriliza-
  tion** [,sterələ'zeɪʃən] *n* : esterilización *f*
  — **sterilize** ['sterə,laɪz] *vt* **-ized; -izing**
  : esterilizar
sterling ['stɜrlɪŋ] *adj* : excelente — **sterling silver** *n* : plata *f* de ley
stern¹ ['stɜrn] *adj* : severo, adusto
stern² *n* : popa *f*
stethoscope ['steθə,skoːp] *n* : estetosco-
  pio *m*
stew ['stuː, 'stjuː] *n* : estofado *m*, guiso *m*
  — ~ *vt* : estofar, guisar — *vi* 1 : cocer
  2 FRET : preocuparse
steward ['stuːərd, 'stjuː-] *n* 1 : administrador *m*, -dora *f* 2 : auxiliar *m* de
  vuelo (en un avión) 3 : camarero *m* (en
  un barco) — **stewardess** ['stuːərdəs,
  'stjuː-] *n* 1 : auxiliar *f* de vuelo, azafata
  f (en un avión) 2 : camarera *f* (en un
  barco)
stick¹ ['stɪk] *n* 1 : palo *m* 2 TWIG : ramita *f* (suelta) 3 WALKING STICK : bastón
  m
stick² *v* **stuck** ['stʌk], **sticking** *vt* 1
  : pegar 2 STAB : clavar 3 PUT : poner 4
  ~ **out** : sacar (la lengua, etc.) — *vi* 1
  : pegarse 2 JAM : atascarse 3 ~
  around : quedarse 4 ~ **out** PROTRUDE
  : sobresalir 5 ~ **out** SHOW : asomar 6
  ~ **up** : sobresalir 7 ~ **up for** : defender — **sticker** ['stɪkər] *n* : etiqueta *f*

adhesiva — **stickler** ['stɪklər] *n* be a ~ for : insistir mucho en — **sticky** ['stɪki] *adj* **stickier; -est** : pegajoso

stiff ['stɪf] *adj* **1** RIGID : rígido, tieso **2** STILTED : forzado **3** STRONG : fuerte **4** DIFFICULT : difícil **5** : entumecido (dícese de músculos) — **stiffen** ['stɪfən] *vt* : fortalecer, hacer más duro — *vi* **1** HARDEN : endurecerse **2** : entumecerse (dícese de músculos) — **stiffness** ['stɪfnəs] *n* : rigidez *f*

stifle ['staɪfəl] *vt* **-fled; -fling** : sofocar

stigmatize ['stɪgmə,taɪz] *vt* **-tized; -tizing** : estigmatizar

still ['stɪl] *adj* **1** : inmóvil **2** SILENT : callado — *adv* **1** : todavía, aún **2** NEVERTHELESS : de todos modos, aún así **3** sit ~! : ¡quédate quieto! — ~ *n* **1** : quietud *f*, calma *f* — **stillborn** ['stɪl,bɔrn] *adj* : nacido muerto — **stillness** ['stɪlnəs] *n* : calma *f*, silencio *m*

stilt ['stɪlt] *n* : zanco *m* — **stilted** ['stɪltəd] *adj* : forzado

stimulate ['stɪmjə,leɪt] *vt* **-lated; -lating** : estimular — **stimulant** ['stɪmjələnt] *n* : estimulante *m* — **stimulation** [,stɪmjə'leɪʃən] *n* : estimulación *f* — **stimulus** ['stɪmjələs] *n, pl* **-li** [-,laɪ] : estímulo *m*

sting ['stɪŋ] *v* **stung** ['stʌŋ]; **stinging** : picar — ~ *n* : picadura *f* — **stinger** ['stɪŋər] *n* : aguijón *m*

stingy ['stɪndʒi] *adj* **stingier; -est** : tacaño — **stinginess** ['stɪndʒinəs] *n* : tacañería *f*

stink ['stɪŋk] *vi* **stank** ['stæŋk] *or* **stunk** ['stʌŋk]; **stunk; stinking** : apestar, oler mal — ~ *n* : hedor *m*, peste *f fam*

stint ['stɪnt] *vi* ~ **on** : escatimar — ~ *n* : período *m*

stipulate ['stɪpjə,leɪt] *vt* **-lated; -lating** : estipular

stir ['stər] *v* **stirred; stirring** *vt* **1** : remover, revolver **2** MOVE : mover **3** INCITE : incitar **4** *or* ~ **up** : despertar (memorias, etc.), provocar (ira, etc.) — *vi* : moverse, agitarse — ~ *n* COMMOTION : revuelo *m*

stirrup ['stərəp, 'stɪr-] *n* : estribo *m*

stitch ['stɪtʃ] *n* **1** : puntada *f* **2** PAIN : punzada *f* (en el costado) — ~ *vt* : coser

stock ['stɑk] *n* **1** INVENTORY : existencias *fpl* **2** SECURITIES : acciones *fpl* **3** ANCESTRY : linaje *m*, estirpe *f* **4** BROTH : caldo *m* **5** out of ~ : agotado **6** take ~ of : evaluar — ~ *vt* : surtir, abastecer — *vi* ~ **up on** : abastecerse de — **stockbroker** ['stɑk,broːkər] *n* : corredor *m*, -dora *f* de bolsa

stocking ['stɑkɪŋ] *n* : media *f*

stock market *n* : bolsa *f* — **stockpile** ['stɑk,paɪl] *n* : reservas *fpl* — ~ *vt* **-piled; -piling** : almacenar — **stocky** ['stɑki] *adj* **stockier; -est** : robusto, fornido

stodgy ['stɑdʒi] *adj* **stodgier; -est 1** DULL : pesado **2** OLD-FASHIONED : anticuado

stoic ['stoːɪk] *n* : estoico *m*, -ca *f* — ~ *or* **stoical** [-ɪkəl] *adj* : estoico — **stoicism** ['stoːə,sɪzəm] *n* : estoicismo *m*

stoke ['stoːk] *vt* **stoked; stoking** : echar carbón o leña a

stole[1] ['stoːl] → **steal**

stole[2] *n* : estola *f*

stolen → **steal**

stomach ['stʌmɪk] *n* : estómago *m* — ~ *vt* : aguantar, soportar — **stomachache** ['stʌmɪk,eɪk] *n* : dolor *m* de estómago

stone ['stoːn] *n* **1** : piedra *f* **2** : hueso *m* (de una fruta) — ~ *vt* **stoned; stoning** : apedrear — **stony** ['stoːni] *adj* **stonier; -est 1** : pedregoso **2 a** ~ **silence** : un silencio sepulcral

stood → **stand**

stool ['stuːl] *n* : taburete *m*

stoop ['stuːp] *vi* **1** : agacharse **2** ~ **to** : rebajarse a — ~ *n* **have a** ~ : ser encorvado

stop ['stɑp] *v* **stopped; stopping** *vt* **1** PLUG : tapar **2** PREVENT : impedir **3** HALT : parar, detener **4** CEASE : dejar de — *vi* **1** : detenerse, parar **2** CEASE : cesar, dejar **3** ~ **by** : visitar — ~ *n* **1** : parada *f*, alto *m* **2** come to a ~ : pararse, detenerse **3** put a ~ to : poner fin a — **stopgap** ['stɑp,gæp] *n* : arreglo *m* provisorio — **stoplight** ['stɑp,laɪt] *n* : semáforo *m* — **stoppage** ['stɑpɪdʒ] *n or* **work** ~ : paro *m* — **stopper** ['stɑpər] *n* : tapón *m*

store ['stor] *vt* **stored; storing** : guardar (comida, etc.), almacenar (datos, mercancías, etc.) — ~ *n* **1** SUPPLY : reserva *f* **2** SHOP : tienda *f* — **storage** ['storɪdʒ] *n* : almacenamiento *m* — **storehouse** ['stor,haʊs] *n* : almacén *m* — **storekeeper** ['stor,kiːpər] *n* : tendero *m*, -ra *f* — **storeroom** ['stor,ruːm, -,rʊm] *n* : almacén *m*

stork ['stork] *n* : cigüeña *f*

storm ['storm] *n* : tormenta *f*, tempestad *f* — ~ *vi* **1** RAGE : ponerse furioso **2** ~ **in/out** : entrar/salir furioso — *vt* ATTACK : asaltar — **stormy** ['stormi] *adj* **stormier; -est** : tormentoso

story[1] ['stori] *n, pl* **stories 1** TALE : cuento *m* **2** ACCOUNT : historia *f* **3** RUMOR : rumor *m*

story² *n* FLOOR : piso *m*, planta *f*

stout ['staut] *adj* 1 BRAVE : valiente 2 RESOLUTE : tenaz 3 STURDY : fuerte 4 FAT : corpulento

stove¹ ['sto:v] *n* 1 : estufa *f* (para calentar) 2 RANGE : cocina *f*

stove² → **stave**

stow ['sto:] *vt* 1 : guardar 2 LOAD : cargar — *vi* ~ **away** : viajar de polizón — **stowaway** ['sto:ə,weɪ] *n* : polizón *m*

straddle ['strædəl] *vt* -**dled; -dling** : sentarse a horcajadas sobre

straggle ['strægəl] *vi* -**gled; -gling** : rezagarse, quedarse atrás — **straggler** ['stræglər] *n* : rezagado *m*, -da *f*

straight ['streɪt] *adj* 1 : recto, derecho 2 : lacio (dícese del pelo) 3 HONEST : franco 4 TIDY : arreglado — ~ *adv* 1 DIRECTLY : derecho 2 EXACTLY : justo 3 CLEARLY : con claridad 4 FRANKLY : con franqueza — **straightaway** ['streɪt'weɪ, -,weɪ] *adv* : inmediatamente — **straighten** ['streɪtən] *vt* 1 : enderezar 2 ~ **up** : arreglar — **straightforward** [streɪt'fɔrwərd] *adj* 1 FRANK : franco 2 CLEAR : claro, sencillo

strain¹ ['streɪn] *n* 1 LINEAGE : linaje *m* 2 STREAK : veta *f* 3 VARIETY : variedad *f* 4 ~**s** *npl* : acordes *mpl* (de música)

strain² *vt* 1 : forzar (la vista o la voz) 2 FILTER : colar 3 : tensar (relaciones, etc.) 4 ~ **a muscle** : sufrir un esguince 5 ~ **oneself** : hacerse daño — *vi* : esforzarse (por) — ~ *n* 1 STRESS : tensión *f* 2 SPRAIN : esguince *m* — **strainer** ['streɪnər] *n* : colador *m*

strait ['streɪt] *n* 1 : estrecho *m* 2 **in dire** ~**s** : en grandes apuros

strand¹ ['strænd] *vt* **be** ~**ed** : quedar(se) varado

strand² *n* 1 : hebra *f* 2 **a** ~ **of hair** : un pelo

strange ['streɪndʒ] *adj* **stranger; -est** 1 : extraño, raro 2 UNFAMILIAR : desconocido — **strangely** ['streɪndʒli] *adv* : de manera extraña — **strangeness** ['streɪndʒnəs] *n* 1 : rareza *f* 2 UNFAMILIARITY : lo desconocido — **stranger** ['streɪndʒər] *n* : desconocido *m*, -da *f*

strangle ['stræŋgəl] *vt* -**gled; -gling** : estrangular

strap ['stræp] *n* 1 : correa *f* 2 **or shoulder** ~ : tirante *m* — ~ *vt* **strapped; strapping** : sujetar con una correa — **strapless** ['stræpləs] *n* : sin tirantes — **strapping** ['stræpɪŋ] *adj* : robusto, fornido

strategy ['strætədʒi] *n*, *pl* -**gies** : estrategia *f* — **strategic** [strə'ti:dʒɪk] *adj* : estratégico

straw ['strɔ] *n* 1 : paja *f* 2 **or drinking** ~ : pajita *f* 3 **the last** ~ : el colmo

strawberry ['strɔ,beri] *n*, *pl* -**ries** : fresa *f*

stray ['streɪ] *n* : animal *m* perdido — ~ *vi* 1 : perderse, extraviarse 2 : apartarse (de un grupo, etc.) 3 DEVIATE : desviarse — ~ *adj* : perdido

streak ['stri:k] *n* 1 : raya *f* 2 VEIN : veta *f* 3 ~ **of luck** : racha *f* de suerte — *vi* ~ **by** : pasar como una flecha

stream ['stri:m] *n* 1 : arroyo *m*, riachuelo *m* 2 FLOW : chorro *m*, corriente *f* — ~ *vi* : correr — **streamer** ['stri:mər] *n* 1 PENNANT : banderín *m* 2 : serpentina *f* (de papel) — **streamlined** ['stri:m-,laɪnd] *adj* 1 : aerodinámico 2 EFFICIENT : eficiente

street ['stri:t] *n* : calle *f* — **streetcar** ['stri:t,kɑr] *n* : tranvía *m* — **streetlight** ['stri:t,laɪt] *n* : farol *m*

strength ['streŋkθ] *n* 1 : fuerza *f* 2 FORTITUDE : fortaleza *f* 3 TOUGHNESS : resistencia *f*, solidez *f* 4 INTENSITY : intensidad *f* 5 ~**s and weaknesses** : virtudes y defectos — **strengthen** ['streŋkθən] *vt* 1 : fortalecer 2 REINFORCE : reforzar 3 INTENSIFY : intensificar

strenuous ['strenjuəs] *adj* 1 : enérgico 2 ARDUOUS : duro, riguroso

stress ['stres] *n* 1 : tensión *f* 2 EMPHASIS : énfasis *m* 3 : acento *m* (en lingüística) — ~ *vt* 1 EMPHASIZE : enfatizar 2 **or** ~ **out** : estresar — **stressful** ['stresfəl] *adj* : estresante

stretch ['stretʃ] *vt* 1 : estirar (músculos, elástico, etc.) 2 EXTEND : extender 3 ~ **the truth** : forzar la verdad — *vi* 1 : estirarse 2 EXTEND : extenderse — ~ *n* 1 : extensión *f* 2 ELASTICITY : elasticidad *f* 3 EXPANSE : tramo *m* 4 : período *m* (de tiempo) — **stretcher** ['stretʃər] *n* : camilla *f*

strew ['stru:] *vt* **strewed; strewed** *or* **strewn** ['stru:n]; **strewing** : esparcir (semillas, etc.), desparramar (papeles, etc.)

stricken ['strɪkən] *adj* ~ **with** : aquejado de (una enfermedad), afligido por (tristeza, etc.)

strict ['strɪkt] *adj* : estricto — **strictly** *adv* ~ **speaking** : en rigor

stride ['straɪd] *vi* **strode** ['stro:d]; **stridden** ['strɪdən]; **striding** : ir dando zancadas — ~ *n* 1 : zancada *f* 2 **make great** ~**s** : hacer grandes progresos

strident ['straɪdənt] *adj* : estridente

strife ['straɪf] *n* : conflictos *mpl*

strike ['straɪk] v **struck** ['strʌk]; **struck; striking** vt 1 HIT : golpear 2 or ~ **against** : chocar contra 3 or ~ **out** DELETE : tachar 4 : dar (la hora) 5 IMPRESS : impresionar 6 : descubrir (oro o petróleo) 7 **it** ~**s me as...** : me parece... 8 ~ **up** START : entablar — vi 1 : golpear 2 ATTACK : atacar 3 : declararse en huelga 4 : sobrevenir (dícese de una enfermedad, etc.) — ~ n 1 BLOW : golpe m 2 : huelga f, paro m Lat (de trabajadores) 3 ATTACK : ataque m — **strikebreaker** ['straɪk-ˌbreɪkər] n : esquirol mf — **striker** ['straɪkər] n : huelgista mf — **striking** ['straɪkɪŋ] adj : notable, llamativo

string ['strɪŋ] n 1 : cordel m 2 : sarta f (de perlas, insultos, etc.), serie f (de eventos, etc.) — ~ vt **strung** ['strʌŋ]; **stringing** 1 : ensartar 2 or ~ **up** : colgar — **string bean** n : habichuela f verde

stringent ['strɪndʒənt] adj : estricto, severo

strip[1] ['strɪp] v **stripped; stripping** vt 1 REMOVE : quitar 2 UNDRESS : desnudar 3 ~ **s.o. of sth** : despojar a algn de algo — vi UNDRESS : desnudarse

strip[2] n : tira f

stripe ['straɪp] n : raya f, lista f — **striped** ['straɪpt, 'straɪpəd] adj : a rayas, rayado

strive ['straɪv] vi **strove** ['stroːv]; **striven** ['strɪvən] or **strived; striving** 1 ~ **for** : luchar por 2 ~ **to** : esforzarse por

strode → **stride**

stroke ['stroːk] vt **stroked; stroking** : acariciar — ~ n 1 : golpe m 2 : derrame m cerebral (en medicina)

stroll ['stroːl] vi : pasearse — ~ n : paseo m — **stroller** ['stroːlər] n : cochecito m (para niños)

strong ['strɔŋ] adj : fuerte — **stronghold** ['strɔŋˌhoːld] n : bastión m — **strongly** ['strɔŋli] adv 1 DEEPLY : profundamente 2 WHOLEHEARTEDLY : totalmente 3 VIGOROUSLY : enérgicamente

strove → **strive**

struck → **strike**

structure ['strʌktʃər] n : estructura f — **structural** ['strʌktʃərəl] adj : estructural

struggle ['strʌgəl] vi **-gled; -gling** 1 : forcejear 2 STRIVE : luchar — ~ n : lucha f

strum ['strʌm] vt **strummed; strumming** : rasguear

strung → **string**

strut ['strʌt] vi **strutted; strutting** : pavonearse — ~ n : puntal m (en construcción)

stub ['stʌb] n : colilla f (de un cigarrillo), cabo m (de un lápiz, etc.), talón m (de un cheque) — ~ vt **stubbed; stubbing** ~ **one's toe** : darse en el dedo

stubble ['stʌbəl] n : barba f de varios días

stubborn ['stʌbərn] adj 1 : terco, obstinado 2 PERSISTENT : tenaz

stucco ['stʌkoː] n, pl **stuccos** or **stuccoes** : estuco m

stuck → **stick** — **stuck-up** ['stʌk'ʌp] adj : engreído, creído fam

stud[1] ['stʌd] n : semental m (animal)

stud[2] n 1 NAIL, TACK : tachuela f, tachón m 2 or ~ **earring** : arete m Lat, pendiente m Spain 3 : montante m (en construcción)

student ['stuːdənt, 'stjuː-] n : estudiante mf; alumno m, -na f (de un colegio) — **studio** ['stuːdiˌoː, 'stjuː-] n, pl **studios** : estudio m — **study** ['stʌdi] n, pl **studies** : estudio m — ~ v **studied; studying** : estudiar — **studious** ['stuːdiəs, 'stjuː-] adj : estudioso

stuff ['stʌf] n 1 : cosas fpl 2 MATTER, SUBSTANCE : cosa f 3 **know one's** ~ : ser experto — ~ vt 1 FILL : rellenar 2 CRAM : meter — **stuffing** ['stʌfɪŋ] n : relleno m — **stuffy** ['stʌfi] adj **stuffier; -est** 1 STODGY : pesado, aburrido 2 : tapado (dícese de la nariz) 3 ~ **rooms** : salas fpl mal ventiladas

stumble ['stʌmbəl] vi **-bled; -bling** 1 : tropezar 2 ~ **across** or **upon** : tropezar con

stump ['stʌmp] n 1 : muñón m (de una pierna, etc.) 2 or **tree** ~ : tocón m — ~ vt : dejar perplejo

stun ['stʌn] vt **stunned; stunning** 1 : aturdir (con un golpe) 2 ASTONISH : dejar atónito

stung → **sting**

stunk → **stink**

stunning ['stʌnɪŋ] adj 1 : increíble, sensacional 2 STRIKING : imponente

stunt[1] ['stʌnt] vt : atrofiar

stunt[2] n : proeza f (acrobática)

stupendous [stʊ'pendəs, stju-] adj : estupendo

stupid ['stuːpəd, 'stjuː-] adj 1 : estúpido 2 SILLY : tonto, bobo — **stupidity** [stʊ-'pɪdəṭi, stju-] n : tontería f, estupidez f

sturdy ['stərdi] adj **sturdier; -est** 1 : fuerte, resistente 2 ROBUST : robusto

stutter ['stʌṭər] vi : tartamudear — ~ n : tartamudeo m

sty ['staɪ] n 1 pl **sties** PIGPEN : pocilga f

2 *pl* **sties** *or* **styes** : orzuelo *m* (en el ojo)

style ['staɪl] *n* **1** : estilo *m* **2** FASHION : moda *f* **3 be in ~** : estar de moda — **~** *vt* **styled; styling** : peinar (pelo), diseñar (vestidos, etc.) — **stylish** ['staɪlɪʃ] *adj* : elegante, chic — **stylist** ['staɪlɪst] *n* : estilista *mf*

suave ['swɑv] *adj* : refinado y afable

sub¹ ['sʌb] *vi* **subbed; subbing** → **substitute** — **~** *n* → **substitute**

sub² *n* → **submarine**

subconscious [səb'kɑntʃəs] *adj* : subconsciente — **~** *n* : subconsciente *m*

subdivide [ˌsʌbdə'vaɪd, 'sʌbdə,vaɪd] *vt* **-vided; -viding** : subdividir — **subdivision** ['sʌbdə,vɪʒən] *n* : subdivisión *f*

subdue [səb'duː, -'djuː] *vt* **-dued; -duing** **1** CONQUER : sojuzgar **2** CONTROL : dominar **3** SOFTEN : atenuar — **subdued** *adj* : apagado

subject ['sʌbdʒɪkt] *n* **1** : sujeto *m* **2** : súbdito *m*, -ta *f* (de un gobierno) **3** TOPIC : tema *m* — **~** *adj* **1** : sometido **2 ~ to** : sujeto a — **~** [səb'dʒɛkt] *vt* **~ to** : someter a — **subjective** [səb'dʒɛktɪv] *adj* : subjetivo

subjunctive [səb'dʒʌŋktɪv] *n* : subjuntivo *m* — **subjunctive** *adj* : subjuntivo

sublime [sə'blaɪm] *adj* : sublime

submarine ['sʌbmə,riːn, ˌsʌbmə'-] *adj* : submarino — **~** *n* : submarino *m*

submerge [səb'mərdʒ] *v* **-merged; -merging** *vt* : sumergir — *vi* : sumergirse

submit [səb'mɪt] *v* **-mitted; -mitting** *vi* YIELD : rendirse **2 ~ to** : someterse a — *vt* : presentar — **submission** [səb'mɪʃən] *n* **1** : sumisión *f* **2** PRESENTATION : presentación *f* — **submissive** [səb'mɪsɪv] *adj* : sumiso

subordinate [sə'bɔrdənət] *adj* : subordinado — **~** *n* : subordinado *m*, -da *f* — **~** [sə'bɔrdən,eɪt] *vt* **-nated; -nating** : subordinar

subpoena [sə'piːnə] *n* : citación *f*

subscribe [səb'skraɪb] *vi* **-scribed; -scribing ~ to** : suscribirse a (una revista, etc.), suscribir (una opinión, etc.) — **subscriber** [səb'skraɪbər] *n* : suscriptor *m*, -tora *f* (de una revista, etc.); abonado *m*, -da *f* (de un servicio) — **subscription** [səb'skrɪpʃən] *n* : suscripción *f*

subsequent ['sʌbsɪkwənt, -sə,kwent] *adj* **1** : subsiguiente **2 ~ to** : posterior a — **subsequently** ['sʌb,kwentli, -kwənt-] *adv* : posteriormente

subservient [səb'sərviənt] *adj* : servil

subside [səb'saɪd] *vi* **-sided; -siding 1**

SINK : hundirse **2** : amainar (dícese de tormentas, pasiones, etc.), remitir (dícese de fiebres, etc.)

subsidiary [səb'sɪdi,eri] *adj* : secundario — **~** *n*, *pl* **-ries** : filial *f*

subsidy ['sʌbsədi] *n*, *pl* **-dies** : subvención *f* — **subsidize** ['sʌbsə,daɪz] *vt* **-dized; -dizing** : subvencionar

subsistence [səb'sɪstəns] *n* : subsistencia *f* — **subsist** [səb'sɪst] *vi* : subsistir

substance ['sʌbstəns] *n* : sustancia *f*

substandard [ˌsʌb'stændərd] *adj* : inferior

substantial [səb'stæntʃəl] *adj* **1** CONSIDERABLE : considerable **2** STURDY : sólido **3** : sustancioso (dícese de una comida, etc.) — **substantially** [səb'stæntʃəli] *adv* : considerablemente

substitute ['sʌbstə,tuːt, -,tjuːt] *n* : sustituto *m*, -ta *f* (de una persona); sucedáneo *m* (de una cosa) — **~** *vt* **-tuted; -tuting** : sustituir — **substitution** [ˌsʌbstə'tuːʃən, -'tjuː-] *n* : sustitución *f*

subterranean [ˌsʌbtə'reɪniən] *adj* : subterráneo

subtitle ['sʌb,taɪtəl] *n* : subtítulo *m*

subtle ['sʌtəl] *adj* **-tler; -tlest** : sutil — **subtlety** ['sʌtəlti] *n*, *pl* **-ties** : sutileza *f*

subtraction [səb'trækʃən] *n* : resta *f* — **subtract** [səb'trækt] *vt* : restar

suburb ['sʌ,bərb] *n* **1** : barrio *m* residencial, suburbio *m* **2 the ~s** : las afueras — **suburban** [sə'bərbən] *adj* : de las afueras (de una ciudad)

subversion [səb'vərʒən] *n* : subversión *f* — **subversive** [səb'vərsɪv] *adj* : subversivo

subway ['sʌb,weɪ] *n* : metro *m*

succeed [sək'siːd] *vt* : suceder a — *vi* : tener éxito (dícese de personas), dar resultado (dícese de planes, etc.) — **success** [sək'sɛs] *n* : éxito *m* — **successful** [sək'sɛsfəl] *adj* : de éxito, exitoso *Lat* — **successfully** *adv* : con éxito

succession [sək'sɛʃən] *n* **1** : sucesión *f* **2 in ~** : sucesivamente, seguidos — **successive** [sək'sɛsɪv] *adj* : sucesivo — **successor** [sək'sɛsər] *n* : sucesor *m*, -sora *f*

succinct [sək'sɪŋkt, sə'sɪŋkt] *adj* : sucinto

succulent ['sʌkjələnt] *adj* : suculento

succumb [sə'kʌm] *vi* : sucumbir

such ['sʌtʃ] *adj* **1** : tal **2** : como **3 ~ a pity!** : ¡qué lástima! — **~** *pron* **1** : tal **2 and ~** : y cosas por el estilo **3 as ~** : como tal — **~** *adv* **1** VERY : muy **2 ~ a nice man!** : ¡qué hombre tan simpático! **3 ~ that** : de tal manera que

suck ['sʌk] vt 1 or ~ on : chupar 2 or ~ up : sorber (bebidas), aspirar (con una máquina) — **sucker** ['sʌkər] n 1 SHOOT : chupón m 2 FOOL : imbécil mf — **suckle** ['sʌkəl] vt -led; -ling : amamantar — **suction** ['sʌkʃən] n : succión f

sudden ['sʌdən] adj 1 : repentino 2 all of a ~ : de repente — **suddenly** ['sʌdənli] adv : de repente

suds ['sʌdz] npl : espuma f (de jabón)

sue ['suː] vt sued; suing : demandar (por)

suede ['sweɪd] n : ante m, gamuza f

suet ['suːət] n : sebo m

suffer ['sʌfər] vi : sufrir — vt 1 : sufrir 2 BEAR : tolerar — **suffering** ['sʌfərɪŋ] n : sufrimiento m

suffice [sə'faɪs] vi -ficed; -ficing : bastar — **sufficient** [sə'fɪʃənt] adj : suficiente — **sufficiently** [sə'fɪʃəntli] adv : (lo) suficientemente

suffix ['sʌˌfɪks] n : sufijo m

suffocate ['sʌfəˌkeɪt] v -cated; -cating vt : asfixiar — vi : asfixiarse — **suffocation** [ˌsʌfə'keɪʃən] n : asfixia f

suffrage ['sʌfrɪdʒ] n : sufragio m

sugar ['ʃʊgər] n : azúcar mf — **sugarcane** ['ʃʊgərˌkeɪn] n : caña f de azúcar — **sugary** ['ʃʊgəri] adj : azucarado

suggestion [səg'dʒɛstʃən, sə-] n 1 : sugerencia f 2 TRACE : indicio m — **suggest** [səg'dʒɛst, sə-] vt 1 : sugerir 2 INDICATE : indicar

suicide ['suːəˌsaɪd] n 1 : suicidio m (acto) 2 : suicida mf (persona) — **suicidal** [ˌsuːə'saɪdəl] adj : suicida

suit ['suːt] n 1 LAWSUIT : pleito m 2 : traje m (ropa) 3 : palo m (de naipes) — ~ vt 1 ADAPT : adaptar 2 BEFIT : ser apropiado para 3 ~ s.o. : convenir a algn (dícese de fechas, etc.), quedar bien a algn (dícese de ropa) — **suitable** ['suːtəbəl] adj : apropiado — **suitcase** ['suːtˌkeɪs] n : maleta f, valija f Lat

suite ['swiːt, for 2 also 'suːt] n 1 : suite f (de habitaciones) 2 : juego m (de muebles)

suitor ['suːtər] n : pretendiente m

sulfur ['sʌlfər] n : azufre m

sulk ['sʌlk] vi : enfurruñarse fam — **sulky** ['sʌlki] adj sulkier; -est : malhumorado

sullen ['sʌlən] adj : hosco

sultry ['sʌltri] adj sultrier; -est 1 : bochornoso 2 SENSUAL : sensual

sum ['sʌm] n : suma f — ~ vt summed; summing ~ up : resumir — **summarize** ['sʌməˌraɪz] v -rized; -rizing : resumir — **summary** ['sʌməri] n, pl -ries : resumen m

summer ['sʌmər] n : verano m

summit ['sʌmət] n : cumbre f

summon ['sʌmən] vt 1 : llamar (a algn), convocar (una reunión) 2 : citar (en derecho) — **summons** ['sʌmənz] n, pl **summonses** SUBPOENA : citación f

sumptuous ['sʌmptʃʊəs] adj : suntuoso

sun ['sʌn] n : sol m — **sunbathe** ['sʌnˌbeɪð] vi -bathed; -bathing : tomar el sol — **sunbeam** ['sʌnˌbiːm] n : rayo m de sol — **sunburn** ['sʌnˌbərn] n : quemadura f de sol

Sunday ['sʌnˌdeɪ, -di] n : domingo m

sundry ['sʌndri] adj : varios, diversos

sunflower ['sʌnˌflaʊər] n : girasol m

sung → **sing**

sunglasses ['sʌnˌglæsəz] npl : gafas fpl de sol, lentes mpl de sol

sunk → **sink** — **sunken** ['sʌŋkən] adj : hundido

sunlight ['sʌnˌlaɪt] n : (luz f del) sol m — **sunny** ['sʌni] adj -nier; -est : soleado — **sunrise** ['sʌnˌraɪz] n : salida f del sol — **sunset** ['sʌnˌsɛt] n : puesta f del sol — **sunshine** ['sʌnˌʃaɪn] n : sol m, luz f del sol — **suntan** ['sʌnˌtæn] n : bronceado m

super ['suːpər] adj : súper fam

superb [sʊ'pərb] adj : magnífico, espléndido

superficial [ˌsuːpər'fɪʃəl] adj : superficial

superfluous [sʊ'pərfluəs] adj : superfluo

superimpose [ˌsuːpərɪm'poːz] vt -posed; -posing : sobreponer

superintendent [ˌsuːpərɪn'tɛndənt] n 1 : superintendente mf (de policía) 2 or building ~ : portero m, -ra f 3 or school ~ : director m, -tora f (de un colegio)

superior [sʊ'pɪriər] adj : superior — ~ n : superior m — **superiority** [sʊˌpɪriˈɔrət̬i] n, pl -ties : superioridad f

superlative [sʊ'pərlət̬ɪv] adj 1 : superlativo (en gramática) 2 EXCELLENT : excepcional — ~ n : superlativo m

supermarket ['suːpərˌmɑrkət] n : supermercado m

supernatural [ˌsuːpər'nætʃərəl] adj : sobrenatural

superpower ['suːpərˌpaʊər] n : superpotencia f

supersede [ˌsuːpər'siːd] vt -seded; -seding : reemplazar, suplantar

supersonic [ˌsuːpər'sɑnɪk] adj : supersónico

superstition [ˌsuːpər'stɪʃən] n : superstición f — **superstitious** [ˌsuːpər'stɪʃəs] adj : supersticioso

supervisor ['suːpərˌvaɪzər] n : supervisor

m, -sora *f* — **supervise** ['su:pər,vaiz] *vt*
-**vised; -vising** : supervisar — **supervision** [,su:pər'viʒən] *n* : supervisión *f*
— **supervisory** [,su:pər'vaizəri] *adj*
: de supervisor

supper ['sʌpər] *n* : cena *f*, comida *f*

supplant [sə'plænt] *vt* : suplantar

supple ['sʌpəl] *adj* **-pler; -plest** : flexible

supplement ['sʌpləmənt] *n* : suplemento *m* — ~ ['sʌplə,ment] *vt* : complementar — **supplementary** [,sʌplə-
'mentəri] *adj* : suplementario

supply [sə'plai] *vt* **-plied; -plying 1**
: suministrar **2** ~ **with** : proveer de —
~ *n*, *pl* **-plies 1** : suministro *m*, provisión *f* **2** ~ **and demand** : oferta y
demanda **3** **supplies** *npl* PROVISIONS
: provisiones *fpl*, víveres *mpl* — **supplier** [sə'plaiər] *n* : proveedor *m*, -dora *f*

support [sə'port] *vt* **1** BACK : apoyar **2**
: mantener (una familia, etc.) **3** PROP
UP : sostener — ~ *n* **1** : apoyo *m*
(moral), ayuda *f* (económica) **2** PROP
: soporte *m* — **supporter** [sə'portər] *n*
: partidario *m*, -ria *f*

suppose [sə'po:z] *vt* -**posed; -posing 1**
: suponer **2 be** ~**d to (do sth)** : tener
que (hacer algo) — **supposedly** *adv*
: supuestamente

suppress [sə'pres] *vt* **1** : reprimir **2**
: suprimir (noticias, etc.) — **suppression** [sə'preʃən] *n* **1** : represión *f* **2**
: supresión *f* (de información)

supreme [su'pri:m] *adj* : supremo — **supremacy** [su'preməsi] *n*, *pl* **-cies** : supremacía *f*

sure ['ʃur] *adj* **surer; -est 1** : seguro **2**
make ~ **that** : asegurarse de que —
~ *adv* **1** OF COURSE : por supuesto,
claro **2 it** ~ **is hot!** : ¡qué calor! —
surely ['ʃurli] *adv* : seguramente

surfing ['sərfiŋ] *n* : surf *m*, surfing *m*

surface ['sərfəs] *n* : superficie *f* — ~ *v*
-**faced; -facing** *vi* : salir a la superficie
— *vt* : revestir

surfeit ['sərfət] *n* : exceso *m*

surfing ['sərfiŋ] *n* : surf *m*, surfing *m*

surge ['sərdʒ] *vi* **surged; surging 1**
SWELL : hincharse (dícese del mar) **2**
SWARM : moverse en tropel — ~ *n* **1**
: oleaje *m* (del mar), oleada *f* (de gente)
2 INCREASE : aumento *m* (súbito)

surgeon ['sərdʒən] *n* : cirujano *m*, -na *f*
— **surgery** ['sərdʒəri] *n*, *pl* **-geries**
: cirugía *f* — **surgical** ['sərdʒikəl] *adj*
: quirúrgico

surly ['sərli] *adj* **surlier; -est** : hosco,
arisco

surmount [sər'maunt] *vt* : superar

surname ['sər,neim] *n* : apellido *m*

surpass [sər'pæs] *vt* : superar

surplus ['sər,plʌs] *n* : excedente *m*

surprise [sə'praiz, sər-] *n* **1** : sorpresa *f* **2**
take by ~ : sorprender — ~ *vt*
-**prised; -prising** : sorprender — **surprising** [sə'praiziŋ, sər-] *adj* : sorprendente

surrender [sə'rendər] *vt* : entregar,
rendir — *vi* : rendirse — ~ *n* : rendición *f* (de una ciudad, etc.), entrega *f*
(de posesiones)

surrogate ['sərəgət, -,geit] *n* : sustituto *m*

surround [sə'raund] *vt* : rodear — **surroundings** [sə'raundiŋz] *npl* : ambiente *m*

surveillance [sər'veiləns, -'veiljəns,
-'veiəns] *n* : vigilancia *f*

survey [sər'vei] *vt* -**veyed; -veying 1**
: medir (un solar) **2** INSPECT : inspeccionar **3** POLL : sondear — ~ ['sər,vei]
n, *pl* **-veys 1** INSPECTION : inspección *f*
2 : medición *f* (de un solar) **3** POLL
: encuesta *f*, sondeo *m* — **surveyor**
[sər'veiər] *n* : agrimensor *m*, -sora *f*

survive [sər'vaiv] *v* -**vived; -viving** *vi*
: sobrevivir — *vt* : sobrevivir a — **survival** [sər'vaivəl] *n* : supervivencia *f* —
survivor [sər'vaivər] *n* : superviviente
mf

susceptible [sə'septəbəl] *adj* ~ **to**
: propenso a — **susceptibility** [sə-
,septə'biləti] *n*, *pl* **-ties** : propensión *f* (a
enfermedades, etc.)

suspect ['sʌs,pekt, sə'spekt] *adj* : sospechoso — ~ ['sʌs,pekt] *n* : sospechoso
m, -sa *f* — ~ [sə'spekt] *vt* **1** : sospechar
(algo), sospechar de (algn)

suspend [sə'spend] *vt* : suspender —
suspense [sə'spens] *n* **1** : incertidumbre *m* **2** : suspenso *m* *Lat*, suspense *m*
Spain (en el cine, etc.) — **suspension**
[sə'spentʃən] *n* : suspensión *f*

suspicion [sə'spiʃən] *n* : sospecha *f* —
suspicious [sə'spiʃəs] *adj* **1** QUESTION-
ABLE : sospechoso **2** DISTRUSTFUL
: suspicaz

sustain [sə'stein] *vt* **1** : sostener **2** SUF-
FER : sufrir

swagger ['swægər] *vi* : pavonearse

swallow[1] ['swɑ:lo:] *v* : tragar — ~ *n*
: trago *m*

swallow[2] *n* : golondrina *f* (pájaro)

swam → **swim**

swamp ['swɑmp] *n* : pantano *m*, ciénaga
f — ~ *vt* : inundar — **swampy**
['swɑmpi] *adj* **swampier; -est** : pantanoso, cenagoso

swan ['swɑn] *n* : cisne *f*

swap ['swɑp] *vt* **swapped; swapping 1**

: intercambiar **2** ~ **sth for sth** : cambiar algo por algo **3** ~ **sth with s.o.** : cambiar algo a algn — ~ *n* : cambio *m*

swarm ['swɔrm] *n* : enjambre *m* — ~ *vi* : enjambrar

swat ['swɑt] *vt* **swatted; swatting** : aplastar (un insecto)

sway ['swei] *v* **1** : balanceo *m* **2** INFLUENCE : influjo *m* — ~ *vi* : balancearse — *vt* : influir en

swear ['swær] *v* **swore** ['swor]; **sworn** ['sworn]; **swearing** *vi* **1** : jurar **2** CURSE : decir palabrotas — *vt* : jurar — **swearword** ['swær,wərd] *n* : palabrota *f*

sweat ['swet] *vi* **sweat** *or* **sweated; sweating** : sudar — ~ *n* : sudor *m* — **sweater** ['swetər] *n* : suéter *m* — **sweatshirt** ['swet,ʃərt] *n* : sudadera *f* — **sweaty** ['sweti] *adj* **sweatier; -est** : sudado

Swedish ['swiːdɪʃ] *adj* : sueco — ~ *n* : sueco *m* (idioma)

sweep ['swiːp] *v* **swept** ['swept]; **sweeping** *vt* **1** : barrer **2** ~ **aside** : apartar **3** ~ **through** : extenderse por — *vi* : barrer — ~ *n* **1** : barrido *m* **2** : movimiento *m* circular (de la mano, etc.) **3** SCOPE : alcance *m* — **sweeping** ['swiːpɪŋ] *adj* **1** WIDE : amplio **2** EXTENSIVE : extenso — **sweepstakes** ['swiːp,steiks] *ns & pl* : lotería *f*

sweet ['swiːt] *adj* **1** : dulce **2** PLEASANT : agradable — ~ *n* : dulce *m* — **sweeten** ['swiːtən] *vt* : endulzar — **sweetener** ['swiːtənər] *n* : endulzante *m* — **sweetheart** ['swiːt,hɑrt] *n* **1** : novio *m*, -via *f* (*used as a form of address*) : cariño *m* — **sweetness** ['swiːtnəs] *n* : dulzura *f* — **sweet potato** *n* : batata *f*, boniato *m*

swell ['swel] *vi* **swelled; swelled** *or* **swollen** ['swoːlən, 'swʌl-]; **swelling 1** *or* ~ **up** : hincharse **2** INCREASE : aumentar, crecer — ~ *n* : oleaje *m* (del mar) — **swelling** ['swelɪŋ] *n* : hinchazón *f*

sweltering ['sweltərɪŋ] *adj* : sofocante

swept → **sweep**

swerve ['swərv] *vi* **swerved; swerving** : virar bruscamente

swift ['swɪft] *adj* : rápido — **swiftly** *adv* : rápidamente

swig ['swɪg] *n* : trago *m* — ~ *vi* **swigged; swigging** : beber a tragos

swim ['swɪm] *vi* **swam** ['swæm]; **swum** ['swʌm]; **swimming 1** : nadar **2** REEL : dar vueltas — ~ *n* **1** : baño *m* **2 go for a** ~ : ir a nadar — **swimmer** ['swɪmər] *n* : nadador *m*, -dora *f*

swindle ['swɪndəl] *vt* **-dled; -dling** : estafar, timar — ~ *n* : estafa *f*, timo *m fam*

swine ['swain] *ns & pl* : cerdo *m*, -da *f*

swing ['swɪŋ] *v* **swung** ['swʌŋ]; **swinging** *vt* **1** : balancear, hacer oscilar **2** MANAGE : arreglar — *vi* **1** : balancearse, oscilar **2** SWIVEL : girar — ~ *n* **1** : vaivén *m*, balanceo *m* **2** SHIFT : cambio *m* **3** : columpio *m* (para niños) **4 in full** ~ : en pleno proceso

swipe ['swaip] *v* **swiped; swiping** *vt* STEAL : birlar *fam*, robar — *vi* ~ **at** : intentar pegar

swirl ['swərl] *vi* : arremolinarse — ~ *n* **1** EDDY : remolino *m* **2** SPIRAL : espiral *f*

swish ['swɪʃ] *vt* : agitar (haciendo un sonido) — *vi* **1** RUSTLE : hacer frufrú **2** ~ **by** : pasar silbando

Swiss ['swɪs] *adj* : suizo

switch ['swɪtʃ] *n* **1** WHIP : vara *f* **2** CHANGE : cambio *m* **3** : interruptor *m*, llave *f* (de la luz, etc.) — ~ *vt* **1** CHANGE : cambiar de **2** EXCHANGE : intercambiar **3** ~ **on** : encender, prender *Lat* **4** ~ **off** : apagar — *vi* **1** : sacudir (la cola, etc.) **2** CHANGE : cambiar **3** SWAP : intercambiarse — **switchboard** ['swɪtʃ,bord] *n* : centralita *f*, conmutador *m Lat*

swivel ['swɪvəl] *vi* **-veled** *or* **-velled; -veling** *or* **-velling** : girar (sobre un pivote)

swollen → **swell**

swoon ['swuːn] *vi* : desvanecerse

swoop ['swuːp] *vi* ~ **down on** : abatirse sobre — ~ *n* : descenso *m* en picada

sword ['sord] *n* : espada *f*

swordfish ['sord,fɪʃ] *n* : pez *m* espada

swore, sworn → **swear**

swum → **swim**

swung → **swing**

syllable ['sɪləbəl] *n* : sílaba *f*

syllabus ['sɪləbəs] *n, pl* **-bi** [-,bai] *or* **-buses** : programa *m* (de estudios)

symbol ['sɪmbəl] *n* : símbolo *m* — **symbolic** [sɪm'bɑlɪk] *adj* : simbólico — **symbolism** ['sɪmbə,lɪzəm] *n* : simbolismo *m* — **symbolize** ['sɪmbə,laiz] *vt* **-ized; -izing** : simbolizar

symmetry ['sɪmətri] *n, pl* **-tries** : simetría *f* — **symmetrical** [sə-'metrɪkəl] *adj* : simétrico

sympathy ['sɪmpəθi] *n, pl* **-thies 1** COMPASSION : compasión *f* **2** UNDERSTANDING : comprensión *f* **3** CONDOLENCES : pésame *m* **4 sympathies** *npl* LOYALTY : simpatías *fpl* — **sympathize** ['sɪmpə,θaiz] *vi* **-thized; -thizing 1** ~ **with** PITY : compadecerse de **2** ~

with UNDERSTAND : comprender — **sympathetic** [ˌsɪmpəˈθeṯɪk] *adj* **1** COMPASSIONATE : compasivo **2** UNDERSTANDING : comprensivo

symphony [ˈsɪmpfəni] *n, pl* **-nies** : sinfonía *f*

symposium [sɪmˈpoːziəm] *n, pl* **-sia** [-ziə] *or* **-siums** : simposio *m*

symptom [ˈsɪmptəm] *n* : síntoma *m* — **symptomatic** [ˌsɪmptəˈmæṯɪk] *adj* : sintomático

synagogue [ˈsɪnəˌgag, -ˌgɔg] *n* : sinagoga *f*

synchronize [ˈsɪŋkrəˌnaɪz, ˈsɪn-] *vt* **-nized; -nizing** : sincronizar

syndrome [ˈsɪndˌroːm] *n* : síndrome *m*

synonym [ˈsɪnəˌnɪm] *n* : sinónimo *m* —

synonymous [səˈnɑnəməs] *adj* : sinónimo

synopsis [səˈnɑpsɪs] *n, pl* **-opses** [-ˌsiːz] : sinopsis *f*

syntax [ˈsɪnˌtæks] *n* : sintaxis *f*

synthesis [ˈsɪnθəsɪs] *n, pl* **-theses** [-ˌsiːz] : síntesis *f* — **synthesize** [ˈsɪnθəˌsaɪz] *vt* **-sized; -sizing** : sintetizar — **synthetic** [sɪnˈθeṯɪk] *adj* : sintético

syphilis [ˈsɪfələs] *n* : sífilis *f*

Syrian [ˈsɪriən] *adj* : sirio

syringe [səˈrɪndʒ, ˈsɪrɪndʒ] *n* : jeringa *f*, jeringuilla *f*

syrup [ˈsərəp, ˈsɪrəp] *n* : jarabe *m*

system [ˈsɪstəm] *n* **1** : sistema *m* **2** BODY : organismo *m* **3 digestive ~** : aparato *m* digestivo — **systematic** [ˌsɪstəˈmæṯɪk] *adj* : sistemático

T

t [ˈtiː] *n, pl* **t's** *or* **ts** [ˈtiːz] : t *f*, vigésima letra del alfabeto inglés

tab [ˈtæb] *n* **1** TAG : etiqueta *f* **2** FLAP : lengüeta *f* **3** ACCOUNT : cuenta *f* **4 keep ~s on** : vigilar

table [ˈteɪbəl] *n* **1** : mesa *f* **2** LIST : tabla *f* **3 ~ of contents** : índice *m* de materias — **tablecloth** [ˈteɪbəlˌklɔθ] *n* : mantel *m* — **tablespoon** [ˈteɪbəlˌspuːn] *n* **1** : cuchara *f* grande **2** : cucharada *f* (cantidad)

tablet [ˈtæblət] *n* **1** PAD : bloc *m* **2** PILL : pastilla *f* **3** *or* **stone ~** : lápida *f*

tabloid [ˈtæˌblɔɪd] *n* : tabloide *m*

taboo [təˈbuː, tæ-] *adj* : tabú — *~ n* : tabú *m*

tacit [ˈtæsɪt] *adj* : tácito

taciturn [ˈtæsɪˌtərn] *adj* : taciturno

tack [ˈtæk] *vt* **1** : fijar con tachuelas **2 ~ on** ADD : añadir — *~ n* **1** : tachuela *f* **2 change ~** : cambiar de rumbo

tackle [ˈtækəl] *n* **1** GEAR : aparejo *m* **2** : placaje *m*, tacle *m Lat* (acción) — *~ vt* **-led; -ling 1** : placar, taclear *Lat* **2** CONFRONT : abordar

tacky [ˈtæki] *adj* **tackier; -est 1** : pegajoso **2** GAUDY : de mal gusto

tact [ˈtækt] *n* : tacto *m* — **tactful** [ˈtæktfəl] *adj* : diplomático, discreto

tactical [ˈtæktɪkəl] *adj* : táctico — **tactic** [ˈtæktɪk] *n* : táctica *f* — **tactics** [ˈtæktɪks] *ns & pl* : táctica *f*

tactless [ˈtæktləs] *adj* : indiscreto

tadpole [ˈtædˌpoːl] *n* : renacuajo *m*

tag¹ [ˈtæg] *n* LABEL : etiqueta *f* — *~ v* **tagged; tagging** *vt* : etiquetar — *vi*

~ along with s.o. : acompañar a algn

tag² *vt* : tocar (en varios juegos)

tail [ˈteɪl] *n* **1** : cola *f* **2 ~s** *npl* : cruz *f* (de una moneda) — *~ vt* FOLLOW : seguir

tailor [ˈteɪlər] *n* : sastre *m*, -tra *f* — *~ vt* **1** : confeccionar (ropa) **2** ADAPT : adaptar

taint [ˈteɪnt] *vt* : contaminar

take [ˈteɪk] *v* **took** [ˈtʊk]; **taken** [ˈteɪkən]; **taking** *vt* **1** : tomar **2** BRING : llevar **3** REMOVE : sacar **4** BEAR : soportar, aguantar **5** ACCEPT : aceptar **6 I ~ it that...** : supongo que... **7 ~ a bath** : bañarse **8 ~ a walk** : dar un paseo **9 ~ back** : retirar (palabras, etc.) **10 ~ in** ALTER : achicar **11 ~ in** GRASP : entender **12 ~ in** TRICK : engañar **13 ~ off** REMOVE : quitar, quitarse (ropa) **14 ~ on** : asumir (una responsabilidad, etc.) **15 ~ out** : sacar **16 ~ over** : tomar el poder de **17 ~ place** : tener lugar **18 ~ up** SHORTEN : acortar **19 ~ up** OCCUPY : ocupar — *vi* **1** : prender (dícese de una vacuna, etc.) **2 ~ off** : despegar (dícese de aviones, etc.) **3 ~ over** : asumir el mando — *~ n* **1** PROCEEDS : ingresos *mpl* **2** : toma *f* (en el cine) — **takeoff** [ˈteɪkˌɔf] *n* : despegue *m* (de un avión, etc.) — **takeover** [ˈteɪkoːvər] *n* : toma *f* (de poder, etc.), adquisición *f* (de una empresa)

talcum powder [ˈtælkəm] *n* : polvos *mpl* de talco

tale [ˈteɪl] *n* : cuento *m*

talent ['tælənt] *n* : talento *m* — **talented** ['tælentəd] *adj* : talentoso

talk ['tɔk] *vi* **1** : hablar **2** ~ **about** : hablar de **3** ~ **to/with** : hablar con — *vt* **1** SPEAK : hablar **2** ~ **over** : hablar de, discutir — *n* **1** CHAT : conversación *f* **2** SPEECH : charla *f* — **talkative** ['tɔkətɪv] *adj* : hablador

tall ['tɔl] *adj* **1** : alto **2** **how** ~ **are you?** : ¿cuánto mides?

tally ['tæli] *n*, *pl* **-lies** : cuenta *f* — ~ *v* **-lied; -lying** *vt* RECKON : calcular — *vi* MATCH : concordar, cuadrar

talon ['tælən] *n* : garra *f*

tambourine [,tæmbə'riːn] *n* : pandereta *f*

tame ['teɪm] *adj* **tamer; -est** **1** : domesticado **2** DOCILE : manso **3** DULL : insípido, soso — ~ *vt* **tamed; taming** : domar

tamper ['tæmpər] *vi* ~ **with** : forzar (una cerradura), amañar (documentos, etc.)

tampon ['tæm,pɑn] *n* : tampón *m*

tan ['tæn] *v* **tanned; tanning** *vt* : curtir (cuero) — *vi* : broncearse — ~ *n* **1** SUNTAN : bronceado *m* **2** : (color *m*) café *m* con leche

tang ['tæŋ] *n* : sabor *m* fuerte

tangent ['tændʒənt] *n* : tangente *f*

tangerine [,tændʒə'riːn, ,tændʒə'-] *n* : mandarina *f*

tangible ['tændʒəbəl] *adj* : tangible

tangle ['tæŋgəl] *v* **-gled; -gling** *vt* : enredar — *vi* : enredarse — ~ *n* : enredo *m*

tango ['tæŋgoː] *n*, *pl* **-gos** : tango *m*

tank ['tæŋk] *n* **1** : tanque *m*, depósito *m* **2** : tanque *m* (militar) — **tanker** ['tæŋkər] *n* **1** : buque *m* tanque **2** *or* ~ **truck** : camión *m* cisterna

tantalizing ['tæntə,laɪzɪŋ] *adj* : tentador

tantrum ['tæntrəm] *n* **throw a** ~ : hacer un berrinche

tap[1] ['tæp] *n* FAUCET : llave *f*, grifo *m* *Spain* — ~ *vt* **tapped; tapping** **1** : sacar (un líquido, etc.), sangrar (un árbol) **2** : intervenir (un teléfono)

tap[2] *vt* **tapped; tapping** STRIKE : tocar, dar un golpecito en — ~ *n* : golpecito *m*, toque *m*

tape ['teɪp] *n* : cinta *f* — ~ *vt* **taped; taping** **1** : pegar con cinta **2** RECORD : grabar — **tape measure** *n* : cinta *f* métrica

taper ['teɪpər] *n* : vela *f* (larga) — ~ *vi* **1** NARROW : estrecharse **2** *or* ~ **off** : disminuir

tapestry ['tæpəstri] *n*, *pl* **-tries** : tapiz *m*

tar ['tɑr] *n* : alquitrán *m* — ~ *vt* **tarred; tarring** : alquitranar

tarantula [tə'ræntʃələ, -'ræntələ] *n* : tarántula *f*

target ['tɑrgət] *n* **1** : blanco *m* **2** GOAL : objetivo *m*

tariff ['tærɪf] *n* : tarifa *f*, arancel *m*

tarnish ['tɑrnɪʃ] *vt* **1** : deslustrar **2** : empañar (una reputación, etc.) — *vi* : deslustrarse

tart[1] ['tɑrt] *adj* SOUR : ácido, agrio

tart[2] *n* : pastel *m*

tartan ['tɑrtən] *n* : tartán *m*

task ['tæsk] *n* : tarea *f*

tassel ['tæsəl] *n* : borla *f*

taste ['teɪst] *v* **tasted; tasting** *vt* TRY : probar — *vi* **1** : saber **2** ~ **like** : saber a — ~ *n* **1** FLAVOR : gusto *m*, sabor *m* **2** **have a** ~ **of** : probar **3** **in good/bad** ~ : de buen/mal gusto — **tasteful** ['teɪstfəl] *adj* : de buen gusto — **tasteless** ['teɪstləs] *adj* **1** : sin sabor **2** COARSE : de mal gusto — **tasty** ['teɪsti] *adj* **tastier; -est** : sabroso

tatters ['tætərz] *npl* : harapos *mpl* — **tattered** ['tætərd] *adj* : harapiento

tattle ['tætəl] *vi* **-tled; -tling** ~ **on s.o.** : acusar a algn

tattoo [tæ'tuː] *vt* : tatuar — ~ *n* : tatuaje *m*

taught → **teach**

taunt ['tɔnt] *n* : pulla *f*, burla *f* — ~ *vt* : mofarse de, burlarse de

taut ['tɔt] *adj* : tirante, tenso

tavern ['tævərn] *n* : taberna *f*

tax ['tæks] *vt* **1** : gravar **2** STRAIN : poner a prueba — ~ *n* **1** : impuesto *m* **2** BURDEN : carga *f* — **taxable** ['tæksəbəl] *adj* : imponible — **taxation** [tæk-'seɪʃən] *n* : impuestos *mpl* — **tax-exempt** ['tæksɪg'zempt, -ɛg-] *adj* : libre de impuestos

taxi ['tæksi] *n*, *pl* **taxis** : taxi *m* — ~ *vi* **taxied; taxiing** *or* **taxying; taxis** *or* **taxies** : rodar por la pista (dícese de un avión)

taxpayer ['tæks,peɪər] *n* : contribuyente *mf*

tea ['tiː] *n* : té *m*

teach ['tiːtʃ] *v* **taught** ['tɔt]; **teaching** *vt* : enseñar, dar clases de (una asignatura) — *vi* : dar clases — **teacher** ['tiːtʃər] *n* : profesor *m*, -sora *f*; maestro *m*, -tra *f* (de niños pequeños) — **teaching** ['tiːtʃɪŋ] *n* : enseñanza *f*

teacup ['tiː,kʌp] *n* : taza *f* de té

team ['tiːm] *n* : equipo *m* — ~ *vi or* ~ **up** : asociarse — **teammate** ['tiːm-,meɪt] *n* : compañero *m*, -ra *f* de equipo — **teamwork** ['tiːm,wərk] *n* : trabajo *m* de equipo

teapot ['tiː,pɑt] *n* : tetera *f*

tear[1] ['tær] v **tore** ['tor]; **torn** ['torn]; **tearing** vt **1** : romper, rasgar **2 ~ apart** : destrozar **3 ~ down** : derribar **4 ~ off** or **~ out** : arrancar **5 ~ up** : romper (papel, etc.) — vi **1** : romperse, rasgarse **2** RUSH : ir a toda velocidad — ~ n : desgarro m, rasgón m

tear[2] ['tɪr] n : lágrima f — **tearful** ['tɪrfəl] adj : lloroso

tease ['tiːz] vt **teased; teasing 1** : tomar el pelo a, burlarse de **2** ANNOY : fastidiar

teaspoon ['tiːˌspuːn] n **1** : cucharita f **2** : cucharadita f (cantidad)

technical ['tɛknɪkəl] adj : técnico — **technicality** [ˌtɛknəˈkælət̬i] n, pl **-ties** : detalle m técnico — **technically** [-kli] adv : técnicamente — **technician** [tɛkˈnɪʃən] n : técnico m, -ca f

technique [tɛkˈniːk] n : técnica f

technological [ˌtɛknəˈlɑdʒɪkəl] adj : tecnológico — **technology** [tɛkˈnɑlədʒi] n, pl **-gies** : tecnología f

teddy bear ['tɛdi] n : oso m de peluche

tedious ['tiːdiəs] adj : tedioso, aburrido — **tedium** ['tiːdiəm] n : tedio m

tee ['tiː] n : tee m (en deportes)

teem ['tiːm] vi **1** POUR : llover a cántaros **2 be ~ing with** : estar repleto de

teenage ['tiːnˌeɪdʒ] or **teenaged** [-ˌeɪdʒd] adj : adolescente — **teenager** ['tiːnˌeɪdʒər] n : adolescente mf — **teens** ['tiːnz] npl : adolescencia f

teepee → tepee

teeter ['tiːt̬ər] vi : tambalearse

teeth → tooth — **teethe** ['tiːð] vi **teethed; teething** : echar los dientes

telecommunication ['tɛləkəˌmjuːnəˈkeɪʃən] n : telecomunicación f

telegram ['tɛləˌgræm] n : telegrama m — **telegraph** ['tɛləˌgræf] n : telégrafo m — ~ v : telegrafiar

telephone ['tɛləˌfoːn] n : teléfono m — ~ v **-phoned; -phoning** : llamar por teléfono

telescope ['tɛləˌskoːp] n : telescopio m

televise ['tɛləˌvaɪz] vt **-vised; -vising** : televisar — **television** ['tɛləˌvɪʒən] n : televisión f

tell ['tɛl] v **told** ['toːld]; **telling** vt **1** : decir **2** RELATE : contar **3** DISTINGUISH : distinguir **4 ~ s.o. off** : regañar a algn — vi **1** : decir **2** KNOW : saber **3** SHOW : tener efecto **4 ~ on s.o.** : acusar a algn — **teller** ['tɛlər] n or **bank ~** : cajero m, -ra f

temp ['tɛmp] n : empleado m, -da f temporal

temper ['tɛmpər] vt MODERATE : temperar — ~ n **1** MOOD : humor m **2 have a bad ~** : tener mal genio **3 lose one's ~** : perder los estribos — **temperament** ['tɛmpərmənt, -prə-, -pərə-] n : temperamento m — **temperamental** [ˌtɛmpərˈmɛntəl, -prə-, -pərə-] adj : temperamental — **temperate** ['tɛmpərət] adj **1** : moderado **2 ~ zone** : zona f templada

temperature ['tɛmpərˌtʃur, -prə-, -pərə-, -tʃər] n **1** : temperatura f **2 have a ~** : tener fiebre

tempest ['tɛmpəst] n : tempestad f

temple ['tɛmpəl] n **1** : templo m **2** : sien f (en anatomía)

tempo ['tɛmpoː] n, pl **-pi** [-piː] or **-pos 1** : tempo m **2** PACE : ritmo m

temporarily [ˌtɛmpəˈrɛrəli] adv : temporalmente — **temporary** ['tɛmpəˌrɛri] adj : temporal

tempt ['tɛmpt] vt : tentar — **temptation** [tɛmpˈteɪʃən] n : tentación f

ten ['tɛn] adj : diez — ~ n : diez m

tenacity [təˈnæsət̬i] n : tenacidad f — **tenacious** [təˈneɪʃəs] adj : tenaz

tenant ['tɛnənt] n : inquilino m, -na f; arrendatario m, -ria f

tend[1] ['tɛnd] v MIND : cuidar

tend[2] vi **~ to** : tender a — **tendency** ['tɛndənt̬si] n, pl **-cies** : tendencia f

tender[1] ['tɛndər] adj **1** : tierno **2** PAINFUL : dolorido

tender[2] vt : presentar — ~ n **1** : oferta f **2 legal ~** : moneda f de curso legal

tenderloin ['tɛndərˌlɔɪn] n : lomo f (de cerdo o vaca)

tenderness ['tɛndərnəs] n : ternura f

tendon ['tɛndən] n : tendón m

tenet ['tɛnət] n : principio m

tennis ['tɛnəs] n : tenis m

tenor ['tɛnər] n : tenor m

tense[1] ['tɛns] n : tiempo m (de un verbo)

tense[2] v **tensed; tensing** vt : tensar — vi : tensarse — ~ adj **tenser; tensest** : tenso — **tension** ['tɛntʃən] n : tensión f

tent ['tɛnt] n : tienda f de campaña

tentacle ['tɛntɪkəl] n : tentáculo m

tentative ['tɛntət̬ɪv] adj **1** HESITANT : vacilante **2** PROVISIONAL : provisional

tenth ['tɛnθ] adj : décimo — ~ n **1** : décimo m, -ma f (en una serie) **2** : décimo m (en matemáticas)

tenuous ['tɛnjʊəs] adj : tenue, endeble

tepid ['tɛpɪd] adj : tibio

term ['tərm] n **1** WORD : término m **2** PERIOD : período m **3 be on good ~s** : tener buenas relaciones **4 in ~s of** : con respecto a — ~ vt : calificar de

terminal ['tərmənəl] *adj* : terminal — ~ *n* 1 : terminal *m* 2 *or* **bus** ~ : terminal *f*

terminate ['tərmə‚neɪt] *v* -**nated;** -**nating** *vi* : terminar(se) — *vt* : poner fin a — **termination** [‚tərmə'neɪʃən] *n* : terminación *f*

termite ['tər‚maɪt] *n* : termita *f*

terrace ['terəs] *n* : terraza *f*

terrain [tə'reɪn] *n* : terreno *m*

terrestrial [tə'restriəl] *adj* : terrestre

terrible ['terəbəl] *adj* : espantoso, terrible — **terribly** ['terəbli] *adv* : terriblemente

terrier ['teriər] *n* : terrier *mf*

terrific [tə'rɪfɪk] *adj* 1 HUGE : tremendo 2 EXCELLENT : estupendo

terrify ['terə‚faɪ] *vt* -**fied;** -**fying** : aterrar, aterrorizar — **terrifying** ['terə‚faɪɪŋ] *adj* : aterrador

territory ['terə‚tori] *n, pl* -**ries** : territorio *m* — **territorial** [‚terə'toriəl] *adj* : territorial

terror ['terər] *n* : terror *m* — **terrorism** ['terər‚ɪzəm] *n* : terrorismo *m* — **terrorist** ['terərɪst] *n* : terrorista *mf* — **terrorize** ['terər‚aɪz] *vt* -**ized;** -**izing** : aterrorizar

terse ['tərs] *adj* **terser; tersest** : seco, lacónico

test ['test] *n* 1 TRIAL : prueba *f* 2 EXAM : examen *m*, prueba *f* 3 : análisis *m* (en medicina) — ~ *vt* 1 TRY : probar 2 QUIZ : analizar (la sangre, etc.), examinar (los ojos, etc.)

testament ['testəmənt] *n* 1 WILL : testamento *m* 2 **the Old/New Testament** : el Antiguo/Nuevo Testamento

testicle ['testɪkəl] *n* : testículo *m*

testify ['testə‚faɪ] *v* -**fied;** -**fying** : testificar

testimony ['testə‚moni] *n, pl* -**nies** : testimonio *m*

test tube *n* : probeta *f*, tubo *m* de ensayo

tetanus ['tetənəs] *n* : tétano *m*

tether ['teðər] *vt* : atar

text ['tekst] *n* : texto *m* — **textbook** ['tekst‚bʊk] *n* : libro *m* de texto

textile ['tek‚staɪl, 'tekstəl] *n* : textil *m*

texture ['tekstʃər] *n* : textura *f*

than ['ðæn] *conj & prep* : que, de (con cantidades)

thank ['θæŋk] *vt* 1 : agradecer, dar (las) gracias a 2 ~ **you!** : ¡gracias! — **thankful** ['θæŋkfəl] *adj* : agradecido — **thankfully** ['θæŋkfəli] *adv* 1 : con agradecimiento 2 FORTUNATELY : gracias a Dios — **thanks** ['θæŋks] *npl* 1 : agradecimiento *m* 2 ~**!** : ¡gracias!

Thanksgiving [θæŋks'gɪvɪŋ, 'θæŋks‚-] *n* : día *m* de Acción de Gracias

that ['ðæt] *pron, pl* **those** ['ðoːz] 1 : ése, ésa, eso 2 (*more distant*) : aquél, aquélla, aquello 3 **is** ~ **you?** : ¿eres tú? 4 **like** ~ : así 5 ~ **is...** : es decir... 6 **those who...** : los que... — ~ *conj* : que — ~ *adj, pl* **those** 1 : ese, esa 2 (*more distant*) : aquel, aquella 3 ~ **one** : ése, ésa — ~ *adv* : tan

thatched ['θætʃt] *adj* : con techo de paja

thaw ['θɔ] *vt* : descongelar (alimentos), derretir (hielo) — *vi* 1 : descongelarse 2 MELT : derretirse — ~ *n* : deshielo *m*

the [ðə, *before vowel sounds usu* ðiː] *art* 1 : el, la, los, las 2 PER : por — ~ *adv* 1 ~ **sooner** ~ **better** : cuanto más pronto, mejor 2 **I like this one** ~ **best** : éste es el que más me gusta

theater *or* **theatre** ['θiːətər] *n* : teatro *m* — **theatrical** [θi'ætrɪkəl] *adj* : teatral

theft ['θeft] *n* : robo *m*, hurto *m*

their ['ðer] *adj* : su, sus, de ellos, de ellas — **theirs** ['ðerz] *pron* 1 : (el) suyo, (la) suya, (los) suyos, (las) suyas 2 **some friends of** ~ : unos amigos suyos, unos amigos de ellos

them ['ðem] *pron* 1 (*used as direct object*) : los, las 2 (*used as indirect object*) : les, se 3 (*used as object of a preposition*) : ellos, ellas

theme ['θiːm] *n* 1 : tema *m* 2 ESSAY : trabajo *m* (escrito)

themselves [ðəm'selvz, ðem-] *pron* 1 (*used reflexively*) : se 2 (*used emphatically*) : ellos mismos, ellas mismas 3 (*used after a preposition*) : sí (mismos, sí (mismas)

then ['ðen] *adv* 1 : entonces 2 NEXT : luego, después 3 BESIDES : además — ~ *adj* : entonces

thence ['ðens, 'θens] *adv* : de ahí (en adelante)

theology [θi'ɑlədʒi] *n, pl* -**gles** : teología *f* — **theological** [‚θiə'lɑdʒɪkəl] *adj* : teológico

theorem ['θiːərəm, 'θɪrəm] *n* : teorema *m* — **theoretical** [‚θiːə'retɪkəl] *adj* : teórico — **theory** ['θiːəri, 'θɪri] *n, pl* -**ries** : teoría *f*

therapeutic [‚θerə'pjuːtɪk] *adj* : terapéutico — **therapist** ['θerəpɪst] *n* : terapeuta *mf* — **therapy** ['θerəpi] *n, pl* -**pies** : terapia *f*

there ['ðer] *adv* 1 *or* **over** — : allí, allá 2 *or* **right** — : ahí 3 **in** — : ahí (dentro) 4 ~**, it's done!** : ¡listo! 5 **up/down** ~ : ahí arriba/abajo 6

who's ~? : ¿quién es? — **~** *pron* **1** **~ is/are** : hay **2 ~ are three of us** : somos tres — **thereabouts** *or* **thereabout** [ˌðærəˈbauts, -ˈbaut, ˈðærə-] *adv or* **~** : por ahí — **thereafter** [ðærˈæftər] *adv* : después — **thereby** [ðærˈbaɪ, ˈðærˌbaɪ] *adv* : así — **therefore** [ˈðærˌfɔr] *adv* : por lo tanto

thermal [ˈθərməl] *adj* : térmico

thermometer [θərˈmɑmətər] *n* : termómetro *m*

thermos [ˈθərməs] *n* : termo *m*

thermostat [ˈθərməˌstæt] *n* : termostato *m*

thesaurus [θɪˈsɔrəs] *n*, *pl* **-sauri** [-ˈsɔrˌaɪ] *or* **-sauruses** [-ˈsɔrəsəz] : diccionario *m* de sinónimos

these → **this**

thesis [ˈθiːsɪs] *n*, *pl* **theses** [ˈθiːˌsiːz] : tesis *f*

they [ˈðeɪ] *pron* **1** : ellos, ellas **2 where are ~?** : ¿dónde están? **3 as ~ say** : como dicen — **they'd** [ˈðeɪd] (*contraction of* **they had** *or* **they would**) → **have, would** — **they'll** [ˈðeɪl, ˈðeɪl] (*contraction of* **they shall** *or* **they will**) → **shall, will** — **they're** [ˈðer] (*contraction of* **they are**) → **be** — **they've** [ˈðeɪv] (*contraction of* **they have**) → **have**

thick [ˈθɪk] *adj* **1** : grueso **DENSE** : espeso **3 a ~ accent** : un acento marcado **4 it's two inches ~** : tiene dos pulgadas de grosor — **~** *n* **in the ~ of** : en medio de — **thicken** [ˈθɪkən] *vt* : espesar — *vi* : espesarse — **thicket** [ˈθɪkət] *n* : matorral *m* — **thickness** [ˈθɪknəs] *n* : grosor *m*, espesor *m*

thief [ˈθiːf] *n*, *pl* **thieves** [ˈθiːvz] : ladrón *m*, -drona *f*

thigh [ˈθaɪ] *n* : muslo *m*

thimble [ˈθɪmbəl] *n* : dedal *m*

thin [ˈθɪn] *adj* **thinner; -est 1** : delgado **2** : ralo (dícese del pelo) **3 WATERY** : claro, aguado **4 FINE** : fino — **~** *v* **thinned; thinning** *vt* **DILUTE** : diluir — *vi* : ralear (dícese del pelo)

thing [ˈθɪŋ] *n* **1** : cosa *f* **2 for one ~** : en primer lugar **3 how are ~s?** : ¿qué tal? **4 it's a good ~ that...** : menos mal que... **5 the important ~ is...** : lo importante es...

think [ˈθɪŋk] *v* **thought** [ˈθɔt]; **thinking** *vt* **1** : pensar **2 BELIEVE** : creer **3 ~ up** : idear — *vi* **1** : pensar **2 ~ about** *or* **~ of CONSIDER** : pensar en **3 ~ of REMEMBER** : acordarse de **4 what do you ~ of it?** : ¿qué te parece? — **thinker** [ˈθɪŋkər] *n* : pensador *m*, -dora *f*

third [ˈθərd] *adj* : tercero — **~** *or* **third-**

ly [-li] *adv* : en tercer lugar — **~** *n* **1** : tercero *m*, -ra *f* (en una serie) **2** : tercero *m* (en matemáticas) — **Third World** *n* : Tercer Mundo *m*

thirst [ˈθərst] *n* : sed *f* — **thirsty** [ˈθərsti] *adj* **thirstier; -est 1** : sediento **2 be ~** : tener sed

thirteen [ˌθərˈtiːn] *adj* : trece — **~** *n* : trece *m* — **thirteenth** [ˌθərˈtiːnθ] *adj* : décimo tercero — **~** *n* **1** : decimotercero *m*, -ra *f* (en una serie) **2** : treceavo *m* (en matemáticas)

thirty [ˈθərti] *adj* : treinta — **~** *n*, *pl* **thirties** : treinta *m* — **thirtieth** [ˈθərtiəθ] *adj* : trigésimo — **~** *n* **1** : trigésimo *m*, -ma *f* (en una serie) **2** : treintavo *m* (en matemáticas)

this [ˈðɪs] *pron*, *pl* **these** [ˈðiːz] **1** : éste, ésta, esto **2 like ~** : así — **~** *adj*, *pl* **these 1** : este, esta **2 ~ one** : éste, ésta **3 ~ way** : por aquí — **~** *adv* **~ big** : así de grande

thistle [ˈθɪsəl] *n* : cardo *m*

thong [ˈθɔŋ] *n* **1** : correa *f* **2 SANDAL** : chancla *f*

thorn [ˈθɔrn] *n* : espina *f* — **thorny** [ˈθɔrni] *adj* : espinoso

thorough [ˈθɔroː] *adj* **1** : meticuloso **2 COMPLETE** : completo — **thoroughly** *adv* **1** : a fondo **2 COMPLETELY** : completamente — **thoroughbred** [ˈθɔroːˌbred] *adj* : de pura sangre — **thoroughfare** [ˈθɔroːˌfær] *n* : vía *f* pública

those → **that**

though [ˈðoː] *conj* : aunque — **~** *adv* **1** : sin embargo **2 as ~** : como si

thought [ˈθɔt] → **think** — **~** *n* **1** : pensamiento *m* **2 IDEA** : idea *f* — **thoughtful** [ˈθɔtfəl] *adj* **1** : pensativo **2 KIND** : amable — **thoughtless** [ˈθɔtləs] *adj* **1 CARELESS** : descuidado **2 RUDE** : desconsiderado

thousand [ˈθauzənd] *adj* : mil — **~** *n*, *pl* **-sands** *or* **-sand** : mil *m* — **thousandth** [ˈθauzəntθ] *adj* : milésimo — **~** *n* **1** : milésimo *m*, -ma *f* (en una serie) **2** : milésimo *m* (en matemáticas)

thrash [ˈθræʃ] *vt* : dar una paliza a — *vi or* **~ around** : agitarse, revolcarse

thread [ˈθred] *n* **1** : hilo *m* **2** : rosca *f* (de un tornillo) — **~** *vt* : enhilar (una aguja), ensartar (cuentas) — **threadbare** [ˈθredˌbær] *adj* : raído

threat [ˈθret] *n* : amenaza *f* — **threaten** [ˈθretən] *v* : amenazar — **threatening** [ˈθretənɪŋ] *adj* : amenazador

three [ˈθriː] *adj* : tres — **~** *n* : tres *m* — **three hundred** *adj* : trescientos — **~** *n* : trescientos *m*

threshold ['θreʃ.ho:ld, -,o:ld] *n* : umbral *m*

threw → **throw**

thrift ['θrɪft] *n* : frugalidad *f* — **thrifty** ['θrɪfti] *adj* **thriftier; -est** : económico, frugal

thrill ['θrɪl] *vt* : emocionar — ~ *n* : emoción *f* — **thriller** ['θrɪlər] *n* : película *f* de suspense *Spain*, película *f* de suspenso *Lat* — **thrilling** ['θrɪlɪŋ] *adj* : emocionante

thrive ['θraɪv] *vi* **throve** ['θro:v] *or* **thrived; thriven** ['θrɪvən] 1 FLOURISH : florecer 2 PROSPER : prosperar

throat ['θro:t] *n* : garganta *f*

throb ['θrab] *vi* **throbbed; throbbing** 1 PULSATE : palpitar 2 VIBRATE : vibrar 3 ~ **with pain** : tener un dolor punzante

throes ['θro:z] *npl* 1 PANGS : agonía *f* 2 **in the** ~ **of** : en medio de

throne ['θro:n] *n* : trono *m*

throng ['θrɔŋ] *n* : muchedumbre *f*, multitud *f*

throttle ['θrɑtəl] *vt* **-tled; -tling** : estrangular — ~ *n* : válvula *f* reguladora

through ['θru:] *prep* 1 : por, a través de 2 BETWEEN : entre 3 BECAUSE OF : a causa de 4 DURING : durante 5 → **throughout** 6 **Monday** ~ **Friday** : de lunes a viernes — ~ *adv* 1 : de un lado a otro (en el espacio), de principio a fin (en el tiempo) 2 COMPLETELY : completamente — ~ *adj* 1 **be** ~ : haber terminado 2 ~ **traffic** : tráfico *m* de paso — **throughout** [θru:'aʊt] *prep* : por todo (un lugar), a lo largo de (un período de tiempo)

throw ['θro:] *v* **threw** ['θru:]; **thrown** ['θro:n]; **throwing** *vt* 1 : tirar, lanzar 2 : proyectar (una sombra) 3 CONFUSE : desconcertar 4 ~ **a party** : dar una fiesta 5 ~ **away** *or* ~ **out** : tirar, botar *Lat* — *vi* ~ **up** VOMIT : vomitar — ~ *n* : tiro *m*, lanzamiento *m*

thrush ['θrʌʃ] *n* : tordo *m*, zorzal *m*

thrust ['θrʌst] *vt* **thrust; thrusting** 1 : empujar (bruscamente) 2 PLUNGE : clavar 3 ~ **upon** : imponer a — ~ *n* 1 : empujón *m* 2 : estocada *f* (en esgrima)

thud ['θʌd] *n* : ruido *m* sordo

thug ['θʌg] *n* : matón *m*

thumb ['θʌm] *n* : (dedo *m*) pulgar *m* — ~ *vt* ~ **through** : hojear — **thumbnail** ['θʌm,neɪl] *n* : uña *f* del pulgar — **thumbtack** ['θʌm,tæk] *n* : tachuela *f*, chinche *f* Lat

thump ['θʌmp] *vt* : golpear — *vi* : latir

con fuerza (dícese del corazón) — ~ *n* : ruido *m* sordo

thunder ['θʌndər] *n* : truenos *mpl* — ~ *vi* : tronar — *vt* SHOUT : bramar — **thunderbolt** ['θʌndər,bo:lt] *n* : rayo *m* — **thunderous** ['θʌndərəs] *adj* : atronador — **thunderstorm** ['θʌndər,stɔrm] *n* : tormenta *f* eléctrica

Thursday ['θərz,deɪ, -di] *n* : jueves *m*

thus ['ðʌs] *adv* 1 : así 2 THEREFORE : por lo tanto

thwart ['θwɔrt] *vt* : frustrar

thyme ['taɪm, 'θaɪm] *n* : tomillo *m*

thyroid ['θaɪ,rɔɪd] *n* : tiroides *mf*

tiara [ti'ærə, -'ɑr-] *n* : diadema *f*

tic ['tɪk] *n* : tic *m* (nervioso)

tick[1] ['tɪk] *n* : garrapata *f* (insecto)

tick[2] *n* 1 : tictac *m* (sonido) 2 CHECK : marca *f* — ~ *vi* : hacer tictac — *vt* 1 *or* ~ **off** CHECK : marcar 2 ~ **off** ANNOY : fastidiar

ticket ['tɪkət] *n* 1 : pasaje *m* (de avión), billete *m* Spain (de tren, avión, etc.), boleto *m* Lat (de tren o autobús) 2 : entrada *f* (al teatro, etc.) 3 FINE : multa *f*

tickle ['tɪkəl] *v* **-led; -ling** 1 : hacer cosquillas a 2 AMUSE : divertir — *vi* : picar — ~ *n* : cosquilleo *m* — **ticklish** ['tɪkəlɪʃ] *adj* 1 : cosquilloso 2 TRICKY : delicado

tidal wave ['taɪdəl] *n* : maremoto *m*

tidbit ['tɪd,bɪt] *n* MORSEL : golosina *f*

tide ['taɪd] *n* : marea *f* — ~ *vt* **tided; tiding** ~ **over** : ayudar a superar un apuro

tidy ['taɪdi] *adj* **-dier; -est** : ordenado, arreglado — ~ *vt* **-died; -dying** *or* ~ **up** : ordenar, arreglar

tie ['taɪ] *n* 1 : atadura *f*, cordón *m* 2 BOND : lazo *m* 3 : empate *m* (en deportes) 4 NECKTIE : corbata *f* — ~ *v* **tied; tying** *or* **tieing** *vt* 1 : atar, amarrar *Lat* 2 ~ **a knot** : hacer un nudo — *vi* : empatar (en deportes)

tier ['tɪr] *n* : nivel *m*, piso (de un pastel), grada *f* (de un estadio)

tiger ['taɪgər] *n* : tigre *m*

tight ['taɪt] *adj* 1 : apretado 2 SNUG : ajustado, ceñido 3 TAUT : tirante 4 STINGY : agarrado 5 SCARCE : escaso 6 **a** ~ **seal** : un cierre hermético 7 **a** ~ **spot** : un aprieto — ~ *adv* **closed** ~ : bien cerrado — **tighten** ['taɪtən] *vt* 1 : apretar 2 TENSE : tensar 3 : hacer más estricto (reglas, etc.) — **tightly** ['taɪtli] *adv* : bien, fuerte — **tightrope** ['taɪt,ro:p] *n* : cuerda *f* floja — **tights** ['taɪts] *npl* : leotardo *m*, mallas *fpl*

tile ['taɪl] *n* 1 : azulejo *m*, baldosa *f* (de

piso) **2** *or* **roofing** ~ : teja *f* — ~ *vt*
tiled; tiling 1 : revestir de azulejos,
embaldosar (un piso) **2** : tejar (un
techo)

till¹ ['tɪl] *prep & conj* → **until**

till² *vt* : cultivar

till³ *n* : caja *f* (registradora)

tilt ['tɪlt] *n* **1** : inclinación *f* **2 at full** ~ : a
toda velocidad — ~ *vt* : inclinar — *vi*
: inclinarse

timber ['tɪmbər] *n* **1** : madera *f* (para
construcción) **2** BEAM : viga *f*

timbre ['tæmbər, 'tɪm-] *n* : timbre *m*

time ['taɪm] *n* **1** : tiempo *m* **2** AGE : época
f **3** : compás *m* (en música) **4 at** ~**s**
: a veces **5 at this** ~ : en este momento **6 for the** ~ **being** : por el momento **7 from** ~ **to** ~ : de vez en
cuando **8 have a good** ~ : pasarlo
bien **9 many** ~**s** : muchas veces **10
on** ~ : a tiempo **11** ~ **after** ~ : una
y otra vez **12 what** ~ **is it?** : ¿qué
hora es? — ~ *vt* **timed; timing**
: tomar el tiempo a (algn), cronome-
trar (una carrera, etc.) — **timeless**
['taɪmləs] *adj* : eterno — **timely** ['taɪm-
li] *adj* **-lier; -est** : oportuno — **timer**
['taɪmər] *n* : temporizador *m*, avisador
m (de cocina) — **times** ['taɪmz] *prep* **3**
~ **4 is 12** : 3 por 4 son 12 — **timetable** ['taɪm,teɪbəl] *n* : horario *m*

timid ['tɪmɪd] *adj* : tímido

tin ['tɪn] *n* **1** : estaño *m* **2** CAN : lata *f*,
bote *m* *Spain* — **tinfoil** ['tɪn,fɔɪl] *n*
: papel *m* (de) aluminio

tinge ['tɪndʒ] *vt* **tinged; tingeing** *or*
tinging ['tɪndʒɪŋ] : matizar — ~ *n* **1**
TINT : matiz *m* **2** TOUCH : dejo *m*

tingle ['tɪŋgəl] *vi* **-gled; -gling** : sentir
(un) hormigueo — ~ *n* : hormigueo
m

tinker ['tɪŋkər] *vi* ~ **with** : intentar
arreglar (con pequeños ajustes)

tinkle ['tɪŋkəl] *vi* **-kled; -kling** : tintinear
— ~ *n* : tintineo *m*

tint ['tɪnt] *n* : tinte *m* — ~ *vt* : teñir

tiny ['taɪni] *adj* **-nier; -est** : diminuto,
minúsculo

tip¹ ['tɪp] *v* **tipped; tipping** *vt* **1** TILT : inclinar **2** *or* ~ **over** : volcar — *vi* : inclinarse

tip² *n* END : punta *f*

tip³ *n* ADVICE : consejo *m* — ~ *vt* ~
off : avisar

tip⁴ *vt* : dar una propina a — ~ *n* GRA-
TUITY : propina *f*

tipsy ['tɪpsi] *adj* **-sier; -est** : achispado

tiptoe ['tɪp,toː] *n* **on** ~ : de puntillas —
~ *vi* **-toed; -toeing** : caminar de puntillas
tillas

tip–top ['tɪp'tɑp, -,tɑp] *adj* : excelente

tire¹ ['taɪr] *n* : neumático *m*, llanta *f* *Lat*

tire² *v* **tired; tiring** *vt* : cansar — *vi*
: cansarse — **tired** ['taɪrd] *adj* **1** ~ **of**
: cansado de, harto de **2** ~ **out** : agotado — **tireless** ['taɪrləs] *adj* : incansable — **tiresome** ['taɪrsəm] *adj* : pesado

tissue ['tɪˌʃuː] *n* **1** : pañuelo *m* de papel **2**
: tejido *m* (en biología)

title ['taɪtəl] *n* : título *m* — ~ *vt* **-tled;
-tling** : titular

to ['tuː] *prep* **1** : a **2** TOWARD : hacia **3** IN
ORDER TO : para **4** UP TO : hasta **5 a
quarter** ~ **seven** : las siete menos
cuarto **6 be nice** ~ **them** : trátalos
bien **7 ten** ~ **the box** : diez por caja **8
the mate** ~ **this shoe** : el compañero de este zapato **9 two** ~ **four
years old** : entre dos y cuatro años de
edad **10 want** ~ **do** : querer hacer —
~ *adv* **1 come** ~ : volver en sí **2** ~
and fro : de un lado a otro

toad ['toːd] *n* : sapo *m*

toast ['toːst] *vt* **1** : tostar (pan, etc.) **2**
: brindar por (una persona) — ~ *n* **1**
: pan *m* tostado, tostadas *fpl* **2** DRINK
: brindis *m* — **toaster** ['toːstər] *n*
: tostador *m*

tobacco [təˈbækoː] *n*, *pl* **-cos** : tabaco *m*

toboggan [təˈbɑgən] *n* : tobogán *m*

today [təˈdeɪ] *adv* : hoy — ~ *n* : hoy *m*

toddler ['tɑdələr] *n* : niño *m* pequeño,
niña *f* pequeña (que comienza a caminar)

toe ['toː] *n* : dedo *m* (del pie) — **toenail**
['toːˌneɪl] *n* : uña *f* (del pie)

together [təˈgeðər] *adv* **1** : juntos **2** ~
with : junto con

toil ['tɔɪl] *n* : trabajo *m* duro — ~ *vi*
: trabajar duro

toilet ['tɔɪlət] *n* **1** BATHROOM : baño *m*,
servicio *m* **2** : inodoro *m* (instalación)
— **toilet paper** *n* : papel *m* higiénico
— **toiletries** ['tɔɪlətriz] *npl* : artículos
mpl de tocador

token ['toːkən] *n* **1** SIGN : muestra *f* **2** ME-
MENTO : recuerdo *m* **3** : ficha *f* (para un
tren, etc.)

told → **tell**

tolerable ['tɑlərəbəl] *adj* : tolerable —
tolerance ['tɑlərənts] *n* : tolerancia *f* —
tolerant ['tɑlərənt] *adj* : tolerante —
tolerate ['tɑlə,reɪt] *vt* **-ated; -ating**
: tolerar

toll¹ ['toːl] *n* **1** : peaje *m* **2 death** ~
: número *m* de muertos **3 take a** ~ **on**
: afectar

toll² *vi* RING : tocar, doblar — ~ *n*
: tañido *m*

tomato [tə'meɪɾo, -'mɑ-] *n, pl* **-toes** : tomate *m*

tomb ['tuːm] *n* : tumba *f*, sepulcro *m* — **tombstone** ['tuːm,stoːn] *n* : lápida *f*

tome ['toːm] *n* : tomo *m*

tomorrow [tə'mɑro] *adv* : mañana — ~ *n* : mañana *m*

ton ['tən] *n* : tonelada *f*

tone ['toːn] *n* : tono *m* — ~ *vt* **toned; toning** *or* ~ **down** : atenuar

tongs ['tɑŋz, 'tɔŋz] *npl* : tenazas *fpl*

tongue ['tʌŋ] *n* : lengua *f*

tonic ['tɑnɪk] *n* **1** : tónico *m* **2** *or* ~ **water** : tónica *f*

tonight [tə'naɪt] *adv* : esta noche — ~ *n* : esta noche *f*

tonsil ['tɑntsəl] *n* : amígdala *f*

too ['tuː] *adv* **1** ALSO : también **2** EXCESSIVELY : demasiado

took → **take**

tool ['tuːl] *n* : herramienta *f* — **toolbox** ['tuːl,bɑks] *n* : caja *f* de herramientas

toot ['tuːt] *vt* : sonar (un claxon, etc.) — ~ *n* **1** WHISTLE : pitido *m* **2** HONK : bocinazo *m*

tooth ['tuːθ] *n, pl* **teeth** ['tiːθ] : diente *m* — **toothache** ['tuːθ,eɪk] *n* : dolor *m* de muelas — **toothbrush** ['tuːθ,brʌʃ] *n* : cepillo *m* de dientes — **toothpaste** ['tuːθ,peɪst] *n* : pasta *f* de dientes, pasta *f* dentífrica

top[1] ['tɑp] *n* **1** : parte *f* superior **2** SUMMIT : cima *f*, cumbre *f* **3** COVER : tapa *f*, cubierta *f* **4 on** ~ **of** : encima de — ~ *vt* **topped; topping 1** COVER : rematar (un edificio, etc.), bañar (un pastel, etc.) **2** SURPASS : superar **3** ~ **off** : llenar — ~ *adj* **1** : de arriba, superior **2** BEST : mejor **3 a** ~ **executive** : un alto ejecutivo

top[2] *n* : trompo *m* (juguete)

topic ['tɑpɪk] *n* : tema *m* — **topical** ['tɑpɪkəl] *adj* : de interés actual

topmost ['tɑp,moːst] *adj* : más alto

topple ['tɑpəl] *v* **-pled; -pling** : caerse — *vt* **1** OVERTURN : volcar **2** OVERTHROW : derrocar

torch ['tɔrtʃ] *n* : antorcha *f*

tore → **tear**[1]

torment ['tɔr,ment] *n* : tormento *m* — ~ [tɔr'ment, 'tɔr-] *vt* : atormentar

torn → **tear**[1]

tornado [tɔr'neɪdo] *n, pl* **-does** *or* **-dos** : tornado *m*

torpedo [tɔr'piːdo] *n, pl* **-does** : torpedo *m* — ~ *vt* : torpedear

torrent ['tɔrənt] *n* : torrente *m*

torrid ['tɔrɪd] *adj* : tórrido

torso ['tɔr,soː] *n, pl* **-sos** *or* **-si** [-,siː] : torso *m*

tortilla [tɔr'tiːjə] *n* : tortilla *f*

tortoise ['tɔrṭəs] *n* : tortuga *f* (terrestre) — **tortoiseshell** ['tɔrṭəsˌʃel] *n* : carey *m*, concha *f*

tortuous ['tɔrtʃuəs] *adj* : tortuoso

torture ['tɔrtʃər] *n* : tortura *f* — ~ *vt* **-tured; -turing** : torturar

toss ['tɔs, 'tɑs] *vt* **1** : tirar, lanzar **2** : mezclar (una ensalada) — *vi* ~ **and turn** : dar vueltas — ~ *n* : lanzamiento *m*

tot ['tɑt] *n* : pequeño *m*, -ña *f*

total ['toːtəl] *adj* : total — ~ *n* : total *m* — ~ *vt* **-taled** *or* **-talled; -taling** *or* **-talling 1** : ascender a **2** *or* ~ **up** : totalizar, sumar

totalitarian [toːˌtæləˈteriən] *adj* : totalitario

tote ['toːt] *vt* **toted; toting** : llevar

totter ['tɑtər] *vi* : tambalearse

touch ['tʌtʃ] *vt* **1** : tocar **2** MOVE : conmover **3** AFFECT : afectar **4** ~ **up** : retocar — *vi* : tocarse — ~ *n* **1** : tacto *m* (sentido) **2** HINT : toque *m* **3** BIT : pizca *f* **4 keep in** ~ : mantenerse en contacto **5 lose one's** ~ : perder la habilidad — **touchdown** ['tʌtʃ,daʊn] *n* : touchdown *m* — **touchy** ['tʌtʃi] *adj* **touchier; -est 1** : delicado **2 be** ~ **about** : picarse a la mención de

tough ['tʌf] *adj* **1** : duro **2** STRONG : fuerte **3** STRICT : severo **4** DIFFICULT : difícil — **toughen** ['tʌfən] *vt* *or* ~ **up** : endurecer — *vi* : endurecerse — **toughness** ['tʌfnəs] *n* : dureza *f*

tour ['tʊr] *n* **1** : viaje *m* (por un país, etc.), visita *f* (a un museo, etc.) **2** : gira *f* (de un equipo, etc.) — ~ *vi* **1** TRAVEL : viajar **2** : hacer una gira (dícese de equipos, etc.) — *vt* : viajar por, recorrer — **tourist** ['tʊrɪst, 'tɔr-] *n* : turista *mf*

tournament ['tɔrnəmənt, 'tʊr-] *n* : torneo *m*

tousle ['taʊzəl] *vt* **-sled; -sling** : despeinar

tout ['taʊt] *vt* : promocionar

tow ['toː] *vt* : remolcar — ~ *n* : remolque *m*

toward ['tord, tə'word] *or* **towards** ['tordz, tə'wordz] *prep* : hacia

towel ['taʊəl] *n* : toalla *f*

tower ['taʊər] *n* : torre *f* — ~ *vi* ~ **over** : descollar sobre — **towering** ['taʊərɪŋ] *adj* : altísimo

town ['taʊn] *n* **1** VILLAGE : pueblo *m* **2** CITY : ciudad *f* — **township** ['taʊnˌʃɪp] *n* : municipio *m*

tow truck ['toːˌtrʌk] *n* : grúa *f*

toxic ['tɑksɪk] *adj* : tóxico

toy ['tɔɪ] *n* : juguete *m* — ~ *vi* ~ **with** : juguetear con

trace ['treɪs] *n* **1** SIGN : rastro *m*, señal *f* **2** HINT : dejo *m* — ~ *vt* **traced; tracing** **1** : calcar (un dibujo, etc.) **2** DRAW : trazar **3** FIND : localizar

track ['træk] *n* **1** : pista *f* **2** PATH : sendero *m* **3** *or* **railroad** ~ : vía *f* (férrea) **4** **keep** ~ **of** : llevar la cuenta de — ~ *vt* TRAIL : seguir la pista de

tract[1] ['trækt] *n* **1** EXPANSE : extensión *f* **2** : tracto *m* (en anatomía)

tract[2] *n* PAMPHLET : folleto *m*

traction ['trækʃən] *n* : tracción *f*

tractor ['træktər] *n* **1** : tractor *m* **2** *or* ~ **-trailer** : camión *m* (con remolque)

trade ['treɪd] *n* **1** PROFESSION : oficio *m* **2** COMMERCE : comercio *m* **3** INDUSTRY : industria *f* **4** EXCHANGE : cambio *m* — ~ *v* **traded; trading** *vi* : comerciar — *vt* ~ **sth with s.o.** : cambiar algo a algn — **trademark** ['treɪd,mɑrk] *n* : marca *f* registrada

tradition [trə'dɪʃən] *n* : tradición *f* — **traditional** [trə'dɪʃənəl] *adj* : tradicional

traffic ['træfɪk] *n* : tráfico *m* — ~ *vi* **trafficked; trafficking** ~ **in** : traficar con — **traffic light** *n* : semáforo *m*

tragedy ['trædʒədi] *n, pl* **-dies** : tragedia *f* — **tragic** ['trædʒɪk] *adj* : trágico

trail ['treɪl] *vi* **1** DRAG : arrastrar **2** LAG : rezagarse **3** ~ **off** : apagarse — *vt* **1** DRAG : arrastrar **2** PURSUE : seguir la pista de — ~ *n* **1** : rastro *m*, huellas *fpl* PATH : sendero *m* — **trailer** ['treɪlər] *n* **1** : remolque *m* **2** : caravana *f* (vivienda)

train ['treɪn] *n* **1** : tren *m* **2** : cola *f* (de un vestido) **3** SERIES : serie *f* **4** ~ **of thought** : hilo *m* (de las ideas) — ~ *vt* **1** : adiestrar, entrenar (atletas, etc.) **2** AIM : apuntar — *vi* : prepararse, entrenarse (en deportes, etc.) — **trainer** ['treɪnər] *n* : entrenador *m*, -dora *f*

trait ['treɪt] *n* : rasgo *m*

traitor ['treɪtər] *n* : traidor *m*, -dora *f*

tramp ['træmp] *vi* : caminar (pesadamente) — ~ *n* VAGRANT : vagabundo *m*, -da *f*

trample ['træmpəl] *vt* **-pled; -pling** : pisotear

trampoline [,træmpə'liːn, 'træmpə,-] *n* : trampolín *m*

trance ['trænts] *n* : trance *m*

tranquillity *or* **tranquility** [træŋ'kwɪləti] *n* : tranquilidad *f* — **tranquil** ['træŋkwəl] *adj* : tranquilo — **tranquilize** ['træŋkwə,laɪz] *vt* **-ized; -izing** : tranquilizar — **tranquilizer** ['træŋkwə,laɪzər] *n* : tranquilizante *m*

transaction [træn'zækʃən] *n* : transacción *f*

transatlantic [,træntsət'læntɪk, ,trænz-] *adj* : transatlántico

transcend [træn'send] *vt* **1** : ir más allá de **2** OVERCOME : superar

transcribe [træn'skraɪb] *vt* **-scribed; -scribing** : transcribir — **transcript** ['træn,skrɪpt] *n* : transcripción *f*

transfer [træns'fər, 'træns,fər] *v* **-ferred; -ferring** *vt* **1** : transferir (fondos, etc.) **2** : trasladar (a un empleado, etc.) — *vi* **1** : cambiarse (de escuelas, etc.) **2** : hacer transbordo (entre trenes, etc.) — ~ ['træns,fər] *n* **1** : transferencia *f* (de fondos, etc.), traslado *m* (de una persona) **2** : boleto *m* (para hacer transbordo) **3** DECAL : calcomanía *f*

transform [træns'fɔrm] *vt* : transformar — **transformation** [,trænsfər'meɪʃən] *n* : transformación *f*

transfusion [træns'fjuːʒən] *n* : transfusión *f*

transgression [træns'greʃən, trænz-] *n* : transgresión *f* — **transgress** [træns'gres, trænz-] *vt* : transgredir

transient ['træntʃənt, 'trænsiənt] *adj* : pasajero

transit ['træntsɪt, 'trænzɪt] *n* **1** : tránsito *m* **2** TRANSPORTATION : transporte *m*

transition [træn'sɪʃən, -'zɪʃ-] *n* : transición *f* — **transitive** ['træntsətɪv, 'trænzə-] *adj* : transitivo — **transitory** ['træntsə,tori, 'trænzə-] *adj* : transitorio

translate [træns'leɪt, trænz-; 'træns,-, 'trænz,-] *vt* **-lated; -lating** : traducir — **translation** [træns'leɪʃən, trænz-] *n* : traducción *f* — **translator** [træns'leɪtər, trænz-; 'træns,-, 'trænz,-] *n* : traductor *m*, -tora *f*

translucent [træns'luːsənt, trænz-] *adj* : translúcido

transmit [træns'mɪt, trænz-] *vt* **-mitted; -mitting** : transmitir — **transmission** [træns'mɪʃən, trænz-] *n* : transmisión *f* — **transmitter** [træns'mɪtər, trænz-; 'træns,-, 'trænz,-] *n* : transmisor *m*

transparent [træns'pærənt] *adj* : transparente — **transparency** [træns'pærəntsi] *n, pl* **-cies** : transparencia *f*

transpire [træns'paɪr] *vi* **-spired; -spiring** **1** TURN OUT : resultar **2** HAPPEN : suceder

transplant [træns'plænt] *vt* : trasplantar — ~ ['træns,plænt] *n* : trasplante *m*

transport [træns'port, 'træns,-] *vt* : transportar — ~ ['træns,port] *n* : transporte *m* — **transportation** [,trænspər'teɪʃən] *n* : transporte *m*

transpose [træns'poːz] *vt* **-posed;**

-posing 1 : trasponer **2** : transportar (en música)

trap ['træp] n : trampa f — ~ vt **trapped; trapping** : atrapar — **trapdoor** ['træp'dor] n : trampilla f

trapeze [træ'pi:z] n : trapecio m

trappings ['træpɪŋz] npl : adornos mpl, atavíos mpl

trash ['træʃ] n : basura f

trauma ['tromə, 'trau-] n : trauma m — **traumatic** [trə'mætɪk, trɔ-, trau-] adj : traumático

travel ['trævəl] vi **-eled** or **-elled; -eling** or **-elling 1** : viajar **2** MOVE : desplazarse — ~ n : viajes mpl — **traveler** or **traveller** ['trævələr] n : viajero m, -ra f

traverse [trə'vərs, træ'vərs, 'trævərs] vt **-versed; -versing** : atravesar

travesty ['trævəsti] n, pl **-ties** : parodia f

trawl ['trɔl] vi : pescar (con red de arrastre) — **trawler** ['trɔlər] n : barco m de pesca

tray ['treɪ] n : bandeja f

treachery ['tretʃəri] n, pl **-eries** : traición f — **treacherous** ['tretʃərəs] adj **1** : traidor **2** DANGEROUS : peligroso

tread ['tred] v **trod** ['trɒd], **trodden** ['trɒdən] or **trod; treading** vt **1** or ~ **on** : pisar **2** ~ **water** : flotar — vi **1** STEP : pisar **2** WALK : caminar — ~ n **1** STEP : paso m **2** : banda f de rodadura (de un neumático) — **treadmill** ['tred,mɪl] n : rueda f de andar

treason ['tri:zən] n : traición f (a la patria)

treasure ['treʒər, 'treɪ-] n : tesoro m — ~ vt **-sured; -suring** : apreciar — **treasurer** ['treʒərər, 'treɪ-] n : tesorero m, -ra f — **treasury** ['treʒəri, 'treɪ-] n, pl **-suries** : erario m, tesoro m

treat ['tri:t] vt **1** : tratar **2** CONSIDER : considerar **3** ~ **s.o. to (dinner, etc.)** : invitar a algn (a cenar, etc.) — ~ n **1** : gusto m, placer m **2 it's my** ~ : invito yo

treatise ['tri:tɪs] n : tratado m

treatment ['tri:tmənt] n : tratamiento m

treaty ['tri:ti] n, pl **-ties** : tratado m

treble ['trebəl] adj **1** TRIPLE : triple **2** : de tiple (en música) — ~ vt **-bled; -bling** : triplicar — **treble clef** : clave f de sol

tree ['tri:] n : árbol m

trek ['trek] vi **trekked; trekking** : viajar (con dificultad) — ~ n : viaje m difícil

trellis ['trelɪs] n : enrejado m

tremble ['trembəl] vi **-bled; -bling** : temblar

tremendous [trɪ'mendəs] adj : tremendo

tremor ['tremər] n : temblor m

trench ['trentʃ] n **1** : zanja f **2** : trinchera f (militar)

trend ['trend] n **1** : tendencia f **2** FASHION : moda f — **trendy** ['trendi] adj **trendier; -est** : de moda

trepidation [,trepə'deɪʃən] n : inquietud f

trespass ['trespəs, -,pæs] vi : entrar ilegalmente (en propiedad ajena)

trial ['traɪəl] n **1** : juicio m, proceso m **2** TEST : prueba f **3** ORDEAL : dura prueba f — ~ adj : de prueba

triangle ['traɪ,æŋgəl] n : triángulo m — **triangular** [traɪ'æŋgjələr] adj : triangular

tribe ['traɪb] n : tribu f — **tribal** ['traɪbəl] adj : tribal

tribulation [,trɪbjə'leɪʃən] n : tribulación f

tribunal [traɪ'bju:nəl, trɪ-] n : tribunal m

tribute ['trɪbju:t] n : tributo m — **tributary** ['trɪbjə,teri] n, pl **-taries** : afluente m

trick ['trɪk] n **1** : trampa f **2** PRANK : broma f **3** KNACK, FEAT : truco m **4** : baza f (en naipes) — ~ vt : engañar — **trickery** ['trɪkəri] n : engaño m

trickle ['trɪkəl] vi **-led; -ling** : gotear — ~ n : goteo m

tricky ['trɪki] adj **trickier; -est 1** SLY : astuto, taimado **2** DIFFICULT : difícil

tricycle ['traɪsɪkəl, -,sɪkəl] n : triciclo m

trifle ['traɪfəl] n **1** TRIVIALITY : nimiedad f **2 a** ~ : un poco — ~ vi **-fled; -fling** ~ **with** : jugar con — **trifling** ['traɪflɪŋ] adj : insignificante

trigger ['trɪgər] n : gatillo m — ~ vt : causar, provocar

trill ['trɪl] n : trino m — ~ vi : trinar

trillion ['trɪljən] n : billón m

trilogy ['trɪlədʒi] n, pl **-gies** : trilogía f

trim ['trɪm] vt **trimmed; trimming 1** : recortar **2** ADORN : adornar — ~ adj **trimmer; trimmest 1** SLIM : esbelto **2** NEAT : arreglado — ~ n **1** : recorte m **2** DECORATION : adornos mpl **3 in** ~ : en buena forma — **trimming** ['trɪmɪŋ] npl **1** : adornos mpl **2** GARNISH : guarnición f

Trinity ['trɪnəti] n : Trinidad f

trinket ['trɪŋkət] n : chuchería f

trio ['tri:,o] n, pl **trios** : trío m

trip ['trɪp] v **tripped; tripping** vi **1** : caminar (a paso ligero) **2** STUMBLE : tropezar **3** ~ **up** : equivocarse — vt **1** ACTIVATE : activar **2** ~ **s.o.** : hacer una zancadilla a algn **3** ~ **s.o. up** : hacer equivocar a algn — ~ n **1** : viaje m **2** STUMBLE : traspié m

tripe ['traɪp] n 1 : mondongo m, callos mpl 2 NONSENSE : tonterías fpl

triple ['trɪpəl] vt -**pled**; -**pling** : triplicar — ~ n : triple m — ~ adj : triple — **triplet** ['trɪplət] n : trillizo m, -za f — **triplicate** ['trɪplɪkət] n : triplicado m

tripod ['traɪpɑd] n : trípode m

trite ['traɪt] adj **triter**; **tritest** : trillado

triumph ['traɪəmpf] n : triunfo m — ~ vi : triunfar — **triumphal** [traɪˈʌmpfəl] adj : triunfal — **triumphant** [traɪˈʌmpfənt] adj : triunfante

trivial ['trɪviəl] adj : trivial — **trivia** ['trɪviə] ns & pl : trivialidades fpl — **triviality** [ˌtrɪviˈæləṭi] n, pl -**ties** : trivialidad f

trod, trodden → **tread**

trolley ['trɑli] n, pl -**leys** : tranvía m

trombone [trɑmˈboːn] n : trombón m

troop ['truːp] n 1 : escuadrón m (de caballería), compañía f (de soldados) 2 ~**s** npl : tropas fpl — ~ vi ~ **in/out** : entrar/salir en tropel — **trooper** ['truːpər] n 1 : soldado m 2 or **state** ~ : policía mf estatal

trophy ['troːfi] n, pl -**phies** : trofeo m

tropic ['trɑpɪk] n 1 : trópico m 2 **the** ~**s** : el trópico — ~ or **tropical** [-pɪkəl] adj : tropical

trot ['trɑt] n : trote m — ~ vi **trotted**; **trotting** : trotar

trouble ['trʌbəl] v -**bled**; -**bling** vt 1 WORRY : preocupar 2 BOTHER : molestar — vi : molestarse — ~ n 1 PROBLEMS : problemas mpl 2 EFFORT : molestia f 3 **be in** ~ : estar en apuros 4 **get in** ~ : meterse en problemas 5 **I had** ~ **doing it** : me costó hacerlo — **troublemaker** ['trʌbəlˌmeɪkər] n : alborotador m, -dora f — **troublesome** ['trʌbəlsəm] adj : problemático

trough ['trɔf] n, pl **troughs** ['trɔfs, 'trɔvz] 1 : depresión f 2 or **feeding** ~ : comedero m 3 or **drinking** ~ : bebedero m

troupe ['truːp] n : compañía f (de teatro)

trousers ['traʊzərz] npl : pantalón m, pantalones mpl

trout ['traʊt] n, pl **trout** : trucha f

trowel ['traʊəl] n : paleta f (de albañil), desplantador m (de jardinero)

truant ['truːənt] n : alumno m, -na f que falta a clase

truce ['truːs] n : tregua f

truck ['trʌk] vt : transportar en camión — ~ n 1 : camión m 2 CART : carro m — **trucker** ['trʌkər] n : camionero m, -ra f

trudge ['trʌdʒ] vi **trudged**; **trudging** : caminar a paso pesado

true ['truː] adj **truer**; **truest** 1 : verdadero 2 LOYAL : fiel 3 GENUINE : auténtico 4 **be** ~ : ser cierto, ser verdad

truffle ['trʌfəl] n : trufa f

truly ['truːli] adv : verdaderamente

trump ['trʌmp] n : triunfo m (en naipes)

trumpet ['trʌmpət] n : trompeta f

trunk ['trʌŋk] n 1 STEM, TORSO : tronco m 2 : trompa f (de un elefante) 3 : baúl m (equipaje) 4 : maletero m (de un auto) 5 ~**s** npl : traje m de baño (de hombre)

truss ['trʌs] n 1 FRAMEWORK : armazón m 2 : braguero m (en medicina)

trust ['trʌst] n 1 CONFIDENCE : confianza f 2 HOPE : esperanza f 3 CREDIT : crédito m 4 : trust m (en finanzas) 5 **in** ~ : en fideicomiso — vi 1 : confiar 2 HOPE : esperar — vt 1 : confiar en, fiarse de (en frases negativas) 2 ~ **s.o. with sth** : confiar algo a algn — **trustee** [ˌtrʌsˈtiː] n : fideicomisario m, -ria f — **trustworthy** ['trʌstˌwərði] adj : digno de confianza

truth ['truːθ] n, pl **truths** ['truːðz, 'truːθs] : verdad f — **truthful** ['truːθfəl] adj : sincero, veraz

try ['traɪ] v **tried**; **trying** vt 1 ATTEMPT : tratar (de), intentar 2 : juzgar (un caso, etc.) 3 TEST : poner a prueba 4 or ~ **out** : probar 5 ~ **on** : probarse (ropa) — vi : hacer un esfuerzo — ~ n, pl **tries** : intento m — **trying** adj 1 ANNOYING : irritante, pesado 2 DIFFICULT : duro — **tryout** ['traɪaʊt] n : prueba f

tsar ['zɑr, 'tsɑr, 'sɑr] → **czar**

T-shirt ['tiːˌʃərt] n : camiseta f

tub ['tʌb] n 1 : cuba f, tina f 2 CONTAINER : envase m 3 BATHTUB : bañera f

tuba ['tuːbə, 'tjuː-] n : tuba f

tube ['tuːb, 'tjuːb] n 1 : tubo m 2 or **inner** ~ : cámara f 3 **the** ~ : la tele

tuberculosis [tʊˌbərkjəˈloːsɪs, tjʊ-] n, pl -**loses** [-ˌsiːz] : tuberculosis f

tubing ['tuːbɪŋ, 'tjuː-] n : tubería f — **tubular** ['tuːbjələr, 'tjuː-] adj : tubular

tuck ['tʌk] vt 1 : meter 2 ~ **away** : guardar 3 ~ **in** : meter por dentro (una blusa, etc.) 4 ~ **s.o. in** : arropar a algn — ~ n : jareta f

Tuesday ['tuːzˌdeɪ, 'tjuːz-, -di] n : martes m

tuft ['tʌft] n : mechón m (de pelo), penacho m (de plumas)

tug ['tʌg] v **tugged**; **tugging** or ~ **at** : tirar de, jalar de — ~ n : tirón m, jalón m — **tugboat** ['tʌgˌboːt] n : remolcador m — **tug-of-war** [ˌtʌgəˈwɔr] n, pl **tugs-of-war** : tira y afloja m

tuition [tuˈɪʃən, tjuː-] n 1 : enseñanza f 2 or ~ **fees** : matrícula f

tulip ['tuːlɪp, 'tjuː-] n : tulipán m

tumble ['tʌmbəl] vi -**bled**; -**bling** : caerse — ~ n : caída f — **tumbler** ['tʌmblər] : vaso m (sin pie)

tummy ['tʌmi] n, pl -**mies** : barriga f, panza f

tumor ['tuːmər 'tjuː-] n : tumor m

tumult ['tuːmʌlt 'tjuː-] n : tumulto m — **tumultuous** [tʊˈmʌltʃuəs, tjuː-] adj : tumultuoso

tuna ['tuːnə 'tjuː-] n, pl -**na** or -**nas** : atún m

tune ['tuːn, 'tjuːn] n 1 MELODY : melodía f 2 SONG : tonada f 3 **in** ~ : afinado 4 **out of** ~ : desafinado — ~ v **tuned**; **tuning** vt : afinar — vi ~ **in** : sintonizar — **tuner** ['tuːnər, 'tjuː-] n 1 : afinador m, -dora f (de pianos, etc.) 2 : sintonizador m (de un receptor)

tunic ['tuːnɪk, 'tjuː-] n : túnica f

tunnel ['tʌnəl] n : túnel m — ~ vi -**neled** or -**nelled**; -**neling** or -**nelling** : hacer un túnel

turban ['tərbən] n : turbante m

turbine ['tərbən, -ˌbaɪn] n : turbina f

turbulent ['tərbjələnt] adj : turbulento — **turbulence** ['tərbjələnts] n : turbulencia f

turf ['tərf] n 1 GRASS : césped m 2 SOD : tepe m

turgid ['tərdʒɪd] adj : ampuloso (dícese de prosa, etc.)

turkey ['tərki] n, pl -**keys** : pavo m

turmoil ['tərˌmɔɪl] n : confusión f

turn ['tərn] vt 1 : hacer girar (una rueda, etc.), volver (la cabeza, una página, etc.) 2 : dar la vuelta a (una esquina) 3 SPRAIN : torcer 4 ~ **down** REFUSE : rechazar 5 ~ **down** LOWER : bajar 6 ~ **in** : entregar 7 ~ **off** : cerrar (una llave), apagar (la luz, etc.) 8 ~ **on** : abrir (una llave), encender, prender Lat (la luz, etc.) 9 ~ **out** EXPEL : echar 10 ~ **out** PRODUCE : producir 11 ~ **out** → **turn off** 12 or ~ **over** FLIP : dar la vuelta a, voltear Lat 13 ~ **over** TRANSFER : entregar 14 ~ **s.o.'s stomach** : revolver el estómago a algn 15 ~ **sth into sth** : convertir algo en algo 16 ~ **up** RAISE : subir — vi 1 ROTATE : girar, dar vueltas 2 BECOME : ponerse 3 SOUR : agriarse 4 RESORT : recurrir 5 ~ **around** : darse la vuelta, volverse 6 ~ **into** : convertirse en 7 ~ **left** : doblar a la izquierda 8 ~ **out** COME : acudir 9 ~ **out** RESULT : resultar 10 ~ **up** APPEAR : aparecer — ~ n 1 : vuelta f 2

CHANGE : cambio m 3 CURVE : curva f 4 **do a good** ~ : hacer un favor 5 **whose** ~ **is it?** : ¿a quién le toca?

turnip ['tərnəp] n : nabo m

turnout ['tərnˌaʊt] n : concurrencia f — **turnover** ['tərnˌoːvər] n 1 : tartaleta f (postre) 2 : volumen m (de ventas) 3 : movimiento f (de personal) — **turnpike** ['tərnˌpaɪk] n : carretera f de peaje — **turntable** ['tərnˌteɪbəl] n : plato m giratorio

turpentine ['tərpənˌtaɪn] n : trementina f

turquoise ['tərˌkɔɪz, -ˌkwɔɪz] n : turquesa f

turret ['tərət] n 1 : torrecilla f 2 : torreta f (de un tanque, etc.)

turtle ['tərtəl] n : tortuga f (marina) — **turtleneck** ['tərtəlˌnɛk] n : cuello m de tortuga

tusk ['tʌsk] n : colmillo m

tussle ['tʌsəl] n : pelea f — ~ vi -**sled**; -**sling** : pelearse

tutor ['tuːtər, 'tjuː-] n : profesor m, -sora f particular — ~ vt : dar clases particulares a

tuxedo [ˌtəkˈsiːdoː] n, pl -**dos** or -**does** : esmoquin m, smoking m

TV [ˌtiːˈviː, ˈtiːˌviː] → **television**

twang ['twæŋ] n 1 : tañido m 2 : acento m nasal (de la voz)

tweak ['twiːk] vt : pellizcar — ~ n : pellizco m

tweed ['twiːd] n : tweed m

tweet ['twiːt] n : gorjeo m, pío m — ~ vi : piar

tweezers ['twiːzərz] npl : pinzas fpl

twelve ['twɛlv] adj : doce — ~ n : doce m — **twelfth** ['twɛlfθ] adj : duodécimo — ~ n 1 : duodécimo m, -ma f (en una serie) 2 : doceavo m (en matemáticas)

twenty ['twʌnti, 'twɛn-] adj : veinte — ~ n, pl -**ties** : veinte m — **twentieth** ['twʌntiəθ, 'twɛn-] adj : vigésimo — ~ n 1 : vigésimo m, -ma f (en una serie) 2 : veinteavo m (en matemáticas)

twice ['twaɪs] adv 1 : dos veces 2 ~ **as much/many as** : el doble de (algo), el doble que (algn)

twig ['twɪg] n : ramita f

twilight ['twaɪˌlaɪt] n : crepúsculo m

twin ['twɪn] n : gemelo m, -la f; mellizo m, -za f — ~ adj : gemelo, mellizo

twine ['twaɪn] n : cordel m, bramante m Spain

twinge ['twɪndʒ] n : punzada f

twinkle ['twɪŋkəl] vi -**kled**; -**kling** 1 : centellear 2 : brillar (dícese de los ojos) — ~ n : centelleo m, brillo m (de los ojos)

twirl ['twərl] *vt* : girar, dar vueltas a — *vi* : girar, dar vueltas — ～ *n* : giro *m*, vuelta *f*

twist ['twɪst] *vt* **1** : retorcer **2** TURN : girar **3** SPRAIN : torcerse **4** : tergiversar (palabras) — *vi* **1** : retorcerse **2** COIL : enrollarse **3** : serpentear (entre montañas, etc.) — ～ *n* **1** BEND : vuelta *f* **2** TURN : giro *m* **3** ～ **of lemon** : rodajita *f* de limón — **twister** ['twɪstər] → **tornado**

twitch ['twɪtʃ] *vi* : moverse (espasmódicamente) — ～ *n* **nervous ～** : tic *m* nervioso

two ['tuː] *adj* : dos — ～ *n, pl* **twos** : dos *m* — **twofold** ['tuːˌfoːld] *adj* : doble — ～ ['tuːˈfoːld] *adv* : al doble — **two**

hundred *adj* : doscientos — ～ *n* : doscientos *m*

tycoon [taɪˈkuːn] *n* : magnate *mf*

tying → **tie**

type ['taɪp] *n* : tipo *m* — ～ *v* **typed; typing** : escribir a máquina — **typewritten** ['taɪpˌrɪtən] *adj* : escrito a máquina — **typewriter** ['taɪpˌraɪtər] *n* : máquina *f* de escribir

typhoon [taɪˈfuːn] *n* : tifón *m*

typical ['tɪpɪkəl] *adj* : típico, característico — **typify** ['tɪpəˌfaɪ] *vt* **-fied; -fying** : tipificar

typist ['taɪpɪst] *n* : mecanógrafo *m*, -fa *f*

typography [taɪˈpɑgrəfi] *n* : tipografía *f*

tyranny ['tɪrəni] *n, pl* **-nies** : tiranía *f* — **tyrant** ['taɪrənt] *n* : tirano *m*, -na *f*

tzar ['zɑr, 'tsɑr, 'sɑr] → **czar**

U

u ['juː] *n, pl* **u's** *or* **us** ['juːz] : u *f*, vigésima primera letra del alfabeto inglés

udder ['ʌdər] *n* : ubre *f*

UFO [ˌjuːˌefˈoː, ˈjuːˌfoː] (*unidentified flying object*) *n, pl* **UFO's** *or* **UFOs** : ovni *m*, OVNI *m*

ugly ['ʌgli] *adj* **uglier; -est** : feo — **ugliness** ['ʌglinəs] *n* : fealdad *f*

ulcer ['ʌlsər] *n* : úlcera *f*

ulterior [ʌlˈtɪriər] *adj* **～ motive** : segunda intención *f*

ultimate ['ʌltəmət] *adj* **1** FINAL : final, último **2** UTMOST : máximo **3** FUNDAMENTAL : fundamental — **ultimately** ['ʌltəmətli] *adv* **1** FINALLY : por último, finalmente **2** EVENTUALLY : a la larga

ultimatum [ˌʌltəˈmeɪtəm, -ˈmɑ-] *n, pl* **-tums** *or* **-ta** [-ˌtə] : ultimátum *m*

ultraviolet [ˌʌltrəˈvaɪələt] *adj* : ultravioleta

umbilical cord [ʌmˈbɪlɪkəl] *n* : cordón *m* umbilical

umbrella [ʌmˈbrelə] *n* : paraguas *m*

umpire ['ʌmˌpaɪr] *n* : árbitro *m*, -tra *f* — ～ *vt* **-pired; -piring** : arbitrar

umpteenth [ˈʌmpˈtiːnθ] *adj* : enésimo

unable [ʌnˈeɪbəl] *adj* **1** : incapaz **2 be ～ to** : no poder

unabridged [ˌʌnəˈbrɪdʒd] *adj* : íntegro

unacceptable [ˌʌnɪkˈseptəbəl] *adj* : inaceptable

unaccountable [ˌʌnəˈkaʊntəd] *adj* : inexplicable

unaccustomed [ˌʌnəˈkʌstəmd] *adj* **be ～ to** : no estar acostumbrado a

unadulterated [ˌʌnəˈdʌltəˌreɪtəd] *adj* : puro

unaffected [ˌʌnəˈfektəd] *adj* **1** : no afectado **2** NATURAL : sin afectación, natural

unafraid [ˌʌnəˈfreɪd] *adj* : sin miedo

unaided [ˌʌnˈeɪdəd] *adj* : sin ayuda

unanimous [juˈnænəməs] *adj* : unánime

unannounced [ˌʌnəˈnaʊnst] *adj* : sin dar aviso

unarmed [ˌʌnˈɑrmd] *adj* : desarmado

unassuming [ˌʌnəˈsuːmɪŋ] *adj* : modesto, sin pretensiones

unattached [ˌʌnəˈtætʃt] *adj* **1** : suelto **2** UNMARRIED : soltero

unattractive [ˌʌnəˈtræktɪv] *adj* : poco atractivo

unauthorized [ˌʌnˈɔːθəˌraɪzd] *adj* : no autorizado

unavailable [ˌʌnəˈveɪləbəl] *adj* : no disponible

unavoidable [ˌʌnəˈvɔɪdəbəl] *adj* : inevitable

unaware [ˌʌnəˈwær] *adj* **1** : inconsciente **2 be ～ of** : ignorar — **unawares** [ˌʌnəˈwærz] *adv* **catch s.o. ～** : agarrar a algn desprevenido

unbalanced [ˌʌnˈbælənst] *adj* : desequilibrado

unbearable [ˌʌnˈbærəbəl] *adj* : inaguantable, insoportable

unbelievable [ˌʌnbəˈliːvəbəl] *adj* : increíble

unbending [ˌʌnˈbendɪŋ] *adj* : inflexible

unbiased [ˌʌnˈbaɪəst] *adj* : imparcial

unborn [ˌʌnˈbɔrn] *adj* : aún no nacido

unbreakable [ˌʌnˈbreɪkəbəl] *adj* : irrompible

unbridled [ʌn'braɪdəld] *adj* : desenfrenado

unbroken [ʌn'broːkən] *adj* 1 INTACT : intacto 2 CONTINUOUS : continuo

unbutton [ʌn'bʌtən] *vt* : desabrochar, desabotonar

uncalled—for [ʌn'kɔld,fɔr] *adj* : inapropiado, innecesario

uncanny [ən'kæni] *adj* -nier; -est : extraño, misterioso

unceasing [ʌn'siːsɪŋ] *adj* : incesante

unceremonious [ʌn,serə'moːniəs] *adj* 1 INFORMAL : poco ceremonioso 2 ABRUPT : brusco

uncertain [ʌn'sərtən] *adj* 1 : incierto 2 in no ~ terms : de forma vehemente — **uncertainty** [ʌn'sərtənti] *n, pl* -ties : incertidumbre *f*

unchanged [ʌn'tʃeɪndʒd] *adj* : igual, sin alterar — **unchanging** [ʌn'tʃeɪdʒɪŋ] *adj* : inmutable

uncivilized [ʌn'sɪvə,laɪzd] *adj* : incivilizado

uncle ['ʌŋkəl] *n* : tío *m*

unclear [ʌn'klɪr] *adj* : poco claro

uncomfortable [ʌn'kʌmpfərtəbəl] *adj* 1 : incómodo 2 DISCONCERTING : inquietante, desagradable

uncommon [ʌn'kamən] *adj* : raro

uncompromising [ʌn'kamprə,maɪzɪŋ] *adj* : intransigente

unconcerned [ʌnkən'sərnd] *adj* : indiferente

unconditional [ʌnkən'dɪʃənəl] *adj* : incondicional

unconscious [ʌn'kantʃəs] *adj* : inconsciente

unconstitutional [ʌn,kantstə'tuːʃənəl, -'tjuː-] *adj* : inconstitucional

uncontrollable [ʌnkən'troːləbəl] *adj* : incontrolable

unconventional [ʌnkən'ventʃənəl] *adj* : poco convencional

uncouth [ʌn'kuːθ] *adj* : grosero

uncover [ʌn'kʌvər] *vt* 1 : destapar 2 REVEAL : descubrir

undecided [ʌndi'saɪdəd] *adj* : indeciso

undeniable [ʌndi'naɪəbəl] *adj* : innegable

under ['ʌndər] *adv* 1 : debajo 2 LESS : menos 3 *or* ~ anesthetic : bajo los efectos de la anestesia — ~ *prep* 1 BELOW, BENEATH : debajo de, abajo de 2 ~ 20 minutes : menos de 20 minutos 3 ~ the circumstances : dadas las circunstancias

underage [ʌndər'eɪdʒ] *adj* : menor de edad

underclothes ['ʌndər,kloːz, -,kloːðz] → **underwear**

undercover [ʌndər'kʌvər] *adj* : secreto

undercurrent ['ʌndər,kərənt] *n* : tendencia *f* oculta

underdeveloped [ʌndərdɪ'veləpt] *adj* : subdesarrollado

underestimate [ʌndər'estə,meɪt] *vt* -mated; -mating : subestimar

underfoot [ʌndər'fut] *adj* : bajo los pies

undergo [ʌndər'goː] *vt* -went [-'went;]; -gone [-'gɔn]; -going : sufrir, experimentar

undergraduate [ʌndər'grædʒuət] *n* : estudiante *m* universitario, estudiante *f* universitaria

underground [ʌndər'graund] *adv* 1 : bajo tierra 2 go ~ : pasar a la clandestinidad — ['ʌndər,graund] *adj* 1 : subterráneo 2 SECRET : secreto, clandestino — ['ʌndər,graund] *n* : movimiento *m* clandestino

undergrowth ['ʌndər'groːθ] *n* : maleza *f*

underhanded [ʌndər'hændəd] *adj* SLY : solapado

underline ['ʌndər,laɪn] *vt* -lined; -lining : subrayar

underlying [ʌndər'laɪɪŋ] *adj* : subyacente

undermine [ʌndər'maɪn] *vt* -mined; -mining : socavar, minar

underneath [ʌndər'niːθ] *adv* : debajo, abajo — ~ *prep* : debajo de, abajo de *Lat*

underpants ['ʌndər,pænts] *npl* : calzoncillos *mpl*, calzones *mpl Lat*

underpass ['ʌndər,pæs] *n* : paso *m* inferior

underprivileged [ʌndər'prɪvlɪdʒd] *adj* : desfavorecido

underrate [ʌndər'reɪt] *vt* -rated; -rating : subestimar

undershirt ['ʌndər,ʃərt] *n* : camiseta *f*

understand [ʌndər'stænd] *v* -stood [-'stʊd]; -standing : comprender, entender — **understandable** [ʌndər'stændəbəl] *adj* : comprensible — **understanding** [ʌndər'stændɪŋ] *adj* : comprensivo, compasivo — ~ *n* 1 : comprensión *f* 2 AGREEMENT : acuerdo *m*

understatement [ʌndər'steɪtmənt] *n* that's an ~ : decir sólo eso es quedarse corto

understudy ['ʌndər,stʌdi] *n, pl* -dies : sobresaliente *mf* (en el teatro)

undertake [ʌndər'teɪk] *vt* -took [-'tʊk]; -taken [-'teɪkən]; -taking : emprender (una tarea), encargarse de (una responsabilidad) — **undertaker** ['ʌndər,teɪkər] *n* : director *m*, -tora *f* de una funeraria — **undertaking** ['ʌndər,teɪkɪŋ, ,ʌndər-] *n* : empresa *f*, tarea *f*

undertone ['ʌndər,toːn] n 1 : voz f baja 2 SUGGESTION : matiz m

undertow ['ʌndər,toː] n : resaca f

underwater [ʌndər'wɔtər, -'wɑ-] adj : submarino — ~ adv : debajo (del agua)

under way [ʌndər'weɪ] adv get ~ : ponerse en marcha

underwear ['ʌndər,wær] n : ropa f interior

underwent → undergo

underworld ['ʌndər,wərld] n the ~ CRIMINALS : la hampa, los bajos fondos

underwriter ['ʌndər,raɪtər, ,ʌndər'-] n : asegurador m, -dora f

undesirable [ʌndɪ'zaɪrəbəl] adj : indeseable

undeveloped [ʌndɪ'veləpt] adj : sin desarrollar

undignified [ʌn'dɪgnəfaɪd] adj : indecoroso

undisputed [ʌndɪ'spjuːtəd] adj : indiscutible

undo [ʌn'duː] vt -did [-'dɪd]; -done [-'dʌn]; -doing 1 UNFASTEN : deshacer, desatar 2 : reparar (daños, etc.)

undoubtedly [ʌn'dautədli] adv : indudablemente

undress [ʌn'drɛs] vt : desnudar — vi : desnudarse

undue [ʌn'duː, -'djuː] adj : indebido, excesivo

undulate [ʌndʒə,leɪt] vi -lated; -lating : ondular

unduly [ʌn'duːli, -'djuː-] adv : excesivamente

undying [ʌn'daɪɪŋ] adj : eterno

unearth [ʌn'ərθ] vt : desenterrar

unearthly [ʌn'ərθli] adj -lier; -est : sobrenatural, de otro mundo

uneasy [ʌn'izi] adj -easier; -est 1 AWKWARD : incómodo 2 WORRIED : inquieto 3 RESTLESS : agitado — **uneasily** [ʌn'izəli] adv : inquietamente — **uneasiness** [ʌn'izinəs] n : inquietud f

uneducated [ʌn'edʒə,keɪtəd] adj : inculto

unemployed [ʌnɪm'plɔɪd] adj : desempleado — **unemployment** [ʌnɪm'plɔɪmənt] n : desempleo m

unerring [ʌn'ərɪŋ, -'ər-] adj : infalible

unethical [ʌn'eθɪkəl] adj : poco ético

uneven [ʌn'ivən] adj 1 : desigual 2 : impar (dícese de un número)

unexpected [ʌnɪk'spɛktəd] adj : inesperado

unfailing [ʌn'feɪlɪŋ] adj 1 CONSTANT : constante 2 INEXHAUSTIBLE : inagotable

unfair [ʌn'fær] adj : injusto — **unfairly** [ʌn'færli] adv : injustamente — **unfairness** [ʌn'færnəs] n : injusticia f

unfaithful [ʌn'feɪθfəl] adj : infiel — **unfaithfulness** [ʌn'feɪθfəlnəs] n : infidelidad f

unfamiliar [ʌnfə'mɪljər] adj 1 : desconocido 2 be ~ with : desconocer

unfasten [ʌn'fæsən] vt 1 : desabrochar (ropa, etc.) 2 UNDO : desatar (una cuerda, etc.)

unfavorable [ʌn'feɪvrəbəl] adj : desfavorable

unfeeling [ʌn'fiːlɪŋ] adj : insensible

unfinished [ʌn'fɪnɪʃd] adj : sin terminar

unfit [ʌn'fɪt] adj 1 UNSUITABLE : impropio 2 UNSUITED : no apto, incapaz

unfold [ʌn'foːld] vt 1 : desplegar, desdoblar 2 REVEAL : revelar (un plan, etc.) — vi 1 : extenderse, desplegarse 2 DEVELOP : desarrollarse

unforeseen [ʌnfor'siː] adj : imprevisto

unforgettable [ʌnfər'gɛtəbəl] adj : inolvidable

unforgivable [ʌnfər'gɪvəbəl] adj : imperdonable

unfortunate [ʌn'fortʃənət] adj 1 UNLUCKY : desgraciado, desafortunado 2 INAPPROPRIATE : inoportuno — **unfortunately** [ʌn'fortʃənətli] adv : desgraciadamente

unfounded [ʌn'faundəd] adj : infundado

unfriendly [ʌn'frendli] adj -lier; -est : poco amistoso

unfurl [ʌn'fərl] vt : desplegar

unfurnished [ʌn'fərnɪʃt] adj : desamueblado

ungainly [ʌn'geɪnli] adj : desgarbado

ungodly [ʌn'gɒdli, -'gɑd-] adj 1 : impío 2 an ~ hour : una hora intempestiva

ungrateful [ʌn'greɪtfəl] adj : desagradecido

unhappy [ʌn'hæpi] adj -pier; -est 1 SAD : infeliz, triste 2 UNFORTUNATE : desafortunado — **unhappily** [ʌn'hæpəli] adv 1 SADLY : tristemente 2 UNFORTUNATELY : desgraciadamente — **unhappiness** [ʌn'hæpinəs] n : tristeza f

unharmed [ʌn'hɑrmd] adj : salvo, ileso

unhealthy [ʌn'helθi] adj -thier; -est 1 : malsano 2 SICKLY : enfermizo

unheard-of [ʌn'hərdəv] adj : sin precedente, insólito

unhook [ʌn'hʊk] vt : desenganchar

unhurt [ʌn'hərt] adj : ileso

unicorn ['juːnə,kɔrn] n : unicornio m

unification [juːnəfə'keɪʃən] n : unificación f

uniform ['juːnə,fɔrm] adj : uniforme —

~ *n* : uniforme *m* — **uniformity** [ju:nə'fɔrməti] *n, pl* **-ties** : uniformidad *f*

unify ['ju:nə,faɪ] *vt* **-fied; -fying** : unificar

unilateral [ju:nə'lætərəl] *adj* : unilateral

unimaginable [ˌʌnɪ'mædʒənəbəl] *adj* : inconcebible

unimportant [ˌʌnɪm'pɔrtənt] *adj* : insignificante

uninhabited [ˌʌnɪn'hæbətəd] *adj* : deshabitado, despoblado

uninjured [ʌn'ɪndʒərd] *adj* : ileso

unintentional [ˌʌnɪn'tentʃənəl] *adj* : involuntario

union ['ju:njən] *n* **1** : unión *f* **2** *or* **labor ~** : sindicato *m*, gremio *m* *Lat*

unique [ju'ni:k] *adj* : único — **uniquely** [ju'ni:kli] *adv* EXCEPTIONALLY : excepcionalmente

unison ['ju:nəsən, -zən] *n* **in ~** : al unísono

unit ['ju:nɪt] *n* **1** : unidad *f* **2** : módulo *m* (de un mobiliario)

unite [ju'naɪt] *v* **united; uniting** *vt* : unir — *vi* : unirse — **unity** ['ju:nəti] *n, pl* **-ties 1** : unidad *f* **2** HARMONY : acuerdo *m*

universe ['ju:nə,vərs] *n* : universo *m* — **universal** [ju:nə'vərsəl] *adj* : universal

university [ju:nə'vərsəti] *n, pl* **-ties** : universidad *f*

unjust [ʌn'dʒʌst] *adj* : injusto — **unjustified** [ʌn'dʒʌstə,faɪd] *adj* : injustificado

unkempt [ʌn'kempt] *adj* **1** : descuidado, desaseado **2** : despeinado (dícese del pelo)

unkind [ʌn'kaɪnd] *adj* : poco amable, cruel — **unkindness** [ʌn'kaɪndnəs] *n* : falta *f* de amabilidad, crueldad *f*

unknown [ʌn'noːn] *adj* : desconocido

unlawful [ʌn'lɔːfəl] *adj* : ilegal

unless [ən'les] *conj* : a menos que, a no ser que

unlike [ʌn'laɪk] *adj* : diferente — **~** *prep* : a diferencia de — **unlikelihood** [ʌn'laɪkli,hʊd] *n* : improbabilidad *f* — **unlikely** [ʌn'laɪkli] *adj* **-lier; -est** : improbable

unlimited [ʌn'lɪmətəd] *adj* : ilimitado

unload [ʌn'loːd] *v* : descargar

unlock [ʌn'lɑk] *vt* : abrir (con llave)

unlucky [ʌn'lʌki] *adj* **-luckier; -est 1** UNFORTUNATE : desgraciado **2** : de mala suerte (dícese de un número, etc.)

unmarried [ʌn'mærid] *adj* : soltero

unmask [ʌn'mæsk] *vt* : desenmascarar

unmistakable [ˌʌnmɪ'steɪkəbəl] *adj* : inconfundible

unnatural [ʌn'nætʃərəl] *adj* **1** : anormal **2** AFFECTED : afectado, forzado

unnecessary [ʌn'nesə,seri] *adj* : innecesario — **unnecessarily** [-ˌnesə'serəli] *adv* : innecesariamente

unnerving [ʌn'nərvɪŋ] *adj* : desconcertante

unnoticed [ʌn'noːtəst] *adj* : inadvertido

unobtainable [ˌʌnəb'teɪnəbəl] *adj* : inasequible

unobtrusive [ˌʌnəb'struːsɪv] *adj* : discreto

unofficial [ˌʌnə'fɪʃəl] *adj* : no oficial

unorthodox [ʌn'ɔrθə,dɑks] *adj* : poco ortodoxo

unpack [ʌn'pæk] *vt* **1** : desempaquetar, desempacar *Lat* (un paquete, etc.) **2** : deshacer (una maleta) — *vi* : deshacer las maletas

unparalleled [ʌn'pærə,leld] *adj* : sin igual

unpleasant [ʌn'plezənt] *adj* : desagradable

unplug [ʌn'plʌɡ] *vt* **-plugged; -plugging** : desconectar, desenchufar

unpopular [ʌn'pɑpjələr] *adj* : poco popular

unprecedented [ʌn'presə,dentəd] *adj* : sin precedente

unpredictable [ˌʌnpri'dɪktəbəl] *adj* : imprevisible

unprepared [ˌʌnpri'pærd] *adj* **1** : no preparado **2** UNREADY : desprevenido

unqualified [ʌn'kwɑlə,faɪd] *adj* **1** : no calificado, sin título **2** COMPLETE : absoluto

unquestionable [ʌn'kwestʃənəbəl] *adj* : indiscutible — **unquestioning** [ʌn'kwestʃənɪŋ] *adj* : incondicional

unravel [ʌn'rævəl] *v* **-eled** *or* **-elled; -eling** *or* **-elling** *vt* : desenmarañar — *vi* : deshacerse

unreal [ʌn'riːl] *adj* : irreal — **unrealistic** [ˌʌn,riː'lɪstɪk] *adj* : poco realista

unreasonable [ʌn'riːzənəbəl] *adj* **1** : irrazonable **2** EXCESSIVE : excesivo

unrecognizable [ʌn'rekəg,naɪzəbəl] *adj* : irreconocible

unrelated [ˌʌnri'leɪtəd] *adj* : no relacionado

unrelenting [ˌʌnri'lentɪŋ] *adj* : implacable

unreliable [ˌʌnri'laɪəbəl] *adj* : que no es de fiar

unrepentant [ˌʌnri'pentənt] *adj* : impenitente

unrest [ʌn'rest] *n* **1** : inquietud *f*, malestar *m* **2** *or* **political ~** : disturbios *mpl*

unripe [ʌn'raɪp] *adj* : verde, no maduro

unrivaled or **unrivalled** [ʌnˈraɪvəld] adj : incomparable, sin par

unroll [ʌnˈroːl] vt : desenrollar — vi : desenrollarse

unruly [ʌnˈruːli] adj : indisciplinado

unsafe [ʌnˈseɪf] adj : inseguro

unsaid [ʌnˈsed] adj : sin decir

unsanitary [ʌnˈsænəˌteri] adj : antihigiénico

unsatisfactory [ʌnˌsætəsˈfæktəri] adj : insatisfactorio

unscathed [ʌnˈskeɪðd] adj : ileso

unscrew [ʌnˈskruː] vt : destornillar

unscrupulous [ʌnˈskruːpjələs] adj : sin escrúpulos

unseemly [ʌnˈsiːmli] adj -lier; -est : indecoroso

unseen [ʌnˈsiːn] adj 1 : no visto 2 UN-NOTICED : inadvertido

unselfish [ʌnˈselfɪʃ] adj : desinteresado

unsettle [ʌnˈsetəl] vt -tled; -tling DIS-TURB : perturbar — **unsettled** [ʌn-ˈsetəld] adj 1 CHANGEABLE : inestable 2 DISTURBED : agitado, inquieto 3 : variable (dícese del tiempo)

unsightly [ʌnˈsaɪtli] adj : feo

unskilled [ʌnˈskɪld] adj : no calificado — **unskillful** [ʌnˈskɪlfəl] adj : torpe, poco hábil

unsociable [ʌnˈsoːʃəbəl] adj : poco sociable

unsound [ʌnˈsaʊnd] adj 1 : defectuoso, erróneo 2 of ~ mind : demente

unspeakable [ʌnˈspiːkəbəl] adj 1 : indecible 2 TERRIBLE : atroz

unstable [ʌnˈsteɪbəl] adj : inestable

unsteady [ʌnˈstedi] adj 1 : inestable 2 SHAKY : tembloroso

unsuccessful [ʌnsəkˈsesfəl] adj 1 : fracasado 2 be ~ : no tener éxito

unsuitable [ʌnˈsuːtəbəl] adj 1 : inadecuado 2 INCONVENIENT : inconveniente

unsure [ʌnˈʃʊr] adj : inseguro

unsuspecting [ʌnsəˈspektɪŋ] adj : confiado

unsympathetic [ʌnˌsɪmpəˈθetɪk] adj : indiferente

unthinkable [ʌnˈθɪŋkəbəl] adj : inconcebible

untidy [ʌnˈtaɪdi] adj : desordenado (dícese de una sala, etc.), desaliñado (dícese de una persona)

untie [ʌnˈtaɪ] vt -tied; -tying or -tieing : desatar

until [ʌnˈtɪl] prep : hasta — ~ conj : hasta que

untimely [ʌnˈtaɪmli] adj 1 PREMATURE : prematuro 2 INOPPORTUNE : inoportuno

untold [ʌnˈtoːld] adj : incalculable

untoward [ʌnˈtord, -ˈtoːrd, -təˈwoːrd] adj 1 ADVERSE : adverso 2 IMPROPER : indecoroso

untroubled [ʌnˈtrʌbəld] adj 1 : tranquilo 2 be ~ by : no estar afectado por

untrue [ʌnˈtruː] adj : falso

unused [ʌnˈjuːzd, in sense 2 usually -ˈjuːst] adj 1 NEW : nuevo 2 be ~ to : no estar acustumbrado a

unusual [ʌnˈjuːʒuəl] adj : poco común, insólito — **unusually** [ʌnˈjuːʒuəl, -ˈjuːʒəli] adv : excepcionalmente

unveil [ʌnˈveɪl] vt 1 : descubrir, revelar

unwanted [ʌnˈwɑntəd] adj : superfluo (dícese de un objeto), no deseado (dícese de un niño, etc.)

unwarranted [ʌnˈwɔrəntəd] adj : injustificado

unwelcome [ʌnˈwelkəm] adj : inoportuno, molesto

unwell [ʌnˈwel] adj be ~ : sentirse mal

unwieldy [ʌnˈwiːldi] adj : difícil de manejar

unwilling [ʌnˈwɪlɪŋ] adj : poco dispuesto — **unwillingly** [ʌnˈwɪlɪŋli] adv : de mala gana

unwind [ʌnˈwaɪnd] v -wound [-ˈwaʊnd]; -winding vt : desenrollar — vi 1 : desenrollarse 2 RELAX : relajarse

unwise [ʌnˈwaɪz] adj : imprudente

unworthy [ʌnˈwərði] adj be ~ of : no ser digno de

unwrap [ʌnˈræp] vt -wrapped; -wrapping : desenvolver

up [ˈʌp] adv 1 ABOVE : arriba 2 UPWARDS : hacia arriba 3 ten miles farther ~ : diez millas más adelante 4 ~ here/there : aquí/allí arriba 5 ~ north : en el norte 6 ~ until : hasta — ~ adj 1 AWAKE : levantado 2 FINISHED : terminado 3 be ~ against : enfrentarse a 4 be ~ on : estar al corriente de 5 it's ~ to you : depende de tí 6 prices are ~ : los precios han aumentado 7 the sun is ~ : ha salido el sol 8 what's ~? : ¿qué pasa? — ~ prep 1 go ~ the river : ir río arriba 2 go ~ the stairs : subir la escalera 3 ~ the coast : a lo largo de la costa — ~ v upped [ˈʌpt]; upping; ups vt : aumentar — vi she ~ and left : agarró y se fue

upbringing [ˈʌpˌbrɪŋɪŋ] n : educación f

upcoming [ˈʌpˌkʌmɪŋ] adj : próximo

update [ʌpˈdeɪt] vt -dated; -dating : poner al día, actualizar — ~ [ˈʌp-ˌdeɪt] n : puesta f al día

upgrade [ˈʌpˌgreɪd, ˌʌpˈ-] vt -graded; -grading : elevar la categoría de (un puesto, etc.), mejorar (una facilidad, etc.)

upheaval [ˌʌpˈhiːvəl] n : trastorno m
uphill [ˌʌpˈhɪl] adv : cuesta arriba — ~
['ʌpˌhɪl] adj 1 : en subida 2 **be an** ~
battle : ser muy difícil
uphold [ʌpˈhoːld] vt **-held; -holding**
: sostener, apoyar
upholstery [ʌpˈhoːlstəri] n, pl **-steries**
: tapicería f
upkeep ['ʌpˌkiːp] n : mantenimiento m
upon [əˈpɔn, əˈpɑn] prep 1 : en, sobre 2
~ **leaving** : al salir
upper ['ʌpər] adj : superior — ~ n
: parte f superior (del calzado, etc.)
uppercase [ˌʌpərˈkeɪs] adj : mayúsculo
upper class n : clase f alta
upper hand n : ventaja f, dominio m
uppermost ['ʌpərˌmoːst] adj : más alto
upright ['ʌpˌraɪt] adj 1 VERTICAL : vertical 2 ERECT : derecho 3 JUST : recto,
honesto — ~ n : montante m, poste f
uprising ['ʌpˌraɪzɪŋ] n : insurrección f,
revuelta f
uproar ['ʌpˌror] n COMMOTION : alboroto
m
uproot [ʌpˈruːt, -ˈrʊt] vt : desarraigar
upset [ʌpˈsɛt] vt **-set; -setting** 1 OVERTURN : volcar 2 DISTRESS : alterar, inquietar 3 DISRUPT : trastornar — ~
adj 1 DISTRESSED : alterado 2 **have an**
~ **stomach** : estar mal del estómago
— ~ ['ʌpˌsɛt] n : trastorno m
upshot ['ʌpˌʃɑt] n : resultado m final
upside down [ˌʌpˌsaɪdˈdaʊn] adv 1 : al
revés 2 **turn** ~ : volver — **upside-down** [ˌʌpˌsaɪdˈdaʊn] adj : al revés
upstairs [ˌʌpˈstærz] adv : arriba — ~
['ʌpˌstærz, ˌʌp-'] adj : de arriba — ~
['ʌpˌstærz, ˌʌp-'] ns & pl : piso m de arriba
upstart ['ʌpˌstɑrt] n : advenedizo m, -za f
upstream ['ʌpˈstriːm] adv : río arriba
upswing ['ʌpˌswɪŋ] n **be on the** ~
: estar mejorándose
up-to-date [ˌʌptəˈdeɪt] adj 1 : corriente,
al día 2 MODERN : moderno
uptown ['ʌpˈtaʊn] adv : hacia la parte
alta de la ciudad, hacia el distrito residencial
upturn ['ʌpˌtərn] n : mejora f, auge m
(económico)
upward ['ʌpwərd] or **upwards** [-wərdz]
adv : hacia arriba — **upward** adj : ascendente, hacia arriba
uranium [jʊˈreɪniəm] n : uranio m
urban ['ərbən] adj : urbano
urbane [ərˈbeɪn] adj : urbano, cortés
urge ['ərdʒ] vt **urged; urging** 1 PRESS
: instar, exhortar 2 ~ **on** : animar —
~ n : impulso m, ganas fpl — **ur-**

gency ['ərdʒəntsi] n, pl **-cies** : urgencia f — **urgent** ['ərdʒənt] adj 1 : urgente 2 **be** ~ : urgir
urine ['jʊrən] n : orina f — **urinate** ['jʊrəˌneɪt] vi **-nated; -nating** : orinar
urn ['ərn] n : urna f
Uruguayan [ˌʊrəˈgwaɪən, ˌjʊr-, -ˈgweɪ-]
adj : uruguayo
us ['ʌs] pron 1 (as direct or indirect object) : nos 2 (as object of a preposition) : nosotros, nosotras 3 **both of** ~
: nosotros dos 4 **it's** ~**!** : ¡somos nosotros!
usage ['juːsɪdʒ, -zɪdʒ] n : uso m
use ['juːz] v **used** ['juːzd, the phrase "used to" is usually 'juːstu]; **using** vt 1
: usar 2 CONSUME : consumir, tomar
(drogas, etc.) 3 ~ **up** : agotar, consumir — vi 1 **she** ~**d to dance**
: acostumbraba bailar 2 **winters** ~**d**
to be colder : los inviernos solían ser
más fríos — ~ ['juːs] n 1 : uso m 2
have no ~ **for** : no necesitar 3 **have**
the ~ **of** : poder usar, tener acceso a
4 **it's no** ~**!** : ¡es inútil! — **used**
['juːzd, in sense 2 usually 'juːst] adj 1
SECONDHAND : usado 2 **be** ~ **to** : estar
acostumbrado a — **useful** ['juːsfəl] adj
: útil, práctico — **usefulness**
['juːsfəlnəs] n : utilidad f — **useless**
['juːsləs] adj : inútil — **user** ['juːzər] n
: usuario m, -ria f
usher ['ʌʃər] vt 1 : acompañar, conducir
2 ~ **in** : hacer entrar — ~ n : acomodador m, -dora f
usual [ˈjuːʒʊəl] adj 1 : habitual, usual 2
as ~ : como de costumbre — **usually** [ˈjuːʒʊəli, ˈjuːʒəli] adv : usualmente
usurp [jʊˈsərp, -ˈzərp] vt : usurpar
utensil [jʊˈtɛntsəl] n : utensilio m
uterus ['juːtʃərəs] n, pl **uteri** [-ˌraɪ] : útero
m, matriz f
utility [juːˈtɪləti] n, pl **-ties** 1 : utilidad f 2
or **public** ~ : empresa f de servicio
público
utilize ['juːtʃəˌlaɪz] vt **-lized; -lizing** : utilizar
utmost ['ʌtˌmoːst] adj 1 FARTHEST : extremo 2 **of the** ~ **importance** : de
suma importancia — ~ n **do one's**
~ : hacer todo lo posible
utopia [juːˈtoːpiə] n : utopía f — **utopian**
[juːˈtoːpiən] adj : utópico
utter¹ ['ʌtər] adj : absoluto, completo
utter² vt : decir, pronunciar (palabras)
— **utterance** ['ʌtərənts] n : declaración f, expresión f
utterly ['ʌtərli] adv : completamente, totalmente

V

v ['viː] *n*, *pl* **v's** *or* **vs** ['viːz] : v *f*, vigésima segunda letra del alfabeto inglés

vacant ['veɪkənt] *adj* **1** AVAILABLE : libre **2** UNOCCUPIED : desocupado **3** : vacante (dícese de un puesto) **4** : ausente (dícese de una mirada) — **vacancy** ['veɪkəntsi] *n*, *pl* **-cies 1** : (puesto *m*) vacante *f* **2** : habitación *f* libre (en un hotel, etc.)

vacate ['veɪkeɪt] *vt* **-cated; -cating** : desalojar, desocupar

vacation [veɪˈkeɪʃən, və-] *n* : vacaciones *fpl*

vaccination [ˌvæksəˈneɪʃən] *n* : vacunación *f* — **vaccinate** ['væksəˌneɪt] *vt* **-nated; -nating** : vacunar — **vaccine** ['vækˌsiːn, 'væk-] *n* : vacuna *f*

vacuum ['vækjuːm, -kjəm] *n*, *pl* **vacuums** *or* **vacua** : vacío *m* — ~ *vt* : pasar la aspiradora por — **vacuum cleaner** *n* : aspiradora *f*

vagina [vəˈdʒaɪnə] *n*, *pl* **-nae** [-ˌniː, -ˌnaɪ] *or* **-nas** : vagina *f*

vagrant ['veɪɡrənt] *n* : vagabundo *m*, -da *f*

vague ['veɪɡ] *adj* **vaguer; -est** : vago, indistinto

vain ['veɪn] *adj* **1** CONCEITED : vanidoso **2 in ~** : en vano

valentine ['væləntaɪn] *n* : tarjeta *f* del día de San Valentín

valiant ['væljənt] *adj* : valiente, valeroso

valid ['væləd] *adj* : válido — **validate** ['væləˌdeɪt] *vt* **-dated; -dating** : validar — **validity** [vəˈlɪdəti, væ-] *n* : validez *f*

valley ['væli] *n*, *pl* **-leys** : valle *m*

valor ['vælər] *n* : valor *m*, valentía *f*

value ['væljuː] *n* : valor *m* — ~ *vt* **-ued; -uing** : valorar — **valuable** ['væljuəbəl, 'væljəbəl] *adj* : valioso — **valuables** *npl* : objetos *mpl* de valor

valve ['vælv] *n* : válvula *f*

vampire ['væmˌpaɪr] *n* : vampiro *m*

van ['væn] *n* : furgoneta *f*, camioneta *f*

vandal ['vændəl] *n* : vándalo *m* — **vandalism** ['vændəlˌɪzəm] *n* : vandalismo *m* — **vandalize** ['vændəlˌaɪz] *vt* : destrozar, destruir

vane ['veɪn] *n or* **weather ~** : veleta *f*

vanguard ['vænˌɡɑrd] *n* : vanguardia *f*

vanilla [vəˈnɪlə, -ˈne-] *n* : vainilla *f*

vanish ['vænɪʃ] *vi* : desaparecer

vanity ['vænəti] *n*, *pl* **-ties 1** : vanidad *f* **2** *or* **~ table** : tocador *m*

vantage point ['væntɪdʒ] *n* : posición *f* ventajosa

vapor ['veɪpər] *n* : vapor *m*

variable ['veriəbəl] *adj* : variable — ~ *n* : variable *f* — **variance** ['veriənts] *n* **at ~ with** : en desacuerdo con — **variant** ['veriənt] *n* : variante *f* — **variation** [ˌveriˈeɪʃən] *n* : variación *f* — **varied** ['verid] *adj* : variado — **variegated** ['veriəˌɡeɪtəd] *adj* : abigarrado, multicolor — **variety** [vəˈraɪəti] *n*, *pl* **-ties 1** : variedad *f* **2** ASSORTMENT : surtido *m* **3** SORT : clase *f* — **various** ['veriəs] *adj* : varios, diversos

varnish ['vɑrnɪʃ] *n* : barniz *f* — ~ *vt* : barnizar

vary ['veri] *v* **varied; varying** : variar

vase ['veɪs, 'veɪz, 'vɑz] *n* **1** : jarrón *m* **2** *or* **flower ~** : florero *m*

vast ['væst] *adj* : vasto, enorme — **vastness** ['væstnəs] *n* : inmensidad *f*

vat ['væt] *n* : cuba *f*

vault[1] ['vɔlt] *vi* LEAP : saltar — ~ *n* : salto *m*

vault[2] *n* **1** DOME : bóveda *f* **2** *or* **bank ~** : cámara *f* acorazada, bóveda *f* de seguridad *Lat* **3** CRYPT : cripta *f*

VCR [ˌviːsiˈɑr] (*videocassette recorder*) *n* : video *m*

veal ['viːl] *n* : (carne *f* de) ternera *f*

veer ['vɪr] *vi* : virar

vegetable ['vedʒtəbəl, 'vedʒətə-] *adj* : vegetal — ~ *n* **1** : vegetal *m* (planta) **2 ~s** *npl* : verduras *fpl* — **vegetarian** [ˌvedʒəˈteriən] *n* : vegetariano *mf* — **vegetation** [ˌvedʒəˈteɪʃən] *n* : vegetación *f*

vehemence ['viːəmənts] *n* : vehemencia *f* — **vehement** ['viːəmənt] *adj* : vehemente

vehicle ['viːəkəl, 'viːˌhɪkəl] *n* : vehículo *m*

veil ['veɪl] *n* : velo *m* — ~ *vt* **1** : cubrir con un velo **2** CONCEAL : velar

vein ['veɪn] *n* **1** : vena *f* **2** : veta *f* (de un mineral, etc.)

velocity [vəˈlɑsəti] *n*, *pl* **-ties** : velocidad *f*

velvet ['vɛlvət] *n* : terciopelo *m* — **velvety** ['vɛlvəti] *adj* : aterciopelado

vending machine ['vɛndɪŋ-] *vt* : máquina *f* expendedora

vendor ['vɛndər] *n* : vendedor *m*, -dora *f*
veneer [və'nɪr] *n* **1** : chapa *f* **2** FACADE : apariencia *f*
venerable ['vɛnərəbəl] *adj* : venerable — **venerate** ['vɛnə,reɪt] *vt* **-ated; -ating** : venerar — **veneration** [,vɛnə'reɪʃən] *n* : veneración *f*
venereal [və'nɪriəl] *adj* : venéreo
venetian blind [və'ni:ʃən-] *n* : persiana *f* veneciana
Venezuelan [,vɛnə'zweɪlən, -zu'eɪ-] *adj* : venezolano
vengeance ['vɛndʒənts] *n* **1** : venganza *f* **2 take ~ on** : vengarse de — **vengeful** ['vɛndʒfəl] *adj* : vengativo
venison ['vɛnəsən, -zən] *n* : (carne *f* de) venado *m*
venom ['vɛnəm] *n* : veneno *m* — **venomous** ['vɛnəməs] *adj* : venenoso
vent ['vɛnt] *vt* : desahogar — **~** *n* **1 or air ~** : rejilla *f* de ventilación **2** OUTLET : desahogo *m* — **ventilate** ['vɛntəl,eɪt] *vt* **-lated; -lating** : ventilar — **ventilation** [,vɛntəl'eɪʃən] *n* : ventilación *f* — **ventilator** ['vɛntəl,eɪtər] *n* : ventilador *m*
ventriloquist [vɛn'trɪləkwɪst] *n* : ventrílocuo *m*, -cua *f*
venture ['vɛntʃər] *v* **-tured; -turing** *vt* **1** RISK : arriesgar **2** : aventurar (una opinión, etc.) — *vi* : atreverse — **~** *n* **1** *or* **business ~** : empresa *f*
venue ['vɛnju:] *n* : lugar *m*
Venus ['vi:nəs] *n* : Venus *m*
veranda *or* **verandah** [və'rændə] *n* : veranda *f*
verb ['vərb] *n* : verbo *m* — **verbal** ['vərbəl] *adj* : verbal — **verbatim** [vər'beɪtəm] *adv* : palabra por palabra — **~** *adj* : literal — **verbose** [vər'bo:s] *adj* : verboso
verdict ['vərdɪkt] *n* **1** : veredicto *m* **2** OPINION : opinión *f*
verge ['vərdʒ] *n* **1** : borde *m* **2 on the ~ of** : a punto de (hacer algo), al borde de (algo) — **~** *vi* **verged; verging ~ on** : rayar en
verify ['vɛrə,faɪ] *vt* **-fied; -fying** : verificar — **verification** [,vɛrəfə'keɪʃən] *n* : verificación *f*
vermin ['vərmən] *ns & pl* : alimañas *fpl*
vermouth [vər'mu:θ] *n* : vermut *m*
versatile ['vərsətəl] *adj* : versátil — **versatility** [,vərsə'tɪləti] *n* : versatilidad *f*
verse ['vərs] *n* **1** LINE : verso *m* **2** POETRY : poesía *f* **3** : versículo *m* (en la Biblia) — **versed** ['vərst] *adj* **be well ~ in** : ser muy versado en
version ['vərʒən] *n* : versión *f*
versus ['vərsəs] *prep* : versus

vertebra ['vərtəbrə] *n, pl* **-brae** [-,breɪ, -,bri:] *or* **-bras** : vértebra *f*
vertical ['vərtɪkəl] *adj* : vertical — **~** *n* : vertical *f*
vertigo ['vərtɪ,go:] *n, pl* **-goes** *or* **-gos** : vértigo *m*
verve ['vərv] *n* : brío *m*
very ['vɛri] *adv* **1** : muy **2 at the ~ least** : por lo menos **3 the ~ same thing** : la misma cosa **4 ~ much** : mucho **5 ~ well** : muy bien — **~** *adj* **verier; -est 1** PRECISE, SAME : mismo **2** MERE : solo, mero **3 the ~ thing** : justo lo que hacía falta
vessel ['vɛsəl] *n* **1** CONTAINER : recipiente *m* **2** SHIP : nave *f*, buque *m* **3 or blood ~** : vaso *m* sanguíneo
vest ['vɛst] *n* **1** : chaleco *m* **2** *Brit* UNDERSHIRT : camiseta *f*
vestibule ['vɛstə,bju:l] *n* : vestíbulo *m*
vestige ['vɛstɪdʒ] *n* : vestigio *m*
vet ['vɛt] *n* **1 → veterinarian 2 → veteran**
veteran ['vɛtərən, 'vɛtrən] *n* : veterano *m*, -na *f*
veterinarian [,vɛtərə'nɛriən, ,vɛtə'nɛr-] *n* : veterinario *m*, -ria *f* — **veterinary** ['vɛtərə,nɛri] *adj* : veterinario
veto ['vi:to:] *n, pl* **-toes** : veto *m* — **~** *vt* : vetar
vex ['vɛks] *vt* ANNOY : irritar
via ['vaɪə, 'vi:ə] *prep* : por, vía
viable ['vaɪəbəl] *adj* : viable
viaduct ['vaɪə,dʌkt] *n* : viaducto *m*
vial ['vaɪəl] *n* : frasco *m*
vibrant ['vaɪbrənt] *adj* : vibrante — **vibrate** ['vaɪbreɪt] *vi* **-brated; -brating** : vibrar — **vibration** [vaɪ'breɪʃən] *n* : vibración *f*
vicar ['vɪkər] *n* : vicario *m*, -ria *f*
vicarious [vaɪ'kæriəs, vɪ-] *adj* : indirecto
vice ['vaɪs] *n* : vicio *m*
vice president *n* : vicepresidente *m*, -ta *f*
vice versa [,vaɪsɪ'vərsə, ,vaɪs'vər-] *adv* : viceversa
vicinity [və'sɪnəti] *n, pl* **-ties 1** : inmediaciones *fpl* **2 in the ~ of** ABOUT : alrededor de
vicious ['vɪʃəs] *adj* **1** SAVAGE : feroz **2** MALICIOUS : malicioso
victim ['vɪktəm] *n* : víctima *f*
victor ['vɪktər] *n* : vencedor *m*, -dora *f*
victory ['vɪktəri] *n, pl* **-ries** : victoria *f* — **victorious** [vɪk'to:riəs] *adj* : victorioso
video ['vɪdi,o:] *n* : video *m*, vídeo *m* *Spain* — **~** *adj* : de video — **videocassette** [,vɪdiokə'sɛt] *n* : videocasete *m* — **videotape** ['vɪdio,teɪp] *n* : video-

cinta f — ~ vt **-taped; -taping** : videograbar

vie ['vaɪ] vi **vied; vying** ['vaɪɪŋ] : competir

Vietnamese [vi̯ˌɛtnə'miːz, -'miːs] adj : vietnamita

view ['vjuː] n 1 : vista f 2 OPINION : opinión f 3 **come into** ~ : aparecer 4 **in** ~ **of** : en vista de (que) — ~ vt 1 : ver 2 CONSIDER : considerar — **viewer** ['vjuːər] n or **television** ~ : televidente mf — **viewpoint** ['vjuː-ˌpɔɪnt] n : punto m de vista

vigil ['vɪdʒəl] n : vela f — **vigilance** ['vɪdʒələnts] n : vigilancia f — **vigilant** ['vɪdʒələnt] adj : vigilante

vigor or Brit **vigour** ['vɪgər] n : vigor m — **vigorous** ['vɪgərəs] adj 1 : enérgico 2 ROBUST : vigoroso

Viking ['vaɪkɪŋ] n : vikingo m, -ga f

vile ['vaɪl] adj **viler; vilest** 1 : vil 2 RE-VOLTING : asqueroso 3 TERRIBLE : horrible

villa ['vɪlə] n : casa f de campo

village ['vɪlɪdʒ] n : pueblo m (grande), aldea f (pequeña) — **villager** ['vɪlɪdʒər] n : vecino m, -na f (de un pueblo); aldeano m, -na f (de una aldea)

villain ['vɪlən] n : villano m, -na f

vindicate ['vɪndəˌkeɪt] vt **-cated; -cating** 1 : vindicar 2 JUSTIFY : justificar

vindictive [vɪn'dɪktɪv] adj : vengativo

vine ['vaɪn] n 1 : enredadera f 2 GRAPE-VINE : vid f

vinegar ['vɪnɪgər] n : vinagre m

vineyard ['vɪnjərd] n : viña f, viñedo m

vintage ['vɪntɪdʒ] n 1 : cosecha f (de vino) 2 ERA : época f — ~ adj 1 : añejo (dícese de un vino) 2 CLASSIC : de época

vinyl ['vaɪnəl] n : vinilo m

viola [vi'oːlə] n : viola f

violate ['vaɪəˌleɪt] vt **-lated; -lating** : violar — **violation** [ˌvaɪə'leɪʃən] n : violación f

violence ['vaɪlənts, 'vaɪə-] n : violencia f — **violent** ['vaɪlənt, 'vaɪə-] adj : violento

violet ['vaɪlət, 'vaɪə-] n : violeta f (flor), violeta m (color)

violin [ˌvaɪə'lɪn] n : violín m — **violinist** [ˌvaɪə'lɪnɪst] n : violinista mf — **violoncello** [ˌvaɪələn'tʃɛloː, -viː-] → cello

VIP [ˌviːˌaɪ'piː] n, pl **VIPs** [-'piːz] : VIP mf

viper ['vaɪpər] n : víbora f

virgin ['vərdʒən] n : virgen mf — ~ adj 1 : virgen (dícese de la lana, etc.) 2 CHASTE : virginal — **virginity** [vər-'dʒɪnəti] n : virginidad f

virile ['vɪrəl, -ˌaɪl] adj : viril — **virility** [və'rɪləti] n : virilidad f

virtual ['vərtʃuəl] adj : virtual — **virtually** ['vərtʃuəli, 'vərtʃəli] adv : prácticamente

virtue ['vərtʃuː] n 1 : virtud f 2 **by** ~ **of** : en virtud de

virtuoso [ˌvərtʃu'oːsoː, -zoː] n, pl **-sos** or **-si** [-ˌsiː, -ˌziː] : virtuoso m, -sa f

virtuous ['vərtʃuəs] adj : virtuoso

virulent ['vɪrələnt, 'vɪrjə-] adj : virulento

virus ['vaɪrəs] n : virus m

visa ['viːzə, -sə] n : visado m, visa f Lat

vis-à-vis [ˌviːzə'viː, -sə-] prep : con respecto a

viscous ['vɪskəs] adj : viscoso

vise ['vaɪs] n : torno m de banco

visible ['vɪzəbəl] adj 1 : visible 2 NO-TICEABLE : evidente — **visibility** [ˌvɪzə-'bɪləti] n, pl **-ties** : visibilidad f

vision ['vɪʒən] n 1 : visión f 2 **have** ~**s of** : imaginarse — **visionary** ['vɪʒə-ˌneri] adj : visionario — ~ n, pl **-ries** : visionario m, -ria f

visit ['vɪzət] vt : visitar — vi 1 : hacer una visita 2 **be** ~**ing** : estar de visita — ~ n : visita f — **visitor** ['vɪzətər] n 1 : visitante mf 2 GUEST : visita f

visor ['vaɪzər] n : visera f

vista ['vɪstə] n : vista f

visual ['vɪʒuəl] adj : visual — **visualize** ['vɪʒuəˌlaɪz] vt **-ized; -izing** : visualizar

vital ['vaɪtəl] adj 1 : vital 2 CRUCIAL : esencial — **vitality** [vaɪ'tæləti] n, pl **-ties** : vitalidad f, energía f

vitamin ['vaɪtəmən] n : vitamina f

vivacious [və'veɪʃəs, vaɪ-] adj : vivaz, animado

vivid ['vɪvəd] adj : vivo (dícese de colores), vívido (dícese de sueños, etc.)

vocabulary [voː'kæbjəˌleri] n, pl **-laries** : vocabulario m

vocal ['voːkəl] adj 1 : vocal 2 OUTSPO-KEN : vociferante — **vocal cords** npl : cuerdas fpl vocales — **vocalist** ['voː-kəlɪst] n : cantante mf, vocalista mf

vocation [voː'keɪʃən] n : vocación f — **vocational** [voː'keɪʃənəl] adj : profesional

vociferous [voː'sɪfərəs] adj : vociferante, ruidoso

vodka ['vɑdkə] n : vodka m

vogue ['voːg] n 1 : moda f, boga f 2 **be in** ~ : estar de moda, estar en boga

voice ['vɔɪs] n : voz f — ~ vt **voiced; voicing** : expresar

void ['vɔɪd] adj 1 INVALID : nulo 2 ~ **of** : falto de — ~ n : vacío m — ~ vt : anular

volatile [ˈvɑlət̬əl] *adj* : volátil — **volatility** [ˌvɑləˈtɪlət̬i] *n* : volatilidad *f*
volcano [vɑlˈkeɪnoː] *n*, *pl* **-noes** *or* **-nos** : volcán *m* — **volcanic** [vɑlˈkænɪk] *adj* : volcánico
volition [voˈlɪʃən] *n* **of one's own ~** : por voluntad propia
volley [ˈvɑli] *n*, *pl* **-leys 1** : descarga *f* (de tiros) **2** : torrente *m* (de insultos, etc.) **3** : volea *f* (en deportes) — **volleyball** [ˈvɑliˌbɔl] *n* : voleibol *m*
volt [ˈvoːlt] *n* : voltio *m* — **voltage** [ˈvoːltɪdʒ] *n* : voltaje *m*
voluble [ˈvɑljəbəl] *adj* : locuaz
volume [ˈvɑljəm, -juːm] *n* : volumen *m* — **voluminous** [vəˈluːmənəs] *adj* : voluminoso
voluntary [ˈvɑlənˌteri] *adj* : voluntario — **volunteer** [ˌvɑlənˈtɪr] *n* : voluntario *m*, -ria *f* — **~** *vt* : ofrecer — *vi* **to ~** : ofrecerse a
voluptuous [vəˈlʌptʃuəs] *adj* : voluptuoso

vomit [ˈvɑmət] *n* : vómito *m* — **~** *v* : vomitar
voracious [vɔˈreɪʃəs, və-] *adj* : voraz
vote [ˈvoːt] *n* **1** : voto *m* **2** SUFFRAGE : derecho *m* al voto — **~** *vi* **voted; voting** : votar — **voter** [ˈvoːt̬ər] *n* : votante *mf* — **voting** [ˈvoːt̬ɪŋ] *n* : votación *f*
vouch [ˈvaʊtʃ] *vi* **~ for** : responder de (algo), responder por (algn) — **voucher** [ˈvaʊtʃər] *n* : vale *m*
vow [ˈvaʊ] *n* : voto *m* — **~** *vt* : jurar
vowel [ˈvaʊəl] *n* : vocal *m*
voyage [ˈvɔɪɪdʒ] *n* : viaje *m*
vulgar [ˈvʌlgər] *adj* **1** COMMON : ordinario **2** CRUDE : grosero, vulgar — **vulgarity** [ˌvʌlˈgærət̬i] *n*, *pl* **-ties** : vulgaridad *f*
vulnerable [ˈvʌlnərəbəl] *adj* : vulnerable — **vulnerability** [ˌvʌlnərəˈbɪlət̬i] *n*, *pl* **-ties** : vulnerabilidad *f*
vulture [ˈvʌltʃər] *n* : buitre *m*
vying → vie

W

w [ˈdʌbəlˌjuː] *n*, *pl* **w's** *or* **ws** [-juːz] : w *f*, vigésima tercera letra del alfabeto inglés
wad [ˈwɑd] *n* : taco *m* (de papel, etc.), fajo *m* (de billetes)
waddle [ˈwɑdəl] *vi* **-dled; -dling** : andar como un pato
wade [ˈweɪd] *v* **waded; wading** *vi* : caminar por el agua — *vt* *or* **~ across** : vadear
wafer [ˈweɪfər] *n* : barquillo *m*
waffle [ˈwɑfəl] *n* : gofre *m* *Spain*, wafle *m* *Lat*
waft [ˈwɑft, ˈwæft] *vt* : llevar por el aire — *vi* : flotar
wag [ˈwæg] *v* **wagged; wagging** *vt* : menear — *vi* : menearse
wage [ˈweɪdʒ] *n* *or* **wages** *npl* : salario *m* — **~** *vt* **waged; waging** **~ war** : hacer la guerra
wager [ˈweɪdʒər] *n* : apuesta *f* — **~** *v* : apostar
wagon [ˈwægən] *n* **1** CART : carrito *m* **2** **→ station wagon**
waif [ˈweɪf] *n* : niño *m* abandonado
wail [ˈweɪl] *vi* : lamentarse — **~** *n* : lamento *m*
waist [ˈweɪst] *n* : cintura *f* — **waistline** [ˈweɪstˌlaɪn] *n* : cintura *f*
wait [ˈweɪt] *vi* : esperar — *vt* **1** AWAIT : esperar **2 ~ tables** : servir a la mesa

— **~** *n* **1** : espera *f* **2 lie in ~** : estar al acecho — **waiter** [ˈweɪt̬ər] *n* : camarero *m*, mozo *m* *Lat* — **waiting room** *n* : sala *f* de espera — **waitress** [ˈweɪtrəs] *n* : camarera *f*, moza *f* *Lat*
waive [ˈweɪv] *vt* **waived; waiving** : renunciar a — **waiver** [ˈweɪvər] *n* : renuncia *f*
wake[1] [ˈweɪk] *v* **woke** [ˈwoːk]; **woken** [ˈwoːkən] *or* **waked; waking** *vi* *or* **~ up** : despertarse — *vt* : despertar — **~** *n* : velatorio *m* (de un difunto)
wake[2] *n* **1** : estela *f* (de un barco) **2 in the ~ of** : tras, como consecuencia de
waken [ˈweɪkən] *vt* : despertar — *vi* : despertarse
walk [ˈwɔk] *vi* **1** : caminar, andar **2** STROLL : pasear **3 too far to ~** : demasiado lejos para ir a pie — *vt* **1** : caminar por (algo) **2** : sacar a pasear (a un perro) — **~** *n* **1** : paseo *m* **2** PATH : camino *m* **3** GAIT : andar *m* — **walker** [ˈwɔkər] *n* **1** : paseante *mf* **2** HIKER : excursionista *mf* — **walking stick** *n* : bastón *m* — **walkout** [ˈwɔkˌaʊt] *n* STRIKE : huelga *f* — **walk out** *vi* **1** STRIKE : declararse en huelga **2** LEAVE : salir, irse **3 ~ on** : abandonar
wall [ˈwɔl] *n* : muro *m* (exterior), pared *f* (interior), muralla *f* (de una ciudad)

wallet ['wɑlət] *n* : billetera *f*, cartera *f*

wallflower ['wɔl,flauər] *n* **be a ~** : comer pavo

wallop ['wɑləp] *vt* : pegar fuerte — **~** *n* : golpe *m* fuerte

wallow ['wɑ,lo] *vi* : revolcarse

wallpaper ['wɔl,peɪpər] *n* : papel *m* pintado — **~** *vt* : empapelar

walnut ['wɔl,nʌt] *n* : nuez *f*

walrus ['wɔlrəs, 'wɑl-] *n*, *pl* **-rus** *or* **-ruses** : morsa *f*

waltz ['wɔlts] *n* : vals *m* — **~** *vi* : valsar

wan ['wɑn] *adj* **wanner; -est** : pálido

wand ['wɑnd] *n* : varita *f* (mágica)

wander ['wɑndər] *vi* **1** : vagar, pasear **2** STRAY : divagar — *vt* : pasear por — **wanderer** ['wɑndərər] *n* : vagabundo *m*, -da *f* — **wanderlust** ['wɑndər,lʌst] *n* : pasión *f* por viajar

wane ['weɪn] *vi* **waned; waning** : menguar — **~** *n* **be on the ~** : estar disminuyendo

want ['wɑnt, 'wɔnt] *vt* **1** DESIRE : querer **2** NEED : necesitar **3** LACK : carecer de — **~** *n* **1** NEED : necesidad *f* **2** LACK : falta *f* **3** DESIRE : deseo *m* — **wanting** ['wɑntɪŋ, 'wɔn-] *adj* **be ~** : carecer

wanton ['wɑntən, 'wɔn-] *adj* **1** LEWD : lascivo **2 ~ cruelty** : crueldad *f* despiadada

war ['wɔr] *n* : guerra *f*

ward ['wɔrd] *n* **1** : sala *f* (de un hospital, etc.) **2** : distrito *m* electoral **3** : pupilo *m*, -la *f* (de un tutor, etc.) — **~** *vt* **off** : protegerse contra — **warden** ['wɔrdən] *n* **1** : guardián *m*, -diana *f* **2** *or* **game ~** : guardabosque *mf* **3** *or* **prison ~** : alcaide *m*

wardrobe ['wɔrd,rob] *n* **1** CLOSET : armario *m* **2** CLOTHES : vestuario *m*

warehouse ['wær,haus] *n* : almacén *m*, bodega *f* *Lat* — **wares** ['wærz] *npl* : mercancías *fpl*

warfare ['wɔr,fær] *n* : guerra *f*

warily ['wærəli] *adv* : cautelosamente

warlike ['wær,laɪk] *adj* : belicoso

warm ['wɔrm] *adj* **1** : caliente **2** LUKEWARM : tibio **3** CARING : cariñoso **4 I feel ~** : tengo calor **5 ~ clothes** : ropa *f* de abrigo — **~** *vt* *or* **~ up** : calentar — *vi* **1** *or* **~ up** : calentarse **2 ~ to** : tomar simpatía a (algn), entusiasmarse con (algo) — **warmblooded** ['wɔrm'blʌdəd] *adj* : de sangre caliente — **warmhearted** ['wɔrm'hɑrtəd] *adj* : cariñoso — **warmly** ['wɔrmli] *adv* : calurosamente **2 dress ~** : abrigarse — **warmth** ['wɔrmθ] *n* **1** : calor *m* **2** AFFECTION : cariño *m*, afecto *m*

warn ['wɔrn] *vt* : advertir, avisar— **warning** ['wɔrnɪŋ] *n* : advertencia *f*, aviso *m*

warp ['wɔrp] *vt* **1** : alabear (madera, etc.) **2** DISTORT : deformar — *vi* : alabearse

warrant ['wɔrənt] *n* **1** : autorización *f* **2 arrest ~** : orden *f* judicial — **~** *vt* : justificar — **warranty** ['wɔrənti, ,wɔrən'ti:] *n*, *pl* **-ties** : garantía *f*

warrior ['wɔriər] *n* : guerrero *m*, -ra *f*

warship ['wɔr,ʃɪp] *n* : buque *m* de guerra

wart ['wɔrt] *n* : verruga *f*

wartime ['wɔr,taɪm] *n* : tiempo *m* de guerra

wary ['wæri] *adj* **warier; -est** : cauteloso

was → **be**

wash ['wɔʃ, 'wɑʃ] *vt* **1** : lavar(se) **2** CARRY : arrastrar **3 ~ away** : llevarse **4 ~ over** : bañar — *vi* : lavarse — **~** *n* **1** : lavado *m* **2** LAUNDRY : ropa *f* sucia — **washable** ['wɔʃəbəl, 'wɑ-] *adj* : lavable — **washcloth** ['wɔʃ,klɔθ, 'wɑʃ-] *n* : toallita *f* (para lavarse) — **washed-out** ['wɔʃ'aut, 'wɑʃt-] *adj* **1** : desvaído (dícese de colores) **2** EXHAUSTED : agotado — **washer** ['wɔʃər, 'wɑ-] *n* **1** → **washing machine 2** : arandela *f* (de una llave, etc.) — **washing machine** *n* : máquina *f* de lavar, lavadora *f* — **washroom** ['wɔʃ,ru:m, 'wɑʃ-, -,rum] *n* : servicios *mpl* (públicos), baño *m*

wasn't ['wɑzənt] (*contraction of* **was not**) → **be**

wasp ['wɑsp] *n* : avispa *f*

waste ['weɪst] *v* **wasted; wasting** *vt* **1** : desperdiciar, derrochar, malgastar **2 ~ time** : perder tiempo — *vi* *or* **~ away** : consumirse — **~** *adj* : de desecho — **~** *n* **1** : derroche *m*, desperdicio *m* **2** RUBBISH : desechos *mpl* **3 a ~ of time** : una pérdida de tiempo — **wastebasket** ['weɪst,bæskət] *n* : papelera *f* — **wasteful** ['weɪstfəl] *adj* : derrochador — **wasteland** ['weɪst,lænd, -lənd] *n* : yermo *m*

watch ['wɑtʃ] *vi* **1** : mirar **2** *or* **keep ~** : velar **3 ~ out!** : ¡ten cuidado!, ¡ojo! — *vt* **1** : mirar **2** *or* **~ over** : vigilar, cuidar **3 ~ what you do** : ten cuidado con lo que haces — **~** *n* **1** : reloj *m* **2** SURVEILLANCE : vigilancia *f* **3** LOOKOUT : guardia *mf* — **watchdog** ['wɑtʃ,dɔg] *n* : perro *m* guardián — **watchful** ['wɑtʃfəl] *adj* : vigilante — **watchman** ['wɑtʃmən] *n*, *pl* **-men** [-mən, -,men] : vigilante *m*, guarda *m* — **watchword** ['wɑtʃ,wərd] *n* : santo *m* y seña

water ['wɔtər, 'wɑ-] *n* : agua *f* — **~** *vt* **1**

: regar (el jardín, etc.) **2 ~ down** DI-
LUTE : diluir, aguar — *vi* **1** : lagrimar
(dícese de los ojos) **2 my mouth is
~ing** : se me hace agua la boca —
watercolor ['wɔtər,kʌlər, 'wɑ-] *n* : acuarela *f* — **watercress** ['wɔtər,kres,
'wɑ-] *n* : berro *m* — **waterfall** ['wɔtər-
,fɔl, 'wɑ-] *n* : cascada *f*, salto *m* de agua
— **water lily** *n* : nenúfar *m* — **water-
logged** ['wɔtər,lɔgd, 'wɔtər,lɑgd] *adj*
: lleno de agua, empapado — **watermelon** ['wɔtər,melən, 'wɑ-] *n* : sandía *f*
— **waterpower** ['wɔtər,pauər, 'wɑ-] *n*
: energía *f* hidráulica — **waterproof**
['wɔtər,pruːf, 'wɑ-] *adj* : impermeable
— **watershed** ['wɔtər,ʃed, 'wɑ-] *n* **1**
: cuenca *f* (de un río) **2** : momento *m*
crítico — **waterskiing** ['wɔtər,skiːɪŋ,
'wɑ-] *n* : esquí *m* acuático — **watertight** ['wɔtər,taɪt, 'wɑ-] *adj* : hermético
— **waterway** ['wɔtər,weɪ, 'wɑ-] *n* : vía *f*
navegable — **waterworks** ['wɔtər-
,wɔrks, 'wɑ-] *npl* : central *f* de abastecimiento de agua — **watery** ['wɔtəri,
'wɑ-] *adj* **1** : acuoso **2** DILUTED : aguado, diluido **3** WASHED-OUT : desvaído
(dícese de colores)
watt ['wɑt] *n* : vatio *m* — **wattage** ['wɑt-
,ɪdʒ] *n* : vataje *m*
wave ['weɪv] *v* **waved; waving** *vi* **1**
: saludar con la mano **2** : flotar (dícese
de una bandera) — *vt* **1** SHAKE : agitar
2 CURL : ondular **3** SIGNAL : hacer
señas a (con la mano) — **~** *n* **1** : ola *f*
(de agua) **2** CURL : onda *f* **3** : onda *f* (en
física) **4** : señal *f* (con la mano) **5**
SURGE : oleada *f* — **wavelength**
['weɪv,leŋkθ] *n* : longitud *f* de onda
waver ['weɪvər] *vi* : vacilar
wax¹ ['wæks] *vi* : crecer (dícese de la
luna)
wax² *n* : cera *f* (para pisos, etc.) — **~** *vt*
: encerar — **waxy** ['wæksi] *adj* **waxier;
-est** : ceroso
way ['weɪ] *n* **1** : camino *m* **2** MEANS
: manera *f*, modo *m* **3 by the ~** : a
propósito, por cierto **4 by ~ of** : vía,
pasando por **5 come a long ~** : hacer
grandes progresos **6 get in the ~**
: meterse en el camino **7 get one's
own ~** : salirse uno con la suya **8
mend one's ~s** : dejar las malas cos-
tumbres **9 out of the ~** REMOTE : remoto, recóndito **10 which ~ did he
go?** : ¿por dónde fue?
we ['wiː] *pron* : nosotros, nosotras
weak ['wiːk] *adj* **1** : débil **2** DILUTED
: aguado **3 a ~ excuse** : una excusa
poco convincente — **weaken** ['wiːkən]
vt : debilitar — *vi* : debilitarse —

weakling ['wiːklɪŋ] *n* : debilucho *m*,
-cha *f* — **weakly** ['wiːkli] *adv* : débilmente — **~** *adj* **weaklier; -est** : enfermizo — **weakness** ['wiːknəs] *n* **1**
: debilidad *f* **2** FLAW : flaqueza *f*, punto
m débil
wealth ['welθ] *n* : riqueza *f* — **wealthy**
['welθi] *adj* **wealthier; -est** : rico
wean ['wiːn] *vt* : destetar
weapon ['wepən] *n* : arma *f*
wear ['wær] *v* **wore** ['wor]; **worn** ['worn];
wearing *vt* **1** : llevar (ropa, etc.),
calzar (zapatos) **2** or **~ away** : desgastar **3 ~ oneself out** : agotarse **4
~ out** : gastar — *vi* **1** LAST : durar **2
~ off** : desaparecer **3 ~ out** : gastarse — **~** *n* **1** USE : uso *m* **2** CLOTHING
: ropa *f* **3 be the worse for ~** : estar
deteriorado — **wear and tear** *n* : desgaste *m*
weary ['wɪri] *adj* **-rier; -est** : cansado —
~ *v* **-ried; -rying** *vt* : cansar — *vi*
: cansarse — **weariness** ['wɪrinəs] *n*
: cansancio *m* — **wearisome** ['wɪri-
səm] *adj* : cansado
weasel ['wiːzəl] *n* : comadreja *f*
weather ['weðər] *n* : tiempo *m* — **~** *vt*
1 WEAR : erosionar, desgastar **2** EN-
DURE, OVERCOME : superar — **weath-
er-beaten** ['weðər,biːtən] *adj* : curtido
— **weatherman** ['weðər,mæn] *n*, *pl*
-men [-mən, -,men] : meteorólogo *m*,
-ga *f* — **weather vane** *n* : veleta *f*
weave ['wiːv] *v* **wove** ['woːv] or
weaved; woven ['woːvən] or **weaved;
weaving** *vt* **1** : tejer (tela) **2** INTERLACE
: entretejer **3 ~ one's way** : abrirse
camino — *vi* : tejer — **~** *n* : tejido *m*
— **weaver** ['wiːvər] *n* : tejedor *m*, -dora
f
web ['web] *n* **1** : telaraña *f* (de araña) **2**
: membrana *f* interdigital (de aves) **3**
NETWORK : red *f*
wed ['wed] *v* **wedded; wedding** *vt*
: casarse con — *vi* : casarse
we'd ['wiːd] (*contraction of* **we had, we
should,** or **we would**) → **have,
should, would**
wedding ['wedɪŋ] *n* : boda *f*, casamiento
m
wedge ['wedʒ] *n* **1** : cuña *f* **2** PIECE : porción *f*, trozo *m* — **~** *vt* **wedged;
wedging 1** : apretar (con una cuña) **2**
CRAM : meter
Wednesday ['wenz,deɪ, -di] *n* : miércoles *m*
wee ['wiː] *adj* **1** : pequeñito **2 in the ~
hours** : a las altas horas
weed ['wiːd] *n* : mala hierba *f* — **~** *vt* **1**
: desherbar **2 ~ out** : eliminar

week ['wiːk] *n* : semana *f* — **weekday** ['wiːkˌdeɪ] *n* : día *m* laborable — **weekend** ['wiːkˌend] *n* : fin *m* de semana — **weekly** ['wiːkli] *adv* : semanalmente — ~ *adj* : semanal — ~ *n, pl* **-lies** : semanario *m*

weep ['wiːp] *v* **wept** ['wept]; **weeping** : llorar — **weeping willow** *n* : sauce *m* llorón — **weepy** ['wiːpi] *adj* **weepier; -est** : lloroso

weigh ['weɪ] *vt* **1** : pesar **2** CONSIDER : sopesar **3** ~ **down** : sobrecargar (con una carga), abrumar (con preocupaciones, etc.) — *vi* : pesar

weight ['weɪt] *n* **1** : peso *m* **2** **gain** ~ : engordar **3** **lose** ~ : adelgazar — **weighty** ['weɪti] *adj* **weightier; -est 1** HEAVY : pesado **2** IMPORTANT : importante, de peso

weird ['wɪrd] *adj* **1** : misterioso **2** STRANGE : extraño

welcome ['welkəm] *vt* **-comed; -coming** : dar la bienvenida a, recibir — ~ *adj* **1** : bienvenido **2 you're** ~ : de nada — ~ *n* : bienvenida *f*, acogida *f*

weld ['weld] *v* : soldar

welfare ['welˌfær] *n* **1** WELL-BEING : bienestar *m* **2** AID : asistencia *f* social

well¹ ['wel] *adv* **better** ['betər]; **best** ['best] **1** : bien **2** CONSIDERABLY : bastante **3 as** ~ : también **4 as** ~ **as** : además de — ~ *adj* : bien — ~ *interj* **1** (*used to introduce a remark*) : bueno **2** (*used to express surprise*) : ¡vaya!

well² *n* : pozo *m* — ~ *vi or* ~ **up** : brotar, manar

we'll ['wiːl, wɪl] (*contraction of* **we shall** *or* **we will**) → **shall, will**

well-being ['wel'biːɪŋ] *n* : bienestar *m* — **well-bred** ['wel'bred] *adj* : fino, bien educado — **well-done** ['wel'dʌn] *adj* **1** : bien hecho **2** : bien cocido (dícese de la carne, etc.) — **well-known** ['wel'noːn] *adj* : famoso, bien conocido — **well-meaning** ['wel'miːnɪŋ] *adj* : bien-intencionado — **well-off** ['wel'ɔf] *adj* : acomodado — **well-rounded** ['wel'raʊndəd] *adj* : completo — **well-to-do** [ˌweltə'duː] *adj* : próspero, adinerado

Welsh ['welʃ] *adj* : galés — ~ *n* **1** : galés *m* (idioma) **2 the** ~ : los galeses

went → **go**

wept → **weep**

were → **be**

we're ['wɪr, 'wər, 'wiːər] (*contraction of* **we are**) → **be**

weren't ['wərənt, 'wɔrnt] (*contraction of* **were not**) → **be**

west ['west] *adv* : al oeste — ~ *adj* : oeste, del oeste — ~ *n* **1** : oeste *m* **2 the West** : el Oeste, el Occidente — **westerly** ['westərli] *adv* & *adj* : del oeste — **western** ['westərn] *adj* **1** : del oeste **2 Western** : occidental — **Westerner** ['westərnər] *n* : habitante *mf* del oeste — **westward** ['westwərd] *adv* & *adj* : hacia el oeste

wet ['wet] *adj* **wetter; wettest 1** : mojado **2** RAINY : lluvioso **3** ~ **paint** : pintura *f* fresca — ~ *vt* **wet** *or* **wetted; wetting** : mojar, humedecer

we've ['wiːv] (*contraction of* **we have**) → **have**

whack ['hwæk] *vt* : golpear fuertemente — ~ *n* : golpe *m* fuerte

whale ['hweɪl] *n, pl* **whales** *or* **whale** : ballena *f*

wharf ['hwɔrf] *n, pl* **wharves** ['hwɔrvz] : muelle *m*, embarcadero *m*

what ['hwɑt, 'hwʌt] *adj* **1** (*used in questions and exclamations*) : qué **2** WHATEVER : cualquier — ~ *pron* **1** (*used in questions*) : qué **2** (*used in indirect statements*) : lo que, que **3** ~ **does it cost?** : ¿cuánto cuesta? **4** ~ **for?** : ¿por qué? **5** ~ **if** : y si — **whatever** [hwɑt'evər, 'hwʌt-] *adj* **1** : cualquier **2 there's no chance** ~ : no hay ninguna posibilidad **3 nothing** ~ : nada en absoluto — ~ *pron* **1** ANYTHING : lo que **2** (*used in questions*) : qué **3** ~ **it may be** : sea lo que sea — **whatsoever** [ˌhwɑtsoʊ'evər, 'hwʌ-] *adj* & *pron* : **whatever**

wheat ['hwiːt] *n* : trigo *m*

wheedle ['hwiːdəl] *vt* **-dled; -dling** : engatusar

wheel ['hwiːl] *n* **1** : rueda *f* **2** *or* **steering** ~ : volante *m* (de automóviles, etc.), timón *m* (de barcos) — ~ *vt* : empujar (algo sobre ruedas) — *vi or* ~ **around** : darse la vuelta — **wheelbarrow** ['hwiːlˌbærˌoː] *n* : carretilla *f* — **wheelchair** ['hwiːlˌtʃær] *n* : silla *f* de ruedas

wheeze ['hwiːz] *vi* **wheezed; wheezing** : resollar — ~ *n* : resuello *m*

when ['hwen] *adv* : cuándo — ~ *conj* **1** : cuando **2 the days** ~ **I clean the house** : los días (en) que limpio la casa — ~ *pron* : cuándo — **whenever** [hwen'evər] *adv* : cuando sea — ~ *conj* **1** : cada vez que **2** ~ **you like** : cuando quieras

where ['hwer] *adv* **1** : dónde **2** ~ **are you going?** : ¿adónde vas? — ~ *conj*

& *pron* : donde — **whereabouts** ['hwerə,bauts] *adv* : (por) dónde — ~ *ns & pl* : paradero *m* — **wherever** [hwer'evər] *adv* 1 : en cualquier parte 2 WHERE : dónde, adónde — ~ *conj* : dondequiera que

whet ['hwet] *vt* **whetted; whetting** 1 : afilar 2 ~ **the appetite** : estimular el apetito

whether ['hweðər] *conj* 1 : si 2 **we doubt ~ he'll show up** : dudamos que aparezca 3 ~ **you like it or not** : tanto si quieras como si no

which ['hwɪtʃ] *adj* 1 : qué, cuál 2 **in ~ case** : en cuyo caso — ~ *pron* 1 (*used in questions*) : cuál 2 (*used in relative clauses*) : que, el (la) cual — **whichever** [hwɪtʃ'evər] *adj* : cualquier — ~ *pron* : el (la) que, cualquiera que

whiff ['hwɪf] *n* 1 PUFF : soplo *m* 2 SMELL : olorcillo *m*

while ['hwaɪl] *n* 1 : rato *m* 2 **be worth one's ~** : valer la pena 3 **in a ~** : dentro de poco — ~ *conj* 1 : mientras 2 WHEREAS : mientras que 3 ALTHOUGH : aunque — ~ *vt* **whiled; whiling** ~ **away the time** : matar el tiempo

whim ['hwɪm] *n* : capricho *m*, antojo *m*

whimper ['hwɪmpər] *vi* : lloriquear— ~ *n* : quejido *m*

whimsical ['hwɪmzɪkəl] *adj* : caprichoso, fantasioso

whine ['hwaɪn] *vi* **whined; whining** 1 : gimotear 2 COMPLAIN : quejarse — ~ *n* : quejido *m*, gemido *m*

whip ['hwɪp] *v* **whipped; whipping** *vt* 1 : azotar 2 BEAT : batir (huevos, crema, etc.) 3 ~ **up** AROUSE : avivar, despertar — *vi* FLAP : agitarse — ~ *n* : látigo *m*

whir ['hwər] *vi* **whirred; whirring** : zumbar — ~ *n* : zumbido *m*

whirl ['hwərl] *vi* 1 : dar vueltas, girar 2 *or* ~ **about** : arremolinarse — ~ *n* 1 : giro *m* 2 SWIRL : torbellino *m* — **whirlpool** ['hwərl,puːl] *n* : remolino *m* — **whirlwind** ['hwərl,wɪnd] *n* : torbellino *m*

whisk ['hwɪsk] *vt* 1 : batir 2 ~ **away** : llevarse — ~ *n or* ~ **egg** ~ : batidor *m* — **whisk broom** *n* : escobilla *f*

whisker ['hwɪskər] *n* 1 : pelo *m* (de la barba) 2 ~**s** *npl* : bigotes *mpl* (de animales)

whiskey *or* **whisky** ['hwɪski] *n, pl* -**keys** *or* -**kies** : whisky *m*

whisper ['hwɪspər] *vi* : cuchichear, susurrar — *vt* : susurrar — ~ *n* : susurro *m*

whistle ['hwɪsəl] *v* -**tled; -tling** *vi* 1 : silbar, chiflar *Lat* 2 : pitar (dícese de un tren, etc.) — *vt* : silbar — ~ *n* 1 : silbido *m*, chiflido *m* (sonido) 2 : silbato *m*, pito *m* (instrumento)

white ['hwaɪt] *adj* **whiter; -est** : blanco — ~ *n* 1 : blanco *m* (color) 2 : clara *f* (de huevos) 3 *or* ~ **person** : blanco *m*, -ca *f* — **white–collar** ['hwaɪt'kɑlər] *adj* 1 : de oficina 2 ~ **worker** : oficinista *mf* — **whiten** ['hwaɪtən] *vt* : blanquear — **whiteness** ['hwaɪtnəs] *n* : blancura *f* — **whitewash** ['hwaɪt,wɔʃ] *vt* 1 : enjalbegar 2 CONCEAL : encubrir (un escándalo, etc.) — ~ *n* 1 : jalbegue *m*, lechada *f* 2 COVER-UP : encubrimiento *m*

whittle ['hwɪtəl] *vt* -**tled; -tling** 1 : tallar (madera) 2 *or* ~ **down** : reducir

whiz *or* **whizz** ['hwɪz] *vi* **whizzed; whizzing** 1 BUZZ : zumbar 2 ~ **by** : pasar muy rápido — ~ *or* **whizz** *n, pl* **whizzes** : zumbido *m* — **whiz kid** *n* : joven *m* prometedor

who ['huː] *pron* 1 (*used in direct and indirect questions*) : quién 2 (*used in relative clauses*) : que, quien — **whodunit** [huː'dʌnɪt] *n* : novela *f* policíaca — **whoever** [huː'evər] *pron* 1 : quienquiera que, quien 2 (*used in questions*) : quién

whole ['hoːl] *adj* 1 : entero 2 INTACT : intacto 3 **a ~ lot** : muchísimo — ~ *n* 1 : todo *m* 2 **as a ~** : en conjunto 3 **on the ~** : en general — **wholehearted** ['hoːl'hɑrtəd] *adj* : sincero — **wholesale** ['hoːl,seɪl] *n* : venta *f* al por mayor — ~ *adj* 1 : al por mayor 2 ~ **slaughter** : matanza *f* sistemática — ~ *adv* : al por mayor — **wholesaler** ['hoːl,seɪlər] *n* : mayorista *mf* — **wholesome** ['hoːlsəm] *adj* : sano — **whole wheat** *adj* : de trigo integral — **wholly** ['hoːli] *adv* : completamente

whom ['huːm] *pron* 1 (*used in direct questions*) : a quién 2 (*used in indirect questions*) : de quién, con quién, en quién 3 (*used in relative clauses*) : que, a quien

whooping cough *n* : tos *f* ferina

whore ['hor] *n* : puta *f*

whose ['huːz] *adj* 1 (*used in questions*) : de quién 2 (*used in relative clauses*) : cuyo — ~ *pron* : de quién

why ['hwaɪ] *adv* : por qué — ~ *n, pl* **whys** : porqué *m* — ~ *conj* : por qué — ~ *interj* (*used to express surprise*) : ¡vaya!, ¡mira!

wick ['wɪk] *n* : mecha *f*

wicked ['wɪkəd] *adj* 1 : malo, malvado 2

MISCHIEVOUS : travieso **3 TERRIBLE** : terrible, horrible — **wickedness** ['wɪkədnəs] n : maldad f

wicker ['wɪkər] n : mimbre m — ~ adj : de mimbre

wide ['waɪd] adj **wider; widest 1** : ancho **2 VAST** : amplio, extenso **3** or ~ **of the mark** : desviado — ~ adv **1** ~ **apart** : muy separados **2 far and** ~ : por todas partes **3** ~ **open** : abierto de par en par — **wide-awake** ['waɪdə'weɪk] adj : (completamente) despierto — **widely** ['waɪdli] adv : extensivamente — **widespread** ['waɪd'sprɛd] adj : extendido

widow ['wɪdoː] n : viuda f — ~ vt : dejar viuda — **widower** ['wɪdowər] n : viudo m

width ['wɪdθ] n : ancho m, anchura f

wield ['wiːld] vt **1** : usar, manejar **2 EXERT** : ejercer

wiener ['wiːnər] → **frankfurter**

wife ['waɪf] n, pl **wives** ['waɪvz] : esposa f, mujer f

wig ['wɪg] n : peluca f

wiggle ['wɪgəl] v **-gled; -gling** vt : menear, contonear — vi : menearse — ~ n : meneo m

wigwam ['wɪg,wɑm] n : wigwam m

wild ['waɪld] adj **1** : salvaje **2 DESOLATE** : agreste **3 UNRULY** : desenfrenado **4 RANDOM** : al azar **5 FRANTIC** : frenético **6 OUTRAGEOUS** : extravagante — ~ adv **1** → **wildly 2 run** ~ : volver al estado silvestre (dícese de las plantas), desmandarse (dícese de los niños) — **wildcat** ['waɪld,kæt] n : gato m montés — **wilderness** ['wɪldərnəs] n : yermo m, desierto m — **wildfire** ['waɪld,faɪr] n **1** : fuego m descontrolado **2 spread like** ~ : propagarse como un reguero de pólvora — **wildflower** ['waɪld,flaʊər] n : flor f silvestre — **wildlife** ['waɪld,laɪf] n : fauna f — **wildly** ['waɪldli] adv **1 FRANTICALLY** : frenéticamente **2 EXTREMELY** : locamente

will[1] ['wɪl] v past **would** ['wʊd]; pres sing & pl **will** vi **WISH** : querer — v aux **1 tomorrow we** ~ **go shopping** : mañana iremos de compras **2 he** ~ **get angry over nothing** : se pone furioso por cualquier cosa **3 I** ~ **go despite them** : iré a pesar de ellos **4 I won't do it** : no lo haré **5 that** ~ **be the mailman** : eso ha de ser el cartero **6 the couch** ~ **hold three people** : en el sofá cabrán tres personas **7 accidents** ~ **happen** : los accidentes ocurrirán **8 you** ~ **do as I say** : harás lo que digo

will[2] n **1** : voluntad f **2 TESTAMENT** : testamento m **3 free** ~ : libre albedrío m — **willful** or **wilful** ['wɪlfəl] adj **1 OBSTINATE** : terco **2 INTENTIONAL** : intencionado — **willing** ['wɪlɪŋ] adj **1** : complaciente **2 be** ~ **to** : estar dispuesto a — **willingly** ['wɪlɪŋli] adv : con gusto — **willingness** ['wɪlɪŋnəs] n : buena voluntad f

willow ['wɪloː] n : sauce m

willpower ['wɪl,paʊər] n : fuerza f de voluntad

wilt ['wɪlt] vi : marchitarse

wily ['waɪli] adj **wilier; -est** : artero, astuto

win ['wɪn] v **won** ['wʌn]; **winning** vi : ganar — vt **1** : ganar, conseguir **2** ~ **over** : ganarse a — ~ n : triunfo m, victoria f

wince ['wɪnts] vi **winced; wincing** : hacer una mueca de dolor — ~ n : mueca f de dolor

winch ['wɪntʃ] n : torno m

wind[1] ['wɪnd] n **1** : viento m **2 BREATH** : aliento m **3 FLATULENCE** : flatulencia f **4 get** ~ **of** : enterarse de

wind[2] ['waɪnd] v **wound** ['waʊnd]; **winding** vi : serpentear — vt **1 COIL** : enrollar **2** ~ **a clock** : dar cuerda a un reloj

windfall ['wɪnd,fɔl] n : beneficio m imprevisto

winding ['waɪndɪŋ] adj : tortuoso

wind instrument n : instrumento m de viento

windmill ['wɪnd,mɪl] n : molino m de viento

window ['wɪn,doː] n : ventana f (de un edificio o una computadora), ventanilla f (de un vehículo), vitrina f (de una tienda) — **windowpane** ['wɪn,doː,peɪn] n : vidrio m — **windowsill** ['wɪn,doː,sɪl] n : repisa f de la ventana

windpipe ['wɪnd,paɪp] n : tráquea f

windshield ['wɪnd,ʃiːld] n **1** : parabrisas m **2** ~ **wiper** : limpiaparabrisas m

window-shop ['wɪndo,ʃɑp] vi **-shopped; -shopping** : mirar las vitrinas

wind up ['waɪnd,ʌp] vt : terminar, concluir — vi : terminar, acabar — **windup** n : conclusión f

windy ['wɪndi] adj **windier; -est 1** : ventoso **2 it's** ~ : hace viento

wine ['waɪn] n : vino m — **wine cellar** n : bodega f

wing ['wɪŋ] n **1** : ala f **2 under s.o.'s** ~ : bajo el cargo de algn — **winged** ['wɪŋd, 'wɪŋəd] adj : alado

wink ['wɪŋk] vi : guiñar — ~ n **1** : guiño m **2 not sleep a** ~ : no pegar el ojo

winner ['wɪnər] n : ganador m, -dora f —

winning ['wɪnɪŋ] *adj* **1** : ganador **2** CHARMING : encantador — **winnings** ['wɪnɪŋz] *npl* : ganancias *fpl*

winter ['wɪntər] *n* — *m* — *adj* : invernal, de invierno — **wintergreen** ['wɪntərˌgriːn] *n* : gaulteria *f* — **wintertime** ['wɪntərˌtaɪm] *n* : invierno *m* — **wintry** ['wɪntri] *adj* **wintrier; -est** : invernal, de invierno

wipe ['waɪp] *vt* **wiped; wiping 1** : limpiar **2** ~ **away** : enjugar (lágrimas), borrar (una memoria) **3** ~ **out** : aniquilar, destruir — ~ *n* : pasada *f* (con un trapo, etc.)

wire ['waɪr] *n* **1** : alambre *m* **2** : cable *m* (eléctrico o telefónico) **3** TELEGRAM : telegrama *m* — ~ *vt* **-wired; wiring 1** : instalar el cableado en (una casa, etc.) **2** BIND : atar con alambre **3** TELEGRAPH : enviar un telegrama a — **wireless** ['waɪrləs] *adj* : inalámbrico — **wiring** ['waɪrɪŋ] *n* : cableado *m* — **wiry** ['waɪri] *adj* **wirier; -est 1** : hirsuto, tieso (dícese del pelo) **2** : esbelto y musculoso (dícese del cuerpo)

wisdom ['wɪzdəm] *n* : sabiduría *f* — **wisdom tooth** *n* : muela *f* de juicio

wise ['waɪz] *adj* **wiser; wisest 1** : sabio **2** SENSIBLE : prudente — **wisecrack** ['waɪzˌkræk] *n* : broma *f*, chiste *m* — **wisely** ['waɪzli] *adv* : sabiamente

wish ['wɪʃ] *vt* **1** : desear **2** ~ **s.o. well** : desear lo mejor a algn — *vi* **1** : pedir (como deseo) **2 as you** ~ : como quieras — ~ *n* **1** : deseo *m* **2 best** ~**es** : muchos recuerdos — **wishbone** ['wɪʃˌboːn] *n* : espoleta *f* — **wishful** ['wɪʃfəl] *adj* **1** : deseoso **2** ~ **thinking** : ilusiones *fpl*

wishy-washy ['wɪʃiˌwɑʃi, -ˌwɔʃi] *adj* : insípido, soso

wisp ['wɪsp] *n* **1** : mechón *m* (de pelo) **2** : voluta *f* (de humo)

wistful ['wɪstfəl] *adj* : melancólico

wit ['wɪt] *n* **1** CLEVERNESS : ingenio *m* **2** HUMOR : agudeza *f* **3 at one's** ~**'s end** : desesperado **4 scared out of one's** ~**s** : muerto de miedo

witch ['wɪtʃ] *n* : bruja *f* — **witchcraft** ['wɪtʃˌkræft] *n* : brujería *f*, hechicería *f*

with ['wɪð, 'wɪθ] *prep* **1** : con **2 I'm going** ~ **you** : voy contigo **3 it varies** ~ **the season** : varía según la estación **4 the girl** ~ **red hair** : la muchacha de pelo rojo **5** ~ **all his work, the business failed** : a pesar de su trabajo, el negocio fracasó

withdraw [wɪð'drɔ, wɪθ-] *v* **-drew** [-'druː]; **-drawn** [-'drɔn]; **-drawing** *vt* : retirar — *vi* : apartarse — **withdraw-**

-al [wɪð'drɔəl, wɪθ-] *n* **1** : retirada *f* **2** : abandono (de drogas, etc.) — **withdrawn** [wɪð'drɔn, wɪθ-] *adj* : introvertido

wither ['wɪðər] *vi* : marchitarse

withhold [wɪθ'hoːld, wɪð-] *vt* **-held** [-'held]; **-holding** : retener (fondos), negar (permiso, etc.)

within [wɪð'ɪn, wɪθ-] *adv* : dentro — ~ *prep* **1** : dentro de **2** (*in expressions of distance*) : a menos de **3** (*in expressions of time*) : dentro de, en menos de **4** ~ **reach** : al alcance de la mano

without [wɪð'aʊt, wɪθ-] *adv* **do** ~ : pasar sin algo — ~ *prep* : sin

withstand [wɪθ'stænd, wɪð-] *vt* **-stood** [-'stʊd]; **-standing 1** BEAR : aguantar **2** RESIST : resistir

witness ['wɪtnəs] *n* **1** : testigo *mf* **2** EVIDENCE : testimonio *m* **3 bear** ~ : atestiguar — ~ *vt* **1** SEE : ser testigo de **2** : atestiguar (una firma, etc.)

witticism ['wɪtəˌsɪzəm] *n* : agudeza *f*, ocurrencia *f*

witty ['wɪti] *adj* **-tier; -est** : ingenioso, ocurrente

wives → wife

wizard ['wɪzərd] *n* **1** : mago *m*, brujo *m* **2 a math** ~ : un genio de matemáticas

wizened ['wɪzənd, 'wiː-] *adj* : arrugado

wobble ['wɑbəl] *vi* **-bled; -bling 1** : tambalearse **2** : temblar (dícese de la voz, etc.) — **wobbly** ['wɑbli] *adj* : cojo

woe ['woː] *n* **1** : aflicción *f* **2** ~**s** *npl* TROUBLES : penas *fpl* — **woeful** ['woːfəl] *adj* : triste

woke, woken → wake

wolf ['wʊlf] *n, pl* **wolves** ['wʊlvz] : lobo *m*, -ba *f* — ~ *vt or* ~ **down** : engullir

woman ['wʊmən] *n, pl* **women** ['wɪmən] : mujer *f* — **womanly** ['wʊmənli] *adj* : femenino

womb ['wuːm] *n* : útero *m*, matriz *f*

won → win

wonder ['wʌndər] *n* **1** MARVEL : maravilla *f* **2** AMAZEMENT : asombro *m* — ~ *v* : preguntarse — **wonderful** ['wʌndərfəl] *adj* : maravilloso, estupendo

won't ['woːnt] (*contraction of* **will not**) → **will**

woo ['wuː] *vt* **1** COURT : cortejar **2** : buscar el apoyo de (clientes, votantes, etc.)

wood ['wʊd] *n* **1** : madera *f* (materia) **2** FIREWOOD : leña *f* **3** *or* ~**s** *npl* FOREST : bosque *m* — ~ *adj* : de madera — **woodchuck** ['wʊdˌtʃʌk] *n* : marmota *f* de América — **wooded** ['wʊdəd] *adj* : arbolado, boscoso — **wooden**

['wʊdən] *adj* : de madera — **woodpecker** ['wʊd.pekər] *n* : pájaro *m* carpintero — **woodshed** ['wʊd.ʃed] *n* : leñera *f* — **woodwind** ['wʊd.wɪnd] *n* : instrumento *m* de viento de madera — **woodwork** ['wʊd.wərk] *n* : carpintería *f*

wool ['wʊl] *n* : lana *f* — **woolen** *or* **woollen** ['wʊlən] *adj* : de lana — **~** *n* 1 : lana *f* (tela) 2 **~s** *npl* : prendas *fpl* de lana — **woolly** ['wʊli] *adj* **-lier; -est** : lanudo

word ['wərd] *n* 1 : palabra *f* 2 NEWS : noticias *fpl* 3 **~s** *npl* : letra *f* (de una canción, etc.) 4 **have ~s with** : reñir con 5 **just say the ~** : no tienes que decirlo 6 **keep one's ~** : cumplir su palabra — **~** *vt* : expresar — **word processing** *n* : procesamiento *m* de textos — **word processor** *n* : procesador *m* de textos — **wordy** ['wərdi] *adj* **wordier; -est** : prolijo

wore → wear

work ['wərk] *n* 1 LABOR : trabajo *m* 2 EMPLOYMENT : trabajo *m*, empleo *m* 3 : obra *f* (de arte, etc.) 4 **~s** *npl* FACTORY : fábrica *f* 5 **~s** *npl* MECHANISM : mecanismo *m* — **~** *v* **worked** ['wərkt] *or* **wrought** ['rɔt]; **working** *vt* 1 : hacer trabajar (a una persona) 2 : manejar, operar (una máquina, etc.) — *vi* 1 : trabajar 2 FUNCTION : funcionar 3 : surtir efecto (dícese de una droga), resultar (dícese de una idea, etc.) — **worked up** *adj* : nervioso — **worker** ['wərkər] *n* : trabajador *m*, -dora *f*; obrero *m*, -ra *f* — **working** ['wərkɪŋ] *adj* 1 : que trabaja (dícese de personas), de trabajo (dícese de la ropa, etc.) 2 **be in ~ order** : funcionar bien — **working class** *n* : clase *f* obrera — **workingman** ['wərkɪŋmæn] *n*, *pl* **-men** [-mən, -men] : obrero *m* — **workman** ['wərkmən] *n*, *pl* **-men** [-mən, -men] 1 : obrero *m* 2 ARTISAN : artesano *m* — **workmanship** ['wərkmən.ʃɪp] *n* : artesanía *f*, destreza *f* — **workout** ['wərk.aʊt] *n* : ejercicios *mpl* (físicos) — **work out** *vt* 1 DEVELOP : elaborar 2 SOLVE : resolver — *vi* 1 TURN OUT : resultar 2 SUCCEED : lograr, salir bien 3 EXERCISE : hacer ejercicio — **workshop** ['wərk.ʃɑp] *n* : taller *m* — **work up** *vt* 1 EXCITE : ponerse como loco 2 GENERATE : desarrollar

world ['wərld] *n* : mundo *m* 2 **think the ~ of s.o.** : tener a algn en alta estima — **~** *adj* : mundial, del mundo — **worldly** ['wərldli] *adj* : mundano —

worldwide ['wərld.waɪd] *adv* : en todo el mundo — **~** *adj* : global, mundial

worm ['wərm] *n* 1 : gusano *m*, lombriz *f* 2 **~s** *npl* : lombrices *fpl* (parásitos)

worn → wear — **worn-out** ['worn.aʊt] *adj* 1 USED : gastado 2 TIRED : agotado

worry ['wəri] *v* **-ried; -rying** *vt* : preocupar, inquietar — *vi* : preocuparse, inquietarse — **~** *n*, *pl* **-ries** : preocupación *f* — **worried** ['wərid] *adj* : preocupado — **worrisome** ['wərisəm] *adj* : inquietante

worse ['wərs] *adv* (*comparative of* **bad** *or of* **ill**) : peor — **~** *adj* (*comparative of* **bad** *or of* **ill**) 1 : peor 2 **from bad to ~** : de mal en peor 3 **get ~** : empeorar — **~** *n* 1 **the ~** : el (la) peor, lo peor 2 **take a turn for the ~** : ponerse peor — **worsen** ['wərsən] *v* : empeorar

worship ['wərʃəp] *v* **-shiped** *or* **-shipped; -shiping** *or* **-shipping** *vt* : adorar — *vi* : practicar una religión — **~** *n* : adoración *f*, culto *m* — **worshiper** *or* **worshipper** ['wərʃəpər] *n* : adorador *m*, -dora *f*

worst ['wərst] *adv* (*superlative of* **ill** *or of* **bad** *or* **badly**) : peor — **~** *adj* (*superlative of* **bad** *or of* **ill**) : peor — **~** *n* **the ~** : lo peor, el (la) peor

worth ['wərθ] *n* 1 : valor *m* (monetario) 2 MERIT : mérito *m*, valía *f* 3 **ten dollars' ~ of gas** : diez dólares de gasolina — **~** *prep* 1 **it's ~ $ 10** : vale $ 10 2 **it's ~ doing** : vale la pena hacerlo — **worthless** ['wərθləs] *adj* 1 : sin valor 2 USELESS : inútil — **worthwhile** ['wərθ'hwaɪl] *adj* : que vale la pena — **worthy** ['wərði] *adj* **-thier; -est** : digno

would ['wʊd] *past of* **will** 1 **he ~ often take his children to the park** : solía llevar a sus hijos al parque 2 **I ~ go if I had the money** : iría yo si tuviera el dinero 3 **I ~ rather go alone** : preferiría ir sola 4 **she ~ have won if she hadn't tripped** : habría ganado si no hubiera tropezado 5 **~ you kindly help me with this?** : ¿tendría la bondad de ayudarme con esto? — **would-be** ['wʊd'bi:] *adj* **a ~ poet** : un aspirante a poeta — **wouldn't** ['wʊd-ənt] (*contraction of* **would not**) → **would**

wound¹ ['wu:nd] *n* : herida *f* — **~** *vt* : herir

wound² → wind

wove, woven → weave

wrangle ['ræŋgəl] *vi* **-gled; -gling** : reñir — **~** *n* : riña *f*, disputa *f*

wrap ['ræp] *vt* **wrapped; wrapping 1**
: envolver **2 ~ up** FINISH : dar fin a —
~ *n* **1** : prenda *f* que envuelve (como
un chal) **2** WRAPPER : envoltura *f* —
wrapper ['ræpər] *n* : envoltura *f*, envoltorio *m* — **wrapping** ['ræpɪŋ] *n*
: envoltura *f*, envoltorio *m*

wrath ['ræθ] *n* : ira *f*, cólera *f* — **wrath-
ful** ['ræθfəl] *adj* : iracundo

wreath ['ri:θ] *n, pl* **wreaths** ['ri:ðz, 'ri:θs]
: corona *f* (de flores, etc.)

wreck ['rɛk] *n* **1** WRECKAGE : restos *mpl*
2 RUIN : ruina *f*, desastre *m* **3 be a
nervous ~** : tener los nervios de-
strozados — **~** *vt* : destrozar (un automóvil), naufragar (un barco) —
wreckage ['rɛkɪʤ] *n* : restos *mpl* (de
un buque naufragado, etc.), ruinas *fpl*
(de un edificio)

wren ['rɛn] *n* : chochín *m*

wrench ['rɛntʃ] *vt* **1** PULL : arrancar (de
un tirón) **2** SPRAIN, TWIST : torcerse
— **~** *n* **1** TUG : tirón *m*, jalón *m* **2** SPRAIN
: torcedura *f* **3** *or* **monkey ~** : llave *f*
inglesa

wrestle ['rɛsəl] *vi* **-tled; -tling** : luchar
— **wrestler** ['rɛsələr] *n* : luchador *m*,
-dora *f* — **wrestling** ['rɛsəlɪŋ] *n* : lucha
f

wretch ['rɛtʃ] *n* : desgraciado *m*, -da *f* —
wretched ['rɛtʃəd] *adj* **1** : miserable **2
~ weather** : tiempo *m* espantoso

wriggle ['rɪgəl] *vi* **-gled; -gling** : retorcerse, menearse

wring ['rɪŋ] *vt* **wrung** ['rʌŋ]; **wringing 1**
or **~ out** : escurrir (el lavado, etc.) **2**

TWIST : retorcer **3** EXTRACT : arrancar
(información, etc.)

wrinkle ['rɪŋkəl] *n* : arruga *f* — **~** *v*
-kled; -kling *vt* : arrugar — *vi* : arrugarse

wrist ['rɪst] *n* : muñeca *f* — **wristwatch**
['rɪst,wɑtʃ] *n* : reloj *m* de pulsera

writ ['rɪt] *n* : orden *f* (judicial)

write ['raɪt] *v* **wrote** ['ro:t]; **written**
['rɪtən]; **writing** : escribir — **write
down** *vt* : apuntar, anotar — **write off**
vt CANCEL : cancelar — **writer** ['raɪtər]
n : escritor *m*, -tora *f*

writhe ['raɪð] *vi* **writhed; writhing** : retorcerse

writing ['raɪtɪŋ] *n* : escritura *f*

wrong ['rɔŋ] *n* **1** INJUSTICE : injusticia *f*,
mal *m* **2** : agravio *m* (en derecho) **3 be
in the ~** : haber hecho mal — **~** *adj*
1 : malo **2** UNSUITABLE : inadecuado, inapropiado **3** INCORRECT : incorrecto,
equivocado **4 be ~** : no tener razón
— **~** *adv* : mal, incorrectamente —
~ *vt* **wronged; wronging** : ofender,
ser injusto con — **wrongful** ['rɔŋfəl]
adj **1** UNJUST : injusto **2** UNLAWFUL
: ilegal — **wrongly** ['rɔŋli] *adv* **1** UN-
JUSTLY : injustamente **2** INCORRECTLY
: mal

wrote → write

wrought iron ['rɔt] *n* : hierro *m* forjado

wrung → wring

wry ['raɪ] *adj* **wrier** ['raɪər]; **wriest**
['raɪəst] : irónico, sardónico (dícese del
humor)

XYZ

x *n, pl* **x's** *or* **xs** ['ɛksəz] : x *f*, vigésima
cuarta letra del alfabeto inglés

xenophobia [,zɛnə'fo:biə, ,zi:-] *n* : xenofobia *f*

Xmas ['krɪsməs] *n* : Navidad *f*

X ray ['ɛks,reɪ] *n* **1** : rayo *m* X **2** *or* **~
photograph** : radiografía *f* — **x-ray**
vt : radiografiar

xylophone ['zaɪlə,fo:n] *n* : xilófono *m*

y ['waɪ] *n, pl* **y's** *or* **ys** ['waɪz] : y *f*,
vigésima quinta letra del alfabeto in-
glés

yacht ['jɑt] *n* : yate *m*

yam ['jæm] *n* **1** : ñame *m* **2** SWEET POTA-
TO : batata *f*, boniato *m*

yank ['jæŋk] *vt* : tirar de, jalar *Lat* — **~**
n : tirón *m*, jalón *m* *Lat*

Yankee ['jæŋki] *n* : yanqui *mf*

yap ['jæp] *vi* **yapped; yapping** : ladrar
— **~** *n* : ladrido *m*

yard ['jɑrd] *n* **1** : yarda *f* (medida) **2**
COURTYARD : patio *m* **3** : jardín *m* (de
una casa) — **yardstick** ['jɑrd,stɪk] *n* **1**
: vara *f* (de medir) **2** CRITERION : criterio *m*

yarn ['jɑrn] *n* **1** : hilado *m* **2** TALE : historia *f*, cuento *m*

yawn ['jɔn] *vi* : bostezar — **~** *n* : bostezo *m*

year ['jɪr] *n* **1** : año *m* **2 she's ten ~s
old** : tiene diez años **3 I haven't seen
them in ~s** : hace siglos que no los
veo — **yearbook** ['jɪr,bʊk] *n* : anuario
m — **yearling** ['jɪrlɪŋ, 'jərlən] *n* : animal *m* menor de dos años — **yearly**
['jɪrli] *adv* **1** : anualmente **2 three**

times ~ : tres veces al año — ~ *adj* : anual

yearn ['jərn] *vi* : anhelar — **yearning** ['jərnɪŋ] *n* : anhelo *m*, ansia *f*

yeast ['ji:st] *n* : levadura *f*

yell ['jel] *vi* : gritar, chillar — *vt* : gritar — ~ *n* : grito *m*, chillido *m*

yellow ['jelo] *adj* : amarillo — ~ *n* : amarillo *m* — **yellowish** ['jeloɪʃ] *adj* : amarillento

yelp ['jelp] *n* : gañido *m* — ~ *vi* : dar un gañido

yes ['jes] *adv* **1** : sí **2 say** ~ : decir que sí — ~ *n* : sí *m*

yesterday ['jestərˌdeɪ, -di] *adv* : ayer — ~ *n* **1** : ayer *m* **2 the day before** ~ : anteayer

yet ['jet] *adv* **1** : aún, todavía **2 has he come** ~ ? : ¿ya ha venido? **3 not** ~ : todavía no **4** ~ **more problems** : más problemas aún **5** NEVERTHELESS : sin embargo — ~ *conj* : pero

yield ['ji:ld] *vt* **1** PRODUCE : producir **2** ~ **the right of way** : ceder el paso — *vi* : ceder — ~ *n* : rendimiento *m*, rédito *m* (en finanzas)

yoga ['joːgə] *n* : yoga *m*

yogurt ['joːgərt] *n* : yogur *m*, yogurt *m*

yoke ['joːk] *n* : yugo *m*

yolk ['joːk] *n* : yema *f* (de un huevo)

you ['ju:] *pron* **1** (*used as subject—familiar*) : tú; vos (*in some Latin American countries*); ustedes *pl*; vosotros, vosotras *pl Spain* **2** (*used as subject—formal*) : usted, ustedes *pl* **3** (*used as indirect object—familiar*) : te, les *pl* (*se before lo, la, los, las*), os *pl Spain* **4** (*used as indirect object—formal*) : lo (*Spain sometimes* le), la; los (*Spain sometimes* les), las *pl* **5** (*used after a preposition—familiar*) : ti; vos (*in some Latin American countries*); ustedes *pl*; vosotros, vosotras *pl Spain* **6** (*used after a preposition—formal*) : usted, ustedes *pl* **7 with** ~ (*familiar*) : contigo; con ustedes *pl*; con vosotros, con vosotras *pl Spain* **8 with** ~ (*formal*) : con usted, con ustedes *pl* **9** ~ **never know** : nunca se sabe — **you'd** ['ju:d, 'jud] (*contraction of* **you had** *or* **you would**) → **have**, **would** — **you'll** ['ju:l, 'jul] (*contraction of* **you shall** *or* **you will**) → **shall**, **will**

young ['jʌŋ] *adj* **younger** ['jʌŋgər]; **youngest** [-gəst] **1** : joven **2 my** ~ **er brother** : mi hermano menor **3 she is the** ~**est** : es la más pequeña **4 the** ~ : los jóvenes — ~ *npl* : jóvenes *mfpl* (de los humanos), crías *fpl* (de

los animales) — **youngster** ['jʌŋkstər] *n* : chico *m*, -ca *f*; joven *mf*

your ['jʊr, 'jɔr, jər] *adj* **1** (*familiar singular*) : tu **2** (*familiar plural*) su, vuestro *Spain* **3** (*formal*) : su **4 on** ~ **left** : a la izquierda

you're ['jʊr, 'jɔr, 'jər, 'ju:r] (*contraction of* **you are**) → **be**

yours ['jʊrz, 'jɔrz] *pron* **1** (*belonging to one person—familiar*) : (el) tuyo (la) tuya, (los) tuyos, (las) tuyas **2** (*belonging to more than one person—familiar*) : (el) suyo, (la) suya, (los) suyos, (las) suyas; (el) vuestro, (la) vuestra, (los) vuestros, (las) vuestras *Spain* **3** (*formal*) : (el) suyo, (la) suya, (los) suyos, (las) suyas

yourself [jər'self] *pron*, *pl* **yourselves** [-'selvz] **1** (*used reflexively—familiar*) : te, se *pl*, os *pl Spain* **2** (*used reflexively—formal*) : se **3** (*used for emphasis*) : tú mismo, tú misma; usted mismo, usted misma; ustedes mismos, ustedes mismas *pl*; vosotros mismos, vosotras mismas *pl Spain*

youth ['ju:θ] *n*, *pl* **youths** ['ju:ðz, 'ju:θs] **1** : juventud *f* **2** BOY : joven *m* **3 today's** ~ : los jóvenes de hoy — **youthful** ['ju:θfəl] *adj* **1** : juvenil, de juventud **2** YOUNG : joven

you've ['ju:v] (*contraction of* **you have**) → **have**

yowl ['jaʊl] *vi* : aullar — ~ *n* : aullido *m*

yucca ['jʌkə] *n* : yuca *f*

Yugoslavian [ju:go'slaviən] *adj* : yugoslavo

yule ['ju:l] *n* CHRISTMAS : Navidad *f* — **yuletide** ['ju:lˌtaɪd] *n* : Navidades *fpl*

z ['zi:] *n*, *pl* **z's** *or* **zs** : z *f*, vigésima sexta letra del alfabeto inglés

zany ['zeɪni] *adj* **-nier; -est** : alocado, disparatado

zeal ['zi:l] *n* : fervor *m*, celo *m* — **zealous** ['zeləs] *adj* : entusiasta

zebra ['zi:brə] *n* : cebra *f*

zenith ['zi:nəθ] *n* **1** : cenit *m* (en astronomía) **2** PEAK : apogeo *m*

zero ['zi:ro, 'zɪro] *n*, *pl* **-ros** : cero *m*

zest ['zest] *n* **1** : gusto *m* **2** FLAVOR : sazón *f*

zigzag ['zɪgˌzæg] *n* : zigzag *m* — ~ *vi* **-zagged; -zagging** : zigzaguear

zinc ['zɪŋk] *n* : cinc *m*, zinc *m*

zip ['zɪp] *v* **zipped; zipping** *vt* *or* ~ **up** : cerrar la cremallera de, cerrar el cierre de *Lat* — *vi* SPEED : pasarse volando — **zip code** *n* : código *m* postal — **zipper** ['zɪpər] *n* : cremallera *f*, cierre *m Lat*

zodiac ['zoːdiˌæk] *n* : zodíaco *m*
zone ['zoːn] *n* : zona *f*
zoo ['zuː] *n, pl* **zoos** : zoológico *m*, zoo
m — **zoology** [zoˈɑlədʒi, zuː-] *n* : zoología *f*

zoom ['zuːm] *vi* : zumbar, ir volando —
~ *n* **1** : zumbido *m* **2** *or* ~ **lens**
: zoom *m*
zucchini [zuˈkiːni] *n, pl* **-ni** *or* **-nis** : calabacín *m*, calabacita *f Lat*

Common Spanish Abbreviations

abr.	abril	**Apr.**	April
A.C., a.C.	antes de Cristo	**BC**	before Christ
a. de J.C.	antes de Jesucristo	**BC**	before Christ
admon., admón.	administración	—	administration
a/f	a favor	—	in favor
ago.	agosto	**Aug.**	August
Apdo.	apartado (de correos)	—	P.O. box
aprox.	aproximadamente	**approx.**	approximately
Aptdo.	apartado (de correos)	—	P.O. box
Arq.	arquitecto	**arch.**	architect
A.T.	Antiguo Testamento	**O.T.**	Old Testament
atte.	atentamente	—	sincerely
atto., atta.	atento, atenta	—	kind, courteous
av., avda.	avenida	**ave.**	avenue
a/v.	a vista	—	on receipt
BID	Banco Interamericano de Desarrollo	**IDB**	Interamerican Development Bank
Bo	banco	—	bank
BM	Banco Mundial	—	World Bank
c/, C/	calle	**st.**	street
C	centígrado, Celsius	**C**	centigrade, Celsius
C.	compañía	**Co.**	company
CA	corriente alterna	**AC**	alternating current
cap.	capítulo	**ch., chap.**	chapter
c/c	cuenta corriente	—	current account, checking account
c.c.	centímetros cúbicos	**cu. cm**	cubic centimeters
CC	corriente continua	**DC**	direct current
c/d	con descuento	—	with discount
Cd.	ciudad	—	city
CE	Comunidad Europea	**EC**	European Community
CEE	Comunidad Económica Europea	**EEC**	European Economic Community
cf.	confróntese	**cf.**	compare
cg.	centígramo	**cg**	centigram
CGT	Confederación General de Trabajadores *o* del Trabajo	—	confederation of workers, workers' union
CI	coeficiente intelectual *o* de inteligencia	**IQ**	intelligence quotient
Cía.	compañía	**Co.**	company
cm.	centímetro	**cm**	centimeter
Cnel.	coronel	**Col.**	colonel
col.	columna	**col.**	column
Col. *Mex*	colonia	—	residential area
Com.	comandante	**Cmdr.**	commander
comp.	compárese	**comp.**	compare
Cor.	coronel	**Col.**	colonel
C.P.	código postal	—	zip code

SPANISH ABBREVIATION AND EXPANSION		ENGLISH EQUIVALENT	
CSF, c.s.f.	coste, seguro y flete	**c.i.f.**	cost, insurance, and freight
cta.	cuenta	**ac., acct.**	account
cte.	corriente	**cur.**	current
c/u	cada uno, cada una	**ea.**	each
CV	caballo de vapor	**hp**	horsepower
D.	Don	—	—
Da., D.ª	Doña	—	—
d.C.	después de Cristo	**AD**	anno Domini (in the year of our Lord)
dcha.	derecha	—	right
d. de J.C.	después de Jesucristo	**AD**	anno Domini (in the year of our lord)
dep.	departamento	**dept.**	department
DF, D.F.	Distrito Federal	—	Federal District
dic.	diciembre	**Dec.**	December
dir.	director, directora	**dir.**	director
dir.	dirección	—	address
Dña.	Doña	—	—
do.	domingo	**Sun.**	Sunday
dpto.	departamento	**dept.**	department
Dr.	doctor	**Dr.**	doctor
Dra.	doctora	**Dr.**	doctor
dto.	descuento	—	discount
E, E.	Este, este	**E**	East, east
Ed.	editorial	—	publishing house
Ed., ed.	edición	**ed.**	edition
edif.	edificio	**bldg.**	building
edo.	estado	**st.**	state
EEUU, EE.UU.	Estados Unidos	**US, U.S.**	United States
ej.	por ejemplo	**e.g.**	for example
E.M.	esclerosis multiple	**MS**	multiple sclerosis
ene.	enero	**Jan.**	January
etc.	etcétera	**etc.**	et cetera
ext.	extensión	**ext.**	extension
F	Fahrenheit	**F**	Fahrenheit
f.a.b.	franco a bordo	**f.o.b.**	free on board
FC	ferrocarril	**RR**	railroad
feb.	febrero	**Feb.**	February
FF AA, FF.AA.	Fuerzas Armadas	—	armed forces
FMI	Fondo Monetario Internacional	**IMF**	International Monetary Fund
g.	gramo	**g., gm, gr.**	gram
G.P.	giro postal	**M.O.**	money order
gr.	gramo	**g., gm, gr.**	gram
Gral.	general	**Gen.**	general
h.	hora	**hr.**	hour
Hnos.	hermanos	**Bros.**	brothers
I + D, I & D, I y D	investigación y desarrollo	**R & D**	research and development
i.e.	esto es, es decir	**i.e.**	that is
incl.	inclusive	**incl.**	inclusive, inclusively

SPANISH ABBREVIATION AND EXPANSION		ENGLISH EQUIVALENT	
Ing.	ingeniero, ingeniera	eng.	engineer
IPC	índice de precios al consumo	CPI	consumer price index
IVA	impuesto al valor agregado	VAT	value-added tax
izq.	izquierda	l.	left
juev.	jueves	Thurs.	Thursday
jul.	julio	Jul.	July
jun.	junio	Jun.	June
kg.	kilogramo	kg	kilogram
km.	kilómetro	km	kilometer
km/h	kilómetros por hora	kph	kilometers per hour
kv, kV	kilovatio	kw, kW	kilowatt
l.	litro	l, lit.	liter
Lic.	licenciado, licenciada	—	—
Ltda.	limitada	Ltd.	limited
lun.	lunes	Mon.	Monday
m	masculino	m	masculine
m	metro	m	meter
m	minuto	m	minute
mar.	marzo	Mar.	March
mart.	martes	Tues.	Tuesday
mg.	miligramo	mg	milligram
miérc.	miércoles	Wed.	Wednesday
min	minuto	min.	minute
mm.	milímetro	mm	millimeter
M-N, m/n	moneda nacional	—	national currency
Mons.	monseñor	Msgr.	monsignor
Mtra.	maestra	—	teacher
Mtro.	maestro	—	teacher
N, N.	Norte, norte	N, no.	North, north
n/o	nuestro	—	our
n.º	número	no.	number
N. de (la) R.	nota de (la) redacción	—	editor's note
NE	nordeste	NE	northeast
NN.UU.	Naciones Unidas	UN	United Nations
NO	noroeste	NW	northwest
nov.	noviembre	Nov.	November
N.T.	Nuevo Testamento	N.T.	New Testament
ntra., ntro.	nuestra, nuestro	—	our
NU	Naciones Unidas	UN	United Nations
núm.	número	num.	number
O, O.	Oeste, oeste	W	West, west
oct.	octubre	Oct.	October
OEA, O.E.A.	Organización de Estados Americanos	OAS	Organization of American States
OMS	Organización Mundial de la Salud	WHO	World Health Organization
ONG	organización no gubernamental	NGO	non-governmental organization
ONU	Organización de las Naciones Unidas	UN	United Nations
OTAN	Organización del Tratado del Atlántico Norte	NATO	North Atlantic Treaty Organization

SPANISH ABBREVIATION AND EXPANSION		ENGLISH EQUIVALENT	
p.	página	p.	page
P, P.	padre	Fr.	father
pág.	página	pg.	page
pat.	patente	pat.	patent
PCL	pantalla de cristal líquido	LCD	liquid crystal display
P.D.	post data	P.S.	postscript
p. ej.	por ejemplo	e.g.	for example
PNB	Producto Nacional Bruto	GNP	gross national product
p°	paseo	Ave.	avenue
p.p.	porte pagado	ppd.	postpaid
PP, p.p.	por poder, por poderes	p.p.	by proxy
prom.	promedio	av., avg.	average
ptas., pts.	pesetas	—	—
q.e.p.d.	que en paz descanse	R.I.P.	may he/she rest in peace
R, R/	remite	—	sender
RAE	Real Academia Española	—	—
ref., ref.ª	referencia	ref.	reference
rep.	república	rep.	republic
r.p.m.	revoluciones por minuto	rpm.	revolutions per minute
rte.	remite, remitente	—	sender
s.	siglo	c., cent.	century
s/	su, sus	—	his, her, your, their
S, S.	Sur, sur	S, so.	South, south
S.	san, santo	St.	saint
S.A.	sociedad anónima	Inc.	incorporated (company)
sáb.	sábado	Sat.	Saturday
s/c	su cuenta	—	your account
SE	sudeste, sureste	SE	southeast
seg.	segundo, segundos	sec.	second, seconds
sep., sept.	septiembre	Sept.	September
s.e.u.o.	salvo error u omisión	—	errors and omissions excepted
Sgto.	sargento	Sgt.	sergeant
S.L.	sociedad limitada	Ltd.	limited (corporation)
S.M.	Su Majestad	HM	His Majesty, Her Majesty
s/n	sin número	—	no (street) number
s.n.m.	sobre el nivel de mar	a.s.l.	above sea level
SO	sudoeste/suroeste	SW	southwest
S.R.C.	se ruega contestación	R.S.V.P.	please reply
ss.	siguientes	—	the following ones
SS, S.S.	Su Santidad	H.H.	His Holiness
Sta.	santa	St.	Saint
Sto.	santo	St.	saint
t, t.	tonelada	t., tn	ton
TAE	tasa anual efectiva	APR	annual percentage rate
tb.	también	—	also
tel., Tel.	teléfono	tel.	telephone
Tm.	tonelada métrica	MT	metric ton
Tn.	tonelada	t., tn	ton
trad.	traducido	tr., trans., transl.	translated
UE	Unión Europea	EU	European Union
Univ.	universidad	Univ., U.	university

SPANISH ABBREVIATION AND EXPANSION		ENGLISH EQUIVALENT	
UPC	unidad procesadora central	**CPU**	central processing unit
Urb.	urbanización	—	residential area
v	versus	**v., vs.**	versus
v	verso	**v., ver., vs.**	verse
v.	véase	**vid.**	see
Vda.	viuda	—	widow
v.g., v.gr.	verbigracia	**e.g.**	for example
vier., viern.	viernes	**Fri.**	Friday
V.M.	Vuestra Majestad	—	Your Majesty
V.^{O}B.^{O}, V.^{O}B.^{O}	visto bueno	—	OK, approved
vol, vol.	volumen	**vol.**	volume
vra., vro.	vuestra, vuestro	—	your

Spanish Numbers

Cardinal Numbers

1	uno	28	veintiocho
2	dos	29	veintinueve
3	tres	30	treinta
4	cuatro	31	treinta y uno
5	cinco	40	cuarenta
6	seis	50	cincuenta
7	siete	60	sesenta
8	ocho	70	setenta
9	nueve	80	ochenta
10	diez	90	noventa
11	once	100	cien
12	doce	101	ciento uno
13	trece	200	doscientos
14	catorce	300	trescientos
15	quince	400	cuatrocientos
16	dieciséis	500	quinientos
17	diecisiete	600	seiscientos
18	dieciocho	700	setecientos
19	diecinueve	800	ochocientos
20	veinte	900	novecientos
21	veintiuno	1,000	mil
22	veintidós	1,001	mil uno
23	veintitrés	2,000	dos mil
24	veinticuatro	100,000	cien mil
25	veinticinco	1,000,000	un millón
26	veintiséis	1,000,000,000	mil millones
27	veintisiete	1,000,000,000,000	un billón

Ordinal Numbers

1st	primero, -ra	17th	decimoséptimo, -ma
2nd	segundo, -da	18th	decimoctavo, -va
3rd	tercero, -ra	19th	decimonoveno, -na; *or*
4th	cuarto, -ta		decimonono, -na
5th	quinto, -ta	20th	vigésimo, -ma
6th	sexto, -ta	21st	vigésimoprimero,
7th	séptimo, -ta		vigésimaprimera
8th	octavo, -ta	30th	trigésimo, -ma
9th	noveno, -na	40th	cuadragésimo, -ma
10th	décimo, -ma	50th	quincuagésimo, -ma
11th	undécimo, -ca	60th	sexagésimo, -ma
12th	duodécimo, -ma	70th	septuagésimo, -ma
13th	decimotercero, -ra	80th	octogésimo, -ma
14th	decimocuarto, -ta	90th	nonagésimo, -ma
15th	decimoquinto, -ta	100th	centésimo, -ma
16th	decimosexto, -ta	1,000th	milésimo, -ma

English Numbers

Cardinal Numbers

1	one	20	twenty
2	two	21	twenty-one
3	three	30	thirty
4	four	40	forty
5	five	50	fifty
6	six	60	sixty
7	seven	70	seventy
8	eight	80	eighty
9	nine	90	ninety
10	ten	100	one hundred
11	eleven	101	one hundred and one
12	twelve	200	two hundred
13	thirteen	1,000	one thousand
14	fourteen	1,001	one thousand and one
15	fifteen	2,000	two thousand
16	sixteen	100,000	one hundred thousand
17	seventeen	1,000,000	one million
18	eighteen	1,000,000,000	one billion
19	nineteen	1,000,000,000,000	one trillion

Ordinal Numbers

1st	first	16th	sixteenth
2nd	second	17th	seventeenth
3rd	third	18th	eighteenth
4th	fourth	19th	nineteenth
5th	fifth	20th	twentieth
6th	sixth	21st	twenty-first
7th	seventh	30th	thirtieth
8th	eighth	40th	fortieth
9th	ninth	50th	fiftieth
10th	tenth	60th	sixtieth
11th	eleventh	70th	seventieth
12th	twelfth	80th	eightieth
13th	thirteenth	90th	ninetieth
14th	fourteenth	100th	hundredth
15th	fifteenth	1,000th	thousandth